Mini-Case: With TIPS, Real Interest Rates Have Become Observable in the United States
Mini-Case: Helping Investors Select Desired Interest-Rate Risk

CHAPTER 5

Mini-Case: The Yield Curve as a Forecasting Tool for Inflation and the Business Cycle

CHAPTER 6

Mini-Case: An Exception That Proves the Rule: Raj Rajaratnam and Galleon
Mini-Case: Should You Hire an Ape as Your Investment Adviser?

CHAPTER 7

Mini-Case: The Enron Implosion
Mini-Case: The Tyranny of Collateral
Mini-Case: The Demise of Arthur Andersen
Mini-Case: Credit Rating Agencies and the 2007–2009 Financial Crisis
Mini-Case: Has Sarbanes-Oxley Led to a Decline in U.S. Capital Markets?

CHAPTER 8

Mini-Case: Collateralized Debt Obligations (CDOs)
Inside the Fed: Was the Fed to Blame for the Housing Price Bubble?
Global: The European Sovereign Debt Crisis

CHAPTER 9

Inside the Fed: The Political Genius of the Founders of the Federal Reserve System
Inside the Fed: The Special Role of the Federal Reserve Bank of New York
Inside the Fed: The Role of the Research Staff
Inside the Fed: The FOMC Meeting
Inside the Fed: Green, Blue, Teal, and Beige: What Do These Colors Mean at the Fed?
Inside the Fed: Styles of Federal Reserve Chairs: Bernanke and Yellen Versus Greenspan
Inside the Fed: The Evolution of the Fed's Communication Strategy

CHAPTER 10

Inside the Fed: A Day at the Trading Desk
Inside the Fed: Fed Lending Facilities During the Global Financial Crisis
Global: The European Central Bank's Monetary Policy Strategy
Inside the Fed: Ben Bernanke and the Federal Reserve's Adoption of Inflation Targeting

CHAPTER 11

Mini-Case: Treasury Bill Auctions Go Haywire
Global: Ironic Birth of the Eurodollar Market

CHAPTER 13

Mini-Case: History of the Dow Jones Industrial Average

CHAPTER 14

E-Finance: Borrowers Shop the Web for Mortgages

CHAPTER 16

Inside the Fed: A Day at the Federal Reserve Bank of New York's Foreign Exchange Desk
Global: Why the Large U.S. Current Account Deficit Worries Economists
Global: Will the Euro Survive?
Global: Argentina's Currency Board
Global: Dollarization

CHAPTER 17

Conflicts of Interest: Barings, Daiwa, Sumitomo, Société Générale, and J.P. Morgan Chase: Rogue Traders and the Principal–Agent Problem

CHAPTER 18

Global: The Spread of Government Deposit Insurance Throughout the World: Is This a Good Thing?
Global: Where is the Basel Accord Heading After the Global Financial Crisis?
Mini-Case: Mark-to-Market Accounting and the Global Financial Crisis
Mini-Case: The Global Financial Crisis and Consumer Protection Regulation
E-Finance: Electronic Banking: New Challenges for Bank Regulation
Global: International Financial Regulation

CHAPTER 19

E-Finance: Will "Clicks" Dominate "Bricks" in the Banking Industry?
E-Finance: Why Are Scandinavians So Far Ahead of Americans in Using Electronic Payments and Online Banking?
E-Finance: Are We Headed for a Cashless Society?
Mini-Case: Bruce Bent and the Money Market Mutual Fund Panic of 2008
E-Finance: Information Technology and Bank Consolidation
Mini-Case: The Global Financial Crisis and the Demise of Large, Free-Standing Investment Banks

CHAPTER 20

Mini-Case: The Long Term Capital Debacle
Conflicts of Interest: Many Mutual Funds Are Caught Ignoring Ethical Standards
Conflicts of Interest: SEC Survey Reports Mutual Fund Abuses Widespread

CHAPTER 21

Mini-Case: Insurance Agent: The Customer's Ally
Conflicts of Interest: The AIG Blowup
Conflicts of Interest: The Subprime Financial Crisis and the Monoline Insurers
Mini-Case: Power to the Pensions

CHAPTER 22

Mini-Case: Example of Using the Limit-Order Book
E-Finance: Venture Capitalists Lose Focus with Internet Companies

CHAPTER 24

Mini-Case: The Hunt Brothers and the Silver Crash

Following the Financial News

CHAPTER 2

Foreign Stock Market Indexes

CHAPTER 4

Forecasting Interest Rates

CHAPTER 5

Yield Curves

CHAPTER 15

Foreign Exchange Rates

CHAPTER 24

Financial Futures
Stock Index Futures

FINANCIAL MARKETS AND INSTITUTIONS

Ninth Edition

The Pearson Series in Finance

Berk/DeMarzo
*Corporate Finance**
*Corporate Finance: The Core**

Berk/DeMarzo/Harford
*Fundamentals of Corporate Finance**

Brooks
*Financial Management: Core Concepts**

Copeland/Weston/Shastri
Financial Theory and Corporate Policy

Dorfman/Cather
Introduction to Risk Management and Insurance

Eakins/McNally
*Corporate Finance Online**

Eiteman/Stonehill/Moffett
Multinational Business Finance

Fabozzi
Bond Markets: Analysis and Strategies

Foerster
*Financial Management: Concepts and Applications**

Frasca
Personal Finance

Gitman/Zutter
*Principles of Managerial Finance**
*Principles of Managerial Finance—Brief Edition**

Haugen
The Inefficient Stock Market: What Pays Off and Why
The New Finance: Overreaction, Complexity, and Uniqueness

Holden
Excel Modeling in Corporate Finance
Excel Modeling in Investments

Hughes/MacDonald
International Banking: Text and Cases

Hull
Fundamentals of Futures and Options Markets
Options, Futures, and Other Derivatives

Keown
*Personal Finance: Turning Money into Wealth**

Keown/Martin/Petty
*Foundations of Finance: The Logic and Practice of Financial Management**

Madura
*Personal Finance**

McDonald
Derivatives Markets
Fundamentals of Derivatives Markets

Mishkin/Eakins
Financial Markets and Institutions

Moffett/Stonehill/Eiteman
Fundamentals of Multinational Finance

Pennacchi
Theory of Asset Pricing

Rejda/McNamara
Principles of Risk Management and Insurance

Smart/Gitman/Joehnk
*Fundamentals of Investing**

Solnik/McLeavey
Global Investments

Titman/Keown/Martin
*Financial Management: Principles and Applications**

Titman/Martin
Valuation: The Art and Science of Corporate Investment Decisions

Weston/Mitchel/Mulherin
Takeovers, Restructuring, and Corporate Governance

*denotes MyFinanceLab titles   Log onto www.myfinancelab.com to learn more.

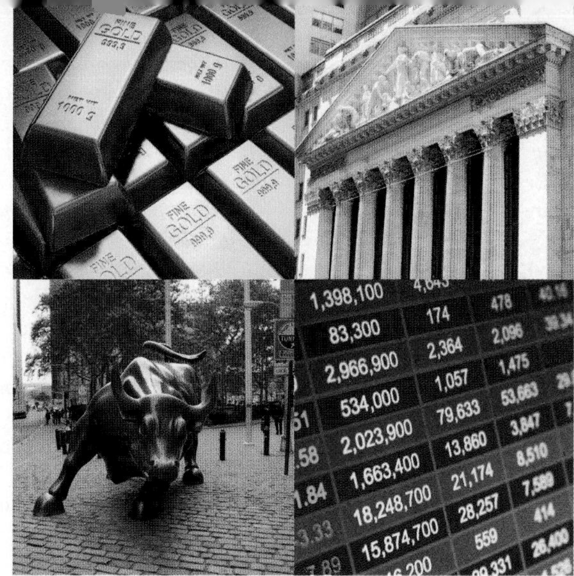

FINANCIAL MARKETS AND INSTITUTIONS

Ninth Edition

Frederic S. Mishkin
Graduate School of Business, Columbia University

Stanley G. Eakins
East Carolina University

New York, NY

Vice President, Business Publishing: Donna Battista
Director of Portfolio Management: Adrienne D'Ambrosio
Senior Portfolio Manager: Christina Masturzo
Vice President, Product Marketing: Roxanne McCarley
Director of Strategic Marketing: Brad Parkins
Strategic Marketing Manager: Deborah Strickland
Product Marketer: Tricia Murphy
Field Marketing Manager: Ramona Elmer
Field Marketing Assistant: Kristen Compton
Product Marketing Assistant: Jessica Quazza
Vice President, Production and Digital Studio, Arts and Business: Etain O'Dea
Director of Production, Business: Jeff Holcomb
Managing Producer, Business: Alison Kalil
Content Producer: Kathryn Brightney
Operations Specialist: Carol Melville
Creative Director: Blair Brown
Manager, Learning Tools: Brian Surette
Content Developer, Learning Tools: Lindsey Sloan
Managing Producer, Digital Studio, Arts and Business: Diane Lombardo
Digital Studio Producer: Melissa Honig
Digital Studio Producer: Alana Coles
Digital Content Team Lead: Noel Lotz
Full-Service Project Management and Composition: Cenveo® Publisher Services
Interior Design: Cenveo® Publisher Services
Cover Design: Cenveo® Publisher Services
Cover Art: Top left: Piboolchai / Shutterstock; top right: TravnikovStudio / Shutterstock; bottom left: Bummi100 / Fotalia; bottom right: Alterov / Shutterstock
Printer/Binder: LSC Communications, Willard
Cover Printer: Phoenix Color

Cataloging-in-Publication Data is on file at the Library of Congress

2 17

ISBN 10: 0-13-451926-4
ISBN 13: 978-0-13-451926-5

To My Dad

—F. S. M.

To My Wife, Laurie

—S. G. E.

Contents in Brief

CHAPTERS ON THE WEB

Contents in Detail

Contents on the Web

The following updated chapters and appendices are available on our Companion Website at www.pearsonhighered.com/mishkin_eakins.

CHAPTER APPENDICES

Preface

A Note from Frederic Mishkin

When I took leave from Columbia University in September 2006 to take a position as a member (governor) of the Board of Governors of the Federal Reserve System, I never imagined how exciting—and stressful—the job was likely to be. How was I to know that, as Alan Greenspan put it, the world economy would be hit by a "once-in-a-century credit tsunami," the global financial crisis of 2007–2009? When I returned to Columbia in September 2008, the financial crisis had reached a particularly virulent stage, with credit markets completely frozen and some of our largest financial institutions in very deep trouble. The global financial crisis, which has been the worst financial crisis the world has experienced since the Great Depression, has completely changed the nature of financial markets and institutions.

Given what has happened, the study of financial markets and institutions has become particularly exciting. I hope that students reading this book will have as much fun learning from it as we have had in writing it.

August 2016

What's New in the Ninth Edition

In addition to the expected updating of all data through 2016 whenever possible, there is major new material in every part of the text.

New Material on Financial Markets and Institutions

In light of ongoing research and changes in financial markets and institutions, we have added the following material to keep the text current:

- A new section on hedge funds (Chapter 2)
- An updated Mini-Case box on negative interest rates in the United States, Europe, and Japan (Chapter 3)
- An updated case on explaining low interest rates in Europe, Japan, and the United States (Chapter 4)
- A new Mini-Case box on the tyranny of collateral (Chapter 7)

- A new section describing securitization and the shadow banking system (Chapter 19)

New Material on Monetary Policy

In the aftermath of the global financial crisis, there have been major changes in the way central banks conduct monetary policy. This has involved the following new material.

- An updated Inside the Fed box on how Janet Yellen's style differs from former Federal Reserve chairs (Chapter 9)
- An updated Inside the Fed box on the evolution of the Fed's communication strategy (Chapter 9)
- A new section on how Federal Reserve actions affect reserves in the banking system (Chapter 10)
- An updated section on forward guidance (Chapter 10)
- A new section on the policy tool, negative interest rates on bank deposits at central banks (Chapter 10)

Appendices on the Web

The Web site for this book, **www.pearsonhighered.com/mishkin_eakins**, has allowed us to retain and add new material for the book by posting content online. The appendices include:

Chapter 4: Models of Asset Pricing

Chapter 4: Applying the Asset Market Approach to a Commodity Market: The Case of Gold

Chapter 4: Loanable Funds Framework

Chapter 4: Supply and Demand in the Market for Money: The Liquidity Preference Framework

Chapter 18: Banking Crises Throughout the World

Chapter 24: More on Hedging with Financial Derivatives

Instructors can either use these appendices in class to supplement the material in the textbook or recommend them to students who want to expand their knowledge of the financial markets and institutions field.

Hallmarks

Although this text has undergone a major revision, it retains the basic hallmarks that make it the best-selling textbook on financial markets and institutions. The ninth edition of *Financial Markets and Institutions* is a practical introduction to the workings of today's financial markets and institutions. Moving beyond the descriptions and definitions provided by other textbooks in the field, *Financial Markets and Institutions* encourages students to understand the connection between the theoretical concepts and their real-world applications. By enhancing students' analytical abilities and concrete problem-solving skills, this textbook prepares students for successful careers in the financial services industry or successful interactions with financial institutions, whatever their jobs.

To prepare students for their future careers, *Financial Markets and Institutions* provides the following features:

- A unifying analytic framework that uses a few basic principles to organize students' thinking. These principles include:
  - Asymmetric information (agency) problems
  - Conflicts of interest
  - Transaction costs
  - Supply and demand
  - Asset market equilibrium
  - Efficient markets
  - Measurement and management of risk
- "The Practicing Manager" sections include nearly 20 hands-on applications that emphasize the financial practitioner's approach to financial markets and institutions.
- A careful step-by-step development of models enables students to master the material more easily.
- A high degree of flexibility allows professors to teach the course in the manner they prefer.
- International perspectives are completely integrated throughout the text.
- "Following the Financial News" is a feature that encourages the reading of a financial newspaper.
- Numerous cases increase students' interest by applying theory to real-world data and examples.
- The text focuses on the impact of electronic (computer and telecommunications) technology on the financial system. The text makes extensive use of the Internet with Web exercises, Web sources for charts and tables, and Web references in the margins. It also features special "E-Finance" boxes that explain how changes in technology have affected financial markets and institutions.

Flexibility

There are as many ways to teach financial markets and institutions as there are instructors. Thus, there is a great need to make a textbook flexible in order to satisfy the diverse needs of instructors, and that has been a primary objective in writing this book. This textbook achieves this flexibility in the following ways:

- Core chapters provide the basic analysis used throughout the book, and other chapters or sections of chapters can be assigned or omitted according to instructor preferences. For example, Chapter 2 introduces the financial system and basic concepts such as transaction costs, adverse selection, and moral hazard. After covering Chapter 2, an instructor can decide to teach a more detailed treatment of financial structure and financial crises using chapters in Part 3 of the text, or cover specific chapters on financial markets or financial institutions in Parts 4 or 5 of the text, or the instructor can skip these chapters and take any of a number of different paths.

- The approach to internationalizing the text using separate, marked international sections within chapters and separate chapters on the foreign exchange market and the international monetary system is comprehensive yet flexible. Although many instructors will teach all the international material, others will choose not to. Instructors who want less emphasis on international topics can easily skip Chapter 15 (on the foreign exchange market) and Chapter 16 (on the international financial system).
- "The Practicing Manager" applications, as well as Part 7 on the management of financial institutions, are self-contained and so can be skipped without loss of continuity. Thus, an instructor wishing to teach a less managerially oriented course, who might want to focus on public policy issues, will have no trouble doing so. Alternatively, Part 7 can be taught earlier in the course, immediately after Chapter 17 on bank management.

The course outlines listed next for a semester teaching schedule illustrate how this book can be used for courses with a different emphasis. More detailed information about how the text can offer flexibility in your course is available in the *Instructor's Manual.*

Financial markets and institutions emphasis: Chapters 1–5, 7–8, 11–13, 17–19, and a choice of five other text chapters
Financial markets and institutions with international emphasis: Chapters 1–5, 7–8, 11–13, 15–19, and a choice of three other text chapters
Managerial emphasis: Chapters 1–5, 17–19, 23–24, and a choice of eight other text chapters
Public policy emphasis: Chapters 1–5, 7–10, 17–18, and a choice of seven other text chapters

Pedagogical Aids

A textbook must be a solid motivational tool. To this end, we have incorporated a wide variety of pedagogical features.

1. **Chapter Previews** at the beginning of each chapter tell students where the chapter is heading, why specific topics are important, and how they relate to other topics in the book.
2. **Cases** demonstrate how the analysis in the book can be used to explain many important real-world situations.
3. **"The Practicing Manager"** is a set of special cases that introduce students to real-world problems that managers of financial institutions have to solve.
4. **Numerical Examples** guide students through solutions to financial problems using formulas, time lines, and calculator key strokes.
5. **"Following the Financial News" boxes** introduce students to relevant news articles and data that are reported daily in financial news sources and explain how to read them.
6. **"Inside the Fed" boxes** give students a feel for what is important in the operation and structure of the Federal Reserve System.
7. **"Global" boxes** include interesting material with an international focus.
8. **"E-Finance" boxes** relate how changes in technology have affected financial markets and institutions.

9. **"Conflicts of Interest" boxes** outline conflicts of interest in different financial service industries.
10. **"Mini-Case" boxes** highlight dramatic historical episodes or apply the theory to the data.
11. **Summary Tables** are useful study aids for reviewing material.
12. **Key Statements** are important points that are set in boldface type so that students can easily find them for later reference.
13. **Graphs** with captions, numbering over 60, help students understand the interrelationship of the variables plotted and the principles of analysis.
14. **Summaries** at the end of each chapter list the chapter's main points.
15. **Key Terms** are important words or phrases that appear in boldface type when they are defined for the first time and are listed at the end of each chapter.
16. **End-of-Chapter Questions** help students learn the subject matter by applying economic concepts and feature a special class of questions that students find particularly relevant, titled "Predicting the Future."
17. **End-of-Chapter Quantitative Problems**, numbering over 250, help students to develop their quantitative skills.
18. **Web Exercises** encourage students to collect information from online sources or use online resources to enhance their learning experience.
19. **Web Sources** report the URL source of the data used to create the many tables and charts.
20. **Marginal Web References** point the student to Web sites that provide information or data that supplement the text material.
21. **Glossary** at the back of the book defines all the key terms.
22. **Full Solutions to the Questions and Quantitative Problems** appear in the *Instructor's Manual* and on the Instructor's Resource Center at **www.pearsonhighered.com/irc**. Professors have the flexibility to share the solutions with their students as they see fit.

Supplementary Materials

The ninth edition of *Financial Markets and Institutions* includes the most comprehensive program of supplementary materials of any textbook in its field. These items are available to qualified domestic adopters but in some cases may not be available to international adopters. These include the following items:

For the Professor

The demands for good teaching at business schools have increased dramatically in recent years. To meet these demands, the ninth edition of *Financial Markets and Institutions* includes the most comprehensive program of supplementary materials of any textbook in its field that should make teaching the course substantially easier. These resources are available at **www.pearsonhighered.com/irc**.

1. **Instructor's Manual:** This manual, prepared by the authors, includes chapter outlines, overviews, teaching tips, and complete solutions to questions and problems in the text.
2. **PowerPoint:** Prepared by John Banko (University of Florida). The presentation, which contains lecture notes and the complete set of figures and tables from

the textbook, contains more than 1,000 slides that comprehensively outline the major points covered in the text.

3. **Test Bank:** Updated and revised for the ninth edition, the Test Bank comprises over 2,500 multiple-choice, true-false, and essay questions. All of the questions from the Test Bank are available in computerized format for use in the TestGen software. The TestGen software is available for both Windows and Macintosh systems.
4. **Mishkin/Eakins Companion Website** (**www.pearsonhighered.com/mishkin_eakins**) features Web chapters on financial crises in emerging economies, savings associations and credit unions, and another on finance companies, Web appendices, and links to relevant data sources and Federal Reserve Web sites.

For the Student

1. **Study Guide:** Updated and revised for the ninth edition by William Gerken, the Study Guide offers chapter summaries, exercises, self-tests, and answers to the exercises and self-tests.
2. **Mishkin/Eakins Companion Website** (**www.pearsonhighered.com/mishkin_eakins**) includes Web chapters on financial crises in emerging economies, savings associations and credit unions, and another on finance companies, Web appendices, glossary flash cards, and links from the textbook.

Acknowledgments

As always in so large a project, there are many people to thank. Our special gratitude goes to Bruce Kaplan, former economics editor at HarperCollins; Donna Battista and Adrienne D'Ambrosio, my former finance editors; Christina Masturzo, my current finance editor at Pearson; and Jane Tufts and Amy Fleischer, our former development editors. We also have been assisted by comments from my colleagues at Columbia and from my students.

In addition, we have been guided in this edition and its predecessors by the thoughtful comments of outside reviewers and correspondents. Their feedback has made this a better book. In particular, we thank:

Ibrahim J. Affanen, Indiana University of Pennsylvania
Vikas Agarwal, Georgia State University
Senay Agca, George Washington University
Aigbe Akhigbe, University of Akron
Ronald Anderson, University of Nevada–Las Vegas
Bala G. Arshanapalli, Indiana University Northwest
Christopher Bain, Ohio State University
James C. Baker, Kent State University
John Banko, University of Central Florida
Mounther H. Barakat, University of Houston–Clear Lake
Joel Barber, Florida International University
Thomas M. Barnes, Alfred University
Marco Bassetto, Northwestern University
Dallas R. Blevins, University of Montevallo
Matej Blusko, University of Georgia
Paul J. Bolster, Northeastern University
Lowell Boudreaux, Texas A&M University–Galveston
Deanne Butchey, Florida International University
Mitch Charklewicz, Central Connecticut State University
Yea-Mow Chen, San Francisco State University
N. K. Chidambaran, Tulane University
Wan-Jiun Paul Chiou, Shippensburg University
Jeffrey A. Clark, Florida State University
Robert Bruce Cochran, San Jose State University
William Colclough, University of Wisconsin–La Crosse
James Conover, University of North Texas
Elizabeth Cooperman, University of Baltimore
Brian Davis, Pennsylvania State University
Carl Davison, Mississippi State University
Cris de la Torre, University of Northern Colorado
Erik Devos, Ohio University at SUNY Binghamton
David Dieterle, Walsh Colege
Alan Durell, Dartmouth College
Franklin R. Edwards, Columbia University
Marty Eichenbaum, Northwestern University
Elyas Elyasiani, Temple University
Edward C. Erickson, California State University–Stanislaus
Kenneth Fah, Ohio Dominican College
J. Howard Finch, Florida Gulf Coast University
E. Bruce Fredrikson, Syracuse University
Cheryl Frohlich, University of North Florida
James Gatti, University of Vermont
Steven Gattuso, Canisius College
Paul Girma, State University of New York–New Paltz
Susan Glanz, St. John's University
Gary Gray, Pennsylvania State University
Wei Guan, University of South Florida–St. Petersburg
Charles Guez, University of Houston
Beverly L. Hadaway, University of Texas
John A. Halloran, University of Notre Dame
Billie J. Hamilton, East Carolina University
John H. Hand, Auburn University
Jeffery Heinfeldt, Ohio Northern University
Tahereh Hojjat, DeSales University
Don P. Holdren, Marshall University
Adora Holstein, Robert Morris College
Sylvia C. Hudgins, Old Dominion University
Jerry G. Hunt, East Carolina University
Boulis Ibrahim, Heroit-Watt University
William E. Jackson, University of North Carolina–Chapel Hill
Joe James, Sam Houston State University
Melvin H. Jameson, University of Nevada–Las Vegas
Kurt Jessewein, Texas A&M International University
Jack Jordan, Seton Hall University
Tejendra Kalia, Worcester State College
Taeho Kim, Thunderbird: The American Graduate School of International Management
Taewon Kim, California State University–Los Angeles
Elinda Kiss, University of Maryland
Glen A. Larsen, Jr., University of Tulsa
James E. Larsen, Wright State University
Rick LeCompte, Wichita State University
Baeyong Lee, Fayetteville State University
Boyden E. Lee, New Mexico State University
Adam Lei, Midwestern State University
Kartono Liano, Mississippi State University
Hao Lin, California State University, Sacramento
John Litvan, Southwest Missouri State
Richard A. Lord, Georgia College
Robert L. Losey, American University
Anthony Loviscek, Seton Hall University
James Lynch, Robert Morris College
Judy E. Maese, New Mexico State University
William Mahnic, Case Western Reserve University
Inayat Mangla, Western Michigan University
William Marcum, Wake Forest University
David A. Martin, Albright College
Lanny Martindale, Texas A&M University
Joseph S. Mascia, Adelphi University
Khalid Metabdin, College of St. Rose

Robert McLeod, University of Alabama
David Milton, Bentley College
A. H. Moini, University of Wisconsin–Whitewater
Russell Morris, Johns Hopkins University
Chee Ng, Fairleigh Dickinson University
Srinivas Nippani, Texas A&M Commerce
Terry Nixon, Indiana University
William E. O'Connell, Jr., The College of William and Mary
Masao Ogaki, Ohio State University
Sam Olesky, University of California–Berkeley
Evren Ors, Southern Illinois University
Coleen C. Pantalone, Northeastern University
Scott Pardee, University of Chicago
Ohaness Paskelian, University of Houston
James Peters, Fairleigh Dickinson University
Fred Puritz, State University of New York–Oneonta
Mahmud Rahman, Eastern Michigan University
Anoop Rai, Hofstra University
Mitchell Ratner, Rider University
David Reps, Pace University–Westchester
Terry Richardson, Bowling Green State University
Harvey Rosenblum, Southern Methodist University
Jack Rubens, Bryant College
Charles B. Ruscher, James Madison University
William Sackley, University of Southern Mississippi
Kevin Salyer, University of California–Davis
Siamack Shojai, Manhattan College
Javadi Siamak, Oklahoma University
Donald Smith, Boston University
Kenneth Smith, University of Texas–Dallas
Sonya Williams Stanton, Ohio State University
Michael Sullivan, Florida International University
Rick Swasey, Northeastern University
Anjan Thackor, University of Michigan
Janet M. Todd, University of Delaware
James Tripp, Western Illinois University
Carlos Ulibarri, Washington State University
Emre Unlu, University of Nebraska–Lincoln
John Wagster, Wayne State University
Bruce Watson, Wellesley College
David A. Whidbee, California State University–Sacramento
Arthur J. Wilson, George Washington University
Shee Q. Wong, University of Minnesota–Duluth
Criss G. Woodruff, Radford University
Tong Yu, University of Rhode Island
Dave Zalewski, Providence College

Finally, I want to thank my wife, Sally, my son, Matthew, and my daughter, Laura, who provide me with a warm and happy environment that enables me to do my work, and my father, Sydney, now deceased, who a long time ago put me on the path that led to this book.

Frederic S. Mishkin

I would like to thank Rick Mishkin for his excellent comments on my contributions. By working with Rick on this text, not only have I gained greater skill as a writer, but I have also gained a friend. I would also like to thank my wife, Laurie, for patiently reading each draft of this manuscript and for helping make this my best work. Through the years, her help and support have made this aspect of my career possible.

Stanley G. Eakins

About the Authors

Frederic S. Mishkin is the Alfred Lerner Professor of Banking and Financial Institutions at the Graduate School of Business, Columbia University. From September 2006 to August 2008, he was a member (governor) of the Board of Governors of the Federal Reserve System.

He is also a research associate at the National Bureau of Economic Research and past president of the Eastern Economics Association. Since receiving his Ph.D. from the Massachusetts Institute of Technology in 1976, he has taught at the University of Chicago, Northwestern University, Princeton University, and Columbia University. He has also received an honorary professorship from the People's (Renmin) University of China. From 1994 to 1997, he was executive vice president and director of research at the Federal Reserve Bank of New York and an associate economist of the Federal Open Market Committee of the Federal Reserve System.

Professor Mishkin's research focuses on monetary policy and its impact on financial markets and the aggregate economy. He is the author of more than 20 books, including *Macroeconomics: Policy and Practice, Second Edition* (Pearson, 2015); *The Economics of Money, Banking and Financial Markets*, Eleventh Edition (Pearson, 2016); *Monetary Policy Strategy* (MIT Press, 2007); *The Next Great Globalization: How Disadvantaged Nations Can Harness Their Financial Systems to Get Rich* (Princeton University Press, 2006); *Inflation Targeting: Lessons from the International Experience* (Princeton University Press, 1999); *Money, Interest Rates, and Inflation* (Edward Elgar, 1993); and *A Rational Expectations Approach to Macroeconometrics: Testing Policy Ineffectiveness and Efficient Markets Models* (University of Chicago Press, 1983). In addition, he has published more than 200 articles in such journals as *American Economic Review*, *Journal of Political Economy*, *Econometrica*, *Quarterly Journal of Economics*, *Journal of Finance*, *Journal of Applied Econometrics*, *Journal of Economic Perspectives*, and *Journal of Money Credit and Banking*.

Professor Mishkin has served on the editorial board of the *American Economic Review* and has been an associate editor at the *Journal of Business and Economic Statistics*, *Journal of Applied Econometrics*, *Journal of Economic Perspectives*, *Journal of Money, Credit and Banking*, and *Journal of International Money and Finance*; he also served as the editor of the Federal Reserve Bank of New York's *Economic Policy Review*. He is currently an associate editor (member of the editorial board) at six academic journals, including *International Finance*; *Finance India*; *Emerging Markets, Finance and Trade*; *Review of Development Finance*, *Borsa Economic Review*, and *PSU Research Review*. He has served as a senior fellow to at the Federal Deposit Insurance Corporation's Center for Banking Research and has been a consultant to the Board of Governors of the Federal Reserve System, the World Bank, and the International Monetary Fund, as well as to many central banks throughout the world. He was also a member of the International Advisory Board to the Financial Supervisory Service of South Korea and an adviser to the Institute for Monetary and Economic Research at the Bank of Korea. He is currently a member of the Economic Advisory Panel and the Monetary Policy Advisory Panel of the Federal Reserve Bank of New York.

Stanley G. Eakins has notable experience as a financial practitioner, serving as vice president and comptroller at the First National Bank of Fairbanks and as a commercial and real estate loan officer. A founder of the Denali Title and Escrow Agency, a title insurance company in Fairbanks, Alaska, he also ran the operations side of a bank and was the chief finance officer for a multimillion-dollar construction and development company.

Professor Eakins received his Ph.D. from Arizona State University. He is the Dean for the College of Business at East Carolina University. His research is focused primarily on the role of institutions in corporate control and how they influence investment practices. He is also interested in integrating multimedia tools into the learning environment and has received grants from East Carolina University in support of this work.

A contributor to journals such as the *Quarterly Journal of Business and Economics*, the *Journal of Financial Research*, and the *International Review of Financial Analysis*, Professor Eakins is also the author of *Corporate Finance Online (CFO)* (Pearson, 2018), a multimedia online text designed from the ground up for electronic delivery.

PART 1 INTRODUCTION

CHAPTER 1

Why Study Financial Markets and Institutions?

> PREVIEW

On the evening news you have just heard that the bond market has been booming. Does this mean that interest rates will fall so that it is easier for you to finance the purchase of a new computer system for your small retail business? Will the economy improve in the future so that it is a good time to build a new building or add to the one you are in? Should you try to raise funds by issuing stocks or bonds, or instead go to the bank for a loan? If you import goods from abroad, should you be concerned that they will become more expensive?

This book provides answers to these questions by examining how financial markets (such as those for bonds, stocks, and foreign exchange) and financial institutions (banks, insurance companies, mutual funds, and other institutions) work. Financial markets and institutions not only affect your everyday life but also involve huge flows of funds—trillions of dollars—throughout our economy, which in turn affect business profits, the production of goods and services, and even the economic well-being of countries other than the United States. What happens to financial markets and institutions is of great concern to politicians and can even have a major impact on elections. The study of financial markets and institutions will reward you with an understanding of many exciting issues. In this chapter we provide a road map of the book by outlining these exciting issues and exploring why they are worth studying.

Why Study Financial Markets?

Parts 2 and 5 of this book focus on **financial markets**, markets in which funds are transferred from people who have an excess of available funds to people who have a shortage. Financial markets, such as bond and stock markets, are crucial to promoting greater economic efficiency by channeling funds from people who do not have a productive use for them to those who do. Indeed, well-functioning financial markets are a key factor in producing high economic growth, and poorly performing financial markets are one reason that many countries in the world remain desperately poor. Activities in financial markets also have direct effects on personal wealth, the behavior of businesses and consumers, and the cyclical performance of the economy.

Debt Markets and Interest Rates

A **security** (also called a *financial instrument*) is a claim on the issuer's future income or **assets** (any financial claim or piece of property that is subject to ownership). A **bond** is a debt security that promises to make payments periodically for a specified period of time.[1] Debt markets, also often referred to generically as the *bond* market, are especially important to economic activity because they enable corporations and governments to borrow in order to finance their activities; the bond market is also where interest rates are determined. An **interest rate** is the cost of borrowing or the price paid for the rental of funds (usually expressed as a percentage of the rental of $100 per year). Many types of interest rates are found in the economy—mortgage interest rates, car loan rates, and interest rates on many types of bonds.

http://research.stlouisfed.org/fred2/

The Federal Reserve Bank of St. Louis' FRED database provides access to daily, weekly, monthly, quarterly, and annual releases and historical data for selected interest rates, foreign exchange rates, and other economic statistics.

Interest rates are important on a number of levels. On a personal level, high interest rates could deter you from buying a house or a car because the cost of financing it would be high. Conversely, high interest rates could encourage you to save because you can earn more interest income by putting aside some of your earnings as savings. On a more general level, interest rates have an impact on the overall health of the economy because they affect not only consumers' willingness to spend or save but also businesses' investment decisions. High interest rates, for example, might cause a corporation to postpone building a new plant that would provide more jobs.

Because changes in interest rates have important effects on individuals, financial institutions, businesses, and the overall economy, it is important to explain fluctuations in interest rates that have been substantial over the past 35 years. For example, the interest rate on three-month Treasury bills peaked at over 16% in 1981. This interest rate fell to 3% in late 1992 and 1993, and then rose to above 5% in the mid to late 1990s. It then fell below 1% in 2004, rose to 5% by 2007, only to fall close to zero from 2008 to 2016.

Because different interest rates have a tendency to move in unison, economists frequently lump interest rates together and refer to "the" interest rate. As Figure 1.1

[1]The definition of *bond* used throughout this book is the broad one in common use by academics, which covers both short- and long-term debt instruments. However, some practitioners in financial markets use the word *bond* to describe only specific long-term debt instruments, such as corporate bonds or U.S. Treasury bonds.

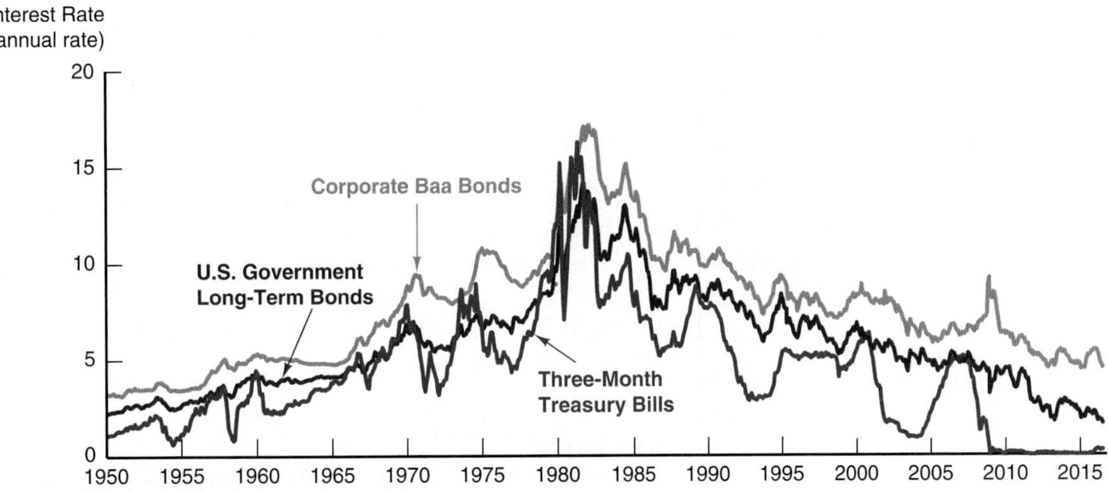

FIGURE 1.1 Interest Rates on Selected Bonds, 1950–2016

Although different interest rates have a tendency to move in unison, they do often differ substantially and the spreads between them fluctuate.

Source: Federal Reserve Bank of St. Louis, FRED database: https://fred.stlouisfed.org/series/TB3MS; https://fred.stlouisfed.org/series/GS10; https://fred.stlouisfed.org/series/BAA.

shows, however, interest rates on various types of bonds can differ substantially. The interest rate on three-month Treasury bills, for example, fluctuates more than the other interest rates and is lower, on average. The interest rate on Baa (medium-quality) corporate bonds is higher, on average, than the other interest rates, and the spread, or difference, between it and U.S. government long-term bonds became larger in the 1970s, narrowed in the 1990s and particularly in the middle 2000s, only to surge to extremely high levels during the global financial crisis of 2007–2009 before narrowing again.

In Chapters 2, 11, 12, and 14 we study the role of debt markets in the economy, and in Chapters 3 through 5 we examine what an interest rate is, how the common movements in interest rates come about, and why the interest rates on different bonds vary.

The Stock Market

A **common stock** (typically just called a **stock**) represents a share of ownership in a corporation. It is a security that is a claim on the earnings and assets of the corporation. Issuing stock and selling it to the public is a way for corporations to raise funds to finance their activities. The stock market, in which claims on the earnings of corporations (shares of stock) are traded, is the most widely followed financial market in almost every country that has one; that's why it is often called simply "the market." A big swing in the prices of shares in the stock market is always a major story on the evening news. People often speculate on where the market is heading and get very excited when they can brag about their latest "big killing," but they become depressed when they suffer a big loss. The attention the market receives can probably be best explained by one simple fact: It is a place where people can get rich—or poor—quickly.

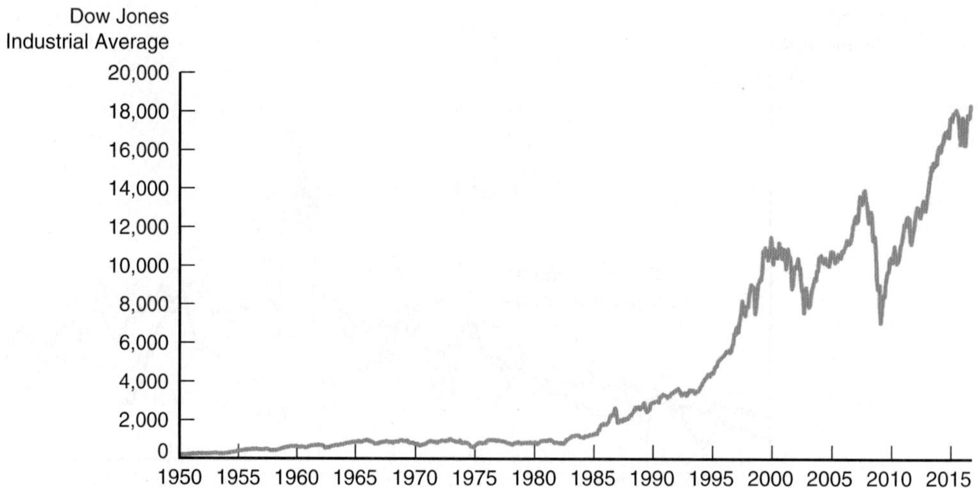

FIGURE 1.2 Stock Prices as Measured by the Dow Jones Industrial Average, 1950–2016

Stock prices are extremely volatile.

Source: Federal Reserve Bank of St. Louis, FRED database: https://fred.stlouisfed.org/series/DJIA.

As Figure 1.2 indicates, stock prices are extremely volatile. After the market rose in the 1980s, on "Black Monday," October 19, 1987, it experienced the worst one-day drop in its entire history, with the Dow Jones Industrial Average (DJIA) falling by 22%. From then until 2000, the stock market experienced one of the great bull markets in its history, with the Dow climbing to a peak of over 11,000. With the collapse of the high-tech bubble in 2000, the stock market fell sharply, dropping by over 30% by late 2002. It then rose above the 14,000 level in 2007, only to fall by over 50% of its value to a low below 7,000 in 2009. Then another bull market began, with the Dow rising above the 18,000 level in 2016. These considerable fluctuations in stock prices affect the size of people's wealth and as a result may affect their willingness to spend.

The stock market is also an important factor in business investment decisions because the price of shares affects the amount of funds that can be raised by selling newly issued stock to finance investment spending. A higher price for a firm's shares means that it can raise a larger amount of funds, which can be used to buy production facilities and equipment.

In Chapter 2 we examine the role that the stock market plays in the financial system, and we return to the issue of how stock prices behave and respond to information in the marketplace in Chapters 6 and 13.

The Foreign Exchange Market

For funds to be transferred from one country to another, they have to be converted from the currency in the country of origin (say, dollars) into the currency of the country they are going to (say, euros). The **foreign exchange market** is where this conversion takes place, so it is instrumental in moving funds between countries. It is also important because it is where the **foreign exchange rate**, the price of one country's currency in terms of another's, is determined.

Figure 1.3 shows the exchange rate for the U.S. dollar from 1973 to 2016 (measured as the value of the U.S. dollar in terms of a basket of major foreign currencies). The fluctuations in prices in this market have also been substantial: The dollar's value reached a low point in the 1978–1980 period and then appreciated dramatically until early 1985. It then declined again, reaching another low in 1995, but appreciated from 1995 to 2001. From 2001 to 2008, the dollar depreciated substantially. After a temporary upturn in 2008 and 2009, the dollar fell back down, but then appreciated from mid-2014 to 2016.

What have these fluctuations in the exchange rate meant to the American public and businesses? A change in the exchange rate has a direct effect on American consumers because it affects the cost of imports. In 2001, when the euro was worth around 85 cents, 100 euros of European goods (say, French wine) cost $85. When the dollar subsequently weakened, raising the cost of a euro to $1.50, the same 100 euros of wine now cost $150. Thus, a weaker dollar leads to more expensive foreign goods, makes vacationing abroad more expensive, and raises the cost of indulging your desire for imported delicacies. When the value of the dollar drops, Americans decrease their purchases of foreign goods and increase their consumption of domestic goods (such as travel in the United States or American-made wine).

Conversely, a strong dollar means that U.S. goods exported abroad will cost more in foreign countries, and hence foreigners will buy fewer of them. Exports of steel, for example, declined sharply when the dollar strengthened in the 1980–1985 and 1995–2001 periods. A strong dollar benefited American consumers by making foreign goods cheaper but hurt American businesses and eliminated some jobs by cutting both domestic and foreign sales of their products. The decline in the value of the dollar from 1985 to 1995 and from 2001 to 2014 had the opposite effect: It

FIGURE 1.3 Exchange Rate of the U.S. Dollar, 1973–2016

The value of the U.S. dollar relative to other currencies has fluctuated substantially over the years.

Source: Federal Reserve Bank of St. Louis, FRED database: https://fred.stlouisfed.org/series/TWEXMMTH.

made foreign goods more expensive but made American businesses more competitive. Fluctuations in the foreign exchange markets thus have major consequences for the American economy.

In Chapter 15 we study how exchange rates are determined in the foreign exchange market, in which dollars are bought and sold for foreign currencies.

Why Study Financial Institutions?

The second major focus of this book is financial institutions. Financial institutions are what make financial markets work. Without them, financial markets would not be able to move funds from people who save to people who have productive investment opportunities. Financial institutions thus play a crucial role in improving the efficiency of the economy.

Structure of the Financial System

The financial system is complex, comprising many types of private-sector financial institutions, including banks, insurance companies, mutual funds, finance companies, and investment banks—all of which are heavily regulated by the government. If you wanted to make a loan to Apple or Amazon, for example, you would not go directly to the president of the company and offer a loan. Instead, you would lend to such companies indirectly through **financial intermediaries**, institutions such as commercial banks, savings and loan associations, mutual savings banks, credit unions, insurance companies, mutual funds, pension funds, and finance companies that borrow funds from people who have saved and in turn make loans to others.

Why are financial intermediaries so crucial to well-functioning financial markets? Why do they give credit to one party but not to another? Why do they usually write complicated legal documents when they extend loans? Why are they the most heavily regulated businesses in the economy?

We answer these questions by developing a coherent framework for analyzing financial structure both in the United States and in the rest of the world in Chapter 7.

Financial Crises

At times, the financial system seizes up and produces **financial crises**, major disruptions in financial markets that are characterized by sharp declines in asset prices and the failures of many financial and nonfinancial firms. Financial crises have been a feature of capitalist economies for hundreds of years and are typically followed by the most serious business cycle downturns. From 2007 to 2009, the U.S. economy was hit by the worst financial crisis since the Great Depression. Defaults in subprime residential mortgages led to major losses in financial institutions, not only producing numerous bank failures but also leading to the demise of Bear Stearns and Lehman Brothers, two of the largest investment banks in the United States. The result of the crisis was the worst recession since World War II, which is now referred to as the "Great Recession."

Why these crises occur and why they do so much damage to the economy is discussed in Chapter 8.

Central Banks and the Conduct of Monetary Policy

www.federalreserve.gov
Access general information as well as monetary policy, banking system, research, and economic data of the Federal Reserve.

The most important financial institution in the financial system is the **central bank**, the government agency responsible for the conduct of monetary policy, which in the United States is the **Federal Reserve System** (also called simply **the Fed**). **Monetary policy** involves the management of interest rates and the quantity of **money**, also referred to as the **money supply** (defined as anything that is generally accepted in payment for goods and services or in the repayment of debt). Because monetary policy affects interest rates, inflation, and business cycles, all of which have a major impact on financial markets and institutions, we study how monetary policy is conducted by central banks in both the United States and abroad in Chapters 9 and 10.

The International Financial System

The tremendous increase in capital flows between countries means that the international financial system has a growing impact on domestic economies. Whether a country fixes its exchange rate to that of another is an important determinant of how monetary policy is conducted. Whether there are capital controls that restrict mobility of capital across national borders has a large effect on domestic financial systems and the performance of the economy. What role international financial institutions such as the International Monetary Fund should play in the international financial system is very controversial. All of these issues are explored in Chapter 16.

Banks and Other Financial Institutions

Banks are financial institutions that accept deposits and make loans. Included under the term *banks* are firms such as commercial banks, savings and loan associations, mutual savings banks, and credit unions. Banks are the financial intermediaries that the average person interacts with most frequently. A person who needs a loan to buy a house or a car usually obtains it from a local bank. Most Americans keep a large proportion of their financial wealth in banks in the form of checking accounts, savings accounts, or other types of bank deposits. Because banks are the largest financial intermediaries in our economy, they deserve careful study. However, banks are not the only important financial institutions. Indeed, in recent years, other financial institutions such as insurance companies, finance companies, pension funds, mutual funds, and investment banks have been growing at the expense of banks, and so we need to study them as well. We study banks and all these other institutions in Parts 6 and 7.

Financial Innovation

In the good old days, when you took cash out of the bank or wanted to check your account balance, you got to say hello to a friendly human. Nowadays, you are more likely to interact with an automatic teller machine (ATM) when withdrawing cash and to use your home computer to check your account balance. **Financial innovation**, the development of new financial products and services, can be an important force for good by making the financial system more efficient. Unfortunately, as we will see in Chapter 8, financial innovation can have a dark side: It can lead to devastating financial crises, such as the one experienced from 2007 to 2009. In Chapter 19 we study why and how financial innovation takes place, with particular emphasis on how the dramatic improvements in information technology have led to new financial products and the ability to deliver financial services electronically, in what has become known as **e-finance**. We also study financial innovation because it shows us how creative thinking on the part of financial institutions can lead to higher profits but can sometimes result in financial disasters. By seeing how and why financial institutions have been creative in the past, we obtain a better grasp of how they may be creative in the future. This knowledge provides us with useful clues about how the financial system may change over time and will help keep our understanding about banks and other financial institutions from becoming obsolete.

Managing Risk in Financial Institutions

In the past ten years, the economic environment has become an increasingly risky place. Interest rates fluctuated wildly, stock markets crashed both here and abroad, speculative crises occurred in the foreign exchange markets, and failures of financial institutions reached levels unprecedented since the Great Depression. To avoid wild swings in profitability (and even possibly failure) resulting from this environment, financial institutions must be concerned with how to cope with increased risk. We look at techniques that these institutions use when they engage in risk management in Chapter 23. Then in Chapter 24, we look at how these institutions make use of new financial instruments, such as financial futures, options, and swaps, to manage risk.

Applied Managerial Perspective

Another reason for studying financial institutions is that they are among the largest employers in the country and frequently pay very high salaries. Hence, some of you have a very practical reason for studying financial institutions: It may help you get a good job in the financial sector. Even if your interests lie elsewhere, you should still care about how financial institutions are run because there will be many times in your life, as an individual, an employee, or the owner of a business, when you will interact with these institutions. Knowing how financial institutions are managed may help you get a better deal when you need to borrow from them or if you decide to supply them with funds.

This book emphasizes an applied managerial perspective in teaching you about financial markets and institutions by including special case applications headed "The Practicing Manager." These cases introduce you to the real-world problems that managers of financial institutions commonly face and need to solve in their day-to-day jobs. For example, how does the manager of a financial institution come up with a new financial product that will be profitable? How does a manager of a financial institution manage the risk that the institution faces from fluctuations in interest rates, stock prices, or foreign exchange rates? Should a manager hire an expert on Federal Reserve policy making, referred to as a "Fed watcher," to help the institution discern where monetary policy might be going in the future?

Not only do "The Practicing Manager" cases, which answer these questions and others like them, provide you with some special analytic tools that you will need if you make your career at a financial institution, but they also give you a feel for what a job as the manager of a financial institution is all about.

How We Will Study Financial Markets and Institutions

Instead of focusing on a mass of dull facts that will soon become obsolete, this textbook emphasizes a unifying, analytic framework for studying financial markets and institutions. This framework uses a few basic concepts to help organize your thinking about the determination of asset prices, the structure of financial markets, bank management, and the role of monetary policy in the economy. The basic concepts are equilibrium, basic supply and demand analysis to explain behavior in financial markets, the search for profits, and an approach to financial structure based on transaction costs and asymmetric information.

The unifying framework used in this book will keep your knowledge from becoming obsolete and make the material more interesting. It will enable you to learn what *really* matters without having to memorize material that you will forget soon after the final exam. This framework will also provide you with the tools needed to understand trends in the financial marketplace and in variables such as interest rates and exchange rates.

To help you understand and apply the unifying analytic framework, simple models are constructed throughout the text in which the variables held constant are carefully delineated, each step in the derivation of the model is clearly and carefully laid out, and the models are then used to explain various phenomena by focusing on changes in one variable at a time, holding all other variables constant.

To reinforce the models' usefulness, this text also emphasizes the interaction of theoretical analysis and empirical data in order to expose you to real-life events and data. To make the study of financial markets and institutions even more relevant and to help you learn the material, the book contains, besides "The Practicing Manager" cases, numerous additional cases and mini-cases that demonstrate how you can use the analysis in the book to explain many real-world situations.

To function better in the real world outside the classroom, you must have the tools to follow the financial news that appears in leading financial publications and on the Web. To help and encourage you to read the financial section of the newspaper, this book contains two special features. The first is a set of special boxed inserts titled "Following the Financial News" that provide detailed information and definitions you need to evaluate the data that are discussed frequently in the media. This book also contains nearly 400 end-of-chapter questions and problems that ask you to apply the analytic concepts you have learned to other real-world issues. Particularly relevant is a special class of problems headed "Predicting the Future." These questions give you an opportunity to review and apply many of the important financial concepts and tools presented throughout the book.

Exploring the Web

The World Wide Web has become an extremely valuable and convenient resource for financial research. We emphasize the importance of this tool in several ways. First, wherever we use the Web to find information to build the charts and tables that appear throughout the text, we include the source site's URL. These sites often contain additional information and are updated frequently. Second, we have added Web exercises to the end of each chapter. These exercises prompt you to visit sites related to the chapter and to work with real-time data and information. We have also supplied Web references to the end of the chapter that list the URLs of sites related to the material being discussed. Visit these sites to further explore a topic you find of particular interest. Web site URLs are subject to frequent change. We have tried to select stable sites, but we realize that even government URLs change. The publisher's Web site (www.pearsonhighered.com/mishkin_eakins) will maintain an updated list of current URLs for your reference.

Collecting and Graphing Data

The following Web exercise is especially important because it demonstrates how to export data from a Web site into Microsoft Excel for further analysis. We suggest you work through this problem on your own so that you will be able to perform this activity when prompted in subsequent Web exercises whenever you want to collect data from the Web and apply it to particular situations.

Web Exercise

You have been hired by Risky Ventures, Inc., as a consultant to help the company analyze interest-rate trends from the beginning of 2015 to the present. Your employers are initially interested in determining the relationship between long- and short-term interest rates in that year. The biggest task you must immediately undertake is collecting market interest-rate data. You know the best source of this information is the Web.

1. You decide that your best indicator of long-term interest rates is that on a 10-year U.S. Treasury note. Your first task is to gather historical data. Go to the Federal Reserve Bank of St. Louis, FRED database, at http://research.stlouisfed.org/fred2/, a terrific resource for economic data. In the search box in the upper right corner, type in "10-year," and then click on "10-Year Treasury Constant Maturity Rate" in the drop down box. The site should look like Figure 1.4.
2. Now that you have located an accurate source of historical interest-rate data, the next step is choosing the sample period and getting it onto a spreadsheet. Check "monthly" under "10-year Treasury Constant Maturity Rate." Change the beginning observation date to 2015, January. Now click on "Edit Graph" and then click on "Add Line." Type in "1-year" in the "Add data series in the graph" box and hit Enter. Click on "1-Year Treasury Constant Maturity Rate: Monthly" and click on "Add Series." Click on "Download" and then on "Excel (data)." Click on "fedgraph.xls" at the bottom and you will now see Figure 1.5.
3. You now want to analyze the interest rates by first graphing them. Put headings such as "10-Year Interest Rate" and "1-Year Interest Rate" at the top of each column of data. Highlight the two columns of interest-rate data you just created in Excel, including the headings. Click on "Insert" on the toolbar and then click on the "Insert Line Chart" icon and the first 2-D Line. Put labels in column A: "Average" and "Standard deviation." In the same row as you put the label "Average," in columns B and C, click on the f_x icon on the Excel toolbar, then click on "AVERAGE" in the Insert Function box and click "OK." Highlight the dates for each of the series from January 2015 to the present and click "OK." In the same row as you put the label "Standard deviation,"

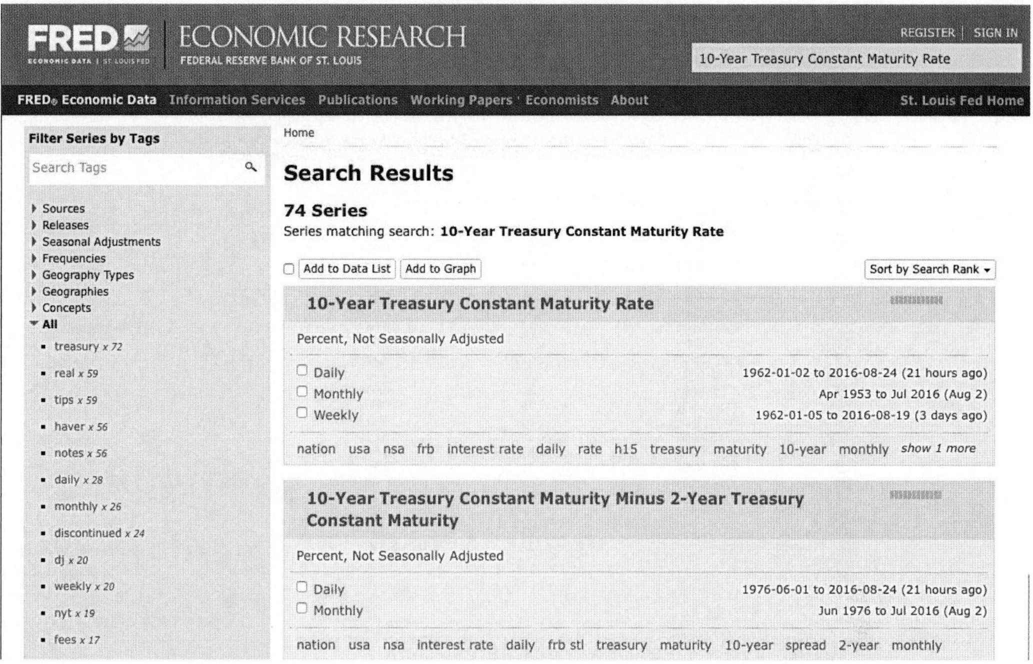

FIGURE 1.4 Federal Reserve Bank of St. Louis, FRED Database

Source: https://fred.stlouisfed.org/series/GS10.

	A	B	C	D	E
1	FRED Graph Observations				
2	Federal Reserve Economic Data				
3	Link: https://fred.stlouisfed.org				
4	Help: https://fred.stlouisfed.org/help-faq				
5	Economic Research Division				
6	Federal Reserve Bank of St. Louis				
7					
8	GS10	10-Year Treasury Constant Maturity Rate, Percent, Monthly, Not Seasonally Adjusted			
9	GS1	1-Year Treasury Constant Maturity Rate, Percent, Monthly, Not Seasonally Adjusted			
10					
11	Frequency: Monthly				
12	observation_date	GS10	GS1		
13	2015-01-01	1.88	0.20		
14	2015-02-01	1.98	0.22		
15	2015-03-01	2.04	0.25		
16	2015-04-01	1.94	0.23		
17	2015-05-01	2.20	0.24		
18	2015-06-01	2.36	0.28		
19	2015-07-01	2.32	0.30		
20	2015-08-01	2.17	0.38		
21	2015-09-01	2.17	0.37		
22	2015-10-01	2.07	0.26		
23	2015-11-01	2.26	0.48		
24	2015-12-01	2.24	0.65		
25	2016-01-01	2.09	0.54		
26	2016-02-01	1.78	0.53		
27	2016-03-01	1.89	0.66		
28	2016-04-01	1.81	0.56		
29	2016-05-01	1.81	0.59		
30	2016-06-01	1.64	0.55		
31	2016-07-01	1.50	0.51		
32					

FIGURE 1.5 Excel Spreadsheet with Interest-Rate Data

Source: Used with permission from Microsoft Corporation; https://fred.stlouisfed.org/series/GS1; https://fred.stlouisfed.org/series/GS10.

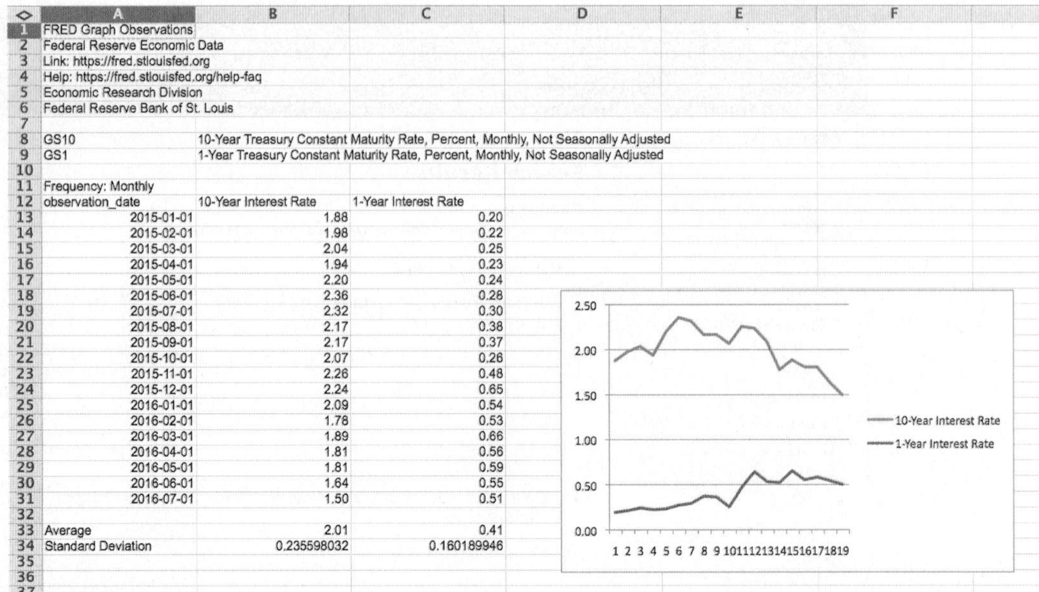

	A	B	C
1	FRED Graph Observations		
2	Federal Reserve Economic Data		
3	Link: https://fred.stlouisfed.org		
4	Help: https://fred.stlouisfed.org/help-faq		
5	Economic Research Division		
6	Federal Reserve Bank of St. Louis		
7			
8	GS10	10-Year Treasury Constant Maturity Rate, Percent, Monthly, Not Seasonally Adjusted	
9	GS1	1-Year Treasury Constant Maturity Rate, Percent, Monthly, Not Seasonally Adjusted	
10			
11	Frequency: Monthly		
12	observation_date	10-Year Interest Rate	1-Year Interest Rate
13	2015-01-01	1.88	0.20
14	2015-02-01	1.98	0.22
15	2015-03-01	2.04	0.25
16	2015-04-01	1.94	0.23
17	2015-05-01	2.20	0.24
18	2015-06-01	2.36	0.28
19	2015-07-01	2.32	0.30
20	2015-08-01	2.17	0.38
21	2015-09-01	2.17	0.37
22	2015-10-01	2.07	0.26
23	2015-11-01	2.26	0.48
24	2015-12-01	2.24	0.65
25	2016-01-01	2.09	0.54
26	2016-02-01	1.78	0.53
27	2016-03-01	1.89	0.66
28	2016-04-01	1.81	0.56
29	2016-05-01	1.81	0.59
30	2016-06-01	1.64	0.55
31	2016-07-01	1.50	0.51
32			
33	Average	2.01	0.41
34	Standard Deviation	0.235598032	0.160189946

FIGURE 1.6 Excel Graph of Interest-Data

Source: Used with permission from Microsoft Corporation.

in columns B and C, click on the f_x icon on the Excel toolbar, then click on "STDEV" in the Insert Function box and click "OK." Highlight the dates for each of the series from January 2015 to the present and click "OK." You should now see Figure 1.6.

Concluding Remarks

The field of financial markets and institutions is an exciting one. Not only will you develop skills that will be valuable in your career, but you will also gain a clearer understanding of events in financial markets and institutions you frequently hear about in the news media. This book will introduce you to many of the controversies that are hotly debated in the current political arena.

SUMMARY

1. Activities in financial markets have direct effects on individuals' wealth, the behavior of businesses, and the efficiency of our economy. Three financial markets deserve particular attention: the bond market (where interest rates are determined), the stock market (which has a major effect on people's wealth and on firms' investment decisions), and the foreign exchange market (because fluctuations in the foreign exchange rate have major consequences for the U.S. economy).

2. Because monetary policy affects interest rates, inflation, and business cycles, all of which have an important impact on financial markets and institutions, we need to understand how monetary policy is conducted by central banks in the United States and abroad.
3. Banks and other financial institutions channel funds from people who might not put them to productive use to people who can do so and thus play a crucial role in improving the efficiency of the economy. When the financial system seizes up and produces a financial crisis, financial firms fail, which causes severe damage to the economy.
4. Understanding how financial institutions are managed is important because there will be many times in your life, as an individual, an employee, or the owner of a business, when you will interact with them. "The Practicing Manager" cases not only provide special analytic tools that are useful if you choose a career with a financial institution but also give you a feel for what a job as the manager of a financial institution is all about.
5. This textbook emphasizes an analytic way of thinking by developing a unifying framework for the study of financial markets and institutions using a few basic principles. This textbook also focuses on the interaction of theoretical analysis and empirical data.

KEY TERMS

assets, p. 2
banks, p. 7
bond, p. 2
central bank, p. 7
common stock (stock), p. 3
e-finance, p. 8
Federal Reserve System (the Fed), p. 7
financial crises, p. 6
financial innovation, p. 7
financial intermediaries, p. 6
financial markets, p. 2
foreign exchange market, p. 4
foreign exchange rate, p. 5
interest rate, p. 2
monetary policy, p. 7
money (money supply), p. 7
security, p. 2

QUESTIONS

1. Explain the link between well-performing financial markets and economic growth. Name one channel through which financial markets might affect economic growth and poverty.
2. When interest rates rise, how might businesses and consumers change their economic behavior?
3. How can a change in interest rates affect the profitability of financial institutions?
4. Why is it that economists often refer to "the" interest rate, while there are many interest rates in any economy?
5. What effect might a fall in stock prices have on business investment?
6. Explain the main difference between a bond and a common stock.
7. How does a decline in the value of the pound sterling affect British consumers?
8. How does an increase in the value of the pound sterling affect American businesses?
9. How can changes in foreign exchange rates affect the profitability of financial institutions?
10. Looking at Figure 1.3, in what years would you have chosen to visit the Grand Canyon in Arizona rather than the Tower of London?
11. Can you think of a reason why people in general do not lend money to one another to buy a house or a car? How would your answer explain the existence of banks?
12. What are the other important financial intermediaries in the economy besides banks?
13. Can you date the latest financial crisis in the United States or in Europe? Are there reasons to think that these crises might have been related? Why?
14. What types of risks do financial institutions face?
15. Why do managers of financial institutions care so much about the activities of the Federal Reserve System?

QUANTITATIVE PROBLEMS

1. The following table lists foreign exchange rates between U.S. dollars and British pounds (GBP) during April.

Date	U.S. Dollars per GBP
4/1	1.9564
4/4	1.9293
4/5	1.914
4/6	1.9374
4/7	1.961
4/8	1.8925
4/11	1.8822
4/12	1.8558
4/13	1.796
4/14	1.7902
4/15	1.7785
4/18	1.7504
4/19	1.7255
4/20	1.6914
4/21	1.672
4/22	1.6684
4/25	1.6674
4/26	1.6857
4/27	1.6925
4/28	1.7201
4/29	1.7512

Which day would have been the best day to convert $200 into British pounds? Which day would have been the worst day? What would be the difference in pounds?

WEB EXERCISES

Working with Financial Market Data

1. In this exercise we will practice collecting data from the Web and graphing it using Excel. Use the example on pages 10–12 as a guide. Go to **https://fred.stlouisfed.org/series/DJIA**, and select "10 year graph" on the top middle. On the far right select "Edit Graph." Choose "modify frequency" and select "Monthly." Click on the X on the top right to return to the graph and then choose "Download" and then "Excel(data)" from the drop down.

a. Using the method presented in this chapter, move the data into an Excel spreadsheet.

b. Using the data from step a, prepare a chart. Use the Chart Wizard to properly label your axes.

2. In Web Exercise 1 you collected and graphed the Dow Jones Industrial Average. Now go to **www.forecasts.org**. Click on "Stock Market Forecast" and then on "Dow Jones Industrial Average" in the left column. Review the forecast in the graph.

a. What is the Dow forecast to be in six months?

b. What percentage increase is forecast for the next six months?

CHAPTER 2

Overview of the Financial System

> PREVIEW

Suppose that you want to start a business that manufactures a recently invented low-cost robot that cleans the house (even does windows), mows the lawn, and washes the car, but you have no funds to put this wonderful invention into production. Walter has plenty of savings that he has inherited. If you and Walter could get together so that he could provide you with the funds, your company's robot would see the light of day, and you, Walter, and the economy would all be better off: Walter could earn a high return on his investment, you would get rich from producing the robot, and we would have cleaner houses, shinier cars, and more beautiful lawns.

Financial markets (bond and stock markets) and financial intermediaries (banks, insurance companies, and pension funds) have the basic function of getting people such as you and Walter together by moving funds from those who have a surplus of funds (Walter) to those who have a shortage of funds (you). More realistically, when Apple invents a better iPad, it may require funds to bring it to market. Similarly, when a local government needs to build a road or a school, it may need more funds than local property taxes provide. Well-functioning financial markets and financial intermediaries are crucial to our economic health.

To study the effects of financial markets and financial intermediaries on the economy, we need to acquire an understanding of their general structure and operation. In this chapter we learn about the major financial intermediaries and the instruments that are traded in financial markets.

This chapter offers a preliminary overview of the fascinating study of financial markets and institutions. We will return to a more detailed treatment of the regulation, structure, and evolution of financial markets and institutions in Parts 3 through 7.

Function of Financial Markets

Financial markets perform the essential economic function of channeling funds from households, firms, and governments that have saved surplus funds by spending less than their income to those that have a shortage of funds because they wish to spend more than their income. This function is shown schematically in Figure 2.1. Those who have saved and are lending funds, the lender-savers, are at the left and those who must borrow funds to finance their spending, the borrower-spenders, are at the right. The principal lender-savers are households, but business enterprises and the government (particularly state and local government), as well as foreigners and their governments, sometimes also find themselves with excess funds and so lend them out. The most important borrower-spenders are businesses and the government (particularly the federal government), but households and foreigners also borrow to finance their purchases of cars, furniture, and houses. The arrows show that funds flow from lender-savers to borrower-spenders via two routes.

In *direct finance* (the route at the bottom of Figure 2.1), borrowers borrow funds directly from lenders in financial markets by selling them *securities* (also called *financial instruments*), which are claims on the borrower's future income or assets. Securities are assets for the person who buys them, but they are **liabilities**

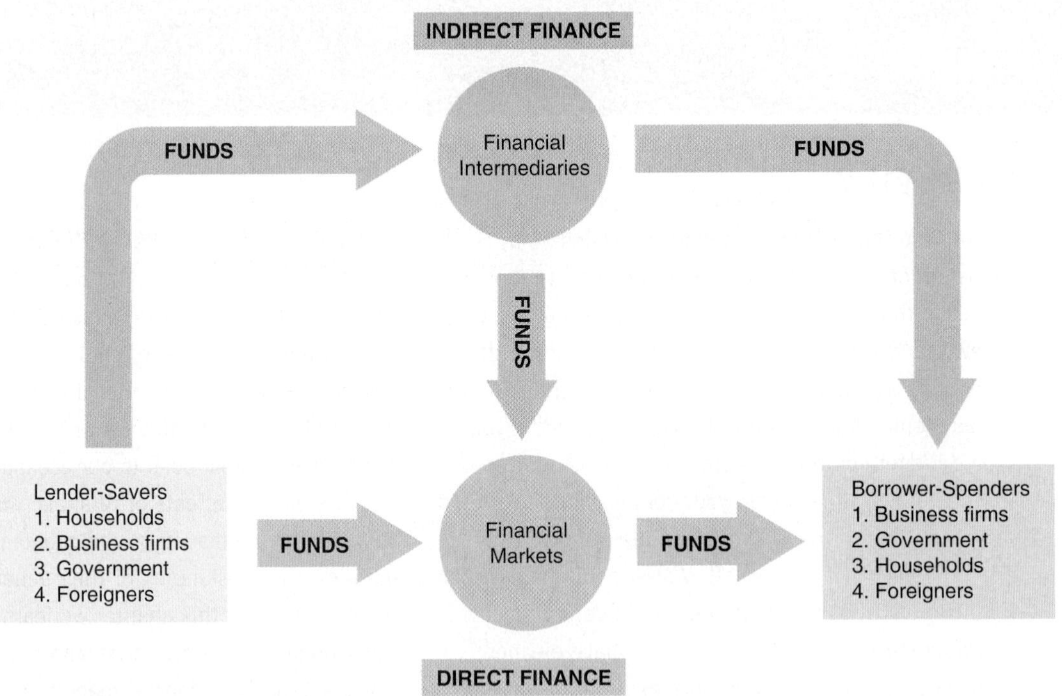

FIGURE 2.1 Flows of Funds Through the Financial System

The arrows show that funds flow from lender-savers to borrower-spenders via two routes: *direct finance*, in which borrowers borrow funds directly from financial markets by selling securities, and *indirect finance*, in which a financial intermediary borrows funds from lender-savers and then uses these funds to make loans to borrower-spenders.

(IOUs or debts) for the individual or firm that sells (issues) them. For example, if General Motors needs to borrow funds to pay for a new factory to manufacture electric cars, it might borrow the funds from savers by selling them a *bond*, a debt security that promises to make payments periodically for a specified period of time, or a *stock*, a security that entitles the owner to a share of the company's profits and assets.

Why is this channeling of funds from savers to spenders so important to the economy? The answer is that the people who save are frequently not the same people who have profitable investment opportunities available to them, the entrepreneurs. Let's first think about this on a personal level. Suppose that you have saved $1,000 this year, but no borrowing or lending is possible because no financial markets are available. If you do not have an investment opportunity that will permit you to earn income with your savings, you will just hold on to the $1,000 and will earn no interest. However, Carl the carpenter has a productive use for your $1,000: He can use it to purchase a new tool that will shorten the time it takes him to build a house, thereby earning an extra $200 per year. If you could get in touch with Carl, you could lend him the $1,000 at a rental fee (interest) of $100 per year, and both of you would be better off. You would earn $100 per year on your $1,000, instead of the zero amount that you would earn otherwise, while Carl would earn $100 more income per year (the $200 extra earnings per year minus the $100 rental fee for the use of the funds).

In the absence of financial markets, you and Carl the carpenter might never get together. You would both be stuck with the status quo, and both of you would be worse off. Without financial markets, it is hard to transfer funds from a person who has no investment opportunities to one who has them. Financial markets are thus essential to promoting economic efficiency.

The existence of financial markets is beneficial even if someone borrows for a purpose other than increasing production in a business. Say that you are recently married, have a good job, and want to buy a house. You earn a good salary, but because you have just started to work, you have not saved much. Over time, you would have no problem saving enough to buy the house of your dreams, but by then you would be too old to get full enjoyment from it. Without financial markets, you are stuck; you cannot buy the house and must continue to live in your tiny apartment.

If a financial market were set up so that people who had built up savings could lend you the funds to buy the house, you would be more than happy to pay them some interest so that you could own a home while you are still young enough to enjoy it. Then, over time, you would pay back your loan. If this loan could occur, you would be better off, as would the persons who made you the loan. They would now earn some interest, whereas they would not if the financial market did not exist.

Now we can see why financial markets have such an important function in the economy. They allow funds to move from people who lack productive investment opportunities to people who have such opportunities. Financial markets are critical for producing an efficient allocation of **capital** (wealth, either financial or physical, that is employed to produce more wealth), which contributes to higher production and efficiency for the overall economy. Indeed, as we will explore in Chapter 8, when financial markets break down during financial crises, as they did during the recent global financial crisis, severe economic hardship results, which can even lead to dangerous political instability.

Well-functioning financial markets also directly improve the well-being of consumers by allowing them to time their purchases better. They provide funds to young people to buy what they need and can eventually afford without forcing them to wait until they have saved up the entire purchase price. Financial markets that are operating efficiently improve the economic welfare of everyone in the society.

Structure of Financial Markets

Now that we understand the basic function of financial markets, let's look at their structure. The following descriptions of several categorizations of financial markets illustrate the essential features of these markets.

Debt and Equity Markets

A firm or an individual can obtain funds in a financial market in two ways. The most common method is to issue a debt instrument, such as a bond or a mortgage, which is a contractual agreement by the borrower to pay the holder of the instrument fixed dollar amounts at regular intervals (interest and principal payments) until a specified date (the maturity date), when a final payment is made. The **maturity** of a debt instrument is the number of years (term) until that instrument's expiration date. A debt instrument is **short-term** if its maturity is less than a year and **long-term** if its maturity is 10 years or longer. Debt instruments with a maturity between one and 10 years are said to be **intermediate-term**.

The second method of raising funds is by issuing **equities**, such as common stock, which are claims to share in the net income (income after expenses and taxes) and the assets of a business. If you own one share of common stock in a company that has issued one million shares, you are entitled to 1 one-millionth of the firm's net income and 1 one-millionth of the firm's assets. Equities often make periodic payments (**dividends**) to their holders and are considered long-term securities because they have no maturity date. In addition, owning stock means that you own a portion of the firm and thus have the right to vote on issues important to the firm and to elect its directors.

The main disadvantage of owning a corporation's equities rather than its debt is that an equity holder is a *residual claimant*; that is, the corporation must pay all its debt holders before it pays its equity holders. The advantage of holding equities is that equity holders benefit directly from any increases in the corporation's profitability or asset value because equities confer ownership rights on the equity holders. Debt holders do not share in this benefit because their dollar payments are fixed. We examine the pros and cons of debt versus equity instruments in more detail in Chapter 7, which provides an economic analysis of financial structure.

The total value of equities in the United States has typically fluctuated between $15 trillion and $40 trillion since 2000, depending on the prices of shares. Although the average person is more aware of the stock market than any other financial market, the size of the debt market is often substantially larger than the size of the equities market: At the end of 2015, the value of debt instruments was $39.7 trillion, while the value of equities was $25.1 trillion.

Primary and Secondary Markets

A **primary market** is a financial market in which new issues of a security, such as a bond or a stock, are sold to initial buyers by the corporation or government agency borrowing the funds. A **secondary market** is a financial market in which securities that have been previously issued can be resold.

GO ONLINE
www.nyse.com
Access the New York Stock Exchange. Find listed companies, quotes, company historical data, real-time market indexes, and more.

The primary markets for securities are not well known to the public because the selling of securities to initial buyers often takes place behind closed doors. An important financial institution that assists in the initial sale of securities in the primary market is the **investment bank**. It does this by **underwriting** securities: It guarantees a price for a corporation's securities and then sells them to the public.

The New York Stock Exchange and NASDAQ (National Association of Securities Dealers Automated Quotation System), in which previously issued stocks are traded, are the best-known examples of secondary markets, although the bond markets, in which previously issued bonds of major corporations and the U.S. government are bought and sold, actually have a larger trading volume. Other examples of secondary markets are foreign exchange markets, futures markets, and options markets. Securities brokers and dealers are crucial to a well-functioning secondary market. **Brokers** are agents of investors who match buyers with sellers of securities; **dealers** link buyers and sellers by buying and selling securities at stated prices.

When an individual buys a security in the secondary market, the person who has sold the security receives money in exchange for the security, but the corporation that issued the security acquires no new funds. A corporation acquires new funds only when its securities are first sold in the primary market. Nonetheless, secondary markets serve two important functions. First, they make it easier and quicker to sell these financial instruments to raise cash; that is, they make the financial instruments more **liquid**. The increased liquidity of these instruments then makes them more desirable and thus easier for the issuing firm to sell in the primary market. Second, they determine the price of the security that the issuing firm sells in the primary market. The investors who buy securities in the primary market will pay the issuing corporation no more than the price they think the secondary market will set for this security. The higher the security's price in the secondary market, the higher the price that the issuing firm will receive for a new security in the primary market, and hence the greater the amount of financial capital it can raise. Conditions in the secondary market are therefore the most relevant to corporations issuing securities. For this reason books like this one, which deal with financial markets, focus on the behavior of secondary markets rather than primary markets.

Exchanges and Over-the-Counter Markets

GO ONLINE
www.nasdaq.com
Access detailed market and security information for the NASDAQ OTC stock exchange.

Secondary markets can be organized in two ways. One method is to organize **exchanges**, where buyers and sellers of securities (or their agents or brokers) meet in one central location to conduct trades. The New York and American Stock Exchanges for stocks and the Chicago Board of Trade for commodities (wheat, corn, silver, and other raw materials) are examples of organized exchanges.

The other method of organizing a secondary market is to have an **over-the-counter (OTC) market**, in which dealers at different locations who have an inventory of securities stand ready to buy and sell securities "over the counter" to anyone who comes to them and is willing to accept their prices. Because over-the-counter dealers are in contact via computers and know the prices set by one another, the OTC market is very competitive and not very different from a market with an organized exchange.

Many common stocks are traded over the counter, although a majority of the largest corporations have their shares traded at organized stock exchanges. The U.S. government bond market, with a larger trading volume than the New York Stock Exchange, by contrast, is set up as an over-the-counter market. Forty or so dealers establish a "market" in these securities by standing ready to buy and sell

U.S. government bonds. Other over-the-counter markets include those that trade other types of financial instruments such as negotiable certificates of deposit, federal funds, banker's acceptances, and foreign exchange.

Money and Capital Markets

Another way of distinguishing between markets is on the basis of the maturity of the securities traded in each market. The **money market** is a financial market in which only short-term debt instruments (generally those with original maturity of less than one year) are traded; the **capital market** is the market in which longer-term debt (generally with original maturity of one year or greater) and equity instruments are traded. Money market securities are usually more widely traded than longer-term securities and so tend to be more liquid. In addition, as we will see in Chapter 3, short-term securities have smaller fluctuations in prices than long-term securities, making them safer investments. As a result, corporations and banks actively use the money market to earn interest on surplus funds that they expect to have only temporarily. Capital market securities, such as stocks and long-term bonds, are often held by financial intermediaries such as insurance companies and pension funds, which have little uncertainty about the amount of funds they will have available in the future.

Internationalization of Financial Markets

The growing internationalization of financial markets has become an important trend. Before the 1980s, U.S. financial markets were much larger than those outside the United States, but in recent years the dominance of U.S. markets has been disappearing. (See the Global box, "Are U.S. Capital Markets Losing Their Edge?") The extraordinary growth of foreign financial markets has been the result of both large increases in the pool of savings in foreign countries such as Japan and the deregulation of foreign financial markets, which has enabled foreign markets to expand their activities. American corporations and banks are now more likely to tap international capital markets to raise needed funds, and American investors often seek investment opportunities abroad. Similarly, foreign corporations and banks raise funds from Americans, and foreigners have become important investors in the United States. A look at international bond markets and world stock markets will give us a picture of how this globalization of financial markets is taking place.

International Bond Market, Eurobonds, and Eurocurrencies

The traditional instruments in the international bond market are known as foreign bonds. **Foreign bonds** are sold in a foreign country and are denominated in that country's currency. For example, if the German automaker Porsche sells a bond in the United States denominated in U.S. dollars, it is classified as a foreign bond. Foreign bonds have been an important instrument in the international capital market for centuries. In fact, a large percentage of U.S. railroads built in the nineteenth century were financed by sales of foreign bonds in Britain.

A more recent innovation in the international bond market is the **Eurobond**, a bond denominated in a currency other than that of the country in which it is

> GLOBAL

Are U.S. Capital Markets Losing Their Edge?

Over the past few decades the United States lost its international dominance in a number of manufacturing industries, including automobiles and consumer electronics, as other countries became more competitive in global markets. Recent evidence suggests that financial markets now are undergoing a similar trend: Just as Ford and General Motors have lost global market share to Toyota and Honda, U.S. stock and bond markets recently have seen their share of sales of newly issued corporate securities slip. The London and Hong Kong stock exchanges now handle a larger share of initial public offerings (IPOs) of stock than does the New York Stock Exchange, which had been by far the dominant exchange in terms of IPO value before 2000. Furthermore, the number of stocks listed on U.S. exchanges has been falling, while stock listings abroad have been growing rapidly: Listings outside the United States are now about ten times greater than those in the United States. Likewise, the portion of new corporate bonds issued worldwide that are initially sold in U.S. capital markets has fallen below the share sold in European debt markets.

Why do corporations that issue new securities to raise capital now conduct more of this business in financial markets in Europe and Asia than in the United States? Among the factors contributing to this trend are quicker adoption of technological innovation by foreign financial markets, tighter immigration controls in the United States following the terrorist attacks in 2001, and perceptions that listing on American exchanges will expose foreign securities issuers to greater risks of lawsuits. Many people see burdensome financial regulation as the main cause, however, and point specifically to the Sarbanes-Oxley Act of 2002. Congress passed this act after a number of accounting scandals involving U.S. corporations and the accounting firms that audited them came to light. Sarbanes-Oxley aims to strengthen the integrity of the auditing process and the quality of information provided in corporate financial statements. The costs to corporations of complying with the new rules and procedures are high, especially for smaller firms, but largely avoidable if firms choose to issue their securities in financial markets outside the United States. For this reason, there is much support for revising Sarbanes-Oxley to lessen its alleged harmful effects and induce more securities issuers back to U.S. financial markets. However, evidence is not conclusive to support the view that Sarbanes-Oxley is the main cause of the relative decline of U.S. financial markets and therefore in need of reform.

Discussion of the relative decline of U.S. financial markets and debate about the factors that are contributing to it likely will continue. Chapter 7 provides more detail on the Sarbanes-Oxley Act and its effects on the U.S. financial system.

sold—for example, a bond denominated in U.S. dollars sold in London. Currently, over 80% of the new issues in the international bond market are Eurobonds, and the market for these securities has grown very rapidly. As a result, the Eurobond market is now larger than the U.S. corporate bond market.

A variant of the Eurobond is **Eurocurrencies**, which are foreign currencies deposited in banks outside the home country. The most important of the Eurocurrencies are **Eurodollars**, which are U.S. dollars deposited in foreign banks outside the United States or in foreign branches of U.S. banks. Because these short-term deposits earn interest, they are similar to short-term Eurobonds. American banks borrow Eurodollar deposits from other banks or from their own foreign branches, and Eurodollars are now an important source of funds for American banks. Note that the euro, the currency used by countries in the European Monetary System, can create some confusion about the terms *Eurobond*, *Eurocurrencies*, and *Eurodollars*. A bond denominated in euros is called a Eurobond only *if it is sold outside the countries that have adopted the euro*. In fact, most Eurobonds are not denominated in euros but are instead denominated in U.S. dollars. Similarly, Eurodollars have nothing to do with euros, but are instead U.S. dollars deposited in banks outside the United States.

World Stock Markets

www.stockcharts.com
This site contains historical stock market index charts for many countries around the world.

Until recently, the U.S. stock market was by far the largest in the world, but foreign stock markets have been growing in importance, with the United States not always number one. The increased interest in foreign stocks has prompted the development in the United States of mutual funds that specialize in trading in foreign stock markets. American investors now pay attention not only to the Dow Jones Industrial Average but also to stock price indexes for foreign stock markets such as the Nikkei 300 Average (Tokyo) and the Financial Times Stock Exchange (FTSE) 100-Share Index (London).

http://quote.yahoo.com/m2?u
Access major world stock indexes, with charts, news, and components.

The internationalization of financial markets is having profound effects on the United States. Foreigners, particularly Chinese investors, not only are providing funds to corporations in the United States but also are helping finance the federal government. Without these foreign funds, the U.S. economy would have grown far less rapidly in the past 20 years. The internationalization of financial markets is also leading the way to a more integrated world economy in which flows of goods and technology between countries are more commonplace. In later chapters, we will encounter many examples of the important roles that international factors play in our economy (see the Following the Financial News box).

Function of Financial Intermediaries: Indirect Finance

As shown in Figure 2.1 (p. 16), funds also can move from lenders to borrowers by a second route called *indirect finance* because it involves a financial intermediary that stands between the lender-savers and the borrower-spenders and helps transfer funds from one to the other. A financial intermediary does this by borrowing funds from the lender-savers and then using these funds to make loans to borrower-spenders. For example, a bank might acquire funds by issuing a liability to the public (an asset for the public) in the form of savings deposits. It might then use the funds to acquire an asset by making a loan to General Motors or by buying a U.S. Treasury bond in the financial market. The ultimate result is that funds have been transferred from the public (the lender-savers) to General Motors or the U.S. Treasury (the borrower-spender) with the help of the financial intermediary (the bank).

The process of indirect finance using financial intermediaries, called **financial intermediation**, is the primary route for moving funds from lenders to borrowers. Indeed, although the media focus much of their attention on securities markets, particularly the stock market, financial intermediaries are a far more important source of financing for corporations than securities markets are. This is true not only for the United States but also for other industrialized countries (see the Global box). Why are financial intermediaries and indirect finance so important in financial markets? To answer this question, we need to understand the role of transaction costs, risk sharing, and information costs in financial markets.

> FOLLOWING THE FINANCIAL NEWS

Foreign Stock Market Indexes

Foreign stock market indexes are published daily in newspapers and Internet sites such as www.finance.yahoo.com.

The most important of these stock market indexes are:

Dow Jones Industrial Average (DJIA) An index of the 30 largest publicly traded corporations in the United States maintained by the Dow Jones Corporation.

S&P 500 An index of 500 of the largest companies traded in the United States maintained by Standard & Poor's.

Nasdaq Composite An index for all the stocks that trade on the Nasdaq stock market, where most of the technology stocks in the United States are traded.

FTSE 100 An index of the 100 most highly capitalized UK companies listed on the London Stock Exchange.

DAX An index of the 30 largest German companies trading on the Frankfurt Stock Exchange.

CAC 40 An index of the largest 40 French companies traded on Euronext Paris.

Hang Seng An index of the largest companies traded on the Hong Kong stock markets.

Strait Times An index of the largest 30 companies traded on the Singapore Exchange.

> GLOBAL

The Importance of Financial Intermediaries Relative to Securities Markets: An International Comparison

Patterns of financing corporations differ across countries, but one key fact emerges: Studies of the major developed countries, including the United States, Canada, the United Kingdom, Japan, Italy, Germany, and France, show that when businesses go looking for funds to finance their activities, they usually obtain them indirectly through financial intermediaries and not directly from securities markets.* Even in the United States and Canada, which have the most developed securities markets in the world, loans from financial intermediaries are far more important for corporate finance than securities markets are. The countries that have made the least use of securities markets are Germany and Japan; in these two countries, financing from financial intermediaries has been almost 10 times greater than that from securities markets. However, after the deregulation of Japanese securities markets in recent years, the share of corporate financing by financial intermediaries has been declining relative to the use of securities markets.

Although the dominance of financial intermediaries over securities markets is clear in all countries, the relative importance of bond versus stock markets differs widely across countries. In the United States the bond market is far more important as a source of corporate finance: On average, the amount of new financing raised using bonds is 10 times the amount raised using stocks. By contrast, countries such as France and Italy make more use of equities markets than of the bond market to raise capital.

* See, for example, Colin Mayer, "Financial Systems, Corporate Finance, and Economic Development," in *Asymmetric Information, Corporate Finance, and Investment*, ed. R. Glenn Hubbard (Chicago: University of Chicago Press, 1990), pp. 307–332.

Transaction Costs

Transaction costs, the time and money spent in carrying out financial transactions, are a major problem for people who have excess funds to lend. As we have seen, Carl the carpenter needs $1,000 for his new tool, and you know that it is an excellent investment opportunity. You have the cash and would like to lend him the money, but to protect your investment, you have to hire a lawyer to write up the loan contract that specifies how much interest Carl will pay you, when he will make these interest payments, and when he will repay you the $1,000. Obtaining the contract will cost you $500. When you figure in this transaction cost for making the loan, you realize that you can't earn enough from the deal (you spend $500 to make perhaps $100) and reluctantly tell Carl that he will have to look elsewhere.

This example illustrates that small savers like you or potential borrowers like Carl might be frozen out of financial markets and thus be unable to benefit from them. Can anyone come to the rescue? Financial intermediaries can.

Financial intermediaries can substantially reduce transaction costs because they have developed expertise in lowering them and because their large size allows them to take advantage of **economies of scale**, the reduction in transaction costs per dollar of transactions as the size (scale) of transactions increases. For example, a bank knows how to find a good lawyer to produce an airtight loan contract, and this contract can be used over and over again in its loan transactions, thus lowering the legal cost per transaction. Instead of a loan contract (which may not be all that well written) costing $500, a bank can hire a topflight lawyer for $5,000 to draw up an airtight loan contract that can be used for 2,000 loans at a cost of $2.50 per loan. At a cost of $2.50 per loan, it now becomes profitable for the financial intermediary to lend Carl the $1,000.

Because financial intermediaries are able to reduce transaction costs substantially, they make it possible for you to provide funds indirectly to people like Carl with productive investment opportunities. In addition, a financial intermediary's low transaction costs mean that it can provide its customers with **liquidity services**, services that make it easier for customers to conduct transactions. For example, banks provide depositors with checking accounts that enable them to pay their bills easily. In addition, depositors can earn interest on checking and savings accounts and yet still convert them into goods and services whenever necessary.

Risk Sharing

Another benefit made possible by the low transaction costs of financial institutions is that they can help reduce the exposure of investors to **risk**—that is, uncertainty about the returns investors will earn on assets. Financial intermediaries do this through the process known as **risk sharing**: They create and sell assets with risk characteristics that people are comfortable with, and the intermediaries then use the funds they acquire by selling these assets to purchase other assets that may have far more risk. Low transaction costs allow financial intermediaries to share risk at low cost, enabling them to earn a profit on the spread between the returns they earn on risky assets and the payments they make on the assets they have sold. This process of risk sharing is also sometimes referred to as **asset transformation** because, in a sense, risky assets are turned into safer assets for investors.

Financial intermediaries also promote risk sharing by helping individuals to diversify and thereby lower the amount of risk to which they are exposed. **Diversification** entails investing in a collection (**portfolio**) of assets whose returns do not always move together, with the result that overall risk is lower than for individual assets. (Diversification is just another name for the old adage, "You shouldn't put all your eggs in one basket.") Low transaction costs allow financial intermediaries to do this by pooling a collection of assets into a new asset and then selling it to individuals.

Asymmetric Information: Adverse Selection and Moral Hazard

The presence of transaction costs in financial markets explains, in part, why financial intermediaries and indirect finance play such an important role in financial markets. An additional reason is that in financial markets, one party often does not know enough about the other party to make accurate decisions. This inequality is called **asymmetric information**. For example, a borrower who takes out a loan usually has better information about the potential returns and risks associated with the investment projects for which the funds are earmarked than the lender does. Lack of information creates problems in the financial system both before and after the transaction is entered into.[1]

Adverse selection is the problem created by asymmetric information *before* the transaction occurs. Adverse selection in financial markets occurs when the potential borrowers who are the most likely to produce an undesirable (*adverse*) outcome—the bad credit risks—are the ones who most actively seek out a loan and are thus most likely to be selected. Because adverse selection makes it more likely that loans might be made to bad credit risks, lenders may decide not to make any loans even though good credit risks exist in the marketplace.

To understand why adverse selection occurs, suppose that you have two aunts to whom you might make a loan—Aunt Louise and Aunt Sheila. Aunt Louise is a conservative type who borrows only when she has an investment she is quite sure will pay off. Aunt Sheila, by contrast, is an inveterate gambler who has just come across a get-rich-quick scheme that will make her a millionaire if she can just borrow $1,000 to invest in it. Unfortunately, as with most get-rich-quick schemes, the probability is high that the investment won't pay off and that Aunt Sheila will lose the $1,000.

Which of your aunts is more likely to call you to ask for a loan? Aunt Sheila, of course, because she has so much to gain if the investment pays off. You, however, would not want to make a loan to her because the probability is high that her investment will turn sour and she will be unable to pay you back.

If you knew both your aunts very well—that is, if your information were not asymmetric—you wouldn't have a problem because you would know that Aunt Sheila is a bad risk and so you would not lend to her. Suppose, though, that you don't know your aunts well. You are more likely to lend to Aunt Sheila than to Aunt Louise because Aunt Sheila would be hounding you for the loan. Because of the possibility of adverse selection, you might decide not to lend to either of your aunts, even though there are times when Aunt Louise, who is an excellent credit risk, might need a loan for a worthwhile investment.

Moral hazard is the problem created by asymmetric information *after* the transaction occurs. Moral hazard in financial markets is the risk (*hazard*) that the borrower might engage in activities that are undesirable (*immoral*) from the lender's point of view because they make it less likely that the loan will be paid back. Because moral hazard lowers the probability that the loan will be repaid, lenders may decide that they would rather not make a loan.

As an example of moral hazard, suppose that you made a $1,000 loan to another relative, Uncle Melvin, who needs the money to purchase a computer so that he can

---

[1]Asymmetric information and the adverse selection and moral hazard concepts are also crucial problems for the insurance industry. See Chapter 21.

set up a business typing students' term papers. Once you have made the loan, however, Uncle Melvin is more likely to slip off to the track and play the horses. If he bets on a 20-to-1 long shot and wins with your money, he is able to pay back your $1,000 and live high off the hog with the remaining $19,000. But if he loses, as is likely, you don't get paid back, and all he has lost is his reputation as a reliable, upstanding uncle. Uncle Melvin therefore has an incentive to go to the track because his gains ($19,000) if he bets correctly are much greater than the cost to him (his reputation) if he bets incorrectly. If you knew what Uncle Melvin was up to, you would prevent him from going to the track, and he would not be able to increase the moral hazard. However, because it is hard for you to keep informed about his whereabouts—that is, because information is asymmetric—there is a good chance that Uncle Melvin will go to the track and you will not get paid back. The risk of moral hazard might therefore discourage you from making the $1,000 loan to Uncle Melvin, even if you were sure that you would be paid back if he used it to set up his business.

The problems created by adverse selection and moral hazard are significant impediments to well-functioning financial markets. Again, financial intermediaries can alleviate these problems.

With financial intermediaries in the economy, small savers can provide their funds to the financial markets by lending these funds to a trustworthy intermediary—say, the Honest John Bank—which in turn lends the funds out either by making loans or by buying securities such as stocks or bonds. Successful financial intermediaries have higher earnings on their investments than do small savers because they are better equipped than individuals to screen out bad credit risks from good ones, thereby reducing losses due to adverse selection. In addition, financial intermediaries have high earnings because they develop expertise in monitoring the parties they lend to, thus reducing losses due to moral hazard. The result is that financial intermediaries can afford to pay lender-savers interest or provide substantial services and still earn a profit.

As we have seen, financial intermediaries play an important role in the economy because they provide liquidity services, promote risk sharing, and solve information problems, thereby allowing small savers and borrowers to benefit from the existence of financial markets. The success of financial intermediaries in performing this role is evidenced by the fact that most Americans invest their savings with them and obtain loans from them. Financial intermediaries play a key role in improving economic efficiency because they help financial markets channel funds from lender-savers to people with productive investment opportunities. Without a well-functioning set of financial intermediaries, it is very hard for an economy to reach its full potential. We will explore further the role of financial intermediaries in the economy in Parts 5 and 6.

Economies of Scope and Conflicts of Interest

Another reason why financial intermediaries play such an important role in the economy is that by providing multiple financial services to their customers, such as offering them bank loans or selling their bonds for them, they can also achieve **economies of scope**; that is, they can lower the cost of information production for each service by applying one information resource to many different services. An investment bank, for example, can evaluate how good a credit risk a corporation is when making a loan to the firm, which then helps the bank decide whether it would be easy to sell the bonds of this corporation to the public.

Although the presence of economies of scope may substantially benefit financial institutions, it also creates potential costs in terms of **conflicts of interest**. Conflicts of interest are a type of moral hazard problem that arises when a person or institution has multiple objectives (interests) and, as a result, has conflicts between those objectives. Conflicts of interest are especially likely to occur when a financial institution provides multiple services. The potentially competing interests of those services may lead an individual or firm to conceal information or disseminate misleading information. We care about conflicts of interest because a substantial reduction in the quality of information in financial markets increases asymmetric information problems and prevents financial markets from channeling funds into the most productive investment opportunities. Consequently, the financial markets and the economy become less efficient. We will discuss conflicts of interest in financial markets in more detail in Parts 3 and 6.

Types of Financial Intermediaries

We have seen why financial intermediaries have such an important function in the economy. Now we look at the principal financial intermediaries themselves and how they perform the intermediation function. They fall into three categories: depository institutions (banks), contractual savings institutions, and investment intermediaries. Table 2.1 provides a guide to the discussion of the financial intermediaries that fit into these three categories by describing their primary liabilities (sources of funds) and assets (uses of funds). The relative size of these intermediaries in the United States is indicated in Table 2.2, which lists the amounts of their assets at the end of 1990, 2000, 2010, and 2015.

Depository Institutions

Depository institutions (for simplicity, we refer to these as *banks* throughout this text) are financial intermediaries that accept deposits from individuals and institutions and make loans. These institutions include commercial banks and the so-called **thrift institutions (thrifts)**: savings and loan associations, mutual savings banks, and credit unions.

Commercial Banks These financial intermediaries raise funds primarily by issuing checkable deposits (deposits on which checks can be written), savings deposits (deposits that are payable on demand but do not allow their owner to write checks), and time deposits (deposits with fixed terms to maturity). They then use these funds to make commercial, consumer, and mortgage loans and to buy U.S. government securities and municipal bonds. Around 5,000 commercial banks are found in the United States, and as a group, they are the largest financial intermediary and have the most diversified portfolios (collections) of assets.

Savings and Loan Associations (S&Ls) and Mutual Savings Banks These depository institutions, of which there are approximately 900, obtain funds primarily through savings deposits (often called *shares*) and time and checkable deposits. In the past, these institutions were constrained in their activities and mostly made mortgage loans for residential housing. Over time, these restrictions have been

TABLE 2.1 Primary Assets and Liabilities of Financial Intermediaries

Type of Intermediary	Primary Liabilities (Sources of Funds)	Primary Assets (Uses of Funds)
Depository institutions (banks)		
Commercial banks	Deposits	Business and consumer loans, mortgages, U.S. government securities, and municipal bonds
Savings and loan associations	Deposits	Mortgages
Mutual savings banks	Deposits	Mortgages
Credit unions	Deposits	Consumer loans
Contractual savings institutions		
Life insurance companies	Premiums from policies	Corporate bonds and mortgages
Fire and casualty insurance companies	Premiums from policies	Municipal bonds, corporate bonds and stock, and U.S. government securities
Pension funds, government retirement funds	Employer and employee contributions	Corporate bonds and stock
Investment intermediaries		
Finance companies	Commercial paper, stocks, bonds	Consumer and business loans
Mutual funds	Shares	Stocks, bonds
Money market mutual funds	Shares	Money market instruments
Hedge funds	Partnership participation	Stocks, bonds, loans, foreign currencies, and many other assets

loosened so the distinction between these depository institutions and commercial banks has blurred. These intermediaries have become more alike and are now more competitive with each other.

Credit Unions These financial institutions, numbering about 7,000, are typically very small cooperative lending institutions organized around a particular group: union members, employees of a particular firm, and so forth. They acquire funds from deposits called *shares* and primarily make consumer loans.

Contractual Savings Institutions

Contractual savings institutions, such as insurance companies and pension funds, are financial intermediaries that acquire funds at periodic intervals on a contractual basis. Because they can predict with reasonable accuracy how much they will have to pay out in benefits in the coming years, they do not have to worry as much as

TABLE 2.2 Principal Financial Intermediaries and Value of Their Assets

	Value of Assets ($ billions, end of year)			
Type of Intermediary	**1990**	**2000**	**2010**	**2015**
Depository institutions (banks)				
Commercial banks, savings and loans, and mutual savings banks	4,779	7,687	15,580	17,368
Credit unions	215	441	912	1,146
Contractual savings institutions				
Life insurance companies	1,367	3,136	5,176	6,350
Fire and casualty insurance companies	533	862	1,242	1,591
Pension funds (private)	1,629	4,355	4,527	8,517
State and local government retirement funds	737	2,293	2,661	5,641
Investment intermediaries				
Finance companies	610	1,140	1,439	1,474
Mutual funds	654	4,435	7,935	12,843
Money market mutual funds	498	1,812	2,755	2,716

Source: Federal Reserve Flow of Funds Accounts: https://www.federalreserve.gov/releases/z1/current/data.htm, Tables L110, L114, L115, L116, L118, L120, L121, L122, L127.

depository institutions about losing funds quickly. As a result, the liquidity of assets is not as important a consideration for them as it is for depository institutions, and they tend to invest their funds primarily in long-term securities such as corporate bonds, stocks, and mortgages.

Life Insurance Companies Life insurance companies insure people against financial hazards following a death and sell annuities (annual income payments upon retirement). They acquire funds from the premiums that people pay to keep their policies in force and use them mainly to buy corporate bonds and mortgages. They also purchase stocks but are restricted in the amount that they can hold. Currently, with $6.4 trillion in assets, they are among the largest of the contractual savings institutions.

Fire and Casualty Insurance Companies These companies insure their policyholders against loss from theft, fire, and accidents. They are very much like life insurance companies, receiving funds through premiums for their policies, but they have a greater possibility of loss of funds if major disasters occur. For this reason, they use their funds to buy more liquid assets than life insurance companies do. Their largest holding of assets consists of municipal bonds; they also hold corporate bonds and stocks and U.S. government securities.

Pension Funds and Government Retirement Funds Private pension funds and state and local retirement funds provide retirement income in the form of annuities to employees who are covered by a pension plan. Funds are acquired by contributions from employers and from employees, who either have a contribution automatically deducted from their paychecks or contribute voluntarily. The largest asset holdings of pension funds are corporate bonds and stocks. The establishment of pension funds has been actively encouraged by the federal government, both through legislation requiring pension plans and through tax incentives to encourage contributions.

Investment Intermediaries

This category of financial intermediaries includes finance companies, mutual funds, money market mutual funds, and investment banks.

Finance Companies Finance companies raise funds by selling commercial paper (a short-term debt instrument) and by issuing stocks and bonds. They lend these funds to consumers (who make purchases of such items as furniture, automobiles, and home improvements) and to small businesses. Some finance companies are organized by a parent corporation to help sell its product. For example, Ford Motor Credit Company makes loans to consumers who purchase Ford automobiles.

Mutual Funds These financial intermediaries acquire funds by selling shares to many individuals and use the proceeds to purchase diversified portfolios of stocks and bonds. Mutual funds allow shareholders to pool their resources so that they can take advantage of lower transaction costs when buying large blocks of stocks or bonds. In addition, mutual funds allow shareholders to hold more diversified portfolios than they otherwise would. Shareholders can sell (redeem) shares at any time, but the value of these shares will be determined by the value of the mutual fund's holdings of securities. Because these fluctuate greatly, the value of mutual fund shares does, too; therefore, investments in mutual funds can be risky.

Money Market Mutual Funds These financial institutions have the characteristics of a mutual fund but also function to some extent as a depository institution because they offer deposit-type accounts. Like most mutual funds, they sell shares to acquire funds that are then used to buy money market instruments that are both safe and very liquid. The interest on these assets is paid out to the shareholders.

A key feature of these funds is that shareholders can write checks against the value of their shareholdings. In effect, shares in a money market mutual fund function like checking account deposits that pay interest. Money market mutual funds have experienced extraordinary growth since 1971, when they first appeared. By the end of 2015, their assets had climbed to nearly $2.7 trillion.

Hedge Funds Hedge funds are a type of mutual fund with special characteristics. Hedge funds are organized as limited partnerships with minimum investments ranging from $100,000 to, more typically, $1 million or more. These limitations mean that hedge funds are subject to much weaker regulation than other mutual funds. Hedge funds invest in many types of assets, with some specializing in stocks, others in bonds, others in foreign currencies, and still others in far more exotic assets.

Investment Banks Despite its name, an investment bank is not a bank or a financial intermediary in the ordinary sense; that is, it does not take in deposits and then lend them out. Instead, an investment bank is a different type of intermediary that helps a corporation issue securities. First it advises the corporation on which type of securities to issue (stocks or bonds); then it helps sell (underwrite) the securities by purchasing them from the corporation at a predetermined price and reselling them in the market. Investment banks also act as deal makers and earn enormous fees by helping corporations acquire other companies through mergers or acquisitions.

Regulation of the Financial System

www.sec.gov
Access the United States Securities and Exchange Commission home page. It contains vast SEC resources, laws and regulations, investor information, and litigation.

The financial system is among the most heavily regulated sectors of the American economy. The government regulates financial markets for two main reasons: to increase the information available to investors and to ensure the soundness of the financial system. We will examine how these two reasons have led to the present regulatory environment. As a study aid, the principal regulatory agencies of the U.S. financial system are listed in Table 2.3.

TABLE 2.3 Principal Regulatory Agencies of the U.S. Financial System

Regulatory Agency	Subject of Regulation	Nature of Regulations
Securities and Exchange Commission (SEC)	Organized exchanges and financial markets	Requires disclosure of information; restricts insider trading
Commodities Futures Trading Commission (CFTC)	Futures market exchanges	Regulates procedures for trading in futures markets
Office of the Comptroller of the Currency	Federally chartered commercial banks and thrift institutions	Charters and examines the books of federally chartered commercial banks and thrift institutions; imposes restrictions on assets they can hold
National Credit Union Administration (NCUA)	Federally chartered credit unions	Charters and examines the books of federally chartered credit unions and imposes restrictions on assets they can hold
State banking and insurance commissions	State-chartered depository institutions	Charter and examine the books of state-chartered banks and insurance companies; impose restrictions on assets they can hold; and impose restrictions on branching
Federal Deposit Insurance Corporation (FDIC)	Commercial banks, mutual savings banks, savings and loan associations	Provides insurance of up to $250,000 for each depositor at a bank; examines the books of insured banks; and imposes restrictions on assets they can hold
Federal Reserve System	All depository institutions	Examines the books of commercial banks that are members of the system; sets reserve requirements for all banks

Increasing Information Available to Investors

Asymmetric information in financial markets means that investors may be subject to adverse selection and moral hazard problems that may hinder the efficient operation of financial markets. Risky firms or outright crooks may be the most eager to sell securities to unwary investors, and the resulting adverse selection problem may keep investors out of financial markets. Furthermore, once an investor has bought a security, thereby lending money to a firm, the borrower may have incentives to engage in risky activities or to commit outright fraud. The presence of this moral hazard problem may also keep investors away from financial markets. Government regulation can reduce adverse selection and moral hazard problems in financial markets and enhance the efficiency of the markets by increasing the amount of information available to investors.

As a result of the stock market crash in 1929 and revelations of widespread fraud in the aftermath, political demands for regulation culminated in the Securities Act of 1933 and the establishment of the Securities and Exchange Commission (SEC). The SEC requires corporations issuing securities to disclose certain information about their sales, assets, and earnings to the public and restricts trading by the largest stockholders (known as *insiders*) in the corporation. By requiring disclosure of this information and by discouraging insider trading, which could be used to manipulate security prices, the SEC hopes that investors will be better informed and protected from some of the abuses in financial markets that occurred before 1933. Indeed, in recent years, the SEC has been particularly active in prosecuting people involved in insider trading.

Ensuring the Soundness of Financial Intermediaries

Asymmetric information can lead to the widespread collapse of financial intermediaries, referred to as a **financial panic**. Because providers of funds to financial intermediaries may not be able to assess whether the institutions holding their funds are sound, if they have doubts about the overall health of financial intermediaries, they may want to pull their funds out of both sound and unsound institutions. The possible outcome is a financial panic that produces large losses for the public and causes serious damage to the economy. To protect the public and the economy from financial panics, the government has implemented six types of regulations.

Restrictions on Entry State banking and insurance commissions, as well as the Office of the Comptroller of the Currency (an agency of the federal government), have created tight regulations governing who is allowed to set up a financial intermediary. Individuals or groups that want to establish a financial intermediary, such as a bank or an insurance company, must obtain a charter from the state or the federal government. Only if they appear to be upstanding citizens with impeccable credentials and a large amount of initial funds will they be given a charter.

Disclosure Reporting requirements for financial intermediaries are stringent. Their bookkeeping must follow certain strict principles, their books are subject to periodic inspection, and they must make certain information available to the public.

Restrictions on Assets and Activities Financial intermediaries are restricted in what they are allowed to do and what assets they can hold. Before you put funds into a bank or some other such institution, you would want to know that your funds are safe and that the bank or other financial intermediary will be able to meet its obligations to you. One way of doing this is to restrict the financial intermediary from engaging in certain risky activities. Legislation passed in 1933 (repealed in 1999) separated commercial banking from the securities industry so that banks could not engage in risky ventures associated with this industry. Another way to limit a financial intermediary's risky behavior is to restrict it from holding certain risky assets, or at least from holding a greater quantity of these risky assets than is prudent. For example, commercial banks and other depository institutions are not allowed to hold common stock because stock prices experience substantial fluctuations. Insurance companies are allowed to hold common stock, but their holdings cannot exceed a certain fraction of their total assets.

Deposit Insurance The government can insure people's deposits so that they do not suffer great financial loss if the financial intermediary that holds these deposits should fail. The most important government agency that provides this type of insurance is the Federal Deposit Insurance Corporation (FDIC), which insures each depositor at a commercial bank, savings and loan association, or mutual savings bank up to a loss of $250,000 per account. Premiums paid by these financial intermediaries go into the FDIC's Deposit Insurance Fund, which is used to pay off depositors if an institution fails. The FDIC was created in 1934 after the massive bank failures of 1930–1933, in which the savings of many depositors at commercial banks were wiped out. The National Credit Union Share Insurance Fund (NCUSIF) provides similar insurance protection for deposits (shares) at credit unions.

Limits on Competition Politicians have often declared that unbridled competition among financial intermediaries promotes failures that will harm the public. Although the evidence that competition does indeed have this effect is extremely weak, state and federal governments at times have imposed restrictions on the opening of additional locations (branches). In the past, banks were not allowed to open branches in other states, and in some states, banks were restricted from opening branches in additional locations.

Restrictions on Interest Rates Competition has also been inhibited by regulations that impose restrictions on interest rates that can be paid on deposits. For decades after 1933, banks were prohibited from paying interest on checking accounts. In addition, until 1986, the Federal Reserve System had the power under *Regulation Q* to set maximum interest rates that banks could pay on savings deposits. These regulations were instituted because of the widespread belief that unrestricted interest-rate competition had contributed to bank failures during the Great Depression. Later evidence does not seem to support this view, and Regulation Q has been abolished (although there are still restrictions on paying interest on checking accounts held by businesses).

In later chapters we will look more closely at government regulation of financial markets and will see whether it has improved their functioning.

Financial Regulation Abroad

Not surprisingly, given the similarity of the economic system here and in Japan, Canada, and the nations of western Europe, financial regulation in these countries is similar to that in the United States. Provision of information is improved by requiring corporations issuing securities to report details about assets and liabilities, earnings, and sales of stock, and by prohibiting insider trading. The soundness of intermediaries is ensured by licensing, periodic inspection of financial intermediaries' books, and provision of deposit insurance (although its coverage is smaller than that in the United States and its existence is often intentionally not advertised).

The major differences between financial regulation in the United States and that found abroad relate to bank regulation. In the past, the United States was the only industrialized country to subject banks to restrictions on branching, which limited their size and confined them to certain geographic regions. (These restrictions were abolished by legislation in 1994.) U.S. banks are also the most restricted in the range of assets they may hold. Banks abroad frequently hold shares in commercial firms; in Japan and Germany, those stakes can be sizable.

SUMMARY

1. The basic function of financial markets is to channel funds from savers who have an excess of funds to spenders who have a shortage of funds. Financial markets can do this either through direct finance, in which borrowers borrow funds directly from lenders by selling them securities, or through indirect finance, which involves a financial intermediary that stands between the lender-savers and the borrower-spenders and helps transfer funds from one to the other. This channeling of funds improves the economic welfare of everyone in society. Because they allow funds to move from people who have no productive investment opportunities to those who have such opportunities, financial markets contribute to economic efficiency. In addition, channeling of funds directly benefits consumers by allowing them to make purchases when they need them most.

2. Financial markets can be classified as debt and equity markets, primary and secondary markets, exchanges and over-the-counter markets, and money and capital markets.

3. An important trend in recent years is the growing internationalization of financial markets. Eurobonds, which are denominated in a currency other than that of the country in which they are sold, are now the dominant security in the international bond market and have surpassed U.S. corporate bonds as a source of new funds. Eurodollars, which are U.S. dollars deposited in foreign banks, are an important source of funds for American banks.

4. Financial intermediaries are financial institutions that acquire funds by issuing liabilities and, in turn, use those funds to acquire assets by purchasing securities or making loans. Financial intermediaries play an important role in the financial system because they reduce transaction costs, allow risk sharing, and solve problems created by adverse selection and moral hazard. As a result, financial intermediaries allow small savers and borrowers to benefit from the existence of financial markets, thereby increasing the efficiency of the economy. However, the economies of scope that help make financial intermediaries successful can lead to conflicts of interest that make the financial system less efficient.

5. The principal financial intermediaries fall into three categories: (a) banks—commercial banks, savings and loan associations, mutual savings banks, and credit unions; (b) contractual savings institutions—life insurance companies, fire and casualty insurance companies, and pension funds; and (c) investment intermediaries—finance companies, mutual funds, money market mutual funds, hedge funds, and investment banks.

6. The government regulates financial markets and financial intermediaries for two main reasons: to increase the information available to investors and to ensure the soundness of the financial system. Regulations include requiring disclosure of information to the public, restrictions on who can set up a financial intermediary, restrictions on the assets financial intermediaries can hold, the provision of deposit insurance, limits on competition, and restrictions on interest rates.

KEY TERMS

adverse selection, p. 25
asset transformation, p. 24
asymmetric information, p. 25
brokers, p. 19
capital, p. 17
capital market, p. 20
conflicts of interest, p. 27
dealers, p. 19
diversification, p. 24
dividends, p. 18
economies of scale, p. 24
economies of scope, p. 26
equities, p. 18
Eurobond, p. 20
Eurocurrencies, p. 21
Eurodollars, p. 21
exchanges, p. 19
financial intermediation, p. 22
financial panic, p. 32
foreign bonds, p. 20
intermediate-term, p. 18
investment bank, p. 19
liabilities, p. 16
liquid, p. 19
liquidity services, p. 24
long-term, p. 18
maturity, p. 18
money market, p. 20
moral hazard, p. 25
over-the-counter (OTC) market, p. 19
portfolio, p. 24
primary market, p. 18
risk, p. 24
risk sharing, p. 24
secondary market, p. 18
short-term, p. 18
thrift institutions (thrifts), p. 27
transaction costs, p. 23
underwriting, p. 19

QUESTIONS

1. Give at least three examples of a situation in which financial markets allow consumers to better time their purchases.
2. If I can buy a car today for $5,000 and it is worth $10,000 in extra income next year to me because it enables me to get a job as a traveling anvil seller, should I take out a loan from Larry the loan shark at a 90% interest rate if no one else will give me a loan? Will I be better or worse off as a result of taking out this loan? Can you make a case for legalizing loan sharking?
3. Some economists suspect that one of the reasons that economies in developing countries grow so slowly is that they do not have well-developed financial markets. Does this argument make sense?
4. The U.S. economy borrowed heavily from the British in the nineteenth century to build a railroad system. What was the principal debt instrument used? Why did this make both countries better off?
5. Suppose that Toyota sells yen-denominated bonds in Tokyo. Is this debt instrument considered a Eurobond? How would your answer change if the bond were sold in New York?
6. If you suspect that a company will go bankrupt next year, which would you rather hold, bonds issued by the company or equities issued by the company? Why?
7. How can the adverse selection problem explain why you are more likely to make a loan to a family member than to a stranger?
8. Maria has accumulated $15,000 in savings and wants to buy shares in a hedge fund. Explain why Maria cannot participate in this particular type of mutual fund.
9. Why do loan sharks worry less bout moral hazard in connection with their borrowers than some other lenders do?
10. If you are an employer, what kinds of moral hazard problems might you worry about with your employees?
11. If there were no asymmetry in the information that a borrower and a lender had, could there still be a moral hazard problem?
12. "In a world without information and transaction costs, financial intermediaries would not exist." Is this statement true, false, or uncertain? Explain your answer.
13. Why might you be willing to make a loan to your neighbor by putting funds in a savings account earning a 5% interest rate at the bank and having the bank lend her the funds at a 10% interest rate rather than lend her the funds yourself?
14. How does risk sharing benefit both financial intermediaries and private investors?
15. Financial regulation is similar, but not exactly the same, in industrialized countries. Discuss why it might be desirable—or undesirable—to have the same financial regulation across industrialized countries.

WEB EXERCISES

The Financial System

1. One of the best sources of information about financial institutions is the U.S. Flow of Funds report produced by the Federal Reserve. This document contains data on most financial intermediaries. Go to **www.federalreserve.gov/releases/Z1/**. Go to the most current release. You may have to install Acrobat Reader if your computer does not already have it; the site has a link to download it for free. Go to the Level Tables and answer the following questions.
   - **a.** What percentage of assets do commercial banks hold in loans? What percentage of assets are held in mortgage loans?
   - **b.** What percentage of assets do savings and loans hold in mortgage loans?
   - **c.** What percentage of assets do credit unions hold in mortgage loans and in consumer loans?
2. The most famous financial market in the world is the New York Stock Exchange. Go to **www.nyse.com**.
   - **a.** What is the mission of the NYSE?
   - **b.** Firms must pay a fee to list their shares for sale on the NYSE. What would be the fee for a firm with 5 million common shares outstanding?

PART 2 FUNDAMENTALS OF FINANCIAL MARKETS

CHAPTER 3

What Do Interest Rates Mean and What Is Their Role in Valuation?

> PREVIEW

Interest rates are among the most closely watched variables in the economy. Their movements are reported almost daily by the news media because they directly affect our everyday lives and have important consequences for the health of the economy. They affect personal decisions such as whether to consume or save, whether to buy a house, and whether to purchase bonds or put funds into a savings account. Interest rates also affect the economic decisions of businesses and households, such as whether to use their funds to invest in new equipment for factories or to save their money in a bank.

Before we can go on with the study of financial markets, we must understand exactly what the phrase *interest rates* means. In this chapter, we see that a concept known as the *yield to maturity* is the most accurate measure of interest rates; the yield to maturity is what financial economists mean when they use the term *interest rate*. We discuss how the yield to maturity is measured on credit market instruments and how it is used to value these instruments. We also see that a bond's interest rate does not necessarily indicate how good an investment the bond is because what it earns (its rate of return) does not necessarily equal its interest rate. Finally, we explore the distinction between real interest rates, which are adjusted for changes in the price level, and nominal interest rates, which are not.

Although learning definitions is not always the most exciting of pursuits, it is important to read carefully and understand the concepts presented in this chapter. Not only are they continually used throughout the remainder of this text, but a firm grasp of these terms will give you a clearer understanding of the role that interest rates play in your life as well as in the general economy.

Measuring Interest Rates

www.bloomberg.com/markets/
Under "Rates & Bonds," you can access information on key interest rates, U.S. Treasuries, government bonds, and municipal bonds.

Different debt instruments have very different streams of cash payments to the holder (known as **cash flows**), with very different timing. Thus, we first need to understand how we can compare the value of one kind of debt instrument with another before we see how interest rates are measured. To do this, we use the concept of *present value*.

Present Value

The concept of **present value (or present discounted value)** is based on the commonsense notion that a dollar of cash flow paid to you one year from now is less valuable to you than a dollar paid to you today: This notion is true because you can deposit a dollar in a savings account that earns interest and have more than a dollar in one year. Economists use a more formal definition, as explained in this section.

Let's look at the simplest kind of debt instrument, which we will call a **simple loan**. In this loan, the lender provides the borrower with an amount of funds (called the *principal*) that must be repaid to the lender at the *maturity date*, along with an additional payment for the interest. For example, if you made your friend Jane a simple loan of \$100 for one year, you would require her to repay the principal of \$100 in one year's time along with an additional payment for interest, say, \$10. In the case of a simple loan like this one, the interest payment divided by the amount of the loan is a natural and sensible way to measure the interest rate. This measure of the so-called *simple interest rate*, i, is

$$i = \frac{\$10}{\$100} = 0.10 = 10\%$$

If you make this \$100 loan, at the end of the year you would have \$110, which can be rewritten as:

$$\$100 \times (1 + 0.10) = \$110$$

If you then lent out the \$110, at the end of the second year you would have:

$$\$110 \times (1 + 0.10) = \$121$$

or, equivalently,

$$\$100 \times (1 + 0.10) \times (1 + 0.10) = \$100 \times (1 + 0.10)^2 = \$121$$

Continuing with the loan again, at the end of the third year you would have:

$$\$121 \times (1 + 0.10) = \$100 \times (1 + 0.10)^3 = \$133$$

Generalizing, we can see that at the end of n years, your \$100 would turn into:

$$\$100 \times (1 + i)^n$$

The amounts you would have at the end of each year by making the \$100 loan today can be seen in the following timeline:

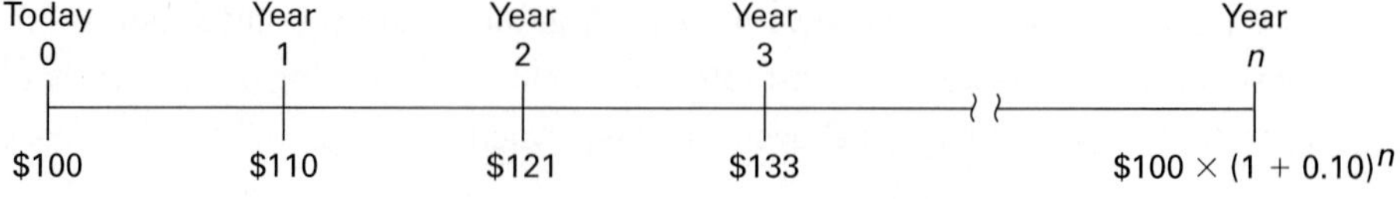

This timeline immediately tells you that you are just as happy having \$100 today as having \$110 a year from now (of course, as long as you are sure that Jane will pay you back). Or that you are just as happy having \$100 today as having \$121 two years from now, or \$133 three years from now, or $\$100 \times (1 + 0.10)^n$ in n years from now. The timeline tells us that we can also work backward from future amounts to the present. For example, $\$133 = \$100 \times (1 + 0.10)^3$ three years from now is worth \$100 today, so that:

$$\$100 = \frac{\$133}{(1 + 0.10)^3}$$

The process of calculating today's value of dollars received in the future, as we have done above, is called *discounting the future*. We can generalize this process by writing today's (present) value of \$100 as PV, writing the future cash flow of \$133 as CF, and replacing 0.10 (the 10% interest rate) by i. This leads to the following formula:

$$PV = \frac{CF}{(1 + i)^n} \tag{1}$$

Intuitively, what Equation 1 tells us is that if you are promised \$1 of cash flow for certain 10 years from now, this dollar would not be as valuable to you as \$1 is today because if you had the \$1 today, you could invest it and end up with more than \$1 in 10 years.

EXAMPLE 3.1

Simple Present Value

What is the present value of \$250 to be paid in two years if the interest rate is 15%?

> Solution

The present value would be \$189.04. Using Equation 1:

$$PV = \frac{CF}{(1 + i)^n}$$

where

CF = cash flow in two years = \$250

i = annual interest rate = 0.15

n = number of years = 2

Thus,

$$PV = \frac{\$250}{(1 + 0.15)^2} = \frac{\$250}{1.3225} = \$189.04$$

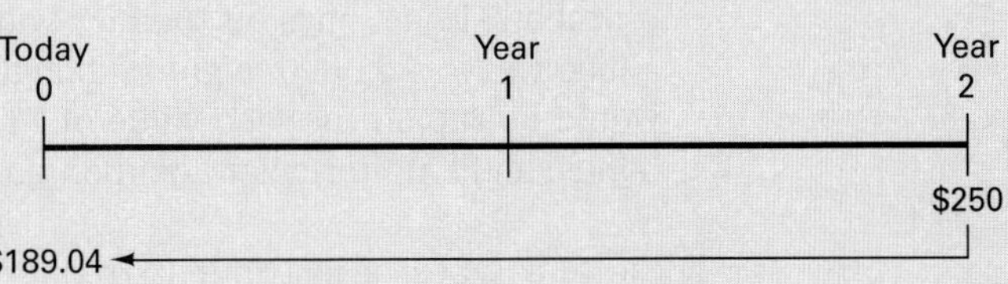

The concept of present value is extremely useful because it enables us to figure out today's value of a credit market instrument at a given simple interest rate i by just adding up the present value of all the future cash flows received. The present value concept allows us to compare the value of two instruments with very different timing of their cash flows.

Four Types of Credit Market Instruments

In terms of the timing of their cash flows, there are four basic types of credit market instruments.

1. A simple loan, which we have already discussed, in which the lender provides the borrower with an amount of funds, which must be repaid to the lender at the maturity date along with an additional payment for the interest. Many money market instruments are of this type, for example, commercial loans to businesses.
2. A **fixed-payment loan** (also called a **fully amortized loan**), in which the lender provides the borrower with an amount of funds, which must be repaid by making the same payment every period (such as a month), consisting of part of the principal and interest for a set number of years. For example, if you borrowed $1,000, a fixed-payment loan might require you to pay $126 every year for 25 years. Installment loans (such as auto loans) and mortgages are frequently of the fixed-payment type.
3. A **coupon bond** pays the owner of the bond a fixed interest payment (coupon payment) every year until the maturity date, when a specified final amount (**face value** or **par value**) is repaid. The coupon payment is so named because the bondholder used to obtain payment by clipping a coupon off the bond and sending it to the bond issuer, who then sent the payment to the holder. On all but the oldest bonds, it is no longer necessary to send in coupons to receive these payments. A coupon bond with $1,000 face value, for example, might pay you a coupon payment of $100 per year for 10 years, and at the maturity date repay you the face value amount of $1,000. (The face value of a bond is usually in $1,000 increments.)

   A coupon bond is identified by three pieces of information. First is the corporation or government agency that issues the bond. Second is the maturity date of the bond. Third is the bond's **coupon rate**, the dollar amount of the yearly coupon payment expressed as a percentage of the face value of the bond. In our example, the coupon bond has a yearly coupon payment of $100 and a face value of $1,000. The coupon rate is then $100/$1,000 = 0.10, or 10%. Capital market instruments such as U.S. Treasury bonds and notes and corporate bonds are examples of coupon bonds.
4. A **discount bond** (also called a **zero-coupon bond**) is bought at a price below its face value (at a discount), and the face value is repaid at the maturity date. Unlike a coupon bond, a discount bond does not make any interest payments; it just pays off the face value. For example, a discount bond with a face value of $1,000 might be bought for $900; in a year's time the owner would be repaid the face value of $1,000. U.S. Treasury bills, U.S. savings bonds, and long-term zero-coupon bonds are examples of discount bonds.

These four types of instruments require payments at different times: Simple loans and discount bonds make payment only at their maturity dates, whereas fixed-payment loans and coupon bonds have payments periodically until maturity. How would you decide which of these instruments would provide you with more income? They all seem so different because they make payments at different times. To solve this problem, we use the concept of present value, explained earlier, to provide us with a procedure for measuring interest rates on these types of instruments.

Yield to Maturity

Of the several common ways of calculating interest rates, the most important is the **yield to maturity**, the interest rate that equates the present value of cash flows received from a debt instrument with its value today. Because the concept behind the calculation of the yield to maturity makes good economic sense, financial economists consider it the most accurate measure of interest rates.

To understand the yield to maturity better, we now look at how it is calculated for the four types of credit market instruments. The key in all these examples to understanding the calculation of the yield to maturity is equating today's value of the debt instrument with the present value of all of its future cash flow payments.

Simple Loan With the concept of present value, the yield to maturity on a simple loan is easy to calculate. For the one-year loan we discussed, today's value is \$100, and the cash flow in one year's time would be \$110 (the repayment of \$100 plus the interest payment of \$10). We can use this information and Equation 1 to solve for the yield to maturity i by recognizing that the present value of the future payments must equal today's value of a loan.

EXAMPLE 3.2

Simple Loan

If Pete borrows \$100 from his sister and next year she wants \$110 back from him, what is the yield to maturity on this loan?

> Solution

The yield to maturity on the loan is 10%.

$$PV = \frac{CF}{(1+i)^n}$$

where

PV = amount borrowed = \$100

CF = cash flow in one year = \$110

n = number of years = 1

Thus,

$$\$100 = \frac{\$110}{(1+i)}$$

$$(1+i)\$100 = \$110$$

$$(1+i) = \frac{\$110}{\$100}$$

$$i = 1.10 - 1 = 0.10 = 10\%$$

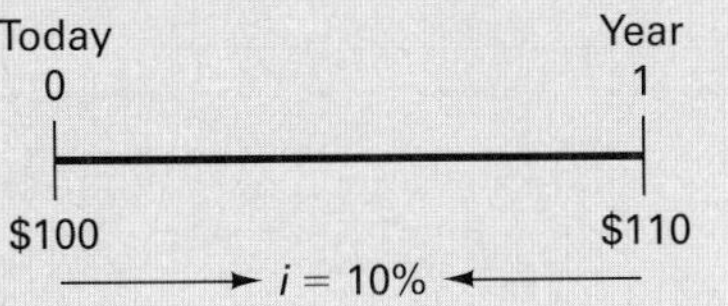

This calculation of the yield to maturity should look familiar because it equals the interest payment of \$10 divided by the loan amount of \$100; that is, it equals the simple interest rate on the loan. An important point to recognize is that ***for simple loans, the simple interest rate equals the yield to maturity***. Hence the same term i is used to denote both the yield to maturity and the simple interest rate.

Fixed-Payment Loan Recall that this type of loan has the same cash flow payment every year throughout the life of the loan. On a fixed-rate mortgage, for example, the borrower makes the same payment to the bank every month until the maturity date, when the loan will be completely paid off. To calculate the yield to maturity for a fixed-payment loan, we follow the same strategy we used for the simple loan—we equate today's value of the loan with its present value. Because the fixed-payment loan involves more than one cash flow payment, the present value of the fixed-payment loan is calculated as the sum of the present values of all cash flows (using Equation 1).

Suppose the loan is \$1,000 and the yearly cash flow payment is \$85.81 for the next 25 years. The present value is calculated as follows: At the end of one year, there is a \$85.81 cash flow payment with a *PV* of $\$85.81/(1 + i)$; at the end of two years, there is another \$85.81 cash flow payment with a *PV* of $\$85.81/(1 + i)^2$; and so on until at the end of the 25th year, the last cash flow payment of \$85.81 with a *PV* of $\$85.81/(1 + i)^{25}$ is made. Making today's value of the loan (\$1,000) equal to the sum of the present values of all the yearly cash flows gives us

$$\$1{,}000 = \frac{\$85.81}{1 + i} + \frac{\$85.81}{(1 + i)^2} + \frac{\$85.81}{(1 + i)^3} + \cdots + \frac{\$85.81}{(1 + i)^{25}}$$

More generally, for any fixed-payment loan,

$$LV = \frac{FP}{1 + i} + \frac{FP}{(1 + i)^2} + \frac{FP}{(1 + i)^3} + \cdots + \frac{FP}{(1 + i)^n} \tag{2}$$

where LV = loan value
FP = fixed yearly cash flow payment
n = number of years until maturity

For a fixed-payment loan amount, the fixed yearly payment and the number of years until maturity are known quantities, and only the yield to maturity is not. So we can solve this equation for the yield to maturity i. Because this calculation is not easy, many pocket calculators have programs that allow you to find i given the loan's numbers for LV, FP, and n. For example, in the case of the 25-year loan with yearly payments of \$85.81, the yield to maturity that solves Equation 2 is 7%. Real estate brokers always have a pocket calculator or an app that can solve such equations so that they can immediately tell the prospective house buyer exactly what the yearly (or monthly) payments will be if the house purchase is financed by a mortgage.

EXAMPLE 3.3

Fixed-Payment Loan

You decide to purchase a new home and need a \$100,000 mortgage. You take out a loan from the bank that has an interest rate of 7%. What is the yearly payment to the bank to pay off the loan in 20 years?

> Solution

The yearly payment to the bank is \$9,439.29.

$$LV = \frac{FP}{1+i} + \frac{FP}{(1+i)^2} + \frac{FP}{(1+i)^3} + \cdots + \frac{FP}{(1+i)^n}$$

where

LV = loan value amount = \$100,000

i = annual interest rate = 0.07

n = number of years = 20

Thus,

$$\$100{,}000 = \frac{FP}{1+0.07} + \frac{FP}{(1+0.07)^2} + \frac{FP}{(1+0.07)^3} + \cdots + \frac{FP}{(1+0.07)^{20}}$$

To find the yearly payment for the loan using a financial calculator:

n = number of years = 20

PV = amount of the loan (LV) = −100,000

FV = amount of the loan after 20 years = 0

i = annual interest rate = .07

Then push the *PMT* button = fixed yearly payment (*FP*) = \$9,439.29.

Coupon Bond To calculate the yield to maturity for a coupon bond, follow the same strategy used for the fixed-payment loan: Equate today's value of the bond with its present value. Because coupon bonds also have more than one cash flow payment, the present value of the bond is calculated as the sum of the present values of all the coupon payments plus the present value of the final payment of the face value of the bond.

The present value of a \$1,000 face value bond with 10 years to maturity and yearly coupon payments of \$100 (a 10% coupon rate) can be calculated as follows: At the end of one year, there is a \$100 coupon payment with a *PV* of $\$100/(1 + i)$; at the end of two years, there is another \$100 coupon payment with a *PV* of $\$100/(1 + i)^2$; and so on until at maturity, there is a \$100 coupon payment with a *PV* of $\$100/(1 + i)^{10}$ plus the repayment of the \$1,000 face value with a *PV* of $\$1{,}000/(1 + i)^{10}$. Setting today's value of the bond (its current price, denoted by *P*) equal to the sum of the present values of all the cash flows for this bond gives

$$P = \frac{\$100}{(1+i)} + \frac{\$100}{(1+i)^2} + \frac{\$100}{(1+i)^3} + \cdots + \frac{\$100}{(1+i)^{10}} + \frac{\$1{,}000}{(1+i)^{10}}$$

More generally, for any coupon bond,[1]

$$P = \frac{C}{(1+i)} + \frac{C}{(1+i)^2} + \frac{C}{(1+i)^3} + \cdots + \frac{C}{(1+i)^n} + \frac{F}{(1+i)^n} \quad (3)$$

[1]Most coupon bonds actually make coupon payments on a semiannual basis rather than once a year as assumed here. The effect on the calculations is only very slight and is ignored here.

where P = price of coupon bond
C = yearly coupon payment
F = face value of the bond
n = years to maturity date

In Equation 3, the coupon payment, the face value, the years to maturity, and the price of the bond are known quantities, and only the yield to maturity is not. Hence we can solve this equation for the yield to maturity i.[2] As in the case of the fixed-payment loan, this calculation is not easy, so business-oriented software and calculators have built-in programs that solve this equation for you.

EXAMPLE 3.4

Coupon Bond

Find the price of a 10% coupon bond with a face value of $1,000, a 12.25% yield to maturity, and eight years to maturity.

> Solution

The price of the bond is $889.20. To solve using a financial calculator,

n = years to maturity = 8
FV = face value of the bond = 1,000
i = annual interest rate = 12.25%
PMT = yearly coupon payments = 100

Then push the *PV* button = price of the bond = $889.20.

Table 3.1 shows the yields to maturity calculated for several bond prices. Three interesting facts emerge:

1. When the coupon bond is priced at its face value, the yield to maturity equals the coupon rate.
2. The price of a coupon bond and the yield to maturity are negatively related; that is, as the yield to maturity rises, the price of the bond falls. If the yield to maturity falls, the price of the bond rises.
3. The yield to maturity is greater than the coupon rate when the bond price is below its face value.

TABLE 3.1 Yields to Maturity on a 10% Coupon Rate Bond Maturing in 10 Years (Face Value = $1,000)

Price of Bond ($)	Yield to Maturity (%)
1,200	7.13
1,100	8.48
1,000	10.00
900	11.75
800	13.81

[2]In other contexts, it is also called the *internal rate of return*.

These three facts are true for any coupon bond and are really not surprising if you think about the reasoning behind the calculation of the yield to maturity. When you put $1,000 in a bank account with an interest rate of 10%, you can take out $100 every year and you will be left with the $1,000 at the end of 10 years. This process is similar to buying the $1,000 bond with a 10% coupon rate analyzed in Table 3.1, which pays a $100 coupon payment every year and then repays $1,000 at the end of 10 years. If the bond is purchased at the par value of $1,000, its yield to maturity must equal the interest rate of 10%, which is also equal to the coupon rate of 10%. The same reasoning applied to any coupon bond demonstrates that if the coupon bond is purchased at its par value, the yield to maturity and the coupon rate must be equal.

It is straightforward to show that the valuation of a bond and the yield to maturity are negatively related. As i, the yield to maturity, rises, all denominators in the bond price formula must necessarily rise. Hence a rise in the interest rate as measured by the yield to maturity means that the value and therefore the price of the bond must fall. Another way to explain why the bond price falls when the interest rate rises is that a higher interest rate implies that the future coupon payments and final payment are worth less when discounted back to the present; hence the price of the bond must be lower.

GO ONLINE
www.teachmefinance.com
Access a review of the key financial concepts: time value of money, annuities, perpetuities, and so on.

The third fact, that the yield to maturity is greater than the coupon rate when the bond price is below its par value, follows directly from facts 1 and 2. When the yield to maturity equals the coupon rate, then the bond price is at the face value; when the yield to maturity rises above the coupon rate, the bond price necessarily falls and so must be below the face value of the bond.

One special case of a coupon bond that is worth discussing because its yield to maturity is particularly easy to calculate is called a **perpetuity**, or a **consol**; it is a perpetual bond with no maturity date and no repayment of principal that makes fixed coupon payments of $C forever. The formula in Equation 3 for the price of a perpetuity, P_c, simplifies to the following:[3]

$$P_c = \frac{C}{i_c} \tag{4}$$

where P_c = price of the perpetuity (consol)
C = yearly payment
i_c = yield to maturity of the perpetuity (consol)

---

[3]The bond price formula for a perpetuity is

$$P_c = \frac{C}{1 + i_c} + \frac{C}{(1 + i_c)^2} + \frac{C}{(1 + i_c)^3} + \cdots$$

which can be written

$$P_c = C(x + x^2 + x^3 + \cdots)$$

in which $x = 1/(1 + i)$. From your high school algebra you might remember the formula for an infinite sum:

$$1 + x + x^2 + x^3 + \cdots = \frac{1}{1 - x} \quad \text{for } x < 1$$

and so

$$P_c = C\left(\frac{1}{1 - x} - 1\right) = C\left[\frac{1}{1 - 1/(1 + i_c)} - 1\right]$$

which by suitable algebraic manipulation becomes

$$P_c = C\left(\frac{1 + i_c}{i_c} - \frac{i_c}{i_c}\right) = \frac{C}{i_c}$$

One nice feature of perpetuities is that you can immediately see that as i_c goes up, the price of the bond falls. For example, if a perpetuity pays \$100 per year forever and the interest rate is 10%, its price will be \$1,000 = \$100/0.10. If the interest rate rises to 20%, its price will fall to \$500 = \$100/0.20. We can also rewrite this formula as

$$i_c = \frac{C}{P_c} \tag{5}$$

EXAMPLE 3.5

Perpetuity

What is the yield to maturity on a bond that has a price of \$2,000 and pays \$100 annually forever?

> Solution

The yield to maturity would be 5%.

$$i_c = \frac{C}{P_c}$$

where

C = yearly payment = \$100

P_c = price of perpetuity (consol) = \$2,000

Thus,

$$i_c = \frac{\$100}{\$2{,}000}$$

$$i_c = 0.05 = 5\%$$

The formula in Equation 5, which describes the calculation of the yield to maturity for a perpetuity, also provides a useful approximation for the yield to maturity on coupon bonds. When a coupon bond has a long term to maturity (say, 20 years or more), it is very much like a perpetuity, which pays coupon payments forever. This is because the cash flows more than 20 years in the future have such small present discounted values that the value of a long-term coupon bond is very close to the value of a perpetuity with the same coupon rate. Thus, i_c in Equation 5 will be very close to the yield to maturity for any long-term bond. For this reason, i_c, the yearly coupon payment divided by the price of the security, has been given the name **current yield** and is frequently used as an approximation to describe interest rates (yields to maturity) on long-term bonds.

Discount Bond The yield-to-maturity calculation for a discount bond is similar to that for the simple loan. Let's consider a discount bond such as a one-year U.S. Treasury bill, which pays a face value of \$1,000 in one year's time. If the current purchase price of this bill is \$900, then equating this price to the present value of the \$1,000 received in one year, using Equation 1, gives

$$\$900 = \frac{\$1{,}000}{1 + i}$$

and solving for i,

$$
\begin{aligned}
(1 + i) \times \$900 &= \$1{,}000 \\
\$900 + \$900i &= \$1{,}000 \\
\$900i &= \$1{,}000 - \$900 \\
i &= \frac{\$1{,}000 - \$900}{\$900} = 0.111 = 11.1\%
\end{aligned}
$$

More generally, for any one-year discount bond, the yield to maturity can be written as

$$i = \frac{F - P}{P} \tag{6}$$

where F = face value of the discount bond
P = current price of the discount bond

In other words, the yield to maturity equals the increase in price over the year $F - P$ divided by the initial price P. In normal circumstances, investors earn positive returns from holding these securities and so they sell at a discount, meaning that the current price of the bond is below the face value. Therefore, $F - P$ should be positive, and the yield to maturity should be positive as well. However, this is not always the case, as extraordinary events in Japan and elsewhere have indicated (see the Global box).

An important feature of this equation is that it indicates that for a discount bond, the yield to maturity is negatively related to the current bond price. This is

> GLOBAL

Negative Interest Rates? Japan First, Then the United States, Then Europe

We normally assume that the yield to maturity must always be positive. A negative yield to maturity would imply that you are willing to pay more for a bond today than you will receive for it in the future (as our formula for yield to maturity on a discount bond demonstrates). A negative yield to maturity therefore seems like an impossibility because you would do better by holding cash that has the same value in the future as it does today.

Events in Japan in the late 1990s and then in the United States during the 2008 global financial crisis and finally in Europe in recent years have demonstrated that this reasoning is not quite correct. In November 1998, the yield to maturity on Japanese six-month Treasury bills became negative, at −0.004%. In September 2008, the yield to maturity on three-month U.S. T-bills fell very slightly below zero for a very brief period. Interest rates that banks are paid on deposits they keep at their central banks became negative first in Sweden in July 2009, followed by Denmark in July 2012, the Eurozone in June 2014, Switzerland in December 2014, and Japan in January 2016. Negative interest rates have rarely occurred in the past. How could this happen in recent years?

As we will see in Chapter 4, a dearth of investment opportunities and very low inflation can drive interest rates to low levels, but these two factors can't explain the negative yield to maturity. The answer is that despite negative interest rates, large investors and banks found it more convenient to hold Treasury bills or keep their funds as deposits at the central bank because they are stored electronically. For that reason, investors and banks were willing to accept negative interest rates, even though in pure monetary terms the investors would be better off holding cash.

the same conclusion that we reached for a coupon bond. For example, Equation 6 shows that a rise in the bond price from \$900 to \$950 means that the bond will have a smaller increase in its price over its lifetime, and the yield to maturity falls from 11.1% to 5.3%. Similarly, a fall in the yield to maturity means that the price of the discount bond has risen.

Summary The concept of present value tells you that a dollar in the future is not as valuable to you as a dollar today because you can earn interest on this dollar. Specifically, a dollar received n years from now is worth only $\$1/(1 + i)^n$ today. The present value of a set of future cash flows on a debt instrument equals the sum of the present values of each of the future cash flows. The yield to maturity for an instrument is the interest rate that equates the present value of the future cash flows on that instrument to its value today. Because the procedure for calculating the yield to maturity is based on sound economic principles, this is the measure that financial economists think most accurately describes the interest rate.

Our calculations of the yield to maturity for a variety of bonds reveal the important fact that ***current bond prices and interest rates are negatively related: When the interest rate rises, the price of the bond falls, and vice versa***.

The Distinction Between Real and Nominal Interest Rates

So far in our discussion of interest rates, we have ignored the effects of inflation on the cost of borrowing. What we have up to now been calling the interest rate makes no allowance for inflation, and it is more precisely referred to as the **nominal interest rate**. We distinguish it from the **real interest rate**, the interest rate that is adjusted by subtracting expected changes in the price level (inflation) so that it more accurately reflects the true cost of borrowing. This interest rate is more precisely referred to as the *ex ante real interest rate* because it is adjusted for *expected* changes in the price level. The *ex ante* real interest rate is most important to economic decisions, and typically it is what financial economists mean when they make reference to the "real" interest rate. The interest rate that is adjusted for *actual* changes in the price level is called the *ex post real interest rate*. It describes how well a lender has done in real terms *after the fact*.

The real interest rate is more accurately defined by the *Fisher equation*, named for Irving Fisher, one of the great monetary economists of the twentieth century. The Fisher equation states that the nominal interest rate i equals the real interest rate i_r plus the expected rate of inflation π^e.[4]

$$i = i_r + \pi^e \tag{7}$$

[4]A more precise formulation of the Fisher equation is

$$i = i_r + \pi^e + (i_r \times \pi^e)$$

because

$$1 + i = (1 + i_r)\,(1 + \pi^e) = 1 + i_r + \pi^e + (i_r \times \pi^e)$$

and subtracting 1 from both sides gives us the first equation. For small values of i_r and π^e, the term $i_r \times \pi^e$ is so small that we ignore it.

Rearranging terms, we find that the real interest rate equals the nominal interest rate minus the expected inflation rate:

$$i_r = i - \pi^e \tag{8}$$

To see why this definition makes sense, let us first consider a situation in which you have made a one-year simple loan with a 5% interest rate ($i = 5\%$) and you expect the price level to rise by 3% over the course of the year ($\pi^e = 3\%$). As a result of making the loan, at the end of the year you expect to have 2% more in **real terms**, that is, in terms of real goods and services you can buy.

In this case, the interest rate you expect to earn in terms of real goods and services is 2%; that is,

$$i_r = 5\% - 3\% = 2\%$$

as indicated by the Fisher definition.

EXAMPLE 3.6

Real and Nominal Interest Rates

What is the real interest rate if the nominal interest rate is 8% and the expected inflation rate is 10% over the course of a year?

> Solution

The real interest rate is –2%. Although you will be receiving 8% more dollars at the end of the year, you will be paying 10% more for goods. The result is that you will be able to buy 2% fewer goods at the end of the year, and you will be 2% worse off in real terms.

$$i_r = i - \pi^e$$

where

$$i = \text{nominal interest rate} = 0.08$$

$$\pi^e = \text{expected inflation rate} = 0.10$$

Thus,

$$i_r = 0.08 - 0.10 = -0.02 = -2\%$$

As a lender, you are clearly less eager to make a loan in Example 3.6 because in terms of real goods and services you have actually earned a negative interest rate of 2%. By contrast, as the borrower, you fare quite well because at the end of the year, the amounts you will have to pay back will be worth 2% less in terms of goods and services—you as the borrower will be ahead by 2% in real terms. ***When the real interest rate is low, there are greater incentives to borrow and fewer incentives to lend.***

The distinction between real and nominal interest rates is important because the real interest rate, which reflects the real cost of borrowing, is likely to be a better indicator of the incentives to borrow and lend. It appears to be a better guide to how people will be affected by what is happening in credit markets. Figure 3.1, which presents estimates from 1953 to 2016 of the real and nominal interest rates on three-month U.S. Treasury bills, shows us that nominal and real rates often do not move together. (This is also true for nominal and real interest rates in the rest

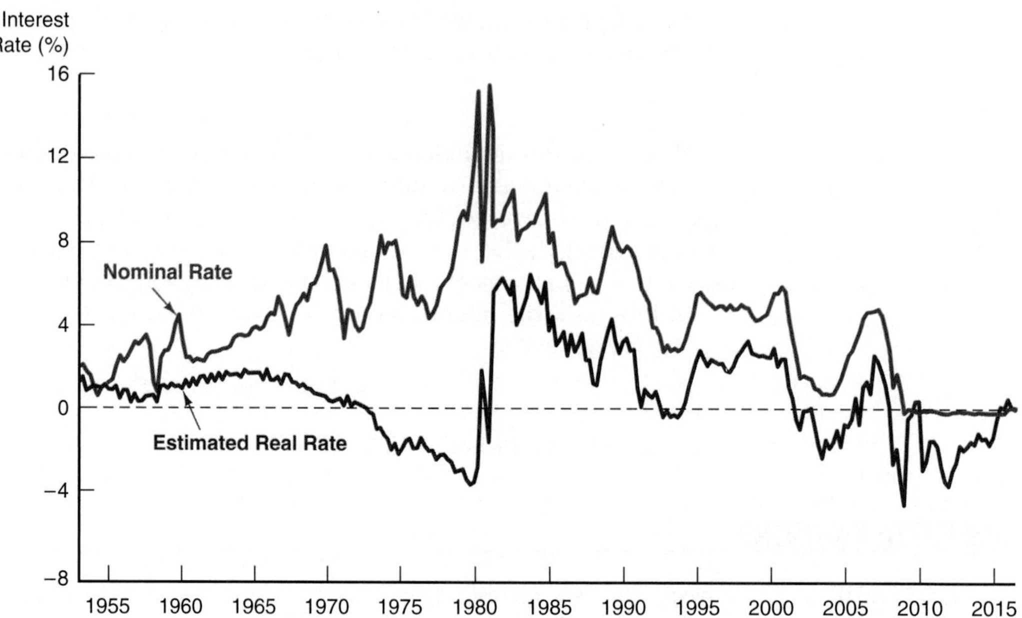

FIGURE 3.1 Real and Nominal Interest Rates (Three-Month Treasury Bill), 1953–2016

Nominal and real interest rates often do not move together. When U.S. nominal rates were high in the 1970s, real rates were actually extremely low—often negative.

Sources: Federal Reserve Bank of St. Louis FRED database: https://fred.stlouisfed.org/series/TB3MS and https://fred.stlouisfed.org/series/CPIAUCSL. The real rate is constructed using the procedure outlined in Frederic S. Mishkin, "The Real Interest Rate: An Empirical Investigation," *Carnegie–Rochester Conference Series on Public Policy* 15 (1981): 151–200. This involves estimating expected inflation as a function of past interest rates, inflation, and time trends and then subtracting the expected inflation measure from the nominal interest rate.

of the world.) In particular, when nominal rates in the United States were high in the 1970s, real rates were actually extremely low, often negative. By the standard of nominal interest rates, you would have thought that credit market conditions were tight in this period because it was expensive to borrow. However, the estimates of the real rates indicate that you would have been mistaken. In real terms, the cost of borrowing was actually quite low.[5]

[5]Because most interest income in the United States is subject to federal income taxes, the true earnings in real terms from holding a debt instrument are not reflected by the real interest rate defined by the Fisher equation but rather by the *after-tax real interest rate*, which equals the nominal interest rate *after income tax payments have been subtracted*, minus the expected inflation rate. For a person facing a 30% tax rate, the after-tax interest rate earned on a bond yielding 10% is only 7% because 30% of the interest income must be paid to the Internal Revenue Service. Thus, the after-tax real interest rate on this bond when expected inflation is 20% equals −13% (= 7% − 20%). More generally, the after-tax real interest rate can be expressed as

$$i(1 - \tau) - \pi^e$$

where τ = the income tax rate.

MINI-CASE

With TIPS, Real Interest Rates Have Become Observable in the United States

When the U.S. Treasury decided to issue TIPS (Treasury Inflation Protection Securities), a version of indexed coupon bonds, it was somewhat late in the game. Other countries such as the United Kingdom, Canada, Australia, and Sweden had beaten the United States to the punch. (In September 1998, the U.S. Treasury also began issuing the Series I savings bond, which provides inflation protection for small investors.)

These indexed securities have successfully acquired a niche in the bond market, enabling governments to raise more funds. In addition, because their interest and principal payments are adjusted for changes in the price level, the interest rate on these bonds provides a direct measure of a real interest rate. These indexed bonds are very useful to policy makers, especially monetary policy makers, because by subtracting their interest rate from a nominal interest rate, they generate more insight into expected inflation, a valuable piece of information. For example, on May 13, 2016, the interest rate on the 10-year Treasury bond was 1.71%, while that on the 10-year TIPS was 0.13%. Thus, the implied expected inflation rate for the next 10 years, derived from the difference between these two rates, was 1.58%. The private sector finds the information provided by TIPS very useful: Many commercial and investment banks routinely publish the expected U.S. inflation rates derived from these bonds.

Until recently, real interest rates in the United States were not observable because only nominal rates were reported. This all changed in January 1997, when the U.S. Treasury began to issue **indexed bonds**, bonds whose interest and principal payments are adjusted for changes in the price level (see the Mini-Case box above).

The Distinction Between Interest Rates and Returns

Many people think that the interest rate on a bond tells them all they need to know about how well off they are as a result of owning it. If Irving the investor thinks he is better off when he owns a long-term bond yielding a 10% interest rate and the interest rate rises to 20%, he will have a rude awakening: As we will shortly see, Irving has lost his shirt! How well a person does by holding a bond or any other security over a particular time period is accurately measured by the **return**, or, in more precise terminology, the **rate of return**. The concept of return discussed here is extremely important because it is used continually throughout the book.

This formula for the after-tax real interest rate also provides a better measure of the effective cost of borrowing for many corporations and individuals in the United States because in calculating income taxes, they can deduct interest payments on loans from their income. Thus, if you face a 30% tax rate and take out a mortgage loan with a 10% interest rate, you are able to deduct the 10% interest payment and thus lower your taxes by 30% of this amount. Your after-tax nominal cost of borrowing is then 7% (10% minus 30% of the 10% interest payment), and when the expected inflation rate is 20%, the effective cost of borrowing in real terms is again −13% (= 7% − 20%).

As the example (and the formula) indicates, after-tax real interest rates are always below the real interest rate defined by the Fisher equation. For a further discussion of measures of after-tax real interest rates, see Frederic S. Mishkin, "The Real Interest Rate: An Empirical Investigation," *Carnegie-Rochester Conference Series on Public Policy* 15 (1981): 151–200.

Make sure that you understand how a return is calculated and why it can differ from the interest rate. This understanding will make the material presented later in the book easier to follow.

For any security, the rate of return is defined as the payments to the owner plus the change in its value, expressed as a fraction of its purchase price. To make this definition clearer, let us see what the return would look like for a \$1,000-face-value coupon bond with a coupon rate of 10% that is bought for \$1,000, held for one year, and then sold for \$1,200. The payments to the owner are the yearly coupon payments of \$100, and the change in its value is \$1,200 − \$1,000 = \$200. Adding these together and expressing them as a fraction of the purchase price of \$1,000 gives us the one-year holding-period return for this bond:

$$\frac{\$100 + \$200}{\$1{,}000} = \frac{\$300}{\$1{,}000} = 0.30 = 30\%$$

You may have noticed something quite surprising about the return that we have just calculated: It equals 30%, yet as Table 3.1 indicates, initially the yield to maturity was only 10%. This discrepancy demonstrates that ***the return on a bond will not necessarily equal the interest rate on that bond***. We now see that the distinction between interest rate and return can be important, although for many securities the two may be closely related.

More generally, the return on a bond held from time t to time $t + 1$ can be written as

$$R = \frac{C + P_{t+1} - P_t}{P_t} \tag{9}$$

where
R = return from holding the bond from time t to time $t + 1$
P_t = price of the bond at time t
P_{t+1} = price of the bond at time $t + 1$
C = coupon payment

EXAMPLE 3.7

Rate of Return

What would the rate of return be on a bond bought for \$1,000 and sold one year later for \$800? The bond has a face value of \$1,000 and a coupon rate of 8%.

> Solution

The rate of return on the bond for holding it one year is −12%.

$$R = \frac{C + P_{t+1} - P_t}{P_t}$$

where

C = coupon payment = \$1,000 × 0.08 = \$80
P_{t+1} = price of the bond one year later = \$800
P_t = price of the bond today = \$1,000

Thus,

$$R = \frac{\$80 + (\$800 - \$1{,}000)}{\$1{,}000} = \frac{-120}{1{,}000} = -0.12 = -12\%$$

A convenient way to rewrite the return formula in Equation 9 is to recognize that it can be split into two terms:

$$R = \frac{C}{P_t} + \frac{P_{t+1} - P_t}{P_t}$$

The first term is the current yield i_c (the coupon payment over the purchase price):

$$\frac{C}{P_t} = i_c$$

The second term is the **rate of capital gain**, or the change in the bond's price relative to the initial purchase price:

$$\frac{P_{t+1} - P_t}{P_t} = g$$

where g = rate of capital gain. Equation 9 can then be rewritten as

$$R = i_c + g \tag{10}$$

which shows that the return on a bond is the current yield i_c plus the rate of capital gain g. This rewritten formula illustrates the point we just discovered. Even for a bond for which the current yield i_c is an accurate measure of the yield to maturity, the return can differ substantially from the interest rate. Returns will differ from the interest rate especially if the price of the bond experiences sizable fluctuations, which then produce substantial capital gains or losses.

To explore this point even further, let's look at what happens to the returns on bonds of different maturities when interest rates rise. Using Equation 10 above, Table 3.2 calculates the one-year return on several 10% coupon rate bonds all purchased at par when interest rates on all these bonds rise from 10% to 20%. Several key findings in this table are generally true of all bonds:

- The only bond whose return equals the initial yield to maturity is one whose time to maturity is the same as the holding period (see the last bond in Table 3.2).
- A rise in interest rates is associated with a fall in bond prices, resulting in capital losses on bonds whose terms to maturity are longer than the holding period.
- The more distant a bond's maturity, the greater the size of the price change associated with an interest-rate change.
- The more distant a bond's maturity, the lower the rate of return that occurs as a result of the increase in the interest rate.
- Even though a bond has a substantial initial interest rate, its return can turn out to be negative if interest rates rise.

At first, it frequently puzzles students that a rise in interest rates can mean that a bond has been a poor investment (as it puzzles poor Irving the investor). The trick to understanding this is to recognize that a rise in the interest rate means that the price of a bond has fallen. A rise in interest rates therefore means that a capital loss has occurred, and if this loss is large enough, the bond can be a poor investment indeed. For example, we see in Table 3.2 that the bond that has 30 years to maturity when purchased has a capital loss of 49.7% when the interest rate rises from 10% to 20%. This loss is so large that it exceeds the current yield of 10%, resulting in a

TABLE 3.2 One-Year Returns on Different-Maturity 10% Coupon Rate Bonds When Interest Rates Rise from 10% to 20%

(1) Years to Maturity When Bond Is Purchased	(2) Initial Current Yield (%)	(3) Initial Price ($)	(4) Price Next Year* ($)	(5) Rate of Capital Gain (%)	(6) Rate of Return (2 + 5) (%)
30	10	1,000	503	–49.7	-39.7
20	10	1,000	516	–48.4	-38.4
10	10	1,000	597	–40.3	-30.3
5	10	1,000	741	–25.9	-15.9
2	10	1,000	917	–8.3	+1.7
1	10	1,000	1,000	0.0	+10.0

*Calculated with a financial calculator using Equation 3.

negative return (loss) of –39.7%. If Irving does not sell the bond, the capital loss is often referred to as a "paper loss." This is a loss nonetheless because if he had not bought this bond and had instead put his money in the bank, he would now be able to buy more bonds at their lower price than he presently owns.

Maturity and the Volatility of Bond Returns: Interest-Rate Risk

The finding that the prices of longer-maturity bonds respond more dramatically to changes in interest rates helps explain an important fact about the behavior of bond markets: ***Prices and returns for long-term bonds are more volatile than those for shorter-term bonds***. Price changes of +20% and −20% within a year, with corresponding variations in returns, are common for bonds more than 20 years away from maturity.

We now see that changes in interest rates make investments in long-term bonds quite risky. Indeed, the riskiness of an asset's return that results from interest-rate changes is so important that it has been given a special name, **interest-rate risk**. Dealing with interest-rate risk is a major concern of managers of financial institutions and investors, as we will see in later chapters (see also the Mini-Case box).

Although long-term debt instruments have substantial interest-rate risk, short-term debt instruments do not. Indeed, bonds with a maturity that is as short as the holding period have no interest-rate risk.[6] We see this for the coupon bond at the

[6]The statement that there is no interest-rate risk for any bond whose time to maturity matches the holding period is literally true only for discount bonds and zero-coupon bonds that make no intermediate cash payments before the holding period is over. A coupon bond that makes an intermediate cash payment before the holding period is over requires that this payment be reinvested at some future date. Because the interest rate at which this payment can be reinvested is uncertain, there is some uncertainty about the return on this coupon bond even when the time to maturity equals the holding period. However, the riskiness of the return on a coupon bond from reinvesting the coupon payments is typically quite small, and so the basic point that a coupon bond with a time to maturity equaling the holding period has very little risk still holds true.

MINI-CASE

Helping Investors Select Desired Interest-Rate Risk

Because many investors want to know how much interest-rate risk they are exposed to, some mutual fund companies try to educate investors about the perils of interest-rate risk, as well as to offer investment alternatives that match their investors' preferences.

Vanguard Group, for example, offers eight high-grade bond mutual funds. In its prospectus, Vanguard separates the funds by the average maturity of the bonds they hold and demonstrates the effect of interest-rate changes by computing the percentage change in bond value resulting from a 1% increase and decrease in interest rates. Three of the funds invest in bonds with average maturities of one to three years, which Vanguard rates as having the lowest interest-rate risk. Three other funds hold bonds with average maturities of five to ten years, which Vanguard rates as having medium interest-rate risk. Two funds hold long-term bonds with maturities of 15 to 30 years, which Vanguard rates as having high interest-rate risk.

By providing this information, Vanguard hopes to increase its market share in the sales of bond funds. Not surprisingly, Vanguard is one of the most successful mutual fund companies in the business.

bottom of Table 3.2, which has no uncertainty about the rate of return because it equals the yield to maturity, which is known at the time the bond is purchased. The key to understanding why there is no interest-rate risk for *any* bond whose time to maturity matches the holding period is to recognize that (in this case) the price at the end of the holding period is already fixed at the face value. The change in interest rates can then have no effect on the price at the end of the holding period for these bonds, and the return will therefore be equal to the yield to maturity known at the time the bond is purchased.

Reinvestment Risk

Up to now, we have been assuming that all holding periods are short and equal to the maturity on short-term bonds and are thus not subject to interest-rate risk. However, if an investor's holding period is longer than the term to maturity of the bond, the investor is exposed to a type of interest-rate risk called **reinvestment risk**. Reinvestment risk occurs because the proceeds from the short-term bond need to be reinvested at a future interest rate that is uncertain.

To understand reinvestment risk, suppose that Irving the investor has a holding period of two years and decides to purchase a $1,000 one-year, 10% coupon rate bond at face value and then purchase another one at the end of the first year. If the initial interest rate is 10%, Irving will have $1,100 at the end of the year. If the interest rate on one-year bonds rises to 20% at the end of the year, as in Table 3.2, Irving will find that buying $1,100 worth of another one-year bond will leave him at the end of the second year with $\$1{,}100 \times (1 + 0.20) = \$1{,}320$. Thus, Irving's two-year return will be $(\$1{,}320 - \$1{,}000)/\$1{,}000 = 0.32 = 32\%$, which equals 14.9% at an annual rate. In this case, Irving has earned more by buying the one-year bonds than if he had initially purchased the two-year bond with an interest rate of 10%. Thus, when Irving has a holding period that is longer than the term to maturity of the bonds he purchases, he benefits from a rise in interest rates. Conversely, if interest rates on one-year bonds fall to 5% at the end of the year, Irving will have only $1,155 at the end of two years: $1,100 × (1 + 0.05). Thus, his two-year return will be ($1,155 − $1,000)/$1,000 = 0.155 = 15.5%, which is 7.2% at an annual rate. With a holding period greater than the term to maturity of the bond, Irving now loses from a fall in interest rates.

We have thus seen that when the holding period is longer than the term to maturity of a bond, the return is uncertain because the future interest rate when reinvestment occurs is also uncertain—in short, there is reinvestment risk. We also see that if the holding period is longer than the term to maturity of the bond, the investor benefits from a rise in interest rates and is hurt by a fall in interest rates.

Summary

The return on a bond, which tells you how good an investment it has been over the holding period, is equal to the yield to maturity in only one special case: when the holding period and the maturity of the bond are identical. Bonds whose term to maturity is longer than the holding period are subject to interest-rate risk: Changes in interest rates lead to capital gains and losses that produce substantial differences between the return and the yield to maturity known at the time the bond is purchased. Interest-rate risk is especially important for long-term bonds, where the capital gains and losses can be substantial. This is why long-term bonds are not considered to be safe assets with a sure return over short holding periods. Bonds whose term to maturity is shorter than the holding period are also subject to reinvestment risk. Reinvestment risk occurs because the proceeds from the short-term bond need to be reinvested at a future interest rate that is uncertain.

THE PRACTICING MANAGER

Calculating Duration to Measure Interest-Rate Risk

Earlier in our discussion of interest-rate risk, we saw that when interest rates change, a bond with a longer term to maturity has a larger change in its price and hence more interest-rate risk than a bond with a shorter term to maturity. Although this is a useful general fact, in order to measure interest-rate risk, the manager of a financial institution needs more precise information on the actual capital gain or loss that occurs when the interest rate changes by a certain amount. To do this, the manager needs to make use of the concept of **duration**, the average lifetime of a debt security's stream of payments.

The fact that two bonds have the same term to maturity does not mean that they have the same interest-rate risk. A long-term discount bond with 10 years to maturity, a so-called zero-coupon bond, makes all of its payments at the end of the 10 years, whereas a 10% coupon bond with 10 years to maturity makes substantial cash payments before the maturity date. Since the coupon bond makes payments earlier than the zero-coupon bond, we might intuitively guess that the coupon bond's *effective maturity*, the term to maturity that accurately measures interest-rate risk, is shorter than it is for the zero-coupon discount bond.

Indeed, this is exactly what we find in Example 3.8.

EXAMPLE 3.8

Rate of Capital Gain

Calculate the rate of capital gain or loss on a 10-year zero-coupon bond for which the interest rate has increased from 10% to 20%. The bond has a face value of $1,000.

> Solution

The rate of capital gain or loss is –49.7%.

$$g = \frac{P_{t+1} - P_t}{P_t}$$

where

$$P_{t+1} = \text{price of the bond one year from now} = \frac{\$1{,}000}{(1 + 0.20)^9} = \$193.81$$

$$P_t = \text{price of the bond today} = \frac{\$1{,}000}{(1 + 0.10)^{10}} = \$385.54$$

Thus,

$$g = \frac{\$193.81 - \$385.54}{\$385.54}$$

$$g = -0.497 = -49.7\%$$

But as we have already calculated in Table 3.2, the capital gain on the 10% 10-year coupon bond is –40.3%. We see that interest-rate risk for the 10-year coupon bond is less than for the 10-year zero-coupon bond, so the effective maturity on the coupon bond (which measures interest-rate risk) is, as expected, shorter than the effective maturity on the zero-coupon bond.

Calculating Duration

To calculate the duration or effective maturity on any debt security, Frederick Macaulay, a researcher at the National Bureau of Economic Research, invented the concept of duration more than half a century ago. Because a zero-coupon bond makes no cash payments before the bond matures, it makes sense to define its effective maturity as equal to its actual term to maturity. Macaulay then realized that he could measure the effective maturity of a coupon bond by recognizing that a coupon bond is equivalent to a set of zero-coupon discount bonds. A 10-year 10% coupon bond with $1,000 face value has cash payments identical to the following set of zero-coupon bonds: a $100 one-year zero-coupon bond (which pays the equivalent of the $100 coupon payment made by the $1,000 10-year 10% coupon bond at the end of one year), a $100 two-year zero-coupon bond (which pays the equivalent of the $100 coupon payment at the end of two years),…, a $100 10-year zero-coupon bond (which pays the equivalent of the $100 coupon payment at the end of 10 years), and a $1,000 10-year zero-coupon bond (which pays back the equivalent of the coupon bond's $1,000 face value). This set of coupon bonds is shown in the following timeline:

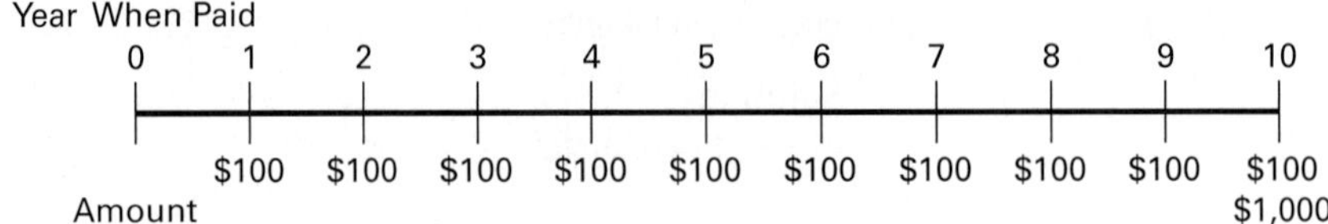

This same set of coupon bonds is listed in column (2) of Table 3.3, which calculates the duration on the 10-year coupon bond when its interest rate is 10%.

To get the effective maturity of this set of zero-coupon bonds, we would want to sum up the effective maturity of each zero-coupon bond, weighting it by the percentage of the total value of all the bonds that it represents. In other words, the duration of this set of zero-coupon bonds is the weighted average of the effective maturities of the individual zero-coupon bonds, with the weights equaling the proportion of the total value represented by each zero-coupon bond. We do this in several steps in Table 3.3. First we calculate the present value of each of the zero-coupon bonds when the interest rate is 10% in column (3). Then in column (4) we divide each of these present values by $1,000, the total present value of the set of zero-coupon bonds, to get the percentage of the total value of all the bonds that each bond represents. Note that the sum of the weights in column (4) must total 100%, as shown at the bottom of the column.

To get the effective maturity of the set of zero-coupon bonds, we add up the weighted maturities in column (5) and obtain the figure of 6.76 years. This figure

TABLE 3.3 Calculating Duration on a $1,000 Ten-Year 10% Coupon Bond When Its Interest Rate Is 10%

(1) Year	(2) Cash Payments (Zero-Coupon Bonds) ($)	(3) Present Value (*PV*) of Cash Payments (i = 10%) ($)	(4) Weights (% of total *PV* = *PV*/$1,000) (%)	(5) Weighted Maturity (1 × 4)/100 (years)
1	100	90.91	9.091	0.09091
2	100	82.64	8.264	0.16528
3	100	75.13	7.513	0.22539
4	100	68.30	6.830	0.27320
5	100	62.09	6.209	0.31045
6	100	56.44	5.644	0.33864
7	100	51.32	5.132	0.35924
8	100	46.65	4.665	0.37320
9	100	42.41	4.241	0.38169
10	100	38.55	3.855	0.38550
10	1,000	385.54	38.554	3.85500
Total		1,000.00	100.000	6.75850

for the effective maturity of the set of zero-coupon bonds is the duration of the 10% 10-year coupon bond because the bond is equivalent to this set of zero-coupon bonds. In short, we see that ***duration is a weighted average of the maturities of the cash payments***.

The duration calculation done in Table 3.3 can be written as follows:

$$DUR = \sum_{t=1}^{n} t \frac{CP_t}{(1+i)^t} \Bigg/ \sum_{t=1}^{n} \frac{CP_t}{(1+i)^t} \tag{11}$$

where
DUR = duration
t = years until cash payment is made
CP_t = cash payment (interest plus principal) at time t
i = interest rate
n = years to maturity of the security

This formula is not as intuitive as the calculation done in Table 3.3, but it does have the advantage that it can easily be programmed into a calculator or computer, making duration calculations very easy.

If we calculate the duration for an 11-year 10% coupon bond when the interest rate is again 10%, we find that it equals 7.14 years, which is greater than the 6.76 years for the 10-year bond. Thus, we have reached the expected conclusion: ***All else being equal, the longer the term to maturity of a bond, the longer its duration.***

You might think that knowing the maturity of a coupon bond is enough to tell you what its duration is. However, that is not the case. To see this and to give you more practice in calculating duration, in Table 3.4 we again calculate the duration

TABLE 3.4 Calculating Duration on a $1,000 Ten-Year 10% Coupon Bond When Its Interest Rate Is 20%

(1) Year	(2) Cash Payments (Zero-Coupon Bonds) ($)	(3) Present Value (*PV*) of Cash Payments (*i* = 20%) ($)	(4) Weights (% of total *PV* = *PV*/$580.76) (%)	(5) Weighted Maturity (1 × 4)/100 (years)
1	100	83.33	14.348	0.14348
2	100	69.44	11.957	0.23914
3	100	57.87	9.965	0.29895
4	100	48.23	8.305	0.33220
5	100	40.19	6.920	0.34600
6	100	33.49	5.767	0.34602
7	100	27.91	4.806	0.33642
8	100	23.26	4.005	0.32040
9	100	19.38	3.337	0.30033
10	100	16.15	2.781	0.27810
10	1,000	161.51	27.808	2.78100
Total		580.76	100.000	5.72204

for the 10-year 10% coupon bond, but when the current interest rate is 20% rather than 10%, as in Table 3.3. The calculation in Table 3.4 reveals that the duration of the coupon bond at this higher interest rate has fallen from 6.76 years to 5.72 years. The explanation is fairly straightforward. When the interest rate is higher, the cash payments in the future are discounted more heavily and become less important in present-value terms relative to the total present value of all the payments. The relative weight for these cash payments drops as we see in Table 3.4, and so the effective maturity of the bond falls. We have come to an important conclusion: ***All else being equal, when interest rates rise, the duration of a coupon bond falls***.

The duration of a coupon bond is also affected by its coupon rate. For example, consider a 10-year 20% coupon bond when the interest rate is 10%. Using the same procedure, we find that its duration at the higher 20% coupon rate is 5.98 years versus 6.76 years when the coupon rate is 10%. The explanation is that a higher coupon rate means that a relatively greater amount of the cash payments is made earlier in the life of the bond, and so the effective maturity of the bond must fall. We have thus established a third fact about duration: ***All else being equal, the higher the coupon rate on the bond, the shorter the bond's duration***.

One additional fact about duration makes this concept useful when applied to a portfolio of securities. Our examples have shown that duration is equal to the weighted average of the durations of the cash payments (the effective maturities of the corresponding zero-coupon bonds). So if we calculate the duration for two different securities, it should be easy to see that the duration of a portfolio of the two securities is just the weighted average of the durations of the two securities, with the weights reflecting the proportion of the portfolio invested in each.

EXAMPLE 3.9

Duration of a Portfolio

A manager of a financial institution is holding 25% of a portfolio in a bond with a five-year duration and 75% in a bond with a 10-year duration. What is the duration of the portfolio?

> Solution

The duration of the portfolio is 8.75 years.

$$(0.25 \times 5) + (0.75 \times 10) = 1.25 + 7.5 = 8.75 \text{ years}$$

We now see that ***the duration of a portfolio of securities is the weighted average of the durations of the individual securities, with the weights reflecting the proportion of the portfolio invested in each***. This fact about duration is often referred to as the *additive property of duration*, and it is extremely useful because it means that the duration of a portfolio of securities is easy to calculate from the durations of the individual securities.

To summarize, our calculations of duration for coupon bonds have revealed four facts:

1. The longer the term to maturity of a bond, everything else being equal, the greater its duration.

2. When interest rates rise, everything else being equal, the duration of a coupon bond falls.
3. The higher the coupon rate on the bond, everything else being equal, the shorter the bond's duration.
4. Duration is additive: The duration of a portfolio of securities is the weighted average of the durations of the individual securities, with the weights reflecting the proportion of the portfolio invested in each.

Duration and Interest-Rate Risk

Now that we understand how duration is calculated, we want to see how it can be used by the practicing financial institution manager to measure interest-rate risk. Duration is a particularly useful concept because it provides a good approximation, particularly when interest-rate changes are small, for how much the security price changes for a given change in interest rates, as the following formula indicates:

$$\%\Delta P \approx -DUR \times \frac{\Delta i}{1+i} \tag{12}$$

where

$\%\Delta P = (P_{t+1} - P_t)/P_t =$ percentage change in the price of the security from t to $t+1 =$ rate of capital gain
$DUR =$ duration
$i =$ interest rate

EXAMPLE 3.10

Duration and Interest-Rate Risk

A pension fund manager is holding a 10-year 10% coupon bond in the fund's portfolio, and the interest rate is currently 10%. What loss would the fund be exposed to if the interest rate rises to 11% tomorrow?

> Solution

The approximate percentage change in the price of the bond is –6.15%.

As the calculation in Table 3.3 shows, the duration of a 10-year 10% coupon bond is 6.76 years.

$$\%\Delta P \approx -DUR \times \frac{\Delta i}{1+i}$$

where

$DUR =$ duration $= 6.76$
$\Delta i =$ change in interest rate $= 0.11 - 0.10 = 0.01$
$i =$ current interest rate $= 0.10$

Thus,

$$\%\Delta P \approx -6.76 \times \frac{0.01}{1+0.10}$$

$$\%\Delta P \approx -0.0615 = -6.15\%$$

EXAMPLE 3.11

Duration and Interest-Rate Risk

Now the pension manager has the option to hold a 10-year coupon bond with a coupon rate of 20% instead of 10%. As mentioned earlier, the duration for this 20% coupon bond is 5.98 years when the interest rate is 10%. Find the approximate change in the bond price when the interest rate increases from 10% to 11%.

> Solution

This time the approximate change in bond price is –5.4%. This change in bond price is much smaller than for the higher-duration coupon bond.

$$\%\Delta P \approx -DUR \times \frac{\Delta i}{1+i}$$

where

$$\begin{aligned} DUR &= \text{duration} &&= 5.98 \\ \Delta i &= \text{change in interest rate} &&= 0.11 - 0.10 = 0.01 \\ i &= \text{current interest rate} &&= 0.10 \end{aligned}$$

Thus,

$$\%\Delta P \approx -5.98 \times \frac{0.01}{1+0.10}$$
$$\%\Delta P \approx -0.054 = -5.4\%$$

The pension fund manager realizes that the interest-rate risk on the 20% coupon bond is less than on the 10% coupon bond, so he switches the fund out of the 10% coupon bond and into the 20% coupon bond.

Examples 3.10 and 3.11 have led the pension fund manager to an important conclusion about the relationship of duration and interest-rate risk: ***The greater the duration of a security, the greater the percentage change in the market value of the security for a given change in interest rates. Therefore, the greater the duration of a security, the greater its interest-rate risk***.

This reasoning applies equally to a portfolio of securities. So by calculating the duration of the fund's portfolio of securities using the methods outlined here, a pension fund manager can easily ascertain the amount of interest-rate risk the entire fund is exposed to. As we will see in Chapter 23, duration is a highly useful concept for the management of interest-rate risk that is widely used by managers of banks and other financial institutions.

SUMMARY

1. The yield to maturity, which is the measure most accurately reflecting the interest rate, is the interest rate that equates the present value of future cash flows of a debt instrument with its value today. Application of this principle reveals that bond prices and interest rates are negatively related: When the interest rate rises, the price of the bond must fall, and vice versa.

2. The real interest rate is defined as the nominal interest rate minus the expected rate of inflation. It is both a better measure of the incentives to borrow and lend and a more accurate indicator of the tightness of credit market conditions than the nominal interest rate.
3. The return on a security, which tells you how well you have done by holding this security over a stated period of time, can differ substantially from the interest rate as measured by the yield to maturity. Long-term bond prices have substantial fluctuations when interest rates change and thus bear interest-rate risk. The resulting capital gains and losses can be large, which is why long-term bonds are not considered to be safe assets with a sure return. Bonds whose maturity is shorter than the holding period are also subject to reinvestment risk, which occurs because the proceeds from the short-term bond need to be reinvested at a future interest rate that is uncertain.
4. Duration, the average lifetime of a debt security's stream of payments, is a measure of effective maturity, the term to maturity that accurately measures interest-rate risk. Everything else being equal, the duration of a bond is greater the longer the maturity of a bond, when interest rates fall, or when the coupon rate of a coupon bond falls. Duration is additive: The duration of a portfolio of securities is the weighted average of the durations of the individual securities, with the weights reflecting the proportion of the portfolio invested in each. The greater the duration of a security, the greater the percentage change in the market value of the security for a given change in interest rates. Therefore, the greater the duration of a security, the greater its interest-rate risk.

KEY TERMS

cash flows, p. 38
coupon bond, p. 40
coupon rate, p. 40
current yield, p. 46
discount bond (zero-coupon bond), p. 40
duration, p. 56
face value (par value), p. 40
fixed-payment loan (fully amortized loan), p. 40
indexed bonds, p. 51
interest-rate risk, p. 54
nominal interest rate, p. 48
perpetuity (consol), p. 45
present value (present discounted value), p. 38
rate of capital gain, p. 53
real interest rate, p. 48
real terms, p. 49
reinvestment risk, p. 55
return (rate of return), p. 51
simple loan, p. 38
yield to maturity, p. 41

QUESTIONS

1. Explain which information you would need to take into consideration when deciding to receive \$5,000 today or \$5,500 one year from today.
2. If there is a decline in interest rates, which would you rather be holding, long-term bonds or short-term bonds? Why? Which type of bond has the greater interest-rate risk?
3. Suppose today you buy a coupon bond that you plan to sell one year later. Which part of the rate of return formula incorporates future changes into the bond's price? *Note:* Check Equations 9 and 10 in this chapter.
4. If mortgage rates rise from 5% to 10%, but the expected rate of increase in housing prices rises from 2% to 9%, are people more or less likely to buy houses?

QUANTITATIVE PROBLEMS

1. Calculate the present value of a \$1,000 zero-coupon bond with five years to maturity if the yield to maturity is 6%.
2. A lottery claims its grand prize is \$10 million, payable over 20 years at \$500,000 per year. If the first payment is made immediately, what is this grand prize really worth? Use an interest rate of 6%.

3. Consider a bond with a 7% annual coupon and a face value of $1,000. Complete the following table.

Years to Maturity	Yield to Maturity	Current Price
3	5	
3	7	
6	7	
9	7	
9	9	

What relationships do you observe between maturity and discount rate and the current price?

4. Consider a coupon bond that has a $1,000 par value and a coupon rate of 10%. The bond is currently selling for $1,150 and has eight years to maturity. What is the bond's yield to maturity?

5. Suppose that a commercial bank wants to buy Treasury bills. These instruments pay $5,000 in one year and are currently selling for $5,012. What is the yield to maturity of these bonds? Is this a typical situation? Why?

6. What is the price of a perpetuity that has a coupon of $50 per year and a yield to maturity of 2.5%? If the yield to maturity doubles, what will happen to its price?

7. Property taxes in DeKalb County are roughly 2.66% of the purchase price every year. If you just bought a $100,000 home, what is the *PV* of all future property tax payments? Assume that the house remains worth $100,000 forever, property tax rates never change, and that a 9% interest rate is used for discounting.

8. Suppose that you want to take out a loan and that your local bank wants to charge you an annual real interest rate equal to 3%. Assuming that the annualized expected rate of inflation over the life of the loan is 1%, determine the nominal interest rate that the bank will charge you. What was the actual real interest rate on the loan if, over the life of the loan, actual inflation is 0.5%?

9. Lucia just bought two coupon bonds, one with a face value of $1,000 and the other with a face value of $5,000. Both bonds have a coupon rate of 5% and sold at par today. Calculate both bonds' current yield and both bonds' rate of return if Lucia is able to sell these bonds one year later for $100 more than the buying price. Can you estimate what happened to the interest rate over that year?

10. You have paid $980.30 for an 8% coupon bond with a face value of $1,000 that matures in five years. You plan on holding the bond for one year. If you want to earn a 9% rate of return on this investment, what price must you sell the bond for? Is this realistic?

11. Calculate the duration of a $1,000, 6% coupon bond with three years to maturity. Assume that all market interest rates are 7%.

12. Consider the bond in the previous question. Calculate the expected price change if interest rates drop to 6.75% using the duration approximation. Calculate the actual price change using discounted cash flow.

13. The duration of a $100 million portfolio is 10 years. Added to the portfolio are $40 million in new securities, increasing the duration of the portfolio to 12.5 years. What is the duration of the $40 million in new securities?

14. A bank has two 3-year commercial loans with a present value of $70 million. The first is a $30 million loan that requires a single payment of $37.8 million in three years, with no other payments till then. The second loan is for $40 million. It requires an annual interest payment of $3.6 million. The principal of $40 million is due in three years.

a. What is the duration of the bank's commercial loan portfolio?

b. What will happen to the value of its portfolio if the general level of interest rates increases from 8% to 8.5%?

15. Consider a bond that promises the following cash flows. The yield to maturity is 12%.

Year	0	1	2	3	4
Promised Payments	160	160	170	180	230

You plan to buy this bond, hold it for 2.5 years, and then sell the bond.

a. What total cash will you receive from the bond after the 2.5 years? Assume that periodic cash flows are reinvested at 12%.

b. If immediately after you buy this bond all market interest rates drop to 11% (including your reinvestment rate), what will be the impact on your total cash flow after 2.5 years? How does this compare to part (a)?

c. Assuming all market interest rates are 12%, what is the duration of this bond?

WEB EXERCISES

Understanding Interest Rates

1. Investigate the data available from the Federal Reserve Bank of St. Louis FRED database at **http://research.stlouisfed.org/fred2/**. Then answer the following questions.

   a. What is the difference in the interest rates on commercial paper for financial firms versus nonfinancial firms?

   b. What was the interest rate on the one-month Eurodollar at the end of 2016?

   c. What is the most recent interest rate reported for the 10-year Treasury note?

CHAPTER 4

Why Do Interest Rates Change?

> PREVIEW

In the early 1950s, nominal interest rates on three-month Treasury bills were about 1% at an annual rate; by 1981 they had reached over 15%. By 2003 they fell to 1%, then rose to over 5% by 2007, and then fell close to zero from 2008 to 2016. What explains these substantial fluctuations in interest rates? One reason we study financial markets and institutions is to provide some answers to this question.

In this chapter we examine why the overall level of *nominal* interest rates (which we refer to simply as "interest rates") changes and the factors that influence their behavior. We learned in Chapter 3 that interest rates are negatively related to the price of bonds, so if we can explain why bond prices change, we can also explain why interest rates fluctuate. Here we will apply supply-and-demand analysis to examine how bond prices and interest rates change.

Determinants of Asset Demand

An **asset** is a piece of property that is a store of value. Items such as money, bonds, stocks, art, land, houses, farm equipment, and manufacturing machinery are all assets. Facing the question of whether to buy and hold an asset or whether to buy one asset rather than another, an individual must consider the following factors:

1. **Wealth**, the total resources owned by the individual, including all assets
2. **Expected return** (the return expected over the next period) on one asset relative to alternative assets
3. **Risk** (the degree of uncertainty associated with the return) of one asset relative to alternative assets
4. **Liquidity** (the ease and speed with which an asset can be turned into cash) relative to alternative assets

Wealth

When we find that our wealth has increased, we have more resources available with which to purchase assets and so, not surprisingly, the quantity of assets we demand increases.[1] Therefore, the effect of changes in wealth on the quantity demanded of an asset can be summarized as follows: ***Holding everything else constant, an increase in wealth raises the quantity demanded of an asset.***

Expected Returns

In Chapter 3 we saw that the return on an asset (such as a bond) measures how much we gain from holding that asset. When we make a decision to buy an asset, we are influenced by what we expect the return on that asset to be. If an ExxonMobil bond, for example, has a return of 15% half of the time and 5% the other half, its expected return (which you can think of as the average return) is 10%. More formally, the expected return on an asset is the weighted average of all possible returns, where the weights are the probabilities of occurrence of that return:

$$R^e = p_1R_1 + p_2R_2 + \cdots + p_nR_n \tag{1}$$

where
R^e = expected return
n = number of possible outcomes (states of nature)
R_i = return in the ith state of nature
p_i = probability of occurrence of the return R_i

[1]Although it is possible that some assets (called *inferior assets*) might have the property that the quantity demanded does not increase as wealth increases, such assets are rare. Hence we will always assume that demand for an asset increases as wealth increases.

EXAMPLE 4.1

Expected Return

What is the expected return on the Exxon-Mobil bond if the return is 12% two-thirds of the time and 8% one-third of the time?

> Solution

The expected return is 10.68%.

$$R^e = p_1R_1 + p_2R_2$$

where

$$\begin{aligned} p_1 &= \text{probability of occurrence of return 1} &&= \tfrac{2}{3} = 0.67 \\ R_1 &= \text{return in state 1} &&= 12\% = 0.12 \\ p_2 &= \text{probability of occurrence of return 2} &&= \tfrac{1}{3} = 0.33 \\ R_2 &= \text{return in state 2} &&= 8\% = 0.08 \end{aligned}$$

Thus,

$$R^e = (.67)(0.12) + (.33)(0.08) = 0.1068 = 10.68\%$$

If the expected return on the Exxon-Mobil bond rises relative to expected returns on alternative assets, holding everything else constant, then it becomes more desirable to purchase it, and the quantity demanded increases. This can occur in either of two ways: (1) when the expected return on the Exxon-Mobil bond rises while the return on an alternative asset—say, stock in IBM—remains unchanged or (2) when the return on the alternative asset, the IBM stock, falls while the return on the Exxon-Mobil bond remains unchanged. To summarize, ***an increase in an asset's expected return relative to that of an alternative asset, holding everything else unchanged, raises the quantity demanded of the asset***.

Risk

The degree of risk or uncertainty of an asset's returns also affects demand for the asset. Consider two assets, stock in Fly-by-Night Airlines and stock in Feet-on-the-Ground Bus Company. Suppose that Fly-by-Night stock has a return of 15% half of the time and 5% the other half of the time, making its expected return 10%, while stock in Feet-on-the-Ground has a fixed return of 10%. Fly-by-Night stock has uncertainty associated with its returns and so has greater risk than stock in Feet-on-the-Ground, whose return is a sure thing.

To see this more formally, we can use a measure of risk called the **standard deviation**. The standard deviation of returns on an asset is calculated as follows. First you need to calculate the expected return, R^e; then you subtract the expected return from each possible return to get a deviation; then you square each deviation and multiply it by the probability of occurrence of that outcome; finally, you add up all these weighted squared deviations and take the square root. The formula for the standard deviation, σ, is thus:

$$\sigma = \sqrt{p_1(R_1 - R^e)^2 + p_2(R_2 - R^e)^2 + \cdots + p_n(R_n - R^e)^2} \quad (2)$$

The higher the standard deviation, σ, the greater the risk of an asset.

EXAMPLE 4.2

Standard Deviation

What is the standard deviation of the returns on the Fly-by-Night Airlines stock and Feet-on-the Ground Bus Company, with the same return outcomes and probabilities described above? Of these two stocks, which is riskier?

> Solution

Fly-by-Night Airlines has a standard deviation of returns of 5%.

$$\sigma = \sqrt{p_1(R_1 - R^e)^2 + p_2(R_2 - R^e)^2}$$
$$R^e = p_1R_1 + p_2R_2$$

where

p_1 = probability of occurrence of return 1 $= \frac{1}{2} = 0.50$

R_1 = return in state 1 $= 15\% = 0.15$

p_2 = probability of occurrence of return 2 $= \frac{1}{2} = 0.50$

R_2 = return in state 2 $= 5\% = 0.05$

R^e = expected return $= (.50)(0.15) + (.50)(0.05) = 0.10$

Thus,

$$\sigma = \sqrt{(.50)(0.15 - 0.10)^2 + (.50)(0.05 - 0.10)^2}$$
$$\sigma = \sqrt{(.50)(0.0025) + (.50)(0.0025)} = \sqrt{0.0025} = 0.05 = 5\%$$

Feet-on-the-Ground Bus Company has a standard deviation of returns of 0%.

$$\sigma = \sqrt{p_1(R_1 - R^e)^2}$$
$$R^e = p_1R_1$$

where

p_1 = probability of occurrence of return 1 $= 1.0$

R_1 = return in state 1 $= 10\% = 0.10$

R^e = expected return $= (1.0)(0.10) = 0.10$

Thus,

$$\sigma = \sqrt{(1.0)(0.10 - 0.10)^2}$$
$$= \sqrt{0} = 0 = 0\%$$

Clearly, Fly-by-Night Airlines is a riskier stock because its standard deviation of returns of 5% is higher than the zero standard deviation of returns for Feet-on-the-Ground Bus Company, which has a certain return.

A *risk-averse* person prefers Feet-on-the-Ground stock (the sure thing) to Fly-by-Night stock (the riskier asset), even though the stocks have the same expected return, 10%. By contrast, a person who prefers risk is a *risk preferer* or *risk lover*. Most people are risk-averse, especially in their financial decisions: Everything else being equal, they prefer to hold the less risky asset. Hence, ***holding everything***

else constant, if an asset's risk rises relative to that of alternative assets, its quantity demanded will fall.[2]

Liquidity

Another factor that affects the demand for an asset is how quickly it can be converted into cash at low cost—its liquidity. An asset is liquid if the market in which it is traded has depth and breadth, that is, if the market has many buyers and sellers. A house is not a very liquid asset because it may be hard to find a buyer quickly; if a house must be sold to pay off bills, it might have to be sold for a much lower price. And the transaction costs in selling a house (broker's commissions, lawyer's fees, and so on) are substantial. A U.S. Treasury bill, by contrast, is a highly liquid asset. It can be sold in a well-organized market with many buyers, so it can be sold quickly at low cost. ***The more liquid an asset is relative to alternative assets, holding everything else unchanged, the more desirable it is, and the greater will be the quantity demanded.***

Theory of Portfolio Choice

All the determining factors we have just discussed can be assembled into the **theory of portfolio choice**, which tells us how much of an asset people want to hold in their portfolio. It states that, holding all the other factors constant:

1. The quantity demanded of an asset is usually positively related to wealth.
2. The quantity demanded of an asset is positively related to its expected return relative to alternative assets.
3. The quantity demanded of an asset is negatively related to the risk of its returns relative to alternative assets.
4. The quantity demanded of an asset is positively related to its liquidity relative to alternative assets.

These results are summarized in Table 4.1.

Supply and Demand in the Bond Market

We approach the analysis of interest-rate determination by studying the supply of and demand for bonds. Because interest rates on different securities tend to move together, in this chapter we will act as if there is only one type of security and a single interest rate in the entire economy. In Chapter 5, we will expand our analysis to look at why interest rates on different securities differ.

The first step is to use the analysis to obtain a **demand curve**, which shows the relationship between the quantity demanded and the price when all other economic variables are held constant (that is, values of other variables are taken as given). You

[2]Diversification, the holding of many risky assets in a portfolio, reduces the overall risk an investor faces. If you are interested in how diversification lowers risk and what effect this has on the price of an asset, you can look at an appendix to this chapter that describes models of asset pricing and is on the book's Web site at www.pearsonhighered.com/mishkin_eakins.

TABLE 4.1 SUMMARY Response of the Quantity of an Asset Demanded to Changes in Wealth, Expected Returns, Risk, and Liquidity

Variable	Change in Variable	Change in Quantity Demanded
Wealth	↑	↑
Expected return relative to other assets	↑	↑
Risk relative to other assets	↑	↓
Liquidity relative to other assets	↑	↑

Note: Only increases in the variables are shown. The effect of decreases in the variables on the change in quantity demanded would be the opposite of those indicated in the far-right column.

may recall from previous finance and economics courses that the assumption that all other economic variables are held constant is called *ceteris paribus*, which means "other things being equal" in Latin.

Demand Curve

To clarify our analysis, let's consider the demand for one-year discount bonds, which make no coupon payments but pay the owner the $1,000 face value in a year. If the holding period is one year, then as we have seen in Chapter 3, the return on the bonds is known absolutely and is equal to the interest rate as measured by the yield to maturity. This means that the expected return on this bond is equal to the interest rate i, which, using Equation 6 in Chapter 3, is

$$i = R^e = \frac{F - P}{P}$$

where
i = interest rate = yield to maturity
R^e = expected return
F = face value of the discount bond
P = initial purchase price of the discount bond

This formula shows that a particular value of the interest rate corresponds to each bond price. If the bond sells for $950, the interest rate and expected return are

$$\frac{\$1{,}000 - \$950}{\$950} = 0.053 = 5.3\%$$

At this 5.3% interest rate and expected return corresponding to a bond price of $950, let us assume that the quantity of bonds demanded is $100 billion, which is plotted as point A in Figure 4.1.

At a price of $900, the interest rate and expected return are

$$\frac{\$1{,}000 - \$900}{\$900} = 0.111 = 11.1\%$$

Because the expected return on these bonds is higher, with all other economic variables (such as income, expected returns on other assets, risk, and liquidity) held constant, the quantity demanded of bonds will be higher as predicted by the theory

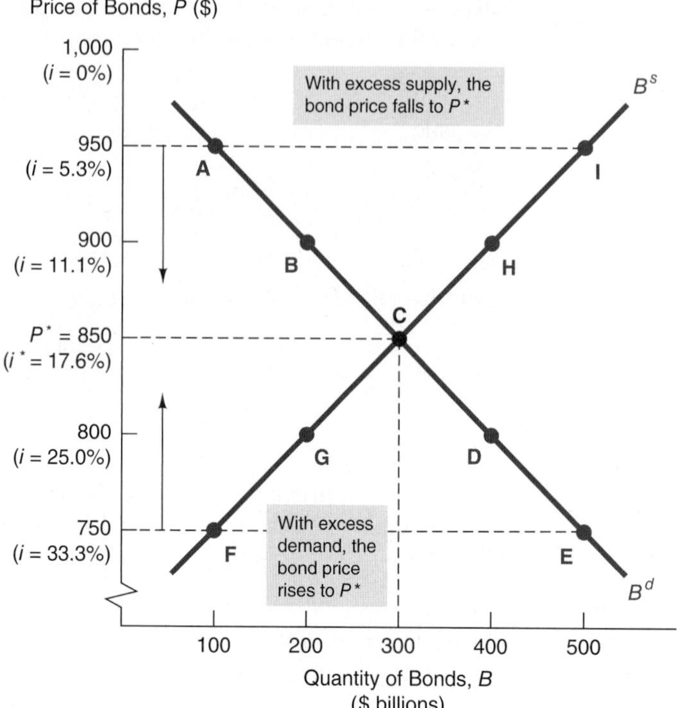

FIGURE 4.1 Supply and Demand for Bonds

Equilibrium in the bond market occurs at point C, the intersection of the demand curve B^d and the bond supply curve B^s. The equilibrium price is $P^* = \$850$, and the equilibrium interest rate is $i^* = 17.6\%$.

of portfolio choice. Point B in Figure 4.1 shows that the quantity of bonds demanded at the price of $900 has risen to $200 billion. Continuing with this reasoning, we see that if the bond price is $850 (interest rate and expected return = 17.6%), the quantity of bonds demanded (point C) will be greater than at point B. Similarly, at the lower prices of $800 (interest rate = 25%) and $750 (interest rate = 33.3%), the quantity of bonds demanded will be even higher (points D and E). The curve B^d, which connects these points, is the demand curve for bonds. It has the usual downward slope, indicating that at lower prices of the bond (everything else being equal), the quantity demanded is higher.[3]

Supply Curve

An important assumption behind the demand curve for bonds in Figure 4.1 is that all other economic variables besides the bond's price and interest rate are held constant. We use the same assumption in deriving a **supply curve**, which shows the

[3]Although our analysis indicates that the demand curve slopes downward, it does not imply that the curve is a straight line. For ease of exposition, however, we will draw demand curves and supply curves as straight lines.

relationship between the quantity supplied and the price when all other economic variables are held constant.

When the price of the bonds is $750 (interest rate = 33.3%), point F shows that the quantity of bonds supplied is $100 billion for the example we are considering. If the price is $800, the interest rate is the lower rate of 25%. Because at this interest rate it is now less costly to borrow by issuing bonds, firms will be willing to borrow more through bond issues, and the quantity of bonds supplied is at the higher level of $200 billion (point G). An even higher price of $850, corresponding to a lower interest rate of 17.6%, results in a larger quantity of bonds supplied of $300 billion (point C). Higher prices of $900 and $950 (which indicate lower interest rates) result in even greater quantities of bonds supplied (points H and I). The B^s curve, which connects these points, is the supply curve for bonds. It has the usual upward slope found in supply curves, indicating that as the price increases (everything else being equal), the quantity supplied increases.

Market Equilibrium

In economics, **market equilibrium** occurs when the amount that people are willing to buy (*demand*) equals the amount that people are willing to sell (*supply*) at a given price. In the bond market, this is achieved when the quantity of bonds demanded equals the quantity of bonds supplied:

$$B^d = B^s \tag{3}$$

In Figure 4.1, equilibrium occurs at point C, where the demand and supply curves intersect at a bond price of $850 (interest rate of 17.6%) and a quantity of bonds of $300 billion. The price of $P^* = \$850$, where the quantity demanded equals the quantity supplied, is called the *equilibrium*, or *market-clearing*, price. Similarly, the interest rate of $i^* = 17.6\%$ that corresponds to this price is called the equilibrium, or market-clearing, interest rate.

The concepts of market equilibrium and equilibrium price or interest rate are useful because the market tends to head toward them. We can see that it does in Figure 4.1 by first looking at what happens when we have a bond price that is above the equilibrium price. When the price of bonds is set too high, at, say, $950, the quantity of bonds supplied at point I is greater than the quantity of bonds demanded at point A. A situation like this, in which the quantity of bonds supplied exceeds the quantity of bonds demanded, is called a condition of **excess supply**. Because people want to sell more bonds than others want to buy, the price of the bonds will fall, which is why the downward arrow is drawn in the figure at the bond price of $950. As long as the bond price remains above the equilibrium price, an excess supply of bonds will continue to be available, and the price will continue to fall. This decline will stop only when the price has reached the equilibrium price of $850, where the excess supply of bonds has been eliminated.

Now let's look at what happens when the price of bonds is below the equilibrium price. If the price of the bonds is set too low, at, say, $750, the quantity demanded at point E is greater than the quantity supplied at point F. This is called a condition of **excess demand**. People now want to buy more bonds than others are willing to sell, so the price of bonds will be driven up, as illustrated by the upward arrow drawn in the figure at the bond price of $750. Only when the excess demand for bonds is eliminated by the price rising to the equilibrium level of $850 is there no further tendency for the price to rise.

We can see that the concept of equilibrium price is a useful one because it indicates where the market will settle. Because each price on the vertical axis of Figure 4.1 corresponds to a particular value of the interest rate, the same diagram also shows that the interest rate will head toward the equilibrium interest rate of 17.6%. When the interest rate is below the equilibrium interest rate, as it is when it is at 5.3%, the price of the bond is above the equilibrium price, and an excess supply of bonds will result. The price of the bond then falls, leading to a rise in the interest rate toward the equilibrium level. Similarly, when the interest rate is above the equilibrium level, as it is when it is at 33.3%, an excess demand for bonds occurs, and the bond price will rise, driving the interest rate back down to the equilibrium level of 17.6%.

Supply-and-Demand Analysis

Our Figure 4.1 is a conventional supply-and-demand diagram with price on the vertical axis and quantity on the horizontal axis. Because the interest rate that corresponds to each bond price is also marked on the vertical axis, this diagram allows us to read the equilibrium interest rate, giving us a model that describes the determination of interest rates. It is important to recognize that a supply-and-demand diagram like Figure 4.1 can be drawn for *any type* of bond because the interest rate and price of a bond are *always* negatively related for all kinds of bonds, whether a discount bond or a coupon bond.

An important feature of the analysis here is that supply and demand are always in terms of *stocks* (amounts *at* a given point in time) of assets, not in terms of *flows* (amounts *per* a given unit of time). The **asset market approach** to understanding behavior in financial markets—which emphasizes stocks of assets rather than flows in determining asset prices—is the dominant methodology used by economists because correctly conducting analyses in terms of flows is very tricky, especially when we encounter inflation.[4]

Changes in Equilibrium Interest Rates

We will now use the supply-and-demand framework for bonds to analyze why interest rates change. To avoid confusion, it is important to make the distinction between *movements along* a demand (or supply) curve and *shifts in* a demand (or supply) curve. When quantity demanded (or supplied) changes as a result of a change in the price of the bond (or, equivalently, a change in the interest rate), we have a *movement along* the demand (or supply) curve. The change in the quantity demanded when we move from point A to B to C in Figure 4.1, for example, is a movement along a demand curve. A *shift in* the demand (or supply) curve, by con-

[4]The asset market approach developed in the text is useful in understanding not only how interest rates behave but also how any asset price is determined. A second appendix to this chapter, which is on this book's Web site at www.pearsonhighered.com/mishkin_eakins, shows how the asset market approach can be applied to understanding the behavior of commodity markets, and in particular, the gold market. The analysis of the bond market that we have developed here has another interpretation that uses a different terminology and framework involving the supply and demand for loanable funds. This loanable funds framework is discussed in a third appendix to this chapter, which is also on the book's Web site.

trast, occurs when the quantity demanded (or supplied) changes *at each given price (or interest rate)* of the bond in response to a change in some other factor besides the bond's price or interest rate. When one of these factors changes, causing a shift in the demand or supply curve, there will be a new equilibrium value for the interest rate.

In the following pages, we will look at how the supply and demand curves shift in response to changes in variables, such as expected inflation and wealth, and what effects these changes have on the equilibrium value of interest rates.

Shifts in the Demand for Bonds

The theory of portfolio choice, which we developed at the beginning of the chapter, provides a framework for deciding which factors cause the demand curve for bonds to shift. These factors include changes in four parameters:

1. Wealth
2. Expected returns on bonds relative to alternative assets
3. Risk of bonds relative to alternative assets
4. Liquidity of bonds relative to alternative assets

To see how a change in each of these factors (holding all other factors constant) can shift the demand curve, let's look at some examples. (As a study aid, Table 4.2 summarizes the effects of changes in these factors on the bond demand curve.)

Wealth When the economy is growing rapidly in a business cycle expansion and wealth is increasing, the quantity of bonds demanded at each bond price (or interest rate) increases, as shown in Figure 4.2. To see how this works, consider point B on the initial demand curve for bonds B_1^d. With higher wealth, the quantity of bonds

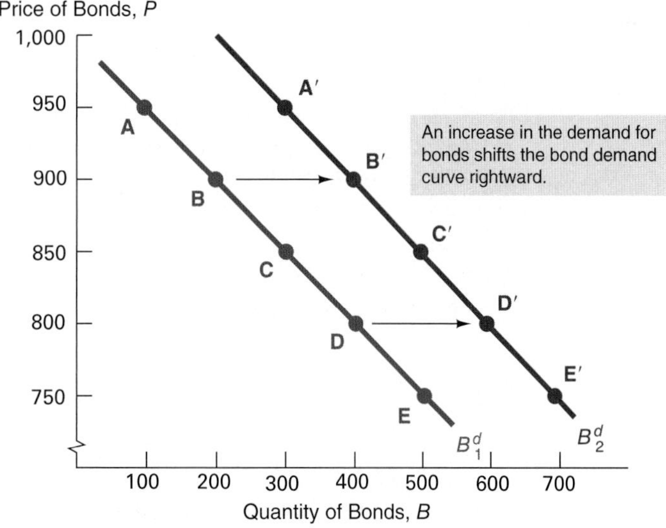

FIGURE 4.2 Shift in the Demand Curve for Bonds
When the demand for bonds increases, the demand curve shifts to the right as shown.

TABLE 4.2 SUMMARY Factors That Shift the Demand Curve for Bonds

Variable	Change in Variable	Change in Quantity Demanded at Each Bond Price	Shift in Demand Curve
Wealth	↑	↑	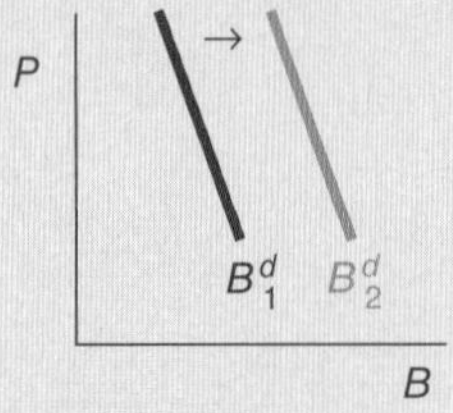 P, B; B_1^d → B_2^d
Expected interest rate	↑	↓	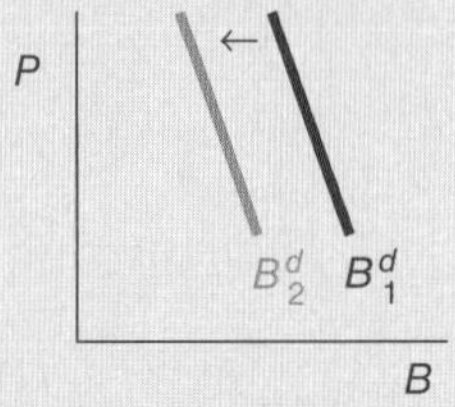 P, B; B_2^d ← B_1^d
Expected inflation	↑	↓	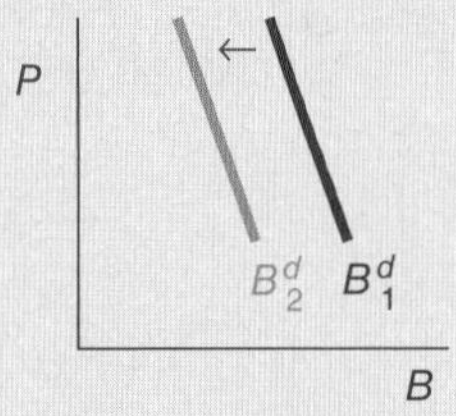 P, B; B_2^d ← B_1^d
Riskiness of bonds relative to other assets	↑	↓	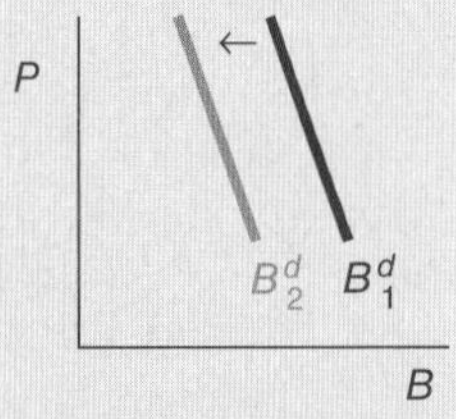 P, B; B_2^d ← B_1^d
Liquidity of bonds relative to other assets	↑	↑	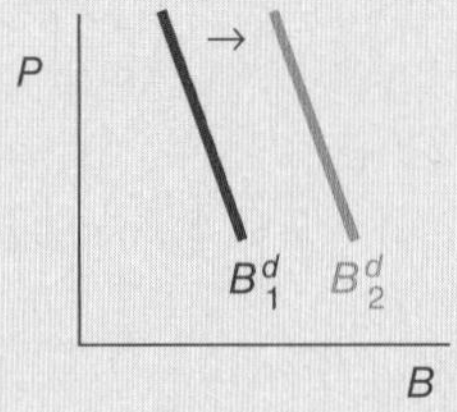 P, B; B_1^d → B_2^d

Note: Only increases in the variables are shown. The effect of decreases in the variables on the change in demand would be the opposite of those indicated in the remaining columns.

demanded at the same price must rise, to point B′. Similarly, for point D the higher wealth causes the quantity demanded at the same bond price to rise to point D′. Continuing with this reasoning for every point on the initial demand curve B_1^d, we can see that the demand curve shifts to the right from B_1^d to B_2^d, as is indicated by the arrows.

The conclusion we have reached is that ***in a business cycle expansion with growing wealth, the demand for bonds rises and the demand curve for bonds shifts to the right***. With the same reasoning applied, ***in a recession, when income and wealth are falling, the demand for bonds falls, and the demand curve shifts to the left***.

Another factor that affects wealth is the public's propensity to save. If households save more, wealth increases and, as we have seen, the demand for bonds rises and the demand curve for bonds shifts to the right. Conversely, if people save less, wealth and the demand for bonds will fall and the demand curve shifts to the left.

Expected Returns For a one-year discount bond and a one-year holding period, the expected return and the interest rate are identical, so nothing besides today's interest rate affects the expected return.

For bonds with maturities of greater than one year, the expected return may differ from the interest rate. For example, we saw in Chapter 3, Table 3.2 that a rise in the interest rate on a long-term bond from 10% to 20% would lead to a sharp decline in price and a very large negative return. Hence, if people began to think that interest rates would be higher next year than they had originally anticipated, the expected return today on long-term bonds would fall, and the quantity demanded would fall at each interest rate. ***Higher expected interest rates in the future lower the expected return for long-term bonds, decrease the demand, and shift the demand curve to the left***.

By contrast, a revision downward of expectations of future interest rates would mean that long-term bond prices would be expected to rise more than originally anticipated, and the resulting higher expected return today would raise the quantity demanded at each bond price and interest rate. ***Lower expected interest rates in the future increase the demand for long-term bonds and shift the demand curve to the right*** (as in Figure 4.2).

Changes in expected returns on other assets can also shift the demand curve for bonds. If people suddenly became more optimistic about the stock market and began to expect higher stock prices in the future, both expected capital gains and expected returns on stocks would rise. With the expected return on bonds held constant, the expected return on bonds today relative to stocks would fall, lowering the demand for bonds and shifting the demand curve to the left.

A change in expected inflation is likely to alter expected returns on physical assets (also called *real assets*) such as automobiles and houses, which affect the demand for bonds. An increase in expected inflation, say, from 5% to 10%, will lead to higher prices on cars and houses in the future and hence higher nominal capital gains. The resulting rise in the expected returns today on these real assets will lead to a fall in the expected return on bonds relative to the expected return on real assets today and thus cause the demand for bonds to fall. Alternatively, we can think of the rise in expected inflation as lowering the real interest rate on bonds, and the resulting decline in the relative expected return on bonds will cause the demand for bonds to fall. ***An increase in the expected rate of inflation lowers the expected return for bonds, causing their demand to decline and the demand curve to shift to the left. Conversely, a decrease in the expected rate of inflation raises the expected return for bonds, causing the demand curve to shift to the right***.

Risk If prices in the bond market become more volatile, the risk associated with bonds increases, and bonds become a less attractive asset. ***An increase in the***

riskiness of bonds causes the demand for bonds to fall and the demand curve to shift to the left.

Conversely, an increase in the volatility of prices in another asset market, such as the stock market, would make bonds more attractive. ***An increase in the riskiness of alternative assets causes the demand for bonds to rise and the demand curve to shift to the right*** (as in Figure 4.2).

Liquidity If more people started trading in the bond market, and as a result it became easier to sell bonds quickly, the increase in their liquidity would cause the quantity of bonds demanded at each interest rate to rise. ***Increased liquidity of bonds results in an increased demand for bonds, and the demand curve shifts to the right*** (see Figure 4.2). ***Similarly, increased liquidity of alternative assets lowers the demand for bonds and shifts the demand curve to the left.*** The reduction of brokerage commissions for trading common stocks that occurred when the fixed-rate commission structure was abolished in 1975, for example, increased the liquidity of stocks relative to bonds, and the resulting lower demand for bonds shifted the demand curve to the left.

Shifts in the Supply of Bonds

Certain factors can cause the supply curve for bonds to shift, among them these:

1. Expected profitability of investment opportunities
2. Expected inflation
3. Government budget

We will look at how the supply curve shifts when each of these factors changes (all others remaining constant). (As a study aid, Table 4.3 summarizes the effects of changes in these factors on the bond supply curve.)

Expected Profitability of Investment Opportunities The more profitable plant and equipment investments that a firm expects it can make, the more willing it will be to borrow to finance these investments. When the economy is growing rapidly, as in a business cycle expansion, investment opportunities that are expected to be profitable abound, and the quantity of bonds supplied at any given bond price will increase (see Figure 4.3). ***Therefore, in a business cycle expansion, the supply of bonds increases, and the supply curve shifts to the right. Likewise, in a recession, when far fewer profitable investment opportunities are expected, the supply of bonds falls, and the supply curve shifts to the left.***

Expected Inflation As we saw in Chapter 3, the real cost of borrowing is more accurately measured by the real interest rate, which equals the (nominal) interest rate minus the expected inflation rate. For a given interest rate (and bond price), when expected inflation increases, the real cost of borrowing falls; hence the quantity of bonds supplied increases at any given bond price. ***An increase in expected inflation causes the supply of bonds to increase and the supply curve to shift to the right*** (see Figure 4.3). ***Conversely, a decrease in expected inflation causes the supply of bonds to decrease and the supply curve shifts to the left.***

Government Budget The activities of the government can influence the supply of bonds in several ways. The U.S. Treasury issues bonds to finance government deficits, the gap between the government's expenditures and its revenues. When

TABLE 4.3 SUMMARY **Factors That Shift the Supply of Bonds**

Variable	Change in Variable	Change in Quantity Supplied at Each Bond Price	Shift in Supply Curve
Profitability of investments	↑	↑	P, B^s_1 → B^s_2, B
Expected inflation	↑	↑	P, B^s_1 → B^s_2, B
Government deficit	↑	↑	P, B^s_1 → B^s_2, B

Note: Only increases in the variables are shown. The effect of decreases in the variables on the change in supply would be the opposite of those indicated in the remaining columns.

these deficits are large, the Treasury sells more bonds, and the quantity of bonds supplied at each bond price increases. ***Higher government deficits increase the supply of bonds and shift the supply curve to the right*** (see Figure 4.3). ***On the other hand, government surpluses, as occurred in the late 1990s, decrease the supply of bonds and shift the supply curve to the left.***

State and local governments and other government agencies also issue bonds to finance their expenditures, and this can affect the supply of bonds as well.

We now can use our knowledge of how supply-and-demand curves shift to analyze how the equilibrium interest rate can change. The best way to do this is to pursue several case applications. In going through these applications, keep two things in mind:

1. When you examine the effect of a variable change, remember we are assuming that all other variables are unchanged; that is, we are making use of the *ceteris paribus* assumption.
2. Remember that the interest rate is negatively related to the bond price, so when the equilibrium bond price rises, the equilibrium interest rate falls. Conversely, if the equilibrium bond price moves downward, the equilibrium interest rate rises.

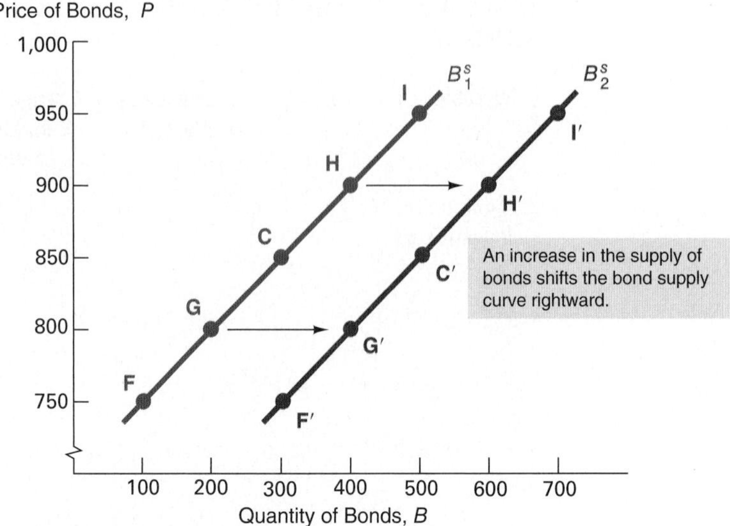

FIGURE 4.3 Shift in the Supply Curve for Bonds

When the supply of bonds increases, the supply curve shifts to the right.

CASE

Changes in the Interest Rate Due to Expected Inflation: The Fisher Effect

We have already done most of the work to evaluate how a change in expected inflation affects the nominal interest rate, in that we have already analyzed how a change in expected inflation shifts the supply and demand curves. Figure 4.4 shows the effect of an increase in expected inflation on the equilibrium interest rate.

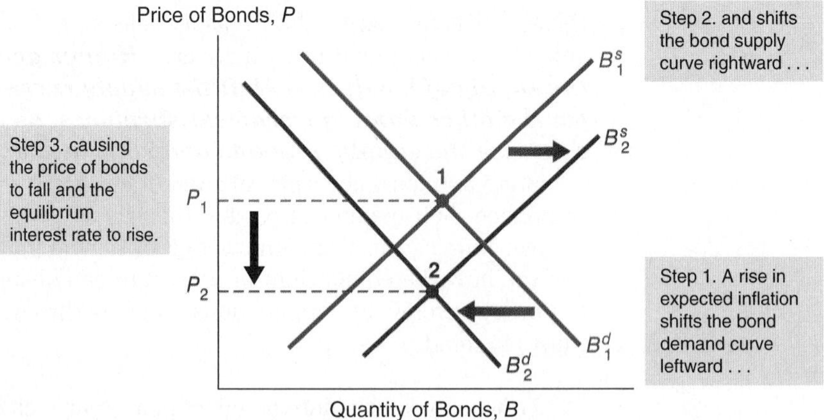

FIGURE 4.4 Response to a Change in Expected Inflation

When expected inflation rises, the supply curve shifts from B_1^s to B_2^s, and the demand curve shifts from B_1^d to B_2^d. The equilibrium moves from point 1 to point 2, with the result that the equilibrium bond price falls from P_1 to P_2 and the equilibrium interest rate rises.

Suppose that expected inflation is initially 5% and the initial supply and demand curves B_1^s and B_1^d intersect at point 1, where the equilibrium bond price is P_1. If expected inflation rises to 10%, the expected return on bonds relative to real assets falls for any given bond price and interest rate. As a result, the demand for bonds falls, and the demand curve shifts to the left, from B_1^d to B_2^d. The rise in expected inflation also shifts the supply curve. At any given bond price and interest rate, the real cost of borrowing has declined, causing the quantity of bonds supplied to increase, and the supply curve shifts to the right, from B_1^s to B_2^s.

When the demand and supply curves shift in response to the change in expected inflation, the equilibrium moves from point 1 to point 2, the intersection of B_2^d and B_2^s. The equilibrium bond price has fallen from P_1 to P_2, and because the bond price is negatively related to the interest rate, this means that the interest rate has risen. (Note that Figure 4.4 has been drawn so that the equilibrium quantity of bonds remains the same for both point 1 and point 2. However, depending on the size of the shifts in the supply and demand curves, the equilibrium quantity of bonds could either rise or fall when expected inflation rises.)

Our supply-and-demand analysis has led us to an important observation: ***When expected inflation rises, interest rates will rise***. This result has been named the **Fisher effect**, after Irving Fisher, the economist who first pointed out the relationship of expected inflation to interest rates. The accuracy of this prediction is shown in Figure 4.5. The interest rate on three-month Treasury bills has usually moved along with the expected inflation rate. Consequently, it is understandable that many economists recommend that inflation be kept low if we want to keep nominal interest rates low.

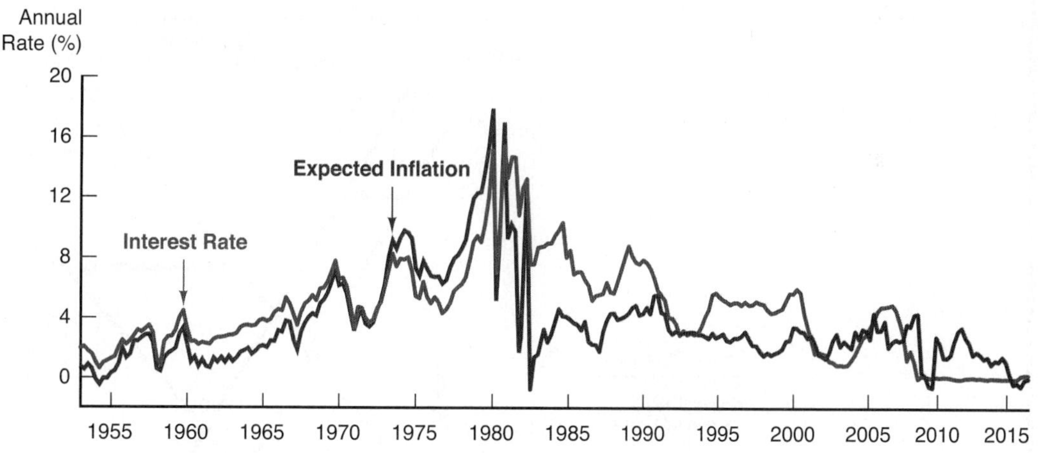

FIGURE 4.5 Expected Inflation and Interest Rates (Three-Month Treasury Bills), 1953–2016

The interest rate on three-month Treasury bills and the expected inflation rate generally move together, as the Fisher effect predicts.

Source: Expected inflation calculated using procedures outlined in Frederic S. Mishkin, "The Real Interest Rate: An Empirical Investigation," *Carnegie-Rochester Conference Series on Public Policy* 15 (1981): 151–200. These procedures involve estimating expected inflation as a function of past interest rates, inflation, and time trends. Nominal three-month Treasury bill rates from Federal Reserve Bank of St. Louis FRED database: https://fred.stlouisfed.org/series/TB3MS and https://fred.stlouisfed.org/series/CPIAUCSL

CASE

Changes in the Interest Rate Due to a Business Cycle Expansion

Figure 4.6 analyzes the effects of a business cycle expansion on interest rates. In a business cycle expansion, the amounts of goods and services being produced in the economy increase, so national income rises. When this occurs, businesses are more willing to borrow because they are likely to have many profitable investment opportunities for which they need financing. Hence at a given bond price, the quantity of bonds that firms want to sell (that is, the supply of bonds) will increase. This means that in a business cycle expansion, the supply curve for bonds shifts to the right (see Figure 4.6), from B_1^s to B_2^s.

Expansion in the economy will also affect the demand for bonds. As the business cycle expands, wealth is likely to increase, and the theory of portfolio choice tells us that the demand for bonds will rise as well. We see this in Figure 4.6, where the demand curve has shifted to the right, from B_1^d to B_2^d.

Given that both the supply and demand curves have shifted to the right, we know that the new equilibrium reached at the intersection of B_2^d and B_2^s must also move to the right. However, depending on whether the supply curve shifts more than the demand curve, or vice versa, the new equilibrium interest rate can either rise or fall.

The supply-and-demand analysis used here gives us an ambiguous answer to the question of what will happen to interest rates in a business cycle expansion. Figure 4.6

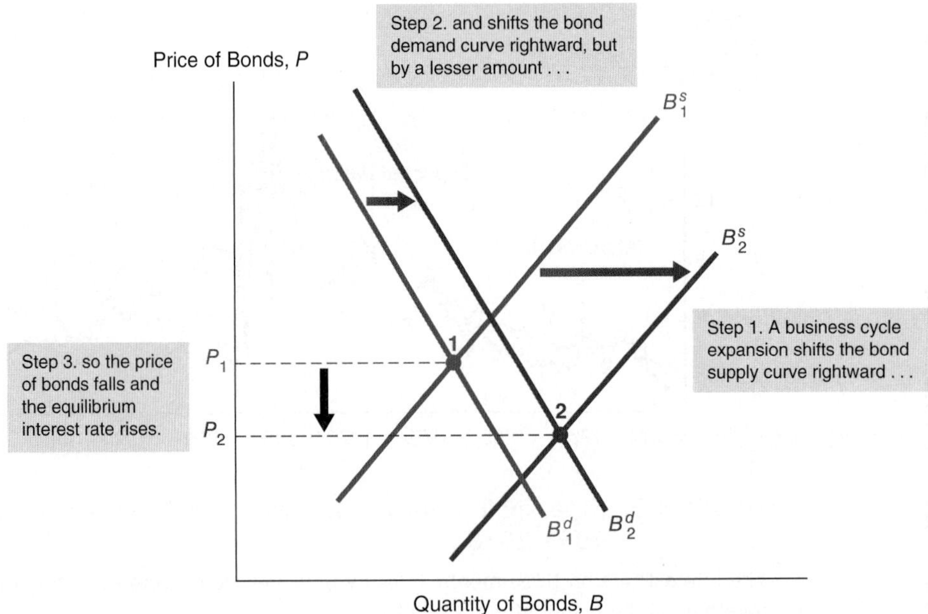

FIGURE 4.6 Response to a Business Cycle Expansion

In a business cycle expansion, when income and wealth are rising, the demand curve shifts rightward from B_1^d to B_2^d and the supply curve shifts rightward from B_1^s to B_2^s. If the supply curve shifts to the right more than the demand curve, as in this figure, the equilibrium bond price moves down from P_1 to P_2, and the equilibrium interest rate rises.

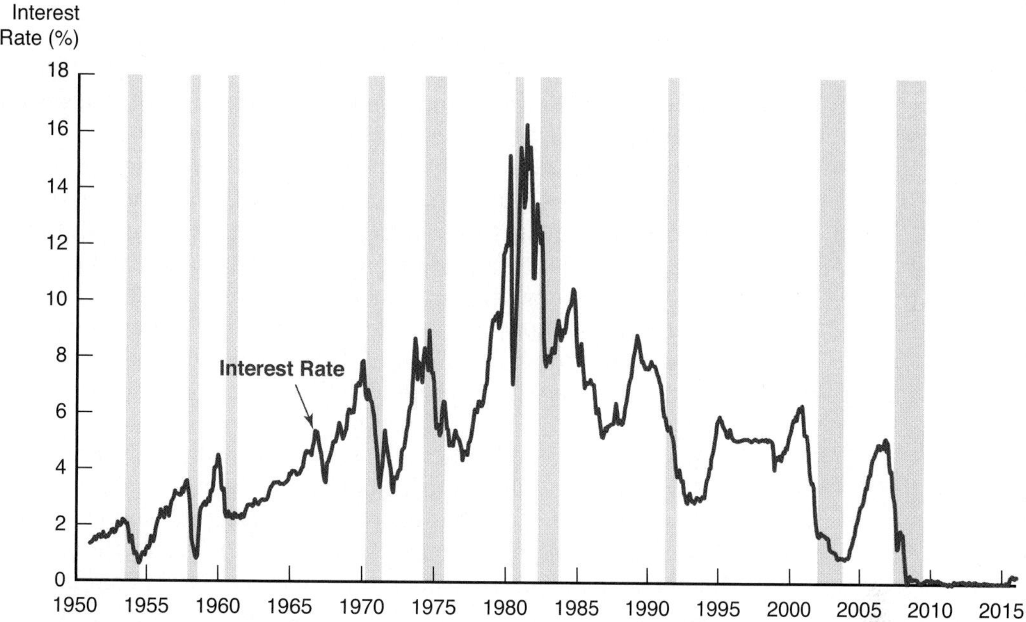

FIGURE 4.7 Business Cycle and Interest Rates (Three-Month Treasury Bills), 1951–2016

Shaded areas indicate periods of recession. The interest rate tends to rise during business cycle expansions and to fall during recessions.

Source: Federal Reserve Bank of St. Louis, FRED database: https://fred.stlouisfed.org/series/TB3MS.

has been drawn so that the shift in the supply curve is greater than the shift in the demand curve, causing the equilibrium bond price to fall to P_2, leading to a rise in the equilibrium interest rate. The reason the figure has been drawn so that a business cycle expansion and a rise in income lead to a higher interest rate is that this is the outcome we actually see in the data. Figure 4.7 plots the movement of the interest rate on three-month U.S. Treasury bills from 1951 to 2016 and indicates when the business cycle is undergoing recessions (shaded areas). As you can see, the interest rate tends to rise during business cycle expansions and falls during recessions, which is what the supply-and-demand diagram indicates.

CASE

Explaining the Current Low Interest Rates in Europe, Japan, and the United States

In the aftermath of the global financial crisis, interest rates in Europe and the United States, as well as in Japan, have fallen to extremely low levels. Indeed, as discussed in Chapter 3, we have seen that interest rates have even sometimes turned negative. Why are interest rates in these countries at such low levels?

The answer is that inflation has fallen to very low levels in all these countries, sometimes even going negative, while at the same time there has been a dearth of attractive investment opportunities. Using these facts, analysis similar to that used in the preceding application explains why interest rates have become so low.

Very low and even negative inflation causes the demand for bonds to rise because the expected return on real assets falls, thereby raising the relative expected return on bonds and in turn causing the demand curve to shift to the right. Low and even negative inflation also raises the real interest rate and therefore the real cost of borrowing for any given nominal rate, thereby causing the supply of bonds to contract and the supply curve to shift to the left. The outcome is then exactly the opposite of that graphed in Figure 4.4: The rightward shift of the demand curve and leftward shift of the supply curve lead to a rise in the bond price and a fall in interest rates.

All of these countries have also been experiencing very low economic growth rates, which has resulted in a lack of profitable investment opportunities. As a result, the supply of bonds has decreased, shifting the supply curve to the left. The leftward shift of the supply curve for bonds leads to a further rise in the bond price and interest rates fall (the opposite outcome to that in Figure 4.6).

Usually, we think that low interest rates are a good thing because they make it cheap to borrow. But the recent episodes of low interest rates in the United States, Europe, and Japan show that just as a fallacy is present in the adage, "You can never be too rich or too thin" (maybe you can't be too rich, but you can certainly be too thin and damage your health), a fallacy is present in always thinking that lower interest rates are better. In the United States, Europe, and Japan, the low and even negative interest rates are a sign that these economies are not doing all that well, with slow growth and inflation that is too low. Only when these economies return to good health will interest rates rise back to more normal levels.

THE PRACTICING MANAGER

Profiting from Interest-Rate Forecasts

Given the importance of interest rates, the media frequently report interest-rate forecasts, as the Following the Financial News box on page 85 indicates. Because changes in interest rates have a major impact on the profitability of financial institutions, financial managers care a great deal about the path of future interest rates. Managers of financial institutions obtain interest-rate forecasts either by hiring their staff economists to generate forecasts or by purchasing forecasts from other financial institutions or economic forecasting firms.

Several methods are used to produce interest-rate forecasts. One of the most popular is based on the supply and demand for bonds framework described here, and it is used by financial institutions such as Citicorp, Morgan Guaranty Trust

Company, and the Prudential Insurance Company.[5] Using this framework, analysts predict what will happen to the factors that affect the supply of and demand for bonds—factors such as the strength of the economy, the profitability of investment opportunities, the expected inflation rate, and the size of government deficits and borrowing. They then use the supply-and-demand analysis outlined in the chapter to come up with their interest-rate forecasts. A variation of this approach makes use of the *Flow of Funds Accounts* produced by the Federal Reserve. These data show the sources and uses of funds by different sectors of the American economy. By looking at how well the supply of credit and the demand for credit by different sectors match up, forecasters attempt to predict future changes in interest rates.

Forecasting done with the supply and demand for bonds framework often does not make use of formal economic models but rather depends on the judgment or "feel" of the forecaster. An alternative method of forecasting interest rates makes use of **econometric models**, models whose equations are estimated with statistical procedures using past data. These models involve interlocking equations that, once input variables such as the behavior of government spending and monetary policy are plugged in, produce simultaneous forecasts of many variables including interest rates. The basic assumption of these forecasting models is that the estimated relationships among variables will continue to hold up in the future. Given this assumption, the forecaster makes predictions of the expected path of the input variables and then lets the model generate forecasts of variables such as interest rates.

Many of these econometric models are quite large, involving hundreds and sometimes over a thousand equations, and consequently require computers to produce their forecasts. Prominent examples of these large-scale econometric models used by the private sector include those developed by Wharton Econometric Forecasting Associates and Macroeconomic Advisors. To generate its interest-rate forecasts, the Board of Governors of the Federal Reserve System uses its own large-scale econometric model, although it uses judgmental forecasts as well.

Managers of financial institutions rely on these forecasts to make decisions about which assets they should hold. A manager who believes a forecast that long-term interest rates will fall in the future would seek to purchase long-term bonds for the asset account because, as we have seen in Chapter 3, the drop in interest rates will produce large capital gains. Conversely, if forecasts say that interest rates are likely to rise in the future, the manager will prefer to hold short-term bonds or loans in the portfolio in order to avoid potential capital losses on long-term securities.

Forecasts of interest rates also help managers decide whether to borrow long-term or short-term. If interest rates are forecast to rise in the future, the financial institution manager will want to lock in today's low interest rates by borrowing long-term; if the forecasts say that interest rates will fall, the manager will seek to borrow short-term in order to take advantage of low interest-rate costs in the future.

Clearly, good forecasts of future interest rates are extremely valuable to the financial institution manager, who, not surprisingly, would be willing to pay a lot for accurate forecasts. Unfortunately, interest-rate forecasting is a perilous business, and even the top forecasters, to their embarrassment, are frequently far off in their forecasts.

[5]Another framework used to produce forecasts of interest rates, developed by John Maynard Keynes, analyzes the supply and demand for money and is called the *liquidity preference framework*. This framework is discussed in a fourth appendix to this chapter, which can be found on the book's Web site at www.pearsonhighered.com/mishkin_eakins.

> FOLLOWING THE FINANCIAL NEWS

Forecasting Interest Rates

Forecasting interest rates is a time-honored profession. Financial economists are hired (sometimes at very high salaries) to forecast interest rates because businesses need to know what the rates will be in order to plan their future spending, and banks and investors require interest-rate forecasts in order to decide which assets to buy. Interest-rate forecasters predict what will happen to the factors that affect the supply and demand for bonds and for money—factors such as the strength of the economy, the profitability of investment opportunities, the expected inflation rate, and the size of government budget deficits and borrowing. They then use the supply-and-demand analysis we have outlined here to come up with their interest-rate forecasts.

The *Wall Street Journal* reports interest-rate forecasts by leading prognosticators twice a year (early January and July) on its Web site.

You can obtain the current URL for the interest-rate forecasts on the Web site www.pearsonhighered.com/mishkin_eakins. In addition to the displayed interest-rate forecast, you can see what the leading economists predict for GDP, inflation, unemployment, and housing.

SUMMARY

1. The theory of portfolio choice tells us that the quantity demanded of an asset is (a) positively related to wealth, (b) positively related to the expected return on the asset relative to alternative assets, (c) negatively related to the riskiness of the asset relative to alternative assets, and (d) positively related to the liquidity of the asset relative to alternative assets.
2. The supply-and-demand analysis for bonds provides a theory of how interest rates are determined. It predicts that interest rates will change when there is a change in demand because of changes in income (or wealth), expected returns, risk, or liquidity, or when there is a change in supply because of changes in the attractiveness of investment opportunities, the real cost of borrowing, or government activities.

KEY TERMS

asset, p. 67
asset market approach, p. 74
demand curve, p. 70
econometric models, p. 85
excess demand, p. 73
excess supply, p. 73
expected return, p. 67
Fisher effect, p. 81
liquidity, p. 67
market equilibrium, p. 73
risk, p. 67
standard deviation, p. 68
supply curve, p. 72
theory of portfolio choice, p. 70
wealth, p. 67

QUESTIONS

1. Explain why you would be more or less willing to buy a share of Verizon stock in the following situations:
   - **a.** Your wealth falls.
   - **b.** You expect it (Verizon stock) to appreciate in value.
   - **c.** The bond market becomes more liquid.
   - **d.** You expect gold to appreciate in value.
   - **e.** Prices in the bond market become more volatile.
2. Explain why you would be more or less willing to buy a house under the following circumstances:
   - **a.** You just inherited $100,000.
   - **b.** Real estate commissions fall from 6% of the sales price to 4% of the sales price.
   - **c.** You expect Verizon stock to double in value next year.
   - **d.** Prices in the stock market become more volatile.
   - **e.** You expect housing prices to fall.
3. Raphael observes that at the current level of interest rates there is an excess supply of bonds, and therefore he anticipates an increase in the price of bonds. Is Raphael correct?
4. I own a professional football team, and I plan to diversify by purchasing shares in either a company that

owns a pro basketball team or a pharmaceutical company. Which of these two investments is more likely to reduce the overall risk I face? Why?

5. Suppose Maria prefers to buy a bond with a 7% expected return and 2% standard deviation of its expected return, while Jennifer prefers to buy a bond with a 4% expected return and 1% standard deviation of its expected return. Can you tell if Maria is more or less risk-averse than Jennifer?

For items 6–13, answer each question by drawing the appropriate supply-and-demand diagrams.

6. An important way in which the Federal Reserve decreases the money supply is by selling bonds to the public. Using a supply-and-demand analysis for bonds, show what effect this action has on interest rates.
7. Using the supply-and-demand for bonds framework, show why interest rates are procyclical (rising when the economy is expanding and falling during recessions).
8. What will happen in the bond market if the government imposes a limit on the amount of daily transactions? Which characteristic of an asset would be affected?
9. How might a sudden increase in people's expectations of future real estate prices affect interest rates?
10. Suppose that many big corporations decide not to issue bonds, since it is now too costly to comply with new financial market regulations. Can you describe the expected effect on interest rates?
11. In the aftermath of the global financial crisis, U.S. government budget deficits increased dramatically, yet interest rates on U.S. Treasury debt fell sharply and stayed low for many years. Does this make sense? Why or why not?
12. How would the demand curve for corporate bonds be affected if news about accounting scandals in major corporations spread? What would be the effect on interest rates?
13. Will there be an effect on interest rates if brokerage commissions on stocks fall? Explain your answer.

Predicting the Future

14. Suppose Great Britain leaves the Eurozone, causing a recession in Europe. Considering that the Eurozone is a big commercial partner of the United States, how do you think this might affect the bond market in the United States? Is the effect on the U.S. interest rate ambiguous or not?
15. The chairman of the Fed announces that interest rates will rise sharply next year, and the market believes him. What will happen to today's interest rate on AT&T bonds, such as the $8\frac{1}{8}$s of 2022?
16. Suppose that people in France decide to permanently increase their savings rate. Predict what will happen to the French bond market in the future. Can France expect higher or lower domestic interest rates?
17. Suppose you are in charge of the financial department of your company and you have to decide whether to borrow short- or long-term. Checking the news, you realize that the government is about to engage in a major infrastructure plan in the near future. Predict what will happen to interest rates. Will you advise borrowing short- or long-term?

QUANTITATIVE PROBLEMS

1. You own a $1,000-par zero-coupon bond that has five years of remaining maturity. You plan on selling the bond in one year and believe that the interest rate next year will have the following probability distribution:

Probability	Interest Rate Next Year (%)
0.1	6.60
0.2	6.75
0.4	7.00
0.2	7.20
0.1	7.45

   a. What is your expected price when you sell the bond?

   b. What is the standard deviation of the bond price?

2. Consider a $1,000-par junk bond paying a 12% annual coupon with two years to maturity. The issuing company has a 20% chance of defaulting this year, in which case the bond would not pay anything. If the company survives the first year, paying the annual coupon payment, it then has a 25% chance of defaulting in the second year. If the company defaults in the second year, neither the final coupon payment nor par value of the bond will be paid.

   a. What price must investors pay for this bond to expect a 10% yield to maturity?

   b. At that price, what is the expected holding period return and standard deviation of returns? Assume that periodic cash flows are reinvested at 10%.

3. Last month, corporations supplied $250 billion in one-year discount bonds to investors at an average market rate of 11.8%. This month, an additional

$25 billion in one-year discount bonds became available, and market rates increased to 12.2%. Assuming that the demand curve remained constant, derive a linear equation for the demand for bonds, using prices instead of interest rates.

4. An economist has concluded that, near the point of equilibrium, the demand curve and supply curve for one-year discount bonds can be estimated using the following equations:

$$B^d\text{: Price} = \frac{-2}{5}\text{Quantity} + 940$$

$$B^s\text{: Price} = \text{Quantity} + 500$$

a. What is the expected equilibrium price and quantity of bonds in this market?

b. Given your answer to part (a), which is the expected interest rate in this market?

5. The demand curve and supply curve are estimated to be the same as in problem 4. Following a dramatic increase in the value of the stock market, many retirees started moving money out of the stock market and into bonds. This resulted in a parallel shift in the demand for bonds, such that the price of bonds at all quantities increased $50. Assuming no change in the supply equation for bonds, what is the new equilibrium price and quantity? What is the new market interest rate?

6. The demand curve and the supply curve are estimated to be the same as in problem 4. As the stock market continued to rise, the Federal Reserve felt the need to increase the interest rates. As a result, the new market interest rate increased to 19.65%, but the equilibrium quantity remained unchanged. What are the new demand and supply equations? Assume parallel shifts in the equations.

WEB EXERCISES

Interest Rates and Inflation

1. One of the largest influences on the level of interest rates is inflation. A number of sites report inflation over time. Go to the Federal Reserve Bank of St. Louis, FRED database Web site at **https://research.stlouisfed.org/fred2/** and find the consumer price index for all urban consumers. Click on percent change from the previous year, which calculates the inflation rate. What has the average rate of inflation been since 1950, 1960, 1970, 1980, and 1990? Which year had the lowest level of inflation? Which year had the highest level of inflation?

2. Increasing prices erode the purchasing power of the dollar. It is interesting to compute what goods would have cost at some point in the past after adjusting for inflation. Go to the Federal Reserve Bank of St. Louis, FRED database website at **https://research.stlouisfed.org/fred2/** and find the consumer price index for all urban consumers. What would a car that cost $25,000 today have cost the year that you were born? (To find this, multiply the $25,000 by the price index in the year you were born and divide by the price index today.)

3. One of the points made in this chapter is that inflation erodes investment returns. Go to **www.moneychimp.com/articles/econ/inflation_calculator.htm** and review how changes in inflation alter your real return. What happens to the adjusted value of an investment compared with its inflation-adjusted value as

a. inflation increases?

b. the investment horizon lengthens?

c. expected returns increase?

WEB APPENDICES

Please visit our Web site at **www.pearsonhighered.com/mishkin_eakins** to read the Web appendices to Chapter 4:

- ***Appendix 1:*** Models of Asset Pricing
- ***Appendix 2:*** Applying the Asset Market Approach to a Commodity Market: The Case of Gold
- ***Appendix 3:*** Loanable Funds Framework
- ***Appendix 4:*** Supply and Demand in the Market for Money: The Liquidity Preference Framework

CHAPTER 5

How Do Risk and Term Structure Affect Interest Rates?

> PREVIEW

In our supply-and-demand analysis of interest-rate behavior in Chapter 4, we examined the determination of just one interest rate. Yet we saw earlier that there are enormous numbers of bonds on which the interest rates can and do differ. In this chapter we complete the interest-rate picture by examining the relationship of the various interest rates to one another. Understanding why they differ from bond to bond can help businesses, banks, insurance companies, and private investors decide which bonds to purchase as investments and which ones to sell.

We first look at why bonds with the same term to maturity have different interest rates. The relationship among these interest rates is called the **risk structure of interest rates**, although risk, liquidity, and income tax rules all play a role in determining the risk structure. A bond's term to maturity also affects its interest rate, and the relationship among interest rates on bonds with different terms to maturity is called the **term structure of interest rates**. In this chapter we examine the sources and causes of fluctuations in interest rates relative to one another and look at a number of theories that explain these fluctuations.

Risk Structure of Interest Rates

Figure 5.1 shows the yields to maturity for several categories of long-term bonds from 1919 to 2016. It shows us two important features of interest-rate behavior for bonds of the same maturity: Interest rates on different categories of bonds differ from one another in any given year, and the spread (or difference) between the interest rates varies over time. The interest rates on municipal bonds, for example, are higher than those on U.S. government (Treasury) bonds in the late 1930s but lower thereafter. In addition, the spread between the interest rates on Baa corporate bonds (riskier than Aaa corporate bonds) and U.S. government bonds is very large during the Great Depression years 1930–1933, is smaller during the 1940s–1960s, and then widens again afterward. Which factors are responsible for these phenomena?

Default Risk

One attribute of a bond that influences its interest rate is its risk of **default**, which occurs when the issuer of the bond is unable or unwilling to make interest payments when promised or to pay off the face value when the bond matures. A corporation suffering big losses, such as the major airline companies like United, Delta, US Airways, and Northwest in the mid-2000s, might be more likely to suspend interest payments on its bonds. The default risk on its bonds would therefore be quite high. By contrast, U.S. Treasury bonds have usually been considered to have no default

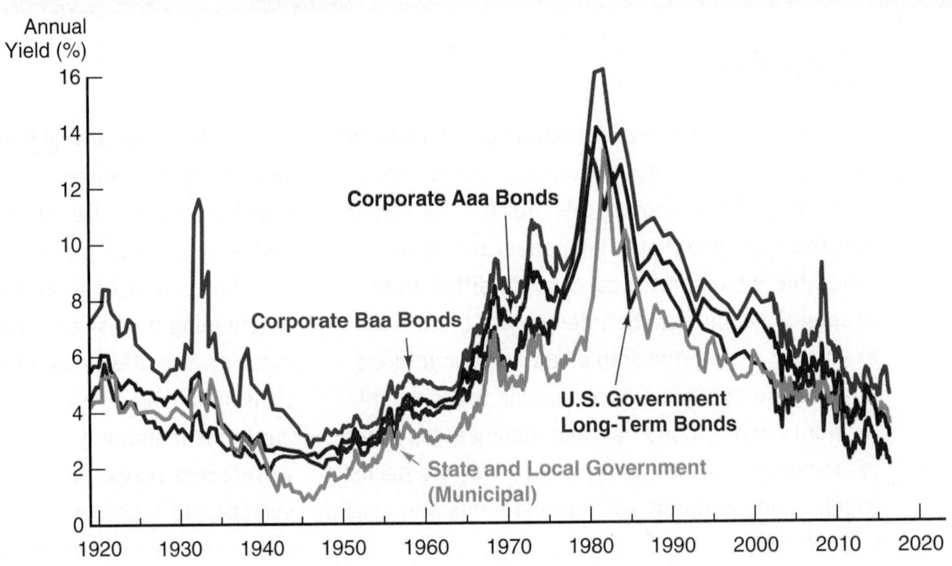

FIGURE 5.1 Long-Term Bond Yields, 1919–2016

Interest rates on different types of bonds differ from one another in any given year, and the spread (or difference) between the interest rates varies over time.

Sources: Board of Governors of the Federal Reserve System, *Banking and Monetary Statistics, 1941–1970*; Federal Reserve Bank of St. Louis FRED database, https://fred.stlouisfed.org/series/GS10, https://fred.stlouisfed.org/series/AAA, https://fred.stlouisfed.org/series/BAA.

risk because the federal government can always increase taxes to pay off its obligations. Bonds like these with no default risk are called **default-free bonds**. (However, during the budget negotiations in Congress in 1995–1996, and then again in 2011–2013, the Republicans threatened to let Treasury bonds default, and this had an impact on the bond market.) The spread between the interest rates on bonds with default risk and default-free bonds, both of the same maturity, called the **risk premium**, indicates how much additional interest people must earn to be willing to hold that risky bond. Our supply-and-demand analysis of the bond market in Chapter 4 can be used to explain why a bond with default risk always has a positive risk premium and why the higher the default risk is, the larger the risk premium will be.

To examine the effect of default risk on interest rates, let's look at the supply-and-demand diagrams for the default-free (U.S. Treasury) and corporate long-term bond markets in Figure 5.2. To make the diagrams somewhat easier to read, let's assume that initially corporate bonds have the same default risk as U.S. Treasury bonds. In this case, these two bonds have the same attributes (identical risk and maturity); their equilibrium prices and interest rates will initially be equal ($P_1^c = P_1^T$ and $i_1^c = i_1^T$), and the risk premium on corporate bonds ($i_1^c - i_1^T$) will be zero.

If the possibility of a default increases because a corporation begins to suffer large losses, the default risk on corporate bonds will increase, and the expected return on these bonds will decrease. In addition, the corporate bond's return will be more uncertain. The theory of portfolio choice predicts that because the expected

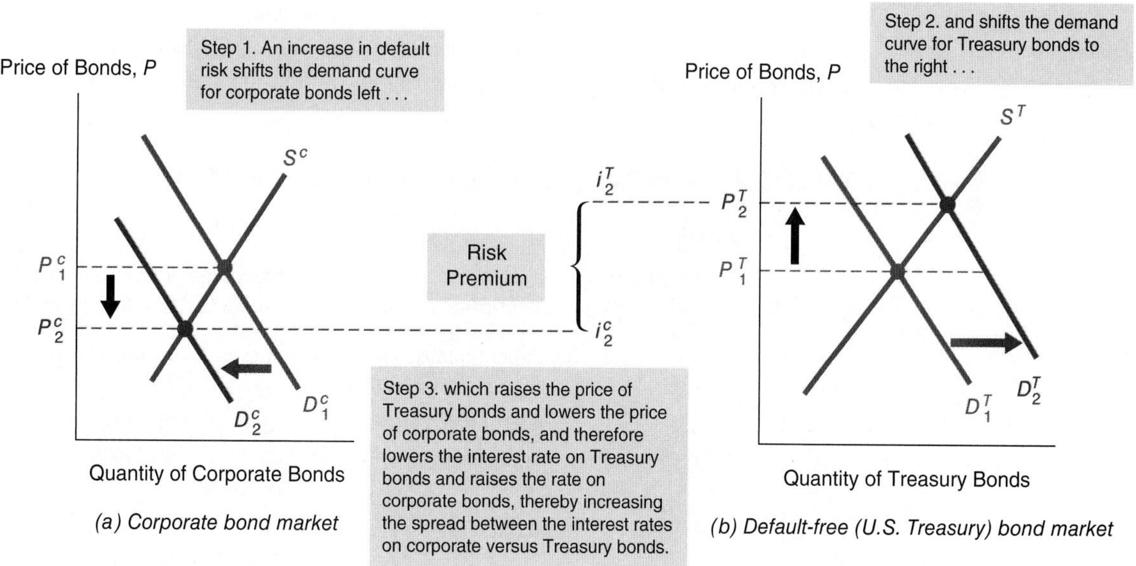

FIGURE 5.2 Response to an Increase in Default Risk on Corporate Bonds

Initially $P_1^c = P_1^T$ and the risk premium is zero. An increase in default risk on corporate bonds shifts the demand curve from D_1^c *to* D_2^c. Simultaneously, it shifts the demand curve for Treasury bonds from D_1^T *to* D_2^T. The equilibrium price for corporate bonds falls from P_1^c *to* P_2^c, and the equilibrium interest rate on corporate bonds rises to i_2^c. In the Treasury market, the equilibrium bond price rises from P_1^T *to* P_2^T and the equilibrium interest rate falls to i_2^T. The brace indicates the difference between i_2^c and i_2^T, the risk premium on corporate bonds. (Note that because P_2^c is lower than P_2^T, i_2^c is greater than i_2^T.)

return on the corporate bond falls relative to the expected return on the default-free Treasury bond while its relative riskiness rises, the corporate bond is less desirable (holding everything else equal), and demand for it will fall. Another way of thinking about this is that if you were an investor, you would want to hold (demand) a smaller amount of corporate bonds. The demand curve for corporate bonds in panel (a) of Figure 5.2 then shifts to the left, from D_1^c to D_2^c.

GO ONLINE
www.federalreserve.gov/Releases/h15/update/
Study how the Federal Reserve reports the yields on different quality bonds. Look at the bottom of the listing of interest rates for AAA- and BBB-rated bonds.

At the same time, the expected return on default-free Treasury bonds increases relative to the expected return on corporate bonds, while their relative riskiness declines. The Treasury bonds thus become more desirable, and demand rises, as shown in panel (b) by the rightward shift in the demand curve for these bonds from D_1^T to D_2^T.

As we can see in Figure 5.2, the equilibrium price for corporate bonds falls from P_1^c to P_2^c, and since the bond price is negatively related to the interest rate, the equilibrium interest rate on corporate bonds rises to i_2^c. At the same time, however, the equilibrium price for the Treasury bonds rises from P_1^T to P_2^T, and the equilibrium interest rate falls to i_2^T. The spread between the interest rates on corporate and default-free bonds—that is, the risk premium on corporate bonds—has risen from zero to $i_2^c - i_2^T$. We can now conclude that ***a bond with default risk will always have a positive risk premium, and an increase in its default risk will raise the risk premium.***

Because default risk is so important to the size of the risk premium, purchasers of bonds need to know whether a corporation is likely to default on its bonds. This information is provided by **credit-rating agencies**, investment advisory firms that rate the quality of corporate and municipal bonds in terms of the probability of default. Table 5.1 provides the ratings and their description for the two largest credit-rating agencies, Moody's Investor Service and Standard and Poor's Corporation. Bonds with relatively low risk of default are called *investment-grade*

TABLE 5.1 Bond Ratings by Moody's and Standard and Poor's

Rating			
Moody's	Standard and Poor's	Descriptions	Examples of Corporations with Bonds Outstanding in 2016
Aaa	AAA	Highest quality (lowest default risk)	Microsoft, Johnson & Johnson
Aa	AA	High quality	Apple, General Electric
A	A	Upper-medium grade	MetLife, Intel Corp., Harley-Davidson
Baa	BBB	Medium grade	McDonald's, Bank of America, Hewlett-Packard, FedEx, Southwest Airlines
Ba	BB	Lower-medium grade	Best Buy, American Airlines, Delta Airlines, United Airlines
B	B	Speculative	Netflix, Rite Aid, J.C. Penney
Caa	CCC, CC	Poor (high default risk)	Sears, Elizabeth Arden
C	D	Highly speculative	Halcon Resources, Seventy-Seven Energy

securities and have a rating of Baa (or BBB) and above. Bonds with ratings below Baa (or BBB) have higher default risk and have been aptly dubbed speculative-grade or **junk bonds**. Because these bonds always have higher interest rates than investment-grade securities, they are also referred to as high-yield bonds.

Next let's look at Figure 5.1 at the beginning of the chapter and see if we can explain the relationship between interest rates on corporate and U.S. Treasury bonds. Corporate bonds always have higher interest rates than U.S. Treasury bonds because they always have some risk of default, whereas U.S. Treasury bonds do not. Because Baa-rated corporate bonds have a greater default risk than the higher-rated Aaa bonds, their risk premium is greater, and the Baa rate therefore always exceeds the Aaa rate. We can use the same analysis to explain the huge jump in the risk premium on Baa corporate bond rates during the Great Depression years 1930–1933 and the rise in the risk premium after 1970 (see Figure 5.1). The depression period saw a very high rate of business failures and defaults. As we would expect, these factors led to a substantial increase in the default risk for bonds issued by vulnerable corporations, and the risk premium for Baa bonds reached unprecedentedly high levels. Since 1970, we have again seen higher levels of business failures and defaults, although they were still well below Great Depression levels. Again, as expected, both default risks and risk premiums for corporate bonds rose, widening the spread between interest rates on corporate bonds and those on Treasury bonds.

Liquidity

Another attribute of a bond that influences its interest rate is its liquidity. As we learned in Chapter 4, a liquid asset is one that can be quickly and cheaply converted

CASE

The Global Financial Crisis and the Baa-Treasury Spread

Starting in August 2007, the collapse of the subprime mortgage market led to large losses in financial institutions (which we will discuss more extensively in Chapter 8). As a consequence of the subprime collapse and the subsequent global financial crisis, many investors began to doubt the financial health of corporations with low credit ratings such as Baa and even the reliability of the ratings themselves. The perceived increase in default risk for Baa bonds made them less desirable at any given interest rate, decreased the quantity demanded, and shifted the demand curve for Baa bonds to the left. As shown in panel (a) of Figure 5.2, the interest rate on Baa bonds should have risen, which is indeed what happened. Interest rates on Baa bonds rose by 280 basis points (2.80 percentage points) from 6.63% at the end of July 2007 to 9.43% at the most virulent stage of the global financial crisis in mid-October 2008. But the increase in perceived default risk for Baa bonds in October 2008 made default-free U.S. Treasury bonds relatively more attractive and shifted the demand curve for these securities to the right—an outcome described by some analysts as a "flight to quality." Just as our analysis predicts in Figure 5.2, interest rates on Treasury bonds fell by 80 basis points, from 4.78% at the end of July 2007 to 3.98% in mid-October 2008. The spread between interest rates on Baa and Treasury bonds rose by 360 basis points, from 1.85% before the crisis to 5.45% afterward.

into cash if the need arises. The more liquid an asset is, the more desirable it is (holding everything else constant). U.S. Treasury bonds are the most liquid of all long-term bonds; because they are so widely traded, they are the easiest to sell quickly and the cost of selling them is low. Corporate bonds are not as liquid because fewer bonds for any one corporation are traded; thus, it can be costly to sell these bonds in an emergency because it might be hard to find buyers quickly.

How does the reduced liquidity of the corporate bonds affect their interest rates relative to the interest rate on Treasury bonds? We can use supply-and-demand analysis with the same figure that was used to analyze the effect of default risk, Figure 5.2, to show that the lower liquidity of corporate bonds relative to Treasury bonds increases the spread between the interest rates on these two bonds. Let's start the analysis by assuming that initially corporate and Treasury bonds are equally liquid and all their other attributes are the same. As shown in Figure 5.2, their equilibrium prices and interest rates will initially be equal: $P_1^c = P_1^T$ and $i_1^c = i_1^T$. If the corporate bond becomes less liquid than the Treasury bond because it is less widely traded, then (as the theory of portfolio choice indicates) demand for it will fall, shifting its demand curve from D_1^c to D_2^c as in panel (a). The Treasury bond now becomes relatively more liquid in comparison with the corporate bond, so its demand curve shifts rightward from D_1^T to D_2^T as in panel (b). The shifts in the curves in Figure 5.2 show that the price of the less liquid corporate bond falls and its interest rate rises, while the price of the more liquid Treasury bond rises and its interest rate falls.

The result is that the spread between the interest rates on the two bond types has increased. Therefore, the differences between interest rates on corporate bonds and Treasury bonds (that is, the risk premiums) reflect not only the corporate bond's default risk but also its liquidity. This is why a risk premium is more accurately a "risk and liquidity premium," but convention dictates that it is called a *risk premium*.

Income Tax Considerations

Returning to Figure 5.1, we are still left with one puzzle—the behavior of municipal bond rates. Municipal bonds are certainly not default-free: State and local governments have defaulted on the municipal bonds they have issued in the past, particularly during the Great Depression and even more recently in San Bernardino, Mammoth Lakes, Stockton (all in California); Jefferson County, Alabama; Harrisburg, Pennsylvania; Central Falls, Rhode Island; and Boise County, Idaho. Also, municipal bonds are not as liquid as U.S. Treasury bonds.

Why is it, then, that these bonds have had lower interest rates than U.S. Treasury bonds for at least 70 years, as indicated in Figure 5.1? The explanation lies in the fact that interest payments on municipal bonds are exempt from federal income taxes, a factor that has the same effect on the demand for municipal bonds as an increase in their expected return.

Let's imagine that you have a high enough income to put you in the 35% income tax bracket, where for every extra dollar of income you have to pay 35 cents to the government. If you own a $1,000-face-value U.S. Treasury bond that sells for $1,000 and has a coupon payment of $100, you get to keep only $65 of the payment after taxes. Although the bond has a 10% interest rate, you actually earn only 6.5% after taxes.

Suppose, however, that you put your savings into a $1,000-face-value municipal bond that sells for $1,000 and pays only $80 in coupon payments. Its interest rate is only 8%, but because it is a tax-exempt security, you pay no taxes on the $80 coupon payment, so you earn 8% after taxes. Clearly, you earn more on the municipal bond after taxes, so you are willing to hold the riskier and less liquid municipal bond even though it has a lower interest rate than the U.S. Treasury bond. (This was not true before World War II, when the tax-exempt status of municipal bonds did not convey much of an advantage because income tax rates were extremely low.)

EXAMPLE 5.1

Income Tax Considerations

Suppose you had the opportunity to buy either a municipal bond or a corporate bond, both of which have a face value and purchase price of $1,000. The municipal bond has coupon payments of $60 and a coupon rate of 6%. The corporate bond has coupon payments of $80 and an interest rate of 8%. Which bond would you choose to purchase, assuming a 40% tax rate?

> Solution

You would choose to purchase the municipal bond because it will earn you $60 in coupon payments and an interest rate after taxes of 6%. Since municipal bonds are tax-exempt, you pay no taxes on the $60 coupon payments and earn 6% after taxes. However, you have to pay taxes on corporate bonds. You will keep only 60% of the $80 coupon payment because the other 40% goes to taxes. Therefore, you receive $48 of the coupon payment and have an interest rate of 4.8% after taxes. Buying the municipal bond would yield you higher earnings.

Another way of understanding why municipal bonds have lower interest rates than Treasury bonds is to use the supply-and-demand analysis depicted in Figure 5.3. We assume that municipal and Treasury bonds have identical attributes and so have the same bond prices as drawn in the figure: $P_1^m = P_1^T$ and the same interest rates. Once the municipal bonds are given a tax advantage that raises their after-tax expected return relative to Treasury bonds and makes them more desirable, demand for them rises, and their demand curve shifts to the right, from D_1^m to D_2^m. The result is that their equilibrium bond price rises from P_1^m to P_2^m and their equilibrium interest rate falls. By contrast, Treasury bonds have now become less desirable relative to municipal bonds; demand for Treasury bonds decreases, and D_1^T shifts to D_2^T. The Treasury bond price falls from P_1^T to P_2^T, and the interest rate rises. The resulting lower interest rates for municipal bonds and higher interest rates for Treasury bonds explain why municipal bonds can have interest rates below those of Treasury bonds.[1]

Summary

The risk structure of interest rates (the relationship among interest rates on bonds with the same maturity) is explained by three factors: default risk, liquidity, and the income tax treatment of a bond's interest payments. As a bond's default risk

[1]In contrast to corporate bonds, Treasury bonds are exempt from state and local income taxes. Using the analysis in the text, you should be able to show that this feature of Treasury bonds provides an additional reason why interest rates on corporate bonds are higher than those on Treasury bonds.

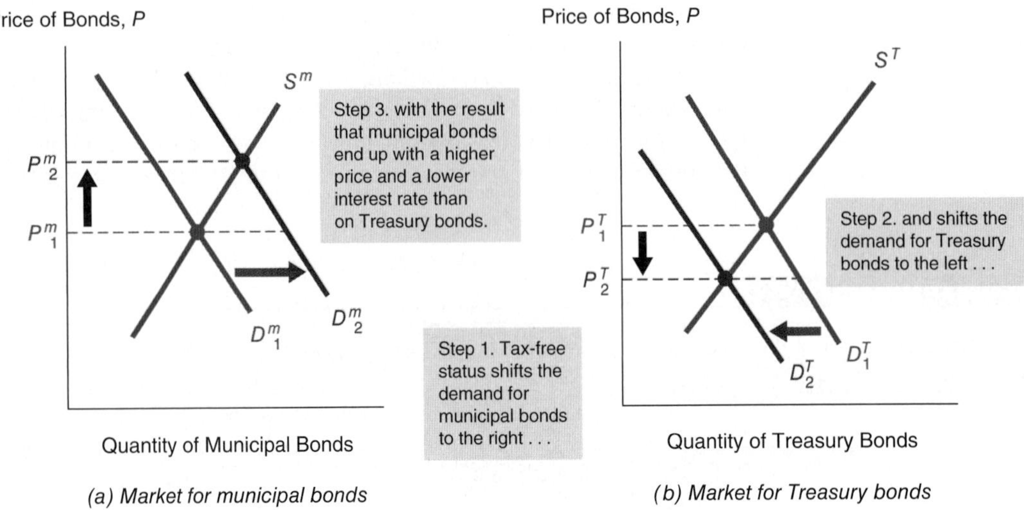

FIGURE 5.3 Interest Rates on Municipal and Treasury Bonds

When the municipal bond is given tax-free status, demand for the municipal bond shifts rightward from D^m_1 to D^m_2 and demand for the Treasury bond shifts leftward from D^T_1 to D^T_2. The equilibrium price of the municipal bond rises from P^m_1 to P^m_2 so its interest rate falls, while the equilibrium price of the Treasury bond falls from P^T_1 to P^T_2 and its interest rate rises. The result is that municipal bonds end up with lower interest rates than those on Treasury bonds.

increases, the risk premium on that bond (the spread between its interest rate and the interest rate on a default-free Treasury bond) rises. The greater liquidity of Treasury bonds also explains why their interest rates are lower than those on less liquid bonds. If a bond has a favorable tax treatment, as do municipal bonds, whose interest payments are exempt from federal income taxes, its interest rate will be lower.

CASE

Effects of the Bush Tax Cut and the Obama Tax Increase on Bond Interest Rates

The Bush tax cut passed in 2001 scheduled a reduction of the top income tax bracket from 39% to 35% over a 10-year period. What was the effect of this income tax decrease on interest rates in the municipal bond market relative to those in the Treasury bond market?

Our supply-and-demand analysis provides the answer. A decreased income tax rate for wealthy people means that the after-tax expected return on tax-free municipal bonds relative to that on Treasury bonds is lower because the interest on Treasury bonds is now taxed at a lower rate. Because municipal bonds now become less desirable, their demand decreases, shifting the demand curve to the left, which lowers their price and raises their interest rate. Conversely, the lower income tax rate makes Treasury bonds more desirable; this change shifts their demand curve to the right, raises their price, and lowers their interest rates.

Our analysis thus shows that the Bush tax cut raised the interest rates on municipal bonds relative to the interest rate on Treasury bonds.

With the Obama tax increase that repealed the Bush tax cuts for high-income taxpayers in 2013, the analysis would be reversed. The Obama tax increase raised the after-tax expected return on tax-free municipal bonds relative to Treasury bonds. Demand for municipal bonds would increase, shifting the demand curve to the right, which raises their price and lowers their interest rate. Conversely, the higher tax rate would make Treasury bonds less desirable, shifting their demand curve to the left, lowering their price, and raising their interest rate. The higher tax rates for high-income households put in place by the Obama administration thus led to lower interest rates on municipal bonds relative to the interest rate on Treasury bonds.

Term Structure of Interest Rates

http://stockcharts.com/charts/YieldCurve.html
Access this site to look at the dynamic yield curve at any point in time since 1995.

We have seen how risk, liquidity, and tax considerations (collectively embedded in the risk structure) can influence interest rates. Another factor that influences the interest rate on a bond is its term to maturity: Bonds with identical risk, liquidity, and tax characteristics may have different interest rates because the time remaining to maturity is different. A plot of the yields on bonds with differing terms to maturity but the same risk, liquidity, and tax considerations is called a **yield curve**, and it describes the term structure of interest rates for particular types of bonds, such as government bonds. The Following the Financial News box on page 98 shows several yield curves for Treasury securities. Yield curves can be classified as upward-sloping, flat, and downward-sloping (the last sort is often referred to as an **inverted yield curve**). When yield curves slope upward, the most usual case, the long-term interest rates are above the short-term interest rates, as in the Following the Financial News box; when yield curves are flat, short- and long-term interest rates are the same; and when yield curves are inverted, long-term interest rates are below short-term interest rates. Yield curves can also have more complicated shapes in which they first slope up and then down, or vice versa. Why do we usually see upward slopes of the yield curve but sometimes other shapes?

Besides explaining why yield curves take on different shapes at different times, a good theory of the term structure of interest rates must explain the following three important empirical facts:

1. As we see in Figure 5.4, interest rates on bonds of different maturities move together over time.
2. When short-term interest rates are low, yield curves are more likely to have an upward slope; when short-term interest rates are high, yield curves are more likely to slope downward and be inverted.
3. Yield curves almost always slope upward, as in the Following the Financial News box.

Three theories have been put forward to explain the term structure of interest rates—that is, the relationship among interest rates on bonds of different maturities

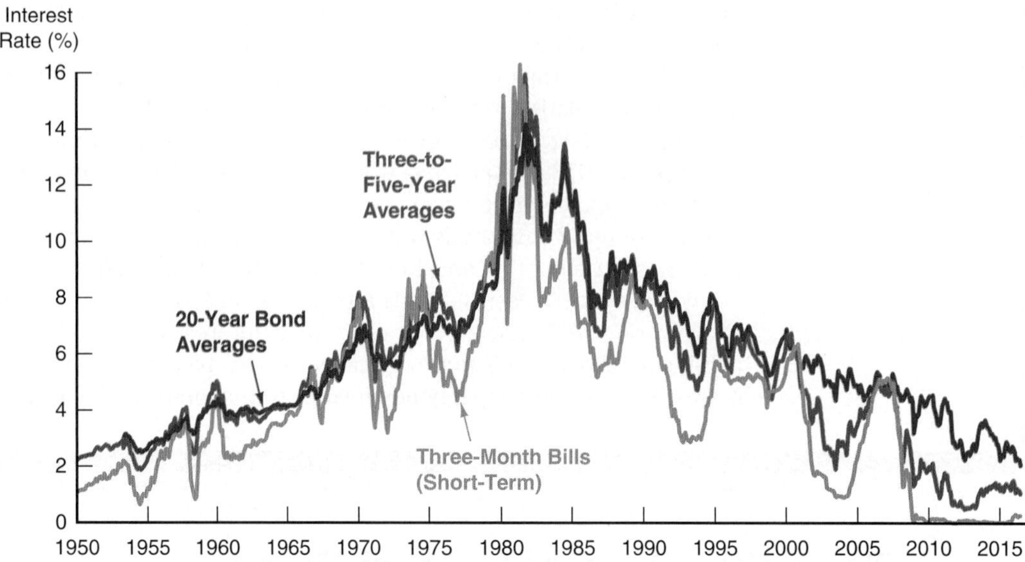

FIGURE 5.4 **Movements over Time of Interest Rates on U.S. Government Bonds with Different Maturities**

Interest rates on bonds of different maturities move together over time.

Source: Federal Reserve Bank of St. Louis, FRED database, https://fred.stlouisfed.org/series/TB3MS; https://fred.stlouisfed.org/series/GS3; https://fred.stlouisfed.org/series/GS5; https://fred.stlouisfed.org/series/GS20: Yield curve, http://finance.yahoo.com/bonds.

reflected in yield curve patterns: (1) the expectations theory, (2) the market segmentation theory, and (3) the liquidity premium theory, each of which is described in the following sections. The expectations theory does a good job of explaining the first two facts on our list, but not the third. The market segmentation theory can account for fact 3 but not the other two facts, which are well explained by the

> FOLLOWING THE FINANCIAL NEWS

Yield Curves

Many newspapers and Internet sites such as www.finance.yahoo.com publish a daily plot of the yield curves for Treasury securities. An example for May 17, 2016, is presented here. The numbers on the vertical axis indicate the interest rate for the Treasury security, and the maturity is given on the horizontal axis, with "m" denoting month and "y" denoting year.

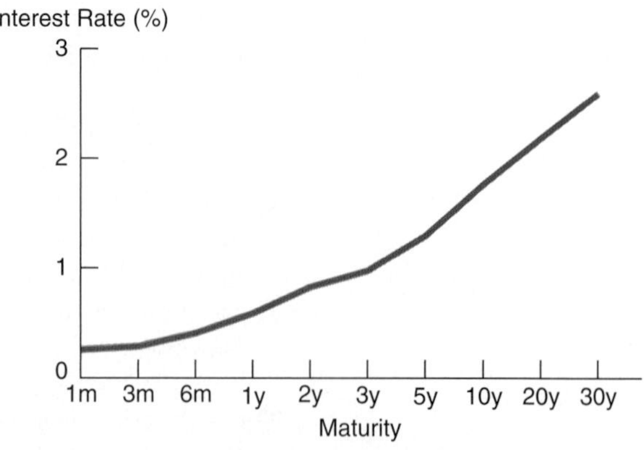

expectations theory. Because each theory explains facts that the other cannot, a natural way to seek a better understanding of the term structure is to combine features of both theories, which leads us to the liquidity premium theory, which can cover all three facts.

If the liquidity premium theory does a better job of explaining the facts and is hence the most widely accepted theory, why do we spend time discussing the other two theories? There are two reasons. First, the ideas in these two theories lay the groundwork for the liquidity premium theory. Second, it is important to see how economists modify theories to improve them when they find that the predicted results are inconsistent with the empirical evidence.

Expectations Theory

The **expectations theory** of the term structure states the following commonsense proposition: The interest rate on a long-term bond will equal an average of the short-term interest rates that people expect to occur over the life of the long-term bond. For example, if people expect that short-term interest rates will be 10% on average over the coming five years, the expectations theory predicts that the interest rate on bonds with five years to maturity will be 10%, too. If short-term interest rates were expected to rise even higher after this five-year period, so that the average short-term interest rate over the coming 20 years is 11%, then the interest rate on 20-year bonds would equal 11% and would be higher than the interest rate on five-year bonds. We can see that the explanation provided by the expectations theory for why interest rates on bonds of different maturities differ is that short-term interest rates are expected to have different values at different future dates.

The key assumption behind this theory is that buyers of bonds do not prefer bonds of one maturity over another, so they will not hold any quantity of a bond if its expected return is less than that of another bond with a different maturity. Bonds that have this characteristic are said to be *perfect substitutes*. What this means in practice is that if bonds with different maturities are perfect substitutes, the expected return on these bonds must be equal.

To see how the assumption that bonds with different maturities are perfect substitutes leads to the expectations theory, let's consider the following two investment strategies:

1. Purchase a one-year bond, and when it matures in one year, purchase another one-year bond.
2. Purchase a two-year bond and hold it until maturity.

Because both strategies must have the same expected return if people are holding both one- and two-year bonds, the interest rate on the two-year bond must equal the average of the two one-year interest rates.

EXAMPLE 5.2

Expectations Theory

The current interest rate on a one-year bond is 9%, and you expect the interest rate on the one-year bond next year to be 11%. What is the expected return over the two years? What interest rate must a two-year bond have to equal the two one-year bonds?

> **Solution**
>
> The expected return over the two years will average 10% per year ([9% + 11%]/2 = 10%). The bondholder will be willing to hold both the one- and two-year bonds only if the expected return per year of the two-year bond equals 10%. Therefore, the interest rate on the two-year bond must equal 10%, the average interest rate on the two one-year bonds. Graphically, we have:

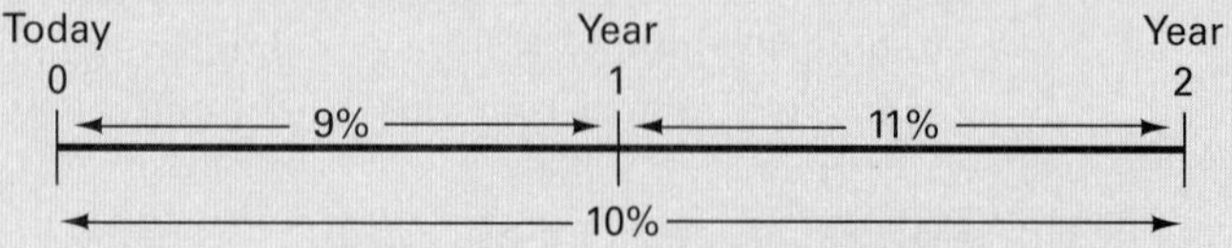

We can make this argument more general. For an investment of $1, consider the choice of holding, for two periods, a two-period bond or two one-period bonds. Using the definitions

$$
\begin{aligned}
i_t &= \text{today's (time } t\text{) interest rate on a one-period bond} \\
i^e_{t+1} &= \text{interest rate on a one-period bond expected for next period (time } t+1\text{)} \\
i_{2t} &= \text{today's (time } t\text{) interest rate on the two-period bond}
\end{aligned}
$$

the expected return over the two periods from investing $1 in the two-period bond and holding it for the two periods can be calculated as

$$(1 + i_{2t})(1 + i_{2t}) - 1 = 1 + 2i_{2t} + (i_{2t})^2 - 1 = 2i_{2t} + (i_{2t})^2$$

After the second period, the $1 investment is worth $(1 + i_{2t})(1 + i_{2t})$. Subtracting the $1 initial investment from this amount and dividing by the initial $1 investment gives the rate of return calculated in the previous equation. Because $(i_{2t})^2$ is extremely small—if $i_{2t} = 10\% = 0.10$, then $(i_{2t})^2 = 0.01$—we can simplify the expected return for holding the two-period bond for the two periods to

$$2i_{2t}$$

With the other strategy, in which one-period bonds are bought, the expected return on the $1 investment over the two periods is

$$(1 + i_t)(1 + i^e_{t+1}) - 1 = 1 + i_t + i^e_{t+1} + i_t(i^e_{t+1}) - 1 = i_t + i^e_{t+1} + i_t(i^e_{t+1})$$

This calculation is derived by recognizing that after the first period, the $1 investment becomes $1 + i_t$, and this is reinvested in the one-period bond for the next period, yielding an amount $(1 + i_t)(1 + i^e_{t+1})$. Then subtracting the $1 initial investment from this amount and dividing by the initial investment of $1 gives the expected return for the strategy of holding one-period bonds for the two periods. Because $i_t(i^e_{t+1})$ is also extremely small—if $i_t = i^e_{t+1} = 0.10$, then $i_t(i^e_{t+1}) = 0.01$—we can simplify this to

$$i_t + i^e_{t+1}$$

Both bonds will be held only if these expected returns are equal—that is, when

$$2i_{2t} = i_t + i^e_{t+1}$$

Solving for i_{2t} in terms of the one-period rates, we have

$$i_{2t} = \frac{i_t + i^e_{t+1}}{2} \quad (1)$$

which tells us that the two-period rate must equal the average of the two one-period rates. Graphically, this can be shown as

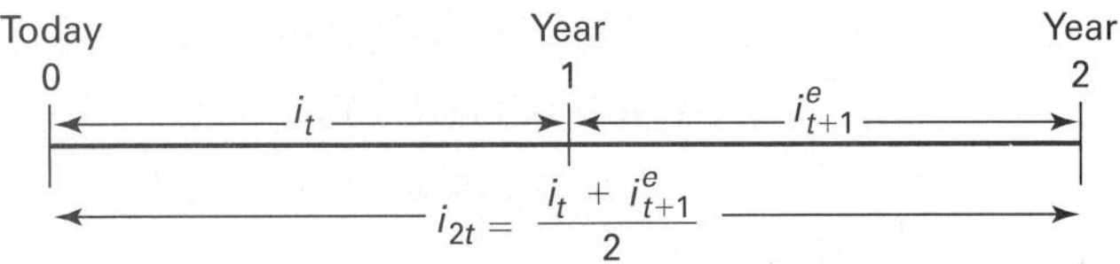

We can conduct the same steps for bonds with a longer maturity so that we can examine the whole term structure of interest rates. Doing so, we will find that the interest rate of i_{nt} on an n-period bond must be

$$i_{nt} = \frac{i_t + i^e_{t+1} + i^e_{t+2} + \cdots + i^e_{t+(n-1)}}{n} \quad (2)$$

Equation 2 states that the n-period interest rate equals the average of the one-period interest rates expected to occur over the n-period life of the bond. This is a restatement of the expectations theory in more precise terms.[2]

EXAMPLE 5.3

Expectations Theory

The one-year interest rates over the next five years are expected to be 5%, 6%, 7%, 8%, and 9%. Given this information, what are the interest rates on a two-year bond and a five-year bond? Explain what is happening to the yield curve.

> Solution

The interest rate on the two-year bond would be 5.5%.

$$i_{nt} = \frac{i_t + i^e_{t+1} + i^e_{t+2} + \cdots + i^e_{t+(n-1)}}{n}$$

where

i_t = year 1 interest rate = 5%

i^e_{t+1} = year 2 interest rate = 6%

n = number of years = 2

Thus,

$$i_{2t} = \frac{5\% + 6\%}{2} = 5.5\%$$

The interest rate on the five-year bond would be 7%.

$$i_{nt} = \frac{i_t + i^e_{t+1} + i^e_{t+2} + \cdots + i^e_{t+(n-1)}}{n}$$

[2]The analysis here has been conducted for discount bonds. Formulas for interest rates on coupon bonds would differ slightly from those used here but would convey the same principle.

where

i_t = year 1 interest rate = 5%

i^e_{t+1} = year 2 interest rate = 6%

i^e_{t+2} = year 3 interest rate = 7%

i^e_{t+3} = year 4 interest rate = 8%

i^e_{t+4} = year 5 interest rate = 9%

n = number of years = 5

Thus,

$$i_{5t} = \frac{5\% + 6\% + 7\% + 8\% + 9\%}{5} = 7.0\%$$

Using the same equation for the one-, three-, and four-year interest rates, you will be able to verify the one-year to five-year rates as 5.0%, 5.5%, 6.0%, 6.5%, and 7.0%, respectively. The rising trend in short-term interest rates produces an upward-sloping yield curve along which interest rates rise as maturity lengthens.

The expectations theory is an elegant theory that explains why the term structure of interest rates (as represented by yield curves) changes at different times. When the yield curve is upward-sloping, the expectations theory suggests that short-term interest rates are expected to rise in the future, as we have seen in our numerical example. In this situation, in which the long-term rate is currently higher than the short-term rate, the average of future short-term rates is expected to be higher than the current short-term rate, which can occur only if short-term interest rates are expected to rise. This result is what we see in our numerical example. When the yield curve is inverted (slopes downward), the average of future short-term interest rates is expected to be lower than the current short-term rate, implying that short-term interest rates are expected to fall, on average, in the future. Only when the yield curve is flat does the expectations theory suggest that short-term interest rates are not expected to change, on average, in the future.

The expectations theory also explains fact 1, which states that interest rates on bonds with different maturities move together over time. Historically, short-term interest rates have had the characteristic that if they increase today, they will tend to be higher in the future. Hence a rise in short-term rates will raise people's expectations of future short-term rates. Because long-term rates are the average of expected future short-term rates, a rise in short-term rates will also raise long-term rates, causing short- and long-term rates to move together.

The expectations theory also explains fact 2, which states that yield curves tend to have an upward slope when short-term interest rates are low and are inverted when short-term rates are high. When short-term rates are low, people generally expect them to rise to some normal level in the future, and the average of future expected short-term rates is high relative to the current short-term rate. Therefore, long-term interest rates will be substantially higher than current short-term rates, and the yield curve would then have an upward slope. Conversely, if short-term rates are high, people usually expect them to come back down. Long-term rates would then drop below short-term rates because the average of expected future short-term rates would be lower than current short-term rates, and the yield curve would slope downward and become inverted.[3]

The expectations theory is an attractive theory because it provides a simple explanation of the behavior of the term structure, but unfortunately it has a major shortcoming: It cannot explain fact 3, which says that yield curves usually slope upward. The typical upward slope of yield curves implies that short-term interest rates are usually expected to rise in the future. In practice, short-term interest rates are just as likely to fall as they are to rise, and so the expectations theory suggests that the typical yield curve should be flat rather than upward-sloping.

Market Segmentation Theory

As the name suggests, the **market segmentation theory** of the term structure sees markets for different-maturity bonds as completely separate and segmented. The interest rate for each bond with a different maturity is then determined by the supply of and demand for that bond, with no effects from expected returns on other bonds with other maturities.

The key assumption in market segmentation theory is that bonds of different maturities are not substitutes at all, so the expected return from holding a bond of one maturity has no effect on the demand for a bond of another maturity. This theory of the term structure is at the opposite extreme to the expectations theory, which assumes that bonds of different maturities are perfect substitutes.

The argument for why bonds of different maturities are not substitutes is that investors have strong preferences for bonds of one maturity but not for another, so they will be concerned with the expected returns only for bonds of the maturity they prefer. This might occur because they have a particular holding period in mind, and if they match the maturity of the bond to the desired holding period, they can obtain a certain return with no risk at all.[4] (We have seen in Chapter 3 that if the term to maturity equals the holding period, the return is known for certain because it equals the yield exactly, and no interest-rate risk exists.) For example, people who have a short holding period would prefer to hold short-term bonds. Conversely, if you were putting funds away for your young child to go to college, your desired holding period might be much longer, and you would want to hold longer-term bonds.

In market segmentation theory, differing yield curve patterns are accounted for by supply-and-demand differences associated with bonds of different maturities. If, as seems sensible, investors desire short holding periods and generally prefer

---

[3]The expectations theory explains another important fact about the relationship between short-term and long-term interest rates. As you can see in Figure 5.4, short-term interest rates are more volatile than long-term rates. If interest rates are *mean-reverting*—that is, if they tend to head back down after they are at unusually high levels or go back up when they are at unusually low levels—then an average of these short-term rates must necessarily have less volatility than the short-term rates themselves. Because the expectations theory suggests that the long-term rate will be an average of future short-term rates, it implies that the long-term rate will have less volatility than short-term rates.

[4]The statement that there is no uncertainty about the return if the term to maturity equals the holding period is literally true only for a discount bond. For a coupon bond with a long holding period, some risk exists because coupon payments must be reinvested before the bond matures. Our analysis here is thus being conducted for discount bonds. However, the gist of the analysis remains the same for coupon bonds because the amount of this risk from reinvestment is small when coupon bonds have the same term to maturity as the holding period.

bonds with shorter maturities that have less interest-rate risk, market segmentation theory can explain fact 3, which states that yield curves typically slope upward. Because in the typical situation the demand for long-term bonds is relatively lower than that for short-term bonds, long-term bonds will have lower prices and higher interest rates, and hence the yield curve will typically slope upward.

Although market segmentation theory can explain why yield curves usually tend to slope upward, it has a major flaw in that it cannot explain facts 1 and 2. First, because it views the market for bonds of different maturities as completely segmented, there is no reason for a rise in interest rates on a bond of one maturity to affect the interest rate on a bond of another maturity. Therefore, it cannot explain why interest rates on bonds of different maturities tend to move together (fact 1). Second, because it is not clear how demand and supply for short- versus long-term bonds change with the level of short-term interest rates, the theory cannot explain why yield curves tend to slope upward when short-term interest rates are low and to be inverted when short-term interest rates are high (fact 2).

Because each of our two theories explains empirical facts that the other cannot, a logical step is to combine the theories, which leads us to the liquidity premium theory.

Liquidity Premium Theory

The **liquidity premium theory** of the term structure states that the interest rate on a long-term bond will equal an average of short-term interest rates expected to occur over the life of the long-term bond plus a liquidity premium (also referred to as a term premium) that responds to supply-and-demand conditions for that bond.

The liquidity premium theory's key assumption is that bonds of different maturities are substitutes, which means that the expected return on one bond *does* influence the expected return on a bond of a different maturity, but it allows investors to prefer one bond maturity over another. In other words, bonds of different maturities are assumed to be substitutes, but not perfect substitutes. Investors tend to prefer shorter-term bonds because these bonds bear less interest-rate risk. For these reasons, investors must be offered a positive liquidity premium to induce them to hold longer-term bonds. Such an outcome would modify the expectations theory by adding a positive liquidity premium to the equation that describes the relationship between long- and short-term interest rates. The liquidity premium theory is thus written as

$$i_{nt} = \frac{i_t + i^e_{t+1} + i^e_{t+2} + \cdots + i^e_{t+(n-1)}}{n} + l_{nt} \tag{3}$$

where l_{nt} is the liquidity (term) premium for the n-period bond at time t, which is always positive and rises with the term to maturity of the bond, n.[5]

[5]Closely related to the liquidity premium theory is the **preferred habitat theory**, which takes a somewhat less direct approach to modifying the expectations hypothesis but comes to a similar conclusion. It assumes that investors have a preference for bonds of one maturity over another, a particular bond maturity (preferred habitat) in which they prefer to invest. Because they prefer bonds of one maturity over another, they will be willing to buy bonds that do not have the preferred maturity (habitat) only if they earn a somewhat higher expected return. Because investors are likely to prefer the habitat of short-term bonds over that of longer-term bonds, they are willing to hold long-term bonds only if they have higher expected returns. This reasoning leads to the same Equation 3 implied by the liquidity premium theory, with a term premium that typically rises with maturity.

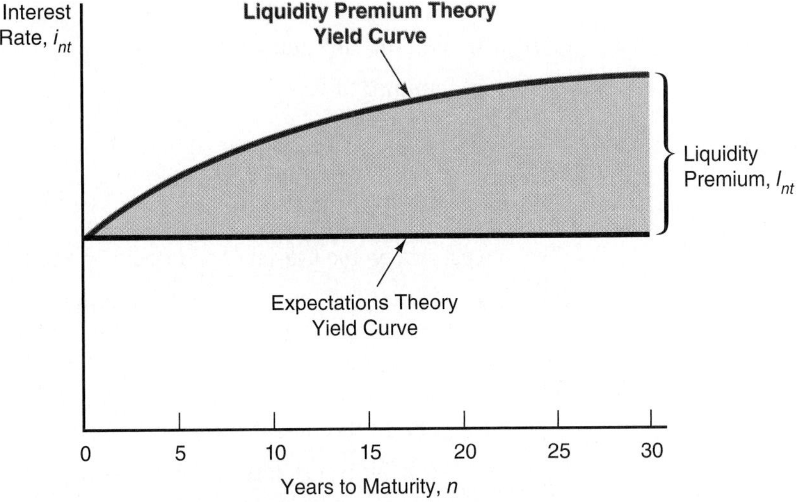

FIGURE 5.5 The Relationship Between the Liquidity Premium and Expectations Theories

Because the liquidity premium is always positive and grows as the term to maturity increases, the yield curve implied by the liquidity premium theory is always above the yield curve implied by the expectations theory and has a steeper slope. For simplicity, the yield curve implied by the expectations theory is drawn under the scenario of unchanging future one-year interest rates.

The relationship between the expectations theory and the liquidity premium theory is shown in Figure 5.5. There we see that because the liquidity premium is always positive and typically grows as the term to maturity increases, the yield curve implied by the liquidity premium theory is always above the yield curve implied by the expectations theory and generally has a steeper slope. (Note that for simplicity we are assuming that the expectations theory yield curve is flat.)

EXAMPLE 5.4

Liquidity Premium Theory

As in Example 3, let's suppose that the one-year interest rates over the next five years are expected to be 5%, 6%, 7%, 8%, and 9%. Investors' preferences for holding short-term bonds have the liquidity premiums for one-year to five-year bonds as 0%, 0.25%, 0.5%, 0.75%, and 1.0%, respectively. What is the interest rate on a two-year bond and a five-year bond? Compare these findings with the answer from Example 5.3 dealing with the pure expectations theory.

> Solution

The interest rate on the two-year bond would be 5.75%.

$$i_{nt} = \frac{i_t + i^e_{t+1} + i^e_{t+2} + \cdots + i^e_{t+(n-1)}}{n} + l_{nt}$$

where

i_t = year 1 interest rate = 5%

i^e_{t+1} = year 2 interest rate = 6%

l_{nt} = liquidity premium = 0.25%

n = number of years = 2

Thus,

$$i_{2t} = \frac{5\% + 6\%}{2} + 0.25\% = 5.75\%$$

The interest rate on the five-year bond would be 8%.

$$i_{nt} = \frac{i_t + i^e_{t+1} + i^e_{t+2} + \cdots + i^e_{t+(n-1)}}{n} + l_{nt}$$

where

i_t = year 1 interest rate = 5%

i^e_{t+1} = year 2 interest rate = 6%

i^e_{t+2} = year 3 interest rate = 7%

i^e_{t+3} = year 4 interest rate = 8%

i^e_{t+4} = year 5 interest rate = 9%

l_{2t} = liquidity premium = 1%

n = number of years = 5

Thus,

$$i_{5t} = \frac{5\% + 6\% + 7\% + 8\% + 9\%}{5} + 1\% = 8.0\%$$

If you did similar calculations for the one-, three-, and four-year interest rates, the one-year to five-year interest rates would be as follows: 5.0%, 5.75%, 6.5%, 7.25%, and 8.0%, respectively. Comparing these findings with those for the pure expectations theory, we can see that the liquidity preference theory produces yield curves that slope more steeply upward because of investors' preferences for short-term bonds.

Let's see if the liquidity premium theory is consistent with all three empirical facts we have discussed. They explain fact 1, which states that interest rates on different-maturity bonds move together over time: A rise in short-term interest rates indicates that short-term interest rates will, on average, be higher in the future, and the first term in Equation 3 then implies that long-term interest rates will rise along with them.

They also explain why yield curves tend to have an especially steep upward slope when short-term interest rates are low and to be inverted when short-term interest rates are high (fact 2). Because investors generally expect short-term interest rates to rise to some normal level when they are low, the average of future expected short-term rates will be high relative to the current short-term rate. With the additional boost of a positive liquidity premium, long-term interest rates will be substantially higher than current short-term rates, and the yield curve will then have a steep upward slope. Conversely, if short-term rates are high, people usually expect them to come back down. Long-term rates will then drop below short-term rates because the average of expected future short-term rates will be so far below current short-term rates that despite positive liquidity premiums, the yield curve will slope downward.

The liquidity premium theory explains fact 3, which states that yield curves typically slope upward, by recognizing that the liquidity premium rises with a bond's maturity because of investors' preferences for short-term bonds. Even if short-term interest rates are expected to stay the same on average in the future, long-term interest rates will be above short-term interest rates, and yield curves will typically slope upward.

How can the liquidity premium theory explain the occasional appearance of inverted yield curves if the liquidity premium is positive? It must be that at times short-term interest rates are expected to fall so much in the future that the average of the expected short-term rates is well below the current short-term rate. Even when the positive liquidity premium is added to this average, the resulting long-term rate will still be lower than the current short-term interest rate.

As our discussion indicates, a particularly attractive feature of the liquidity premium theory is that it tells you what the market is predicting about future short-term interest rates just from the slope of the yield curve. A steeply rising yield curve, as in panel (a) of Figure 5.6, indicates that short-term interest rates are expected to rise in the future. A moderately steep yield curve, as in panel (b), indicates that short-term interest rates are not expected to rise or fall much in the future. A flat yield curve, as in panel (c), indicates that short-term rates are expected to fall moderately in the future. Finally, an inverted yield curve, as in panel (d), indicates that short-term interest rates are expected to fall sharply in the future.

Evidence on the Term Structure

In the 1980s, researchers examining the term structure of interest rates questioned whether the slope of the yield curve provides information about movements of future short-term interest rates.[6] They found that the spread between long- and short-term interest rates does not always help predict future short-term interest rates, a finding that may stem from substantial fluctuations in the liquidity (term) premium for long-term bonds. More recent research using more discriminating tests now favors a different view. It shows that the term structure contains quite a bit of information for the very short run (over the next several months) and the long run (over several years) but is unreliable at predicting movements in interest rates over the intermediate term (the time in between).[7] Research also finds that the yield curve helps forecast future inflation and business cycles (see the Mini-Case box on page 109).

---

[6]Robert J. Shiller, John Y. Campbell, and Kermit L. Schoenholtz, "Forward Rates and Future Policy: Interpreting the Term Structure of Interest Rates," *Brookings Papers on Economic Activity* 1 (1983): 173–217; N. Gregory Mankiw and Lawrence H. Summers, "Do Long-Term Interest Rates Overreact to Short-Term Interest Rates?" *Brookings Papers on Economic Activity* 1 (1984): 223–242.

[7]Eugene Fama, "The Information in the Term Structure," *Journal of Financial Economics* 13 (1984): 509–528; Eugene Fama and Robert Bliss, "The Information in Long-Maturity Forward Rates," *American Economic Review* 77 (1987): 680–692; John Y. Campbell and Robert J. Shiller, "Cointegration and Tests of the Present Value Models," *Journal of Political Economy* 95 (1987): 1062–1088; John Y. Campbell and Robert J. Shiller, "Yield Spreads and Interest Rate Movements: A Bird's Eye View," *Review of Economic Studies* 58 (1991): 495–514.

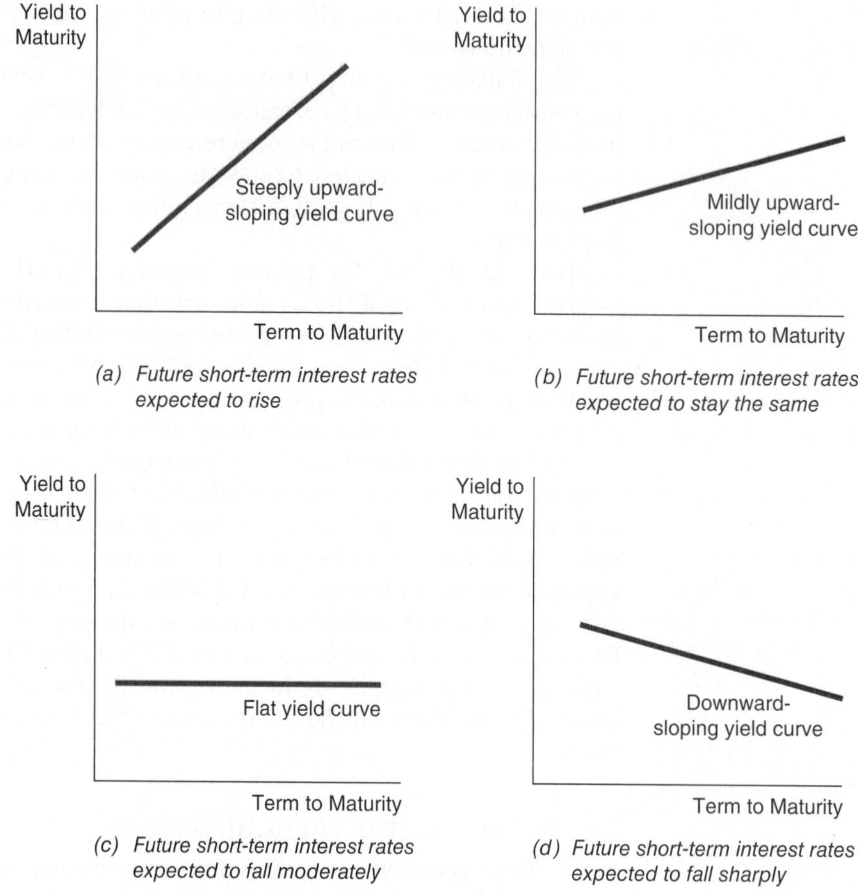

FIGURE 5.6 Yield Curves and the Market's Expectations of Future Short-Term Interest Rates According to the Liquidity Premium Theory

A steeply rising yield curve, as in panel (a), indicates that short-term interest rates are expected to rise in the future. A moderately steep yield curve, as in panel (b), indicates that short-term interest rates are not expected to rise or fall much in the future. A flat yield curve, as in panel (c), indicates that short-term interest rates are expected to fall moderately in the future. Finally, an inverted yield curve, as in panel (d), indicates that short-term interest rates are expected to fall sharply in the future.

Summary

The liquidity premium theory is the most widely accepted theory of the term structure of interest rates because it explains the major empirical facts about the term structure so well. It combines the features of both the expectations theory and the market segmentation theory by asserting that a long-term interest rate will be the sum of a liquidity (term) premium and the average of the short-term interest rates that are expected to occur over the life of the bond.

The liquidity premium theory explains the following facts:

1. Interest rates on bonds of different maturities tend to move together over time.
2. Yield curves usually slope upward.

> MINI-CASE

The Yield Curve as a Forecasting Tool for Inflation and the Business Cycle

Because the yield curve contains information about future expected interest rates, it should also have the capacity to help forecast inflation and real output fluctuations. To see why, recall from Chapter 4 that rising interest rates are associated with economic booms and falling interest rates with recessions. When the yield curve is either flat or downward-sloping, it suggests that future short-term interest rates are expected to fall and, therefore, that the economy is more likely to enter a recession. Indeed, the yield curve is found to be an accurate predictor of the business cycle.[a]

In Chapter 3, we also learned that a nominal interest rate is composed of a real interest rate and expected inflation, implying that the yield curve contains information about both the future path of nominal interest rates and future inflation. A steep upward-sloping yield curve predicts a future increase in inflation, while a flat or downward-sloping yield curve forecasts a future decline in inflation.[b]

The ability of the yield curve to forecast business cycles and inflation is one reason why the slope of the yield curve is part of the toolkit of many economic forecasters and is often viewed as a useful indicator of the stance of monetary policy, with a steep yield curve indicating loose policy and a flat or downward-sloping yield curve indicating tight policy.

[a]For example, see Arturo Estrella and Frederic S. Mishkin, "Predicting U.S. Recessions: Financial Variables as Leading Indicators," *Review of Economics and Statistics* 80 (February 1998): 45–61.

[b]Frederic S. Mishkin, "What Does the Term Structure Tell Us About Future Inflation?" *Journal of Monetary Economics* 25 (January 1990): 77–95; and Frederic S. Mishkin, "The Information in the Longer-Maturity Term Structure About Future Inflation," *Quarterly Journal of Economics* 55 (August 1990): 815–828.

3. When short-term interest rates are low, yield curves are more likely to have a steep upward slope, whereas when short-term interest rates are high, yield curves are more likely to be inverted.

The theory also helps us predict the movement of short-term interest rates in the future. A steep upward slope of the yield curve means that short-term rates are expected to rise, a mild upward slope means that short-term rates are expected to remain the same, a flat slope means that short-term rates are expected to fall moderately, and an inverted yield curve means that short-term rates are expected to fall sharply.

CASE

Interpreting Yield Curves, 1980–2016

Figure 5.7 illustrates several yield curves that have appeared for U.S. government bonds since 1980. What do these yield curves tell us about the public's expectations of future movements of short-term interest rates?

The steep inverted yield curve that occurred on January 15, 1981, indicated that short-term interest rates were expected to decline sharply in the future. For longer-term interest rates with their positive liquidity premium to be well below the short-term interest rate, short-term interest rates must be expected to decline so sharply that their average is far below the current short-term rate. Indeed, the public's expectations of sharply lower short-term interest rates evident in the yield

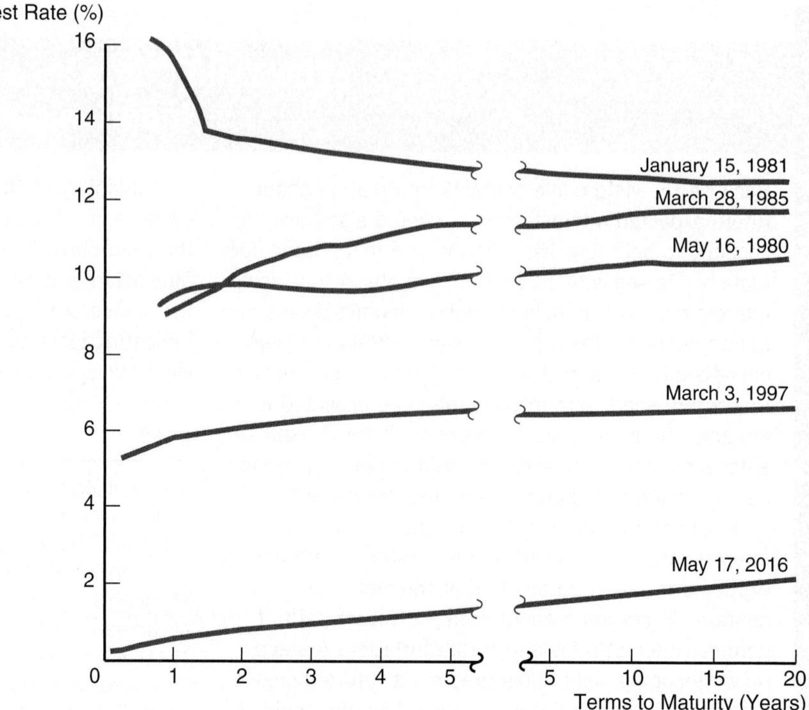

FIGURE 5.7 Yield Curves for U.S. Government Bonds

Yield curves for U.S. government bonds for different dates from 1981 to 2016.

Sources: Federal Reserve Bank of St. Louis; FRED database, https://fred.stlouisfed.org/series/TB3MS, https://fred.stlouisfed.org/series/GS3, https://fred.stlouisfed.org/series/GS5, https://fred.stlouisfed.org/series/GS20.

curve were realized soon after January 15; by March, three-month Treasury bill rates had declined from the 16% level to 13%.

The steep upward-sloping yield curve on March 28, 1985, and May 17, 2016, indicated that short-term interest rates would climb in the future. The long-term interest rate is higher than the short-term interest rate when short-term interest rates are expected to rise because their average plus the liquidity premium will be higher than the current short-term rate. The moderately upward-sloping yield curves on May 16, 1980, and March 3, 1997, indicated that short-term interest rates were expected neither to rise nor to fall in the near future. In this case, their average remains the same as the current short-term rate, and the positive liquidity premium for longer-term bonds explains the moderate upward slope of the yield curve.

THE PRACTICING MANAGER

Using the Term Structure to Forecast Interest Rates

As was discussed in Chapter 4, interest-rate forecasts are extremely important to managers of financial institutions because future changes in interest rates have a significant impact on the profitability of their institutions. Furthermore, interest-rate forecasts are needed when managers of financial institutions have to set interest rates on loans that are promised to customers in the future. Our discussion of the term structure of interest rates has indicated that the slope of the yield curve provides general information about the market's prediction of the future path of interest rates. For example, a steeply upward-sloping yield curve indicates that short-term interest rates are predicted to rise in the future, and a downward-sloping yield curve indicates that short-term interest rates are predicted to fall. However, a financial institution manager needs much more specific information on interest-rate forecasts than this. Here we show how the manager of a financial institution can generate specific forecasts of interest rates using the term structure.

To see how this is done, let's start the analysis using the approach we took in developing the pure expectations theory. Recall that because bonds of different maturities are perfect substitutes, we assumed that the expected return over two periods from investing \$1 in a two-period bond, which is $(1 + i_{2t})(1 + i_{2t}) - 1$, must equal the expected return from investing \$1 in one-period bonds, which is $(1 + i_t)(1 + i^e_{t+1}) - 1$. This is shown graphically as follows:

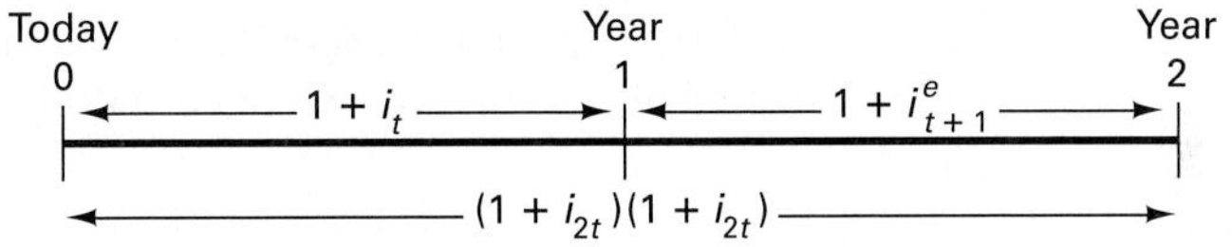

Today 0 —— $1 + i_t$ —— Year 1 —— $1 + i^e_{t+1}$ —— Year 2

←—— $(1 + i_{2t})(1 + i_{2t})$ ——→

In other words,

$$(1 + i_t)(1 + i^e_{t+1}) - 1 = (1 + i_{2t})(1 + i_{2t}) - 1$$

Through some tedious algebra we can solve for i^e_{t+1}:

$$i^e_{t+1} = \frac{(1 + i_{2t})^2}{1 + i_t} - 1 \tag{4}$$

This measure of i^e_{t+1} is called the **forward rate** because it is the one-period interest rate that the pure expectations theory of the term structure indicates is expected to prevail one period in the future. To differentiate forward rates derived from the term structure from actual interest rates that are observed at time t, we call these observed interest rates **spot rates**.

Going back to Example 3, which we used to discuss the pure expectations theory earlier in this chapter, at time t the one-year interest rate is 5% and the two-year rate is 5.5%. Plugging these numbers into Equation 4 yields the following estimate of the forward rate one period in the future:

$$i^e_{t+1} = \frac{(1 + 0.055)^2}{1 + 0.05} - 1 = 0.06 = 6\%$$

Not surprisingly, this 6% forward rate is identical to the expected one-year interest rate one year in the future that we used in Example 3. This is exactly what we should find, as our calculation here is just another way of looking at the pure expectations theory.

We can also compare holding the three-year bond against holding a sequence of one-year bonds, which reveals the following relationship:

$$(1 + i_t)(1 + i^e_{t+1})(1 + i^e_{t+2}) - 1 = (1 + i_{3t})(1 + i_{3t})(1 + i_{3t}) - 1$$

and plugging in the estimate for i^e_{t+1} derived in Equation 4, we can solve for i^e_{t+2}:

$$i^e_{t+2} = \frac{(1 + i_{3t})^3}{(1 + i_{2t})^2} - 1$$

Continuing with these calculations, we obtain the general solution for the forward rate n periods into the future:

$$i^e_{t+n} = \frac{(1 + i_{n+1t})^{n+1}}{(1 + i_{nt})^n} - 1 \quad (5)$$

Our discussion indicated that the pure expectations theory is not entirely satisfactory because investors must be compensated with liquidity premiums to induce them to hold longer-term bonds. Hence we need to modify our analysis, as we did when discussing the liquidity premium theory, by allowing for these liquidity premiums in estimating predictions of future interest rates.

Recall from the discussion of those theories that because investors prefer to hold short-term rather than long-term bonds, the n-period interest rate differs from that indicated by the pure expectations theory by a liquidity premium of l_{nt}. So to allow for liquidity premiums, we need merely subtract l_{nt} from i_{nt} in our formula to derive i^e_{t+n}:

$$i^e_{t+n} = \frac{(1 + i_{n+1t} - l_{n+1t})^{n+1}}{(1 + i_{nt} - l_{nt})^n} - 1 \quad (6)$$

This measure of i^e_{t+n} is referred to, naturally enough, as the *adjusted forward-rate forecast*.

In the case of i^e_{t+1}, Equation 6 produces the following estimate:

$$i^e_{t+1} = \frac{(1 + i_{2t} - l_{2t})^2}{1 + i_t} - 1$$

Using Example 4 in our discussion of the liquidity premium theory, at time t the l_{2t} liquidity premium is 0.25%, $l_{1t} = 0$, the one-year interest rate is 5%, and the two-year interest rate is 5.75%. Plugging these numbers into our equation yields the following adjusted forward-rate forecast for one period in the future:

$$i^e_{t+1} = \frac{(1 + 0.0575 - 0.0025)^2}{1 + 0.05} - 1 = 0.06 = 6\%$$

which is the same as the expected interest rate used in Example 3, as it should be.

Our analysis of the term structure thus provides managers of financial institutions with a fairly straightforward procedure for producing interest-rate forecasts. First they need to estimate l_{nt}, the values of the liquidity premiums for various n. Then they need merely apply the formula in Equation 6 to derive the market's forecasts of future interest rates.

EXAMPLE 5.5

Forward Rate

A customer asks a bank if it would be willing to commit to making the customer a one-year loan at an interest rate of 8% one year from now. To compensate for the costs of making the loan, the bank needs to charge one percentage point more than the expected interest rate on a Treasury bond with the same maturity if it is to make a profit. If the bank manager estimates the liquidity premium to be 0.4%, and the one-year Treasury bond rate is 6% and the two-year bond rate is 7%, should the manager be willing to make the commitment?

> Solution

The bank manager is unwilling to make the loan because at an interest rate of 8%, the loan is likely to be unprofitable to the bank.

$$i^e_{t+n} = \frac{(1 + i_{n+1t} - l_{n+1t})^{n+1}}{(1 + i_{nt} - l_{nt})^n} - 1$$

where

$$\begin{aligned} i_{n+1t} &= \text{two-year bond rate} = 0.07 \\ l_{n+1t} &= \text{liquidity premium} = 0.004 \\ i_{nt} &= \text{one-year bond rate} = 0.06 \\ l_{1t} &= \text{liquidity premium} = 0 \\ n &= \text{number of years} = 1 \end{aligned}$$

Thus,

$$i^e_{t+1} = \frac{(1 + 0.07 - 0.004)^2}{1 + 0.06} - 1 = 0.072 = 7.2\%$$

The market's forecast of the one-year Treasury bond rate one year in the future is therefore 7.2%. Adding the 1% necessary to make a profit on the one-year loan means that the loan is expected to be profitable only if it has an interest rate of 8.2% or higher.

As we will see in Chapter 6, the bond market's forecasts of interest rates may be the most accurate ones possible. If this is the case, the estimates of the market's forecasts of future interest rates using the simple procedure outlined here may be the best interest-rate forecasts that a financial institution manager can obtain.

SUMMARY

1. Bonds with the same maturity will have different interest rates because of three factors: default risk, liquidity, and tax considerations. The greater a bond's default risk, the higher its interest rate relative to other bonds; the greater a bond's liquidity, the lower its interest rate; and bonds with tax-exempt status will have lower interest rates than they otherwise would. The relationship among interest rates on bonds with the same maturity that arise because of these three factors is known as the *risk structure of interest rates*.

2. Several theories of the term structure provide explanations of how interest rates on bonds with different terms to maturity are related. The expectations theory views long-term interest rates as equaling the average of future short-term interest rates expected to occur over the life of the bond. By contrast, the market segmentation theory treats the determination of interest rates for each bond's maturity as the outcome of supply and demand in that market only. Neither of these theories by itself can explain the fact that interest rates on bonds of different maturities

move together over time and that yield curves usually slope upward.

3. The liquidity premium theory combines the features of the other two theories and, by so doing, is able to explain the facts just mentioned. It views long-term interest rates as equaling the average of future short-term interest rates expected to occur over the life of the bond plus a liquidity premium. This theory allows us to infer the market's expectations about the movement of future short-term interest rates from the yield curve. A steeply upward-sloping curve indicates that future short-term rates are expected to rise; a mildly upward-sloping curve that short-term rates are expected to stay the same; a flat curve that short-term rates are expected to decline slightly; and an inverted yield curve that a substantial decline in short-term rates is expected in the future.

KEY TERMS

credit-rating agencies, p. 92
default, p. 90
default-free bonds, p. 91
expectations theory, p. 99
forward rate, p. 111
inverted yield curve, p. 97
junk bonds, p. 93
liquidity premium theory, p. 104
market segmentation theory, p. 103
preferred habitat theory, p. 104
risk premium, p. 91
risk structure of interest rates, p. 89
spot rate, p. 111
term structure of interest rates, p. 89
yield curve, p. 97

QUESTIONS

1. Which should have the higher risk premium on its interest rates, a corporate bond with a Moody's Baa rating or a corporate bond with a C rating? Why?
2. Do you think that a U.S. Treasury bill will have a risk premium that is higher than, lower than, or the same as that of a similar security (in terms of maturity and liquidity) issued by the government of Colombia?
3. Risk premiums on corporate bonds are usually anti-cyclical; that is, they decrease during business cycle expansions and increase during recessions. Why is this so?
4. "If bonds of different maturities are close substitutes, their interest rates are more likely to move together." Is this statement true, false, or uncertain? Explain your answer.
5. Just before the collapse of the subprime mortgage market in 2007, the most important credit-rating agencies rated mortgage-backed securities with Aaa and AAA ratings. Explain how it was possible that a few months into 2008, the same securities had the lowest possible ratings. Should we always trust credit-rating agencies?
6. If a yield curve looks like the one shown here, what is the market predicting about the movement of future short-term interest rates? What might the yield curve indicate about the market's predictions concerning the inflation rate in the future?

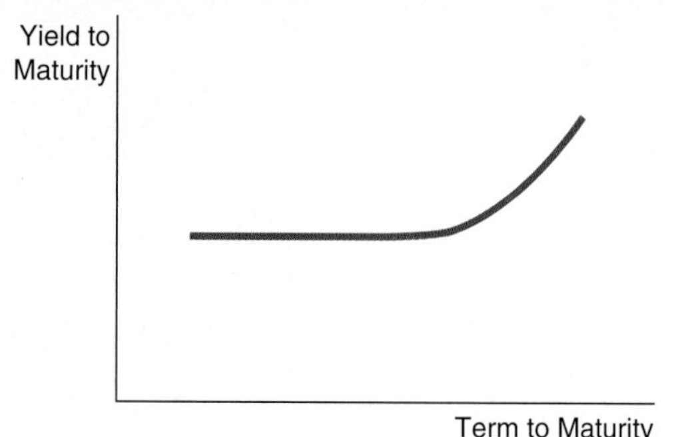

7. If a yield curve looks like the one below, what is the market predicting about the movement of future short-term interest rates? What might the yield curve indicate about the market's predictions concerning the inflation rate in the future?

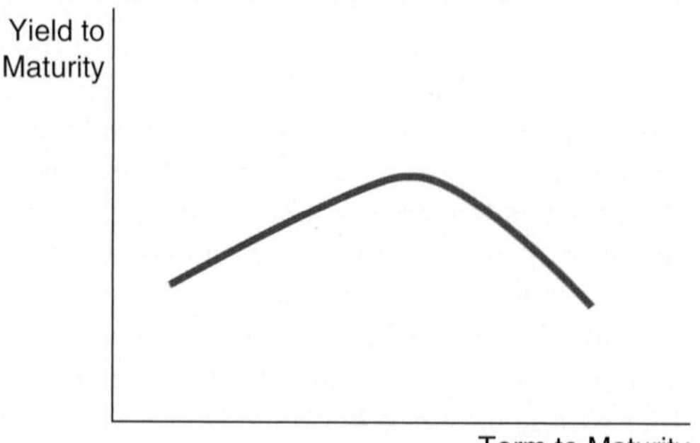

8. Suppose that the volume of corporate bonds traded declines. What would be the impact on the corporate bond risk premium? Which characteristics of a corporate bond might be affected?

Predicting the Future

9. Predict what will happen to interest rates on a corporation's bonds if the federal government guarantees today that it will pay creditors if the corporation goes bankrupt in the future. What will happen to the interest rates on Treasury securities?

10. Predict what would happen to the risk premiums of municipal bonds if the federal government guarantees today that it will pay creditors if municipal governments default on their payments. Do you think that it will then make sense for municipal bonds to be exempt from income taxes?

11. If the income tax exemption on municipal bonds were abolished, what would happen to the interest rates on these bonds? What effect would it have on interest rates on U.S. Treasury securities?

QUANTITATIVE PROBLEMS

1. Assuming that the expectations theory is the correct theory of the term structure, calculate the interest rates in the term structure for maturities of one to five years, and plot the resulting yield curves for the following series of one-year interest rates over the next five years:

   a. 5%, 7%, 7%, 7%, 7%

   b. 5%, 4%, 4%, 4%, 4%

   How would your yield curves change if people preferred shorter-term bonds over longer-term bonds?

2. Government economists have forecasted one-year T-bill rates for the following five years, as follows:

Year	1-Year Rate (%)
1	4.25
2	5.15
3	5.50
4	6.25
5	7.10

   You have a liquidity premium of 0.25% for the next two years and 0.50% thereafter. Would you be willing to purchase a four-year T-bond at a 5.75% interest rate?

3. How does the after-tax yield on a $1,000,000 municipal bond with a coupon rate of 8% paying interest annually compare with that of a $1,000,000 corporate bond with a coupon rate of 10% paying interest annually? Assume that you are in the 25% tax bracket.

4. Consider the decision to purchase either a five-year corporate bond or a five-year municipal bond. The corporate bond is a 12% annual coupon bond with a par value of $1,000. It is currently yielding 11.5%. The municipal bond has an 8.5% annual coupon and a par value of $1,000. It is currently yielding 7%. Which of the two bonds would be more beneficial to you? Assume that your marginal tax rate is 35%.

5. A municipal bond and a corporate bond of equal risk, liquidity, and maturity yield 6% and 10%, respectively. For which values of marginal tax rates would you prefer to buy the municipal bond?

6. One-year T-bill rates are expected to steadily increase by 150 basis points per year over the next six years. Determine the required interest rate on a three-year T-bond and a six-year T-bond if the current interest rate on one-year Treasury bonds is 7.5%. Assume that the expectations hypothesis for interest rates holds.

7. Short-term (one-year) interest rates over the next 6 years will be 0.5%, 0.6%, 0.7%, 0.76%, 0.80%, and 0.84%. Using the expectations theory, what will be the interest rates on three-, four-, and six-year bonds?

8. The one-year interest rate over the next 10 years will be 3%, 4.5%, 6%, 7.5%, 9%, 10.5%, 13%, 14.5%, 16%, and 17.5%. Assume that investors prefer holding short-term bonds so that a liquidity premium of 10 basis points is required for each year of a bond's maturity. What will be the interest rates on a three-year bond, a six-year bond, and a nine-year bond?

9. Suppose that the expectations theory is true and that you can buy a three-year bond with an interest rate of 6% or three consecutive one-year bonds with interest rates of 4%, 5%, and 6%. Which option would you choose to undertake?

10. Little Monsters, Inc., borrowed $1,000,000 for two years from NorthernBank, Inc., at an 11.5% interest rate. The current risk-free rate is 2%, and Little Monsters' condition warrants a default risk premium of 3% and a liquidity risk premium of 2%. The liquidity premium for a two-year loan is 1%, and inflation

is expected to be 3% next year. What does this information imply about the rate of inflation in the second year?

11. One-year T-bill rates are 2% currently. If interest rates are expected to go up after three years by 2% every year, what should be the required interest rate on a 10-year bond issued today? Assume that the expectations theory holds.

12. Short-term (one-year) interest rates over the next 3 years are expected to be 2%, 3%, and 3.55%. If you are ready to buy a three-year bond that yields 3%, what is your minimum required liquidity premium for this period?

13. At your favorite bond store, Bonds-R-Us, you see the following prices:

    One-year $100 zero selling for $90.19

    Three-year 10% coupon $1,000 par bond selling for $1,000

    Two-year 10% coupon $1,000 par bond selling for $1,000

    Assume that the expectations theory for the term structure of interest rates holds, no liquidity premium exists, and the bonds are equally risky. What is the implied one-year rate two years from now?

14. You observe the following market interest rates, for both borrowing and lending:

    One-year rate = 5%

    Two-year rate = 6%

    One-year rate one year from now = 7.25%

    How can you take advantage of these rates to earn a riskless profit? Assume that the expectations theory for interest rates holds.

15. Predict the one-year interest rate three years from today if interest rates are 4%, 4.5%, 4.75%, and 5% for bonds with one to four years to maturity and the respective liquidity premiums are 0%, 0.1%, 0.15%, and 0.2%.

WEB EXERCISES

The Risk and Term Structures of Interest Rates

1. The amount of additional interest investors receive due to the various risk premiums changes over time. Sometimes the risk premiums are much larger than at other times. For example, the default risk premium was very small in the late 1990s, when the economy was so healthy that business failures were rare. This risk premium increases during recessions.

    Go to the Federal Reserve Bank of St. Louis FRED database at **http://research.stlouisfed.org/fred2/** and find the interest-rate listings for AAA- and Baa-rated bonds at three points in time: the most recent; August 1, 2007; and October 1, 2008. Prepare a graph that shows these three time periods (see Figure 5.1 for an example). Are the risk premiums stable or do they change over time?

2. Figure 5.7 shows a number of yield curves at various points in time. Go to **www.treasury.gov**, and in the "Resource Center" at the top of the page click on "Data and Charts Center." Find the Treasury yield curve. Does the current yield curve fall above or below the most recent one listed in Figure 5.7? Is the current yield curve flatter or steeper than the most recent one reported in Figure 5.7?

3. Investment companies attempt to explain to investors the nature of the risk the investor incurs when buying shares in their mutual funds. For example, go to **https://personal.vanguard.com/us/funds/vanguard/all?sort=name&sortorder=asc**.

    a. Select the bond fund you would recommend to an investor who has a very low tolerance for risk. Justify your answer.

    b. Select the bond fund you would recommend to an investor who has a higher tolerance for risk and a long investment horizon. Justify your answer.

CHAPTER 6

Are Financial Markets Efficient?

> PREVIEW

Throughout our discussion of how financial markets work, you may have noticed that the subject of expectations keeps cropping up. Expectations of returns, risk, and liquidity are central elements in the demand for assets; expectations of inflation have a major impact on bond prices and interest rates; expectations about the likelihood of default are the most important factor that determines the risk structure of interest rates; and expectations of future short-term interest rates play a central role in determining the term structure of interest rates. Not only are expectations critical in understanding behavior in financial markets, but as we will see later in this book, they are also central to our understanding of how financial institutions operate.

To understand how expectations are formed so that we can understand how securities prices move over time, we look at the efficient market hypothesis. In this chapter we examine the basic reasoning behind the efficient market hypothesis in order to explain some puzzling features of the operation and behavior of financial markets. You will see, for example, why changes in stock prices are unpredictable and why listening to a stockbroker's hot tips may not be a good idea.

Theoretically, the efficient market hypothesis should be a powerful tool for analyzing behavior in financial markets. But to establish that it is in reality a useful tool, we must compare the theory with the data. Does the empirical evidence support the theory? Though mixed, the available evidence indicates that for many purposes, this theory is a good starting point for analyzing expectations.

The Efficient Market Hypothesis

To understand how expectations affect securities prices, we need to look at how information in the market affects these prices. To do this we examine the **efficient market hypothesis** (also referred to as the **theory of efficient capital markets**), which states that prices of securities in financial markets fully reflect all available information. But what does this mean?

You may recall from Chapter 3 that the rate of return from holding a security equals the sum of the capital gain on the security (the change in the price) plus any cash payments, divided by the initial purchase price of the security:

$$R = \frac{P_{t+1} - P_t + C}{P_t} \tag{1}$$

where R = rate of return on the security held from time t to time $t+1$ (say, the end of 2017 to the end of 2018)

P_{t+1} = price of the security at time $t+1$, the end of the holding period

P_t = the price of the security at time t, the beginning of the holding period

C = cash payment (coupon or dividend payments) made in the period t to $t+1$

Let's look at the expectation of this return at time t, the beginning of the holding period. Because the current price and the cash payment C are known at the beginning, the only variable in the definition of the return that is uncertain is the price next period, P_{t+1}.[1] Denoting the expectation of the security's price at the end of the holding period as P^e_{t+1}, the expected return R^e is

$$R^e = \frac{P^e_{t+1} - P_t + C}{P_t}$$

The efficient market hypothesis views expectations as equal to optimal forecasts using all available information. What exactly does this mean? An optimal forecast is the best guess of the future using all available information. This does not mean that the forecast is perfectly accurate, but only that it is the best possible given the available information. This can be written more formally as

$$P^e_{t+1} = P^{of}_{t+1}$$

which in turn implies that the expected return on the security will equal the optimal forecast of the return:

$$R^e = R^{of} \tag{2}$$

Unfortunately, we cannot observe either R^e or P^e_{t+1}, so the equations above by themselves do not tell us much about how the financial market behaves. However, if we can devise some way to measure the value of R^e, these equations will have important implications for how prices of securities change in financial markets.

[1]There are cases in which C might not be known at the beginning of the period, but that does not make a substantial difference to the analysis. We would in that case assume that not only price expectations but also the expectations of C are optimal forecasts using all available information.

The supply-and-demand analysis of the bond market developed in Chapter 4 shows us that the expected return on a security (the interest rate in the case of the bond examined) will have a tendency to head toward the equilibrium return that equates the quantity demanded to the quantity supplied. Supply-and-demand analysis enables us to determine the expected return on a security with the following equilibrium condition: The expected return on a security R^e equals the equilibrium return R^*, which equates the quantity of the security demanded to the quantity supplied; that is,

$$R^e = R^* \tag{3}$$

The academic field of finance explores the factors (risk and liquidity, for example) that influence the equilibrium returns on securities. For our purposes, it is sufficient to know that we can determine the equilibrium return and thus determine the expected return with the equilibrium condition.

We can derive an equation to describe pricing behavior in an efficient market by using the equilibrium condition to replace R^e with R^* in Equation 2. In this way we obtain

$$R^{of} = R^* \tag{4}$$

This equation tells us that ***current prices in a financial market will be set so that the optimal forecast of a security's return using all available information equals the security's equilibrium return.*** Financial economists state it more simply: A security's price fully reflects all available information in an efficient market.

EXAMPLE 6.1

The Efficient Market Hypothesis

Suppose that a share of Microsoft had a closing price yesterday of \$90, but new information was announced after the market closed that caused a revision in the forecast of the price for next year to go to \$120. If the annual equilibrium return on Microsoft is 15%, what does the efficient market hypothesis indicate the price will go to today when the market opens? (Assume that Microsoft pays no dividends.)

> Solution

The price would rise to \$104.35 after the opening.

$$R^{of} = \frac{P^{of}_{t+1} - P_t + C}{P_t} = R^*$$

where

$$\begin{aligned}
R^{of} &= \text{optimal forecast of the return} = 15\% &&= 0.15\\
R^{*} &= \text{equilibrium return} = 15\% &&= 0.15\\
P^{of}_{t+1} &= \text{optimal forecast of price next year} &&= \$120\\
P_t &= \text{price today after opening}\\
C &= \text{cash (dividend) payment} &&= 0
\end{aligned}$$

Thus,

$$0.15 = \frac{\$120 - P_t}{P_t}$$

$$P_t \times 0.15 = \$120 - P_t$$

$$P_t(1.15) = \$120$$

$$P_t = \$104.35$$

Rationale Behind the Hypothesis

To see why the efficient market hypothesis makes sense, we make use of the concept of **arbitrage**, in which market participants (*arbitrageurs*) eliminate **unexploited profit opportunities**, meaning returns on a security that are larger than what is justified by the characteristics of that security. Arbitrage is of two types: *pure arbitrage*, in which the elimination of unexploited profit opportunities involves no risk, and the type of arbitrage we discuss here, in which the arbitrageur takes on some risk when eliminating the unexploited profit opportunities. To see how arbitrage leads to the efficient market hypothesis, suppose that, given its risk characteristics, the normal return on a security, say, Exxon-Mobil common stock, is 10% at an annual rate, and its current price P_t is lower than the optimal forecast of tomorrow's price P^e_{t+1} so that the optimal forecast of the return at an annual rate is 50%, which is greater than the equilibrium return of 10%. We are now able to predict that, on average, Exxon-Mobil's return would be abnormally high, so there is an unexpected profit opportunity. Knowing that, on average, you can earn such an abnormally high rate of return on Exxon-Mobil because $R^{of} > R^*$, you would buy more, which would in turn drive up its current price relative to the expected future price P^e_{t+1}, thereby lowering R^{of}. When the current price had risen sufficiently so that R^{of} equals R^* and the efficient market condition (Equation 4) is satisfied, the buying of Exxon-Mobil will stop, and the unexploited profit opportunity will have disappeared.

Similarly, a security for which the optimal forecast of the return is −5% while the equilibrium return is 10% ($R^{of} < R^*$) would be a poor investment because, on average, it earns less than the equilibrium return. In such a case, you would sell the security and drive down its current price relative to the expected future price until R^{of} rose to the level of R^* and the efficient market condition is again satisfied. What we have shown can be summarized as follows:

$$\left.\begin{matrix} R^{of} > R^* \rightarrow P_t\uparrow \rightarrow R^{of}\downarrow \\ R^{of} < R^* \rightarrow P_t\downarrow \rightarrow R^{of}\uparrow \end{matrix}\right\} \text{until } R^{of} = R^*$$

Another way to state the efficient market condition is this: ***In an efficient market, all unexploited profit opportunities will be eliminated.***

An extremely important factor in this reasoning is that ***not everyone in a financial market must be well informed about a security for its price to be driven to the point at which the efficient market condition holds.*** Financial markets are structured so that many participants can play. As long as a few (who are often referred to as "smart money") keep their eyes open for unexploited profit opportunities, they will eliminate the profit opportunities that appear because in so doing, they make a profit. The efficient market hypothesis makes sense because it does not require everyone in a market to be cognizant of what is happening to every security.

Evidence on the Efficient Market Hypothesis

Early evidence on the efficient market hypothesis was quite favorable to it, but in recent years deeper analysis of the evidence suggests that the hypothesis may not always be entirely correct. Let's first look at the earlier evidence in favor of the hypothesis and then examine some of the more recent evidence that casts some doubt on it.

Evidence in Favor of Market Efficiency

Evidence in favor of market efficiency has examined the performance of investment analysts and mutual funds, whether stock prices reflect publicly available information, the random-walk behavior of stock prices, and the success of so-called technical analysis.

Performance of Investment Analysts and Mutual Funds We have seen that one implication of the efficient market hypothesis is that when purchasing a security, you cannot expect to earn an abnormally high return, a return greater than the equilibrium return. This implies that it is impossible to beat the market. Many studies shed light on whether investment advisers and mutual funds (some of which charge steep sales commissions to people who purchase them) beat the market. One common test that has been performed is to take buy and sell recommendations from a group of advisers or mutual funds and compare the performance of the resulting selection of stocks with the market as a whole. Sometimes the advisers' choices have even been compared to a group of stocks chosen by putting a copy of the financial page of the newspaper on a dartboard and throwing darts. The *Wall Street Journal*, for example, used to have a regular feature called "Investment Dartboard" that compared how well stocks picked by investment advisers did relative to stocks picked by throwing darts. Did the advisers win? To their embarrassment, the dartboard beat them as often as they beat the dartboard. Furthermore, even when the comparison included only advisers who had been successful in the past in predicting the stock market, the advisers still didn't regularly beat the dartboard.

Consistent with the efficient market hypothesis, mutual funds are also not found to beat the market. Mutual funds not only do not outperform the market on average, but when they are separated into groups according to whether they had the highest or lowest profits in a chosen period, the mutual funds that did well in the first period did not beat the market in the second period.[2]

---

[2]An early study that found that mutual funds do not outperform the market is Michael C. Jensen, "The Performance of Mutual Funds in the Period 1945–64," *Journal of Finance* 23 (1968): 389–416. More recent studies on mutual fund performance are Mark Grimblatt and Sheridan Titman, "Mutual Fund Performance: An Analysis of Quarterly Portfolio Holdings," *Journal of Business* 62 (1989): 393–416; R. A. Ippolito, "Efficiency with Costly Information: A Study of Mutual Fund Performance, 1965–84," *Quarterly Journal of Economics* 104 (1989): 1–23; J. Lakonishok, A. Shleifer, and R. Vishny, "The Structure and Performance of the Money Management Industry," *Brookings Papers on Economic Activity, Microeconomics* (1992); and B. Malkiel, "Returns from Investing in Equity Mutual Funds, 1971–1991," *Journal of Finance* 50 (1995): 549–572.

MINI-CASE

An Exception That Proves the Rule: Raj Rajaratnam and Galleon

The efficient market hypothesis indicates that investment advisers should not have the ability to beat the market. Yet that is exactly what Raj Rajaratnam and his Galleon Group were able to do until 2009, when he was charged by the Securities and Exchange Commission with making unfair profits (estimated to be on the order of $60 million) by trading on inside information. Rajaratnam was convicted in May 2011 of insider trading and was sentenced to 11 years in prison and a fine of $150 million. If the stock market is efficient, can the SEC legitimately claim that Rajaratnam was able to beat the market? The answer is yes.

Rajaratnam and his Galleon Group made millions in profits for himself and his clients by investing in the stocks of firms on which he allegedly received inside information—from Rajat Gupta and Anil Kumar of McKinsey and Company, Robert Moffat of IBM, and Rajiv Goel and Roomy Khan of Intel Capital—about outside investments and other activities at specific firms. Rajaratnam and Galleon Group's ability to make millions year after year in the 2000s is an exception that proves the rule that financial analysts cannot continually outperform the market; yet it supports the efficient markets claim that only information unavailable to the market enables an investor to do so. Rajaratnam profited from knowing about inside information before the rest of the market; this information was known to him but unavailable to the market.

http://stocks.tradingcharts.com
Access detailed stock quotes, charts, and historical stock data.

The conclusion from the study of investment advisers and mutual fund performance is this: ***Having performed well in the past does not indicate that an investment adviser or a mutual fund will perform well in the future.*** This is not pleasing news to investment advisers, but it is exactly what the efficient market hypothesis predicts. It says that some advisers will be lucky and some will be unlucky. Being lucky does not mean that a forecaster actually has the ability to beat the market. (An exception that proves the rule is discussed in the Mini-Case box.)

Do Stock Prices Reflect Publicly Available Information? The efficient market hypothesis predicts that stock prices will reflect all publicly available information. Thus, if information is already publicly available, a positive announcement about a company will not, on average, raise the price of its stock because this information is already reflected in the stock price. Early empirical evidence also confirmed this conjecture from the efficient market hypothesis: Favorable earnings announcements or announcements of stock splits (a division of a share of stock into multiple shares, which is usually followed by higher earnings) do not, on average, cause stock prices to rise.[3]

Random-Walk Behavior of Stock Prices The term **random walk** describes the movements of a variable whose future changes cannot be predicted (are random) because, given today's value, the variable is just as likely to fall as to rise. An important implication of the efficient market hypothesis is that stock prices should approximately follow a random walk; that is, ***future changes in stock prices should, for all practical purposes, be unpredictable.*** The random-walk implication of the efficient market hypothesis is the one most commonly mentioned

[3]Ray Ball and Philip Brown, "An Empirical Evaluation of Accounting Income Numbers," *Journal of Accounting Research* 6 (1968): 159–178; Eugene F. Fama, Lawrence Fisher, Michael C. Jensen, and Richard Roll, "The Adjustment of Stock Prices to New Information," *International Economic Review* 10 (1969): 1–21.

in the press because it is the most readily comprehensible to the public. In fact, when people mention the "random-walk theory of stock prices," they are in reality referring to the efficient market hypothesis.

The case for random-walk stock prices can be demonstrated. Suppose that people could predict that the price of Happy Feet Corporation (HFC) stock would rise 1% in the coming week. The predicted rate of capital gains and rate of return on HFC stock would then be over 50% at an annual rate. Since this is very likely to be far higher than the equilibrium rate of return on HFC stock ($R^{of} > R^*$), the efficient market hypothesis indicates that people would immediately buy this stock and bid up its current price. The action would stop only when the predictable change in the price dropped to near zero so that $R^{of} = R^*$.

Similarly, if people could predict that the price of HFC stock would fall by 1%, the predicted rate of return would be negative and less than the equilibrium return ($R^{of} < R^*$), and people would immediately sell. The current price would fall until the predictable change in the price rose back to near zero, where the efficient market condition again holds. The efficient market hypothesis suggests that the predictable change in stock prices will be near zero, leading to the conclusion that stock prices will generally follow a random walk.[4]

Financial economists have used two types of tests to explore the hypothesis that stock prices follow a random walk. In the first, they examine stock market records to see if changes in stock prices are systematically related to past changes and hence could have been predicted on that basis. The second type of test examines the data to see if publicly available information other than past stock prices could have been used to predict changes. These tests are somewhat more stringent because additional information (money supply growth, government spending, interest rates, corporate profits) might be used to help forecast stock returns. Early results from both types of tests generally confirmed the efficient market view that stock prices are not predictable and follow a random walk.[5]

Technical Analysis A popular technique used to predict stock prices, called technical analysis, is to study past stock price data and search for patterns such as trends and regular cycles. Rules for when to buy and sell stocks are then established on the basis of the patterns that emerge. The efficient market hypothesis suggests that technical analysis is a waste of time. The simplest way to understand why is

---

[4]Note that the random-walk behavior of stock prices is only an *approximation* derived from the efficient market hypothesis. It would hold exactly only for a stock for which an unchanged price leads to its having the equilibrium return. Then, when the predictable change in the stock price is exactly zero, $R^{of} = R^*$.

[5]The first type of test, using only stock market data, is referred to as a test of *weak-form efficiency* because the information that can be used to predict stock prices is restricted solely to past price data. The second type of test is referred to as a test of *semistrong-form efficiency* because the information set is expanded to include all publicly available information, not just past stock prices. A third type of test is called a test of *strong-form efficiency* because the information set includes insider information, known only to the owners of the corporation, as when they plan to declare a high dividend. Strong-form tests do sometimes indicate that insider information can be used to predict changes in stock prices. This finding does not contradict the efficient markets theory because the information is not available to the market and hence cannot be reflected in market prices. In fact, there are strict laws against using insider information to trade in financial markets. For an early survey on the three forms of tests, see Eugene F. Fama, "Efficient Capital Markets: A Review of Theory and Empirical Work," *Journal of Finance* 25 (1970): 383–416.

to use the random-walk result derived from the efficient market hypothesis that holds that past stock price data cannot help predict changes. Therefore, technical analysis, which relies on such data to produce its forecasts, cannot successfully predict changes in stock prices.

CASE

Should Foreign Exchange Rates Follow a Random Walk?

Although the efficient market hypothesis is usually applied to the stock market, it can also be used to show that foreign exchange rates, like stock prices, should generally follow a random walk. To see why this is the case, consider what would happen if people could predict that a currency would appreciate by 1% in the coming week. By buying this currency, they could earn a greater than 50% return at an annual rate, which is likely to be far above the equilibrium return for holding a currency. As a result, people would immediately buy the currency and bid up its current price, thereby reducing the expected return. The process would stop only when the predictable change in the exchange rate dropped to near zero so that the optimal forecast of the return no longer differed from the equilibrium return. Likewise, if people could predict that the currency would depreciate by 1% in the coming week, they would sell it until the predictable change in the exchange rate was again near zero. The efficient market hypothesis therefore implies that future changes in exchange rates should, for all practical purposes, be unpredictable; in other words, exchange rates should follow random walks. This is exactly what empirical evidence finds.[*]

[*]See Richard A. Meese and Kenneth Rogoff, "Empirical Exchange Rate Models of the Seventies: Do They Fit Out of Sample?" *Journal of International Economics* 14 (1983): 3–24.

Two types of tests bear directly on the value of technical analysis. The first performs the empirical analysis described earlier to evaluate the performance of any financial analyst, technical or otherwise. The results are exactly what the efficient market hypothesis predicts: Technical analysts fare no better than other financial analysts; on average, they do not outperform the market, and successful past forecasting does not imply that their forecasts will outperform the market in the future. The second type of test takes the rules developed in technical analysis for when to buy and sell stocks and applies them to new data.[6] The performance of these rules is then evaluated by the profits that would have been made using them. These tests also discredit technical analysis: It does not outperform the overall market.

[6]Sidney Alexander, "Price Movements in Speculative Markets: Trends or Random Walks?" *Industrial Management Review*, May 1961, pp. 7–26; and Sidney Alexander, "Price Movements in Speculative Markets: Trends or Random Walks? No. 2" in *The Random Character of Stock Prices*, ed. Paul Cootner (Cambridge, Mass.: MIT Press, 1964), pp. 338–372. More recent evidence also seems to discredit technical analysis, for example, F. Allen and R. Karjalainen, "Using Genetic Algorithms to Find Technical Trading Rules," *Journal of Financial Economics* (1999) 51: 245–271. However, some other research is more favorable to technical analysis, e.g., P. Sullivan, A. Timmerman, and H. White, "Data-Snooping, Technical Trading Rule Performance and the Bootstrap," Centre for Economic Policy Research Discussion Paper No. 1976, 1998.

Evidence Against Market Efficiency

All the early evidence supporting the efficient market hypothesis appeared to be overwhelming, causing Eugene Fama, later a winner of the Nobel Prize, to state in his famous 1970 survey of the empirical evidence on the efficient market hypothesis, "The evidence in support of the efficient markets model is extensive, and (somewhat uniquely in economics) contradictory evidence is sparse."[7] However, in recent years, the theory has begun to show a few cracks, referred to as anomalies, and empirical evidence indicates that the efficient market hypothesis may not always be generally applicable.

Small-Firm Effect One of the earliest reported anomalies in which the stock market did not appear to be efficient is called the *small-firm effect*. Many empirical studies have shown that small firms have earned abnormally high returns over long periods of time, even when the greater risk for these firms has been taken into account.[8] The small-firm effect seems to have diminished in recent years, but it is still a challenge to the theory of efficient markets. Various theories have been developed to explain the small-firm effect, suggesting that it may be due to rebalancing of portfolios by institutional investors, tax issues, low liquidity of small-firm stocks, large information costs in evaluating small firms, or an inappropriate measurement of risk for small-firm stocks.

January Effect Over long periods of time, stock prices have tended to experience an abnormal price rise from December to January that is predictable and hence inconsistent with random-walk behavior. This so-called **January effect** seems to have diminished in recent years for shares of large companies but still occurs for shares of small companies.[9] Some financial economists argue that the January effect is due to tax issues. Investors have an incentive to sell stocks before the end of the year in December because they can then take capital losses on their tax return and reduce their tax liability. Then when the new year starts in January, they can repurchase the stocks, driving up their prices and producing abnormally high returns. Although this explanation seems sensible, it does not explain why institutional investors such as private pension funds, which are not subject to income taxes, do not take advantage of the abnormal returns in January and buy stocks in December, thus bidding up their price and eliminating the abnormal returns.[10]

---

[7]Eugene F. Fama, "Efficient Capital Markets: A Review of Theory and Empirical Work," *Journal of Finance* 25 (1970): 383–416.

[8]For example, see Marc R. Reinganum, "The Anomalous Stock Market Behavior of Small Firms in January: Empirical Tests of Tax Loss Selling Effects," *Journal of Financial Economics* 12 (1983): 89–104; Jay R. Ritter, "The Buying and Selling Behavior of Individual Investors at the Turn of the Year," *Journal of Finance* 43 (1988): 701–717; and Richard Roll, "Vas Ist Das? The Turn-of-the-Year Effect: Anomaly or Risk Mismeasurement?" *Journal of Portfolio Management* 9 (1988): 18–28.

[9]For example, see Donald B. Keim, "The CAPM and Equity Return Regularities," *Financial Analysts Journal* 42 (May–June 1986): 19–34.

[10]Another anomaly that makes the stock market seem less than efficient is the fact that the *Value Line Survey*, one of the most prominent investment advice newsletters, has produced stock recommendations that have yielded abnormally high returns on average. See Fischer Black, "Yes, Virginia, There Is Hope: Tests of the Value Line Ranking System," *Financial Analysts Journal* 29 (September–October 1973): 10–14, and Gur Huberman and Shmuel Kandel, "Market Efficiency and Value Line's Record," *Journal of Business* 63 (1990): 187–216. Whether the excellent performance of the *Value Line Survey* will continue in the future is, of course, a question mark.

Market Overreaction Recent research suggests that stock prices may overreact to news announcements and that the pricing errors are corrected only slowly.[11] When corporations announce a major change in earnings, say, a large decline, the stock price may overshoot, and after an initial large decline, it may rise back to more normal levels over a period of several weeks. This violates the efficient market hypothesis because an investor could earn abnormally high returns, on average, by buying a stock immediately after a poor earnings announcement and then selling it after a couple of weeks when it has risen back to normal levels.

Excessive Volatility A closely related phenomenon to market overreaction is that the stock market appears to display excessive volatility; that is, fluctuations in stock prices may be much greater than is warranted by fluctuations in their fundamental value. In an important paper, Nobel Prize winner Robert Shiller of Yale University found that fluctuations in the S&P 500 stock index could not be justified by the subsequent fluctuations in the dividends of the stocks making up this index. There has been much subsequent technical work criticizing these results, but Shiller's work, along with research that finds that there are smaller fluctuations in stock prices when stock markets are closed, has produced a consensus that stock market prices appear to be driven by factors other than fundamentals.[12]

Mean Reversion Some researchers have also found that stock returns display **mean reversion**: Stocks with low returns today tend to have high returns in the future, and vice versa. Hence stocks that have done poorly in the past are more likely to do well in the future because mean reversion indicates that there will be a predictable positive change in the future price, suggesting that stock prices are not a random walk. Other researchers have found that mean reversion is not nearly as strong in data after World War II and so have raised doubts about whether it is currently an important phenomenon. The evidence on mean reversion remains controversial.[13]

New Information Is Not Always Immediately Incorporated into Stock Prices Although it is generally found that stock prices adjust rapidly to new

---

[11]Werner F. M. De Bondt and Richard Thaler, "Further Evidence on Investor Overreaction and Stock Market Seasonality," *Journal of Finance* 62 (1987): 557–580.

[12]Robert Shiller, "Do Stock Prices Move Too Much to Be Justified by Subsequent Changes in Dividends?" *American Economic Review* 71 (1981): 421–436, and Kenneth R. French and Richard Roll, "Stock Return Variances: The Arrival of Information and the Reaction of Traders," *Journal of Financial Economics* 17 (1986): 5–26.

[13]Evidence for mean reversion has been reported by James M. Poterba and Lawrence H. Summers, "Mean Reversion in Stock Prices: Evidence and Implications," *Journal of Financial Economics* 22 (1988): 27–59; Eugene F. Fama and Kenneth R. French, "Permanent and Temporary Components of Stock Prices," *Journal of Political Economy* 96 (1988): 246–273; and Andrew W. Lo and A. Craig MacKinlay, "Stock Market Prices Do Not Follow Random Walks: Evidence from a Simple Specification Test," *Review of Financial Studies* 1 (1988): 41–66. However, Myung Jig Kim, Charles R. Nelson, and Richard Startz, "Mean Reversion in Stock Prices? A Reappraisal of the Evidence," *Review of Economic Studies* 58 (1991): 515–528, question whether some of these findings are valid. For an excellent summary of this evidence, see Charles Engel and Charles S. Morris, "Challenges to Stock Market Efficiency: Evidence from Mean Reversion Studies," Federal Reserve Bank of Kansas City *Economic Review*, September–October 1991, pp. 21–35. See also N. Jegadeesh and Sheridan Titman, "Returns to Buying Winners and Selling Losers: Implications for Stock Market Efficiency," *Journal of Finance* 48 (1993): 65–92, which shows that mean reversion also occurs for individual stocks.

information, as is suggested by the efficient market hypothesis, recent evidence suggests that, inconsistent with the efficient market hypothesis, stock prices do not instantaneously adjust to profit announcements. Instead, on average stock prices continue to rise for some time after the announcement of unexpectedly high profits, and they continue to fall after surprisingly low profit announcements.[14]

Overview of the Evidence on the Efficient Market Hypothesis

As you can see, the debate on the efficient market hypothesis is far from over. The evidence seems to suggest that the efficient market hypothesis may be a reasonable starting point for evaluating behavior in financial markets. However, there do seem to be important violations of market efficiency that suggest that the efficient market hypothesis may not be the whole story and so may not be generalizable to all behavior in financial markets.

THE PRACTICING MANAGER

Practical Guide to Investing in the Stock Market

The efficient market hypothesis has numerous applications to the real world. It is especially valuable because it can be applied directly to an issue that concerns managers of financial institutions (and the general public as well): how to make profits in the stock market. A practical guide to investing in the stock market, which we develop here, provides a better understanding of the use and implications of the efficient market hypothesis.

How Valuable Are Published Reports by Investment Advisers?

Suppose that you have just read in the "Heard on the Street" column of the *Wall Street Journal* that investment advisers are predicting a boom in oil stocks because an oil shortage is developing. Should you proceed to withdraw all your hard-earned savings from the bank and invest it in oil stocks?

The efficient market hypothesis tells us that when purchasing a security, we cannot expect to earn an abnormally high return, a return greater than the equilibrium return. Information in newspapers and in the published reports of investment advisers is readily available to many market participants and is already reflected in market prices. So acting on this information will not yield abnormally high returns, on average. As we have seen, the empirical evidence for the most part confirms that recommendations from investment advisers cannot help us outperform the general market. Indeed, as the Mini-Case box on page 128 suggests, human investment advisers in San Francisco do not on average even outperform an orangutan!

[14]For example, see R. Ball and P. Brown, "An Empirical Evaluation of Accounting Income Numbers," *Journal of Accounting Research* (1968) 6: 159–178; L. Chan, N. Jegadeesh, and J. Lakonishok, "Momentum Strategies," *Journal of Finance* (1996) 51: 1681–1713; and Eugene Fama, "Market Efficiency, Long-Term Returns and Behavioral Finance," *Journal of Financial Economics* (1998) 49: 283–306.

> MINI-CASE

Should You Hire an Ape as Your Investment Adviser?

The *San Francisco Chronicle* came up with an amusing way of evaluating how successful investment advisers are at picking stocks. They asked eight analysts to pick five stocks at the beginning of the year and then compared the performance of their stock picks to those chosen by Jolyn, an orangutan living at Marine World/Africa USA in Vallejo, California. Consistent with the results found in the "Investment Dartboard" feature of the *Wall Street Journal*, Jolyn beat the investment advisers as often as they beat her. Given this result, you might be just as well off hiring an orangutan as your investment adviser as you would hiring a human being!

Probably no other conclusion is met with more skepticism by students than this one when they first hear it. We all know or have heard of somebody who has been successful in the stock market for a period of many years. We wonder, how could someone be so consistently successful if he or she did not really know how to predict when returns would be abnormally high? The following story, reported in the press, illustrates why such anecdotal evidence is not reliable.

A get-rich-quick artist invented a clever scam. Every week, he wrote two letters. In letter A, he would pick team A to win a particular football game, and in letter B, he would pick the opponent, team B. A mailing list would then be separated into two groups, and he would send letter A to the people in one group and letter B to the people in the other. The following week he would do the same thing but would send these letters only to the group who had received the first letter with the correct prediction. After doing this for 10 games, he had a small cluster of people who had received letters predicting the correct winning team for every game. He then mailed a final letter to them, declaring that since he was obviously an expert predictor of the outcome of football games (he had picked winners 10 weeks in a row) and since his predictions were profitable for the recipients who bet on the games, he would continue to send his predictions only if he were paid a substantial amount of money. When one of his clients figured out what he was up to, the con man was prosecuted and thrown in jail!

What is the lesson of the story? Even if no forecaster is an accurate predictor of the market, there will always be a group of consistent winners. A person who has done well regularly in the past cannot guarantee that he or she will do well in the future. Note that there will also be a group of persistent losers, but you rarely hear about them because no one brags about a poor forecasting record.

Should You Be Skeptical of Hot Tips?

Suppose that your broker phones you with a hot tip to buy stock in the Happy Feet Corporation (HFC) because it has just developed a product that is completely effective in curing athlete's foot. The stock price is sure to go up. Should you follow this advice and buy HFC stock?

The efficient market hypothesis indicates that you should be skeptical of such news. If the stock market is efficient, it has already priced HFC stock so that its expected return will equal the equilibrium return. The hot tip is not particularly valuable and will not enable you to earn an abnormally high return.

You might wonder, though, if the hot tip is based on new information and would give you an edge on the rest of the market. If other market participants have gotten this information before you, the answer is no. As soon as the information hits the street, the unexploited profit opportunity it creates will be quickly eliminated. The stock's price will already reflect the information, and you should expect to realize only the equilibrium return. But if you are one of the first to know the new information (as Raj Rajaratnam was—see the Mini-Case box on page 122), it can do you some good. Only then can you be one of the lucky ones who, on average, will earn an abnormally high return by helping eliminate the unexploited profit opportunity by buying HFC stock.

Do Stock Prices Always Rise When There Is Good News?

If you follow the stock market, you might have noticed a puzzling phenomenon: When good news about a stock, such as a particularly favorable earnings report, is announced, the price of the stock frequently does not rise. The efficient market hypothesis and the random-walk behavior of stock prices explain this phenomenon.

Because changes in stock prices are unpredictable, when information is announced that has already been expected by the market, the stock price will remain unchanged. The announcement does not contain any new information that should lead to a change in stock prices. If this were not the case and the announcement led to a change in stock prices, it would mean that the change was predictable. Because that is ruled out in an efficient market, ***stock prices will respond to announcements only when the information being announced is new and unexpected***. If the news is expected, there will be no stock price response. This is exactly what the evidence that we described earlier suggests will occur—that stock prices reflect publicly available information.

Sometimes a stock price declines when good news is announced. Although this seems somewhat peculiar, it is completely consistent with the workings of an efficient market. Suppose that although the announced news is good, it is not as good as expected. HFC's earnings may have risen 15%, but if the market expected earnings to rise by 20%, the new information is actually unfavorable, and the stock price declines.

Efficient Markets Prescription for the Investor

What does the efficient market hypothesis recommend for investing in the stock market? It tells us that hot tips, investment advisers' published recommendations, and technical analysis—all of which make use of publicly available information—cannot help an investor outperform the market. Indeed, it indicates that anyone without better information than other market participants cannot expect to beat the market. So what is an investor to do?

The efficient market hypothesis leads to the conclusion that such an investor (and almost all of us fit into this category) should not try to outguess the market by constantly buying and selling securities. This process does nothing but boost the income of brokers, who earn commissions on each trade.* Instead, the investor

*The investor may also have to pay Uncle Sam capital gains taxes on any profits that are realized when a security is sold—an additional reason why continual buying and selling does not make sense.

should pursue a "buy and hold" strategy—purchase stocks and hold them for long periods of time. This will lead to the same returns, on average, but the investor's net profits will be higher because fewer brokerage commissions will have to be paid.**

It is frequently a sensible strategy for a small investor, whose costs of managing a portfolio may be high relative to its size, to buy into a mutual fund rather than individual stocks. Because the efficient market hypothesis indicates that no mutual fund can consistently outperform the market, an investor should not buy into one that has high management fees or that pays sales commissions to brokers but rather should purchase a no-load (commission-free) mutual fund that has low management fees.

As we have seen, the evidence indicates that it will not be easy to beat the prescription suggested here, although some of the anomalies to the efficient market hypothesis suggest that an extremely clever investor (which rules out most of us) may be able to outperform a buy-and-hold strategy.

**The investor can also minimize risk by holding a diversified portfolio. The investor will be better off by pursuing a buy-and-hold strategy with a diversified portfolio or with a mutual fund that has a diversified portfolio.

Why the Efficient Market Hypothesis Does Not Imply That Financial Markets Are Efficient

Many financial economists take the efficient market hypothesis one step further in their analysis of financial markets. Not only do they believe that expectations in financial markets are rational—that is, equal to optimal forecasts using all available information—but they also add the condition that prices in financial markets reflect the true fundamental (intrinsic) value of the securities. In other words, all prices are always correct and reflect **market fundamentals** (items that have a direct impact on future income streams of the securities) and so financial markets are efficient.

This stronger view of market efficiency has several important implications in the academic field of finance. First, it implies that in an efficient capital market, one investment is as good as any other because the securities' prices are correct. Second, it implies that a security's price reflects all available information about the intrinsic value of the security. Third, it implies that security prices can be used by managers of both financial and nonfinancial firms to assess their cost of capital (cost of financing their investments) accurately and hence that security prices can be used to help them make the correct decisions about whether a specific investment is worth making. This stronger version of market efficiency is a basic tenet of much analysis in the finance field.

The efficient market hypothesis may be misnamed, however. It does not imply the stronger view of market efficiency but rather just that prices in markets like the stock market are unpredictable. Indeed, as the following application suggests, the existence of market crashes and **bubbles**, in which the prices of assets rise well above their fundamental values, casts serious doubt on the stronger view that financial markets are efficient but provides less of an argument against the basic lessons of the efficient market hypothesis.

CASE

What Do Stock Market Crashes Tell Us About the Efficient Market Hypothesis?

On October 19, 1987, dubbed "Black Monday," the Dow Jones Industrial Average declined more than 20%, the largest one-day decline in U.S. history. The collapse of the high-tech companies' share prices from their peaks in March 2000 caused the heavily tech-laden NASDAQ index to fall from about 5,000 in March 2000 to about 1,500 in 2001 and 2002, for a decline of well over 60%. These stock market crashes have caused many economists to question the validity of the efficient market hypothesis. They do not believe that an efficient market could have produced such massive swings in share prices. To what degree should these stock market crashes make us doubt the validity of the efficient market hypothesis?

Nothing in the efficient market hypothesis rules out large changes in stock prices. A large change in stock prices can result from new information that produces a dramatic decline in optimal forecasts of the future valuation of firms. However, economists are hard pressed to come up with fundamental changes in the economy that can explain the Black Monday and tech crashes. One lesson from these crashes is that factors other than market fundamentals probably have an effect on asset prices. Indeed, as we will explore in Chapters 7 and 8, there exist good reasons to believe that there are impediments to financial markets working well. Hence these crashes have convinced many economists that the stronger version of the efficient market hypothesis, which states that asset prices reflect the true fundamental (intrinsic) value of securities, is incorrect. They attribute a large role in determination of asset prices to market psychology and to the institutional structure of the marketplace. However, nothing in this view contradicts the basic reasoning behind the weaker version of the efficient market hypothesis—that market participants eliminate unexploited profit opportunities. Even though stock market prices may not always solely reflect market fundamentals, as long as stock market crashes are unpredictable, the basic lessons of the efficient market hypothesis hold.

However, other economists believe that market crashes and bubbles suggest that unexploited profit opportunities may exist and that the efficient market hypothesis might be fundamentally flawed. The controversy over the efficient market hypothesis continues.

Behavioral Finance

Doubts about the efficiency of financial markets, particularly after the stock market crash of 1987, led economists such as Nobel Prize winner Robert Shiller to develop a new field of study, **behavioral finance**, which applies concepts from other social sciences, such as anthropology, sociology, and particularly psychology, to understand the behavior of securities prices.[15]

[15]Surveys of this field can be found in Hersh Shefrin, *Beyond Greed and Fear: Understanding of Behavioral Finance and the Psychology of Investing* (Boston: Harvard Business School Press, 2000); Andrei Shleifer, *Inefficient Markets* (Oxford: Oxford University Press, 2000); and Robert J. Shiller, "From Efficient Market Theory to Behavioral Finance," Cowles Foundation Discussion Paper No. 1385 (October 2002).

As we have seen, the efficient market hypothesis assumes that unexploited profit opportunities are eliminated by "smart money." But can smart money dominate ordinary investors so that financial markets are efficient? Specifically, the efficient market hypothesis suggests that smart money sells when a stock price goes up irrationally, with the result that the stock falls back down to what is justified by fundamentals. However, for this to occur, smart money must be able to engage in **short sales**, in which they borrow stock from brokers and then sell it in the market, with the hope that they earn a profit by buying the stock back again ("covering the short") after it has fallen in price. However, work by psychologists suggests that people are subject to loss aversion: That is, they are more unhappy when they suffer losses than they are happy from making gains. Short sales can result in losses way in excess of an investor's initial investment if the stock price climbs sharply above the price at which the short sale is made (and these losses have the possibility of being unlimited if the stock price climbs to astronomical heights). Loss aversion can thus explain an important phenomenon: Very little short selling actually takes place. Short selling may also be constrained by rules restricting it because it seems unsavory that someone would make money from another person's misfortune. The fact that there is so little short selling can explain why stock prices sometimes get overvalued. Not enough short selling can take place by smart money to drive stock prices back down to their fundamental value.

Psychologists have also found that people tend to be overconfident in their own judgments (just as in "Lake Wobegon," everyone believes he or she is above average). As a result, it is no surprise that investors tend to believe they are smarter than other investors. These "smart" investors not only assume the market often doesn't get it right but also are willing to trade on the basis of these beliefs. This can explain why securities markets have so much trading volume, something that the efficient market hypothesis does not predict.

Overconfidence and social contagion provide an explanation for stock market bubbles. When stock prices go up, investors attribute their profits to their intelligence and talk up the stock market. This word-of-mouth enthusiasm and the media then can produce an environment in which even more investors think stock prices will rise in the future. The result is then a so-called positive feedback loop in which prices continue to rise, producing a speculative bubble, which finally crashes when prices get too far out of line with fundamentals.[16]

The field of behavioral finance is a young one, but it holds out hope that we might be able to explain some features of securities markets' behavior that are not well explained by the efficient market hypothesis.

---

[16]See Robert J. Shiller, *Irrational Exuberance* (New York: Broadway Books, 2001).

SUMMARY

1. The efficient market hypothesis states that current security prices will fully reflect all available information because in an efficient market, all unexploited profit opportunities are eliminated. The elimination of unexploited profit opportunities necessary for a financial market to be efficient does not require that all market participants be well informed.

2. The evidence on the efficient market hypothesis is quite mixed. Early evidence on the performance of investment analysts and mutual funds, whether stock prices reflect publicly available information, the random-walk behavior of stock prices, or the success of so-called technical analysis, was quite favorable to the efficient market hypothesis. However, in

recent years, evidence on the small-firm effect, the January effect, market overreaction, excessive volatility, mean reversion, and that new information is not always incorporated into stock prices suggests that the hypothesis may not always be entirely correct. The evidence seems to suggest that the efficient market hypothesis may be a reasonable starting point for evaluating behavior in financial markets, but it may not be generalizable to all behavior in financial markets.

3. The efficient market hypothesis indicates that hot tips, investment advisers' published recommendations, and technical analysis cannot help an investor outperform the market. The prescription for investors is to pursue a buy-and-hold strategy—purchase stocks and hold them for long periods of time. Empirical evidence generally supports these implications of the efficient market hypothesis in the stock market.

4. The existence of market crashes and bubbles has convinced many financial economists that the stronger version of the efficient market hypothesis, which states that asset prices reflect the true fundamental (intrinsic) value of securities, is not correct. It is far less clear that stock market crashes show that the efficient market hypothesis is wrong. Even if the stock market were driven by factors other than fundamentals, the crashes do not clearly demonstrate that many of the basic lessons of the efficient market hypothesis are no longer valid as long as the crashes could not have been predicted.

5. The new field of behavioral finance applies concepts from other social sciences, such as anthropology, sociology, and particularly psychology, to understand the behavior of securities prices. Loss aversion, overconfidence, and social contagion can explain why trading volume is so high, stock prices get overvalued, and speculative bubbles occur.

KEY TERMS

arbitrage, p. 120
behavioral finance, p. 131
bubbles, p. 130
efficient market hypothesis, p. 118
January effect, p. 125
market fundamentals, p. 130
mean reversion, p. 126
random walk, p. 122
short sales, p. 132
theory of efficient capital markets, p. 118
unexploited profit opportunities, p. 120

QUESTIONS

1. "Forecasters' predictions of inflation are notoriously inaccurate, so their expectations of inflation cannot be optimal." Is this statement true, false, or uncertain? Explain your answer.
2. "Whenever it is snowing when Joe Commuter gets up in the morning, he misjudges how long it will take him to drive to work. Otherwise, his expectations of the driving time are perfectly accurate. Considering that it snows only once every 10 years where Joe lives, Joe's expectations are almost always perfectly accurate." Are Joe's expectations optimal? Why or why not?
3. Suppose that you decide to play a game. You buy stock by throwing a dice a few times, using that method to select which stock to buy. After 10 months you calculate the return on your investment and the return earned by someone who followed "expert" advice during the same period. If both returns are similar, would this constitute evidence in favor of or against the efficient market hypothesis?
4. "If stock prices did not follow a random walk, there would be unexploited profit opportunities in the market." Is this statement true, false, or uncertain? Explain your answer.
5. Suppose that increases in the money supply lead to a rise in stock prices. Does this mean that when you see that the money supply has had a sharp rise in the past week, you should go out and buy stocks? Why or why not?
6. Suppose that you are asked to forecast future stock prices of ABC Corporation, so you proceed to collect all available information. The day you announce your forecast, competitors of ABC Corporation announce a plan to merge and reshape the structure of the industry. Would your forecast be considered optimal?
7. If my broker has been right in her five previous buy and sell recommendations, should I continue listening to her advice?
8. Can a person with optimal expectations expect the price of Google to rise by 10% in the next month?

9. Suppose that in every last week of November stock prices go up by an average of 3%. Would this constitute evidence in favor of or against the efficient market hypothesis?

10. "An efficient market is one in which no one ever profits from having better information than the rest." Is this statement true, false, or uncertain? Explain your answer.

11. If higher money growth is associated with higher future inflation and if announced money growth turns out to be extremely high but is still less than the market expected, what do you think would happen to long-term bond prices?

12. "Foreign exchange rates, like stock prices, should follow a random walk." Is this statement true, false, or uncertain? Explain your answer.

13. Assume that the efficient market hypothesis holds. Marcos has been recently hired by a brokerage firm and claims that he now has access to the best market information. However, he is the "new guy," and no one at the firm tells him much about the business. Would you expect Marcos's clients to be better or worse off than the rest of the firm's clients?

14. Suppose that you work as a forecaster of future monthly inflation rates and that your last 6 forecasts have been off by minus 1%. Can you say that your expectations are optimal?

QUANTITATIVE PROBLEMS

1. A company has just announced a 3-for-1 stock split, effective immediately. Prior to the split, the company had a market value of $5 billion with 100 million shares outstanding. Assuming that the split conveys no new information about the company, what is the value of the company, the number of shares outstanding, and price per share after the split? If the actual market price immediately following the split is $17.00 per share, what does this tell us about market efficiency?

2. If the public expects a corporation to lose $5 a share this quarter and it actually loses $4, which is still the largest loss in the history of the company, what does the efficient market hypothesis say will happen to the price of the stock when the $4 loss is announced?

WEB EXERCISES

The Efficient Market Hypothesis

1. Visit **http://research.stlouisfed.org/fred2/**. Click on "Category," then "Financial Indicators," then "Stock Market Indexes." Review the indices for the DJIA, the S&P 500, and the Wilshire 5000 Market Index. Which index appears most volatile? In which index would you rather have invested in 1985 if the investment had been allowed to compound until now?

2. The Internet is a great source of information on stock prices and stock price movements. Go to **http://finance.yahoo.com** and in Search Finance enter Dow Jones Industrial Average and click to view current data on the Dow Jones Industrial Average. Click on "Historical Prices" and change the time range, and observe the stock trend over various intervals. Have stock prices been going down over the past day, week, three months, and year?

PART 3 FUNDAMENTALS OF FINANCIAL INSTITUTIONS

CHAPTER 7

Why Do Financial Institutions Exist?

> PREVIEW

A healthy and vibrant economy requires a financial system that moves funds from people who save to people who have productive investment opportunities. But how does the financial system make sure that your hard-earned savings get channeled to those with productive investment opportunities?

This chapter answers that question by providing a theory for understanding why financial institutions exist to promote economic efficiency. The theoretical analysis focuses on a few simple but powerful economic concepts that enable us to explain features of our financial markets, such as why financial contracts are written as they are, and why financial intermediaries are more important than securities markets for getting funds to borrowers.

Basic Facts About Financial Structure Throughout The World

The financial system is complex in both structure and function throughout the world. It includes many types of institutions: banks, insurance companies, mutual funds, stock and bond markets, and so on—all of which are regulated by government. The financial system channels trillions of dollars per year from savers to people with productive investment opportunities. If we take a close look at financial structure all over the world, we find eight basic facts, some of which are quite surprising, that we need to explain to understand how the financial system works.

The bar chart in Figure 7.1 shows how American businesses financed their activities using external funds (those obtained from outside the business itself) in the period 1970–2000 and compares U.S. data with those of Germany, Japan, and Canada. The Bank Loans category is made up primarily of loans from depository institutions; Nonbank Loans is composed primarily of loans by other financial intermediaries; the Bonds category includes marketable debt securities such as corporate bonds and commercial paper; and Stock consists of new issues of new equity (stock market shares).

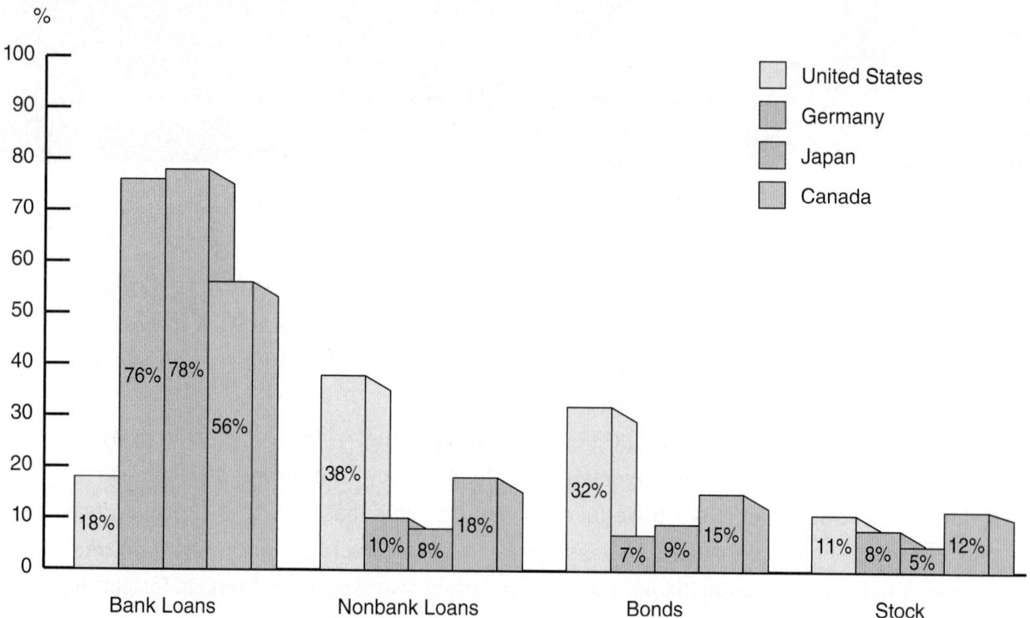

FIGURE 7.1 Sources of External Funds for Nonfinancial Businesses: A Comparison of the United States with Germany, Japan, and Canada

The Bank Loans category is made up primarily of loans from depository institutions; Nonbank Loans is composed primarily of loans by other financial intermediaries; the Bonds category includes marketable debt securities such as corporate bonds and commercial paper; and Stock consists of new issues of new equity (stock market shares).

Sources: Andreas Hackethal and Reinhard H. Schmidt, "Financing Patterns: Measurement Concepts and Empirical Results," Johann Wolfgang Goethe-Universitat Working Paper No. 125, January 2004. The data are from 1970–2000 and are gross flows as percentages of the total, not including trade and other credit data, which are not available.

Now let's explore the eight facts.

1. ***Stocks are not the most important source of external financing for businesses.*** Because so much attention in the media is focused on the stock market, many people have the impression that stocks are the most important sources of financing for American corporations. However, as we can see from the bar chart in Figure 7.1, the stock market accounted for only a small fraction of the external financing of American businesses in the 1970–2000 period: 11%.[1] Similarly small figures apply in the other countries presented in Figure 7.1 as well. Why is the stock market less important than other sources of financing in the United States and other countries?
2. ***Issuing marketable debt and equity securities is not the primary way in which businesses finance their operations.*** Figure 7.1 shows that bonds are a far more important source of financing than stocks in the United States (32% versus 11%). However, stocks and bonds combined (43%), which make up the total share of marketable securities, still supply less than one-half of the external funds corporations need to finance their activities. The fact that issuing marketable securities is not the most important source of financing is true elsewhere in the world as well. Indeed, as we see in Figure 7.1, other countries have a much smaller share of external financing supplied by marketable securities than does the United States. Why don't businesses use marketable securities more extensively to finance their activities?
3. ***Indirect finance, which involves the activities of financial intermediaries, is many times more important than direct finance, in which businesses raise funds directly from lenders in financial markets.*** Direct finance involves the sale to households of marketable securities such as stocks and bonds. The 43% share of stocks and bonds as a source of external financing for American businesses actually greatly overstates the importance of direct finance in our financial system. Since 1970 less than 5% of newly issued corporate bonds and commercial paper and less than one-third of stocks have been sold directly to American households. The rest of these securities have been bought primarily by financial intermediaries such as insurance companies, pension funds, and mutual funds. These figures indicate that direct finance is used in less than 10% of the external funding of American business. Because in most countries marketable securities are an even less important source of finance than in the United States, direct

[1] The 11% figure for the percentage of external financing provided by stocks is based on the flows of external funds to corporations. However, this flow figure is somewhat misleading because when a share of stock is issued, it raises funds permanently, whereas when a bond is issued, it raises funds only temporarily until they are paid back at maturity. To see this, suppose that a firm raises $1,000 by selling a share of stock and another $1,000 by selling a $1,000 one-year bond. In the case of the stock issue, the firm can hold on to the $1,000 it raised this way, but to hold on to the $1,000 it raised through debt, it has to issue a new $1,000 bond every year. If we look at the flow of funds to corporations over a 30-year period, as in Figure 7.1, the firm will have raised $1,000 with a stock issue only once in the 30-year period, while it will have raised $1,000 with debt 30 times, once in each of the 30 years. Thus, it will look as though debt is 30 times more important than stocks in raising funds, even though our example indicates that they are actually equally important for the firm.

finance is also far less important than indirect finance in the rest of the world. Why are financial intermediaries and indirect finance so important in financial markets? In recent years, however, indirect finance has been declining in importance. Why is this happening?

4. ***Financial intermediaries, particularly banks, are the most important source of external funds used to finance businesses.*** As we can see in Figure 7.1, the primary source of external funds for businesses throughout the world comprises loans made by banks and other nonbank financial intermediaries such as insurance companies, pension funds, and finance companies (56% in the United States, but more than 70% in Germany, Japan, and Canada). In other industrialized countries, bank loans are the largest category of sources of external finance (more than 70% in Germany and Japan and more than 50% in Canada). Thus, the data suggest that banks in these countries have the most important role in financing business activities. In developing countries, banks play an even more important role in the financial system than they do in industrialized countries. What makes banks so important to the workings of the financial system? Although banks remain important, their share of external funds for businesses has been declining in recent years. What is driving this decline?
5. ***The financial system is among the most heavily regulated sectors of the economy.*** The financial system is heavily regulated in the United States and all other developed countries. Governments regulate financial markets primarily to promote the provision of information and to ensure the soundness (stability) of the financial system. Why are financial markets so extensively regulated throughout the world?
6. ***Only large, well-established corporations have easy access to securities markets to finance their activities.*** Individuals and smaller businesses that are not well established are less likely to raise funds by issuing marketable securities. Instead, they most often obtain their financing from banks. Why do only large, well-known corporations find it easier to raise funds in securities markets?
7. ***Collateral is a prevalent feature of debt contracts for both households and businesses.*** Collateral is property that is pledged to a lender to guarantee payment in the event that the borrower is unable to make debt payments. Collateralized debt (also known as **secured debt** to contrast it with **unsecured debt**, such as credit card debt, which is not collateralized) is the predominant form of household debt and is widely used in business borrowing as well. The majority of household debt in the United States consists of collateralized loans: Your automobile is collateral for your auto loan, and your house is collateral for your mortgage. Commercial and farm mortgages, for which property is pledged as collateral, make up one-quarter of borrowing by nonfinancial businesses; corporate bonds and other bank loans also often involve pledges of collateral. Why is collateral such an important feature of debt contracts?
8. ***Debt contracts typically are extremely complicated legal documents that place substantial restrictions on the behavior of the borrower.*** Many students think of a debt contract as a simple IOU that can be written on a single piece of paper. The reality of debt contracts is far different, however. In all countries, bond or loan contracts typically are long legal documents with provisions (called **restrictive covenants**) that restrict and specify certain

activities that the borrower can engage in. Restrictive covenants are not just a feature of debt contracts for businesses; for example, personal automobile loan and home mortgage contracts have covenants that require the borrower to maintain sufficient insurance on the automobile or house purchased with the loan. Why are debt contracts so complex and restrictive?

As you may recall from Chapter 2, an important feature of financial markets is that they have substantial transaction and information costs. An economic analysis of how these costs affect financial markets provides us with explanations of the eight facts, which in turn enable a much deeper understanding of how our financial system works. In the next section, we examine the impact of transaction costs on the structure of our financial system. Then we turn to the effect of information costs on financial structure.

Transaction Costs

Transaction costs are a major problem in financial markets. An example will make this clear.

How Transaction Costs Influence Financial Structure

Say you have $5,000 you would like to invest, and you think about investing in the stock market. Because you have only $5,000, you can buy only a small number of shares. Even if you use online trading, your purchase is so small that the brokerage commission for buying the stock you picked will be a large percentage of the purchase price of the shares. If instead you decide to buy a bond, the problem is even worse because the smallest denomination for some bonds you might want to buy is as much as $10,000, and you do not have that much to invest. You are disappointed and realize that you will not be able to use financial markets to earn a return on your hard-earned savings. You can take some consolation, however, in the fact that you are not alone in being stymied by high transaction costs. This is a fact of life for many of us: Only around one-half of American households own any securities.

You also face another problem related to transaction costs. Because you have only a small amount of funds available, you can make only a restricted number of investments because a large number of small transactions would result in very high transaction costs. That is, you have to put all your eggs in one basket, and your inability to diversify will subject you to a lot of risk.

How Financial Intermediaries Reduce Transaction Costs

This example of the problems posed by transaction costs and the example outlined in Chapter 2 when legal costs kept you from making a loan to Carl the Carpenter illustrate that small savers like you are frozen out of financial markets and are unable to benefit from them. Fortunately, financial intermediaries, an important part of the financial structure, have evolved to reduce transaction costs and allow small savers and borrowers to benefit from the existence of financial markets.

Economies of Scale One solution to the problem of high transaction costs is to bundle the funds of many investors together so that they can take advantage of *economies of scale*, the reduction in transaction costs per dollar of investment as the size (scale) of transactions increases. Bundling investors' funds together reduces transaction costs for the individual investors. Economies of scale exist because the total cost of carrying out a transaction in financial markets increases only a little as the size of the transaction grows. For example, the cost of arranging a purchase of 10,000 shares of stock is not much greater than the cost of arranging a purchase of 50 shares of stock.

The presence of economies of scale in financial markets helps explain why financial intermediaries developed and have become such an important part of our financial structure. The clearest example of a financial intermediary that arose because of economies of scale is a mutual fund. A *mutual fund* is a financial intermediary that sells shares to individuals and then invests the proceeds in bonds or stocks. Because it buys large blocks of stocks or bonds, a mutual fund can take advantage of lower transaction costs. These cost savings are then passed on to individual investors after the mutual fund has taken its cut in the form of management fees for administering their accounts. An additional benefit for individual investors is that a mutual fund is large enough to purchase a widely diversified portfolio of securities. The increased diversification for individual investors reduces their risk, making them better off.

Economies of scale are also important in lowering the costs of things such as information technology that financial institutions need to accomplish their tasks. Once a large mutual fund has invested a lot of money in setting up a telecommunications system, for example, the system can be used for a huge number of transactions at a low cost per transaction.

Expertise Financial intermediaries are also better able to develop expertise to lower transaction costs. Their expertise in information technology enables them to offer customers convenient services like being able to call a toll-free number for information on how well their investments are doing and to write checks on their accounts.

An important outcome of a financial intermediary's low transaction costs is the ability to provide its customers with *liquidity services*, services that make it easier for customers to conduct transactions. Money market mutual funds, for example, not only pay shareholders high interest rates but also allow them to write checks for convenient bill paying.

Asymmetric Information: Adverse Selection and Moral Hazard

The presence of transaction costs in financial markets explains in part why financial intermediaries and indirect finance play such an important role in financial markets (fact 3). To understand financial structure more fully, however, we turn to the role of information in financial markets.

Asymmetric information—a situation that arises when one party's insufficient knowledge about the other party involved in a transaction makes it impossible to make accurate decisions when conducting the transaction—is an important aspect of financial markets. For example, managers of a corporation know whether they are honest and have better information about how well their business is doing than the stockholders do. The presence of asymmetric information leads to adverse selection and moral hazard problems, which were introduced in Chapter 2.

Adverse selection is an asymmetric information problem that occurs *before* the transaction: Potential bad credit risks are the ones who most actively seek out loans. Thus, the parties who are the most likely to produce an undesirable outcome are the ones most likely to want to engage in the transaction. For example, big risk takers or outright crooks might be the most eager to take out a loan because they know that they are unlikely to pay it back. Because adverse selection increases the chances that a loan might be made to a bad credit risk, lenders might decide not to make any loans, even though good credit risks can be found in the marketplace.

Moral hazard arises *after* the transaction occurs: The lender runs the risk that the borrower will engage in activities that are undesirable from the lender's point of view because they make it less likely that the loan will be paid back. For example, once borrowers have obtained a loan, they may take on big risks (which have possible high returns but also run a greater risk of default) because they are playing with someone else's money. Because moral hazard lowers the probability that the loan will be repaid, lenders may decide that they would rather not make a loan.

The analysis of how asymmetric information problems affect economic behavior is called **agency theory**. We will apply this theory here to explain why financial structure takes the form it does, thereby explaining the facts outlined at the beginning of the chapter. In the next chapter, we will use the same theory to understand financial crises.

The Lemons Problem: How Adverse Selection Influences Financial Structure

Access **http://www.nobelprize.org/nobel_prizes/economic-sciences/laureates/2001/** and find a complete discussion of the lemons problem on a site dedicated to Nobel Prize winners.

A particular aspect of the way the adverse selection problem interferes with the efficient functioning of a market was outlined in a famous article by Nobel Prize winner George Akerlof. It is called the "lemons problem" because it resembles the problem created by lemons in the used-car market.[2] Potential buyers of used cars are frequently unable to assess the quality of the car; that is, they can't tell whether a particular used car is one that will run well or a lemon that will continually give them grief. The price that a buyer pays must therefore reflect the *average* quality of the cars in the market, somewhere between the low value of a lemon and the high value of a good car.

The owner of a used car, by contrast, is more likely to know whether the car is a peach or a lemon. If the car is a lemon, the owner is more than happy to sell it at the price the buyer is willing to pay, which, being somewhere between the value of a lemon and a good car, is greater than the lemon's value. However, if the car is a

[2] George Akerlof, "The Market for 'Lemons': Quality, Uncertainty and the Market Mechanism," *Quarterly Journal of Economics* 84 (1970): 488–500. Two important papers that have applied the lemons problem analysis to financial markets are Stewart Myers and N. S. Majluf, "Corporate Financing and Investment Decisions When Firms Have Information That Investors Do Not Have," *Journal of Financial Economics* 13 (1984): 187–221; and Bruce Greenwald, Joseph E. Stiglitz, and Andrew Weiss, "Information Imperfections in the Capital Market and Macroeconomic Fluctuations," *American Economic Review* 74 (1984): 194–199.

peach, the owner knows that the car is undervalued at the price the buyer is willing to pay, and so the owner may not want to sell it. As a result of this adverse selection, few good used cars will come to the market. Because the average quality of a used car available in the market will be low and because few people want to buy a lemon, there will be few sales. The used-car market will function poorly, if at all.

Lemons in the Stock and Bond Markets

A similar lemons problem arises in securities markets—that is, the debt (bond) and equity (stock) markets. Suppose that our friend Irving the investor, a potential buyer of securities such as common stock, can't distinguish between good firms with high expected profits and low risk and bad firms with low expected profits and high risk. In this situation, Irving will be willing to pay only a price that reflects the *average* quality of firms issuing securities—a price that lies between the value of securities from bad firms and the value of those from good firms. If the owners or managers of a good firm have better information than Irving and *know* that they have a good firm, they know that their securities are undervalued and will not want to sell them to Irving at the price he is willing to pay. The only firms willing to sell Irving securities will be bad firms (because his price is higher than the securities are worth). Our friend Irving is not stupid; he does not want to hold securities in bad firms, and hence he will decide not to purchase securities in the market. In an outcome similar to that in the used-car market, this securities market will not work very well because few firms will sell securities in it to raise capital.

The analysis is similar if Irving considers purchasing a corporate debt instrument in the bond market rather than an equity share. Irving will buy a bond only if its interest rate is high enough to compensate him for the average default risk of the good and bad firms trying to sell the debt. The knowledgeable owners of a good firm realize that they will be paying a higher interest rate than they should, so they are unlikely to want to borrow in this market. Only the bad firms will be willing to borrow, and because investors like Irving are not eager to buy bonds issued by bad firms, they will probably not buy any bonds at all. Few bonds are likely to sell in this market, so it will not be a good source of financing.

The analysis we have just conducted explains fact 2—why marketable securities are not the primary source of financing for businesses in any country in the world. It also partly explains fact 1—why stocks are not the most important source of financing for American businesses. The presence of the lemons problem keeps securities markets such as the stock and bond markets from being effective in channeling funds from savers to borrowers.

Tools to Help Solve Adverse Selection Problems

In the absence of asymmetric information, the lemons problem goes away. If buyers know as much about the quality of used cars as sellers, so that all involved can tell a good car from a bad one, buyers will be willing to pay full value for good used cars. Because the owners of good used cars can now get a fair price, they will be willing to sell them in the market. The market will have many transactions and will do its intended job of channeling good cars to people who want them.

Similarly, if purchasers of securities can distinguish good firms from bad, they will pay the full value of securities issued by good firms, and good firms will sell their securities in the market. The securities market will then be able to move funds to the good firms that have the most productive investment opportunities.

Private Production and Sale of Information The solution to the adverse selection problem in financial markets is to eliminate asymmetric information by furnishing the people supplying funds with full details about the individuals or firms seeking to finance their investment activities. One way to get this material to saver-lenders is to have private companies collect and produce information that distinguishes good from bad firms and then sell it. In the United States, companies such as Standard & Poor's, Moody's, and Value Line gather information on firms' balance sheet positions and investment activities, publish these data, and sell them to subscribers (individuals, libraries, and financial intermediaries involved in purchasing securities).

The system of private production and sale of information does not completely solve the adverse selection problem in securities markets, however, because of the **free-rider problem**. The free-rider problem occurs when people who do not pay for information take advantage of the information that other people have paid for. The free-rider problem suggests that the private sale of information will be only a partial solution to the lemons problem. To see why, suppose that you have just purchased information that tells you which firms are good and which are bad. You believe that this purchase is worthwhile because you can make up the cost of acquiring this information, and then some, by purchasing the securities of good firms that are undervalued. However, when our savvy (free-riding) investor Irving sees you buying certain securities, he buys right along with you, even though he has not paid for any information. If many other investors act as Irving does, the increased demand for the undervalued good securities will cause their low price to be bid up immediately to reflect the securities' true value. Because of all these free riders, you can no longer buy the securities for less than their true value. Now because you will not gain any profits from purchasing the information, you realize that you never should have paid for this information in the first place. If other investors come to the same realization, private firms and individuals may not be able to sell enough of this information to make it worth their while to gather and produce it. The weakened ability of private firms to profit from selling information will mean that less information is produced in the marketplace, so adverse selection (the lemons problem) will still interfere with the efficient functioning of securities markets.

Government Regulation to Increase Information The free-rider problem prevents the private market from producing enough information to eliminate all the asymmetric information that leads to adverse selection. Could financial markets benefit from government intervention? The government could, for instance, produce information to help investors distinguish good from bad firms and provide it to the public free of charge. This solution, however, would involve the government in releasing negative information about firms, a practice that might be politically difficult. A second possibility (and one followed by the United States and most governments throughout the world) is for the government to regulate securities markets in a way that encourages firms to reveal honest information about themselves so that investors can determine how good or bad the firms are. In the United States, the Securities and Exchange Commission (SEC) is the government agency that requires firms selling their securities to have independent **audits**, in which accounting firms certify that the firm is adhering to standard accounting principles and disclosing accurate information about sales, assets, and earnings. Similar regulations are found in other countries. However, disclosure requirements do not always work well, as the collapse of Enron and accounting scandals at other corporations, such as WorldCom and Parmalat (an Italian company), suggest (see the Mini-Case box, "The Enron Implosion").

The asymmetric information problem of adverse selection in financial markets helps explain why financial markets are among the most heavily regulated sectors in the economy (fact 5). Government regulation to increase information for investors is needed to reduce the adverse selection problem, which interferes with the efficient functioning of securities (stock and bond) markets.

Although government regulation lessens the adverse selection problem, it does not eliminate it. Even when firms provide information to the public about their sales, assets, or earnings, they still have more information than investors: A lot more is involved in knowing the quality of a firm than statistics can provide. Furthermore, bad firms have an incentive to make themselves look like good firms because this would enable them to fetch a higher price for their securities. Bad firms will slant the information they are required to transmit to the public, thus making it harder for investors to sort out the good firms from the bad.

Financial Intermediation So far we have seen that private production of information and government regulation to encourage provision of information lessen, but do not eliminate, the adverse selection problem in financial markets. How, then, can the financial structure help promote the flow of funds to people with productive investment opportunities when asymmetric information exists? A clue is provided by the structure of the used-car market.

An important feature of the used-car market is that most used cars are not sold directly by one individual to another. An individual who considers buying a used car might pay for privately produced information by subscribing to a magazine like

> MINI-CASE

The Enron Implosion

Until 2001 Enron Corporation, a firm that specialized in trading in the energy market, appeared to be spectacularly successful. It had a quarter of the energy-trading market and was valued as high as $77 billion in August 2000 (just a little over a year before its collapse), making it the seventh-largest corporation in the United States at that time. However, toward the end of 2001, Enron came crashing down. In October 2001, Enron announced a third-quarter loss of $618 million and disclosed accounting "mistakes." The SEC then engaged in a formal investigation of Enron's financial dealings with partnerships led by its former finance chief. It became clear that Enron was engaged in a complex set of transactions by which it was keeping substantial amounts of debt and financial contracts off its balance sheet. These transactions enabled Enron to hide its financial difficulties. Despite securing as much as $1.5 billion of new financing from J. P. Morgan Chase and Citigroup, the company was forced to declare bankruptcy in December 2001, up to that point the largest bankruptcy in U.S. history.

The Enron collapse illustrates that government regulation can lessen asymmetric information problems but cannot eliminate them. Managers have tremendous incentives to hide their companies' problems, making it hard for investors to know the true value of the firm.

The Enron bankruptcy not only increased concerns in financial markets about the quality of accounting information supplied by corporations but also led to hardship for many of the firm's former employees, who found that their pensions had become worthless. Outrage against the duplicity of executives at Enron was high, and several of them were sent to jail.

Consumer Reports to find out if a particular make of car has a good repair record. Nevertheless, reading *Consumer Reports* does not solve the adverse selection problem because even if a particular make of car has a good reputation, the specific car someone is trying to sell could be a lemon. The prospective buyer might also take the used car to a mechanic for an inspection. But what if the prospective buyer doesn't know a mechanic who can be trusted or if the mechanic would charge a high fee to evaluate the car?

Because these roadblocks make it hard for individuals to acquire enough information about used cars, most used cars are not sold directly by one individual to another. Instead, they are sold by an intermediary, a used-car dealer who purchases used cars from individuals and resells them to other individuals. Used-car dealers produce information in the market by becoming experts in determining whether a car is a peach or a lemon. Once they know that a car is good, they can sell it with some form of a guarantee: either a guarantee that is explicit, such as a warranty, or an implicit guarantee, in which they stand by their reputation for honesty. People are more likely to purchase a used car because of a dealer's guarantee, and the dealer is able to make a profit on the production of information about automobile quality by being able to sell the used car at a higher price than the dealer paid for it. If dealers purchase and then resell cars on which they have produced information, they avoid the problem of other people free-riding on the information they produced.

Just as used-car dealers help solve adverse selection problems in the automobile market, financial intermediaries play a similar role in financial markets. A financial intermediary, such as a bank, becomes an expert in producing information about firms, so that it can sort out good credit risks from bad ones. Then it can acquire funds from depositors and lend them to the good firms. Because the bank is able to lend mostly to good firms, it is able to earn a higher return on its loans than the interest it has to pay to its depositors. The resulting profit that the bank earns gives it the incentive to engage in this information production activity.

An important element in the bank's ability to profit from the information it produces is that it avoids the free-rider problem by primarily making private loans rather than by purchasing securities that are traded in the open market. Because a private loan is not traded, other investors cannot watch what the bank is doing and bid up the loan's price to the point that the bank receives no compensation for the information it has produced. The bank's role as an intermediary that holds mostly nontraded loans is the key to its success in reducing asymmetric information in financial markets.

Our analysis of adverse selection indicates that financial intermediaries in general—and banks in particular, because they hold a large fraction of nontraded loans—should play a greater role in moving funds to corporations than securities markets do. Our analysis thus explains facts 3 and 4: why indirect finance is so much more important than direct finance and why banks are the most important source of external funds for financing businesses.

Another important fact that is explained by the analysis here is the greater importance of banks in the financial systems of developing countries. As we have seen, when the quality of information about firms is better, asymmetric information problems will be less severe, and it will be easier for firms to issue securities. Information about private firms is harder to collect in developing countries than in industrialized countries; therefore, the smaller role played by securities markets leaves a greater role for financial intermediaries such as banks. A corollary of this analysis is that as information about firms becomes easier to acquire, the role of banks should decline. A major development in the past 30 years in the United States has been huge improvements in information technology. Thus, the analysis here suggests that the lending role of financial institutions, such as banks in the United States, should have declined, and this is exactly what has occurred (see Chapter 19).

Our analysis of adverse selection also explains fact 6, which questions why large firms are more likely to obtain funds from securities markets, a direct route, rather than from banks and financial intermediaries, an indirect route. The better known a corporation is, the more information about its activities is available in the marketplace. Thus, it is easier for investors to evaluate the quality of the corporation and determine whether it is a good firm or a bad one. Because investors have fewer worries about adverse selection with well-known corporations, they will be willing to invest directly in their securities. Our adverse selection analysis thus suggests that a pecking order for firms that can issue securities should be in place. The larger and more established a corporation is, the more likely it will be to issue securities to raise funds, a view that is known as the **pecking order hypothesis**. This hypothesis is supported in the data and is what fact 6 describes.

Collateral and Net Worth Adverse selection interferes with the functioning of financial markets only if a lender suffers a loss when a borrower is unable to make loan payments and thereby defaults.

Collateral, property promised to the lender if the borrower defaults, reduces the consequences of adverse selection because it reduces the lender's losses in the event of a default. If a borrower defaults on a loan, the lender can sell the collateral and use the proceeds to make up for the losses on the loan. For example, if you fail to make your mortgage payments, the lender can take the title to your house, auction it off, and use the receipts to pay off the loan. Lenders are thus more willing to make loans secured by collateral, and borrowers are willing to supply collateral because the reduced risk for the lender makes it more likely they will get the loan in the first place and perhaps at a better loan rate. The presence of adverse selection in credit markets thus provides an explanation for why collateral is an important feature of debt contracts (fact 7).

Net worth (also called **equity capital**), the difference between a firm's assets (what it owns or is owed) and its liabilities (what it owes), can perform a similar role to that of collateral. If a firm has a high net worth, then even if it engages in investments that cause it to have negative profits and so defaults on its debt payments, the lender can take title to the firm's net worth, sell it off, and use the proceeds to recoup some of the losses from the loan. In addition, the more net worth a firm has in the first place, the less likely it is to default, because the firm has a cushion of assets that it can use to pay off its loans. Hence, when firms seeking credit have high net worth, the consequences of adverse selection are less important and lenders are more willing to make loans. This analysis lies behind the often-heard lament, "Only the people who don't need money can borrow it!"

Summary So far we have used the concept of adverse selection to explain seven of the eight facts about financial structure introduced earlier: The first four emphasize the importance of financial intermediaries and the relative unimportance of securities markets for the financing of corporations; the fifth, that financial markets are among the most heavily regulated sectors of the economy; the sixth, that only large, well-established corporations have access to securities markets; and the seventh, that collateral is an important feature of debt contracts. In the next section, we will see that the other asymmetric information concept of moral hazard provides additional reasons for the importance of financial intermediaries and the relative unimportance of securities markets for the financing of corporations, the prevalence of government regulation, and the importance of collateral in debt contracts. In addition, the concept of moral hazard can be used to explain our final fact (fact 8): why debt contracts are complicated legal documents that place substantial restrictions on the behavior of the borrower.

How Moral Hazard Affects the Choice Between Debt and Equity Contracts

Moral hazard is the asymmetric information problem that occurs after the financial transaction takes place, when the seller of a security may have incentives to hide information and engage in activities that are undesirable for the purchaser of the security. Moral hazard has important consequences for whether a firm finds it easier to raise funds with debt than with equity contracts.

Moral Hazard in Equity Contracts: The Principal–Agent Problem

Equity contracts, such as common stock, are claims to a share in the profits and assets of a business. Equity contracts are subject to a particular type of moral hazard called the **principal–agent problem**. When managers own only a small fraction of the firm they work for, the stockholders who own most of the firm's equity (called the *principals*) are not the same people as the managers of the firm, who are the *agents* of the owners. This separation of ownership and control involves moral hazard, in that the managers in control (the agents) may act in their own interest rather than in the interest of the stockholder-owners (the principals) because the managers have less incentive to maximize profits than the stockholder-owners do.

To understand the principal–agent problem more fully, suppose that your friend Steve asks you to become a silent partner in his ice cream store. The store requires an investment of $10,000 to set up and Steve has only $1,000. So you purchase an equity stake (stock shares) for $9,000, which entitles you to 90% of the ownership of the firm, while Steve owns only 10%. If Steve works hard to make tasty ice cream, keeps the store clean, smiles at all the customers, and hustles to wait on tables quickly, after all expenses (including Steve's salary), the store will have $50,000 in profits per year, of which Steve receives 10% ($5,000) and you receive 90% ($45,000).

But if Steve doesn't provide quick and friendly service to his customers, uses the $50,000 in income to buy artwork for his office, and even sneaks off to the beach while he should be at the store, the store will not earn any profit. Steve can earn the additional $5,000 (his 10% share of the profits) over his salary only if he works hard and forgoes unproductive investments (such as art for his office). Steve might decide that the extra $5,000 just isn't enough to make him expend the effort to be a good manager; he might decide that it would be worth his while only if he earned an extra $10,000. If Steve feels this way, he does not have enough incentive to be a good manager and will end up with a beautiful office, a good tan, and a store that doesn't show any profits. Because the store won't show any profits, Steve's decision not to act in your interest will cost you $45,000 (your 90% of the profits if he had chosen to be a good manager instead).

The moral hazard arising from the principal–agent problem might be even worse if Steve were not totally honest. Because his ice cream store is a cash business, Steve has the incentive to pocket $50,000 in cash and tell you that the profits were zero. He now gets a return of $50,000 and you get nothing.

Further indications that the principal–agent problem created by equity contracts can be severe are provided by past scandals in corporations such as Enron and Tyco International, in which managers were found to have diverted funds for their personal use. Besides pursuing personal benefits, managers might also pursue corporate strategies (such as the acquisition of other firms) that enhance their personal power but do not increase the corporation's profitability.

The principal–agent problem would not arise if the owners of a firm had complete information about what the managers were up to and could prevent wasteful expenditures or fraud. The principal–agent problem, which is an example of moral hazard, arises only because a manager, such as Steve, has more information about his activities than the stockholder does—that is, information is asymmetric. The principal–agent problem would not occur if Steve alone owned the store and ownership and control were not separated. If this were the case, Steve's hard work and avoidance of unproductive investments would yield him a profit (and extra income) of $50,000, an amount that would make it worth his while to be a good manager.

Tools to Help Solve the Principal–Agent Problem

Production of Information: Monitoring You have seen that the principal–agent problem arises because managers have more information about their activities and actual profits than stockholders do. One way for stockholders to reduce this moral hazard problem is for them to engage in a particular type of information production, the monitoring of the firm's activities: auditing the firm frequently and checking on what the management is doing. The problem is that the monitoring process can be expensive in terms of time and money, as reflected in the name economists give it, **costly state verification**. Costly state verification makes the equity contract less desirable, and it explains, in part, why equity is not a more important element in our financial structure.

As with adverse selection, the free-rider problem decreases the amount of information production undertaken to reduce the moral hazard (principal–agent) problem. In this example, the free-rider problem decreases monitoring. If you know that other stockholders are paying to monitor the activities of the company you hold shares in, you can take a free ride on their activities. Then you can use the money you save by not engaging in monitoring to vacation on a Caribbean island. If you can do this, though, so can other stockholders. Perhaps all the stockholders will go to the islands, and no one will spend any resources on monitoring the firm. The moral hazard problem for shares of common stock will then be severe, making it hard for firms to issue them to raise capital (providing an additional explanation for fact 1).

Government Regulation to Increase Information As with adverse selection, the government has an incentive to try to reduce the moral hazard problem created by asymmetric information, which provides another reason why the financial system is so heavily regulated (fact 5). Governments everywhere have laws to force firms to adhere to standard accounting principles that make profit verification easier. They also pass laws to impose stiff criminal penalties on people who commit the fraud of hiding and stealing profits. However, these measures can be only partly effective. Catching this kind of fraud is not easy; fraudulent managers have the incentive to make it very hard for government agencies to find or prove fraud.

Financial Intermediation Financial intermediaries have the ability to avoid the free-rider problem in the face of moral hazard, and this is another reason that indirect finance is so important (fact 3). One financial intermediary that helps reduce the moral hazard arising from the principal–agent problem is the **venture capital firm**. Venture capital firms pool the resources of their partners and use the funds to help budding entrepreneurs start new businesses. In exchange for the use of the venture capital, the firm receives an equity share in the new business. Because verification of earnings and profits is so important in eliminating moral hazard, venture capital firms usually insist on having several of their own people participate as members of the managing body of the firm, the board of directors, so that they can keep a close watch on the firm's activities. When a venture capital firm supplies start-up funds, the equity in the firm is private, that is, not marketable to anyone *except* the venture capital firm.[3] Thus, other investors are unable to take a free ride on the venture capital firm's verification activities. As a result of this arrangement, the venture capital firm is able to garner the full benefits of its verification activities and is given the appropriate incentives to reduce the moral hazard problem. Venture capital firms have been important in the development of the high-tech sector in the United States, which has resulted in job creation, economic growth, and increased international competitiveness.

Debt Contracts Moral hazard arises with an equity contract, which is a claim on profits in all situations, whether the firm is making or losing money. If a contract could be structured so that moral hazard would exist only in certain situations, the need to monitor managers would be reduced, and the contract would be more attractive than the equity contract. The debt contract has exactly these attributes because it is a contractual agreement by the borrower to pay the lender *fixed* dollar amounts at periodic intervals. When the firm has high profits, the lender receives the contractual payments and does not need to know the exact profits of the firm. If the managers are hiding profits or are pursuing activities that are personally beneficial but don't increase profitability, the lender doesn't care as long as these activities do not interfere with the ability of the firm to make its debt payments on time. Only when the firm cannot meet its debt payments, thereby being in a state of default, is there a need for the lender to verify the state of the firm's profits. Only in this situation do lenders involved in debt contracts need to act more like equity holders to get their fair share; now they must know how much income the firm has.

---

[3] Private equity firms also engage in private equity investment and solve the free-rider problem in a similar way to venture capital firms. Venture capital firms invest in new businesses, and then when the company matures, sell shares to the public. However, in contrast to venture capital firms, which take new companies public, private equity firms take older public companies private; that is, they purchase all the publicly traded shares and retire them. They then exercise control over the company using similar methods to those of venture capital firms.

The less frequent need to monitor the firm, and thus the lower cost of state verification, helps explain why debt contracts are used more frequently than equity contracts to raise capital. The concept of moral hazard therefore helps explain fact 1, why stocks are not the most important source of financing for businesses.[4]

How Moral Hazard Influences Financial Structure in Debt Markets

Even with the advantages just described, debt contracts are still subject to moral hazard. Because a debt contract requires the borrowers to pay out a fixed amount and lets them keep any profits above this amount, the borrowers have an incentive to take on investment projects that are riskier than the lenders would like.

For example, suppose that because you are concerned about the problem of verifying the profits of Steve's ice cream store, you decide not to become an equity partner. Instead, you lend Steve the $9,000 he needs to set up his business and have a debt contract that pays you an interest rate of 10%. As far as you are concerned, this is a surefire investment because demand for ice cream in your neighborhood is strong and steady. However, once you give Steve the funds, he might use them for purposes other than what you intended. Instead of opening up the ice cream store, Steve might use your $9,000 loan to invest in chemical research equipment because he thinks he has a 1-in-10 chance of inventing a diet ice cream that tastes every bit as good as the premium brands but has no fat or calories.

Obviously, this is a very risky investment, but if Steve is successful, he will become a multimillionaire. He has a strong incentive to undertake the riskier investment with your money because the gains to him would be so large if he succeeded. You would clearly be very unhappy if Steve used your loan for the riskier investment because if he were unsuccessful, which is highly likely, you would lose most, if not all, of the money you gave him. And if he were successful, you wouldn't share in his success—you would still get only a 10% return on the loan because the principal and interest payments are fixed. Because of the potential moral hazard (that Steve might use your money to finance a very risky venture), you would probably not make the loan to Steve, even though an ice cream store in the neighborhood is a good investment that would provide benefits for everyone.

Tools to Help Solve Moral Hazard in Debt Contracts

Net Worth and Collateral When borrowers have more at stake because their net worth (the difference between their assets and their liabilities) is high or the collateral they have pledged to the lender is valuable, the risk of moral hazard—the temptation to act in a manner that lenders find objectionable—will be greatly reduced because the borrowers themselves have a lot to lose. Another way to say this is that if borrowers have more "skin in the game" because they have higher net worth or pledge collateral, they are likely to take less risk at the lender's expense.

[4] Another factor that encourages the use of debt contracts rather than equity contracts in the United States is our tax code. Debt interest payments are a deductible expense for American firms, whereas dividend payments to equity shareholders are not.

Let's return to Steve and his ice cream business. Suppose that the cost of setting up either the ice cream store or the research equipment is $100,000 instead of $10,000. So Steve needs to put $91,000 (instead of $1,000) of his own money into the business in addition to the $9,000 supplied by your loan. Now if Steve is unsuccessful in inventing the no-calorie nonfat ice cream, he has a lot to lose—the $91,000 of net worth ($100,000 in assets minus the $9,000 loan from you). He will think twice about undertaking the riskier investment and is more likely to invest in the ice cream store, which is more of a sure thing. Hence, when Steve has more of his own money (net worth) in the business, and hence more skin in the game, you are more likely to make him the loan. Similarly, if you have pledged your house as collateral, you are less likely to go to Las Vegas and gamble away your earnings that month because you might not be able to make your mortgage payments and might lose your house.

One way of describing the solution that high net worth and collateral provides to the moral hazard problem is to say that it makes the debt contract **incentive compatible**; that is, it aligns the incentives of the borrower with those of the lender. The greater the borrower's net worth and collateral pledged, the greater the borrower's incentive to behave in the way that the lender expects and desires, the smaller the moral hazard problem in the debt contract, and the easier it is for the firm or household to borrow. Conversely, when the borrower's net worth and collateral are lower, the moral hazard problem is greater, and it is harder to borrow.

Monitoring and Enforcement of Restrictive Covenants As the example of Steve and his ice cream store shows, if you could make sure that Steve doesn't invest in anything riskier than the ice cream store, it would be worth your while to make him the loan. You can ensure that Steve uses your money for the purpose *you* want it to be used for by writing provisions (restrictive covenants) into the debt contract that restrict his firm's activities. By monitoring Steve's activities to see whether he is complying with the restrictive covenants and enforcing the covenants if he is not, you can make sure that he will not take on risks at your expense. Restrictive covenants are directed at reducing moral hazard either by ruling out undesirable behavior or by encouraging desirable behavior. There are four types of restrictive covenants that achieve this objective:

1. ***Covenants to discourage undesirable behavior.*** Covenants can be designed to lower moral hazard by keeping the borrower from engaging in the undesirable behavior of undertaking risky investment projects. Some covenants mandate that a loan can be used only to finance specific activities, such as the purchase of particular equipment or inventories. Others restrict the borrowing firm from engaging in certain risky business activities, such as purchasing other businesses.
2. ***Covenants to encourage desirable behavior.*** Restrictive covenants can encourage the borrower to engage in desirable activities that make it more likely that the loan will be paid off. One restrictive covenant of this type requires the breadwinner in a household to carry life insurance that pays off the mortgage upon that person's death. Restrictive covenants of this type for businesses focus on encouraging the borrowing firm to keep its net worth high because higher borrower net worth reduces moral hazard and makes it less likely that the lender will suffer losses. These restrictive covenants typically specify that the firm must maintain minimum holdings of certain assets relative to the firm's size.

3. ***Covenants to keep collateral valuable.*** Because collateral is an important protection for the lender, restrictive covenants can encourage the borrower to keep the collateral in good condition and make sure that it stays in the possession of the borrower. This is the type of covenant ordinary people encounter most often. Automobile loan contracts, for example, require the car owner to maintain a minimum amount of collision and theft insurance and prevent the sale of the car unless the loan is paid off. Similarly, the recipient of a home mortgage must have adequate insurance on the home and must pay off the mortgage when the property is sold.
4. ***Covenants to provide information.*** Restrictive covenants also require a borrowing firm to provide information about its activities periodically in the form of quarterly accounting and income reports, thereby making it easier for the lender to monitor the firm and reduce moral hazard. This type of covenant may also stipulate that the lender has the right to audit and inspect the firm's books at any time.

We now see why debt contracts are often complicated legal documents with numerous restrictions on the borrower's behavior (fact 8): Debt contracts require complicated restrictive covenants to lower moral hazard.

Financial Intermediation Although restrictive covenants help reduce the moral hazard problem, they do not eliminate it. It is almost impossible to write covenants that rule out *every* risky activity. Furthermore, borrowers may be clever enough to find loopholes in restrictive covenants that make them ineffective.

Another problem with restrictive covenants is that they must be monitored and enforced. A restrictive covenant is meaningless if the borrower can violate it knowing that the lender won't check up or is unwilling to pay for legal recourse. Because monitoring and enforcement of restrictive covenants are costly, the free-rider problem arises in the debt securities (bond) market just as it does in the stock market. If you know that other bondholders are monitoring and enforcing the restrictive covenants, you can free-ride on their monitoring and enforcement. But other bondholders can do the same thing, so the likely outcome is that not enough resources are devoted to monitoring and enforcing the restrictive covenants. Moral hazard therefore continues to be a severe problem for marketable debt.

As we have seen before, financial intermediaries—particularly banks—have the ability to avoid the free-rider problem as long as they make primarily private loans. Private loans are not traded, so no one else can free-ride on the intermediary's monitoring and enforcement of the restrictive covenants. The intermediary making private loans thus receives the benefits of monitoring and enforcement and will work to shrink the moral hazard problem inherent in debt contracts. The concept of moral hazard has provided us with additional reasons why financial intermediaries play a more important role in channeling funds from savers to borrowers than marketable securities do, as described in facts 3 and 4.

Summary

The presence of asymmetric information in financial markets leads to adverse selection and moral hazard problems that interfere with the efficient functioning of those markets. Tools to help solve these problems involve the private production and sale of information, government regulation to increase information in financial markets, the importance of collateral and net worth to debt contracts, and the use of monitoring and restrictive covenants. A key finding from our analysis is that the existence of the free-rider problem for traded securities such as stocks and bonds indicates that financial intermediaries—particularly banks—should play a greater role than securities markets in financing the activities of businesses. Economic analysis of the consequences of adverse selection and moral hazard has helped explain the basic features of our financial system and has provided solutions to the eight facts about our financial structure outlined at the beginning of this chapter.

To help you keep track of all the tools that help solve asymmetric information problems, Table 7.1 summarizes the asymmetric information problems and tools that help solve them. In addition, it notes how these tools and asymmetric information problems explain the eight facts of financial structure described at the beginning of the chapter.

TABLE 7.1 SUMMARY Asymmetric Information Problems and Tools to Solve Them

Asymmetric Information Problem	Tools to Solve It	Explains Fact Number
Adverse selection	Private production and sale of information	1, 2
	Government regulation to increase information	5
	Financial intermediation	3, 4, 6
	Collateral and net worth	7
Moral hazard in equity contracts (principal–agent problem)	Production of information: monitoring	1
	Government regulation to increase information	5
	Financial intermediation	3
	Debt contracts	1
Moral hazard in debt contracts	Collateral and net worth	6, 7
	Monitoring and enforcement of restrictive covenants	8
	Financial intermediation	3, 4

Note: List of facts:

1. Stocks are not the most important source of external financing.
2. Marketable securities are not the primary source of finance.
3. Indirect finance is more important than direct finance.
4. Banks are the most important source of external funds.
5. The financial system is heavily regulated.
6. Only large, well-established firms have access to securities markets.
7. Collateral is prevalent in debt contracts.
8. Debt contracts have numerous restrictive covenants.

CASE

Financial Development and Economic Growth

Recent research has found that an important reason many developing countries experience very low rates of growth is that their financial systems are underdeveloped.* The economic analysis of financial structure helps explain how an underdeveloped financial system leads to a low state of economic development and economic growth.

The financial systems in developing countries face several difficulties that keep them from operating efficiently. As we have seen, two important tools used to help solve adverse selection and moral hazard problems in credit markets are collateral and restrictive covenants. In many developing countries, the system of property rights (the rule of law, constraints on government expropriation, absence of corruption) functions poorly, making it hard to use these two tools effectively.

As is discussed in the Mini-Case box, "The Tyranny of Collateral," the weak system of property rights in developing countries impedes the use of collateral, making the adverse selection problem worse because the lender will need even more information about the quality of the borrower so that it can screen out a good loan from a bad one. The result is that it will be harder for lenders to channel funds to borrowers with the most productive investment opportunities. There will be less productive investment, and hence a slower-growing economy.

Similarly, a poorly developed or corrupt legal system may make it extremely difficult for lenders to enforce restrictive covenants. Thus, they may have a much more limited ability to reduce moral hazard on the part of borrowers and so will be less willing to lend. Again the outcome will be less productive investment and a lower growth rate for the economy. The importance of an effective legal system in promoting economic growth suggests that lawyers play a more positive role in the economy than we give them credit for.

Governments in developing countries often use their financial systems to direct credit to themselves or to favored sectors of the economy by setting interest rates at artificially low levels for certain types of loans, by creating development finance institutions to make specific types of loans, or by directing existing institutions to lend to certain entities. As we have seen, private institutions have an incentive to solve adverse selection and moral hazard problems and lend to borrowers with the most productive investment opportunities. Governments have less incentive to do so because they are not driven by the profit motive and thus their directed credit programs may not channel funds to sectors that will produce high growth for the economy. The outcome is again likely to result in less efficient investment and slower growth.

In addition, banks in many developing countries are owned by their governments. Again, because of the absence of the profit motive, these **state-owned banks** have little incentive to allocate their capital to the most productive uses. Not surprisingly, the primary loan customer of these state-owned banks is often the government, which does not always use the funds wisely for productive investments to promote growth.

---

* See World Bank, *Finance for Growth: Policy Choices in a Volatile World* (World Bank and Oxford University Press, 2001) for a survey of the literature linking economic growth with financial development and a list of additional references.

We have seen that government regulation can increase the amount of information in financial markets to make them work more efficiently. Many developing countries have an underdeveloped regulatory apparatus that retards the provision of adequate information to the marketplace. For example, these countries often have weak accounting standards, making it very hard to ascertain the quality of a borrower's balance sheet. As a result, asymmetric information problems are more severe, and the financial system is severely hampered in channeling funds to the most productive uses.

The institutional environment of a poor legal system, weak accounting standards, inadequate government regulation, and government intervention through directed credit programs and state ownership of banks all help explain why many countries stay poor while others, unhindered by these impediments, grow richer.

> MINI-CASE

The Tyranny of Collateral

To use property, such as land or capital, as collateral, a person must legally own it. Unfortunately, as Hernando De Soto documents in his book *The Mystery of Capital*, it is extremely expensive and time consuming for the poor in developing countries to make their ownership of property legal. Obtaining legal title to a dwelling on urban land in the Philippines, for example, involved 168 bureaucratic steps and fifty-three public and private agencies, and the process took thirteen to twenty-five years. For desert land in Egypt, obtaining legal title took seventy-seven steps, thirty-one public and private agencies, and five to fourteen years. To legally buy government land in Haiti, an ordinary citizen had to go through 176 steps over nineteen years. These barriers do not mean the poor do not invest: They still build houses and buy equipment even if they don't have legal title to these assets. By De Soto's calculations, the "total value of the real estate held but not legally owned by the poor of the Third World and former communist nations is at least $9.3 trillion."*

Without legal title, however, none of this property can be used as collateral to borrow funds, a requirement for most lenders. Even when people have legal title to their property, the legal system in most developing countries is so inefficient that collateral does not mean much. Typically, creditors must first sue the defaulting debtor for payment, which takes several years, and then, once obtaining a favorable judgment, the creditor has to sue again to obtain title to the collateral. This process often takes in excess of five years. By the time the lender acquires the collateral, it is likely to have been neglected or stolen and thus has little value. In addition, governments often block lenders from foreclosing on borrowers in politically powerful sectors of a society, such as agriculture.

When the financial system is unable to use collateral effectively, the adverse selection problem will be worse because the lender will need even more information about the quality of the borrower to distinguish a good loan from a bad one. Little lending will take place, especially in transactions that involve collateral, such as mortgages. In Peru, for example, the value of mortgage loans relative to the size of the economy is less than one-twentieth that in the United States.

The poor in developing countries have an even harder time obtaining loans because it is too costly for them to get title to their property and they therefore have no collateral to offer, resulting in what Raghuram Rajan, the governor of India's central bank, and Luigi Zingales, of the University of Chicago, refer to as the "tyranny of collateral."** Even when poor people have a good idea for a business and are willing to work hard, they cannot get the funds to finance it, making it difficult for them to escape poverty.

---

* Hernando De Soto, *The Mystery of Capital: Why Capitalism Triumphs in the West and Fails Everywhere Else* (New York: Basic Books, 2000), 35.

** Raghuram Rajan and Luigi Zingales, *Saving Capitalism from the Capitalists: Unleashing the Power of Financial Markets to Create Wealth and Spread Opportunity* (New York: Crown Business, 2003).

CASE

Is China a Counter-Example to the Importance of Financial Development?

Although China appears to be on its way to becoming an economic powerhouse, its financial development remains in the early stages. The country's legal system is weak, so that financial contracts are difficult to enforce, while accounting standards are lax, so that high-quality information about creditors is hard to find. Regulation of the banking system is still in its formative stages, and the banking sector is dominated by large state-owned banks. Yet the Chinese economy has enjoyed one of the highest growth rates in the world over the past 20 years. How has China been able to grow so rapidly given its low level of financial development?

As noted above, China is in an early state of development, with a per capita income that is around one-fifth of the per capita income in the United States. With an extremely high savings rate, averaging around 40% over the past two decades, the country has been able to rapidly build up its capital stock and shift a massive pool of underutilized labor from the subsistence-agriculture sector into higher-productivity activities that use capital. Even though available savings have not been allocated to their most productive uses, the huge increase in capital combined with the gains in productivity from moving labor out of low-productivity, subsistence agriculture have been enough to produce high growth.

As China gets richer, however, this strategy is unlikely to continue to work. The Soviet Union provides a graphic example. In the 1950s and 1960s, the Soviet Union shared many characteristics with modern-day China: high growth fueled by a high savings rate, a massive buildup of capital, and shifts of a large pool of underutilized labor from subsistence agriculture to manufacturing. During this high-growth phase, however, the Soviet Union was unable to develop the institutions needed to allocate capital efficiently. As a result, once the pool of subsistence laborers was used up, the Soviet Union's growth slowed dramatically and it was unable to keep up with the Western economies. Today no one considers the Soviet Union to have been an economic success story, and its inability to develop the institutions necessary to sustain financial development and growth was an important reason for the demise of this superpower.

To move into the next stage of development, China will need to allocate its capital more efficiently, which requires that it must improve its financial system. The Chinese leadership is well aware of this challenge: The government has announced that state-owned banks are being put on the path to privatization. In addition, the government is engaged in legal reform to make financial contracts more enforceable. New bankruptcy law is being developed so that lenders have the ability to take over the assets of firms that default on their loan contracts. Whether the Chinese government will succeed in developing a first-rate financial system, thereby enabling China to join the ranks of developed countries, is a big question mark.

Conflicts of Interest

Earlier in this chapter, we saw how financial institutions play an important role in the financial system. Specifically, their expertise in interpreting signals and collecting information from their customers gives them a cost advantage in the production of information. Furthermore, because they are collecting, producing, and distributing this information, financial institutions can use the information over and over again in as many ways as they would like, thereby realizing economies of scale. By providing multiple financial services to their customers, such as offering them bank loans or selling their bonds for them, they can also achieve **economies of scope**; that is, they can lower the cost of information production for each service by applying one information resource to many different services. A bank, for example, can evaluate how good a credit risk a corporation is when making a loan to the firm, which then helps the bank decide whether it would be easy to sell the bonds of this corporation to the public. Additionally, by providing multiple financial services to their customers, financial institutions develop broader and longer-term relationships with firms. These relationships both reduce the cost of producing information and increase economies of scope.

What Are Conflicts of Interest and Why Do We Care?

Although the presence of economies of scope may substantially benefit financial institutions, it also creates potential costs in terms of **conflicts of interest**. Conflicts of interest are a type of moral hazard problem that arise when a person or institution has multiple objectives (interests) and, as a result, has conflicts among those objectives. Conflicts of interest are especially likely to occur when a financial institution provides multiple services. The potentially competing interests of those services may lead individuals who work for financial institutions to conceal information or disseminate misleading information. Here we use the analysis of asymmetric information problems to understand why conflicts of interest are important, why they arise, and what can be done about them.

We care about conflicts of interest because a substantial reduction in the quality of information in financial markets increases asymmetric information problems and prevents financial markets from channeling funds into the most productive investment opportunities. Consequently, the financial markets and the economy become less efficient.

Why Do Conflicts of Interest Arise?

Three types of financial service activities have led to prominent conflicts-of-interest problems in financial markets in recent years: underwriting and research in investment banks, auditing and consulting in accounting firms, and credit assessment and consulting in credit-rating agencies. Why do combinations of these activities so often produce conflicts of interest?

Underwriting and Research in Investment Banking Investment banks perform two tasks: They *research* companies issuing securities, and they *underwrite* these securities by selling them to the public on behalf of the issuing corporations.

Investment banks often combine these distinct financial services because information synergies are possible: That is, information produced for one task may also be useful in the other task. A conflict of interest arises between the brokerage and underwriting services because the banks are attempting to simultaneously serve two client groups—the security-issuing firms and the security-buying investors. These client groups have different information needs. Issuers benefit from optimistic research, whereas investors desire unbiased research. However, the same information will be produced for both groups to take advantages of economies of scope. When the potential revenues from underwriting greatly exceed the brokerage commissions from selling, the bank will have a strong incentive to alter the information provided to investors to favor the issuing firm's needs or else risk losing the firm's business to competing investment banks. For example, an internal Morgan Stanley memo excerpted in the *Wall Street Journal* on July 14, 1992, stated, "Our objective...is to adopt a policy, fully understood by the entire firm, including the Research Department, that we do not make negative or controversial comments about our clients as a matter of sound business practice."

Because of directives like this one, analysts in investment banks might distort their research to please issuers, and indeed this seems to have happened during the stock market tech boom of the 1990s. Such actions undermine the reliability of the information that investors use to make their financial decisions and, as a result, diminish the efficiency of securities markets.

Another common practice that exploits conflicts of interest is **spinning**. Spinning occurs when an investment bank allocates hot, but underpriced, **initial public offerings (IPOs)**—that is, shares of newly issued stock—to executives of other companies in return for their companies' future business with the investment banks. Because hot IPOs typically immediately rise in price after they are first purchased, spinning is a form of kickback meant to persuade executives to use that investment bank. When the executive's company plans to issue its own shares, he or she will be more likely to go to the investment bank that distributed the hot IPO shares, which is not necessarily the investment bank that would get the highest price for the company's securities. This practice may raise the cost of capital for the firm, thereby diminishing the efficiency of the capital market.

Auditing and Consulting in Accounting Firms Traditionally, an auditor checks the books of companies and monitors the quality of the information produced by firms to reduce the inevitable information asymmetry between the firm's managers and its shareholders. In auditing, threats to truthful reporting arise from several potential conflicts of interest. The conflict of interest that has received the most attention in the media occurs when an accounting firm provides its client with both auditing services and nonaudit consulting services such as advice on taxes, accounting, management information systems, and business strategy. Supplying clients with multiple services allows for economies of scale and scope but creates two potential sources of conflicts of interest. First, auditors may be willing to skew their judgments and opinions to win consulting business from these same clients. Second, auditors may be auditing information systems or tax and financial plans put in place by their nonaudit counterparts within the firm and therefore may be reluctant to criticize the systems or advice. Both types of conflicts may lead to biased audits, with the result that less reliable information is available in financial markets and investors find it difficult to allocate capital efficiently.

> MINI-CASE

The Demise of Arthur Andersen

In 1913 Arthur Andersen, a young accountant who had denounced the slipshod and deceptive practices that enabled companies to fool the investing public, founded his own firm. Up until the early 1980s, auditing was the most important source of profits within this firm. However, by the late 1980s, the consulting part of the business experienced high revenue growth with high profit margins, while audit profits slumped in a more competitive market. Consulting partners began to assert more power within the firm, and the resulting internal conflicts split the firm in two. Arthur Andersen (the auditing service) and Andersen Consulting were established as separate companies in 2000.

During the period of increasing conflict before the split, Andersen's audit partners had been under increasing pressure to focus on boosting revenue and profits from audit services. Many of Arthur Andersen's clients that later went bust—Enron, WorldCom, Qwest, and Global Crossing—were also the largest clients in Arthur Andersen's regional offices. The combination of intense pressure to generate revenue and profits from auditing and the fact that some clients dominated regional offices translated into tremendous incentives for regional office managers to provide favorable audit stances for these large clients. The loss of a client like Enron or WorldCom would have been devastating for a regional office and its partners, even if that client contributed only a small fraction of the overall revenue and profits of Arthur Andersen.

The Houston office of Arthur Andersen, for example, ignored problems in Enron's reporting. Arthur Andersen was indicted in March 2002 and then convicted in June 2002 for obstruction of justice for impeding the SEC's investigation of the Enron collapse. Its conviction—the first ever against a major accounting firm—barred Arthur Andersen from conducting audits of publicly traded firms. This development contributed to the firm's demise.

Another conflict of interest arises when an auditor provides an overly favorable audit to solicit or retain audit business. The unfortunate collapse of Arthur Andersen—once one of the five largest accounting firms in the United States—suggests that this may be the most dangerous conflict of interest (see the Mini-Case box , "The Demise of Arthur Andersen").

Credit Assessment and Consulting in Credit-Rating Agencies Investors use credit ratings (e.g., Aaa or Baa) that reflect the probability of default to determine the creditworthiness of particular debt securities. As a consequence, debt ratings play a major role in the pricing of debt securities and in the regulatory process. Conflicts of interest can arise when multiple users with divergent interests (at least in the short term) depend on the credit ratings. Investors and regulators are seeking a well-researched, impartial assessment of credit quality; the issuer needs a favorable rating. In the credit-rating industry, the issuers of securities pay a rating firm such as Standard & Poor's or Moody's to have their securities rated. Because the issuers are the parties paying the credit-rating agency, investors and regulators worry that the agency may bias its ratings upward to attract more business from the issuer.

Another kind of conflict of interest may arise when credit-rating agencies also provide ancillary consulting services. Debt issuers often ask rating agencies to advise them on how to structure their debt issues, usually with the goal of securing a favorable rating. In this situation, the credit-rating agencies would be auditing their own work and would experience a conflict of interest similar to the one found in accounting firms that provide both auditing and consulting services. Furthermore, credit-rating agencies may deliver favorable ratings to garner new clients for the ancillary

> MINI-CASE

Credit-Rating Agencies and the 2007–2009 Financial Crisis

The credit-rating agencies have come under severe criticism for the role they played during the 2007–2009 financial crisis. Credit-rating agencies advised clients on how to structure complex financial instruments that paid out cash flows from subprime mortgages. At the same time, they were rating these identical products, leading to the potential for severe conflicts of interest. Specifically, the large fees they earned from advising clients on how to structure products that they were rating meant they did not have sufficient incentives to make sure their ratings were accurate.

When housing prices began to fall and subprime mortgages began to default, it became crystal clear that the ratings agencies had done a terrible job of assessing the risk in the subprime products they had helped to structure. Many AAA-rated products had to be downgraded over and over again until they reached junk status. The resulting massive losses on these assets were one reason why so many financial institutions that were holding them got into trouble, with absolutely disastrous consequences for the economy, as discussed in the next chapter.

Criticisms of the credit-rating agencies led the SEC to propose comprehensive reforms in 2008. The SEC concluded that the credit-rating agencies' models for rating subprime products were not fully developed and that conflicts of interest may have played a role in producing inaccurate ratings. To address conflicts of interest, the SEC prohibited credit-rating agencies from structuring the same products they rate, prohibited anyone who participates in determining a credit rating from negotiating the fee that the issuer pays for it, and prohibited gifts from bond issuers to those who rate them in any amount over $25. To make credit-rating agencies more accountable, the SEC's new rules also required more disclosure of how the credit-rating agencies determine ratings. For example, credit-rating agencies were required to disclose historical ratings performance, including the dates of downgrades and upgrades, information on the underlying assets of a product that were used by the credit-rating agencies to rate a product, and the kind of research they used to determine the rating. In addition, the SEC required the rating agencies to differentiate the ratings on structured products from those issued on bonds. The expectation is that these reforms will bring increased transparency to the ratings process and reduce conflicts of interest that played such a large role in the subprime debacle.

---

consulting business. The possible decline in the quality of credit assessments issued by rating agencies could increase asymmetric information in financial markets, thereby diminishing their ability to allocate credit. Such conflicts of interest came to the forefront because of the damaged reputations of the credit-rating agencies during the financial crisis of 2007–2009 (see the Mini-Case box, "Credit-Rating Agencies and the 2007–2009 Financial Crisis").

What Has Been Done to Remedy Conflicts of Interest?

Two major policy measures were implemented to deal with conflicts of interest: the Sarbanes-Oxley Act and the Global Legal Settlement.

Sarbanes-Oxley Act of 2002 The public outcry over the corporate and accounting scandals led in 2002 to the passage of the Public Accounting Reform and Investor Protection Act, more commonly referred to as the Sarbanes-Oxley Act, after its two principal authors in Congress. This act increased supervisory oversight to monitor and prevent conflicts of interest:

- It established a Public Company Accounting Oversight Board (PCAOB), overseen by the SEC, to supervise accounting firms and ensure that audits are independent and controlled for quality.
- It increased the SEC's budget to supervise securities markets.

Sarbanes-Oxley also directly reduced conflicts of interest:

- It made it illegal for a registered public accounting firm to provide any non-audit service to a client contemporaneously with an audit (as determined by the PCAOB).

Sarbanes-Oxley provided incentives for investment banks not to exploit conflicts of interest:

- It beefed up criminal charges for white-collar crime and obstruction of official investigations.

Sarbanes-Oxley also had measures to improve the quality of information in the financial markets:

- It required a corporation's chief executive officer (CEO) and chief financial officer (CFO), as well as its auditors, to certify that periodic financial statements and disclosures of the firm (especially regarding off-balance-sheet transactions) are accurate (Section 404).
- It required members of the audit committee (the subcommittee of the board of directors that oversees the company's audit) to be "independent"; that is, they cannot be managers in the company or receive any consulting or advisory fee from the company.

Global Legal Settlement of 2002 The second major policy measure arose out of a lawsuit brought by New York Attorney General Eliot Spitzer against the 10 largest investment banks (Bear Stearns, Credit Suisse First Boston, Deutsche Bank, Goldman Sachs, J. P. Morgan, Lehman Brothers, Merrill Lynch, Morgan Stanley, Salomon Smith Barney, and UBS Warburg). A global settlement was reached on December 20, 2002, with these investment banks by the SEC, the New York attorney general, NASD, NASAA, NYSE, and state regulators. Like Sarbanes-Oxley, this settlement directly reduced conflicts of interest:

- It required investment banks to sever the links between research and securities underwriting.
- It banned spinning.

The Global Legal Settlement also provided incentives for investment banks not to exploit conflicts of interest:

- It imposed $1.4 billion of fines on the accused investment banks.

MINI-CASE

Has Sarbanes-Oxley Led to a Decline in U.S. Capital Markets?

There has been much debate in the United States in recent years regarding the impact of Sarbanes-Oxley, especially Section 404, on U.S. capital markets. Section 404 requires both management and company auditors to certify the accuracy of their financial statements. There is no question that Sarbanes-Oxley has led to increased costs for corporations, and this is especially true for smaller firms with revenues of less than $100 million, where the compliance costs have been estimated to exceed 1% of sales. These higher costs could result in smaller firms listing abroad and discourage IPOs in the United States, thereby shrinking U.S. capital markets relative to those abroad. However, improved accounting standards could work to encourage stock market listings and IPOs because better information could raise the valuation of common stocks.

Critics of Sarbanes-Oxley have cited it, as well as higher litigation and weaker shareholder rights, as the cause of declining U.S. stock listings and IPOs, but other factors are likely at work. The European financial system experienced a major liberalization in the 1990s, along with the introduction of the euro, that helped make its financial markets more integrated and efficient. As a result, it became easier for European firms to list in their home countries. The fraction of European firms that list in their home countries has risen to over 90% currently from around 60% in 1995. As the importance of the United States in the world economy has diminished because of the growing importance of other economies, the U.S. capital markets have become less dominant over time. This process is even more evident in the corporate bond market. In 1995 corporate bond issues were double that of Europe, while issues of corporate bonds in Europe now exceed those in the United States.

The global settlement had measures to improve the quality of information in financial markets:

- It required investment banks to make their analysts' recommendations public.
- Over a five-year period, investment banks were required to contract with at least three independent research firms that would provide research to their brokerage customers.

The most controversial elements of the Sarbanes-Oxley Act and the Global Legal Settlement were the separation of functions (research from underwriting, and auditing from nonaudit consulting). Although such a separation of functions may reduce conflicts of interest, it might also diminish economies of scope and thus potentially lead to a reduction of information in financial markets. In addition, there is a serious concern that implementation of these measures, particularly Sarbanes-Oxley, is too costly and is leading to a decline in U.S. capital markets (see the Mini-Case box "Has Sarbanes-Oxley Led to a Decline in U.S. Capital Markets?").

SUMMARY

1. There are eight basic facts about U.S. financial structure. The first four emphasize the importance of financial intermediaries and the relative unimportance of securities markets for the financing of corporations; the fifth recognizes that financial markets are among the most heavily regulated sectors of the economy; the sixth states that only large, well-established corporations have access to securities markets; the seventh indicates that collateral is an important feature of debt contracts; and the eighth presents debt contracts as complicated legal documents that place substantial restrictions on the behavior of the borrower.

2. Transaction costs freeze many small savers and borrowers out of direct involvement with financial markets. Financial intermediaries can take advantage of economies of scale and are better able to develop expertise to lower transaction costs, thus enabling their savers and borrowers to benefit from the existence of financial markets.
3. Asymmetric information results in two problems: adverse selection, which occurs before the transaction, and moral hazard, which occurs after the transaction. Adverse selection refers to the fact that bad credit risks are the ones most likely to seek loans, and moral hazard refers to the risk of the borrower's engaging in activities that are undesirable from the lender's point of view.
4. Adverse selection interferes with the efficient functioning of financial markets. Tools to help reduce the adverse selection problem include private production and sale of information, government regulation to increase information, financial intermediation, and collateral and net worth. The free-rider problem occurs when people who do not pay for information take advantage of information that other people have paid for. This problem explains why financial intermediaries, particularly banks, play a more important role in financing the activities of businesses than securities markets do.
5. Moral hazard in equity contracts is known as the principal–agent problem because managers (the agents) have less incentive to maximize profits than stockholders (the principals). The principal–agent problem explains why debt contracts are so much more prevalent in financial markets than equity contracts. Tools to help reduce the principal–agent problem include monitoring, government regulation to increase information, and financial intermediation.
6. Tools to reduce the moral hazard problem in debt contracts include collateral and net worth, monitoring and enforcement of restrictive covenants, and financial intermediaries.
7. Conflicts of interest arise when financial service providers or their employees are serving multiple interests and have incentives to misuse or conceal information needed for the effective functioning of financial markets. We care about conflicts of interest because they can substantially reduce the amount of reliable information in financial markets, thereby preventing them from channeling funds to parties with the most productive investment opportunities. Three types of financial service activities have had the greatest potential for conflicts of interest: underwriting and research in investment banking, auditing and consulting in accounting firms, and credit assessment and consulting in credit-rating agencies. Two major policy measures have been implemented to deal with conflicts of interest: the Sarbanes-Oxley Act of 2002 and the Global Legal Settlement of 2002, which arose from a lawsuit by the New York attorney general against the 10 largest investment banks.

KEY TERMS

agency theory, p. 141
audits, p. 143
collateral, p. 146
conflicts of interest, p. 157
costly state verification, p. 148
economies of scope, p. 157
equity capital, p. 146
free-rider problem, p. 143
incentive compatible, p. 151
initial public offerings (IPOs), p. 158
net worth (equity capital), p. 146
pecking order hypothesis, p. 146
principal–agent problem, p. 147
restrictive covenants, p. 138
secured debt, p. 138
spinning, p. 158
state-owned banks, p. 154
unsecured debt, p. 138
venture capital firm, p. 149

QUESTIONS

1. How can economies of scale help explain the existence of financial intermediaries?
2. Explain why dating can be considered a method to solve the adverse selection problem.
3. Would moral hazard and adverse selection still arise in financial markets if information were not asymmetric? Explain.
4. How do standard accounting principles help financial markets work more efficiently?
5. Suppose you have data about two groups of countries, one with efficient legal systems and the other with slow, costly, and inefficient legal systems. Which group of countries would you expect to exhibit higher living standards?
6. Which relationship would you expect to exist between measures of corruption and living standards at the country level? Explain by which channel corruption might affect living standards.

7. How can the existence of asymmetric information provide a rationale for government regulation of financial markets?
8. Would you be more willing to lend to a friend if she put all of her life savings into her business than you would if she had not done so? Why?
9. Suppose you are applying for a mortgage loan. The loan officer tells you that if you get the loan, the bank will keep the house title until you pay back the loan. Which problem of asymmetric information is the bank trying to solve?
10. "The more collateral there is backing a loan, the less the lender has to worry about adverse selection." Is this statement true, false, or uncertain? Explain your answer.
11. How does the free-rider problem aggravate adverse selection and moral hazard problems in financial markets?
12. Explain how the separation of ownership and control in American corporations might lead to poor management.
13. Which specific asymmetric information problem do credit-rating agencies help to reduce in the bond market? Explain the effect of the subprime mortgage crisis on the trustworthiness of these agencies and on the quality of information.
14. How does the provision of several types of financial services by one firm lead to conflicts of interest?
15. Suppose that in a given bond market, there is currently no information that can help potential bond buyers to distinguish between bonds. Which bond issuers have an incentive to disclose information about their companies? Explain why.
16. Describe two conflicts of interest that occur when underwriting and research are provided by a single investment firm.
17. Which problem of asymmetric information are prospective employers trying to solve when they ask applicants to go through a job interview. Is that the end of the information asymmetry?
18. Describe two conflicts of interest that occur in accounting firms.
19. Which provisions of Sarbanes-Oxley do you think are beneficial, and which are not?
20. Lucia, Cecilia, and Julia have to do a midterm project. While Lucia works hard on the project for two weeks, Cecilia and Julia do not even answer the phone. The project is a success and everybody gets an A. How would you refer to Cecilia and Julia? What do you think might happen if the same three classmates are assigned to do a final project?

QUANTITATIVE PROBLEMS

1. You are in the market for a used car. At a used car lot, you know that the blue book value for the cars you are looking at is between $20,000 and $24,000. If you believe the dealer knows *as much* about the car as you, how much are you willing to pay? Why? Assume that you care only about the expected value of the car you buy and that the car values are symmetrically distributed.
2. Now, you believe the dealer knows *more* about the cars than you. How much are you willing to pay? Why? How can this be resolved in a competitive market?
3. You wish to hire Ricky to manage your Dallas operations. The profits from the operations depend partially on how hard Ricky works, as follows.

	Probabilities	
	Profit = $10,000	Profit = $50,000
Lazy	60%	40%
Hard worker	20%	80%

If Ricky is lazy, he will surf the Internet all day, and he views this as a zero cost opportunity. However, Ricky would view working hard as a "personal cost" valued at $1,000. What fixed percentage of the profits should you offer Ricky? Assume Ricky cares only about his expected payment less any "personal cost."

4. You own a house worth $400,000 that is located on a river. If the river floods moderately, the house will be completely destroyed. This happens about once every 50 years. If you build a seawall, the river would have to flood heavily to destroy your house, which happens only about once every 200 years. What would be the annual premium for an insurance policy that offers full insurance? For a policy that pays only 75% of the home value, what are your expected costs with and without a seawall? Do the different policies provide an incentive to be safer (i.e., to build the seawall)?

WEB EXERCISES

Why Do Financial Institutions Exist?

1. In this chapter we discuss the lemons problem and its effect on the efficient functioning of a market. This theory was initially developed by George Akerlof. Go to **http://www.nobelprize.org/nobel_prizes/economic-sciences/laureates/2001/**. This site reports that Akerlof, Spence, and Stiglitz were awarded the Nobel Prize in economics in 2001 for their work. Read this report down through the section on George Akerlof. Summarize his research ideas in one page.
2. This chapter discusses how an understanding of adverse selection and moral hazard can help us better understand financial crises. The greatest financial crisis faced by the United States was the Great Depression from 1929 to 1933. Go to **www.amatecon.com/greatdepression.html**. This site contains a brief discussion of the factors that led to the Great Depression. Write a one-page summary explaining how adverse selection and moral hazard contributed to the Great Depression.

CHAPTER 8

Why Do Financial Crises Occur and Why Are They So Damaging to the Economy?

> PREVIEW

Financial crises are major disruptions in financial markets characterized by sharp declines in asset prices and firm failures. Beginning in August 2007, defaults in the mortgage market for subprime borrowers (borrowers with weak credit records) sent a shudder through the financial markets, leading to the worst global financial crisis since the Great Depression. Alan Greenspan, former Chairman of the Fed, described the 2007–2009 financial crisis as a "once-in-a-century credit tsunami." Wall Street firms and commercial banks suffered losses amounting to hundreds of billions of dollars. Households and businesses found they had to pay higher rates on their borrowings—and it was much harder to get credit. World stock markets crashed, with U.S. shares falling by as much as half from their peak in October 2007. Many financial firms, including commercial banks, investment banks, and insurance companies, went belly up. A recession began in December 2007. By the fall of 2008, the economy was in a tailspin, with the recession, which ended in June of 2009, being the most severe since World War II. It is now known as the Great Recession.

Why did this financial crisis occur? Why have financial crises been so prevalent throughout U.S. history, as well as in so many other countries, and what insights do they provide on the current crisis? Why are financial crises almost always followed by severe contractions in economic activity, as occurred during the Great Recession? We will examine these questions in this chapter by developing a framework to understand the dynamics of financial crises. Building on Chapter 7, we make use of the economic analysis of the effects of asymmetric information (adverse selection and moral hazard) on financial markets and the economy, to see why financial crises occur and why they have such devastating effects on the economy. We will then apply the analysis to explain the course of events in a number of past financial crises throughout the world, including the most recent global financial crisis.

What Is a Financial Crisis?

We established in Chapter 7 that a fully functioning financial system is critical to a robust economy. The financial system performs the essential function of channeling funds to individuals or businesses with productive investment opportunities. If capital goes to the wrong uses or does not flow at all, the economy will operate inefficiently or go into an economic downturn.

Agency Theory and the Definition of a Financial Crisis

Academic finance literature calls the analysis of how asymmetric information problems can generate adverse selection and moral hazard problems *agency theory*. Agency theory provides the basis for our definition of a financial crisis. Asymmetric information problems act as a barrier to financial markets channeling funds efficiently from savers to households and firms with productive investment opportunities and are often described by economists as **financial frictions**. When financial frictions increase, it is harder for lenders to ascertain the creditworthiness of borrowers. They need to charge a higher interest rate to protect themselves against the possibility that the borrower may not pay back the loan, which leads to a higher *credit spread*, the difference between the interest rate on loans to businesses and the interest rate on completely safe assets that are sure to be paid back, such as default-free U.S. Treasury bills, notes, and bonds.

A **financial crisis** occurs when information flows in financial markets experience a particularly large disruption, with the result that financial frictions and credit spreads increase sharply and financial markets stop functioning. Then economic activity will collapse.

Dynamics of Financial Crises

As earth-shaking and headline-grabbing as the most recent financial crisis was, it was only one of a number of financial crises that have hit industrialized countries like the United States over the years. These experiences have helped economists uncover insights into present-day economic turmoil.

Financial crises in advanced economies have progressed in two and sometimes three stages. To understand how these crises have unfolded, refer to Figure 8.1, which traces the stages and sequence of financial crises in advanced economies.[1]

Stage One: Initial Phase

Financial crises can begin in several ways: credit and asset-price booms and busts or a general increase in uncertainty caused by failures of major financial institutions.

Credit Boom and Bust The seeds of a financial crisis are often sown when an economy introduces new types of loans or other financial products, known as

---

[1]A Web chapter available at the companion Web site, www.pearsonhighered.com/mishkin, extends the analysis to *emerging market economies,* economies in an early stage of market development that have recently opened up to the flow of goods, services, and capital from the rest of the world.

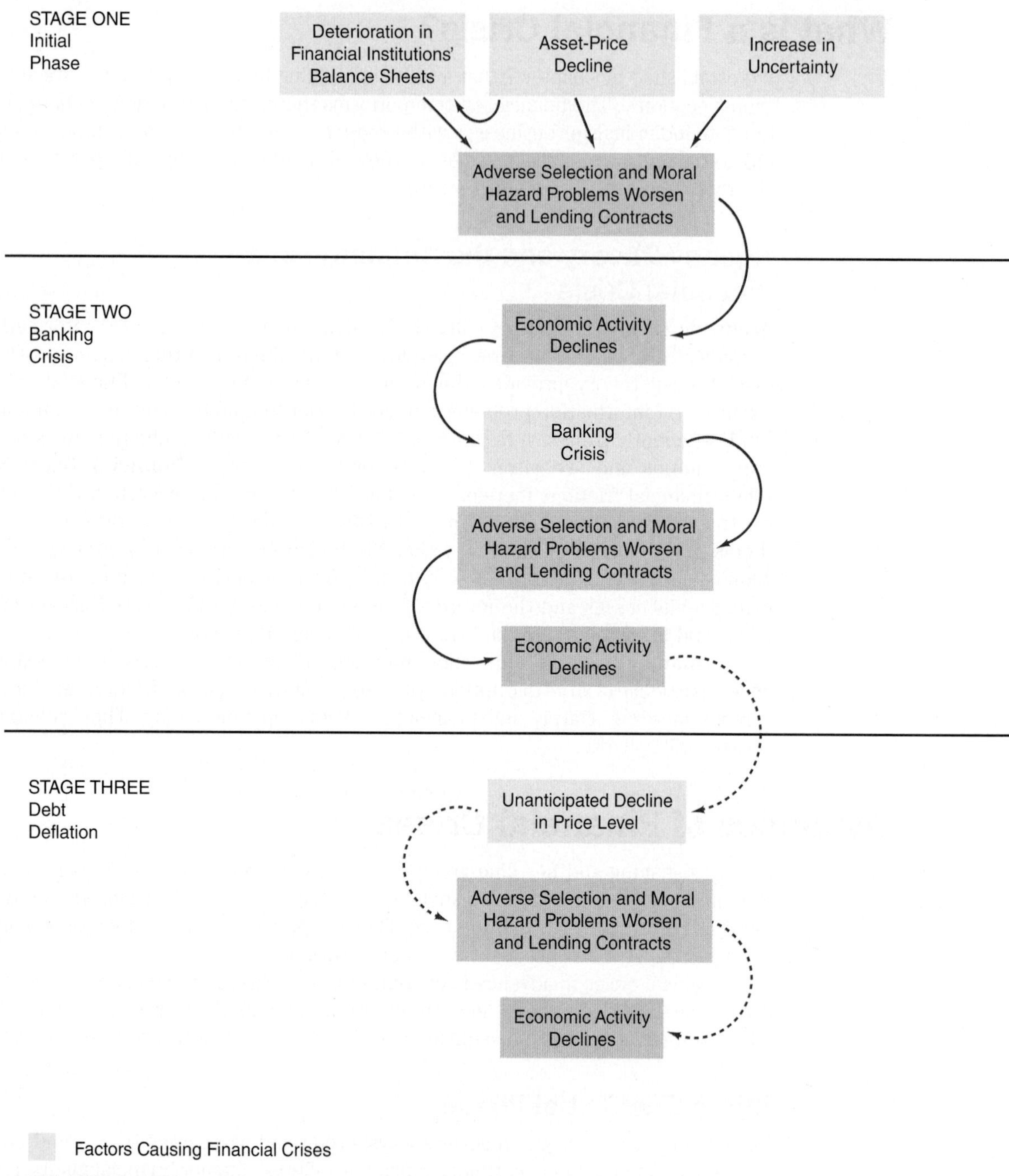

FIGURE 8.1 Sequence of Events in Financial Crises in Advanced Economies

The solid arrows trace the sequence of events during a typical financial crisis; the dotted arrows show the additional set of events that occur if the crisis develops into a debt deflation. The sections separated by the dashed horizontal lines show the different stages of a financial crisis.

financial innovation, or when countries engage in **financial liberalization**, the elimination of restrictions on financial markets and institutions. In the long run, financial liberalization can promote financial development and lead to a well-run financial system that allocates capital efficiently. However, financial liberalization has a dark side: In the short run, it can prompt financial institutions to go on a lending spree, called a **credit boom**. Unfortunately, lenders may not have the expertise, or the incentives, to manage risk appropriately in these new lines of business. Even with proper management, credit booms eventually outstrip the ability of institutions—and government regulators—to screen and monitor credit risks, leading to overly risky lending.

Government safety nets, such as deposit insurance, weaken market discipline and increase the moral hazard incentive for banks to take on greater risk than they otherwise would. Because lender-savers know that government-guaranteed insurance protects them from losses, they will supply even undisciplined banks with funds. Banks and other financial institutions can make risky, high-interest loans to borrower-spenders. They will walk away with nice profits if the loans are repaid, and rely on government deposit insurance, funded by taxpayers, if borrower-spenders default. Without proper monitoring, risk taking grows unchecked.

Eventually, losses on loans begin to mount, and the value of the loans (on the asset side of the balance sheet) falls relative to liabilities, thereby driving down the net worth (capital) of banks and other financial institutions. With less capital, these financial institutions cut back on their lending to borrower-spenders, a process called **deleveraging**. Furthermore, with less capital, banks and other financial institutions become riskier, causing lender-savers and other potential lenders to these institutions to pull out their funds. Fewer funds means fewer loans to fund productive investments and a credit freeze: The lending boom turns into a lending crash.

When financial institutions stop collecting information and making loans, financial frictions rise, limiting the financial system's ability to address the asymmetric information problems of adverse selection and moral hazard (as shown in the arrow pointing from the first factor, "Deterioration in Financial Institutions' Balance Sheets," in the top row of Figure 8.1). As loans become scarce, borrower-spenders are no longer able to fund their productive investment opportunities and they decrease their spending, causing economic activity to contract.

Asset-Price Boom and Bust Prices of assets such as equity shares and real estate can be driven by investor psychology well above their **fundamental economic values**, that is, their values based on realistic expectations of the assets' future income streams. The rise of asset prices above their fundamental economic values is an **asset-price bubble**. Examples of asset-price bubbles are the tech stock market bubble of the late 1990s and the early 2000s housing price bubble that we will discuss later in this chapter. Asset-price bubbles are often also driven by credit booms, in which the large increase in credit is used to fund purchases of assets, thereby driving up their price.

When the bubble bursts and asset prices realign with fundamental economic values, stock and real estate prices tumble, companies see their net worth (the difference between their assets and their liabilities) decline, and the value of collateral they can pledge drops. Now these companies have less at stake because they have less "skin in the game" and so they are more likely to make risky investments because they have less to lose, the problem of moral hazard. As a result, financial institutions tighten lending standards for borrower-spenders and lending contracts (as shown by the downward arrow pointing from the second factor, "Asset-Price Decline," in the top row of Figure 8.1).

The asset-price bust also causes a decline in the value of financial institutions' assets, thereby causing a decline in their net worth and hence a deterioration in their balance sheets (shown by the arrow from the second factor to the first factor in the top row of Figure 8.1), which causes them to deleverage, steepening the decline in economic activity.

Increase in Uncertainty U.S. financial crises have usually begun in periods of high uncertainty, such as just after the start of a recession, a crash in the stock market, or the failure of a major financial institution. Crises began after the failure of Ohio Life Insurance and Trust Company in 1857; Jay Cooke and Company in 1873; Grant and Ward in 1884; the Knickerbocker Trust Company in 1907; the Bank of the United States in 1930; and Bear Stearns, Lehman Brothers, and AIG in 2008. With information hard to come by in a period of high uncertainty, financial frictions increase, reducing lending and economic activity (as shown by the arrow pointing from the last factor, "Increase in Uncertainty," in the top row of Figure 8.1).

Stage Two: Banking Crisis

Deteriorating balance sheets and tougher business conditions lead some financial institutions into insolvency, when net worth becomes negative. Unable to pay off depositors or other creditors, some banks go out of business. If severe enough, these factors can lead to a **bank panic**, in which multiple banks fail simultaneously. The source of the contagion is asymmetric information. In a panic, depositors, fearing for the safety of their deposits (in the absence of or with limited amounts of deposit insurance) and not knowing the quality of banks' loan portfolios, withdraw their deposits to the point that the banks fail. Uncertainty about the health of the banking system in general can lead to runs on banks, both good and bad, which will force banks to sell off assets quickly to raise the necessary funds. These **fire sales** of assets may cause their prices to decline so much that the bank becomes insolvent, even if the resulting contagion can then lead to multiple bank failures and a full-fledged bank panic.

With fewer banks operating, information about the creditworthiness of borrower-spenders disappears. Increasingly severe adverse selection and moral hazard problems in financial markets increase financial frictions and deepen the financial crisis, causing declines in asset prices and the failure of firms throughout the economy that lack funds for productive investment opportunities. Figure 8.1 represents this progression in the stage two portion. Bank panics were a feature of all U.S. financial crises during the nineteenth and twentieth centuries, occurring every twenty years or so until World War II—1819, 1837, 1857, 1873, 1884, 1893, 1907, and 1930–1933. (The 1933 establishment of federal deposit insurance, which protects depositors from losses, has prevented subsequent bank panics in the United States.)

Eventually, public and private authorities shut down insolvent firms and sell them off or liquidate them. Uncertainty in financial markets declines, the stock market recovers, and balance sheets improve. Financial frictions diminish and the financial crisis subsides. With the financial markets able to operate well again, the stage is set for an economic recovery.

Stage Three: Debt Deflation

If, however, the economic downturn leads to a sharp decline in the price level, the recovery process can be short-circuited. In stage three in Figure 8.1, **debt deflation** occurs when a substantial unanticipated decline in the price level sets in, leading to a further deterioration in firms' net worth because of the increased burden of indebtedness.

In economies with moderate inflation, which characterizes most advanced countries, many debt contracts with fixed interest rates are typically of fairly long maturity, ten years or more. Because debt payments are contractually fixed in nominal terms, an unanticipated decline in the price level raises the value of borrowing firms' liabilities in real terms (increases the burden of the debt) but does not raise the real value of borrowing firms' assets. The borrowing firm's net worth in real terms (the difference between assets and liabilities in real terms) thus declines.

To better understand how this decline in net worth occurs, consider what happens if a firm in 2018 has assets of $100 million (in 2018 dollars) and $90 million of long-term liabilities, so that it has $10 million in net worth (the difference between the value of assets and liabilities). If the price level falls by 10% in 2019, the real value of the liabilities would rise to $99 million in 2018 dollars, while the real value of the assets would likely remain unchanged at $100 million. The result would be that real net worth in 2018 dollars would fall from $10 million to $1 million ($100 million minus $99 million).

The substantial decline in real net worth of borrowers from a sharp drop in the price level causes an increase in adverse selection and moral hazard problems facing lenders. Lending and economic activity decline for a long time. The most significant financial crisis that displayed debt deflation was the Great Depression, the worst economic contraction in U.S. history.

CASE

The Mother of All Financial Crises: The Great Depression

With our framework for understanding financial crises in place, we are prepared to analyze how a financial crisis unfolded during the Great Depression and how it led to the worst economic downturn in U.S. history.

Stock Market Crash

In 1928 and 1929, prices doubled in the U.S. stock market. Federal Reserve officials viewed the stock market boom as excessive speculation. To curb it, they pursued a tightening of monetary policy to raise interest rates to limit the rise in stock prices. The Fed got more than it bargained for when the stock market crashed in October 1929, falling by 40% by the end of 1929, as shown in Figure 8.2.

Bank Panics

By the middle of 1930, stocks recovered almost half of their losses and credit market conditions stabilized. What might have been a normal recession turned into something far worse, however, when severe droughts in the Midwest led to

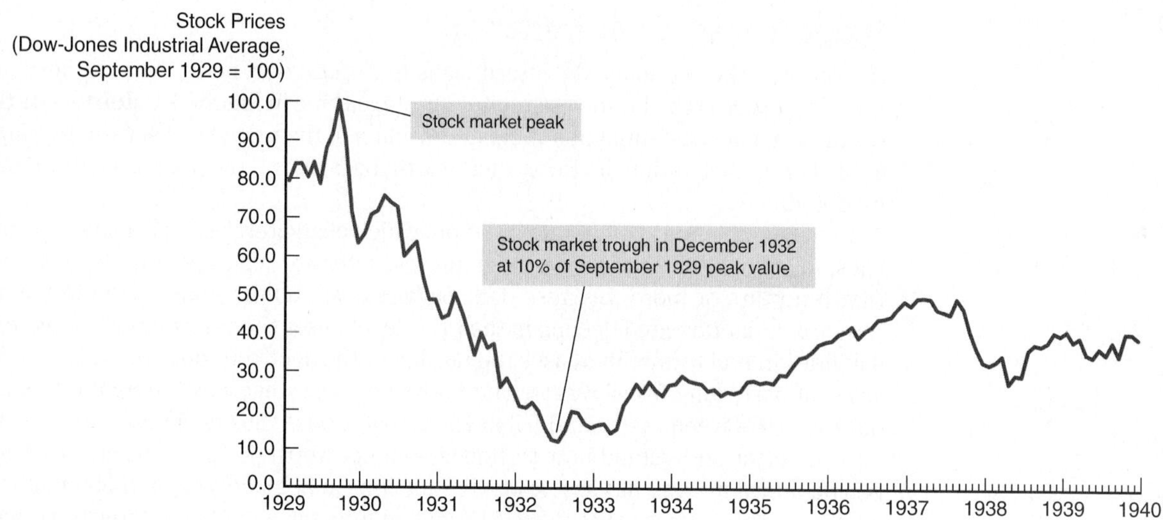

FIGURE 8.2 Stock Price Data During the Great Depression Period

Stock prices crashed in 1929, falling by 40% by the end of 1929, and then continued to fall to only 10% of their peak value by 1932.

Source: Federal Reserve Bank of St. Louis, FRED database: https://fred.stlouisfed.org/series/M1109AUSM293NNBR.

a sharp decline in agricultural production, with the result that farmers could not pay back their bank loans. The resulting defaults on farm mortgages led to large loan losses on bank balance sheets in agricultural regions. The weakness of the economy and the banks in agricultural regions in particular prompted substantial withdrawals from banks, building to a full-fledged panic in November and December 1930, with the stock market falling sharply. For more than two years, the Fed sat idly by through one bank panic after another, the most severe spate of panics in U.S. history. After what would be the era's final panic in March 1933, President Franklin Delano Roosevelt declared a bank holiday, a temporary closing of all banks. "The only thing we have to fear is fear itself," Roosevelt told the nation in his first inaugural address. The damage was done, however, and more than one-third of U.S. commercial banks had failed.

Continuing Decline in Stock Prices

Stock prices kept falling. By mid-1932, stocks had declined to 10% of their value at the 1929 peak (as shown in Figure 8.2), and the increase in uncertainty from the unsettled business conditions created by the economic contraction worsened adverse selection and moral hazard problems in financial markets. With a greatly reduced number of financial intermediaries still in business, adverse selection and moral hazard problems intensified even further. Financial markets struggled to channel funds to borrower-spenders with productive investment opportunities. As our analysis predicts, the amount of outstanding commercial loans fell by half from 1929 to 1933, and investment spending collapsed, declining by 90% from its 1929 level.

A manifestation of the rise in financial frictions is that lenders began charging businesses much higher interest rates to protect themselves from credit losses. The resulting rise in **credit spread**—the difference between the interest rate on loans to households and businesses and the interest rate on completely safe assets that are sure to be paid back, such as U.S. Treasury securities—is shown in Figure 8.3, which displays the difference between interest rates on corporate bonds with a Baa (medium-quality) credit rating and similar-maturity Treasury bonds.

Debt Deflation

The ongoing deflation that started in 1930 eventually led to a 25% decline in the price level. This deflation short-circuited the normal recovery process that occurs in most recessions. The huge decline in prices triggered a debt deflation in which net worth fell because of the increased burden of indebtedness borne by firms. The decline in net worth and the resulting increase in adverse selection and moral hazard problems in the credit markets led to a prolonged economic contraction in which unemployment rose to 25% of the labor force. The financial crisis in the Great Depression was the worst ever experienced in the United States, and it explains why the economic contraction was also the most severe ever experienced by the nation.

International Dimensions

Although the Great Depression started in the United States, it was not just a U.S. phenomenon. Bank panics in the United States also spread to the rest of the world,

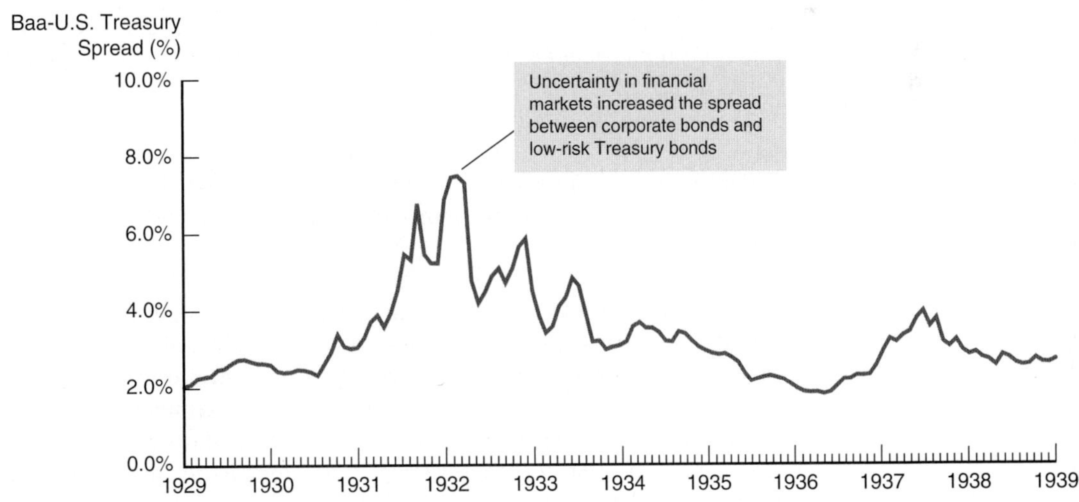

FIGURE 8.3 Credit Spreads During the Great Depression

Credit spreads (the difference between rates on Baa corporate bonds and U.S. Treasury bonds) rose sharply during the Great Depression.

Source: Federal Reserve Bank of St. Louis, FRED database: https://fred.stlouisfed.org/series/M13036USM193NNBR, https://fred.stlouisfed.org/series/LTGOVTBD.

and the contraction of the U.S. economy sharply decreased the demand for foreign goods. The worldwide depression caused great hardship, with millions upon millions of people out of work, and the resulting discontent led to the rise of fascism and World War II. The consequences of the Great Depression financial crisis were disastrous.

CASE

The Global Financial Crisis of 2007–2009

Most economists thought that financial crises of the type experienced during the Great Depression were a thing of the past for advanced countries like the United States. Unfortunately, the financial crisis that engulfed the world in 2007–2009 proved them wrong.

Causes of the 2007–2009 Financial Crisis

We begin our look at the 2007–2009 financial crisis by examining three central factors: financial innovation in mortgage markets, agency problems in mortgage markets, and the role of asymmetric information in the credit-rating process.

Financial Innovation in the Mortgage Markets Before 2000, only the most credit-worthy (prime) borrowers could obtain residential mortgages. Advances in computer technology and new statistical techniques, known as data mining, however, led to enhanced, quantitative evaluation of the credit risk for a new class of risky residential mortgages. Households with credit records could now be assigned a numerical credit score, known as a FICO score (named after the Fair Isaac Corporation, which developed it), that would predict how likely they would be to default on their loan payments. In addition, by lowering transactions costs, computer technology enabled the bundling of smaller loans (like mortgages) into standard debt securities, a process known as **securitization**. These factors made it possible for banks to offer **subprime mortgages** to borrowers with less-than-stellar credit records.

The ability to cheaply quantify the default risk of the underlying high-risk mortgages and bundle them in standardized debt securities called **mortgage-backed securities** provided a new source of financing for these mortgages. Financial innovation didn't stop there. **Financial engineering**, the development of new, sophisticated financial instruments, led to **structured credit products** that pay out income streams from a collection of underlying assets, designed to have particular risk characteristics that appeal to investors with differing preferences. The most notorious of these products were **collateralized debt obligations (CDOs)** (discussed in the Mini-Case box, "Collateralized Debt Obligations (CDOs)").

Agency Problems in the Mortgage Markets The mortgage brokers that originated the loans often did not make a strong effort to evaluate whether the borrower could pay off the loan, since they would quickly sell (distribute) the loans

MINI-CASE

Collateralized Debt Obligations (CDOs)

The creation of a collateralized debt obligation involves a corporate entity called a *special purpose vehicle (SPV)*, which buys a collection of assets such as corporate bonds and loans, commercial real estate bonds, and mortgage-backed securities. The SPV then separates the payment streams (cash flows) from these assets into a number of buckets that are referred to as tranches. The highest-rated tranches, called super senior tranches, are the ones that are paid off first and so have the least risk. The super senior CDO is a bond that pays out these cash flows to investors, and because it has the least risk, it also has the lowest interest rate. The next bucket of cash flows, known as the senior tranche, is paid out next; the senior CDO has a little more risk and pays a higher interest rate. The next tranche of payment streams, the mezzanine tranche of the CDO, is paid out after the super senior and senior tranches and so it bears more risk and has an even higher interest rate. The lowest tranche of the CDO is the equity tranche; this is the first set of cash flows that are not paid out if the underlying assets go into default and stop making payments. This tranche has the highest risk and is often not traded.

If all of this sounds complicated, it is. There were even CDO^2s and CDO^3s that sliced and diced risk even further, paying out the cash flows from CDOs to CDO^2s and from CDO^2s to CDO^3s. Although financial engineering has the potential benefit of creating products and services that match investors' risk appetites, it too has a dark side. Structured products like CDOs, CDO^2s, and CDO^3s can get so complicated that it can be hard to value cash flows of the underlying assets for a security or to determine who actually owns these assets. Indeed, at a speech given in October 2007, Ben Bernanke, the chairman of the Federal Reserve, joked that he "would like to know what those damn things are worth." In other words, the increased complexity of structured products can actually reduce the amount of information in financial markets, thereby worsening asymmetric information in the financial system and increasing the severity of adverse selection and moral hazard problems.

to investors in the form of mortgage-backed securities. This **originate-to-distribute business model** was exposed to the **principal–agent problem** of the type discussed in Chapter 7, in which the mortgage brokers acted as agents for investors (the principals) but did not have the investors' best interests at heart. Once the mortgage broker earns his or her fee, why should the broker care if the borrower makes good on his or her payment? The more volume the broker originates, the more he or she makes.

Not surprisingly, adverse selection became a major problem. Risk-loving investors lined up to obtain loans to acquire houses that would be very profitable if housing prices went up, knowing they could "walk away," i.e., default on their loans, if housing prices went down. The principal–agent problem also created incentives for mortgage brokers to encourage households to take on mortgages they could not afford or to commit fraud by falsifying information on a borrower's mortgage applications in order to qualify them for mortgages. Compounding this problem was lax regulation of originators, who were not required to disclose information to borrowers that would have helped them assess whether they could afford the loans.

The agency problems went even deeper. Commercial and investment banks, which were earning large fees by underwriting mortgage-backed securities and structured credit products like CDOs, also had weak incentives to make sure that the ultimate holders of the securities would be paid off. **Financial derivatives**, financial instruments whose payoffs are linked to (i.e., derived from) previously issued securities, also were an important source of excessive risk taking. Large fees from writing financial insurance contracts called **credit default swaps**, which provide payments to holders of bonds if they default, also drove units of insurance companies like AIG to write hundreds of billions of dollars' worth of these risky contracts.

Asymmetric Information and Credit-Rating Services Credit-rating agencies, who rate the quality of debt securities in terms of the probability of default, were another contributor to asymmetric information in financial markets. The rating agencies advised clients on how to structure complex financial instruments, like CDOs, at the same time they were rating these identical products. The rating agencies were thus subject to conflicts of interest because the large fees they earned from advising clients on how to structure products they were rating meant that they did not have sufficient incentives to make sure their ratings were accurate. The result was wildly inflated ratings that enabled the sale of complex financial products that were far riskier than investors recognized.

Effects of the 2007–2009 Financial Crisis

Consumers and businesses alike suffered as a result of the 2007–2009 financial crisis. The impact of the crisis was most evident in five key areas: the U.S. residential housing market, financial institutions' balance sheets, the shadow banking system, global financial markets, and the headline-grabbing failures of major firms in the financial industry.

Residential Housing Prices: Boom and Bust The subprime mortgage market took off after the recession ended in 2001. By 2007, it had become over a trillion-dollar market. The development of the subprime mortgage market was encouraged by politicians because it led to a "democratization of credit" and helped raise U.S. homeownership rates to the highest levels in history. The asset-price boom in housing (see Figure 8.4), which took off after the 2000–2001 recession was over, also helped stimulate the growth of the subprime mortgage market. High housing prices meant that subprime borrowers could refinance their houses with even larger loans when their homes appreciated in value. With housing prices rising, subprime borrowers were also unlikely to default because they could always sell their house to pay off the loan, making investors happy because the securities backed by cash flows from subprime mortgages would have less risk and higher returns. The growth of the subprime mortgage market, in turn, increased the demand for houses and so fueled the boom in housing prices, resulting in a housing price bubble.

Further stimulus to the housing market came from low interest rates on residential mortgages, which were the result of several different forces. First was the huge capital inflows into the United States from countries like China and India. Second was congressional legislation that encouraged Fannie Mae and Freddie Mac to purchase trillions of dollars of mortgage-backed securities.[2] Third was easy Federal Reserve monetary policy to lower interest rates. The resulting low cost of financing housing purchases then further stimulated the demand for housing, pushing up housing prices. (A highly controversial issue is whether the Federal Reserve was to blame for the housing price bubble, and this is discussed in the Inside the Fed box.)

[2]For a discussion of the government's role in encouraging the boom which led to the bust in the housing market, see Thomas Sowell, *The Housing Boom and Bust*, Revised Edition (New York, Basic Books, 2010).

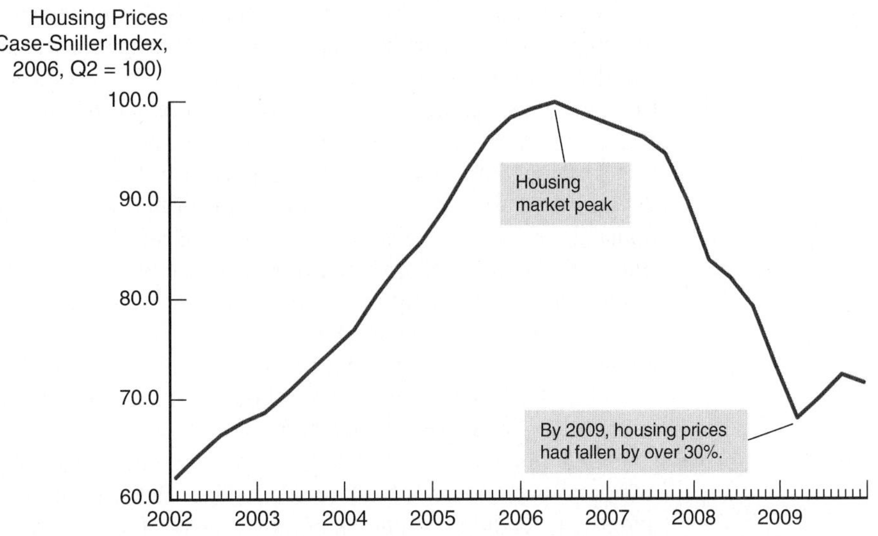

FIGURE 8.4 Housing Prices and the Financial Crisis of 2007–2009

Housing prices boomed from 2002 to 2006, fueling the market for subprime mortgages and forming an asset-price bubble. Housing prices began declining in 2006, falling by more than 30% subsequently, which led to defaults by subprime mortgage holders.

Source: Case-Shiller 20-City Composite Home Price Index in Federal Reserve Bank of St. Louis, FRED database: https://fred.stlouisfed.org/series/SPCS20RSA.

INSIDE THE FED

Was the Fed to Blame for the Housing Price Bubble?

Some economists—most prominently, John Taylor of Stanford University—have argued that the low-rate interest policy of the Federal Reserve in the 2003–2006 period caused the housing price bubble.* Taylor argues that the low federal funds rate led to low mortgage rates that stimulated housing demand and encouraged the issuance of subprime mortgages, both of which led to rising housing prices and a bubble.

In a speech given in January 2010, Federal Reserve Chairman Ben Bernanke countered this argument.** He concluded that monetary policy was not to blame for the housing price bubble. First, he said, it is not at all clear that the federal funds rate was too low during the 2003–2006 period. Rather, the culprits were the proliferation of new mortgage products that lowered mortgage payments, a relaxation of lending standards that brought more buyers into the housing market, and capital inflows from countries such as China and India. Bernanke's speech was very controversial, and the debate over whether monetary policy was to blame for the housing price bubble continues to this day.

*John Taylor, "Housing and Monetary Policy," in Federal Reserve Bank of Kansas City, *Housing, Housing Finance and Monetary Policy* (Kansas City: Federal Reserve Bank of Kansas City, 2007), 463–476.

**Ben S. Bernanke, "Monetary Policy and the Housing Bubble," speech given at the annual meeting of the American Economic Association, Atlanta, Georgia, January 3, 2010, www.federalreserve.gov/newsevents/speech/bernanke20100103a.htm.

As housing prices rose and profitability for mortgage originators and lenders was high, the underwriting standards for subprime mortgages fell to lower and lower standards. High-risk borrowers were able to obtain mortgages, and the amount of the mortgage relative to the value of the house, the loan-to-value ratio (LTV), rose. Borrowers were often able to get piggyback, second, and third mortgages on top of their original 80% loan-to-value mortgage, so that they had to put almost no money down. When asset prices rise too far out of line with fundamentals—in the case of housing, how much housing costs if purchased relative to the cost of renting it, or the cost of houses relative to households' median income—they must come down. Eventually, the housing price bubble burst. With housing prices falling after their peak in 2006 (see Figure 8.4), the rot in the financial system caused by questionable lending practices began to be revealed. The decline in housing prices led to many subprime borrowers finding that their mortgages were "underwater"—that is, the value of the house fell below the amount of the mortgage. When this happened, struggling homeowners had tremendous incentives to walk away from their homes and just send the keys back to the lender. Defaults on mortgages shot up sharply, eventually leading to millions of mortgages in foreclosure.

Deterioration of Financial Institutions' Balance Sheets The decline in U.S. housing prices led to rising defaults on mortgages. As a result, the value of mortgage-backed securities and CDOs collapsed, leaving banks and other financial institutions with a lower value of assets and thus a decline in net worth. With weakened balance sheets, these banks and other financial institutions began to deleverage, selling off assets and restricting the availability of credit to both households and businesses. With no one else able to step in to collect information and make loans, the reduction in bank lending meant that financial frictions increased in financial markets.

Run on the Shadow Banking System The sharp decline in the value of mortgages and other financial assets triggered a run on the **shadow banking system**, composed of hedge funds, investment banks, and other nondepository financial firms, which are not as tightly regulated as banks. Funds from shadow banks flowed through the financial system and for many years supported the issuance of low-interest-rate mortgages and auto loans.

These securities were funded primarily by **repurchase agreements (repos)**, short-term borrowing that, in effect, uses assets like mortgage-backed securities as collateral. Rising concern about the quality of a financial institution's balance sheet led lenders to require larger amounts of collateral, known as **haircuts**. For example, if a borrower took out a $100 million loan in a repo agreement, it might have to post $105 million of mortgage-backed securities as collateral, and the haircut is then 5%.

With rising defaults on mortgages, the value of mortgage-backed securities fell, which then led to a rise in haircuts. At the start of the crisis, haircuts were close to zero, but they eventually rose to nearly 50%.[3] The result was that the same amount of collateral would allow financial institutions to borrow only half as much. Thus, to raise funds, financial institutions had to engage in fire sales and sell off their assets very rapidly. Because selling assets quickly requires lowering their price, the fire sales led to a further decline in financial institutions' asset values. This decline lowered the value of collateral further, raising haircuts and thereby forcing financial

[3]See Gary Gorton and Andrew Metrick, "Securitized Banking and the Run on Repo," *Journal of Financial Economics* 104 (2012): 425–451.

institutions to scramble even more for liquidity. The result was similar to the run on the banking system that occurred during the Great Depression, causing massive deleveraging that resulted in a restriction of lending and a decline in economic activity.

The decline in asset prices in the stock market (which fell by over 50% from October 2007 to March 2009, as shown in Figure 8.5) and the more than 30% drop in residential house prices (shown in Figure 8.4), along with the fire sales resulting from the run on the shadow banking system, weakened both firms' and households' balance sheets. This worsening of financial frictions manifested itself in widening credit spreads, causing higher costs of credit for households and businesses and tighter lending standards. The resulting decline in lending meant that both consumption expenditure and investment fell, causing the economy to contract.

Global Financial Markets Although the problem originated in the United States, the wake-up call for the financial crisis came from Europe, a sign of how extensive the globalization of financial markets had become. After Fitch and Standard & Poor's announced ratings downgrades on mortgage-backed securities and CDOs totaling more than $10 billion, on August 7, 2007, a French investment house, BNP Paribas, suspended redemption of shares held in some of its money market funds, which had sustained large losses. The run on the shadow banking system began, only to become worse and worse over time. Despite huge injections of liquidity into the financial system by the European Central Bank and the Federal Reserve, banks began to horde cash and were unwilling to lend to each other. The drying up of credit led to the first major bank failure in the United Kingdom in over 100 years, when Northern Rock,

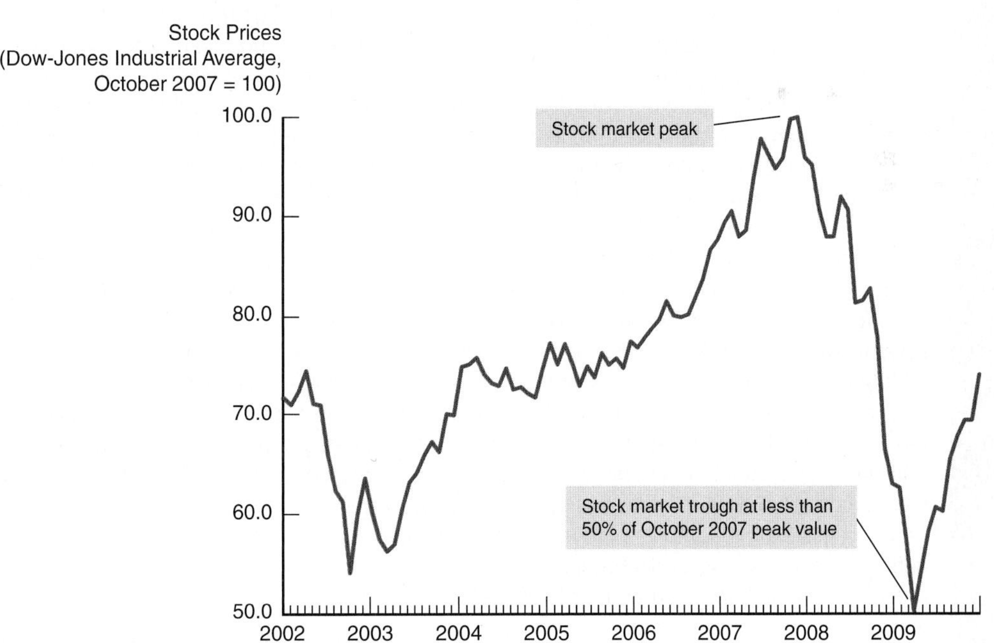

FIGURE 8.5 Stock Prices and the Financial Crisis of 2007–2009

Stock prices fell by 50% from October 2007 to March 2009.

Source: Federal Reserve Bank of St. Louis, FRED database, https://fred.stlouisfed.org/series/DJIA.

which had relied on short-term borrowing in the repo market rather than deposits for its funding, collapsed in September 2007. A string of other European financial institutions then failed as well. Particularly hard hit were countries like Greece, Ireland, Portugal, Spain, and Italy, which led to a sovereign debt crisis, which is described in the Global box, "The European Sovereign Debt Crisis."

Failure of High-Profile Firms The impact of the financial crisis on firms' balance sheets forced major players in the financial markets to take drastic action. In March 2008, Bear Stearns, the fifth-largest investment bank in the United States, which had invested heavily in subprime-related securities, had a run on its repo funding and was forced to sell itself to J. P. Morgan for less than 5% of what it had been worth just a year earlier. To broker the deal, the Federal Reserve had to take over $30 billion of Bear Stearns's hard-to-value assets. In July Fannie Mae and Freddie

> GLOBAL

The European Sovereign Debt Crisis

The global financial crisis in 2007–2009 led not only to a worldwide recession but also to a sovereign debt crisis that threatens to destabilize Europe. Up until 2007, all the countries that had adopted the euro found their interest rates converging to very low levels; but with the global financial crisis, several of these countries were hit very hard with the contraction in economic activity reducing tax revenues, while government bailouts of failed financial institutions required additional government outlays. The resulting surge in budget deficits then led to suspicions that the governments in these hard-hit countries would default on their debt. The result was a surge in interest rates that threatened to spiral out of control.*

Greece was the first domino to fall in Europe. With a weakening economy reducing tax revenue and increasing spending demands, the Greek government in September 2009 was projecting a budget deficit for the year of 6% of GDP and a debt-to-GDP ratio near 100%. However, when a new government was elected in October, it revealed that the budget situation was far worse than anyone had imagined because the previous government had provided misleading numbers both about the budget deficit, which was at least double the 6% number, and about the amount of government debt, which was ten percentage points higher than previously reported. Despite austerity measures to dramatically cut government spending and raise taxes, interest rates on Greek debt soared, eventually rising to nearly 40%, and the debt-to-GDP ratio climbed to 160% of GDP in 2012. Even with bailouts from other European countries and liquidity support from the European Central Bank, Greece was forced to write down the value of its debt held in private hands by more than half, and the country was subject to civil unrest, with massive strikes and the resignation of the prime minister.

The sovereign debt crisis spread from Greece to Ireland, Portugal, Spain, and Italy, with their governments forced to embrace austerity measures to shore up their public finances, while interest rates climbed to double-digit levels. Only with a speech in July 2012 by Mario Draghi, the president of the European Central Bank, in which he stated that the ECB was ready to do "whatever it takes" to save the euro, did the markets begin to calm down. Nonetheless, despite a sharp decline in interest rates in those countries, the countries experienced severe recessions, with unemployment rates rising to double-digit levels and Spain's unemployment rate exceeding 25%. The stresses that the European sovereign debt crisis produced for the Eurozone has raised doubts about the euro's survival, a topic we return to in Chapter 15.

*For a discussion of the dynamics of sovereign debt crises and case studies of the European debt crisis, see David Greenlaw, James D. Hamilton, Frederic S. Mishkin, and Peter Hooper, "Crunch Time: Fiscal Crises and the Role of Monetary Policy," *U.S. Monetary Policy Forum* (Chicago: Chicago Booth Initiative on Global Markets, 2013).

Mac, the two privately owned government-sponsored enterprises that together insured over $5 trillion of mortgages or mortgage-backed assets, were propped up by the U.S. Treasury and the Federal Reserve after suffering substantial losses from their holdings of subprime securities. In early September 2008 they were then put into conservatorship (in effect run by the government).

On Monday, September 15, 2008, after suffering losses in the subprime market, Lehman Brothers, the fourth-largest investment bank by asset size with over $600 billion in assets and 25,000 employees, filed for bankruptcy, making it the largest bankruptcy filing in U.S. history. The day before, Merrill Lynch, the third-largest investment bank, which had also suffered large losses on its holding of subprime securities, announced its sale to Bank of America for a price 60% below its value a year earlier. On Tuesday, September 16, AIG, an insurance giant with assets of over $1 trillion, suffered an extreme liquidity crisis when its credit rating was downgraded. It had written over $400 billion of insurance contracts (credit default swaps) that had to make payouts on possible losses from subprime mortgage securities. The Federal Reserve then stepped in with an $85 billion loan to keep AIG afloat (with total government loans later increased to $173 billion).

Height of the 2007–2009 Financial Crisis

The financial crisis reached its peak in September 2008 after the House of Representatives, fearing the wrath of constituents who were angry about bailing out Wall Street, voted down a $700 billion bailout package proposed by the Bush administration. The Emergency Economic Stabilization Act finally passed nearly a week later. The stock market crash accelerated, with the week beginning October 6, 2008, showing the worst weekly decline in U.S. history. Credit spreads went through the roof over the next three weeks, with the spread between Baa corporate bonds (just above investment grade) and U.S. Treasury bonds going to over 5.5 percentage points (550 basis points), as illustrated by Figure 8.6.

The impaired financial markets and surging interest rates faced by borrower-spenders led to sharp declines in consumer spending and investment. Real GDP declined sharply, falling at a −1.3% annual rate in the third quarter of 2008 and then at a −5.4% and −6.4% annual rate in the next two quarters. The unemployment rate shot up, going over the 10% level in late 2009. The recession that started in December 2007 became the worst economic contraction in the United States since World War II and as a result is now referred to as the "Great Recession."

Starting in March 2009, a bull market in stocks got under way (see Figure 8.5), and credit spreads began to fall (Figure 8.6).[4] With the recovery in financial markets, the economy started to recover but, unfortunately, the pace of the recovery has been slow.

---

[4]The financial market recovery was aided by the U.S. Treasury's requirement announced in February 2009 that the nineteen largest banking institutions undergo what became known as the *bank stress tests* (the Supervisory Capital Assessment Program, or SCAP). The stress tests were a supervisory assessment, led by the Federal Reserve in cooperation with the Office of the Comptroller of the Currency and the FDIC, of the balance sheet position of these banks to ensure that they had sufficient capital to withstand bad macroeconomic outcomes. The Treasury announced the results in early May and they were well received by market participants, allowing these banks to raise substantial amounts of capital from private capital markets. The stress tests were a key factor that helped increase the amount of information in the marketplace, thereby reducing asymmetric information and adverse selection and moral hazard problems.

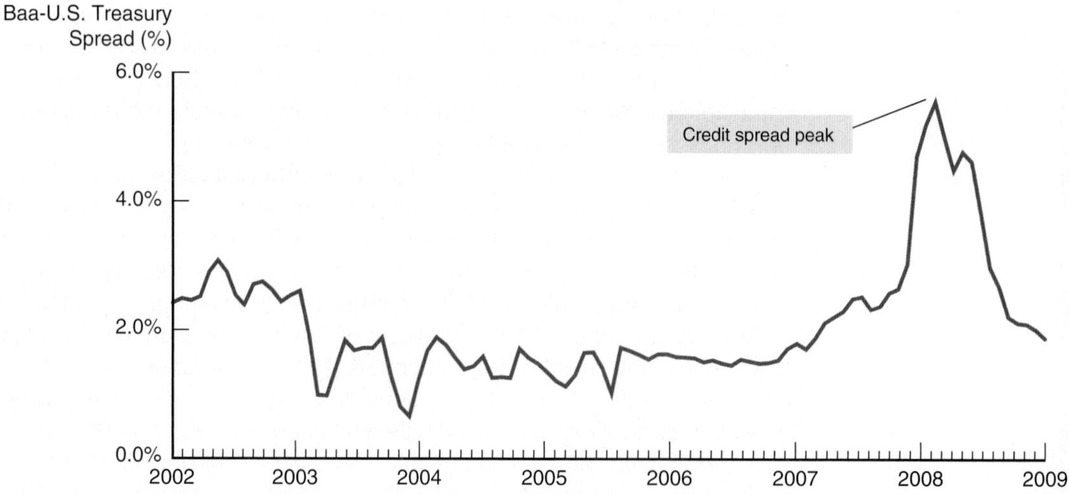

FIGURE 8.6 Credit Spreads and the 2007–2009 Financial Crisis

Credit spreads (the difference between rates on Baa corporate bonds and U.S. Treasury bonds) rose by more than 4 percentage points (400 basis points) during the crisis. Debate over the bailout package and the stock market crash caused credit spreads to peak in December 2008.

Source: Federal Reserve Bank of St. Louis, FRED database, https://fred.stlouisfed.org/series/BAA10Y.

SUMMARY

1. A financial crisis occurs when a particularly large disruption to information flows occurs in financial markets, with the result that financial frictions and credit spreads increase sharply, thereby rendering financial markets incapable of channeling funds to households and firms with productive investment opportunities, and causing a sharp contraction in economic activity.
2. Financial crises can start in advanced countries like the United States in several possible ways: credit and asset-price booms and busts or a general increase in uncertainty when major financial institutions fail. The result is a substantial increase in adverse selection and moral hazard problems that lead to a contraction of lending and a decline in economic activity. The worsening business conditions and deterioration in bank balance sheets then trigger the second stage of the crisis, the simultaneous failure of many banking institutions, a banking crisis. The resulting decrease in the number of banks causes a loss of their information capital, leading to a further decline of lending and a spiraling down of the economy. In some instances, the resulting economic downturn leads to a sharp slide in prices, which increases the real liabilities of firms and households and therefore lowers their net worth, leading to a debt deflation. The further decline in borrowers' net worth worsens adverse selection and moral hazard problems, so that lending, investment spending, and aggregate economic activity remain depressed for a long time.
3. The most significant financial crisis in U.S. history, that which led to the Great Depression, involved several stages: a stock market crash, bank panics, worsening of asymmetric information problems, and finally a debt deflation.
4. The global financial crisis of 2007–2009 was triggered by mismanagement of financial innovations involving subprime residential mortgages and the bursting of a housing price bubble. The crisis spread globally, with substantial deterioration in banks' and other financial institutions' balance sheets, a run on the shadow banking system, the failure of many high-profile firms, and sharp declines in economic activity.

KEY TERMS

asset-price bubble, p. 169
bank panic, p. 170
collateralized debt obligations (CDOs), p. 174
credit boom, p. 169
credit default swaps, p. 176
credit spreads, p. 173
debt deflation, p. 171
deleveraging, p. 169
financial crisis, p. 167
financial derivatives, p. 175
financial engineering, p. 174
financial frictions, p. 167
financial innovation, p. 169
financial liberalization, p. 169
fire sales, p. 170
fundamental economic values, p. 169
haircuts, p. 178
mortgage-backed securities, p. 174
originate-to-distribute business model, p. 175
principal–agent problem, p. 175
repurchase agreements (repos), p. 178
securitization, p. 174
shadow banking system, p. 178
structured credit products, p. 174
subprime mortgages, p. 174

QUESTIONS

1. How does the concept of asymmetric information help to define a financial crisis?
2. How can a bursting of an asset-price bubble in the stock market help trigger a financial crisis?
3. Can you think of a reason why emerging market economies should be very careful when engaging in financial innovation and financial liberalization?
4. Define "financial frictions" in your own terms and explain why an increase in financial frictions is a key element in financial crises.
5. How does a deterioration in balance sheets of financial institutions cause a decline in economic activity?
6. How does a general increase in uncertainty as a result of a failure of a major financial institution lead to an increase in adverse selection and moral hazard problems?
7. What is a credit spread? Why do credit spreads rise during financial crises?
8. Some countries do not advertise that a system of deposit insurance like the FDIC in the United States exists in their banking system. Explain why some countries would want to do that.
9. Describe the process of "securitization" in your own words. Was this process solely responsible for the Great Recession financial crisis of 2007–2009?
10. Provide one argument in favor of and one against the idea that the Fed was responsible for the housing price bubble of the early 2000s.
11. What role do weak financial regulation and supervision play in causing financial crises?
12. Describe two similarities and two differences between the U.S. experiences during the Great Depression and those during the Great Recession financial crisis of 2007–2009.
13. What technological innovations led to the development of the subprime mortgage market?
14. Why is the originate-to-distribute business model subject to the principal–agent problem?
15. True, false, or uncertain: Deposit insurance always and everywhere prevents financial crises.
16. How did a decline in housing prices help trigger the subprime financial crisis starting in 2007?
17. What is the shadow banking system, and why was it an important part of the 2007–2009 financial crisis?
18. Why would haircuts on collateral increase sharply during a financial crisis? How would this lead to fire sales on assets?
19. Why are more resources not devoted to adequate, prudential supervision of the financial system to limit excessive risk taking, when it is clear that this supervision is needed to prevent financial crises?
20. How did the global financial crisis promote a sovereign debt crisis in Europe?
21. How can a sovereign debt crisis make an economic contraction more likely?

WEB EXERCISES

1. This chapter discusses how an understanding of adverse selection and moral hazard can help us better understand financial crises. The greatest financial crisis faced by the United States was the Great Depression of 1929–1933. Go to **www.amatecon.com/greatdepression.html**. This site contains a

brief discussion of the factors that led to the Great Depression. Write a one-page summary explaining how adverse selection and moral hazard contributed to the Great Depression.

2. Go to the International Monetary Fund's Financial Crisis page at **www.imf.org/external/np/exr/key/finstab.htm**. Report on the most recent three countries that the IMF has given emergency loans to in response to a financial crisis. According to the IMF, what caused the crisis in each country?

WEB REFERENCES

www.amatecon.com/gd/gdtimeline.html

A timeline of the Great Depression.

www.imf.org

The International Monetary Fund is an organization of 185 countries that works on global policy coordination (both monetary and trade), stable and sustainable economic prosperity, and the reduction of poverty.

PART 4 CENTRAL BANKING AND THE CONDUCT OF MONETARY POLICY

CHAPTER 9

Central Banks and the Federal Reserve System

> PREVIEW

Among the most important players in financial markets throughout the world are central banks, the government authorities in charge of monetary policy. Central banks' actions affect interest rates, the amount of credit, and the money supply, all of which have direct impacts not only on financial markets but also on aggregate output and inflation. To understand the role that central banks play in financial markets and the overall economy, we need to understand how these organizations work. Who controls central banks and determines their actions? What motivates their behavior? Who holds the reins of power?

In this chapter we look at the institutional structure of major central banks and focus particularly on the Federal Reserve System, the most important central bank in the world. We start by focusing on the elements of the Fed's institutional structure that determine where the true power within the Federal Reserve System lies. By understanding who makes the decisions, we will have a better idea of how they are made. We then look at several other major central banks, particularly the European Central Bank, and see how they are organized. With this information, we will be better able to comprehend the actual conduct of monetary policy described in the following chapter.

Origins of the Federal Reserve System

Of all the central banks in the world, the Federal Reserve System probably has the most unusual structure. To understand why this structure arose, we must go back to before 1913, when the Federal Reserve System was created.

Before the twentieth century, a major characteristic of American politics was the fear of centralized power, as seen in the checks and balances of the Constitution and the preservation of states' rights. This fear of centralized power was one source of the American resistance to the establishment of a central bank. Another source was the traditional American distrust of moneyed interests, the most prominent symbol of which was a central bank. The open hostility of the American public to the existence of a central bank resulted in the demise of the first two experiments in central banking, whose function was to police the banking system: The First Bank of the United States was disbanded in 1811, and the national charter of the Second Bank of the United States expired in 1836 after its renewal was vetoed in 1832 by President Andrew Jackson.

The termination of the Second Bank's national charter in 1836 created a severe problem for American financial markets because there was no lender of last resort that could provide liquidity to the banking system to avert a bank panic. Hence, in the nineteenth and early twentieth centuries, nationwide bank panics became a regular event, occurring every 20 years or so, culminating in the panic of 1907. The 1907 panic resulted in such widespread bank failures and such substantial losses to depositors that the public was finally convinced that a central bank was needed to prevent future panics.

The hostility of the American public to banks and centralized authority created great opposition to the establishment of a single central bank like the Bank of England. Fear was rampant that the moneyed interests on Wall Street (including the largest corporations and banks) would be able to manipulate such an institution to gain control over the economy and that federal operation of the central bank might result in too much government intervention in the affairs of private banks. Serious disagreements existed over whether the central bank should be a private bank or a government institution. Because of the heated debates on these issues, a compromise was struck. In the great American tradition, Congress wrote an elaborate system of checks and balances into the Federal Reserve Act of 1913, which created the Federal Reserve

> INSIDE THE FED

The Political Genius of the Founders of the Federal Reserve System

The history of the United States has been one of public hostility to banks and especially to a central bank. How were the politicians who founded the Federal Reserve able to design a system that has become one of the most prestigious institutions in the United States?

The answer is that the founders recognized that if power was too concentrated in either Washington, D.C., or New York, cities that Americans often love to hate, an American central bank might not have enough public support to operate effectively. They thus decided to set up a decentralized system with 12 Federal Reserve banks spread throughout the country to make sure that all regions of the country were represented in monetary policy deliberations. In addition, they made the Federal Reserve banks quasi-private institutions overseen by directors from the private sector living in each district who represent views from their region and are in close contact with the president of their district's Federal Reserve bank. The unusual structure of the Federal Reserve System has promoted a concern in the Fed with regional issues, as is evident in Federal Reserve bank publications. Without this unusual structure, the Federal Reserve System might have been far less popular with the public, making the institution far less effective.

System with its twelve regional Federal Reserve banks (see the Inside the Fed box, "The Political Genius of the Founders of the Federal Reserve System").

Structure of the Federal Reserve System

Access **http://www.federalreserve.gov/pubs/frseries/frseri.htm** for information on the structure of the Federal Reserve System.

The writers of the Federal Reserve Act wanted to diffuse power along regional lines, between the private sector and the government, and among bankers, business people, and the public. This initial diffusion of power has resulted in the evolution of the Federal Reserve System to include the following entities: the **Federal Reserve banks**, the **Board of Governors of the Federal Reserve System**, the **Federal Open Market Committee (FOMC)**, the Federal Advisory Council, and around 3,000 member commercial banks. Figure 9.1 outlines the relationships of these

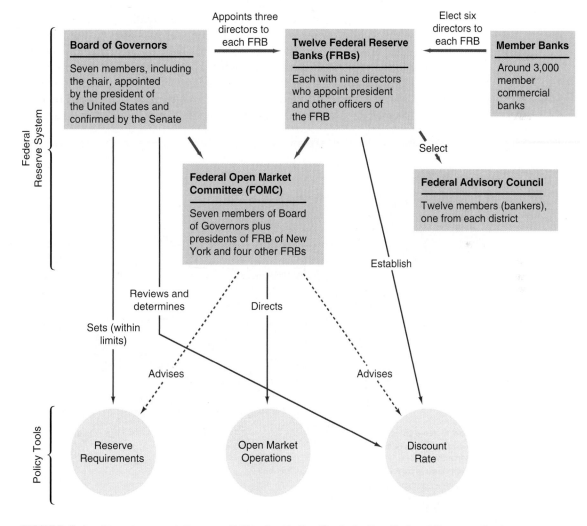

FIGURE 9.1 Structure and Responsibility for Policy Tools in the Federal Reserve System

The figure illustrates the relationships of the Federal Reserve banks, the Board of Governors of the Federal Reserve System, and the FOMC to the three policy tools of the Fed (open market operations, the discount rate, and reserve requirements). Dashed lines indicate that the FOMC "advises" on the setting of reserve requirements and the discount rate.

entities to one another and to the three policy tools of the Fed (open market operations, the discount rate, and reserve requirements) discussed in Chapter 10.

Federal Reserve Banks

GO ONLINE

Access **www.federalreserve.gov/otherfrb.htm** for addresses and phone numbers of Federal Reserve Banks and branches and links to the main pages of the 12 reserve banks and Board of Governors.

Each of the 12 Federal Reserve districts defined by the Federal Reserve Act of 1913 has one main Federal Reserve bank, which may have branches in other cities in the district. The locations of these districts, the Federal Reserve banks, and their branches are shown in Figure 9.2. The three largest Federal Reserve banks in terms of assets are those of New York, Chicago, and San Francisco—combined they hold more than 50% of the assets (discount loans, securities, and other holdings) of the Federal Reserve System. The New York bank, with around one-quarter of the assets, is the most important of the Federal Reserve banks (see the Inside the Fed box, "The Special Role of the Federal Reserve Bank of New York").

Each of the Federal Reserve banks is a quasi-public (part private, part government) institution owned by the private commercial banks in the district that are members of the Federal Reserve System. These member banks have purchased stock in their district Federal Reserve bank (a requirement of membership), and the dividends paid by that stock are limited by law to 6% annually. The member banks elect six directors for each district bank; three more are appointed by the Board of Governors. The directors of a district bank are classified into three categories: A, B,

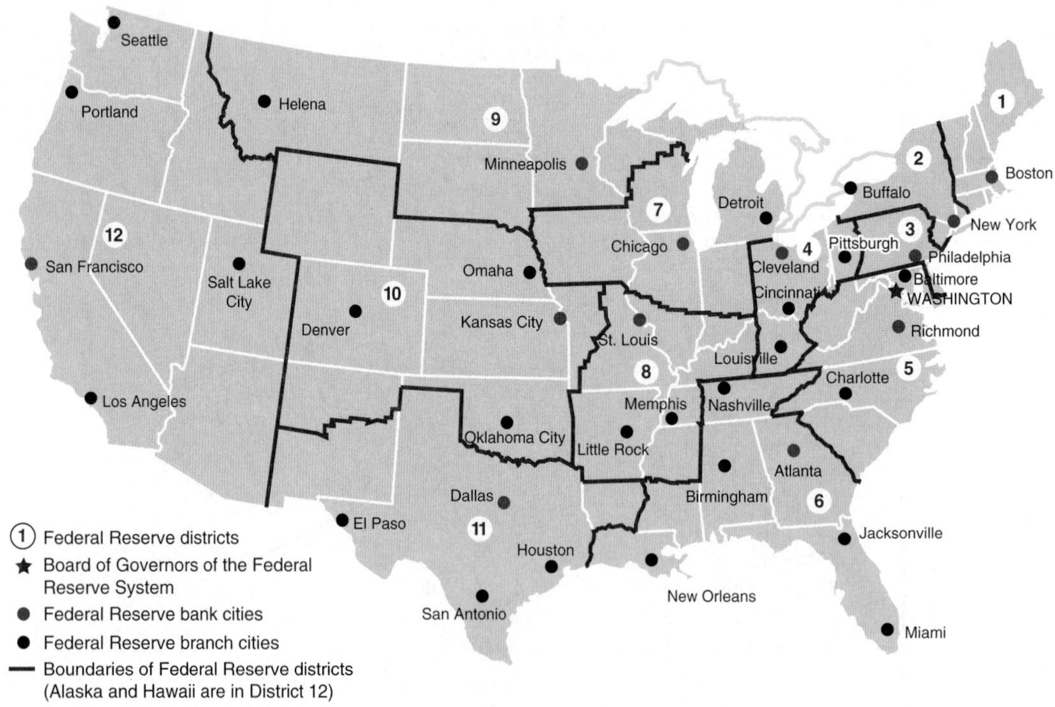

FIGURE 9.2 Federal Reserve System

The locations of the Federal Reserve districts, the Federal Reserve banks, and their branches.

Sources: Federal Reserve *Bulletin.*

INSIDE THE FED

The Special Role of the Federal Reserve Bank of New York

The Federal Reserve Bank of New York plays a special role in the Federal Reserve System for several reasons. First, its district contains many of the largest commercial banks in the United States, the safety and soundness of which are paramount to the health of the U.S. financial system. The Federal Reserve Bank of New York conducts examinations of bank holding companies and state-chartered member banks in its district, making it the supervisor of some of the most important financial institutions in our financial system. Not surprisingly, given this responsibility, the bank supervision group is one of the largest units of the New York Fed and is by far the largest bank supervision group in the Federal Reserve System.

The second reason for the New York Fed's special role is its active involvement in the bond and foreign exchange markets. The New York Fed houses the open market desk, which conducts open market operations—the purchase and sale of bonds—that determine the amount of reserves in the banking system. Because of this involvement in the Treasury securities market, as well as its walking-distance location near the New York and American Stock Exchanges, the officials at the Federal Reserve Bank of New York are in constant contact with the major domestic financial markets in the United States. In addition, the Federal Reserve Bank of New York houses the foreign exchange desk, which conducts foreign exchange interventions on behalf of the Federal Reserve System and the U.S. Treasury. Its involvement in these financial markets means that the New York Fed is an important source of information on what is happening in domestic and foreign financial markets, particularly during crisis periods such as the one we experienced from 2007 to 2009, as well as a liaison between officials in the Federal Reserve System and private participants in the markets.

The third reason for the Federal Reserve Bank of New York's prominence is that it is the only Federal Reserve bank to be a member of the Bank for International Settlements (BIS). Thus, the president of the New York Fed, along with the chair of the Board of Governors, represents the Federal Reserve System in its regular monthly meetings with other major central bankers at the BIS. This close contact with foreign central bankers and interaction with foreign exchange markets means that the New York Fed has a special role in international relations, both with other central bankers and with private market participants. Adding to its prominence in international circles, the New York Fed is the repository for more than $100 billion of the world's gold, an amount greater than the gold at Fort Knox.

Finally, the president of the Federal Reserve Bank of New York is the only permanent voting member of the FOMC among the Federal Reserve bank presidents, serving as the vice-chair of the committee. Thus, he or she and the chair and vice-chair of the Board of Governors are the three most important officials in the Federal Reserve System.

and C. The three A directors (elected by the member banks) are professional bankers, and the three B directors (also elected by the member banks) are prominent leaders from industry, labor, agriculture, or the consumer sector. The three C directors, who are appointed by the Board of Governors to represent the public interest, are not allowed to be officers, employees, or stockholders of banks. The directors oversee the activities of the district bank, but their most important job is to appoint the president of the bank (subject to the approval of the Board of Governors). Up until 2010, all nine directors participated in this decision, but the Dodd-Frank legislation in July 2010 excluded the three class A directors from involvement in choosing the president of the bank. Congress viewed it as inappropriate for bankers to be involved in choosing the president of the Federal Reserve bank that would have supervisory oversight of these same banks.

The twelve Federal Reserve banks are involved in monetary policy in several ways:

- Their directors legally "establish" the discount rate (although the discount rate is in practice set at a fixed amount over the federal funds rate target).
- They decide which banks, member and nonmember alike, can obtain discount loans from the Federal Reserve bank.
- Their directors select one commercial banker from each bank's district to serve on the Federal Advisory Council, which consults with the Board of Governors and provides information that helps in the conduct of monetary policy.
- Five of the 12 bank presidents each have a vote on the Federal Open Market Committee, which directs **open market operations** (the purchase and sale of government securities that affect both interest rates and the amount of reserves in the banking system). As explained in the Inside the Fed box, "The Special Role of the Federal Reserve Bank of New York," because the president of the New York Fed is a permanent member of the FOMC, he or she always has a vote on the FOMC, making it the most important of the banks; the other four votes allocated to the district banks rotate annually among the remaining 11 presidents.

The 12 Federal Reserve banks perform the following functions:

- Clear checks and hold reserve deposits of banks in their districts
- Issue new currency and withdraw damaged currency from circulation
- Administer and make discount loans to banks in their districts
- Evaluate proposed mergers and applications for banks to expand their activities
- Act as liaisons between the business community and the Federal Reserve System
- Examine bank holding companies and state-chartered member banks
- Collect data on local business conditions
- Use their staffs of professional economists to research topics related to the conduct of monetary policy

Member Banks

All *national banks* (commercial banks chartered by the Office of the Comptroller of the Currency) are required to be members of the Federal Reserve System. Commercial banks chartered by the states are not required to be members, but they can choose to join. Currently about 38% of the commercial banks in the United States are members of the Federal Reserve System, having declined from a peak figure of 49% in 1947.

Before 1980, only member banks were required to keep reserves as deposits at the Federal Reserve banks. Nonmember banks were subject to reserve requirements determined by their states, which typically allowed them to hold much of their reserves in interest-bearing securities. Because at the time no interest was paid on reserves deposited at the Federal Reserve banks, it was costly to be a member of the system, and as interest rates rose, the relative cost of membership rose, and more and more banks left the system.

This decline in Fed membership was a major concern of the Board of Governors: One reason was that it lessened the Fed's control over the money supply, making it more difficult for the Fed to conduct monetary policy. The chair of the Board of Governors repeatedly called for new legislation requiring all commercial banks to be members of the Federal Reserve System. One result of the Fed's pressure on Congress was a provision in the Depository Institutions Deregulation and Monetary Control Act of 1980: All depository institutions became subject (by 1987) to the same requirements to keep deposits at the Fed, so member and nonmember banks would be on an equal footing in terms of reserve requirements. In addition, all depository institutions were given access to the Federal Reserve facilities, such as the discount window (discussed in Chapter 10) and Fed check clearing, on an equal basis. These provisions ended the decline in Fed membership and reduced the distinction between member and nonmember banks.

Board of Governors of the Federal Reserve System

GO ONLINE

Access **http://www.federalreserve.gov/aboutthefed/bios/board/default.htm** for lists of all the members of the Board of Governors of the Federal Reserve since its inception.

At the head of the Federal Reserve System is the seven-member Board of Governors, headquartered in Washington, D.C. Each governor is appointed by the president of the United States and confirmed by the Senate. To limit the president's control over the Fed and insulate the Fed from other political pressures, the governors can serve one nonrenewable, 14-year term plus part of another term, with one governor's term expiring every other January.[1] The governors (many are professional economists) are required to come from different Federal Reserve districts to prevent the interests of one region of the country from being overrepresented. The chair of the Board of Governors is chosen from among the seven governors and serves a four-year, renewable term. It is expected that once a new chair is chosen, the old chair resigns from the Board of Governors, even if there are many years left to his or her term as a governor.

The Board of Governors is actively involved in decisions concerning the conduct of monetary policy in the following ways.

- All seven governors are members of the FOMC and vote on the conduct of open market operations. Because only 12 voting members are on this committee (seven governors and five presidents of the district banks), the Board has the majority of the votes.
- It sets reserve requirements (within limits imposed by legislation) and effectively controls the fixed amount over the federal funds rate the discount rate is set by the "review and determination" process, whereby it approves or disapproves the discount rate "established" by the Federal Reserve banks.

[1]Although technically the governor's term is nonrenewable, a governor can resign just before the term expires and then be reappointed by the president. This explains how one governor, William McChesney Martin, Jr., served for 28 years. Since Martin, the chair from 1951 to 1970, retired from the Board in 1970, the practice of allowing a governor to, in effect, serve a second full term has not been continued, and this is why Alan Greenspan had to retire from the Board after his fourteen-year term expired in 2006.

- The chair of the Board advises the president of the United States on economic policy, testifies in Congress, and speaks for the Federal Reserve System to the media.

The Board of Governors has other duties not directly related to the conduct of monetary policy, which are as follows.

- Sets margin requirements, the fraction of the purchase price of securities that has to be paid for with cash rather than borrowed funds.
- Sets the salary of the president and all officers of each Federal Reserve bank and reviews each bank's budget.
- Approves bank mergers and applications for new activities, specifies the permissible activities of bank holding companies, and supervises the activities of foreign banks in the United States.
- Has a staff of professional economists (larger than those of individual Federal Reserve banks), which provides economic analysis that the Board of Governors uses in making its decisions (see the Inside the Fed box, "The Role of the Research Staff").

Federal Open Market Committee (FOMC)

Access **www.federalreserve.gov/fomc** and find general information on the FOMC, as well as its schedule of meetings, statements, minutes, and transcripts; information on its members; and the "beige book."

The Federal Open Market Committee (FOMC) usually meets eight times a year (about every six weeks) and makes decisions regarding the conduct of open market operations and the setting of the policy interest rate, the **federal funds rate**, which is the interest rate on overnight loans from one bank to another. (How the FOMC meeting is conducted is discussed in the Inside the Fed box, "The FOMC Meeting," and the documents produced for the meeting are described in the other Inside the Fed box, "Green, Blue, Teal, and Beige: What Do These Colors Mean at the Fed?") Indeed, the FOMC is often referred to as the "Fed" in the press: For example, when the media say that the Fed is meeting, they actually mean that the FOMC is meeting. The committee consists of the seven members of the Board of Governors, the president of the Federal Reserve Bank of New York, and the presidents of four other Federal Reserve banks. The chair of the Board of Governors also presides as the chair of the FOMC. Even though only the presidents of five of the Federal Reserve banks are voting members of the FOMC, the other seven presidents of the district banks attend FOMC meetings and participate in discussions. Hence they have some input into the committee's decisions.

Because in the past open market operations were the most important policy tool the Fed had for controlling interest rates and the money supply and because it is where decisions about **tightening of monetary policy** (a rise in the federal funds rate) or an **easing of monetary policy** (a lowering of the federal funds rate) are made, the FOMC is necessarily the focal point for policy making in the Federal Reserve System. Although reserve requirements and the discount rate are not actually set by the FOMC, decisions in regard to these policy tools are effectively made there, and this is why Figure 9.1 has dashed lines indicating that the FOMC "advises" on the setting of reserve requirements and the discount rate. The FOMC does not actually carry out securities purchases or sales. Instead, it issues directives to the trading desk at the Federal Reserve Bank of New York, where the manager for domestic open market operations supervises a roomful of people who execute the

> INSIDE THE FED

The Role of the Research Staff

The Federal Reserve System is the largest employer of economists not just in the United States, but in the world. The system's research staff has approximately 1,000 people, about half of whom are economists. Of these 500 economists, about 250 are at the Board of Governors, 100 are at the Federal Reserve Bank of New York, and the remainder are at the other Federal Reserve banks. What do all these economists do?

The most important task of the Fed's economists is to follow the incoming data on the economy from government agencies and private-sector organizations and provide guidance to the policy makers on where the economy may be heading and what the impact of monetary policy actions on the economy might be. Before each FOMC meeting, the research staff at each Federal Reserve bank briefs its president and the senior management of the bank on its forecast for the U.S. economy and the issues that are likely to be discussed at the meeting. The research staff also provides briefing materials or a formal briefing on the economic outlook for the bank's region, something that each president discusses at the FOMC meeting. Meanwhile, at the Board of Governors, economists maintain a large econometric model (a model whose equations are estimated with statistical procedures) that helps them produce their forecasts of the national economy, and they, too, brief the governors on the national economic outlook.

The research staffers at the banks and the Board also provide support for the bank supervisory staff, tracking developments in the banking sector and other financial markets and institutions and supplying bank examiners with technical advice that they might need in the course of their examinations. Because the Board of Governors has to decide on whether to approve bank mergers, the research staffs at both the Board and the bank in whose district the merger is to take place prepare information on what effect the proposed merger might have on the competitive environment. To ensure compliance with the Community Reinvestment Act, economists also analyze a bank's performance in its lending activities in different communities.

Because of increased influence of developments in foreign countries on the U.S. economy, members of the research staff, particularly those at the New York Fed and the Board, produce reports on the major foreign economies. They also conduct research on developments in the foreign exchange market because of its growing importance in the monetary policy process, and to support the activities of the foreign exchange desk. Economists help support the operation of the open market desk by projecting banks' reserves growth and the growth of monetary aggregates.

Staff economists also engage in basic research on the effects of monetary policy on output and inflation, developments in the labor markets, international trade, international capital markets, banking and other financial institutions, financial markets, and the regional economy, among other topics. This research is published widely in academic journals and in Reserve bank publications. (Federal Reserve bank reviews are a good source of supplemental material for finance students.)

Another important activity of the research staff primarily at the Reserve banks is in the public education area. Staff economists are called on frequently to make presentations to the board of directors at their banks or to make speeches to the public in their district.

purchases and sales of the government or agency securities. The manager communicates daily with the FOMC members and their staffs concerning the activities of the trading desk.

Why the Chair of the Board of Governors Really Runs the Show

At first glance, the chair of the Board of Governors is just one of 12 voting members of the FOMC and has no legal authority to exercise control over this body. So why do the media pay so much attention to every word the chair speaks? Does the

> INSIDE THE FED

The FOMC Meeting

The FOMC meeting takes place in the boardroom on the second floor of the main building of the Board of Governors in Washington, D.C. The seven governors and the 12 Reserve Bank presidents, along with the secretary of the FOMC, the Board's director of the Research and Statistics Division and his deputy, and the directors of the Monetary Affairs and International Finance Divisions, sit around a massive conference table. Although only five of the Reserve Bank presidents have voting rights on the FOMC at any given time, all actively participate in the deliberations. Seated around the sides of the room are the directors of research at each of the Reserve banks and other senior board and Reserve Bank officials, who, by tradition, do not speak at the meeting.

The meeting starts with a quick approval of the minutes of the previous meeting of the FOMC. The first substantive agenda item is the report by the manager of system open market operations on foreign currency and domestic open market operations and other issues related to these topics. After the governors and Reserve Bank presidents finish asking questions and discussing these reports, a vote is taken to ratify them.

The next stage in the meeting is a presentation of the Board staff's national economic forecast by the director of the Research and Statistics Division at the Board. After the governors and Reserve Bank presidents have queried the division director about the forecast, the *go-round* occurs: Each bank president presents an overview of economic conditions in his or her district and the bank's assessment of the national outlook, and each governor, including the chair, gives a view of the national outlook. By tradition, remarks avoid the topic of monetary policy at this time.

The agenda then turns to current monetary policy and the domestic policy directive. The Board's director of the Monetary Affairs Division leads off the discussion by outlining the different scenarios for monetary policy actions and may describe an issue relating to how monetary policy should be conducted. After a question-and-answer period, each of the FOMC members, as well as the nonvoting bank presidents, expresses his or her views on monetary policy and on the monetary policy statement. The chair then summarizes the discussion and proposes specific wording for the monetary policy statement and the directive on the federal funds rate target transmitted to the open market desk, indicating whether the federal funds target is to be raised or lowered, say, by ¼ of a percentage point. The secretary of the FOMC formally reads the proposed statement and the members of the FOMC vote.* A public announcement about the monetary policy statement is made around 2:15 p.m.**

*The decisions expressed in the directive may not be unanimous, and the dissenting views are made public. However, except in rare cases, the chair's vote is always on the winning side.

**Half of the meetings have a somewhat different format. Rather than starting Tuesday morning at 9:00 A.M., like the other meetings, they start in the afternoon on Tuesday and go over into Wednesday, with the usual announcement around 2:15 P.M.. These longer meetings also consider the longer-term economic outlook and special topics.

chair really call the shots at the Fed? If so, why does the chair have so much power?

The chair does indeed run the show. He or she is the spokesperson for the Fed and negotiates with Congress and the president of the United States. He or she also exercises control by setting the agenda of Board and FOMC meetings. The chair also influences the Board through the force of stature and personality. Chairs of the Board of Governors (including Marriner S. Eccles, William McChesney Martin, Jr., Arthur Burns, Paul A. Volcker, Alan Greenspan, Ben Bernanke, and Janet Yellen) have typically had strong personalities and have wielded great power.

The chair also exercises power by supervising the Board's staff of professional economists and advisers. Because the staff gathers information for the Board and conducts the analyses the Board uses in its decisions, it has some influence over

> INSIDE THE FED

Green, Blue, Teal, and Beige: What Do These Colors Mean at the Fed?

Three research documents play an important role in the monetary policy process and at Federal Open Market Committee meetings. Up until 2010, a detailed national forecast for the next three years, generated by the Federal Reserve Board of Governors' Research and Statistics Division, was placed between green covers and was thus known as the "green book." Projections for the monetary aggregates prepared by the Monetary Affairs Division of the Board of Governors, along with typically three alternative scenarios for monetary policy decisions (labeled A, B, and C), were contained in the "blue book" in blue covers. Both books were distributed to all participants in FOMC meetings. Starting in 2010, the green and the blue books were combined into the "teal book" with teal covers: Teal is the color that is a combination of green and blue.* The "beige book," with beige covers, is produced by the Reserve banks and details evidence gleaned either from surveys or from talks with key businesses and financial institutions on the state of the economy in each of the Federal Reserve districts. This is the only one of the books that is distributed publicly, and it often receives a lot of attention in the press.

*These FOMC documents are made public after five years and their content can be found at http://www.federalreserve.gov/monetarypolicy/fomc.htm.

monetary policy. In addition, in the past, several appointments to the Board itself have come from within the ranks of its professional staff, making the chair's influence even farther-reaching and longer-lasting than a four-year term. The chair's style also matters, as the Inside the Fed box, "Styles of Federal Reserve Chairs: Bernanke and Yellen Versus Greenspan," suggests.

> INSIDE THE FED

Styles of Federal Reserve Chairs: Bernanke and Yellen Versus Greenspan

Every Federal Reserve chair has a different style that affects how policy decisions are made at the Fed. There has been much discussion of how recent chairs of the Fed, Ben Bernanke and Janet Yellen, differ from Alan Greenspan, who was the chair of the Federal Reserve Board for 19 years, from 1987 until 2006.

Alan Greenspan dominated the Fed like no prior Federal Reserve chair. His background was very different from that of Bernanke and Yellen, who spent most of the early part of their careers in academia. Greenspan, a disciple of Ayn Rand, was a strong advocate for laissez-faire capitalism and headed a very successful economic consulting firm, Townsend-Greenspan.* Greenspan was never an economic theorist but is rather famous for immersing himself in the data—literally so, because he was known to have done this in his bathtub at the beginning of the day—and often focused on rather obscure data series to come up with his forecasts. As a result, Greenspan did not rely exclusively on the Federal Reserve Board staff's forecast in making his policy decisions. A prominent example occurred during 1997, when the Board staff was forecasting a surge in inflation, which would have required a tightening of monetary policy. Yet Greenspan believed that inflation would not rise and convinced the FOMC not to tighten monetary

*For biographical information on Alan Greenspan and Ben Bernanke, see their books, Alan Greenspan, *The Age of Turbulence: Adventures in a New World* (New York: Penguin Press, 2007), and Ben S. Bernanke, *The Courage to Act: A Memoir of a Crisis and Its Aftermath* (New York: W. W. Norton, 2015).

policy. Greenspan proved to be right and was dubbed the "maestro" by the media.

Bernanke, in contrast, before going to Washington as a governor of the Fed in 2002, and then as the chair of the Council of Economic Advisors in 2005, and finally back to the Fed as chair in 2006, spent his entire career as a professor, first at Stanford University's Graduate School of Business and then in the Economics Department at Princeton University, where he became chair. Similarly, Janet Yellen was a professor for twenty years at Harvard University and then the University of California, before working in the Federal Reserve System as a member of the Board of Governors from 1994 to 1997, president of the Federal Reserve Bank of San Francisco from 2004 to 2010, and then vice-chair of the Federal Reserve from 2010 to 2014. Because Bernanke and Yellen did not make their names as economic forecasters, the Board staff's forecast now plays a much greater role in decision making at the FOMC. In contrast to Greenspan's approach, Bernanke and Yellen's background as top academic economists meant that they focus on analytics in making their decisions. The result is a much greater use of model simulations in guiding policy discussions.

The style of policy discussions has also changed with the new chair. Greenspan exercised extensive control of the discussion at the FOMC. During the Greenspan era, the discussion was formal, with each participant speaking after being put on a list by the secretary of the FOMC. Under Bernanke and Yellen, there is more give and take. They both have encouraged so-called two-handed interventions. When a participant wants to go out of turn to ask a question or make a point about something that one of the other participants has just said, he or she raises two hands and is then acknowledged by the chair and called on to speak.

The order of the discussion at the FOMC has also changed in a very subtle but extremely important way. Under Greenspan, after the other FOMC participants had expressed their views on the economy, Greenspan would present his views on the state of the economy and then would make a recommendation for what monetary policy action should be taken. This required that the other participants would then just agree or disagree with the chair's recommendation in the following round of discussion about monetary policy. In contrast, usually Bernanke did not, and Yellen does not, make a recommendation for monetary policy immediately after other FOMC participants have expressed their views on the economy. Instead, they summarize what they have heard from the other participants, add some comments of their own, and then wait until after they have heard the views of all the other participants about monetary policy before making their policy recommendation. The process under Greenspan meant that the chair was pretty much making the decision about policy, whereas Bernanke and Yellen's procedure is more democratic and enables participants to have greater influence over the chair's vote.

Another big difference in style is in terms of transparency. Greenspan was famous for being obscure, and even quipped at a congressional hearing, "I guess I should warn you, if I turn out to be particularly clear, you've probably misunderstood what I've said." Bernanke and Yellen try to be particularly clear speakers. Although advances in transparency were made under Greenspan, he adopted more transparent communication reluctantly. Bernanke and Yellen have been much stronger supporters of transparency, having advocated that the Fed announce its inflation objective and having launched a major initiative in 2006 to study Federal Reserve communications that resulted in substantial increases in Fed transparency (as discussed in the Inside the Fed box on the evolution of the Fed's communication strategy on page 201).

How Independent Is the Fed?

When we look in the next chapter at how the Federal Reserve conducts monetary policy, we will want to know why it decides to take certain policy actions but not others. To understand its actions, we must understand the incentives that motivate the Fed's behavior. How free is the Fed from presidential and congressional pressures? Do economic, bureaucratic, or political considerations guide it? Is the Fed truly independent of outside pressures?

Stanley Fischer, who was a professor at MIT and is now the vice-chair of the Federal Reserve, has defined two types of independence of central banks: **instrument independence**, the ability of the central bank to set monetary policy instruments, and **goal independence**, the ability of the central bank to set the goals of monetary policy. The Federal Reserve has both types of independence and is remarkably free of the political pressures that influence other government agencies. Not only are the members of the Board of Governors appointed for a 14-year term (and so cannot be ousted from office) but also the term is technically not renewable, eliminating some of the incentive for the governors to curry favor with the president and Congress.

Probably even more important to its independence from the whims of Congress is the Fed's independent and substantial source of revenue from its holdings of securities and, to a lesser extent, from its loans to banks. In 2015, for example, the Fed had net earnings after expenses of slightly over $100 billion—not a bad living if you can find it! Because it returns the bulk of these earnings to the Treasury, it does not get rich from its activities, but this income gives the Fed an important advantage over other government agencies: It is not subject to the appropriations process usually controlled by Congress. Indeed, the General Accounting Office, the auditing agency of the federal government, cannot currently audit the monetary policy or foreign exchange market functions of the Federal Reserve. Because the power to control the purse strings is usually synonymous with the power of overall control, this feature of the Federal Reserve System contributes to its independence more than any other factor.

Yet the Federal Reserve is still subject to the influence of Congress because the legislation that structures it is written by Congress and is subject to change at any time. When legislators are upset with the Fed's conduct of monetary policy, they frequently threaten to weaken its independence. A recent example was a bill sponsored by Representative Ron Paul in 2009 to subject the Fed's monetary policy actions to audits by the General Accounting Office (GAO). Threats like this are a powerful club to wield, and it certainly has some effect in keeping the Fed from straying too far from congressional wishes.

Congress has also passed legislation to make the Federal Reserve more accountable for its actions. Under the Humphrey-Hawkins Act of 1978 and later legislation, the Federal Reserve is required to issue a *Monetary Policy Report to the Congress* semiannually, with accompanying testimony by the chair of the Board of Governors, to explain how the conduct of monetary policy is consistent with objectives given by the Federal Reserve Act.

The president can also influence the Federal Reserve. First, because congressional legislation can affect the Fed directly or affect its ability to conduct monetary policy, the president can be a powerful ally through his influence on Congress. Second, although ostensibly a president might be able to appoint only one or two members to the Board of Governors during each presidential term, in actual practice the president appoints members far more often. One reason is that most governors do not serve out a full 14-year term. (Governors' salaries are substantially below what they can earn in the private sector or even at universities, thus providing an incentive for them to return to academia or take private-sector jobs before their term expires.) In addition, the president is able to appoint a new chair of the Board of Governors every four years, and a chair who is not reappointed is expected to resign from the Board so that a new member can be appointed.

The power that the president enjoys through his appointments to the Board of Governors is limited, however. Because the term of the chair is not necessarily concurrent with that of the president, a president may have to deal with a chair of the Board of Governors appointed by a previous administration. Alan Greenspan, for example, was appointed chair in 1987 by President Ronald Reagan and was reappointed to another term by a Republican president, George H. W. Bush, in 1992. When Bill Clinton, a Democrat, became president in 1993, Greenspan had several years left to his term. Clinton was put under tremendous pressure to reappoint Greenspan when his term expired and did so in 1996 and again in 2000, even though Greenspan is a Republican.[2] George W. Bush, a Republican, then reappointed Greenspan in 2004, while Barack Obama, a Democrat, reappointed Ben Bernanke, a Republican, in 2010.

You can see that the Federal Reserve has extraordinary independence for a government agency. Nonetheless, the Fed is not free from political pressures. Indeed, to understand the Fed's behavior, we must recognize that public support for the actions of the Federal Reserve plays a very important role.[3]

Should the Fed Be Independent?

As we have seen, the Federal Reserve is probably the most independent government agency in the United States; this is also true for central banks in most other countries. Every few years, the question arises in Congress whether the independence given the Fed should be curtailed. Politicians who strongly oppose a Fed policy often want to bring it under their supervision, to impose a policy more to their liking. Should the Fed be independent, or would we be better off with a central bank under the control of the president or Congress?

The Case for Independence

The strongest argument for an independent central bank rests on the view that subjecting it to more political pressures would impart an inflationary bias to monetary policy. In the view of many observers, politicians in a democratic society are shortsighted because they are driven by the need to win their next election. With this as the primary goal, they are unlikely to focus on long-run objectives, such as promoting a stable price level. Instead, they will seek short-run solutions to problems, such as high unemployment and high interest rates, even if the short-run solutions have undesirable long-run consequences. For example, high money growth might lead initially to a drop in interest rates but might cause an increase later as inflation heats up. Would a Federal Reserve under the control of Congress or the president be more likely to pursue a policy of excessive money growth when interest rates are high, even though it would eventually lead to inflation and even higher

---

[2]Similarly, William McChesney Martin, Jr., the chair from 1951 to 1970, was appointed by President Truman (Dem.) but was reappointed by Presidents Eisenhower (Rep.), Kennedy (Dem.), Johnson (Dem.), and Nixon (Rep.). Also, Paul Volcker, the chair from 1979 to 1987, was appointed by President Carter (Dem.) but was reappointed by President Reagan (Rep.). Ben Bernanke was appointed by President Bush (Rep.) but was reappointed by President Obama (Dem.).

[3]An inside view of how the Fed interacts with the public and the politicians can be found in Bob Woodward, *Maestro: Greenspan's Fed and the American Boom* (New York: Simon and Schuster, 2000), and David Wessel, *In Fed We Trust* (New York: Random House, 2009).

interest rates in the future? The advocates of an independent Federal Reserve say yes. They believe that a politically insulated Fed is more likely to be concerned with long-run objectives and thus be a defender of a sound dollar and a stable price level.

A variation on the preceding argument is that the political process in America could lead to a **political business cycle**, in which just before an election, expansionary policies are pursued to lower unemployment and interest rates. After the election, the bad effects of these policies—high inflation and high interest rates—come home to roost, requiring contractionary policies that politicians hope the public will forget before the next election. There is some evidence that such a political business cycle exists in the United States, and a Federal Reserve under the control of Congress or the president might make the cycle even more pronounced.

Putting the Fed under the control of the Treasury (making it more subject to influence by the president) is also considered dangerous because the Fed can be used to facilitate Treasury financing of large budget deficits by its purchases of Treasury bonds.[4] Treasury pressure on the Fed to "help out" might lead to more inflation in the economy. An independent Fed is better able to resist this pressure from the Treasury.

Another argument for central bank independence is that control of monetary policy is too important to leave to politicians, a group that has repeatedly demonstrated a lack of expertise at making hard decisions on issues of great economic importance, such as reducing the budget deficit or reforming the banking system. Another way to state this argument is in terms of the principal–agent problem discussed in Chapter 7. Both the Federal Reserve and politicians are agents of the public (the principals) and, as we have seen, both politicians and the Fed have incentives to act in their own interest rather than in the interest of the public. The argument supporting Federal Reserve independence is that the principal–agent problem is worse for politicians than for the Fed because politicians have fewer incentives to act in the public interest.

Indeed, some politicians may prefer to have an independent Fed, which can be used as a public "whipping boy" to take some of the heat off their backs. It is possible that a politician who in private opposes an inflationary monetary policy will be forced to support such a policy in public for fear of not being reelected. An independent Fed can pursue policies that are politically unpopular yet in the public interest.

The Case Against Independence

Proponents of a Fed under the control of the president or Congress argue that it is undemocratic to have monetary policy (which affects everyone in the economy) controlled by an elite group responsible to no one. The current lack of accountability of the Federal Reserve has serious consequences: If the Fed performs badly, no provision is in place for replacing its officials (as there is with politicians). True, the Fed needs to pursue long-run objectives, but elected officials of Congress vote on long-run issues also (foreign policy, for example). If we push the argument further that policy is always performed better by elite groups like the Fed, we end up with such conclusions as the Joint Chiefs of Staff should determine military budgets or

---

[4]The Federal Reserve Act prohibited the Fed from buying Treasury bonds directly from the Treasury (except to roll over maturing securities); instead, the Fed buys Treasury bonds on the open market. One possible reason for this prohibition is consistent with the foregoing argument: The Fed would find it harder to facilitate Treasury financing of large budget deficits.

the IRS should set tax policies with no oversight from the president or Congress. Would you advocate this degree of independence for the Joint Chiefs or the IRS?

The public holds the president and Congress responsible for the economic well-being of the country, yet they lack control over the government agency that may well be the most important factor in determining the health of the economy. In addition, to achieve a cohesive program that will promote economic stability, monetary policy must be coordinated with fiscal policy (management of government spending and taxation). Only by placing monetary policy under the control of the politicians who also control fiscal policy can these two policies be prevented from working at cross-purposes.

Another argument against Federal Reserve independence is that an independent Fed has not always used its freedom successfully. The Fed failed miserably in its stated role as lender of last resort during the Great Depression, and its independence certainly didn't prevent it from pursuing an overly expansionary monetary policy in the 1960s and 1970s that contributed to rapid inflation in this period.

Our earlier discussion also suggests that the Federal Reserve is not immune from political pressures. Its independence may encourage it to pursue a course of narrow self-interest rather than the public interest.

No consensus has yet been reached on whether central bank independence is a good thing, although public support for independence of the central bank seems to have been growing in both the United States and abroad. As you might expect, people who like the Fed's policies are more likely to support its independence, while those who dislike its policies advocate a less independent Fed.

Central Bank Independence and Macroeconomic Performance Throughout the World

We have seen that advocates of an independent central bank believe that macroeconomic performance will be improved by making the central bank more independent. Empirical evidence seems to support this conjecture: When central banks are ranked from least independent to most independent, inflation performance is found to be the best for countries with the most independent central banks. Although a more independent central bank appears to lead to a lower inflation rate, this is not achieved at the expense of poorer real economic performance. Countries with independent central banks are no more likely to have high unemployment or greater output fluctuations than countries with less independent central banks.

Explaining Central Bank Behavior

One view of government bureaucratic behavior is that bureaucracies serve the public interest (this is the *public interest view*). Yet some economists have developed a theory of bureaucratic behavior that indicates other factors influencing how bureaucracies operate. The *theory of bureaucratic behavior* suggests that the objective of a bureaucracy is to maximize its own welfare, just as a consumer's behavior is motivated by the maximization of personal welfare and a firm's behavior is motivated by the maximization of profits. The welfare of a bureaucracy is related to its power and prestige. Thus this theory suggests that an important factor affecting a central bank's behavior is its attempt to increase its power and prestige.

What predictions does this view of a central bank like the Fed indicate? One is that the Federal Reserve will fight vigorously to preserve its autonomy, a prediction verified time and time again as the Fed has continually counterattacked congressional attempts to control its budget. In fact, it is extraordinary how effectively the Fed has been able to mobilize a lobby of bankers and business people to preserve its independence when threatened.

Another prediction is that the Federal Reserve will try to avoid conflict with powerful groups that might threaten to curtail its power and reduce its autonomy. The Fed's behavior may take several forms. One possible factor explaining why the Fed is sometimes slow to increase interest rates and thus smooth out their fluctuations is that it wishes to avoid a conflict with the president and Congress over increases in interest rates. The desire to avoid conflict with Congress and the president may also explain why in the past the Fed has not embraced transparency (see the Inside the Fed box, "The Evolution of the Fed's Communication Strategy").

> INSIDE THE FED

The Evolution of the Fed's Communication Strategy

As the theory of bureaucratic behavior predicts, the Fed has incentives to hide its actions from the public and from politicians to avoid conflicts with them. In the past, this motivation led to a penchant for secrecy in the Fed, about which one former Fed official remarked that "a lot of staffers would concede that [secrecy] is designed to shield the Fed from political oversight."* For example, the Fed pursued an active defense of delaying its release of FOMC directives to Congress and the public. However, in 1994 it began to reveal the FOMC directives immediately after each FOMC meeting. In 1999 it also began to immediately announce the "bias" toward which direction monetary policy was likely to go, later expressed as the balance of risks in the economy. In 2002 the Fed started to report the roll call vote on the federal funds rate target taken at the FOMC meeting. In December 2004, it moved up the release date of the minutes of FOMC meetings to three weeks after the meeting from six weeks, its previous policy.

The Fed has dramatically increased its transparency in recent years but was slower to do so than many other central banks. One important trend toward greater transparency is the announcement by a central bank of a specific numerical objective for inflation, often referred to as an inflation target, which will be discussed in the following chapter. Alan Greenspan was strongly opposed to the Fed's moving in this direction, but Chair Bernanke and Janet Yellen, who was the chair of an internal Federal Reserve subcommittee that proposed new communication policies, were much more favorably disposed, having advocated the announcement of a specific numerical inflation objective in their writings and speeches.

In November 2007, the Federal Reserve announced major enhancements to its communication strategy. First, the forecast horizon for the FOMC's projections under "appropriate policy" for inflation, unemployment, and GDP growth, which were mandated by the Humphrey-Hawkins legislation in 1978, was extended from two calendar years to three, with long-run projections added in 2009. In 2011, the Fed announced a further move toward increased transparency: After the FOMC meetings in April, June, November, and January, the chair of the Federal Reserve would give a press conference intended to further enhance the clarity and timeliness of the Federal Reserve's monetary policy communication.

Starting in August 2011, the Fed provided forward guidance on the target for the federal funds rate with FOMC statements that often specified levels of the federal funds rate that would be likely to occur on specific calendar dates. Starting in January 2012, the FOMC provided even more information about the future path of its policy interest rate by providing the FOMC participants' forecasts of the appropriate level of the target for the federal funds rate. At the same meeting, the FOMC adopted a numerical inflation objective of 2% to improve the control of inflation by anchoring inflation expectations more firmly.

---

*Quoted in "Monetary Zeal: How the Federal Reserve Under Volcker Finally Slowed Down Inflation," *Wall Street Journal*, December 7, 1984, p. 23.

The desire of the Fed to hold as much power as possible also explains why it vigorously pursued a campaign to gain control over more banks. The campaign culminated in legislation that expanded jurisdiction of the Fed's reserve requirements to *all* banks (not just the member commercial banks) by 1987.

The theory of bureaucratic behavior seems applicable to the Federal Reserve's actions, but we must recognize that this view of the Fed as being solely concerned with its own self-interest is too extreme. Maximizing one's welfare does not rule out altruism. (You might give generously to a charity because it makes you feel good about yourself, but in the process you are helping a worthy cause.) The Fed is surely concerned that it conduct monetary policy in the public interest. However, much uncertainty and disagreement exist over what monetary policy should be.[5] When it is unclear what is in the public interest, other motives may influence the Fed's behavior. In these situations, the theory of bureaucratic behavior may be a useful guide to predicting what motivates the Fed and other central banks.

Structure and Independence of the European Central Bank

Access **http://www.ecb.europa.eu/home/html/index.en.html** for details of the European Central Bank.

Until recently, the Federal Reserve had no rivals in terms of its importance in the central banking world. However, this situation changed in January 1999 with the full operational start-up of the European Central Bank (ECB) and European System of Central Banks (ESCB), which now conducts monetary policy for countries that are members of the European Monetary Union. These countries, taken together, have a population exceeding that in the United States and a GDP comparable to that of the United States. The Maastricht Treaty, which established the ECB and ESCB, patterned these institutions after the Federal Reserve in that central banks for each country (referred to as *National Central Banks*, or *NCBs*) have a similar role to that of the Federal Reserve banks. The European Central Bank, which is housed in Frankfurt, Germany, has an Executive Board that is similar in structure to the Board of Governors of the Federal Reserve; it is made up of the president (similar to the chair), the vice-president (similar to the vice-chair), and four other members (similar to the governors), who are appointed to eight-year, nonrenewable terms. The Governing Council, which comprises the Executive Board and the presidents of the National Central Banks, is similar to the FOMC and makes the decisions on monetary policy. While the presidents of the National Central Banks are appointed by their countries' governments, the members of the Executive Board are appointed by a committee consisting of the heads of state of all the countries that are part of the European Monetary Union.

Differences Between the European System of Central Banks and the Federal Reserve System

In the popular press, the European System of Central Banks is usually referred to as the European Central Bank (ECB), even though it would be more accurate to

[5]Economists are not sure how to measure money. So even if economists agreed that controlling the quantity of money is the appropriate way to conduct monetary policy (a controversial position), the Fed cannot be sure which monetary aggregate it should control.

refer to it as the *Eurosystem*, just as it would be more accurate to refer to the Federal Reserve System rather than the Fed. Although the structure of the Eurosystem is similar to that of the Federal Reserve System, some important differences distinguish the two. First, the budgets of the Federal Reserve Banks are controlled by the Board of Governors, whereas the National Central Banks control their own budgets *and* the budget of the ECB in Frankfurt. The ECB in the Eurosystem therefore has less power than does the Board of Governors in the Federal Reserve System. Second, the monetary operations of the Eurosystem are conducted by the National Central Banks in each country, so monetary operations are not centralized as they are in the Federal Reserve System.

Governing Council

Just as there is a focus on meetings of the FOMC in the United States, there is a similar focus in Europe on meetings of the Governing Council, which meets monthly at the ECB in Frankfurt to make decisions on monetary policy. Currently, 17 countries are members of the European Monetary Union, and the head of each of the 17 National Central Banks has one vote in the Governing Council; each of the six Executive Board members also has one vote. In contrast to FOMC meetings, which staff from both the Board of Governors and individual Federal Reserve banks attend, only the 23 members of the Governing Council attend the meetings, with no staff present.

The Governing Council has decided that although its members have the legal right to vote, no formal vote will actually be taken; instead, the Council operates by consensus. One reason the Governing Council has decided not to take votes is because of worries that the casting of individual votes might lead the heads of National Central Banks to support a monetary policy that would be appropriate for their individual countries but not necessarily for the countries in the European Monetary Union as a whole. This problem is less severe for the Federal Reserve: Although Federal Reserve bank presidents do live in different regions of the country, all have the same nationality and are more likely to take a national view in monetary policy decisions rather than a regional view.

Just as the Federal Reserve releases the FOMC's decision on the setting of the policy interest rate (the federal funds rate) immediately after the meeting is over, the ECB does the same after the Governing Council meeting concludes (announcing the target for a similar short-term interest rate for interbank loans). In addition, immediately after every monetary policy meeting of the Governing Council, the president and vice president of the ECB hold a press conference in which they take questions from the news media. (A similar press conference is held by the Federal Reserve chair, but it is less frequent, only four times a year.) The large number of members in the Governing Council presents a particular dilemma. The current size of the Governing Council (twenty-five voting members) is substantially larger than the FOMC (twelve voting members). Many commentators have wondered whether the Governing Council is already too unwieldy—a situation that would get considerably worse as more countries join the European Monetary Union. To deal with this potential problem, the Governing Council has decided on a complex system of rotation, somewhat like that for the FOMC, in which National Central Banks from the larger countries will vote more often than National Central Banks from the smaller countries.

How Independent Is the ECB?

Although the Federal Reserve is a highly independent central bank, the Maastricht Treaty, which established the Eurosystem, has made the latter the most independent central bank in the world. Like the Board of Governors, the members of the Executive Board have long terms (eight years), while heads of National Central Banks are required to have terms at least five years long. Like the Fed, the Eurosystem determines its own budget, and the governments of the member countries are not allowed to issue instructions to the ECB. These elements of the Maastricht Treaty make the ECB highly independent.

The Maastricht Treaty specifies that the overriding, long-term goal of the ECB is price stability, which means that the goal for the Eurosystem is more clearly specified than it is for the Federal Reserve System. However, the Maastricht Treaty did not specify exactly what "price stability" means. The Eurosystem has defined the quantitative goal for monetary policy to be an inflation rate slightly less than 2%. In one way, the ECB is substantially more goal-independent than the Federal Reserve System: The Eurosystem's charter cannot be changed by legislation; it can be changed only by revision of the Maastricht Treaty—a difficult process because *all* signatories to the treaty must agree to accept any proposed change.

Structure and Independence of Other Foreign Central Banks

Here we examine the structure and degree of independence of three other important foreign central banks: the Bank of Canada, the Bank of England, and the Bank of Japan.

Bank of Canada

Access **www.bank-banque-canada.ca/** and find details on the Bank of Canada.

Canada was late in establishing a central bank: The Bank of Canada was founded in 1934. Its directors are appointed by the government to three-year terms, and they appoint the governor, who has a seven-year term. A governing council, consisting of the four deputy governors and the governor, is the policy-making body comparable to the FOMC that makes decisions about monetary policy.

The Bank Act was amended in 1967 to give the ultimate responsibility for monetary policy to the government. So on paper, the Bank of Canada is not as instrument-independent as the Federal Reserve. In practice, however, the Bank of Canada does essentially control monetary policy. In the event of a disagreement between the bank and the government, the minister of finance can issue a directive that the bank must follow. However, because the directive must be in writing and specific and applicable for a specified period, it is unlikely that such a directive would be issued, and none has been to date. The goal for monetary policy, a target for inflation, is set jointly by the Bank of Canada and the government, so the Bank of Canada has less goal independence than the Fed.

Bank of England

Access **www.bankofengland.co.uk** for details on the Bank of England.

Founded in 1694, the Bank of England is the second oldest central bank (with the Riksbank of Sweden, the oldest). The Bank Act of 1946 gave the government statutory authority over the Bank of England. The Court (equivalent to a board of directors) of the Bank of England is made up of the governor and two deputy governors, who are appointed for five-year terms, and 16 nonexecutive directors, who are appointed for three-year terms.

Until 1997, the Bank of England was the least independent of the central banks examined in this chapter because the decision to raise or lower interest rates resided not within the Bank of England but with the Chancellor of the Exchequer (the equivalent of the U.S. Secretary of the Treasury). All of this changed when the new Labour government came to power in May 1997. At this time, the Chancellor of the Exchequer, Gordon Brown, made a surprise announcement that the Bank of England would henceforth have the power to set interest rates. However, the Bank was not granted total instrument independence: The government can overrule the Bank and set rates "in extreme economic circumstances" and "for a limited period." Nonetheless, as in Canada, because overruling the Bank would be so public and is supposed to occur only in highly unusual circumstances and for a limited time, it is likely to be a rare occurrence.

Because the United Kingdom is not a member of the European Monetary Union, the Bank of England makes its monetary policy decisions independently from the European Central Bank. The decision to set interest rates resides in the Monetary Policy Committee, made up of the governor, two deputy governors, two members appointed by the governor after consultation with the chancellor (normally central bank officials), plus four outside economic experts appointed by the chancellor. (Surprisingly, two of the four outside experts initially appointed to this committee were not British citizens—one was Dutch and the other American—and some later appointments have also not been British, including the current Governor, Mark Carney, who is Canadian.) The inflation target for the Bank of England is set by the Chancellor of the Exchequer, so the Bank of England is also less goal-independent than the Fed.

Bank of Japan

Access **www.boj.or.jp/en/index.htm** for details on the Bank of Japan.

The Bank of Japan (Nippon Ginko) was founded in 1882 during the Meiji Restoration. Monetary policy is determined by the Policy Board, which is composed of the governor; two vice-governors; and six outside members, all of whom are appointed by the cabinet, approved by the parliament, and serve for five-year terms.

Until 1998, the Bank of Japan was not formally independent of the government and the ultimate power resided with the Ministry of Finance. However, the Bank of Japan Law, which took effect in that year and was the first major change in the powers of the Bank of Japan in 55 years, changed this situation. In addition to stipulating that the objective of monetary policy is to attain price stability, the law granted greater instrument and goal independence to the Bank of Japan. Before this, the government had two voting members on the Policy Board, one from the Ministry of Finance and the other from the Economic Planning Agency. Now the government may send two representatives from these agencies to board meetings, but they no longer have voting rights, although they do have the ability to request delays in monetary policy decisions. In addition, the Ministry of Finance lost its authority to oversee many operations of the Bank of Japan, particularly the right to dismiss senior officials. However, the Ministry of Finance continues to have control over the part of the Bank's budget that is unrelated to monetary policy, and the recent episode in which the new Abe government put pressure on the Bank of Japan to adopt a 2% inflation target against the wishes of its current Governor, who then resigned, suggests that the Bank of Japan's independence is limited.

The Trend Toward Greater Independence

As our survey of the structure and independence of the major central banks indicates, in recent years we have been seeing a remarkable trend toward increasing independence. It used to be that the Federal Reserve was substantially more independent than almost all other central banks, with the exception of those in Germany and Switzerland. Now the newly established European Central Bank is far more independent than the Fed, and greater independence has been granted to central banks like the Bank of England and the Bank of Japan, putting them more on a par with the Fed, as well as to central banks in such diverse countries as New Zealand, Sweden, and the euro nations. Both theory and experience suggest that more independent central banks produce better monetary policy, thus providing an impetus for this trend.

SUMMARY

1. The Federal Reserve System was created in 1913 to lessen the frequency of bank panics. Because of public hostility to central banks and the centralization of power, the Federal Reserve System was created with many checks and balances to diffuse power.
2. The formal structure of the Federal Reserve System consists of 12 regional Federal Reserve banks, about 3,000 member commercial banks, the Board of Governors of the Federal Reserve System, the Federal Open Market Committee (FOMC), and the Federal Advisory Council.
3. Although on paper the Federal Reserve System appears to be decentralized, in practice it has come to function as a unified central bank controlled by the Board of Governors, especially the Board's chair.
4. The Federal Reserve is more independent than most agencies of the U.S. government, but it is still subject to political pressures because the legislation that structures the Fed is written by Congress and can be changed at any time.
5. The case for an independent Federal Reserve rests on the view that curtailing the Fed's independence and subjecting it to more political pressures would impart an inflationary bias to monetary policy. An independent Fed can afford to take the long view and not respond to short-run problems that will result in expansionary monetary policy and a political business cycle. The case against an independent Fed holds that it is undemocratic to have monetary policy (so important to the public) controlled by an elite that is not accountable to the public. An independent Fed also makes the coordination of monetary and fiscal policy difficult.
6. The theory of bureaucratic behavior suggests that one factor driving central banks' behavior might be an attempt to increase their power and prestige. This view explains many central bank actions, although central banks may also act in the public interest.
7. The European System of Central Banks has a similar structure to that of the Federal Reserve System, with each member country having a National Central Bank, and an Executive Board of the European Central Bank being located in Frankfurt, Germany. The Governing Council, which is made up of the six members of the Executive Board (which includes the president of the European Central Bank) and the presidents of the National Central Banks, makes the decisions on monetary policy. The Eurosystem, which was established under the terms of the Maastricht Treaty, is even more independent than the Federal Reserve System because its charter cannot be changed by legislation. Indeed, it is the most independent central bank in the world.
8. There has been a remarkable trend toward increasing independence of central banks throughout the world. Greater independence has been granted to central banks such as the Bank of England and the Bank of Japan in recent years, as well as to other central banks in such diverse countries as New Zealand and Sweden. Both theory and experience suggest that more independent central banks produce better monetary policy, which maintains low inflation while avoiding high unemployment and output fluctuations.

KEY TERMS

Board of Governors of the Federal Reserve System, p. 187
easing of monetary policy, p. 192
federal funds rate, p. 192
Federal Open Market Committee (FOMC), p. 187
Federal Reserve banks, p. 187
goal independence, p. 197
instrument independence, p. 197
open market operations, p. 190
political business cycle, p. 199
tightening of monetary policy, p. 192

QUESTIONS AND PROBLEMS

1. Why was the Federal Reserve System set up with 12 regional Federal Reserve banks rather than one central bank, as in other countries?
2. What political realities might explain why the Federal Reserve Act of 1913 placed two Federal Reserve banks in Missouri?
3. "The Federal Reserve System resembles the U.S. Constitution in that it was designed with many checks and balances." Discuss.
4. In what ways can the regional Federal Reserve banks influence the conduct of monetary policy?
5. Which entities in the Federal Reserve System control the discount rate? Reserve requirements? Open market operations?
6. Do you think that the 14-year nonrenewable terms for governors effectively insulate the Board of Governors from political pressure?
7. Compare the structure and independence of the Federal Reserve System and the European System of Central Banks.
8. The Fed is the most independent of all U.S. government agencies. What is the main difference between it and other government agencies that explains the Fed's greater independence?
9. What is the primary tool that Congress uses to exercise some control over the Fed?
10. What are the fundamental differences between the styles of Greenspan and Bernanke and Yellen as chairs of the Fed? Do you think that the recent trend toward increased use of formal econometric analysis when making decisions about monetary policy is a good idea or not?
11. People in general welcome actions that promote transparency, and in particular when they involve public or quasi-public institutions. Can you think of a reason why a more transparent communication strategy might be detrimental to the Fed's objectives?
12. Why might eliminating the Fed's independence lead to a more pronounced political business cycle?
13. William does not feel comfortable with the current level of the Fed's independence. Put yourself in William's shoes and state an argument against the current level of the Fed's independence.
14. How would you argue in favor of the current trend toward central banks' independence?
15. The Fed promotes secrecy by not releasing the minutes of the FOMC meetings to Congress or the public immediately. Discuss the pros and cons of this policy.

WEB EXERCISES

Structures of the Federal Reserve System and the European System of Central Banks

1. Go to **http://www.federalreserve.gov/aboutthefed/**. Click on "The Federal Reserve Board" and choose "Board Members." Find biographical data of members of the Board of Governors by following the link on their names. Are there currently 7 members appointed, or are there empty seats?
2. Go to **https://www.ecb.europa.eu/ecb/orga/escb/html/index.en.html**. Click on "Organisation" and choose "Independence." What is the main argument used to defend the ECB's political independence?

CHAPTER 10

Conduct of Monetary Policy

> PREVIEW

Understanding the conduct of monetary policy is important because it affects not only interest rates but also the level of economic activity and hence our well-being. To explore this subject, we look first at how the Fed affects liquidity in the banking system, thereby affecting interest rates. Then we examine in detail how the Fed and other central banks use the tools of monetary policy and what goals they establish for monetary policy. Then we look at how central banks conduct monetary policy to achieve these goals, with the hope that it will give us some clues to where monetary policy may head in the future.

How Fed Actions Affect Reserves in the Banking System

All banks have an account at the Fed in which they hold deposits. **Reserves** consist of deposits at the Fed plus currency that is physically held by banks (called vault cash because it is stored in bank vaults). Reserves are assets for the banks but liabilities for the Fed because the banks can demand payment on them at any time and the Fed is obliged to satisfy its obligation by paying with Federal Reserve notes. The amount of reserves in the banking system is important because these reserves can be lent out, and thus when the Fed takes actions to increase these reserves, it increases liquidity in the banking system.

Total reserves can be divided into two categories: reserves that the Fed requires banks to hold (**required reserves**) and any additional reserves the banks choose to hold (**excess reserves**). For example, the Fed imposes regulations, called **reserve requirements**, making it obligatory for banking institutions to keep a certain fraction of their deposits as reserves with the Fed. For example, the Fed might require that for every dollar of deposits at a depository institution, a certain fraction (say, 10 cents) must be held as reserves. This fraction (10%) is called the **required reserve ratio**.

The Fed injects reserves into the banking system in two ways, through **open market operations**, the central bank's purchase or sale of securities in the open market, or by making loans to banks, which are referred to as **discount loans**.

Open Market Operations

Open market operations are the primary determinant of changes in reserves in the banking system. Federal Reserve purchasse and sales of bonds are always done with **primary dealers**, government securities dealers who operate out of private banking institutions. To see how open market operations work, we need to look at what happens to the Fed's **balance sheet**, its holdings of assets and liabilities. To understand how these actions affect the Fed's balance sheet, we use a tool called a **T-account**. A T-account is a simplified balance sheet, with lines in the form of a T, that lists only the changes that occur in balance sheet items starting from some initial balance sheet position. Let's use T-accounts to examine what happens when the Fed conducts an open market purchase in which $100 million of bonds are bought from primary dealers.

When the primary dealer sells the $100 million of bonds to the Fed, the Fed adds $100 million to the dealer's deposit account at the Fed, so that reserves in the banking system go up by $100 million. The banking system's T-account after this transaction is

Banking System

Assets		Liabilities
Securities	−$100 m	
Reserves (deposits at the Fed)	+$100 m	

The effect on the Fed's balance sheet is that it has gained $100 million of securities in its assets column, whereas reserves have increased by $100 million, as shown in its liabilities column:

Federal Reserve System			
Assets		**Liabilities**	
Securities	+$100 m	Reserves	+$100 m

As you can see, the result of the Fed's open market purchase is an expansion of the Fed's balance sheet with an increase in both its holdings of securities and reserves. The size of the banking system's balance sheet has not changed, with total assets remaining the same. However, the banking system's holdings of deposits at the Fed has increased, and since these can be lent out, liquidity in the banking system has increased.

Another way of looking at what has happened is to recognize that open market purchases of bonds expand reserves because the central bank pays for the bonds with reserves. ***An open market purchase leads to an expansion of reserves in the banking system.***

Similar reasoning indicates that when a central bank conducts an open market sale, reserves in the banking system fall because primary dealers pay for these bonds with their deposits held at the Fed (reserves). Thus, ***an open market sale leads to a contraction of reserves in the banking system.***

Discount Lending

Access **http://www.federalreserve.gov/releases/h3/** and view historic and current data on the aggregate reserves of depository institutions and the monetary base.

Open market operations are not the only way the Federal Reserve can affect the amount of reserves.

Reserves are also changed when the Fed makes a discount loan to a bank, also referred to as *borrowings from the Fed*, or alternatively, as *borrowed reserves*. During normal times, the Fed makes loans only to banking institutions and the interest rate charged banks for these loans is called the **discount rate**. (As we will discuss later in the chapter, during the recent financial crisis, the Fed made loans to other financial institutions.)

For example, suppose that the Fed makes a $100 million discount loan to the First National Bank. The Fed then credits $100 million to the bank's reserve account. The effects on the balance sheets of the banking system and the Fed are illustrated by the following T-accounts:

Banking System		Federal Reserve System	
Assets	**Liabilities**	**Assets**	**Liabilities**
Reserves +$100 m	Loans (borrowings from the Fed) +$100 m	Discount loans +$100 m	Reserves +$100 m

We thus see that ***a discount loan leads to an expansion of reserves, which can be lent out, thereby leading to an expansion of liquidity in the***

banking system. Similar reasoning indicates that ***when a bank repays its discount loan and so reduces the total amount of discount lending, the amount of reserves decreases along with liquidity in the banking system.***

The Market for Reserves and the Federal Funds Rate

We have just seen how open market operations and Federal Reserve lending affect the balance sheet of the Fed and the amount of reserves. Now we will analyze the market for reserves to see how the resulting changes in reserves affect the **federal funds rate**, the interest rate on overnight loans of reserves from one bank to another. The federal funds rate is particularly important in the conduct of monetary policy because it is the interest rate that the Fed tries to influence directly. Thus, it is indicative of the Fed's stance on monetary policy.

Demand and Supply in the Market for Reserves

The analysis of the market for reserves proceeds in a similar fashion to the analysis of the bond market we conducted in Chapter 4. We derive a demand and supply curve for reserves. Then the market equilibrium in which the quantity of reserves demanded equals the quantity of reserves supplied determines the federal funds rate, the interest rate charged on the loans of these reserves.

Demand Curve To derive the demand curve for reserves, we need to ask what happens to the quantity of reserves demanded, holding everything else constant, as the federal funds rate changes. Recall from the earlier section that the amount of reserves can be split into two components: (1) required reserves, which equal the required reserve ratio times the amount of deposits on which reserves are required, and (2) excess reserves, the additional reserves banks choose to hold. Therefore, the quantity of reserves demanded equals required reserves plus the quantity of excess reserves demanded. Excess reserves are insurance against deposit outflows, and the cost of holding these excess reserves is their opportunity cost, the interest rate that could have been earned on lending these reserves out, minus the interest rate that is earned on these reserves, i_{or}.

Before 2008 the Federal Reserve did not pay interest on reserves, but since the autumn of 2008 the Fed has paid interest on reserves at a level that is set at a fixed amount below the federal funds rate target and therefore changes when the target changes. When the federal funds rate is above the rate paid on excess reserves, i_{or}, as the federal funds rate decreases, the opportunity cost of holding excess reserves falls. Holding everything else constant, including the quantity of required reserves, the quantity of reserves demanded rises.

Consequently, the demand curve for reserves, R^d, slopes downward when the federal funds rate is above i_{or}, as Figure 10.1 shows. If, however, the federal funds rate begins to fall below the interest rate paid on reserves i_{or}, banks would not lend in the overnight market at a lower interest rate. Instead, they would just keep on adding to their holdings of excess reserves indefinitely. The result is that the demand curve for reserves, R^d, becomes flat (infinitely elastic) at i_{or} in Figure 10.1.

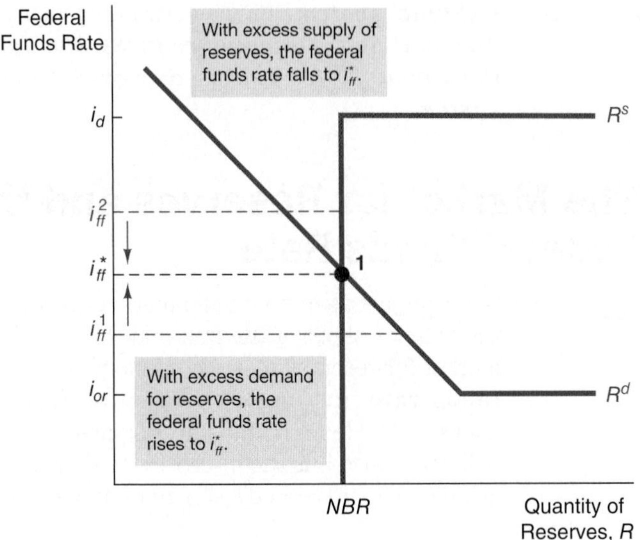

FIGURE 10.1 Equilibrium in the Market for Reserves

Equilibrium occurs at the intersection of the supply curve R^s and the demand curve R^d at point 1 and an interest rate of i^*_{ff}.

Supply Curve The supply of reserves, R^s, can be broken into two components: the amount of reserves that are supplied by the Fed's open market operations, *nonborrowed reserves* (*NBR*), and the amount of reserves borrowed from the Fed, called *borrowed reserves* (*BR*). The primary cost of borrowing from the Fed is the interest rate the Fed charges on these loans, the discount rate (i_d). Because borrowing federal funds from other banks is a substitute for borrowing (taking out discount loans) from the Fed, if the federal funds rate i_{ff} is below the discount rate i_d, then banks will not borrow from the Fed and borrowed reserves will be zero because borrowing in the federal funds market is cheaper. Thus, as long as i_{ff} remains below i_d, the supply of reserves will just equal the amount of nonborrowed reserves supplied by the Fed, *NBR*, and so the supply curve will be vertical, as shown in Figure 10.1. However, if the federal funds rate were to rise even infinitesimally above the discount rate, banks would want to keep borrowing more and more at i_d and then lending out the proceeds in the federal funds market at the higher rate, i_{ff}. The result is that the federal funds rate can never rise above the discount rate and the supply curve becomes flat (infinitely elastic) at i_d, as shown in Figure 10.1.

Access **www.economagic.com/** for a comprehensive listing of sites that offer a wide variety of economic summary data and graphs.

Market Equilibrium Market equilibrium occurs when the quantity of reserves demanded equals the quantity supplied, $R^s = R^d$. Equilibrium therefore occurs at the intersection of the demand curve R^d and the supply curve R^s at point 1, with an equilibrium federal funds rate of i^*_{ff}. When the federal funds rate is above the equilibrium rate at i^2_{ff}, more reserves are supplied than demanded (excess supply) and so the federal funds rate falls to i^*_{ff}, as shown by the downward arrow. When the federal funds rate is below the equilibrium rate at i^1_{ff}, more reserves are demanded than supplied (excess demand) and so the federal funds rate rises, as shown by the upward arrow. (Note that Figure 10.1 is drawn so that i_d is above i^*_{ff} because the

Federal Reserve typically keeps the discount rate substantially above the target for the federal funds rate.)

How Changes in the Tools of Monetary Policy Affect the Federal Funds Rate

GO ONLINE
Access **www.federalreserve.gov/fomc/fundsrate.htm**. This site lists historical federal funds rates and discusses Federal Reserve targets.

Now that we understand how the federal funds rate is determined, we can examine how changes in the four tools of monetary policy—open market operations, discount lending, reserve requirements, and the interest rate paid on reserves—affect the market for reserves and the equilibrium federal funds rate. The first two tools, open market operations and discount lending, affect the federal funds rate by injecting reserves into the banking system, thereby changing the supply of reserves, while the third tool, reserve requirements, affects the federal funds rate by changing the demand for reserves, and the fourth tool affects the federal funds rate by changing the interest rate paid on reserves.

Open Market Operations The effect of an open market operation depends on whether the supply curve initially intersects the demand curve in its downward-sloped section versus its flat section. Panel (a) of Figure 10.2 shows what happens if the intersection initially occurs on the downward-sloped section of the demand curve. We have already seen that an open market purchase leads to a greater quantity of reserves supplied; this is true at any given federal funds rate because of the higher

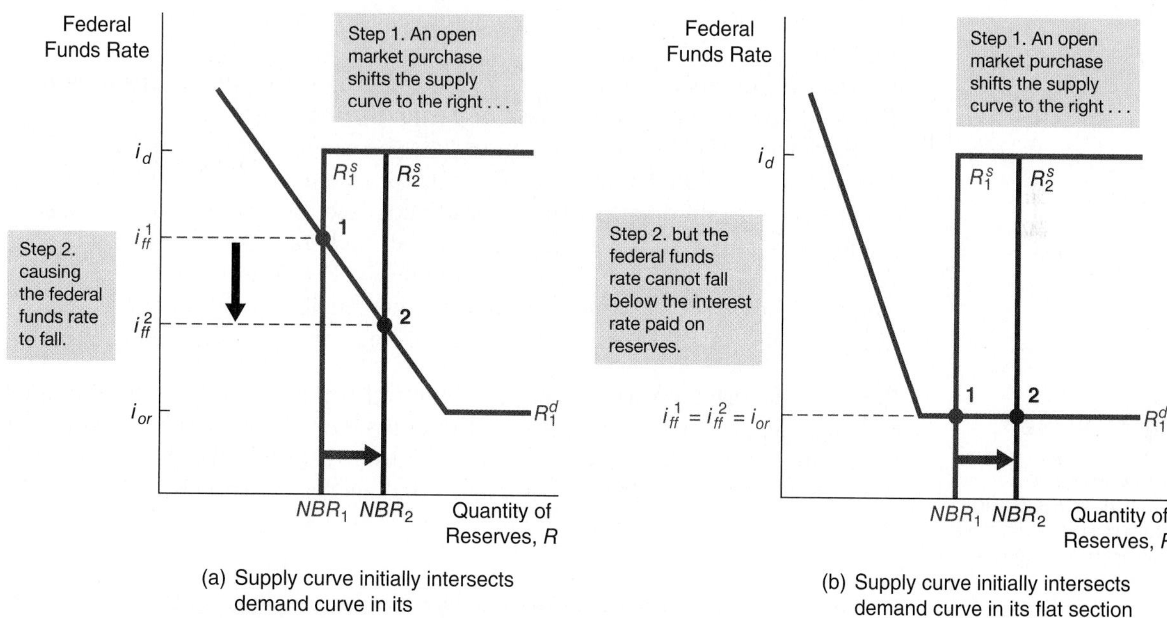

(a) Supply curve initially intersects demand curve in its downward-sloping section

(b) Supply curve initially intersects demand curve in its flat section

FIGURE 10.2 Response to an Open Market Operation

An open market purchase increases nonborrowed reserves and hence the reserves supplied, and shifts the supply curve from R_1^s to R_2^s. In panel (a), the equilibrium moves from point 1 to point 2, lowering the federal funds rate from i_{ff}^1 to i_{ff}^2. In panel (b), the equilibrium moves from point 1 to point 2, but the federal funds rate remains unchanged, $i_{ff}^1 = i_{ff}^2 = i_{or}$.

amount of nonborrowed reserves, which rises from NBR_1 to NBR_2. An open market purchase therefore shifts the supply curve to the right from R_1^s to R_2^s and moves the equilibrium from point 1 to point 2, lowering the federal funds rate from i_{ff}^1 to i_{ff}^2. The same reasoning implies that an open market sale decreases the quantity of nonborrowed reserves supplied, shifts the supply curve to the left, and causes the federal funds rate to rise. Because this is the typical situation—since the Fed usually keeps the federal funds rate target above the interest rate paid on reserves—the conclusion is that ***an open market purchase causes the federal funds rate to fall, whereas an open market sale causes the federal funds rate to rise.***

Access **www.frbdiscountwindow.org/** and find detailed information on the operation of the discount window and data on current and historical interest rates.

However, if the supply curve initially intersects the demand curve on its flat section, as in panel (b) of Figure 10.2, open market operations have no effect on the federal funds rate. To see this, let's again look at an open market purchase that raises the quantity of reserves supplied, which shifts the supply curve from R_1^s to R_2^s, but now where initially $i_{ff}^1 = i_{or}$. The shift in the supply curve moves the equilibrium from point 1 to point 2, but the federal funds rate remains unchanged at i_{or} because ***the interest rate paid on reserves, i_{or}, sets a floor for the federal funds rate.***[1]

Discount Lending The effect of a discount rate change depends on whether the demand curve initially intersects the supply curve in its vertical section versus its flat section. Panel (a) of Figure 10.3 shows what happens if the intersection occurs in the vertical section of the supply curve so there is no discount lending and borrowed reserves, BR, are zero. In this case, when the discount rate is lowered by the Fed from i_d^1 to i_d^2, the horizontal section of the supply curve falls, as in R_2^s, but the intersection of the supply and demand curves remains at point 1. Thus, in this case, no change occurs in the equilibrium federal funds rate, which remains at i_{ff}^1. Because this is the typical situation—since the Fed now usually keeps the discount rate above its target for the federal funds rate—the conclusion is that ***most changes in the discount rate have no effect on the federal funds rate.***

However, if the demand curve intersects the supply curve on its flat section, so there is some discount lending (i.e., $BR > 0$), as in panel (b) of Figure 10.3, changes in the discount rate do affect the federal funds rate. In this case, initially discount lending is positive and the equilibrium federal funds rate equals the discount rate, $i_{ff}^1 = i_d^1$. When the discount rate is lowered by the Fed from i_d^1 to i_d^2, the horizontal section of the supply curve R_2^S falls, moving the equilibrium from point 1 to point 2, and the equilibrium federal funds rate falls from i_{ff}^1 to $i_{ff}^2 (= i_d^2)$ in panel (b).

Access **http://www.federalreserve.gov/monetarypolicy/reservereq.htm** to find historical data and a discussion about reserve requirements.

Reserve Requirements When the required reserve ratio increases, required reserves increase and hence the quantity of reserves demanded increases for any given interest rate. Thus, a rise in the required reserve ratio shifts the demand curve to the right from R_1^d to R_2^d in Figure 10.4, moves the equilibrium from point 1

[1] The federal funds rate can be slightly below the floor set by the interest rate paid on reserves because some big lenders in the federal funds market, particularly Fannie Mae and Freddie Mac, are not banking institutions and so cannot keep deposits in the Federal Reserve and get paid the Fed's interest rate on reserves. Thus if they have excess funds to lend in the federal funds market, they may have to accept a federal funds rate lower than the interest rate the Fed pays on reserves. To make sure that the federal funds rate does not fall much below the floor set by the interest rate on reserves, the Federal Reserve has set up another borrowing facility, the *reverse repo facility*, in which these nonbank lenders can lend to the Fed and earn an interest rate that is close to the interest rate the Fed pays on reserves.

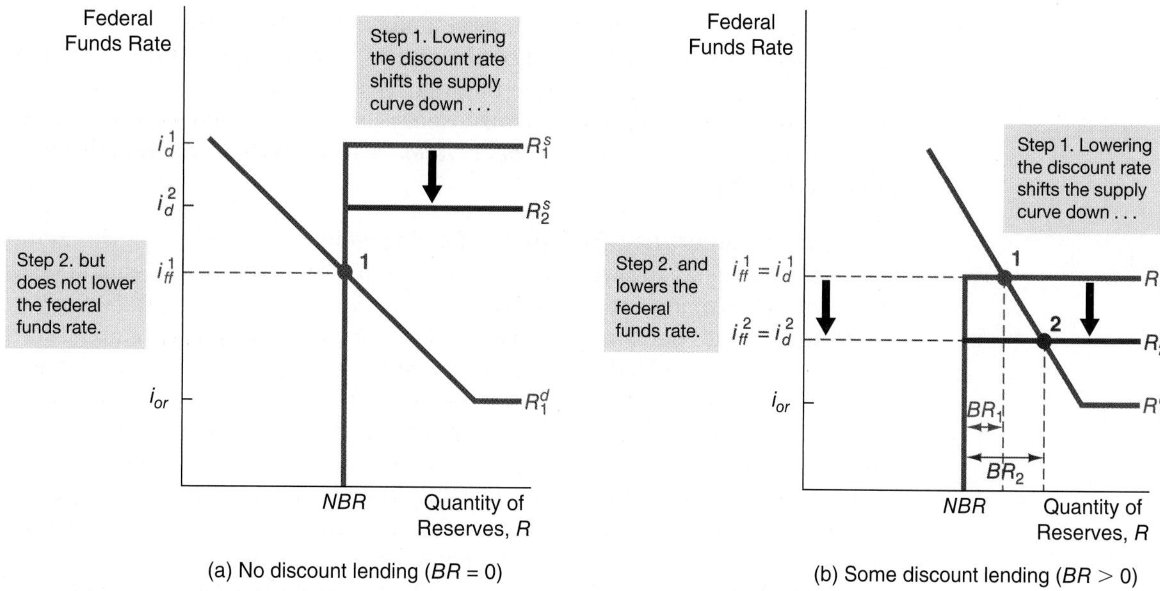

FIGURE 10.3 Response to a Change in the Discount Rate

In panel (a) when the discount rate is lowered by the Fed from i_d^1 to i_d^2, the horizontal section of the supply curve falls, as in R_2^s, and the equilibrium federal funds rate remains unchanged at i_{ff}^1. In panel (b) when the discount rate is lowered by the Fed from i_d^1 to i_d^2, the horizontal section of the supply curve R_2^s falls, and the equilibrium federal funds rate falls from i_{ff}^1 to i_{ff}^2 as borrowed reserves increase.

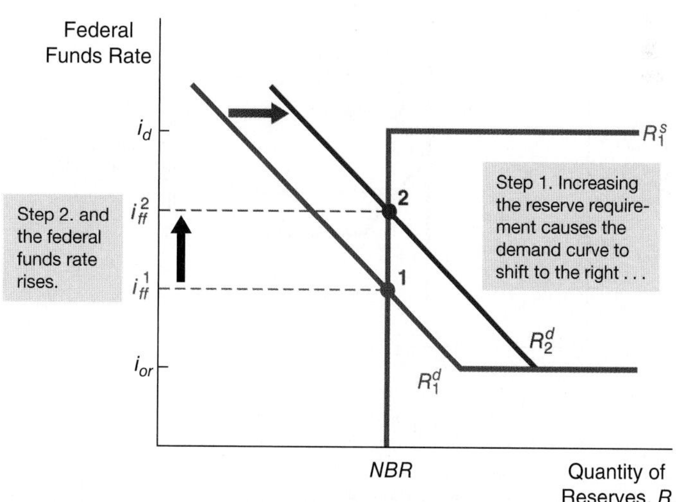

FIGURE 10.4 Response to a Change in Required Reserves

When the Fed raises reserve requirements, required reserves increase, which increases the demand for reserves. The demand curve shifts from R_1^d to R_2^d, the equilibrium moves from point 1 to point 2, and the federal fund rate rises from i_{ff}^1 to i_{ff}^2.

to point 2, and in turn raises the federal funds rate from i_{ff}^1 to i_{ff}^2. The result is that ***when the Fed raises reserve requirements, the federal funds rate rises.***

Conversely, a decline in the required reserve ratio lowers the quantity of reserves demanded, shifts the demand curve to the left, and causes the federal funds rate to fall. ***When the Fed decreases reserve requirements, the federal funds rate falls.***

Interest on Reserves The effect of a change in the interest rate the Fed pays on reserves depends on whether the supply curve intersects the demand curve in its downward-sloping versus its flat section. Panel (a) of Figure 10.5 shows what happens if the intersection occurs on the demand curve's downward-sloping section, where the equilibrium federal funds rate is above the interest rate paid on reserves. In this case, when the interest rate on reserves is raised from i_{or}^1 to i_{or}^2, the horizontal section of the demand curve rises, as in R_2^d, but the intersection of the supply and demand curves remains at point 1. However, if the supply curve intersects the demand curve on its flat section, where the equilibrium federal funds rate is at the interest rate paid on reserves, as in panel (b) of Figure 10.5, a rise in the interest rate on reserves from i_{or}^1 to i_{or}^2 moves the equilibrium to point 2, where the equilibrium federal funds rate rises from $i_{ff}^1 = i_{or}^1$ to $i_{ff}^2 = i_{or}^2$. ***When the federal funds rate is at the interest rate paid on reserves, a rise in the interest rate on reserves raises the federal funds rate.*** Conversely, in this situation, ***a fall in the interest rate paid on reserves lowers the federal funds rate.***

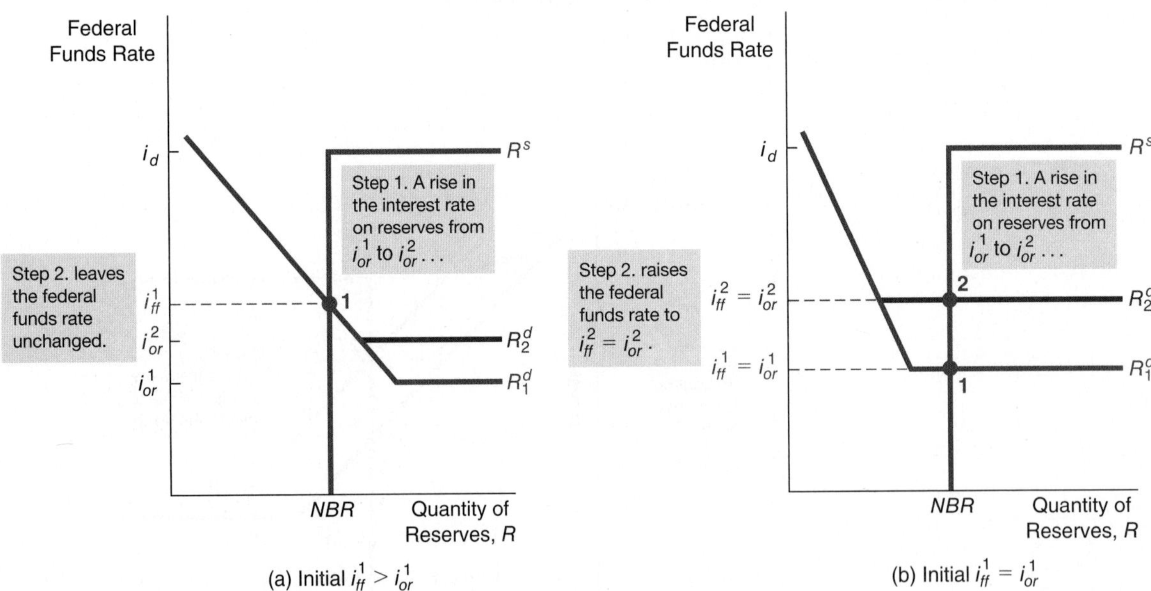

FIGURE 10.5 Response to a Change in the Interest Rate on Reserves

In panel (a) when the equilibrium federal funds rate is above the interest rate paid on reserves, a rise in the interest rate on reserves from i_{or}^1 to i_{or}^2 raises the horizontal section of the demand curve, as in R_2^d, but the equilibrium federal funds rate remains unchanged at i_{ff}^1. In panel (b) when the equilibrium federal funds rate is at the interest rate paid on reserves, a rise in the interest rate on reserves from i_{or}^1 to i_{or}^2 raises the equilibrium federal funds rate $i_{ff}^1 = i_{or}^1$ to $i_{ff}^2 = i_{or}^2$.

CASE

How the Federal Reserve's Operating Procedures Limit Fluctuations in the Federal Funds Rate

An important advantage of the Fed's current procedures for operating the discount window and paying interest on reserves is that they limit fluctuations in the federal funds rate. We can use our supply-and-demand analysis of the market for reserves to see why.

Suppose that initially the equilibrium federal funds rate is at the federal funds rate target of i^*_{ff} in Figure 10.6. If the demand for reserves has a large unexpected increase, the demand curve would shift to the right to $R^{d''}$, where it now intersects the supply curve for reserves on the flat portion where the equilibrium federal funds rate, i''_{ff}, equals the discount rate, i_d. No matter how far the demand curve shifts to the right, the equilibrium federal funds rate, i''_{ff}, will stay at i_d because borrowed reserves will just continue to increase, matching the increase in demand. Similarly, if the demand for reserves has a large unexpected decrease, the demand curve would shift to the left to $R^{d'}$, and the supply curve intersects the demand curve on its flat portion where the equilibrium federal funds rate, i'_{ff}, equals the interest rate paid on reserves i_{or}. No matter how far the demand curve shifts to the left, the equilibrium federal funds rate i'_{ff} will stay at i_{or} because excess reserves will just keep on

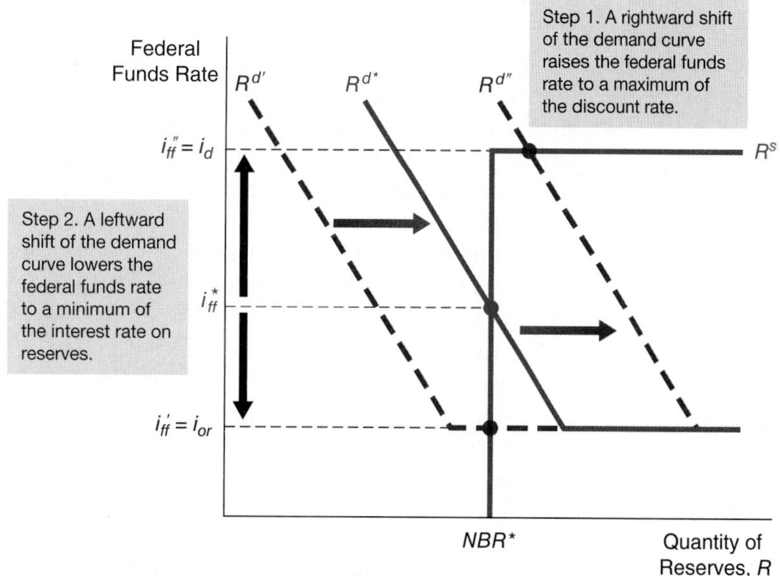

FIGURE 10.6 How the Federal Reserve's Operating Procedures Limit Fluctuations in the Federal Funds Rate

A shift to the right in the demand curve for reserves to $R^{d''}$ will raise the equilibrium federal funds rate to a maximum of $i''_{ff} = i_d$ while a shift to the left of the demand curve to $R^{d'}$ will lower the federal funds rate to a minimum of $i'_{ff} = i_{or}$.

increasing so that the quantity demanded of reserves equals the quantity of nonborrowed reserves supplied.*

Our analysis therefore shows that the ***Federal Reserve's operating procedures limit the fluctuations of the federal funds rate to between i_{or} and i_d.*** If the range between i_{or} and i_d is kept narrow enough, then the fluctuations around the target rate will be small.

*Note that, as discussed in footnote 1, the federal funds rate can be slightly below the floor of the interest rate paid on reserves.

Conventional Monetary Policy Tools

During normal times, the Federal Reserve uses four tools of monetary policy—open market operations, discount lending, reserve requirements, and paying interest on reserves—to control the interest rates, and these are referred to as **conventional monetary policy tools**. We will look at each of them in turn to see how the Fed wields them in practice and how relatively useful each tool is.

Open Market Operations

Open market operations were the primary monetary policy tool used by the Fed to set interest rates before the global financial crisis of 2007–2009. Open market operations are of two types: **Dynamic open market operations** are intended to change the level of reserves and **defensive open market operations** are intended to offset movements in other factors that affect reserves. The Fed conducts open market operations in U.S. Treasury and government agency securities, especially U.S. Treasury bills. The Fed conducts most of its open market operations in Treasury securities because the market for these securities is the most liquid and has the largest trading volume. It has the capacity to absorb the Fed's substantial volume of transactions without experiencing excessive price fluctuations that would disrupt the market.

Access **www.federalreserve.gov/fomc** for a discussion about the Federal Open Market Committee, list of current members, meeting dates, and other current information.

As we saw in Chapter 9, the decision-making authority for open market operations is the Federal Open Market Committee (FOMC), which sets a target for the federal funds rate. The actual execution of these operations, however, is conducted by the trading desk at the Federal Reserve Bank of New York. The best way to see how these transactions are executed is to look at a typical day at the trading desk, located in a newly built trading room on the ninth floor of the Federal Reserve Bank of New York, whose operations are described by the Inside the Fed box, "A Day at the Trading Desk."

Temporary open-market operations are the main way the Fed affects reserves in the banking system, and they are of two basic types. In a **repurchase agreement** (often called a **repo**), the Fed purchases securities with an agreement that the seller will repurchase them in a short period of time, anywhere from one to fifteen days from the original date of purchase. Because the effects on reserves of a repo are reversed on the day the agreement matures, a repo is actually a temporary open market purchase and is an especially desirable way of conducting a defensive open market purchase that will be reversed shortly. When the Fed wants to conduct a temporary open market sale, it engages in a **matched sale–purchase transaction**

> INSIDE THE FED

A Day at the Trading Desk

The manager of domestic open market operations supervises the analysts and traders who execute the purchases and sales of securities in the drive to hit the federal funds rate target. To get a grip on what might happen in the federal funds market that day, her workday starts early in the morning, around 7:30 a.m., when her staff begins with a review of developments in the federal funds market the previous day and with an update on the actual amount of reserves in the banking system the day before. Then her staff produces updated reports that contain detailed forecasts of what will be happening to some of the short-term factors affecting the supply and demand of reserves.

This information will help the manager of domestic open market operations and her staff decide how large a change in nonborrowed reserves is needed to reach the federal funds rate target. If the amount of reserves in the banking system is too large, many banks will have excess reserves to lend that other banks may have little desire to hold, and the federal funds rate will fall. If the level of reserves is too low, banks seeking to borrow reserves from the few banks that have excess reserves to lend may push the funds rate higher than the desired level. Also during the morning, the staff will monitor the behavior of the federal funds rate and contact some of the major participants in the funds market, which may provide independent information about whether a change in reserves is needed to achieve the desired level of the federal funds rate.

Members of the manager's staff also contact several representatives of the primary dealers that the open market desk trades with. Her staff finds out how the dealers view market conditions to get a feel for what may happen to the prices of the securities they trade in over the course of the day. They also call the Treasury to get updated information on the expected level of Treasury balances at the Fed to refine their estimates of the supply of reserves.

Members of the Monetary Affairs Division at the Board of Governors are then contacted, and the New York Fed's forecasts of reserve supply and demand are compared with the Board's. On the basis of these projections and the observed behavior of the federal funds market, the desk will formulate and propose a course of action to be taken that day, which may involve plans to add reserves to or drain reserves from the banking system through open market operations. If an operation is contemplated, the type, size, and maturity will be discussed.

About 9 a.m., a daily conference call takes place linking the desk with the Office of the Director of Monetary Affairs at the Board of Governors and with one of the four voting Reserve Bank presidents outside of New York. During the call, a member of the open market operations unit will outline the desk's proposed reserve management strategy for the day. After the plan is approved, it is announced to the markets at 9:30 a.m. and the desk is instructed to execute immediately any temporary open market operations that were planned for that day.

At times, the desk may see the need to address a persistent reserve shortage or surplus and wish to arrange an operation that will have a more permanent impact on the supply of reserves. This operation, referred to as an *outright operation*, involves a straightforward purchase or sale of securities that is not self-reversing, and it is traditionally executed later in the day when temporary operations are not being conducted.

(sometimes called a **reverse repo**), in which the Fed sells securities and the buyer agrees to sell them back to the Fed in the near future.

Discount Policy and the Lender of Last Resort

The facility at which banks can borrow reserves from the Federal Reserve is called the **discount window**. The easiest way to understand how the Fed affects the volume of borrowed reserves is by looking at how the discount window operates.

Operation of the Discount Window The Fed's discount loans to banks are of three types: primary credit, secondary credit, and seasonal credit.[2] *Primary credit* is the discount lending that plays the most important role in monetary policy. Healthy banks are allowed to borrow all they want at very short maturities (usually overnight) from the primary credit facility, and it is therefore referred to as a **standing lending facility**. The interest rate on these loans is the discount rate, and as we mentioned before, it is set higher than the federal funds rate target, usually by 100 basis points (one percentage point) because the Fed prefers that banks borrow from each other in the federal funds market so that they continually monitor each other for credit risk. As a result, in most circumstances the amount of discount lending under the primary credit facility is very small. If the amount is so small, why does the Fed have this facility?

The answer is that the facility is intended to be a backup source of liquidity for sound banks so that the federal funds rate never rises too far above the federal funds target set by the FOMC. We have already seen how this works in Figure 10.6. When the demand for reserves has a large unexpected increase, no matter how far the demand curve shifts to the right, the equilibrium federal funds rate i_{ff}'' will stay at i_d because borrowed reserves will just continue to increase, and the federal funds rate can rise no further. The primary credit facility has thus put a ceiling on the federal funds rate at i_d.

Secondary credit is given to banks that are in financial trouble and are experiencing severe liquidity problems. The interest rate on secondary credit is set at 50 basis points (0.5 percentage point) above the discount rate. The interest rate on these loans is set at a higher, penalty rate to reflect the less-sound condition of these borrowers. *Seasonal credit* is given to meet the needs of a limited number of small banks in vacation and agricultural areas that have a seasonal pattern of deposits. The interest rate charged on seasonal credit is tied to the average of the federal funds rate and certificate of deposit rates. The Federal Reserve has questioned the need for the seasonal credit facility because of improvements in credit markets and is thus contemplating eliminating it in the future.

Lender of Last Resort In addition to its use as a tool to influence the amount of reserves and interest rates, discounting is important in preventing and coping with financial panics. When the Federal Reserve System was created, its most important role was intended to be **lender of last resort;** to prevent bank failures from spinning out of control, it was to provide reserves to banks when no one else would, thereby preventing bank and financial panics. Discounting is a particularly effective way to provide reserves to the banking system during a banking crisis because reserves are immediately channeled to the banks that need them most.

Using the discount tool to avoid financial panics by performing the role of lender of last resort is an extremely important requirement of successful monetary policy making. Financial panics can severely damage the economy because they interfere

[2] The procedures for administering the discount window were changed in January 2003. The primary credit facility replaced an adjustment credit facility whose discount rate was typically set below market interest rates, so banks were restricted in their access to this credit. In contrast, now healthy banks can borrow all they want from the primary credit facility. The secondary credit facility replaced the extended credit facility, which focused somewhat more on longer-term credit extensions. The seasonal credit facility remains basically unchanged.

with the ability of financial intermediaries and markets to move funds to people with productive investment opportunities (as discussed in Chapter 8).

Unfortunately, the discount tool has not always been used by the Fed to prevent financial panics, as the massive failures during the Great Depression attest. The Fed learned from its mistakes of that period and has performed admirably in its role of lender of last resort in the post–World War II period. The Fed has used its discount lending weapon several times to avoid bank panics by extending loans to troubled banking institutions, thereby preventing further bank failures.

At first glance, it might seem that the presence of the FDIC, which insures depositors up to a limit of $250,000 per account from losses due to a bank's failure, would make the lender-of-last-resort function of the Fed superfluous. This is not the case for two reasons. First, it is important to recognize that the FDIC's insurance fund amounts to about 1% of the amount of these deposits outstanding. If a large number of banks failed, the FDIC would not be able to cover all the depositors' losses. Indeed, the large number of bank failures in the 1980s and early 1990s led to large losses and a shrinkage in the FDIC's insurance fund, which reduced the FDIC's ability to cover depositors' losses. This fact has not weakened the confidence of small depositors in the banking system because the Fed has been ready to stand behind the banks to provide whatever reserves are needed to prevent bank panics. Second, the $1.7 trillion of large-denomination deposits in the banking system are not guaranteed by the FDIC because they exceed the $250,000 limit. A loss of confidence in the banking system could still lead to runs on banks from the large-denomination depositors, and bank panics could still occur despite the existence of the FDIC. The importance of the Federal Reserve's role as lender of last resort is, if anything, more important today because of the high number of bank failures experienced in the 1980s, early 1990s, and during the financial crisis of 2007–2009. Not only can the Fed be a lender of last resort to banks, but it can also play the same role for the financial system as a whole. The existence of the Fed's discount window can help prevent and cope with financial panics that are not triggered by bank failures, as was the case during the global financial crisis from 2007 through 2009.

Although the Fed's role as the lender of last resort has the benefit of preventing bank and financial panics, it does have a cost. If a bank expects that the Fed will provide it with discount loans when it gets into trouble, it will be willing to take on more risk knowing that the Fed will come to the rescue. The Fed's lender-of-last-resort role has thus created a moral hazard problem similar to the one created by deposit insurance (discussed in Chapter 18): Banks take on more risk, thus exposing the deposit insurance agency, and hence taxpayers, to greater losses. The moral hazard problem is most severe for large banks, which may believe that the Fed and the FDIC view them as "too big to fail"; that is, they will always receive Fed loans when they are in trouble because their failure would be likely to precipitate a bank panic.

Similarly, Federal Reserve actions to prevent financial panic may encourage financial institutions other than banks to take on greater risk. They, too, expect the Fed to ensure that they could get loans if a financial panic seems imminent. When the Fed considers using the discount weapon to prevent panics, it therefore needs to consider the trade-off between the moral hazard cost of its role as lender of last resort and the benefit of preventing financial panics. This trade-off explains why the Fed must be careful not to perform its role as lender of last resort too frequently.

Reserve Requirements

Changes in reserve requirements affect the demand for reserves: A rise in reserve requirements means that banks must hold more reserves, and a reduction means that they are required to hold less. The Depository Institutions Deregulation and Monetary Control Act of 1980 provided a simpler scheme for setting reserve requirements. All depository institutions, including commercial banks, savings and loan associations, mutual savings banks, and credit unions, are subject to the same reserve requirements: Required reserves on all checkable deposits—including non-interest-bearing checking accounts, NOW accounts, super-NOW accounts, and ATS (automatic transfer savings) accounts—are equal to 0% of a bank's first $15.2 million of checkable deposits, 3% of a bank's checkable deposits from $15.2 million to $110.2 million,[3] and 10% of checkable deposits over $110.2 million, and the percentage set initially at 10% can be varied between 8% and 14% at the Fed's discretion. In extraordinary circumstances, the percentage can be raised as high as 18%.

Reserve requirements have rarely been used as a monetary policy tool because raising them can cause immediate liquidity problems for banks with low excess reserves. When the Fed increased these requirements in the past, it usually softened the blow by conducting open market purchases or by making the discount loan window (borrowed reserves) more available, thereby providing reserves to banks that needed them. Continually fluctuating reserve requirements would also create more uncertainty for banks and make their liquidity management more difficult.

Interest on Reserves

Because the Fed only started paying interest on reserves in 2008, this tool of monetary policy does not have a long history. For the same reason that the Fed sets the discount rate above the federal funds target—that is, to encourage borrowing and lending in the federal funds market so that banks monitor each other—the Fed typically sets the interest rate on reserves to be below the federal funds target. In this case interest on reserves will not be used as a tool of monetary policy but instead will just help provide a floor under the federal funds rate. However, in the aftermath of the global financial crisis, banks have accumulated huge quantities of excess reserves, and in this situation, to increase the federal funds rate would require massive amounts of open market operations to remove these reserves from the banking system. The interest-on-reserves tool can come to the rescue because raising this interest rate can instead be used to raise the federal funds rate, as is illustrated in panel (b) of Figure 10.5. Indeed, this tool of monetary policy was extensively used when the Fed wanted to raise the federal funds rate and exit from maintaining it at zero in December 2015.

Nonconventional Monetary Policy Tools and Quantitative Easing

Although in normal times, conventional monetary policy tools, which raise or lower interest rates, are enough to stabilize the economy, when the economy experiences a full-scale financial crisis like the one we have recently experienced, conventional

[3] The $15.2 and $110.2 million figure is for the 2016 year. Each year, the figure is adjusted upward (or downward) by 80% of the previous year's percentage increase (or decrease) in checkable deposits in the United States. See www.federalreserve.gov/pubs/supplement/2007/02/200702statsup.pdf.

monetary policy tools cannot do the job for two reasons. First, the financial system seizes up to such an extent that it becomes unable to allocate capital to productive uses, and so investment spending and the economy collapse along the lines we discussed in Chapter 8. Second, the negative shock to the economy can lead to the **zero-lower-bound problem**, in which the central bank is unable to lower the policy interest rate further because it has hit a floor of zero, as occurred at the end of 2008. The zero-lower-bound problem occurs because people can always earn more from holding bonds than holding cash, and therefore nominal interest rates cannot be too far below zero. For both these reasons, central banks need non-interest-rate tools, known as **nonconventional monetary policy tools**, to stimulate the economy. These nonconventional monetary policy tools take four forms: (1) liquidity provision, (2) asset purchases, (3) forward guidance and (4) negative interest rates on bank deposits at a central bank.

Liquidity Provision

Because conventional monetary policy actions were not sufficient to heal the financial markets and contain the financial crisis, the Federal Reserve implemented unprecedented increases in its lending facilities to provide liquidity to the financial markets.

1. **Discount window expansion** At the outset of the crisis in mid-August 2007 the Fed lowered the discount rate (the interest rate on loans it makes to banks) to 50 basis points (0.50 percentage point) above the federal funds rate target from the normal 100 basis points. It then lowered it further in March 2008 to only 25 basis points above the federal funds rate target. However, since borrowing from the discount window has a "stigma" because it suggests that the borrowing bank may be desperate for funds and thus in trouble, its use was limited during the crisis.
2. **Term auction facility** To encourage additional borrowing, in December 2007 the Fed set up a temporary Term Auction Facility (TAF), in which it made loans at a rate determined through competitive auctions. It was more widely used than the discount window facility because it enabled banks to borrow at a rate lower than the discount rate, and it was determined competitively, rather than being set at a penalty rate. The TAF auctions started at amounts of $20 billion, but as the crisis worsened, the Fed raised the amounts dramatically, with a total outstanding of over $400 billion. (The European Central Bank conducted similar operations, with one auction in June 2008 of over 400 billion euros.)
3. **New lending programs** The Fed broadened its provision of liquidity to the financial system well outside its traditional lending to banking institutions. These actions included lending to investment banks, as well as lending to promote purchases of commercial paper, mortgage-backed securities, and other asset-backed securities. In addition, the Fed engaged in lending to J.P. Morgan to assist in its purchase of Bear Stearns and to AIG to prevent its failure. The enlargement of the Fed's lending programs during the 2007–2009 financial crisis was indeed remarkable, expanding the Fed's balance sheet by over $1 trillion by the end of 2008, with the balance-sheet expansion continuing afterward. The number of new programs over the course of the crisis spawned a whole new set of abbreviations, including the TAF, TSLF,

PDCF, AMLF, CPFF, MMIFF, and TALF. These facilities are described in more detail in the Inside the Fed box, "Fed Lending Facilities During the Global Financial Crisis."

INSIDE THE FED

Fed Lending Facilities During the Global Financial Crisis

During the global financial crisis, the Federal Reserve became very creative in assembling a host of new lending facilities to help restore liquidity to different parts of the financial system. The new facilities, the dates they were created, and their functions are listed in the table below.

Lending Facility	Date of Creation	Function
Term Auction Facility (TAF)	December 12, 2007	Made borrowing from the Fed more widely used; extended loans of fixed amounts to banks at interest rates that were determined by competitive auction rather than being set by the Fed, as with normal discount lending
Term Securities Lending Facility (TSLF)	March 11, 2008	Provided sufficient Treasury securities to act as collateral in credit markets; lent Treasury securities to primary dealers for terms longer than overnight against a broad range of collateral
Swap Lines	March 11, 2008	Lent dollars to foreign central banks in exchange for foreign currencies so that these central banks could in turn make dollar loans to their domestic banks
Loans to J.P. Morgan to buy Bear Stearns	March 14, 2008	Bought $30 billion of Bear Stearns assets through nonrecourse loans to J.P. Morgan to facilitate its purchase of Bear Stearns
Primary Dealer Credit Facility (PDCF)	March 16, 2008	Lent to primary dealers (including investment banks) so that they could borrow on similar terms to banks using the traditional discount window facility
Loans to AIG	September 16, 2008	Loaned $85 billion to AIG
Asset-Backed Commercial Paper Money Market Mutual Fund Liquidity Facility (AMLF)	September 19, 2008	Lent to primary dealers so that they could purchase asset-backed commercial paper from money market mutual funds so that these funds could sell this paper to meet redemptions from their investors
Commercial Paper Funding Facility (CPFF)	October 7, 2008	Financed purchase of commercial paper from issuers
Money Market Investor Funding Facility (MMIFF)	October 21, 2008	Lent to special-purpose vehicles so that they could buy a wider range of money market mutual fund assets
Term Asset-Backed Securities Loan Facility (TALF)	November 25, 2008	Lent to issuers of asset-backed securities against these securities as collateral to improve functioning of this market

Large-Scale Asset Purchases

The Fed's open market operations normally involve only purchase of government securities, particularly those that are short-term. However, during the crisis the Fed started three new large-scale asset purchase programs (often referred to as LSAPs) to lower interest rates for particular types of credit. Because, as we have seen earlier in the chapter, Federal Reserve asset purchases lead to an expansion of its balance sheet, these asset purchase programs have been given the name **quantitative easing (QE)**.

1. In November 2008 the Fed set up a Government Sponsored Entities Purchase Program, more commonly referred to as *QE1*, in which the Fed eventually purchased $1.25 trillion of mortgage-backed securities (MBS) guaranteed by Fannie Mae and Freddie Mac. Through these purchases, the Fed hoped to prop up the MBS market and to lower interest rates on residential mortgages to stimulate the housing market.
2. In November 2010 the Fed announced that it would purchase $600 billion of long-term Treasury securities at a rate of about $75 billion per month. This purchase program, which became known as *QE2* (which stands for Quantitative Easing 2, not the Cunard cruise ship) was intended to lower long-term interest rates. Although *short-term* interest rates on Treasury securities hit a floor of zero during the global financial crisis, *long-term* interest rates did not. Since investment projects have a long life, long-term interest rates are more relevant than short-term ones to investment decisions. The Fed's purchase of long-term Treasuries to lower long-term interest rates could therefore help stimulate investment spending and the economy.
3. In September 2012 the Federal Reserve announced a third asset-purchase program, which has become known as *QE3*, which combined elements of QE1 and QE2 by conducting purchases of $40 billion of mortgage-backed securities and $45 billion of long-term Treasuries. However, QE3 differed in one major way from the previous QE programs in that it was not for a fixed dollar amount but instead was open-ended, with the purchase plan continuing "if the outlook for the labor market does not improve substantially."

The result of these programs of liquidity provision and asset purchases resulted in an unprecedented quadrupling of the Federal Reserve's balance sheet (shown in Figure 10.7).

Quantitative Easing Versus Credit Easing

These quantitative easing programs resulted in an unprecedented expansion of the Federal Reserve's balance sheet from about $900 billion to over $4 trillion by 2016. Because this increase in reserves increases liquidity in the banking system, enabling banks to lend more, it could be a powerful force to stimulate the economy and possibly produce inflation down the road.

There are reasons to be very skeptical. First, because the federal funds rate had already hit the zero-lower-bound when it fell to zero, the expansion of the balance sheet and the monetary base could not lower short-term interest rates any further and thereby stimulate the economy. Second, the increase in reserves did not result in an increase in lending because banks just added to their holdings of excess

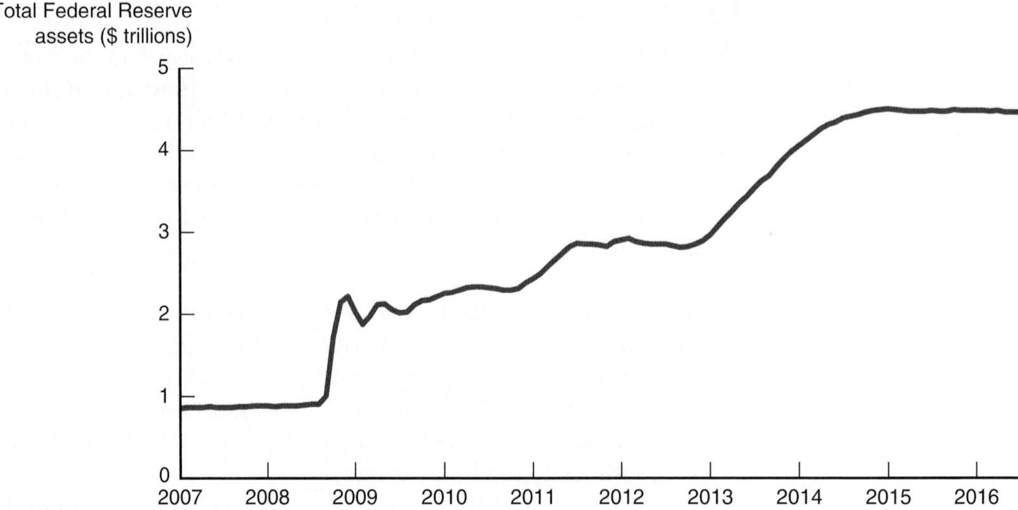

FIGURE 10.7 The Expansion of the Federal Reserve's Balance Sheet During and After the Global Financial Crisis: Total Federal Reserve Assets, 2007–2016

The size of the Federal Reserve's balance sheet more than quadrupled in the aftermath of the global financial crisis.

Source: Federal Reserve Bank of St. Louis, FRED database: https://fred.stlouisfed.org/series/WALCL#0.

reserves instead of making loans. A similar phenomenon seems to have occurred when the Bank of Japan engaged in quantitative easing after the bubble burst in the stock and real estate markets; yet not only did the economy not recover, but inflation even turned negative.

Does skepticism about quantitative easing mean that the Fed's nonconventional monetary policy actions would be ineffective at stimulating the economy? The Fed chair at the time, Ben Bernanke, argued that the answer is no because the Fed's policies were directed not at expanding the Fed's balance sheet but rather at **credit easing**—that is, altering the composition of the Fed's balance sheet in order to improve the functioning of particular segments of the credit markets. Indeed, Chair Bernanke was adamant that the Fed's policies should not be characterized as quantitative easing.

Altering the composition of the Fed's balance sheet can stimulate the economy in several ways. First, when the Fed provides liquidity to a particular segment of the credit markets that has seized up, it can help unfreeze the market and thereby enable it to allocate capital to productive uses and consequently stimulate the economy. Second, when the Fed purchases particular securities, it increases the demand for those securities and, as we saw in Chapter 5, it can lower the interest rates on those securities relative to other securities. Thus, even if short-term interest rates have hit a floor of zero, asset purchases can lower interest rates for borrowers in particular credit markets and thereby stimulate spending. For example, purchases of mortgage-backed securities appear to have lowered their interest rates on these securities and led to a substantial decline in residential mortgage rates. Purchase of long-term government securities could also lower their interest rates relative to short-term interest rates, and because long-term interest rates are likely to be more relevant to investment decisions, these asset market purchases could boost investment spending. Recent research appears to support this viewpoint, with estimates of the decline in long-term interest rates from the Fed's asset purchase programs on the order of 100 basis points (one percentage point).[4]

Forward Guidance

Although short-term interest rates could not be driven below zero in the aftermath of the global financial crisis, the Federal Reserve could take another route to lower long-term interest rates, which, as we have mentioned above, would stimulate the economy. This route involved a commitment by the Fed to keep the federal funds rate at zero for a long period of time in order to lower the market's expectations of future short-term interest rates, thereby causing the long-term interest rate to fall. This strategy is referred to as **forward guidance**.

The Fed pursued this forward guidance strategy when it announced after its FOMC meeting on December 16, 2008, that not only would it lower the federal funds rate target to between zero and ¼%, but also that "the Committee anticipates that weak economic conditions are likely to warrant exceptionally low levels of the federal funds rate for some time." The Fed then continued to use this language in its FOMC statements for several years afterward and then moved to announcing specific dates, eventually with the statement that "the exceptionally low levels of the federal funds rate are likely to be warranted until mid-2015." Although long-term interest rates on Treasury securities did subsequently fall with these announcements, it is not clear how much of this decline was due to the Fed's forward guidance versus weakness in the economy.

There are two types of commitments to future policy actions: conditional and unconditional. The commitment to keep the federal funds rate at zero for an extended period starting in 2008 was *conditional* because it mentioned that the decision was predicated on a weak economy going forward. If economic circumstances changed, the FOMC was indicating that it might abandon the commitment. Alternatively, the Fed could have made an *unconditional* commitment by just stating that it would keep the federal funds rate at zero for an extended period without indicating that this decision was based on the state of the economy. An unconditional commitment has the advantage of being stronger than a conditional commitment because it does not suggest that the commitment will be abandoned and so is likely to have a larger effect on long-term interest rates. Unfortunately, it has the disadvantage that even if circumstances change in such a way that it would be better to abandon the commitment, the Fed may feel it cannot go back on its word and do so.

The problem of an unconditional commitment is illustrated by the Fed's experience in the 2003–2006 period. In 2003 the Fed became worried that inflation was too low and that the probability of a deflation was significant. At the August 12, 2003, FOMC meeting, the FOMC stated, "In these circumstances, the Committee believes that policy accommodation can be maintained for a considerable period." Then when the Fed started to tighten policy at its June 30, 2004, FOMC meeting, it

---

[4] See, for example, Joseph Gagnon, Mathew Raskin, Julie Remache, and Brian Sack, "Large Scale Asset Purchases by the Federal Reserve: Did They Work?" *Federal Reserve Bank of New York Economic Policy Review*, 17, no. 1 (May 2011): 41–59.

changed its statement to "policy accommodation can be removed at a pace that is likely to be measured." Then for the next ten FOMC meetings through June 2006, the Fed raised the federal funds rate target by exactly ¼ percentage point at every meeting. The market interpreted the FOMC's statements as indicating an unconditional commitment, and this is why the Fed may have been constrained not to deviate from ¼ percentage point moves at every FOMC meeting. In retrospect, this commitment led to monetary policy that was too easy for too long, with inflation subsequently rising to well above desirable levels and, as discussed in Chapter 8, it may have helped promote the housing bubble whose bursting led to such devastating consequences for the economy.

When the Fed announced a specific date for exiting from exceptionally low rates, many market participants viewed this announcement as an unconditional commitment, despite the Federal Reserve's objections. To avoid the problems with an unconditional commitment, in December 2012 the Fed changed its statement to be more clearly conditional by indicating that the "exceptionally low range for the federal funds rate will be appropriate at least as long as the unemployment rate remains above 6-½ percent, inflation between one and two years ahead is projected to be no more than a half percentage point above the Committee's 2 percent longer-run goal, and longer-term inflation expectations continue to be well anchored." With the unemployment rate approaching the 6-½ % mark, at its March 2014 meeting the FOMC dropped forward guidance based on unemployment and inflation thresholds. Subsequently, it announced that it would determine the timing and size of changes in the target for the federal funds rate taking "into account a wide range of information, including measures of labor market conditions, indicators of inflation pressures and inflation expectations, and readings on financial and international developments."

Negative Interest Rates on Banks' Deposits

With inflation very low and their economies weak after the global financial crisis, central banks in Europe and Japan recently began experimenting with a new nonconventional monetary policy tool, setting interest rates on deposits held by banks at their central banks to be negative. In other words, banks now had to pay their central bank to keep deposits in the central bank. The central bank of Sweden was the first to set negative interest rates on bank deposits in July 2009, followed by the central bank of Denmark in July 2012, the ECB in June 2014, the central bank of Switzerland in December 2014, and the Bank of Japan in January 2016.

Setting negative interest rates on banks' deposits is supposed to work to stimulate the economy by encouraging banks to lend out the deposits they were keeping at the central bank, thereby encouraging households and businesses to spend more. However, there are doubts that negative interest rates on deposits will have the intended, expansionary effect.

First, banks might not lend out their deposits at the central bank, but instead move them into cash. There would be some cost to doing so because banks would have to build more vaults and hire security guards to protect the cash. Nonetheless, they still might prefer to do this rather than lend them out.

Second, charging banks interest on their deposits might be very costly to banks if they still have to pay positive interest rates to their depositors. In this case, bank profitability would fall. The result might then make banks less likely to lend. So instead of being expansionary, negative interest rates on banks' deposits could cause banks to cut back on lending and therefore be contractionary.

The jury is still out on whether negative interest rates on bank deposits held at central banks will stimulate the economy as intended. Indeed, doubts about the effectiveness of this nonconventional monetary policy tool led Janet Yellen, the chair of the Board of Governors of the Federal Reserve, to announce in 2016 that the Fed was not considering using this tool to stimulate the economy. However, the Federal Reserve's views might change if the U.S. economy became much weaker and if the experience with negative interest rates in other countries suggested that this tool is effective in stimulating spending.

Monetary Policy Tools of the European Central Bank

Like the Federal Reserve, the European System of Central Banks (which is usually referred to as the European Central Bank) signals the stance of its monetary policy by setting a **target financing rate**, which in turn sets a target for the **overnight cash rate**. Like the federal funds rate, the overnight cash rate is the interest rate for very short-term interbank loans. The monetary policy tools used by the European Central Bank are similar to those used by the Federal Reserve and involve open market operations, lending to banks, and reserve requirements.

Access **http://www.federalreserve.gov/aboutthefed/**. The Federal Reserve provides links to other central bank Web pages.

Open Market Operations

Like the Federal Reserve, the European Central Bank uses open market operations as its primary tool for conducting monetary policy and setting the overnight cash rate at the target financing rate. **Main refinancing operations** are the predominant form of open market operations and are similar to the Fed's repo transactions. They involve weekly **reverse transactions** (purchase or sale of eligible assets under repurchase or credit operations against eligible assets as collateral) that are reversed within two weeks. Credit institutions submit bids, and the European Central Bank decides which bids to accept. Like the Federal Reserve, the European Central Bank accepts the most attractively priced bids and makes purchases or sales to the point where the desired amount of reserves is supplied. In contrast to the Federal Reserve, which conducts open market operations in one location at the Federal Reserve Bank of New York, the European Central Bank decentralizes its open market operations by having them be conducted by the individual national central banks.

A second category of open market operations is the **longer-term refinancing operations**, which are a much smaller source of liquidity for the euro-area banking system and are similar to the Fed's outright purchases or sales of securities. These operations are carried out monthly and typically involve purchases or sales of securities with a maturity of three months. They are not used for signaling the monetary policy stance but are aimed at providing euro-area banks with additional longer-term refinancing.

Lending to Banks

As for the Fed, the next most important tool of monetary policy for the European Central Bank involves lending to banking institutions, which is carried out by the national central banks, just as discount lending is performed by the individual

Federal Reserve Banks. This lending takes place through a standing lending facility called the **marginal lending facility**. There, banks can borrow (against eligible collateral) overnight loans from the national central banks at the **marginal lending rate**, which is set at 100 basis points above the target financing rate. The marginal lending rate provides a ceiling for the overnight market interest rate in the European Monetary Union, just as the discount rate does in the United States.

Interest on Reserves

As in the United States, Canada, Australia, and New Zealand, the Eurosystem has another standing facility, the **deposit facility**, in which banks are paid an interest rate that is typically 100 basis points below the target financing rate. The prespecified interest rate on the deposit facility provides a floor for the overnight market interest rate, while the marginal lending rate sets a ceiling. The interest rate on reserves set by the European Central Bank is not always positive. As discussed above, the European Central Bank set the interest rate on reserves to negative values starting in June 2014.

Reserve Requirements

Like the Federal Reserve, the European Central Bank imposes reserve requirements such that all deposit-taking institutions are required to hold 2% of the total amount of checking deposits and other short-term deposits in reserve accounts with national central banks. All institutions that are subject to minimum reserve requirements have access to the European Central Bank's standing lending facilities and participate in open market operations.

The Price Stability Goal and the Nominal Anchor

Over the past few decades, policy makers throughout the world have become increasingly aware of the social and economic costs of inflation and more concerned with maintaining a stable price level as a goal of economic policy. Indeed, **price stability**, which central bankers define as low and stable inflation, is increasingly viewed as the most important goal of monetary policy. Price stability is desirable because a rising price level (inflation) creates uncertainty in the economy, and that uncertainty might hamper economic growth. For example, when the overall level of prices is changing, the information conveyed by the prices of goods and services is harder to interpret, which complicates decision making for consumers, businesses, and government, thereby leading to a less efficient financial system.

Not only do public opinion surveys indicate that the public is hostile to inflation, but a growing body of evidence also suggests that inflation leads to lower economic growth.[5] The most extreme example of unstable prices is *hyperinflation*, such as Argentina, Brazil, and Russia have experienced in the recent past. Hyperinflation has proved to be very damaging to the workings of the economy.

Inflation also makes it difficult to plan for the future. For example, it is more difficult to decide how much to put aside to provide for a child's college education

---

[5] For example, see Stanley Fischer, "The Role of Macroeconomic Factors in Growth," *Journal of Monetary Economics* 32 (1993): 485–512.

in an inflationary environment. Furthermore, inflation can strain a country's social fabric: Conflict might result because each group in the society may compete with other groups to make sure that its income keeps up with the rising level of prices.

The Role of a Nominal Anchor

Because price stability is so crucial to the long-run health of an economy, a central element in successful monetary policy is the use of a **nominal anchor**, a nominal variable such as the inflation rate or the money supply, which ties down the price level to achieve price stability. Adherence to a nominal anchor that keeps the nominal variable within a narrow range promotes price stability by directly promoting low and stable inflation expectations. A more subtle reason for a nominal anchor's importance is that it can limit the **time-inconsistency problem**, in which monetary policy conducted on a discretionary, day-by-day basis leads to poor long-run outcomes.[6]

The Time-Inconsistency Problem

The time-inconsistency problem is something we deal with continually in everyday life. We often have a plan that we know will produce a good outcome in the long run, but when tomorrow comes, we just can't help ourselves and we renege on our plan because doing so has short-run gains. For example, we make a New Year's resolution to go on a diet, but soon thereafter we can't resist having one more bite of that rocky road ice cream—and then another bite, and then another bite—and the weight begins to pile back on. In other words, we find ourselves unable to *consistently* follow a good plan over *time*; the good plan is said to be *time-inconsistent* and will soon be abandoned.

Monetary policy makers also face the time-inconsistency problem. They are always tempted to pursue a discretionary monetary policy that is more expansionary than firms or people expect because such a policy would boost economic output (or lower unemployment) in the short run. The best policy, however, is *not* to pursue expansionary policy because decisions about wages and prices reflect workers' and firms' expectations about policy; when they see a central bank pursuing expansionary policy, workers and firms will raise their expectations about inflation, driving wages and prices up. The rise in wages and prices will lead to higher inflation but will not result in higher output on average.

A central bank will have better inflation performance in the long run if it does not try to surprise people with an unexpectedly expansionary policy but instead keeps inflation under control. However, even if a central bank recognizes that discretionary policy will lead to a poor outcome (high inflation with no gains in output), it still may not be able to pursue the better policy of inflation control because politicians are likely to apply pressure on the central bank to try to boost output with overly expansionary monetary policy.

---

[6] The time-inconsistency problem was first outlined in papers by Nobel Prize winners Finn Kydland and Edward Prescott, "Rules Rather Than Discretion: The Inconsistency of Optimal Plans," *Journal of Political Economy* 85 (1977): 473–491; Guillermo Calvo, "On the Time Consistency of Optimal Policy in the Monetary Economy," *Econometrica* 46 (November 1978): 1411–1428; and Robert J. Barro and David Gordon, "A Positive Theory of Monetary Policy in a Natural Rate Model," *Journal of Political Economy* 91 (August 1983): 589–610.

A clue to how we should deal with the time-inconsistency problem comes from how-to books on parenting. Parents know that giving in to a child to keep him from acting up will produce a very spoiled child. Nevertheless, when a child throws a tantrum, many parents give him what he wants just to shut him up. Because parents don't stick to their "do not give in" plan, the child expects that he will get what he wants if he behaves badly, so he will throw tantrums over and over again. Parenting books suggest a solution to the time-inconsistency problem (although they don't call it that): Parents should set behavior rules for their children and stick to them.

A nominal anchor is like a behavior rule. Just as rules help to prevent the time-inconsistency problem in parenting by helping adults resist pursuing the discretionary policy of giving in, a nominal anchor can help prevent the time-inconsistency problem in monetary policy by providing an expected constraint on discretionary policy.

Other Goals of Monetary Policy

Although price stability is the primary goal of most central banks, five other goals are continually mentioned by central bank officials when they discuss the objectives of monetary policy: (1) high employment, (2) economic growth, (3) stability of financial markets, (4) interest-rate stability, and (5) stability in foreign exchange markets.

High Employment and Output Stability

High employment is a worthy goal for two main reasons: (1) The alternative situation—high unemployment—causes much human misery, and (2) when unemployment is high, the economy has both idle workers and idle resources (closed factories and unused equipment), resulting in a loss of output (lower GDP).

Although it is clear that high employment is desirable, how high should it be? At what point can we say that the economy is at full employment? At first, it might seem that full employment is the point at which no worker is out of a job—that is, when unemployment is zero. But this definition ignores the fact that some unemployment, called *frictional unemployment*, which involves searches by workers and firms to find suitable matchups, is beneficial to the economy. For example, a worker who decides to look for a better job might be unemployed for a while during the job search. Workers often decide to leave work temporarily to pursue other activities (raising a family, travel, returning to school), and when they decide to reenter the job market, it may take some time for them to find the right job.

Another reason that unemployment is not zero when the economy is at full employment is *structural unemployment*, a mismatch between job requirements and the skills or availability of local workers. Clearly, this kind of unemployment is undesirable. Nonetheless, it is something that monetary policy can do little about.

This goal for high employment is not an unemployment level of zero but a level above zero consistent with full employment at which the demand for labor equals the supply of labor. This level is called the **natural rate of unemployment**.

Although this definition sounds neat and authoritative, it leaves a troublesome question unanswered: What unemployment rate is consistent with full employment? In some cases, it is obvious that the unemployment rate is too high: The unemployment rate in excess of 20% during the Great Depression, for example, was clearly far too high. In the early 1960s, on the other hand, policy makers thought that a reasonable goal was 4%, a level that was probably too low because it led to accelerating inflation. Current estimates of the natural rate of unemployment place it between 4.5% and 6%, but even this estimate is subject to much uncertainty and disagreement. It is possible, for example, that appropriate government policy, such as the provision of better information about job vacancies or job training programs, might decrease the natural rate of unemployment.

The high employment goal can be thought of in another way. Because the level of unemployment is tied to the level of economic activity in the economy, a level of output is produced at the natural rate of unemployment, which naturally enough is referred to as the **natural rate of output** but is more often referred to as **potential output**.

Trying to achieve the goal of high employment thus means that central banks should try to move the level of output toward the natural rate of output. In other words, they should try to stabilize the level of output around its natural rate.

Economic Growth

The goal of steady economic growth is closely related to the high employment goal because businesses are more likely to invest in capital equipment to increase productivity and economic growth when unemployment is low. Conversely, if unemployment is high and factories are idle, it does not pay for a firm to invest in additional plants and equipment. Although the two goals are closely related, policies can be specifically aimed at promoting economic growth by directly encouraging firms to invest or by encouraging people to save, which provides more funds for firms to invest. In fact, this approach is the stated purpose of *supply-side economics* policies, which are intended to spur economic growth by providing tax incentives for businesses to invest in facilities and equipment and for taxpayers to save more. Active debate continues over what role monetary policy can play in boosting growth.

Stability of Financial Markets

Financial crises can interfere with the ability of financial markets to channel funds to people with productive investment opportunities and lead to a sharp contraction in economic activity. The promotion of a more stable financial system in which financial crises are avoided is thus an important goal for a central bank. Indeed, as discussed in Chapter 9, the Federal Reserve System was created in response to the bank panic of 1907 to promote financial stability.

Interest-Rate Stability

Interest-rate stability is desirable because fluctuations in interest rates can create uncertainty in the economy and make it harder to plan for the future. Fluctuations in interest rates that affect consumers' willingness to buy houses, for example, make it more difficult for consumers to decide when to purchase a house and for construction firms to plan how many houses to build. A central bank may also want to reduce upward movements in interest rates for the reasons we discussed in Chapter 9: Upward movements in interest rates generate hostility toward central banks and lead to demands that their power be curtailed.

The stability of financial markets is also fostered by interest-rate stability because fluctuations in interest rates create great uncertainty for financial institutions. An increase in interest rates produces large capital losses on long-term bonds and mortgages, losses that can cause the failure of the financial institutions holding them. In recent years, more pronounced interest-rate fluctuations have been a particularly severe problem for savings and loan associations and mutual savings banks, many of which got into serious financial trouble in the 1980s and early 1990s.

Stability in Foreign Exchange Markets

With the increasing importance of international trade to the U.S. economy, the value of the dollar relative to other currencies has become a major consideration for the Fed. A rise in the value of the dollar makes American industries less competitive with those abroad, and declines in the value of the dollar stimulate inflation in the United States. In addition, preventing large changes in the value of the dollar makes it easier for firms and individuals purchasing or selling goods abroad to plan ahead. Stabilizing extreme movements in the value of the dollar in foreign exchange markets is thus an important goal of monetary policy. In other countries, which are even more dependent on foreign trade, stability in foreign exchange markets takes on even greater importance.

Should Price Stability Be the Primary Goal of Monetary Policy?

In the long run, no inconsistency exists between the price stability goal and the other goals mentioned earlier. The natural rate of unemployment is not lowered by high inflation, so higher inflation cannot produce lower unemployment or more employment in the long run. In other words, there is no long-run trade-off between inflation and employment. In the long run, price stability promotes economic growth as well as financial and interest-rate stability. Although price stability is consistent with the other goals in the long run, in the short run price stability often conflicts with the goals of high employment and interest-rate stability. For example, when the economy is expanding and unemployment is falling, the economy may become overheated, leading to a rise in inflation. To pursue the price stability goal, a central bank would prevent this overheating by raising interest rates, an action that would initially lower employment and increase interest-rate instability. How should a central bank resolve this conflict among goals?

Hierarchical vs. Dual Mandates

Because price stability is crucial to the long-run health of the economy, many countries have decided that price stability should be the primary, long-run goal for central banks. For example, the Maastricht Treaty, which created the European Central Bank, states, "The primary objective of the European System of Central Banks [ESCB] shall be to maintain price stability. Without prejudice to the objective of price stability, the ESCB shall support the general economic policies in the Community," which include objectives such as "a high level of employment" and "sustainable and noninflationary growth." Mandates of this type, which put the goal of price stability first and then say that as long as it is achieved other goals can be pursued, are known as **hierarchical mandates**. They are the directives governing the behavior of central banks such as the Bank of England, the Bank of Canada, and the Reserve Bank of New Zealand, as well as for the European Central Bank.

In contrast, the legislation defining the mission of the Federal Reserve states, "The Board of Governors of the Federal Reserve System and the Federal Open Market Committee shall maintain long-run growth of the monetary and credit aggregates commensurate with the economy's long-run potential to increase production, so as to promote effectively the goals of maximum employment, stable prices, and moderate long-term interest rates." Because, as we learned in Chapter 4, long-term interest rates will be high if inflation is high, to achieve moderate long-term interest rates, inflation must be low. Thus, in practice, the Fed has a **dual mandate** to achieve two co-equal objectives: price stability and maximum employment.

Is it better for an economy to operate under a hierarchical mandate or a dual mandate?

Price Stability as the Primary, Long-Run Goal of Monetary Policy

Because no inconsistency exists between achieving price stability in the long run and the natural rate of unemployment, these two types of mandates are not very different *if* maximum employment is defined as the natural rate of unemployment. In practice, however, a substantial difference between these two mandates could exist because the public and politicians may believe that a hierarchical mandate puts too much emphasis on inflation control and not enough on reducing business cycle fluctuations.

Because low and stable inflation rates promote economic growth, central bankers have come to realize that price stability should be the primary, long-run goal of monetary policy. Nevertheless, because output fluctuations should also be a concern of monetary policy, the goal of price stability should be seen as primary only in the long run. Attempts to keep inflation at the same level in the short run no matter what would likely lead to excessive output fluctuations.

As long as price stability is a long-run but not short-run goal, central banks can focus on reducing output fluctuations by allowing inflation to deviate from the long-run goal for short periods and, therefore, can operate under a dual mandate. However, if a dual mandate leads a central bank to pursue short-run expansionary policies that increase output and employment without worrying about the long-run consequences for inflation, the time-inconsistency problem may recur. Concerns that a dual mandate might lead to overly expansionary policy is a key reason why central bankers often favor hierarchical mandates in which the pursuit of price stability takes precedence. Hierarchical mandates can also be a problem if they lead to a central bank behaving as what the former Governor of the Bank of England, Mervyn King, referred to as an "inflation nutter"—that is, a central bank that focuses solely on inflation control, even in the short run, and so undertakes policies that lead to large output fluctuations. The choice of which type of mandate is better for a central bank ultimately depends on the subtleties of how it will work in practice. Either type of mandate is acceptable as long as it operates to make price stability the primary goal in the long run, but not the short run.

In the following section, we examine the most prominent monetary policy strategy that monetary policy makers use today to achieve price stability: inflation targeting. This strategy features a strong nominal anchor and has price stability as the primary, long-run goal of monetary policy.

GLOBAL

The European Central Bank's Monetary Policy Strategy

The European Central Bank (ECB) pursues a hybrid monetary policy strategy that includes some elements of inflation targeting.* Like inflation targeting, the ECB has an announced goal for inflation over the medium term of "below, but close to, 2%." The ECB's strategy has two key "pillars." First, monetary and credit aggregates are assessed for "their implications for future inflation and economic growth." Second, many other economic variables are used to assess the future economic outlook.

The ECB's strategy is somewhat unclear and has been subject to criticism for this reason. Although the "below, but close to, 2%" goal for inflation sounds like an inflation target, the ECB has repeatedly stated that it does not have an inflation target. This central bank seems to have decided to try to "have its cake and eat it, too" by not committing too strongly to an inflation-targeting strategy. The resulting difficulty of assessing the ECB's strategy has the potential to reduce the accountability of the institution.

*For a description of the ECB's monetary policy strategy, go to the ECB's Web site at www.ecb.int.

Inflation Targeting

The recognition that price stability should be the primary long-run goal of monetary policy and the value of having a nominal anchor to achieve this goal has led to a monetary policy strategy known as inflation targeting. **Inflation targeting** involves several elements: (1) public announcement of medium-term numerical targets for inflation; (2) an institutional commitment to price stability as the primary, long-run goal of monetary policy and a commitment to achieve the inflation goal; (3) an information-inclusive approach in which many variables are used in making decisions about monetary policy; (4) increased transparency of the monetary policy strategy through communication with the public and the markets about the plans and objectives of monetary policy makers; and (5) increased accountability of the central bank for attaining its inflation objectives. New Zealand was the first country to formally adopt inflation targeting in 1990, followed by Canada in 1991, the United Kingdom in 1992, Sweden and Finland in 1993, and Australia and Spain in 1994. Israel, Chile, and Brazil, among others, have also adopted a form of inflation targeting.[7]

As the Global box, "The European Central Bank's Monetary Policy Strategy," suggests, the European Central Bank also follows a variant of inflation targeting. One country that was late to the party of inflation targeting was the United States, but this changed in January 2012, as is discussed in the Inside the Fed box, "Ben Bernanke and the Federal Reserve's Adoption of Inflation Targeting."

Advantages of Inflation Targeting

Inflation targeting has the key advantage that it is readily understood by the public and is thus highly transparent. Also, because an explicit numerical inflation target

[7] If you are interested in a more detailed discussion of experiences with inflation targeting in these and other countries, see Ben S. Bernanke, Thomas Laubach, Frederic S. Mishkin, and Adam S. Posen, *Inflation Targeting: Lessons from the International Experience* (Princeton, N.J.: Princeton University Press, 1999).

> INSIDE THE FED

Ben Bernanke and the Federal Reserve's Adoption of Inflation Targeting

Ben Bernanke, a former professor at Princeton University, became the new Federal Reserve chairman in February 2006, after serving as a member of the Board of Governors from 2002 to 2005 and then as the chairman of the president's Council of Economic Advisors. Bernanke is a world-renowned expert on monetary policy and, while serving as an academic, wrote extensively on inflation targeting, including articles and a book written with the author of this text.*

Bernanke's writings indicated that he was a strong proponent of inflation targeting and increased transparency in central banks. In an important speech given at a conference at the Federal Reserve Bank of St. Louis in 2004 he described how the Federal Reserve might move toward inflation targeting by announcing a numerical value for its long-run inflation goal.** Bernanke emphasized that announcing a numerical objective for inflation would be completely consistent with the Fed's dual mandate of achieving price stability and maximum employment. Therefore, it might be called a *mandate-consistent inflation objective* because the goal for measured inflation would be set above zero to avoid deflations that have harmful effects on employment and because measured inflation is likely to be biased upward. In addition, it would not be intended to be a short-run target that might lead to control of inflation that is too tight at the expense of overly high employment fluctuations.

After becoming Fed chairman, Bernanke made it clear that any movement toward inflation targeting must result from a consensus within the Federal Reserve and be consistent with the dual mandate given to the Fed by Congress. After Chairman Bernanke set up a subcommittee to discuss Federal Reserve communication, which included discussions about announcing a specific numerical inflation objective, the FOMC made partial steps in the direction of inflation targeting with its new communication strategy first outlined in November 2007 (with an amendment in January 2009) that provided FOMC participants' inflation projections for one, two, and three years ahead as well as for the longer term. The inflation projections for the longer term are produced under an assumption of "appropriate policy" and so reflect each participant's long-run inflation objective. Because the long-run inflation projections of all the FOMC participants ended up being close to 2%, the FOMC finally moved to inflation targeting in January 2012 by agreeing to a single numerical value of the inflation objective, 2% on the PCE deflator. However, the FOMC also made it clear that it would be pursuing a flexible form of inflation targeting consistent with its dual mandate because it not only would seek to achieve its inflation target but would also focus on promoting maximum sustainable employment.

*Ben S. Bernanke and Frederic S. Mishkin, "Inflation Targeting: A New Framework for Monetary Policy," *Journal of Economic Perspectives,* 11, no. 2 (1997); Ben S. Bernanke, Frederic S. Mishkin, and Adam S. Posen, "Inflation Targeting: Fed Policy After Greenspan," *Milken Institute Review* (Fourth Quarter, 1999): 48–56; Ben S. Bernanke, Frederic S. Mishkin, and Adam S. Posen, "What Happens When Greenspan Is Gone," *Wall Street Journal* (January 5, 2000): A22; and Ben S. Bernanke, Thomas Laubach, Frederic S. Mishkin, and Adam S. Posen, *Inflation Targeting: Lessons from the International Experience* (Princeton, N.J.: Princeton University Press, 1999).

**Ben S. Bernanke, "Inflation Targeting," Federal Reserve Bank of St. Louis, *Review,* 86, no. 4 (July/August 2004): 165–168.

increases the accountability of the central bank, inflation targeting has the potential to reduce the likelihood that the central bank will fall into the time-inconsistency trap of trying to expand output and employment in the short run by pursuing overly expansionary monetary policy. A key advantage of inflation targeting is that it can help focus the political debate on what a central bank can do in the long run, that is, control inflation, rather than what it cannot do, permanently increase economic growth and the number of jobs through expansionary monetary policy. Thus, inflation targeting has the potential to reduce political pressures on the central bank to pursue inflationary monetary policy and thereby to reduce the likelihood of the time-inconsistency problem.

The performance of inflation-targeting regimes has been quite good. Inflation-targeting countries seem to have significantly reduced both the rate of inflation and inflation expectations beyond what would likely have occurred in the absence of inflation targets. Furthermore, once down, inflation in these countries has stayed down; following disinflations, the inflation rate in targeting countries has not bounced back up during subsequent cyclical expansions of the economy.

Disadvantages of Inflation Targeting

Critics of inflation targeting cite four disadvantages of this monetary policy strategy: delayed signaling, too much rigidity, the potential for increased output fluctuations, and low economic growth. We look at each in turn and examine the validity of these criticisms.

Delayed Signaling Inflation is not easily controlled by the monetary authorities, and because of the long lags in the effects of monetary policy, inflation outcomes are revealed only after a substantial lag. Thus, an inflation target is unable to send immediate signals to both the public and markets about the stance of monetary policy.

Too Much Rigidity Some economists have criticized inflation targeting because they believe it imposes a rigid rule on monetary policy makers and limits their ability to respond to unforeseen circumstances. However, useful policy strategies exist that are "rule-like," in that they involve forward-looking behavior that limits policy makers from systematically engaging in policies with undesirable long-run consequences. Such policies avoid the time-inconsistency problem and would best be described as "constrained discretion."

Indeed, inflation targeting can be described exactly in this way. Inflation targeting, as actually practiced, is far from rigid and is better described as "flexible inflation targeting." First, inflation targeting does not prescribe simple and mechanical instructions on how the central bank should conduct monetary policy. Rather, it requires the central bank to use all available information to determine which policy actions are appropriate to achieve the inflation target. Unlike simple policy rules, inflation targeting never requires the central bank to focus solely on one key variable. Second, inflation targeting as practiced contains a substantial degree of policy discretion. Inflation targets have been modified depending on economic circumstances, as we have seen. Moreover, central banks under inflation-targeting regimes have left themselves considerable scope to respond to output growth and fluctuations through several devices.

Potential for Increased Output Fluctuations An important criticism of inflation targeting is that a sole focus on inflation may lead to monetary policy that is too tight when inflation is above target and thus may lead to larger output fluctuations. Inflation targeting does not, however, require a sole focus on inflation—in fact, experience has shown that inflation targeters display substantial concern about output fluctuations.

Inflation targeters have chosen inflation targets above zero (typically around 2%), and this reflects the concern of monetary policy makers that particularly low inflation can have substantial negative effects on real economic activity. Deflation (negative inflation in which the price level actually falls) is especially to be feared because of the possibility that it may promote financial instability and precipitate a severe economic contraction (Chapter 8). The deflation in Japan in recent years has been an important factor in the weakening of the Japanese financial system and economy. Targeting inflation rates of above zero makes periods of deflation less likely. This is one reason why economists, both within and outside Japan, called for the Bank of Japan to adopt an inflation target at levels of 2%, which finally occurred in 2013.

Inflation targeting also does not ignore traditional stabilization goals. Central bankers in inflation-targeting countries continue to express their concern about fluctuations in output and employment, and the ability to accommodate short-run stabilization goals to some degree is built into all inflation-targeting regimes. All inflation-targeting countries have been willing to minimize output declines by gradually lowering medium-term inflation targets toward the long-run goal.

Low Economic Growth Another common concern about inflation targeting is that it will lead to low growth in output and employment. Although inflation reduction has been associated with below-normal output during disinflationary phases in inflation-targeting regimes, once low inflation levels were achieved, output and employment returned to levels at least as high as they were before. A conservative conclusion is that once low inflation is achieved, inflation targeting is not harmful to the real economy. Given the strong economic growth after disinflation in many countries (such as New Zealand) that have adopted inflation targets, a case can be made that inflation targeting promotes real economic growth, in addition to controlling inflation.

Should Central Banks Respond to Asset-Price Bubbles? Lessons from the Global Financial Crisis

Over the centuries, economies have been periodically subject to *asset-price bubbles*, pronounced increases in asset prices that depart from fundamental values, which eventually burst resoundingly. The story of the 2007–2009 financial crisis, discussed in Chapter 8, indicates how costly these bubbles can be. The bursting of the asset-price bubble in the housing market severely disrupted the financial system, leading to an economic downturn, a rise in unemployment, distressed communities, and direct hardship for families forced to leave their homes after foreclosures.

The high cost of asset-price bubbles raises a key question for monetary policy strategy: What should central banks do about them? Should they use monetary policy to try to pop bubbles? Are there regulatory measures they can take to rein in asset-price bubbles? To answer these questions, we need to ask whether different bubbles require different responses.

Because asset prices affect business and household spending and hence economic activity, monetary policy certainly needs to respond to asset prices in order to stabilize the economy. Hence, the issue of how monetary policy should respond to asset-price movements is not whether it should respond at all, but whether it should respond at a level over and above that called for in terms of the objectives of stabilizing inflation and employment. Another way of defining the issue is whether monetary policy should try to pop, or slow, the growth of possibly developing asset-price bubbles to minimize later damage to the economy when these bubbles burst. Alternatively, rather than respond directly to possible asset-price bubbles, should the monetary authorities respond to asset-price declines only after a bubble bursts, to stabilize both output and inflation? These opposing positions have been characterized as *leaning* against asset-price bubbles versus *cleaning up* after the bubble bursts, and so the debate over what to do about asset-price bubbles is often referred to as the "lean versus clean" debate.

Two Types of Asset-Price Bubbles

There are two types of asset-price bubbles: one that is driven by credit and a second that is driven purely by overly optimistic expectations (which former chairman of the Fed, Alan Greenspan, referred to as "irrational exuberance").

Credit-Driven Bubbles When a credit boom begins, it can spill over into an asset-price bubble: Easier credit can be used to purchase particular assets and thereby raise their prices. The rise in asset values, in turn, encourages further lending for these assets, either because it increases the value of collateral, making it easier to borrow, or because it raises the value of capital at financial institutions, which gives them more capacity to lend. The lending for these assets can then increase demand for them further and hence raise their prices even more. This feedback loop—in which a credit boom drives up asset prices, which in turn fuels the credit boom, which drives asset prices even higher, and so on—can generate a bubble in which asset prices rise well above their fundamental values.

Credit-driven bubbles are particularly dangerous, as the recent global financial crisis has demonstrated. When asset prices come back down to Earth and the bubble bursts, the collapse in asset prices then leads to a reversal of the feedback loop in which loans go sour, lenders cut back on credit supply, the demand for assets declines further, and prices drop even more. These were exactly the dynamics in housing markets during the global financial crisis. Driven by a credit boom in subprime lending, housing prices rose way above fundamental values, but when housing prices crashed, credit shriveled up and housing prices plummeted.

The resulting losses on subprime loans and securities eroded the balance sheets of financial institutions, causing a decline in credit (deleveraging) and a sharp fall in business and household spending, and therefore in economic activity. As we saw during the 2007–2009 financial crisis, the interaction between housing prices and the health of financial institutions following the collapse of the housing price bubble endangered the operation of the financial system as a whole and had dire consequences for the economy.

Bubbles Driven Solely by Irrational Exuberance **Bubbles** that are driven solely by overly optimistic expectations, but that are not associated with a credit boom, pose much less risk to the financial system. For example, the bubble in technology stocks in the late 1990s described in Chapter 6 was not fueled by credit, and the bursting of the tech-stock bubble was not followed by a marked deterioration in financial institutions' balance sheets. The bursting of the tech-stock bubble thus did not have a very severe impact on the economy, and the recession that followed was quite mild. Bubbles driven solely by irrational exuberance are therefore far less dangerous than those driven by credit booms.

The Debate over Whether Central Banks Should Try to Pop Bubbles

Whether central banks should try to pop, or prick, bubbles was actively debated before the crisis. Alan Greenspan argued against, and his position held great sway in central banking circles before the global financial crisis. However, the crisis has led to reevaluation of this viewpoint, and we look at the pro and con arguments below.

Con: Why Central Banks Should Not Try to Pop Bubbles Alan Greenspan's arguments that central banks should not take actions to prick bubbles became known as the "Greenspan doctrine." His position reflected five arguments.

1. Asset-price bubbles are nearly impossible to identify. If central banks or government officials knew that a bubble was in progress, why wouldn't market participants know as well? If so, then a bubble would be unlikely to develop because market participants would know that prices were getting out of line with fundamentals. Unless central bank or government officials are smarter than market participants, which is unlikely given the especially high wages that savvy market participants garner, they will be unlikely to identify when bubbles of this type are occurring.
2. Although some economic analysis suggests that raising interest rates can diminish rises in asset prices, raising interest rates may be very ineffective in restraining the bubble because market participants expect such high rates of return from buying bubble-driven assets. Furthermore, raising interest rates has often been found to cause a bubble to burst more severely, thereby increasing damage to the economy. Another way of saying this is that bubbles are departures from normal behavior, and it is unrealistic to expect that the usual tools of monetary policy will be effective in abnormal conditions.
3. Many different asset prices exist, and at any one time a bubble may be present in only a fraction of assets. Monetary policy actions are a very blunt instrument in such a case, as such actions would be likely to affect asset prices in general, rather than the specific assets that are experiencing a bubble.
4. Monetary policy actions to prick bubbles can have harmful effects on the aggregate economy. If interest rates are raised significantly to curtail a bubble, the economy will slow, people will lose jobs, and inflation can fall below its desirable level. Indeed, as the first two arguments suggest, the rise in interest rates necessary to prick a bubble may be so high that it can only be done at great cost to workers and the economy. This is not to say that monetary policy should not respond to asset prices per se. The level of asset prices does affect household and business spending and thus the evolution of the economy. Monetary policy should react to fluctuations in asset prices to the extent that they affect inflation and economic activity.
5. As long as the central bank responds in a timely fashion, by easing monetary policy aggressively after an asset bubble bursts, the harmful effects of a bursting bubble could be kept at a manageable level. Indeed, the Greenspan Fed acted exactly in this way after the stock market crash of 1987 and the bursting of the tech bubble in the stock market in 2000. Aggressive easing after the stock market bubbles burst in 1987 and 2000 was highly successful. The economy did not enter a recession after the stock market crash of 1987, whereas the recession was very mild after the tech bubble burst in 2000.

Pro: Why Central Banks Should Try to Pop Bubbles In contrast to the Greenspan doctrine, the recent crisis has clearly demonstrated that the bursting of credit-driven bubbles can be not only extremely costly but also very hard to clean up after. The global financial crisis has therefore provided a much stronger case for trying to pop potential bubbles.

However, the distinction between the two types of bubbles, one of which (credit-driven) is much more costly than the other, suggests that the lean versus clean debate may have been miscast. Rather than leaning against potential asset-price bubbles, which would include both credit-driven and irrational exuberance-type bubbles, the case is much stronger for leaning against credit bubbles, which would involve leaning against credit-driven asset-price bubbles but not irrational exuberance asset-price bubbles. In addition, it is much easier to identify credit bubbles than asset-price bubbles. When asset-price bubbles are rising rapidly at the same time that credit is booming, the likelihood is greater that asset prices are deviating from fundamentals because laxer credit standards are driving asset prices upward. In this case, central bank or government officials have a greater likelihood of identifying that a bubble is in progress; this was indeed the case during the housing market bubble in the United States because these officials did have information that lenders had weakened lending standards and that credit extension in the mortgage markets was rising at abnormally high rates.

The case for leaning against credit bubbles seems strong, but what policies will be most effective in restraining credit bubbles?

Macroprudential Policies First, it is important to recognize that the key principle to consider in designing effective policies to lean against credit bubbles is to curb excessive risk taking. Only when this risk taking is excessive are credit bubbles likely to develop, and so it is natural to look to prudential regulatory measures to constrain credit bubbles. Regulatory policy to affect what is happening in credit markets in the aggregate is referred to as **macroprudential regulation**, and it does seem to be the right tool for reigning in credit-driven bubbles.

Financial regulation and supervision, either by central banks or by other government entities, with the usual elements of a well-functioning prudential regulatory and supervisory system, as described in Chapter 18, can prevent excessive risk taking that can trigger a credit boom, which in turn leads to an asset-price bubble. These elements include adequate disclosure and capital requirements, prompt corrective action, close monitoring of financial institutions' risk management procedures, and close supervision to enforce compliance with regulations. More generally, regulation should focus on preventing leverage cycles. As the global financial crisis demonstrated, the rise in asset prices that accompanied the credit boom resulted in higher capital buffers at financial institutions, supporting further lending in the context of unchanging capital requirements, which led to higher asset prices, and so on; in the bust, the value of the capital dropped precipitously, leading to a cut in lending. Capital requirements that are countercyclical, that is, adjusted upward during a boom and downward during a bust, might help eliminate the pernicious feedback loops that promote credit-driven bubbles.

A rapid rise in asset prices accompanied by a credit boom provides a signal that market failures or poor financial regulation and supervision might be causing a bubble to form. Central banks and other government regulators could then consider implementing policies to rein in credit growth directly or implement measures to make sure credit standards are sufficiently high.

Monetary Policy The fact that the low interest-rate policies of the Federal Reserve from 2002 to 2005 were followed by excessive risk taking suggests to many that overly easy monetary policy might promote financial instability, as was discussed in Chapter 8. Although it is far from clear that the Federal Reserve is primarily to blame for the housing bubble, research does suggest that low interest rates can encourage excessive risk taking in what has been called the "risk-taking channel of monetary policy." Low interest rates may increase the incentives for asset managers in financial institutions to search for yield and hence increase risk taking. Low interest rates may also increase the demand for assets, raising their prices and leading to increased valuation of collateral, which in turn encourages lenders to lend to riskier borrowers.

The risk-taking channel of monetary policy suggests that monetary policy should be used to lean against credit bubbles. However, many of the objections to using monetary policy to prick bubbles behind the Greenspan doctrine are still valid, so wouldn't it be better to use macroprudential supervision to constrain credit bubbles, leaving monetary policy to focus on price and output stability?

This argument would be quite strong if macroprudential policies were able to do the job. However, there are doubts on this score. Prudential supervision is subject to more political pressure than monetary policy because it affects the bottom line of financial institutions more directly. Thus they have greater incentives to lobby politicians to discourage macroprudential policies that would rein in credit bubbles, particularly during a credit bubble when they are making the most money. In addition, financial institutions are often very good at finding loopholes to avoid regulation and so macroprudential supervision may not be effective. The possibility that macroprudential policies may not be implemented sufficiently well to constrain credit bubbles suggests that monetary policy may have to be used instead.

An important lesson from the global financial crisis is that central banks and other regulators should not have a laissez-faire attitude and let credit-driven bubbles proceed without any reaction. How to do this well, however, is indeed a daunting task.

THE PRACTICING MANAGER

Using a Fed Watcher

As we have seen, the most important player in the determination of the U.S. interest rates is the Federal Reserve. When the Fed wants to inject reserves into the system, it conducts open market purchases of bonds, which cause their prices to increase and their interest rates to fall, at least in the short term. To withdraw reserves from the system, the Fed sells bonds, thereby depressing their price and raising their interest rates. From a longer-run perspective, if the Fed pursues an expansionary monetary policy with low interest rates initially, inflation will eventually rise and interest rates will eventually rise as well. Contractionary monetary policy is likely to lower inflation in the long run and lead to lower long-run interest rates.

Access **www.federalreserve.gov/pf/pf.htm** and review what the Federal Reserve reports as its primary purposes and functions.

Knowing what actions the Fed might be taking can thus help financial institution managers predict the future course of interest rates with greater accuracy. Because, as we have seen, changes in interest rates have a major impact on a financial institution's profitability, the managers of these institutions are particularly interested in scrutinizing the Fed's behavior. To help in this task, managers hire so-called Fed watchers, experts on Federal Reserve behavior who may have worked in the Federal Reserve System and so have an insider's view of Federal Reserve operations.

Divining what the Fed is up to is by no means easy. The Fed does not disclose the content of the minutes of FOMC meetings at which it decides the course of monetary policy until three weeks after each meeting. In addition, the Fed does not provide information on the amount of certain transactions and frequently tries to obscure from the market whether it is injecting reserves into the banking system by making open market purchases and sales simultaneously.

Fed watchers, with their specialized knowledge of the ins and outs of the Fed, scrutinize the public pronouncements of Federal Reserve officials to get a feel for where monetary policy is heading. They also carefully study the data on past Federal Reserve actions and current events in the bond markets to determine what the Fed is up to.

If a Fed watcher tells a financial institution manager that Federal Reserve concerns about inflation are high and the Fed will pursue a tight monetary policy and raise short-term interest rates in the near future, the manager may decide immediately to acquire funds at the currently low interest rates in order to keep the cost of funds from rising. If the financial institution trades foreign exchange, the rise in interest rates and the attempt by the Fed to keep inflation down might lead the manager to instruct traders to sell foreign currencies and purchase dollars in the foreign exchange market. As we will see in Chapter 15, these actions by the Fed would be likely to cause the value of the dollar to appreciate, so the purchase of dollars by the financial institution should lead to substantial profits.

If, conversely, the Fed watcher thinks that the Fed is worried about a weak economy and will thus pursue an expansionary policy and lower interest rates, the financial institution manager will take very different actions. Now the manager might instruct loan officers to make as many loans as possible so as to lock in the higher interest rates that the financial institution can earn currently. Or the manager might buy bonds, anticipating that interest rates will fall and their prices will rise, giving the institution a nice profit. The more expansionary policy is also likely to lower the value of the dollar in the foreign exchange market, so the financial institution manager might tell foreign exchange traders to buy foreign currencies and sell dollars in order to make a profit when the dollar falls in the future.

A Fed watcher who is right is a very valuable commodity to a financial institution. Successful Fed watchers are actively sought out by financial institutions and often earn high salaries, well into the six-figure range.

SUMMARY

1. Central banks affect the amount of reserves in the banking system through either open market operations or discount lending. Conduct of monetary policy involves actions that affect the Federal Reserve's balance sheet. Open market purchases lead to an expansion of reserves and liquidity in the banking system. An increase in discount loans also leads to an expansion of reserves and liquidity in the banking system.
2. A supply-and-demand analysis of the market for reserves yields the following results: When the Fed

makes an open market purchase or lowers reserve requirements, the federal funds rate declines. When the Fed makes an open market sale or raises reserve requirements, the federal funds rate rises. Changes in the discount rate and the interest rate paid on reserves may also affect the federal funds rate.

3. Conventional monetary policy tools include open market operations, discount policy, reserve requirements, and interest on reserves. Open market operations were the primary tool used by the Fed to implement monetary policy before the global financial crisis. Discount policy has the advantage of enabling the Fed to perform its role of lender of last resort. Reserve requirements have rarely been used as a monetary policy tool. Raising interest rates on reserves to increase the federal funds rate has the advantage that it avoids the need to conduct massive open market operations to reduce reserves when banks have accumulated large amounts of excess reserves.

4. Conventional monetary policy tools are ineffective when the zero-lower-bound problem occurs, in which the central bank is unable to lower interest rates because they have hit a floor of zero. In this situation, central banks use nonconventional monetary policy tools, which involve liquidity provision, asset purchases, forward guidance, and negative interest rates on banks' deposits at the central bank. Liquidity provision and asset purchases lead to an expansion of the central bank balance sheet, which is referred to as *quantitative easing*. Expansion of the central bank balance sheet by itself is unlikely to have a large impact on the economy, but changing the composition of the balance sheet, which is what liquidity provision and asset purchases accomplished and is referred to as *credit easing*, can have a large impact by improving the function of credit markets. Negative interest rates on banks' deposits at the central bank might help stimulate the economy by encouraging banks to lend out their reserves. However, this expansionary effect might not occur because banks choose to move their deposits at the central bank into cash or because negative interest rates might hurt bank profitability, thereby discouraging banks from lending.

5. The monetary policy tools used by the European Central Bank are similar to those used by the Federal Reserve System and involve open market operations, lending to banks, interest on reserves, and reserve requirements. Main financing operations—open market operations in repos that are typically reversed within two weeks—are the primary tool to set the overnight cash rate at the target financing rate. The European Central Bank also operates standing lending facilities that ensure that the overnight cash rate remains within 100 basis points of the target financing rate.

6. The six basic goals of monetary policy are price stability (the primary goal), high employment, economic growth, interest-rate stability, stability of financial markets, and stability in foreign exchange markets.

7. A nominal anchor is a key element in monetary policy strategy. It helps promote price stability by tying down inflation expectations and limiting the time-inconsistency problem, in which monetary policy makers conduct monetary policy in a discretionary way that might provide short-term benefits but produces poor long-run outcomes.

8. Inflation targeting has several advantages: (1) It is readily understood by the public and is highly transparent; (2) it increases accountability of the central bank; (3) it makes it less likely the central bank will fall into the time-inconsistency trap of pursuing overly expansionary monetary policy; (4) it helps focus the debate on what central banks can do in the long run, that is control inflation; and (5) it appears to ameliorate the effects of inflationary shocks. It does have some disadvantages, however: (1) Inflation is not easily controlled by the monetary authorities, so that an inflation target is unable to send immediate signals to both the public and markets; (2) it might impose a rigid rule on policy makers, although this has not been the case in practice; and (3) a sole focus on inflation may lead to larger output fluctuations, although this has also not been the case in practice.

9. The lessons from the global financial crisis suggest that monetary policy should lean against credit booms but not asset-price bubbles.

10. Because predicting the Federal Reserve's actions can help managers of financial institutions predict the course of interest rates, which has a major impact on financial institutions' profitability, such managers value the services of Fed watchers, who are experts on Federal Reserve behavior.

KEY TERMS

balance sheet, p. 209
bubbles, p. 240
conventional monetary policy tools, p. 218
credit easing, p. 226
defensive open market operations, p. 218

deposit facility, p. 230
discount loans, p. 209
discount rate, p. 210
discount window, p. 219
dual mandate, p. 235
dynamic open market operations, p. 218
excess reserves, p. 209
federal funds rate, p. 211
forward guidance, p. 227
hierarchical mandate, p. 234
inflation targeting, p. 236
lender of last resort, p. 220
longer-term refinancing operations, p. 229
macroprudential regulation, p. 242
main refinancing operations, p. 229
marginal lending facility, p. 230
marginal lending rate, p. 230
matched sale–purchase transaction, p. 218
natural rate of output, p. 233
natural rate of unemployment, p. 232
nominal anchor, p. 231
nonconventional monetary policy tools, p. 223
open market operations, p. 209
overnight cash rate, p. 229
potential output, p. 233
price stability, p. 230
primary dealers, p. 209
quantitative easing, p. 225
repurchase agreement (repo), p. 218
required reserve ratio, p. 209
required reserves, p. 209
reserve requirements, p. 209
reserves, p. 209
reverse repo, p. 219
reverse transactions, p. 229
standing lending facility, p. 220
T-account, p. 209
target financing rate, p. 229
time-inconsistency problem, p. 231
zero-lower-bound problem, p. 223

QUESTIONS

1. During the implementation of programs now known as QE programs, between 2008 and 2012, many forecasters claimed that these programs would result in high inflation rates in the future. In light of the evolution of the inflation rate in the United States, determine if these forecasts were correct or not.
2. In which economic conditions would a central bank want to use a "forward guidance" strategy? Based on your previous answer, can we easily measure the effects of such a strategy?
3. "Discounting is no longer needed because the presence of the FDIC eliminates the possibility of bank panics." Is this statement true, false, or uncertain? Explain your answer.
4. With the onset of the global financial crisis, assets on the Federal Reserve's balance sheet increased dramatically, from approximately \$900 billion in 2007 to over \$4 trillion in 2016. Many of the assets held are longer-term securities acquired through various loan programs instituted as a result of the crisis. In this situation, how could reverse repos (matched sale–purchase transactions) help the Fed reduce its assets held in an orderly fashion while reducing potential inflationary problems?
5. Why was the Term Auction Facility more widely used by financial institutions than the discount window during the global financial crisis?
6. What are the advantages and disadvantages of *quantitative easing* as an alternative to conventional monetary policy when short-term interest rates are at the zero-lower-bound?
7. Why is the composition of the Fed's balance sheet a potentially important aspect of monetary policy during a crisis?
8. How do the monetary policy tools of the European System of Central Banks compare to the monetary policy tools of the Fed? Does the ECB have a discount lending facility? Does the ECB pay banks interest on their deposits?
9. The benefits of using Fed discount operations to prevent bank panics are straightforward. What are the costs?
10. What is the main rationale behind paying negative interest rates to banks for keeping their deposits at central banks in Sweden, Switzerland, and Japan? What could happen to these economies if banks decide to loan their excess reserves, but no good investment opportunities exist?
11. Give an example of the time-inconsistency problem that you experience in your everyday life.
12. What incentives arise for a central bank to fall into the time-inconsistency trap of pursuing overly expansionary monetary policy?
13. Suppose your boss asks you to write a report with two conditions: It has to be clear (i.e., well written) and it has to be completed by the end of the day. Do these instructions constitute a dual mandate or a hierarchical mandate? Suppose that in the short run (during the first month) you fail to meet one of the conditions (you either write a proper report or are late, or vice versa). Do you see a conflict between these two conditions in the long run?

14. Why might inflation targeting increase support for the independence of the central bank to conduct monetary policy?
15. "Because inflation targeting focuses on achieving the inflation target, it will lead to excessive output fluctuations." Is this statement true, false, or uncertain? Explain your answer.
16. "A central bank with a dual mandate will achieve lower unemployment in the long run than a central bank with a hierarchical mandate in which price stability takes precedence." Is this statement true, false, or uncertain?
17. A central bank decides to issue a statement declaring that it will not try to eliminate asset-price bubbles. Can you think of a negative consequence of this statement for the central bank's ability to conduct monetary policy?
18. If higher inflation is bad, then why might it be more advantageous to have a higher inflation target than a lower target closer to zero?
19. Why aren't most central banks more proactive at trying to use monetary policy to eliminate asset-price bubbles?
20. Why would it be better to *lean* against credit-driven bubbles and *clean* after other types of asset bubbles crash?
21. Describe in your own terms the concept of macroprudential regulation. Why might this approach be an important element in preventing credit bubbles?

QUANTITATIVE PROBLEMS

1. Consider a bank policy to maintain 12% of deposits as reserves. The bank currently has $10 million in deposits and holds $400,000 in excess reserves. What is the required reserve on a new deposit of $50,000?
2. Estimates of unemployment for the upcoming year have been developed as follows:

Economy	Probability	Unemployment Rate (%)
Bust	0.15	20
Average	0.50	10
Good	0.20	5
Boom	0.15	1

What is the expected unemployment rate? The standard deviation?

3. Suppose a bank currently has $150,000 in deposits and $15,000 in reserves. The required reserve ratio is 10% (so this bank holds no excess reserves). If there is a deposit outflow (i.e., someone withdraws funds from her account) for $5,000, would this bank still comply with the Fed's requirement of keeping 10% of its deposits in the form of reserves? What would be the cost for this bank to comply with this regulation if the bank decides to borrow from another bank to eliminate its reserve shortage? Assume a federal funds rate of 0.25%.
4. Refer to the previous problem. What would be the cost for this bank to comply with its required reserves if the bank decides to borrow from the Fed at a discount rate of 0.75%? Can you now explain why excess reserves serve as insurance against deposit outflows?
5. The short-term nominal interest rate is 5%, with an expected inflation of 2%. Economists forecast that next year's nominal rate will increase by 100 basis points, but inflation will fall to 1.5%. What is the expected change in real interest rates?

WEB EXERCISES

Conduct of Monetary Policy: Tools, Goals, Strategy, and Tactics

1. Go to **www.federalreserve.gov/releases/h15/update/**. Define the federal funds rate. What is the current federal funds rate? Define the discount rate. What is the current Federal Reserve discount rate? Have short-term rates increased or declined since the end of 2005?
2. The Federal Open Market Committee (FOMC) meets about every six weeks to assess the state of

the economy and to decide what actions the central bank should take. The minutes of this meeting are released three weeks after the meeting; however, a brief press release is made available immediately. Find the schedule of minutes and press releases at **www.federalreserve.gov/fomc/**.

a. When was the last scheduled meeting of the FOMC? When is the next meeting?

b. Review the press release from the last meeting. What did the committee decide to do about short-term interest rates?

c. Review the most recently published meeting minutes. What areas of the economy seemed to be of most concern to the committee members?

3. It is possible to access other central bank Web sites to learn about their structure. One example is the European Central Bank. Go to **www.ecb.int**. On the ECB home page, find information about the ECB's strategy for monetary policy.

4. Many countries have central banks that are responsible for their nation's monetary policy. Go to **www.bis.org/cbanks.htm** and select one of the central banks (for example, Norway). Review that bank's Web site to determine its policies regarding application of monetary policy. How does this bank's policies compare to those of the U.S. central bank?

PART 5 FINANCIAL MARKETS

CHAPTER 11

The Money Markets

> PREVIEW

If you were to review the annual report of Alphabet (holding company for Google) for 2016, you would find that the company had over $14 billion in cash. The firm also listed $58 billion in short-term securities. The firm chose to hold over $72 billion in highly liquid short-term assets in order to be ready to take advantage of investment opportunities and to avoid the risks associated with other types of investments. Alphabet will have much of these funds invested in the money markets. Recall that money market securities are short-term, low-risk, and very liquid. Because of the high degree of safety and liquidity these securities exhibit, they are close to being money, hence their name. The money markets have been active since the early 1800s but have become much more important since 1970, when interest rates rose above historic levels. In fact, the rise in short-term rates, coupled with a regulated ceiling on the rate that banks could pay for deposits, resulted in a rapid outflow of funds from financial institutions in the late 1970s and early 1980s. This outflow caused many banks and savings and loans to fail. The industry regained its health only after massive changes were made to bank regulations with regard to money market interest rates.

This chapter carefully reviews the money markets and the securities that are traded there. In addition, we discuss why the money markets are important to our financial system.

The Money Markets Defined

The term *money market* is actually a misnomer. Money—currency—is not traded in the money markets. Because the securities that do trade there are short-term and highly liquid, however, they are close to being money. Money market securities, which are discussed in detail here, have three basic characteristics in common:

- They are usually sold in large denominations.
- They have low default risk.
- They mature in one year or less *from their original issue date*. Most money market instruments mature in less than 120 days.

Money market transactions do not take place in any one particular location or building. Instead, traders usually arrange purchases and sales between participants over the phone and complete them electronically. Because of this characteristic, money market securities usually have an active *secondary market*. This means that after the security has been sold initially, it is relatively easy to find buyers who will purchase it in the future. An active secondary market makes money market securities very flexible instruments to use to fill short-term financial needs. For example, Microsoft's annual report states, "We consider all highly liquid interest-earning investments with a maturity of 3 months or less at date of purchase to be cash equivalents."*

Another characteristic of the money markets is that they are **wholesale markets**. This means that most transactions are very large, usually in excess of $1 million. The size of these transactions prevents most individual investors from participating directly in the money markets. Instead, dealers and brokers, operating in the trading rooms of large banks and brokerage houses, bring customers together. These traders will buy or sell $50 or $100 million in mere seconds—certainly not a job for the faint of heart!

As you may recall from Chapter 2, flexibility and innovation are two important characteristics of any financial market, and the money markets are no exception. Despite the wholesale nature of the money market, innovative securities and trading methods have been developed to give small investors access to money market securities. We will discuss these securities and their characteristics later in the chapter, and again in Chapter 20, where we show how they are used by the mutual fund industry.

Why Do We Need the Money Markets?

In a totally unregulated world, the money markets should not be needed. The banking industry exists primarily to provide short-term loans and to accept short-term deposits. Banks should have an efficiency advantage in gathering information, an advantage that should eliminate the need for the money markets. Thanks to continuing relationships with customers, banks should be able to offer loans more cheaply than diversified markets, which must evaluate each borrower every time a new security is offered. Furthermore, short-term securities offered for sale in the money markets are neither as liquid nor as safe as deposits placed in banks and thrifts. Given the advantages that banks have, why do the money markets exist at all?

---

*Excerpt from Accounting Policies, Microsoft Corporation 2012 Annual Report. Published by Microsoft Corporation, © 2012.

The banking industry exists primarily to mediate the asymmetric information problem between saver-lenders and borrower-spenders, and banks can earn profits by capturing economies of scale while providing this service. However, the banking industry is subject to more regulations and governmental costs than are the money markets. In situations where the asymmetric information problem is not severe, the money markets have a distinct cost advantage over banks in providing short-term funds.

Money Market Cost Advantages

Interest-rate regulations were a competitive obstacle for banks. One of the principal purposes of the banking regulations of the 1930s was to reduce competition among banks. Regulators felt that with less competition banks were less likely to fail. The cost to consumers of the greater profits banks earned because of the lack of free market competition was justified by the greater economic stability that a healthy banking system would provide.

One way that banking profits were ensured was by regulations that set a ceiling on the rate of interest that banks could pay for funds, known as Regulation Q. The Glass-Steagall Act of 1933 prohibited payment of interest on checking accounts and limited the interest that could be paid on time deposits. The limits on interest rates were not particularly relevant until the late 1950s. Figure 11.1 shows that the limits became especially troublesome to banks in the late 1970s and early 1980s when inflation pushed short-term interest rates above the level that banks could

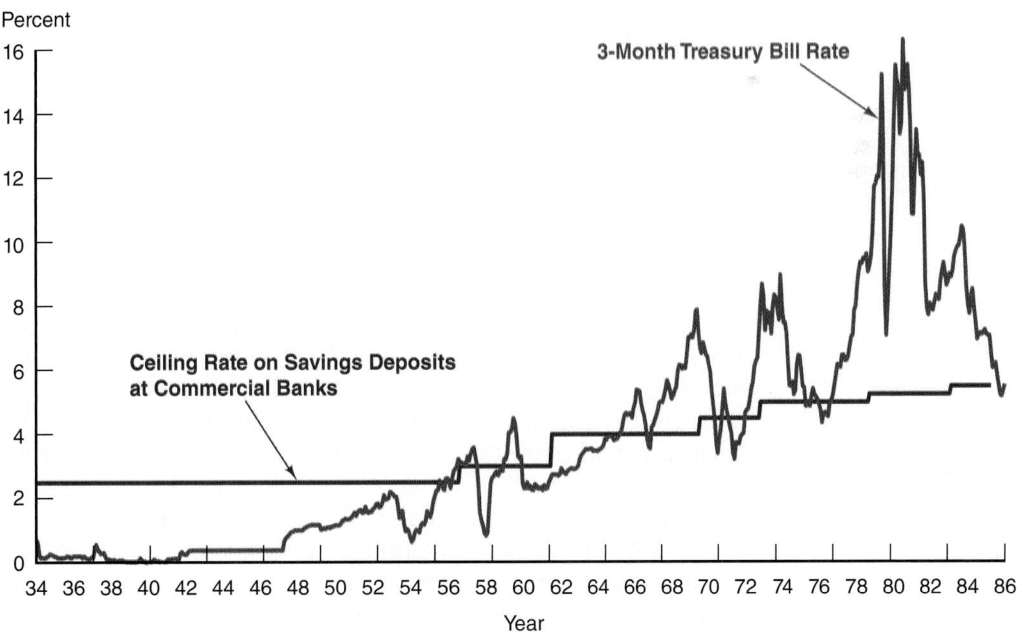

FIGURE 11.1 Three-Month Treasury Bill Rate and Ceiling Rate on Savings Deposits at Commercial Banks, 1933 to 1986

Source: http://www.stlouisfed.org/default.cfm.

legally pay. Investors pulled their money out of banks and put it into money market security accounts offered by many brokerage firms. These new investors caused the money markets to grow rapidly. Commercial bank interest-rate ceilings were removed in March 1986, but by then the retail money markets were well established.

Banks continue to provide valuable intermediation, as we will see in several later chapters. In some situations, however, the cost structure of the banking industry makes it unable to compete effectively in the market for short-term funds against the less restricted money markets.

The Purpose of the Money Markets

The well-developed secondary market for money market instruments makes the money market an ideal place for a firm or financial institution to "warehouse" surplus funds until they are needed. Similarly, the money markets provide a low-cost source of funds to firms, the government, and intermediaries that need a short-term infusion of funds.

The goal of most investors in the money market who are temporarily warehousing funds is not to earn particularly high returns on their funds. Rather, they use the money market as an interim investment that provides a higher return than holding cash or money in banks. They may feel that market conditions are not right to warrant the purchase of additional stock, or they may expect interest rates to rise and hence not want to purchase bonds. It is important to keep in mind that holding idle surplus cash is expensive for an investor because cash balances earn no income for the owner. Idle cash represents an *opportunity cost* in terms of lost interest income. Recall from Chapter 4 that an asset's opportunity cost is the amount of interest sacrificed by not holding an alternative asset. The money markets provide a means to invest idle funds and to reduce this opportunity cost.

Investment advisers often hold some funds in the money market so that they will be able to act quickly to take advantage of investment opportunities they might identify. Most investment funds and financial intermediaries also hold money market securities to meet investment or deposit outflows.

The sellers of money market securities find that the money market provides a low-cost source of temporary funds. Table 11.1 shows the interest rates available on a variety of money market instruments sold by different firms and institutions. For example, banks may borrow excess reserves (we will define the money market securities later in this chapter) to obtain funds in the money market to meet short-term reserve requirement shortages. The government funds a large portion of the U.S. debt with Treasury bills. Finance companies like GMAC (General Motors Acceptance Company) may enter the money market to raise the funds that it uses to make car loans.[1]

Why do corporations and the U.S. government sometimes need to get their hands on funds quickly? The primary reason is that cash inflows and outflows are rarely synchronized. Government tax revenues, for example, usually come only at certain times of the year, but expenses are incurred all year long. The government can borrow short-term funds that it will pay back when it receives tax revenues.

---

[1]GMAC was once a wholly owned subsidiary of General Motors that provided financing options exclusively for GM car buyers. In December 2008 it became an independent bank holding company.

TABLE 11.1 Sample Money Market Rates, May 13, 2016

Instrument	Interest Rate (%)
Prime rate	3.50
Federal funds	0.37
Commercial paper	0.55
London interbank offer rate	0.44
Eurodollar	0.48
Treasury bills (4 week)	0.24

Source: Federal Reserve Statistical Bulletin, http://www.federalreserve.gov/releases/h15/data.htm and Libor: http://www.fedprimerate.com/libor/libor_rates_history.htm.

Businesses also face problems caused by revenues and expenses occurring at different times. The money markets provide an efficient, low-cost way of solving these problems.

Who Participates in the Money Markets?

An obvious way to discuss the players in the money market would be to list those who borrow and those who lend. The problem with this approach is that most money market participants operate on both sides of the market. For example, any large bank will borrow aggressively in the money market by selling large commercial CDs. At the same time, it will lend short-term funds to businesses through its commercial lending departments. Nevertheless, we can identify the primary money market players—the U.S. Treasury, the Federal Reserve System, commercial banks, businesses, investments and securities firms, and individuals—and discuss their roles (summarized in Table 11.2).

U.S. Treasury Department

The U.S. Treasury Department is unique because it is always a demander of money market funds and never a supplier. The U.S. Treasury is the largest of all money market borrowers worldwide. It issues Treasury bills (often called T-bills) and other securities that are popular with other money market participants. Short-term issues enable the government to raise funds until tax revenues are received. The Treasury also issues T-bills to replace maturing issues.

Federal Reserve System

The Fed holds vast quantities of Treasury securities that it sells if it believes interest rates should be raised. Similarly, the Fed will purchase Treasury securities if it believes interest rates should be lowered. The Fed's responsibility for interest rates makes it the most influential participant in the U.S. money market. The Federal Reserve's role in controlling the economy through open market operations was discussed in detail in Chapters 9 and 10.

TABLE 11.2 Money Market Participants

Participant	Role
U.S. Treasury Department	Sells U.S. Treasury securities to fund the national debt
Federal Reserve System	Buys and sells U.S. Treasury securities as its primary method of controlling interest rates
Commercial banks	Buy U.S. Treasury securities; sell certificates of deposit and make short-term loans; offer individual investors accounts that invest in money market securities
Businesses	Buy and sell various short-term securities as a regular part of their cash management
Investment companies (brokerage firms)	Trade on behalf of commercial accounts
Finance companies (commercial leasing companies)	Lend funds to individuals
Insurance companies (property and casualty insurance companies)	Maintain liquidity needed to meet unexpected demands
Pension funds	Maintain funds in money market instruments in readiness for investment in stocks and bonds
Individuals	Buy money market mutual funds
Money market mutual funds	Allow small investors to participate in the money market by aggregating their funds to invest in large-denomination money market securities

Commercial Banks

Commercial banks hold a percentage of U.S. government securities second only to pension funds. This is partly because of regulations that limit the investment opportunities available to banks. Specifically, banks are prohibited from owning risky securities, such as stocks or corporate bonds. There are no restrictions against holding Treasury securities because of their low risk and high liquidity.

Banks are also the major issuer of negotiable certificates of deposit (CDs), banker's acceptances, federal funds, and repurchase agreements (we will discuss these securities in the next section). In addition to using money market securities to help manage their own liquidity, many banks trade on behalf of their customers.

Not all commercial banks deal in the secondary money market for their customers. The ones that do are among the largest in the country and are often referred to as *money center banks*. The biggest money center banks include Citigroup, Bank of America, J.P. Morgan, and Wells Fargo.

Businesses

Many businesses buy and sell securities in the money markets. Such activity is usually limited to major corporations because of the large dollar amounts involved.

As discussed earlier, the money markets are used extensively by businesses both to warehouse surplus funds and to raise short-term funds. We will discuss the specific money market securities that businesses issue later in this chapter.

Investment and Securities Firms

The other financial institutions that participate in the money markets are listed in Table 11.2.

Investment Companies Large diversified brokerage firms are active in the money markets. The largest of these include Bank of America, Merrill Lynch, Barclays Capital, Credit Suisse, and Goldman Sachs. The primary function of these dealers is to "make a market" for money market securities by maintaining an inventory from which to buy or sell. These firms are very important to the liquidity of the money market because they ensure that sellers can readily market their securities. We discuss investment companies in Chapter 22.

Finance Companies Finance companies raise funds in the money markets primarily by selling commercial paper. They then lend the funds to consumers for the purchase of durable goods such as cars, boats, and home improvements. Finance companies and related firms are discussed in Chapter 27 (on the Web at www.pearsonhighered.com/mishkin_eakins).

Insurance Companies Property and casualty insurance companies must maintain liquidity because of their unpredictable need for funds. For example, when tornadoes and flooding hit the Midwest in December 2015, more than 1,000 homes were destroyed and 50 lives lost. Insurance companies paid out over a billion dollars in benefits to policyholders. To meet this demand for funds, the insurance companies sold some of their money market securities to raise cash. Insurance companies are discussed in Chapter 21.

Pension Funds Pension funds invest a portion of their cash in the money markets so that they can take advantage of investment opportunities that they may identify in the stock or bond markets. Like insurance companies, pension funds must have sufficient liquidity to meet their obligations. However, because their obligations are reasonably predictable, large money market security holdings are unnecessary. Pension funds are discussed in Chapter 21.

Individuals

When inflation rose in the late 1970s, the interest rates that banks were offering on deposits became unattractive to individual investors. At this same time, brokerage houses began promoting money market mutual funds, which paid much higher rates.

Due to regulations that capped the rate they could pay on deposits, banks could not stop large amounts of cash from moving to mutual funds. To combat this flight of money from banks, the authorities revised the regulations. Banks quickly raised rates in an attempt to recapture individual investors' dollars. This halted the rapid movement of funds, but money market mutual funds remain a popular individual investment option. The advantage of mutual funds is that they give investors with relatively small amounts of cash access to large-denomination securities.

Money Market Instruments

A variety of money market instruments are available to meet the diverse needs of market participants. One security will be perfect for one investor; a different security may be best for another. In this section we gain a greater understanding of money market security characteristics and how money market participants use them to manage their cash.

Treasury Bills

To finance the national debt, the U.S. Treasury Department issues a variety of debt securities. The most widely held and most liquid security is the Treasury bill. Treasury bills are sold with 4-, 13-, 26-, and 52-week maturities. The Treasury bill had a minimum denomination of $1,000 until 2008, at which time new $100 denominations became available. The Federal Reserve is the Treasury's agent for the distribution of all government securities. It has set up a direct purchase option that individuals may use to purchase Treasury bills over the Internet. First available in September 1998, this method of buying securities represented an effort to make Treasury securities more widely available.

The government does not actually pay interest on Treasury bills. Instead, they are issued at a discount from par (their value at maturity). The investor's yield comes from the increase in the value of the security between the time it was purchased and the time it matures.

CASE

Discounting the Price of Treasury Securities to Pay the Interest

Most money market securities do not pay interest. Instead, the investor pays less for the security than it will be worth when it matures, and the increase in price provides a return. This is called **discounting** and is common to short-term securities because it simplifies the distribution at maturity. (We discussed discounting in Chapter 3.)

Table 11.3 shows the results of a typical Treasury bill auction as reported on the Treasury direct web site. If we look at the first listing we see that the 28-day Treasury bill sold for $99.981333 per $100. This means that a $1,000 bill was discounted to $999.81. The table also reports the discount rate and the investment rate. The discount rate is computed as

$$i_{discount} = \frac{F - P}{F} \times \frac{360}{n} \tag{1}$$

where $i_{discount}$ = annualized discount rate
P = purchase price
F = face or maturity value
n = number of days until maturity

Notice a few features about this equation. First, the return is computed using the face amount in the denominator. You will actually pay less than the face amount, since this is sold as a discount instrument, so the return is underestimated. Second,

TABLE 11.3 Recent Bill Auction Results

Security Term	Issue Date	Maturity Date	Discount Rate	Investment Rate	Price per $100	CUSIP
28 day	5/19/2016	6/16/2016	0.240	0.243	99.981333	912796HX0
91 day	5/19/2016	8/18/2016	0.275	0.279	99.930486	912796HA0
182 day	5/19/2016	11/17/2016	0.370	0.376	99.812944	912796JU4
28 day	5/12/2016	6/9/2016	0.245	0.248	99.980944	912796HW2
91 day	5/12/2016	8/11/2016	0.240	0.243	99.939333	912796JF7

Source: http://www.treasurydirect.gov/RI/OFBills.

a 360-day year (30 × 12) is used when annualizing the return. This also underestimates the return when compared to using a 365-day year.

The investment rate is computed as

$$i_{investment} = \frac{F - P}{P} \times \frac{365}{n} \tag{2}$$

The investment rate is a more accurate representation of what an investor will earn, since it uses the actual number of days per year and the true initial investment in its calculation. Note that when computing the investment rate the Treasury uses the actual number of days in the following year. This means that there are 366 days in leap years.

EXAMPLE 11.1

Discount and Investment Rate Percent Calculations

You submit a noncompetitive bid to purchase a 28-day $1,000 Treasury bill, and you find that you are buying the bond for $999.81333. What are the discount rate and the investment rate?

> Solution

Discount rate

$$i_{discount} = \frac{\$1000 - \$999.81333}{\$1000} \times \frac{360}{28}$$

$$i_{discount} = .00240 = .240\%$$

Investment rate

$$i_{investment} = \frac{\$1000 - \$999.81333}{999.81333} \times \frac{365}{28}$$

$$i_{investment} = .00243 = .243\%$$

These solutions for the discount rate and the investment rate match those reported by Treasury direct for the first Treasury bill in Table 11.3.

Access **www.treasurydirect.gov**. Visit this site to study how Treasury securities are auctioned.

Risk Treasury bills have virtually zero default risk because even if the government ran out of money, it could simply print more to redeem them when they mature. The risk of unexpected changes in inflation is also low because of the short term to maturity. The market for Treasury bills is extremely deep and liquid. A **deep market** is one with many different buyers and sellers. A **liquid market** is one in which securities can be bought and sold quickly and with low transaction costs. Investors in markets that are deep and liquid have little risk that they will not be able to sell their securities when they want to.

On a historical note, the budget debates in 1978, 1996, and again in 2013 caused the government to temporarily shut down, nearly leading to default on its debt, despite the long-held belief that such a thing could not happen. If the stalemates had lasted much longer, we would have witnessed the first-ever U.S. government security default. We can only speculate what the long-term effect on interest rates will be if the market decides to add a default risk premium to all government securities.

Treasury Bill Auctions Each week the Treasury announces how many and what kind of Treasury bills it will offer for sale. The Treasury accepts the bids offering the highest price. The Treasury accepts competitive bids in ascending order of yield until the accepted bids reach the offering amount. Each accepted bid is then awarded at the highest yield paid to any accepted bid.

As an alternative to the **competitive bidding** procedure just outlined, the Treasury also permits **noncompetitive bidding**. When competitive bids are offered, investors state both the amount of securities desired and the price they are willing to pay. By contrast, noncompetitive bids include only the amount of securities the investor wants. The Treasury accepts all noncompetitive bids. The price is set as the highest yield paid to any accepted competitive bid. Thus, noncompetitive bidders pay the same price paid by competitive bidders. The significant difference between the two methods is that competitive bidders may or may not end up buying securities, whereas the noncompetitive bidders are guaranteed to do so.

In 1976 the Treasury switched the entire marketable portion of the federal debt over to **book entry** securities, replacing engraved pieces of paper. In a book entry system, ownership of Treasury securities is documented only in the Fed's computer: Essentially, a ledger entry replaces the actual security. This procedure reduces the cost of issuing Treasury securities as well as the cost of transferring them as they are bought and sold in the secondary market.

The Treasury auction of securities is supposed to be highly competitive and fair. To ensure proper levels of competition, no one dealer is allowed to purchase more than 35% of any one issue. About 40 primary dealers regularly participate in the auction. Salomon Smith Barney was caught violating the limits on the percentage of one issue a dealer may purchase, with serious consequences. (See the Mini-Case box "Treasury Bill Auctions Go Haywire.")

Treasury Bill Interest Rates Treasury bills are very close to being risk-free. As expected for a risk-free security, the interest rate earned on Treasury bill securities is among the lowest in the economy. Investors in Treasury bills have found that in some years their earnings did not even compensate them for changes in purchasing power due to inflation. Figure 11.2 shows the interest rate on Treasury bills and the inflation rate over the period 1973–2016. As discussed in Chapter 3, the *real*

MINI-CASE

Treasury Bill Auctions Go Haywire

Every Thursday the Treasury announces how many 28-day, 91-day, and 182-day Treasury bills it will offer for sale. Buyers must submit bids by the following Monday, and awards are made the next morning. The Treasury accepts the bids offering the highest price.

The Treasury auction of securities is supposed to be highly competitive and fair. To ensure proper levels of competition, no one dealer is allowed to purchase more than 35% of any one issue. About 40 primary dealers regularly participate in the auction.

In 1991 the disclosure that Salomon Smith Barney had broken the rules to corner the market cast the fairness of the auction in doubt. Salomon Smith Barney purchased 35% of the Treasury securities in its own name by submitting a relatively high bid. It then bought additional securities in the names of its customers, often without their knowledge or consent. Salomon then bought the securities from the customers. As a result of these transactions, Salomon cornered the market and was able to charge a monopoly-like premium. The investigation of Salomon Smith Barney revealed that during one auction in May 1991, the brokerage managed to gain control of 94% of an $11 billion issue. During the scandal that followed this disclosure, John Gutfreund, the firm's chairman, and several other top executives with Salomon retired. The Treasury has instituted new rules since then to ensure that the market remains competitive.

rate of interest has occasionally been less than zero. Several times since 1973 the inflation rate matched or exceeded the earnings on T-bills. Clearly, the T-bill is not an investment to be used for anything but temporary storage of excess funds because it may not even keep up with inflation.

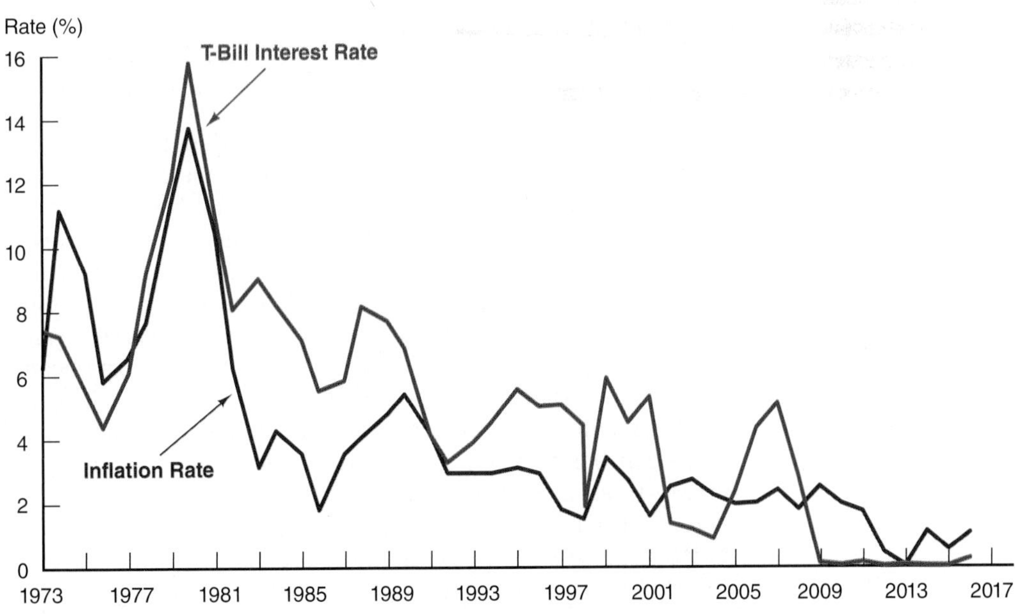

FIGURE 11.2 Treasury Bill Interest Rate and the Inflation Rate, January 1973–January 2016

Source: http://www.federalreserve.gov/releases and CPI: ftp://ftp.bls.gov/pub/special.requests/cpi/cpiai.txt.

Federal Funds

Federal funds are short-term funds transferred (loaned or borrowed) between financial institutions, usually for a period of one day. The term *federal funds* (or *fed funds*) is misleading. Fed funds really have nothing to do with the federal government. The term comes from the fact that these funds are held at the Federal Reserve bank. The fed funds market began in the 1920s when banks with excess reserves loaned them to banks that needed them. The interest rate for borrowing these funds was close to the rate that the Federal Reserve charged on discount loans.

Purpose of Fed Funds The Federal Reserve has set minimum reserve requirements that all banks must maintain. To meet these reserve requirements, banks must keep a certain percentage of their total deposits with the Federal Reserve. The main purpose for fed funds is to provide banks with an immediate infusion of reserves. Banks can borrow directly from the Federal Reserve, but the Fed actively discourages banks from regularly borrowing from it. One indication of the popularity of fed funds is that on a typical day a quarter of a trillion dollars in fed funds will change hands.

Terms for Fed Funds Fed funds are usually overnight investments. Banks analyze their reserve position on a daily basis and either borrow or invest in fed funds, depending on whether they have deficit or excess reserves. Suppose that a bank finds that it has $50 million in excess reserves. It will call its correspondent banks (banks that have reciprocal accounts) to see if they need reserves that day. The bank will sell its excess funds to the bank that offers the highest rate. Once an agreement has been reached, the bank with excess funds will communicate to the Federal Reserve bank instructions to take funds out of its account at the Fed and deposit the funds in the borrower's account. The next day, the funds are transferred back, and the process begins again.

Most fed funds borrowings are unsecured. Typically, the entire agreement is established by direct communication between buyer and seller.

Federal Funds Interest Rates The forces of supply and demand set the fed funds interest rate. This is a competitive market that analysts watch closely for indications of what is happening to short-term rates. The fed funds rate reported by the press is known as the *effective rate*, which is defined in the *Federal Reserve Bulletin* as the weighted average of rates on trades through New York brokers.

The Federal Reserve cannot directly control fed funds rates. It can and does indirectly influence them by adjusting the level of reserves available to banks in the system. The Fed can increase the amount of money in the financial system by buying securities, as was demonstrated in Chapter 10. When investors sell securities to the Fed, the proceeds are deposited in their banks' accounts at the Federal Reserve. These deposits increase the supply of reserves in the financial system and lower interest rates. If the Fed removes reserves by selling securities, fed funds rates will increase. The Fed, through its open market committee (FOMC), will often announce its intention to raise or lower the fed funds rate in advance. Though these rates directly affect few businesses or consumers, analysts consider them an important indicator of the direction in which the Federal Reserve wants the economy to move. Figure 11.3 compares the fed funds rate with the T-bill rate over the period January 1990 to April 2016. Clearly, the two track together.

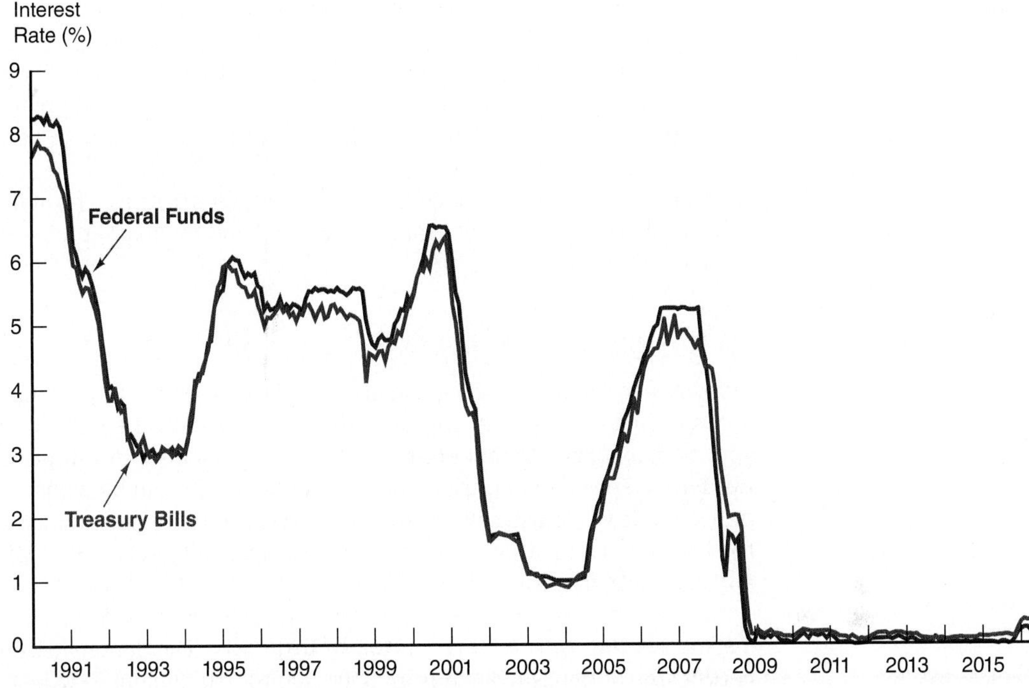

FIGURE 11.3 Federal Funds and Treasury Bill Interest Rates, January 1990–April 2016

Source: http://www.federalreserve.gov/releases/h15/data.htm.

Repurchase Agreements

Repurchase agreements (repos) work much the same as fed funds except that nonbanks can participate. A firm can sell Treasury securities in a repurchase agreement whereby the firm agrees to buy back the securities at a specified future date. Most repos have a very short term, the most common being for 3 to 14 days. There is a market, however, for one- to three-month repos.

The Use of Repurchase Agreements Government securities dealers frequently engage in repos. The dealer may sell the securities to a bank with the promise to buy the securities back the next day. This makes the repo essentially a short-term collateralized loan. Securities dealers use the repo to manage their liquidity and to take advantage of anticipated changes in interest rates.

The Federal Reserve also uses repos in conducting monetary policy. We presented the details of monetary policy in Chapter 10. Recall that the conduct of monetary policy typically requires that the Fed adjust bank reserves on a temporary basis. To accomplish this adjustment, the Fed will buy or sell Treasury securities in the repo market. The maturities of Federal Reserve repos never exceed 15 days.

Interest Rate on Repos Because repos are collateralized with Treasury securities, they are usually low-risk investments and therefore have low interest rates. Though rare, losses have occurred in these markets. For example, in 1985 ESM Government Securities and Bevill, Bresler & Schulman declared bankruptcy. These firms had used the same securities as collateral for more than one loan. The resulting losses to municipalities that had purchased the repos exceeded $500 million. Such losses also caused the failure of the state-insured thrift insurance system in Ohio.

More recently, the financial crisis of 2007–2008 impacted the repo market when the value of the securitizing collateral came under scrutiny. The ability of borrowers to issue short-term debt was rapidly curtailed and the market collapsed for a period of time.

Negotiable Certificates of Deposit

A negotiable certificate of deposit is a bank-issued security that documents a deposit and specifies the interest rate and the maturity date. Because a maturity date is specified, a CD is a **term security** as opposed to a **demand deposit**: Term securities have a specified maturity date; demand deposits can be withdrawn at any time. A negotiable CD is also called a **bearer instrument**. This means that whoever holds the instrument at maturity receives the principal and interest. The CD can be bought and sold until maturity.

Terms of Negotiable Certificates of Deposit The denominations of negotiable certificates of deposit range from $100,000 to $10 million. Few negotiable CDs are denominated less than $1 million. The reason that these instruments are so large is that dealers have established the round lot size to be $1 million. A round lot is the minimum quantity that can be traded without incurring higher than normal brokerage fees.

Negotiable CDs typically have a maturity of one to four months. Some have six-month maturities, but there is little demand for ones with longer maturities.

History of the CD Citibank issued the first large certificates of deposit in 1961. The bank offered the CD to counter the long-term trend of declining demand deposits at large banks. Corporate treasurers were minimizing their cash balances and investing their excess funds in safe, income-generating money market instruments such as T-bills. The attraction of the CD was that it paid a market interest rate. There was a problem, however. The rate of interest that banks could pay on CDs was restricted by Regulation Q. As long as interest rates on most securities were low, this regulation did not affect demand. But when interest rates rose above the level permitted by Regulation Q, the market for these certificates of deposit evaporated. In response, banks began offering the certificates overseas, where they were exempt from Regulation Q limits. In 1970 Congress amended Regulation Q to exempt certificates of deposit over $100,000. By 1972 the CD represented approximately 40% of all bank deposits. The certificate of deposit is now the second most popular money market instrument, behind only the T-bill.

Interest Rate on CDs The rates paid on negotiable CDs are negotiated between the bank and the customer. They are similar to the rate paid on other money market instruments because the level of risk is relatively low. Large money center banks can offer rates a little lower than other banks because many investors in the market believe that the government would never allow one of the nation's largest banks to fail. This belief makes these banks' obligations less risky.

Access **www.federalreserve.gov/releases/CP/**. Find detailed information on commercial paper, including criteria used for calculating commercial paper interest rates, outstanding volume, and historical discount rates.

Commercial Paper

Commercial paper securities are unsecured promissory notes, issued by corporations, that mature in no more than 270 days. Because these securities are unsecured, only the largest and most creditworthy corporations issue commercial paper. The interest rate the corporation is charged reflects the firm's level of risk.

Terms and Issuance Commercial paper always has an original maturity of less than 270 days. This is to avoid the need to register the security issue with the Securities and Exchange Commission. (To be exempt from SEC registration, the issue must have an original maturity of less than 270 days and be intended for current transactions.) Most commercial paper actually matures in 20 to 45 days. Like T-bills, most commercial paper is issued on a discounted basis.

About 60% of commercial paper is sold directly by the issuer to the buyer. The balance is sold by dealers in the commercial paper market. A strong secondary market for commercial paper does not exist. A dealer will redeem commercial paper if a purchaser has a dire need for cash, though this is generally not necessary.

History of Commercial Paper Commercial paper has been used in various forms since the 1920s. In 1969 a tight-money environment caused bank holding companies to issue commercial paper to finance new loans. In response, to keep control over the money supply, the Federal Reserve imposed reserve requirements on bank-issued commercial paper in 1970. These reserve requirements removed the major advantage to banks of using commercial paper. Bank holding companies still use commercial paper to fund leasing and consumer finance.

The use of commercial paper increased substantially in the early 1980s because of the rising cost of bank loans. Figure 11.4 graphs the interest rate on commercial paper against the bank prime rate for the period January 1990–April 2016. Commercial paper has become an important alternative to bank loans primarily because of its lower cost.

Market for Commercial Paper Nonbank corporations use commercial paper extensively to finance the loans that they extend to their customers. For example, General Motors Acceptance Corporation (GMAC) borrows money by issuing commercial paper and uses the money to make loans to consumers. Similarly, GE Capital and Chrysler Credit use commercial paper to fund loans made to consumers. The total number of firms issuing commercial paper varies between 600 and 800, depending on the level of interest rates. Most of these firms use one of about 30 commercial paper dealers who match up buyers and sellers. The large New York City money center banks are very active in this market. Some of the larger issuers of commercial paper choose to distribute their securities with **direct placements**. In a direct placement, the issuer bypasses the dealer and sells directly to the end investor. The advantage of this method is that the issuer saves the 0.125% commission that the dealer charges.

Most issuers of commercial paper back up their paper with a line of credit at a bank. This means that in the event the issuer cannot pay off or roll over the maturing paper, the bank will lend the firm funds for this purpose. The line of credit reduces the risk to the purchasers of the paper and so lowers the interest rate. The bank that provides the backup line of credit agrees in advance to make a loan to the issuer if needed to pay off the outstanding paper. The bank charges a fee of 0.5% to

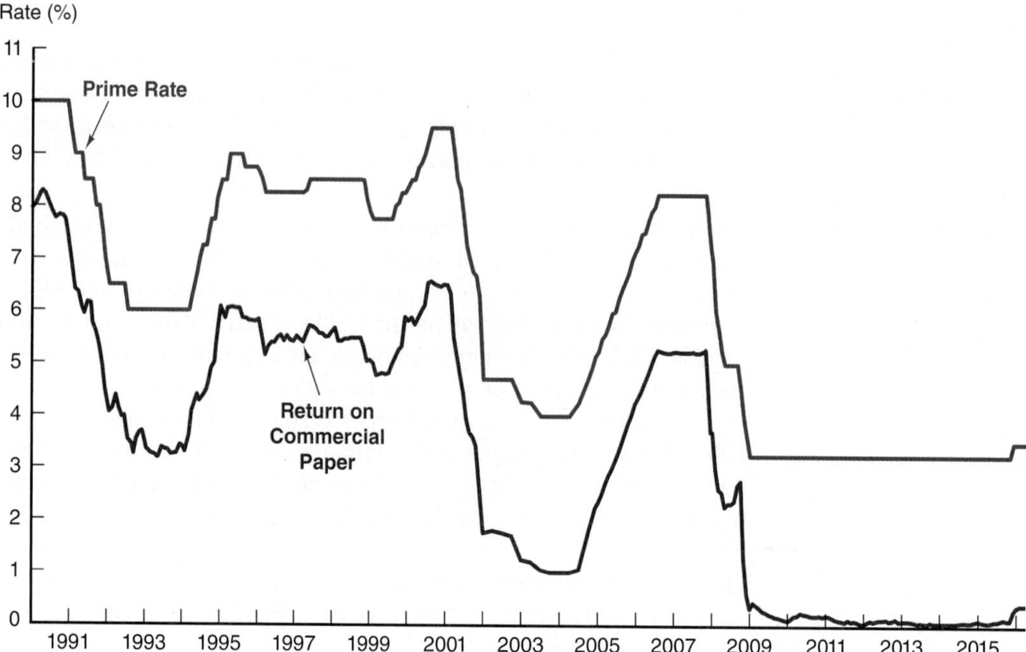

FIGURE 11.4 Return on Commercial Paper and the Prime Rate, 1990–April 2016

Source: http://www.federalreserve.gov/releases/h15/data/Monthly/H15_PRIME_NA.txt.

1% for this commitment. Issuers pay this fee because they are able to save more than this in lowered interest costs by having the line of credit.

Commercial banks were the original purchasers of commercial paper. Today the market has greatly expanded to include large insurance companies, nonfinancial businesses, bank trust departments, and government pension funds. These firms are attracted by the relatively low default risk, short maturity, and somewhat higher yields these securities offer. In 2016 there was about $1 trillion in commercial paper outstanding (see Figure 11.5).

The Role of Asset-Backed Commercial Paper in the Financial Crisis A special type of commercial paper known as **asset-backed commercial paper**, or ABCPs, comprises short-term securities with more than half having maturities of 1 to 4 days. The average maturity is 30 days. ABCPs differ from conventional commercial paper in that they are backed (secured) by some bundle of assets. In 2004–2007 these assets were mostly securitized mortgages. The majority of the sponsors of the ABCP programs had credit ratings from major rating agencies; however, the quality of the pledged assets was usually poorly understood. The size of the ABCP market nearly doubled between 2004 and 2007 to about $1 trillion as the securitized mortgage market exploded.

When the poor quality of the subprime mortgages used to secure ABCP was exposed in 2007–2008, a run on ABCPs began. Unlike commercial bank deposits, there was no deposit insurance backing these investments. Investors attempted to sell them into a saturated market. The problems extended to money market mutual

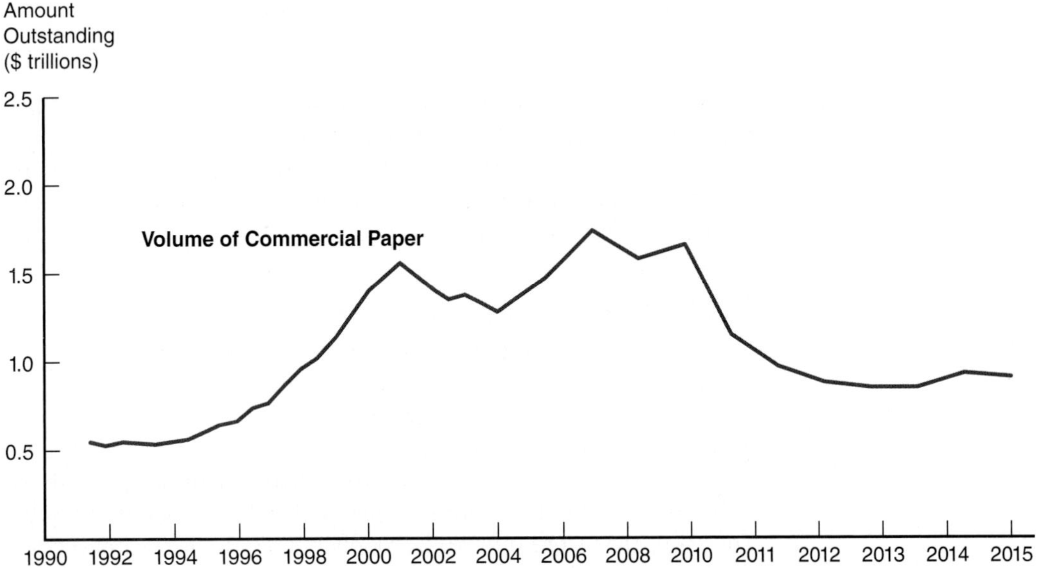

FIGURE 11.5 Volume of Commercial Paper Outstanding, 1990 to 2016

Source: http://www.federalreserve.gov/releases/cp/yrend.htm.

funds, which found that the issuers of ABCP had exercised their option to extend the maturities at low rates. Withdrawals from money market mutual funds threatened to cause them to "break the buck," where a dollar held in the fund can be redeemed only at something less than a dollar, say, 90 cents. In September 2008 the Federal Reserve set up a guarantee program to prevent the collapse of the money market mutual fund market and to allow for an orderly liquidation of their ABCP holdings.[2]

Banker's Acceptances

A banker's acceptance is an order to pay a specified amount of money to the bearer on a given date. Banker's acceptances have been in use since the twelfth century. However, they were not major money market securities until the volume of international trade ballooned in the 1960s. They are used to finance goods that have not yet been transferred from the seller to the buyer. For example, suppose that Builtwell Construction Company wants to buy a bulldozer from Komatsu in Japan. Komatsu does not want to ship the bulldozer without being paid because Komatsu has never heard of Builtwell and realizes that it would be difficult to collect if payment were not forthcoming. Similarly, Builtwell is reluctant to send money to Japan before receiving the equipment. A bank can intervene in this standoff by issuing a banker's

[2]For more detail on ABCPs and their role in the subprime crisis, see "The Evolution of a Financial Crisis: Panic in the Asset-Backed Commercial Paper Market," by Daniel Covitz, Nellie Liang, and Gustavo Suarez, working paper from the Federal Reserve Board.

acceptance whereby the bank in essence substitutes its creditworthiness for that of the purchaser.

Because banker's acceptances are payable to the bearer, they can be bought and sold until they mature. They are sold on a discounted basis like commercial paper and T-bills. Dealers in this market match up firms that want to discount a banker's acceptance (sell it for immediate payment) with companies wishing to invest in banker's acceptances. Interest rates on banker's acceptances are low because the risk of default is very low.

Eurodollars

Many contracts around the world call for payment in U.S. dollars due to the dollar's stability. For this reason, many foreign companies and governments choose to hold dollars. Prior to World War II, most of these deposits were held in New York money center banks. However, as a result of the Cold War that followed, there was fear that deposits held on U.S. soil could be expropriated. Some large London banks responded to this opportunity by offering to hold dollar-denominated deposits in British banks. These deposits were dubbed Eurodollars (see the following Global box).

The Eurodollar market has continued to grow rapidly. The primary reason is that depositors often receive a higher rate of return on a dollar deposit in the Eurodollar market than in their domestic market. At the same time the borrower is often able to receive a more favorable rate in the Eurodollar market than in their domestic market. This is because multinational banks are not subject to the same regulations restricting U.S. banks and because they are willing and able to accept narrower spreads between the interest paid on deposits and the interest earned on loans.

London Interbank Market Some large London banks act as brokers in the interbank Eurodollar market. Recall that fed funds are used by banks to make up temporary shortfalls in their reserves. Eurodollars are an alternative to fed funds. Banks from around the world buy and sell overnight funds in this market. The rate paid by banks buying funds is the **London interbank bid rate (LIBID)**. Funds are offered for sale in this market at the **London interbank offer rate (LIBOR)**. Because many banks participate in this market, it is extremely competitive. The spread between the bid and the offer rate seldom exceeds 0.125%. Eurodollar deposits are time deposits, which means that they cannot be withdrawn for a specified period of

> GLOBAL

Ironic Birth of the Eurodollar Market

One of capitalism's great ironies is that the Eurodollar market, one of the most important financial markets used by capitalists, was fathered by the Soviet Union. In the early 1950s, during the height of the Cold War, the Soviets had accumulated a substantial amount of dollar balances held by banks in the United States. Because the Russians feared that the U.S. government might freeze these assets in the United States, they wanted to move the deposits to Europe, where they would be safe from expropriation. (This fear was not unjustified—consider the U.S. freeze on Iranian assets in 1979 and Iraqi assets in 1990.) However, they also wanted to keep the deposits in dollars so that they could be used in their international transactions. The solution was to transfer the deposits to European banks but to keep the deposits denominated in dollars. When the Soviets did this, the Eurodollar was born.

time. Although the most common time period is overnight, different maturities are available. Each maturity has a different rate.

The overnight LIBOR and the fed funds rate tend to be very close to each other. This is because they are near-perfect substitutes. Suppose that the fed funds rate exceeds the overnight LIBOR. Banks that need to borrow funds will borrow overnight Eurodollars, thus tending to raise rates, and banks with funds to lend will lend fed funds, thus tending to lower rates. The demand-and-supply pressure will cause a rapid adjustment that will drive the two rates together.

At one time, most short-term loans with adjustable interest rates were tied to the Treasury bill rate. However, the market for Eurodollars is so broad and deep that it has recently become the standard rate against which others are compared. For example, the U.S. commercial paper market now quotes rates as a spread over LIBOR rather than over the T-bill rate.

The Eurodollar market is not limited to London banks anymore. The primary brokers in this market maintain offices in all of the major financial centers worldwide.

Eurodollar Certificates of Deposit Because Eurodollars are time deposits with fixed maturities, they are to a certain extent illiquid. As usual, the financial markets created new types of securities to combat this problem. These new securities were transferable negotiable certificates of deposit (negotiable CDs). Because most Eurodollar deposits have a relatively short term to begin with, the market for Eurodollar negotiable CDs is relatively limited, constituting less than 10% of the amount of regular Eurodollar deposits. The market for the negotiable CDs is still thin.

Other Eurocurrencies The Eurodollar market is by far the largest short-term security market in the world. This is due to the international popularity of the U.S. dollar for trade. However, the market is not limited to dollars. It is possible to have an account denominated in Japanese yen held in a London or New York bank. Such an account would be termed a Euroyen account. Other Euro currencies are possible as well. Keep in mind that if market participants have a need for a particular security and are willing to pay for it, the financial markets stand ready and willing to create it.

Comparing Money Market Securities

Although money market securities share many characteristics, such as liquidity, safety, and short maturities, they all differ in some aspects.

Interest Rates

Figure 11.6 compares the interest rates on many of the money market instruments we have discussed. The most notable feature of this graph is that all of the money market instruments appear to move very closely together over time. This is because all have very low risk and a short term. They all have deep markets and so are priced competitively. In addition, because these instruments have so many of the same risk and term characteristics, they are close substitutes. Consequently, if one rate should temporarily depart from the others, market supply-and-demand forces would soon cause a correction. It is also noteworthy how rapidly these rates responded to the

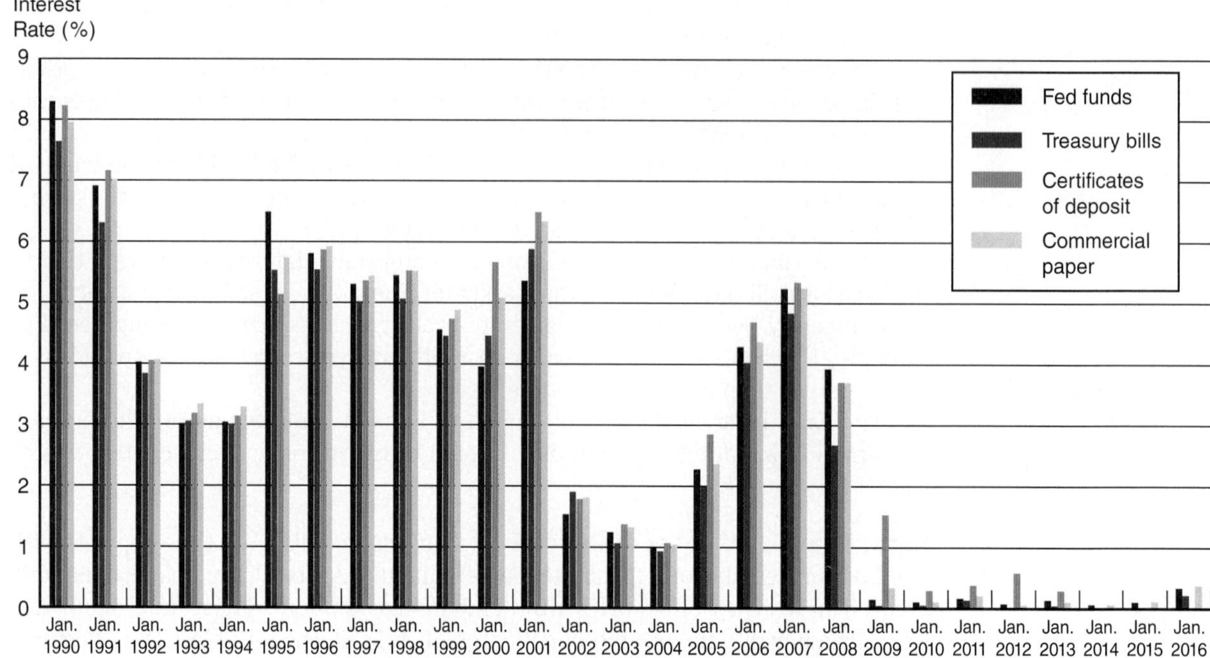

FIGURE 11.6 **Interest Rates on Money Market Securities, 1990–2016**

Source: http://www.federalreserve.gov/releases/h15/data.htm.

global recession that followed the 2007–2008 financial crisis. Money market rates were still at historic lows years later.

Liquidity

As we discussed in Chapter 4, the *liquidity* of a security refers to how quickly, easily, and cheaply it can be converted into cash. Typically, the depth of the secondary market where the security can be resold determines its liquidity. For example, the secondary market for Treasury bills is extensive and well developed. As a result, Treasury bills can be converted into cash quickly and with little cost. By contrast, there is no well-developed secondary market for commercial paper. Most holders of commercial paper hold the securities until maturity. In the event that a commercial paper investor needed to sell the securities to raise cash, it is likely that brokers would charge relatively high fees.

In some ways, the depth of the secondary market is not as critical for money market securities as it is for long-term securities such as stocks and bonds. This is because money market securities are short-term to start with. Nevertheless, many investors desire *liquidity intervention*: They seek an intermediary to provide liquidity where it did not previously exist. This is one function of money market mutual funds (discussed in Chapter 20).

Table 11.4 summarizes the types of money market securities and the depth of the secondary market.

TABLE 11.4 Money Market Securities and Their Markets

Money Market Security	Issuer	Buyer	Usual Maturity	Secondary Market
Treasury bills	U.S. government	Consumers and companies	4, 13, 26, and 52 weeks	Excellent
Federal funds	Banks	Banks	1 to 7 days	None
Repurchase agreements	Businesses and banks	Businesses and banks	1 to 15 days	Good
Negotiable certificates of deposit	Large money center banks	Businesses	14 to 120 days	Good
Commercial paper	Finance companies and businesses	Businesses	1 to 270 days	Poor
Banker's acceptance	Banks	Businesses	30 to 180 days	Good
Eurodollar deposits	Non-U.S. banks	Businesses, governments, and banks	1 day to 1 year	Poor

How Money Market Securities Are Valued

Suppose that you work for Merrill Lynch and that it is your job to submit the bid for Treasury bills this week. How would you know what price to submit? Your first step would be to determine the yield that you require. Let us assume that, based on your understanding of interest rates learned in Chapters 3 and 4, you decide you need a 2% return. To simplify our calculations, let us also assume we are bidding on securities with a one-year maturity. We know that our Treasury bill will pay $1,000 when it matures, so to compute how much we will pay today we find the present value of $1,000. The process of computing a present value was discussed in Example 1 in Chapter 3. The formula is

$$PV = \frac{FV}{(1 + i)^n}$$

In this example $FV = \$1000$, the interest rate $= 0.02$, and the period until maturity is 1, so

$$\text{Price} = \frac{\$1,000}{(1 + 0.02)} = \$980.39$$

Note what happens to the price of the security as interest rates rise. Since we are dividing by a larger number, the current price will decrease. For example, if interest rates rise to 3%, the value of the security would fall to $970.87 [$1,000/(1.03) = $970.87].

This method of discounting the future maturity value back to the present is the method used to price most money market securities.

SUMMARY

1. Money market securities are short-term instruments with an original maturity of less than one year. These securities include Treasury bills, commercial paper, federal funds, repurchase agreements, negotiable certificates of deposit, banker's acceptances, and Eurodollars.
2. Money market securities are used to "warehouse" funds until needed. The returns earned on these investments are low due to their low risk and high liquidity.
3. Many participants in the money markets both buy and sell money market securities. The U.S. Treasury, commercial banks, businesses, and individuals all benefit by having access to low-risk short-term investments.
4. Interest rates on all money market securities tend to follow one another closely over time. Treasury bill returns are the lowest because they are virtually devoid of default risk. Banker's acceptances and negotiable certificates of deposit are next lowest because they are backed by the creditworthiness of large money center banks.

KEY TERMS

asset-backed commercial paper (ABCP), p. 264
bearer instrument, p. 262
book entry, p. 258
competitive bidding, p. 258
deep market, p. 258
demand deposit, p. 262
direct placements, p. 263
discounting, p. 256
liquid market, p. 258
London interbank bid rate (LIBID), p. 266
London interbank offer rate (LIBOR), p. 266
noncompetitive bidding, p. 258
term security, p. 262
wholesale markets, p. 250

QUESTIONS

1. What characteristics define the money markets?
2. Describe at least two distinct benefits that money markets offer to their participants.
3. Why does the existence of banks banks not eliminate the need for money markets?
4. Explain why asymmetric information problems do not prevent money market participants from buying and selling money market instruments.
5. What motivated regulators to impose interest ceilings on bank savings accounts? What effect did this eventually have on the money markets?
6. Explain why the U.S. Treasury has to make every possible effort to keep its T-bill auctions competitive.
7. Why do businesses use the money markets?
8. What purpose initially motivated Merrill Lynch to offer money market mutual funds to its customers?
9. Why do property and casualty insurance companies invest more funds than life insurance companies in the money markets?
10. The interest rate on negotiable CDs is usually very close to the T-bill interest rate; however, the gap between these rates increased substantially between March 2008 and mid-2009. Why do you think this happened?
11. Distinguish between competitive bidding and noncompetitive bidding for Treasury securities.
12. Who lends or borrows federal funds, and what is the usual purpose of these funds?
13. Does the Federal Reserve *directly* set the federal funds interest rate? How does the Fed influence this rate?
14. Suppose the U.S. government defaults on its payments (i.e., cannot pay T-bills at their maturity date). What would be the effect on the T-bill rate? What would be the effect on the interest rates of other money market instruments?
15. Why are banker's acceptances so popular for international transactions?

QUANTITATIVE PROBLEMS

1. What would be the underestimation of your earnings as an investor if you use the discount rate instead of the investment rate to measure the return on your investment if you buy a $5,000 T-bill that matures in 91 days for $4,999.55?
2. What are the annualized discount rate and your annualized investment rate on a Treasury bill that you purchase for $9,940 that will mature in 91 days for $10,000?
3. If you want to earn an annualized discount rate of 3.5%, what is the most you can pay for a 91-day Treasury bill that pays $5,000 at maturity?
4. What is the minimum discount rate you will accept if you want to earn at least a 0.25% annualized investment rate on a 182-day $1,000 T-bill?
5. The price of 182-day commercial paper is $7,840. If the annualized investment rate is 4.093%, what will the paper pay at maturity?
6. Your minimum discount rate bid of 0.35% for a $10,000 T-bill that matures in 91 days has been accepted. Calculate your annualized investment rate.
7. The price of $8,000 face value commercial paper is $7,930. If the annualized discount rate is 4%, when will the paper mature? If the annualized investment rate is 4%, when will the paper mature?
8. A $5,000 commercial paper issued by CMF Corp. matures in 182 days and sells for $4,995. The investment rate on same maturity T-bills is currently 0.1%. Would you state that commercial paper issued by CMF Corp. is default free?
9. The annualized discount rate on a particular money market instrument is 3.75%. The face value is $200,000, and it matures in 51 days. What is its price? What would be the price if it had 71 days to maturity?
10. The annualized yield is 3% for 91-day commercial paper and 3.5% for 182-day commercial paper. What is the expected 91-day commercial paper rate 91 days from now?
11. In a Treasury auction of $2.1 billion par value 91-day T-bills, the following bids were submitted:

Bidder	Bid Amount ($ million)	Price per $100
1	500.0	99.40
2	750.0	99.01
3	1.5	99.25
4	1.0	99.36
5	600.0	99.39

If only these competitive bids are received, who will receive T-bills, in what quantity, and at what price?

12. If the Treasury also received $750 million in noncompetitive bids, who will receive T-bills, in what quantity, and at what price? (Refer to the table in problem 11.)

WEB EXERCISES

The Money Markets

1. Up-to-date interest rates are available from the Federal Reserve at **http://www.federalreserve.gov/releases**. Locate the current rate on the following securities:

   a. Prime rate

   b. Federal funds

   c. Commercial paper (financial)

   d. Certificates of deposit

   e. Discount rate

   f. One-month Eurodollar deposits

   Compare the rates for items a–c to those reported in Table 11.1. Have short-term rates generally increased or decreased?
2. The Treasury conducts auctions of money market treasury securities at regular intervals. Go to **http://treasurydirect.gov/instit/instit.htm?upcoming** and locate the schedule of auctions. When is the next auction of 4-week bills? When is the next auction of 13- and 26-week bills? How often are these securities auctioned?

CHAPTER 12

The Bond Market

> PREVIEW

The last chapter discussed short-term securities that trade in a market we call the money market. This chapter talks about the first of several securities that trade in a market we call the capital market. Capital markets are for securities with an original maturity that is greater than one year. These securities include bonds, stocks, and mortgages. We will devote an entire chapter to each major type of capital market security due to their importance to investors, businesses, and the economy. This chapter begins with a brief introduction on how the capital markets operate before launching into the study of bonds. In the next chapter we will study stocks and the stock market. We will conclude our look at the capital markets in Chapter 14 with mortgages.

Purpose of the Capital Market

Firms that issue capital market securities and the investors who buy them have very different motivations than those who operate in the money markets. Firms and individuals use the money markets primarily to warehouse funds for short periods of time until a more important need or a more productive use for the funds arises. By contrast, firms and individuals use the capital markets for long-term investments.

Suppose that after a careful financial analysis, your firm determines that it needs a new plant to meet the increased demand for its products. This analysis will be made using interest rates that reflect the *current* long-term cost of funds to the firm. Now suppose that your firm chooses to finance this plant by issuing money market securities, such as commercial paper. As long as interest rates do not rise, all is well: When these short-term securities mature, they can be reissued at the same interest rate. However, if interest rates rise, as they did dramatically in 1980, the firm will still have to reissue, now at a higher rate. It may find that it does not have the cash flows or income to support the plant at this increased rate. If long-term securities, such as bonds or stock, had been used, the increased interest rates would not have been as critical. The primary reason that individuals and firms choose to borrow long-term is to reduce the risk that interest rates will rise before they pay off their debt. This reduction in risk comes at a cost, however. As you may recall from Chapter 5, most long-term interest rates are higher than short-term rates due to risk premiums. Despite the need to pay higher interest rates to borrow in the capital markets, these markets remain very active.

Capital Market Participants

The primary issuers of capital market securities are federal and local governments and corporations. The federal government issues long-term notes and bonds to fund the national debt. State and municipal governments also issue long-term notes and bonds to finance capital projects, such as school and prison construction. Governments never issue stock because they cannot sell ownership claims.

Corporations issue both bonds and stock. One of the most difficult decisions a firm faces can be whether it should finance its growth with debt or equity. The distribution of a firm's capital between debt and equity is called its capital structure. Corporations may enter the capital markets because they do not have sufficient capital to fund their investment opportunities. Alternatively, firms may choose to enter the capital markets because they want to preserve their capital to protect against unexpected needs. In either case, the availability of efficiently functioning capital markets is crucial to the continued health of the business sector. This was dramatically demonstrated during the 2008–2009 financial crisis. With the near collapse of the bond and stock markets, funds for business expansion dried up. This led to reduced business activity, high unemployment, and slow growth. Only after market confidence was restored did a recovery begin.

The largest purchasers of capital market securities are households. Frequently, individuals and households deposit funds in financial institutions that use the funds to purchase capital market instruments such as bonds or stock.

Capital Market Trading

Capital market trading occurs in either the *primary market* or the *secondary market*. The primary market is where new issues of stocks and bonds are introduced. Investment funds, corporations, and individual investors can all purchase securities offered in the primary market. You can think of a primary market transaction as one where the issuer of the security actually receives the proceeds of the sale. When firms sell securities for the very first time, the issue is an **initial public offering (IPO)**. Subsequent sales of a firm's new stocks or bonds to the public are simply primary market transactions (as opposed to an initial one).

The capital markets have well-developed secondary markets. A secondary market is where the sale of previously issued securities takes place. Secondary markets are critical in capital markets because most investors plan to sell long-term bonds at some point before they mature. There are two types of exchanges in the secondary market for capital securities: *organized exchanges* and *over-the-counter exchanges*. Whereas most money market transactions originate over the phone, most capital market transactions, measured by volume, occur in organized exchanges. An organized exchange has a building where securities (including stocks, bonds, options, and futures) trade. Exchange rules govern trading to ensure the efficient and legal operation of the exchange, and the exchange's board constantly reviews these rules to ensure that they result in competitive trading.

Find listed companies, member information, real-time market indices, and current stock quotes at **www.nyse.com**.

Types of Bonds

Bonds are securities that represent a debt owed by the issuer to the investor. Bonds obligate the issuer to pay a specified amount at a given date, generally with periodic interest payments. The par, face, or maturity value of the bond (they all mean the same thing) is the amount that the issuer must pay at maturity. The **coupon rate** is the rate of interest that the issuer must pay, and this periodic interest payment is often called the coupon payment. This rate is usually fixed for the duration of the bond and does not fluctuate with market interest rates. If the repayment terms of a bond are not met, the holder of a bond has a claim on the assets of the issuer. Look at the bond in Figure 12.1. The face value of the bond is given in the upper-right corner. The interest rate of $8\frac{5}{8}\%$, along with the maturity date, is reported several times on the face of the bond.

Long-term bonds traded in the capital market include long-term government notes and bonds, municipal bonds, and corporate bonds.

Treasury Notes and Bonds

The U.S. Treasury issues notes and bonds to finance the national debt. The difference between a note and a bond is that notes have an original maturity of 1 to 10 years while bonds have an original maturity of 10 to 30 years. (Recall from Chapter 11 that Treasury *bills* mature in less than one year.) The Treasury currently issues notes with 2-, 3-, 5-, 7-, and 10-year maturities. The Treasury resumed issuing 30-year bonds in February 2006. Table 12.1 summarizes the maturity differences among Treasury securities. The prices of Treasury notes, bonds, and bills are quoted as a percentage of $100 face value.

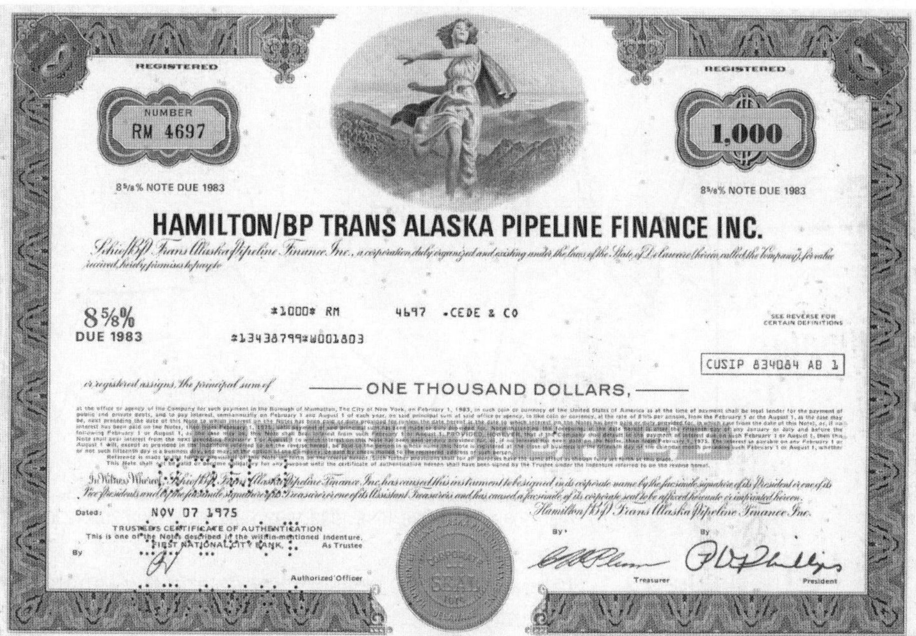

FIGURE 12.1 Hamilton/BP Corporate Bond

Federal government notes and bonds are free of default risk because the government can always print money to pay off the debt if necessary. This does *not* mean that these securities are risk-free. We will discuss interest-rate risk applied to bonds later in this chapter.

Treasury Bond Interest Rates

Treasury bonds have very low interest rates because they have no default risk.[1] Although investors in 10-year Treasury bonds earned less than the rate of inflation during the 1970s and early 1980s (see Figure 12.2), since then the interest rate on those bonds has been above the inflation rate and is also above the interest rate on money market securities because of interest-rate risk.

TABLE 12.1 Treasury Securities

Type	Maturity
Treasury bill	Less than 1 year
Treasury note	1 to 10 years
Treasury bond	10 to 30 years

[1]We noted in Chapter 11 that Treasury bills were also considered risk-free of default except that budget stalemates in 1996, 2011, and 2013 almost caused default. The same small chance of default applies to Treasury bonds.

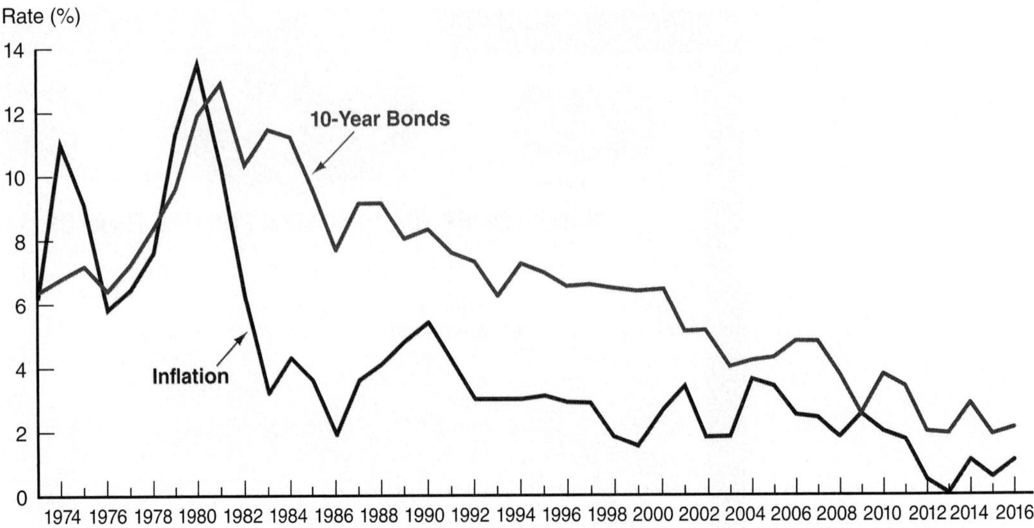

FIGURE 12.2 **Interest Rate on Treasury Bonds and the Inflation Rate, 1973–2016 (January of each year)**

Source: http://www.federalreserve.gov/releases and https://www.treasury.gov/resource-center/data-chart-center/interest-rates/Pages/TextView.aspx?data=reallongtermrate.

Figure 12.3 plots the yield on 20-year Treasury bonds against the yield on 90-day Treasury bills. Two things are noteworthy in this graph. First, in most years, the rate of return on the short-term bill is below that on the 20-year bond. Second, short-term rates are more volatile than long-term rates. Short-term rates are more influenced by the expected rate of inflation. Investors in long-term securities expect

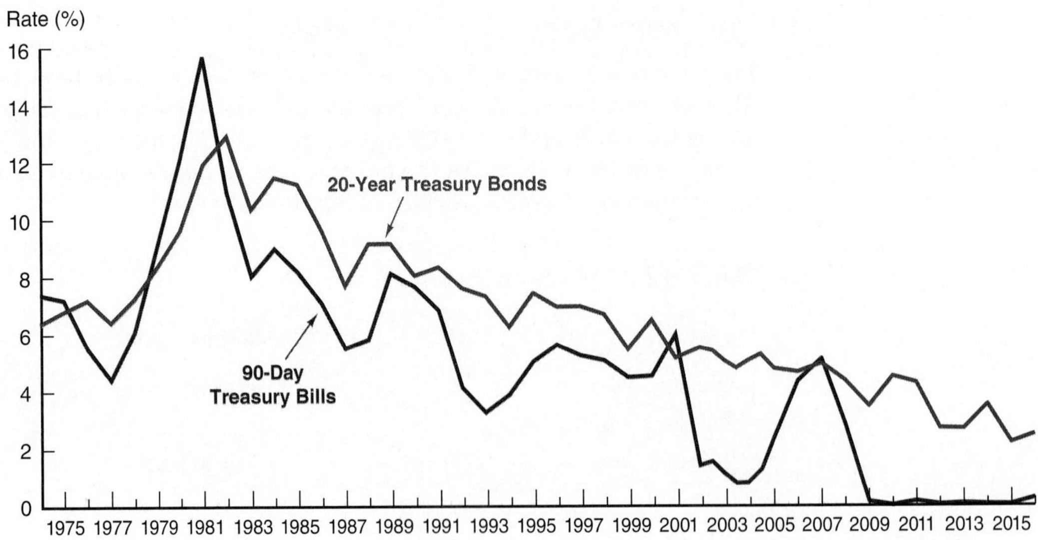

FIGURE 12.3 **Interest Rate on Treasury Bills and Treasury Bonds, 1974–2016 (January of each year)**

Source: http://www.federalreserve.gov/releases/h15/data.htm.

extremely high or low inflation rates to return to more normal levels, so long-term rates do not typically change as much as short-term rates.

Treasury Inflation-Protected Securities (TIPS)

In 1997 the Treasury Department began offering an innovative bond designed to remove inflation risk from holding treasury securities. The inflation-indexed bonds have an interest rate that does not change throughout the term of the security. However, the principal amount used to compute the interest payment does change based on the consumer price index. At maturity, the securities are redeemed at the greater of their inflation-adjusted principal or par amount at original issue.

The advantage of inflation-indexed securities, also referred to as inflation-protected securities, is that they give both individual and institutional investors a chance to buy a security whose value won't be eroded by inflation. These securities can be used by retirees who want to hold a very low-risk portfolio. They are offered by the Treasury with maturities of 5, 10, and 30 years.

Treasury STRIPS

In addition to bonds, notes, and bills, in 1985 the Treasury began issuing to depository institutions bonds in book entry form called **Separate Trading of Registered Interest and Principal Securities**, more commonly called **STRIPS**. Recall from Chapter 11 that to be sold in book entry form means that no physical document exists; instead, the security is issued and accounted for electronically. This allowed for the creation of a new security. A STRIPS separates the periodic interest payments from the final principal repayment. When a Treasury fixed-principal or inflation-indexed note or bond is "stripped," each interest payment and the principal payment becomes a separate zero-coupon security. Each component has its own identifying number and maturity and can be held or traded separately. For example, a Treasury note with five years remaining to maturity consists of a single principal payment at maturity and 10 interest payments, one every six months for five years. When this note is stripped, each of the 10 interest payments and the principal payment becomes a separate security. Thus, the single Treasury note becomes 11 securities that can be traded individually. STRIPS are also called **zero-coupon securities** because the only time an investor receives a payment during the life of each STRIPS component is when it matures.

Before the government introduced these securities, the private sector had created them indirectly. In the early 1980s, Merrill Lynch created the Treasury Investment Growth Fund (TIGRs, pronounced "tigers"), in which it purchased Treasury securities and then stripped them to create principal-only securities and interest-only securities. Currently, more than $50 billion in stripped Treasury securities are outstanding.

Agency Bonds

Congress has authorized a number of U.S. agencies, also known as government-sponsored enterprises (GSEs), to issue bonds. The government does not explicitly guarantee agency bonds, though most investors feel that the government would not allow the agencies to default. Issuers of agency bonds include the Student Loan Marketing Association (Sallie Mae), the Farmers Home Administration, the Federal

Housing Administration, the Veterans Administrations, and the Federal Land Banks. These agencies issue bonds to raise funds that are used for purposes that Congress has deemed to be in the national interest. For example, Sallie Mae helps provide student loans to increase access to college.

The risk on agency bonds is actually very low. They are usually secured by the loans that are made with the funds raised by the bond sales. In addition, the federal agencies may use their lines of credit with the Treasury Department should they have trouble meeting their obligations. Finally, it is unlikely that the federal government would permit its agencies to default on their obligations. This was evidenced by the bailout of the Federal National Mortgage Association (Fannie Mae) and the Federal Home Loan Mortgage Corporation (Freddie Mac) in 2008. Faced with portfolios of subprime mortgage loans, they were at risk of defaulting on their bonds before the government stepped in to guarantee payment. The bailout is discussed in the following case.

CASE

The 2007–2009 Financial Crisis and the Bailout of Fannie Mae and Freddie Mac

Because it encouraged excessive risk taking, the peculiar structure of Fannie Mae and Freddie Mac—private companies sponsored by the government—was an accident waiting to happen. Many economists predicted exactly what came to pass: a government bailout of both companies, with huge potential losses for American taxpayers.

As we will discuss in Chapter 18, when there is a government safety net for financial institutions, there needs to be appropriate government regulation and supervision to make sure these institutions do not take on excessive risk. Fannie and Freddie were given a federal regulator and supervisor, the Office of Federal Housing Enterprise Oversight (OFHEO), as a result of legislation in 1992, but this regulator was quite weak, with only a limited ability to rein them in. This outcome was not surprising: These firms had strong incentives to resist effective regulation and supervision because it would cut into their profits. This is exactly what they did: Fannie and Freddie were legendary for their lobbying machine in Congress, and they were not apologetic about it. In 1999 Franklin Raines, at the time Fannie's CEO, said, "We manage our political risk with the same intensity that we manage our credit and interest-rate risks."* Between 1998 and 2008 Fannie and Freddie jointly spent over $170 million on lobbyists, and from 2000 to 2008 they and their employees made over $14 million in political campaign contributions.

Their lobbying efforts paid off: Attempts to strengthen their regulator, OFHEO, in both the Clinton and Bush administrations came to naught, and remarkably this was even true after major accounting scandals at both firms were revealed in 2003 and 2004, in which they cooked the books to smooth out earnings. (It was only in July 2008, after the cat was let out of the bag and Fannie and Freddie were in serious trouble, that legislation was passed to put into place a stronger regulator, the Federal Housing Finance Agency, to supersede OFHEO.)

---

* Quoted in Nile Stephen Campbell, "Fannie Mae Officials Try to Assuage Worried Investors," *Real Estate Finance Today,* May 10, 1999.

With a weak regulator and strong incentives to take on risk, Fannie and Freddie grew like crazy, and by 2008 had purchased or were guaranteeing over $5 trillion of mortgages or mortgage-backed securities. The accounting scandals might even have pushed them to take on more risk. In the 1992 legislation, Fannie and Freddie had been given a mission to promote affordable housing. What better way to do this than to purchase subprime and Alt-A mortgages or mortgage-backed securities (discussed in Chapter 8)? The accounting scandals made this motivation even stronger because they weakened the political support for Fannie and Freddie, giving these companies even greater incentives to please Congress and support affordable housing by the purchase of these assets. By the time the subprime financial crisis hit in force, they had over $1 trillion of subprime and Alt-A assets on their books. Furthermore, they had extremely low ratios of capital relative to their assets: Indeed, their capital ratios were far lower than for other financial institutions like commercial banks.

By 2008, after many subprime mortgages went into default, Fannie and Freddie had booked large losses. Their small capital buffer meant that they had little cushion to withstand these losses, and investors started to pull their money out. With Fannie and Freddie playing such a dominant role in mortgage markets, the U.S. government could not afford to have them go out of business because this would have had a disastrous effect on the availability of mortgage credit, which would have had further devastating effects on the housing market. With bankruptcy imminent, the Treasury stepped in with a pledge to provide up to $200 billion of taxpayer money to the companies if needed. This largess did not come for free. The federal government in effect took over these companies by putting them into conservatorship, requiring that their CEOs step down, and by having their regulator, the Federal Housing Finance Agency, oversee the companies' day-to-day operations. In addition, the government received around $1 billion of senior preferred stock and the right to purchase 80% of the common stock if the companies recovered. After the bailout, the prices of both companies' common stock were less than 2% of what they had been worth only a year earlier.

The sad saga of Fannie Mae and Freddie Mac illustrates how dangerous it was for the government to set up GSEs that were exposed to a classic conflict-of-interest problem because they were supposed to serve two masters: As publicly traded corporations, they were expected to maximize profits for their shareholders, but as government agencies, they were obliged to work in the interests of the public. In the end, neither the public nor the shareholders were well served. With the housing market recovery, Fannie Mae and Freddy Mac have been able to pay dividends back to the government on its $187 billion investment. By October of 2016, the two agencies had paid $250 billion in dividends to the treasury.

Municipal Bonds

Municipal bonds are securities issued by local, county, and state governments. The proceeds from these bonds are used to finance public interest projects, such as schools, utilities, and transportation systems. Interest earned on municipal bonds that are issued to pay for essential public projects are exempt from federal taxation. As we saw in Chapter 5, this allows the municipality to borrow at a lower cost

Access **www.bloomberg.com/markets/rates/index.html** for details on the latest municipal bond events, experts' insights and analyses, and a municipal bond yields table.

because investors will be satisfied with lower interest rates on tax-exempt bonds. You can use the following equation to determine what tax-free rate of interest is equivalent to a taxable rate:

$$\text{Equivalent tax-free rate} = \text{taxable interest rate} \times (1 - \text{marginal tax rate})$$

EXAMPLE 12.1

Municipal Bonds

Suppose that the interest rate on a taxable corporate bond is 5% and that the marginal tax is 28%. Suppose a tax-free municipal bond with a rate of 3.75% was available. Which security would you choose?

> Solution

The tax-free equivalent municipal interest rate is 3.6%.

$$\text{Equivalent tax-free rate} = \text{taxable interest rate} \times (1 - \text{marginal tax rate})$$

where

$$\text{Taxable interest rate} = 0.05$$

$$\text{Marginal tax rate} = 0.28$$

Thus,

$$\text{Equivalent tax-free rate} = 0.05 \times (1 - .28) = 0.036 = 3.6\%$$

Since the tax-free municipal bond rate (3.75%) is higher than the equivalent tax-free rate (3.6%), choose the municipal bond.

There are two types of municipal bonds: general obligation bonds and revenue bonds. **General obligation bonds** do not have specific assets pledged as security or a specific source of revenue allocated for their repayment. Instead, they are backed by the "full faith and credit" of the issuer. This phrase means that the issuer promises to use every resource available to repay the bond as promised. Most general obligation bond issues must be approved by the taxpayers because the taxing authority of the government is pledged for their repayment.

Revenue bonds, by contrast, are backed by the cash flow of a particular revenue-generating project. For example, revenue bonds may be issued to build a toll road, with the tolls being pledged as repayment. If the revenues are not sufficient to repay the bonds, they may go into default, and investors may suffer losses. This occurred on a large scale in 1983, when the Washington Public Power Supply System (since called "WHOOPS") used revenue bonds to finance the construction of two nuclear power plants. As a result of falling energy prices and tremendous cost overruns, the plants never became operational, and buyers of these bonds lost $2.25 billion. This remains the largest public debt default on record. Revenue bonds tend to be issued more frequently than general obligation bonds (see Figure 12.4). Note that the low interest rates seen in recent years have prompted municipalities to issue near record amounts of bonds.

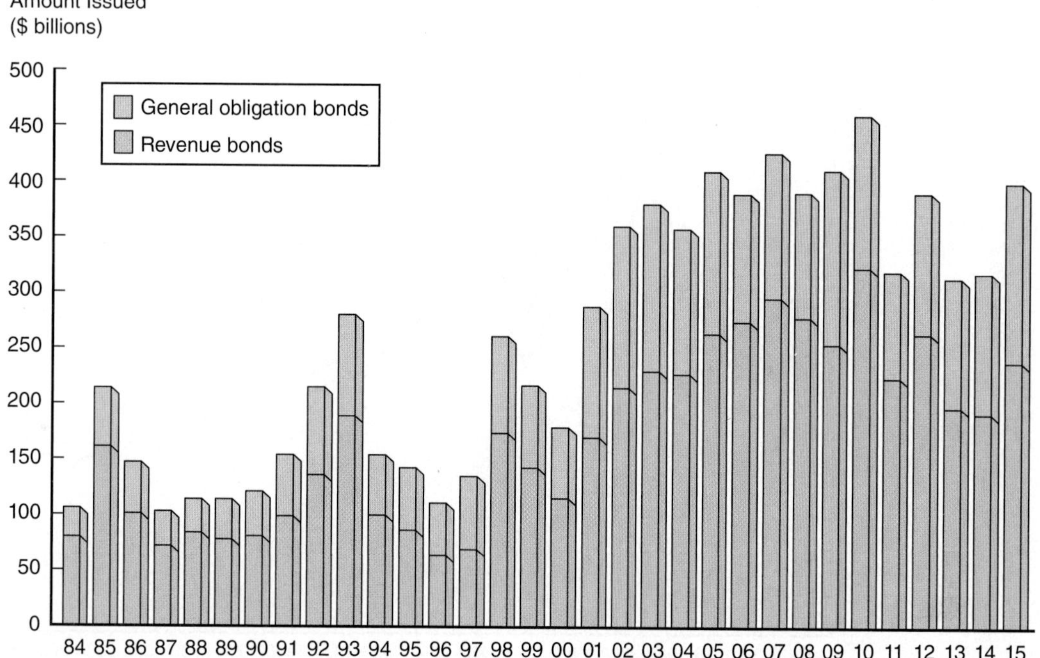

FIGURE 12.4 Issuance of Revenue and General Obligation Bonds, 1984–2015 (End of year)

Source: http://www.federalreserve.gov/econresdata/releases/govsecure/current.htm.

Risk in the Municipal Bond Market

Municipal bonds are not default-free. For example, a study by Fitch Ratings reported a 0.63% default rate on municipal bonds. Default rates are higher during periods when the economy is weak. Clearly, governments are not exempt from financial distress. Unlike the federal government, local governments cannot print money, and there are real limits on how high they can raise taxes without driving the population away.

Corporate Bonds

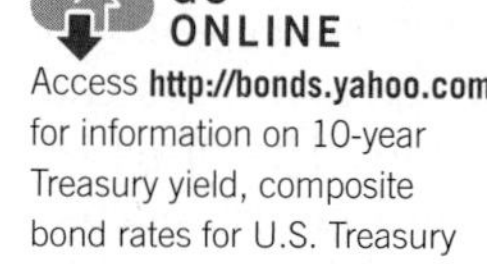

Access **http://bonds.yahoo.com** for information on 10-year Treasury yield, composite bond rates for U.S. Treasury bonds, municipal bonds, and corporate bonds.

When large corporations need to borrow funds for long periods of time, they may issue bonds. Most corporate bonds have a face value of $1,000 and pay interest semiannually (twice per year). Most are also callable, meaning that the issuer may redeem the bonds prior to maturity after a specified date.

The **bond indenture** is a contract that states the lender's rights and privileges and the borrower's obligations. Any collateral offered as security to the bondholders is also described in the indenture.

The degree of risk varies widely among different bond issues because the risk of default depends on the company's health, which can be affected by a number of variables. The interest rate on corporate bonds varies with the level of risk, as we discussed in Chapter 5. Figure 12.5 shows that bonds with lower risk and a higher

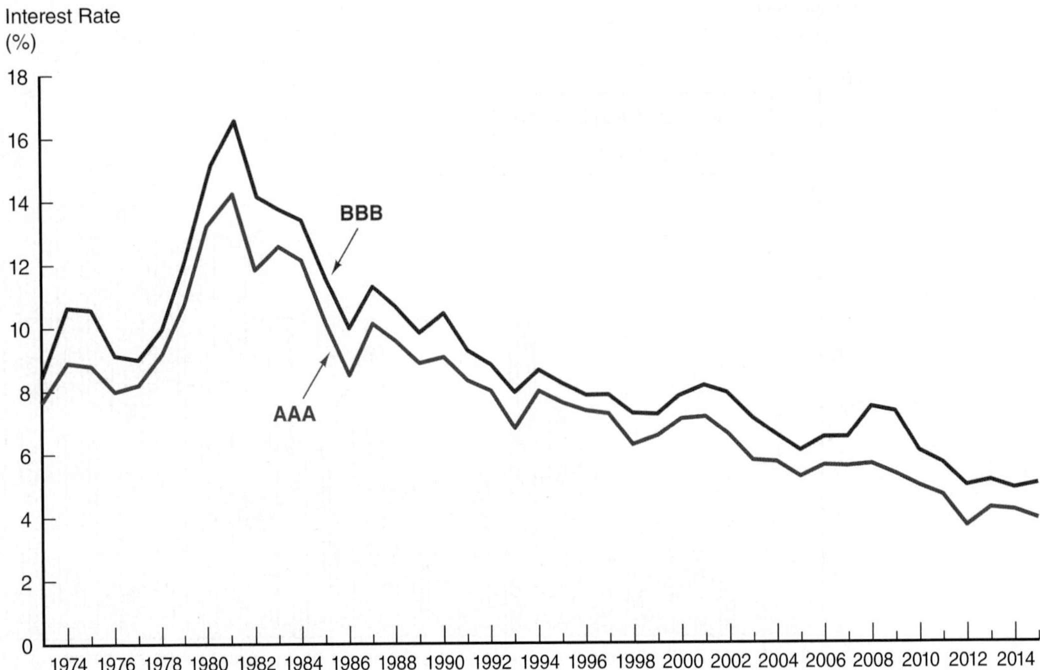

FIGURE 12.5 Corporate Bond Interest Rates, 1973–2015 (End of year)

Source: http://www.federalreserve.gov/releases/h15/data.htm.

rating (AAA being the highest) have lower interest rates than more risky bonds (BBB). The spread between the differently rated bonds varies over time. The spread between AAA and BBB rated bonds has historically averaged a little over 1%. As the financial crisis unfolded, investors seeking safety caused the spread to hit a record 3.38% in December 2008. A bond's interest rate also depends on its features and characteristics, which are described in the following sections.

Characteristics of Corporate Bonds

At one time bonds were sold with attached coupons that the owner of the bond clipped and mailed to the firm to receive interest payments. These were called *bearer bonds* because payments were made to whoever had physical possession of the bonds. The Internal Revenue Service did not care for this method of payment, however, because it made tracking interest income difficult. Bearer bonds have now been largely replaced by **registered bonds**, which do not have coupons. Instead, the owner must register with the firm to receive interest payments. The firms are required to report to the IRS the name of the person who receives interest income. Despite the fact that bearer bonds with attached coupons have been phased out, the interest paid on bonds is still called the "coupon interest payment," and that interest payment divided by a bond's par value is the coupon interest rate.

Restrictive Covenants A corporation's financial managers are hired, fired, and compensated at the direction of the board of directors, which represents the corporation's *stockholders*. This arrangement implies that the managers will be more interested in protecting stockholders than in protecting bondholders. You should recognize this as an example of the moral hazard problem introduced in Chapter 2 and discussed further in Chapter 7. Managers might not use the funds provided by the bonds as the bondholders might prefer. Since bondholders cannot look to managers for protection when the firm gets into trouble, they must impose rules and restrictions on managers designed to protect the bondholders' interests. These are known as **restrictive covenants**. They usually limit the amount of dividends the firm can pay (to conserve cash for interest payments to bondholders) and the ability of the firm to issue additional debt. Other financial policies, such as the firm's involvement in mergers, may also be restricted. Restrictive covenants are included in the bond indenture. Typically, the interest rate is lower the more restrictions are placed on management through these covenants because the bonds will be considered safer by investors.

Call Provisions Most corporate indentures include a **call provision**, which states that the issuer has the right to force the holder to sell the bond back. The call provision usually requires a waiting period between the time the bond is initially issued and the time when it can be called. The price bondholders are paid for the bond is usually set at the bond's par price or slightly higher (usually by one year's interest cost). For example, a 10% coupon rate $1,000 bond may have a call price of $1,100.

If interest rates fall, the price of the bond will rise. If rates fall enough, the price will rise above the call price, and the firm will call the bond. Because call provisions put a limit on the amount that bondholders can earn from the appreciation of a bond's price, investors do not like call provisions.

A second reason that issuers of bonds include call provisions is to make it possible for them to buy back their bonds according to the terms of the **sinking fund**. A sinking fund is a requirement in the bond indenture that the firm pay off a portion of the bond issue each year. This provision is attractive to bondholders because it reduces the probability of default when the issue matures. Because a sinking fund provision makes the issue more attractive, the firm can reduce the bond's interest rate.

A third reason firms usually issue only callable bonds is that firms may have to retire a bond issue if the covenants of the issue restrict the firm from some activity that it feels is in the best interest of stockholders. Suppose that a firm needed to borrow additional funds to expand its storage facilities. If the firm's bonds carried a restriction against adding debt, the firm would have to retire its existing bonds before issuing new bonds or taking out a loan to build the new warehouse.

Finally, a firm may choose to call bonds if it wishes to alter its capital structure. A maturing firm with excess cash flow may wish to reduce its debt load if few attractive investment opportunities are available.

Because bondholders do not generally like call provisions, callable bonds must have a higher yield than comparable noncallable bonds. Despite the higher cost, firms still typically issue callable bonds because of the flexibility this feature provides the firm.

Conversion Some bonds can be converted into shares of common stock. This feature permits bondholders to share in the firm's good fortunes if the stock price rises. Most convertible bonds will state that the bond can be converted into a certain number of common shares at the discretion of the bondholder. The conversion ratio will be such that the price of the stock must rise substantially before conversion is likely to occur.

Issuing convertible bonds is one way firms avoid sending a negative signal to the market. In the presence of asymmetric information between corporate insiders and investors, when a firm chooses to issue stock, the market usually interprets this action as indicating that the stock price is relatively high or that it is going to fall in the future. The market makes this interpretation because it believes that managers are most concerned with looking out for the interests of existing stockholders and will not issue stock when it is undervalued. If managers believe that the firm will perform well in the future, they can, instead, issue convertible bonds. If the managers are correct and the stock price rises, the bondholders will convert to stock at a relatively high price that managers believe is fair. Alternatively, bondholders have the option not to convert if managers turn out to be wrong about the company's future.

Bondholders like a conversion feature. It is very similar to buying just a bond but receiving both a bond and a stock option (stock options are discussed fully in Chapter 24). The price of the bond will reflect the value of this option and so will be higher than the price of comparable nonconvertible bonds. The higher price received for the bond by the firm implies a lower interest rate.

Types of Corporate Bonds

A variety of corporate bonds are available. They are usually distinguished by the type of collateral that secures the bond and by the order in which the bond is paid off if the firm defaults.

Secured Bonds Secured bonds are ones with collateral attached. *Mortgage bonds* are used to finance a specific project. For example, a building may be the collateral for bonds issued for its construction. In the event that the firm fails to make payments as promised, mortgage bondholders have the right to liquidate the property in order to be paid. Because these bonds have specific property pledged as collateral, they are less risky than comparable unsecured bonds. As a result, they will have a lower interest rate.

Equipment trust certificates are bonds secured by tangible non-real-estate property, such as heavy equipment and airplanes. Typically, the collateral backing these bonds is more easily marketed than the real property backing mortgage bonds. As with mortgage bonds, the presence of collateral reduces the risk of the bonds and so lowers their interest rates.

Unsecured Bonds *Debentures* are long-term unsecured bonds that are backed only by the general creditworthiness of the issuer. No specific collateral is pledged to repay the debt. In the event of default, the bondholders must go to court to seize assets. Collateral that has been pledged to other debtors is not available to the holders of debentures. Debentures usually have an attached contract that spells out the terms of the bond and the responsibilities of management. The contract attached to the debenture is called an *indenture*. (Be careful not to confuse the terms *debenture* and *indenture*.) Debentures have lower priority than secured bonds if the firm defaults. As a result, they will have a higher interest rate than otherwise comparable secured bonds.

Subordinated debentures are similar to debentures except that they have a lower priority claim. This means that in the event of a default, subordinated debenture holders are paid only after nonsubordinated bondholders have been paid in full. As a result, subordinated debenture holders are at greater risk of loss.

Variable-rate bonds (which may be secured or unsecured) are a financial innovation spurred by increased interest-rate variability in the 1980s and 1990s. The interest rate on these securities is tied to another market interest rate, such as the rate on Treasury bonds, and is adjusted periodically. The interest rate on the bonds will change over time as market rates change.

Junk Bonds Recall from Chapter 5 that all bonds are rated by various credit-rating agencies according to their default risk. These companies study the issuer's financial characteristics and make a judgment about the issuer's possibility of default. A bond with a rating of AAA has the highest grade possible. Bonds *at or above* Moody's Baa or Standard and Poor's BBB rating are considered to be of investment grade. Those rated *below* this level are usually considered speculative (see Table 12.2). Speculative-grade bonds are often called **junk bonds**. Before the late 1970s, primary issues of speculative-grade securities were very rare; almost all new bond issues consisted of investment-grade bonds. If companies ran into financial difficulties, their bond ratings would fall, sometimes into the junk bond range. Holders of these downgraded bonds found that they were difficult to sell because no well-developed secondary market existed. It is easy to understand why investors would be leery of these securities, as they were usually unsecured.

In 1977 Michael Milken, at the investment banking firm of Drexel Burnham Lambert, recognized that there were many investors who would be willing to take on greater risk if they were compensated with greater returns. First, however, Milken had to address two problems that hindered the market for low-grade bonds. The first was that they suffered from poor liquidity. Whereas underwriters of investment-grade bonds continued to make a market after the bonds were issued, no such market maker existed for junk bonds. Drexel agreed to assume this role as market maker for junk bonds. Making a market meant that Drexel agreed to stand ready to buy or sell these bonds at all times. That ensured the existence of a secondary market, an important consideration for investors, who seldom want to hold the bonds to maturity.

The second problem with the junk bond market was that a very real chance existed that the issuing firms would default on their bond payments. By comparison, the default risk on investment-grade securities was negligible. To reduce the probability of losses, Milken acted much as a commercial bank for junk bond issuers. He would renegotiate the firm's debt or advance additional funds if needed to prevent the firm from defaulting. Milken's efforts substantially reduced the default risk, and the demand for junk bonds soared.

During the early and mid-1980s, many firms took advantage of junk bonds to finance the takeover of other firms. When a firm greatly increases its debt level (by issuing junk bonds) to finance the purchase of another firm's stock, the increase in leverage makes the bonds high risk. Frequently, part of the acquired firm is eventually sold to pay down the debt incurred by issuing the junk bonds. Some 1,800 firms accessed the junk bond market during the 1980s.

Milken and his brokerage firm were very well compensated for their efforts. Milken earned a fee of 2% to 3% of each junk bond issue, which made Drexel the

TABLE 12.2 Debt Rating Descriptions

Standard & Poor's	Moody's	Definition
AAA	Aaa	Best quality and highest rating. Capacity to pay interest and repay principal is extremely strong. Smallest degree of investment risk.
AA	Aa	High quality. Very strong capacity to pay interest and repay principal and differs from AAA/Aaa in a small degree.
A	A	Strong capacity to pay interest and repay principal. Possess many favorable investment attributes and are considered upper-medium-grade obligations. Somewhat more susceptible to the adverse effects of changes in circumstances and economic conditions.
BBB	Baa	Medium-grade obligations. Neither highly protected nor poorly secured. Adequate capacity to pay interest and repay principal. May lack long-term reliability and protective elements to secure interest and principal payments.
BB	Ba	Moderate ability to pay interest and repay principal. Have speculative elements and future cannot be considered well assured. Adverse business, economic, and financial conditions could lead to inability to meet financial obligations.
B	B	Lack characteristics of desirable investment. Assurance of interest and principal payments over long period of time may be small. Adverse conditions likely to impair ability to meet financial obligations.
CCC	Caa	Poor standing. Identifiable vulnerability to default and dependent on favorable business, economic, and financial conditions to meet timely payment of interest and repayment of principal.
CC	Ca	Represent obligations that are speculative to a high degree. Issues often default and have other marked shortcomings.
C	C	Lowest-rated class of bonds. Have extremely poor prospects of attaining any real investment standard. May be used to cover a situation where bankruptcy petition has been filed, but debt service payments are continued.
CI		Reserved for income bonds on which no interest is being paid.
D		Payment default.
NR		No public rating has been requested.
(+) or (−)		Ratings from AA to CCC may be modified by the addition of a plus or minus sign to show relative standing within the major rating categories.

Source: Federal Reserve Bulletin.

most profitable firm on Wall Street in 1987. Milken's personal income between 1983 and 1987 was in excess of $1 billion.

Unfortunately for holders of junk bonds, both Milken and Drexel were caught and convicted of insider trading. With Drexel unable to support the junk bond market, 250 companies defaulted between 1989 and 1991. Drexel itself filed bankruptcy in 1990 due to losses on its own holdings of junk bonds. Milken was sentenced to three years in prison for his part in the scandal. *Fortune* magazine reported that Milken's personal fortune still exceeded $400 million.[2]

The junk bond market had largely recovered since its low in 1990, but the financial crisis in 2008 again reduced the demand for riskier securities. This market behavior was rational, considering that in 2008 the default rate on speculative-grade bonds was three times that of investment-grade bonds.

Financial Guarantees for Bonds

Financially weaker security issuers frequently purchase **financial guarantees** to lower the risk of their bonds. A financial guarantee ensures that the lender (bond purchaser) will be paid both principal and interest in the event the issuer defaults. Large, well-known insurance companies write what are actually insurance policies to back bond issues. With such a financial guarantee, bond buyers no longer have to be concerned with the financial health of the bond issuer. Instead, they are interested only in the strength of the insurer. Essentially, the credit rating of the insurer is substituted for the credit rating of the issuer. The resulting reduction in risk lowers the interest rate demanded by bond buyers. Of course, issuers must pay a fee to the insurance company for the guarantee. Financial guarantees make sense only when the cost of the insurance is less than the interest savings that result.

In 1995 J.P. Morgan introduced a new way to insure bonds called the **credit default swap (CDS)**. In its simplest form a CDS provides insurance against default in the principal and interest payments of a credit instrument. Say you decided to buy a GE bond and wanted to insure yourself against any losses that might occur should GE have problems. You could buy a CDS from a variety of sources that would provide this protection.

In 2000 Congress passed the Commodity Futures Modernization Act, which removed derivative securities, such as CDSs, from regulatory oversight. Additionally, it preempted states from enforcing gaming laws on these types of securities. The effect of this regulation was to make it possible for investors to speculate on the possibility of default on securities they did not own. Consider the idea that you could buy life insurance on anyone you felt looked unhealthy. Insurance laws prevent this type of speculation by requiring that you must be in a position to suffer a loss before you can purchase insurance. The Commodity Futures Modernization Act removed this requirement for derivative securities. Thus, speculators could, in essence, legally bet on whether a firm or security would fail in the future.

Between 2000 and 2008, major CDS players included AIG, Lehman Brothers, and Bear Stearns. The amount of CDSs outstanding mushroomed to over $62 trillion by its peak in 2008. To put that figure in context, the Gross National Product of the entire world is around $50 trillion. In 2008 Lehman Brothers failed, Bear Stearns

[2] A complete history of Milken was reported in *Fortune* (September 30, 1996): 80–105.

TABLE 12.3 Sample Violations and Fines in the Bond Market

Violation	Fine
Excessive trading	$5,000 to $110,000
Excessive markups	$5,000 to $146,000
Failure to supervise	$5,000 to $73,000
Fraud/Misrepresentation	$2,500 to $146,000
Late reporting	$5,000 to $146,000
Net capital deficiencies	$1,000 to $73,000
Outside business activities	$2,500 to $73,000
Recordkeeping violations	$1,000 to $146,000
Sale of unregistered securities	$2,500 to $73,000
Unsuitable recommendations	$2,500 to $110,000

was acquired by J.P. Morgan for pennies on the dollar, and AIG required a $182 billion government bailout. This topic is discussed in greater detail in Chapter 21, "Insurance and Pension Funds."

Oversight of the Bond Markets

Stocks typically sell in public markets where bid and ask prices are readily available and transparent. By contrast, bonds typically trade over the counter, where transaction details can be hidden from the public. To open this market to scrutiny, in 2002 the Securities and Trade Commission created a trade reporting and compliance engine (**TRACE**). TRACE has two significant missions:

1. Rules that say which bond transactions must be publicly reported.
2. The establishment of a trading platform that makes transaction data readily available to the public.

TRACE is under the Financial Industry Regulatory Authority (**FINRA**). All companies that trade securities are required to be members of FINRA. FINRA was formerly the National Association of Securities Dealers (NASD). In 2007 it was created to consolidate the regulatory and oversight functions of NASD with those of the New York Stock Exchange.

The most common violations of rules that result in fines or charges relate to anti–money laundering, the distribution of securities, quality of markets, reporting and recordkeeping, sales practices, and supervision. Sample violations and the range of fines that can be assessed are shown in Table 12.3.

Current Yield Calculation

Chapter 3 introduced interest rates and described the concept of yield to maturity. If you buy a bond and hold it until it matures, you will earn the yield to maturity. This represents the most accurate measure of the yield from holding a bond.

Current Yield

The **current yield** is an approximation of the yield to maturity on coupon bonds that is often reported because it is easily calculated. It is defined as the yearly coupon payment divided by the price of the security,

$$i_c = \frac{C}{P} \tag{1}$$

where i_c = current yield
P = price of the coupon bond
C = yearly coupon payment

This formula is identical to the formula in Equation 5 of Chapter 3, which describes the calculation of the yield to maturity for a perpetuity. Hence for a perpetuity, the current yield is an exact measure of the yield to maturity. When a coupon bond has a long term to maturity (say, 20 years or more), it is very much like a perpetuity, which pays coupon payments forever. Thus, you would expect the current yield to be a rather close approximation of the yield to maturity for a long-term coupon bond, and you can safely use the current yield calculation instead of looking up the yield to maturity in a bond table. However, as the time to maturity of the coupon bond shortens (say, it becomes less than five years), it behaves less and less like a perpetuity and so the approximation afforded by the current yield becomes worse and worse.

We have also seen that when the bond price equals the par value of the bond, the yield to maturity is equal to the coupon rate (the coupon payment divided by the par value of the bond). Because the current yield equals the coupon payment divided by the bond price, the current yield is also equal to the coupon rate when the bond price is at par. This logic leads us to the conclusion that when the bond price is at par, the current yield equals the yield to maturity. This means that the nearer the bond price is to the bond's par value, the better the current yield will approximate the yield to maturity.

The current yield is negatively related to the price of the bond. In the case of our 10% coupon rate bond, when the price rises from $1,000 to $1,100, the current yield falls from 10% (= $100/$1,000) to 9.09% (= $100/$1,100). As Table 3.1 in Chapter 3 indicates, the yield to maturity is also negatively related to the price of the bond; when the price rises from $1,000 to $1,100, the yield to maturity falls from 10% to 8.48%. In this we see an important fact: The current yield and the yield to maturity always move together; a rise in the current yield always signals that the yield to maturity has also risen.

EXAMPLE 12.2

Current Yield

What is the current yield for a bond that has a par value of $1,000 and a coupon interest rate of 10.95%? The current market price for the bond is $921.01.

> Solution

The current yield is 11.89%.

$$i_c = \frac{C}{P}$$

where

C = yearly payment $= 0.1095 \times \$1{,}000 = \$109.50$

P = price of the bond $= \$921.01$

Thus,

$$i_c = \frac{\$109.50}{\$921.01} = 0.1189 = 11.89\%$$

The general characteristics of the current yield (the yearly coupon payment divided by the bond price) can be summarized as follows: ***The current yield better approximates the yield to maturity when the bond's price is nearer to the bond's par value and the maturity of the bond is longer. It becomes a worse approximation when the bond's price is further from the bond's par value and the bond's maturity is shorter.*** Regardless of whether the current yield is a good approximation of the yield to maturity, a change in the current yield *always* signals a change in the same direction of the yield to maturity.

Finding the Value of Coupon Bonds

Before we look specifically at how to price bonds, let us first look at the general theory behind computing the price of any business asset. Luckily, the value of all financial assets is found the same way. The current price is the present value of all future cash flows. Recall the discussion of present value from Chapter 3. If you have the present value of a future cash flow, you can exactly reproduce that future cash flow by investing the present value amount at the discount rate. For example, the present value of \$100 that will be received in one year is \$90.90 if the discount rate is 10%. An investor is completely indifferent between having the \$90.90 today or having the \$100 in one year. This is because the \$90.90 can be invested at 10% to provide \$100.00 in the future ($\$90.90 \times 1.10 = \$100$). This represents the essence of value. The current price must be such that the seller is indifferent between continuing to receive the cash flow stream provided by the asset and receiving the offer price.

One question we might ask is why prices fluctuate if everyone knows how value is established. It is because not everyone agrees about what the future cash flows are going to be. Let us summarize how to find the value of a security:

1. Identify the cash flows that result from owning the security.
2. Determine the discount rate required to compensate the investor for holding the security.
3. Find the present value of the cash flows estimated in step 1 using the discount rate determined in step 2.

The rest of this chapter focuses on how one important asset is valued: bonds. In the next chapter we discuss stock valuation. The unifying theme is that prices (value) are always determined the same way. They are simply the present value of the future cash flows. This concept applies to bonds, stocks, businesses, buildings, and any other investment.

Finding the Price of Semiannual Bonds

Recall that a bond usually pays interest semiannually in an amount equal to the coupon interest rate times the face amount (or par value) of the bond. When the bond matures, the holder will also receive a lump sum payment equal to the face amount. Most corporate bonds have a face amount of $1,000. Basic bond terminology is reviewed in Table 12.4.

The issuing corporation will usually set the coupon rate close to the rate available on other similar outstanding bonds at the time the bond is offered for sale. Unless the bond has an adjustable rate, the coupon interest payment remains unchanged throughout the life of the bond.

The first step in finding the value of the bond is to identify the cash flows the holder of the bond will receive. The value of the bond is the present value of these cash flows. The cash flows consist of the interest payments and the final lump sum repayment.

In the second step these cash flows are discounted back to the present using an interest rate that represents the yield currently available on other bonds of like risk and maturity.

The technique for computing the price of a simple bond with annual cash flows was discussed in detail in Chapter 3. Let us now look at a more realistic example. Most bonds pay interest semiannually. To adjust the cash flows for semiannual payments, divide the coupon payment by 2, since only half of the annual payment is paid each six months. Similarly, to find the interest rate effective during one-half of the year, the market interest rate must be divided by 2. The final adjustment is to

TABLE 12.4 Bond Terminology

Coupon interest rate	The stated annual interest rate on the bond. It is usually fixed for the life of the bond.
Current yield	The coupon interest payment divided by the current market price of the bond.
Face amount	The maturity value of the bond. The holder of the bond will receive the face amount from the issuer when the bond matures. *Face amount* is synonymous with *par value*.
Indenture	The contract that accompanies a bond and specifies the terms of the loan agreement. It includes management restrictions, called covenants.
Market rate	The interest rate currently in effect in the market for securities of similar risk and maturity. The market rate is used to value bonds.
Maturity	The number of years or periods until the bond matures and the holder is paid the face amount.
Par value	The same as *face amount*, the maturity value of the bond.
Yield to maturity	The yield an investor will earn if the bond is purchased at the current market price and held until maturity.

double the number of periods because there will be two periods per year. Equation 2 shows how to compute the price of a semiannual bond:[3]

$$P_{semi} = \frac{C/2}{1+i/2} + \frac{C/2}{(1+i/2)^2} + \frac{C/2}{(1+i/2)^3} + \cdots + \frac{C/2}{(1+i/2)^{2n}} + \frac{F}{(1+i/2)^{2n}} \quad (2)$$

where
P_{semi} = price of semiannual coupon bond
C = yearly coupon payment
F = face value of the bond
n = years to maturity date
i = annual market interest rate

EXAMPLE 12.3

Bond Valuation, Semiannual Payment Bond

Let us compute the price of a sample bond. Suppose the bonds have a 10% coupon rate, a $1,000 par value (maturity value), and mature in two years. Assume semiannual compounding and that market rates of interest are 12%.

> **Solution**

1. Begin by identifying the cash flows. Compute the coupon interest payment by multiplying 0.10 times $1,000 to get $100. Since the coupon payment is made each six months, it will be one-half of $100, or $50. The final cash flow consists of repayment of the $1,000 face amount of the bond. This does not change because of semiannual payments.
2. We need to know what market rate of interest is appropriate to use for computing the present value of the bond. We are told that bonds being issued today with similar risk and maturity have coupon rates of 12%. Divide this amount by 2 to get the interest rate over six months. This provides an interest rate of 6%.
3. Find the present value of the cash flows. Note that with semiannual compounding the number of periods must be doubled. This means that we discount the bond payments for four periods.

Solution: Equation

$$P = \frac{\$100/2}{(1+.06)} + \frac{\$100/2}{(1+.06)^2} + \frac{\$100/2}{(1+.06)^3} + \frac{\$100/2}{(1+.06)^4} + \frac{\$1{,}000}{(1+.06)^4}$$

$$P = \$47.17 + \$44.50 + \$41.98 + \$39.60 + \$792.10 = \$965.35$$

Solution: Financial Calculator

$N = 4$

$FV = \$1{,}000$

[3] There is a theoretical argument for discounting the final cash flow using the full-year interest rate with the original number of periods. Derivative securities are sold, in which the principal and interest cash flows are separated and sold to different investors. The fact that one investor is receiving semiannual interest payments should not affect the value of the principal-only cash flow. However, virtually every text, calculator, and spreadsheet computes bond values by discounting the final cash flow using the same interest rate and number of periods as is used to compute the present value of the interest payments. To be consistent, we will use that method in this text.

$I = 6\%$

$PMT = \$50$

Compute PV = price of bond = $965.35.

Note that the most common mistake students make is to confuse when to use the coupon rate and when to use the market rate. The coupon rate is used only to compute the interest payments that will be received. The market rate is used to discount the interest payment back to the present.

Notice that the market price for the bond in Example 3 is below the $1,000 par value of the bond. When the bond sells for less than the par value, it is selling at a **discount**. When the market price exceeds the par value, the bond is selling at a **premium**.

What determines whether a bond will sell for a premium or a discount? Suppose that you are asked to invest in an old bond that has a coupon rate of 10% and $1,000 par. You would not be willing to pay $1,000 for this bond if new bonds with similar risk were available yielding 12%. The seller of the old bond would have to lower the price on the 10% bond to make it an attractive investment. In fact, the seller would have to lower the price until the yield earned by a buyer of the old bond equaled the yield on similar new bonds. This means that as interest rates in the market rise, the value of bonds with fixed coupon rates falls. Similarly, as interest rates available in the market on new bonds fall, the value of old fixed-coupon-rate bonds rises.

Investing in Bonds

Bonds represent one of the most popular long-term alternatives to investing in stocks (see Figure 12.6). Bonds are lower risk than stocks because they have a higher priority of payment. This means that when the firm is having difficulty meeting its obligations, bondholders get paid before stockholders. Additionally, should the firm have to liquidate, bondholders must be paid before stockholders.

Even healthy firms with sufficient cash flow to pay both bondholders and stockholders frequently have very volatile stock prices. This volatility scares many investors out of the stock market. Bonds are the most popular alternative. They offer relative security and dependable cash payments, making them ideal for retired investors and those who want to live off their investments.

Many investors think that bonds represent a very low risk investment, since the cash flows are relatively certain. It is true that high-grade bonds seldom default; however, bond investors face fluctuations in price due to market interest-rate movements in the economy. As interest rates rise and fall, the value of bonds changes in the opposite direction. As discussed in Chapter 3, the possibility of suffering a loss because of interest-rate changes is called **interest-rate risk**. The longer the time until the bond matures, the greater will be the change in price. This does not cause a loss to those investors who do not sell their bonds; however, many investors do not hold their bonds until maturity. If they attempt to sell their bonds after interest rates have risen, they will receive less than they paid. Interest-rate risk is an important consideration when deciding whether to invest in bonds.

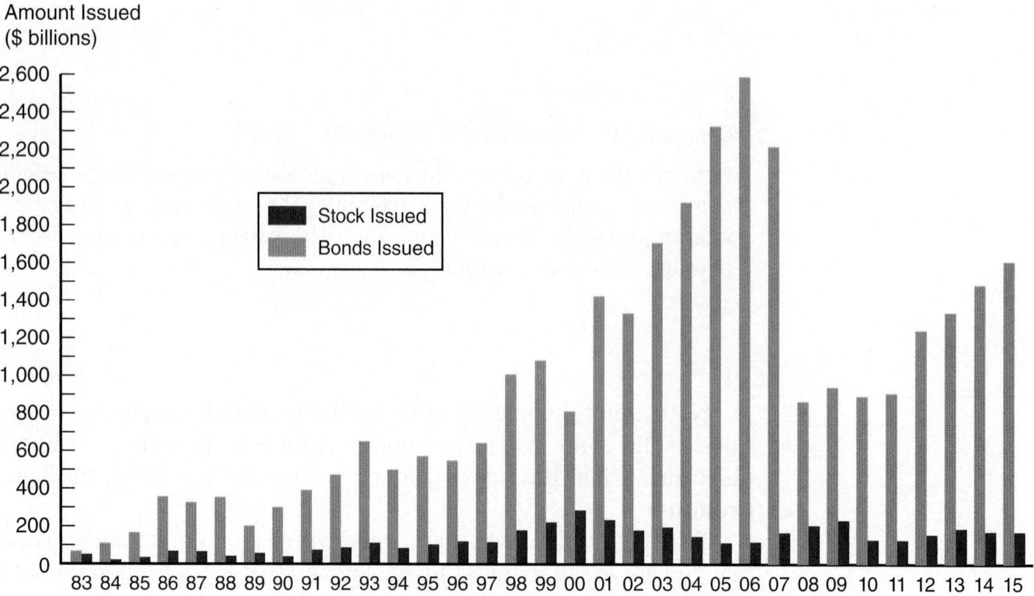

FIGURE 12.6 Bonds and Stocks Issued, 1983–2015

Source: http://www.federalreserve.gov/econresdata/releases/corpsecure/current.htm.

SUMMARY

1. The capital markets exist to provide financing for long-term capital assets. Households, often through investments in pension and mutual funds, are net investors in the capital markets. Corporations and the federal and state governments are net users of these funds.
2. The three main capital market instruments are bonds, stocks, and mortgages. Bonds represent borrowing by the issuing firm. Stock represents ownership in the issuing firm. Mortgages are long-term loans secured by real property. Only corporations can issue stock. Corporations and governments can issue bonds. In any given year, far more funds are raised with bonds than with stock.
3. Firm managers are hired by stockholders to protect and increase their wealth. Bondholders must rely on a contract called an indenture to protect their interests. Bond indentures contain covenants that restrict the firm from activities that increase risk and hence the chance of defaulting on the bonds. Bond indentures also contain many provisions that make them more or less attractive to investors, such as a call option, convertibility, or a sinking fund.
4. The value of any business asset is computed the same way, by computing the present value of the cash flows that will go to the holder of the asset. For example, a commercial building is valued by computing the present value of the net cash flows the owner will receive. We compute the value of bonds by finding the present value of the cash flows, which consist of periodic interest payments and a final principal payment.
5. The value of bonds fluctuates with current market prices. If a bond has an interest payment based on a 5% coupon rate, no investor will buy it at face value if new bonds are available for the same price with interest payments based on 8% coupon interest. To sell the bond, the holder will have to discount the price until the yield to the holder equals 8%. The amount of the discount is greater the longer the term to maturity.

KEY TERMS

bond indenture, p. 281
call provision, p. 283
coupon rate, p. 274
credit default swap (CDS), p. 287
current yield, p. 289
discount, p. 293
financial guarantees, p. 287
FINRA, p. 288
general obligation bonds, p. 280
initial public offering (IPO), p. 274
initial public offering, p. 274
interest-rate risk, p. 293
junk bonds, p. 285
premium, p. 293
registered bonds, p. 282
restrictive covenants, p. 283
revenue bonds, p. 280
Separate Trading of Registered Interest and Principal Securities (STRIPS), p. 277
sinking fund, p. 283
TRACE, p. 288
zero-coupon securities, p. 277

QUESTIONS

1. Contrast investors' use of capital markets with their use of money markets.
2. What are the primary capital market securities, and who are the primary purchasers of these securities?
3. What two characteristics make bonds a more popular long-term alternative to investing in stocks?
4. Does it seem right to you that one could buy insurance on anyone who looks unhealthy? Why?
5. The U.S. Treasury issues bills, notes, and bonds. How do these three securities differ?
6. As interest rates in the market change over time, the market price of bonds rises and falls. The change in the value of bonds due to changes in interest rates is a risk incurred by bond investors. What is this risk called?
7. Explain how the creation of TRACE relates to asymmetric information problems in the bond markets.
8. A call provision on a bond allows the issuer to redeem the bond at will. Investors do not like call provisions and so require higher interest on callable bonds. Why do issuers continue to issue callable bonds anyway?
9. What is a sinking fund? Do investors like bonds that contain this feature? Why?
10. Why do you think that all companies that trade securities are required to be members of FINRA?
11. Describe the two ways whereby capital market securities pass from the issuer to the public.

QUANTITATIVE PROBLEMS

1. A bond makes an annual \$80 interest payment (8% coupon). The bond has five years before it matures, at which time it will pay \$1,000. Assuming a discount rate of 10%, what should be the price of the bond? (Review Chapters 3 and 12.)
2. Calculate the price of a bond that matures in 8 years, has a face value of \$5,000, and has a coupon rate of 2% (paid semiannually) if the market interest rate is 1%. What is the price of the bond if the market interest rate drops to 0.5%?
3. Consider the two bonds described below:

	Bond A	Bond B
Maturity (years)	15	20
Coupon rate (%) (paid semiannually)	10	6
Par value	\$1,000	\$1,000

   a. If both bonds had a required return of 8%, what would the bonds' prices be?
   b. Describe what it means if a bond sells at a discount, at a premium, and at its face amount (par value). Are these two bonds selling at a discount, premium, or par?
   c. If the required return on the two bonds rose to 10%, what would the bonds' prices be?
4. A two-year \$1,000 par zero-coupon bond is currently priced at \$819.00. A two-year \$1,000 annuity is currently priced at \$1,712.52. If you want to invest \$50,000 in one of the two securities, which is a better buy? (Hint: Compute the yield of each security.)
5. Consider the following cash flows. All market interest rates are 12%.

Year	0	1	2	3	4
Cash Flow		160	170	180	230

a. What price would you pay for these cash flows? What total wealth do you expect after 2.5 years if you sell the rights to the remaining cash flows? Assume interest rates remain constant.

b. Immediately after buying these cash flows, all market interest rates drop to 11%. What is the impact on your total wealth after 2.5 years?

6. The yield on a corporate bond is 10%, and it is currently selling at par. The marginal tax rate is 20%. A par value municipal bond with a coupon rate of 8.50% is available. Which security is a better buy?

7. Suppose a municipal bond offers a yield to maturity of 5% and a same maturity corporate bond offers a 4% yield. For which values of the marginal tax rate would an investor prefer to buy the corporate bond?

8. M&E, Inc., has an outstanding convertible bond. The bond can be converted into 20 shares of common equity (currently trading at $52/share). The bond has five years of remaining maturity, a $1,000 par value, and a 6% annual coupon. M&E's straight debt is currently trading to yield 5%. What is the minimum price of the bond?

9. Assume the debt in the previous question is trading at $1,035. How can you earn a riskless profit from this situation (arbitrage)?

10. Consider two $10,000 face-value corporate bonds. One is currently selling for $9,980 and matures in 15 years. The other bond sells for $9,350 and matures in 3 years. Calculate the current yield for both bonds if both have a coupon rate equal to 5%. Which current yield is a better approximation of the yield to maturity? (Assume a yearly coupon payment.)

11. A $5,000 corporate bond with an 8.625% coupon rate sells above par. Is the current yield higher, lower, or equal to the coupon rate? Is the current yield higher, lower, or equal to the yield to maturity?

12. A one-year discount bond with a face value of $1,000 was purchased for $900. What is the yield to maturity? What is the yield on a discount basis? (See Chapters 3 and 12.)

13. A corporate bond sells at par and has a current yield equal to 5.625%. Another bond sells for $10,075, has a face value of $10,000, and has a coupon rate equal to 5.5%. Which bond has a higher yield to maturity?

14. Your company owns the following bonds:

Bond	Market Value	Duration
A	$13 million	2
B	$18 million	4
C	$20 million	3

If general interest rates rise from 8% to 8.5%, what is the approximate change in the value of the portfolio? (Review Chapter 3.)

WEB EXERCISE

The Bond Market

1. Stocks tend to get more publicity than bonds, but many investors, especially those nearing or in retirement, find that bonds are more consistent with their risk preferences. Go to **http://finance.yahoo.com/calculator/index**. Under Retirement find the calculator "How should I allocate my assets?" After answering the questionnaire, discuss whether you agree with the recommended asset destination.

CHAPTER

13

The Stock Market

> PREVIEW

In the last chapter we identified the capital markets as the place where long-term securities trade. We then examined the bond market and discussed how bond prices are established. In this chapter we continue our investigation of the capital markets by taking a close look at the stock market. The market for stocks is undoubtedly the one that receives the most attention and scrutiny. Great fortunes are made and lost as investors attempt to anticipate the market's ups and downs. We have witnessed an unprecedented period of volatility over the last decade. Stock indexes hit record highs in the late 1990s, largely led by technology companies, and then fell precipitously in 2000. By 2007 they had returned to record highs before falling back to 1997 levels in 2009. Since then the markets have fully recovered and reached new record highs. In this chapter we look at how this important market works.

We begin by discussing the markets where stocks trade. We then examine the fundamental theories that underlie the valuation of stocks. These theories are critical to an understanding of the forces that cause the value of stocks to rise and fall minute by minute and day by day. We will learn that determining a value for a common stock is very difficult and that it is this difficulty that leads to so much volatility in the stock markets.

Investing in Stocks

A share of stock in a firm represents ownership. A stockholder owns a percentage interest in a firm, consistent with the percentage of outstanding stock held.

Investors can earn a return from stock in one of two ways. Either the price of the stock rises over time or the firm pays the stockholder dividends. Frequently, investors earn a return from both sources. Stock is riskier than bonds because stockholders have a lower priority than bondholders when the firm is in trouble, dividends are less assured, and stock price increases are not guaranteed. Despite these risks, it is possible to make a great deal of money by investing in stock, whereas that is very unlikely by investing in bonds. Another distinction between stock and bonds is that stock does not mature.

Ownership of stock gives the stockholder certain rights regarding the firm. One is the right of a *residual claimant*: Stockholders have a claim on all assets and income left over after all other claimants have been satisfied. If nothing is left over, they get nothing. As noted, however, it is possible to get rich as a stockholder if the firm does well.

Most stockholders have the *right to vote* for directors and on certain issues, such as amendments to the corporate charter and whether new shares should be issued.

Notice that the stock certificate shown in Figure 13.1 does not list a maturity date, face value, or an interest rate, which were indicated on the bond shown in Chapter 12.

Common Stock vs. Preferred Stock

There are two types of stock, common and preferred. A share of common stock in a firm represents an ownership interest in that firm. **Common stockholders** vote,

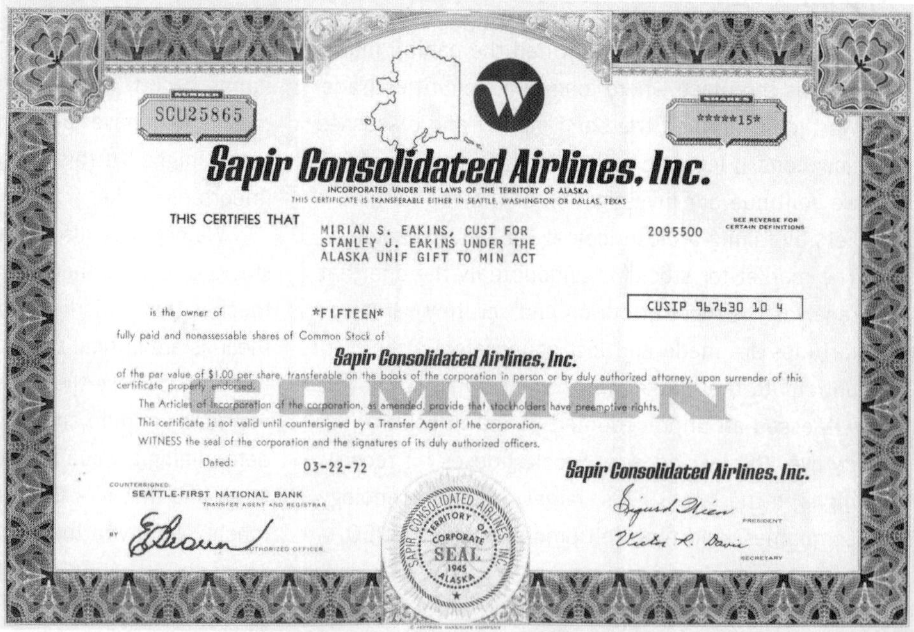

SCU25865

*****15*

Sapir Consolidated Airlines, Inc.

INCORPORATED UNDER THE LAWS OF THE TERRITORY OF ALASKA

THIS CERTIFIES THAT

MIRIAN S. EAKINS, CUST FOR
STANLEY J. EAKINS UNDER THE
ALASKA UNIF GIFT TO MIN ACT

2095500

CUSIP 967630 10 4

is the owner of *FIFTEEN*

fully paid and nonassessable shares of Common Stock of

Sapir Consolidated Airlines, Inc.

of the par value of $1.00 per share, transferable on the books of the corporation in person or by duly authorized attorney, upon surrender of this certificate properly endorsed.

The Articles of Incorporation of the corporation, as amended, provide that stockholders have preemptive rights.

This certificate is not valid until countersigned by a Transfer Agent of the corporation.

WITNESS the seal of the corporation and the signatures of its duly authorized officers.

Dated: 03-22-72

COMMON

SEATTLE-FIRST NATIONAL BANK

Sapir Consolidated Airlines, Inc.

SAPIR CONSOLIDATED AIRLINES, INC. TERRITORY OF ALASKA CORPORATE SEAL 1945

FIGURE 13.1 Sapir Consolidated Airlines Stock

receive dividends, and hope that the price of their stock will rise. There are various classes of common stock, usually denoted type A, type B, and so on. Unfortunately, the type does not have any meaning that is standard across all companies. The differences among the types usually involve either the distribution of dividends or voting rights. It is important for an investor in stocks to know exactly what rights go along with the shares of stock being contemplated.

Preferred stock is a form of equity from a legal and tax standpoint. However, it differs from common stock in several important ways. First, because preferred stockholders receive a fixed dividend that never changes, a share of preferred stock is as much like a bond as it is like common stock. Second, because the dividend does not change, the price of preferred stock is relatively stable. Third, preferred stockholders do not usually vote unless the firm has failed to pay the promised dividend. Finally, preferred stockholders hold a claim on assets that has priority over the claims of common shareholders but after that of creditors such as bondholders.

Less than 25% of new equity issues are preferred stock, and only about 5% of all capital is raised using preferred stock. This may be because preferred dividends are not tax-deductible to the firm like bond interest payments. Consequently, preferred stock usually has a higher cost than debt, even though it shares many of the characteristics of a bond.

How Stocks Are Sold

Literally billions of shares of stock are sold each business day in the United States. The orderly flow of information, stock ownership, and funds through the stock markets is a critical feature of well-developed and efficient markets. This efficiency encourages investors to buy stocks and to provide equity capital to businesses with valuable growth opportunities. We traditionally discuss stocks as trading either on an organized exchange or over the counter. Recently, this distinction is blurring as electronic trading grows in both volume and influence.

Organized Securities Exchanges Historically, the New York Stock Exchange (NYSE) has been the best known of the organized exchanges. The NYSE first began trading in 1792, when 24 brokers began trading a few stocks on Wall Street. The NYSE is still the world's largest and most liquid equities exchange. The traditional definition of an organized exchange is that there is a specified location where buyers and sellers meet on a regular basis to trade securities using an open-outcry auction model. As more sophisticated technology has been adapted to securities trading, this model is becoming less frequently used. The NYSE currently advertises itself as a hybrid market that combines aspects of electronic trading and traditional auction-market trading. In March of 2006, the NYSE merged with Archipelago, an Electronic Communication Network (ECN) firm. On April 4, 2007, the NYSE Euronext was created by the combination of the NYSE Group and Euronext N.V. NYSE Euronext completed acquisition of the American stock exchange in 2009. In November 2013, Intercontinental Exchange (ICE) purchased NYSE Euronext for about $8.2 billion.

Find listed companies, member information, real-time market indices, and current stock quotes at **www.nyse.com**.

There are also major organized stock exchanges around the world. The most active exchange in the world is the Nikkei in Tokyo. Other major exchanges include the London Stock Exchange in England, the DAX in Germany, and the Toronto Stock Exchange in Canada.

To have a stock listed for trading on one of the organized exchanges, a firm must file an application and meet certain criteria set by the exchange designed to enhance trading. For example, the NYSE encourages only the largest firms to list so that transaction volume will be high. There are several ways to meet the minimum listing requirements. Generally, the firm must have substantial earnings and market value (greater than $10 million per year and $100 million market value).

Over 8,000 companies around the world list their shares on the NYSE Euronext. The average firm on the exchange has a market value of $19.6 billion. On October 28, 1998, the NYSE volume topped 1 billion shares for the first time.[1] By 2016, daily volume was usually in excess of 4 billion shares with more than 10 billion shares being traded on peak days.

Regional exchanges, such as the Philadelphia, are even easier to list on. Some firms choose to list on more than one exchange, believing that more exposure will increase the demand for their stock and hence its price. Many firms also believe that there is a certain amount of prestige in being listed on one of the major exchanges. They may even include this fact in their advertising. There is little conclusive research to support this belief, however. Microsoft, for example, is not listed on any organized exchange, yet its stock had a total market value of around $400 billion in 2016.

Over-the-Counter Markets If Microsoft's stock is not traded on any of the organized stock exchanges, where does it sell its stock? Securities not listed on one of the exchanges trade in the over-the-counter (OTC) market. This market is not organized in the sense of having a building where trading takes place. Instead, trading occurs over sophisticated telecommunications networks. One such network is called the **National Association of Securities Dealers Automated Quotation System (NASDAQ)**. This system, introduced in 1971, provides current bid and ask prices on about 3,000 actively traded securities. Dealers "make a market" in these stocks by buying for inventory when investors want to sell and selling from inventory when investors want to buy. These dealers provide small stocks with the liquidity that is essential to their acceptance in the market. Total volume on the NASDAQ is usually slightly lower than on the NYSE; however, NASDAQ volume has been growing and occasionally exceeds NYSE volume.

Not all publicly traded stocks list on one of the organized exchanges or on NASDAQ. Securities that trade very infrequently or trade primarily in one region of the country are usually handled by the regional offices of various brokerage houses. These offices often maintain small inventories of regionally popular securities. Dealers that make a market for stocks that trade in low volume are very important to the success of the over-the-counter market. Without these dealers standing ready to buy or sell shares, investors would be reluctant to buy shares of stock in regional or unknown firms, and it would be very difficult for start-up firms to raise needed capital. Recall from Chapter 4 that the more liquid an asset is, the greater its quantity demanded. By providing liquidity intervention, dealers increase demand for thinly traded securities.

Organized vs. Over-the-Counter Trading There is a significant difference between how organized and OTC exchanges operate. Organized exchanges are characterized as auction markets that use floor traders who specialize in particular stocks. These specialists oversee and facilitate trading in a group of stocks. Floor

---

[1] *NYSE Fact Book,* www.nyse.com.

traders, representing various brokerage firms with buy and sell orders, meet at the trading post on the exchange and learn about current bid and ask prices. These quotes are called out loud. In about 90% of trades, the specialist matches buyers with sellers. In the other 10%, the specialists may intervene by taking ownership of the stock themselves or by selling stock from inventory. It is the specialist's duty to maintain an orderly market in the stock even if that means buying stock in a declining market.

Few orders on the New York Stock Exchange are filled by floor traders personally approaching the specialist on the exchange. Most orders are filled electronically via the **super display book (SDBK)**. This system bypasses the floor trader and routes the order to the specialist directly. The system will automatically match buy orders with sell orders without intervention. Only complex institutional orders continue to be executed by floor traders on the exchange. This system allows for rapid execution of the high volume of trades made daily.

Whereas organized exchanges have specialists who facilitate trading, over-the-counter markets have market makers. Rather than trade stocks in an auction format, they trade on an electronic network where bid and ask prices are set by the market makers. There are usually multiple market makers for any particular stock. They each enter their bid and ask quotes. Once this is done, they are obligated to buy or sell at least 1,000 securities at that price. Once a trade has been executed, they may enter a new bid and ask quote. Market makers are important to the economy in that they ensure there is continuous liquidity for every stock, even those with little transaction volume. Market makers are compensated by the spread between the **bid price** (the price they pay for stocks) and **ask price** (the price they sell the stocks for). They also receive commissions on trades.

Although NASDAQ, the NYSE, and the other exchanges are heavily regulated, they are still public for-profit businesses. They have shareholders, directors, and officers who are interested in market share and generating profits. This means that the NYSE is vigorously competing with NASDAQ for the high-volume stocks that generate the big fees. For example, the NYSE has been trying to entice Microsoft to leave the NASDAQ and list with them for many years.

Alternative Trading Systems (ATSs) and Multilateral Trading Facilities (MTFs) ATSs are trading systems that bypass traditional exchanges and allow for buyers and sellers of securities to deal directly with each other. ATSs and MFTs are typically used for large transactions among institutional investors. A subset of these trading facilities consists of Electronic Communications Networks (ECNs), which are ATSs that are fully electronic. ECNs have been challenging both NASDAQ and the organized exchanges for business in recent years. An ECN is an electronic network that brings together major brokerages and traders so that they can trade among themselves and bypass the middleman. ECNs have a number of advantages that have led to their rapid growth.

- *Transparency:* All unfilled orders are available for review by ECN traders. This provides valuable information about supply and demand that traders can use to set their strategy. Although some exchanges make this information available, it is not always as current or complete as what the ECN provides.
- *Cost reduction:* Because the middleman and the commission are cut out of the deal, transaction costs can be lower for trades executed over an ECN. The spread is usually reduced and sometimes eliminated.

- *Faster execution:* Since ECNs are fully automated, trades are matched and confirmed faster than can be done when there is human involvement. For many traders this is not of great significance, but for those trying to trade on small price fluctuations, this is critical.
- *After-hours trading:* Prior to the advent of ECNs only institutional traders had access to trading securities after the exchanges had closed for the day. Many news reports and information become available after the major exchanges have closed, and small investors were locked out of trading on this data. Since ECNs never close, trading can continue around the clock.

Along with the advantages of ECNs there are disadvantages. The primary one is that they work well only for stocks with substantial volume. Since ECNs require there to be a seller to match against each buyer and vice versa, thinly traded stocks may go long intervals without trading. One of the largest ECNs is Instinet. It is mainly for institutional traders. Instinet also owns Island, which is for active individual traders.

The major exchanges are fighting the ECNs by expanding their own automatic trading systems. For example, the NYSE recently announced changes to its own Direct+ order routing system and merged with Archipelago to give it an established place in this market. Although the NYSE still dominates the American stock market in terms of share and dollar volume, its live auction format may not survive technological challenges for many more years.

Exchange Traded Funds Exchange traded funds (ETFs) have become the latest market innovation to capture investor interest. They were first introduced in 1990 and by 2015 there were over 1,500 separate ETFs were being traded. In their simplest form, ETFs are formed when a basket of securities is purchased and a stock is created based on this basket that is traded on an exchange. The makeup and structure are continuing to evolve, but ETFs share the following features:

1. They are listed and traded as individual stocks on a stock exchange.
2. They are indexed rather than actively managed.
3. Their value is based on the underlying net asset value of the stocks held in the index basket. The exact content of the basket is public so that intraday arbitrage keeps the ETF price close to the implied value.

In many ways ETFs resemble stock index mutual funds in that they track the performance of some index, such as the S&P 500 or the Dow Jones Industrial Average. They differ in that ETFs trade like stocks, so they allow for limit orders, short sales, stop-loss orders, and the ability to buy on margin. ETFs tend to have lower management fees than do comparable index mutual funds. For example, the Vanguard extended market ETF reports an expense ratio of .08% compared to an expense ratio of .25% for its extended market index mutual fund. Another advantage of ETFs is that they usually have no minimum investment amount, whereas mutual funds often require $3,000–$5,000 minimums.

The primary disadvantage of ETFs is that since they trade like stocks, investors have to pay a broker commission each time they buy or sale shares. This provides a cost disadvantage compared to mutual funds for those who want to frequently invest small amounts, such as through a 401(k).

ETFs feature some of the more exotic names found in finance, including Vipers, Diamonds, Spiders, and Qubes. These names are derived from the index that is tracked or the name of the issuing firm. For example, Diamonds are indexed to the Dow Jones Industrial Average, Spiders track the S&P 500, and Qubes follow the NASDAQ (ticker symbol QQQQ). Vipers are Vanguard's ETFs. The list of available indexes that can be tracked by purchasing ETFs is rapidly expanding to include virtually every sector, commodity, and investment style (value, growth, capitalization, etc.). Their popularity is likely to increase as more investors learn about how they can be effectively used as a low-cost way to help diversify a portfolio.

Computing the Price of Common Stock

One basic principle of finance is that the value of any investment is found by computing the value today of all cash flows the investment will generate over its life. For example, a commercial building will sell for a price that reflects the net cash flows (rents minus expenses) it is projected to have over its useful life. Similarly, we value common stock as the value in today's dollars of all future cash flows. The cash flows a stockholder may earn from stock are dividends, the sales price, or both.

To develop the theory of stock valuation, we begin with the simplest possible scenario. This assumes that you buy the stock, hold it for one period to get a dividend, then sell the stock. We call this the *one-period valuation model*. It is useful for building an understanding of how stock is valued.

The One-Period Valuation Model

GO ONLINE
Access **http://stockcharts.com/freecharts/historical** for detailed stock quotes, charts, and historical stock data.

Suppose that you have some extra money to invest for one year. After a year you will need to sell your investment to pay tuition. After watching *Wall Street Week* on TV you decide that you want to buy Intel Corp. stock. You call your broker and find that Intel is currently selling for $50 per share and pays $0.16 per year in dividends. The analyst on *Wall Street Week* predicts that the stock will be selling for $60 in one year. Should you buy this stock?

To answer this question, you need to determine whether the current price accurately reflects the analyst's forecast. To value the stock today, you need to find the present discounted value of the expected cash flows (future payments) using the formula in Equation 1 of Chapter 3 in which the discount factor used to discount the cash flows is the required return on investments in equity. The cash flows consist of one dividend payment plus a final sales price, which, when discounted back to the present, leads to the following equation that computes the current price of the stock.

$$P_0 = \frac{D_1}{(1 + k_e)} + \frac{P_1}{(1 + k_e)} \tag{1}$$

where

P_0 = the current price of the stock. The zero subscript refers to time period zero, or the present.
D_1 = the dividend paid at the end of year 1.
k_e = the required return on investments in equity.
P_1 = the price at the end of the first year. This is the assumed sales price of the stock.

EXAMPLE 13.1

Stock Valuation: One-Period Model

Find the value of the Intel stock given the figures reported above. You will need to know the required return on equity to find the present value of the cash flows. Since a stock is more risky than a bond, you will require a higher return than that offered in the bond market. Assume that after careful consideration you decide that you would be satisfied to earn 12% on the investment.

> Solution

Putting the numbers into Equation 1 yields the following:

$$P_0 = \frac{.16}{1 + 0.12} + \frac{\$60}{1 + 0.12} = \$.14 + \$53.57 = \$53.71$$

Based on your analysis, you find that the stock is worth $53.71. Since the stock is currently available for $50 per share, you would choose to buy it. Why is the stock selling for less than $53.71? It may be because other investors place a different risk on the cash flows or estimate the cash flows to be less than you do.

The Generalized Dividend Valuation Model

The one-period *dividend* valuation model can be extended to any number of periods. The concept remains the same. The value of stock is the present value of all future cash flows. The only cash flows that an investor will receive are dividends and a final sales price when the stock is ultimately sold. The generalized formula for stock can be written as in Equation 2.

$$P_0 = \frac{D_1}{(1 + k_e)^1} + \frac{D_2}{(1 + k_e)^2} + \cdots + \frac{D_n}{(1 + k_e)^n} + \frac{P_n}{(1 + k_e)^n} \tag{2}$$

If you were to attempt to use Equation 2 to find the value of a share of stock, you would soon realize that you must first estimate the value the stock will have at some point in the future before you can estimate its value today. In other words, you must find P_n in order to find P_0. However, if P_n is far in the future, it will not affect P_0. For example, the present value of a share of stock that sells for $50 seventy-five years from now using a 12% discount rate is just one cent $[\$50/(1.12^{75}) = \$0.01]$. *This means that the current value of a share of stock can be found as simply the present value of the future dividend stream.* The **generalized dividend model** is rewritten in Equation 3 without the final sales price.

$$P_0 = \sum_{t=1}^{\infty} \frac{D_t}{(1 + k_e)^t} \tag{3}$$

Consider the implications of Equation 3 for a moment. The generalized dividend model says that the price of stock is determined only by the present value of the dividends and that nothing else matters. Many stocks do not pay dividends, so how is it that these stocks have value? *Buyers of the stock expect that the firm will pay dividends someday.* Most of the time a firm institutes dividends as soon as it has completed the rapid growth phase of its life cycle. The stock price increases as the time approaches for the dividend stream to begin.

The generalized dividend valuation model requires that we compute the present value of an infinite stream of dividends, a process that could be difficult, to say the least. Therefore, simplified models have been developed to make the calculations easier. One such model is the **Gordon growth model**, which assumes constant dividend growth.

The Gordon Growth Model

Many firms strive to increase their dividends at a constant rate each year. Equation 4 rewrites Equation 3 to reflect this constant growth in dividends.

$$P_0 = \frac{D_0 \times (1+g)^1}{(1+k_e)^1} + \frac{D_0 \times (1+g)^2}{(1+k_e)^2} + \cdots + \frac{D_0 \times (1+g)^\infty}{(1+k_e)^\infty} \tag{4}$$

where D_0 = the most recent dividend paid.
g = the expected constant growth rate in dividends.
k_e = the required return on an investment in equity.

Equation 4 has been simplified using some algebra to obtain Equation 5.[2]

$$P_0 = \frac{D_0 \times (1+g)}{(k_e - g)} = \frac{D_1}{(k_e - g)} \tag{5}$$

This model is useful for finding the value of stock, given a few assumptions:

1. *Dividends are assumed to continue growing at a constant rate forever.* Actually, as long as they are expected to grow at a constant rate for an extended period of time (even if not forever), the model should yield reasonable results. This is because errors about distant cash flows become small when discounted to the present.
2. *The growth rate is assumed to be less than the required return on equity,* k_e. Myron Gordon, in his development of the model, demonstrated that this is a reasonable assumption. In theory, if the growth rate were faster than the rate demanded by holders of the firm's equity, in the long run the firm would grow impossibly large.

---

[2] To generate Equation 5 from Equation 4, first multiply both sides of Equation 4 by $(1 + k_e)/(1 + g)$ and subtract Equation 4 from the result. This yields

$$\frac{P_0 \times (1+k_e)}{(1+g)} - P_0 = D_0 - \frac{D_0 \times (1+g)^\infty}{(1+k_e)^\infty}$$

Assuming that k_e is greater than g, the term on the far right will approach zero and can be dropped. Thus, after factoring P_0 out of the left side,

$$P_0 \times \left[\frac{1+k_e}{1+g} - 1\right] = D_0$$

Next, simplify by combining terms to

$$P_0 \times \frac{(1+k_e) - (1+g)}{(1+g)} = D_0$$

$$P_0 = \frac{D_0 \times (1+g)}{k_e - g} = \frac{D_1}{k_e - g}$$

EXAMPLE 13.2

Stock Valuation: Gordon Growth Model

Find the current market price of Coca-Cola stock, assuming dividends grow at a constant rate of 10.95%, $D_0 = \$1.00$, and the required return is 13%.

> **Solution**

$$P_0 = \frac{D_0 \times (1 + g)}{k_e - g}$$

$$P_0 = \frac{\$1.00 \times (1.1095)}{.13 - .1095}$$

$$P_0 = \frac{\$1.1095}{0.0205} = \$54.12$$

Coca-Cola stock should sell for $54.12 if the assumptions regarding the constant growth rate and required return are correct.

Price Earnings Valuation Method

Theoretically, the best method of stock valuation is the dividend valuation approach. Sometimes, however, it is difficult to apply. If a firm is not paying dividends or has a very erratic growth rate, the results may not be satisfactory. Other approaches to stock valuation are sometimes applied. Among the more popular is the price/earnings multiple.

The **price earnings ratio (PE)** is a widely watched measure of how much the market is willing to pay for $1 of earnings from a firm. The PE ratio can be used to estimate the value of a firm's stock. Note that algebraically the product of the PE ratio times expected earnings is the firm's stock price.

$$\frac{P}{E} \times E = P \tag{6}$$

Firms in the same industry are expected to have similar PE ratios in the long run. The value of a firm's stock can be found by multiplying the average industry PE times the expected earnings per share. A high PE has two interpretations.

1. A higher-than-average PE may mean that the market expects earnings to rise in the future. This would return the PE to a more normal level.
2. A high PE may alternatively indicate that the market feels the firm's earnings are very low risk and is therefore willing to pay a premium for them.

EXAMPLE 13.3

Stock Valuation: PE Ratio Approach

The average industry PE ratio for restaurants similar to Applebee's, a pub restaurant chain, is 23. What is the current price of Applebee's if earnings per share are projected to be $1.13?

> **Solution**

Using Equation 6 and the data given we find:

$$P_0 = P/E \times E$$

$$P_0 = 23 \times \$1.13 = \$26$$

The PE ratio approach is especially useful for valuing privately held firms and firms that do not pay dividends. The weakness of the PE approach to valuation is that by using an industry average PE ratio, firm-specific factors that might contribute to a long-term PE ratio above or below the average are ignored in the analysis. A skilled analyst will adjust the PE ratio up or down to reflect unique characteristics of a firm when estimating its stock price.

How the Market Sets Security Prices

Suppose you go to an auto auction. The cars are available for inspection before the auction begins, and you find a little Mazda Miata that you like. You test-drive it in the parking lot and notice that it makes a few strange noises, but you decide that you would still like the car. You decide \$5,000 would be a fair price that would allow you to pay some repair bills should the noises turn out to be serious. You see that the auction is ready to begin, so you go in and wait for the Miata to enter.

Suppose there is another buyer who also spots the Miata. He test-drives the car and recognizes that the noises are simply the result of worn brake pads that he can fix himself at a nominal cost. He decides that the car is worth \$7,000. He also goes in and waits for the Miata to enter.

Who will buy the car and for how much? Suppose only the two of you are interested in the Miata. You begin the bidding at \$4,000. He ups your bid to \$4,500. You bid your top price of \$5,000. He counters with \$5,100. The price is now higher than you are willing to pay, so you stop bidding. The car is sold to the more informed buyer for \$5,100.

This simple example raises a number of points. First, the price is set by the buyer willing to pay the highest price. The price is not necessarily the highest price the asset could fetch, but it is incrementally greater than what any other buyer is willing to pay.

Second, the market price will be set by the buyer who can take best advantage of the asset. The buyer who purchased the car knew that he could fix the noise easily and cheaply. Because of this, he was willing to pay more for the car than you were. The same concept holds for other assets. For example, a piece of property or a building will sell to the buyer who can put the asset to the most productive use. Consider why one company often pays a substantial premium over current market prices to acquire ownership of another (target) company. The acquiring firm may believe that it can put the target firm's assets to work better than they are currently and that this justifies the premium price.

Finally, the example shows the role played by information in asset pricing. Superior information about an asset can increase its value by reducing its risk. When you consider buying a stock, there are many unknowns about the future cash flows. The buyer who has the best information about these cash flows will discount them at a lower interest rate than will a buyer who is very uncertain.

Now let us apply these ideas to stock valuation. Suppose that you are considering the purchase of stock expected to pay dividends of \$2 next year ($D_1 = \$2$). The firm is expected to grow at 3% infinitively ($g = 3\%$). You are quite *uncertain* about both the constancy of the dividend stream and the accuracy of the estimated growth rate. To compensate yourself for this risk, you require a return of 15%.

Now suppose Jennifer, another investor, has spoken with industry insiders and feels more confident about the projected cash flows. Jennifer requires only a 12% return because her perceived risk is lower than yours. Bud, on the other hand, is dating the CEO of the company. He knows with near certainty what the future of the firm actually is. He thinks that both the estimated growth rate and the estimated cash flows are lower than what they will *actually* be in the future. Because he sees almost no risk in this investment, he requires only a 7% return.

What are the values each investor will give to the stock? Applying the Gordon growth model yields the following stock prices.

Investor	Discount Rate	Stock Price
You	15%	\$16.67
Jennifer	12%	\$22.22
Bud	7%	\$50.00

You are willing to pay \$16.67 for the stock. Jennifer would pay up to \$22.22, and Bud would pay \$50. The investor with the lowest perceived risk is willing to pay the most for the stock. If there were no other traders, the market price would be just above \$22.22. If you already held the stock, you would sell it to Bud.

The point of this section is that the players in the market, bidding against each other, establish the market price. When new information is released about a firm, expectations change, and with them, prices change. New information can cause changes in expectations about the level of future dividends or the risk of those dividends. Since market participants are constantly receiving new information and constantly revising their expectations, it is reasonable that stock prices are constantly changing as well.

Errors in Valuation

In this chapter we learned about several asset valuation models. An interesting exercise is to apply these models to real firms. Students who do this find that computed stock prices do not match market prices much of the time. Students often question whether the models are wrong or incomplete or whether they are simply being used incorrectly. There are many opportunities for errors in applying the models. These include problems estimating growth, estimating risk, and forecasting dividends.

Problems with Estimating Growth

The constant growth model requires the analyst to estimate the constant rate of growth the firm will experience. You may estimate future growth by computing the historical growth rate in dividends, sales, or net profits. This approach fails to consider any changes in the firm or economy that may affect the growth rate. Robert Haugen, a professor of finance at the University of California, writes in his book, *The New Finance*, that competition will prevent high-growth firms from being able to maintain their historical growth rate. He demonstrates that, despite this, the stock prices of historically high-growth firms tend to reflect a continuation of the high growth rate. The result is that investors in these firms receive lower returns than they would by investing in mature, slower-growing firms. This just points out that even the experts

TABLE 13.1 Stock Prices for a Security with D_0 = \$2.00, k_e = 15%, and Constant Growth Rates as Listed

Growth (%)	Price ($)
1	14.43
3	17.17
5	21.00
10	44.00
11	55.50
12	74.67
13	113.00
14	228.00

have trouble estimating future growth rates. Table 13.1 shows the stock price for a firm with a 15% required return, a $2 dividend, and a range of different growth rates. The stock price varies from $14.43 at 1% growth to $228.00 at 14% growth rate. Estimating growth at 13% instead of 12% results in a $38.33 price difference.

Problems with Estimating Risk

The dividend valuation model requires the analyst to estimate the required return for the firm's equity. Table 13.2 shows how the price of a share of stock offering a $2 dividend and a 5% growth rate changes with different estimates of the required return. Clearly, stock price is highly dependent on the required return, despite our uncertainty regarding how it is found.

Problems with Forecasting Dividends

Even if we are able to accurately estimate a firm's growth rate and its required return, we are still faced with the problem of determining how much of the firm's earnings will be paid as dividends. Clearly, many factors can influence the dividend payout ratio. These will include the firm's future growth opportunities and management's concern over future cash flows.

TABLE 13.2 Stock Prices for a Security with D_0 = \$2.00, g = 5%, and Required Returns as Listed

Required Return (%)	Price ($)
10	42.00
11	35.00
12	30.00
13	26.25
14	23.33
15	21.00

Putting all of these concerns together, we see that stock analysts are seldom very certain that their stock price projections are accurate. This is why stock prices fluctuate so widely on news reports. For example, information that the economy is slowing can cause analysts to revise their growth expectations. When this happens across a broad spectrum of stocks, major market indexes can change.

Does all this mean that you should not invest in the market? No, it only means that short-term fluctuations in stock prices are expected and natural. Over the long term, the stock price will adjust to reflect the true earnings of the firm. If high-quality firms are chosen for your portfolio, they should provide fair returns over time.

CASE

The 2007–2009 Financial Crisis and the Stock Market

The subprime financial crisis that started in August 2007 led to one of the worst bear markets in the past 50 years. Our analysis of stock price valuation, again using the Gordon growth model, can help us understand how this event affected stock prices.

The subprime financial crisis had a major negative impact on the economy, leading to a downward revision of the growth prospects for U.S. companies, thus lowering the dividend growth rate (g) in the Gordon model. The resulting increase in the denominator in Equation 5 would lead to a decline in P_0 and hence a decline in stock prices.

Increased uncertainty for the U.S. economy and the widening credit spreads resulting from the subprime crisis would also raise the required return on investment in equity. A higher k_e also leads to an increase in the denominator in Equation 5, a decline in P_0, and a general fall in stock prices.

In the early stages of the financial crisis, the decline in growth prospects and credit spreads were moderate and so, as the Gordon model predicts, the stock market decline was also moderate. However, when the crisis entered a particularly virulent stage, credit spreads shot through the roof, the economy tanked, and as the Gordon model predicts, the stock market crashed. Between January 6, 2009, and March 6, 2009, the Dow Jones Industrial Average fell from 9,015 to 6,547. Between October 2007 (high of 14,066) and March 2009, the market lost 53% of its value. Within a year the index was back over 10,000.

CASE

The September 11 Terrorist Attack, the Enron Scandal, and the Stock Market

In 2001 two big shocks hit the stock market: the September 11 terrorist attack and the Enron scandal. Our analysis of stock price evaluation, again using the Gordon growth model, can help us understand how these events affected stock prices.

The September 11 terrorist attack raised the possibility that terrorism against the United States would paralyze the country. These fears led to a downward revision of the growth prospects for U.S. companies, thus lowering the dividend growth rate g

in the Gordon model. The resulting rise in the denominator in Equation 5 should lead to a decline in P_0 and hence a decline in stock prices.

Increased uncertainty for the U.S. economy would also raise the required return on investment in equity. A higher k_e also leads to a rise in the denominator in Equation 5, a decline in P_0, and a general fall in stock prices. As the Gordon model predicts, the stock market fell by over 10% immediately after September 11.

Subsequently, the U.S. successes against the Taliban in Afghanistan and the absence of further terrorist attacks reduced market fears and uncertainty, causing g to recover and k_e to fall. The denominator in Equation 5 then fell, leading to a recovery in P_0 and the stock market in October and November. However, by the beginning of 2002, the Enron scandal and disclosures that many companies had overstated their earnings caused many investors to doubt the formerly rosy forecast of earnings and dividend growth for corporations. The resulting revision of g downward, and the rise in k_e because of increased uncertainty about the quality of accounting information, should have led to a rise in the denominator in the Gordon Equation 5, thereby lowering P_0 for many companies and hence the overall stock market. As predicted by our analysis, this is exactly what happened. The stock market recovery was aborted and it entered a downward slide.

Stock Market Indexes

A stock market index is used to monitor the behavior of a group of stocks. By reviewing the average behavior of a group of stocks, investors are able to gain some insight as to how a broad group of stocks may have performed. Various stock market indexes are reported to give investors an indication of the performance of different groups of stocks. The most commonly quoted index is the Dow Jones Industrial Average (DJIA), an index based on the performance of the stocks of 30 large companies. The following Mini-Case box provides more background on this famous index. Table 13.3 lists the 30 stocks that made up the index in June 2013.

> MINI-CASE

History of the Dow Jones Industrial Average

The Dow Jones Industrial Average (DJIA) is an index composed of 30 "blue chip" industrial firms. On May 26, 1896, Charles H. Dow added up the prices of 12 of the best-known stocks and created an average by dividing by the number of stocks. In 1916 eight more stocks were added, and in 1928 the 30-stock average made its debut.

Today the editors of the *Wall Street Journal* select the firms that make up the DJIA. They take a broad view of the type of firm that is considered "industrial": In essence, it is almost any company that is not in the transportation or utility business (because there are also Dow Jones averages for those kinds of stocks). In choosing a new company for DJIA, they look among substantial industrial companies with a history of successful growth and wide interest among investors. The components of the DJIA are changed periodically. For example, recently ATT and Bank of America were replaced with Apple and Nike.

Most market watchers agree that the DJIA is not the best indicator of the market's overall day-to-day performance. Indeed, it varies substantially from broader-based stock indexes in the short run. It continues to be followed so closely primarily because it is the oldest index and was the first to be quoted by other publications. It continues to be popular because it tracks the performance of the overall markets reasonably well over the long run.

TABLE 13.3 The Thirty Companies That Make Up the Dow Jones Industrial Average

Company	Stock Symbol
3M Co.	MMM
Apple Inc.	AAPL
American Express Co.	AXP
Boeing Co.	BA
Caterpillar Inc.	CAT
Chevron	CVX
Cisco Systems	CSCO
Coca-Cola Co.	KO
E.I. DuPont de Nemours	DD
Exxon Mobil Corp.	XOM
General Electric Co.	GE
Goldman Sachs	GS
Home Depot Inc.	HD
International Business Machines	IBM
Intel Corp.	INTC
Johnson & Johnson	JNJ
JP Morgan Chase & Co.	JPM
McDonald's Corp.	MCD
Merck & Co. Inc.	MRK
Microsoft Corp.	MSFT
Nike	NKE
Pfizer Inc.	PFE
Procter & Gamble Co.	PG
Travelers Corp.	TRV
United Technologies Corp.	UTX
United Health Group	UNH
Verizon Communications Inc.	VZ
Visa International	V
Wal-Mart Stores Inc.	WMT
Walt Disney Co.	DIS

Access a wealth of information about the current DJIA and its history at **www.djindexes.com**.

Other indexes, such as Standard & Poor's 500 Index, the NASDAQ composite, and the NYSE composite, may be more useful for following the performance of different groups of stocks. Figure 13.2 shows the DJIA since 1980.

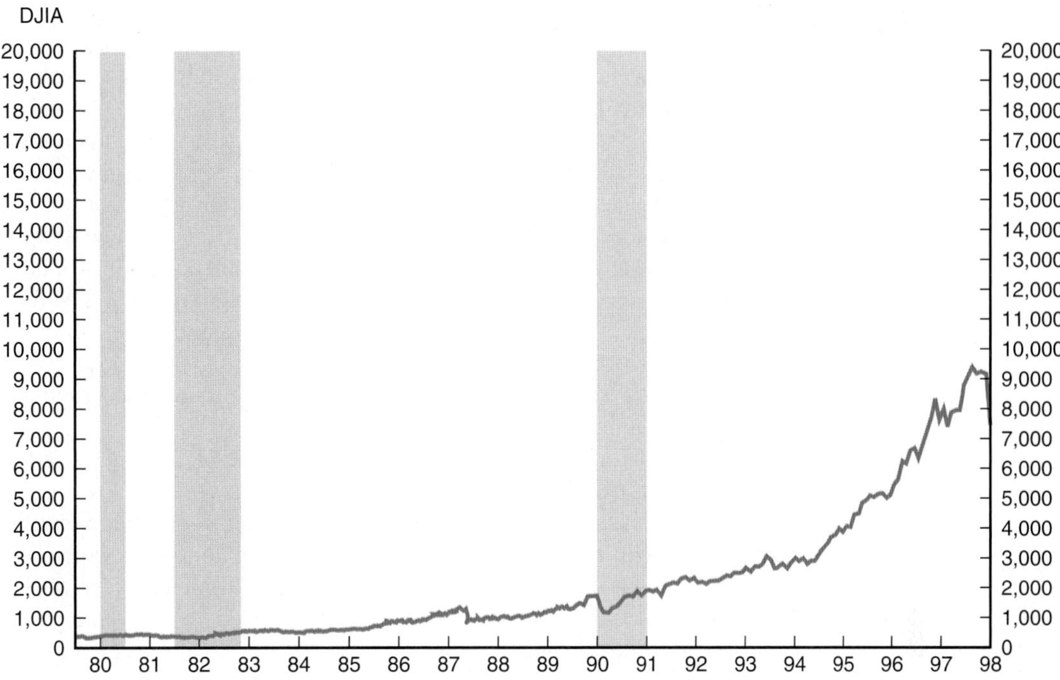

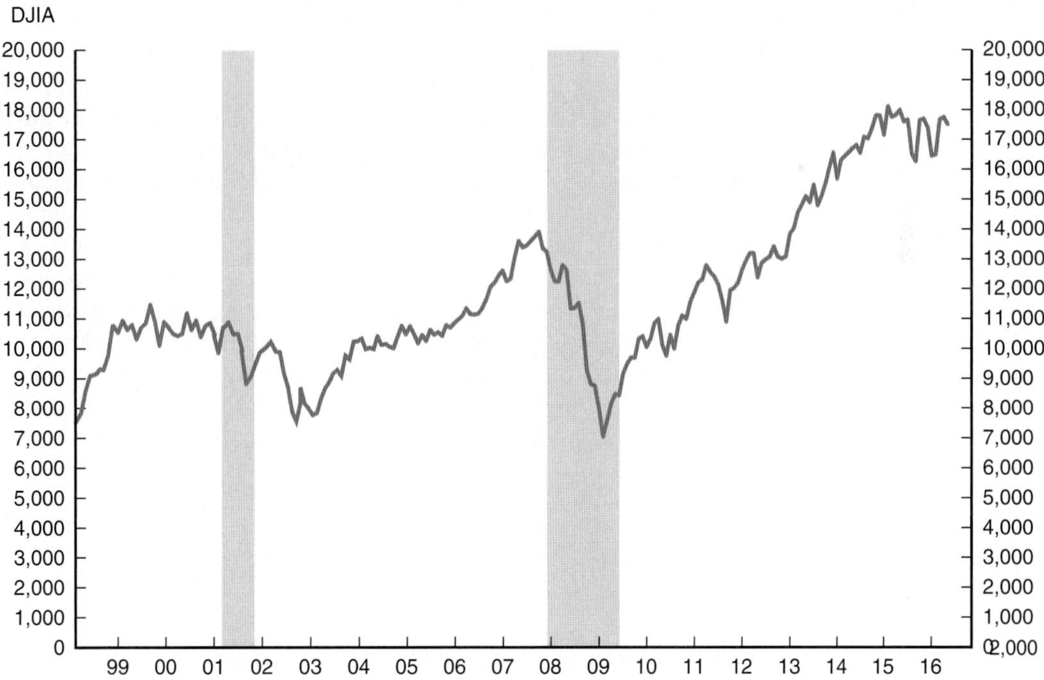

FIGURE 13.2 Dow Jones Industrial Averages, 1980–2016. Blue bars indicate recessions.

Source: http://finance.yahoo.com/q/hp?s=%5EDJI&a=09&b=1&c=2007&d=03&e=13&f=2010&g=m.

Buying Foreign Stocks

In Chapter 4 we learned that diversification of a portfolio reduces risk. A fully diversified portfolio not only will hold securities across a broad swath of domestic industries, but will also hold securities from around the world. When one country is suffering from a recession, others may be booming. If inflationary concerns in the United States cause stock prices to drop, falling inflation in Japan may cause Japanese stocks to rise.

The problem with buying foreign stocks is that most foreign companies are not listed on any of the U.S. stock exchanges, so the purchase of shares is difficult. Intermediaries have found a way to solve this problem by selling **American depository receipts (ADRs)**. A U.S. bank buys the shares of a foreign company and places them in its vault. The bank then issues receipts against these shares, and these receipts can be traded domestically, usually on the NASDAQ. Trade in ADRs is conducted entirely in U.S. dollars, and the bank converts stock dividends into U.S. currency. One advantage of the ADR is that it allows foreign firms to trade in the United States without the firms having to meet the disclosure rules required by the SEC.

As the worldwide recession of 2008 demonstrated, while volatility peculiar to one country can be reduced by diversification, the degree of economic interconnectivity among nations means that some risk always remains. Nevertheless, interest is particularly keen in the stocks of firms in emerging economies such as Mexico, Brazil, and South Korea.

Regulation of the Stock Market

Properly functioning capital markets are a hallmark of an economically advanced economy. For an economy to flourish, firms must be able to raise funds to take advantage of growth opportunities as they become available. Firms raise funds in the capital markets, and for these to function properly investors must be able to trust the information that is released about the firms that are using them. Markets can collapse in the absence of this trust. The most notable example of this in the United States was the Great Depression. During the 1920s, about $50 billion in new securities were offered for sale. By 1932, half had become worthless. The public's confidence in the capital markets justifiably plummeted, and lawmakers agreed that for the economy to recover, public faith had to be restored. Following a series of investigative hearings, Congress passed the Securities Act of 1933 and, shortly after, the Securities Act of 1934. The main purpose of these laws was to (1) require firms to tell the public the truth about their businesses and (2) require brokers, dealers, and exchanges to treat investors fairly. Congress established the Securities and Exchange Commission (SEC) to enforce these laws.

The Securities and Exchange Commission

The SEC Web site states the following:

> The primary mission of the U.S. Securities and Exchange Commission is to protect investors and maintain the integrity of the securities markets.[3]

It accomplishes this daunting task primarily by ensuring a constant, timely, and accurate flow of information to investors, who can then judge for themselves if a

[3] *Source:* www.sec.gov/about/whatwedo.shtml.

company's securities are a good investment. Thus, the SEC is primarily focused on promoting disclosure of information and reducing asymmetric information rather than determining the strength or well-being of any particular firm. The SEC brings 400 to 500 civil enforcement actions against individuals and companies each year in its effort to maintain the quality of the information provided to investors.

The SEC is organized around five divisions and 12 offices and employs about 4,600 people. One way to understand how it accomplishes its goals is to review the duties assigned to each division.

- The Division of Corporate Finance is responsible for collecting the many documents that public companies are required to file. These include annual reports, registration statements, quarterly filings, and many others. The division reviews these filings to check for compliance with the regulations. It does not verify the truth or accuracy of filings.
- The Division of Trading and Markets establishes and maintains standards for an orderly and efficient market by regulating the major securities market participants. This is the division that reviews and approves new rules and changes to existing rules.
- The Division of Investment Management oversees and regulates the investment management industry. This includes oversight of the mutual fund industry. Just as the Division of Market Regulation establishes rules governing the markets, the Division of Investment Management establishes rules governing investment companies.
- The Division of Enforcement investigates the violation of any of the rules and regulations established by the other divisions. The Division of Enforcement conducts its own investigations into various types of securities fraud and acts on tips provided by the SEC's other divisions.
- The Division of Economic Risk and Analysis provides data and analysis to all of the divisions as needed. Among its responsibilities is to advise the divisions about the economic impact of proposed rules.

Later, in Chapter 20 we discuss specific instances where the SEC has addressed fraud and violations of ethical standards.

SUMMARY

1. There are both organized and over-the-counter exchanges. Organized exchanges are distinguished by a physical building where trading takes place. The over-the-counter market operates primarily over phone lines and computer links. Typically, larger firms trade on organized exchanges and smaller firms trade in the over-the-counter market, though there are many exceptions to this rule. In recent years, alternative trading systems through ECNs have begun to capture a significant portion of business traditionally belonging to the stock exchanges. These electronic networks are likely to become increasingly significant players in the future.
2. Stocks are valued as the present value of the dividends. Unfortunately, we do not know precisely what these dividends will be. This introduces a great deal of error into the valuation process. The Gordon growth model is a simplified method of computing stock value that depends on the assumption that the dividends are growing at a constant rate forever. Given our uncertainty regarding future dividends, this assumption is often the best we can do.
3. An alternative method for estimating a stock price is to multiply the firm's earnings per share times the industry price earnings ratio. This ratio can be adjusted up or down to reflect specific characteristics of the firm.
4. The interaction among traders in the market is what actually sets prices on a day-to-day basis. The trader

that values the security the most, either because of less uncertainty about the cash flows or because of greater estimated cash flows, will be willing to pay the most. As new information is released, investors will revise their estimates of the true value of the security and will either buy or sell it, depending upon how the market price compares to their estimated valuation. Because small changes in estimated growth rates or required return result in large changes in price, it is not surprising that the markets are often volatile.

KEY TERMS

American depository receipts (ADRs), p. 314
ask price, p. 301
bid price, p. 301
common stockholder, p. 298
generalized dividend model, p. 304
Gordon growth model, p. 305
National Association of Securities Dealers Automated Quotation System (NASDAQ), p. 300
preferred stock, p. 299
price earnings ratio (PE), p. 306
super display book (SDBK), p. 301

QUESTIONS

1. What basic principle of finance can be applied to the valuation of any investment asset?
2. Identify the cash flows available to an investor in stock. How reliably can these cash flows be estimated? Compare the problem of estimating stock cash flows to estimating bond cash flows. Which security would you predict to be more volatile?
3. Discuss the benefits and potential risks of using the SDBK system in organized exchanges.
4. What is the National Association of Securities Dealers Automated Quotation System (NASDAQ)?
5. It is not uncommon for weather conditions to affect harvests differently across the world. How can you incorporate this information if you are a specialist in trading stock of food manufacturing companies?
6. Review the list of firms now included in the Dow Jones Industrial Average listed in Table 13.3. How many firms appear to be technology related? Discuss what this means in terms of the risk of the index.

QUANTITATIVE PROBLEMS

eBay, Inc., went public in September 1998. The following information on shares outstanding was listed in the final prospectus filed with the SEC.[4]

In the IPO, eBay issued 3,500,000 new shares. The initial price to the public was \$18.00 per share. The final first-day closing price was \$44.88.

1. If the investment bankers retained \$1.26 per share as fees, what were the net proceeds to eBay? What was the market capitalization of the new shares of eBay?
2. Two common statistics in IPOs are *underpricing* and *money left on the table.* Underpricing is defined as percentage change between the offering price and the first-day closing price. Money left on the table is the difference between the first-day closing price and the offering price, multiplied by the number of shares offered. Calculate the underpricing and money left on the table for eBay. What does this suggest about the efficiency of the IPO process?
3. The shares of Misheak, Inc., are expected to generate the following possible returns over the next 12 months:

Return (%)	Probability
–5	.10
5	.25
10	.30
15	.25
25	.10

If the stock is currently trading at \$25 per share, what is the expected price in one year? Assume that the stock pays no dividends.

4. Sine Corp. stock sells for \$75.00 and currently pays an annual dividend of \$2.50 per share. Calculate analysts' projected price one year from today if the expected one-year return is currently 3%.
5. Suppose Microsoft, Inc., is trading at \$27.29 per share. It pays an annual dividend of \$0.32 per share,

[4] This information is summarized from http://www.sec.gov/Archives/edgar/data/1065088/0001012870-98-002475.txt.

and analysts have set a one-year target price around \$33.30 per share. What is the expected return of this stock?

6. LaserAce is selling at \$22.00 per share. The most recent annual dividend paid was \$0.80. Using the Gordon growth model, if the market requires a return of 11%, what is the expected dividend growth rate for LaserAce?

7. ANCAP Oil Co. stock has a PE ratio equal to 22, whereas VRC Oil has a PE ratio equal to 20. Both firms' earnings per share are \$1.12. Calculate both firms' stock prices.

8. Refer to the previous exercise. Calculate the premium paid by investors to hold ANCAP Oil Co. shares instead of VRC Oil shares. Which company do you think is a safer investment?

9. Gordon & Co.'s stock has just paid its annual dividend of \$1.10 per share. Analysts believe that Gordon will maintain its historic dividend growth rate of 3%. If the required return is 8%, what is the expected price of the stock next year?

10. Macro Systems just paid an annual dividend of \$0.32 per share. Its dividend is expected to double for the next four years (D_1 through D_4), after which it will grow at a more modest pace of 1% per year. If the required return is 13%, what is the current price?

11. Nat-T-Cat Industries just went public. As a growing firm, it is not expected to pay a dividend for the first five years. After that, investors expect Nat-T-Cat to pay an annual dividend of \$1.00 per share (i.e., $D_6 = 1.00$), with no growth. If the required return is 10%, what is the current stock price?

12. Calculate the stock price of OSE Water Co. if the difference between the required rate of return on this investment and the expected growth rate of dividends is 3.6% and dividends per share are \$1.728.

13. Refer to the previous exercise. What is the implicit required rate of return if dividends are expected to grow at a 5% annual rate?

14. Consider the following security information for four securities making up an index:

Security	Price Time = 0	Price Time = 1	Shares Outstanding (millions)
1	8	13	20
2	22	25	50
3	35	30	120
4	50	55	75

What is the change in the value of the index from Time = 0 to Time = 1 if the index is calculated using a value-weighted arithmetic mean?

15. An index had an average (geometric) mean return over 20 years of 3.8861%. If the beginning index value was 100, what was the final index value after 20 years?

16. Calculate the dividend paid by a share of stock that you buy today for \$55 and you expect to sell one year from today at \$56 if you want to earn a one-year return equal to 3.5%.

17. The projected earnings per share for Risky Ventures, Inc., is \$3.50. The average PE ratio for the industry composed of Risky Ventures' closest competitors is 21. After careful analysis, you decide that Risky Ventures is a little more risky than average, so you decide a PE ratio of 23 better reflects the market's perception of the firm. Estimate the current price of the firm's stock.

WEB EXERCISES

The Stock Market

1. Visit **http://www.forecasts.org/index.htm**. Click "Stock Index Data" at the very top of the page, and then click "U.S. Stock Indices–monthly." Review the indexes for the DJIA, the S&P 500, and the NASDAQ composite. Which index appears most volatile? In which index would you have rather invested in 1985 if the investment had been allowed to compound until now?

2. There are a number of indexes that track the performance of the stock market. It is interesting to review how well they track along with each other. Go to **http://bloomberg.com**. Click the "Stocks" tab at the top of the screen. The graph will display the DJIA, the S&P 500, and the NASDAQ composite. Set the time frame at the top of the chart to five years.

   a. Which index has been most volatile over the past five years?

   b. Which index has posted the greatest gains over the past five years?

   c. Now adjust the time frame to intraday. Which index has performed the best today? Which has been most volatile?

CHAPTER 14

The Mortgage Markets

> PREVIEW

Part of the classic American dream is to own one's own home. With the price of the average house now over $232,500[1], few of us could hope to do this until late in life if we were not able to borrow the bulk of the purchase price. Similarly, businesses rely on borrowed capital far more than on equity investment to finance their growth. Many small firms do not have access to the bond market and must find alternative sources of funds. Consider the state of the mortgage loan markets 100 years ago. They were organized mostly to accommodate the needs of businesses and the very wealthy. Much has changed since then. The purpose of this chapter is to discuss these changes.

Chapter 11 discussed the *money markets*, the markets for short-term funds. Chapters 12 and 13 discussed the *bond* and *stock markets.* This chapter discusses the *mortgage markets*, where borrowers—individuals, businesses, and governments—can obtain long-term collateralized loans. From one perspective, the mortgage markets form a subcategory of the capital markets because mortgages involve long-term funds. But the mortgage markets differ from the stock and bond markets in important ways. First, the usual borrowers in the capital markets are government entities and businesses, whereas the usual borrowers in the mortgage markets are individuals. Second, mortgage loans are made for varying amounts and maturities, depending on the borrowers' needs, features that cause problems for developing a secondary market.

In this chapter we will identify the characteristics of typical residential mortgages, discuss the usual terms and types of mortgages available, and review who provides and services these loans. We will also continue the discussion of issues in the mortgage-backed security market and the crash of the subprime mortgage market begun in Chapter 8.

[1] *Source:* National Association of Realtors: https://ycharts.com/indicators/sources/nar.

What Are Mortgages?

A **mortgage** is a long-term loan secured by real estate. A developer may obtain a mortgage loan to finance the construction of an office building, or a family may obtain a mortgage loan to finance the purchase of a home. In either case, the loan is **amortized**: The borrower pays it off over time in some combination of principal and interest payments that result in full payment of the debt by maturity. Table 14.1 shows the distribution of mortgage loan borrowers. Because over 72% of mortgage loans finance residential home purchases, that will be the primary focus of this chapter.

One way to understand the modern mortgage is to review its history. Originally, many states had laws that prevented banks from funding mortgages so that banks would not tie up their funds in long-term loans. The National Banking Act of 1863 further restricted mortgage lending. As a result, most mortgage contracts in the past were arranged between individuals, usually with the help of a lawyer who brought the parties together and drew up the papers. Such loans were generally available only to the wealthy and socially connected. As the demand for long-term funds increased, however, more mortgage brokers surfaced. They often originated loans in the rapidly developing western part of the country and sold them to savings banks and insurance companies in the East.

By 1880 mortgage bankers had learned to streamline their operations by selling bonds to raise the long-term funds they lent. They would gather a portfolio of mortgage contracts and use them as security for an issue of bonds that were sold publicly. Many of these loans were used to finance agricultural expansion in the Midwest. Unfortunately, an agricultural recession in the 1890s resulted in many defaults. Land prices fell, and a large number of the mortgage bankers went bankrupt. It became very difficult to obtain long-term loans until after World War I, when national banks were authorized to make mortgage loans. This regulatory change caused a tremendous real estate boom, and mortgage lending expanded rapidly.

The mortgage market was again devastated by the Great Depression in the 1930s. Millions of borrowers were without work and were unable to make their loan payments. This led to foreclosures and land sales that caused property values to collapse. Mortgage-lending institutions were again hit hard, and many failed.

One reason that so many borrowers defaulted on their loans was the type of mortgage loan they had. Most mortgages in this period were **balloon loans**: The borrower paid only interest for three to five years, at which time the entire loan amount became due. The lender was usually willing to renew the debt with some

TABLE 14.1 Mortgage Loan Borrowing, 2016

Type of Property	Mortgage Loans Issued ($ billions)	Proportion of Total (%)
One- to four-family dwelling	9,986	72.38
Multifamily dwelling	1,099	7.97
Commercial building	2,506	18.16
Farm	205	1.49

Source: http://www.federalreserve.gov/econresdata/releases/mortoutstand/current.htm.

reduction in principal. However, if the borrower were unemployed, the lender would not renew, and the borrower would default.

As part of the recovery program from the Depression, the federal government stepped in and restructured the mortgage market. The government took over delinquent balloon loans and allowed borrowers to repay them over long periods of time. It is no surprise that these new types of loans were very popular. The surviving savings and loans began offering home buyers similar loans, and the high demand contributed to restoring the health of the mortgage industry.

Characteristics of the Residential Mortgage

Access **www.interest.com** to track mortgage rates and shop for mortgage rates in different geographic areas.

The modern mortgage lender has continued to refine the long-term loan to make it more desirable to borrowers. Even in the past 20 years, both the nature of the lenders and the instruments have undergone substantial changes. One of the biggest changes is the development of an active secondary market for mortgage contracts. We will examine the nature of mortgage loan contracts and then look at their secondary market.

Twenty years ago, savings and loan institutions and the mortgage departments of large banks originated most mortgage loans. Some were maintained in-house by the originator while others were sold to one of a few firms. These firms closely tracked delinquency rates and would refuse to continue buying loans from banks where delinquencies were very high. More recently, many loan production offices arose that competed in real estate financing. Some of these offices are subsidiaries of banks, and others are independently owned. As a result of the competition for mortgage loans, borrowers could choose from a variety of terms and options. Many of these mortgage businesses were organized around the originate-to-distribute model where the broker originated the loan and sold (distributed) it to an investor as quickly as possible. This model increased the principal–agent problem, since the originator had little concern whether the loan was actually paid off.

Mortgage Interest Rates

The interest rate borrowers pay on their mortgages is probably the most important factor in their decision of how much and from whom to borrow. The interest rate on the loan is determined by three factors: current long-term market rates, the life (term) of the mortgage, and the number of discount points paid.

1. *Market rates.* Long-term market rates are determined by the supply of and demand for long-term funds, which are in turn influenced by a number of global, national, and regional factors. As Figure 14.1 shows, mortgage rates tend to stay above the less risky Treasury bonds most of the time but tend to track along with them.
2. *Term.* Longer-term mortgages have higher interest rates than shorter-term mortgages. The usual mortgage lifetime is either 15 or 30 years. Lenders also offer 20-year loans, though they are not as popular. Because interest-rate risk falls as the term to maturity decreases, the interest rate on the 15-year loan will be substantially less than on the 30-year loan. For example, in May 2016, the average 30-year mortgage rate was 3.79%, and the 15-year rate was 2.99%.

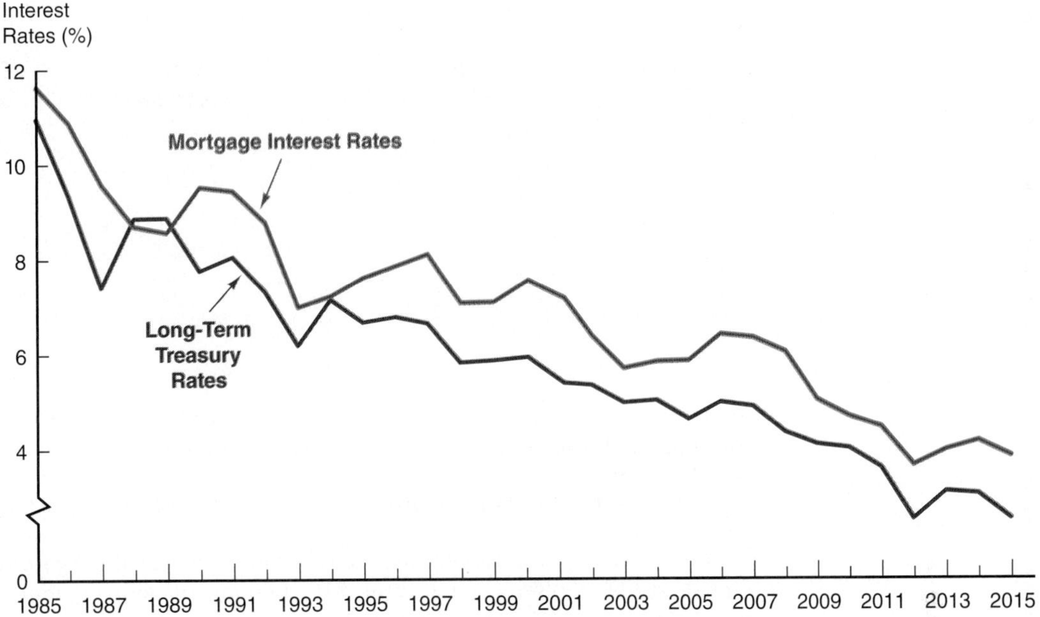

FIGURE 14.1 Mortgage Rates and Long-Term Treasury Interest Rates, 1985–2016

Source: http://www.federalreserve.gov/releases/h15/data.htm.

3. *Discount points.* **Discount points** (or simply *points*) are interest payments made at the beginning of a loan. A loan with one discount point means that the borrower pays 1% of the loan amount at *closing*, the moment when the borrower signs the loan paper and receives the proceeds of the loan. In exchange for the points, the lender reduces the interest rate on the loan. In considering whether to pay points, borrowers must determine whether the reduced interest rate over the life of the loan fully compensates for the increased up-front expense. To make this determination, borrowers must take into account how long they will hold on to the loan. Typically, discount points should not be paid if the borrower will pay off the loan in five years or less. This breakeven point is not surprising, since the average home sells every five years.

CASE

The Discount Point Decision

Suppose that you are offered two loan alternatives. In the first, you pay no discount points and the interest rate is 12%. In the second, you pay 2 discount points but receive a lower interest rate of 11.5%. Which alternative do you choose?

To answer this question, you must first compute the effective annual rate without discount points. Since the loan is compounded monthly, you pay 1% per month. Because of the compounding, the effective annual rate is greater than the simple

TABLE 14.2 Effective Rate of Interest on a Loan at 12% with 2 Discount Points

Year of Prepayment	Effective Rate of Interest (%)	Year of Prepayment	Effective Rate of Interest (%)
1	14.54	6	12.65
2	13.40	7	12.60
3	13.02	10	12.52
4	12.84	15	12.45
5	12.73	30	12.42

annual rate. To compute the effective rate, raise 1 plus the monthly rate to the 12th power and subtract 1. The effective annual rate on the no-point loan is thus

$$\text{Effective annual rate} = (1.01)^{12} - 1 = 0.1268 = 12.68\%$$

Because of monthly compounding, a 12% annual percentage rate has an effective annual rate of 12.68%. On a 30-year, $100,000 mortgage loan, your payment will be $1,028.61 as found on a financial calculator.

Now compute the effective annual rate if you pay 2 discount points. Let's assume that the amount of the loan is still $100,000. If you pay 2 points, instead of receiving $100,000, you will receive only $98,000 ($100,000 – $2,000). Your payment is computed on the $100,000 but at the lower interest rate. Using a financial calculator, we find that the monthly payment is $990.29 and your monthly rate is 0.9804%.* The effective annual rate after compounding is

$$\text{Effective annual rate} = (1.009804)^{12} - 1 = 0.1242 = 12.42\%$$

As a result of paying the 2 discount points, the effective annual rate has dropped from 12.68% to 12.42%. On the surface, it would seem like a good idea to pay the points. The problem is that these calculations were made assuming the loan would be held for the life of the loan, 30 years. What happens if you sell the house before the loan matures?

If the loan is paid off early, the borrower will benefit from the lower interest rate for a shorter length of time, and the discount points are spread over a shorter period of time. The result of these two factors is that the effective interest rate rises the shorter the time the loan is held before being paid. This relationship is demonstrated in Table 14.2. If the 2-point loan is held for 15 years, the effective rate is 12.45%. At 10 years, the effective rate is up to 12.52%. Even at 6 years, when the effective rate is 12.65%, paying the discount points has saved the borrower money. However, if the loan is paid off at 5 years, the effective rate is 12.73%, which is higher than the 12.68% effective rate if no points were paid.**

---

*See Chapter 3 for a discussion on how loan payments are computed.

**For example, to compute the effective rate if the loan is prepaid after two years, find the *FV* if $I = 11.5\%$, $PV = 100{,}000$, $N = 360$, and $PMT = 990.29$. Now set *PV* equal to 98,000 and compute *I*. Divide this *I* by 12, add 1, and raise the result to the 12th power.

Loan Terms

Mortgage loan contracts contain many legal and financial terms, most of which protect the lender from financial loss.

Collateral One characteristic common to mortgage loans is the requirement that collateral, usually the real estate being financed, be pledged as security. The lending institution will place a **lien** against the property, and this remains in effect until the loan is paid off. A lien is a public record that attaches to the title of the property, advising that the property is security for a loan, and it gives the lender the right to sell the property if the underlying loan defaults.

No one can buy the property and obtain clear title to it without paying off this lien. For example, if you purchased a piece of property with a loan secured by a lien, the lender would file notice of this lien at the public recorder's office. The lien gives notice to the world that if there is a default on the loan, the lender has the right to seize the property. If you try to sell the property without paying off the loan, the lien would remain attached to the title or deed to the property. Since the lender can take the property away from whoever owns it, no one would buy it unless you paid off the loan. The existence of liens against real estate explains why a title search is an important part of any mortgage loan transaction. During the title search, a lawyer or title company searches the public record for any liens. Title insurance is then sold that guarantees the buyer that the property is free of *encumbrances*, any questions about the state of the title to the property, including the existence of liens.

Down Payments To obtain a mortgage loan, the lender also requires the borrower to make a **down payment** on the property, that is, to pay a portion of the purchase price. The balance of the purchase price is paid by the *loan proceeds*. Down payments (like liens) are intended to make the borrower less likely to default on the loan. A borrower who does not make a down payment could walk away from the house and the loan and lose nothing. Furthermore, if real estate prices drop even a small amount, the balance due on the loan will exceed the value of the collateral. As we discussed in Chapters 2 and 8, the down payment reduces *moral hazard* for the borrower. The amount of the down payment depends on the type of mortgage loan. Beginning in the mid-2000s the required down payment was often circumvented with piggyback loans whereby a second mortgage was added to the first so that 100% financing was provided. We saw in the housing downturn beginning in 2006 that many borrowers recognized their property was worth less than they owed and default rates skyrocketed.

Private Mortgage Insurance Another way that lenders protect themselves against default is by requiring the borrower to purchase **private mortgage insurance (PMI)**. PMI is an insurance policy that guarantees to make up any discrepancy between the value of the property and the loan amount, should a default occur. For example, if the balance on your loan was \$120,000 at the time of default and the property was worth only \$100,000, PMI would pay the lending institution \$20,000. The default still appears on the credit record of the borrower, but the lender avoids sustaining the loss. PMI is usually required on loans that have less than a 20% down payment. If the loan-to-value ratio falls because of payments being made or because the value of the property increases, the borrower can request that the PMI requirement be dropped. PMI usually costs between \$20 and \$30 per month for a \$100,000 loan.

Ideally, PMI should have protected investors against losses on mortgage investments, and it did until recently. As we will discuss later, relaxed lending standards led to a competitive mortgage market where lenders found ways to attract customers with questionable practices. One such method was to structure loans to avoid PMI. PMI is usually required only on the first mortgage. By structuring loans so that the first mortgage loan was set at 80% loan-to-value with a second mortgage covering the remaining 20%, PMI was avoided. Of course, the lender suffered the loss when the borrower defaulted.

Borrower Qualification Historically, before granting a mortgage loan, the lender would determine whether the borrower qualified for it. Qualifying for a mortgage loan was different from qualifying for a bank loan because most lenders sold their mortgage loans to one of a few federal agencies in the secondary mortgage market. These agencies established very precise guidelines that had to be followed before they would accept the loan. If the lender gave a mortgage loan to a borrower who did not fit these guidelines, the lender would not be able to resell the loan. That tied up the lender's funds.

The rules for qualifying a borrower were complex and constantly changing, but a rule of thumb was that the loan payment, including taxes and insurance, should not exceed 25% of gross monthly income. Furthermore, the sum of the monthly payments on all loans to the borrower, including car loans and credit cards, should not exceed 36% of gross monthly income. For example, if you earn $60,000 per year ($5,000 per month) and do not have any other debt, your payment should not exceed $5,000 × .25 = $1,250. At a 4% interest rate you would qualify for a loan of about $200,000.

Lenders will also order a credit report from one of the major credit-reporting agencies. The credit score is based on a model that weights a number of variables found to be predictors of creditworthiness. The most common score is called the FICO, named after its creator, Fair Isaac Company. **FICO scores** may range from a low of 300 to a maximum of 850. Scores above 720 are considered good, while scores below 660 were likely to cause problems obtaining a loan. The FICO score is determined by your payment history, outstanding debt, length of credit history, number of recent credit applications, and types of credit and loans you have. It is interesting to note that simply applying for and holding a number of credit cards can significantly affect your FICO score.

When the competition to originate mortgage loans grew in the mid-2000s, a variety of mortgage loans were offered that circumvented traditional lending practices. For example, borrowers were offered No Doc loans (sometimes called NINJA loans for No Income, No Job, and No Assets) in which income or assets were not required on the loan application. The rationale for these loans was a mistaken belief that real estate prices would not decline and so the collateral was strong enough to justify the loans. These lending practices have been largely abandoned as the search for quality borrowers has replaced the need for loan volume.

Mortgage Loan Amortization

Mortgage loan borrowers agree to pay a monthly amount of principal and interest that will fully amortize the loan by its maturity. "Fully amortize" means that the payments will pay off the outstanding indebtedness by the time the loan matures. During the early years of the loan, the lender applies most of the payment to the

TABLE 14.3 Amortization of a 30-Year, $130,000 Loan at 8.5%

Payment Number	Beginning Balance of Loan	Monthly Payment	Amount Applied to Interest	Amount Applied to Principal	Ending Balance of Loan
1	130,000.00	999.59	920.83	78.75	129,921.24
24	128,040.25	999.59	906.95	92.66	127,947.62
60	124,256.74	999.59	880.15	119.43	124,137.31
120	115,365.63	999.59	817.17	182.41	115,183.22
180	101,786.23	999.59	720.99	278.60	101,507.63
240	81,046.41	999.59	574.08	425.51	80,620.90
360	991.77	999.59	7.82	991.77	0

interest on the loan and a small amount to the outstanding principal balance. Many borrowers are surprised to find that after years of making payments, their loan balance has not dropped appreciably.

Table 14.3 shows the distribution of principal and interest for a 30-year, $130,000 loan at 8.5% interest. Only $78.75 of the first payment is applied to reduce the loan balance. At the end of two years, the balance due is still $127,947, and at the end of five years, the balance due is $124,137. Put another way, of $59,975.40 in loan payments made during the first five years, only $5,862.69 is applied to the principal. Over the life of the $130,000 loan, a total of $229,850 in interest will be paid.

If the loan in Table 14.3 had been financed for 15 years instead of for 30, the payment would have increased by about $280 per month to $1,279.59, but the interest savings over the life of the loan would be nearly $130,000. It is no wonder why so many borrowers prefer the shorter-term loans.

Types of Mortgage Loans

A number of types of mortgage loans are available in the market. Different borrowers may qualify for different ones. A skilled mortgage banker can help find the best type of mortgage loan for each particular situation.

Insured and Conventional Mortgages

Mortgages are classified as either *insured* or *conventional*. **Insured mortgages** are originated by banks or other mortgage lenders but are guaranteed by either the Federal Housing Administration (FHA) or the Veterans Administration (VA). Applicants for FHA and VA loans must meet certain qualifications, such as having served in the military or having income below a given level, and can borrow only up to a certain amount. The FHA or VA then guarantees the bank making the loans against any losses—meaning that the agency guarantees that it will pay off the mortgage loan if the borrower defaults. One important advantage to a borrower who qualifies for an FHA or VA loan is that only a very low or zero down payment is required.

Conventional mortgages are originated by the same sources as insured loans but are not guaranteed. Private mortgage companies now insure many conventional loans against default. As we noted, most lenders require the borrower to obtain private mortgage insurance on all loans with a loan-to-value ratio exceeding 80%.

Fixed- and Adjustable-Rate Mortgages

In standard mortgage contracts, borrowers agree to make regular payments on the principal and interest they owe to lenders. As we saw earlier, the interest rate significantly affects the size of this monthly payment. In *fixed-rate mortgages*, the interest rate and the monthly payment do not vary over the life of the mortgage.

The interest rate on *adjustable-rate mortgages* (ARMs) is tied to some market interest rate and therefore changes over time. ARMs usually have limits, called *caps*, on how high (or low) the interest rate can move in one year and during the term of the loan. A typical ARM might tie the interest rate to the average Treasury bill rate plus 2%, with caps of 2% per year and 6% over the lifetime of the mortgage. Caps make ARMs more palatable to borrowers.

Borrowers tend to prefer fixed-rate loans to ARMs because ARMs may cause financial hardship if interest rates rise. However, fixed-rate borrowers do not benefit if rates fall unless they are willing to refinance their mortgage (pay it off by obtaining a new mortgage at a lower interest rate). The fact that individuals are risk-averse means that fear of hardship most often overwhelms anticipation of savings.

Lenders, by contrast, prefer ARMs because ARMs lessen interest-rate risk. Recall from Chapter 3 that interest-rate risk is the risk that rising interest rates will cause the value of debt instruments to fall. The effect on the value of the debt is greatest when the debt has a long term to maturity. Since mortgages are usually long-term, their value is very sensitive to interest-rate movements. Lending institutions can reduce the sensitivity of their portfolios by making ARMs instead of standard fixed-rate loans.

Seeing that lenders prefer ARMs and borrowers prefer fixed-rate mortgages, lenders must entice borrowers by offering lower initial interest rates on ARMs than on fixed-rate loans. For example, in May 2016 the reported interest rate for 30-year fixed-rate mortgage loans was 3.79%. The rate at that time for 5-year adjustable-rate mortgages was 2.63%. The rate on the ARM would have to rise 1.16% before the borrower of the ARM would be in a worse position than the fixed-rate borrower.

Other Types of Mortgages

As the market for mortgage loans became more competitive, lenders offered more innovative mortgage contracts in an effort to attract borrowers. We discuss some of these mortgages here.

Graduated-Payment Mortgages (GPMs) Graduated-payment mortgages are useful for home buyers who expect their incomes to rise. The GPM has lower payments in the first few years; then the payments rise. The early payments may not even be sufficient to cover the interest due, in which case the principal balance increases. As time passes, the borrower expects income to increase so that the higher payment will not be a burden.

The advantage of the GPM is that borrowers will qualify for a larger loan than if they requested a conventional mortgage. This may help buyers purchase adequate housing now and avoid the need to move to more expensive homes as their family size increases. The disadvantage is that the payments escalate whether or not the borrower's income does.

Growing-Equity Mortgages (GEMs) Lenders designed the growing-equity mortgage loan to help the borrower pay off the loan in a shorter period of time. With a GEM, the payments will initially be the same as on a conventional mortgage. However, over time the payment will increase. This increase will reduce the principal more quickly than the conventional payment stream would. For example, a typical contract may call for level payments for the first two years. The payments may increase by 5% per year for the next five years, then remain the same until maturity. The result is to reduce the life of the loan from 30 years to about 17.

GEMs are popular among borrowers who expect their incomes to rise in the future. It gives them the benefit of a small payment at the beginning while still retiring the debt early. Although the increase in payments is *required* in GEMs, most mortgage loans have no prepayment penalty. This means that a borrower with a 30-year loan could create a GEM by simply increasing the monthly payments beyond what is required and designating that the excess be applied entirely to the principal.

The GEM is similar to the graduated-payment mortgage; the difference is that the goal of the GPM is to help the borrower qualify by reducing the first few years' payments. The loan still pays off in 30 years. The goal of the GEM is to let the borrower pay off early.

Second Mortgages (Piggyback) Second mortgages are loans that are secured by the same real estate that is used to secure the first mortgage. The second mortgage is junior to the original loan. This means that should a default occur, the second mortgage holder will be paid only after the original loan has been paid off and only if sufficient funds are available from selling the property.

Originally second mortgages had two purposes. The first is to give borrowers a way to use the equity they have in their homes as security for another loan. An alternative to the second mortgage would be to refinance the home at a higher loan amount than is currently owed. The cost of obtaining a second mortgage is often much lower than refinancing.

Another purpose of the second mortgage is to take advantage of one of the few remaining tax deductions available to the middle class. The interest on loans secured by residential real estate is tax-deductible (the tax laws allow borrowers to deduct the interest on the primary residence and one vacation home). No other kind of consumer loan has this tax deduction. Many banks now offer lines of credit secured by second mortgages. In most cases, the value of the security is not of great interest to the bank. Consumers prefer that the line of credit be secured so that they can deduct the interest on the loan from their taxes.

As mentioned earlier, a contributing factor in the mortgage market collapse was the use of second mortgage loans to reduce or eliminate the need for a down payment. Borrowers who had no real equity in the home were more willing to walk away once its value dropped or their income fell. An appropriate use of the second mortgage is where a borrower has had a home loan for a number of years and has built up real equity, meaning that the true market value of the home is much greater than the balance owed on the loan.

Reverse Annuity Mortgages (RAMs) The reverse annuity mortgage is an innovative method for retired people to live on the equity they have in their homes. The contract for a RAM has the bank advancing funds on a monthly schedule. This increasing-balance loan is secured by the real estate. The borrower does not make

TABLE 14.4 Summary of Mortgage Types

Type	Description
Conventional mortgage	Loan is not guaranteed; usually requires private mortgage insurance; 5% to 20% down payment
Insured mortgage	Loan is guaranteed by FHA or VA; low or zero down payment
Adjustable-rate mortgage (ARM)	Interest rate is tied to some other security and is adjusted periodically; size of adjustment is subject to annual limits
Graduated-payment mortgage (GPM)	Initial low payment increases each year; loan amortizes in 30 years
Growing-equity mortgage (GEM)	Initial payment increases each year; loan amortizes in less than 30 years
Second mortgage	Loan is secured by a second lien against the real estate; often used for lines of credit or home improvement loans
Reverse annuity mortgage	Lender disburses a monthly payment to the borrower on an increasing-balance loan; loan comes due when the real estate is sold

any payments against the loan. When the borrower dies, the borrower's estate sells the property to retire the debt.

The advantage of the RAM is that it allows retired people to use the equity in their homes without the necessity of selling it. For retirees in need of supplemental funds to meet living expenses, the RAM can be a desirable option.

Between 2004 and 2008 various mortgage loan options were offered that were intended to allow almost any borrower to qualify. The argument at the time was that home prices have usually gone up and if a borrower could not continue to afford the mortgage, they could simply sell the home at a profit. When the housing bubble burst and prices fell, this was not an option and many loans defaulted. Since 2008, the mortgage industry has largely stopped offering these high-risk loan options.

The various mortgage types are summarized in Table 14.4.

Mortgage-Lending Institutions

Originally, the thrift industry was established with the mandate from Congress to provide mortgage loans to families. Congress gave these institutions the ability to attract depositors by allowing S&Ls to pay slightly higher interest rates on deposits. For many years, the thrift industry did its job well. Thrifts raised short-term funds by attracting deposits and used these funds to make long-term mortgage loans. The early growth of the housing industry owes much of its success to these institutions. (The thrift industry is discussed further in Web Chapter 25.)

Until the 1970s, interest rates remained relatively stable, and when fluctuations did occur, they tended to be small and short-lived. But in the 1970s, interest rates rose rapidly, along with inflation, and thrifts became the victims of interest-rate risk. As market interest rates rose, the value of their fixed-rate mortgage loan portfolios fell. Because of the losses the thrifts suffered, they stopped being the primary source of mortgage loans.

Another serious problem with the early mortgage market was that thrift institutions were restricted from nationwide branching by federal and state laws and were forbidden to lend outside their normal lending territory, about 100 miles around

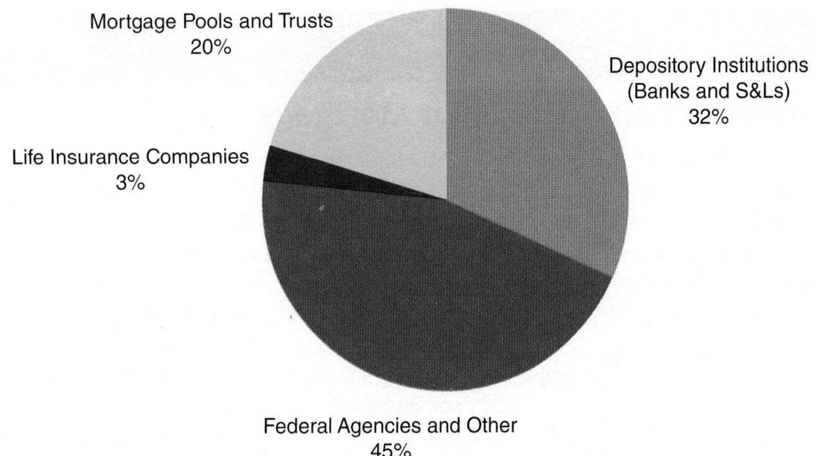

FIGURE 14.2 Share of the Mortgage Market Held by Major Mortgage-Lending Institutions

Source: http://www.federalreserve.gov/econresdata/releases/mortoutstand/current.htm.

their offices. So even if an institution appeared very diversified, with thousands of different loans, all of the loans were from the same region. When that region had economic problems, many of the loans would default at the same time. For example, Texas and Oklahoma experienced a recession in the mid-1980s due to falling oil prices. Many mortgage loans defaulted because real estate values fell at the same time as the region's unemployment rate rose. That other areas of the country remained healthy was of no help to local lenders.

Figure 14.2 shows the share of the total mortgage market held by the major mortgage-lending institutions in the United States. Currently the largest investors are Federal Agencies. This is a change from several years ago, when Mortgage Pools and Trust had over 50% of the market.

Loan Servicing

Many of the institutions making mortgage loans do not want to hold large portfolios of long-term securities. Commercial banks, for example, obtain their funds from short-term sources. Investing in long-term loans would subject them to unacceptably high interest-rate risk. Commercial banks, thrifts, and most other loan originators do, however, make money through the fees that they earn by packaging loans for other investors to hold. Loan origination fees are typically 1% of the loan amount, though this varies with the market.

Once a loan has been made, many lenders immediately sell the loan to another investor. The borrower may not even be aware that the original lender transferred the loan. By selling the loan, the originator frees up funds that can be lent to another borrower, thereby generating additional fee income.

Some of the originators also provide servicing of the loan. The loan-servicing agent collects payments from the borrower, passes the principal and interest on to the investor, keeps required records of the transaction, and maintains **reserve accounts**. Reserve accounts are established for most mortgage loans to permit the

> E-FINANCE

Borrowers Shop the Web for Mortgages

One business area that has been significantly affected by the Web is mortgage banking. Historically, borrowers went to local banks, savings and loans, and mortgage banking companies to obtain mortgage loans. These offices packaged the loans and resold them. In recent years, hundreds of new Web-based mortgage banking companies have emerged.

The mortgage market is well suited to providing online service for several reasons. First, it is information-based and no products have to be shipped or inventoried. Second, the product (a loan) is homogeneous across providers. A borrower does not really care who provides the money as long as it is provided efficiently. Third, because home buyers tend not to obtain mortgage loans very often, they have little loyalty to any local lender. Finally, online lenders can often offer loans at lower cost because they can operate with lower overhead than firms that must greet the public.

The online mortgage market makes it much easier for borrowers to shop interest rates and terms. By filling out one application, a borrower can obtain a number of alternative loan options from various Web service companies. Borrowers can then select the option that best suits their requirements.

Online mortgage firms, such as Lending Tree, have made mortgage lending more competitive. This may lead to lower rates and better service. It has also led lenders to offer an often confusing array of loan alternatives that most borrowers have difficulty interpreting. This makes comparison shopping more difficult than simply comparing interest rates.

Borrowers using online services to shop for loans must be aware that scam artists have found this an easy way to obtain personal information. They set up a bogus loan site and offer extremely attractive interest rates to draw in customers. Once they have collected all the information needed to wipe out your checking, savings, and credit card accounts, they close their site and open another.

---

lender to make tax and insurance payments for the borrower. Lenders prefer to make these payments because they protect the security of the loan. Loan-servicing agents usually earn 0.5% per year of the total loan amount for their efforts.

In summary, there are three distinct elements to most mortgage loans:

1. The originator packages the loan for an investor.
2. The investor holds the loan.
3. The servicing agent handles the paperwork.

One, two, or three different intermediaries may provide these functions for any particular loan.

Mortgage loans are increasingly obtained from the Web. The E-Finance box discusses this new source of mortgage loans.

Secondary Mortgage Market

The federal government founded the secondary market for mortgages. As we noted earlier, the mortgage market had all but collapsed during the Great Depression. To help spur the nation's economic activity, the government established several agencies to buy mortgages. The Federal National Mortgage Association (Fannie Mae) was set up to buy mortgages from thrifts so that these institutions could make more mortgage loans. This agency would fund these purchases by selling bonds to the public.

At about the same time, the Federal Housing Administration was established to insure certain mortgage contracts. This made it easier to sell the mortgages because the buyer did not have to be concerned with the borrower's credit history or the value of the collateral. A similar insurance program was set up through the Veterans Administration to insure loans to veterans after World War II.

One advantage of the insured loans was that they were required to be written on a standard loan contract. This standardization was an important factor in the growth of the secondary market for mortgages.

As the secondary market for mortgage contracts took shape, a new intermediary, the mortgage bank, emerged. Because this firm did not accept deposits, it was able to open offices across the country. The mortgage bank originated the loans, funding them initially with its own capital. After a group of similar loans were made, they would be bundled and sold, either to one of the federal agencies or to an insurance or pension fund. There were several advantages to the mortgage banks. Because of their size, they were able to capture economies of scale in loan origination and servicing. They were also able to bundle loans from different regions, which helped reduce their risk. The increased competition for loans among these intermediaries led to lower rates for borrowers.

Securitization of Mortgages

Intermediaries still faced several problems when trying to sell mortgages. The first was that mortgages are usually too small to be wholesale instruments. The average new home mortgage loan is now about $250,000. This is far below the $5 million round lot established for commercial paper, for example. Many institutional investors do not want to deal in such small denominations.

The second problem with selling mortgages in the secondary market was that they were not standardized. They have different times to maturity, interest rates, and contract terms. That makes it difficult to bundle a large number of mortgages together.

Third, mortgage loans are relatively costly to service. Compare the servicing a mortgage loan requires to that of a corporate bond. The lender must collect monthly payments, often pay property taxes and insurance premiums, and service reserve accounts. None of this is required if a bond is purchased.

Finally, mortgages have unknown default risk. Investors in mortgages do not want to expend energy evaluating the credit of borrowers. These problems inspired the creation of the **mortgage-backed security**, also known as a **securitized mortgage**.

What Is a Mortgage-Backed Security?

By the late 1960s, the secondary market for mortgages was declining, mostly because fewer veterans were obtaining guaranteed loans. The government reorganized Fannie Mae and also created two new agencies: the Government National Mortgage Association (GNMA, or Ginnie Mae) and the Federal Home Loan Mortgage Corporation (FHLMC, or Freddie Mac). These three agencies were now able to offer new securities backed by both insured and, for the first time, uninsured mortgages.

An alternative to selling mortgages directly to investors is to create a new security backed by (secured by) a large number of mortgages assembled into what is called a *mortgage pool*. A trustee, such as a bank or a government agency, holds the mortgage pool, which serves as collateral for the new security. This process is called *securitization*. The most common type of mortgage-backed security is the **mortgage pass-through**, a security that has the borrower's mortgage payments pass through the trustee before being disbursed to the investors in the mortgage pass-through. If borrowers prepay their loans, investors receive more principal than expected. For example, investors may buy mortgage-backed securities on which the average interest rate is 6%. If interest rates fall and borrowers refinance at lower rates, the securities will pay off early. The possibility that mortgages will prepay and force investors to seek alternative investments, usually with lower returns, is called *prepayment risk*.

As is evident in Figure 14.3, the dollar volume of outstanding mortgage pools increased steadily from 1984 to 2009. The reason that mortgage pools became so popular was that they permitted the creation of new securities (like mortgage pass-throughs) that made investing in mortgage loans much more efficient. For example, an institutional investor could invest in one large mortgage pass-through secured by a mortgage pool rather than invest in many small and dissimilar mortgage contracts.

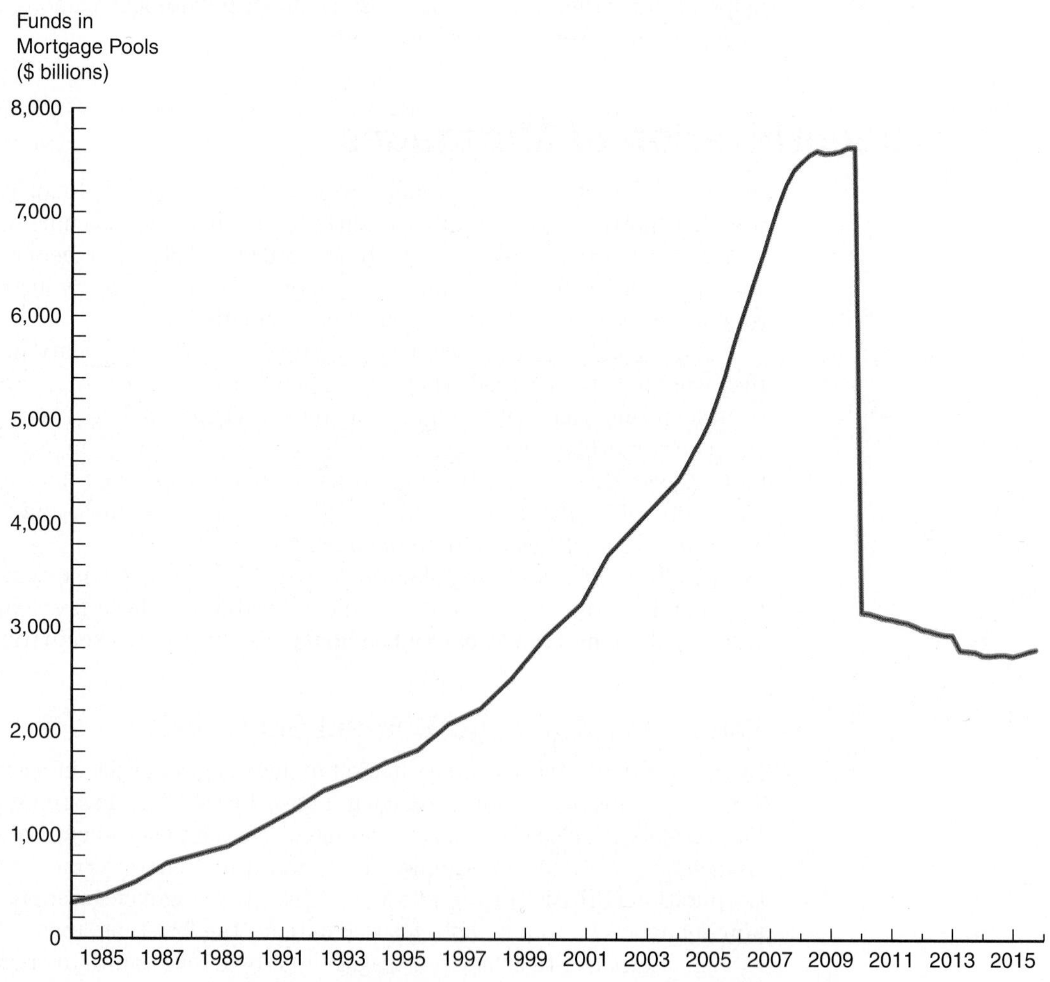

FIGURE 14.3 Value of Mortgage Principal Held in Mortgage Pools, 1984–2016

Source: http://www.federalreserve.gov/econresdata/releases/mortoutstand/current.htm.

The slump in the real estate market and losses to mortgage pool investors led to a sharp decline in their popularity after 2009, and this market has not yet recovered.

Types of Pass-Through Securities

There are several types of mortgage pass-through securities: GNMA pass-throughs, FHLMC pass-throughs, and private pass-throughs.

Government National Mortgage Association (GNMA) Pass-Throughs Ginnie Mae began guaranteeing pass-through securities in 1968. Since then, the popularity of these instruments increased dramatically.

A variety of financial intermediaries, including commercial banks and mortgage companies, originate Ginnie Mae mortgages. Ginnie Mae aggregates these mortgages into a pool and issues pass-through securities that are collateralized by the interest and principal payments from the mortgages. Ginnie Mae also guarantees the pass-through securities against default. The usual minimum denomination for pass-throughs is $25,000. The minimum pool size is $1 million. One pool may back up many pass-through securities.

Federal Home Loan Mortgage Corporation (FHLMC) Pass-Throughs Freddie Mac was created to assist savings and loan associations, which are not eligible to originate Ginnie Mae–guaranteed loans. Freddie Mac purchases mortgages for its own account and also issues pass-through securities similar to those issued by Ginnie Mae. Pass-through securities issued by Freddie Mac are called *participation certificates* (PCs). Freddie Mac pools are distinct from Ginnie Mae pools in that they contain conventional (nonguaranteed) mortgages, are not federally insured, contain mortgages with different rates, are larger (ranging up to several hundred million dollars), and have a minimum denomination of $100,000.

One innovation in the FHLMC pass-through market has been the **collateralized mortgage obligation (CMO)**. CMOs are securities classified by when prepayment is likely to occur. These differ from traditional mortgage-backed securities in that they are offered in different maturity groups. These securities help reduce prepayment risk, which is a problem with other types of pass-through securities.

CMOs backed by a particular mortgage pool are divided into tranches (French for "slices"). When principal is repaid, the investors in the first tranche are paid first, then those in the second tranche, and so on. Investors choose a tranche that matches their maturity requirements. For example, if they will need cash from their investment in a few years, they purchase tranche 1 or 2 CMOs. If they want the investment to be long-term, they can purchase CMOs from the last tranche. There is a distinct risk differential between tranches as well. Those paid off first are less likely to see a default than those paid off last.

Even when an investor purchases a CMO, there are no guarantees about how long the investment will last. If interest rates fall significantly, many borrowers will pay off their mortgages early by refinancing at lower rates.

Real estate mortgage investment conduits (REMICs) were authorized by the 1986 Tax Reform Act to allow originators to pass through all interest payments tax free. Only their legal and tax consequences distinguish REMICs from CMOs.

Private Pass-Throughs (PIPs) In addition to the agency pass-throughs, intermediaries in the private sector have offered privately issued pass-through securities. The first of these PIPs was offered by BankAmerica in 1977.

One mortgage market opportunity available to private institutions is for mortgages larger than the maximum size set by the government. These so-called *jumbo mortgages* are often bundled into pools to back private pass-throughs.

Subprime Mortgages and CDOs

Subprime loans are those made to borrowers who do not qualify for loans at the going market rate of interest because of a poor credit rating or because the loan is larger than justified by their income. There can be subprime car loans or credit cards, but subprime mortgages were highly publicized due to the high default rates realized when real estate values began dropping in 2006.

Before the securitized market made it easy to bundle and sell mortgages, if you did not meet the qualifications for one of the major mortgage agencies, you were unlikely to be able to buy a house. These qualifications were strictly enforced, and each element was verified to ensure compliance. Once it became possible to sell bundles of loans to other investors, different lending rules emerged. These new rules gave rise to a new class of mortgage loans known as subprime mortgages.

According to the Mortgage Bankers Association, in 2000 about 70% of all loans were conventional prime, 20% were FHA, 8% were VA, and only 2% were subprime. In 2006, 70% were still conventional prime, but now fully 17% were subprime, with the balance being FHA and VA. The FICO score is computed for virtually every borrower. This score is computed by the different credit-rating agencies as an index of credit risk. Though each agency uses a slightly different algorithm, all include payment history, level of current debt, length of credit history, types of credit held, and the number of new credit inquiries made as criteria for rating creditworthiness. The average subprime FICO score was 624 versus 742 for prime mortgage loans.

Several innovative lending practices led to this increase in lending to less creditworthy borrowers. First, 2/28 ARMs (sometimes called "teaser" loans) became popular. These loans freeze the interest rate for 2 years, and then it increases, often substantially, after that. Piggyback loans, No Doc, or NINJA (no income no asset loans), and variations on the graduated payment mortgage, as discussed in an earlier section, encouraged borrowers to commit to larger loans than they could realistically handle.

Many saw the increase in mortgage loans to less creditworthy borrowers as progress. If home ownership is the goal of every American, then relaxed lending standards allowed more families to reach their goal. Additionally, the increased demand for housing fueled economic growth and increased employment in the building industry. The downside was that the competitive nature of the market led mortgage salespeople to target less financially sophisticated borrowers who were less able to properly evaluate their ability to repay the loans. Furthermore, the relaxed lending standards allowed speculators to obtain loans without investing any equity.

The growth of the subprime mortgage was in part fueled by the creation of the structured credit products such as the collateralized debt obligation (CDO). These securities were first introduced in Chapter 8 as providing a source of funds for high-risk investments. A CDO is similar to the CMO discussed above, except that rather than slice the pool of securities by maturity as with the CMO, the CDO usually creates tranches based on risk class. While CDOs can be backed by corporate bonds, real estate investment trust (REIT) debt, or other assets, mortgage-backed securities are common.

When real estate values were rapidly increasing, borrowers could easily sell their property if they found themselves unable to make the payments. Once the real estate market cooled in 2006 and 2007, it became much more difficult to sell property and many borrowers were forced into default and bankruptcy. As discussed more fully in Chapter 8, subprime lending was ultimately a leading cause of the financial crisis of 2007–2008 and led to a global recession.

The Real Estate Bubble

The mortgage market was heavily influenced by the real estate boom and bust between the years 2000 and 2008. Between 2000 and 2005 home prices increased an average of 8% per year. They increased 17% in 2005 alone. The run-up in prices was caused by two factors. The first was the increase in subprime loans discussed previously. With more people now qualifying for loans, there was increased demand. This meant that over a very short period many new buyers were now qualified to purchase homes. While home construction increased, it could not keep pace with demand.

Real estate speculators were a second driver of the price bubble. People of all walks of life started noticing that quick and apparently easy money was to be made by buying real estate for the purpose of resale. The ability to obtain zero down loans allowed them to buy property easily and with little committed capital. They could then resell the property at a higher price. Many development projects were sold out before they were even started. The buyers were often speculators with no intention of occupying the property. Condominiums were especially popular, since they did not require much upkeep by the owner until the next sale could be arranged. At times, speculators were selling to other speculators as the demand drove up prices.

As with most speculative bubbles, at some point the process ends. Default rates on the subprime mortgages increased, and the extent of speculation started to make the news. Those left owning properties bought at the height of the market suffered losses, including lending institutions and investors in mortgage-backed securities.

In the aftermath of a mortgage-fueled financial meltdown, lending policies have largely returned to selecting capable borrowers. One indication of this is the decline in global CDO issuance. It peaked at $520 billion in 2006. By 2009 it had fallen to $4.3 billion. The market recovered somewhat such that between 2013 and 2015 it was hovering around $100 billion.[2]

The securitized mortgage was initially hailed as a method for reducing the risk to lenders by allowing them to sell off a portion of their loan portfolio. The lender could continue making loans without having to retain the risk. Unfortunately, this led to increased moral hazard. By separating the lender from the risk, riskier loans were issued than would have been had the securitized mortgage channel not existed. Individual firm risk may have been reduced, but systemic risk greatly increased.

---

[2] *Source:* http://www.sifma.org/research/statistics.aspx.

SUMMARY

1. Mortgages are long-term loans secured by real estate. Both individuals and businesses obtain mortgage loans to finance real estate purchases.
2. Mortgage interest rates are relatively low due to competition among various institutions that want to make mortgage loans. In addition to keeping interest rates low, the competition has resulted in a variety of terms and options for mortgage loans. For example, borrowers may choose to obtain a 30-year fixed-rate loan or an adjustable-rate loan that has its interest rate tied to the Treasury bill rate.
3. Several features of mortgage loans are designed to reduce the likelihood that the borrower will default. For example, a down payment is usually required so that the borrower will suffer a loss if the lender repossesses the property. Most lenders also require that the borrower purchase private mortgage insurance unless the loan-to-value ratio drops below 80%.
4. A variety of mortgages are available to meet the needs of most borrowers. The graduated-payment mortgage has low initial payments that increase over time. The growing-equity mortgage has increasing payments that cause the loan to be paid off in a shorter period than a level-payment loan. Reverse annuity mortgages allow retired people to live on the equity they have in their homes. The growing loan balance is secured by the real estate.
5. Securitized mortgages have become a common investment security as institutional investors look for attractive investment opportunities. Securitized mortgages are securities collateralized by a pool of mortgages. The payments on the pool are passed through to the investors. Ginnie Mae, Freddie Mac, and private banks issue pass-through securities. Securitized mortgage securities separate the lending risk from the lender and lead to increasingly risky loans.
6. Subprime loans increased in volume from being a negligible portion of the mortgage loan volume in the 1990s to 17% by 2006. Zero-down loans along with underqualified borrowers led to speculative growth in home prices and a subsequent collapse when default rates and lack of real demand became public.

KEY TERMS

amortized, p. 319
balloon loans, p. 319
collateralized mortgage obligation (CMO), p. 333
conventional mortgages, p. 325
discount points, p. 321
down payment, p. 323
FICO scores, p. 324
insured mortgages, p. 325
lien, p. 323
mortgage, p. 319
mortgage pass-through, p. 332
mortgage-backed security, p. 331
private mortgage insurance (PMI), p. 323
reserve accounts, p. 329
securitized mortgage, p. 331
subprime loans, p. 334

QUESTIONS

1. Explain why it was so complicated to take out a mortgage loan to buy a house from a commercial bank in the 1870s.
2. Most mortgage loans once had balloon payments; now most current mortgage loans fully amortize. What is the difference between a balloon loan and an amortizing loan?
3. Based on the history review of the mortgage market presented at the beginning of the chapter, can we say that the originate-to-distribute model is a recent business model?
4. What are discount points, and why do some mortgage borrowers choose to pay them?
5. Suppose you want to take out a loan to buy a house in town and you want to use your farm land as collateral, but you do not have the land title. Your family has lived there for 150 years, and everybody knows it is your land. What are your chances of getting the loan? Would you say this is a prevalent problem around the world?
6. What is the purpose of requiring that a borrower make a down payment before receiving a loan?
7. What kind of insurance do lenders usually require of borrowers who have less than an 80% loan-to-value ratio?
8. Lenders tend not to be as flexible about the qualifications required of mortgage customers as they can be for other types of bank loans. Why is this so?
9. In which circumstances would it be appropriate to take out a second mortgage?

10. Interpret what is meant when a lender quotes the terms on a loan as "floating with the T-bill plus 2 with caps of 2 and 6."
11. The monthly payments on both graduated-payment loans and growing-equity loans increase over time. Despite this similarity, the two types of loans have different purposes. What is the motivation behind each type of loan?
12. Many banks offer lines of credit that are secured by a second mortgage (or lien) on real property. These loans have been very popular among bank customers. Why are homeowners so willing to pledge their homes as security for these lines of credit?
13. The reverse annuity mortgage (RAM) allows retired people to live off the equity they have in their homes without having to sell the home. Explain how a RAM works.
14. Which type of mortgage would you choose if you were an advanced student at the UCLA School of Medicine with the prospect of a $150,000 salary as soon as you graduate?
15. Describe how a mortgage pass-through works.

QUANTITATIVE PROBLEMS

1. Compute the required monthly payment on a $150,000 30-year fixed-rate mortgage with a nominal interest rate of 8%. What is the balance due at the end of the first year?
2. Refer to problem 1. What is the total amount of interest paid over the life of the loan?
3. Compute the face value of a 30-year fixed-rate mortgage with a monthly payment of $1,200, assuming a nominal interest rate of 6%. Compute the face value if the interest rate is now 7%. What is the difference in maximum house prices if both mortgages require 5% down?
4. Consider a $180,000 30-year fixed-rate mortgage with a nominal interest rate of 6%. Suppose that after paying the first 12 monthly payments, the borrower decides that she cannot pay more than $900 per month. Determine the number of months necessary to pay off the mortgage.
5. Consider a 30-year fixed-rate mortgage for $200,000 at a nominal rate of 8%. A mortgage broker closes this deal on August 30. If the broker wants to sell this mortgage to a bank on August 31 and rates have decreased to 7.5%, how much would this broker ask for the mortgage?
6. Consider a 30-year fixed-rate mortgage of $100,000 at a nominal rate of 9%. What is the duration of the loan? If interest rates increase to 9.5% immediately after the mortgage is made, how much is the loan worth to the lender?
7. Consider a 5-year balloon loan for $250,000. The bank requires a monthly payment equal to $1,450, and the interest rate is 6%. How much will the borrower owe when the balloon payment is due?
8. A 30-year variable-rate mortgage offers a first-year teaser rate of 2%. After that, the rate starts at 4.5%, adjusted based on actual interest rates. The maximum rate over the life of the loan is 10.5%, and the rate can increase by no more than 200 basis points a year. If the mortgage is for $250,000, what is the monthly payment during the first year? Second year? What is the maximum payment during the fourth year? What is the maximum payment ever?
9. Consider a 30-year fixed-rate mortgage for $500,000 at a nominal rate of 6%. What is the difference in required payments between a monthly payment and a bimonthly payment (payments made twice a month)?
10. Consider the following options available to a mortgage borrower:

	Loan Amount ($)	Interest Rate (%)	Type of Mortgage	Discount Points
Option 1	100,000	6.75	30-year fixed	none
Option 2	150,000	6.25	30-year fixed	1
Option 3	125,000	6.0	30-year fixed	2

What is the effective annual rate for each option?
11. Two mortgage options are available: a 15-year fixed-rate loan at 6% with no discount points, and a 15-year fixed-rate loan at 5.75% with 1 discount point. Assuming you will not pay off the loan early, which alternative is best for you? Assume a $100,000 mortgage.
12. Two mortgage options are available: a 30-year fixed-rate loan at 6% with no discount points, and a 30-year fixed-rate loan at 5.75% with 1 discount point. How long do you have to stay in the house for the mortgage with points to be a better option? Assume a $100,000 mortgage.

13. Two mortgage options are available: a 30-year fixed-rate loan at 6% with no discount points, and a 30-year fixed-rate loan at 5.75% with points. If you are planning on living in the house for 12 years, what is the most you are willing to pay in points for the 5.75% mortgage? Assume a $100,000 mortgage.

14. A mortgage on a house worth $350,000 requires what down payment to avoid PMI insurance?

15. Consider a 30-year graduated-payment mortgage on a $250,000 mortgage with yearly payments. The stated interest rate on the mortgage is 6%, but the first annual payment is calculated assuming a 3% rate for the life of the loan. Thereafter, the annual payment will grow by 3.151222%. Develop an amortization table for this loan, assuming the initial payment is based on 30 years and the loan pays off in 15.

16. Consider a growing-equity mortgage on a $250,000 mortgage with yearly payments. The stated interest rate on the mortgage is 6%, but this only applies to the first annual payment. Thereafter, the annual payment will grow by 5.5797%. Develop an amortization table for this loan, assuming the initial payment is based on 30 years and the loan pays off in 15 years.

17. Rusty Nail owns his house free and clear, and it's worth $400,000. To finance his retirement, he acquires a reverse annuity mortgage (RAM) from his bank. The RAM provides a fixed monthly payment over 15 years on 70% of the value of his home at 5%. The payments are made at the beginning of the month. How much does Rusty get each month?

18. You are working with a pool of 1,000 mortgages. Each mortgage is for $100,000 and has a stated annual interest rate (nominal) of 6.00%. The mortgages are all 30-year fixed-rate and fully amortizing. Mortgage-servicing fees are currently 0.25% annually. Complete the following table.

Month	(1) Beginning Balance	(2) Required Payment	(3) Interest	(4) Principal	(5) Expected Prepayment	(6) Servicing Fees	(7) Ending Balance
1	100,000,000		500,000	99,551	16,665		
2					33,322		99,750,430

WEB EXERCISES

The Mortgage Markets

1. You may be looking into acquiring a home in the near future. One common question you may have is how large a mortgage loan you can afford. Go to **http://interest.com** and click on the "Mortgage" tab and then on "calculators." Choose the "mortgage required income calculator." Input your expected future salary data. How large a mortgage can you afford according to the calculator? Increase your debt to see the impact on the amount of mortgage loan you will qualify for.

2. One of the more difficult decisions faced by homeowners is whether it pays to refinance a mortgage loan when rates have dropped. Go to **http://interest.com** and click on the calculator labeled "Refinance interest savings calculator." Compute how long it will take to recoup the interest of refinancing your mortgage loan. Assume you obtained a 30-year $130,000 loan four years ago at 7%. Now rates have dropped and your income is higher. Determine how much you will save if you get a new loan for 15 years at 6.25%.

CHAPTER 15

The Foreign Exchange Market

> PREVIEW

In the mid-1980s, American businesses became less competitive with their foreign counterparts; after that, their competitiveness increased. Did this swing in competitiveness occur primarily because American management fell down on the job in the 1980s and then got its act together afterward? Not really. American business became less competitive in the 1980s because American dollars became worth more in terms of foreign currencies, making American goods more expensive relative to foreign goods. Afterward, the value of the U.S. dollar had fallen appreciably from its highs in the mid-1980s, making American goods cheaper and American businesses more competitive.

The price of one currency in terms of another is called the **exchange rate**. As you can see in Figure 15.1, exchange rates are highly volatile. The exchange rate affects the economy and our daily lives, because when the U.S. dollar becomes more valuable relative to foreign currencies, foreign goods become cheaper for Americans and American goods become more expensive for foreigners. When the U.S. dollar falls in value, foreign goods become more expensive for Americans and American goods become cheaper for foreigners.

We begin our study of international finance by examining the **foreign exchange market**, the financial market where exchange rates are determined.

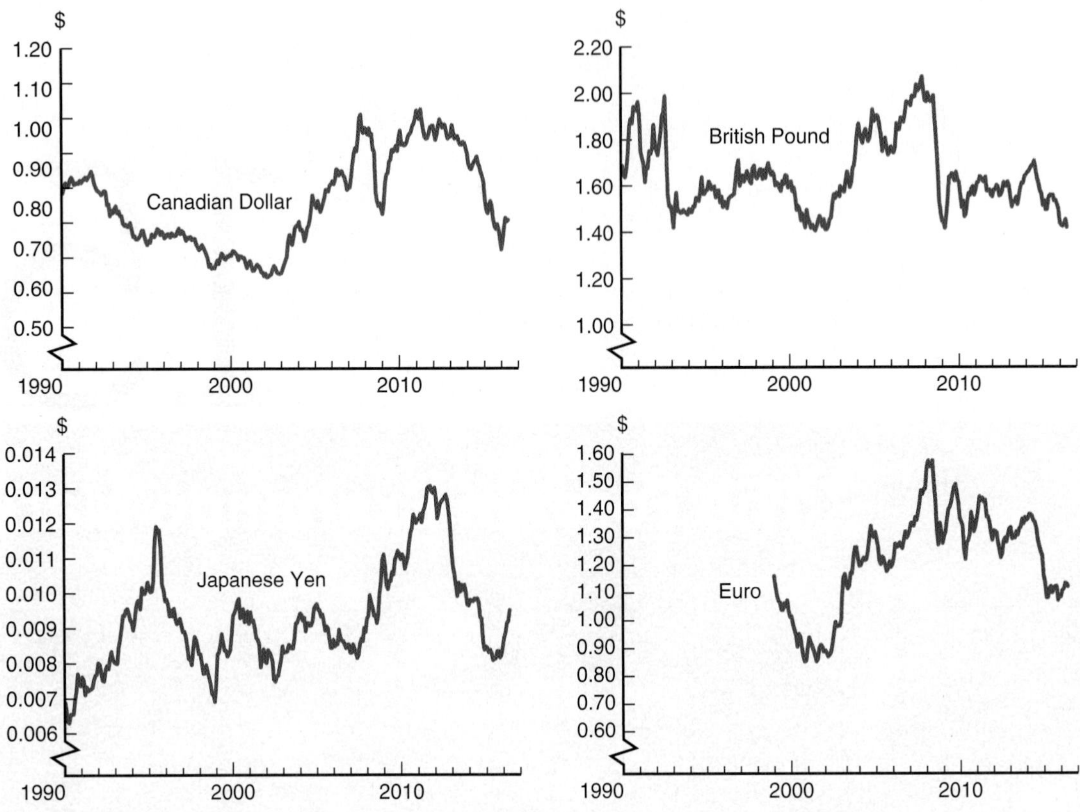

FIGURE 15.1 Exchange Rates, 1990–2016

Exchange rates are highly volatile. Note that exchange rates are quoted as $/currency, so that a rise in these plots indicates a strengthening of the foreign currency (weakening of the dollar).

Source: Federal Reserve Bank of St. Louis FRED database: https://fred.stlouisfed.org/series/EXCAUS; https://fred.stlouisfed.org/series/EXUSUK; https://fred.stlouisfed.org/series/EXJPUS; https://fred.stlouisfed.org/series/EXUSEU.

Foreign Exchange Market

Access **http://www.newyorkfed.org/markets/foreignex.html** and get detailed information about the foreign exchange market in the United States.

Most countries of the world have their own currencies: The United States has its dollar; the European Monetary Union, its euro; Brazil, its real; and China, its yuan. Trade between countries involves the mutual exchange of different currencies (or, more usually, bank deposits denominated in different currencies). When an American firm buys foreign goods, services, or financial assets, for example, U.S. dollars (typically, bank deposits denominated in U.S. dollars) must be exchanged for foreign currency (bank deposits denominated in the foreign currency).

The trading of currencies and bank deposits denominated in particular currencies takes place in the foreign exchange market. Transactions conducted in the foreign exchange market determine the rates at which currencies are exchanged, which in turn determine the cost of purchasing foreign goods and financial assets.

What Are Foreign Exchange Rates?

There are two kinds of exchange rate transactions. The predominant ones, called **spot transactions**, involve the immediate (two-day) exchange of bank deposits. **Forward transactions** involve the exchange of bank deposits at some specified future date. The **spot exchange rate** is the exchange rate for the spot transaction, and the **forward exchange rate** is the exchange rate for the forward transaction.

When a currency increases in value, it experiences **appreciation**; when it falls in value and is worth fewer U.S. dollars, it undergoes **depreciation**. At the beginning of 1999, for example, the euro was valued at \$1.18 and, as indicated in the Following the Financial News box, on June 16, 2016, it was valued at \$1.11. The euro *depreciated* by 6%: $(1.11 - 1.18)/1.18 = -0.06 = -6\%$. Equivalently, we could say that the U.S. dollar, which went from a value of 0.85 euro per dollar at the beginning of 1999 to a value of 0.90 euro per dollar on June 16, 2016, *appreciated* by 6%: $(0.90 - 0.85)/0.85 = 0.06 = 6\%$.

Why Are Exchange Rates Important?

Access **http://quotes.ino.com/chart/** and click "Foreign Exchange" to get market rates and time charts for the exchange rate of the U.S. dollar to major world currencies.

Exchange rates are important because they affect the relative price of domestic and foreign goods. The dollar price of French goods to an American is determined by the interaction of two factors: the price of French goods in euros and the euro–dollar exchange rate.

Suppose that Wanda the wine taster, an American, decides to buy a bottle of 1961 (a very good year) Château Lafite Rothschild to complete her wine cellar. If the price of the wine in France is 1,000 euros and the exchange rate is \$1.11 to the euro, the wine will cost Wanda \$1,110 (1,000 euros × \$1.11/euro). Now suppose that Wanda delays her purchase by two months, at which time the euro has appreciated to \$1.40 per euro. If the domestic price of the bottle of Lafite Rothschild remains 1,000 euros, its dollar cost will have risen from \$1,110 to \$1,400.

The same currency appreciation, however, makes the price of foreign goods in that country less expensive. At an exchange rate of \$1.11 per euro, a Dell computer priced at \$2,000 costs Pierre the programmer 1,802 euros; if the exchange rate increases to \$1.40 per euro, the computer will cost only 1,429 euros.

A depreciation of the euro lowers the cost of French goods in America but raises the cost of American goods in France. If the euro drops in value to \$1.00, Wanda's

> FOLLOWING THE FINANCIAL NEWS

Foreign Exchange Rates

Foreign exchange rates are published daily in newspapers and Internet sites such as www.finance.yahoo.com. Exchange rates for a currency such as the euro are quoted in two ways: U.S. dollars per unit of domestic currency or domestic currency per U.S. dollar. For example, on June 16, 2016, the euro exchange rate was quoted as \$1.1132 per euro and 0.8983 euro per dollar. Americans generally would regard the exchange rate with the euro as \$1.11 per euro, while Europeans think of it as 0.90 euro per dollar.

Exchange rates are quoted for the spot transaction (the spot exchange rate) and for forward transactions (the forward exchange rates) that will take place one month, three months, and six months in the future.

bottle of Lafite Rothschild will cost her only $1,000 instead of $1,110, and the Dell computer will cost Pierre 2,000 euros rather than 1,800.

Such reasoning leads to the following conclusion: ***When a country's currency appreciates (rises in value relative to other currencies), the country's goods abroad become more expensive and foreign goods in that country become cheaper (holding domestic prices constant in the two countries). Conversely, when a country's currency depreciates, its goods abroad become cheaper and foreign goods in that country become more expensive.***

Depreciation of a currency makes it easier for domestic manufacturers to sell their goods abroad and makes foreign goods less competitive in domestic markets. From 2002 to 2016, the dollar depreciated, which helped U.S. industries sell more goods, but it hurt American consumers because foreign goods were more expensive. The prices of French wine and cheese and the cost of vacationing abroad all rose as a result of the weak dollar.

How Is Foreign Exchange Traded?

You cannot go to a centralized location to watch exchange rates being determined; currencies are not traded on exchanges such as the New York Stock Exchange. Instead, the foreign exchange market is organized as an over-the-counter market in which several hundred dealers (mostly banks) stand ready to buy and sell deposits denominated in foreign currencies. Because these dealers are in constant telephone and computer contact, the market is very competitive; in effect, it functions no differently from a centralized market.

An important point to note is that although banks, companies, and governments talk about buying and selling currencies in foreign exchange markets, they do not take a fistful of dollar bills and sell them for British pound notes. Rather, most trades involve the buying and selling of bank deposits denominated in different currencies. So when we say that a bank is buying dollars in the foreign exchange market, what we actually mean is that the bank is buying *deposits denominated in dollars*. The volume in this market is colossal, exceeding $5 trillion per day.

Trades in the foreign exchange market consist of transactions in excess of $1 million. The market that determines the exchange rates in the Following the Financial News box is not where one would buy foreign currency for a trip abroad. Instead, we buy foreign currency in the retail market from dealers such as American Express or from banks. Because retail prices are higher than wholesale, when we buy foreign exchange, we obtain fewer units of foreign currency per dollar—that is, we pay a higher price for foreign currency—than the exchange rates quoted in the newspaper indicate.

Exchange Rates in the Long Run

Like the price of any good or asset in a free market, exchange rates are determined by the interaction of supply and demand. To simplify our analysis of exchange rates in a free market, we divide it into two parts. First, we examine how exchange rates are determined in the long run; then we use our knowledge of the long-run determinants of the exchange rate to help us understand how they are determined in the short run.

Law of One Price

The starting point for understanding how exchange rates are determined is a simple idea called the **law of one price**: If two countries produce an identical good, and transportation costs and trade barriers are very low, the price of the good should be the same throughout the world no matter which country produces it. Suppose that American steel costs $100 per ton and identical Japanese steel costs 10,000 yen per ton. For the law of one price to hold, the exchange rate between the yen and the dollar must be 100 yen per dollar ($0.01 per yen), so that one ton of American steel sells for 10,000 yen in Japan (the price of Japanese steel) and one ton of Japanese steel sells for $100 in the United States (the price of U.S. steel). If the exchange rate were 200 yen to the dollar, Japanese steel would sell for $50 per ton in the United States or half the price of American steel, and American steel would sell for 20,000 yen per ton in Japan, twice the price of Japanese steel. Because American steel is identical to Japanese steel but would be more expensive in both countries, the demand for American steel would go to zero. Given a fixed dollar price for American steel, the resulting excess supply of American steel will be eliminated only if the exchange rate falls to 100 yen per dollar, making the price of American steel and Japanese steel the same in both countries.

EXAMPLE 15.1

Law of One Price

Recently, the yen price of Japanese steel has increased by 10% (to 11,000 yen) relative to the dollar price of American steel (unchanged at $100). By what amount must the dollar increase or decrease in value for the law of one price to hold true?

> Solution

For the law of one price to hold, the exchange rate must rise to 110 yen per dollar, which is a 10% appreciation of the dollar.

The exchange rate rises to 110 yen so that the price of Japanese steel in dollars remains unchanged at $100 (11,000 yen/110 yen per dollar). In other words, the 10% depreciation of the yen (10% appreciation of the dollar) just offsets the 10% increase in the yen price of the Japanese steel.

Theory of Purchasing Power Parity

GO ONLINE

Access the purchasing power parities home page at **http://www.oecd.org/std/prices-ppp/** and find details about the PPP program overview, statistics, research, publications, and OECD meetings on PPP.

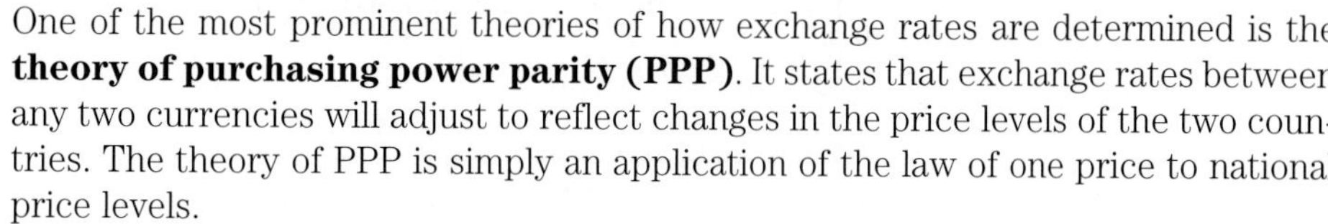

One of the most prominent theories of how exchange rates are determined is the **theory of purchasing power parity (PPP)**. It states that exchange rates between any two currencies will adjust to reflect changes in the price levels of the two countries. The theory of PPP is simply an application of the law of one price to national price levels.

As Example 15.1 illustrates, if the law of one price holds, a 10% rise in the yen price of Japanese steel results in a 10% appreciation of the dollar. Applying the law of one price to the price levels in the two countries produces the theory of purchasing power parity, which maintains that if the Japanese price level rises 10% relative to the U.S. price level, the dollar will appreciate by 10%. As our U.S./Japanese example illustrates, ***the theory of PPP suggests that if one country's price level rises relative to another's, its currency should depreciate (the other country's currency should appreciate).***

Another way of thinking about purchasing power parity is through a concept called the **real exchange rate**, the rate at which domestic goods can be exchanged for foreign goods. In effect, it is the price of domestic goods relative to the price of foreign goods denominated in the domestic currency. For example, if a basket of goods in New York costs \$50, while the cost of the same basket of goods in Tokyo costs \$75 because it costs 7,500 yen while the exchange rate is at 100 yen per dollar, then the real exchange rate is 0.66 (= \$50/\$75). The real exchange rate is below 1.0, indicating that it is cheaper to buy the basket of goods in the United States than in Japan. At the time of publication, the real exchange rate for the U.S. dollar is low against many other currencies, and this is why we see New York overwhelmed by so many foreign tourists going on shopping sprees. The real exchange rate indicates whether a currency is relatively cheap or not.

Another way of describing the theory of PPP is to say that it predicts that the real exchange rate is always equal to 1.0, so that the purchasing power of the dollar is the same as that of other currencies such as the yen or the euro.

As you can see in Figure 15.2, this prediction of the theory of PPP is borne out in the long run. From 1973 to 2016, the British price level rose 69% relative to the U.S. price level, and as the theory of PPP predicts, the dollar appreciated against sterling, though by 70%, almost the same as the increase predicted by PPP.

Yet, as the same figure indicates, PPP theory often has little predictive power in the short run. From early 1985 to the end of 1987, for example, the British price level rose relative to that of the United States. Instead of appreciating, as PPP theory predicts, the U.S. dollar actually depreciated by 40% against the pound. So even though PPP theory provides some guidance to the long-run movement of exchange

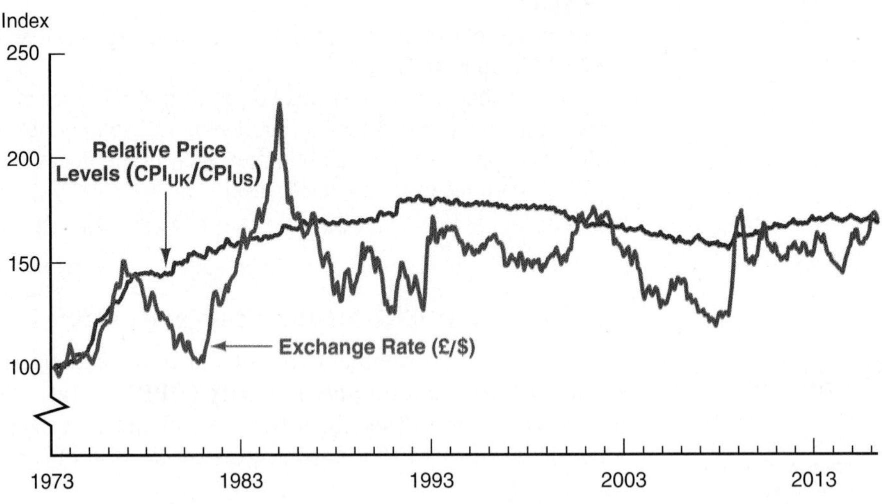

FIGURE 15.2 Purchasing Power Parity, United States/United Kingdom, 1973–2016 (Index: March 1973 = 100)

Over the whole period, the rise in the British price level relative to the U.S. price level is associated with a rise in the value of the dollar, as PPP predicts. However, the PPP relationship does not hold over shorter periods.

Source: Federal Reserve Bank of St. Louis FRED database: https://fred.stlouisfed.org/series/CP0000GBM086NEST; https://fred.stlouisfed.org/series/CPIAUCNS; https://fred.stlouisfed.org/series/EXUSUK.

rates, it is not perfect and in the short run is a particularly poor predictor. What explains PPP theory's failure to predict well?

Why the Theory of Purchasing Power Parity Cannot Fully Explain Exchange Rates

The PPP conclusion that exchange rates are determined solely by changes in relative price levels rests on the assumption that all goods are identical in both countries and that transportation costs and trade barriers are very low. When this assumption is true, the law of one price states that the relative prices of all these goods (that is, the relative price level between the two countries) will determine the exchange rate. The assumption that goods are identical may not be too unreasonable for American and Japanese steel, but is it a reasonable assumption for American and Japanese cars? Is a Toyota the equivalent of a Chevrolet?

Because Toyotas and Chevys are obviously not identical, their prices do not have to be equal. Toyotas can be more expensive relative to Chevys, and both Americans and Japanese will still purchase Toyotas. Because the law of one price does not hold for all goods, a rise in the price of Toyotas relative to Chevys will not necessarily mean that the yen must depreciate by the amount of the relative price increase of Toyotas over Chevys.

Furthermore, PPP theory does not take into account that many goods and services (whose prices are included in a measure of a country's price level) are not traded across borders. Housing, land, and services such as restaurant meals, haircuts, and golf lessons are not traded goods. So even though the prices of these items might rise and lead to a higher price level relative to another country's, the exchange rate would experience little direct effect.

Factors That Affect Exchange Rates in the Long Run

In the long run, four major factors affect the exchange rate: relative price levels, tariffs and quotas, preferences for domestic versus foreign goods, and productivity. We examine how each of these factors affects the exchange rate while holding the others constant.

The basic reasoning proceeds along the following lines: Anything that increases the demand for domestically produced goods that are traded relative to foreign traded goods tends to appreciate the domestic currency because domestic goods will continue to sell well even when the value of the domestic currency is higher. Similarly, anything that increases the demand for foreign goods relative to domestic goods tends to depreciate the domestic currency because domestic goods will continue to sell well only if the value of the domestic currency is lower. In other words, ***if a factor increases the demand for domestic goods relative to foreign goods, the domestic currency will appreciate; if a factor decreases the relative demand for domestic goods, the domestic currency will depreciate.***

Relative Price Levels In line with PPP theory, when prices of American goods rise (holding prices of foreign goods constant), the demand for American goods falls and the dollar tends to depreciate so that American goods can still sell well. By contrast, if prices of Japanese goods rise so that the relative prices of American goods fall, the demand for American goods increases, and the dollar tends to appreciate because American goods will continue to sell well even with a higher value of the domestic currency. ***In the long run, a rise in a country's price level (relative to the foreign price level) causes its currency to depreciate, and a fall in the country's relative price level causes its currency to appreciate.***

Trade Barriers Barriers to free trade such as **tariffs** (taxes on imported goods) and **quotas** (restrictions on the quantity of foreign goods that can be imported) can affect the exchange rate. Suppose that the United States increases its tariff or puts a lower quota on Japanese steel. These increases in trade barriers increase the demand for American steel, and the dollar tends to appreciate because American steel will still sell well even with a higher value of the dollar. ***Increasing trade barriers causes a country's currency to appreciate in the long run.***

Preferences for Domestic Versus Foreign Goods If the Japanese develop an appetite for American goods—say, for Florida oranges and American movies—the increased demand for American goods (exports) tends to appreciate the dollar because the American goods will continue to sell well even at a higher value for the dollar. Likewise, if Americans decide that they prefer Japanese cars to American cars, the increased demand for Japanese goods (imports) tends to depreciate the dollar. ***Increased demand for a country's exports causes its currency to appreciate in the long run; conversely, increased demand for imports causes the domestic currency to depreciate.***

Productivity When productivity in a country rises, it tends to rise in domestic sectors that produce traded goods rather than nontraded goods. Higher productivity, therefore, is associated with a decline in the price of domestically produced traded goods relative to foreign traded goods. As a result, the demand for traded domestic goods rises, and the domestic currency tends to appreciate. If, however, a country's productivity lags behind that of other countries, its traded goods become relatively more expensive, and the currency tends to depreciate. ***In the long run, as a country becomes more productive relative to other countries, its currency appreciates.***[1]

Our long-run theory of exchange rate behavior is summarized in Table 15.1. We use the convention that the exchange rate E is quoted so that an appreciation of the currency corresponds to a rise in the exchange rate. In the case of the United States, this means that we are quoting the exchange rate as units of foreign currency per dollar (say, yen per dollar).[2]

---

[1]A country might be so small that a change in productivity or the preferences for domestic or foreign goods would have no effect on prices of these goods relative to foreign goods. In this case, changes in productivity or changes in preferences for domestic or foreign goods affect the country's income but will not necessarily affect the value of the currency. In our analysis, we are assuming that these factors can affect relative prices and consequently the exchange rate.

[2]Exchange rates can be quoted either as units of foreign currency per domestic currency or as units of domestic currency per foreign currency. In professional writing, many economists quote exchange rates as units of domestic currency per foreign currency so that an appreciation of the domestic currency is portrayed as a fall in the exchange rate. The opposite convention is used in the text here because it is more intuitive to think of an appreciation of the domestic currency as a rise in the exchange rate.

TABLE 15.1 Summary Factors That Affect Exchange Rates in the Long Run
SUMMARY

Factor	Change in Factor	Response of the Exchange Rate, E^*
Domestic price level[†]	↑	↓
Trade barriers[†]	↑	↑
Import demand	↑	↓
Export demand	↑	↑
Productivity[†]	↑	↑

[*]Units of foreign currency per dollar: ↑ indicates domestic currency appreciation; ↓, depreciation.
[†]Relative to other countries.

Note: Only increases (↑) in the factors are shown; the effects of decreases in the variables on the exchange rate are the opposite of those indicated in the "Response" column.

Exchange Rates in the Short Run: A Supply and Demand Analysis

GO ONLINE
Access **www.federalreserve.gov/releases/** and study how the Federal Reserve reports current and historical exchange rates for many countries.

We have developed a theory of the long-run behavior of exchange rates. However, because factors driving long-run changes in exchange rates move slowly over time, if we are to understand why exchange rates exhibit such large changes (sometimes several percent) from day to day, we must develop a supply-and-demand analysis of how current exchange rates (spot exchange rates) are determined in the short run.

The key to understanding the short-run behavior of exchange rates is to recognize that an exchange rate is the price of domestic assets (bank deposits, bonds, equities, etc., denominated in the domestic currency) in terms of foreign assets (similar assets denominated in the foreign currency). Because the exchange rate is the price of one asset in terms of another, the natural way to investigate the short-run determination of exchange rates is to use an asset market approach that relies heavily on the theory of portfolio choice developed in Chapter 4 in which we outlined the determinants of asset demand. As you will see, however, the long-run determinants of the exchange rate we have just outlined also play an important part in the short-run asset market approach.

In the past, supply-and-demand approaches to exchange rate determination emphasized the role of import and export demand. The more modern asset market approach used here emphasizes stocks of assets rather than the flows of exports and imports over short periods because export and import transactions are small relative to the amount of domestic and foreign assets at any given time. For example, foreign exchange transactions in the United States each year are well over 25 times greater than the amount of U.S. exports and imports. Thus, over short periods, decisions to hold domestic or foreign assets have a much greater role in exchange rate determination than the demand for exports and imports does.

Supply Curve for Domestic Assets

We start by discussing the supply curve. In this analysis we treat the United States as the home country, so domestic assets are denominated in dollars. For simplicity,

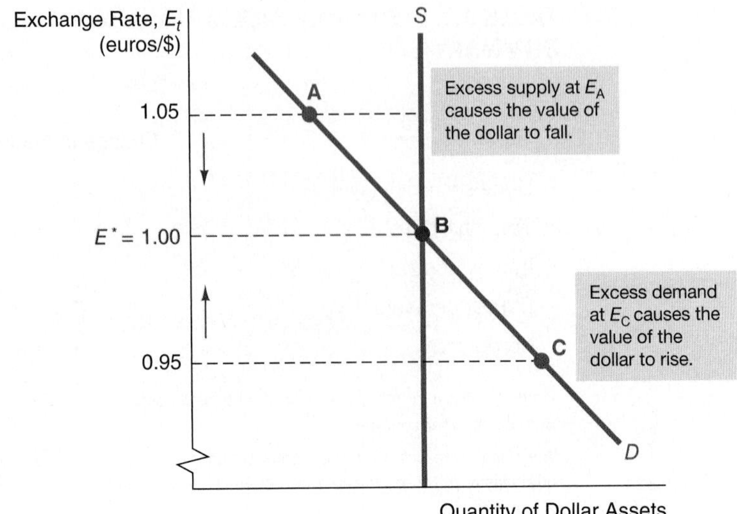

FIGURE 15.3 Equilibrium in the Foreign Exchange Market
Equilibrium in the foreign exchange market occurs at point B, the intersection of the demand curve *D* and the supply curve *S*. The equilibrium exchange rate is $E^* = 1$ euro per dollar.

we use euros to stand for any foreign country's currency, so foreign assets are denominated in euros.

The quantity of dollar assets supplied is primarily the quantity of bank deposits, bonds, and equities in the United States, and for all practical purposes we can take this amount as fixed with respect to the exchange rate. The quantity supplied at any exchange rate does not change, so the supply curve, *S*, is vertical, as shown in Figure 15.3.

Demand Curve for Domestic Assets

The demand curve traces out the quantity demanded at each current exchange rate by holding everything else constant, particularly the expected future value of the exchange rate. We write the current exchange rate (the spot exchange rate) as E_t, and the expected exchange rate for the next period as E^e_{t+1}. As the theory of portfolio choice suggests, the most important determinant of the quantity of domestic (dollar) assets demanded is the relative expected return of domestic assets. Let's see what happens as the current exchange rate E_t falls.

Suppose we start at point A in Figure 15.3, where the current exchange rate is at 1.05 euros per dollar. With the future expected value of the exchange rate held constant at E^e_{t+1}, a lower value of the exchange rate—say, at $E^* = 1$ euro per dollar—implies that the dollar is expected to rise more in value, that is, appreciate. The greater the expected rise (appreciation) of the dollar, the higher the relative expected return on dollar (domestic) assets. The theory of portfolio choice then tells us that because dollar assets are now more desirable to hold, the quantity of dollar assets demanded will rise, as is shown by point B in Figure 15.3. If the current exchange rate is even lower at 0.95 euro per dollar, there is an even higher expected appreciation of the dollar, a higher expected return, and therefore an even greater quantity of dollar assets demanded. This effect is shown in point C in Figure 15.3. The resulting demand curve, D, which connects these points, is downward-sloping, indicating that at lower current values of the dollar (everything else being equal), the quantity demanded of dollar assets is higher.

Equilibrium in the Foreign Exchange Market

As in the usual supply-and-demand analysis, the market is in equilibrium when the quantity of dollar assets demanded equals the quantity supplied. In Figure 15.3, equilibrium occurs at point B, the intersection of the demand and supply curves. At point B, the exchange rate is $E^* = 1$ euro per dollar.

Suppose that the exchange rate is at 1.05 euros per dollar, which is higher than the equilibrium exchange rate of 1 euro per dollar. As we can see in Figure 15.3, the quantity of dollar assets supplied is then greater than the quantity demanded, a condition of excess supply. Given that more people want to sell dollar assets than want to buy them, the value of the dollar will fall. As long as the exchange rate remains above the equilibrium exchange rate, an excess supply of dollar assets will continue to be available, and the dollar will fall in value until it reaches the equilibrium exchange rate of 1 euro per dollar.

Similarly, if the exchange rate is less than the equilibrium exchange rate at 0.95 euro per dollar, the quantity of dollar assets demanded will exceed the quantity supplied, a condition of excess demand. Given that more people want to buy dollar assets than want to sell them, the value of the dollar will rise until the excess demand disappears and the value of the dollar is again at the equilibrium exchange rate of 1 euro per dollar.

Explaining Changes in Exchange Rates

Access **http://fx.sauder.ubc.ca**. The Pacific Exchange Rate Service at the University of British Columbia's Sauder School of Business provides information on how market conditions are affecting exchange rates and allows easy plotting of exchange rate data.

The supply-and-demand analysis of the foreign exchange market can explain how and why exchange rates change. We have simplified this analysis by assuming the amount of dollar assets is fixed: The supply curve is vertical at a given quantity and does not shift. Under this assumption, we need to look at only those factors that shift the demand curve for dollar assets to explain how exchange rates change over time.

Shifts in the Demand for Domestic Assets

As we have seen, the quantity of domestic (dollar) assets demanded depends on the relative expected return of dollar assets. To see how the demand curve shifts, we need to ask how the quantity demanded changes, holding the current exchange rate, E_t, constant, when other factors change over time.

For insight into which direction the demand curve shifts, suppose you are an investor who is considering putting funds into domestic (dollar) assets. When a factor changes, decide whether at a given level of the current exchange rate, holding all other variables constant, you would earn a higher or lower expected return on dollar assets versus foreign assets. This decision tells you whether you want to hold more or fewer dollar assets and thus whether the quantity demanded increases or decreases at each level of the exchange rate. Knowing the direction of the change in the quantity demanded at each exchange rate indicates which way the demand curve shifts. In other words, if the relative expected return of dollar assets rises, holding the current exchange rate constant, the demand curve shifts to the right. If the relative expected return falls, the demand curve shifts to the left.

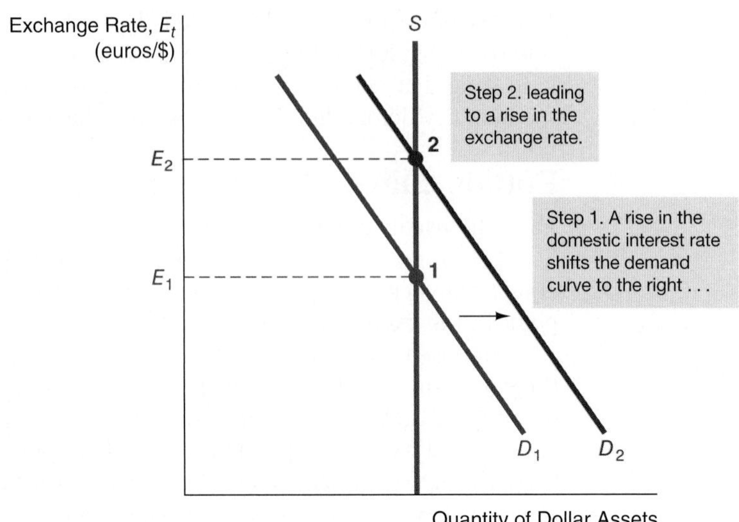
Exchange Rate, E_t (euros/$)
S
Step 2. leading to a rise in the exchange rate.
2
E_2
Step 1. A rise in the domestic interest rate shifts the demand curve to the right . . .
1
E_1
D_1
D_2
Quantity of Dollar Assets

FIGURE 15.4 Response to an Increase in the Domestic Interest Rate, i^D

When the domestic interest rate i^D increases, the relative expected return on domestic (dollar) assets increases and the demand curve shifts to the right. The equilibrium exchange rate rises from E_1 to E_2.

Domestic Interest Rate, i^D Suppose that dollar assets pay an interest rate of i^D. When the domestic interest rate on dollar assets, i^D, rises, holding the current exchange rate E_t and everything else constant, the return on dollar assets increases relative to foreign assets, so people will want to hold more dollar assets. The quantity of dollar assets demanded increases at every value of the exchange rate, as shown by the rightward shift of the demand curve from D_1 to D_2 in Figure 15.4. The new equilibrium is reached at point 2, the intersection of D_2 and S, and the equilibrium exchange rate rises from E_1 to E_2. ***An increase in the domestic interest rate i^D shifts the demand curve for domestic assets, D, to the right and causes the domestic currency to appreciate ($E\uparrow$).***

Conversely, if i^D falls, the relative expected return on dollar assets falls, the demand curve shifts to the left, and the exchange rate falls. ***A decrease in the domestic interest rate i^D shifts the demand curve for domestic assets, D, to the left and causes the domestic currency to depreciate ($E\downarrow$).***

Foreign Interest Rate, i^F Suppose that the foreign asset pays an interest rate of i^F. When the foreign interest rate, i^F, rises, holding the current exchange rate and everything else constant, the return on foreign assets rises relative to dollar assets. Thus the relative expected return on dollar assets falls. Now people want to hold fewer dollar assets, and the quantity demanded decreases at every value of the exchange rate. This scenario is shown by the leftward shift of the demand curve from D_1 to D_2 in Figure 15.5. The new equilibrium is reached at point 2, when the value of the dollar has fallen. Conversely, a decrease in i^F raises the relative expected return on dollar assets, shifts the demand curve to the right, and raises the exchange rate. To summarize, ***an increase in the foreign interest rate i^F shifts the demand curve for domestic assets, D, to the left and causes the domestic currency to depreciate; a fall in the foreign interest rate i^F shifts the demand curve D to the right and causes the domestic currency to appreciate.***

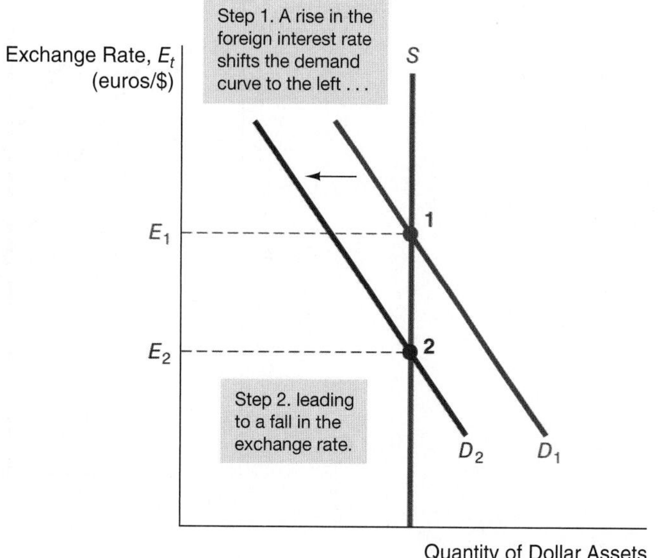

FIGURE 15.5 Response to an Increase in the Foreign Interest Rate, i^F

When the foreign interest rate i^F increases, the relative expected return on domestic (dollar) assets falls and the demand curve shifts to the left. The equilibrium exchange rate falls from E_1 to E_2.

Changes in the Expected Future Exchange Rate, E^e_{t+1} Expectations about the future value of the exchange rate play an important role in shifting the current demand curve because the return on domestic assets, like that for any durable good, depends on the future resale price. Any factor that causes the expected future exchange rate, E^e_{t+1}, to rise increases the expected appreciation of the dollar. The result is a higher relative expected return on dollar assets, which increases the demand for dollar assets at every exchange rate, thereby shifting the demand curve to the right from D_1 to D_2 in Figure 15.6. The equilibrium exchange rate rises to point 2 at the intersection of the D_2 and S curves. ***A rise in the expected future exchange rate, E^e_{t+1}, shifts the demand curve to the right and causes an appreciation of the domestic currency. Using the same reasoning, a fall in the expected future exchange rate, E^e_{t+1}, shifts the demand curve to the left and causes a depreciation of the currency.***

Earlier we discussed the determinants of the exchange rate in the long run: the relative price level, relative tariffs and quotas, import and export demand, and relative productivity (refer to Table 15.1). These four factors influence the expected future exchange rate. The theory of purchasing power parity suggests that if a higher American price level relative to the foreign price level is expected to persist, the dollar will depreciate in the long run. A higher expected relative American price level should thus have a tendency to lower E^e_{t+1}, lower the relative expected return on dollar assets, shift the demand curve to the left, and then lower the current exchange rate.

Similarly, the other long-run determinants of the exchange rate can influence the relative expected return on dollar assets and the current exchange rate. Briefly, the following changes, all of which increase the demand for domestic goods relative to foreign goods, will raise E^e_{t+1}: (1) expectations of a fall in the American price level relative to the foreign price level, (2) expectations of higher American trade barriers relative to

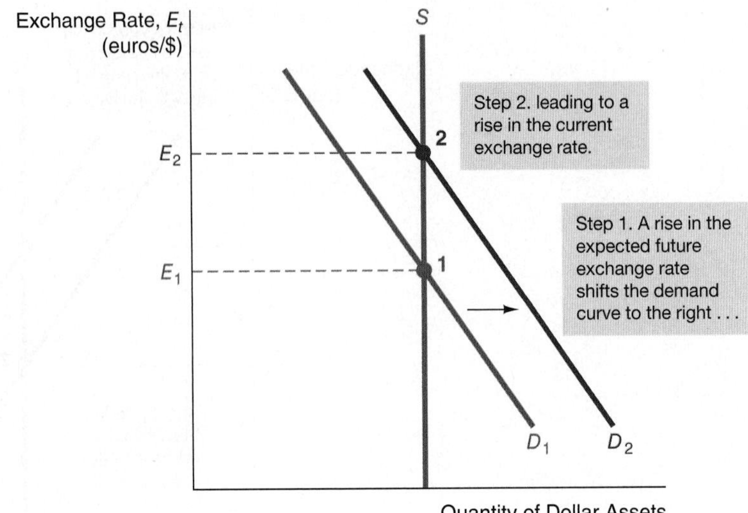

FIGURE 15.6 Response to an Increase in the Expected Future Exchange Rate, E^e_{t+1}
When the expected future exchange rate increases, the relative expected return on domestic (dollar) assets rises and the demand curve shifts to the right. The equilibrium exchange rate rises from E_1 to E_2.

foreign trade barriers, (3) expectations of lower American import demand, (4) expectations of higher foreign demand for American exports, and (5) expectations of higher American productivity relative to foreign productivity. By increasing E^e_{t+1}, all of these changes increase the relative expected return on dollar assets, shift the demand curve to the right, and cause an appreciation of the domestic currency, the dollar.

Recap: Factors That Change the Exchange Rate

Summary Table 15.2 outlines all the factors that shift the demand curve for domestic assets and thereby cause the exchange rate to change. Shifts in the demand curve occur when one factor changes, holding everything else constant, including the current exchange rate. Again, the theory of portfolio choice tells us that changes in the relative expected return on dollar assets are the source of shifts in the demand curve.

Let's review what happens when each of the seven factors in Table 15.2 changes. Remember that to understand which direction the demand curve shifts, consider what happens to the relative expected return on dollar assets when the factor changes. If the relative expected return rises, holding the current exchange rate constant, the demand curve shifts to the right. If the relative expected return falls, the demand curve shifts to the left.

1. When the interest rates on domestic assets, i^D, rise, the expected return on dollar assets rises at each exchange rate and so the quantity demanded increases. The demand curve therefore shifts to the right, and the equilibrium exchange rate rises, as is shown in the first row of Table 15.2.
2. When the foreign interest rate i^F rises, the return on foreign assets rises, so the relative expected return on dollar assets falls. The quantity demanded of

TABLE 15.2 SUMMARY **Summary Factors That Shift the Demand Curve for Domestic Assets and Affect the Exchange Rate**

Factor	Change in Factor	Change in Quantity Demanded of Domestic Assets at Each Exchange Rate	Response of Exchange Rate, E_t
Domestic interest rate, i^D 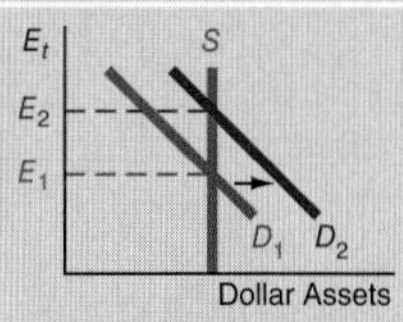	↑	↑	↑
Foreign interest rate, i^F 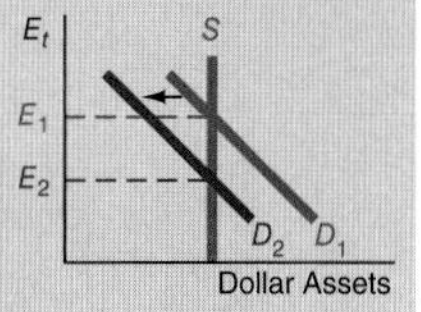	↑	↓	↓
Expected domestic price level* 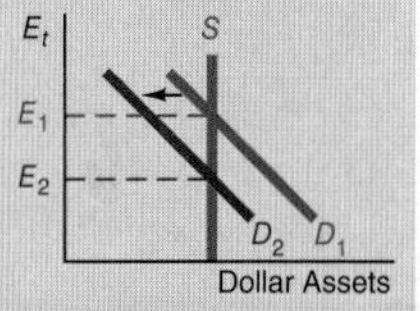	↑	↓	↓
Expected trade barriers* 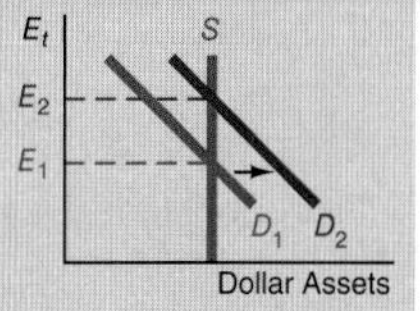	↑	↑	↑
Expected import demand 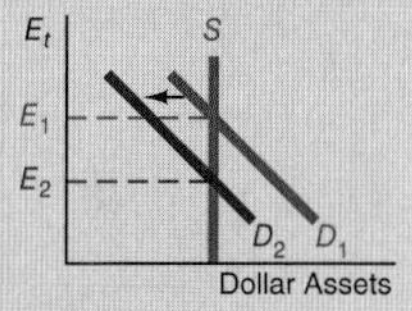	↑	↓	↓
Expected export demand 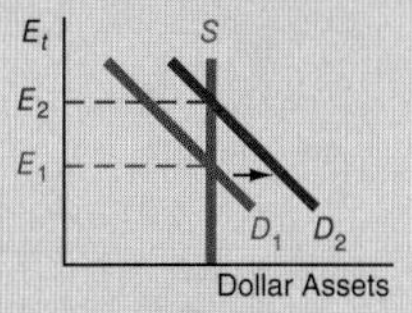	↑	↑	↑
Expected productivity* 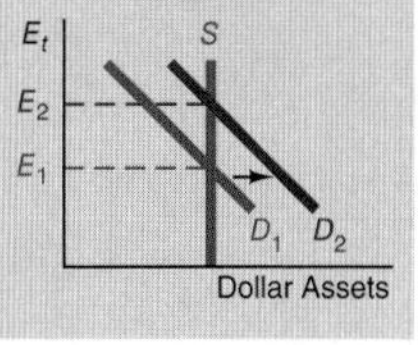	↑	↑	↑

*Relative to other countries.

Note: Only increases (↑) in the factors are shown; the effects of decreases in the variables on the exchange rate are the opposite of those indicated in the "Response" column.

dollar assets then falls, the demand curve shifts to the left, and the exchange rate declines, as in the second row of Table 15.2.

3. When the expected price level is higher, our analysis of the long-run determinants of the exchange rate indicates that the value of the dollar will fall in the future. The expected return on dollar assets thus falls, the quantity

demanded declines, the demand curve shifts to the left, and the exchange rate falls, as in the third row of Table 15.2.

4. With higher expected trade barriers, the value of the dollar is higher in the long run and the expected return on dollar assets is higher. The quantity demanded of dollar assets thus rises, the demand curve shifts to the right, and the exchange rate rises, as in the fourth row of Table 15.2.
5. When expected import demand rises, we expect the exchange rate to depreciate in the long run, so the expected return on dollar assets falls. The quantity demanded of dollar assets at each value of the current exchange rate therefore falls, the demand curve shifts to the left, and the exchange rate declines, as in the fifth row of Table 15.2.
6. When expected export demand rises, the opposite occurs because the exchange rate is expected to appreciate in the long run. The expected return on dollar assets rises, the demand curve shifts to the right, and the exchange rate rises, as in the sixth row of Table 15.2.
7. With higher expected domestic productivity, the exchange rate is expected to appreciate in the long run, so the expected return on domestic assets rises. The quantity demanded at each exchange rate therefore rises, the demand curve shifts to the right, and the exchange rate rises, as in the seventh row of Table 15.2.

CASE

Effect of Changes in Interest Rates on the Equilibrium Exchange Rate

Our analysis has revealed the factors that affect the value of the equilibrium exchange rate. Now we use this analysis to take a close look at the response of the exchange rate to changes in interest rates.

Changes in domestic interest rates i^D are often cited as a major factor affecting exchange rates. For example, we see headlines in the financial press like this one: "Dollar Recovers as Interest Rates Edge Upward." But is the view presented in this headline always correct?

Not necessarily, because to analyze the effects of interest rate changes, we must carefully distinguish the sources of the changes. The Fisher equation (Chapter 3) states that a nominal interest rate such as i^D equals the *real* interest rate plus expected inflation: $i = i_r + \pi^e$. The Fisher equation thus indicates that the interest rate i^D can change for two reasons: Either the real interest rate i_r changes or the expected inflation rate π^e changes. The effect on the exchange rate is quite different, depending on which of these two factors is the source of the change in the nominal interest rate.

Suppose that the domestic real interest rate increases so that the nominal interest rate i^D rises while expected inflation remains unchanged. In this case, it is reasonable to assume that the expected future exchange rate is unchanged because expected inflation is unchanged. In this case, the increase in i^D increases the relative expected return on dollar assets, raises the quantity of dollar assets demanded at each level of the exchange rate, and shifts the demand curve to the right. We end up with the situation depicted in Figure 15.4, which analyzes an increase in i^D, holding everything else constant. Our model of the foreign exchange market produces the following result: ***When domestic real interest rates rise, the domestic currency appreciates.***

When the nominal interest rate rises because of an increase in expected inflation, we get a different result from the one shown in Figure 15.4. The rise in expected

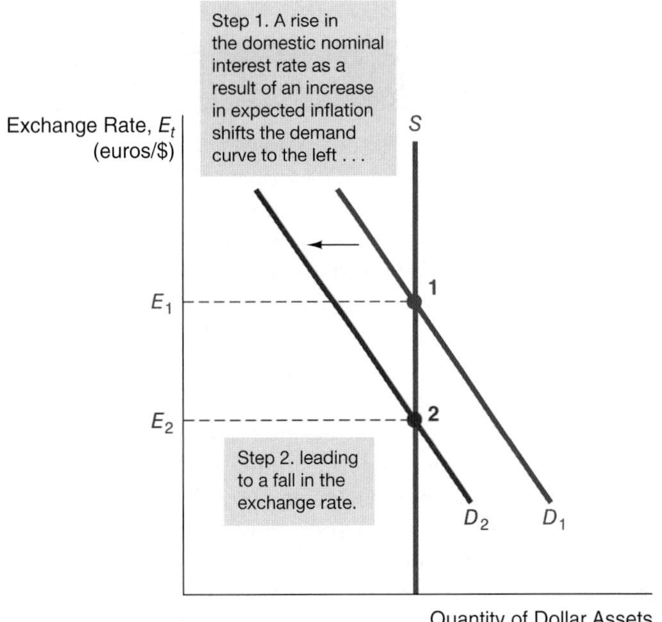

FIGURE 15.7 Effect of a Rise in the Domestic Interest Rate as a Result of an Increase in Expected Inflation

Because a rise in domestic expected inflation leads to a decline in expected dollar appreciation that is larger than the increase in the domestic interest rate, the relative expected return on domestic (dollar) assets falls. The demand curve shifts to the left, and the equilibrium exchange rate falls from E_1 to E_2.

domestic inflation leads to a decline in the expected appreciation of the dollar, which is typically thought to be larger than the increase in the domestic interest rate i^D.* As a result, at any given exchange rate, the relative expected return on domestic (dollar) assets falls, the demand curve shifts to the left, and the exchange rate falls from E_1 to E_2, as shown in Figure 15.7. Our analysis leads to this conclusion: ***When domestic interest rates rise due to an expected increase in inflation, the domestic currency depreciates.***

Because this conclusion is completely different from the one reached when the rise in the domestic interest rate is associated with a higher real interest rate, we must always distinguish between *real* and *nominal* measures when analyzing the effects of interest rates, either domestic or foreign, on exchange rates.

---

*This conclusion is standard in asset market models of exchange rate determination; see Rudiger Dornbusch, "Expectations and Exchange Rate Dynamics," *Journal of Political Economy* 84 (1976): 1061–1076. It is also consistent with empirical evidence that suggests that nominal interest rates do not rise one-for-one with increases in expected inflation. See Frederic S. Mishkin, "The Real Interest Rate: An Empirical Investigation," *Carnegie-Rochester Conference Series on Public Policy* 15 (1981): 151–200; and Lawrence Summers, "The Nonadjustment of Nominal Interest Rates: A Study of the Fisher Effect," in *Macroeconomics, Prices and Quantities*, ed. James Tobin (Washington, DC: Brookings Institution, 1983), pp. 201–240.

CASE

Why Are Exchange Rates So Volatile?

The high volatility of foreign exchange rates surprises many people. Forty or so years ago, economists generally believed that allowing exchange rates to be determined in the free market would not lead to large fluctuations in their values. Recent experience has proved them wrong. If we return to Figure 15.1, we see that exchange rates over the 1990–2016 period have been very volatile.

The asset market approach to exchange rate determination that we have outlined here gives a straightforward explanation of volatile exchange rates. Because expected appreciation of the domestic currency affects the expected return on domestic assets, expectations about the price level, inflation, trade barriers, productivity, import demand, export demand, and future monetary policy play important roles in determining the exchange rate. When expectations about any of these variables change, as they do—and often at that—our model indicates that the expected return on domestic assets, and therefore on the exchange rate, will be immediately affected. Because expectations on all these variables change with just about every bit of news that appears, it is not surprising that the exchange rate is volatile.

Because earlier models of exchange rate behavior focused on goods markets rather than asset markets, they did not emphasize changing expectations as a source of exchange rate movements, and so these earlier models could not predict substantial fluctuations in exchange rates. The failure of earlier models to explain volatility is one reason why they are no longer so popular. The more modern approach developed here emphasizes that the foreign exchange market is like any other asset market in which expectations of the future matter. The foreign exchange market, like other asset markets such as the stock market, displays substantial price volatility, and foreign exchange rates are notoriously hard to forecast.

CASE

The Dollar and Interest Rates

In the chapter preview we mentioned that the dollar rose substantially from 1980 to 1985, and declined thereafter. We can use our analysis of the foreign exchange market to understand exchange rate movements and help explain the dollar's rise in the early 1980s and its fall thereafter.

Some important information for tracing the dollar's changing value is presented in Figure 15.8, which plots measures of real and nominal interest rates and the value of the dollar in terms of a basket of foreign currencies (called an **effective exchange rate index**). We can see that the value of the dollar and the measure of real interest rates tend to rise and fall together. In the late 1970s, real interest rates were at low levels, and so was the value of the dollar. Beginning in 1980, however, real interest

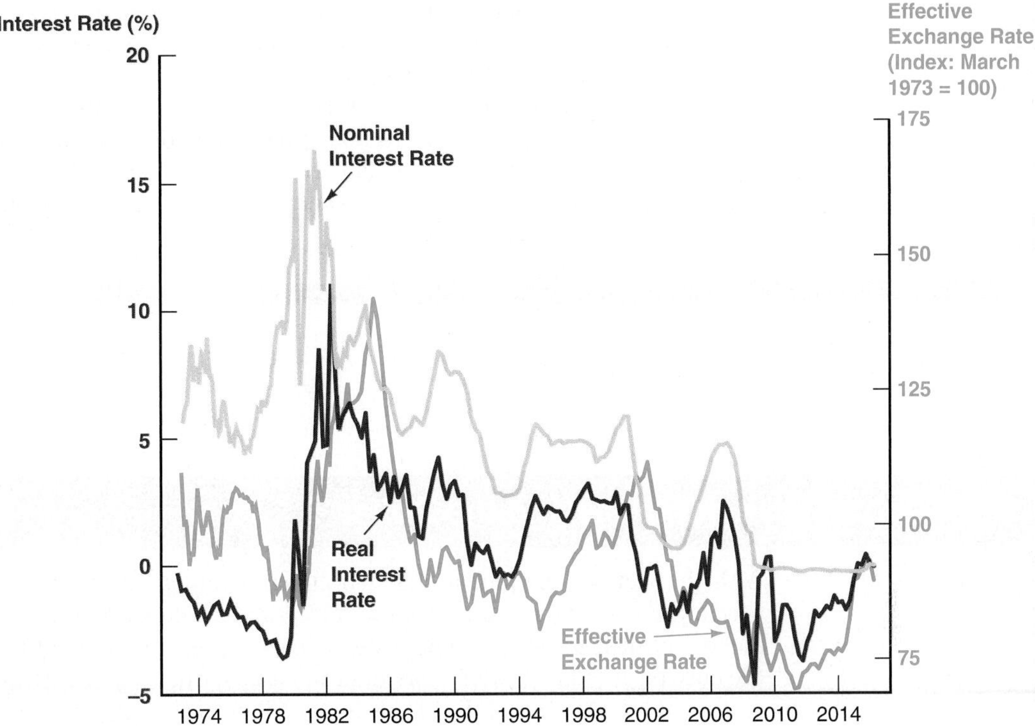

FIGURE 15.8 Value of the Dollar and Interest Rates, 1973–2016

The correspondence between nominal interest rates and exchange rate movements is not nearly as close as that between real interest rates and exchange rate movements.

Source: Federal Reserve Bank of St. Louis FRED database: https://fred.stlouisfed.org/series/TWEXMMTH; https://fred.stlouisfed.org/series/TB3MS; real interest rate from Figure 3.1 in Chapter 3.

rates in the United States began to climb sharply, and at the same time so did the dollar. After 1984, the real interest rate declined substantially, as did the dollar.

Our model of exchange rate determination helps explain the rise in the dollar in the early 1980s and its fall thereafter. As Figure 15.4 indicates, a rise in the U.S. real interest rate raises the relative expected return on dollar assets, which leads to purchases of dollar assets that raise the exchange rate. This is exactly what happened in the 1980–1984 period. The subsequent fall in U.S. real interest rates then reduced the relative expected return on dollar assets, which lowered the demand for them and thus lowered the exchange rate.

The plot of *nominal* interest rates in Figure 15.8 also demonstrates that the correspondence between nominal interest rates and exchange rate movements is not nearly as close as that between *real* interest rates and exchange rate movements. This is also exactly what our analysis predicts. The rise in nominal interest rates in the late 1970s was not reflected in a corresponding rise in the value of the dollar; indeed, the dollar actually fell in the late 1970s. Figure 15.8 explains why the rise in nominal rates in the late 1970s did not produce a rise in the dollar. As a comparison of the real and nominal interest rates in the late 1970s indicates, the rise in nominal interest rates reflected an increase in expected inflation, not an increase in real interest rates. As our analysis in Figure 15.7 demonstrates, the rise in nominal interest rates stemming from a rise in expected inflation should lead to a decline in the dollar, and that is exactly what happened.

If there is a moral to the story, it is that a failure to distinguish between real and nominal interest rates can lead to poor predictions of exchange rate movements: The weakness of the dollar in the late 1970s and the strength of the dollar in the early 1980s can be explained by movements in *real* interest rates but not by movements in *nominal* interest rates.

CASE

The Global Financial Crisis and the Dollar

With the start of the global financial crisis in August 2007, the dollar began an accelerated decline in value, falling by 9% against the euro until mid-July of 2008, and 6% against a wider basket of currencies. After hitting an all-time low against the euro on July 11, the dollar suddenly shot upward, by over 20% against the euro by the end of October and 15% against a wider basket of currencies. What is the relationship between the global financial crisis and these large swings in the value of the dollar?

During 2007 the negative effects of the global financial crisis on economic activity were mostly confined to the United States. The Federal Reserve acted aggressively to lower interest rates to counter the contractionary effects, decreasing the federal funds rate target by 325 basis points from September 2007 to April 2008. In contrast, other central banks like the ECB did not see the need to lower interest rates, particularly because high energy prices had led to a surge in inflation. The relative expected return on dollar assets thus declined, shifting the demand curve for dollar assets to the left, as in Figure 15.5, leading to a decline in the equilibrium exchange rate. Our analysis of the foreign exchange market thus explains why the early phase of the global financial crisis led to a decline in the value of the dollar.

We now turn to the rise in the value of the dollar. Starting in the summer of 2008, the effects of the global financial crisis on economic activity began to spread more widely throughout the world. Foreign central banks started to cut interest rates, with the expectation that further rate cuts would follow, as indeed did occur. The expected decline in foreign interest rates then increased the relative expected return of dollar assets, leading to a rightward shift in the demand curve, and a rise in the value of the dollar, as shown in Figure 15.4. Another factor driving the dollar upward was the "flight to quality" when the global financial crisis reached a particularly virulent stage in September and October of 2008. Both Americans and foreigners now wanted to put their money in the safest assets possible: U.S. Treasury securities. The resulting increase in the demand for dollar assets provided an additional reason for the demand curve for dollar assets to shift out to the right, thereby helping to produce a sharp appreciation of the dollar.

THE PRACTICING MANAGER

Profiting from Foreign Exchange Forecasts

Managers of financial institutions care a great deal about what foreign exchange rates will be in the future because these rates affect the value of assets on their balance sheet that are denominated in foreign currencies. In addition, financial institutions often engage in trading foreign exchange, both for their own account and for their customers. Forecasts of foreign exchange rates can thus have a big impact on the profits that financial institutions make on their foreign exchange trading operations.

Managers of financial institutions obtain foreign exchange forecasts either by hiring their own staff economists to generate them or by purchasing forecasts from other financial institutions or economic forecasting firms. In predicting exchange rate movements, forecasters look at the factors mentioned in this chapter. For example, if they expect domestic real interest rates to rise, they will predict, in line with our analysis, that the domestic currency will appreciate; conversely, if they expect domestic inflation to increase, they will predict that the domestic currency will depreciate.

Managers of financial institutions, particularly those engaged in international banking, rely on foreign exchange forecasts to make decisions about which assets denominated in foreign currencies they should hold. For example, if a financial institution manager has a reliable forecast that the euro will appreciate in the future but the yen will depreciate, the manager will want to sell off assets denominated in yen and instead purchase assets denominated in euros. Alternatively, the manager might instruct loan officers to make more loans denominated in euros and fewer loans denominated in yen. Likewise, if the yen is forecast to appreciate and the euro to depreciate, the manager would want to switch out of euro-denominated assets into yen-denominated assets and would want to make more loans in yen and fewer in euros.

If the financial institution has a foreign exchange trading operation, a forecast of an appreciation of the yen means that the financial institution manager should tell foreign exchange traders to buy yen. If the forecast turns out to be correct, the higher value of the yen means that the trader can sell the yen in the future and pocket a tidy profit. If the euro is forecast to depreciate, the trader can sell euros and buy them back in the future at a lower price if the forecast turns out to be correct, and again the financial institution will make a profit.

Accurate foreign exchange rate forecasts can thus help a financial institution manager generate substantial profits for the institution. Unfortunately, exchange rate forecasters are no more or less accurate than other economic forecasters, and they often make large errors. Reports on foreign exchange rate forecasts and how well forecasters are doing appear from time to time in the *Wall Street Journal* and in the trade magazine *Euromoney*.

SUMMARY

1. Foreign exchange rates (the price of one country's currency in terms of another's) are important because they affect the price of domestically produced goods sold abroad and the cost of foreign goods bought domestically.
2. The theory of purchasing power parity suggests that long-run changes in the exchange rate between the currencies of two countries are determined by changes in the relative price levels in the two countries. Other factors that affect exchange rates in the long run are tariffs and quotas, import demand, export demand, and productivity.
3. In the short run, exchange rates are determined by changes in the relative expected return on domestic assets, which cause the demand curve to shift. Any factor that changes the relative expected return on domestic assets will lead to changes in the exchange rate. Such factors include changes in the interest rates on domestic and foreign assets as well as changes in any of the factors that affect the long-run exchange rate and hence the expected future exchange rate.
4. The asset market approach to exchange rate determination can explain both the volatility of exchange rates and the rise of the dollar in the 1980–1984 period and its subsequent fall in value, as well as changes in the value of the dollar during the global financial crisis.
5. Forecasts of foreign exchange rates are very valuable to managers of financial institutions because these rates influence decisions about which assets denominated in foreign currencies the institutions should hold and what kinds of trades should be made by their traders in the foreign exchange market.

KEY TERMS

QUESTIONS

1. Suppose that you are considering going on vacation abroad and that the euro has appreciated by 15% with respect to the U.S. dollar. Would you be more or less willing to visit Rome and Paris?
2. "A country is always worse off when its currency is weak (falls in value)." Is this statement true, false, or uncertain? Explain your answer.
3. When the U.S. dollar depreciates, what happens to exports and imports in the United States?
4. If the Japanese price level rises by 5% relative to the price level in the United States, what does the theory of purchasing power parity predict will happen to the value of the Japanese yen in terms of dollars?
5. If the demand for a country's exports falls at the same time that tariffs on imports are raised, will the country's currency tend to appreciate or depreciate in the long run?
6. In the mid to late 1970s, the yen appreciated relative to the dollar even though Japan's inflation rate was higher than America's. How can this be explained by an improvement in the productivity of Japanese industry relative to American industry?

Predicting the Future

Answer the remaining questions by drawing the appropriate exchange market diagrams.

7. The president of the United States announces that he will reduce inflation with a new anti-inflation program. If the public believes him, predict what will happen to the exchange rate for the U.S. dollar.
8. If the British central bank prints money to reduce unemployment, what will happen to the value of the pound in the short run and the long run?
9. If the Indian government unexpectedly announces that it will be imposing higher tariffs on foreign goods one year from now, what will happen to the value of the Indian rupee today?

10. Investors around the world decide to buy T-Bills, since no other instrument is safe to hold anymore. Predict what will happen to the U.S. exchange rate.

11. If American auto companies make a breakthrough in automobile technology and are able to produce a car that gets 60 miles to the gallon, what will happen to the U.S. exchange rate?

12. If Mexicans go on a spending spree and buy twice as much French perfume, Japanese TVs, English sweaters, Swiss watches, and Italian wine, what will happen to the value of the Mexican peso?

13. If expected inflation drops in Europe so that interest rates fall there, predict what will happen to the exchange rate for the U.S. dollar.

14. If the European central bank decides to raise interest rates to fight inflation, what will happen to the value of the U.S. dollar?

15. On June 23, 2016, the United Kingdom voted on whether to remain or leave the European Union. From June 16 to June 23 the exchange rate between the British pound and the dollar increased from 1.4075 US/GBP to 1.4800 US/GBP (Source: FRED database). What can you say about the market expectations regarding the result of the referendum and its impact on the UK economy?

QUANTITATIVE PROBLEMS

1. Calculate the appreciation of the U.S. dollar and the depreciation of the Japanese yen if the exchange rate between the U.S. dollar and the Japanese yen went from 110 ¥/US to 120 ¥/US.

2. An investor in England purchased a 91-day T-bill for $987.65. At that time, the exchange rate was $1.75 per pound. At maturity, the exchange rate was $1.83 per pound. What was the investor's holding period return in pounds?

3. An investor in Canada purchased 100 shares of IBM on January 1 at $93.00 per share. IBM paid an annual dividend of $0.72 on December 31. The stock was sold that day as well for $100.25. The exchange rate was $0.68 per Canadian dollar on January 1 and $0.71 per Canadian dollar on December 31. What is the investor's total return in Canadian dollars?

4. The current exchange rate is 0.75 euro per dollar, but you believe the dollar will decline to 0.67 euro per dollar. If a euro-denominated bond is yielding 2%, what return do you expect in U.S. dollars?

5. The six-month forward rate between the British pound and the U.S. dollar is $1.75 per pound. If six-month interest rates are 3% in the United States and 150 basis points higher in England, what is the current exchange rate?

6. If the Canadian dollar to U.S. dollar exchange rate is 1.28 and the British pound to U.S. dollar exchange rate is 0.62, what must the Canadian dollar to British pound exchange rate be?

7. The New Zealand dollar to U.S. dollar exchange rate is 1.36, and the British pound to U.S. dollar exchange rate is 0.62. If you found that the British pound to New Zealand dollar were trading at 0.49, what would you do to earn a riskless profit?

8. A rare French cheese sells for 60.00 euros per pound. Assuming a very similar cheese in Wisconsin sells for $55.00 per pound, what is the exchange rate between the euro and the U.S. dollar according to the law of one price?

9. The Argentinian peso trades at 0.067 peso per U.S. dollar. How many Argentinian pesos would you tip a taxi driver if you give her a $5 bill?

10. The annual inflation rate in Venezuela was 200% during 2015. For the same year, the U.S. annual inflation rate was 1%. If the Venezuelan bolivar traded at 0.10 U.S. dollar in 2015, what was the expected exchange rate between these two currencies for 2016?

11. The current exchange rate between the United States and Britain is $1.825 per pound. The six-month forward rate between the British pound and the U.S. dollar is $1.79 per pound. What is the percentage difference between current six-month U.S. and British interest rates?

12. Suppose that a Big Mac sells for 40.90 Norwegian kroners in Oslo and that the exchange rate is 8.18 kroners per U.S. dollar. If a Big Mac sells for $4.35 in New York, can you say that the law of one price holds?

13. If the price level recently increased by 20% in England while falling by 5% in the United States, how much must the exchange rate change if PPP holds? Assume that the current exchange rate is 0.55 pound per dollar.

14. A one-year CD in Europe is currently paying 5%, and the exchange rate is currently 0.99 euro per dollar. If you believe the exchange rate will be 1.04 euros per dollar one year from now, what is the expected return in terms of dollars?

15. Short-term interest rates are 2% in Japan and 4% in the United States. The current exchange rate is 120 yen per dollar. What is the expected forward exchange rate?

16. Short-term interest rates are 2% in Japan and 4% in the United States. The current exchange rate is 120 yen per dollar. If you can enter into a forward exchange rate of 115 yen per dollar, how can you arbitrage the situation?

17. The interest rate in the United States is 4%, and the euro is trading at 1 euro per dollar. The euro is expected to depreciate to 1.1 euros per dollar. Calculate the interest rate in Germany.

WEB EXERCISES

The Foreign Exchange Market

1. The Federal Reserve maintains a Web site that lists the exchange rates between the U.S. dollar and many other currencies. Go to **http://www.newyorkfed.org/markets/foreignex.html**. Go to the historical data from 2000 and later and find the euro.
   - **a.** What has the percentage change in the euro–dollar exchange rate been between the euro's introduction and now?
   - **b.** What has been the annual percentage change in the euro–dollar exchange rate for each year since the euro's introduction?

2. International travelers and business people frequently need to accurately convert from one currency to another. It is often easy to find the rate needed to convert the U.S. dollar into another currency. It can be more difficult to find exchange rates between two non-U.S. currencies. Go to **www.oanda.com/convert/classic**. This site lets you convert from any currency into any other currency. How many Lithuanian litas can you currently buy with one Chilean peso?

APPENDIX TO CHAPTER 15

The Interest Parity Condition

All the results in the text can be derived with a concept that is widely used in international finance. The **interest parity condition** shows the relationship between domestic interest rates, foreign interest rates, and the expected appreciation of the domestic currency. To derive this condition, we examine how expected returns on domestic and foreign assets are compared.

Comparing Expected Returns on Domestic and Foreign Assets

As in the chapter, we treat the United States as the home country, so domestic assets are denominated in dollars. For simplicity, we use euros to stand for any foreign country's currency, so foreign assets are denominated in euros. To illustrate further, suppose that dollar assets pay an interest rate of i^D and do not have any possible capital gains, so that they have an expected return payable in dollars of i^D. Similarly, foreign assets have an interest rate of i^F and an expected return payable in the foreign currency, euros, of i^F. To compare the expected returns on dollar assets and foreign assets, investors must convert the returns into the currency unit they use.

First let us examine how François the foreigner compares the returns on dollar assets and foreign assets denominated in his currency, the euro. When he considers the expected return on dollar assets in terms of euros, he recognizes that it does not equal i^D; instead, the expected return must be adjusted for any expected appreciation or depreciation of the dollar. If François expects the dollar to appreciate by 3%, for example, the expected return on dollar assets in terms of euros would be 3% higher than i^D because the dollar is expected to become worth 3% more in terms of euros. Thus, if the interest rate on dollar assets is 4%, with an expected 3% appreciation of the dollar, the expected return on dollar assets in terms of euros is 7%: the 4% interest rate plus the 3% expected appreciation of the dollar. Conversely, if the dollar were expected to depreciate by 3% over the year, the expected return on dollar assets in terms of euros would be only 1%: the 4% interest rate minus the 3% expected depreciation of the dollar.

Writing the current exchange rate (the spot exchange rate) as E_t and the expected exchange rate for the next period as E^e_{t+1}, the expected rate of appreciation of the dollar is $(E^e_{t+1} - E_t)/E_t$. Our reasoning indicates that the expected return on dollar assets R^D in terms of foreign currency can be written as the sum of the interest rate on dollar assets plus the expected appreciation of the dollar.[1]

$$R^D \text{ in terms of euros} = i^D + \frac{E^e_{t+1} - E_t}{E_t}$$

However, François's expected return on foreign assets R^F in terms of euros is just i^F. Thus, in terms of euros, the relative expected return on dollar assets (that is, the difference between the expected return on dollar assets and euro assets) is calculated by subtracting i^F from the expression above to yield

$$\text{Relative } R^D = i^D - i^F + \frac{E^e_{t+1} - E_t}{E_t} \tag{A1}$$

As the relative expected return on dollar assets increases, foreigners will want to hold more dollar assets and fewer foreign assets.

Next let us look at the decision to hold dollar assets versus euro assets from Al, the American's point of view. Following the same reasoning we used to evaluate the decision for François, we know that the expected return on foreign assets R^F in terms of dollars is the interest rate on foreign assets i^F plus the expected

---

[1] This expression is actually an approximation of the expected return in terms of euros, which can be more precisely calculated by thinking how a foreigner invests in dollar assets. Suppose that François decides to put one euro into dollar assets. First he buys $1/E_t$ of U.S. dollar assets (recall that E_t, the exchange rate between dollar and euro assets, is quoted in euros per dollar), and at the end of the period he is paid $(1 + i^D)(1/E_t)$ in dollars. To convert this amount into the number of euros he expects to receive at the end of the period, he multiplies this quantity by E^e_{t+1}. François's expected return on his initial investment of one euro can thus be written as $(1 + i^D)(E^e_{t+1}/E_t)$ minus his initial investment of one euro:

$$(1 + i^D)\left(\frac{E^e_{t+1}}{E_t}\right) - 1$$

This expression can be rewritten as

$$i^D\left(\frac{E^e_{t+1}}{E_t}\right) + \frac{E^e_{t+1} - E_t}{E_t},$$

which is approximately equal to the expression in the text because E^e_{t+1}/E_t is typically close to 1. To see this, consider our example in which $i^D = 0.04$; $(E^e_{t+1} - E_t)/E_t = 0.03$, so $E^e_{t+1}/E_t = 1.03$. Then François's expected return on dollar assets is $0.04 \times 1.03 + 0.03 = 0.0712 = 7.12\%$, rather than the 7% reported in the text.

appreciation of the foreign currency, equal to minus the expected appreciation of the dollar, $-(E^e_{t+1} - E_t)/E_t$.

$$R^F \text{ in terms of dollars } = i^F - \frac{E^e_{t+1} - E_t}{E_t}$$

If the interest rate on euro assets is 5%, for example, and the dollar is expected to appreciate by 3%, then the expected return on euro assets in terms of dollars is 2%. Amy earns the 5% interest rate, but she expects to lose 3% because she expects the euro to be worth 3% less in terms of dollars as a result of the dollar's appreciation.

Amy's expected return on the dollar assets R^D in terms of dollars is just i^D. Hence, in terms of dollars, the relative expected return on dollar assets is calculated by subtracting the expression just given from i^D to obtain

$$\text{Relative } R^D = i^D - \left(i^F - \frac{E^e_{t+1} - E_t}{E_t}\right) = i^D - i^F + \frac{E^e_{t+1} - E_t}{E_t}$$

This equation is the same as Equation A1 describing François's relative expected return on dollar assets (calculated in terms of euros). The key point here is that the relative expected return on dollar assets is the same—whether it is calculated by François in terms of euros or by Equation Al in terms of dollars. Thus, as the relative expected return on dollar assets increases, both foreigners and domestic residents respond in exactly the same way—both will want to hold more dollar assets and fewer foreign assets.

Interest Parity Condition

We currently live in a world in which there is **capital mobility**: Foreigners can easily purchase American assets, and Americans can easily purchase foreign assets. If there are few impediments to capital mobility and we are looking at assets that have similar risk and liquidity—say, foreign and American bank deposits—then it is reasonable to assume that the assets are perfect substitutes (that is, equally desirable). When capital is mobile and when assets are perfect substitutes, if the expected return on dollar assets is above that on foreign assets, both foreigners and Americans will want to hold only dollar assets and will be unwilling to hold foreign assets. Conversely, if the expected return on foreign assets is higher than on dollar assets, both foreigners and Americans will not want to hold any dollar assets and will want to hold only foreign assets. For existing supplies of both dollar assets and foreign assets to be held, it must therefore be true that there is no difference in their expected returns; that is, the relative expected return in Equation A1 must equal zero. This condition can be rewritten as

$$i^D = i^F - \frac{E^e_{t+1} - E_t}{E_t} \tag{A2}$$

This equation, which is called the interest parity condition, states that the domestic interest rate equals the foreign interest rate minus the expected appreciation of the domestic currency. Equivalently, this condition can be stated in a more intuitive way: The domestic interest rate equals the foreign interest rate plus the expected appreciation of the foreign currency. If the domestic interest rate is higher than the foreign interest rate, there is a positive expected appreciation of the foreign currency, which compensates for the lower foreign interest rate.

EXAMPLE A15.1

Interest Parity Condition

If interest rates in the United States and Japan are 6% and 3%, respectively, what is the expected rate of appreciation of the foreign (Japanese) currency?

> Solution

The expected appreciation of the foreign currency is 3%.

$$i^D = i^F - \frac{E^e_{t+1} - E_t}{E_t}$$

where

i^D = interest rate on dollars = 6%

i^F = interest rate on foreign currency = 3%

Thus,

$$6\% = 3\% - \frac{E^e_{t+1} - E_t}{E_t}$$

$$-\frac{E^e_{t+1} - E_t}{E_t} = \text{rate of appreciation of the foreign currency}$$

$$= 6\% - 3\% = 3\%$$

There are several ways to look at the interest parity condition. First, recognize that interest parity means simply that the expected returns are the same on both dollar assets and foreign assets. To see this, note that the left side of the interest parity condition (Equation A2) is the expected return on dollar assets, while the right side is the expected return on foreign assets, both calculated in terms of a single currency, the U.S. dollar. Given our assumption that domestic and foreign assets are perfect substitutes (equally desirable), the interest parity condition is an equilibrium condition for the foreign exchange market. Only when the exchange rate is such that expected returns on domestic and foreign assets are equal—that is, when interest parity holds—will investors be willing to hold both domestic and foreign assets.

With some algebraic manipulation, we can rewrite the interest parity condition in Equation A2 as

$$E_t = \frac{E^e_{t+1}}{i^F - i^D + 1}$$

This equation produces exactly the same results that we find in the supply-and-demand analysis in the text: If i^D rises, the denominator falls and so E_t rises. If i^F rises, the denominator rises and so E_t falls. If E^e_{t+1} rises, the numerator rises and so E_t rises.

CHAPTER 16

The International Financial System

> PREVIEW

Thanks to the growing interdependence between the U.S. economy and the economies of the rest of the world, the international financial system now plays a more prominent role in economic events in the United States. In this chapter we see how fixed and managed exchange rate systems work and how they can provide substantial profit opportunities for financial institutions. We also look at the controversies over what role capital controls and the International Monetary Fund should play in the international financial system.

Intervention in the Foreign Exchange Market

In Chapter 15 we analyzed the foreign exchange market as if it were a completely free market that responds to all market pressures. Like many other markets, however, the foreign exchange market is not free of government intervention; central banks regularly engage in international financial transactions called **foreign exchange interventions** to influence exchange rates. In our current international environment, exchange rates fluctuate from day to day, but central banks attempt to influence their countries' exchange rates by buying and selling currencies. We can use the exchange rate analysis we developed in Chapter 15 to explain the effect of central bank intervention on the foreign exchange market.

Foreign Exchange Intervention and Reserves in the Banking System

The first step in understanding how central bank intervention in the foreign exchange market affects exchange rates is to see the effect on reserves in the banking system from a central bank sale in the foreign exchange market of some of its holdings of assets denominated in a foreign currency. These holdings of assets denominated in foreign currency are called **international reserves**, which are different from the *reserves* in the banking system, the deposits banks keep in their local Federal Reserve banks. Suppose that the Fed decides to sell $1 billion of its foreign assets, which it always does by selling them to the banks. (This transaction is conducted at the foreign exchange desk at the Federal Reserve Bank of New York—see the Inside the Fed box.)

The Fed's sale of international reserves has two effects. First, it reduces the Fed's holding of international reserves by $1 billion. Second, when the Fed sells its international reserves to banks, it subtracts the amount of their $1 billion purchase from their reserve deposits held at the Fed. In other words, the sale of international reserves is, in effect, a purchase of dollars held by banks in their reserve accounts and is thus usually referred to as purchase of dollars. This transaction is shown in the following T-account for the Federal Reserve:

Federal Reserve System			
Assets		**Liabilities**	
Foreign assets (international reserves)	–$1 billion	Reserves (bank deposits with the Fed)	–$1 billion

We have thus reached an important conclusion: ***A Fed purchase of dollars and corresponding sale of foreign assets in the foreign exchange market leads to an equal decline in its international reserves and in reserves (banks' deposits at the Fed).*** We could have reached the same conclusion by a more direct route. A central bank sale of a foreign asset is no different from an open market sale of a government bond. We learned in our exploration of monetary policy in Chapter 10 that an open market sale leads to an equal decline in reserves, and this is also true for a central bank sale of its foreign assets.

By similar reasoning, a central bank purchase of foreign assets paid for by selling domestic currency, like an open market purchase, leads to an equal rise in reserves. Thus, we reach the following conclusion: ***A central bank's sale of domestic currency to purchase foreign assets in the foreign exchange***

INSIDE THE FED

A Day at the Federal Reserve Bank of New York's Foreign Exchange Desk

Although the U.S. Treasury is primarily responsible for foreign exchange policy, decisions to intervene in the foreign exchange market are made jointly by the U.S. Treasury and the Federal Reserve's FOMC (Federal Open Market Committee). The actual conduct of foreign exchange intervention is the responsibility of the foreign exchange desk at the Federal Reserve Bank of New York, which is right next to the open market desk.

The manager of foreign exchange operations at the New York Fed supervises the traders and analysts who follow developments in the foreign exchange market. Every morning at 7:30, a trader on staff who has arrived at the New York Fed in the predawn hours speaks on the telephone with counterparts at the U.S. Treasury and provides an update on overnight activity in overseas financial and foreign exchange markets. Later in the morning, at 9:30, the manager and his or her staff hold a conference call with senior staff at the Board of Governors of the Federal Reserve in Washington. In the afternoon, at 2:30, they have a second conference call, which is a joint briefing of officials at the board and the Treasury. Although by statute the Treasury has the lead role in setting foreign exchange policy, it strives to reach a consensus among all three parties—the Treasury, the Board of Governors, and the Federal Reserve Bank of New York. If they decide that a foreign exchange intervention is necessary that day—an unusual occurrence, as a year may go by without a U.S. foreign exchange intervention—the manager instructs his traders to carry out the agreed-on purchase or sale of foreign currencies. Because funds for exchange rate intervention are held separately by the Treasury (in its Exchange Stabilization Fund) and the Federal Reserve, the manager and his or her staff are not trading the funds of the Federal Reserve Bank of New York; rather, they act as an agent for the Treasury and the FOMC in conducting these transactions.

As part of their duties, before every FOMC meeting, the staff helps prepare a lengthy document full of data for the FOMC members, other Reserve bank presidents, and Treasury officials. It describes developments in the domestic and foreign markets over the previous five or six weeks, a task that keeps them especially busy right before the FOMC meeting.

market results in an equal rise in its international reserves and reserves in the banking system.

The intervention we have just described, in which a central bank allows the purchase or sale of domestic currency to have an effect on reserves, is called an **unsterilized foreign exchange intervention**. But what if the central bank does not want the purchase or sale of domestic currency to affect reserves? All it has to do is to counter the effect of the foreign exchange intervention by conducting an offsetting open market operation in the government bond market. For example, in the case of a $1 billion purchase of dollars by the Fed and a corresponding $1 billion sale of foreign assets, which, as we have seen, would decrease reserves by $1 billion, the Fed can conduct an open market purchase of $1 billion of government bonds, which would increase reserves by $1 billion. The resulting T-account for the foreign exchange intervention and the offsetting open market operation leaves reserves in the banking system unchanged:

Federal Reserve System			
Assets		**Liabilities**	
Foreign assets (international reserves)	–$1 billion	Reserves	0
Government bonds	+$1 billion		

A foreign exchange intervention with an offsetting open market operation that leaves reserves unchanged is called a **sterilized foreign exchange intervention**.

Now that we understand that there are two types of foreign exchange interventions—unsterilized and sterilized—let's look at how each affects the exchange rate.

Unsterilized Intervention

Intuition might lead you to suspect that if a central bank wants to raise the value of the domestic currency, it should buy its currency in the foreign exchange market and sell foreign assets. Indeed, this intuition is correct for the case of an unsterilized intervention.

Recall that in an unsterilized intervention, if the Federal Reserve decides to buy dollars and therefore sells foreign assets in exchange for dollar assets, this works just like an open market sale of bonds to decrease reserves. Hence the purchase of dollars leads to a decrease in reserves and hence a decrease in liquidity in the banking system, which as we saw in Chapter 10 raises the domestic interest rate. We thus find ourselves analyzing a similar situation to that described in Figure 15.4 in Chapter 15, which is reproduced here as Figure 16.1.[1] The decrease in reserves and liquidity in the banking system causes the interest rate on dollar assets to rise and so increases the relative expected return on dollar assets. The demand curve shifts to the right from D_1 to D_2, and the exchange rate rises to E_2.

Our analysis leads us to the following conclusion about unsterilized interventions in the foreign exchange market: ***An unsterilized intervention in which domestic currency is bought and foreign assets are sold leads to a fall in international reserves, a fall in reserves, a rise in domestic interest rates, and an appreciation of the domestic currency.***

The reverse result is found for an unsterilized intervention in which domestic currency is sold and foreign assets are purchased. The sale of domestic currency and purchase of foreign assets (increasing international reserves) works like an open market purchase to increase reserves. The increase in reserves and liquidity in the banking system lowers the interest rate on dollar assets. The resulting decrease in the relative expected return on dollar assets means that people will buy fewer dollar assets, so the demand curve shifts to the left and the exchange rate falls. ***An unsterilized intervention in which domestic currency is sold and foreign assets are purchased leads to a rise in international reserves, a rise in reserves, a fall in domestic interest rates, and a depreciation of the domestic currency.***

Sterilized Intervention

The key point to remember about a sterilized intervention is that the central bank engages in offsetting open market operations, so that there is no impact on reserves.

---

[1]An unsterilized intervention, in which the Fed buys dollars, decreases the amount of dollar assets slightly because it leads to a decrease in banks' deposits at the Fed while leaving the amount of government bonds in the hands of the public unchanged. The curve depicting the supply of dollar assets would thus shift to the left slightly, which also works toward raising the exchange rate, yielding the same conclusion derived from Figure 16.1. Because the resulting fall in reserves is only a minuscule fraction of the total amount of dollar assets outstanding, the supply curve would shift by an imperceptible amount. This is why Figure 16.1 is drawn with the supply curve unchanged.

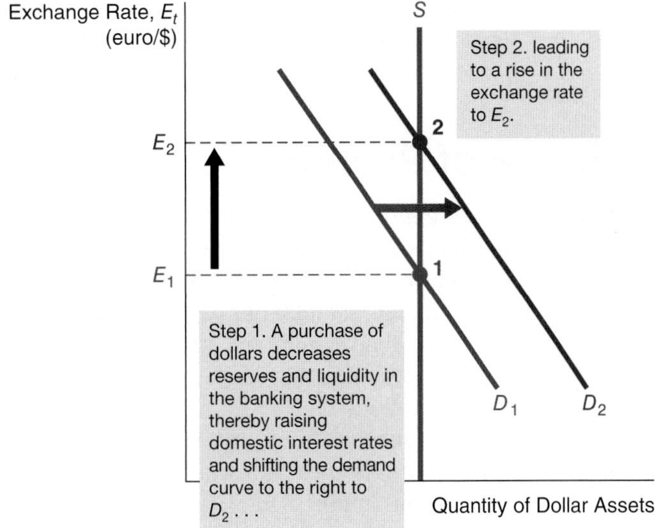
Exchange Rate, E_t (euro/$)
S
Step 2. leading to a rise in the exchange rate to E_2.
2
E_2
E_1
1
Step 1. A purchase of dollars decreases reserves and liquidity in the banking system, thereby raising domestic interest rates and shifting the demand curve to the right to D_2 . . .
D_1
D_2
Quantity of Dollar Assets

FIGURE 16.1 Effect of an Unsterilized Purchase of Dollars and Sale of Foreign Assets

A purchase of dollars and the consequent open market sale of foreign assets decreases reserves in the banking system. The resulting rise in domestic interest rates raises the relative expected return on dollar assets. The demand curve shifts to the right, from D_1 to D_2, and the equilibrium exchange rate rises from E_1 to E_2.

In the context of the model of exchange rate determination we have developed here, it is straightforward to show that a sterilized intervention has almost *no effect* on the exchange rate. A sterilized intervention leaves reserves unchanged and thus has no direct way of affecting interest rates.[2] Because the relative expected return on dollar assets is unaffected, the demand curve would remain at D_1 in Figure 16.1, and the exchange rate would remain unchanged at E_1.

At first it might seem puzzling that a central bank purchase or sale of domestic currency that is sterilized does not lead to a change in the exchange rate. A central bank purchase of domestic currency cannot raise the exchange rate because with no effect on reserves in the banking system or interest rates, any resulting rise in the exchange rate would mean that an excess supply of dollar assets would arise.

---

[2]A sterilized intervention changes the amount of foreign securities relative to domestic securities in the hands of the public, called a *portfolio balance effect*. Through this effect, the central bank might be able to affect the interest differential between domestic and foreign assets, which in turn affects the relative expected return of domestic assets. Empirical evidence has not revealed this portfolio balance effect to be significant. However, a sterilized intervention *could* indicate what central banks want to happen to the future exchange rate and so might provide a signal about the course of future monetary policy. In this way a sterilized intervention could lead to shifts in the demand curve for domestic assets and ultimately affect the exchange rate. However, the future change in monetary policy—not the sterilized intervention—is the source of the exchange rate effect. For a further discussion of the signaling and portfolio balance effects and the possible differential effects of sterilized versus unsterilized intervention, see Paul Krugman and Maurice Obstfeld, *International Economics*, 9th ed. (Boston: Addison-Wesley, 2012).

With more people willing to sell dollar assets than to buy them, the exchange rate would have to fall back to its initial equilibrium level, where the demand and supply curves intersect.

Balance of Payments

Because international financial transactions such as foreign exchange interventions have considerable effects on monetary policy, it is worth knowing how these transactions are measured. The **balance of payments** is a bookkeeping system for recording all receipts and payments that have a direct bearing on the movement of funds between a nation (private sector and government) and foreign countries. Here we examine the key items in the balance of payments that you often hear about in the media.

GO ONLINE
Access **http://research.stlouisfed.org/fred2**. This Web site contains exchange rates, balance of payments, and trade data.

The **current account** shows international transactions that involve current flows of funds into and out of a country. The difference between merchandise exports and imports, the net receipts from trade, is called the **trade balance**, but more accurately is referred to as the **merchandise trade balance**. When merchandise imports are greater than exports (by $762 billion in 2015), we have a trade deficit; if exports are greater than imports, we have a trade surplus. Since a country produces not only goods but also services, a more accurate view of what is happening to a country's international trade would include the balance on services as well as on goods. This balance of trade in both goods and services is referred to as **net exports**. Because the United States exports more services than it imports (by $262 billion), net exports has a deficit of $500 billion versus a merchandise trade deficit of $762 billion. Additional items included in the current account are the net receipts (cash flows received from abroad minus cash flows sent abroad) from investment income and transfers. In 2015, for example, net investment income was $182 billion for the United States because Americans received more investment income from abroad than they paid out. Transfers are funds sent by domestic residents and the government to foreigners and include remittances of domestic workers to foreigners (usually relatives), pensions, and foreign aid. Because Americans made more transfers to foreigners than foreigners made to the United States, net transfers were negative $145 billion. The sum of these two items plus the merchandise trade balance and the balance on services is the current account balance, which in 2015 showed a deficit of −$463 billion (−$762 + $262 + $182 − $145).

The current account balance is an important number because it tells us whether the United States (private sector and government combined) is increasing or decreasing its claims on foreign wealth. A surplus indicates that America has positive net receipts on a current basis and thus is increasing its claims on foreign wealth by holding more foreign assets (a good thing for Americans). A current account deficit (as in 2015) indicates that the United States has negative net receipts on a current basis and must finance them by borrowing abroad, thus reducing its claims on foreign wealth by increasing foreigners' claims on the United States.[3] The large

[3]The current account balance can also be viewed as showing the amount by which total saving exceeds private sector and government investment in the United States. Total U.S. saving equals the increase in total wealth held by the U.S. private sector and government. Total investment equals the increase in the U.S. capital stock (wealth physically in the United States). The difference between them is the increase in U.S. claims on foreign wealth.

> GLOBAL

Why the Large U.S. Current Account Deficit Worries Economists

The large U.S. current account deficits in recent years—in 2015 it was $463 billion, 2.6% of GDP—worries economists for several reasons. First, it indicates that at current exchange rate values, foreigners' demand for U.S. exports is far less than Americans' demand for imports. As we saw in the previous chapter, low demand for U.S. exports and high U.S. demand for imports may lead to a future decline in the value of the U.S. dollar.

Second, the current account deficit means that foreigners' claims on U.S. assets are growing, and these claims will have to be paid back at some point. Americans are mortgaging their future to foreigners; when the bill comes due, Americans will be poorer. Furthermore, if Americans have a greater preference for dollar assets than foreigners do, the movement of American wealth to foreigners could decrease the demand for dollar assets over time, also causing the dollar to depreciate.

The hope is that the eventual decline in the dollar resulting from the large U.S. current account deficits will be a gradual one, occurring over a period of several years. If the decline is precipitous, however, it could disrupt financial markets and hurt the U.S. economy.

U.S. current account deficit in recent years, which is now over $400 billion, has raised serious concerns that these large deficits may have negative consequences for the U.S. economy (see the Global box, "Why the Large U.S. Current Account Deficit Worries Economists").

Exchange Rate Regimes in the International Financial System

Exchange rate regimes in the international financial system are classified into two basic types: fixed and floating. In a **fixed exchange rate regime**, the value of a currency is pegged relative to the value of another currency (called the **anchor currency**) so that the exchange rate is fixed in terms of the anchor currency. In a **floating exchange rate regime**, the value of a currency is allowed to fluctuate against all other currencies. When countries intervene in foreign exchange markets in an attempt to influence their exchange rates by buying and selling foreign assets, the regime is referred to as a **managed float regime** (or a **dirty float**).

Fixed Exchange Rate Regimes

After World War II, the victors set up a fixed exchange rate system that became known as the **Bretton Woods system**, after the New Hampshire town in which the agreement was negotiated in 1944. The Bretton Woods system remained in effect until 1971.

The Bretton Woods agreement created the **International Monetary Fund (IMF)**, headquartered in Washington, D.C., which had 30 original member countries in 1945 and currently has over 185. The IMF was given the task of promoting the growth of world trade by setting rules for the maintenance of fixed exchange rates and by making loans to countries that were experiencing balance-of-payments difficulties. As part of its role of monitoring the compliance of member countries with its rules, the IMF also took on the job of collecting and standardizing international economic data.

The Bretton Woods agreement also set up the International Bank for Reconstruction and Development, commonly referred to as the **World Bank**. Headquartered in Washington, D.C., it provides long-term loans to help developing countries build dams, roads, and other physical capital that would contribute to their economic development. The funds for these loans are obtained primarily by issuing World Bank bonds, which are sold in the capital markets of the developed countries. In addition, the General Agreement on Tariffs and Trade (GATT), headquartered in Geneva, Switzerland, was set up to monitor rules for the conduct of trade between countries (tariffs and quotas). The GATT has since evolved into the **World Trade Organization (WTO)**.

Because the United States emerged from World War II as the world's largest economic power, with over half of the world's manufacturing capacity and the greater part of the world's gold, the Bretton Woods system of fixed exchange rates was based on the convertibility of U.S. dollars into gold (for foreign governments and central banks only) at $35 per ounce. The fixed exchange rates were to be maintained by intervention in the foreign exchange market by central banks in countries besides the United States that bought and sold dollar assets, which they held as international reserves. The U.S. dollar, which was used by other countries to denominate the assets that they held as international reserves, was called the **reserve currency**. Thus, an important feature of the Bretton Woods system was the establishment of the United States as the reserve currency country. Even after the breakup of the Bretton Woods system, the U.S. dollar has kept its position as the reserve currency in which most international financial transactions are conducted.

The fixed exchange rate, which was a feature of the Bretton Woods system, was finally abandoned in 1973. From 1979 to 1990, however, the European Union instituted among its members its own fixed exchange rate system, the European Monetary System (EMS). In the *exchange rate mechanism (ERM)* in this system, the exchange rate between any pair of currencies of the participating countries was not supposed to fluctuate outside narrow limits, called the "snake." In practice, all of the countries in the EMS pegged their currencies to the German mark.

How a Fixed Exchange Rate Regime Works

Figure 16.2 shows how a fixed exchange rate regime works in practice by using the supply-and-demand analysis of the foreign exchange market we learned in the previous chapter. Panel (a) describes a situation in which the domestic currency is fixed relative to an anchor currency at E_{par}, while the demand curve has shifted left to D_1, perhaps because foreign interest rates have risen, thereby lowering the relative expected return of domestic assets. At E_{par} the exchange rate is now *overvalued*: The demand curve D_1 intersects the supply curve at exchange rate E_1, which is lower than the fixed (par) value of the exchange rate E_{par}. To keep the exchange rate at E_{par}, the central bank must intervene in the foreign exchange market to purchase domestic currency by selling foreign assets. This action, like an open market sale, means that reserves and liquidity in the banking system decline, driving up the interest rate on domestic assets, i^D.[4] This increase in the domestic interest rate

[4] Because the exchange rate will continue to be fixed at E_{par}, the expected future exchange rate remains unchanged and so does not need to be addressed in the analysis.

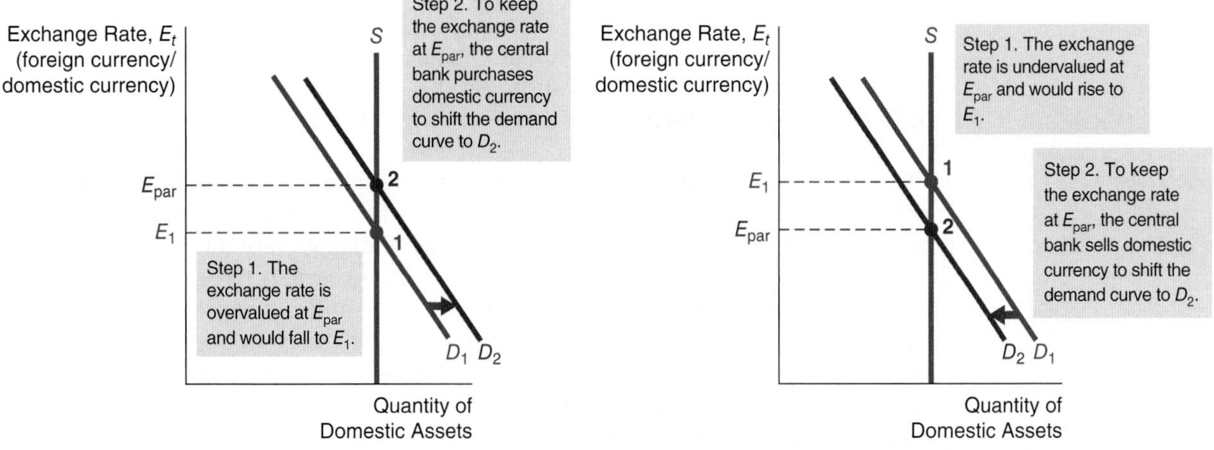

FIGURE 16.2 Intervention in the Foreign Exchange Market Under a Fixed Exchange Rate Regime
In panel (a), the exchange rate at E_{par} is overvalued. To keep the exchange rate at E_{par} (point 2), the central bank must purchase domestic currency to shift the demand curve to D_2. In panel (b), the exchange rate at E_{par} is undervalued, so the central bank must sell domestic currency to shift the demand curve to D_2 and keep the exchange rate at E_{par} (point 2).

raises the relative expected return on domestic assets, shifting the demand curve to the right. The central bank will continue purchasing domestic currency until the demand curve reaches D_2 and the equilibrium exchange rate is at E_{par} at point 2 in panel (a).

We have thus come to the conclusion that ***when the domestic currency is overvalued, the central bank must purchase domestic currency to keep the exchange rate fixed, but as a result it loses international reserves.***

Panel (b) in Figure 16.2 describes the situation in which the demand curve has shifted to the right to D_1 because the relative expected return on domestic assets has risen and hence the exchange rate is undervalued: The initial demand curve D_1 intersects the supply curve at exchange rate E_1, which is above E_{par}. In this situation, the central bank must sell domestic currency and purchase foreign assets. This action works like an open market purchase to increase reserves and lower the interest rate on domestic assets, i^D. The central bank keeps selling domestic currency and lowering i^D until the demand curve shifts all the way to D_2, where the equilibrium exchange rate is at E_{par}—point 2 in panel (b). Our analysis thus leads us to the following result: ***When the domestic currency is undervalued, the central bank must sell domestic currency to keep the exchange rate fixed, but as a result, it gains international reserves.***

Devaluation and Revaluation As we have seen, if a country's currency is overvalued, its central bank's attempts to keep the currency from depreciating will result in a loss of international reserves. If the country's central bank eventually runs out of international reserves, it cannot keep its currency from depreciating, and a **devaluation** must occur, in which the par exchange rate is reset at a lower level.

If, by contrast, a country's currency is undervalued, its central bank's intervention to keep the currency from appreciating leads to a gain of international reserves. As we will see shortly, the central bank might not want to acquire these international reserves, and so it might want to reset the par value of its exchange rate at a higher level (a **revaluation**).

Perfect Capital Mobility If perfect capital mobility exists—that is, if there are no barriers to domestic residents purchasing foreign assets or foreigners purchasing domestic assets—then a sterilized exchange rate intervention cannot keep the exchange rate at E_{par} because, as we saw earlier, the relative expected return of domestic assets is unaffected. For example, if the exchange rate is overvalued, a sterilized purchase of domestic currency will leave the relative expected return and the demand curve unchanged—so pressure for a depreciation of the domestic currency is not removed. If the central bank keeps purchasing its domestic currency but continues to sterilize, it will just keep losing international reserves until it finally runs out of them and is forced to let the value of the currency seek a lower level.

The Policy Trilemma

One important implication of the foregoing analysis is that a country that ties its exchange rate to an anchor currency of a larger country loses control of its monetary policy. If the larger country pursues a more contractionary monetary policy and raises interest rates, this would lead to lower expected inflation in the larger country, thus causing an appreciation of the larger country's currency and a depreciation of the smaller country's currency. The smaller country, having locked in its exchange rate to the anchor currency, will now find its currency overvalued and will therefore have to sell the anchor currency and buy its own to keep its currency from depreciating. The result of this foreign exchange intervention after a rise in the anchor country's interest rates will then be a decline in the smaller country's international reserves, a decline in the amount of reserves in its banking system, and a corresponding rise in domestic interest rates. Sterilization of this foreign exchange intervention is not an option because this would just lead to a continuing loss of international reserves until the smaller country was forced to devalue its currency. The smaller country no longer controls its monetary policy because movements in its interest rates are completely determined by movements in the larger country's interest rates.

Our analysis therefore indicates that a country (or a currency union like the Eurozone) can't pursue the following three policies at the same time: (1) free capital mobility, (2) a fixed exchange rate, and (3) an independent monetary policy. Economists call this result the **policy trilemma** (or, more graphically, the **impossible trinity**). Figure 16.3 illustrates the policy trilemma. A country can choose only two of the three options, which are denoted by each side of the triangle. In option 1, a country (or monetary union) chooses to have capital mobility and an independent monetary policy but not a fixed exchange rate. The Eurozone and the United States have made this choice. Hong Kong and Belize have chosen option 2, in which there is free capital mobility and the exchange rate is fixed, so the country does not have an independent monetary policy. Other countries, like China, have chosen option 3, in which they have a fixed exchange

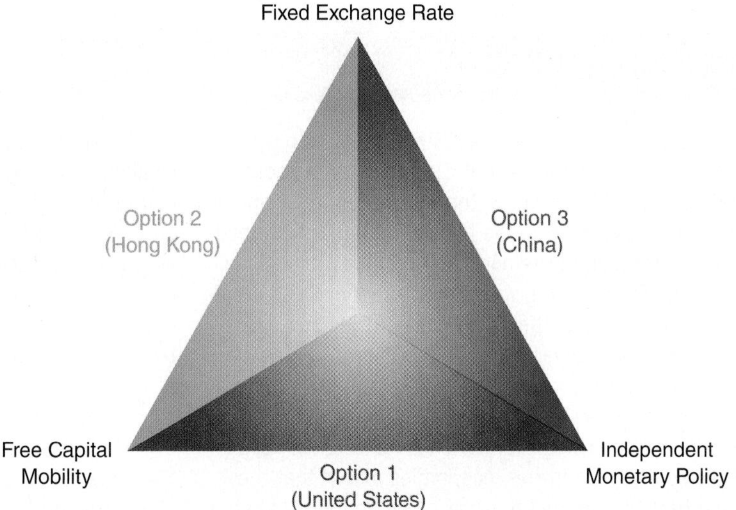

FIGURE 16.3 The Policy Trilemma

A country (or monetary union) cannot pursue the following three policies at the same time: (1) free capital mobility, (2) a fixed exchange rate, and (3) an independent monetary policy. Instead, it must choose two of the three policies on each side of the triangle.

rate and pursue an independent monetary policy but do not have free capital mobility because they have **capital controls**, restrictions on the free movement of capital across the borders.

The policy trilemma thus leaves countries with a difficult choice. Do they accept exchange rate volatility (option 1), give up on independent monetary policy (option 2), or restrict capital flows (option 3)?

Monetary Unions

A variant of a fixed exchange rate regime is a **monetary union** (or **currency union**) in which a group of countries decide to adopt a common currency, thereby fixing their exchange rates vis-à-vis each other. One of the early examples of a monetary union occurred when the thirteen colonies formed the United States in 1787 and gave up their individual currencies for the U.S. dollar. The most recent monetary union is the European Monetary Union (EMU), in which eleven initial countries adopted a new currency, the euro, in January 1999.

The key economic advantage of a monetary union is that it makes trade across borders easier because goods and services in all the member countries are now priced in the same currency. However, as we have seen above, as with any fixed exchange rate regime and free capital mobility, a currency union means that individual countries no longer have their own independent monetary policy to deal with shortfalls of aggregate demand. This disadvantage of a currency union has raised questions about whether the Eurozone will break up, as the Global box "Will the Euro Survive?" indicates.

GLOBAL

Will the Euro Survive?

The global financial crisis of 2007–2009 led to economic contraction throughout Europe, with the countries in the southern part of the Eurozone hit especially hard. Unemployment in the hard-hit countries climbed much faster than in the northern countries, especially Germany. Furthermore, with the contraction in their economies, many of the southern countries began to experience large government budget deficits and sovereign debt crises, in which investors pulled back from purchasing these countries' bonds, sending interest rates to extremely high levels. The resulting collapse of the southern countries' economies meant that they could benefit from much easier monetary policy to stimulate economic activity, but this option was unavailable because the European Central Bank had to conduct monetary policy for the Eurozone as a whole, which was not suffering as badly as the southern countries.

The straightjacket of the euro has resulted in a weakening of support for the euro in the southern countries, and there is increasing talk of exiting the euro. Support for the euro has also weakened in the stronger, northern countries because they have been called on to provide bailouts to the weaker member countries. With the prospect that the stronger countries might want to exit in order to limit their transfer of funds to the weaker countries, and the weaker countries to exit so they can boost their economies by more expansionary monetary policy and depreciation of their currency if they abandon the euro, there are doubts the European Monetary Union can survive. However, the euro is seen as an important step in the creation of a more united and powerful Europe, and this political consideration has generated strong forces to retain the monetary union.

Currency Boards and Dollarization

Smaller countries are often willing to tie their exchange rate to that of a larger country in order to inherit the more disciplined monetary policy of their bigger neighbor, thus ensuring a low inflation rate. An extreme example of such a strategy is the **currency board**, in which the domestic currency is backed 100% by a foreign currency (say, dollars) and in which the note-issuing authority, whether the central bank or the government, establishes a fixed exchange rate to this foreign currency and stands ready to exchange domestic currency for the foreign currency at this rate whenever the public requests it. Currency boards have been established in countries such as Hong Kong (1983), Argentina (1991), Estonia (1992), Lithuania (1994), Bulgaria (1997), and Bosnia (1998). (Argentina's currency board, which operated from 1991 to 2002, is one of the most interesting and is described in the Global box, "Argentina's Currency Board.") An even more extreme strategy is **dollarization**, in which a country abandons its currency altogether and adopts that of another country, typically the U.S. dollar (see the Global box, "Dollarization").

Speculative Attacks

A serious shortcoming of fixed exchange rate systems such as the Bretton Woods system or the European Monetary System is that they can lead to foreign exchange crises involving a **speculative attack** on a currency—massive sales of a weak currency or purchases of a strong currency that cause a sharp change in the exchange rate. In the following case, we use our model of exchange rate determination to understand how the September 1992 exchange rate crisis that rocked the European Monetary System came about.

GLOBAL

Argentina's Currency Board

Argentina has had a long history of monetary instability, with inflation rates fluctuating dramatically and sometimes surging to beyond 1,000% per year. To end this cycle of inflationary surges, Argentina decided to adopt a currency board in April 1991. The Argentine currency board worked as follows: Under Argentina's convertibility law, the peso/dollar exchange rate was fixed at one to one, and a member of the public could go to the Argentine central bank and exchange a peso for a dollar, or vice versa, at any time.

The early years of Argentina's currency board looked stunningly successful. Inflation, which had been running at an 800% annual rate in 1990, fell to less than 5% by the end of 1994, and economic growth was rapid, averaging almost 8% per year from 1991 to 1994. In the aftermath of the Mexican peso crisis, however, concern about the health of the Argentine economy resulted in the public pulling money out of the banks (deposits fell by 18%) and exchanging pesos for dollars, thus causing a contraction of reserves in the Argentine banking system and a rise in Argentine interest rates. The result was a sharp drop in Argentine economic activity, with real GDP shrinking by more than 5% in 1995 and the unemployment rate jumping above 15%. Only in 1996 did the economy begin to recover.

Because the central bank of Argentina had no control over monetary policy under the currency board system, it was relatively helpless to counteract the contractionary monetary policy stemming from the public's behavior. Furthermore, because the currency board did not allow the central bank to create pesos and lend them to the banks, it had very little capability to act as a lender of last resort. With help from international agencies, such as the IMF, the World Bank, and the Inter-American Development Bank, which lent Argentina more than $5 billion in 1995 to help shore up its banking system, the currency board survived.

However, in 1998 Argentina entered another recession, which was both severe and very long lasting. By the end of 2001, unemployment reached nearly 20%, a level comparable to that experienced in the United States during the Great Depression of the 1930s. The result was civil unrest and the fall of the elected government, as well as a major banking crisis and a default on nearly $150 billion of government debt. Because the Central Bank of Argentina had no control over monetary policy under the currency board system, it was unable to use monetary policy to expand the economy and get out of its recession, nor could it act as a lender of last resort to prop up its banks. In January 2002, the currency board finally collapsed and the peso depreciated by more than 70%. The result was a full-scale financial crisis, with inflation shooting up and an extremely severe depression. Clearly, the Argentine public is not as enamored of its currency board as it once was.*

*The Argentine financial crisis is described in detail in Web Chapter 25, "Financial Crises in Emerging Market Economies," which can be found on this book's Web site at www.pearsonhighered.com/mishkin_eakins.

Managed Float

With the demise of the Bretton Woods system, most exchange rates currently change daily in response to market forces, yet many central banks have not been willing to give up their option of intervening in the foreign exchange market. Preventing large changes in exchange rates makes it easier for firms and individuals purchasing or selling goods abroad to plan into the future. Furthermore, countries with surpluses in their current account balances frequently do not want to see their currencies appreciate because it makes their goods more expensive abroad and foreign goods cheaper in their country. Because an appreciation might hurt sales for domestic businesses and increase unemployment, surplus countries have often sold their currency in the foreign exchange market and acquired international reserves.

GLOBAL

Dollarization

Dollarization, which involves the adoption of another country's currency, usually the U.S. dollar (but other sound currencies like the euro and the yen are also possibilities), is a more extreme version of a fixed exchange rate than is a currency board. A currency board can be abandoned, allowing a change in the value of the currency, but a change of value is impossible with dollarization: A dollar bill is always worth one dollar whether it is held in the United States or outside it. Panama has been dollarized since the inception of the country in the early twentieth century, while El Salvador and Ecuador have recently adopted dollarization.

Dollarization, like a currency board, prevents a central bank from creating inflation. Another key advantage is that it completely avoids the possibility of a speculative attack on the domestic currency (because there is none) that is still a danger even under a currency board arrangement. However, like a currency board, dollarization does not allow a country to pursue its own monetary policy or have a lender of last resort. Dollarization has one additional disadvantage not characteristic of a currency board: Because a country adopting dollarization no longer has its own currency, it loses the revenue that a government receives by issuing money, which is called *seigniorage*. Because governments (or their central banks) do not have to pay interest on their currency, they earn revenue (seigniorage) by using this currency to purchase income-earning assets such as bonds. In the case of the Federal Reserve in the United States, this revenue is usually in excess of $20 billion dollars per year. If an emerging-market country dollarizes and gives up its currency, it needs to make up this loss of revenue somewhere, which is not always easy for a poor country.

CASE

The Foreign Exchange Crisis of September 1992

In the aftermath of German reunification in October 1990, the German central bank, the Bundesbank, faced rising inflationary pressures, with inflation having accelerated from below 3% in 1990 to near 5% by 1992. To dampen inflation, the Bundesbank raised German interest rates to near double-digit levels. Figure 16.4 shows the consequences of these actions by the Bundesbank in the foreign exchange market for British pounds. Note that in the diagram, the pound is the domestic currency and the German mark (deutsche mark, DM, Germany's currency before the advent of the euro in 1999) is the foreign currency.

The increase in German interest rates i^F lowered the relative expected return of British pound assets and shifted the demand curve to D_2 in Figure 16.4. The intersection of the supply and demand curves at point 2 was now below the lower exchange rate limit at that time (2.778 marks per pound, denoted E_{par}). To increase the value of the pound relative to the mark and to restore the mark/pound exchange rate to within the exchange rate mechanism limits, one of two things had to happen. The Bank of England would have to pursue a contractionary monetary policy, thereby raising British interest rates sufficiently to shift the demand curve back to D_1 so that the equilibrium would remain at point 1, where the exchange rate would remain at E_{par}. Alternatively, the Bundesbank would have to pursue an expansionary monetary policy, thereby lowering German interest rates. Lower German interest rates would raise the relative expected return on British assets and shift the demand curve back to D_1 so that the exchange rate would be at E_{par}.

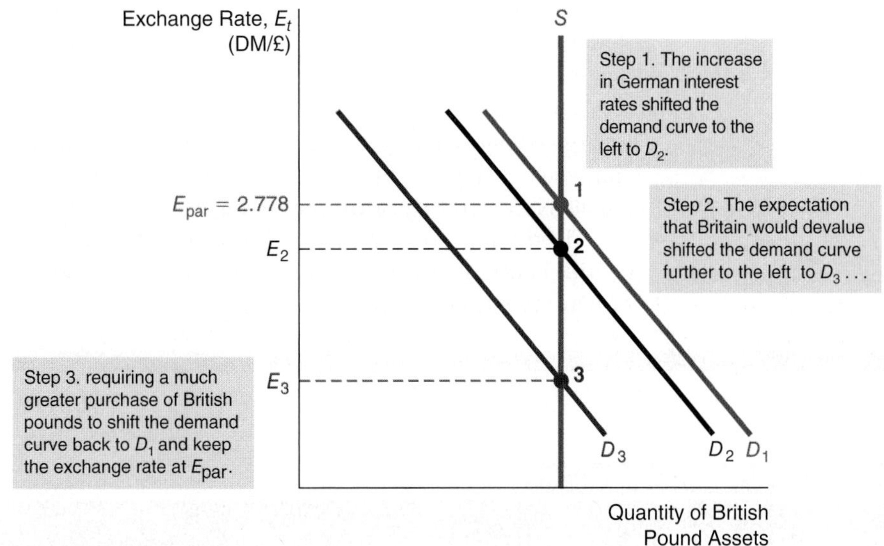

FIGURE 16.4 Foreign Exchange Market for British Pounds in 1992

The realization by speculators that the United Kingdom would soon devalue the pound decreased the relative expected return on British pound assets, resulting in a leftward shift of the demand curve from D_2 to D_3. The result was the need for a much greater purchase of pounds by the British central bank to raise the interest rate so that the demand curve would shift back to D_1 and keep the exchange rate E_{par} at 2.778 German marks per pound.

The catch was that the Bundesbank, whose primary goal was fighting inflation, proved unwilling to pursue an expansionary monetary policy, and the British, who were facing their worst recession in the postwar period, proved unwilling to pursue a contractionary monetary policy to prop up the pound. This impasse became clear when in response to great pressure from other members of the EMS, the Bundesbank was willing to lower its lending rates by only a token amount on September 16 after a speculative attack was mounted on the currencies of the Scandinavian countries. So at some point in the very near future, the value of the pound would have to decline to point 2. Speculators now knew that depreciation of the pound was imminent. As a result, the relative expected return of the pound immediately fell sharply, shifting the demand curve left to D_3 in Figure 16.4.

As a result of the large leftward shift of the demand curve, a huge excess supply of pound assets now existed at the par exchange rate E_{par}, which caused a massive sell-off of pounds (and purchases of marks) by speculators on September 16. The need for the British central bank to intervene to raise the value of the pound now became much greater and required a huge rise in British interest rates. After a major intervention effort on the part of the Bank of England, which included a rise in its lending rate from 10% to 15%, which still wasn't enough, the British were finally forced to give up on that day: They pulled out of the ERM indefinitely and allowed the pound to depreciate by 10% against the mark.

Speculative attacks on other currencies forced devaluation of the Spanish peseta by 5% and the Italian lira by 15%. To defend its currency, the Swedish central bank was forced to raise its daily lending rate to the astronomical level of 500%! By the time the crisis was over, the British, French, Italian, Spanish, and Swedish central banks had intervened to the tune of $100 billion; the Bundesbank alone had laid out $50 billion for foreign exchange intervention. Because foreign exchange crises lead to large changes in central banks' holdings of international reserves and thus significantly affect the official reserve asset items in the balance of payments, these crises are also referred to as **balance-of-payments crises**.

The attempt to prop up the European Monetary System was not cheap for these central banks. It is estimated that they lost $4 to $6 billion as a result of exchange rate intervention during the crisis.

THE PRACTICING MANAGER

Profiting from a Foreign Exchange Crisis

Large banks and other financial institutions often conduct foreign exchange trading operations that generate substantial profits for their parent institution. When a foreign exchange crisis like the one that occurred in September 1992 comes along, foreign exchange traders and speculators are presented with a golden opportunity. The foregoing analysis of this crisis helps explain why.

As we saw in Figure 16.4, the high German interest rates resulted in a situation in which the British pound was overvalued, in that the equilibrium exchange rate in the absence of intervention by the British and German central banks was below the lower exchange rate limit of 2.778 German marks per British pound. Once foreign exchange traders realized that the central banks would not be willing to intervene sufficiently or alter their policies to keep the value of the pound above the 2.778-mark-per-pound lower limit, the traders were presented with a "heads I win, tails you lose" bet. They knew that there was only one direction in which the exchange rate could go—down—and so they were almost sure to make money by buying marks and selling pounds. Our analysis of Figure 16.4 reflects this state of affairs; another way of looking at this one-sided bet is to recognize that it implies that the expected return on mark-denominated deposits increased sharply, shifting the demand curve far to the left to D_3 in Figure 16.4.

Savvy foreign exchange traders, who read the writing on the wall early in September 1992, sold pounds and bought marks. When the pound depreciated 10% against the mark after September 16, they made huge profits because the marks they had bought could now be sold at a price 10% higher. Foreign exchange traders at Citibank are reported to have made $200 million in the week of the September 1992 exchange rate crisis—not bad for a week's work! But these profits pale in comparison to those made by George Soros, an investment fund manager whose funds are reported to have run up profits of $1 billion during the crisis. (However, Soros gave some of these profits back in 1994 when he acknowledged that he had suffered a $600 million loss from trades on the yen.) Clearly, foreign exchange trading can be a highly profitable enterprise for financial institutions, particularly during foreign exchange rate crises.

CASE

How Did China Accumulate over $3 Trillion of International Reserves?

By the end of 2016, China had accumulated more than $3 trillion of international reserves. How did the Chinese get their hands on this vast amount of foreign assets? After all, China is not yet a rich country.

The answer is that China pegged its exchange rate to the U.S. dollar at a fixed rate of 8.28 yuan (also called renminbi) to the dollar in 1994. Because of China's rapidly growing productivity and an inflation rate that was lower than that in the United States, the long-run value of the yuan increased, leading to a higher relative expected return for yuan assets and a rightward shift of the demand for yuan assets. As a result, the Chinese found themselves in the situation depicted in panel (b) of Figure 16.2, in which the yuan is undervalued. To keep the yuan from appreciating above E_{par} to E_1 in the figure, the Chinese central bank engaged in massive purchases of U.S. dollar assets. Today the Chinese government is one of the largest holders of U.S. government bonds in the world.

The pegging of the yuan to the U.S. dollar created several problems for Chinese authorities. First, the Chinese now own a lot of U.S. assets, particularly U.S. Treasury securities, which have very low returns. Second, the undervaluation of the yuan has meant that Chinese goods are so cheap abroad that many countries have threatened to erect trade barriers against these goods if the Chinese government does not allow an upward revaluation of the yuan. Third, the Chinese purchase of dollar assets has resulted in a substantial increase in reserves in the Chinese banking system, which has the potential to produce high inflation in the future. Because the Chinese authorities have created substantial roadblocks to capital mobility, they have been able to sterilize most of their exchange rate interventions while maintaining the exchange rate peg. Nevertheless, they still worry about inflationary pressures. In July 2005 China finally made its peg somewhat more flexible by letting the value of the yuan rise 2.1%. The central bank also indicated that it would no longer fix the yuan to the U.S. dollar but would instead maintain its value relative to a basket of currencies. Why did the Chinese authorities maintain this exchange rate peg for so long despite the problems? One answer is that they wanted to keep their export sector humming by keeping the prices of their export goods low. A second answer might be that they wanted to accumulate a large amount of international reserves as a "war chest" that could be sold to buy yuan in the event of a speculative attack against the yuan at some future date. Given the pressure on the Chinese government to further revalue its currency from government officials in the United States and Europe, further adjustments in China's exchange rate policy are likely.

Countries with balance-of-payments deficits do not want to see their currency lose value because it makes foreign goods more expensive for domestic consumers and can stimulate inflation. To keep the value of the domestic currency high, deficit countries have often bought their own currency in the foreign exchange market and given up international reserves.

The current international financial system is a hybrid of a fixed and a flexible exchange rate system. Rates fluctuate in response to market forces but are not determined solely by them. Furthermore, many countries continue to keep the value of their currency fixed against other currencies.

Capital Controls

Emerging market countries are countries that have recently opened up to flows of goods, services, and capital from the rest of the world. Politicians and some economists have advocated that emerging market countries avoid financial instability by restricting capital mobility. Are capital controls a good idea?

Controls on Capital Outflows

Capital outflows can promote financial instability in emerging market countries because when domestic residents and foreigners pull their capital out of a country, the resulting capital outflow forces a country to devalue its currency. This risk is why some politicians in emerging market countries have found capital controls particularly attractive. For example, Prime Minister Mahathir of Malaysia instituted capital controls in 1998 to restrict outflows in the aftermath of the East Asian crisis.

Although these controls sound like a good idea, they suffer from several disadvantages. First, empirical evidence indicates that controls on capital outflows are seldom effective during a crisis because the private sector finds ingenious ways to evade them and has little difficulty moving funds out of the country. Second, the evidence suggests that capital flight may even increase after controls are put into place because confidence in the government is weakened. Third, controls on capital outflows often lead to corruption, as government officials get bribed to look the other way when domestic residents are trying to move funds abroad. Fourth, controls on capital outflows may lull governments into thinking they do not have to take the steps to reform their financial systems to deal with the crisis, with the result that opportunities to improve the functioning of the economy are lost.

Controls on Capital Inflows

Although most economists find the arguments against controls on capital outflows persuasive, controls on capital inflows receive more support. Supporters reason that if speculative capital cannot come in, then it cannot go out suddenly and create a crisis. Our analysis of the financial crises in East Asia in Web Chapter 25 provides support for this view by suggesting that capital inflows can lead to a lending boom and excessive risk taking on the part of banks, which then helps trigger a financial crisis.

However, controls on capital inflows have the undesirable feature that they may block those funds from entering a country that would be used for productive investment opportunities. Although such controls may limit the fuel supplied to lending booms through capital flows, over time they produce substantial distortions and misallocation of resources as households and businesses try to get around them. Indeed, as with controls on capital outflows, controls on capital inflows can lead to corruption. Serious doubts arise over whether capital controls can be effective in today's environment, in which trade is open and where many financial instruments make it easier to get around these controls.

On the other hand, a strong case can be made for improving bank regulation and supervision so that capital inflows are less likely to produce a lending boom and encourage excessive risk taking by banking institutions. For example, restricting banks in how fast their borrowing can grow might substantially limit capital inflows. Supervisory controls that focus on the sources, rather than the symptoms, of financial fragility can enhance the efficiency of the financial system rather than hamper it.

The Role of the IMF

The International Monetary Fund was originally set up under the Bretton Woods system to help countries deal with balance-of-payments problems and stay with the fixed exchange rates by lending to deficit countries. When the Bretton Woods system of fixed exchange rates collapsed in 1971, the IMF took on new roles.

Although the IMF no longer attempts to encourage fixed exchange rates, its role as an international lender has become more important recently. This role first came to the fore in the 1980s during the Third World debt crisis, in which the IMF assisted developing countries in repaying their loans. The financial crises in Mexico in 1994–1995 and in East Asia in 1997–1998 led to huge loans by the IMF to these and other affected countries to help them recover from their financial crises and to prevent the spread of these crises to other countries. Then starting in 2010, the IMF made large loans to Greece, Ireland, and Portugal to help them avoid a default on their government debt. This role, in which the IMF acts like an international lender of last resort to cope with financial instability, is indeed highly controversial.

Should the IMF Be an International Lender of Last Resort?

We have seen that when a central bank engages in a lender-of-last-resort operation, as the Federal Reserve did during the recent global financial crisis, it can minimize the severity of the financial crisis and even sometimes prevent it from happening. When the IMF acts as an international lender of last resort, it can have similar benefits, particularly when the central bank of the country it is lending to does not have the capacity to cope with the crisis.

However, when the IMF acts as an international lender of last resort it can lead to serious moral hazard problems. First, it may encourage governments to be profligate because they know that they are likely to be bailed out by the IMF. Second, governments use IMF funds to protect depositors and other creditors of banking institutions from losses. This safety net creates a moral hazard problem: Because the depositors and other creditors do not suffer losses when banks get into trouble, they have less incentive to monitor these banking institutions and withdraw their funds if the institutions are taking on too much risk.

An international lender of last resort must find ways to limit these moral hazard problems, or it can actually make the situation worse. The international lender of last resort can make it clear that it will extend liquidity only to governments that both put their fiscal houses in order and implement measures to prevent excessive risk taking by financial institutions. Critics of the IMF, however, believe that the IMF has not put enough pressure on the governments to which it lends to contain these two moral hazard problems. They thus argue that the IMF should abandon its role as an international lender of last resort. The IMF has also been criticized for imposing so-called austerity programs that force borrowing governments to cut government spending, raise taxes, and raise interest rates. These austerity programs can be highly contractionary, leading to high unemployment and even possibly political instability.

The debate on whether the world will be better off with the IMF operating as an international lender of last resort is currently a hot one. Much attention is being focused on making the IMF more effective in performing this role, and redesign of the IMF is at the center of proposals for a new international financial architecture to help reduce international financial instability.

SUMMARY

1. An unsterilized central bank intervention in which the domestic currency is sold to purchase foreign assets leads to a gain in international reserves, an increase in reserves in the banking system, a fall in interest rates, and a depreciation of the domestic currency. Available evidence suggests, however, that sterilized central bank interventions have little long-term effect on the exchange rate.
2. The balance of payments is a bookkeeping system for recording all payments between a country and foreign countries that have a direct bearing on the movement of funds between them. The current account balance, which is the sum of the merchandise trade balance, the balance on services, net income, and transfers, shows the total of net receipts on a current basis. It also indicates what is happening to claims on foreign wealth, with a current account surplus indicating that claims on foreign wealth are increasing, and a deficit indicating that claims on foreign wealth are decreasing.
3. After World War II, the Bretton Woods system and the IMF were established to promote a fixed exchange rate system in which the U.S. dollar, the reserve currency, was convertible into gold. The Bretton Woods system collapsed in 1971. We now have an international financial system that has elements of a managed float and a fixed exchange rate system. Some exchange rates fluctuate from day to day, although central banks intervene in the foreign exchange market, while other exchange rates are fixed.
4. Controls on capital outflows receive support because they may prevent domestic residents and foreigners from pulling capital out of a country during a crisis and make devaluation less likely. Controls on capital inflows make sense under the theory that if speculative capital cannot flow in, then it cannot go out suddenly and create a crisis. However, capital controls suffer from several disadvantages: They are seldom effective, they lead to corruption, and they may allow governments to avoid taking the steps needed to reform their financial systems to deal with the crisis.
5. The IMF has recently taken on the role of an international lender of last resort. Because central banks in emerging market countries are unlikely to be able to perform a lender-of-last-resort operation successfully, an international lender of last resort like the IMF is needed to prevent financial instability. However, the IMF's role as an international lender of last resort creates a serious moral hazard problems that can encourage excessive risk taking and make a financial crisis more likely, but refusing to lend may be politically hard to do. In addition, the IMF needs to be able to provide liquidity quickly during a crisis to keep manageable the amount of funds lent.

KEY TERMS

anchor currency, p. 373
balance of payments, p. 372
balance-of-payments crises, p. 382
Bretton Woods system, p. 373
capital controls, p. 377
currency board, p. 378
currency union, p. 377
current account, p. 372
devaluation, p. 375
dollarization, p. 378
emerging market countries, p. 384
fixed exchange rate regime, p. 373
floating exchange rate regime, p. 373
foreign exchange interventions, p. 368
impossible trinity, p. 376
International Monetary Fund (IMF), p. 373
international reserves, p. 368
managed float regime (dirty float), p. 373
merchandise trade balance, p. 372
monetary union, p. 377

QUESTIONS

1. If the Federal Reserve sells dollars in the foreign exchange market but conducts an offsetting open market operation to sterilize the intervention, what will be the effect on international reserves, reserves in the banking system, and the exchange rate?
2. If the Federal Reserve buys dollars in the foreign exchange market but does not sterilize the intervention, what will be the effect on international reserves, reserves in the banking system, and the exchange rate?
3. For each of the following, identify whether they increase or decrease the balance on current account.
   - **a.** An American's purchase of an airline ticket from Air France
   - **b.** A Japanese's purchase of California oranges
   - **c.** $50 million of foreign aid to Honduras
   - **d.** A worker in California who sends money to his or her parents in Mexico
   - **e.** The services an American accounting firm provides to a German firm
4. Suppose that you travel to Cali (Colombia), where the fixed exchange rate is 1 USD to 2,900 Colombian pesos. As you enter a McDonald's restaurant, you realize you need 17,400 Colombian pesos to buy a Big Mac. Assuming a Big Mac sells for $5 in the United States, would you say that the Colombian peso is over- or undervalued?
5. Refer to the previous exercise. Which type of foreign market intervention must the central bank of Colombia conduct to keep the exchange rate at a level where the currency is not under- or overvalued?
6. What would be the effect of a devaluation on a country's imports and exports? If a country imports most of the goods included in the basket of goods and services used to calculate the CPI, what do you think the effect will be on this country's inflation rate?
7. If a country's par exchange rate was undervalued during the Bretton Woods fixed exchange rate regime, what kind of intervention would that country's central bank be forced to undertake, and what effect would it have on its international reserves and reserves in the banking system?
8. Why might a country that is suffering a recession not want to intervene in the foreign exchange market if its currency is overvalued? Assume this country participates in a fixed exchange rate regime.
9. "If a country wants to keep its exchange rate from changing, it must give up some control over its monetary policy." Is this statement true, false, or uncertain? Explain your answer.
10. Why can balance-of-payments deficits force some countries to implement a contractionary monetary policy?
11. "Balance-of-payments deficits always cause a country to lose international reserves." Is this statement true, false, or uncertain? Explain your answer.
12. How can persistent U.S. balance-of-payments deficits stimulate world inflation?
13. Why did the exchange rate peg lead to difficulties for the countries in the ERM when German reunification occurred?
14. Why is it that in a pure flexible exchange rate system, the foreign exchange market has no direct effects on the reserves in the banking system. Does this mean that the foreign exchange market has no effect on monetary policy?
15. "The abandonment of fixed exchange rates after 1973 has meant that countries have pursued more independent monetary policies." Is this statement true, false, or uncertain? Explain your answer.
16. Are controls on capital outflows a good idea? Why or why not?
17. Discuss the pros and cons of controls on capital inflows.
18. Why might central banks in emerging market countries find that engaging in a lender-of-last-resort operation might be counterproductive? Does this provide a rationale for having an international lender of last resort like the IMF?
19. The IMF does not enjoy a great reputation in many countries that were recipients of IMF loans or bailouts. Explain why many citizens were not happy with the role played by the IMF.
20. What steps should an international lender of last resort take to limit moral hazard?

QUANTITATIVE PROBLEMS

1. Calculate the overvaluation of the Thai baht (THB) if you can get 34.6 THB per USD at the exchange counter, but a lunch menu that costs 25 USD in Boston sells for 948.25 THB in Bangkok.
2. Suppose that for a given country the demand for imports can be expressed as $IM = 1{,}250 + 0.05E$ and the demand for exports can be expressed as $X = 750 - 0.08E$, where E is the exchange rate (units of foreign currency per unit of domestic currency). Calculate the trade balance when $E = 200$. Calculate the new trade balance if this country devalues its currency 20%.
3. If the interest rate is 4% on euro deposits and 2% on dollar deposits, while the euro is trading at $1.30 per euro, what does the market expect the exchange rate to be one year from now?
4. If the dollar begins trading at $1.30 per euro, with the same interest rates given in problem 3, and the ECB raises interest rates so that the rate on euro deposits rises by 1 percentage point, what will happen to the exchange rate (assuming that the expected future exchange rate is unchanged)?

WEB EXERCISE

The International Financial System

1. The International Monetary Fund stands ready to help nations facing monetary crises. Go to **www.imf.org**. Click on the tab labeled "About the IMF." What is the stated purpose of the IMF? How many nations participate, and when was it established?

PART 6 THE FINANCIAL INSTITUTIONS INDUSTRY

CHAPTER 17

Banking and the Management of Financial Institutions

> PREVIEW

Because banking plays such a major role in channeling funds to borrowers with productive investment opportunities, this financial activity is important in ensuring that the financial system and the economy run smoothly and efficiently. In the United States, banks (depository institutions) supply on the order of $10 trillion in credit annually. They provide loans to businesses, help us finance our college educations or the purchase of a new car or home, and provide us with services such as checking and savings accounts.

In this chapter, we examine how banking is conducted to earn the highest profits possible: how and why banks make loans, how they acquire funds and manage their assets and liabilities (debts), and how they earn income. Although we focus on commercial banking because this is the most important financial intermediary activity, many of the same principles are applicable to other types of financial intermediation.

The Bank Balance Sheet

To understand how banking works, we start by looking at the bank **balance sheet**, a list of the bank's assets and liabilities. As the name implies, this list balances; that is, it has the characteristic that

$$\text{total assets} = \text{total liabilities} + \text{capital}$$

GO ONLINE
Access **http://investor.bankofamerica.com/phoenix.zhtml?c=71595&p=irol-reportsannual&cm_re=EBZ-Corp_SocialResponsibility-_-About_Us-_-EI38LTOOOD_About_Us_Reports#fbid=OCD9gCcbS6u**. Click on Annual Reports to view the balance sheet.

A bank's balance sheet is also a list of its *sources* of bank funds (liabilities) and *uses* to which the funds are put (assets). Banks obtain funds by borrowing and by issuing other liabilities such as deposits. They then use these funds to acquire assets such as securities and loans. Banks make profits by charging an interest rate on their asset holdings of securities and loans that is higher than the interest and other expenses on their liabilities. The balance sheet of all commercial banks in 2016 appears in Table 17.1.

Liabilities

A bank acquires funds by issuing (selling) liabilities, such as deposits, which are the *sources of funds* the bank uses. The funds obtained from issuing liabilities are used to purchase income-earning assets.

Checkable Deposits Checkable deposits are bank accounts that allow the owner of the account to write checks to third parties. Checkable deposits include all accounts on which checks can be drawn: non-interest-bearing checking accounts (demand deposits), interest-bearing NOW (negotiable order of withdrawal) accounts, and money market deposit accounts (MMDAs). Introduced with the Depository Institutions Act in 1982, MMDAs have features similar to those of money market mutual funds and are included in the checkable deposits category. However, MMDAs are not subject to reserve requirements (discussed later in the chapter) as checkable deposits are. Table 17.1 shows that the category of checkable deposits makes up 10%

TABLE 17.1 Balance Sheet of All Commercial Banks (items as a percentage of the total, June, 2016)

Assets		Liabilities	
Reserves and cash items	16	Checkable deposits	10
Securities		Nontransaction deposits	
U.S. government and agency	14	Small-denomination time deposits	50
State and local government and other securities	6	(<$100,000) + savings deposits	
Loans		Large-denomination time deposits	10
Commercial and industrial	13	Borrowings	19
Real estate	25	Bank capital	11
Consumer	8		
Other	9		
Other assets (for example, physical capital)	8		
Total	100	Total	100

Source: http://www.federalreserve.gov/releases/h8/ and http://www.federalreserve.gov/releases/h6/.

of bank liabilities. Once, checkable deposits were the most important source of bank funds (more than 60% of bank liabilities in 1960), but with the appearance of new, more attractive financial instruments, such as money market deposit accounts, the share of checkable deposits in total bank liabilities has shrunk over time.

Checkable deposits and money market deposit accounts are payable on demand; that is, if a depositor shows up at the bank and requests payment by making a withdrawal, the bank must pay the depositor immediately. Similarly, if a person who receives a check written on an account from a bank presents that check at the bank, it must pay the funds out immediately (or credit them to that person's account).

A checkable deposit is an asset for the depositor because it is part of his or her wealth. Because the depositor can withdraw funds and the bank is obligated to pay, checkable deposits are a liability for the bank. They are usually the lowest-cost source of bank funds because depositors are willing to forgo some interest to have access to a liquid asset that can be used to make purchases. The bank's costs of maintaining checkable deposits include interest payments and the costs incurred in servicing these accounts—processing, preparing, and sending out monthly statements, providing efficient tellers (human or otherwise), maintaining an impressive building and conveniently located branches, and advertising and marketing to entice customers to deposit their funds with a given bank. In recent years, interest paid on deposits (checkable and nontransaction) has accounted for around 5% of bank operating expenses, whereas the costs involved in servicing accounts (employee salaries, building rent, and so on) have been approximately 50% of operating expenses.

Nontransaction Deposits Nontransaction deposits are the primary source of bank funds (60% of bank liabilities in Table 17.1). Owners cannot write checks on nontransaction deposits, but the interest rates paid on these deposits are usually higher than those on checkable deposits. There are two basic types of nontransaction deposits: savings accounts and time deposits (also called certificates of deposit, or CDs).

Savings accounts were once the most common type of nontransaction deposit. In these accounts, to which funds can be added or from which funds can be withdrawn at any time, transactions and interest payments are recorded in a monthly statement or in a passbook held by the owner of the account.

Time deposits have a fixed maturity length, ranging from several months to over five years, and assess substantial penalties for early withdrawal (the forfeiture of several months' interest). Small-denomination time deposits (deposits of less than $100,000) are less liquid for the depositor than passbook savings, earn higher interest rates, and are a more costly source of funds for the banks.

Large-denomination time deposits (CDs) are available in denominations of $100,000 or more and are typically bought by corporations or other banks. Large-denomination CDs are negotiable; like bonds, they can be resold in a secondary market before they mature. For this reason, negotiable CDs are held by corporations, money market mutual funds, and other financial institutions as alternative assets to Treasury bills and other short-term bonds. Since 1961, when they first appeared, negotiable CDs have become an important source of bank funds (10%).

Borrowings Banks also obtain funds by borrowing from the Federal Reserve System, the Federal Home Loan banks, other banks, and corporations. Borrowings from the Fed are called **discount loans** (also known as *advances*). Banks also borrow reserves overnight in the federal (fed) funds market from other U.S. banks and financial institutions. Banks borrow funds overnight to have enough deposits at the Federal Reserve to meet the amount required by the Fed. (The *federal funds* designation is somewhat confusing because these loans are not made by the federal government or by the Federal Reserve, but rather by banks to other banks.) Other sources of borrowed funds are loans made to banks by their parent companies (bank holding companies), loan arrangements with corporations (such as repurchase agreements), and borrowings of Eurodollars (deposits denominated in U.S. dollars residing in foreign banks or foreign branches of U.S. banks). Borrowings have become a more important source of bank funds over time: In 1960 they made up only 2% of bank liabilities; currently, they are 19% of bank liabilities.

Bank Capital The final category on the liabilities side of the balance sheet is bank capital, the bank's net worth, which equals the difference between total assets and liabilities (11% of bank assets in Table 17.1). A bank's capital is raised by selling new equity (stock) or from retained earnings. Bank capital is a cushion against a drop in the value of its assets, which could force the bank into insolvency (having liabilities in excess of assets, meaning that the bank can be forced into liquidation).

Assets

A bank uses the funds that it has acquired by issuing liabilities to purchase income-earning assets. Bank assets are thus naturally referred to as *uses of funds*, and the interest income earned on them are what enable banks to make profits.

Reserves All banks hold some of the funds they acquire as deposits in an account at the Fed. **Reserves** are these deposits plus currency that is physically held by banks (called **vault cash** because it is stored in bank vaults). Although reserves earn a low interest rate, banks hold them for two reasons. First, some reserves, called **required reserves**, are held because of **reserve requirements**, the regulation that for every dollar of checkable deposits at a bank, a certain fraction (10 cents, for example) must be kept as reserves. This fraction (10% in the example) is called the **required reserve ratio**. Banks hold additional reserves, called **excess reserves**, because they are the most liquid of all bank assets and a bank can use them to meet its obligations when funds are withdrawn, either directly by a depositor or indirectly when a check is written on an account.

Cash Items in Process of Collection Suppose that a check written on an account at another bank is deposited in your bank and the funds for this check have not yet been received (collected) from the other bank. The check is classified as a cash item in process of collection, and it is an asset for your bank because it is a claim on another bank for funds that will be paid within a few days.

Deposits at Other Banks Many small banks hold deposits in larger banks in exchange for a variety of services, including check collection, foreign exchange transactions, and help with securities purchases. This is an aspect of a system called *correspondent banking*.

Collectively, reserves, cash items in process of collection, and deposits at other banks are referred to as *cash items*. In Table 17.1, reserves and cash terms together constitute 16% of total assets.

Securities A bank's holdings of securities are an important income-earning asset: Securities (made up entirely of debt instruments for commercial banks, because banks are not allowed to hold stock) account for 20% of bank assets in Table 17.1, and they provide commercial banks with about 10% of their revenue. These securities can be classified into three categories: U.S. government and agency securities, state and local government securities, and other securities. The U.S. government and agency securities are the most liquid because they can be easily traded and converted into cash with low transaction costs. Because of their high liquidity, short-term U.S. government securities are called **secondary reserves**.

Banks hold state and local government securities because state and local governments are more likely to do business with banks that hold their securities. State and local government and other securities, although tax deductible, are both less marketable (less liquid) and riskier than U.S. government securities, primarily because of default risk: There is some possibility that the issuer of the securities may not be able to make its interest payments or pay back the face value of the securities when they mature.

Loans Banks make their profits primarily by issuing loans. In Table 17.1, some 56% of bank assets are in the form of loans, and in recent years they have generally produced more than half of bank revenues. A loan is a liability for the individual or corporation receiving it, but an asset for a bank, because it provides income to the bank. Loans are typically less liquid than other assets because they cannot be turned into cash until the loan matures. If the bank makes a one-year loan, for example, it cannot get its funds back until the loan comes due in one year. Loans also have a higher probability of default than other assets. Because of the lack of liquidity and higher default risk, the bank earns its highest return on loans.

As you saw in Table 17.1, the largest categories of loans for commercial banks are commercial and industrial loans made to businesses and real estate loans. Commercial banks also make consumer loans and lend to each other. The bulk of these interbank loans are overnight loans lent in the federal funds market. The major difference in the balance sheets of the various depository institutions is primarily in the type of loan in which they specialize. Savings and loans and mutual savings banks, for example, specialize in residential mortgages, while credit unions tend to make consumer loans.

Other Assets The physical capital (bank buildings, computers, and other equipment) owned by the banks is included in this category.

Basic Banking

Before proceeding to a more detailed study of how a bank manages its assets and liabilities to make the highest profit, you should understand the basic operation of a bank.

In general terms, banks make profits by selling liabilities with one set of characteristics (a particular combination of liquidity, risk, size, and return) and using the proceeds to buy assets with a different set of characteristics. This process is often referred to as *asset transformation*. For example, a savings deposit held by one person can provide the funds that enable the bank to make a mortgage loan to another person. The bank has, in effect, transformed the savings deposit (an asset held by the depositor) into a mortgage loan (an asset held by the bank). Another way this process of asset transformation is described is to say that the bank "borrows short and lends long" because it makes long-term loans and funds them by issuing short-dated deposits.

The process of transforming assets and providing a set of services (check clearing, record keeping, credit analysis, and so forth) is like any other production process in a firm. If the bank produces desirable services at low cost and earns substantial income on its assets, it earns profits; if not, the bank suffers losses.

Let's say that Jane Brown has heard that the First National Bank provides excellent service, so she opens a checking account with a $100 bill. She now has a $100 checkable deposit at the bank, which shows up as a $100 liability on the bank's balance sheet. The bank now puts her $100 bill into its vault so that the bank's assets rise by the $100 increase in vault cash. The T-account for the bank looks like this:

First National Bank			
Assets		**Liabilities**	
Vault cash	+$100	Checkable deposits	+$100

Because vault cash is also part of the bank's reserves, we can rewrite the T-account as follows:

Assets		**Liabilities**	
Reserves	+$100	Checkable deposits	+$100

Note that Jane Brown's opening of a checking account leads to *an increase in the bank's reserves equal to the increase in checkable deposits*.

If Jane had opened her account with a $100 check written on an account at another bank, say, the Second National Bank, we would get the same result. The initial effect on the T-account of the First National Bank is as follows:

Assets		**Liabilities**	
Cash items in process of collection	+$100	Checkable deposits	+$100

Checkable deposits increase by $100 as before, but now the First National Bank is owed $100 by the Second National Bank. This asset for the First National Bank is entered in the T-account as $100 of cash items in process of collection because the First National Bank will now try to collect the funds that it is owed. It could go directly to the Second National Bank and ask for payment of the funds, but if the two banks are in separate states, that would be a time-consuming and costly process. Instead, the First National Bank deposits the check in its account at the Fed, and the Fed collects the funds from the Second National Bank. The result is that the Fed transfers $100 of reserves from the Second National Bank to the First National Bank, and the final balance sheet positions of the two banks are as follows:

First National Bank				**Second National Bank**			
Assets		**Liabilities**		**Assets**		**Liabilities**	
Reserves	+$100	Checkable deposits	+$100	Reserves	–$100	Checkable deposits	–$100

The process initiated by Jane Brown can be summarized as follows: When a check written on an account at one bank is deposited in another, the bank receiving the deposit gains reserves equal to the amount of the check, while the bank on which the check is written sees its reserves fall by the same amount. Therefore, ***when a bank receives additional deposits, it gains an equal amount of reserves; when it loses deposits, it loses an equal amount of reserves.***

Now that you understand how banks gain and lose reserves, we can examine how a bank rearranges its balance sheet to make a profit when it experiences a change in its deposits. Let's return to the situation when the First National Bank has just received the extra $100 of checkable deposits. As you know, the bank is obliged to keep a certain fraction of its checkable deposits as required reserves. If the fraction (the required reserve ratio) is 10%, the First National Bank's required reserves have increased by $10, and we can rewrite its T-account as follows:

First National Bank			
Assets		**Liabilities**	
Required reserves	+$10	Checkable deposits	+$100
Excess reserves	+$90		

Let's see how well the bank is doing as a result of the additional checkable deposits. Servicing the extra $100 of checkable deposits is costly because the bank must keep records, pay tellers, pay for check clearing, and so forth. The bank is taking a loss! The situation is even worse if the bank makes interest payments on the deposits, as with NOW accounts. If it is to make a profit, the bank must put to productive use all or part of the $90 of excess reserves it has available. One way to do this is to invest in securities. The other is to make loans; as we have seen, loans account for over half of the total value of bank assets (uses of funds). Because lenders are subject to the asymmetric information problems of adverse selection and moral hazard (discussed in Chapter 7), banks take steps to reduce the incidence and severity of these problems. Bank loan officers evaluate potential borrowers using what are called the "five Cs": character, capacity (ability to repay), collateral, conditions (in the local and national economies), and capital (net worth) before they agree to lend. (Chapter 23 provides a more detailed discussion of the methods banks use to reduce the risk involved in lending.)

Let us assume that the bank chooses not to hold any excess reserves but to make loans instead. The T-account then looks like this:

First National Bank			
Assets		**Liabilities**	
Required reserves	+$10	Checkable deposits	+$100
Loans	+$90		

The bank is now making a profit because it holds short-term liabilities such as checkable deposits and uses the proceeds to buy longer-term assets such as loans with higher interest rates. As mentioned earlier, this process of asset transformation is frequently described by saying that banks are in the business of "borrowing short and lending long." For example, if the loans have an interest rate of 10% per year, the bank earns $9 in income from its loans over the year. If the $100 of checkable deposits is in a NOW account with a 5% interest rate and it costs another $3 per year to service the account, the cost per year of these deposits is $8. The bank's profit on the new deposits is then $1 per year, plus any interest that is paid on required reserves.

General Principles of Bank Management

Now that you have some idea of how a bank operates, let's look at how a bank manages its assets and liabilities to earn the highest possible profit. The bank manager has four primary concerns. The first is to make sure that the bank has enough ready cash to pay its depositors when there are **deposit outflows**—that is, when deposits are lost because depositors make withdrawals and demand payment. To keep enough cash on hand, the bank must engage in **liquidity management**, the acquisition of sufficiently liquid assets to meet the bank's obligations to depositors. Second, the bank manager must pursue an acceptably low level of risk by acquiring assets that have a low rate of default and by diversifying asset holdings (**asset management**). The third concern is to acquire funds at low cost (**liability management**). Finally, the manager must decide the amount of capital the bank should maintain and then acquire the needed capital (**capital adequacy management**).

To understand bank and other financial institution management fully, we must go beyond the general principles of bank asset and liability management described next and look in more detail at how a financial institution manages its assets. Chapter 23 provides an in-depth discussion of how a financial institution manages **credit risk**, the risk arising because borrowers may default, and how it manages **interest-rate risk**, the riskiness of earnings and returns on bank assets that results from interest-rate changes.

Liquidity Management and the Role of Reserves

Let us see how a typical bank, the First National Bank, can deal with deposit outflows that occur when its depositors withdraw cash from checking or savings accounts or write checks that are deposited in other banks. In the example that follows, we assume that the bank has ample excess reserves and that all deposits have the same required reserve ratio of 10% (the bank is required to keep 10% of its time and checkable deposits as reserves). Suppose that the First National Bank's initial balance sheet is as follows:

Assets		Liabilities	
Reserves	$20 million	Deposits	$100 million
Loans	$80 million	Bank capital	$ 10 million
Securities	$10 million		

The bank's required reserves are 10% of $100 million, or $10 million. Given that it holds $20 million of reserves, the First National Bank has excess reserves of $10 million. If a deposit outflow of $10 million occurs, the bank's balance sheet becomes

Assets		Liabilities	
Reserves	$10 million	Deposits	$90 million
Loans	$80 million	Bank capital	$10 million
Securities	$10 million		

The bank loses $10 million of deposits *and* $10 million of reserves, but because its required reserves are now 10% of only $90 million ($9 million), its reserves still exceed this amount by $1 million. In short, ***if a bank has ample excess reserves, a deposit outflow does not necessitate changes in other parts of its balance sheet.***

The situation is quite different when a bank holds insufficient excess reserves. Let's assume that instead of initially holding $10 million in excess reserves, the First National Bank makes additional loans of $10 million, so that it holds no excess reserves. Its initial balance sheet would then be

Assets		Liabilities	
Reserves	$10 million	Deposits	$100 million
Loans	$90 million	Bank capital	$ 10 million
Securities	$10 million		

When it suffers the $10 million deposit outflow, its balance sheet becomes

Assets		Liabilities	
Reserves	$ 0	Deposits	$90 million
Loans	$90 million	Bank capital	$10 million
Securities	$10 million		

After $10 million has been withdrawn from deposits and hence reserves, the bank has a problem: It has a reserve requirement of 10% of $90 million, or $9 million, but it has no reserves! To eliminate this shortfall, the bank has four basic options. One is to acquire reserves to meet a deposit outflow by borrowing them from other banks in the federal funds market or by borrowing from corporations.[1] If the First National Bank acquires the $9 million shortfall in reserves by borrowing it from other banks or corporations, its balance sheet becomes

Assets		Liabilities	
Reserves	$ 9 million	Deposits	$90 million
Loans	$90 million	Borrowings from other banks or corporations	$ 9 million
Securities	$10 million	Bank capital	$10 million

[1]One way the First National Bank can borrow from other banks and corporations is by selling negotiable certificates of deposit. This method for obtaining funds is discussed in the section on liability management.

The cost of this activity is the interest rate on these borrowings, such as the federal funds rate.

A second alternative is for the bank to sell some of its securities to help cover the deposit outflow. For example, it might sell $9 million of its securities and deposit the proceeds with the Fed, resulting in the following balance sheet:

Assets		Liabilities	
Reserves	$ 9 million	Deposits	$90 million
Loans	$90 million	Bank capital	$10 million
Securities	$ 1 million		

The bank incurs some brokerage and other transaction costs when it sells these securities. The U.S. government securities that are classified as secondary reserves are very liquid, so the transaction costs of selling them are quite modest. However, the other securities the bank holds are less liquid, and the transaction cost can be appreciably higher.

A third way that the bank can meet a deposit outflow is to acquire reserves by borrowing from the Fed. In our example, the First National Bank could leave its security and loan holdings the same and borrow $9 million in discount loans from the Fed. Its balance sheet would then be

Assets		Liabilities	
Reserves	$ 9 million	Deposits	$90 million
Loans	$90 million	Borrowings from the Fed	$ 9 million
Securities	$10 million		
		Bank capital	$10 million

The cost associated with discount loans is the interest rate that must be paid to the Fed (called the **discount rate**).

Finally, a bank can acquire the $9 million of reserves to meet the deposit outflow by reducing its loans by this amount and depositing the $9 million it then receives with the Fed, thereby increasing its reserves by $9 million. This transaction changes the balance sheet as follows:

Assets		Liabilities	
Reserves	$ 9 million	Deposits	$90 million
Loans	$81 million	Bank capital	$10 million
Securities	$10 million		

The First National Bank is once again in good shape because its $9 million of reserves satisfies the reserve requirement.

However, this process of reducing its loans is the bank's costliest way of acquiring reserves when a deposit outflow occurs. If the First National Bank has numerous short-term loans renewed at fairly short intervals, it can reduce its total amount of loans outstanding fairly quickly by *calling in* loans—that is, by not renewing some loans when they come due. Unfortunately for the bank, this is likely to antagonize the customers whose loans are not being renewed because they have not done anything to deserve such treatment. Indeed, they are likely to take their business elsewhere in the future, a very costly consequence for the bank.

A second method for reducing its loans is for the bank to sell them off to other banks. Again, this is very costly because other banks do not know how risky these loans are and so may not be willing to buy the loans at their full value. (This is just the lemons adverse selection problem described in Chapter 7.)

The foregoing discussion explains why banks hold excess reserves even though loans or securities earn a higher return. When a deposit outflow occurs, holding excess reserves allows the bank to escape the costs of (1) borrowing from other banks or corporations, (2) selling securities, (3) borrowing from the Fed, or (4) calling in or selling off loans. ***Excess reserves are insurance against the costs associated with deposit outflows. The higher the costs associated with deposit outflows, the more excess reserves banks will want to hold.***

Just as you and I would be willing to pay an insurance company to insure us against a casualty loss such as the theft of a car, a bank is willing to pay the cost of holding excess reserves (the opportunity cost, that is, the earnings forgone by not holding income-earning assets such as loans or securities) to ensure against losses due to deposit outflows. Because excess reserves, like insurance, have a cost, banks also take other steps to protect themselves; for example, they might shift their holdings of assets to more liquid securities (secondary reserves).

Asset Management

Now that you understand why a bank has a need for liquidity, we can examine the basic strategy a bank pursues in managing its assets. To maximize its profits, a bank must simultaneously seek the highest returns possible on loans and securities, reduce risk, and make adequate provisions for liquidity by holding liquid assets. Banks try to accomplish these three goals in four basic ways.

First, banks try to find borrowers who will pay high interest rates and are unlikely to default on their loans. They seek out loan business by advertising their borrowing rates and by approaching corporations directly to solicit loans. It is up to the bank's loan officer to decide if potential borrowers are good credit risks who will make interest and principal payments on time (i.e., engage in screening to reduce the adverse selection problem). Typically, banks are conservative in their loan policies; the default rate is usually less than 1%. It is important, however, that banks not be so conservative that they miss out on attractive lending opportunities that earn high interest rates.

Second, banks try to purchase securities with high returns and low risk. Third, in managing their assets, banks must attempt to lower risk by diversifying. They accomplish this by purchasing many different types of assets (short- and long-term, U.S. Treasury, and municipal bonds) and approving many types of loans to a number of customers. Banks that have not sufficiently sought the benefits of diversification often come to regret it later. For example, banks that had overspecialized in making loans to energy companies, real estate developers, or farmers suffered huge losses in the 1980s with the slump in energy, property, and farm prices. Indeed, many of these banks went broke because they had "put too many eggs in one basket."

Finally, the bank must manage the liquidity of its assets so that it can satisfy its reserve requirements without bearing huge costs. This means that it will hold liquid securities even if they earn a somewhat lower return than other assets. The bank must decide, for example, how much in excess reserves must be held to avoid costs from a deposit outflow. In addition, it will want to hold U.S. government securities as secondary reserves so that even if a deposit outflow forces some costs on the bank, these will not be terribly high. Again, it is not wise for a bank to be too conservative. If it avoids all costs associated with deposit outflows by holding only excess reserves, the bank suffers losses because reserves earn no interest, while the bank's liabilities are costly to maintain. The bank must balance its desire for liquidity against the increased earnings that can be obtained from less liquid assets such as loans.

Liability Management

Before the 1960s, liability management was a staid affair: For the most part, banks took their liabilities as fixed and spent their time trying to achieve an optimal mix of assets. There were two main reasons for the emphasis on asset management. First, more than 60% of the sources of bank funds were obtained through checkable (demand) deposits that by law could not pay any interest. Thus, banks could not actively compete with one another for these deposits by paying interest on them, and so their amount was effectively a given for an individual bank. Second, because the markets for making overnight loans between banks were not well developed, banks rarely borrowed from other banks to meet their reserve needs.

Starting in the 1960s, however, large banks (called **money center banks**) in key financial centers, such as New York, Chicago, and San Francisco, began to explore ways in which the liabilities on their balance sheets could provide them with reserves and liquidity. This move led to an expansion of overnight loan markets, such as the federal funds market, and the development of new financial instruments such as negotiable CDs (first developed in 1961), which enabled money center banks to acquire funds quickly.[2]

This new flexibility in liability management meant that banks could take a different approach to bank management. They no longer needed to depend on checkable deposits as the primary source of bank funds and as a result no longer treated their sources of funds (liabilities) as given. Instead, they aggressively set target goals for their asset growth and tried to acquire funds (by issuing liabilities) as they were needed.

For example, today, when a money center bank finds an attractive loan opportunity, it can acquire funds by selling a negotiable CD. Or, if it has a reserve shortfall, it can borrow funds from another bank in the federal funds market without incurring high transaction costs. The federal funds market can also be used to finance loans. Because of the increased importance of liability management, most banks now manage both sides of the balance sheet together in an *asset–liability management (ALM) committee*.

The greater emphasis on liability management explains some of the important changes over the past three decades in the composition of banks' balance sheets.

[2]Because small banks are not as well known as money center banks and so might be a higher credit risk, they find it harder to raise funds in the negotiable CD market. Hence, they do not engage nearly as actively in liability management.

While negotiable CDs and bank borrowings have greatly increased in importance as a source of bank funds in recent years (rising from 2% of bank liabilities in 1960 to 29% in 2016), checkable deposits have decreased in importance (from 61% of bank liabilities in 1960 to 10% in 2016). Newfound flexibility in liability management and the search for higher profits have also stimulated banks to increase the proportion of their assets held in loans, which earn higher income (from 46% of bank assets in 1960 to 56% in 2016).

Capital Adequacy Management

Banks have to make decisions about the amount of capital they need to hold for three reasons. First, bank capital helps prevent *bank failure*, a situation in which the bank cannot satisfy its obligations to pay its depositors and other creditors and so goes out of business. Second, the amount of capital affects returns for the owners (equity holders) of the bank. Third, a minimum amount of bank capital (bank capital requirements) is required by regulatory authorities.

How Bank Capital Helps Prevent Bank Failure Let's consider two banks with identical balance sheets, except that High Capital Bank has a ratio of capital to assets of 10% while Low Capital Bank has a ratio of 4%.

High Capital Bank				Low Capital Bank			
Assets		Liabilities		Assets		Liabilities	
Reserves	$10 million	Deposits	$90 million	Reserves	$10 million	Deposits	$96 million
Loans	$90 million	Bank capital	$10 million	Loans	$90 million	Bank capital	$ 4 million

Suppose that both banks got caught up in the euphoria of the real estate market, only to find that $5 million of their real estate loans became worthless later. When these bad loans are written off (valued at zero), the total value of assets declines by $5 million. As a consequence, bank capital, which equals total assets minus liabilities, also declines by $5 million. The balance sheets of the two banks now look like this:

High Capital Bank				Low Capital Bank			
Assets		Liabilities		Assets		Liabilities	
Reserves	$10 million	Deposits	$90 million	Reserves	$10 million	Deposits	$96 million
Loans	$85 million	Bank capital	$ 5 million	Loans	$85 million	Bank capital	–$ 1 million

High Capital Bank takes the $5 million loss in stride because its initial cushion of $10 million in capital means that it still has a positive net worth (bank capital) of $5 million after the loss. Low Capital Bank, however, is in big trouble. The value of its assets has fallen below its liabilities, and its net worth is now –$1 million. Because the bank has a negative net worth, it is insolvent: It does not have sufficient assets to pay off all holders of its liabilities. When a bank becomes insolvent, government regulators close the bank, its assets are sold off, and its managers are fired. Because the owners of Low Capital Bank will find their investment wiped out, they would clearly have preferred the bank to have had a large enough cushion of bank capital to absorb the losses, as was the case for High Capital Bank. We therefore see an important rationale for a bank to maintain a sufficient level of capital: ***A bank maintains bank capital to lessen the chance that it will become insolvent.***

How the Amount of Bank Capital Affects Returns to Equity Holders Because owners of a bank must know whether their bank is being managed well, they need good measures of bank profitability. A basic measure of bank profitability is the **return on assets (ROA)**, the net profit after taxes per dollar of assets:

$$\text{ROA} = \frac{\text{net profit after taxes}}{\text{assets}}$$

The return on assets provides information on how efficiently a bank is being run because it indicates how much profit is generated on average by each dollar of assets.

However, what the bank's owners (equity holders) care about most is how much the bank is earning on their equity investment. This information is provided by the other basic measure of bank profitability, the **return on equity (ROE)**, the net profit after taxes per dollar of equity (bank) capital:

$$\text{ROE} = \frac{\text{net profit after taxes}}{\text{equity capital}}$$

There is a direct relationship between the return on assets (which measures how efficiently the bank is run) and the return on equity (which measures how well the owners are doing on their investment). This relationship is determined by the **equity multiplier (EM)**, the amount of assets per dollar of equity capital:

$$\text{EM} = \frac{\text{assets}}{\text{equity capital}}$$

To see this, we note that

$$\frac{\text{net profit after taxes}}{\text{equity capital}} = \frac{\text{net profit after taxes}}{\text{assets}} \times \frac{\text{assets}}{\text{equity capital}}$$

which, using our definitions, yields

$$\text{ROE} = \text{ROA} \times \text{EM} \tag{1}$$

The formula in Equation 1 tells us what happens to the return on equity when a bank holds a smaller amount of capital (equity) for a given amount of assets. As we have seen, High Capital Bank initially has \$100 million of assets and \$10 million of equity, which gives it an equity multiplier of 10 (\$100 million/\$10 million). Low Capital Bank, by contrast, has only \$4 million of equity, so its equity multiplier is higher, equaling 25 (\$100 million/\$4 million). Suppose that these banks have been equally well run so that they both have the same return on assets, 1%. The return on equity for High Capital Bank equals $1\% \times 10 = 10\%$, whereas the return on equity for Low Capital Bank equals $1\% \times 25 = 25\%$. The equity holders in Low Capital Bank are clearly a lot happier than the equity holders in High Capital Bank because they are earning more than twice as high a return. We now see why owners of a bank may not want it to hold too much capital. ***Given the return on assets, the lower the bank capital, the higher the return for the owners of the bank.***

Trade-off Between Safety and Returns to Equity Holders We now see that bank capital has both benefits and costs. Bank capital benefits the owners of a bank in that it makes their investment safer by reducing the likelihood of bankruptcy. But bank capital is costly because the higher it is, the lower will be the return on equity for a given return on assets. In determining the amount of bank capital, managers must decide how much of the increased safety that comes with higher capital (the benefit) they are willing to trade off against the lower return on equity that comes with higher capital (the cost).

In more uncertain times, when the possibility of large losses on loans increases, bank managers might want to hold more capital to protect the equity holders. Conversely, if they have confidence that loan losses won't occur, they might want to reduce the amount of bank capital, have a higher equity multiplier, and thereby increase the return on equity.

Bank Capital Requirements Banks also hold capital because they are required to do so by regulatory authorities. Because of the high costs of holding capital for the reasons just described, bank managers often want to hold less bank capital relative to assets than is required by the regulatory authorities. In this case, the amount of bank capital is determined by the bank capital requirements. We discuss the details of bank capital requirements and their important role in bank regulation in Chapter 18.

THE PRACTICING MANAGER

Strategies for Managing Bank Capital

Mona, the manager of the First National Bank, has to make decisions about the appropriate amount of bank capital. Looking at the balance sheet of the bank, which, like High Capital Bank, has a ratio of bank capital to assets of 10% ($10 million of capital and $100 million of assets), Mona is concerned that the large amount of bank capital is causing the return on equity to be too low. She concludes that the bank has a capital surplus and should increase the equity multiplier to increase the return on equity.

To lower the amount of capital relative to assets and raise the equity multiplier, she can do any of three things: (1) She can reduce the amount of bank capital by buying back some of the bank's stock. (2) She can reduce the bank's capital by paying out higher dividends to its stockholders, thereby reducing the bank's retained earnings. (3) She can keep bank capital constant but increase the bank's assets by acquiring new funds—say, by issuing CDs—and then seeking out loan business or purchasing more securities with these new funds. Because the manager thinks that it would enhance her position with the stockholders, she decides to pursue the second alternative and raise the dividend on the First National Bank stock.

Now suppose that the First National Bank is in a situation similar to that of Low Capital Bank and has a ratio of bank capital to assets of 4%. The bank manager now might worry that the bank is short on capital relative to assets because it does not have a sufficient cushion to prevent bank failure. To raise the amount of capital relative to assets, she now has the following three choices: (1) She can raise capital for the bank by having it issue equity (common stock). (2) She can raise capital by reducing the bank's dividends to shareholders, thereby increasing retained earnings that it can put into its capital account. (3) She can keep capital at the same level but reduce the bank's assets by making fewer loans or by selling off securities and then using the proceeds to reduce its liabilities. Suppose that raising bank capital is not easy to do at the current time because capital markets are tight or because shareholders will protest if their dividends are cut. Then Mona might have to choose the third alternative and decide to shrink the size of the bank.

In past years, many banks experienced capital shortfalls and had to restrict asset growth, as Mona might have to do if the First National Bank were short of capital. The important consequences of this for the credit markets are illustrated in the case that follows.

CASE

How a Capital Crunch Caused a Credit Crunch During the Global Financial Crisis

The dramatic slowdown in the growth of credit in the wake of the financial crisis starting in 2007 triggered a "credit crunch" in which credit was hard to get. As a result, the performance of the economy in 2008 and 2009 was very poor. What caused the credit crunch?

Our analysis of how a bank manages its capital indicates that the 2008–2009 credit crunch was caused, at least in part, by the capital crunch, in which shortfalls of bank capital led to slower credit growth.

As we discussed in Chapter 8, there was a major boom and bust in the housing market that led to huge losses for banks from their holdings of securities backed by residential mortgages. In addition, banks had to take back onto their balance sheets many of the structured investment vehicles (SIVs) they had sponsored. The losses that reduced bank capital, along with the need for more capital to support the assets coming back onto their balance sheets, led to capital shortfalls: Banks had to either raise new capital or restrict asset growth by cutting back on lending. Banks did raise some capital, but with the growing weakness of the economy, raising new capital was extremely difficult, so banks also chose to tighten their lending standards and reduce lending. Both of these helped produce a weak economy in 2008 and 2009.

Off-Balance-Sheet Activities

Although asset and liability management has traditionally been the major concern of banks, in the more competitive environment of recent years banks have been aggressively seeking out profits by engaging in off-balance-sheet activities.

Off-balance-sheet activities involve trading financial instruments and generating income from fees and loan sales, activities that affect bank profits but do not appear on bank balance sheets. Indeed, off-balance-sheet activities have been growing in importance for banks: The income from these activities as a percentage of assets has increased more than fivefold since 1980.

Loan Sales

One type of off-balance-sheet activity that has grown in importance in recent years involves income generated by loan sales. A **loan sale**, also called a *secondary loan participation*, involves a contract that sells all or part of the cash stream from a specific loan and thereby removes the loan from the bank's balance sheet. Banks earn profits by selling loans for an amount slightly greater than that of the original loan. Because the high interest rate on these loans makes them attractive, institutions are willing to buy them, even though the higher price means that they earn a slightly lower interest rate than the original interest rate on the loan, usually on the order of 0.15 percentage point.

Generation of Fee Income

Another type of off-balance-sheet activity involves the generation of income from fees that banks receive for providing specialized services to their customers, such as making foreign exchange trades on a customer's behalf, servicing a mortgage-backed security by collecting interest and principal payments and then paying them out, guaranteeing debt securities such as banker's acceptances (by which the bank promises to make interest and principal payments if the party issuing the security cannot), and providing backup lines of credit. There are several types of backup lines of credit. The most important is the **loan commitment**, under which for a fee the bank agrees to provide a loan at the customer's request, up to a given dollar amount, over a specified period of time. Credit lines are also now available to bank depositors with "overdraft privileges"—these bank customers can write checks in excess of their deposit balances and, in effect, write themselves a loan. Other lines of credit for which banks get fees include standby letters of credit to back up issues of commercial paper and other securities and credit lines (called *note issuance facilities*, NIFs, and *revolving underwriting facilities*, RUFs) for underwriting Euronotes, which are medium-term Eurobonds.

Off-balance-sheet activities involving guarantees of securities and backup credit lines increase the risk a bank faces. Even though a guaranteed security does not appear on a bank balance sheet, it still exposes the bank to default risk: If the issuer of the security defaults, the bank is left holding the bag and must pay off the security's owner. Backup credit lines also expose the bank to risk because the bank may be forced to provide loans when it does not have sufficient liquidity or when the borrower is a very poor credit risk.

Trading Activities and Risk Management Techniques

As we will see in Chapter 24, banks' attempts to manage interest-rate risk have led them to trading in financial futures, options for debt instruments, and interest-rate swaps. Banks engaged in international banking also conduct transactions in the foreign exchange market. All transactions in these markets are off-balance-sheet activities because they do not have a direct effect on the bank's balance sheet. Although bank trading in these markets is often directed toward reducing risk or facilitating other bank business, banks may also try to outguess the markets and engage in speculation. This speculation can be a very risky business and indeed has led to bank insolvencies, the most dramatic being the failure of Barings, a British bank, in 1995.

GO ONLINE
Access **www.federalreserve.gov/boarddocs/SupManual/default.htm#trading**. The Federal Reserve Bank Trading and Capital Market Activities Manual offers an in-depth discussion of a wide range of risk management issues encountered in trading operations.

Trading activities, although often highly profitable, are dangerous because they make it easy for financial institutions and their employees to make huge bets quickly. A particular problem for management of trading activities is that the principal–agent problem, discussed in Chapter 7, is especially severe. Given the ability to place large bets, a trader (the agent), whether she trades in bond markets, in foreign exchange markets, or in financial derivatives, has an incentive to take on excessive risks: If her trading strategy leads to large profits, she is likely to receive a high salary and bonuses, but if she takes large losses, the financial institution (the principal) will have to cover them. As the Barings Bank failure in 1995 so forcefully demonstrated, a trader subject to the principal–agent problem can take an institution that is quite healthy and drive it into insolvency very rapidly (see the Conflicts of Interest box).

> CONFLICTS OF INTEREST

Barings, Daiwa, Sumitomo, Société Générale, and J.P. Morgan Chase: Rogue Traders and the Principal–Agent Problem

The demise of Barings, a venerable British bank more than a century old, is a sad morality tale of how the principal–agent problem operating through a rogue trader can take a financial institution that has a healthy balance sheet one month and turn it into an insolvent tragedy the next.

In July 1992 Nick Leeson, Barings' new head clerk at its Singapore branch, began to speculate on the Nikkei, the Japanese version of the Dow Jones stock index. By late 1992, Leeson had suffered losses of $3 million, which he hid from his superiors by stashing the losses in a secret account. He even fooled his superiors into thinking he was generating large profits, thanks to a failure of internal controls at his firm, which allowed him to execute trades on the Singapore exchange *and* oversee the bookkeeping of those trades. (As anyone who runs a cash business, such as a bar, knows, there is always a lower likelihood of fraud if more than one person handles the cash. Similarly, for trading operations, you never mix management of the back room with management of the front room; this principle was grossly violated by Barings' management.)

Things didn't get better for Leeson, who by late 1994 had losses exceeding $250 million. In January and February 1995, he bet the bank. On January 17, 1995, the day of the earthquake in Kobe, Japan, he lost $75 million, and by the end of the week had lost more than $150 million. When the stock market declined on February 23, leaving him with a further loss of $250 million, he called it quits and fled Singapore. Three days later, he turned himself in at the Frankfurt airport. By the end of his wild ride, Leeson's losses, $1.3 billion in all, ate up Barings' capital and caused the bank to fail. Leeson was subsequently convicted and sent to jail in Singapore for his activities. He was released in 1999 and apologized for his actions.

Our asymmetric information analysis of the principal–agent problem explains Leeson's behavior and the danger of Barings' management lapse. Letting Leeson control both his own trades and the back room increased asymmetric information because it reduced the principal's (Barings') knowledge about Leeson's trading activities. This lapse increased the moral hazard incentive for him to take risks at the bank's expense, as he was now less likely to be caught. Furthermore, once he had experienced large losses, he had even greater incentives to take on even higher risk because if his bets worked out, he could reverse his losses and keep in good standing with the company, whereas if his bets soured, he had little to lose because he was out of a job anyway. Indeed, the bigger his losses, the more he had to gain by bigger bets, which explains the escalation of the amount of his trades as his losses mounted. If Barings' managers had understood the principal–agent problem, they would have been more vigilant at finding out what Leeson was up to, and the bank might still be here today.

Unfortunately, Nick Leeson is no longer a rarity in the rogue traders' billionaire club, those who have lost more than $1 billion. Over 11 years, Toshihide Iguchi, an officer in the New York branch of Daiwa Bank, also had control of both the bond trading operation and the back room, and he racked up $1.1 billion in losses over the period. In July 1995 Iguchi disclosed his losses to his superiors, but the management of the bank did not disclose them to its regulators. The result was that Daiwa was slapped with a $340 million fine and the bank was thrown out of the country by U.S. bank regulators.

Yasuo Hamanaka is another member of the billionaire club. In July 1996 he topped Leeson's and Iguchi's record, losing $2.6 billion for his employer, the Sumitomo Corporation, one of Japan's top trading companies. J. Jerome Kerviel's loss for his bank, Société Générale, in January 2008 set the all-time record for a rogue trader: His unauthorized trades cost the bank $7.2 billion. Even the highly successful J.P. Morgan Chase bank experienced in 2012 over a $2 billion trading loss by Bruno Iksill, who was colorfully nicknamed "the London Whale."

The moral of these stories is that management of firms engaged in trading activities must reduce the principal–agent problem by closely monitoring their traders' activities, or the rogues' gallery will continue to grow.

To reduce the principal–agent problem, managers of financial institutions must set up internal controls to prevent debacles like the one at Barings. Such controls include the complete separation of the people in charge of trading activities from those in charge of the bookkeeping for trades. In addition, managers must set limits on the total amount of traders' transactions and on the institution's risk exposure. Managers must also scrutinize risk assessment procedures using the latest computer technology. One such method involves the value-at-risk approach. In this approach, the institution develops a statistical model with which it can calculate the maximum loss that its portfolio is likely to sustain over a given time interval, dubbed the value at risk, or VAR. For example, a bank might estimate that the maximum loss it would be likely to sustain over one day with a probability of 1 in 100 is $1 million; the $1 million figure is the bank's calculated value at risk. Another approach is called "stress testing." In this approach, a manager asks models what would happen if a doomsday scenario occurs; that is, she looks at the losses the institution would sustain if an unusual combination of bad events occurred. With the value-at-risk approach and stress testing, a financial institution can assess its risk exposure and take steps to reduce it.

U.S. bank regulators have become concerned about the increased risk that banks are facing from their off-balance-sheet activities and, as we will see in Chapter 18, are encouraging banks to pay increased attention to risk management. In addition, the Bank for International Settlements is developing additional bank capital requirements based on value-at-risk calculations for a bank's trading activities.

Measuring Bank Performance

To understand how well a bank is doing, we need to start by looking at a bank's income statement, the description of the sources of income and expenses that affect the bank's profitability.

Bank's Income Statement

The end-of-year 2015 income statement for all federally insured commercial banks and savings institutions appears in Table 17.2.

Operating Income **Operating income** is the income that comes from a bank's ongoing operations. Most of a bank's operating income is generated by interest on its assets, particularly loans. As we see in Table 17.2, in 2015 interest income represented 65.4% of commercial banks' operating income. Interest income fluctuates with the level of interest rates, and so its percentage of operating income is highest when interest rates are at peak levels. That is exactly what happened in 1981, when interest rates rose above 15% and interest income rose to 93% of total bank operating income.

TABLE 17.2 Income Statement for All Federally Insured Commercial Banks and Savings Institutions, 2015

	Amount ($ billions)		Share of Operating Income or Expenses (%)	
Operating Income				
Interest income		478.5		65.4
Interest on loans	382.0		52.2	
Interest on securities	70.5		9.6	
Other interest	26.0		3.6	
Noninterest income		253.3		34.6
Service charges on deposit accounts	34.6		4.7	
Other noninterest income	218.7		29.9	
Total operating income		731.8		100.0
Operating Expenses				
Interest expense		46.5		9.3
Interest on deposits	29.0		5.8	
Interest on fed funds	1.5		0.3	
Other	16.0		3.2	
Noninterest expenses		417.3		83.3
Salaries and employee benefits	192.9		38.5	
Premises and equipment	45.0		9.0	
Other	179.4		35.8	
Provisions for loan losses		37.0		7.4
Total operating expense		500.8		100.0
Net Operating Income		231.0		
Gain or loss on securities		3.6		
Extraordinary items net		–0.1		
Income taxes		–70.6		
Net Income		163.9		

Source: http://www2.fdic.gov/SDI/main.asp.

Noninterest income, which made up 34.6% of operating income in 2015, is generated partly by service charges on deposit accounts, but the bulk of it comes from the off-balance-sheet activities mentioned earlier, which generate fees or trading profits for the bank. The importance of these off-balance-sheet activities to bank profits has been growing in recent years. Whereas in 1980 other noninterest income from off-balance-sheet activities represented only 5% of operating income, it reached 29.9% in 2015.

Operating Expenses **Operating expenses** are the expenses incurred in conducting the bank's ongoing operations. An important component of a bank's operating expenses is the interest payments that it must make on its liabilities, particularly on its deposits. Just as interest income varies with the level of interest rates, so do interest expenses. Interest expenses as a percentage of total operating expenses reached a peak of 74% in 1981, when interest rates were at their highest, and fell to 9.3% in 2015 as interest rates moved lower. Noninterest expenses include the costs of running a banking business: salaries for tellers and officers, rent, maintenance and utilities for bank buildings, purchases of equipment such as desks and vaults, and servicing costs of equipment such as computers.

The final item listed under operating expenses is provisions for loan losses. When a bank has a bad debt or anticipates that a loan might become a bad debt, it can write up the loss as a current expense in its income statement under the "provision for loan losses" heading. Provisions for loan losses are directly related to loan loss reserves. When a bank wants to increase its loan loss reserves account by, say, $1 million, it does this by adding $1 million to its provisions for loan losses. Loan loss reserves rise when this is done because by increasing expenses when losses have not yet occurred, earnings are being set aside to deal with the losses in the future.

Provisions for loan losses have been a major element in fluctuating bank profits in recent years. The 1980s brought the third-world debt crisis; a sharp decline in energy prices in 1986, which caused substantial losses on loans to energy producers; and a collapse in the real estate market. As a result, provisions for loan losses were particularly high in the late 1980s, reaching a peak of 13% of operating expenses in 1987. After that, losses on loans began to subside, but they rose sharply during the 2007–2009 financial crisis. In 2009 provisions for loan losses reached a new peak of 32.7% of operating expenses. In 2015, provisions for loan losses were down to 7.4% of operating expenses.

Income Subtracting the $500.8 billion in operating expenses from the $731.8 billion of operating income in 2015 yields net operating income of $231.0 billion. Net operating income is closely watched by bank managers, bank shareholders, and bank regulators because it indicates how well the bank is doing on an ongoing basis.

Two items, gains (or losses) on securities sold by banks ($3.6 billion) and net extraordinary items, which are events or transactions that are both unusual and infrequent ($–0.1 billion), are added to the net operating income figure to get the $234.5 billion figure for net income before taxes. Net income before taxes is more commonly referred to as profits before taxes. Subtracting the $70.6 billion of income taxes then results in $163.9 billion of net income. Net income, more commonly referred to as profits after taxes, is the figure that tells us most directly how well the bank is doing because it is the amount that the bank has available to keep as retained earnings or to pay out to stockholders as dividends.

Measures of Bank Performance

Although net income gives us an idea of how well a bank is doing, it suffers from one major drawback: It does not adjust for the bank's size, thus making it hard to compare how well one bank is doing relative to another. A basic measure of bank profitability that corrects for the size of the bank is the return on assets (ROA), mentioned earlier, which divides the net income of the bank by the amount of its assets. ROA is a useful measure of how well a bank manager is doing on the job because it indicates how well a bank's assets are being used to generate profits. For 2015, the total assets of all federally insured banking institutions amounted to \$15,759 billion, so using the \$163.9 billion net income figure from Table 17.2 gives us a return on assets of

$$\text{ROA} = \frac{\text{net income}}{\text{assets}} = \frac{163.9}{15{,}759} = 0.0104 = 1.04\%$$

Although ROA provides useful information about bank profitability, we have already seen that it is not what the bank's owners (equity holders) care about most. They are more concerned about how much the bank is earning on their equity investment, an amount that is measured by the return on equity (ROE), the net income per dollar of equity capital. For 2015, the average equity capital for all federally insured banking institutions was \$1,762 billion, so the ROE was therefore

$$\text{ROE} = \frac{\text{net income}}{\text{capital}} = \frac{163.9}{1{,}762} = 0.0930 = 9.30\%$$

Another commonly watched measure of bank performance is called the **net interest margin (NIM)**, the difference between interest income and interest expenses as a percentage of total assets:

$$\text{NIM} = \frac{\text{interest income} - \text{interest expenses}}{\text{assets}}$$

As we have seen, one of a bank's primary intermediation functions is to issue liabilities and use the proceeds to purchase income-earning assets. If a bank manager has done a good job of asset and liability management such that the bank earns substantial income on its assets and has low costs on its liabilities, profits will be high. How well a bank manages its assets and liabilities is affected by the spread between the interest earned on the bank's assets and the interest costs on its liabilities. This spread is exactly what the net interest margin measures. If the bank is able to raise funds with liabilities that have low interest costs and is able to acquire assets with high interest income, the net interest margin will be high, and the bank is likely to be highly profitable. If the interest cost of its liabilities rises relative to the interest earned on its assets, the net interest margin will fall, and bank profitability will suffer.

Recent Trends in Bank Performance Measures

Table 17.3 provides measures of return on assets (ROA), return on equity (ROE), and the net interest margin (NIM) for all federally insured banking institutions from 1980 to 2015. Because the relationship between bank equity capital and total assets for all commercial banks remained fairly stable in the 1980s, both the ROA and ROE measures of bank performance move closely together and indicate that from the

TABLE 17.3 Measures of Performance for all Federally Insured Institutions, 1980–2015

Year	Return on Assets (ROA) (%)	Return on Equity (ROE) (%)	Net Interest Margin (NIM) (%)
1980	0.77	13.38	3.33
1981	0.79	13.68	3.31
1982	0.73	12.55	3.39
1983	0.68	11.60	3.34
1984	0.66	11.04	3.47
1985	0.72	11.67	3.62
1986	0.64	10.30	3.48
1987	0.09	1.54	3.40
1988	0.82	13.74	3.57
1989	0.50	7.92	3.58
1990	0.49	7.81	3.50
1991	0.53	8.25	3.60
1992	0.94	13.86	3.89
1993	1.23	16.30	3.97
1994	1.20	15.00	3.95
1995	1.17	14.66	4.29
1996	1.19	14.45	4.27
1997	1.23	14.69	4.21
1998	1.18	13.30	3.47
1999	1.31	15.31	4.07
2000	1.19	14.02	3.95
2001	1.15	13.09	3.90
2002	1.30	14.08	3.96
2003	1.38	15.05	3.73
2004	1.28	13.20	3.54
2005	1.30	12.73	3.50
2006	1.28	12.31	3.31
2007	0.81	7.75	3.29
2008	0.03	0.35	3.16
2009	0.08	0.73	3.49
2010	0.65	5.85	3.76
2011	0.88	7.79	3.60
2012	1.00	8.90	3.42
2013	1.07	9.54	3.26
2014	1.01	9.01	3.14
2015	1.04	9.30	3.07

Source: https://fdic.gov/bank/analytical/qbp/2016mar/qbp.pdf.

early to the late 1980s, there was a sharp decline in bank profitability. The rightmost column, net interest margin, indicates that the spread between interest income and interest expenses remained fairly stable throughout the 1980s and even improved in the late 1980s and early 1990s, which should have helped bank profits. The NIM measure thus tells us that the poor bank performance in the late 1980s was not the result of interest-rate movements.

The explanation of the weak performance of commercial banks in the late 1980s is that they had made many risky loans in the early 1980s that turned sour. The resulting huge increase in loan loss provisions in that period directly decreased net income and hence caused the fall in ROA and ROE. (Why bank profitability deteriorated and the consequences for the economy are discussed in Chapters 18 and 19.)

Beginning in 1992, bank performance improved substantially. The return on equity rose to nearly 14% in 1992 and remained above 12% in the 1993–2006 period. Similarly, the return on assets rose from the 0.5% level in the 1990–1991 period to well over the 1% level during 1993–2006. The performance measures in Table 17.3 suggest that the banking industry returned to health. Then, however, with the onset of the 2007–2009 financial crisis, bank profitability deteriorated dramatically, with the ROE falling to a low of 0.35% in 2008 and ROA falling to 0.03%. In recent years, bank profitability has improved, but is still not as strong as it was before the crisis, with the return on equity at 9.3% in 2015 and the return on assets, 1.0%.

SUMMARY

1. The balance sheet of commercial banks can be thought of as a list of the sources and uses of bank funds. The bank's liabilities are its sources of funds, which include checkable deposits, time deposits, discount loans from the Fed, borrowings from other banks and corporations, and bank capital. The bank's assets are its uses of funds, which include reserves, cash items in process of collection, deposits at other banks, securities, loans, and other assets (mostly physical capital).

2. Banks make profits through the process of asset transformation: They borrow short (accept deposits) and lend long (make loans). When a bank takes in additional deposits, it gains an equal amount of reserves; when it pays out deposits, it loses an equal amount of reserves.

3. Although more liquid assets tend to earn lower returns, banks still desire to hold them. Specifically, banks hold excess and secondary reserves because they provide insurance against the costs of a deposit outflow. Banks manage their assets to maximize profits by seeking the highest returns possible on loans and securities while at the same time trying to lower risk and making adequate provisions for liquidity. Although liability management was once a staid affair, large (money center) banks now actively seek out sources of funds by issuing liabilities such as negotiable CDs or by actively borrowing from other banks and corporations. Banks manage the amount of capital they hold to prevent bank failure and to meet bank capital requirements set by the regulatory authorities. However, they do not want to hold too much capital because by so doing they will lower the returns to equity holders.

4. Off-balance-sheet activities consist of trading financial instruments and generating income from fees and loan sales, all of which affect bank profits but are not visible on bank balance sheets. Because these off-balance-sheet activities expose banks to increased risk, bank management must pay particular attention to risk assessment procedures and internal controls to restrict employees from taking on too much risk.

5. A bank's net operating income equals operating income minus operating expenses. Adding gains (or losses) on securities and net extraordinary items to net operating income and then subtracting taxes yields net income (profits after taxes). Additional measures of bank performance include the return on assets (ROA), the return on equity (ROE), and the net interest margin (NIM).

KEY TERMS

asset management, p. 396
balance sheet, p. 390
capital adequacy management, p. 396
credit risk, p. 396
deposit outflows, p. 396
discount loans, p. 391
discount rate, p. 398
equity multiplier (EM), p. 402
excess reserves, p. 392
interest-rate risk, p. 396
liability management, p. 396
liquidity management, p. 396
loan commitment, p. 405
loan sale, p. 405
money center banks, p. 400
net interest margin (NIM), p. 410
off-balance-sheet activities, p. 405
operating expenses, p. 409
operating income, p. 408
required reserve ratio, p. 392
required reserves, p. 392
reserve requirements, p. 392
reserves, p. 392
return on assets (ROA), p. 402
return on equity (ROE), p. 402
secondary reserves, p. 393
vault cash, p. 392

QUESTIONS

1. Some central banks do not pay interest on required reserves. Some bankers see this as a tax on their business. Can you explain why?
2. If no decent lending opportunity arises in the economy, and the central bank pays an interest rate on reserves that is similar to other low-risk investments, do you think banks will be willing to hold large amounts of excess reserves.
3. If the bank you own has no excess reserves and a sound customer comes in asking for a loan, should you automatically turn the customer down, explaining that you don't have any excess reserves to loan out? Why or why not? What options are available for you to provide the funds your customer needs?
4. Why has the development of overnight loan markets made it more likely that banks will hold fewer excess reserves?
5. If you are a banker and expect interest rates to rise in the future, would you want to make short-term or long-term loans?
6. "Bank managers should always seek the highest return possible on their assets." Is this statement true, false, or uncertain? Explain your answer.
7. "Banking has become a more dynamic industry because of more active liability management." Is this statement true, false, or uncertain? Explain your answer.
8. After July 2010, bank customers using a debit card had to specifically opt-in to the bank's overdraft protection plan. Explain the effect of this regulation on bank's noninterest income.
9. Which components of operating expenses experience the greatest fluctuations? Why?
10. Why do equity holders care more about ROE than about ROA?
11. Explain how the net interest margin (NIM) would respond to increased competition for funds by the financial intermediation industry.
12. If a bank doubles the amount of its capital and ROA stays constant, what will happen to ROE?
13. If a bank finds that its ROE is too low because it has too much bank capital, what can it do to raise its ROE?
14. What are the benefits and costs for a bank when it decides to increase the amount of its bank capital?
15. If a bank is falling short of meeting its capital requirements by $1 million, what three things can it do to rectify the situation?

QUANTITATIVE PROBLEMS

1. Angus Bank holds no excess reserves but complies with the reserve requirement. The required reserves ratio is 9%, and reserves are currently $27 million. Determine the amount of deposits, the reserve shortage created by a deposit outflow of $5 million, and the cost of the reserve shortage if Angus Bank borrows in the federal funds market (assume the federal funds rate is 0.25%).
2. Excess reserves act as insurance against deposit outflows. Suppose that on a yearly basis Malcom Bank holds $12 million in excess reserves and $88 million in required reserves. Suppose that Malcom Bank can earn 3.5% on its loans and that the interest paid on (total) reserves is 0.2%. What would be the cost of this insurance policy?
3. Nice Horizon Bank has the following measures of bank profitability: EM = 14 and ROA = 1.05%. Gold Coast Bank's measures are EM = 12.3 and ROA = 1.15%. Which bank has a higher ROE?

4. Refer to the previous problem. Calculate both banks' net profit after taxes and equity capital if both banks' assets are equal to $120 million.
5. Victory Bank reports an EM of 25, while Batovi Bank reports an EM equal to 14. Which bank is better prepared to respond against large losses on loans?
6. A bank is considering two investment portfolios composed of a mix of government securities (federal and municipal securities). The first portfolio has a return of 6% with probability 0.9 and returns of 5% and 7% with 0.05 probability. The second portfolio has a return of 5% with probability 0.5 and a return of 7% with probability 0.5. Which portfolio has the best combination of return, risk, and liquidity?

The remaining questions relate to the first month's operations of NewBank.

7. NewBank started its first day of operations with $6 million in capital. $100 million in checkable deposits is received. The bank issues a $25 million commercial loan and another $25 million in mortgages, with the following terms:
   - Mortgages: 100 standard 30-year fixed-rate mortgages with a nominal annual rate of 5.25% each for $250,000
   - Commercial loan: 3-year loan, simple interest paid monthly at 0.75% per month

   If required reserves are 8%, what do the bank balance sheets look like? Ignore any loan loss reserves.
8. NewBank decides to invest $45 million in 30-day T-bills. The T-bills are currently trading at $4,986.70 (including commissions) for a $5,000 face value instrument. How many do they purchase? What does the balance sheet look like?
9. On the third day of operations, deposits fall by $5 million. What does the balance sheet look like? Are there any problems?
10. To meet any shortfall in the previous problem, NewBank will borrow in the federal funds market. Management decides to borrow the needed funds for the remainder of the month (now 29 days). The required yield on a discount basis is 2.9%. What does the balance sheet look like after this transaction?
11. The end of the month finally arrives for NewBank, and it receives all the required payments from its mortgages, commercial loans, and T-bills. How much cash was received? How are these transactions recorded?
12. NewBank also pays off its federal funds borrowed. How much cash is owed? How is this recorded?
13. What does the month-end balance sheet for NewBank look like?
14. Calculate NewBank's ROA and NIM for its first month. Assume that net interest equals earnings before taxes, and that NewBank is in the 34% tax bracket.
15. Calculate NewBank's ROE and final balance sheet.
16. If NewBank were required to establish a loan loss reserve at 0.25% of the loan value for commercial loans, how would this be recorded? Recalculate NewBank's ROE and final balance sheet, including its tax liabilities.
17. If NewBank's target ROE is 4.5%, how much net fee income must it generate to meet this target?
18. After making payments for three years, one of the mortgage borrowers defaults on the mortgage. NewBank immediately takes possession of the house and sells it at auction for $175,000. Legal fees amount to $25,000. If no loan loss reserve was established for the mortgage loans, how is this event recorded?

WEB EXERCISES

Banking and the Management of Financial Institutions

1. Table 17.1 reports the balance sheet of all commercial banks based on aggregate data found in the Federal Reserve *Bulletin*. Compare this table to the balance sheet reported by BB&T in its latest annual report, which can be found at **http://www.bbt.com/bbt/about/investorrelations/default.html**. Does BB&T have more or less of its portfolio in loans than the average bank? Which type of loan is most common?
2. It is relatively easy to find up-to-date information on banks because of their extensive reporting requirements. Go to **http://www2.fdic.gov/qbp/**. This site is sponsored by the Federal Deposit Insurance Corporation. You will find summary data on financial institutions. Go to the most recent Quarterly Banking Profile. Scroll down and open Table 1-A.
   - **a.** Have banks' return on assets been increasing or decreasing over the past few years?
   - **b.** Has the core capital been increasing, and how does it compare to the capital ratio reported in Table 17.1 in the text?
   - **c.** How many institutions are currently reporting to the FDIC?

CHAPTER 18

Financial Regulation

> PREVIEW

As we have seen in previous chapters, the financial system is among the most heavily regulated sectors of the economy, and banks are among the most heavily regulated of financial institutions. In this chapter, we develop a framework to see why regulation of the financial system takes the form it does.

Unfortunately, the regulatory process may not always work very well, as evidenced by the recent global and other financial crises, not only in the United States but in many countries throughout the world. Here we also use our analysis of financial regulation to explain the worldwide crises in banking and to consider how the regulatory system can be reformed to prevent future disasters.

Asymmetric Information as a Rationale for Financial Regulation

Access **http://www.newyorkfed.org/banking/supervisionregulate.html** to view bank regulation information.

In earlier chapters, we have seen how asymmetric information—the fact that different parties in a financial contract do not have the same information—leads to adverse selection and moral hazard problems that have an important impact on our financial system. The concepts of asymmetric information, adverse selection, and moral hazard are especially useful in understanding why governments pursue financial regulation.

Government Safety Net

Access **http://www.federalreserve.gov/bankinforeg/** for regulatory publications of the Federal Reserve Board.

As we saw in Chapter 7, financial intermediaries, like banks, are particularly well suited to solving adverse selection and moral hazard problems because they make private loans that help avoid the free-rider problem. However, this solution to the free-rider problem creates another asymmetric information problem because depositors lack information about the quality of these private loans. This asymmetric information problem leads to other problems that interfere with the proper functioning of the financial system.

Bank Panics and the Need for Deposit Insurance Before the FDIC (Federal Deposit Insurance Corporation) started operations in 1934, a **bank failure** (in which a bank is unable to meet its obligations to pay its depositors and other creditors and so must go out of business) meant that depositors would have to wait until the bank was liquidated (until its assets had been turned into cash) to get their deposit funds; at that time, they would be paid only a fraction of the value of their deposits. Because they couldn't know if bank managers were taking on too much risk or were outright crooks, depositors would be reluctant to put money in the bank, thus making banking institutions less viable. Second, depositors' lack of information about the quality of bank assets can lead to a **bank panic**, in which many banks fail simultaneously. Because the simultaneous failure of many banks leads to a sharp decline in bank lending, bank panics have serious harmful consequences for the economy.

To understand why bank panics occur, consider the following situation. Deposit insurance does not exist, and an adverse shock hits the economy. As a result of the shock, 5% of banks have such large losses on loans that they become insolvent (have a negative net worth and so are bankrupt). Because of asymmetric information, depositors are unable to tell whether their bank is a good bank or one of the 5% that are insolvent. Depositors at bad *and* good banks recognize that they may not get back 100 cents on the dollar for their deposits and therefore are inclined to withdraw them. Indeed, because banks operate on a "sequential service constraint" (a first-come, first-served basis), depositors have a very strong incentive to be first to show up at the bank because if they are last in line, the bank may have paid out all its funds and they will get nothing. The incentive to "run" to the bank to be first is why withdrawals when there is fear about the health of a bank is described as a "bank run." Uncertainty about the health of the banking system in general can lead to runs on both good and bad banks, and the failure of one bank can hasten the failure of others (referred to as the *contagion effect*). If nothing is done to restore the public's confidence, a bank panic can ensue.

Indeed, bank panics were a fact of American life in the nineteenth and early twentieth centuries, with major panics occurring every 20 years or so in 1819, 1837,

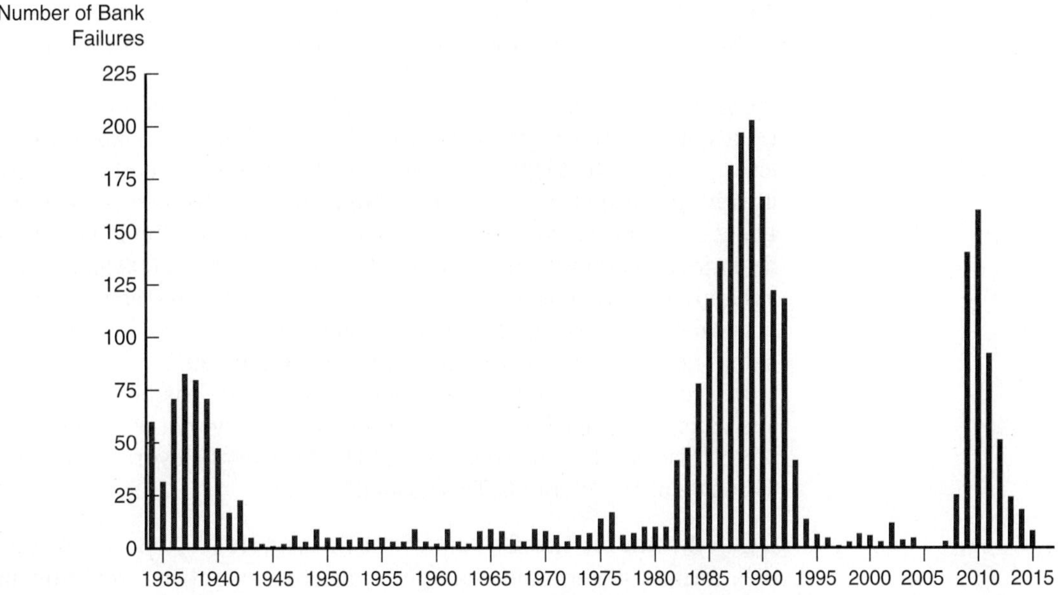

FIGURE 18.1 **Bank Failures in the United States, 1934–2015**

Bank failures were a rarity from 1934 to 1980, averaging fewer than 15 per year, but in the periods 1982–1993 and 2009–2010, they rose to levels more than 10 times greater.

Source: www.fdic.gov/bank/historical/bank/index.html.

1857, 1873, 1884, 1893, 1907, and 1930–1933. Bank failures were a serious problem even during the boom years of the 1920s, when the number of bank failures averaged around 600 per year.

A government safety net for depositors can short-circuit runs on banks and bank panics, and by providing protection for the depositor, it can overcome reluctance to put funds in the banking system. One form of safety net is deposit insurance, such as that provided by the Federal Deposit Insurance Corporation (FDIC) in the United States. The FDIC guarantees that current depositors will be paid off in full on the first $250,000 they have deposited in a bank if the bank fails. With fully insured deposits, depositors don't need to run to the bank to make withdrawals—even if they are worried about the bank's health—because their deposits will be worth 100 cents on the dollar no matter what. From 1930 to 1933, the years immediately preceding the creation of the FDIC, the number of bank failures averaged more than 2,000 per year. After the establishment of the FDIC in 1934, bank failures averaged fewer than 15 per year until 1981. However, as shown in Figure 18.1, in the periods 1982–1983 and 2009–2010, they rose to levels more than ten times higher.

Access **http://www.fdic.gov/bank/individual/failed/** for information on bank failures in any year.

The FDIC uses two primary methods to handle a failed bank. In the first, called the *payoff method*, the FDIC allows the bank to fail and pays off deposits up to the $250,000 insurance limit (with funds acquired from the insurance premiums paid by the banks that have bought FDIC insurance). After the bank has been liquidated, the FDIC lines up with other creditors of the bank and is paid its share of the proceeds from the liquidated assets. Typically, when the payoff method is used, account holders with deposits in excess of the $250,000 limit get back more than 90 cents on the dollar, although the process can take several years to complete.

In the second method, called the *purchase and assumption method*, the FDIC reorganizes the bank, typically by finding a willing merger partner who assumes (takes over) all of the failed bank's liabilities so that no depositor or other creditor loses a penny. The FDIC often sweetens the pot for the merger partner by providing it with subsidized loans or by buying some of the failed bank's weaker loans. The net effect of the purchase and assumption method is that the FDIC has guaranteed *all* liabilities and deposits, not just deposits under the $250,000 limit. The purchase and assumption method is typically more costly for the FDIC than the payoff method but nevertheless was the FDIC's more common procedure for dealing with a failed bank before new banking legislation was introduced in 1991.

In recent years, government deposit insurance has been growing in popularity and has spread to many countries throughout the world. Whether this trend is desirable is discussed in the Global box, "The Spread of Government Deposit Insurance Throughout the World: Is This a Good Thing?"

Other Forms of the Government Safety Net Deposit insurance is not the only form of government safety net. In other countries, governments have often stood ready to provide support to domestic banks facing runs even in the absence of explicit deposit insurance. Furthermore, banks are not the only financial intermediaries that can pose a systemic threat to the financial system. When financial institutions are very large or highly interconnected with other financial

GLOBAL

The Spread of Government Deposit Insurance Throughout the World: Is This a Good Thing?

For the first 30 years after federal deposit insurance was established in the United States, only six countries emulated the United States and adopted deposit insurance. However, this began to change in the late 1960s, with the trend accelerating in the 1990s, when the number of countries adopting deposit insurance topped 70. Government deposit insurance has taken off throughout the world because of growing concern about the health of banking systems, particularly after the increasing number of banking crises in recent years (documented at the end of this chapter). Has this spread of deposit insurance been a good thing? Has it helped improve the performance of the financial system and prevent banking crises?

The answer seems to be *no* under many circumstances. Research at the World Bank has found that, on average, the adoption of explicit government deposit insurance is associated with less banking sector stability and a higher incidence of banking crises.* Furthermore, on average, deposit insurance seems to retard financial development. However, these negative effects of deposit insurance occur only in countries with weak institutional environments: an absence of rule of law, ineffective regulation and supervision of the financial sector, and high corruption. This situation is exactly what might be expected because, as we will see later in this chapter, a strong institutional environment is needed to limit the moral hazard incentives for banks to engage in the excessively risky behavior encouraged by deposit insurance. The problem is that development of a strong institutional environment may be very difficult to achieve in many emerging market countries. We are left with the following conclusion: Adoption of deposit insurance may be exactly the wrong medicine for promoting stability and efficiency of banking systems in emerging market countries.

*See World Bank, *Finance for Growth: Policy Choices in a Volatile World* (Oxford: World Bank and Oxford University Press, 2001).

institutions or markets, their failure has the potential to bring down the entire financial system. Indeed, this is exactly what happened with Bear Stearns and Lehman Brothers, two investment banks, and AIG, an insurance company, during the recent financial crisis in 2008.

One way in which governments provide support is through lending from the central bank to troubled institutions, as the Federal Reserve did during the global financial crisis (discussed in Chapter 10). This form of support is often referred to as the "lender of last resort" role of the central bank. In other cases, funds are provided directly to troubled institutions, as was done by the U.S. Treasury and by other governments in 2008 during a particularly virulent phase of the 2007–2009 financial crisis. Governments can also take over (nationalize) troubled institutions and guarantee that all creditors' loans will be paid in full.

Moral Hazard and the Government Safety Net Although a government safety net can help protect depositors and other creditors and prevent, or ameliorate, financial crises, it is a mixed blessing. The most serious drawback of the government safety net stems from moral hazard, the incentives of one party in a transaction to engage in activities detrimental to the other party. Moral hazard is an important concern in insurance arrangements in general because the existence of insurance provides increased incentives for taking risks that might result in an insurance payoff. For example, some drivers with automobile collision insurance that has a low deductible might be more likely to drive recklessly because if they get into an accident, the insurance company pays most of the costs for damage and repairs.

Moral hazard is a prominent concern associated with government arrangements to provide safety nets. With a safety net, depositors and creditors know they will not suffer losses if a financial institution fails, so they do not impose the discipline of the marketplace on these institutions by withdrawing funds when they suspect that the financial institution is taking on too much risk. Consequently, financial institutions with a government safety net have an incentive to take on greater risks than they otherwise would, because taxpayers will foot the bill if the bank subsequently goes belly up. Financial institutions can place the following bet: "Heads I win, tails the taxpayer loses."

Adverse Selection and the Government Safety Net A further problem with a government safety net like deposit insurance is adverse selection, the fact that the people who are most likely to produce the adverse outcome insured against (bank failure) are the same people who most want to take advantage of the insurance. For example, bad drivers are more likely than good drivers to take out automobile collision insurance with a low deductible. Because depositors and creditors protected by a government safety net have little reason to impose discipline on financial institutions, risk-loving entrepreneurs might find the financial industry a particularly attractive one—they know they will be able to engage in highly risky activities. Even worse, because protected depositors and creditors have so little reason to monitor the financial institution's activities, without government intervention outright crooks might also find finance an attractive industry for their activities because it is easy for them to get away with fraud and embezzlement.

Too Big to Fail The moral hazard created by a government safety net and the desire to prevent financial institution failures have presented financial regulators with a particular quandary, the **too-big-to-fail problem**, in which regulators are reluctant to close down large financial institutions and impose losses on the institutions' depositors and creditors because doing so might precipitate a financial crisis. The too-big-to-fail problem arose when Continental Illinois, once one of the 10 largest banks in the United States, became insolvent in May 1984. Not only did the FDIC guarantee depositors up to the $100,000 limit (the maximum at the time), but it also guaranteed accounts exceeding $100,000 and even prevented losses for Continental Illinois bondholders. Shortly thereafter, the Comptroller of the Currency (the regulator of national banks) testified to Congress that 11 of the largest banks would receive a treatment similar to that received by Continental Illinois. Although the comptroller did not use the term "too big to fail" (it was actually used by Congressman Stewart McKinney in those congressional hearings), this term is now applied to a policy in which the government provides guarantees of repayment of large uninsured creditors of the largest banks, so that no depositor or creditor suffers a loss, even when the depositors and creditors are not automatically entitled to this guarantee. The FDIC does this by using the purchase-and-assumption method, giving the insolvent bank a large infusion of capital and then finding a willing merger partner to take over the bank and its deposits. The too-big-to-fail policy was extended to big banks that were not even among the 11 largest. (Note that "too big to fail" is a somewhat misleading term because when a financial institution is closed or merged into another financial institution, the managers are usually fired and the stockholders in the financial institution lose their investment.)

One problem with the too-big-to-fail policy is that it increases the moral hazard incentives for big banks. If the FDIC were willing to close a bank using the payoff method, paying depositors only up to the current $250,000 limit, large depositors with more than $250,000 would suffer losses if the bank failed. Thus they would have an incentive to monitor the bank by examining the bank's activities closely and pulling their money out if the bank was taking on too much risk. To prevent such a loss of deposits, the bank would be more likely to engage in less risky activities. However, once large depositors know that a bank is too big to fail, they have no incentive to monitor the bank and pull out their deposits when it takes on too much risk: No matter what the bank does, large depositors will not suffer losses. The result of the too-big-to-fail policy is that big financial institutions might take on even greater risks, thereby making bank failures more likely.

Similarly, the too-big-to-fail policy increases the moral hazard incentives for nonbank financial institutions that are extended a government safety net. Knowing that the financial institution will be bailed out, creditors have little incentive to monitor the institution and pull their money out when the institution is taking on excessive risk. As a result, large or interconnected financial institutions are more likely to engage in highly risky activities, making a financial crisis more likely.

Indeed, financial institutions that were considered too big to fail—including Bear Stearns, Lehman Brothers, and AIG—did take on excessive risk in the run up to the global financial crisis, and their subsequent collapse helped trigger the worst financial crisis since the Great Depression.

Financial Consolidation and the Government Safety Net With financial innovation and the passage of the Riegle-Neal Interstate Banking and Branching Efficiency Act of 1994 and the Gramm-Leach-Bliley Financial Services Modernization Act in 1999, financial consolidation has been proceeding at a rapid pace, leading to both larger and more complex financial organizations. Financial consolidation poses two challenges to financial regulation because of the existence of the government safety net. First, the increased size of financial institutions resulting from financial consolidation increases the too-big-to-fail problem because there are now more large institutions whose failure would expose the financial system to systemic (systemwide) risk. Thus more financial institutions are likely to be treated as too big to fail, and the increased moral hazard incentives for these large institutions to take on greater risk increases the fragility of the financial system. Second, financial consolidation of banks with other financial services firms means that the government safety net may be extended to new activities such as securities underwriting, insurance, or real estate activities, as occurred during the global financial crisis. This situation increases incentives for greater risk taking in these activities, which can also weaken the fabric of the financial system. Limiting the moral hazard incentives for the larger, more complex financial organizations that have arisen as a result of recent changes in legislation is one of the key issues facing banking regulators in the aftermath of the global financial crisis.

Types of Financial Regulation

There are nine basic types of financial regulation aimed at lessening asymmetric information problems and excessive risk taking in the financial system: (1) restrictions on asset holdings, (2) capital requirements, (3) prompt corrective action, (4) chartering and examination, (5) assessment of risk management, (6) disclosure requirements, (7) consumer protection, (8) restrictions on competition, and (9) macroprudential regulation.

Restrictions on Asset Holdings

As we have seen, the moral hazard associated with a government safety net encourages too much risk taking on the part of financial institutions. Bank regulations that restrict asset holdings are directed at minimizing this moral hazard, which can cost the taxpayers dearly.

Even in the absence of a government safety net, financial institutions still have the incentive to take on too much risk. Risky assets may provide the financial institution with higher earnings when they pay off, but if they do not pay off and the institution fails, depositors and creditors are left holding the bag. If depositors and creditors were able to monitor the bank easily by acquiring information on its risk-taking activities, they would immediately withdraw their funds if the institution was taking on too much risk. To prevent such a loss of funds, the institution would be more likely to reduce its risk-taking activities. Unfortunately, acquiring information on an institution's activities to learn how much risk it is taking can be a difficult task. Hence most depositors and many creditors are incapable of imposing discipline that might prevent financial institutions from engaging in risky activities. A strong rationale for government regulation to reduce risk taking on the part of financial institutions therefore existed even before the establishment of government safety nets like federal deposit insurance.

Because banks are most prone to panics, they are subjected to strict regulations to restrict their holding of risky assets such as common stocks. Bank regulations also promote diversification, which reduces risk by limiting the dollar amount of loans in particular categories or to individual borrowers. With the extension of the government safety net during the 2007–2009 financial crisis, it is likely that nonbank financial institutions may face greater restrictions on their holdings of risky assets. The danger exists, however, that these restrictions may become so onerous that the efficiency of the financial system will be impaired.

Capital Requirements

Government-imposed capital requirements are another way of minimizing moral hazard at financial institutions. When a financial institution is forced to hold a large amount of equity capital, the institution has more to lose if it fails and is thus more likely to pursue less risky activities. In addition, as was illustrated in Chapter 17, capital functions as a cushion when bad shocks occur, making it less likely that the financial institution will fail, thereby directly adding to the safety and soundness of financial institutions.

Capital requirements for banks and investment banks take two forms. The first type is based on the **leverage ratio**, the amount of capital divided by the bank's total assets. To be classified as well capitalized, a bank's leverage ratio must exceed 5%; a lower leverage ratio, especially one below 3%, triggers increased regulatory restrictions on the bank. Through most of the 1980s, minimum bank capital in the United States was set solely by specifying a minimum leverage ratio.

In the wake of the Continental Illinois and savings and loans bailouts, regulators in the United States and the rest of the world became increasingly worried about banks' holdings of risky assets and about the increase in banks' off-balance-sheet activities. **Off-balance-sheet activities** do not appear on the bank balance sheet but nevertheless expose banks to risk involving trading financial instruments and generating income from fees. An agreement among banking officials from industrialized nations set up the **Basel Committee on Banking Supervision** (so named because it meets under the auspices of the Bank for International Settlements in Basel, Switzerland), which has implemented the **Basel Accord**, which deals with a second type of capital requirements, risk-based capital requirements. The initial Basel Accord, which still applies to all but the largest banks in the United States, requires that banks hold as capital at least 8% of their risk-weighted assets; it was adopted by more than 100 countries, including the United States. Assets were allocated into four categories, each with a different weight to reflect the degree of credit risk. The first category carried a zero weight and included items that have little default risk, such as reserves and government securities issued by the Organization for Economic Cooperation and Development (OECD—industrialized) countries. The second category had a 20% weight and included claims on banks in OECD countries. The third category had a weight of 50% and included municipal bonds and residential mortgages. The fourth category had the maximum weight of 100% and included loans to consumers and corporations. Off-balance-sheet activities were treated in a similar manner. They are assigned a credit-equivalent percentage that converted them to on-balance-sheet items to which the appropriate risk weight applied.

Over time, the limitations of the Basel Accord became apparent because the regulatory measure of bank risk as stipulated by the risk weights differed substantially from the actual risk the bank faced. This discrepancy resulted in **regulatory arbitrage**, a practice in which banks keep on their books assets that have the same risk-based capital requirement but are relatively risky, such as a loan to a company with a very low credit rating, while taking off their books low-risk assets, such as a loan to a company with a very high credit rating. The Basel Accord thus led to increased risk taking, the opposite of its intent. To address these limitations, the Basel Committee on Bank Supervision came up with a new capital accord, referred to as Basel 2. However, in the aftermath of the global financial crisis, the committee developed an even newer accord, which the media has dubbed "Basel 3." These accords are described in the Global box, "Where Is the Basel Accord Heading After the Global Financial Crisis?"

Prompt Corrective Action

If the amount of a financial institution's capital falls to low levels, two serious problems result. First, the bank is more likely to fail because it has a smaller capital cushion if it suffers loan losses or other asset write-downs. Second, with less capital, a financial institution has less "skin in the game" and is therefore more likely to take on excessive risks. In other words, the moral hazard problem becomes more severe, making it more likely that the institution will fail and the taxpayer will be left holding the bag. To prevent this, the Federal Deposit Insurance Corporation Improvement Act of 1991 adopted prompt corrective action provisions that require the FDIC to intervene earlier and more vigorously when a bank gets into trouble.

Banks in the United States are now classified into five groups based on bank capital. Group 1, classified as "well capitalized," comprises banks that significantly exceed minimum capital requirements and are allowed privileges such as the ability to do some securities underwriting. Banks in group 2, classified as "adequately capitalized," meet minimum capital requirements and are not subject to corrective actions but are not allowed the privileges of the well-capitalized banks. Banks in group 3, "undercapitalized," fail to meet capital requirements. Banks in groups 4 and 5 are "significantly undercapitalized" and "critically undercapitalized," respectively, and are not allowed to pay interest on their deposits at rates that are higher than average. In addition, for group 3 banks, the FDIC is required to take prompt corrective actions such as requiring them to submit a capital restoration plan, restrict their asset growth, and seek regulatory approval to open new branches or develop new lines of business. Banks that are so undercapitalized as to have equity capital that amounts to less than 2% of assets fall into group 5, and the FDIC must take steps to close them down.

Financial Supervision: Chartering and Examination

Overseeing who operates financial institutions and how they are operated, referred to as **financial supervision** or **prudential supervision**, is an important method for reducing adverse selection and moral hazard in the financial industry. Because financial institutions can be used by crooks or overambitious entrepreneurs to engage in highly speculative activities, such undesirable people would be eager to run a financial institution. Chartering financial institutions is one method for preventing this adverse selection problem; through chartering, proposals for new institutions are screened to prevent undesirable people from controlling them.

Regular on-site examinations, which allow regulators to monitor whether the institution is complying with capital requirements and restrictions on asset holdings, also function to limit moral hazard. Bank examiners give banks a *CAMELS rating*. The acronym is based on the six areas assessed: capital adequacy, asset quality,

> GLOBAL

Where Is the Basel Accord Heading After the Global Financial Crisis?

Starting in June 1999, the Basel Committee on Banking Supervision released several proposals to reform the original 1988 Basel Accord. These efforts culminated in what bank supervisors refer to as Basel 2, which is based on three pillars.

1. Pillar 1 links capital requirements for large, internationally active banks more closely to actual risk of three types: market risk, credit risk, and operational risk. It does so by specifying many more categories of assets with different risk weights in its standardized approach. Alternatively, it allows sophisticated (typically the largest) banks to pursue an internal ratings-based approach that permits these banks to use their own models of credit risk.
2. Pillar 2 focuses on strengthening the supervisory process, particularly in assessing the quality of risk management in banking institutions and evaluating whether these institutions have adequate procedures in place for determining how much capital they need.
3. Pillar 3 focuses on improving market discipline through increased disclosure of details about a bank's credit exposures, its amount of reserves and capital, the officials who control the bank, and the effectiveness of its internal rating system.

Although Basel 2 made strides toward limiting excessive risk taking by internationally active banking institutions, it greatly increased the complexity of the accord. The document describing the original Basel Accord was 26 pages, whereas the final draft of Basel 2 exceeded 500 pages. The original timetable called for the completion of the final round of consultation by the end of 2001, with the new rules taking effect by 2004. However, criticism from banks, trade associations, and national regulators led to several postponements. The final draft was not published until June 2004, and Basel 2 began to be implemented at the start of 2008 by European banks, but full implementation in the United States did not occur until 2009. Only the dozen or so largest U.S. banks are subject to Basel 2: All others are allowed to use a simplified version of the standards it imposes.

The global financial crisis, however, revealed many limitations of the new accord. First, Basel 2 did not require banks to have sufficient capital to weather the financial disruption that occurred during this period. Second, risk weights in the standardized approach are heavily reliant on credit ratings, which proved to be extremely unreliable in the run-up to the financial crisis. Third, Basel 2 is very procyclical. That is, it demands that banks hold less capital when times are good but more when times are bad, thereby exacerbating credit cycles. Because the probability of default and expected losses on different classes of assets rises during bad times, Basel 2 may require more capital at exactly the time when capital is most short. This has been a particularly serious concern in the aftermath of the 2007–2009 financial crisis. As a result of this crisis, banks' capital balances eroded, leading to a cutback on lending that was a big drag on the economy. Basel 2 has made this cutback in lending even worse, doing yet more harm to the economy. Fourth, Basel 2 did not focus sufficiently on the dangers of a possible drying up of liquidity, a problem that brought down financial institutions during the financial crisis.

As a result of these limitations, in 2010 the Basel Committee developed a new accord, Basel 3. It beefs up capital standards by not only raising them substantially but also improving the quality of the capital, makes them less procyclical by raising capital requirements in good times and lowering them in bad, makes new rules on the use of credit ratings, and requires financial institutions to have more stable funding so that they are better able to withstand liquidity shocks. Measures to achieve these objectives are highly controversial because of concerns that tightening up capital standards might cause banks to restrict their lending, which would make it harder for economies throughout the world to recover from the recent deep recession. Basel 3 is being implemented slowly over time, with the target for full implementation extending out to the end of 2019. Whether Basel 3 will be fully in place by that date and be successful in restraining risk taking is highly uncertain.

management, earnings, liquidity, and sensitivity to market risk. With this information about a bank's activities, regulators can enforce regulations by taking such formal actions as *cease and desist orders* to alter the bank's behavior or even close a bank if its CAMELS rating is sufficiently low. Actions taken to reduce moral hazard by restricting banks from taking on too much risk help reduce the adverse selection problem further because with less opportunity for risk taking, risk-loving entrepreneurs will be less likely to be attracted to the banking industry. Note that the methods regulators use to cope with adverse selection and moral hazard have their counterparts in private financial markets (see Chapters 7 and 23). Chartering is similar to the screening of potential borrowers, regulations restricting risky asset holdings are similar to restrictive covenants that prevent borrowing firms from engaging in risky investment activities, capital requirements act like restrictive covenants that require minimum amounts of net worth for borrowing firms, and regular examinations are similar to the monitoring of borrowers by lending institutions.

A bank obtains a charter either from the Comptroller of the Currency (in the case of a national bank) or from a state banking authority (in the case of a state bank). To obtain a charter, the people planning to organize the bank must submit an application that shows how they plan to operate the bank. In evaluating the application, the regulatory authority looks at whether the bank is likely to be sound by examining the quality of the bank's intended management, the likely earnings of the bank, and the amount of the bank's initial capital. Before 1980 the chartering agency typically explored the issue of whether the community needed a new bank. Often a new bank charter would not be granted if existing banks in a community would be hurt by its presence. Today this anticompetitive stance (justified by the desire to prevent failures of existing banks) is no longer as strong in the chartering agencies.

Once a bank has been chartered, it is required to file periodic (usually quarterly) *call reports* that reveal the bank's assets and liabilities, income and dividends, ownership, foreign exchange operations, and other details. The bank is also subject to examination by the bank regulatory agencies to ascertain its financial condition at least once a year. To avoid duplication of effort, the three federal agencies work together and usually accept each other's examinations. This means that, typically, national banks are examined by the Office of the Comptroller of the Currency, state banks that are members of the Federal Reserve System are examined by the Fed, and insured nonmember state banks are examined by the FDIC.

Bank examinations are conducted by bank examiners, who sometimes make unannounced visits to the bank (so that nothing can be "swept under the rug" in anticipation of their examination). The examiners study a bank's books to see whether it is complying with the rules and regulations that apply to its holdings of assets. If a bank is holding securities or loans that are too risky, the bank examiner can force the bank to get rid of them. If a bank examiner decides that a loan is unlikely to be repaid, the examiner can force the bank to declare the loan worthless (to write off the loan, which reduces the bank's capital). If, after examining the bank, the examiner feels that it does not have sufficient capital or has engaged in dishonest practices, the bank can be declared a "problem bank" and will be subject to more frequent examinations.

Assessment of Risk Management

Traditionally, on-site examinations have focused primarily on assessment of the quality of a financial institution's balance sheet at a point in time and whether it complies with capital requirements and restrictions on asset holdings. Although the traditional focus is still important in reducing excessive risk taking by financial institutions, it is no longer thought to be adequate in today's world, in which financial innovation has produced new markets and instruments that make it easy for financial institutions and their employees to make huge bets easily and quickly. In this new financial environment, a financial institution that is healthy at a particular point in time can be driven into insolvency extremely rapidly from trading losses, as forcefully demonstrated by the failure of Barings in 1995 (discussed in Chapter 17). Thus an examination that focuses only on a financial institution's position at a point in time may not be effective in indicating whether it will, in fact, be taking on excessive risk in the near future.

This change in the financial environment has resulted in a major shift in thinking about the prudential supervisory process throughout the world. Bank examiners, for example, are now placing far greater emphasis on evaluating the soundness of a bank's management processes with regard to controlling risk. This shift in thinking was reflected in a new focus on risk management by the Federal Reserve System, starting with 1993 guidelines to examiners on trading and derivatives activities. The focus was expanded and formalized in the Trading Activities Manual issued early in 1994, which provided bank examiners with tools to evaluate risk management systems. In late 1995, the Federal Reserve and the Comptroller of the Currency announced that they would be assessing risk management processes at the banks they supervise. Now bank examiners give a separate risk management rating from 1 to 5 that feeds into the overall management rating as part of the CAMELS system. Four elements of sound risk management are assessed to arrive at the risk management rating: (1) the quality of oversight provided by the board of directors and senior management, (2) the adequacy of policies and limits for all activities that present significant risks, (3) the quality of the risk measurement and monitoring systems, and (4) the adequacy of internal controls to prevent fraud or unauthorized activities on the part of employees.

This shift toward focusing on management processes is also reflected in guidelines adopted by the U.S. bank regulatory authorities to deal with interest-rate risk. These guidelines require the bank's board of directors to establish interest-rate risk limits, appoint officials of the bank to manage this risk, and monitor the bank's risk exposure. The guidelines also require that senior management of a bank develop formal risk management policies and procedures to ensure that the board of directors' risk limits are not violated and to implement internal controls to monitor interest-rate risk and compliance with the board's directives. Particularly important is the implementation of **stress testing**, which calculates losses under dire scenarios, and **value-at-risk (VaR) calculations**, which measure the size of the loss on a trading portfolio that might happen 1% of the time—say, over a two-week period. In addition to these guidelines, bank examiners will continue to consider interest-rate risk in deciding the bank's capital requirements.

Disclosure Requirements

The free-rider problem described in Chapter 7 indicates that individual depositors and creditors will not have enough incentive to produce private information about the quality of a financial institution's assets. To ensure that better information is available in the marketplace, regulators can require that financial institutions adhere to certain standard accounting principles and disclose a wide range of information that helps the market assess the quality of an institution's portfolio and the amount of its exposure to risk. More public information about the risks incurred by financial institutions and the quality of their portfolios can better enable stockholders, creditors, and depositors to evaluate and monitor financial institutions and so act as a deterrent to excessive risk taking.

Disclosure requirements are a key element of financial regulation. Basel 2 puts a particular emphasis on disclosure requirements, with one of its three pillars focusing on increasing market discipline by mandating increased disclosure by banking institutions of their credit exposure, amount of reserves, and capital. The Securities Act of 1933 and the Securities and Exchange Commission (SEC), which was established in 1934, also impose disclosure requirements on any corporation, including financial institutions, that issues publicly traded securities. In addition, the SEC has required financial institutions to provide additional disclosure regarding their off-balance-sheet positions and more information about how they value their portfolios.

Regulation to increase disclosure is needed to limit incentives to take on excessive risk and to upgrade the quality of information in the marketplace so that investors can make informed decisions, thereby improving the ability of financial markets to allocate capital to its most productive uses. The efficiency of markets is assisted by the SEC's disclosure requirements mentioned above, as well as its regulation of brokerage firms, mutual funds, exchanges, and credit-rating agencies to ensure that they produce reliable information and protect investors. The Sarbanes-Oxley Act of 2002, discussed in Chapter 7, took disclosure of information even further by increasing the incentives to produce accurate audits of corporate income statements and balance sheets, established the Public Company Accounting Oversight Board (PCAOB) to oversee the audit industry, and put in place regulations to limit conflicts of interest in the financial services industry.

Particularly controversial in the wake of the global financial crisis is the move to so-called **mark-to-market accounting**, also called **fair-value accounting**, in which assets are valued in the balance sheet at what they could sell for in the market (see the Mini-Case box, "Mark-to-Market Accounting and the Global Financial Crisis").

Consumer Protection

The existence of asymmetric information also suggests that consumers may not have enough information to protect themselves fully in financial dealings. Consumer protection regulation has taken several forms. The Consumer Protection Act of 1969 (more commonly referred to as the Truth in Lending Act) requires all lenders, not just banks, to provide information to consumers about the cost of borrowing, including the disclosure of a standardized interest rate (called the *annual percentage rate*, or *APR*) and the total finance charges on the loan. The Fair Credit Billing Act of 1974 requires creditors, especially credit card issuers, to provide information on the method of assessing finance charges and requires that billing complaints be handled quickly.

Congress also passed legislation to reduce discrimination in credit markets. The Equal Credit Opportunity Act of 1974 and its extension in 1976 forbid discrimination by lenders based on race, gender, marital status, age, or national origin. This act is administered by the Federal Reserve under Regulation B. The Community Reinvestment Act (CRA) of 1977 was enacted to prevent "redlining," a lender's refusal to lend in a particular area (marked off by a hypothetical red line on a map). The Community Reinvestment Act requires that banks show that they lend in all

> MINI-CASE

Mark-to-Market Accounting and the Global Financial Crisis

The controversy over mark-to-market accounting has made accounting a hot topic. Mark-to-market accounting was made standard practice in the U.S. accounting industry in 1993. The rationale behind mark-to-market accounting is that market prices provide the best basis for estimating the true value of assets, and hence capital, in the firm. Before mark-to-market accounting, firms relied on traditional historical-cost (book value) accounting in which the value of an asset was set at its initial purchase price. The problem with historical-cost accounting is that fluctuations in the value of assets and liabilities because of changes in interest rates or default are not reflected in the calculation of the firm's equity capital. Yet changes in the market value of assets and liabilities—and hence changes in the market value of equity capital—are what indicates if a firm is in good shape or, alternatively, if it is getting into trouble and may therefore be more susceptible to moral hazard.

Mark-to-market accounting, however, is subject to a major flaw. At times markets stop working, as occurred during the global financial crisis. The price of an asset sold at a time of financial distress does not reflect its fundamental value. That is, the fire-sale liquidation value of an asset can at times be well below the present value of its expected future cash flows. Many people, particularly bankers, have criticized mark-to-market accounting, claiming that it has been an important factor driving the recent global financial crisis. They claim that the seizing up of financial markets has led to market prices being well below their fundamental values. Mark-to-market accounting requires that the financial firms' assets be marked down in value. This markdown creates a shortfall in capital that leads to a cutback in lending, which causes a further deterioration in asset prices, which in turn causes a further cutback in lending. The resulting adverse feedback loop can then make the financial crisis even worse. Although the criticisms of mark-to-market accounting have some validity, some of the criticism by bankers is self-serving. The criticism was made only when asset values were falling and when mark-to-market accounting was painting a bleaker picture of banks' balance sheets, as opposed to when asset prices were booming and mark-to-market accounting made banks' balance sheets look very good.

The criticisms of mark-to-market accounting led to a congressional focus on mark-to-market accounting that resulted in a provision in the Emergency Economic Stabilization Act of 2008 that required the SEC, in consultation with the Federal Reserve and the U.S. Treasury, to submit a study of mark-to-market accounting applicable to financial institutions. Who knew that accounting could get even politicians worked up!

areas in which they take deposits, and if banks are found to be in noncompliance with the act, regulators can reject their applications for mergers, branching, or other new activities.

The global financial crisis has illustrated the need for greater consumer protection because so many borrowers took out loans with terms they did not understand and that were well beyond their means to repay. The result was millions of foreclosures, with many households losing their homes. Because weak consumer protection regulation played a prominent role in this crisis, demands to strengthen this regulation have been increasing, as is discussed in the Mini-Case box, "The Global Financial Crisis and Consumer Protection Regulation."

Restrictions on Competition

Increased competition can also increase moral hazard incentives for financial institutions to take on more risk. Declining profitability as a result of increased competition could tip the incentives of financial institutions toward assuming greater risk in

MINI-CASE

The Global Financial Crisis and Consumer Protection Regulation

Because of the principal–agent problem inherent in the originate-to-distribute model for subprime mortgages discussed in Chapters 8 and 14, incentives were weak for mortgage originators, typically mortgage brokers who were virtually unregulated, to ensure that subprime borrowers had an ability to pay back their loans. After all, mortgage brokers keep their large fees from mortgage originations even if sometime down the road the borrowers default on their loans and lose their houses. With these incentives, mortgage brokers weakened their underwriting standards, leading to subprime mortgage products such as "no-doc loans," more pejoratively referred to as "liar loans," in which borrowers did not have to produce documentation about their assets or income. A particular infamous variant of the no-doc loan was dubbed the NINJA loan because it was issued to borrowers with No Income, No Job, and No Assets. Mortgage brokers also had incentives to put households into very complicated mortgage products that borrowers could not understand and couldn't afford to pay. In some cases, mortgage brokers even engaged in fraud by falsifying information on borrowers' mortgage applications in order to qualify them for mortgage loans.

Lax consumer protection regulation was an important factor in producing the global financial crisis. Mortgage originators were not required to disclose information to borrowers that would have helped them understand complicated mortgage products and whether they could afford to repay them. Outrage over the surge of foreclosures has been an important stimulus for new regulation to provide better information to mortgage borrowers and to ban unfair and deceptive practices. Under Regulation Z of the Truth in Lending Act, in July 2008 the Federal Reserve issued a final rule for subprime mortgage loans with the following four elements: (1) a ban on lenders making loans without regard to borrowers' ability to repay the loan from income and assets other than the home's value, (2) a ban on no-doc loans, (3) a ban on prepayment penalties (i.e., a penalty for paying back the loan early) if the interest payment can change in the first four years of the loan, and (4) a requirement that lenders establish an escrow account for property taxes and homeowner's insurance to be paid into on a monthly basis. In addition, the rule stipulated the following new regulations for all mortgage loans, not just subprime mortgages: (1) a prohibition on mortgage brokers coercing a real estate appraiser to misstate a home's value, (2) a prohibition on putting one late fee on top of another and a requirement to credit consumers' loan payments as of the date of receipt, (3) a requirement for lenders to provide a good-faith estimate of the loan costs within three days after a household applies for a loan, and (4) a ban on a number of misleading advertising practices, including representing that a rate or payment is "fixed" when the payment can change.

Because the view was held that more needed to be done, the Obama administration and Congress have stepped in by creating a new consumer protection agency as part of the financial reform legislation of 2010: This is discussed later in the chapter. The mandate of this agency is to further strengthen consumer protection regulation on subprime mortgages and other financial products.

an effort to maintain former profit levels. Thus governments in many countries have instituted regulations to protect financial institutions from competition. These regulations have taken two forms in the United States in the past. First were restrictions on branching, which are described in Chapter 19, which reduced competition between banks, but these were eliminated in 1994. The second form involved preventing nonbank institutions from competing with banks by engaging in banking business, as embodied in the Glass-Steagall Act, which was repealed in 1999.

Although restrictions on competition propped up the health of banks, they also had serious disadvantages: They led to higher charges to consumers and decreased the efficiency of banking institutions, which did not have to compete as vigorously.

Thus, although the existence of asymmetric information provided a rationale for anticompetitive regulations, it did not mean that they would be beneficial. Indeed, in recent years, the impulse of governments in industrialized countries to restrict competition has been waning. Electronic banking has raised a new set of concerns for regulators to deal with. See the E-Finance box for a discussion of this challenge.

Macroprudential Versus Microprudential Supervision

Before the global financial crisis, the regulatory authorities engaged in **microprudential supervision**, which focuses on the safety and soundness of *individual* financial institutions. Microprudential supervision looks at each institution separately and assesses the riskiness of its activities and whether it complies with disclosure requirements. Most important, it checks whether that institution satisfies capital *ratios* and, if not, either it engages in prompt corrective action to force the institution to raise its capital ratios or the supervisor closes it down, along the lines we have discussed.

Discussion of the global financial crisis in Chapter 8 reveals that a focus on microprudential supervision is not enough to prevent financial crises. The run on the shadow banking system illustrates how the problems of one financial institution can harm other financial institutions that are otherwise healthy. When the troubled financial institution is forced to engage in fire sales and sell off assets to meet target

> E-FINANCE

Electronic Banking: New Challenges for Bank Regulation

The advent of electronic banking has raised new concerns for banking regulation, specifically about security and privacy. Worries about the security of electronic banking and e-money are an important barrier to their increased use. With electronic banking, you might worry that criminals can access your bank account and steal your money by moving your balances to someone else's account. Private solutions to deal with this problem have arisen with the development of more secure encryption technologies to prevent this kind of fraud. However, because bank customers are not knowledgeable about computer security issues, there is a role for the government in regulating electronic banking to make sure that encryption procedures are adequate. Similar encryption issues apply to e-money, so requirements that banks make it difficult for criminals to engage in digital counterfeiting make sense. To meet these challenges, bank examiners in the United States assess how a bank deals with the special security issues raised by electronic banking and also oversee third-party providers of electronic banking platforms. Also, because consumers want to know that electronic banking transactions are executed correctly, bank examiners assess the technical skills of banks in setting up electronic banking services and the bank's capabilities for dealing with problems. Another security issue of concern to bank customers is the validity of digital signatures. The Electronic Signatures in Global and National Commerce Act of 2000 makes electronic signatures as legally binding as written signatures in most circumstances.

Electronic banking also raises serious privacy concerns. Because electronic transactions can be stored on databases, banks are able to collect a huge amount of information about their customers—their assets, creditworthiness, purchases, and so on—that can be sold to other financial institutions and businesses. This potential invasion of our privacy rightfully makes us very nervous. To protect customers' privacy, the Gramm-Leach-Bliley Act of 1999 has limited the distribution of these data, but it does not go as far as the European Data Protection Directive, which prohibits the transfer of information about online transactions. How to protect consumers' privacy in our electronic age is one of the great challenges our society faces, so privacy regulations for electronic banking are likely to evolve over time.

capital ratios or haircut requirements, this leads to a decline in asset values. This decline in asset values then causes other institutions to engage in fire sales, leading to a rapid deleveraging process and a systemic crisis. In situations like this, even institutions that would normally be healthy and have high capital ratios may find themselves in trouble.

The global financial crisis has therefore made it clear that there is a need for **macroprudential supervision**, which focuses on the safety and soundness of the financial system *in the aggregate*. Rather than focus on the safety and soundness of individual institutions, macroprudential supervision seeks to mitigate systemwide fire sales and deleveraging by assessing the overall capacity of the financial system to avoid them. In addition, because many institutions that were well capitalized faced liquidity shortages and found that their access to short-term funding was cut off, macroprudential supervision focuses not only on capital adequacy as a whole but also on whether the financial system has sufficient liquidity.

Macroprudential policies can take several forms. The run-up to the global financial crisis included a so-called **leverage cycle**, in which there was a feedback loop from a boom in issuing credit, which led to higher asset prices, which resulted in higher capital buffers at financial institutions, which supported further lending in the context of unchanging capital requirements, which then raised asset prices further, and so on; in the bust phase of the cycle, the value of the capital dropped precipitously, leading to a cut in lending. To short-circuit this leverage cycle, macroprudential policies would make capital requirements countercyclical; that is, they would be adjusted upward during a boom and downward during a bust. In addition, during the upward swing in the leverage cycle, macroprudential policies might involve forcing financial institutions to tighten credit standards or even direct limits on the growth of credit. In the downward swing, macroprudential supervision might be needed to force the banking system as a whole to raise an aggregate amount of new capital so that banks would not curtail lending in order to reduce the level of their assets and raise capital ratios. To ensure that financial institutions have enough liquidity, macroprudential policies could require that financial institutions have a sufficiently low *net stable funding ratio* (NSFR), which is the percentage of the institution's short-term funding in relation to total funding. Macroprudential policies of the type discussed here are being considered as part of the Basel 3 framework but have not yet been completely worked out.

Summary

Asymmetric information analysis explains the types of financial regulations that are needed to reduce moral hazard and adverse selection problems in the financial system. However, understanding the theory behind regulation does not mean that regulation and supervision of the financial system are easy in practice. Getting regulators and supervisors to do their jobs properly is difficult for several reasons. First, as we will see in the discussion of financial innovation in Chapter 19, financial institutions, in their search for profits, have strong incentives to avoid existing regulations by loophole mining. Thus regulation applies to a moving target: Regulators are continually playing cat-and-mouse with financial institutions—financial institutions think up clever ways to avoid regulations, which then lead regulators to modify their regulation activities. Regulators continually face new challenges in a dynamically changing financial system—and unless they can respond rapidly, they may not be able to keep financial institutions from taking on excessive risk. This problem can be exacerbated if regulators and supervisors do not have the resources or expertise to keep up with clever people in financial institutions seeking to circumvent the existing regulations.

Financial regulation and supervision are difficult for two other reasons. In the regulation and supervision game, the devil is in the details. Subtle differences in the details may have unintended consequences; unless regulators get the regulation and supervision just right, they may be unable to prevent excessive risk taking. In addition, regulated firms may lobby politicians to lean on regulators and supervisors to go easy on them.

For all of these reasons, there is no guarantee that regulators and supervisors will be successful in promoting a healthy financial system. These same problems bedevil financial regulators in other countries, as the Global box, "International Financial Regulation," indicates. Indeed, as we will see, financial regulation and supervision have not always worked well, leading to banking crises in the United States and throughout the world.

Because so many laws regulating the financial system have been passed in the United States, it is hard to keep track of them all. As a study aid, Table 18.1 lists the major financial legislation since the beginning of the twentieth century and its key provisions.

> GLOBAL

International Financial Regulation

Because asymmetric information problems in the banking industry are a fact of life throughout the world, financial regulation in other countries is similar to that in the United States. Financial institutions are chartered and supervised by government regulators, just as they are in the United States. Disclosure requirements for financial institutions and corporations issuing securities are similar in other developed countries. Deposit insurance is also a feature of the regulatory systems in most other countries, although its coverage is often smaller than in the United States and is intentionally not advertised. We have also seen that capital requirements are in the process of being standardized across countries in compliance with agreements like the Basel Accord.

Particular problems in financial regulation occur when financial institutions operate in many countries and thus can readily shift their business from one country to another. Financial regulators closely examine the domestic operations of financial institutions in their country, but they often do not have the knowledge or ability to keep a close watch on operations in other countries, either by domestic institutions' foreign affiliates or by foreign institutions with domestic branches. In addition, when a financial institution operates in many countries, it is not always clear which national regulatory authority should have primary responsibility for keeping the institution from engaging in overly risky activities.

The difficulties inherent in international financial regulation were highlighted by the collapse of the Bank of Credit and Commerce International (BCCI). BCCI, which was operating in more than 70 countries, including the United States and the United Kingdom, was supervised by Luxembourg, a tiny country unlikely to be up to the task. When massive fraud was discovered, the Bank of England closed BCCI down, but not before depositors and stockholders were exposed to huge losses. Cooperation among regulators in different countries and standardization of regulatory requirements provide potential solutions to the problems of international financial regulation. The world has been moving in this direction through agreements like the Basel Accord and oversight procedures announced by the Basel Committee in July 1992, which require a bank's worldwide operations to be under the scrutiny of a single home-country regulator with enhanced powers to acquire information on the bank's activities. The Basel Committee also ruled that regulators in other countries can restrict the operations of a foreign bank if they believe it lacks effective oversight. Whether agreements of this type will solve the problem of international financial regulation in the future is an open question.

TABLE 18.1 Major Financial Legislation in the United States

Federal Reserve Act (1913)

Created the Federal Reserve System

McFadden Act of 1927

Effectively prohibited banks from branching across state lines

Put national and state banks on equal footing regarding branching

Banking Acts of 1933 (Glass-Steagall) and 1935

Created the FDIC

Separated banking from the securities industry

Prohibited interest on checkable deposits and restricted such deposits to commercial banks

Put interest-rate ceilings on other deposits

Securities Act of 1933 and Securities Exchange Act of 1934

Required that investors receive financial information on securities offered for public sale

Prohibited misrepresentations and fraud in the sale of securities

Created the Securities and Exchange Commission (SEC)

Investment Company Act of 1940 and Investment Advisers Act of 1940

Regulated investment companies, including mutual funds

Regulated investment advisers

Bank Holding Company Act and Douglas Amendment (1956)

Clarified the status of bank holding companies (BHCs)

Gave the Federal Reserve regulatory responsibility for BHCs

Depository Institutions Deregulation and Monetary Control Act (DIDMCA) of 1980

Gave thrift institutions wider latitude in activities

Approved NOW and sweep accounts nationwide

Phased out interest-rate ceilings on deposits

Imposed uniform reserve requirements on depository institutions

Eliminated usury ceilings on loans

Increased deposit insurance to $100,000 per account

Depository Institutions Act of 1982 (Garn–St. Germain)

Gave the FDIC and the Federal Savings and Loan Insurance Corporation (FSLIC) emergency powers to merge banks and thrifts across state lines

Allowed depository institutions to offer money market deposit accounts (MMDAs)

Granted thrifts wider latitude in commercial and consumer lending

Competitive Equality in Banking Act (CEBA) of 1987

Provided $10.8 billion to the FSLIC

Made provisions for regulatory forbearance in depressed areas

(continued)

TABLE 18.1 Major Financial Legislation in the United States (*continued*)

Financial Institutions Reform, Recovery, and Enforcement Act (FIRREA) of 1989

Provided funds to resolve S&L failures

Eliminated the FSLIC and the Federal Home Loan Bank Board

Created the Office of Thrift Supervision to regulate thrifts

Created the Resolution Trust Corporation to resolve insolvent thrifts

Raised deposit insurance premiums

Reimposed restrictions on S&L activities

Federal Deposit Insurance Corporation Improvement Act (FDICIA) of 1991

Recapitalized the FDIC

Limited brokered deposits and the too-big-to-fail policy

Set provisions for prompt corrective action

Instructed the FDIC to establish risk-based premiums

Increased examinations, capital requirements, and reporting requirements

Included the Foreign Bank Supervision Enhancement Act (FBSEA), which strengthened the Fed's authority to supervise foreign banks

Riegle-Neal Interstate Banking and Branching Efficiency Act of 1994

Overturned prohibition of interstate banking

Allowed branching across state lines

Gramm-Leach-Bliley Financial Services Modernization Act of 1999

Repealed Glass-Steagall and removed the separation of banking and securities industries

Sarbanes-Oxley Act of 2002

Created Public Company Accounting Oversight Board (PCAOB)

Prohibited certain conflicts of interest

Required certification by CEO and CFO of financial statements and independence of audit committee

Federal Deposit Insurance Reform Act of 2005

Merged the Bank Insurance Fund and the Savings Association Insurance Fund

Increased deposit insurance on individual retirement accounts to $250,000 per account

Authorized FDIC to revise its system of risk-based premiums

Dodd-Frank Wall Street Reform and Consumer Protection Act of 2010

Created Consumer Financial Protection Bureau to regulate mortgages and other financial products

Required routine derivatives to be cleared through central clearinghouses and exchanges

Provided new government resolution authority to allow government takeovers of financial holding companies

Created Financial Stability Oversight Council to regulate systemically important financial institutions

Banned banks from proprietary trading and owning large percentage of hedge funds

Banking Crises Throughout the World in Recent Years

Because misery loves company, it may make you feel better to know that the United States was not alone in suffering banking crises even before the global financial crisis of 2007–2009. Indeed, as Figure 18.2 and Table 18.2 illustrate, banking crises have struck a large number of countries throughout the world since the 1980s, and many of them have been substantially worse than the ones the United States experienced.

"Déjà Vu All Over Again"

In banking crises in different countries, history keeps repeating itself. The parallels between the banking crisis episodes in all these countries are remarkably similar, creating a feeling of déjà vu. They all started with financial liberalization or innovation, with weak bank regulatory systems and a government safety net. Although financial liberalization is generally a good thing because it promotes competition and

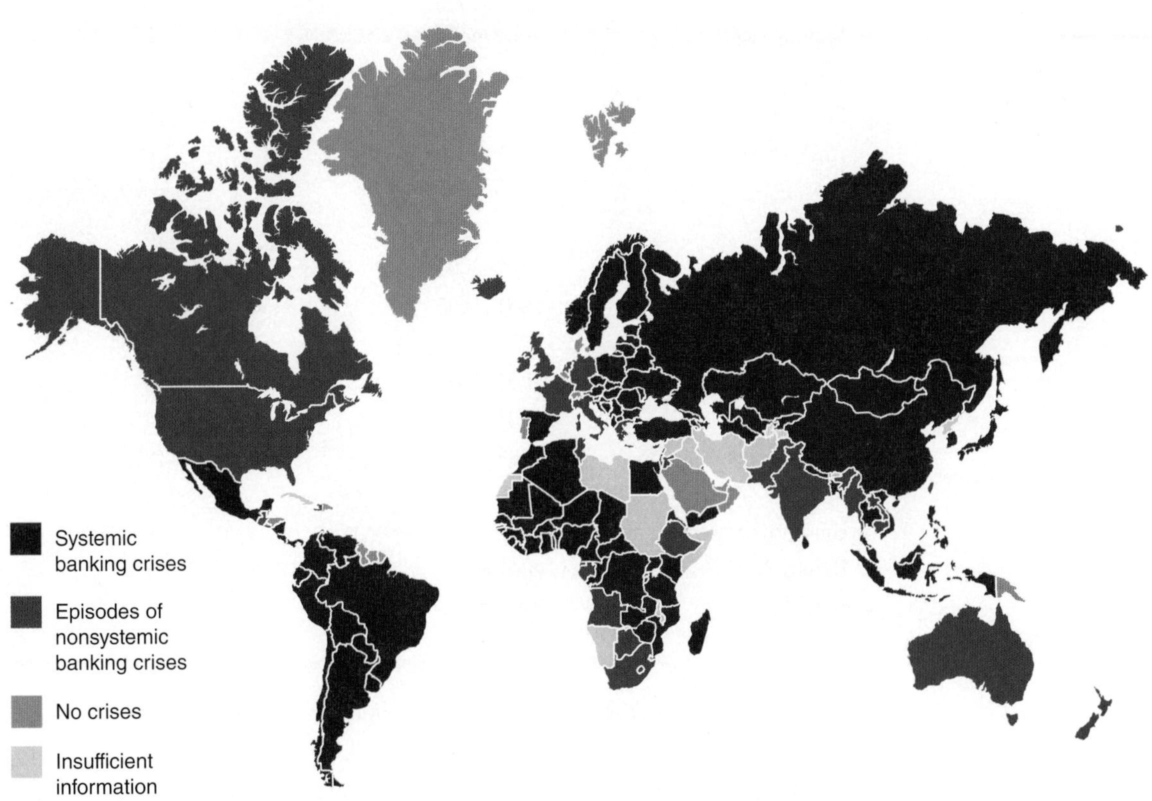

FIGURE 18.2 Banking Crises Throughout the World Since 1970

Banking crises have been very common throughout the world.

Source: Luc Laeven and Fabian Valencia, "Systemic Banking Crises Database: An Update," IMF Working Paper No. WP/12/163 (June 2012).

TABLE 18.2 The Cost of Rescuing Banks in a Number of Countries

Country	Date	Fiscal Cost as Percentage of GDP
Indonesia	1997–2001	57
Argentina	1980–1982	55
Iceland	2008	44
Jamaica	1996–1998	44
Thailand	1997–2000	44
Chile	1981–1985	43
Ireland	2008–	41*
Macedonia	1993–1995	32
Turkey	2000–2001	32
South Korea	1997–1998	31
Israel	1977	30
Ecuador	1998–2002	22
Mexico	1994–1996	19
China	1998	18
Malaysia	1997–1999	16
Philippines	1997–2001	13
Brazil	1994–1998	13
Finland	1991–1995	13
Argentina	2001–2003	10
Jordan	1989–1991	10
Hungary	1991–1995	10
Czech Republic	1996–2000	7
Sweden	1991–1995	4
United States	1988	4
Norway	1991–1993	
Luxembourg	2008–	8*
Netherlands	2008–	13*
Belgium	2008–	6*
United Kingdom	2008–	8*
United States	2007	4
Germany	2008–	1*

Source: Luc Laeven and Fabian Valencia, "Systemic Banking Crises Database: An Update," IMF Working Paper No. WP/12/163 (June 2012).

Note: An * indicates that the fiscal cost has been estimated only up to 2012.

can make a financial system more efficient, it can lead to an increase in moral hazard, with more risk taking on the part of banks if regulation and supervision are lax; the result can then be banking crises.[1]

[1]A Web appendix to this chapter, which can be found on this book's Web site at www.pearsonhighered.com/mishkin_eakins, discusses in detail many of the episodes of banking crises listed in Table 18.2.

However, the banking crisis episodes listed in Table 18.2 do differ in that deposit insurance has not played an important role in many of the countries experiencing banking crises. For example, the size of the Japanese equivalent of the FDIC, the Deposit Insurance Corporation, was so tiny relative to the FDIC that it did not play a prominent role in the banking system and exhausted its resources almost immediately with the first bank failures. This example indicates that deposit insurance is not to blame for some of these banking crises. However, what is common to all the countries discussed here is the existence of a government safety net, in which the government stands ready to bail out banks whether deposit insurance is an important feature of the regulatory environment or not. It is the existence of a government safety net, and not deposit insurance per se, that increases moral hazard incentives for excessive risk taking on the part of banks.

The Dodd-Frank Wall Street Reform and Consumer Protection Act of 2010

Dodd-Frank

The global financial crisis raised calls for a new regulatory structure to make a repeat of the crisis less likely. The result was The Dodd-Frank bill, which was passed in July 2010 after more than a year of discussion. It is the most comprehensive financial reform legislation since the Great Depression. It addresses five categories of regulation, which are discussed next.

Consumer Protection This legislation creates a new Consumer Financial Protection Bureau that is funded and housed within the Federal Reserve, although it is a completely independent agency. It has the authority to examine and enforce regulations for all businesses engaged in issuing residential mortgage products that have more than $10 billion in assets, as well as for issuers of other financial products marketed to poor people. It requires lenders to make sure there is an ability to repay residential mortgages by requiring verification of income, credit history, and job status. It also bans payments to brokers for pushing borrowers into higher-priced loans. It allows states to impose stricter consumer protection laws on national banks and gives state attorneys-general power to enforce certain rules issued by the new bureau. It also permanently increases the level of federal deposit insurance to $250,000.

Resolution Authority Although before this legislation the FDIC had the ability to seize failing banks and wind them down, the government did not have such a resolution authority over the largest financial institutions—those structured as holding companies. Indeed, the U.S. Treasury and the Federal Reserve argued that one reason they were unable to rescue Lehman Brothers and instead had to let it go into bankruptcy was that they did not have the legal means to take Lehman over and break it up. The Dodd-Frank bill now provides the U.S. government with this authority for financial firms that are deemed **systemic**, that is, firms who pose a risk to the overall financial system because their failure would cause widespread damage. It also gives regulators the right to levy fees on financial institutions with more than $50 billion in assets to recoup any losses.

Systemic Risk Regulation The bill creates a Financial Stability Oversight Council, chaired by the Treasury secretary, which would monitor markets for asset-price bubbles and the buildup of systemic risk. In addition, it would designate which financial firms are systemically important and so would receive the official designation of **systemically important financial institutions (SIFIs)**. These firms would be subject to additional regulation by the Federal Reserve, which would include higher capital standards and stricter liquidity requirements, as well as requirements that they draw up a "living will," that is, a plan for orderly liquidation if the firm gets into financial difficulties.

Volcker Rule Banks would be limited in the extent of their **proprietary trading**, that is, trading with their own money, and would be allowed to own only a small percentage of hedge and private equity funds. These provisions are named after Paul Volcker, a former Chairman of the Board of Governors of the Federal Reserve, who argued that banks should not be allowed to take large trading risks when they receive the benefits of federal deposit insurance.

Derivatives Financial instruments whose payoffs are linked to (i.e., derived from) previously issued securities are known as **financial derivatives**. As is discussed in Chapter 8, derivatives such as credit default ended up being "weapons of mass destruction" that helped lead to a financial meltdown when AIG had to be rescued after making overly extensive use of them. To prevent this from happening again, the Dodd-Frank bill requires many standardized derivative products to be traded on exchanges and cleared through clearinghouses to reduce the risk of losses if one counterparty in the derivative transaction goes bankrupt. More customized derivative products would be subject to higher capital requirements. Banks would be banned from some of their derivatives-dealing operations such as those involving riskier swaps. In addition, the bill imposes capital and margin requirements on firms dealing in derivatives and forces them to disclose more information about their activities.

Too-Big-to-Fail and Future Regulation

The Dodd-Frank bill leaves out many details of future regulation and there are doubts that it has dealt sufficiently with the too-big-to fail problem, which we have seen was an important factor that led to the global financial crisis. Here we discuss possible measures to reduce the too-big-to-fail problem and several areas where regulation may be heading in the future.

What Can Be Done About the Too-Big-to-Fail Problem?

Three approaches to solving the too-big-to-fail problem have been actively debated.

Break Up Large, Systemically Important Financial Institutions One way to eliminate the too-big-to-fail problem is to make sure that no financial institutions are so large that they can bring down the financial system. Then regulators will no longer see the need to bail out these institutions, thereby subjecting them to market discipline. One way to shrink these institutions is to reimpose the restrictions in place before Glass-Steagall was repealed, thereby forcing these large SIFIs to break up their different activities into smaller, cohesive companies. Alternatively, regulations could specify that no financial institution can have assets over a specified maximum limit, forcing SIFIs to break up into smaller pieces.

Not surprisingly, both of these approaches have been vehemently opposed by the largest financial institutions. Although breaking up SIFIs would eliminate the too-big-to-fail problem, if there are synergies that enable large institutions to manage risk better or provide financial services at a lower cost, doing so might decrease the efficiency of the financial system.

Higher Capital Requirements Because institutions that are too big to fail have incentives to take on excessive risk, another way to reduce their risk taking is to impose on them higher capital requirements. With higher capital, not only will these institutions have a larger buffer to withstand losses if they occur but they will have more to lose and hence have more "skin in the game," thereby reducing moral hazard and giving them less incentive to take on excessive risk. Another way of describing this approach is to say that higher capital requirements reduce the subsidy to risk taking for institutions that are too big to fail. In addition, because risk taking by SIFIs is far greater during booms, capital requirements could be increased when credit is expanding rapidly and reduced when credit is contracting. By so doing, capital requirements would become more countercyclical and could help restrain the boom-bust credit cycle.

The Swiss central bank has been a leader in this kind of approach: It has the highest capital requirements among advanced countries for its largest banks and raises them when credit markets become particularly frothy. Legislation has been proposed in the U.S. Congress to double capital requirements for large financial institutions, again something that these institutions vigorously oppose.

Leave It to Dodd-Frank Another view is that Dodd-Frank has effectively eliminated the too-big-to-fail problem by making it harder for the Federal Reserve to bail out financial institutions, by increasing stricter regulations for SIFIs, and through application of the Volcker rule. Indeed, the authors of the bill have declared that Dodd-Frank would "end too big to fail, as we know it." Although provisions in Dodd-Frank do take away some of the incentives for excessive risk taking by large, systemically important financial institutions, there are doubts that this bill completely removes the too-big-to fail problem.

Other Issues for Future Regulation

The Dodd-Frank bill leaves out many details of future regulation and does not address some important regulatory issues at all. Here we examine three areas where regulation may be heading.

Compensation in the Financial Services Industry As we saw in Chapter 8, the high fees and executive compensation that have so outraged the public created incentives for the financial industry to push out securities that turned out to be much riskier than advertised and have proved to be disastrous. Regulators, particularly at the Federal Reserve, are closely studying regulations to modify compensation in the financial services industry to reduce risk taking. For example, regulators are in the process of issuing requirements that bonuses be paid out for a number of years after they have been earned and only if the firm has remained in good health. Such "clawbacks" will encourage employees to reduce the riskiness of their activities so that they are more likely to be paid these bonuses in the future.

Government-Sponsored Enterprises (GSEs) A major gap in the Dodd-Frank bill is that it does not address privately owned government-sponsored enterprises such as Fannie Mae and Freddie Mac. As we saw in Chapter 8, both of these firms got into serious financial trouble and had to be taken over by the government. The likely result is that taxpayers will be on the hook for several hundred billion dollars. To prevent this from occurring again, the government might take any of four routes:

1. Fully privatize GSEs by taking away their government sponsorship, thereby removing the implicit backing for their debt.
2. Completely nationalize them by taking away their private status and make them government agencies.
3. Leave them as privately owned GSEs but strengthen regulations to restrict the amount of risk they take and to impose higher capital standards.
4. Leave them as privately owned GSEs but force them to shrink dramatically so they no longer expose the taxpayer to huge losses or pose a systemic risk to the financial system when they fail.

Credit-Rating Agencies Regulations to restrict conflicts of interest at credit-rating agencies and to give them greater incentives to provide reliable ratings have already been strengthened in the aftermath of the global financial crisis, but even more is likely to be done. The inaccurate ratings provided by credit-rating agencies helped promote risk taking throughout the financial system and led to investors' not having the information they needed to make informed choices about their investments. The reliance on credit ratings in the Basel 2 capital requirements may also have to be rethought, given the poor performance of credit-rating agencies in recent years.

The Danger of Overregulation As a result of the global financial crisis, the world of financial regulation will never be the same. Although it is clear that more regulation is needed to prevent such a crisis from occurring again, the danger is substantial that too much or poorly designed regulation could hamper the efficiency of the financial system. If new regulations choke off financial innovation that can benefit both households and businesses, economic growth in the future will suffer.

SUMMARY

1. The concepts of asymmetric information, adverse selection, and moral hazard help explain why governments pursue financial regulation.
2. There are nine basic types of financial regulation aimed at lessening asymmetric information problems and excessive risk taking in financial systems: (1) restrictions on financial institutions' asset holdings, (2) capital requirements, (3) prompt corrective action, (4) chartering and examination, (5) assessment of risk management, (6) disclosure requirements, (7) consumer protection, (8) restrictions on competition, and (9) macroprudential supervision.
3. The parallels between the banking crisis episodes that have occurred in countries throughout the world are striking, indicating that similar forces are at work.
4. The Dodd-Frank Act of 2010 is the most comprehensive financial reform legislation since the Great Depression. It has provisions in five areas: (1) consumer protection, (2) resolution authority, (3) systemic risk regulation, (4) proprietary trading, and (5) derivatives. Future regulation needs to address five issues: (1) the too-big-to-fail problem, either by breaking up large financial institutions or imposing higher capital requirements on them; (2) compensation at financial firms; (3) GSEs; (4) credit-rating agencies; and (5) the dangers of overregulation.

KEY TERMS

QUESTIONS

1. Give one example each of moral hazard and adverse selection in private insurance arrangements.
2. If casualty insurance companies provided fire insurance without restrictions, what kind of adverse selection and moral hazard problems might result?
3. Creation of the FDIC encouraged reluctant depositors to put their money into the banking system. Aside from the benefit of reducing the probability of a bank run, what other positive impact has this policy had in the performance of the overall economy?
4. Suppose that you have $300,000 in deposits at a bank. After careful consideration, the FDIC decides that this bank is now insolvent. Which method would you like to see the FDIC apply? What if your deposit were $200,000?
5. What are the costs and benefits of a too-big-to-fail policy?
6. What special problem do off-balance-sheet activities present to bank regulators, and what have they done about it?
7. Would you recommend the adoption of a system of deposit insurance, like the FDIC in the United States, in a country with weak institutions, prevalent corruption, and ineffective regulation of the financial sector?
8. What forms does bank supervision take, and how do they promote a safe and sound banking system?
9. What steps were taken in the FDICIA legislation of 1991 to improve the functioning of federal deposit insurance?
10. Why has the trend in bank supervision moved away from a focus on capital requirements to a focus on risk management?
11. Suppose that after a few mergers and acquisitions, only one bank holds 70% of all deposits in the United States. Would you say that this bank would be considered too big to fail? What does this tell you about the ongoing process of financial consolidation and the government safety net?
12. In what way might consumer protection regulations negatively affect a financial intermediary's profits? Can you think of a positive effect of such regulations on profits?
13. Do you think that removing the impediments to a nationwide banking system will be beneficial to the economy? Explain.
14. How could higher deposit insurance premiums for banks with riskier assets benefit the economy?
15. Given the set of new regulations included in the Dodd-Frank Act of 2010, do you think this was an easy bill to pass? Discuss reasons why financial industry lobbyists argued against the passing of such regulations.

QUANTITATIVE PROBLEMS

1. Consider a failing bank. A deposit of $350,000 is worth how much if the FDIC uses the *payoff* method given the typical recovery rate? How much is the same deposit worth if the *purchase-and-assumption* method is used? Which is more costly to taxpayers?
2. Consider a bank with the following balance sheet:

Assets		Liabilities	
Required reserves	$17 million	Checkable deposits	$205 million
Excess reserves	$3 million	Bank capital	$10 million

Assets		Liabilities
Municipal bonds	$65 million	
Residential mortgages	$70 million	
Commercial loans	$60 million	

Calculate the bank's risk-weighted assets.

3. Refer to the previous problem. Is this bank complying with the risk-weighted capital requirements set by Basel 1?

Problems 4 through 11 relate to a sequence of transactions at Oldhat Financial.

4. Oldhat Financial started its first day of operations with $9 million in capital. $130 million in checkable deposits are received. The bank issues a $25 million commercial loan and another $50 million in mortgages, with the following terms:
   - Mortgages: 200 standard 30-year, fixed-rate with a nominal annual rate of 5.25% each for $250,000.
   - Commercial loan: Three-year loan, simple interest paid monthly at 0.75% per month.

   a. If required reserves are 8%, what does the bank balance sheet look like? Ignore any loan loss reserves.

   b. How well capitalized is the bank?

5. Calculate the risk-weighted assets and risk-weighted capital ratio after Oldhat's first day.
6. The next day, terrible news hits the mortgage markets, and mortgage rates jump to 13%. What is the market value of Oldhat's mortgages? What is Oldhat's "market value" capital ratio?
7. Bank regulators force Oldhat to sell its mortgages to recognize the fair market value. What is the accounting transaction? How does this affect its capital position?
8. Congress allowed Oldhat to amortize the loss over the remaining life of the mortgage. If this technique had been used in the sale, how would the transaction have been recorded? What would be the annual adjustment? What does Oldhat's balance sheet look like? What is the capital ratio?
9. Oldhat decides to invest the $77 million in excess reserves in commercial loans. What will be the impact on its capital ratio? Its risk-weighted capital ratio?
10. The bad news about the mortgages is featured in the local newspaper, causing a minor bank run. $6 million in deposits is withdrawn. Examine the bank's condition after this occurs.
11. Oldhat borrows $5.5 million in the overnight federal funds market to meet its reserve requirement. What is the new balance sheet for Oldhat? How well capitalized is the bank?

WEB EXERCISES

Banking Regulation

1. Go to **http://www.fdic.gov/regulations/laws/**. This site reports on the most significant pieces of legislation affecting banks since the 1800s. Summarize the most recently enacted bank regulation listed on this site.
2. The Office of the Comptroller of the Currency is responsible for many of the regulations affecting bank operations. Go to **www.occ.treas.gov/**. Click on "Law and Regulations" in the far-right column under Legal & Licensing. Now click on the 12 CFR Parts 1 to 199. What does Part 1 cover? How many parts are there in 12 CFR? Open Part 18. What topic does it cover? Summarize its purpose.

WEB APPENDIX

Please visit our Web site at www.pearsonhighered.com/mishkin_eakins to read the Web appendix to Chapter 18:

- **Appendix:** Banking Crises Throughout the World

CHAPTER 19

Banking Industry: Structure and Competition

> PREVIEW

The operations of individual banks (how they acquire, use, and manage funds to make a profit) are roughly similar throughout the world. In all countries, banks are financial intermediaries in the business of earning profits. When you consider the structure and operation of the banking industry as a whole, however, the United States is in a class by itself. In most countries, four or five large banks typically dominate the banking industry, but in the United States there are on the order of 6,000 banks.

Is more better? Does this diversity mean that the American banking system is more competitive and therefore more economically efficient and sound than banking systems in other countries? What in the American economic and political system explains this large number of banking institutions? In this chapter we try to answer these questions by examining the historical trends in the banking industry and its overall structure.

We start by examining the historical development of the banking system. We then go on to look at the banking industry in detail. In addition to looking at our domestic banking system, we also examine the forces behind the growth in international banking to see how it has affected us in the United States. Finally, we examine how financial innovation has increased the competitive environment for the banking industry and is causing fundamental changes in it.

Historical Development of the Banking System

The modern banking industry in the United States began when the Bank of North America was chartered in Philadelphia in 1782. With the success of this bank, other banks opened for business, and the American banking industry was off and running. (As a study aid, Figure 19.1 provides a time line of the most important dates in the history of American banking before World War II.)

A major controversy involving the industry in its early years was whether the federal government or the states should charter banks. The Federalists, particularly Alexander Hamilton, advocated greater centralized control of banking and federal chartering of banks. Their efforts led to the creation, in 1791, of the Bank of the United States, which had elements of both a private bank and a central bank, a government institution that has responsibility for the amount of money and credit supplied in the economy as a whole. Agricultural and other interests, however, were quite suspicious of centralized power and hence advocated chartering by the states. Furthermore, their distrust of moneyed interests in the big cities led to political pressures to eliminate the Bank of the United States, and in 1811 their efforts met with success, when its charter was not renewed. Because of abuses by state banks and the clear need for a central bank to help the federal government raise funds during the War of 1812, Congress was stimulated to create the Second Bank of the United States in 1816. Tensions between advocates and opponents of centralized banking power were a recurrent theme during the operation of this second attempt at central banking in the United States, and with the election of Andrew Jackson, a

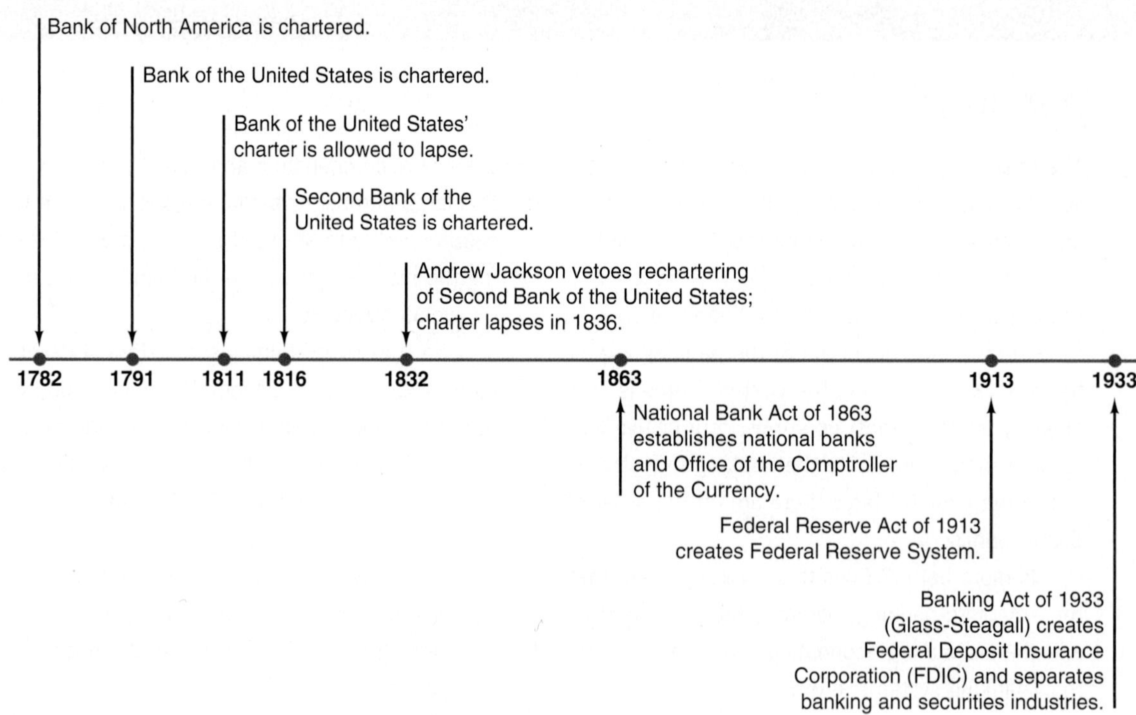

FIGURE 19.1 Time Line of the Early History of Banking in the United States
The most important dates in the history of American banking before World War II.

strong advocate of states' rights, the fate of the Second Bank was sealed. After the election in 1832, Jackson vetoed the rechartering of the Second Bank of the United States as a national bank, and its charter lapsed in 1836.

Until 1863 all banks in the United States were chartered by the banking commission of the state in which each operated. No national currency existed, and banks obtained funds primarily by issuing *banknotes* (currency circulated by the banks that could be redeemed for gold). Because banking regulations were extremely lax in many states, banks regularly failed due to fraud or lack of sufficient bank capital; their banknotes became worthless.

To eliminate the abuses of the state-chartered banks (called **state banks**), the National Bank Act of 1863 (and subsequent amendments to it) created a new banking system of federally chartered banks (called **national banks**), supervised by the Office of the Comptroller of the Currency, a department of the U.S. Treasury. This legislation was originally intended to dry up sources of funds to state banks by imposing a prohibitive tax on their banknotes while leaving the banknotes of the federally chartered banks untaxed. The state banks cleverly escaped extinction by acquiring funds through deposits. As a result, today the United States has a **dual banking system** in which banks supervised by the federal government and banks supervised by the states operate side by side.

Central banking did not reappear in this country until the Federal Reserve System (the Fed) was created in 1913 to promote an even safer banking system. All national banks were required to become members of the Federal Reserve System and became subject to a new set of regulations issued by the Fed. State banks could choose (but were not required) to become members of the system, and most did not because of the high costs of membership stemming from the Fed's regulations.

Access **www.fdic.gov/bank/** to learn how the FDIC gathers data about individual financial institutions and the banking industry.

During the Great Depression years 1930–1933, some 9,000 bank failures wiped out the savings of many depositors at banks. To prevent future depositor losses from such failures, banking legislation in 1933 established the Federal Deposit Insurance Corporation (FDIC), which provided federal insurance on bank deposits. Member banks of the Federal Reserve System were required to purchase FDIC insurance for their depositors, and non–Federal Reserve banks could choose to buy this insurance (almost all of them did). The purchase of FDIC insurance made banks subject to another set of regulations imposed by the FDIC.

Because investment banking activities of the banks were blamed for many bank failures, provisions in the banking legislation in 1933 (also known as the Glass-Steagall Act) prohibited banks from underwriting or dealing in corporate securities (though allowing them to sell new issues of government securities) and limited banks to the purchase of debt securities approved by the bank regulatory agencies. Likewise, it prohibited investment banks from engaging in banking activities. In effect, the Glass-Steagall Act separated the activities of banks from those of the securities industry.

Under the conditions of the Glass-Steagall Act, which was repealed in 1999, banks had to sell off their investment banking operations. The First National Bank of Boston, for example, spun off its investment banking operations into the First Boston Corporation, now part of one of the most important investment banking firms in America, Credit Suisse First Boston. Investment banking firms typically discontinued their deposit business, although J.P. Morgan discontinued its investment banking business and reorganized as a bank; however, some senior officers of J.P. Morgan went on to organize Morgan Stanley, another one of the largest investment banking firms today.

Multiple Regulatory Agencies

Bank regulation in the United States has developed into a crazy quilt of multiple regulatory agencies with overlapping jurisdictions. The Office of the Comptroller of the Currency has the primary supervisory responsibility for the 1,000 national commercial banks, which own more than half of the assets in the banking system, and also 400 or so savings and loans and mutual savings banks with national charters. The Federal Reserve and the state banking authorities have joint primary responsibility for the 2,000 state banks that are members of the Federal Reserve System. The Fed also has regulatory responsibility over companies that own one or more banks (called **bank holding companies**) and secondary responsibility for the national banks. The FDIC and the state banking authorities jointly supervise the 2,300 state banks that have FDIC insurance but are not members of the Federal Reserve System. The state banking authorities have sole jurisdiction over state banks without FDIC insurance. (Such banks hold less than 0.2% of the deposits in the banking system.)

Access **http://www.fdic.gov/bank/statistical/** to learn about the number of employees and the current profitability of banking institutions.

If you find the U.S. bank regulatory system confusing, imagine how confusing it is for the banks, which have to deal with multiple regulatory agencies. Several proposals have been raised by the U.S. Treasury to rectify this situation by centralizing the regulation of all depository institutions under one independent agency. However, none of these proposals has been successful in Congress, and whether there will be regulatory consolidation in the future is highly uncertain.

Financial Innovation and the Growth of the Shadow Banking System

Although banking institutions are still the most important financial institutions in the U.S. economy, in recent years the traditional banking business of making loans that are funded by deposits has been in decline. Some of this business has been replaced by the **shadow banking system**, in which bank lending has been replaced by lending via the securities market with the involvement of a number of different financial institutions.

To understand how the banking industry has evolved over time, we must first understand the process of financial innovation, which has transformed the entire financial system. Like other industries, the financial industry is in business to earn profits by selling its products. If a soap company perceives that a need exists in the marketplace for a laundry detergent with fabric softener, it develops a product to fit the need. Similarly, to maximize their profits, financial institutions develop new products to satisfy their own needs as well as those of their customers; in other words, innovation—which can be extremely beneficial to the economy—is driven by the desire to get (or stay) rich. This view of the innovation process leads to the following simple analysis: ***A change in the financial environment will stimulate a search by financial institutions for innovations that are likely to be profitable.***

Starting in the 1960s, individuals and financial institutions operating in financial markets were confronted with drastic changes in the economic environment: Inflation and interest rates climbed sharply and became harder to predict, a situation that changed demand conditions in financial markets. The rapid advance in computer technology changed supply conditions. In addition, financial regulations became more burdensome. Financial institutions found that many of the old ways of doing business were no longer profitable; the financial services and products they had been offering to the public were not selling. Many financial intermediaries found that they were no longer able to acquire funds with their traditional financial instruments, and without these funds they would soon be out of business. To survive in the new economic environment, financial institutions had to research and develop new products and services that would meet customer needs and prove profitable, a process referred to as **financial engineering**. In their case, necessity was the mother of innovation.

Our discussion of why financial innovation occurs suggests that there are three basic types of financial innovation: responses to changes in demand conditions, responses to changes in supply conditions, and avoidance of regulations. These three motivations often interact to produce particular financial innovations. Now that we have a framework for understanding why financial institutions produce innovations, let's look at examples of how financial institutions in their search for profits have produced financial innovations of the three basic types.

Responses to Changes in Demand Conditions: Interest Rate Volatility

The most significant change in the economic environment that altered the demand for financial products in recent years has been the dramatic increase in the volatility of interest rates. In the 1950s, the interest rate on three-month Treasury bills fluctuated between 1% and 3.5%; in the 1970s, it fluctuated between 4% and 11.5%; in the 1980s, it ranged from 5% to more than 15%. Large fluctuations in interest rates lead to substantial capital gains or losses and greater uncertainty about returns on investments. Recall that the risk related to the uncertainty about interest-rate movements and returns is called *interest-rate risk*, and high volatility of interest rates, such as we saw in the 1970s and 1980s, leads to a higher level of interest-rate risk.

We would expect the increase in interest-rate risk to increase the demand for financial products and services that could reduce the risk. This change in the economic environment would thus stimulate a search for profitable innovations by financial institutions that meet this new demand and would spur the creation of new financial instruments that help lower interest-rate risk. Two examples of financial innovations that appeared in the 1970s confirm this prediction: the development of adjustable-rate mortgages and financial derivatives.

Adjustable-Rate Mortgages Like other investors, financial institutions find that lending is more attractive if interest-rate risk is lower. They would not want to make a mortgage loan at a 10% interest rate and two months later find that they could obtain 12% in interest on the same mortgage. To reduce interest-rate risk, in 1975 savings and loans in California began to issue adjustable-rate mortgages, that is, mortgage loans on which the interest rate changes when a market interest rate (usually the Treasury bill rate) changes. Initially, an adjustable-rate mortgage might have a 5% interest rate. In six months, this interest rate might increase or decrease by the amount of the increase or decrease in, say, the six-month Treasury bill rate, and the mortgage payment would change. Because adjustable-rate mortgages allow mortgage-issuing institutions to earn higher interest rates on mortgages when rates rise, profits remain high during these periods.

This attractive feature of adjustable-rate mortgages encouraged mortgage-issuing institutions to issue adjustable-rate mortgages with lower initial interest rates than on conventional fixed-rate mortgages, making them popular with many households. However, because the mortgage payment on a variable-rate mortgage can increase, many households continue to prefer fixed-rate mortgages. Hence, both types of mortgages are widespread.

Financial Derivatives Given the greater demand for the reduction of interest-rate risk, commodity exchanges such as the Chicago Board of Trade recognized that if they could develop a product that would help investors and financial institutions to protect themselves from, or **hedge**, interest-rate risk, then they could make profits by selling this new instrument. **Futures contracts**, in which the seller agrees to provide a certain standardized commodity to the buyer on a specific future date at an agreed-on price, had been around for a long time. Officials at the Chicago Board of Trade realized that if they created futures contracts in financial instruments, which are called *financial derivatives* because their payoffs are linked to (i.e., derived from) previously issued securities, they could be used to hedge risk. Thus, in 1975 financial derivatives were born.

Responses to Changes in Supply Conditions: Information Technology

The most important source of the changes in supply conditions that stimulate financial innovation has been the improvement in computer and telecommunications technology. This technology, called *information technology*, has had two effects. First, it has lowered the cost of processing financial transactions, making it profitable for financial institutions to create new financial products and services for the public. Second, it has made it easier for investors to acquire information, thereby making it easier for firms to issue securities. The rapid developments in information technology have resulted in many new financial products and services that we examine here.

Bank Credit and Debit Cards Credit cards have been around since well before World War II. Many individual stores (Sears, Macy's, Goldwater's) institutionalized charge accounts by providing customers with credit cards that allowed them to make purchases at these stores without cash. Nationwide credit cards were not established until after World War II, when Diners Club developed one to be used in restaurants all over the country (and abroad). Similar credit card programs were started by American Express and Carte Blanche, but because of the high cost of operating these programs, cards were issued only to selected persons and businesses that could afford expensive purchases.

A firm issuing credit cards earns income from loans it makes to credit card holders and from payments made by stores on credit card purchases (a percentage of the purchase price, say, 5%). A credit card program's costs arise from loan defaults, stolen cards, and the expense involved in processing credit card transactions.

Seeing the success of Diners Club, American Express, and Carte Blanche, bankers wanted to share in the profitable credit card business. Several banks attempted to expand the credit card business to a wider market in the 1950s, but the cost per transaction of running these programs was so high that their early attempts failed.

In the late 1960s, improved computer technology, which lowered the transaction costs for providing credit card services, made it more likely that bank credit card programs would be profitable. The banks tried to enter this business again, and this time their efforts led to the creation of two successful bank credit card programs: BankAmericard (originally started by the Bank of America but now an independent organization called Visa) and MasterCharge (now MasterCard, run by the Interbank Card Association). These programs have become phenomenally successful; around 400 million of their cards are in use. Indeed, bank credit cards have been so profitable that nonfinancial institutions such as Sears (which launched the Discover card), General Motors, and AT&T have also entered the credit card business. Consumers have benefited because credit cards are more widely accepted than checks to pay for purchases (particularly abroad), and they allow consumers to take out loans more easily.

The success of bank credit cards led these institutions to come up with a new financial innovation, *debit cards*. Debit cards often look just like credit cards and can be used to make purchases in an identical fashion. However, in contrast to credit cards, which extend the purchaser a loan that does not have to be paid off immediately, a debit card purchase is immediately deducted from the card holder's bank account. Debit cards depend even more on low costs of processing transactions because their profits are generated entirely from the fees paid by merchants on debit card purchases at their stores. Debit cards have grown extremely popular in recent years.

Electronic Banking The wonders of modern computer technology have also enabled banks to lower the cost of bank transactions by having the customer interact with an electronic banking (e-banking) facility rather than with a human being. One important form of an e-banking facility is the **automated teller machine (ATM)**, an electronic machine that allows customers to get cash, make deposits, transfer funds from one account to another, and check balances. The ATM has the advantage that it does not have to be paid overtime and never sleeps, thus being available for use 24 hours a day. Not only does this result in cheaper transactions for the bank, but it also provides more convenience for the customer. Because of their low cost, ATMs can be put at locations other than a bank or its branches, further increasing customer convenience. The low cost of ATMs has meant that they have sprung up everywhere and now number more than 500,000 in the United States alone. Furthermore, it is now as easy to get foreign currency from an ATM when you are traveling in Europe as it is to get cash from your local bank.

With the drop in the cost of telecommunications, banks have developed another financial innovation, *home banking*. It is now cost-effective for banks to set up an electronic banking facility in which the bank's customer is linked up with the bank's computer to carry out transactions by using either a telephone or a personal computer. Now a bank's customers can conduct many of their bank transactions without ever leaving the comfort of home. The advantage for the customer is the convenience of home banking, while banks find that the cost of transactions is substantially less than having the customer come to the bank. The success of ATMs and home banking has led to another innovation, the **automated banking machine (ABM)**, which combines in one location an ATM, an Internet connection to the bank's Web site, and a telephone link to customer service.

With the decline in the price of personal computers and their increasing presence in the home, we have seen a further innovation in the home banking area, the appearance of a new type of banking institution, the **virtual bank**, a bank that has no physical location but rather exists only in cyberspace. In 1995 Security First

Network Bank, based in Atlanta but now owned by Royal Bank of Canada, became the first virtual bank, offering an array of banking services on the Internet—accepting checking account and savings deposits, selling certificates of deposit, issuing ATM cards, providing bill-paying facilities, and so on. The virtual bank thus takes home banking one step further, enabling the customer to have a full set of banking services at home 24 hours a day. In 1996 Bank of America and Wells Fargo entered the virtual banking market, to be followed by many others, with Bank of America now being the largest Internet bank in the United States. Will virtual banking be the predominant form of banking in the future (see the E-Finance box, "Will 'Clicks' Dominate 'Bricks' in the Banking Industry?")?

Electronic Payment The development of inexpensive computers, smart phones, and the spread of the Internet now make it very cheap for banks to allow their customers to make bill payments electronically. Whereas in the past you had to pay your bills by mailing a check, now banks provide a Web site or an app in which you just log on, make a few clicks, and your payment is transmitted electronically. Not only do you save the cost of the stamp, but paying bills now becomes (almost) a pleasure, requiring little effort. Electronic payment systems provided by banks now even allow you to avoid the step of having to log on to pay the bill. Instead, recurring bills can be automatically deducted from your bank account without your having to do a thing. Providing these services increases profitability for banks in two ways. First, payment of a bill electronically means that banks don't need people to process what would have otherwise been a paper transaction. Estimates of the

> E-FINANCE

Will "Clicks" Dominate "Bricks" in the Banking Industry?

With the advent of virtual banks ("clicks") and the convenience they provide, a key question is whether they will become the primary form in which banks do their business, eliminating the need for physical bank branches ("bricks") as the main delivery mechanism for banking services. Indeed, will stand-alone Internet banks be the wave of the future?

The answer seems to be no. Early Internet-only banks such as Wingspan (owned by Bank One), First-e (Dublin-based), and Egg (a British Internet-only bank owned by Prudential) had disappointing revenue growth and profits. The result was that pure online banking has not been the success that proponents had hoped for and these stand-alone Internet banks have been merged into larger banking organizations. Why has Internet banking been a disappointment?

Internet banking has several strikes against it. First, bank depositors want to know that their savings are secure, and so are reluctant to put their money into new institutions without a long track record. Second, customers worry about the security of their online transactions and whether their transactions will truly be kept private. Traditional banks are viewed as being more secure and trustworthy in terms of releasing private information. Third, customers may prefer services provided by physical branches. For example, banking customers prefer purchasing long-term savings products face-to-face. Fourth, Internet banking has run into technical problems—server crashes, slow connections over phone lines, mistakes in conducting transactions—that will probably diminish over time as technology improves.

The wave of the future thus does not appear to be pure Internet banks. Instead it looks as though "clicks and bricks" will be the predominant form of banking, in which online banking is used to complement the services provided by traditional banks. Nonetheless, the delivery of banking services is undergoing massive changes, with more and more banking services delivered over the Internet and the number of physical bank branches likely to decline in the future.

cost savings for banks when a bill is paid electronically rather than by a check exceed one dollar. Second, the extra convenience for you, the customer, means that you are more likely to open an account with the bank. Electronic payment is thus becoming far more common in the United States, but Americans are far behind Europeans, particularly Scandinavians, in their use of electronic payments (see the E-Finance box, "Why Are Scandinavians So Far Ahead of Americans in Using Electronic Payments and Online Banking?").

E-Money Electronic payments technology not only can substitute for checks but can, in the form of **electronic money** (or **e-money**), money that exists only in electronic form, substitute for cash as well. The first form of e-money is a stored-value card. The simplest form of a stored-value card is purchased for a preset dollar amount that the consumer spends down. The more sophisticated stored-value card is known as a **smart card**. It contains its own computer chip so that it can be loaded with digital cash from the owner's bank account whenever needed. Smart cards can be loaded from ATM machines, from personal computers with a smart card reader, or from specially equipped telephones.

A second form of electronic money is often referred to as **e-cash**, and it is used on the Internet to purchase goods or services. A consumer gets e-cash by setting up

> E-FINANCE

Why Are Scandinavians So Far Ahead of Americans in Using Electronic Payments and Online Banking?

Americans are the biggest users of checks in the world. Over 10 billion checks are written every year in the United States, and the majority of noncash transactions are conducted with paper. In contrast, in most countries of Europe, the bulk of noncash transactions are electronic, with Finland and Sweden having the greatest proportion of online banking customers of any countries in the world. Indeed, if you were Finnish or Swedish, instead of writing a check, you would be far more likely to pay your bills online, using a personal computer or even a mobile phone. Why do Europeans and especially Scandinavians so far outpace Americans in the use of electronic payments? First, Europeans got used to making payments without checks even before the advent of the personal computer. Europeans have long made use of *giro* payments, in which banks and post offices transfer funds for customers to pay bills. Second, Europeans—and particularly Scandinavians—are much greater users of mobile phones and the Internet than are Americans. Finland has the highest per capita use of mobile phones in the world, and Finland and Sweden lead the world in the percentage of the population that accesses the Internet. Maybe these usage patterns stem from the low population densities of these countries and the cold and dark winters that keep Scandinavians inside at their PCs. For their part, Scandinavians would rather take the view that their high-tech culture is the product of their good education systems and the resulting high degree of computer literacy, the presence of top technology companies such as Finland's Nokia and Sweden's Ericsson, and government policies promoting the increased use of personal computers, such as Sweden's tax incentives for companies to provide their employees with home computers. The wired populations of Finland and Sweden are (percentage-wise) the biggest users of online banking in the world. Americans are clearly behind the curve in their use of electronic payments, which has imposed a high cost on the U.S. economy. Switching from checks to electronic payments might save the U.S. economy tens of billions of dollars per year, according to some estimates. Indeed, the U.S. federal government is trying to switch all its payments to electronic ones by directly depositing them into bank accounts, in an effort to reduce its expenses. Can Americans be weaned from paper checks and fully embrace the world of high-tech electronic payments?

> E-FINANCE

Are We Headed for a Cashless Society?

Predictions of a cashless society have been around for decades, but they have not come to fruition. For example, *Business Week* predicted in 1975 that electronic means of payment "would soon revolutionize the very concept of money itself," only to reverse itself several years later. Pilot projects in recent years with smart cards to convert consumers to the use of e-money have not been a success. Mondex, one of the widely touted, early stored-value cards, was launched in Great Britain in 1995, but it is not widely used. In Germany and Belgium, millions of people carry bank cards with computer chips embedded in them that enable them to make use of e-money, but very few use them. Why has the movement to a cashless society been so slow in coming?

Although e-money might be more convenient and may be more efficient than a payments system based on paper, several factors work against the disappearance of the paper system. First, it is very expensive to set up the computer, card reader, and telecommunications networks necessary to make electronic money the dominant form of payment. Second, electronic means of payment raise security and privacy concerns. We often hear media reports that an unauthorized hacker has been able to access a computer database and to alter information stored there. Because this is not an uncommon occurrence, unscrupulous persons might be able to access bank accounts in electronic payments systems and steal funds by moving them from someone else's accounts into their own. The prevention of this type of fraud is no easy task, and a whole new field of computer science has developed to cope with security issues. A further concern is that the use of electronic means of payment leaves an electronic trail that contains a large amount of personal data on buying habits. There are worries that government, employers, and marketers might be able to access these data, thereby encroaching on our privacy.

The conclusion from this discussion is that although the use of e-money will surely increase in the future, to paraphrase Mark Twain, "The reports of cash's death are greatly exaggerated."

an account with a bank that has links to the Internet and then has the e-cash transferred to her PC. When she wants to buy something with e-cash, she surfs to a store on the Web and clicks the "buy" option for a particular item, whereupon the e-cash is automatically transferred from her computer to the merchant's computer. The merchant can then have the funds transferred from the consumer's bank account to his before the goods are shipped.

Given the convenience of e-money, you might think that we would move quickly to the cashless society in which all payments were made electronically. However, this hasn't happened, as discussed in the E-Finance box, "Are We Headed for a Cashless Society?"

Junk Bonds Before the advent of computers and advanced telecommunications, it was difficult to acquire information about the financial situation of firms that might want to sell securities. Because of the difficulty in screening out bad from good credit risks, the only firms that were able to sell bonds were very well-established corporations that had high credit ratings.[1] Before the 1980s, then, only corporations that could issue bonds with ratings of Baa or above could raise funds by selling newly issued bonds. Some firms that had fallen on bad times, known as *fallen angels*, had previously issued long-term corporate bonds which had ratings that had now fallen below Baa, bonds that were pejoratively dubbed "junk bonds."

[1]The discussion of adverse selection problems in Chapter 7 provides a more detailed analysis of why only well-established firms with high credit ratings were able to sell securities.

With the improvement in information technology in the 1970s, it became easier for investors to acquire financial information about corporations, making it easier to screen out bad from good credit risks. With easier screening, investors were more willing to buy long-term debt securities from less well-known corporations with lower credit ratings. With this change in supply conditions, we would expect that some smart individual would pioneer the concept of selling new public issues of junk bonds, not for fallen angels but for companies that had not yet achieved investment-grade status. This is exactly what Michael Milken of Drexel Burnham Lambert, an investment banking firm, started to do in 1977. Junk bonds became an important factor in the corporate bond market, with the amount outstanding exceeding $200 billion by the late 1980s. Although there was a sharp slowdown in activity in the junk bond market after Milken was indicted for securities law violations in 1989, it heated up again in the 1990s and 2000s.

Commercial Paper Market *Commercial paper* is a short-term debt security issued by large banks and corporations. The commercial paper market has undergone tremendous growth since 1970, when there was $33 billion outstanding, to around $1 trillion outstanding at the end of 2015. Indeed, commercial paper has been one of the fastest-growing money market instruments.

Improvements in information technology also help provide an explanation for the rapid rise of the commercial paper market. We have seen that the improvement in information technology made it easier for investors to screen out bad from good credit risks, thus making it simpler for corporations to issue debt securities. Not only did this make it easier for corporations to issue long-term debt securities in the junk bond market, but it also meant that they could raise funds by issuing short-term debt securities such as commercial paper with greater ease. Many corporations that used to do their short-term borrowing from banks now frequently raise short-term funds in the commercial paper market instead. The development of money market mutual funds has been another factor in the rapid growth of the commercial paper market. Because money market mutual funds need to hold liquid, high-quality, short-term assets such as commercial paper, the growth of assets in these funds to around $2.6 trillion has created a ready market in commercial paper. The growth of pension and other large funds that invest in commercial paper has also stimulated the growth of this market.

Securitization and the Shadow Banking System

One of the most important financial innovations in the past two decades arising from improvements in both transaction and information technology is securitization. **Securitization** is the process of bundling small and otherwise illiquid financial assets (such as residential mortgages, auto loans, and credit card receivables), which have typically been the bread and butter of banking institutions, into marketable capital market securities. Securitization is the fundamental building block of the shadow banking system.

How the Shadow Banking System Works In traditional banking, one entity engages in the process of asset transformation—that is, issuing liabilities with one set of desirable characteristics for holders (say, deposits with high liquidity and low risk) to fund the purchase of assets with a different set of characteristics (say, loans with low liquidity and high returns). Securitization, on the other hand, is a process of asset transformation that involves a number of different financial institutions working together that are part of the shadow banking system. In other words, asset transformation done by securitization and the shadow banking system is not done "under one roof," as in traditional banking.

For example, a mortgage broker (who more generally is referred to as a *loan originator*) will arrange for a residential mortgage loan to be made by a financial institution, which will service the loan (that is, collect the interest and principal payments). This *servicer* then sells the mortgage to another financial institution that bundles the mortgage with a large number of other residential mortgages. The *bundler* takes the interest and principal payments on the portfolio of mortgages and then "passes them through" (pays them out) to third parties. The bundler goes to a *distributor* (typically an investment bank), which will design a security that divides the portfolio of loans into standardized amounts. Then the distributor sells the claims to these interest and principal payments as securities, mostly to other financial intermediaries that are also part of the shadow banking system, such as a money market mutual fund or a pension fund. Schematically, the securitization process is described by the following sequence:

Loan origination => servicing => bundling => distribution

Because the securitization process involves the origination of loans and then, finally, the distribution of securities, securitization is also characterized as an **originate-to-distribute** business model.

At each step of the securitization process, the loan originator, servicer, bundler, and distributor earn a fee. These four institutions have specialized in each element of the financial intermediation process. The shadow banking system, which comprises all of the financial institutions involved in the securitization process, can thus be very profitable if transactions costs and the costs of collecting information are low. Advances in information technology have therefore been critical to the growth of securitization and the shadow banking system. Lower costs of acquiring information make it far easier to sell capital market securities, while lower transactions costs make it cheaper for financial institutions to collect interest and principal payments on bundled loans and then pay them out to the securities holders.

Subprime Mortgage Market A particularly important financial innovation that developed in the 2000s as a result of securitization and the shadow banking system was the **subprime mortgage**, a new class of residential mortgages to borrowers with less than stellar credit records. Before 2000, only the most credit-worthy (prime) borrowers could obtain residential mortgages. Advances in computer technology and new statistical techniques, known as data mining, however, led to enhanced, quantitative evaluation of the credit risk for residential mortgages. Households with credit records could now be assigned a numerical credit score, known as a FICO score (named after the Fair Isaac Corporation, which developed it), that would predict how likely they would be to default on their loan payments. Because it now became easier to assess the risk in a pool of subprime mortgages, it became possible to bundle them in a mortgage-backed security, providing a new source of funding for these mortgages. The result was an explosion of subprime mortgage lending, which as we saw in Chapter 8 was a key factor that led to the global financial crisis from 2007 to 2009.

Avoidance of Existing Regulations

The process of financial innovation we have discussed so far is much like innovation in other areas of the economy: It occurs in response to changes in demand and supply conditions. However, because the financial industry is more heavily regulated than other industries, government regulation is a much greater spur to innovation in this industry. Government regulation leads to financial innovation by creating incentives for firms to skirt regulations that restrict their ability to earn profits. Edward Kane, an economist at Boston College, describes this process of avoiding regulations as "loophole mining." The economic analysis of innovation suggests that when the economic environment changes such that regulatory constraints are so burdensome that large profits can be made by avoiding them, loophole mining and innovation are more likely to occur.

Because banking is one of the most heavily regulated industries in America, loophole mining is especially likely to occur. The rise in inflation and interest rates from the late 1960s to 1980 made the regulatory constraints imposed on this industry even more burdensome, leading to financial innovation.

Two sets of regulations have seriously restricted the ability of banks to make profits: reserve requirements that force banks to keep a certain fraction of their deposits as reserves (vault cash and deposits in the Federal Reserve System) and restrictions on the interest rates that can be paid on deposits. For the following reasons, these regulations have been major forces behind financial innovation.

1. *Reserve requirements.* The key to understanding why reserve requirements led to financial innovation is to recognize that they act, in effect, as a tax on deposits. Because up until 2008 the Fed did not pay interest on reserves, the opportunity cost of holding them was the interest that a bank could otherwise earn by lending the reserves out. For each dollar of deposits, reserve requirements therefore imposed a cost on the bank equal to the interest rate, i, that could be earned if the reserves could be lent out times the fraction of deposits required as reserves, r. The cost of $i \times r$ imposed on the bank is just like a tax on bank deposits of $i \times r$ per dollar of deposits.

   It is a great tradition to avoid taxes if possible, and banks also play this game. Just as taxpayers look for loopholes to lower their tax bills, banks seek to increase their profits by mining loopholes and by producing financial innovations that allow them to escape the tax on deposits imposed by reserve requirements.
2. *Restrictions on interest paid on deposits.* Until 1980, legislation prohibited banks in most states from paying interest on checking account deposits, and through Regulation Q, the Fed set maximum limits on the interest rate that could be paid on time deposits. To this day, banks are not allowed to pay interest on corporate checking accounts. The desire to avoid these **deposit rate ceilings** also led to financial innovations.

   If market interest rates rose above the maximum rates that banks paid on time deposits under Regulation Q, depositors withdrew funds from banks to put them into higher-yielding securities. This loss of deposits from the banking system restricted the amount of funds that banks could lend (called **disintermediation**) and thus limited bank profits. Banks had an incentive to get around deposit rate ceilings because by so doing, they could acquire more funds to make loans and earn higher profits.

We can now look at how the desire to avoid restrictions on interest payments and the tax effect of reserve requirements led to two important financial innovations.

Money Market Mutual Funds Money market mutual funds issue shares that are redeemable at a fixed price (usually $1) by writing checks. For example, if you buy 5,000 shares for $5,000, the money market fund uses these funds to invest in short-term money market securities (Treasury bills, certificates of deposit, commercial paper) that provide you with interest payments. In addition, you are able to write checks up to the $5,000 held as shares in the money market fund. Although money market fund shares effectively function as checking account deposits that earn interest, they are not legally deposits and so are not subject to reserve requirements or prohibitions on interest payments. For this reason, they can pay higher interest rates than deposits at banks.

The first money market mutual fund was created by two Wall Street mavericks, Bruce Bent and Henry Brown, in 1970. However, the low market interest rates from 1970 to 1977 (which were just slightly above Regulation Q ceilings of 5.25% to 5.5%) kept them from being particularly advantageous relative to bank deposits. In early 1978 the situation changed rapidly as inflation rose and market interest rates began to climb over 10%, well above the 5.5% maximum interest rates payable on savings accounts and time deposits under Regulation Q. In 1977 money market mutual funds had assets of less than $4 billion; in 1978 their assets climbed to close to $10 billion; in 1979, to more than $40 billion; and in 1982, to $230 billion. Currently, their assets are around $2.8 trillion. To say the least, money market mutual funds have been a successful financial innovation, which is exactly what we would have predicted to occur in the late 1970s and early 1980s when interest rates soared beyond Regulation Q ceilings.

In a supreme irony, risky investments by a money market mutual fund founded by Bruce Bent almost brought down the money market mutual fund industry during the global financial crisis in 2008 (see the Mini-Case box, "Bruce Bent and the Money Market Mutual Fund Panic of 2008").

Sweep Accounts Another innovation that enables banks to avoid the "tax" from reserve requirements is the **sweep account**. In this arrangement, any balances above a certain amount in a corporation's checking account at the end of a business day are "swept out" of the account and invested in overnight securities that pay interest. Because the "swept out" funds are no longer classified as checkable deposits, they are not subject to reserve requirements and thus are not "taxed." They also have the advantage that they allow banks in effect to pay interest on these checking accounts, which otherwise is not allowed under existing regulations. Because sweep accounts have become so popular, they have lowered the amount of required reserves to the degree that most banking institutions do not find reserve requirements binding: In other words, they voluntarily hold more reserves than they are required to.

The financial innovations of sweep accounts and money market mutual funds are particularly interesting because they were stimulated not only by the desire to avoid a costly regulation but also by a change in supply conditions—in this case, information technology. Without low-cost computers to inexpensively process the additional transactions required by these accounts, these innovations would not have been profitable and therefore would not have been developed. Technological factors often combine with other incentives, such as the desire to get around a regulation, to produce innovation.

> MINI-CASE

Bruce Bent and the Money Market Mutual Fund Panic of 2008

Bruce Bent, one of the originators of money market mutual funds, almost brought down the industry during the global financial crisis in the fall of 2008. Mr. Bent told his shareholders in a letter written in July 2008 that the fund was managed on a basis of "unwavering discipline focused on protecting your principal." He also wrote the Securities and Exchange Commission in September 2007, "When I first created the money market fund back in 1970, it was designed with the tenets of safety and liquidity." He added that these principles had "fallen by the wayside as portfolio managers chased the highest yield and compromised the integrity of the money fund." Alas, Bent did not follow his own advice, and his fund, the Reserve Primary Fund, bought risky assets so that its yield was higher than the industry average.

When Lehman Brothers went into bankruptcy on September 15, 2008, the Reserve Primary Fund, with assets over $60 billion, was caught holding the bag on $785 million of Lehman's debt, which then had to be marked down to zero. The resulting losses meant that on September 16, Bent's fund could no longer afford to redeem its shares at the par value of $1, a situation known as "breaking the buck." Bent's shareholders began to pull their money out of the fund, causing it to lose 90% of its assets.

The fear that this could happen to other money market mutual funds led to a classic panic in which shareholders began to withdraw their funds at an alarming rate. The whole money market mutual fund industry looked as though it could come crashing down. To prevent this, the Federal Reserve and the U.S. Treasury rode to the rescue on September 19. The Fed set up a facility, discussed in Chapter 10, to make loans to purchase commercial paper from money market mutual funds so they could meet the demands for redemptions from their investors. The Treasury then put in a temporary guarantee for all money market mutual fund redemptions and the panic subsided.

Not surprisingly, given the extension of a government safety net to the money market mutual fund industry, there are calls to regulate this industry more heavily. The money market mutual fund industry will never be the same.

THE PRACTICING MANAGER

Profiting from a New Financial Product: A Case Study of Treasury Strips

We have seen that the advent of high-speed computers, which lowered the cost of processing financial transactions, led to such financial innovations as bank credit and debit cards. Because there is money to be made from financial innovation, it is important for managers of financial institutions to understand the thinking that goes into producing new, highly profitable financial products that take advantage of computer technology. To illustrate how financial institution managers can figure out ways to increase profits through financial innovation, we look at Treasury strips, a financial instrument first developed in 1982 by Salomon Brothers and Merrill Lynch. (Indeed, this innovation was so successful that the U.S. Treasury copied it when they issued STRIPS in 1985, as discussed in Chapter 12.)

One problem for investors in long-term coupon bonds, even when they have a long holding period, is that there is some uncertainty in their returns arising from what is called *reinvestment risk*. Even if an investor holding a long-term coupon bond has a holding period of 10 years, the return on the bond is not certain. The problem is that coupon payments are made before the bond matures in 10 years, and these coupon payments must be reinvested. Because the interest rates at which the coupon payments will be reinvested fluctuate, the eventual return on the bond fluctuates as well. In contrast, long-term zero-coupon bonds have no reinvestment risk because they make no cash payments before the bond matures. The return on a zero-coupon bond if it is held to maturity is known at the time of purchase. The absence of reinvestment risk is an attractive feature of zero-coupon bonds, and as a result, investors are willing to accept a slightly lower interest rate on them than on coupon bonds, which do bear some reinvestment risk.

The fact that zero-coupon bonds have lower interest rates, along with the ability to use computers to create so-called hybrid securities, which are securities derived from other underlying securities, gave employees of Salomon Brothers and Merrill Lynch a brilliant idea for making profits. They could use computers to separate ("strip") a long-term Treasury coupon bond into a set of zero-coupon bonds, which, naturally enough, are called *Treasury strips*. The lower interest rates on the more desirable Treasury strip zero-coupon bonds would mean that the value of these bonds would exceed the price of the underlying long-term Treasury bond, allowing Salomon Brothers and Merrill Lynch to make a profit by purchasing the long-term Treasury bond, separating it into Treasury strips, and selling them off as zero-coupon bonds.

To see in more detail how their thinking worked, let's look more closely at a $1 million 10-year Treasury bond with a coupon rate of 10% whose yield to maturity is also 10%, so it is selling at par. The cash payments for this bond are listed in the second column of Table 19.1. To make things simple, let's assume that the yield curve is absolutely flat so that the interest rate used to discount all the future cash payments is the same. Because zero-coupon bonds, which have no reinvestment risk, are more desirable than the 10-year Treasury coupon bond, the interest rate on the zero-coupon bonds is 9.75%, a little lower than the 10% interest rate on the coupon bond.

How would Fran, a smart and sophisticated financial institution manager, figure out if she could make a profit from creating and selling the Treasury strips? Her first step is to figure out what the zero-coupon Treasury strips would sell for. She would find this easy to do if she had read the chapter in this text on "What Do Interest Rates Mean?": She would use the present value equation from that chapter

$$PV = \frac{CF}{(1 + i)^n} \tag{1}$$

and she would figure out that each of the Treasury strip zero-coupon bonds would sell for its present discounted value:

$$\frac{\text{Cash payment in year } n}{(1 + 0.09752)^n}$$

The results of this calculation for each year are listed in column (4) of Table 19.1. When Fran adds up the values of the collection of the Treasury strip zero-coupon bonds, she gets a figure of $1,015,528, which is greater than the $1 million purchase price of the Treasury bond. As long as it costs less than $15,528 to collect the payments from the Treasury and then pass them through to the owners of the zero-coupon strips, which is likely to be the case, since computer technology makes the cost of conducting these financial transactions low, the zero-coupon strips will be profitable for her financial institution. Fran would thus recommend that her firm go ahead and market the new financial product. Because the financial institution can now generate much higher profits by selling substantial numbers of Treasury strips, it would amply reward Fran with a spanking new red BMW and a $100,000 bonus!

TABLE 19.1 Market Value of Treasury Strip Zero-Coupon Bonds Derived from a $1 Million 10-Year Treasury Bond with a 10% Coupon Rate and Selling at Par

(1) Year	(2) Cash Payment ($)	(3) Interest Rate on Zero-Coupon Bond (%)	(4) Present Discounted Value of Zero-Coupon Bond ($)
1	100,000	9.75	91,116
2	100,000	9.75	83,022
3	100,000	9.75	75,646
4	100,000	9.75	68,926
5	100,000	9.75	62,802
6	100,000	9.75	57,223
7	100,000	9.75	52,140
8	100,000	9.75	47,508
9	100,000	9.75	43,287
10	100,000	9.75	39,442
10	1,000,000	9.75	394,416
Total			$1,015,528

Financial Innovation and the Decline of Traditional Banking

The traditional financial intermediation role of banking has been to make long-term loans and to fund them by issuing short-term deposits, a process of asset transformation commonly referred to as "borrowing short and lending long." Here we examine how financial innovations have created a more competitive environment for the banking industry, causing the industry to change dramatically, with its traditional banking business going into decline.

In the United States, the importance of banks as a source of funds to nonfinancial borrowers has shrunk dramatically. As we can see in Figure 19.2, in 1974 banks provided over 40% of these funds; by 2016 their market share was down to slightly above 20%.

To understand why traditional banking business has declined in size, we need to look at how the financial innovations described earlier have caused banks to suffer declines in their cost advantages in acquiring funds—that is, on the liabilities side of their balance sheet—while at the same time they have lost income advantages on the assets side of their balance sheet. The simultaneous decline of cost and income advantages has resulted in reduced profitability of traditional banking and an effort by banks to leave this business and engage in new and more profitable activities.

Decline in Cost Advantages in Acquiring Funds (Liabilities) Until 1980 banks were subject to deposit rate ceilings that restricted them from paying

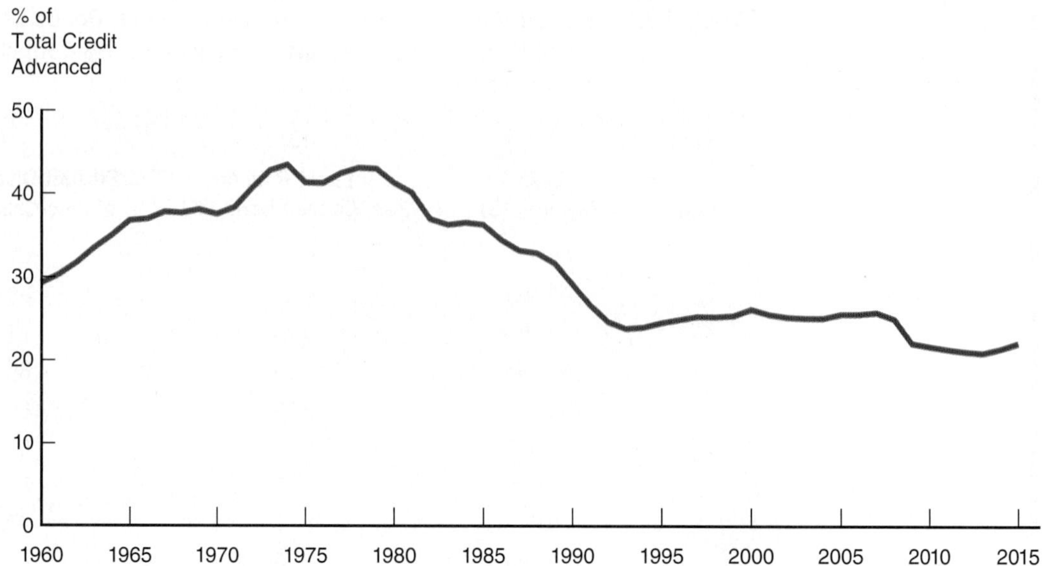

FIGURE 19.2 Bank Share of Total Nonfinancial Borrowing, 1960–2016

In 1974 banks provided over 40% of these funds; by 2016 their market share was down to slightly above 20%.

Source: www2.fdic.gov/hsob/index.asp

interest on checkable deposits and (under Regulation Q) limited them to paying a maximum interest rate of a little more than 5% on time deposits. Until the 1960s, these restrictions worked to the banks' advantage because their major source of funds (in excess of 60%) was checkable deposits, and the zero interest cost on these deposits meant that the banks had a very low cost of funds. Unfortunately, this cost advantage for banks did not last. The rise in inflation beginning in the late 1960s led to higher interest rates, which made investors more sensitive to yield differentials on different assets. The result was the *disintermediation* process, in which people began to take their money out of banks, with their low interest rates on both checkable and time deposits, and began to seek out higher-yielding investments. At the same time, attempts to get around deposit rate ceilings and reserve requirements led to the financial innovation of money market mutual funds, which put the banks at an even further disadvantage because depositors could now obtain checking account-like services while earning high interest on their money market mutual fund accounts. One manifestation of these changes in the financial system was that the low-cost source of funds, checkable deposits, declined dramatically in importance for banks, falling from more than 60% of bank liabilities to around 10% today.

The growing difficulty for banks in raising funds led to their supporting legislation in the 1980s that eliminated Regulation Q ceilings on time deposit interest rates and allowed checkable deposit accounts that paid interest. Although these changes in regulation helped make banks more competitive in their quest for funds, it also meant that their cost of acquiring funds had risen substantially, thereby reducing their earlier cost advantage over other financial institutions.

Decline in Income Advantages on Uses of Funds (Assets) The loss of cost advantages on the liabilities side of the balance sheet for American banks is one reason that they have become less competitive, but they have also been hit by a decline in income advantages on the assets side from the financial innovations we discussed earlier—junk bonds, securitization, and the rise of the commercial paper market. The resulting loss of income advantages for banks relative to these innovations has resulted in a loss of market share and has led to the growth of the shadow banking system, which has made use of these innovations to enable borrowers to bypass the traditional banking system.

We have seen that improvements in information technology have made it easier for firms to issue securities directly to the public. This has meant that instead of going to banks to finance short-term credit needs, many of the banks' best business customers now find it cheaper to go instead to the commercial paper market for funds.

The emergence of the junk bond market has also eaten into banks' loan business. Improvements in information technology have made it easier for corporations to sell their bonds to the public directly, thereby bypassing banks. Although *Fortune* 500 companies started taking this route in the 1970s, now lower-quality corporate borrowers are using banks less often because they have access to the junk bond market.

We have also seen that improvements in computer technology have led to the growth of the shadow banking system and securitization, whereby illiquid financial assets such as bank loans and mortgages are transformed into marketable securities. Computers enable other financial institutions to originate loans because they can now accurately evaluate credit risk with statistical methods, while computers have lowered transaction costs, making it possible to bundle these loans and sell them as securities. When default risk can be easily evaluated with computers, banks no longer have an advantage in making loans. Without their former advantages, banks have lost loan business to other financial institutions even though the banks themselves are involved in the process of securitization. Securitization has been a particular problem for mortgage-issuing institutions such as S&Ls because most residential mortgages are now securitized.

Banks' Responses In any industry, a decline in profitability usually results in exit from the industry (often due to widespread bankruptcies) and a shrinkage of market share. This occurred in the banking industry in the United States during the 1980s via consolidations and bank failures (discussed in the previous chapter).

In an attempt to survive and maintain adequate profit levels, many U.S. banks face two alternatives. First, they can attempt to maintain their traditional lending activity by expanding into new and riskier areas of lending. For example, U.S. banks increased their risk taking by placing a greater percentage of their total funds in commercial real estate loans, traditionally a riskier type of loan. In addition, they increased lending for corporate takeovers and leveraged buyouts, which are highly leveraged transaction loans. The decline in the profitability of banks' traditional business may thus have helped lead to the crisis in banking in the 1980s and early 1990s that we discussed in the last chapter, as well as the global financial crisis that started in 2007, discussed in Chapter 8.

The second way banks have sought to maintain former profit levels is to pursue new off-balance-sheet activities that are more profitable and in effect embrace the shadow banking system. U.S. banks did this starting in the early 1980s, increasing the share of their income from off-balance-sheet, non-interest-income activities by more than fivefold. This strategy, however, has generated concerns about what activities are proper for banks and whether nontraditional activities might be riskier and, therefore, result in excessive risk taking by banks.

The decline of banks' traditional business has thus meant that the banking industry has been driven to seek out new lines of business. This search for business opportunities could be beneficial because by so doing, banks can keep vibrant and healthy. Indeed, bank profitability was high up until 2007, and nontraditional, off-balance-sheet activities played an important role in high bank profits. However, the new directions in banking have led to increased risk taking, and thus the decline in traditional banking has required regulators to be more vigilant. It also poses new challenges for bank regulators, who, as we saw in Chapter 18, must now be far more concerned about banks' off-balance-sheet activities.

Decline of Traditional Banking in Other Industrialized Countries Forces similar to those in the United States have been leading to the decline of traditional banking in other industrialized countries. The loss of banks' monopoly power over depositors and borrowers has occurred outside the United States as well. Financial innovation and deregulation are occurring worldwide and have created attractive alternatives for both depositors and borrowers. In Japan, for example, deregulation opened a wide array of new financial instruments to the public, causing a disintermediation process similar to that in the United States. In European countries, innovations have steadily eroded the barriers that have traditionally protected banks from competition.

In other countries, banks also faced increased competition from the expansion of securities markets and the growth of the shadow banking system. Both financial deregulation and fundamental economic forces in other countries have improved the availability of information in securities markets, making it easier and less costly for firms to finance their activities by issuing securities rather than going to banks. Further, even in countries where securities markets have not grown, banks have still lost loan business because their best corporate customers have had increasing access to foreign and offshore capital markets, such as the Eurobond market. In smaller economies, like that of Australia, which still do not have as well-developed corporate bond or commercial paper markets, banks have lost loan business to international securities markets. In addition, the same forces that drove the securitization process in the United States have been at work in other countries and have undercut the profitability of traditional banking in these countries as well. The United States has not been unique in seeing its banks face a more difficult competitive environment. Thus, although the decline of traditional banking occurred earlier in the United States than in other countries, the same forces have caused a decline in traditional banking abroad.

Structure of the U.S. Banking Industry

There are currently 6,000 banks in the United States, far more than in any other country in the world. As Table 19.2 indicates, we have an extraordinary number of small banks. A remarkable 32.1% of the banks have less than $100 million in assets. Far more typical is the size distribution in Canada or the United Kingdom, where five or fewer banks dominate the industry. In contrast, the 10 largest banks in the United States (listed in Table 19.3) together hold around 50% of the assets in their industry.

TABLE 19.2 Size Distribution of All FDIC-Insured Banking Institutions, March 31, 2016

Assets	Number of Banks	Share of Banks (%)	Share of Assets Held (%)
Less than $100 million	1,663	27.2	0.6
$100 million–$1 billion	3,734	61.0	7.2
$1 billion–$10 billion	616	10.1	10.6
More than $10 billion	109	1.7	81.6
Total	6,122	100.00	100.00

Source: http://www2.fdic.gov/sdi/main.asp.

TABLE 19.3 Ten Largest U.S. Banks, 2016

Bank	Assets ($ billions)	Share of All Bank Assets (%)
1. J.P. Morgan Chase	1,915	12.2
2. Bank of America	1,639	10.4
3. Wells Fargo and Co.	1,611	10.3
4. Citigroup	1,300	8.3
5. U.S. Bank	417	2.7
6. PNC Bank	348	2.2
7. Bank of New York Mellon	319	2.0
8. Capital One	273	1.7
9. TD Bank	246	1.6
10. State Street Bank and Co.	241	1.5
Total	8,309	50.9

Source: http://www.federalreserve.gov/Releases/Lbr/current/default.htm.

Most industries in the United States have far fewer firms than the banking industry; typically, large firms tend to dominate these industries to a greater extent than in the banking industry. (Consider the computer software industry, which is dominated by Microsoft, or the automobile industry, which is dominated by General Motors, Ford, Toyota, and Honda.) Does the large number of banks and the absence of a few dominant firms suggest that banking is more competitive than other industries?

Restrictions on Branching

The presence of so many banks in the United States actually reflects past regulations that restricted the ability of these financial institutions to open **branches** (additional offices for the conduct of banking operations). Each state had its own regulations on the type and number of branches that a bank could open. Regulations on both coasts, for example, tended to allow banks to open branches throughout a state; in the middle part of the country, regulations on branching were more restrictive. The McFadden Act of 1927, which was designed to put national banks and state banks on an equal footing (and the Douglas Amendment of 1956, which closed a loophole in the McFadden Act), effectively prohibited banks from branching across state lines and forced all national banks to conform to the branching regulations of the state where their headquarters were located.

The McFadden Act and state branching regulations constituted strong anticompetitive forces in the banking industry, allowing many small banks to stay in existence because larger banks were prevented from opening a branch nearby. If competition is beneficial to society, why have regulations restricting branching arisen in America? The simplest explanation is that the American public has historically been hostile to large banks. States with the most restrictive branching regulations were typically ones in which populist antibank sentiment was strongest in the nineteenth century. (These states usually had large farming populations whose relations with banks periodically became tempestuous when banks would foreclose on farmers who couldn't pay their debts.) The legacy of nineteenth-century politics was a banking system with restrictive branching regulations and hence an inordinate number of small banks. However, as we will see later in this chapter, branching restrictions have been eliminated, and we have moved toward nationwide banking.

Response to Branching Restrictions

An important feature of the U.S. banking industry is that competition can be repressed by regulation but not completely quashed. As we saw earlier in this chapter, the existence of restrictive regulation stimulates financial innovations that get around these regulations in the banks' search for profits. Regulations restricting branching have stimulated similar economic forces and have promoted the development of two financial innovations: bank holding companies and automated teller machines.

Bank Holding Companies A holding company is a corporation that owns several different companies. This form of corporate ownership has important advantages for banks. It has allowed them to circumvent restrictive branching regulations because the holding company can own a controlling interest in several banks even if branching is not permitted. Furthermore, a bank holding company can engage in other activities related to banking, such as the provision of investment advice, data processing and transmission services, leasing, credit card services, and servicing of loans in other states.

The growth of the bank holding companies has been dramatic over the past three decades. Today, bank holding companies own almost all large banks, and more than 90% of bank deposits are held in banks owned by holding companies.

Automated Teller Machines Another financial innovation that avoided the restrictions on branching is the automated teller machine (ATM). Banks realized that if they did not own or rent the ATM but instead let it be owned by someone else and paid for each transaction with a fee, the ATM would probably not be considered a branch of the bank and thus would not be subject to branching regulations. This is exactly what the regulatory agencies and courts in most states concluded. Because they enable banks to widen their markets, a number of these shared facilities (such as Cirrus and NYCE) have been established nationwide. Furthermore, even when an ATM is owned by a bank, states typically have special provisions that allow wider establishment of ATMs than is permissible for traditional "brick and mortar" branches.

As we saw earlier in this chapter, avoiding regulation was not the only reason for the development of the ATM. The advent of cheaper computer and telecommunications technology enabled banks to provide ATMs at low cost, making them a profitable innovation. This example further illustrates that technological factors often combine with incentives such as the desire to avoid restrictive regulations like branching restrictions to produce financial innovation.

Bank Consolidation and Nationwide Banking

As we can see in Figure 19.3, after a remarkable period of stability from 1934 to the mid-1980s, the number of banks began to fall dramatically. Why has this sudden decline taken place?

The banking industry hit some hard times in the 1980s and early 1990s, with bank failures running at a rate of over 100 per year from 1985 to 1992 and from 2009 to 2010 (more on this later in the chapter; also see Chapter 18). But bank failures are only part of the story. In the years 1985–1992, the number of insured banks declined by 3,000—more than double the number of failures. And in the period

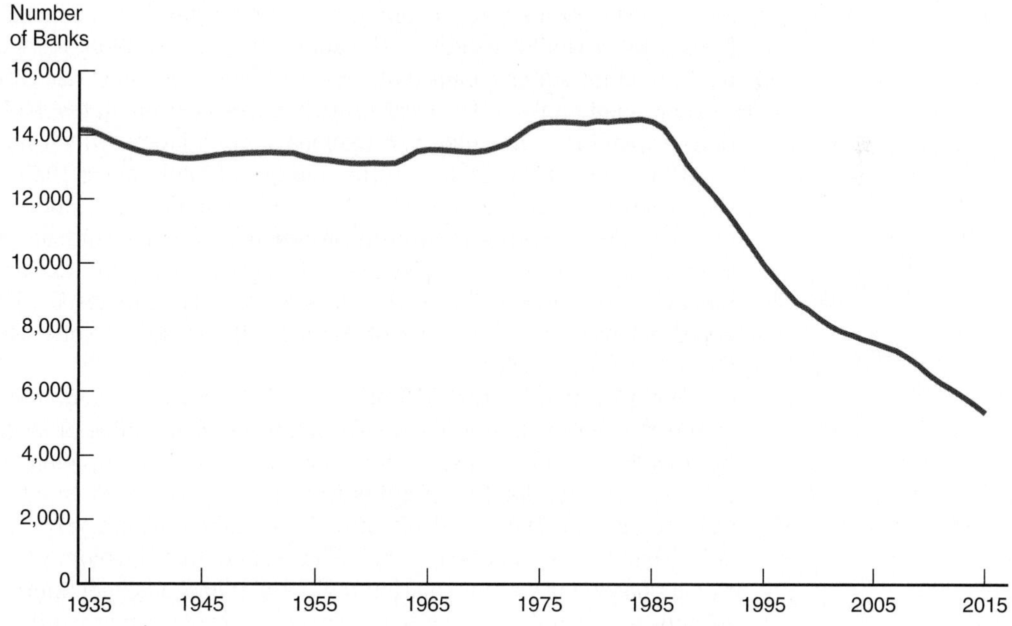

FIGURE 19.3 Number of Insured Banks in the United States, 1934–2016

After a period of stability from 1934 to the mid-1980s, the number of banks began to fall dramatically.

Source: https://www5.fdic.gov/hsob/HSOBRpt.asp..

1992–2007, when the banking industry returned to health, the number of insured banks decreased by a little over 3,800, less than 5% of which were bank failures, and most of these were of small banks. Thus we see that bank failures played an important, though not predominant, role in reducing the number of banks in the 1985–1992 period and an almost negligible role through 2007. The global financial crisis has, however, led to additional declines in the number of banks because of bank failures.

So what explains the rest of the story? The answer is bank consolidation. Banks have been merging to create larger entities or have been buying up other banks. This gives rise to a new question: Why has bank consolidation been taking place in recent years?

As we have seen, loophole mining by banks reduced the effectiveness of branching restrictions, with the result that many states recognized that it would be in their best interest if they allowed ownership of banks across state lines. The result was the formation of reciprocal regional compacts in which banks in one state are allowed to own banks in other states in the region. In 1975 Maine enacted the first interstate banking legislation that allowed out-of-state bank holding companies to purchase banks in that state. In 1982 Massachusetts enacted a regional compact with other New England states to allow interstate banking, and many other regional compacts were adopted thereafter until by the early 1990s, almost all states allowed some form of interstate banking.

Access **www2.fdic.gov/SDI/SOB** to gather statistics on the banking industry.

With the barriers to interstate banking breaking down in the early 1980s, banks recognized that they could gain the benefits of diversification because they would now be able to make loans in many states rather than just one. This gave them the advantage that if one state's economy was weak, another state in which they operated might have a strong economy, thus decreasing the likelihood that loans in different states would default at the same time. In addition, allowing banks to own banks in other states meant that they could increase their size through out-of-state acquisition of banks or by merging with banks in other states. Mergers and acquisitions explain the first phase of banking consolidation, which has played such an important role in the decline in the number of banks since 1985. Another result of the loosening of restrictions on interstate branching is the development of a new class of banks, the **superregional banks**, bank holding companies that have begun to rival the money center banks in size but whose headquarters are not in one of the money center cities (New York, Chicago, and San Francisco). Examples of these superregional banks are Bank of America of Charlotte, North Carolina, and Banc One of Columbus, Ohio.

Not surprisingly, the advent of the Web and improved computer technology is another factor driving bank consolidation. Economies of scale have increased because large up-front investments are required to set up many information technology platforms for financial institutions (see the E-Finance box, "Information Technology and Bank Consolidation"). To take advantage of these economies of scale, banks have needed to get bigger, and this development has led to additional consolidation. Information technology has also been increasing **economies of scope**, the ability to use one resource to provide many different products and services. For example, details about the quality and creditworthiness of firms not only inform decisions about whether to make loans to them but also can be useful in determining at what price their shares should trade. Similarly, once you have marketed one financial product to an investor, you probably know how to market another. Business people describe economies of scope by saying there are

> E-FINANCE

Information Technology and Bank Consolidation

Achieving low costs in banking requires huge investments in information technology. In turn, such enormous investments require a business line of very large scale. This has been particularly true in the credit card business in recent years, in which huge technology investments have been made to provide customers with convenient Web sites and to develop better systems to handle processing and risk analysis for both credit and fraud risk. The result has been substantial consolidation: As recently as 1995, the top five banking institutions issuing credit cards held less than 40% of total credit card debt, while today this number is more than 60%. Information technology has also spurred increasing consolidation of the bank custody business. Banks hold the actual certificate for investors when they purchase a stock or bond and provide data on the value of these securities and the amount of risk an investor is facing. Because this business is also computer-intensive, it requires very large-scale investments in computer technology for the bank to offer these services at competitive rates. The percentage of assets at the top 10 custody banks has therefore risen from 40% in 1990 to more than 90% today.

The increasing importance of e-finance, in which the computer is playing a more central role in delivering financial services, is bringing tremendous changes to the structure of the banking industry. Although many banks are more than willing to offer a full range of products to their customers, most no longer find it profitable to produce all of them. Instead, they are contracting out the business, a practice that will lead to further consolidation of technology-intensive banking businesses in the future.

"synergies" between different lines of business, and information technology is making these synergies more likely. The result is that consolidation is taking place not only to make financial institutions bigger but also to increase the combination of products and services they can provide. This consolidation has had two consequences. First, different types of financial intermediaries are encroaching on each other's territory, making them more alike. Second, consolidation has led to the development of large, complex banking organizations. This development has been facilitated by the repeal of the Glass-Steagall restrictions on combinations of banking and other financial service industries discussed in the next section.

The Riegle-Neal Interstate Banking and Branching Efficiency Act of 1994

Banking consolidation was given further stimulus by the passage in 1994 of the Riegle-Neal Interstate Banking and Branching Efficiency Act. This legislation expanded the regional compacts to the entire nation and overturned the McFadden Act and Douglas Amendment's prohibition of interstate banking. Not only does this act allow bank holding companies to acquire banks in any other state, notwithstanding any state laws to the contrary, but bank holding companies can also merge the banks they own into one bank with branches in different states. States also have the option of opting out of interstate branching, a choice only Texas has made.

The Riegle-Neal Act finally established the basis for a true nationwide banking system. Although interstate banking was accomplished previously by out-of-state purchase of banks by bank holding companies, until 1994 interstate branching was virtually nonexistent because very few states had enacted interstate branching legislation. Allowing banks to conduct interstate banking through branching is especially important because many bankers feel that economies of scale cannot be fully exploited through the bank holding company structure, but only through branching networks in which all of the bank's operations are fully coordinated.

Nationwide banks now emerged. Starting with the merger in 1998 of Bank of America and NationsBank, which created the first bank with branches on both coasts, consolidation in the banking industry has led to banking organizations with operations in almost all 50 states.

What Will the Structure of the U.S. Banking Industry Look Like in the Future?

Now that true nationwide banking in the United States is a reality, the benefits of bank consolidation for the banking industry have increased substantially, driving the next phase of mergers and acquisitions and accelerating the decline in the number of banks. With great changes occurring in the structure of this industry, the question naturally arises: What will the industry look like in 10 years?

One view is that the industry will become more like that in many other countries and we will end up with only a couple of hundred banks. A more extreme view is that the industry will look like that of Canada or the United Kingdom, with a few large banks dominating the industry. Most experts come up with a different answer. The structure of the U.S. banking industry will still be unique, but not to the degree it once was. The consolidation surge is likely to settle down as the U.S. banking industry approaches several thousand, rather than several hundred, banks.

Banking consolidation will result not only in a smaller number of banks, but as the mergers between Chase Manhattan Bank and Chemical Bank and between Bank of America and NationsBank suggest, it will result in a shift in assets from smaller banks to larger banks as well. Indeed, the United States now has several trillion-dollar banks (e.g., Citibank, J.P. Morgan Chase, and Bank of America).

Are Bank Consolidation and Nationwide Banking Good Things?

Advocates of nationwide banking believe that it will produce more efficient banks and a healthier banking system less prone to bank failures. However, critics of bank consolidation fear that it will eliminate small banks, referred to as **community banks**, and that this will result in less lending to small businesses. In addition, they worry that a few banks will come to dominate the industry, making the banking business less competitive.

Most economists are skeptical of these criticisms of bank consolidation. As we have seen, research indicates that even after bank consolidation is completed, the United States will still have plenty of banks. The banking industry will thus remain highly competitive, probably even more so than now, considering that banks that had been protected from competition from out-of-state banks now have to compete with them vigorously to stay in business.

It also does not look as though community banks will disappear. When New York state liberalized its branching laws in 1962, there were fears that community banks upstate would be driven from the market by the big New York City banks. Not only did this not happen, but some of the big boys found that the small banks were able to run rings around them in the local markets. Similarly, California, which has had unrestricted statewide branching for a long time, continues to have a thriving population of community banks.

Economists see some important benefits from bank consolidation and nationwide banking. The elimination of geographic restrictions on banking increases competition and drives inefficient banks out of business, enhancing the efficiency of the banking sector. The move to larger banking organizations also means that there is some increase in efficiency because they can take advantage of economies of scale and scope. The increased diversification of banks' loan portfolios may lower the probability of a banking crisis in the future. In the 1980s and early 1990s, bank failures were often concentrated in states with weak economies. For example, after the decline in oil prices in 1986, all of the major banks in Texas, which had been very profitable, found themselves in trouble. At that time, banks in New England were doing fine. However, when the 1990–1991 recession hit New England hard, some New England banks started failing. With nationwide banking, a bank could make loans in both New England and Texas and would thus be less likely to fail because when loans go sour in one location, they would likely be doing well in the other. Thus, nationwide banking is seen as a major step toward creating a banking system that is less vulnerable to banking crises.

Two concerns remain about the effects of bank consolidation—that it may lead to a reduction in lending to small businesses and that banks rushing to expand into new geographic markets may take increased risks, leading to bank failures. The jury is still out on these concerns, but most economists see the benefits of bank consolidation and nationwide banking as outweighing the costs.

Separation of the Banking and Other Financial Service Industries

Another important feature of the structure of the banking industry in the United States until recently was the separation of the banking and other financial services industries—such as securities, insurance, and real estate—mandated by the Glass-Steagall Act of 1933. As pointed out earlier in the chapter, Glass-Steagall allowed banks to sell new offerings of government securities but prohibited them from underwriting corporate securities or from engaging in brokerage activities. It also prevented banks from engaging in insurance and real estate activities. In turn, it prevented investment banks and insurance companies from engaging in banking activities and thus protected banks from competition.

Erosion of Glass-Steagall

Despite the Glass-Steagall prohibitions, the pursuit of profits and financial innovation stimulated both banks and other financial institutions to bypass the intent of the Glass-Steagall Act and encroach on each other's traditional territory. Brokerage firms engaged in the traditional banking business of issuing deposit instruments with the development of money market mutual funds and cash management accounts. After the Federal Reserve used a loophole in Section 20 of the

Glass-Steagall Act in 1987 to allow bank holding companies to underwrite previously prohibited classes of securities, banks began to enter this business. The loophole allowed affiliates of approved banks to engage in underwriting activities as long as the revenue didn't exceed a specified amount, which started at 10% but was raised to 25% of the affiliates' total revenue. After the U.S. Supreme Court validated the Fed's action in July 1988, the Federal Reserve allowed J.P. Morgan, a bank holding company, to underwrite corporate debt securities (in January 1989) and to underwrite stocks (in September 1990), with the privilege later extended to other bank holding companies. The regulatory agencies also allowed banks to engage in some real estate and insurance activities.

The Gramm-Leach-Bliley Financial Services Modernization Act of 1999: Repeal of Glass-Steagall

Because restrictions on banks' securities and insurance activities put American banks at a competitive disadvantage relative to foreign banks, bills to overturn Glass-Steagall appeared in almost every session of Congress in the 1990s. With the merger in 1998 of Citicorp, the second-largest bank in the United States, and Travelers Group, an insurance company that also owned the third-largest securities firm in the country (Salomon Smith Barney), the pressure to abolish Glass-Steagall became overwhelming. Legislation to eliminate Glass-Steagall finally came to fruition in 1999. This legislation, the Gramm-Leach-Bliley Financial Services Modernization Act of 1999, allows securities firms and insurance companies to purchase banks, and allows banks to underwrite insurance and securities and engage in real estate activities. Under this legislation, states retain regulatory authority over insurance activities, while the Securities and Exchange Commission continues to have oversight of securities activities. The Office of the Comptroller of the Currency has the authority to regulate bank subsidiaries engaged in securities underwriting, but the Federal Reserve continues to have the authority to oversee the bank holding companies under which all real estate and insurance activities and large securities operations will be housed.

Implications for Financial Consolidation

As we have seen, the Riegle-Neal Interstate Banking and Branching Efficiency Act of 1994 stimulated consolidation of the banking industry. The financial consolidation process was further hastened by the Gramm-Leach-Bliley Act of 1999 because the way is now open to consolidation in terms not only of the number of banking institutions, but also across financial service activities. Given that information technology is increasing economies of scope, mergers of banks with other financial service firms like that of Citicorp and Travelers have become increasingly common, and more mega-mergers are likely to be on the way. Banking institutions are becoming not only larger but also increasingly complex organizations, engaging in the full gamut of financial service activities. The trend toward larger and more complex banking organizations was accelerated by the global financial crisis of 2007–2009 (see the Mini-Case box, "The Global Financial Crisis and the Demise of Large, Free-Standing Investment Banks").

MINI-CASE

The Global Financial Crisis and the Demise of Large, Free-Standing Investment Banks

Although the move toward bringing financial service activities into larger, complex banking organizations was inevitable after the demise of Glass-Steagall, no one expected it to occur as rapidly as it did in 2008. Over a six-month period from March to September 2008, all five of the largest, free-standing investment banks ceased to exist in their old form. When Bear Stearns, the fifth-largest investment bank, revealed its large losses from investments in subprime mortgage securities, it had to be bailed out by the Fed in March 2008; the price it paid was a forced sale to J.P. Morgan for less than one-tenth what it had been worth only a year or so before. The Bear Stearns bailout made it clear that the government safety net had been extended to investment banks. The trade-off is that investment banks will be subject to more regulation, along the lines of banks, in the future.

Next to go was Lehman Brothers, the fourth-largest investment bank, which declared bankruptcy on September 15. Only one day before, Merrill Lynch, the third-largest investment bank, which also suffered large losses on its holdings of subprime securities, announced its sale to Bank of America for less than half of its year-earlier price. Within a week Goldman Sachs and Morgan Stanley, the first- and second-largest investment banks, both of which had smaller exposure to subprime securities, nevertheless saw the writing on the wall. They realized that they would soon become regulated on a similar basis and decided to become bank holding companies so they could access insured deposits, a more stable funding base.

It was the end of an era. Large, free-standing investment banking firms are now a thing of the past.

Separation of Banking and Other Financial Services Industries Throughout the World

Not many other countries in the aftermath of the Great Depression followed the lead of the United States in separating the banking and other financial services industries. In fact, in the past this separation was the most prominent difference between banking regulation in the United States and in other countries. Around the world, there are three basic frameworks for the banking and securities industries.

The first framework is *universal banking*, which exists in Germany, the Netherlands, and Switzerland. It provides no separation at all between the banking and securities industries. In a universal banking system, banks provide a full range of banking, securities, real estate, and insurance services, all within a single legal entity. Banks are allowed to own sizable equity shares in commercial firms, and often they do.

The *British-style universal banking system*, the second framework, is found in the United Kingdom and countries with close ties to it, such as Canada and Australia, and now the United States. The British-style universal bank engages in securities underwriting, but it differs from the German-style universal bank in three ways: Separate legal subsidiaries are more common, bank equity holdings of commercial firms are less common, and combinations of banking and insurance firms are less common.

The third framework features some legal separation of the banking and other financial services industries, as in Japan. A major difference between the U.S. and Japanese banking systems is that Japanese banks are allowed to hold substantial equity stakes in commercial firms, whereas American banks cannot. Although the banking and securities industries are legally separated in Japan, banks are increasingly being allowed to engage in securities activities and, like U.S. banks, are becoming more like British-style universal banks.

Thrift Industry

Not surprisingly, the regulation and structure of the thrift industry (savings and loan associations, mutual savings banks, and credit unions) closely parallel the regulation and structure of the commercial banking industry.[2]

Savings and Loan Associations

Just as there is a dual banking system for commercial banks, savings and loan associations (S&Ls) can be chartered either by the federal government or by the states. Most S&Ls, whether state or federally chartered, are members of the Federal Home Loan Bank System (FHLBS). Established in 1932, the FHLBS was styled after the Federal Reserve System. It has 12 district Federal Home Loan banks, which are supervised by the Office of Thrift Supervision.

Federal deposit insurance up to $250,000 per account for S&Ls is provided by the FDIC. The Office of the Comptroller of the Currency regulates federally insured S&Ls by setting minimum capital requirements, requiring periodic reports, and examining the S&Ls. It is also the chartering agency for federally chartered S&Ls, and for these S&Ls it approves mergers and sets the rules for branching.

The FHLBS, like the Fed, makes loans to the members of the system (obtaining funds for this purpose by issuing bonds). However, in contrast to the Fed's discount loans, which are expected to be repaid quickly, the loans from the FHLBS often need not be repaid for long periods of time. In addition, the rates charged to S&Ls for these loans are often below the rates that the S&Ls must pay when they borrow in the open market. In this way, the FHLBS loan program provides a subsidy to the savings and loan industry (and implicitly to the housing industry, since most of the S&L loans are for residential mortgages).

The savings and loans experienced serious difficulties in the 1980s (discussed in Web Chapter 26). Because savings and loans now engage in many of the same activities as commercial banks, the charter and regulatory apparatus for S&Ls is now similar to that of commercial banks.

Mutual Savings Banks

Of the 400 or so mutual savings banks, which are similar to S&Ls but are jointly owned by the depositors, approximately half are chartered by states. Although the mutual savings banks are primarily regulated by the states in which they are located, the majority have their deposits insured by the FDIC up to the limit of $250,000 per account; these banks are also subject to many of the FDIC's regulations for state-chartered banks. As a rule, the mutual savings banks whose deposits are not insured by the FDIC have their deposits insured by state insurance funds.

---

[2]See Web Chapter 26, which can be found at www.pearsonhighered.com/mishkin_eakins, for a far more in-depth discussion of the regulation and structure of the thrift industry.

Credit Unions

Credit unions are small cooperative lending institutions organized around a particular group of individuals with a common bond (e.g., union members or employees of a particular firm). They are the only depository institutions that are tax-exempt and can be chartered either by the states or by the federal government; more than half are federally chartered. The National Credit Union Administration (NCUA) issues federal charters and regulates federally chartered credit unions by setting minimum capital requirements, requiring periodic reports, and examining the credit unions. Federal deposit insurance (up to the $250,000-per-account limit) is provided to both federally chartered and state-chartered credit unions by a subsidiary of the NCUA, the National Credit Union Share Insurance Fund (NCUSIF). Because the majority of credit union lending is for consumer loans with fairly short terms to maturity, these institutions did not suffer the financial difficulties of the S&Ls and mutual savings banks.

Because their members share a common bond, credit unions are typically quite small; most hold less than $10 million of assets. In addition, their ties to a particular industry or company make them more likely to fail when large numbers of workers in that industry or company are laid off and have trouble making loan payments. Recent regulatory changes allow individual credit unions to cater to a more diverse group of people by interpreting the common bond requirement less strictly, and this has encouraged an expansion in the size of credit unions that may help reduce credit union failures in the future.

International Banking

In 1960 only eight U.S. banks operated branches in foreign countries, and their total assets were less than $4 billion. Currently, around 100 American banks have branches abroad, with assets totaling more than $1.5 trillion. The spectacular growth in international banking can be explained by three factors.

First is the rapid growth in international trade and multinational (worldwide) corporations that has occurred since 1960. When American firms operate abroad, they need banking services in foreign countries to help finance international trade. For example, they might need a loan in a foreign currency to operate a factory abroad. And when they sell goods abroad, they need to have a bank exchange the foreign currency they have received for their goods into dollars. Although these firms could use foreign banks to provide them with these international banking services, many of them prefer to do business with the U.S. banks with which they have established long-term relationships and which understand American business customs and practices. As international trade has grown, international banking has grown with it.

Second, American banks have been able to earn substantial profits by being very active in global investment banking, in which they underwrite foreign securities. They also sell insurance abroad, and they derive substantial profits from these investment banking and insurance activities.

Third, American banks have wanted to tap into the large pool of dollar-denominated deposits in foreign countries known as Eurodollars. To understand the structure of U.S. banking overseas, let's first look at the Eurodollar market, an important source of growth for international banking.

Eurodollar Market

Eurodollars are created when deposits in accounts in the United States are transferred to a bank outside the country and are kept in the form of dollars. For example, if Rolls-Royce PLC deposits a $1 million check, written on an account at an American bank, in its bank in London—specifying that the deposit is payable in dollars—$1 million in Eurodollars is created.[3] More than 90% of Eurodollar deposits are time deposits; more than half of them are certificates of deposit with maturities of 30 days or more. The total amount of Eurodollars outstanding is on the order of $5 trillion, making the Eurodollar market one of the most important financial markets in the world economy.

Why would companies such as Rolls-Royce want to hold dollar deposits outside the United States? First, the dollar is the most widely used currency in international trade, so Rolls-Royce might want to hold deposits in dollars to conduct its international transactions. Second, Eurodollars are "offshore" deposits—they are held in countries that will not subject them to regulations such as reserve requirements or restrictions (called *capital controls*) on taking the deposits outside the country.[4]

The main center of the Eurodollar market is London, a major international financial center for hundreds of years. Eurodollars are also held outside Europe in locations that provide offshore status to these deposits—for example, Singapore, the Bahamas, and the Cayman Islands.

The minimum transaction in the Eurodollar market is typically $1 million, and approximately 75% of Eurodollar deposits are held by banks. Plainly, you and I are unlikely to come into direct contact with Eurodollars. Rather than using an intermediary and borrowing all the deposits from foreign banks, American banks decided that they could earn higher profits by opening their own branches abroad to attract these deposits. Consequently, the Eurodollar market was an important stimulus to U.S. banking overseas.

Structure of U.S. Banking Overseas

U.S. banks have most of their foreign branches in Latin America, the Far East, the Caribbean, and London. The largest volume of assets is held by branches in London because it is a major international financial center and the central location for the Eurodollar market. Latin America and the Far East have many branches because of the importance of U.S. trade with these regions. Parts of the Caribbean (especially the Bahamas and the Cayman Islands) have become important as tax havens, with minimal taxation and few restrictive regulations. In actuality, the bank branches in the Bahamas and the Cayman Islands are "shell operations" because they function primarily as bookkeeping centers and do not provide normal banking services.

---

[3]Note that the London bank keeps the $1 million on deposit at the American bank, so the creation of Eurodollars has not caused a reduction in the amount of bank deposits in the United States.

[4]Although most offshore deposits are denominated in dollars, some are denominated in other currencies. Collectively, these offshore deposits are referred to as Eurocurrencies. A Japanese yen-denominated deposit held in London, for example, is called a Euroyen.

An alternative corporate structure for U.S. banks that operate overseas is the **Edge Act corporation**, a special subsidiary engaged primarily in international banking. U.S. banks (through their holding companies) can also own a controlling interest in foreign banks and in foreign companies that provide financial services, such as finance companies. The international activities of U.S. banking organizations are governed primarily by the Federal Reserve's Regulation K.

In late 1981, the Federal Reserve approved the creation of **international banking facilities (IBFs)** within the United States that can accept time deposits from foreigners but are not subject to either reserve requirements or restrictions on interest payments. IBFs are also allowed to make loans to foreigners, but they are not allowed to make loans to domestic residents. States have encouraged the establishment of IBFs by exempting them from state and local taxes. In essence, IBFs are treated like foreign branches of U.S. banks and are not subject to domestic regulations and taxes. The purpose of establishing IBFs is to encourage American and foreign banks to do more banking business in the United States rather than abroad. From this point of view, IBFs were a success: Their assets climbed to nearly $200 billion in the first two years, and are over $1 trillion currently.

Foreign Banks in the United States

The growth in international trade has not only encouraged U.S. banks to open offices overseas, but also encouraged foreign banks to establish offices in the United States. Foreign banks have been extremely successful in the United States. Currently, they hold 25% of total U.S. domestic bank assets and do a large portion of all U.S. bank lending, with over a 20% market share for commercial and industrial loans.

Foreign banks engage in banking activities in the United States by operating an agency office of the foreign bank, a subsidiary U.S. bank, or a branch of the foreign bank. An agency office can lend and transfer funds in the United States, but it cannot accept deposits from domestic residents. Agency offices have the advantage of not being subject to regulations that apply to full-service banking offices (such as requirements for FDIC insurance). A subsidiary U.S. bank is just like any other U.S. bank (it may even have an American-sounding name) and is subject to the same regulations, but it is owned by the foreign bank. A branch of a foreign bank bears the foreign bank's name and is usually a full-service office. Foreign banks may also form Edge Act corporations and IBFs.

The internationalization of banking, both by U.S. banks going abroad and by foreign banks entering the United States, has meant that financial markets throughout the world have become more integrated. As a result, there is a growing trend toward international coordination of bank regulation, one example of which is the Basel Accords to standardize minimum bank capital requirements in industrialized countries, discussed in Chapter 18. Financial market integration has also encouraged bank consolidation abroad, culminating in the creation of the first trillion-dollar bank with the proposed merger of the Industrial Bank of Japan, Dai-Ichi Kangyo Bank, and Fuji Bank, announced in August 1999, but which took place in 2002. Another development has been the importance of foreign banks in international banking. As is shown in Table 19.4, in 2015, eight of the 10 largest banking groups in the world were foreign.

TABLE 19.4 Ten Largest Banks in the World, 2015

Bank	Assets (U.S. $ billions)
1. Industrial & Commercial Bank of China, China	3,545
2. China Construction Bank Corp., China	2,966
3. Agricultural Bank of China, China	2,853
4. Mitsubishi UFK Financial Group Japan	2,655
5. Bank of China, China, China	2,640
6. HSBC Holdings, United Kingdom	2,596
7. J.P. Morgan Chase and Co., United States	2,424
8. BNP Paribas, France	2,404
9. Bank of America, United States	2,186
10. Deutsche Bank, Germany	1,973

Source: http://www.relbanks.com/worlds-top-banks/assets.

SUMMARY

1. The history of banking in the United States has left us with a dual banking system, with banks chartered by the states and the federal government. Multiple agencies regulate banks: the Office of the Comptroller, the Federal Reserve, the FDIC, and the state banking authorities.
2. A change in the economic environment will stimulate financial institutions to search for financial innovations. Changes in demand conditions, especially an increase in interest-rate risk; changes in supply conditions, especially improvements in information technology; and the desire to avoid costly regulations have been major driving forces behind financial innovation. Financial innovation has caused banks to suffer declines in cost advantages in acquiring funds and in income advantages on their assets. The resulting squeeze has hurt profitability in banks' traditional lines of business and has led to a decline in traditional banking and to the rise of shadow banking.
3. Restrictive state branching regulations and the McFadden Act, which prohibited branching across state lines, led to a large number of small banks. The large number of banks in the United States reflected the past *lack* of competition, not the presence of vigorous competition. Bank holding companies and ATMs were important responses to branching restrictions that weakened the restrictions' anticompetitive effect.
4. Since the mid-1980s, bank consolidation has been occurring at a rapid pace. The first phase of bank consolidation was the result of bank failures and the reduced effectiveness of branching restrictions. The second phase has been stimulated by information technology and the Riegle-Neal Interstate Banking and Branching Efficiency Act of 1994, which establishes the basis for a nationwide banking system. Once banking consolidation has settled down, we are likely to be left with a banking system with several thousand banks. Most economists believe that the benefits of bank consolidation and nationwide banking will outweigh the costs.
5. The Glass-Steagall Act separated banking from the securities industry. Legislation in 1999, however, repealed the Glass-Steagall Act, removing the separation of these industries.
6. The regulation and structure of the thrift industry (savings and loan associations, mutual savings banks, and credit unions) parallel closely the regulation and structure of the commercial banking industry. Savings and loans are primarily regulated by the Office of the Comptroller of the Currency, and deposit insurance is administered by the FDIC. Mutual savings banks are regulated by the states, and federal deposit insurance is provided by the FDIC. Credit unions are regulated by the National Credit Union Administration, and

deposit insurance is provided by the National Credit Union Share Insurance Fund.

7. With the rapid growth of world trade since 1960, international banking has grown dramatically. U.S. banks engage in international banking activities by opening branches abroad, owning controlling interests in foreign banks, forming Edge Act corporations, and operating international banking facilities (IBFs) located in the United States. Foreign banks operate in the United States by owning a subsidiary American bank or by operating branches or agency offices in the United States.

KEY TERMS

automated banking machine (ABM), p. 449
automated teller machine (ATM), p. 449
bank holding companies, p. 446
branches, p. 463
community banks, p. 468
deposit rate ceilings, p. 455
disintermediation, p. 455
dual banking system, p. 445
e-cash, p. 451
economies of scope, p. 466
Edge Act corporation, p. 475
electronic money (e-money), p. 451
financial engineering, p. 447
futures contracts, p. 448
hedge, p. 448
international banking facilities (IBFs), p. 475
national banks, p. 445
originate-to-distribute, p. 454
securitization, p. 453
shadow banking system, p. 446
smart card, p. 451
state banks, p. 445
subprime mortgage, p. 454
superregional banks, p. 466
sweep account, p. 456
virtual bank, p. 449

QUESTIONS

1. Do you think that before the National Bank Act of 1863 the prevailing conditions in the banking industry fostered or hindered trade across states in the United States?
2. Which regulatory agency has the primary responsibility for supervising the following categories of banks?
   a. National banks
   b. Bank holding companies
   c. Non-Federal-Reserve-member state banks
   d. Federal-Reserve-member state banks
3. "The banking industry in Canada is less competitive than the banking industry in the United States because in Canada only a few large banks dominate the industry, while in the United States there are around 6,000 banks." Is this statement true, false, or uncertain? Explain your answer.
4. In light of the recent financial crisis of 2007–2009, do you think that the firewall created by the Glass-Steagall Act of 1933 between commercial banking and the securities industry proved to be a good thing or not?
5. Why has there been such a dramatic increase in bank holding companies?
6. What incentives have regulatory agencies created to encourage international banking? Why have they done this?
7. How could the approval of international banking facilities (IBFs) by the Fed in 1981 have reduced employment in the banking industry in Europe?
8. State the relationship between the process of bank consolidation and the too-big-to-fail policy.
9. If reserve requirements were eliminated in the future, as some economists advocate, what effects would this have on the size of money market mutual funds?
10. Why have banks been losing cost advantages in acquiring funds in recent years?
11. "If inflation had not risen in the 1960s and 1970s, the banking industry might be healthier today." Is this statement true, false, or uncertain? Explain your answer.
12. Given the role of the loan originator in the securitization process of a mortgage loan described in the text, do you think the loan originator will be worried about the ability of a household to meet its monthly mortgage payments?
13. "The invention of the computer is the major factor behind the decline of the banking industry." Is this statement true, false, or uncertain? Explain your answer.
14. How did competitive forces lead to the repeal of the Glass-Steagall Act's separation of the banking and the securities industries?
15. How does the Dodd-Frank Act of 2010 compare to the Glass-Steagall Act of 1933?

WEB EXERCISES

Banking Industry: Structure and Competition

1. Go to **www2.fdic.gov/SDI/SOB**. Select "Historical Statistics on Banking," then "Commercial Bank Reports." Finally, choose "Number of Institutions, Branches and Total Offices." In looking at the trend in bank branches, does the public appear to have more or less access to banking facilities? How many banks were there in 1934, and how many are there now? Does the table indicate that the trend toward consolidation is continuing?
2. Despite the regulations that protect banks from failure, some do fail. Go to **www2.fdic.gov/hsob/**. Select the tab labeled "Bank Failures." How many bank failures occurred in the United States during the most recent complete calendar year? What were the total assets held by the banks that failed? How many banks failed in 1937?

CHAPTER 20

The Mutual Fund Industry

> PREVIEW

Suppose you decide that you want to begin investing for retirement. You would probably want to hold some money in a diversified portfolio of stocks. You might want to put some money in bonds. You might even want to hold stock in some foreign companies. Now suppose your budget will let you invest only $25 per week. How are you going to build this retirement fund? You will probably not want to buy individual stocks, and with only $25 to spend at a time, you will not be able to buy bonds. The solution to your problem is to invest in mutual funds.

Mutual funds pool the resources of many small investors by selling them shares in the fund and using the proceeds to buy securities. Through the asset transformation process of issuing shares in small denominations and buying large blocks of securities, mutual funds can take advantage of volume discounts on brokerage commissions and can purchase diversified portfolios of securities. Mutual funds allow small investors to obtain the benefits of lower transaction costs in purchasing securities and to take advantage of a reduction in risk by diversifying their portfolios.

In this chapter we will study why mutual funds have become so popular in recent years, the types of mutual funds, how mutual funds are regulated, and, finally, how conflicts of interest in the mutual fund industry have led to many scandals, fines, and indictments since 2001.

The Growth of Mutual Funds

Mutual funds have become the investment vehicle of choice for many investors. At the beginning of 2016, 54% of retirement funds were invested in mutual funds. Thirty-one percent of the entire U.S. stock market was held by mutual funds by the beginning of 2016, and 43% of all U.S. households held stock in them. Given the pervasive nature of those intermediaries, we should wonder exactly what service they provide that has caused them to grow from $292 billion in assets to nearly $16 trillion in assets over just the past 25 years.

The First Mutual Funds

GO ONLINE
Access the mutual fund factbook found at **www.icifactbook.org**, which provides extensive statistics on the mutual fund industry.

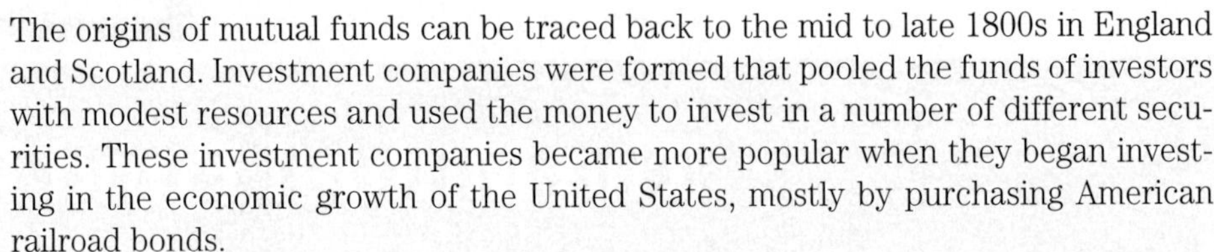

The origins of mutual funds can be traced back to the mid to late 1800s in England and Scotland. Investment companies were formed that pooled the funds of investors with modest resources and used the money to invest in a number of different securities. These investment companies became more popular when they began investing in the economic growth of the United States, mostly by purchasing American railroad bonds.

The first fund in which new shares were issued as new money was invested—the dominant structure seen today—was introduced in Boston in 1824. This fund allowed for continuous offering of shares, the ability to cash out of the fund at any time, and a set of restrictions on investments aimed at protecting investors from losses.

The stock market crash of 1929 set mutual fund growth back for several decades because small investors distrusted stock investments generally and mutual funds in particular. The Investment Company Act of 1940, which required much more disclosure of fees and investment policies, reinvigorated the industry, and mutual funds began a steady growth.

Benefits of Mutual Funds

There are five principal benefits that attract investors to mutual funds:

1. Liquidity intermediation
2. Denomination intermediation
3. Diversification
4. Cost advantages
5. Managerial expertise

Liquidity intermediation means that investors can convert their investments into cash quickly and at a low cost. If you buy a CD or a bond, there can be early redemption penalties or transaction fees imposed if you need your funds before the securities mature. Additionally, if you bought a $10,000 CD, you must redeem the whole security even if you require only $5,000 to meet your current needs. Mutual funds allow investors to buy and redeem at any time and in any amount. Some funds are designed especially to meet short-term transaction requirements and have no fees associated with redemption, whereas others are designed for longer-term investment and may have redemption fees if they are held only a short time.

Denomination intermediation allows small investors access to securities they would be unable to purchase without the mutual fund. For example, in Chapter 11 we learned that most money market securities are available only in large denominations, often in excess of $100,000. By pooling money, the mutual fund can purchase these securities on behalf of investors.

Diversification is an important advantage to investing in mutual funds. As we learned in Chapter 4, your risk can be lowered by holding a portfolio of diversified securities. Small investors buying stocks individually may find it difficult to acquire enough securities in enough different industries to capture this benefit. Additionally, mutual funds provide a low-cost way to diversify into foreign stocks. It can be difficult and expensive to invest in a foreign security not listed on U.S. exchanges.

Significant *cost advantages* may accrue to mutual fund investors. Institutional investors negotiate much lower transaction fees than are available to individual investors. Additionally, large block trades of 100,000 shares or more trade according to a different fee structure than do smaller trades. By buying securities through a mutual fund, investors can share in these lower fees.

One of the main features that has driven mutual fund growth has been access to *managerial expertise*. Despite the fact that research discussed in Chapter 6 has consistently demonstrated that mutual funds do not outperform a random pick from the market, many investors prefer to rely on professional money managers to select their stocks. The failure of mutual funds to post greater-than-average returns should not come as a surprise given our discussion of market efficiency. Still, the financial markets remain something of a mystery to a large number of investors. These investors are willing to pay fees to let someone else choose their stocks.

The increase in the number of defined-contribution pension plans has also been a factor in mutual fund growth. In the past, most pension plans either invested on behalf of the employee and guaranteed a return or required employees to invest in company stock. Now, most new pension plans require the employee to invest his or her own pension dollars. With pension investments being made every payday, the mutual fund provides the perfect pension conduit. Currently, about 57% of all retirement dollars are invested in mutual funds. This amount is likely to grow as more pension plans convert from the defined-benefit to the defined-contribution structure.

Table 20.1 shows the total net assets and number of mutual funds since 1970. There are currently about 7,500 separate mutual funds for investors to choose from. This means there are more separate mutual funds than there are stocks trading on the New York and NASDAQ stock exchanges combined.

In a little over 40 years the amount invested in mutual funds has increased from $47 billion to over $15 trillion. To put this figure in perspective, this is about the same as the amount deposited in all commercial banks in the United States.

Ownership of Mutual Funds

An estimated 53 million, or 44%, of households own mutual funds. By the beginning of 2015, 89% of mutual fund shares were owned by households, with the rest held by fiduciaries and other business organizations. This represents a tremendous increase since 1980, when only 5.7% of households held mutual fund shares (see Figure 20.1). The median mutual fund investor is middle class, 51 years old, married, employed, and possesses financial assets of $190,000. About 48% are college graduates. The median household income is $87,500, and fully 93% cite preparing for retirement as one of their main reasons for holding shares.

TABLE 20.1 Total Industry Net Assets and Number of Mutual Funds

Year	Net Assets ($ millions)	Number of Funds
1970	47,618	361
1971	55,045	392
1972	59,830	410
1973	46,518	421
1974	35,776	431
1975	45,874	426
1976	51,276	452
1977	48,936	477
1978	55,837	505
1979	94,511	526
1980	134,760	564
1981	241,365	665
1982	296,678	857
1983	292,985	1,026
1984	370,680	1,243
1985	495,385	1,528
1986	715,667	1,835
1987	769,171	2,312
1988	809,370	2,737
1989	980,671	2,935
1990	1,065,194	3,079
1991	1,393,189	3,403
1992	1,642,543	3,824
1993	2,069,960	4,534
1994	2,155,320	5,325
1995	2,811,290	5,725
1996	3,525,800	6,248
1997	4,468,200	6,684
1998	5,525,209	7,314
1999	6,846,339	7,791
2000	6,964,630	8,155
2001	6,974,910	8,305
2002	6,383,480	8,243
2003	7,402,420	8,125
2004	8,095,080	8,040
2005	8,891,110	7,974
2006	10,396,510	8,117
2007	12,000,640	8,026

TABLE 20.1 Total Industry Net Assets and Number of Mutual Funds (*continued*)

Year	Net Assets ($ millions)	Number of Funds
2008	9,602,600	8,022
2009	11,120,730	7,691
2010	11,831,880	8,022
2011	11,627,360	7,588
2012	13,045,220	7,590
2013	15,050,820	7,715
2014	15,875,270	7,928
2015	15,651,960	8,116

Source: https://www.ici.org/pdf/2016_factbook.pdf

Mutual funds accounted for $7.1 trillion, or 30%, of the U.S. retirement market at the beginning of 2016. This represents 40% of all mutual fund assets.

Deposits into retirement mutual funds come from two sources: employer-sponsored defined-contribution plans, especially 401(k) plans, and individual retirement accounts (IRAs). Figure 20.2 shows the average asset allocation of all 401(k) mutual fund accounts. The bulk of retirement assets are in equity funds, followed by guaranteed investment contracts, bond funds, and company stock.

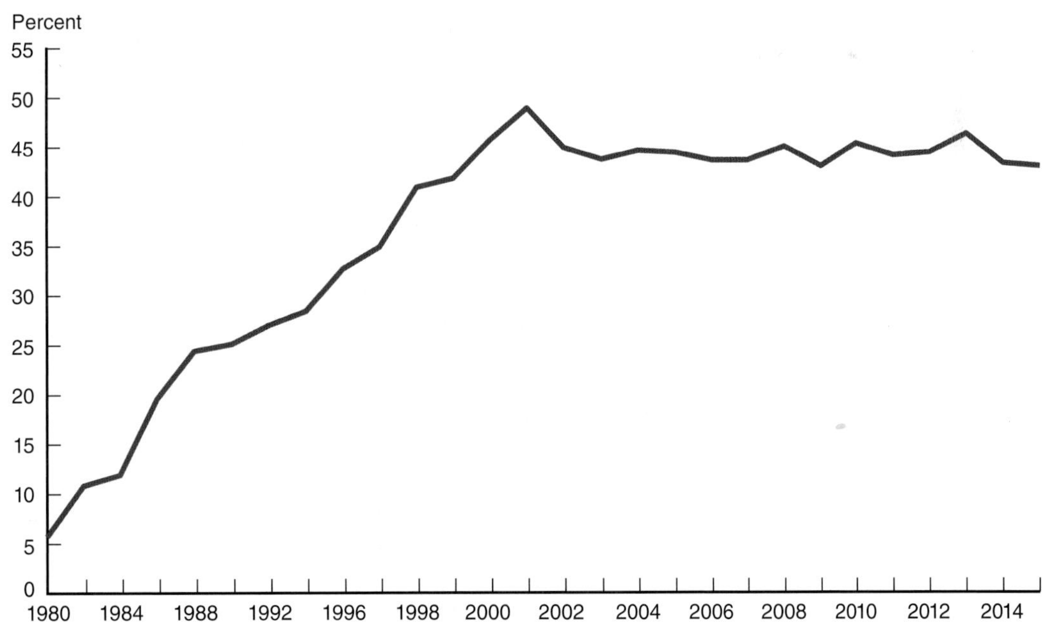

FIGURE 20.1 Household Ownership of Mutual Funds

Data Source: Investment Company Institute, *2016 Investment Company Fact Book* (Washington, DC: ICI), https://www.ici.org/pdf/2016_factbook.pdf.

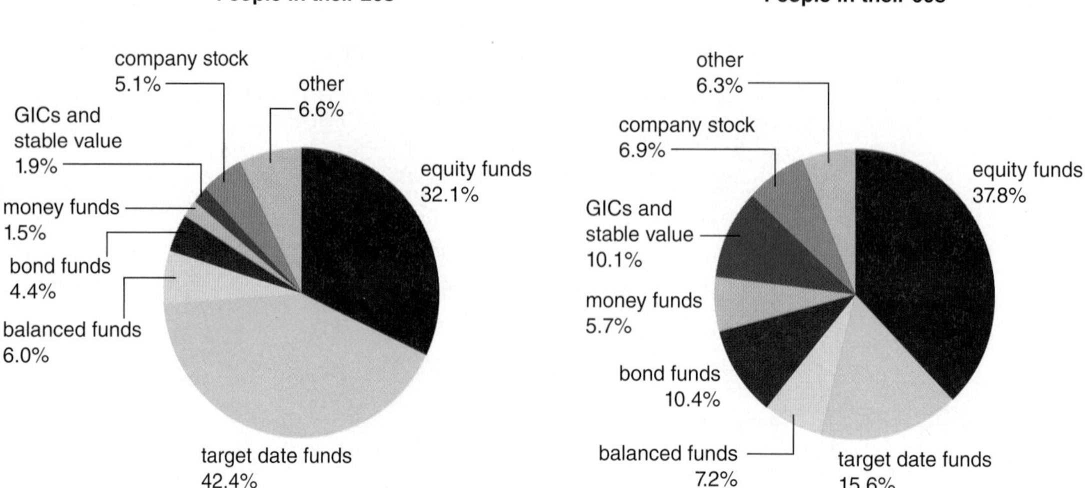

FIGURE 20.2 Average Asset Allocation for All 401(k) Plan Balances

Source: Investment Company Institute, *2016 Investment Company Fact Book*, (Washington, DC: ICI), https://www.ici.org/pdf/2016_factbook.pdf. Reprinted with permission.

Mutual Fund Structure

Mutual fund companies frequently offer a number of separate mutual funds. They are called *complexes* and are defined as a group of funds under substantially common management, composed of one or more families of funds. The advantage to investors of fund complexes is that investments can usually be transferred among different funds within a family very easily and quickly. Additionally, account information can be summarized by the complex to help investors keep their assets organized.

In this section we will look at how mutual funds are structured and at the types of investments the funds hold.

Open- Versus Closed-End Funds

Mutual funds are structured in two ways. The first funds were what are now called **closed-end funds**. In a closed-end fund, a fixed number of nonredeemable shares are sold at an initial offering and are then traded in the over-the-counter market like common stock. The market price of these shares fluctuates with the value of the assets held by the funds. The market value of the shares may be above or below the value of the assets held by the fund, depending on the market's assessment of how likely managers are to pick stocks that will increase fund value.

The problem with closed-end funds is that once shares have been sold, the fund cannot take in any more investment dollars. Thus, to grow the fund managers must start a whole new fund. The advantage of closed-end funds to managers is that investors cannot make withdrawals. The only way investors have of getting money out of their investment in the fund is to sell shares.

Today, the closed-end fund has been largely replaced with the **open-end fund**. Investors can contribute to an open-end fund at any time. The fund simply increases the number of shares outstanding. Another feature of open-end funds is that the fund agrees to buy back shares from investors at any time. Each day the fund's net asset value is computed based on the number of shares outstanding and the net assets of the fund. All shares bought and sold that day are traded at the same net asset value. See the Case for a complete discussion of computing the net asset value.

Open-end mutual funds have a couple of advantages that have contributed to the growth of mutual funds. First, because the fund agrees to redeem shares at any time, the investment is very liquid. As discussed earlier, this liquidity intermediation has great value to investors. Second, the open-end structure allows mutual funds to grow unchecked. As long as investors want to put money into the fund, it can expand to accommodate them. For example, the Vanguard S&P 500 index fund has holdings of about $140 billion. These advantages explain why 98% of all mutual fund dollars are invested in open-end funds.

CASE

Calculating a Mutual Fund's Net Asset Value

If you invest in a mutual fund, you will receive periodic statements summarizing the activity in your account. The statement will show funds that were added to your investment balance, funds that were withdrawn, and any earnings that have accrued. One term on the statement that is critical to understanding the investment's performance is the **net asset value (NAV)**. The net asset value is the total value of the mutual fund's stocks, bonds, cash, and other assets minus any liabilities such as accrued fees, divided by the number of shares outstanding. An example will make this clear. Suppose that a mutual fund has the following assets and liabilities:

Stock (at current market value)	$20,000,000
Bonds (at current market value)	$10,000,000
Cash	$ 500,000
Total value of assets	$30,500,000
Liabilities	−$ 300,000
Net worth	$30,200,000

The net asset value is computed by dividing the net worth by the number of shares outstanding. If 10 million shares are outstanding, the net asset value is $3.02 ($30,200,000/10,000,000 = $3.02).

The net asset value rises and falls as the value of the underlying assets changes. For example, suppose that the value of the stock portfolio held by the mutual fund rises by 10% and the value of the bond portfolio falls by 2% over the course of a year. If the cash and liabilities and the number of shares outstanding are unchanged, the new net asset value will be

Stock (at current market value)	$22,000,000
Bonds (at current market value)	$ 9,800,000
Cash	$ 500,000
Total value of assets	$32,300,000
Liabilities	−$ 300,000
Net worth	$32,000,000

$$\text{NAV} = \frac{\$32{,}000{,}000}{10{,}000{,}000} = \$3.20$$

The yield on your investment in the mutual fund is then

$$\text{Yield} = \frac{\$3.20 - \$3.02}{\$3.02} = \frac{\$0.18}{\$3.02} = 5.96\%$$

When you buy and sell shares in the mutual fund, you do so at the current NAV.

Organizational Structure

Regardless of whether a fund is organized as a closed- or an open-end fund, it will have the same basic organizational structure. The investors in the fund are the shareholders. In the same way that shareholders of corporations receive the residual income of a company, the shareholders of a mutual fund receive the earnings, after expenses, of the mutual fund.

The board of directors oversees the fund's activities and sets policy. They are also responsible for appointing the investment adviser, usually a separate company, to manage the portfolio of investments and a principal underwriter, who sells the fund shares. SEC regulation requires that a majority of the directors be independent of the mutual fund.

The investment advisers manage the fund in accordance with the fund's stated objectives and policies. The investment advisers actually pick the securities that will be held by the fund and make both buy and sell decisions. It is their expertise that determines the success of the fund.

In addition to the investment advisers, the fund will contract with other firms to provide additional services. These will include underwriters, transfer agents, and custodians. Contracts will also be arranged with an independent public accountant. Large funds may arrange for some of these functions to be done in-house, whereas other funds will use all outside companies. Figure 20.3 shows the organizational structure of a mutual fund.

Investment Objective Classes

Four primary classes of mutual funds are available to investors. They are (1) stock funds (also called equity funds), (2) bond funds, (3) hybrid funds, and (4) money market funds. Figure 20.4 shows the distribution of assets among these types of funds. The largest class is the equity funds, followed by the bond funds, then the money market funds.

Equity Funds

Equity funds share a common theme in that they all invest in stock. After that, they can have very different objectives. The three classes reported by the Investment Company Institute are capital appreciation funds, world funds, and total return funds. Capital appreciation funds are the largest, with about 44% of all equity mutual fund assets. These funds seek rapid capital appreciation (increases in share prices)

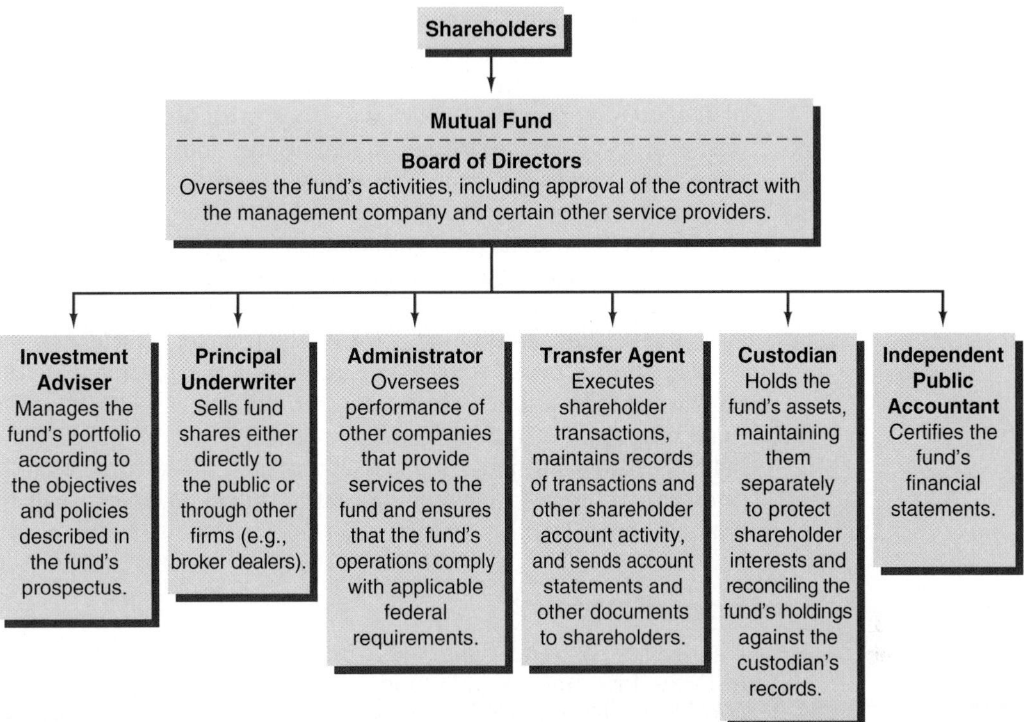

FIGURE 20.3 The Organizational Structure of a Mutual Fund

Source: Investment Company Institute, *2016 Investment Company Fact Book* (Washington, DC: ICI), https://www.ici.org/pdf/2016_factbook.pdf.

and are not concerned with dividends. Many of these funds are relatively risky in that the fund managers are attempting to select companies incurring rapid growth. For example, many capital appreciation mutual funds invested heavily in high technology and Internet stocks during the 1990s.

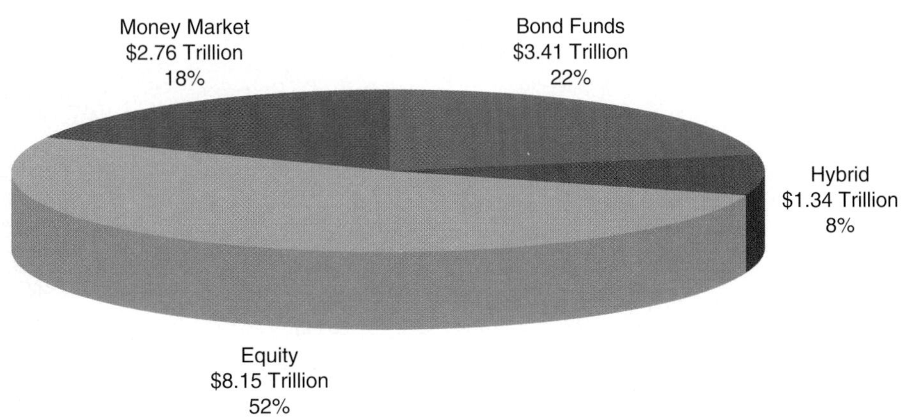

FIGURE 20.4 Distribution of Assets Among Types of Mutual Funds

Source: Investment Company Institute, *2016 Investment Company Fact Book* (Washington, DC: ICI), https://www.ici.org/pdf/2016_factbook.pdf.

Total return funds represent about 29% of equity mutual fund assets. The goal of these funds is to seek a combination of current income and capital appreciation. They will include both mature firms that are paying dividends and growth companies that are expected to post large stock price increases. Total return funds are expected to be less risky than capital appreciation funds, since they will include more large established firms. This was borne out in 2000 when capital appreciation funds lost 16.5% of their assets and total return funds lost only 5.7%.

World equity funds invest primarily in stocks of foreign companies. These funds allow investors easy access to international diversification. Many financial planners recommend that investors hold at least a small portion of their investments in foreign stocks. These world funds provide the primary vehicle.

The three types of equity funds presented here oversimplify the range of stock mutual funds available to investors. For example, the Vanguard family of mutual funds offers over 60 different stock funds. Each one differs in its stated goals. Some hold stock from specific industries; others hold stock with certain historical growth rates. Others are chosen by their PE ratio. Mutual fund companies try to offer a fund that will appeal to every investor's needs.

Bond Funds

Figure 20.5 shows the major types of bond funds tracked by the Investment Company Institute. Investment Grade funds invest in high-quality, relatively low-risk securities. These will typically be high-grade bonds offered by large corporations. The quality of these investments will be high, but the returns may be lower. Investors are trading safety for greater returns.

Government bonds are also popular. These are essentially default risk-free but have relatively low returns. The state and municipal (muni) bonds are tax-free.

Bonds are not as risky as stocks, and so it is not usually as important that investors diversify across a large number of different bonds. Additionally, it is relatively

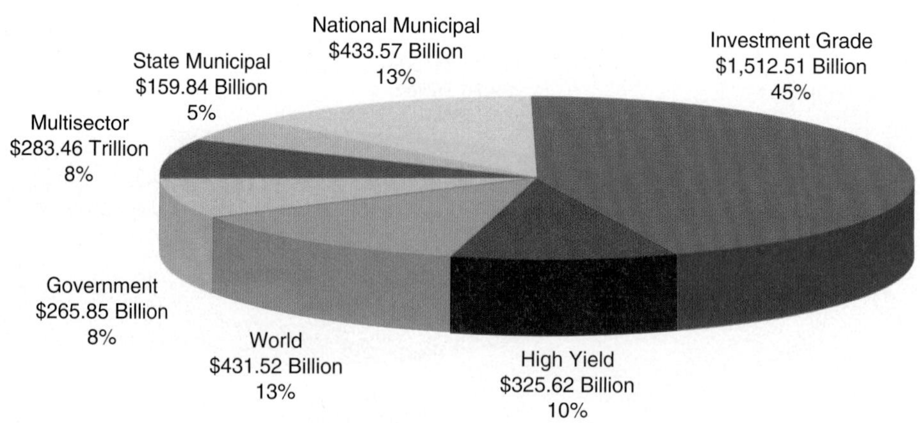

FIGURE 20.5 Assets Invested in Different Types of Bond Mutual Funds

Source: Investment Company Institute, *2016 Investment Company Fact Book* (Washington, DC: ICI), http://www.icifactbook.org/pdf/13_fb_table04.pdf. Data tables, table 4.

easy to buy and sell bonds through the secondary market. As a result, it is not surprising that bond mutual funds hold less than half of the assets held by stock mutual funds. Still, many investors value the liquidity intervention and automatic reinvestment features provided by bond mutual funds.

Hybrid Funds

Hybrid funds combine stocks and bonds into one fund. The idea is to provide an investment that diversifies across different types of securities as well as across different issuers of a particular type of security. Thus, if an investor found a hybrid fund that held the percentage of stocks and bonds he wanted, he could own just one fund instead of several. Despite this apparent convenience, most investors still prefer to choose separate funds. Only about 7% of all mutual fund accounts are hybrid accounts.

Money Market Funds

Access the most recent statistics on the net assets of money market mutual funds at **www.ici.org**.

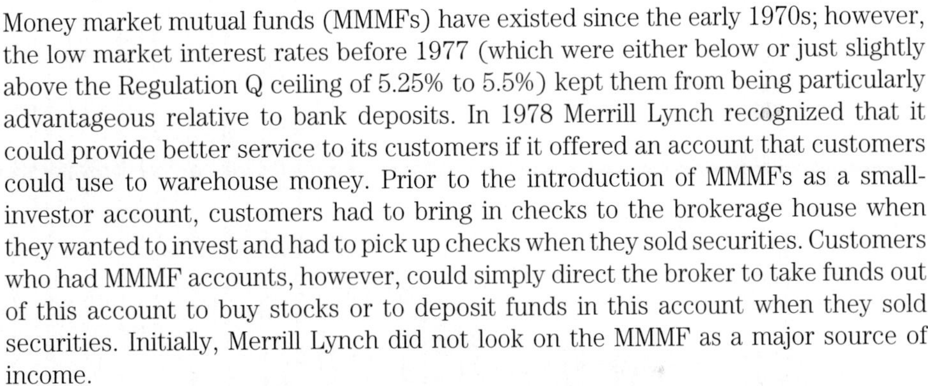

Money market mutual funds (MMMFs) have existed since the early 1970s; however, the low market interest rates before 1977 (which were either below or just slightly above the Regulation Q ceiling of 5.25% to 5.5%) kept them from being particularly advantageous relative to bank deposits. In 1978 Merrill Lynch recognized that it could provide better service to its customers if it offered an account that customers could use to warehouse money. Prior to the introduction of MMMFs as a small-investor account, customers had to bring in checks to the brokerage house when they wanted to invest and had to pick up checks when they sold securities. Customers who had MMMF accounts, however, could simply direct the broker to take funds out of this account to buy stocks or to deposit funds in this account when they sold securities. Initially, Merrill Lynch did not look on the MMMF as a major source of income.

In the early 1980s inflation and interest rates skyrocketed. Regulation Q restricted banks from paying more than 5.25% in interest on savings accounts. With interest rates in the money markets exceeding 15%, investors flocked to MMMFs. Figure 20.6 shows the growth of MMMFs since 1975. Note that with low interest rates on money market securities in the past several years, deposits have dropped significantly.

All MMMFs are open-end investment funds that invest only in money market securities. Most funds do not charge investors any fee for purchasing or redeeming shares. The funds usually have a minimum initial investment of $500 to $2,000. The funds' yields depend entirely on the performance of the securities purchased.

An important feature of MMMFs is that many have check-writing privileges. They often do not charge a fee for writing checks or have any minimum check amount as long as the balance in the account is above the stated level. This convenience, along with market interest rates, makes the accounts very popular with small investors.

Investors often take their money out of federally insured banks and thrifts and put it into uninsured MMMFs. An important question is why they are so willing to take this extra level of risk. The reason is that the extra risk has historically been really very small. The money invested in MMMFs is in turn invested in money market instruments. Treasury bills, U.S. agency issues, and repurchase agreements

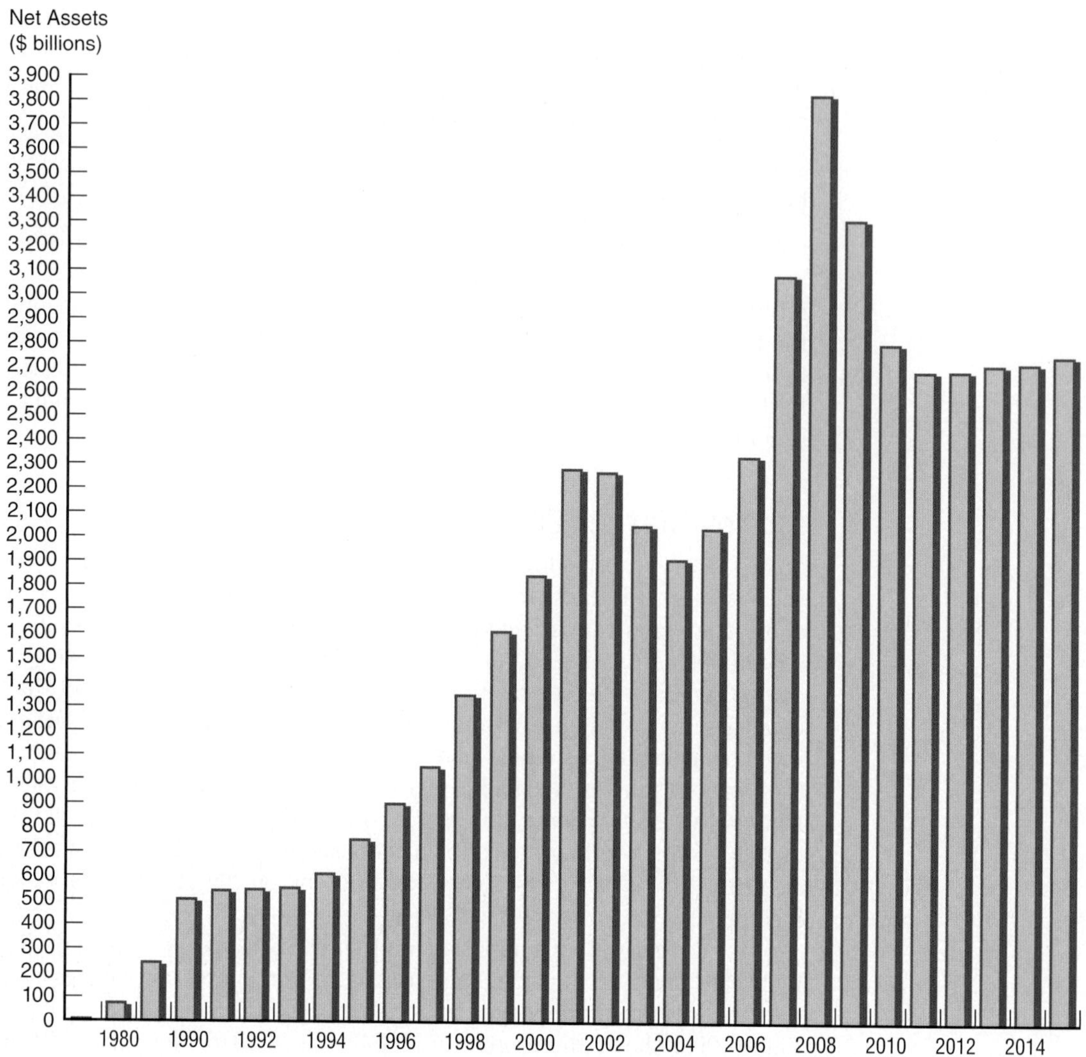

FIGURE 20.6 Net Assets of Money Market Mutual Funds

Source: Investment Company Institute, *2016 Investment Company Fact Book* (Washington, DC: ICI), https://www.ici.org/pdf/2016_factbook.pdf.

make up the bulk of these funds. Figure 20.7 shows the distribution of money market fund assets. Because the risk of default on these securities was thought to be very low, the risk of MMMFs was considered very low. Investors recognized this and so were willing to abandon the safety of banks for higher returns.

This confidence was shaken during the credit crisis when there was a short period during which mutual funds were unable to redeem their holdings of commercial paper. Even though commercial paper is short-term and issued by typically strong companies, the near panic situation in the markets caused the market for these securities to evaporate. The day after Lehman Brothers Holdings, Inc., declared bankruptcy on September 15, 2008, the Reserve Primary Fund "broke the

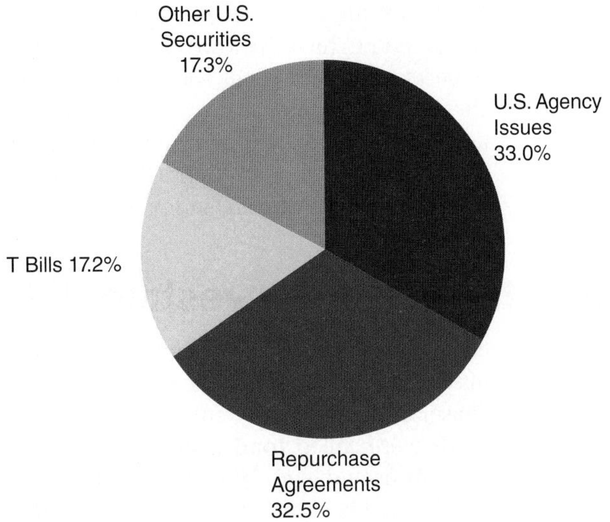

FIGURE 20.7 Average Distribution of Money Market Fund Assets, 2016

Source: Investment Company Institute, *2016 Investment Company Fact Book* (Washington, DC: ICI), https://www.ici.org/pdf/2016_factbook.pdf. Table 40, page 211.

buck" by failing to redeem money market accounts at the $1.00 NAV. This initiated a run around the world on money market funds, with rapid withdrawals threatening the liquidity of hundreds of other funds. Two days later the Treasury announced a Temporary Guarantee Program for money market funds, and the Fed agreed to finance the purchase of asset-backed commercial paper from money market funds. The effect of these actions restored confidence. and by October 2008, investors had added $149 billion in new cash. This trend continued such that by January 2009, total assets in MMMFs were nearly $2.7 trillion.

Index Funds

A special kind of mutual fund that does not fit any of the classes discussed previously, yet represents an alternative investment style, is the index fund. Traditional funds employ investment managers who select stocks and bonds for the fund's portfolio. If we believe in the concept of market efficiency discussed in Chapter 6, we would conclude that investment managers are not likely to pick stocks any better than could a dart thrown at the stock pages of the *Wall Street Journal*. If investment managers are not superior stock pickers, then we might ask why one should pay them a fee to provide a service that may not have any marginal benefit.

Many investors want the benefits of mutual fund investing without the cost of paying for investment manager services. The answer is the index fund. An index fund contains the stocks in an index. For example, the mammoth Vanguard S&P 500 index fund contains the 500 stocks in that index. The stocks are held in a proportion such that changes to the fund value closely match changes to the index level. There are many other index funds available that mimic the behavior of various stock and bond indexes.

Index funds do not require managers to choose securities. As a result, these funds tend to have far lower fees than other actively managed funds. Some financial experts even argue that these funds will outperform most fund managers because they will ignore the fads, trends, emotions, and hysteria that often cloud investment adviser and individual investor judgment. In an interesting admission, the recently retired founder and former CEO of the Vanguard Group of mutual funds, John Bogle, stated he was an "index investor."[1]

Fee Structure of Investment Funds

Originally, most shares of mutual funds were sold by brokers who received a commission for their efforts. Because this commission was paid at the time of the purchase and immediately subtracted from the redemption value of the shares, these funds were called **load funds**. If the fee is charged when the funds are deposited, it is a front-end load. Most front-end loads are between 1% and 2%, but some exceed 6%. If a fee is charged when funds are taken out (usually a declining fee over five years), it is a **deferred load**. The primary purpose of loads is to provide compensation for sales brokers. An additional motivation, especially for deferred-load funds, is to discourage early withdrawal of deposits.

Beginning in the 1980s, funds that did not charge a direct load (or fee) appeared. These are called **no-load funds**. Most no-load funds can be purchased directly by individual investors, and no intermediary is required. Currently about 55% of equity funds and 65% of bond funds are no load. Many investors have realized that when the initial deposit is immediately reduced, it can take a long time to catch up to the returns offered by no-load funds. The shares of front-end-loaded funds are termed Class A shares. Shares in deferred-load funds are termed Class B shares. Class C shares are issued for no-load funds.

Regardless of whether a load is charged, all mutual fund accounts are subject to a variety of fees. One of the primary factors that an investor should consider before choosing a mutual fund is the level of fees the fund charges. The fees are taken out of portfolio income before it is passed on to the investor. Since the investor is not directly charged the fees, many will not realize that they have even been subtracted. The usual fees charged by mutual funds are the following:

- A *contingent deferred sales charge* imposed at the time of redemption is an alternative way to compensate financial professionals for their services. This fee typically applies for the first few years of ownership and then disappears.
- A *redemption fee* is a back-end charge for redeeming shares. It is expressed as a dollar amount or a percentage of the redemption price.
- An *exchange fee* may be charged when transferring money from one fund to another within the same fund family.
- An *account maintenance fee* is charged by some funds to maintain low balance accounts.
- *12b-1 fees*, if any, are deducted from the fund's assets to pay marketing and advertising expenses or, more commonly, to compensate sales professionals. By law, 12b-1 fees cannot exceed 1% of the fund's average net assets per year.

---

[1]Keynote speech by John Bogle, founder and former CEO of the Vanguard Group, before the American Business Editors and Writers Personal Finance Workshop, Denver, Colorado, October 27, 2003.

Clearly, there are many opportunities for mutual fund managers to charge investors for the right to invest. Investors should very carefully evaluate a mutual fund's fee structure before investing, since these fees can range from 0.25% to as much as 8% per year. No research supports the argument that investors get better returns by investing in funds that charge higher fees. On the contrary, most high-fee mutual funds fail to do as well, after expenses, as low-fee funds.

Over the past 20 years, competition within the mutual fund industry has produced substantially lower costs. Between 1990 and 2012, the average total shareholder cost of equity mutual funds decreased by more than 20%. The cost of bond funds dropped by 31%. One factor undoubtedly contributing to this reduction is the requirement by the SEC that mutual funds clearly disclose all fees and costs that investors will incur. The SEC further requires mutual funds to include in their prospectus a standardized sample account where $10,000 is invested for one, three, five, and ten years. The analysis shows investors exactly what fees they will be subject to if they choose the fund. The fee disclosure requirement makes it very easy for investors to compare funds, and therefore increases competition among them.

Regulation of Mutual Funds

Mutual funds are regulated under four federal laws designed to protect investors. The Securities Act of 1933 mandates that funds make certain disclosures. The Securities Exchange Act of 1934 set out antifraud rules covering the purchase and sale of fund shares. The Investment Company Act of 1940 requires all funds to register with the SEC and to meet certain operating standards. Finally, the Investment Advisers Act of 1940 regulates fund advisers.

As part of this government regulation, all funds must provide two types of documents free of charge: a prospectus and a shareholder report. A mutual fund's prospectus describes the fund's goals, fees and expenses, and investment strategies and risks; it also gives information on how to buy and sell shares. The SEC requires a fund to provide a full prospectus either before an investment or together with the confirmation statement of an initial investment.

Annual and semiannual shareholder reports discuss the fund's recent performance and include other important information, such as the fund's financial statements. By examining these reports, an investor can learn if a fund has been effective in meeting the goals and investment strategies described in the fund's prospectus.

In addition, investors are sent a yearly statement detailing the federal tax status of distributions received from the fund. Mutual fund shareholders are taxed on the fund's income directly, as if the shareholders held the underlying securities themselves. Similarly, any tax-exempt income received by a fund is generally passed on to the shareholders as tax exempt.

Investment funds are run by brokerage houses and by institutional investors, who now control over 50% of the outstanding stock in the United States. Over 70% of the total daily volume in stocks is due to institutions initiating trades. Many of the mutual funds are run by brokerage houses; others are run by independent investment advisers. Because of the volume of stock controlled by these investors, there is tremendous competition for their business. This has led to significant cost cutting and to the proliferation of alternative methods of trading. For example, computerized trading that eliminates the broker from the transaction accounts for a growing percentage of the activity in stocks.

Mutual funds are the only companies in America that are required by law to have independent directors. The SEC believes that independent directors play a critical role in the governance of mutual funds. In January 2001, the SEC adopted substantive rule amendments designed to enhance the independence of investment company directors and provide investors with more information to assess directors' independence. These rules require that:

- Independent directors constitute at least a majority of the fund's board of directors.
- Independent directors select and nominate other independent directors.
- Any legal counsel for the fund's independent directors be an independent legal counsel.

In addition, SEC rules require that mutual funds publish extensive information about directors, including their business experience and fund shares held. This system of overseeing the interests of mutual fund shareholders has helped the industry avoid systemic problems and contributed significantly to public confidence in mutual funds.

Hedge Funds

Hedge funds are a special type of mutual fund that have received considerable attention at least partly due to the near collapse of Long Term Capital Management in 1998. In Chapter 24 we discuss how financial markets can use hedges to reduce risk in a wide variety of situations. These risk-reducing strategies should not be confused with hedge funds. Although hedge funds often attempt to be market-neutral, meaning protected from changes in the overall market, they are not riskless.

To illustrate a typical type of transaction conducted by hedge funds, consider a trade made by Long Term Capital Management in 1994. The fund managers noted that $29\frac{1}{2}$-year U.S. Treasury bonds seemed cheap relative to 30-year Treasury securities. The managers figured that the value of the two bonds would converge over time. After all, these securities have nearly identical risk, since the maturity risk difference between $29\frac{1}{2}$-year securities and 30-year securities is insignificant. To make money from the temporary divergence of the bond prices, the fund bought $2 billion of the $29\frac{1}{2}$-year bonds and sold short $2 billion of the 30-year bonds. (Selling short means that the fund borrowed bonds it did not own and sold them. Later the fund must cover its short position by buying the bonds back, hopefully at a lower price.) The net investment by Long Term Capital was $12 million. Six months later, the fund covered its short position by buying 30-year bonds and sold its $29\frac{1}{2}$-year bonds. This transaction yielded a $25 million profit.[2]

In the transaction, the managers did not care whether the overall bond market rose or fell. In this sense, the transaction was market-neutral. All that was required for a profit was that the prices of the bonds converge, an event that occurred as predicted. Hedge fund managers scour the world in their search for pricing anomalies between related securities. Figure 20.8 shows a situation where hedge funds could invest. Securities A and B move in lockstep over time. At some point they diverge, creating an opportunity. The hedge fund would buy security B, because it

[2]*Wall Street Journal*, November 16, 1998, p. A18.

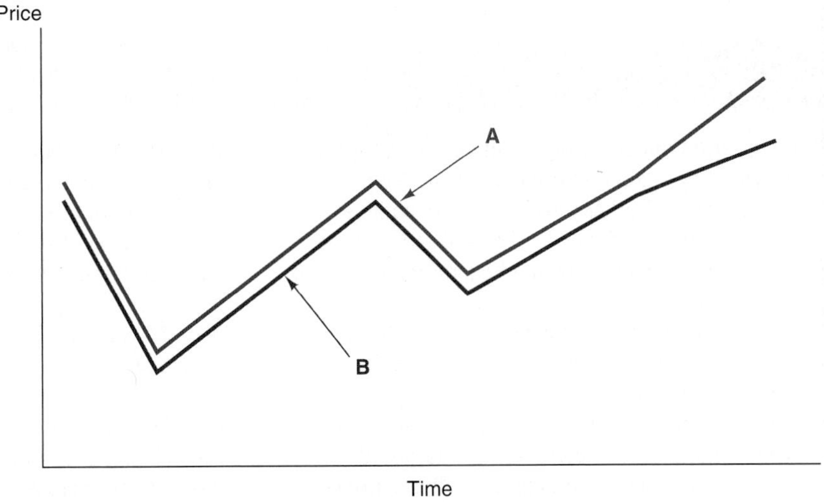

FIGURE 20.8 The Price of Two Similar Securities

Hedge funds search for related securities that historically move in lockstep but have temporarily diverted. In this example, the hedge fund would sell security A short and buy security B.

is expected to increase relative to A, and would sell A short. The fund managers hope that the gain on security B will be greater than the loss on security A. At times, the search for opportunities leads hedge funds to adopt exotic approaches that are not easily available elsewhere, from investing in distressed securities to participating in venture-capital financing.

In addition to investing money contributed by individuals and institutions, hedge funds often set up lines of credit to use in leveraging their investments. For instance, in our example, Long Term Capital earned \$25 million on an investment of \$12 million, a 108% return [(\$25 million − \$12 million)/\$12 million = 1.08 = 108%]. Suppose that half of the \$12 million had been borrowed funds. Ignoring interest cost, the return on invested equity would then be 317% [(\$25 million − \$6 million)/\$6 million = 3.17 = 317%]. Long Term Capital advertised that it was leveraged 20 to 1; however, by the time of the crisis, the figure was actually closer to 50 to 1. The Mini-Case box discusses how Long Term Capital eventually required a private rescue plan to prevent its failure.

Hedge funds accumulate money from many people and invest on their behalf, but several features distinguish them from traditional mutual funds. First, hedge funds have a minimum investment requirement of between \$100,000 and \$20 million, with the typical minimum investment being \$1 million. Long Term Capital Management required a \$10 million minimum investment. Most hedge funds are set up as limited partnerships. Federal law limits hedge funds to no more than 99 limited partners with steady annual incomes of \$200,000 or more or a net worth of \$1 million, excluding their homes. Funds may have up to 499 limited partners if each has \$5 million in invested assets. All of these restrictions are aimed at allowing hedge funds to exist largely unregulated, on the theory that the rich can look out for themselves. Many of the 4,000 funds are domiciled offshore to escape all regulatory restrictions.

MINI-CASE

The Long Term Capital Debacle

Long Term Capital Management was a hedge fund managed by a group that included two Nobel Prize winners and 25 other PhDs. It made headlines in September 1998 because it required a private rescue plan organized by the Federal Reserve Bank of New York.

The experience of Long Term Capital Management demonstrates that hedge funds are not risk-free, despite their being market-neutral. Long Term Capital expected that the spread between long-term Treasury bonds and long-term corporate bonds would narrow. Shortly after Long Term Capital made their investment, many stock markets around the world plunged, causing a flight to quality. Investors bid up the price of Treasury securities while the price of corporate securities fell. This is exactly the opposite of what Long Term Capital Management had predicted. As losses mounted, Long Term Capital's lenders required that the fund increase its equity position.

By mid-September, the fund was unable to raise sufficient equity to meet the demands of its creditors. Faced with the potential collapse of the fund, together with its highly leveraged investment portfolio consisting of nearly $80 billion in equities and over $1 trillion of notional value in derivatives, the Federal Reserve stepped in to prevent the fund from failing. The Fed's rationale was that a sudden liquidation of the Long Term Capital Management portfolio would create unacceptable systemic risk. Tens of billions of dollars' worth of illiquid securities would be dumped on an already jittery market, causing potentially huge losses to numerous lenders and other institutions. A group consisting of banks and brokerage firms contributed $3.6 billion to a rescue plan that prevented the fund's failure.

The Fed's involvement in organizing the rescue of Long Term Capital is controversial, despite no public funds being expended. Some critics argue that the intervention increases moral hazard by weakening the discipline imposed by the market on fund managers. However, others say that the tremendous economic damage the fund's failure would have caused was unacceptable.

Hedge funds have continued to fail in the years since the Long Term Capital bailout. In September 2006, Amaranth Advisors lost its bet on natural gas futures and dropped $6 billion in one week. This is currently the largest hedge fund collapse in history. Other funds have suffered significant losses for their investors, including Advanced Investment Management (lost $415 million), Bayou Management, LLC (lost $450 million), and Lipper Convertibles (lost $315 million). Hedge funds are a high-risk game for well-heeled investors.

Second, hedge funds are unique in that they usually require investors to commit their money for long periods of time, often several years. The purpose of this requirement is to give managers breathing room to attempt long-range strategies.

Hedge funds often charge large fees to investors. The typical fund charges a 1% annual asset management fee plus 20% of profits. Some charge significantly more. For example, Long Term Capital Management charged investors a 2% management fee and took 25% of profits.

Despite the argument that the wealthy do not need regulatory protection from the risk incurred by hedge fund investments, the SEC passed regulation in 2006 requiring that hedge fund advisers register. The SEC cited two concerns prompting the new move. First, they were concerned about the growing incidence of fraudulent conduct by hedge fund advisers. Second, they expressed concern that more investors were participating in hedge funds through "retailization," and that this justified increased oversight. By requiring advisers to register, the SEC can conduct on-site examinations. The SEC argues these examinations are necessary to protect the nation's securities market as well as hedge fund investors.

Conflicts of Interest in the Mutual Fund Industry

In Chapter 7 we discussed conflicts of interest in the financial industry. We concluded that many of the corporate governance breakdowns observed recently were due to the principal–agent relationship. This section extends that discussion to mutual funds, which have been subject to scandals, fines, and indictments. Several top mutual funds managers and CEOs have even been sentenced to jail time.

Investor confidence in the stability and integrity of the mutual fund industry is critical. A large portion of the population is now responsible for planning their own retirement, and most of these investments are being funneled into various funds. If these funds take advantage of investors or fail to provide the returns they should, people will find themselves unable to retire or having to scale back their retirement plans. No one argues that mutual funds can or should guarantee any specific return. They should, however, treat all investors equally and accurately disclose risk and fees. They must also follow the policies and rules they publish as governing the management of each fund.

Sources of Conflicts of Interest

Conflicts of interest arise when there is asymmetric information and the principal's and agent's interests are not closely aligned. The governance structure of mutual funds creates such a situation. Investors in a mutual fund are the shareholders. They elect directors, who are supposed to look out for their interest. The directors in turn select investment advisers, who actually run the mutual fund. However, given the large number of shareholders in the typical fund, there is a free-rider problem that prevents them from monitoring either the directors or the investment advisers.

Shareholders depend on directors to monitor investment advisers. Unfortunately, recent evidence demonstrates that directors' efforts have not been sufficient to prevent abuses. The incentive structure for compensating investment advisers does not ensure that they will be motivated to maximize shareholder wealth. In the absence of monitoring, investment advisers will attempt to increase their own fees and income, even at the expense of shareholders. For example, suppose an institutional investor offers to make a large deposit into the fund in exchange for special trading privileges not afforded other investors. Since investment advisers are compensated as a percentage of the funds under management, they may choose to provide the special treatment because it increases their income. The recent negative publicity about mutual funds is due to this type of misaligned interest. The Conflicts of Interest box discusses some of the better-known mutual fund scandals.

Mutual Fund Abuses

Until 2001 the mutual fund industry could brag that it had not been touched by scandal for more than 60 years. This changed when the New York attorney general began investigating tips that mutual funds were engaging in various activities that undermined their fiduciary duty to shareholders, violated their own policies, and in some cases broke SEC laws. Most of the abuses centered on two activities: late trading and market timing, both of which take advantage of the structure of open-end

> CONFLICTS OF INTEREST

Many Mutual Funds Are Caught Ignoring Ethical Standards

Some of the best-known names in the mutual fund industry have come under attack by the New York attorney general's office and the SEC. Over 300 lawsuits against 18 firms were filed and consolidated in federal court in Baltimore. The mutual funds are eager to settle the suits and to get the bad publicity behind them. Nine firms agreed to pay $1.6 billion in restitution to investors and an additional $855 million in fee reductions. Among the larger settlements were the following:

- The Alliance Capital Management Corp. was charged with allowing traders to engage in market timing. The firm cut fees by $350 million and paid $250 million in fines and restitution to shareholders.
- Bank of America, which was implicated along with Canary Capital Partners in late trading and market timing, agreed to fee reductions of $160 million and fines and restitution of $375 million.
- Janus Capital Management LLC reduced fees by $125 million and paid fines and restitution of $100 million.
- Putnam Investments, the fifth-largest family of funds, agreed to pay $10 million in fee reductions and $100 million in fines and restitution.

In addition to the fines, restitution, and fee reductions, some individual investment managers were charged with criminal activity. The vice-chairperson of Fred Alger & Company, James Connelly Jr., was sentenced to one to three years in jail for his involvement in preferential treatment and self-dealing in the mutual fund.

Source: Wall Street Journal, July 14, 2004, p. C1.

---

mutual funds that provide daily liquidity to shareholders by marking all trades to the NAV as of the close of business at 4:00 p.m.

1. *Late trading.* Late trading refers to the practice of allowing trades that are received after 4:00 p.m. to trade at the 4:00 price when they should trade at the next day's price. Suppose that on Wednesday at 4:00 p.m. the NAV for a technology fund is $20. Now suppose that news is received by traders at 6:00 p.m. that HP, Intel, and Microsoft have reported their income surged 50% over the last quarter. Traders, knowing the industry impact this will have, may want to enter buy orders for the fund at the $20 price. They are sure the NAV on Thursday will be substantially higher and they can earn a quick profit. A late trader can trade at the stale 4:00 p.m. price and buy or sell the funds the next day at a profit.

   The attorney general reported in hearings before Congress that "late trading is like betting on a horse race after the horses have crossed the finish line." It is illegal under SEC regulations. The reason it went undetected for many years is that certain late trades were regularly accepted and were legal. If a broker received a buy order from a client at 2:00, the order might not get consolidated with other orders and transmitted to the fund by 4:00. Since the investor placed the order before the market closed, the investor could not benefit from the late trade. Late trades were simply an opportunity to catch up with order processing. It was when large investors took advantage of their special arrangements at the expense of other shareholders that the legal line was crossed.
2. *Market timing.* Market timing, though technically legal, is considered unethical and is expressly forbidden by virtually all mutual funds' policy

standards. Market timing involves taking advantage of time zone differences that allow arbitrage opportunities, especially in foreign stocks. Mutual funds will set their 4:00 closing NAV using the most recent available foreign prices. However, these prices may be very stale. Japan, for example, closes nine hours earlier. If news is released in Japan that is not reflected in their closing prices, arbitrage opportunities exist by buying at the stale prices embedded in the NAV.

Most mutual funds have fees that are supposed to discourage these kinds of rapid in-and-out trades. However, if an investor such as Bank of America places large deposits in the fund, these fees can be waived. This is exactly what Edward J. Stern and his hedge fund Canary Capital Partners LLC did. In September 2003 Stern settled with the attorney general for $40 million in fines for allowing both late trading and market timing by Bank of America.

To better understand how shareholders in mutual funds are hurt by market timing and late trading, suppose a technology fund holds stock in various firms with a total current market value of $350. Further suppose you own one of 10 shares outstanding in the fund. The NAV of the fund will be $35 per share ($350/10). Now suppose that after the market closes the tech industry announces better-than-expected earnings that everyone agrees will drive the value of shares held by the fund to $400 when the market opens the next morning. The NAV of your share would be $40 ($400/10). However, if another investor with special privileges is allowed to buy a share in the fund for $35 after hours, your NAV will be diluted. The $35 received by the fund from the privileged investor will have to be held as cash, since the market is closed and no additional stock can be purchased by the fund. As a result, the value of the fund's assets the next morning will be $435 ($400 in stock and $35 in cash). The NAV will be $435/11 = $39.54 instead of $40. All of the original investors in the fund will have lost $0.46 per share, while the privileged investor will have gained $4.54 ($39.54 − $35.00).

The costs to investors of market timing and late trading are very hard to estimate, since no reliable statistics are available on how frequently these abuses were practiced. Recent academic studies have estimated the losses to long-term

> CONFLICTS OF INTEREST

SEC Survey Reports Mutual Fund Abuses Widespread

When the New York attorney general announced that his office was going to indict a number of mutual fund managers in September 2003, he caught many regulators off guard. Their focus had been on security abuses by corporations. The revelation that the mutual fund industry might also be dirty resulted in rapidly called hearings before Congress. At these hearings Stephen Cutler, the chief of enforcement for the SEC, presented results that showed that illegal trading in mutual funds was more widespread than anyone had imagined. In a sample of the largest 88 mutual fund companies, which represented 90% of the industry's assets, the SEC said that about 25% of the broker-dealers were allowed to make illegal late trades. Additionally, half the funds let some privileged shareholders engage in market timing trades. Finally, the research showed that more than 30% of the funds admitted that their managers had shared sensitive portfolio information with favored shareholders.

investors to be as high as $4.9 billion.[3] See the Conflicts of Interest box for a discussion of how widespread mutual fund abuses may be.

Government Response to Abuses

Arthur Levitt, former chairman of the SEC, admitted that, despite the scope of the scandal, he had not seen it coming. In fact, the SEC, which is supposed to watch the mutual fund industry, was not the agency that initially investigated the abuses. It was New York State Attorney General Eliot Spitzer who caught the SEC unaware by filing indictments against many of the major players in the mutual fund industry. Now that the issues are commonly recognized, both the SEC and Congress are attempting to ensure the safety of these funds.

- *More independent directors.* Funds are now required to have an independent board chairman and a majority of the board must be independent. In addition, the independent board members must hold annual executive sessions outside the presence of fund managers. The legislation also requires that these independent board members have authority to hire staff to support their oversight efforts.
- *Hardening of the 4:00 p.m. valuation rule.* By more strictly enforcing the rule that trades received after 4:00 be traded at the next day's NAV rather than at the stale NAV, late trading activities should be prevented. These proposals, however, are controversial because they penalize investors whose trades do not get completed due to trading backlogs. They also fail to prevent market timing arbitrage across time zones.
- *Increased and enforced redemption fees.* Most funds already have a policy against market timing and have a redemption fee that is imposed for shares that are sold within 60 or 90 days of purchase. These fees are usually discretionary and were waived in the cases where abuses occurred. The problem with mandatory fees is that they may penalize the investor who needs to make an unexpected withdrawal due to an emergency. This penalty makes mutual funds less attractive and, critics contend, would reduce their popularity. As a result of this argument, a voluntary redemption fee rule was adopted. The rule requires that the board consider whether they should impose the fee to protect shareholders from market timing abuses.
- *Increased transparency.* Other regulations follow the most common approach taken by the SEC—increased disclosure of operating practices to the public. Directors are required to more clearly and openly reveal any relationships that exist between fund owners and investment managers. Investment managers are required to more clearly disclose compensation arrangements and how fees are charged. Additionally, more information is required about compensation arrangements between the mutual fund and sales brokers. This strategy leaves it to the market to discipline firms that seek to exploit conflicts of interest.

---

[3]See Eric Zitzewitz, *Journal of Law, Economics & Organization* 19, no. 2 (2003): 245–280; Jason Greene and Charles Hodges, *Journal of Financial Economics* 65 (2002): 131–158; and Goetzmann, Ivkovic, and Rouwenhorst, *Journal of Financial and Quantitative Analysis* 36, no. 3 (September 2001): 287–309.

SUMMARY

1. Mutual funds have grown rapidly over the past two decades. The growth has been partly fueled by the increase in the number of investors who are responsible for managing their own retirement. Increased liquidity and diversification, among other factors, have also been important. There are currently about 7,500 separate mutual funds with over $13 trillion in net assets.
2. Mutual funds can be organized as either open- or closed-end funds. Closed-end funds issue stock in the fund at an initial offering and do not accept additional funds. Most new funds are organized as open-end funds and issue additional shares when new money is received. The net asset value (NAV) of the shares is computed each day. All trades conducted that day are at the NAV.
3. The primary classes of mutual funds are stock funds, bond funds, hybrid funds, and money market funds. Stock and bond funds can be either actively managed by investment managers or structured as index funds that contain the securities in some index, such as the S&P 500.
4. Hedge funds attempt to earn returns by trading on deviations between historical relationships among securities' prices and current market conditions.
5. The mutual fund industry has been subject to widely publicized scandals for violating SEC regulations and internal policy. Most abuses centered on market timing and late trading by investors receiving privileged treatment in exchange for large deposits with the funds. Conflicts of interest created by fee structures that reward investment managers more for total assets than for returns are partly responsible.

KEY TERMS

closed-end funds, p. 484
deferred load, p. 492
diversification, p. 481
hedge funds, p. 494
load funds, p. 492
net asset value (NAV), p. 485
no-load funds, p. 492
open-end fund, p. 484

QUESTIONS

1. What features of mutual funds and the investment environment have led to mutual funds' rapid growth in the past two decades?
2. Suppose that you can deposit at most $300 per month for your savings and that you want to buy securities that are available only in large denominations. What benefit of mutual funds would be particularly attractive to you?
3. After reading Chapter 6, William realizes that there is no point in paying fees to mutual fund managers for them to choose which stock or securities to buy for him. However, after carefully reviewing his decision, he decides to buy shares in a mutual fund. Could you explain the reasons behind his final decision?
4. Distinguish between an open- and closed-end mutual fund.
5. Discuss why a mutual fund family may find it beneficial to offer 50 or 60 different stock mutual funds.
6. How does an index fund differ from an actively managed fund?
7. Suppose a mutual fund advertises a yearly return of 12%, for which it charges an upfront fee (a percentage of your initial investment). Another fund advertises the same return, but it charges a 3% fee each year. Assuming both funds can achieve the 12% advertised return, which one would you choose if you are 25 years old and starting to save for your retirement? Which option would you choose if you are 55 and are starting to save for your retirement?
8. Considering the evolution of mutual funds fees over the past 20 years, would you say that competition among mutual funds has been a good thing or not?
9. What distinguishes a hedge fund from other types of mutual funds?
10. What prompted the growth of money market mutual funds?
11. Recall that under the provisions of the Dodd-Frank Act of 2010, systemically important financial institutions (SIFIs) are required to maintain capital reserves (potentially up to 8% of the fund's assets). Explain the impact on mutual funds' performance if they are designated as SIFIs.
12. What is the primary source of the conflict of interest between shareholders and investment managers?
13. What is *late trading* when applied to mutual funds?
14. What is *market timing* when applied to mutual funds?
15. What regulatory changes have been adopted or are being considered to deal with abuses in the mutual fund industry?

QUANTITATIVE PROBLEMS

1. A mutual fund charges a 4.2% front-end load. Determine the maximum annual expense ratio you will be willing to pay if you do not want to pay more than 1.7% in fees per year (assume you will hold the fund for 30 years).
2. A mutual fund reported year-end total assets of $2,347,000,000. Determine the expense ratio if total fees amounted to $18,580,000.
3. A mutual fund offers "A" shares, which have a 5% front-end load and an expense ratio of 0.76%. The fund also offers "B" shares, which have a 3% back-end load and an expense ratio of 0.87%. Which shares make more sense for an investor looking over an 18-year horizon?
4. Calculate the NAV of the following fund, assuming 3,500 shares are outstanding. Calculate the percentage change in the NAV of the fund if stock C climbs to $33.41.

Stock	Shares owned	Price
A	500	$5.74
B	6,000	$65.10
C	3,000	$12.04
Cash	n.a.	$4,368.40

5. Calculate the NAV of the following fund if 5,000,000 shares are outstanding. Assuming you bought shares in this fund a year ago at $5.06, determine the yield on your investment.

Stock (at current market value)	$15,000,000
Bonds (at current market value)	$12,000,000
Cash	$800,000
Total value of assets	$27,800,000
Liabilities	– $200,000
Net worth	$27,600,000

Questions 6–12 trace a sequence of transactions involving a single mutual fund.

6. On December 31 a mutual fund has the following assets and prices at 4:00 p.m.

Stock	Shares owned	Price
1	1,000	$1.97
2	5,000	$48.26
3	1,000	$26.44
4	10,000	$67.49
5	3,000	$2.59

Calculate the net asset value (NAV) for the fund. Assume that 8,000 shares are outstanding for the fund.

7. An investor sends the fund a check for $50,000. If there is no front-end load, calculate the new number of shares and price per share. Assume the manager purchases 1,800 shares of stock 3, and the rest is held as cash.
8. On January 2 the prices at 4:00 p.m. are as follows:

Stock	Shares owned	Price
1	1,000	$2.03
2	5,000	$51.37
3	2,800	$29.08
4	10,000	$67.19
5	3,000	$4.42
Cash	n.a.	$2,408.00

Calculate the net asset value (NAV) for the fund.

9. Assume the new investor then sells the 420 shares. What is his profit? What is the annualized return? The fund sells 800 shares of stock 4 to raise the needed funds. Assume 250 trading days per year.
10. To discourage short-term investing in its fund, the fund now charges a 5% front-end load and a 2% back-end load. The same investor decides to put $50,000 back into the fund. Calculate the new number of shares outstanding. Assume the fund manager buys back as many round-lot shares (multiples of 100) of stock 4 with the cash.
11. On January 3 the prices at 4:00 p.m. are as follows:

Stock	Shares owned	Price
1	1,000	$1.92
2	5,000	$51.18
3	2,800	$29.08
4	9,900	$67.19
5	3,000	$4.51
Cash	n.a.	$5,353.40

Calculate the new NAV.

12. Unhappy with the results, the new investor then sells the 389.09 shares. What is his profit? What is the new fund value?

WEB EXERCISES

Investment Banks, Brokerage Firms, and Mutual Funds

1. Morningstar is the best-known company that specializes in analysis and review of mutual funds. There are a number of Web sites that report Morningstar's results. Go to **www.quicken.com/investments/mutualfunds/finder**. Perform the EasyStep Search according to your own preferences for investment. Can you find funds that provide the return you want with the expense ratio you are willing to pay?
2. The mutual fund industry publishes a fact book containing exhaustive data on the historic and current state of mutual funds. Go to **www.ici.org**, click on Research and Statistics, then on Fact Books.
   a. Section 1 provides an overview of the mutual fund industry. Select and report on one statistic not reported in this textbook.
   b. Section 2 reports on trends in the mutual fund industry. Discuss the relationship between the return on equity and flows to equity mutual funds.
   c. According to Chapter 4, what percentage of mutual funds assets are currently owned by households?
   d. According to Chapter 4, what is the average annual income of an investor in mutual funds?

CHAPTER 21

Insurance Companies and Pension Funds

> PREVIEW

In this chapter we continue our discussion of financial institutions by looking at two nonbank institutions: insurance companies and pension funds. Insurance is an important industry in the United States. Most people hold one or more types of insurance policies (health, life, homeowners, automobile, disability, and so on), and the annual revenues of insurance companies exceed $915 billion. Insurance companies are also a major employer, especially of business majors. Figure 21.1 shows the number of persons employed by the insurance industry between 1960 and 2015. The numbers rose rapidly during the 1960s, 1970s, and early 1980s. (Currently, well over 2 million Americans are employed in the insurance industry.) Until very recently the rate of growth has slowed, however. There are a couple of possible explanations for this. First, technology has streamlined claims processing so that fewer back-office workers are needed. Second, competition by other financial institutions such as commercial banks and brokerage houses may be cutting into some of the business traditionally reserved for insurance companies.

One major competitor to insurance has been the private, company-sponsored pension plan. Better-educated and longer-lived workers are putting more money into pension funds than ever before. Over 65 million individuals are now invested in a private pension fund. These plans are also reviewed in this chapter.

Insurance companies and pension funds are considered financial intermediaries for several reasons. First, they receive investment funds from their customers. For example, when a person buys a whole life insurance policy, the person receives a life insurance benefit and accumulates a cash balance. Many people use insurance companies as their primary investment avenue. Similarly, private pension funds also take in investment dollars from their customers. Second, both of these institutions place their money in a variety of money-earning investments. Insurance companies and pension funds make large commercial mortgage loans, invest in stocks, and buy bonds. Thus, these institutions are financial intermediaries in that they take in funds from one sector and invest it in another.

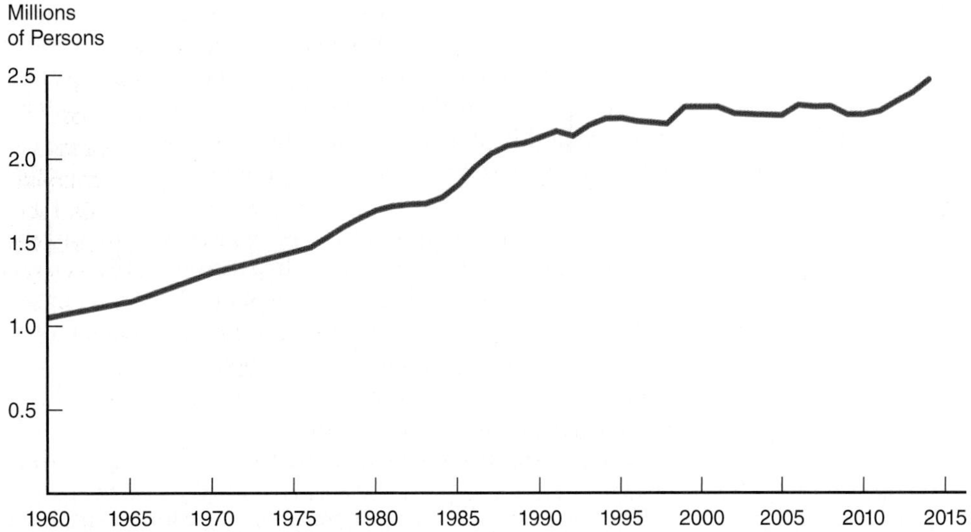

FIGURE 21.1 Number of Persons Employed in the U.S. Insurance Industry, 1960–2015

Source: https://www.acli.com/.

Insurance Companies

Insurance companies are in the business of assuming risk on behalf of their customers in exchange for a fee, called a *premium*. Insurance companies make a profit by charging premiums that are sufficient to pay the expected claims to the company plus a profit. Why do people pay for insurance when they know that over the lifetime of their policy, they will probably pay more in premiums than the expected amount of any loss they will suffer? Because most people are risk-averse: They would rather pay a **certainty equivalent** (the insurance premium) than accept the gamble that they will lose their house or their car. Thus, it is because people are risk-averse that they prefer to buy insurance and know with certainty what their wealth will be (their current wealth minus the insurance premium) than to run the risk that their wealth may fall.

Consider how people's lives would change if insurance were not available. Instead of knowing that the insurance company would help if an emergency occurred, everyone would have to set aside reserves. These reserves could not be invested long-term but would have to be kept in an extremely liquid form. Furthermore, people would be constantly worried that their reserves would be inadequate to pay for catastrophic events such as the loss of their house to fire, the theft of their car, or the death of the family breadwinner. Insurance allows us the peace of mind that a single event can have only a limited financial impact on our lives.

Fundamentals of Insurance

Although there are many types of insurance and insurance companies, all insurance is subject to several basic principles.

1. There must be a relationship between the *insured* (the party covered by insurance) and the *beneficiary* (the party who receives the payment should a loss occur). In addition, the beneficiary must be someone who may suffer

potential harm. For example, you could not take out a policy on your neighbor's teenage driver because you are unlikely to suffer harm if the teenager gets into an accident. The reason for this rule is that insurance companies do not want people to buy policies as a way of gambling. We will discuss how credit default swaps violate this rule later.

2. The insured must provide full and accurate information to the insurance company.
3. The insured is not to profit as a result of insurance coverage.
4. If a third party compensates the insured for the loss, the insurance company's obligation is reduced by the amount of the compensation.
5. The insurance company must have a large number of insureds so that the risk can be spread out among many policies.
6. The loss must be quantifiable. For example, an oil company could not buy a policy on an unexplored oil field.
7. The insurance company must be able to compute the probability of the loss.

The purpose of these principles is to maintain the integrity of the insurance process. Without them, people might be tempted to use insurance companies to gamble or speculate on future events. Taken to an extreme, this behavior could undermine the ability of insurance companies to protect persons in real need. In addition, these principles provide a way to spread the risk among many policies and to establish a price for each policy that will provide an expectation of a profitable return. Despite following these guidelines, insurance companies suffer greatly from the problems of asymmetric information that we first described in Chapter 2.

Adverse Selection and Moral Hazard in Insurance

Recall that adverse selection occurs when the individuals most likely to benefit from a transaction are the ones who most actively seek out the transaction and are thus most likely to be selected. In Chapter 2 we discussed adverse selection in the context of borrowers with the worst credit being the ones who most actively seek loans. The problem also occurs in the insurance market. Who is more likely to apply for health insurance, someone who is seldom sick or someone with chronic health problems? Who is more likely to buy flood insurance, someone who lives on a mountain or someone who lives in a river valley? In both cases, the party more likely to suffer a loss is the party likely to seek insurance. The implication of adverse selection is that loss probability statistics gathered for the entire population may not accurately reflect the loss potential for the persons who actually want to buy policies.

In addition to the adverse selection problem, moral hazard plagues the insurance industry. Moral hazard occurs when the insured fails to take proper precautions to avoid losses because losses are covered by insurance. For example, moral hazard may cause you not to lock your car doors if you will be reimbursed by insurance if the car is stolen. When hurricanes are approaching, many yacht owners do not take down their old canvas covers because they hope the covers will be destroyed by the hurricane, in which case the owners can file a claim with the insurance company and get money to buy new covers. Those with new canvas will take precautions to protect it.

One way that insurance companies combat moral hazard is by requiring a **deductible**. A deductible is the amount of any loss that must be paid by the insured before the insurance company will pay anything. For example, if new canvas yacht covers cost $5,000 and the yacht owner has $1,000 deductible, the owner will pay the first $1,000 of the loss and the insurance company will pay $4,000. In addition to deductibles, there may be other terms in the insurance contract aimed at reducing risk. For example, a business insured against fire may be required to install and maintain a sprinkler system on its premises to reduce the loss should a fire occur.

Although contract terms and deductibles help with the moral hazard problem, these issues remain a constant difficulty for insurance companies. The insurance industry's reaction to moral hazard and adverse selection are discussed in greater detail in "The Practicing Manager" later in this chapter.

Selling Insurance

Another problem common to insurance companies is that people often fail to seek as much insurance as they actually need. Human nature tends to cause people to ignore their mortality, for example. For this reason, insurance, unlike many banking services, does not sell itself. Instead, insurance companies must hire large sales forces to sell their products. The expense of marketing may account for up to 20% of the cost of a policy. A good sales force can convince people to buy insurance coverage that they never would have pursued on their own yet may need.

Insurance is unique in that agents sell a product that commits the company to a risk. The relationship between the agent and the company varies: *Independent agents* may sell insurance for a number of different companies. They do not have loyalty to any one firm and simply try to find the best product for their customer. There are in excess of 60,000 independent agents in the United States. *Exclusive agents* sell the insurance products for only one insurance company.

Most agents, whether independent or exclusive, are compensated by being paid a commission. The agents themselves are usually not at all concerned with the level of risk of any one policy because they have little to lose if a loss occurs. (Rarely are commissions influenced by the claims submitted by an agent's customers.) To keep control of the risk that agents are incurring on behalf of the company, insurance companies employ **underwriters**, people who review and sign off on each policy an agent writes and who have the authority to turn down a policy if they deem the risk unacceptable. If underwriters have questions about the quality of customers, they may order an independent inspector to review the property being insured or request additional medical information about a customer. A final decision to accept the policy may depend on the inspector's report (see the Mini-Case box below).

> MINI-CASE

Insurance Agent: The Customer's Ally

An underwriter working for Prudential Insurance was responsible for a number of agents selling property insurance in Southern California in 1985. One agent sold a large number of fire insurance policies and was always careful to document clearly when a fire hydrant was on the property by including it in a photograph attached to the policy application. The agent made a mistake on one policy, however, when he included his car in a picture of a different view of the property. The picture showed a plastic fire hydrant lying in the open trunk of his car. He had been putting this fire hydrant on property for years when he needed to give a low quote to get business.

The agent was neither fired nor sued. He was simply advised to halt the practice, and his policies continued to be accepted by the company.

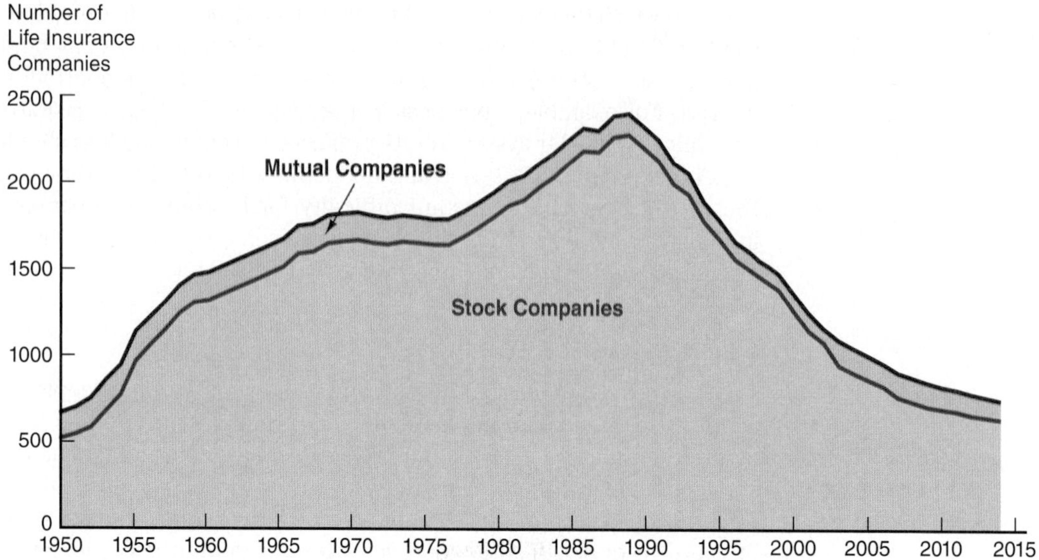

FIGURE 21.2 Number of Life Insurance Companies in the United States, 1950–2014

Source: https://www.acli.com, Life Insurance Fact Book.

Growth and Organization of Insurance Companies

Figure 21.2 shows the number of life insurance companies from 1950 to 2014. There was a steady increase in the number until 1988. Since then the number has fallen steadily. Another interesting point to note about Figure 21.2 is that insurance companies can be organized as either *stock* or *mutual* firms. A **stock company** is owned by stockholders and has the objective of making a profit.

Mutual insurance companies are owned by the policyholders. The objective of mutual insurance firms is to provide insurance at the lowest possible cost to the insured. Policyholders are paid dividends that reflect the surplus of premiums over costs. Because the policyholders share in reducing the cost of insurance, there may be some reduction in the moral hazard that most insurance companies face. A unique feature of mutual insurance dividends is that they are not taxed like dividends received from other types of corporations. The Internal Revenue Service regards the dividends as refunds of overcharges on insurance premiums.

Most new insurance companies organize as stock corporations. As Figure 21.2 shows, relatively few insurance companies are organized as mutuals.

Types of Insurance

Insurance is classified by which type of undesirable event is insured. The most common types are health, life, and property and casualty insurance. In its simplest form, life insurance provides income for the heirs of the deceased. Many insurance companies offer policies that provide retirement benefits as well as life insurance. In this case, the premium combines the cost of the life insurance with a savings program. The cost of life insurance depends on such factors as the age of the insured, average life expectancies, the health and lifestyle of the insured (whether the insured smokes, engages in a dangerous hobby such as skydiving, and so on), and the insurance company's operating costs.

Property and casualty insurance protects property (houses, cars, boats, and so on) against losses due to accidents, fire, disasters, and other calamities. Marine insurance, for example, which insures against the loss of a ship and its cargo, is the oldest form of insurance, predating even life insurance. Property and casualty policies tend to be short-term contracts subject to frequent renewal. Another significant distinction between life insurance policies and property and casualty policies is that the latter do not have a savings component. Property and casualty premiums are based simply on the probability of sustaining the loss. That is why car insurance premiums are higher if a driver has had speeding tickets, has caused accidents, or lives in a high-crime area. Each of these events increases the likelihood that the insurance company will have to pay a claim.

Life Insurance

Life is assumed to unfold in a predictable sequence: You work for a number of years while saving for retirement; then you retire, live off the fruits of your earlier labor, and die at a ripe old age. The problem is that you could die too young and not have time to provide for your loved ones, or you could live too long and run out of retirement assets. Either option is very unappealing to most people. The purpose of life insurance is to relieve some of the concern associated with either eventuality. Although insurance cannot make you comfortable with the idea of a premature death, it can at least allow you the peace of mind that comes with knowing that you have provided for your heirs. Life insurance companies also want to help people save for their retirement. In this way, the insurance company provides for the customer's whole life.

The basic products of life insurance companies are life insurance proper, disability insurance, annuities, and health insurance. Life insurance pays off if you die, protecting those who depend on your continued earnings. As mentioned, the person who receives the insurance payment after you die is called the *beneficiary* of the policy. Disability insurance replaces part of your income should you become unable to continue working due to illness or an accident. An **annuity** is an insurance product that will help if you live longer than you expect. For an initial fixed sum or stream of payments, the insurance company agrees to pay you a fixed amount for as long as you live. If you live a short life, the insurance company pays out less than expected. Conversely, if you live unusually long, the insurance company may pay out much more than expected.

Notice one curiosity among these various types of insurance: Although predicting any one individual's life expectancy or probability of being disabled is very difficult, when many people are insured, the actual amount to be paid out by the insurance company can be predicted very accurately. Insurance companies collect and analyze statistics on life expectancies, health claims, disability claims, and other relevant matters.

For example, a life insurance company can predict with a high degree of accuracy when death benefits must be paid by using *actuarial tables* that predict life expectancies. Table 21.1 lists the expected life of persons at various ages. A 25-year-old female can expect to live another 56.9 years; a 25-year-old male, however, can expect to live only another 52.5 years.

TABLE 21.1 Life Expectancy at Various Ages in the United States, 2013

Age	Male	Female
1	75.78	80.49
5	71.87	76.56
15	61.96	66.64
25	52.47	56.85
35	43.17	47.19
45	33.98	37.73
55	25.41	28.74
65	17.75	20.32
75	11.03	12.83
85	5.84	6.92
95	2.82	3.34
100	2.12	2.45
105	1.6	1.78
110	1.18	1.26
115	0.84	0.85

Source: https://www.ssa.gov/oact/STATS/table4c6.html. Social Security Administration Actualarial Life Table.

The **law of large numbers** says that when many people are insured, the probability distribution of the losses will assume a normal probability distribution, a distribution that allows accurate predictions. This distribution is important: Because insurance companies insure so many millions of people, the law of large numbers tends to make the company's predictions quite accurate and allows companies to price the policies so that they can earn a profit.

Life insurance policies protect against an interruption in the family's stream of income. The broad categories of life insurance products are *term*, *whole life*, and *universal life*.

Term Life The simplest form of life insurance is the *term insurance policy*, which pays out if the insured dies while the policy is in force. This form of policy contains no savings element. Once the policy period expires, there are no residual benefits. As the insured ages, the probability of death increases, so the cost of the policy rises. For example, Table 21.2 shows the estimated premiums for a 40-year-old male nonsmoker for $100,000 of term life insurance from a major insurance company. The premium for the first year is $134. This rises to $147 when the insured is 41 years old, $153 when the insured is 42, and so on. By the time the insured is 60 years old, $100,000 of life insurance costs $810 per year. Of course, rates vary among insurance companies, but these sample rates demonstrate how the annual cost of a term policy rises with the age of the insured.

Some term policies fix the premiums for a set number of years, usually five or ten. Alternatively, *decreasing term policies* have a constant premium, but the amount of the insurance coverage declines each year.

TABLE 21.2 Typical Annual Premiums on a $100,000 Term Policy for a 40-Year-Old Male Nonsmoker

Age of Insured (years)	Cost ($)
40	134
41	147
42	153
45	192
50	286
55	461
60	810

Term policies have been historically hard to sell because once they expire, the policyholder has nothing to show for the premium paid. This problem is solved with whole life policies.

Whole Life A *whole life insurance* policy pays a death benefit if the policyholder dies. Whole life policies usually require the insured to pay a level premium for the duration of the policy. In the beginning, the insured pays more than if a term policy had been purchased. This overpayment accumulates as a cash value that can be borrowed by the insured at reasonable rates.

Survivorship benefits also contribute to the accumulated cash values. When members of the insured pool die, any remaining cash values are divided among the survivors. If the policyholder lives until the policy matures, it can be surrendered for its cash value. This cash value can be used to purchase an annuity. In this way, the whole life policy is advertised as covering the insured for the duration of his or her life.

Universal Life In the late 1970s, whole life policies fell into disfavor because the rates of return earned on the policy premiums were well below rates available on other investments. For example, say that an investor bought a term policy instead of a whole life policy and invested the difference in the premiums. If she did this each year for the term of the whole life policy, she would be able to pay for term insurance and still have a much greater amount in her investment account than if she had initially purchased the whole life policy. Investment advisers and insurance agents began steering customers away from whole life policies. The sales pitch became "buy term and invest the difference." Because the agents were also selling other investments, they did not suffer from this change in insurance plans. To combat the flow of funds out of their companies, insurance firms introduced the *universal life policy*.

Universal life policies combine the benefits of the term policy with those of the whole life policy. The major benefit of the universal life policy is that the cash value accumulates at a much higher rate.

The universal life policy is structured to have two parts, one for the term life insurance and one for savings. One important advantage that universal life policies have over many alternative investment plans is that the interest earned on the savings portion of the account is tax-exempt until withdrawn. To keep this favorable tax treatment, the cash value of the policy cannot exceed the death benefit.

Universal life policies were introduced in the early 1980s when interest rates were at record high levels. They immediately became very popular and by 1984 accounted for almost a third of the volume of life insurance sold. Later, as interest rates fell, their popularity ebbed.

Annuities If we think of term life insurance as insuring against death, the annuity can be viewed as insuring against life. As we noted earlier, one risk people have is outliving their retirement funds. If they live longer than they projected when they initially retired, they could spend all of their money and end up in poverty. One way to avoid this outcome is by purchasing annuities. Once an annuity has been purchased for a fixed amount, it makes payments as long as the beneficiary lives.

Annuities are particularly susceptible to the adverse selection problem. When people retire, they know more about their life expectancy than the insurance company knows. People who are in good health, have a family history of longevity, and have attended to their health all of their lives are more likely to live longer and hence to want to buy an annuity more than people in poor or average health. To avoid this problem, insurance companies tend to price individual annuities expensively. Most annuities are sold to members of large groups where all employees covered by a particular pension plan automatically receive their benefit distribution by purchasing an annuity from the insurance company. Because the annuity is automatic, the adverse selection problem is eliminated.

Assets and Liabilities of Life Insurance Companies Life insurance companies derive funds from two sources. First, they receive premiums that represent future obligations that must be met when the insured dies. Second, they receive premiums paid into pension funds managed by the life insurance company. These funds are long-term in nature.

Since life insurance liabilities are predictable and long-term, life insurance companies can invest in long-term assets. Figure 21.3 shows the distribution of assets of the average life insurance company at the beginning of 2015. Most of the assets are in long-term investments such as bonds.

Insurance companies have also invested heavily in mortgages and real estate over the years. In 2015, about 9% of life insurance assets were invested either in

FIGURE 21.3 Distribution of Life Insurance Company Assets (2015)

Source: Life Insurance Company Fact Book, 2015, Table 2.1 (American Council of Life Insurers), https://www.acli.com/Tools/Industry%20Facts/Life%20Insurers%20Fact%20Book/Pages/RP12.

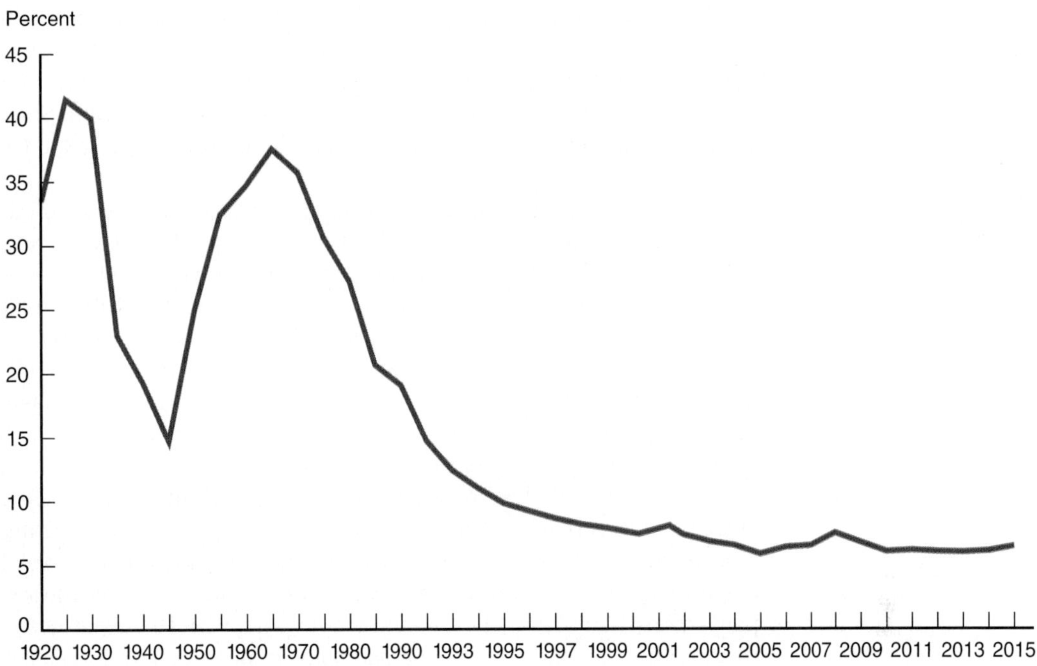

FIGURE 21.4 Percentage of Life Insurance Company Assets Invested in Mortgages, 1920–2015

Source: Federal Reserve Flow of Funds Accounts, Table L117, http://www.federalreserve.gov/releases/z1/Current/z1.pdf.

mortgage loans or directly in real estate. This percentage is down substantially from historic levels. Figure 21.4 displays the percentage of assets invested in mortgages from 1920 to 2015. The decline in mortgage investment, which represents a shift to lower-risk assets, has been offset by increased investment in corporate securities and government bonds.

The shift to less risky investments may be the result of losses suffered by some insurance companies in the late 1980s. As insurance companies competed against mutual funds and money market funds for retirement dollars, they found that they needed higher-return investments. This led some insurance companies to invest in real estate and junk bonds. Deteriorating real estate values brought on by overbuilding during the 1980s caused some firms to suffer large losses. The combination of large real estate losses and junk bond investment contributed to the failure of several large firms in 1991, including Executive Life, with assets of $15 billion, and Mutual Benefit Life, with assets of $14 billion.

Health Insurance

Individual health insurance coverage is very vulnerable to adverse selection problems. People who know that they are likely to become ill are the most likely to seek health insurance coverage. This causes individual health insurance to be very expensive. Most policies are offered through company-sponsored programs in which the company pays all or part of the employee's policy premium.

Most life insurance companies also offer health insurance. Health insurance premiums account for about 24% of premium income. Life insurance companies compete with Blue Cross and Blue Shield organizations, nonprofit firms that are sponsored by hospitals. Blue Cross usually covers hospital care, and Blue Shield, doctors' services. One national agency coordinates and monitors the 73 Blue Cross/Blue Shield organizations.

The government is also involved in health insurance through Medicare and Medicaid. Medicare provides medical coverage for the elderly, and Medicaid provides coverage for people on welfare or who have very limited assets.

Health insurance was a major political issue in the 1992 presidential election and continues to be the subject of regulation and debate. One reason for the extensive debate over medical insurance has been the spiraling costs of health care. For the last several decades, the cost of health care has risen much faster than the cost of living and real wages. One factor contributing to this increase is the more sophisticated and expensive treatments constantly being offered. For example, studies have shown that cholesterol-reducing drugs can reduce the likelihood of cardiovascular trouble across a broad portion of the population. These drugs cost about $3 per day and did not even exist 40 years ago. Insurance companies have dealt with these rising costs in a number of ways. For example, today the risk of most company-sponsored plans is borne by the company, with the insurance company administering the plan and covering catastrophic expenses. This increases the sponsoring company's incentive to maintain a healthy workforce and to encourage responsible use of medical facilities by its employees. For example, many large firms have found it cost-effective to employ physician assistants on site to reduce medical fees and absenteeism and to offer other incentives—onsite gym facilities, onsite Weight Watchers meetings and benefits for various health stats, e.g., healthy weight, nonsmoker, etc.

Another way that insurance companies are attempting to deal with increased medical costs is by controlling them. This is done by negotiating contracts with physician groups to provide services at reduced cost and through *managed care*, where approval is required before services can be rendered. *Health maintenance organizations* (*HMOs*) shift the risk from the insurance company to the provider. The insurance company pays the HMO a fixed payment per person covered in exchange for medical services. One problem many people find with the HMO form of health care is that the provider has an incentive to limit medical services. Regulation was required, for example, to ensure mothers stay at least 48 hours in the hospital following a delivery.

Following a lengthy and contentious national debate, the Patient Protection and Affordable Care Act was signed into law on March 23, 2010. This bill is expected to expand health coverage to include an additional 32 million Americans who are currently uninsured. Some of the more controversial provisions of this bill include:

- Options to purchase insurance through state-based exchanges
- Subsidies for low-income people to help acquire insurance
- Limits on insurance companies denying coverage due to preexisting conditions
- Requirement that insurance companies allow children to stay on their parents' plans until age 26
- Requirement that everyone must purchase insurance or face a fine that will be phased in over several years.

Property and Casualty Insurance

Property and casualty insurance was the earliest form of insurance. It began in the Middle Ages when merchants sent ships off to foreign ports to trade. A merchant, though willing to accept the risk that the trading might not turn a profit, was often unwilling to accept the risk that the ship might sink or be captured by pirates. To reduce such risks, merchants began to band together and insure each other's ships against loss. The process became more sophisticated as time went on, and insurance policies were written that were then traded in the major commercial centers of the time.

In 1666 the Great Fire of London did much to advance the case for fire insurance. The first fire insurance company was founded in London in 1680. In the United States, the first fire insurance company was formed by a group led by Benjamin Franklin in 1752. By the beginning of the nineteenth century, the assets of property and casualty insurance firms exceeded even those of commercial banks, making these firms the most important financial intermediary. The invention of the automobile did a great deal to spur the growth of property and casualty insurance companies during the twentieth century.

Property and Casualty Insurance Today

Property and casualty insurance protects against losses from fire, theft, storm, explosion, and even neglect. **Property insurance** protects businesses and other property owners from the impact of risk associated with owning property. This includes replacement and loss of earnings from income-producing property as well as financial losses to owners of residential property. **Casualty insurance** (or **liability insurance**) protects against liability for harm the insured may cause to others as a result of product failure or accidents. For example, part of your car insurance is property insurance (which pays if your car is damaged) and part is casualty insurance (which pays if you cause an accident).

Property and casualty insurance is different from life insurance. First, policies tend to be short-term, usually for one year or less. Second, whereas life insurance is limited to insuring against one event, property and casualty companies insure against many different events. Finally, the amount of the potential loss is much more difficult to predict than for life insurance. These characteristics cause property and casualty companies to hold more liquid assets than those of life insurance companies. The wide range of losses means that property and casualty firms must maintain substantial liquidity.

Property insurance can be provided in either **named-peril policies** or **open-peril policies**. Named-peril policies insure against loss only from perils that are specifically named in the policy, whereas open-peril policies insure against all perils except those specifically excluded by the policy. For example, many homeowners in low-lying areas are required to buy flood insurance. This insurance covers only losses due to flooding, so it is a named-peril policy. A homeowner's insurance policy, which protects the house from fire, hurricane, tornado, and other damage, is an example of an open-peril policy.

Casualty or liability insurance also protects against financial losses because of a claim of negligence. Liability insurance is bought not only by manufacturers who might be sued because of product defects but also by many types of professionals, including physicians, lawyers, and building contractors. Whereas the risk exposure in property insurance policies is relatively easy to predict, since it is usually limited to the value of the property, liability risk exposure is much more difficult to determine.

Liability risk exposure can have long lag times (often referred to as "tails"). This means that a liability claim may be filed long after the policy expires. Consider liability claims filed against the manufacturers of light airplanes. In the 1950s, 1960s, and 1970s, Cessna and Piper produced airplanes that are still being used today. The companies often get sued when one of these 40- or 50-year-old planes crash. Insurance premiums grew so large in the 1980s due to the extensive lag time that both Cessna and Piper had to stop producing private airplanes. The cost of the liability insurance put the price of the planes out of reach of most private pilots.

There has been extensive publicity about high liability awards given by juries. These awards have often been well above what the insurance companies could have predicted. Liability insurance premiums continue to rise as a result. Some states have attempted to limit liability awards in an effort to contain these insurance costs.

Reinsurance One way that insurance companies may reduce their risk exposure is to obtain **reinsurance**. Reinsurance allocates a portion of the risk to another company in exchange for a portion of the premium. Reinsurance allows insurance companies to write larger policies because a portion of the policy is actually held by another firm.

About 10% of all property and casualty insurance is reinsured. Smaller insurance firms obtain reinsurance more frequently than large firms. You can think of it as insurance for the insurance company.

Since the originator of the policy usually has more to lose than the reinsurer, the moral hazard and adverse selection problems are small. This means that little specific information about the risk being reinsured is required. As a result of the simplified information requirements, the reinsurance market consists of relatively standardized contracts.

Terrorism Risk Insurance Act of 2002 The September 11, 2001, terrorist attacks led the insurance industry to rethink its exposure to losses that could potentially destroy even the best-capitalized insurance company. Following an intensive lobbying effort by the insurance industry, new legislation was passed on November 26, 2002, limiting the amount insurance firms would be required to pay out in the event of future attacks. The Terrorism Risk Insurance Act is annually renewed to adjust the limits on the exposure insurance companies face. Should an act of terrorism occur, as defined in the legislation, the government will pay 90% of the losses. Losses in excess of $100 billion are not covered.

Insurance Regulation

Insurance companies are subject to less federal regulation than many other financial institutions. In fact, the McCarran-Ferguson Act of 1945 explicitly exempts insurance from federal regulation. The primary federal regulator is the Internal Revenue Service, which administers special taxation rules.

Most insurance regulation occurs at the state level. Not only must an insurance company follow the standards set by the state in which it is chartered, but it must also comply with the regulations set in any state in which it does business. New York requires that any insurance company doing business in the state comply with its investment standards. Because New York is such a big market, regardless of home state, virtually every company complies. This makes the New York State regulations almost the same as national regulations.

The purpose of most regulations is to protect policyholders from losses due to the insolvency of the company. To accomplish this, insurance companies are restricted as to their asset composition and minimum capital ratio. All states also require that insurance agents and brokers obtain state licenses to sell each kind of insurance: life, property and casualty, and health. These licenses are to ensure that all agents have a minimum level of knowledge about the products they sell.

THE PRACTICING MANAGER

Insurance Management

Insurance companies, like banks, are in the financial intermediation business of transforming one type of asset into another for the public. Insurance companies use the premiums paid on policies to invest in assets such as bonds, stocks, mortgages, and other loans; the earnings from these assets are then used to pay out claims on the policies. In effect, insurance companies transform assets such as bonds, stocks, and loans into insurance policies that provide a set of services (for example, claim adjustments, savings plans, friendly insurance agents). If the insurance company's production process of asset transformation efficiently provides its customers with adequate insurance services at low cost and if it can earn high returns on its investments, it will make profits; if not, it will suffer losses.

In Chapters 2 and 7 the concepts of adverse selection and moral hazard allowed us to understand why financial intermediaries such as insurance companies are important in the economy. Here we use the adverse selection and moral hazard concepts to explain many management practices specific to the insurance industry.

In the case of an insurance policy, moral hazard arises when the existence of insurance encourages the insured party to take risks that increase the likelihood of an insurance payoff. For example, a person covered by burglary insurance might not take as many precautions to prevent a burglary because the insurance company will reimburse most of the losses if a theft occurs. Adverse selection holds that the people most likely to receive large insurance payoffs are the ones who will want to purchase insurance the most. For example, a person suffering from a terminal disease would want to take out the biggest life and medical insurance policies possible, thereby exposing the insurance company to potentially large losses. Minimizing adverse selection and moral hazard to reduce these payouts is therefore an extremely important goal for insurance companies, and this goal explains the insurance practices we discuss here.

Screening

To reduce adverse selection, insurance companies try to screen out poor insurance risks from good ones. Effective information collection procedures are therefore an important principle of insurance management.

When you apply for auto insurance, the first thing your insurance agent does is ask you questions about your driving record (number of speeding tickets and accidents), the type of car you are insuring, and certain personal matters (age, marital status). If you are applying for life insurance, you go through a similar grilling, but you are asked even more personal questions about such things as your health, smoking habits, and drug and alcohol use. The life insurance company even orders a medical evaluation (usually done by an independent company) that involves taking blood and urine samples. The insurance company uses the information you provide to allocate you to a risk class—a statistical estimate of how likely you are to have an insurance claim. Based on this information, the insurance company can decide whether to accept you for the insurance or to turn you down because you pose too high a risk and thus would be an unprofitable customer for the insurance company.

Risk-Based Premium

Charging insurance premiums on the basis of how much risk a policyholder poses for the insurance company is a time-honored principle of insurance management. Adverse selection explains why this principle is so important to insurance company profitability.

To understand why an insurance company finds it necessary to have risk-based premiums, let's examine an example of risk-based insurance premiums that at first glance seems unfair. Harry and Sally, both with no accidents or speeding tickets, apply for auto insurance. Harry, however, is 20 years old, while Sally is 40. Normally, Harry will be charged a much higher premium than Sally. Insurance companies do this because young males have a much higher accident rate than older females. Suppose, though, that one insurance company did not base its premiums on a risk classification but rather just charged a premium based on the average combined risk for those it insures. Then Sally would be charged too much and Harry too little. Sally could go to another insurance company and get a lower rate, while Harry would sign up for the insurance. Because Harry's premium isn't high enough to cover the accidents he is likely to have, on average the company would lose money on Harry. Only with a premium based on a risk classification, so that Harry is charged more, can the insurance company make a profit.*

Restrictive Provisions

Restrictive provisions in policies are another insurance management tool for reducing moral hazard. Such provisions discourage policyholders from engaging in risky activities that make an insurance claim more likely. One type of restrictive provision keeps the policyholder from benefiting from behavior that makes a claim more likely. For example, life insurance companies have provisions in their policies that eliminate death benefits if the insured person commits suicide. Restrictive provisions may also require certain behavior on the part of the insured that makes a claim less likely. A company renting motor scooters may be required to provide helmets for renters in order to be covered for any liability associated with the rental. The role of restrictive provisions is not unlike that of restrictive covenants on debt contracts described in Chapter 7: Both serve to reduce moral hazard by ruling out undesirable behavior.

Prevention of Fraud

Insurance companies also face moral hazard because an insured person has an incentive to lie to the company and seek a claim even if the claim is not valid. For example, a person who has not complied with the restrictive provisions of an insurance

*You may recognize that the example here is in fact an example of the lemons problem described in Chapter 7.

contract may still submit a claim. Even worse, a person may file claims for events that did not actually occur. Thus, an important management principle for insurance companies is conducting investigations to prevent fraud so that only policyholders with valid claims receive compensation.

Cancellation of Insurance

Being prepared to cancel policies is another insurance management tool. Insurance companies can discourage moral hazard by threatening to cancel a policy when the insured person engages in activities that make a claim more likely. If your auto insurance company makes it clear that if a driver gets too many speeding tickets, coverage will be canceled, you will be less likely to speed.

Deductibles

The deductible is the fixed amount by which the insured's loss is reduced when a claim is paid off. A $250 deductible on an auto policy, for example, means that if you suffer a loss of $1,000 because of an accident, the insurance company will pay you only $750. Deductibles are an additional management tool that helps insurance companies reduce moral hazard. With a deductible, you experience a loss along with the insurance company when you make a claim. Because you also stand to lose when you have an accident, you have an incentive to drive more carefully. A deductible thus makes a policyholder act more in line with what is profitable for the insurance company; moral hazard has been reduced. And because moral hazard has been reduced, the insurance company can lower the premium by more than enough to compensate the policyholder for the existence of the deductible.

Another function of the deductible is to eliminate the administrative costs of small losses by forcing the insured to bear these losses.

Coinsurance

When a policyholder shares a percentage of the losses along with the insurance company, their arrangement is called **coinsurance**. For example, some medical insurance plans provide coverage for 80% of medical bills, and the insured person pays 20% after a certain deductible has been met. Coinsurance works to reduce moral hazard in exactly the same way that a deductible does. A policyholder who suffers a loss along with the insurance company has less incentive to take actions, such as going to the doctor unnecessarily, that involve higher claims. Coinsurance is thus another useful management tool for insurance companies.

Limits on the Amount of Insurance

Another important principle of insurance management is that there should be limits on the amount of insurance provided, even though a customer is willing to pay for more coverage. The higher the insurance coverage, the more the insured person can gain from risky activities that make an insurance claim more likely and hence the greater the moral hazard. For example, if Zelda's car were insured for more than its true value, she might not take proper precautions to prevent its theft, such as making sure that the key is always removed or putting in an alarm system. If her car were stolen, she would come out ahead because the excessive insurance payoff would allow her to buy an even better car. By contrast, when the insurance payment is lower than the value of her car, she will suffer a loss if it is stolen and will thus take the proper precautions to prevent this from happening. Insurance companies must always make sure that their coverage is not so high that moral hazard leads to large losses.

Summary

Effective insurance management requires several practices: information collection and screening of potential policyholders, risk-based premiums, restrictive provisions, prevention of fraud, cancellation of insurance, deductibles, coinsurance, and limits on the amount of insurance. All of these practices reduce moral hazard and adverse selection by making it harder for policyholders to benefit from engaging in activities that increase the amount and likelihood of claims. With smaller benefits available, the poor insurance risks (those who are more likely to engage in the activities in the first place) see less benefit from the insurance and are thus less likely to seek it out.

Credit Default Swaps

CDSs have been mentioned several times earlier in this text, but it is appropriate to discuss them in the context of insurance. A credit default swap (CDS) is insurance against default on a financial instrument, usually some kind of securitized bond. Typically, the holder of debt will buy a CDS from an investment or insurance company, such as AIG, to shift the risk of default to a third party. When the probability of default is low, the cost of the CDS is similarly low. By lowering the risk of these insured bonds with default insurance, the market price of the bonds would increase.

Between 1995 and 2009 the amount of CDSs exploded, along with the marketing of securitized mortgages. By their peak in 2008 there were about $62 trillion of CDSs outstanding (note that the gross domestic product of the entire world is about $60 trillion). A London subsidiary of the giant insurance company, AIG, was issuing vast amounts. Since most players in the market did not anticipate the collapse of the real estate and mortgage bond markets, few saw great risk in the CDSs being issued around the world. One reason for the growth was that there was no real regulatory restraint.

At the beginning of this chapter, we noted that one of the primary tenets of insurance is that before you can buy an insurance policy, you must have something to lose. You cannot buy insurance on your neighbor just because you think he has been looking unhealthy lately. The CDSs market allowed speculators to do just that with companies. If they saw a company that looked unhealthy, even though they may not hold any interest in the firm, they could buy insurance against its failure. Many likened this to gambling, and in fact, Congress passed a law that exempted CDSs from state gaming laws as part of the Commodity Futures Modernization Act of 2000.

As the mortgage crisis unfolded, the true risk that had been accepted by issuers of CDSs became clear, which led to their near bankruptcy and eventual need for a $182 billion bailout of AIG.

> CONFLICTS OF INTEREST

The AIG Blowup

American International Group, better known as AIG, was a trillion-dollar insurance giant and before 2008 was one of the 20 largest companies in the world. A small separate unit, AIG's Financial Products division, went into the credit default swap business in a big way, insuring over $400 billion of securities, of which $57 billion was debt securities backed by subprime mortgages. Lehman Brothers' troubles and eventual bankruptcy on September 15, 2008, revealed that subprime securities were worth much less than they were being valued on the books, and investors came to the realization that AIG's losses, which had already been substantial in the first half of the year, could bankrupt the company. Lenders to AIG then pulled back with a vengeance, and AIG could not raise enough capital to stay afloat.

On September 16 the Federal Reserve and the U.S. Treasury decided to rescue AIG because its failure was deemed potentially catastrophic for the financial system. Not only were banks and mutual funds large holders of AIG's debt, but the bankruptcy of AIG would have rendered all the credit default swaps it had sold worthless, thereby imposing huge losses on financial institutions which had bought them. The Federal Reserve set up an $85 billion credit facility (later raised to $182 billion) to provide liquidity to AIG. The rescue did not come cheap however. AIG was charged a very high interest rate on the loans from the Fed, and the government was given the rights to an 80% stake in the company if it survived. Maurice Greenberg, the former CEO of the company, described the government's actions as a "nationalization" of AIG.

Insurance companies have never been viewed as posing a risk to the financial system as a whole and this is why their regulation has been left to insurance commissions in each state. Since the problems at AIG nearly brought down the U.S. financial system, this view is no longer tenable. The insurance industry will never be the same.

Monoline Insurance Instead of providing credit insurance with CDSs, an insurance company may supply it directly, just as with any insurance policy. However, insurance regulations do not allow property/casualty insurance companies, life insurance companies, or insurance companies with multiple lines of business to underwrite credit insurance. **Monoline insurance companies**, which specialize in credit insurance alone, are therefore the only insurance companies that are allowed to provide insurance that guarantees the timely repayment of bond principal and interest when a debt issuer defaults. These insurance companies, such as Ambac Financial Group and MBIA, have become particularly important in the municipal bond market, where they insure a large percentage of these securities. When a municipal security with a lower credit rating, say an A rating, has an insurance policy from a monoline insurer, it takes on the credit rating of the monoline insurer, say AAA. This lowers the interest cost for the municipality and so makes it worthwhile for the municipality to pay premiums for this insurance policy. Of course, to do this, the monoline insurers need to have a very high credit rating. When the monoline insurers experienced credit downgrades during the subprime financial crisis, not only did they suffer, but so did the municipal bond market (see the Conflicts of Interest box, "The Subprime Financial Crisis and the Monoline Insurers").

Pensions

A **pension plan** is an asset pool that accumulates over an individual's working years and is paid out during the nonworking years. Pension plans represent the fastest-growing financial intermediary. There are a number of reasons for this rapid growth.

> CONFLICTS OF INTEREST

The Subprime Financial Crisis and the Monoline Insurers

One spillover from the subprime financial crisis was a hit to the monoline insurers, with spillover effects in the municipal bond market. Unfortunately for the monoline insurers, they insured not only municipal bonds but also debt securities backed by subprime mortgages. With rising defaults on these mortgages, monoline insurers started to take big losses, resulting in credit downgrades from their AAA status. This weakened the value of their insurance guarantees, not only on subprime securities but on municipal securities as well. As the subprime crisis got into full swing, the markets took the view that monoline insurance was not worth much and so municipal bonds began to trade at lower prices based solely on the municipality's credit rating. The result was that state and local governments now found their interest costs rising. They were hit by a double whammy from the subprime financial crisis of higher borrowing costs and lower tax revenues because of their state's weaker economies. The result was not only weaker state and local finances but also cutbacks in spending for roads, schools, and hospitals.

As the United States became more urban, people realized that they could not rely on their children to care for them in their retirement. In a rural culture, families tend to stay together on the farm. The property passes from generation to generation with an implicit understanding that the younger generations will care for the older ones. When families became more dispersed and moved off farms, both the opportunity for and the expectation of extensive financial support of the older generations declined.

A second factor contributing to the growth of pension plans is that people are living longer and retiring younger. Again, in the rural setting, people often remained productive well into their retirement years. Many companies in urban America, however, encourage older workers to retire. They are often earning high wages as a result of seniority, yet may be less productive than younger workers. The result of this trend toward younger retirement and longer lives is that the average person can expect to spend more years in retirement. These years must be funded somehow, and the pension plan is often the vehicle of choice.

Types of Pensions

Pension plans can be categorized in several ways. They may be defined-benefit or defined-contribution plans, and they may be public or private.

Defined-Benefit Pension Plans

Under a **defined-benefit plan**, the plan sponsor promises the employees a specific benefit when they retire. The payout is usually determined with a formula that uses the number of years worked and the employee's final salary. For example, a pension benefit may be calculated by the following formula:

$$\text{Annual payment} = 2\% \times \text{average of final 3 years' income} \times \text{years of service}$$

In this case, if a worker had been employed for 35 years and the average wages during the last three years were \$50,000, the annual pension benefit would be

$$0.02 \times \$50{,}000 \times 35 = \$35{,}000 \text{ per year}$$

The defined-benefit plan puts the burden on the employer to provide adequate funds to ensure that the agreed payments can be made. External audits of pension plans are required to determine whether sufficient funds have been contributed by the company. If sufficient funds are set aside by the firm for this purpose, the plan is **fully funded**. If more than enough funds are available, the plan is **overfunded**. Often, insufficient funds are available and the fund is **underfunded**. For example, if Jane Brown contributes \$100 per year into her pension plan and the interest rate is 10%, after 10 years, the contributions and their interest earnings would be worth \$1,753.[1] If the defined benefit on her pension plan is \$1,753 or less after 10 years, the plan is fully funded because her contributions and earnings will cover this payment in full. But if the defined benefit is \$2,000, the plan is underfunded because her contributions and earnings do not cover this amount. Underfunding is most common when the employer fails to contribute adequately to the plan. Surprisingly, it is not illegal for a firm to sponsor an underfunded plan.

Defined-Contribution Pension Plans

As the name implies, instead of defining what the pension plan will pay, **defined-contribution plans** specify only what will be contributed to the fund. The retirement benefits depend entirely on the earnings of the fund. Corporate sponsors of defined-contribution plans usually put a fixed percentage of each employee's wages into the pension fund each pay period. In some instances, the employee also contributes to the plan. An insurance company or fund manager acts as trustee and invests the fund's assets. Frequently, employees are allowed to specify how the funds in their individual accounts will be invested. For example, an employee who is a conservative investor may prefer government securities, while one who is a more aggressive investor may prefer to have his or her retirement funds invested in corporate stock. When the employee retires, the balance in the pension account can be transferred into an annuity or some other form of distribution.

Defined-contribution pension plans are becoming increasingly popular. Many existing defined-benefit plans are converting to this form, and virtually all new plans are established as defined-contribution. One reason the defined-contribution plan is becoming so popular is that the onus is put on the employee rather than the employer to look out for the pension plan's performance. This reduces the liability of the employer.

One problem is that plan participants may not understand the need to diversify their holdings. For example, many firms actively encourage employees to invest in company stock. The firm's motivation is to better align employee interest with that of stockholders. The downside is that employees suffer twice should the firm fail. First, they lose their jobs, and second, their retirement portfolios evaporate. The collapse of Enron Inc. brought this issue forcibly to the public's attention. Another problem with defined-contribution plans is that many employees are not familiar enough with investments to make wise long-term choices.

---

[1]The \$100 contributed in year 1 would become worth $\$100 \times (1 + 0.10)^{10} = \$259.37$ at the end of 10 years; the \$100 contributed in year 2 would become worth $\$100 \times (1 + 0.10)^{9} = \$235.79$; and so on until the \$100 contributed in year 10 would become worth $\$100 \times (1 + 0.10) = \$110$. Adding these together, we get the total value of these contributions and their earnings at the end of 10 years as \$1,753.

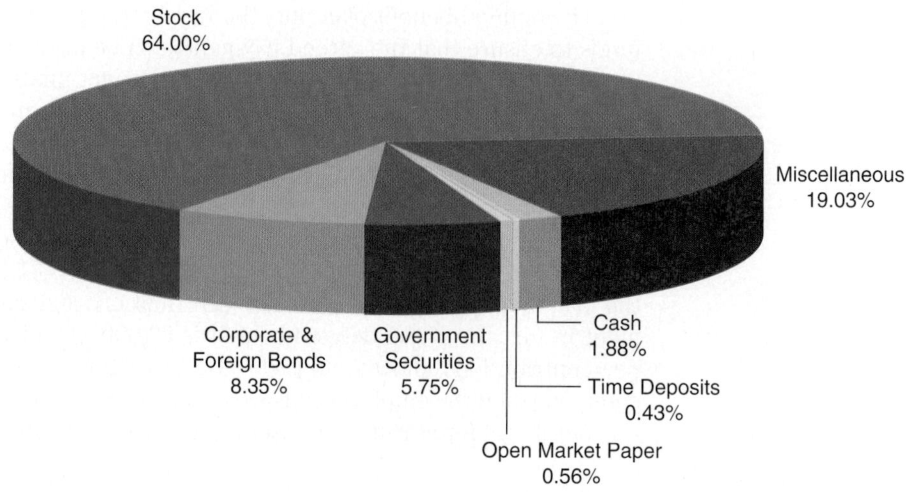

FIGURE 21.5 Distribution of Private Pension Plan Assets (end of 2015)

Source: http://www.federalreserve.gov/releases/z1/current/z1.pdf, Table L116.

Private and Public Pension Plans

Private pension plans, sponsored by employers, groups, and individuals, have grown rapidly as people have become more concerned about the viability of Social Security and more sophisticated about preparing for retirement. In the past, private pension plans invested mostly in government securities and corporate bonds. Although these instruments are still important pension plan assets, corporate stocks, mortgages, open market paper, and time deposits now play a significant role. Figure 21.5 shows the distribution of private pension plan assets. They are now the largest institutional investor in the stock market. This makes pension plan managers a potentially powerful force if they choose to exercise control over firm management (see the Mini-Case box, "Power to the Pensions").

> MINI-CASE

Power to the Pensions

One ramification of the growth of pension plans and other institutional investors is that the managers of these funds have the ability to exercise substantial control over corporate management. Clearly, when a pension fund manager, who controls many thousands of shares, calls a corporate officer, the officer is going to listen. Evidence suggests that fund managers actively apply the power they have to influence corporate management. For example, pension funds recently defeated management-sponsored antitakeover proxy proposals at Honeywell. And Texaco agreed to name a director from candidates submitted by the huge California Public Employees Retirement System. In addition, the stated mission of the Council of Institutional Investors is to "encourage trustees to take an active role in assuring that corporate actions are not taken at the expense of shareholders." It is possible that these actions will work to benefit shareholders, who do not individually wield enough clout to exert control. However, the clout shareholders wield when their shares are placed into a fund manager's hands may be sufficient to improve corporate management significantly.

An alternative to privately sponsored pension plans are the public plans, though in many cases there is very little difference between the two. A **public pension plan** is one that is sponsored by a governmental body.

Find detailed information on your Social Security benefits at **www.ssa.gov/**.

The largest of the public plans is the Federal Old Age Survivors and Disability Insurance Program (often called simply Social Security). This pension plan was established in 1935 to provide a safety net for aging Americans and is a "pay-as-you-go" system—money that workers contribute today pays benefits to current recipients. Future generations will be called on to pay benefits to the individuals who are currently contributing. Many people fear that the fund will be unable to meet its obligations by the time they retire. This fear is based on problems that the fund encountered in the 1970s and on the realization that a large number of people from the baby boom generation (born between 1946 and 1964) will swell the ranks of retirees in the rapidly approaching future.

The amount of the Social Security benefits a retiree receives is based on the person's earnings history. Workers contribute 6.2% of wages up to a current maximum wage of $118,500 (as of 2016). Employers contribute the same amount. There is a certain amount of redistribution in the benefits, with low-income workers receiving a relatively larger return on their investment than high-income workers. One way to evaluate the amount of the benefits of a pension plan is to determine how the monthly benefits compare to preretirement income. This replacement ratio ranged from 49% for someone earning $15,000 a year to 24% for someone earning $53,400.

Figure 21.6 shows that the total assets in the Social Security fund decreased in the late 1970s and early 1980s at the same time that the number of insured people was increasing. This situation led to a restructuring that included raising the program's contributions and reducing the program's benefits. To build public confidence, the Social Security system has started accumulating reserves to be used as the baby boom generation begins retiring.

The problem is that the 77 million baby boomers born between 1946 and 1964 are reaching their normal retirement ages. Meanwhile, the number of workers supporting each one of those retirees will fall from 3.3 to 2.1 by 2035. By 2021 the government predicts that costs will exceed revenues, leading to a reduction in the asset balance. Until recently the government issued a predicted date when the trust fund would be depleted. There are so many variables that affect this date that it now states a range of dates. It currently predicts that the Social Security trust fund will be depleted between 2028 and 2044 with a 95% probability (see Figure 21.7). After that, taxes would cover only 75% of benefits.

Access **www.ssab.gov** for the Social Security advisory board. This site will report the most current estimates for when the trust fund will be depleted.

A number of proposals are being considered to help keep Social Security viable for the future. The idea that AARP polling finds as the least objectionable is to raise the cap on the maximum amount that workers have to pay into the fund in any given year. The maximum wage that was taxed in 2016 was $118,500, which represents only 85% of all income. This is down from a tax on 90% of income in 1983. It is likely that this will be one area for change.

Another possible change concerns the minimum age when one can start receiving benefits. This was changed in 1984 to gradually rise so that those born after 1960 cannot start receiving full benefits until they are age 67. The original retirement age of 65 dates back to 1874, when a railroad company established a pension plan. The basis of this decision was that 65 was considered to be the maximum age at which one could safely operate a train. This rule was later incorporated into the Federal Railroad Retirement Act of 1934, which was used to support that retirement age when the Social Security Act was written. Since few Americans are required to

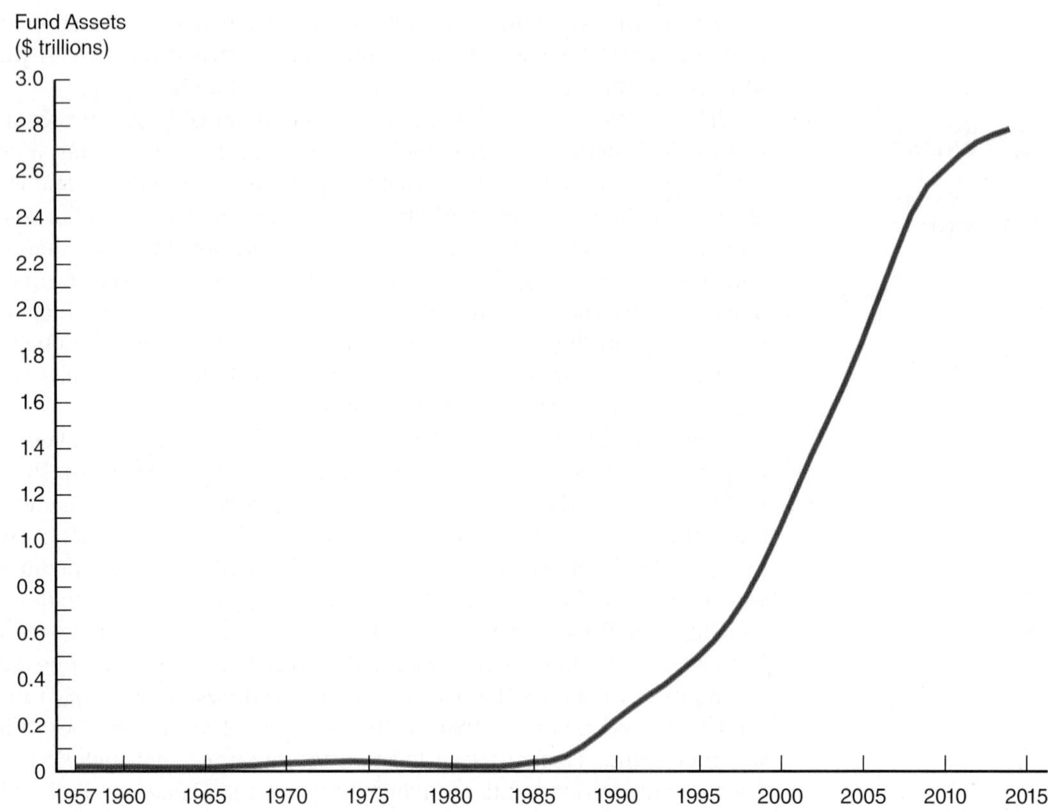

FIGURE 21.6 Social Security Fund Assets, 1957–2016

Source: http://www.ssa.gov/OACT/STATS/table4a3.html.

operate trains any more, there is some justification for reevaluating the retirement age. The good news is that relatively small changes to the retirement age have a large impact on the Social Security fund balance.

Another proposal generating support is to alter the way that cost-of-living adjustments to Social Security payments are calculated. Currently the benefit payments are adjusted annually based on the consumer price index (CPI). Economists argue that this overstates true inflation because it ignores consumers' switching to less expensive alternatives. While admitting some validity to this, critics argue that the CPI underestimates the increase in medical costs, which make up a large portion of retirees' budgets.

Still another suggestion is to recognize that beneficiaries are living longer than in the past and to adjust benefit payments to stretch them over a longer period of time.

Prior to the stock market falling in 2000, many investors were calling for the privatization of Social Security. The biggest obstacle to privatization is that funds diverted into private accounts would not be available to pay current retirees' benefits. This exacerbates the looming problem rather than solving it. Analysts estimate that the cost of transitioning to a fully funded privatized plan would be enormous—about $100 billion. Over time, analysts argue, privatization would gradually transform

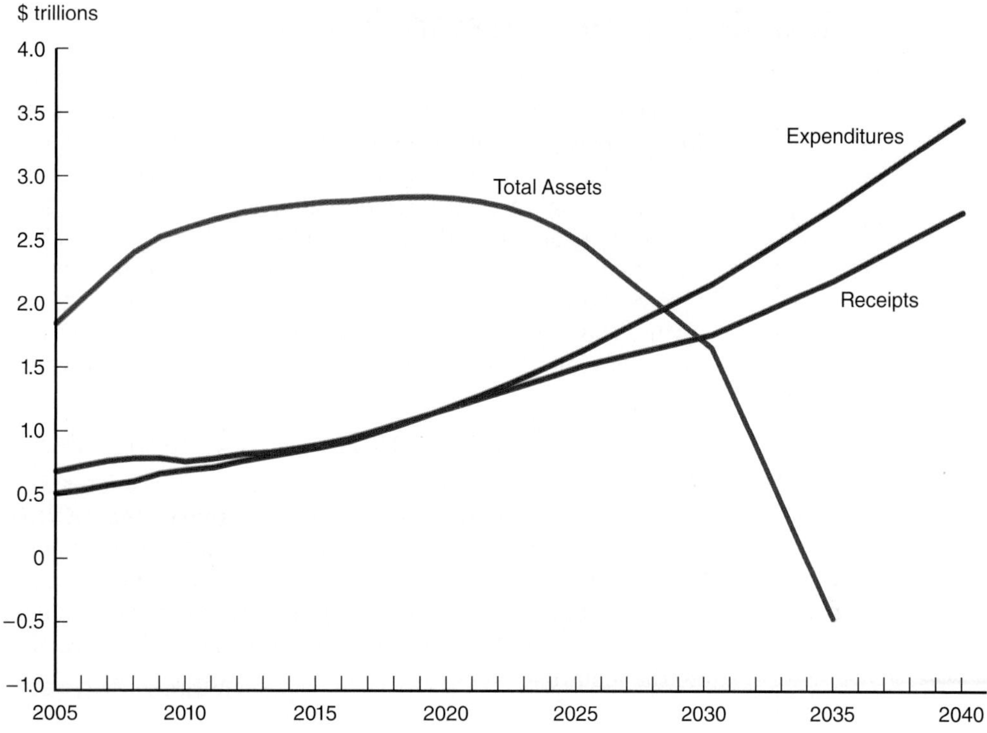

FIGURE 21.7 Projected Social Security Trust Fund Assets

Source: http://www.ssab.gov/Details-Page/ArticleID/207/Social-Security-Why-Action-Should-be-Taken-Soon-December-2010.

Social Security from an unfunded, pay-as-you-go system to a fully funded pension with real assets. However, falling stock prices in 2000–2002 and again in 2007–2009 have reduced support for all privatization options.

In the short term, Social Security reform is more likely to take the form of an increase in tax, a reduction in benefits, a delay in receiving benefits, or all three. For example, the age at which benefits begin is already scheduled to increase from 65 to 67. Some plans suggest delaying benefits until age 70.

We must remember that estimates on the health of Social Security are based on current facts as they are known. Many factors can change to cause the estimates to change. For example, research on cures for cancer has received a great deal of publicity recently. If a cure for any major cause of death is found, the fund will be in greater trouble than currently thought.

It is extremely difficult to make accurate estimates on the health of the Social Security system. In 1995, for example, the Social Security Administration estimated that the fund would be depleted by 2029, instead of the the mid 2030s currently projected. Many factors affect the fund balance including life expectancies, birth rates, and even the rate of legal and illegal immigration. While it would be political disaster for the government to allow the program to fail, current workers should realize that they should not rely on it to provide the majority of their retirement cash flow. In the future, the proportion of preretirement income it replaces may well continue to decrease.

Regulation of Pension Plans

For many years, pension plans were relatively free of government regulation. Many companies provided pension benefits as rewards for long years of good service and used the benefits as an incentive. Frequently, pension benefits were paid out of current income. When the firm failed or was acquired by another firm, the benefits ended. During the Great Depression, widespread pension plan failures led to increased regulation and to the establishment of the Social Security system.

A major U.S. Supreme Court decision in 1949 established that pension benefits were a legitimate part of collective bargaining, the negotiation of contracts by unions. This decision led to a great increase in the number of plans in existence as unions pressured employers to establish such plans for union members.

Employee Retirement Income Security Act

The most important and most comprehensive legislation affecting pension funds is the **Employee Retirement Income Security Act (ERISA)**, passed in 1974. ERISA set certain standards that must be followed by all pension plans. Failure to follow the provisions of the act may cause a plan to lose its advantageous tax status. The motivation for the act was that many workers who had contributed to plans for years were losing their benefits when plans failed. The principal features of the act are the following:

Access **www.pbgc.gov** for additional information about the Pension Benefit Guarantee Corporation.

- ERISA established guidelines for funding.
- It provided that employees switching jobs may transfer their credits from one employer plan to the next.
- Plans must have minimum vesting requirements. *Vesting* refers to how long an employee must work for the company to be eligible for pension benefits. The maximum permissible vesting period is seven years, though most plans allow for vesting in less time. Employee contributions are always immediately vested.
- It increased the disclosure requirements for pension plans, providing employees with more ample information about the health and investments of their pension plans.
- It assigned the responsibility of regulatory oversight to the Department of Labor.

Access **www.pbgc/gov/docs/2005databook.pdf** for details on extensive statistics on the health of PBGC.

ERISA also established the **Pension Benefit Guarantee Corporation** (PBGC or simply called **Penny Benny**), a government agency that performs a role similar to that of the FDIC. It insures pension benefits up to a limit (currently just over $57,000 per year per person) if a company with an underfunded pension plan goes bankrupt or is unable to meet its pension obligations for other reasons. Penny Benny charges pension plans a premium to pay for this insurance, but it can also borrow funds up to $100 million from the U.S. Treasury. Penny Benny currently pays benefits to about 887,000 retirees from more than 4,500 failed pension plans.

Over 66% of defined-benefit pension plan assets are invested in stocks. When the market prices were high, most defined-benefit pension plans were adequately funded. However, the market fall in 2009 along with low interest rates and a weak economy have put many pension plans in jeopardy. As a result, in 2015 PBGC was in the red by $76.3 billion.

The accounting for pension plans makes it very difficult to accurately assess whether a fund is over- or underfunded. The assumptions behind such calculations are subject to constant revision and argument. Cash-strapped firms have tremendous incentive to underfund their pension plans, and Congress is reluctant to enforce higher payments that could put a firm at greater risk of failure.

The Pension Benefit Guaranty Corporation is rapidly facing a funding crisis that could have far-reaching effects. Many defined-benefit pension funds are in severe trouble due to the increasing life spans of their pensioners, increased medical costs, and weak corporate income that has made it difficult to keep up with funding obligations. Currently, the airline and steel industries are responsible for the bulk of PBGC's claims. For example, United Airlines terminated its defined benefit program in 2005. Since then, PBGC has paid over $7.6 billion in claims to 122,000 vested United participants. Figure 21.8 shows annual payments made since 1980 to failed plan participants.

Many firms with defined-benefit plans find it hard to compete against firms with much lower cost defined-contribution plans. This competitive disadvantage increases the likelihood that the firms may not survive to pay down their deficits. For example, General Motors' profit margin per car is about 0.5%. Without the burden of pension and retiree health care costs, the margin would be about 5.5%. Morgan Stanley estimates that the benefits cost is $1,784 per car for GM, while it is only $200 per car for Toyota.

Firms often fail when they face a cost disadvantage. Due to higher costs, including pension obligations, Bethlehem Steel, LTV, and National Steel all filed for bankruptcy in 2002 and terminated their pension plans. PBGC is now paying over 200,000 former steel workers' benefits. International Steel Group Inc. (ISG) has acquired the

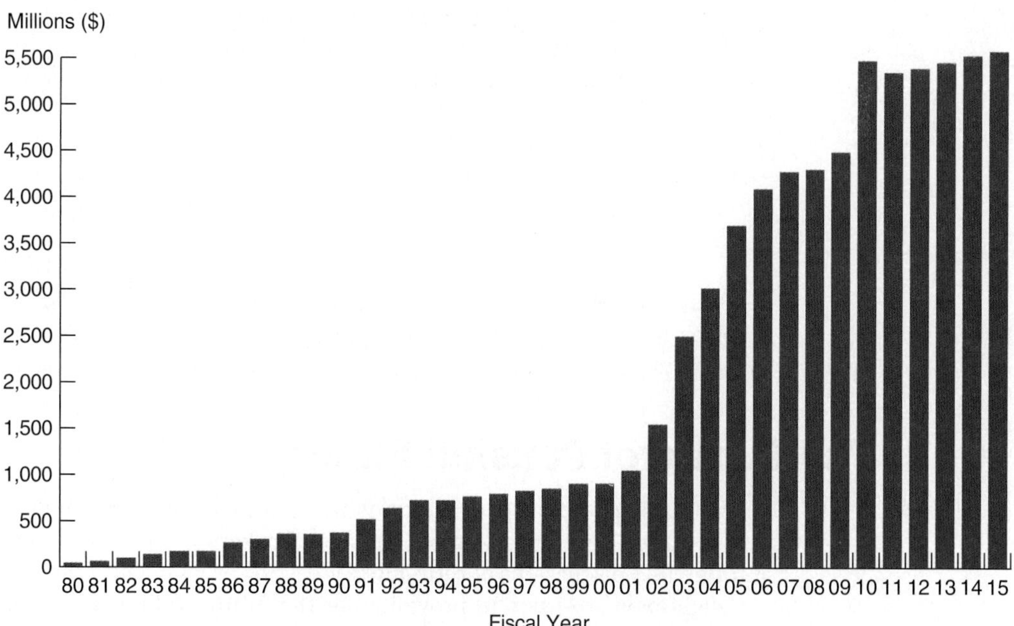

FIGURE 21.8 Total PBGC Benefit Payments

Source: http://www.pbgc.gov/documents/2015-annual-report.pdf#page=7.

mills of these old steel companies and is now the largest steel producer in the country. Its defined-contribution cost for employees is about $45 million. Prior to its bankruptcy, Bethlehem Steel alone was paying out $500 million a year in pension benefits.

If firms with defined benefit plans continue to fail, PBGC will be forced to assume their pension funds' liabilities. These obligations could quickly surpass the financial resources available to PBGC if the economy remains weak. In that event, taxpayers may be called upon to make up the difference.

The government is not strictly responsible for backing up PBGC; however, most observers feel it could not politically allow pensioners to lose their benefits. The temporary fix is to allow firms to use a higher interest rate in their pension calculations so that their pension liability is reduced. The hope is that the economy will continue to revive, stocks will rise, and interest rates increase. This same technique (called regulatory forbearance) was used to prolong the savings and loan crisis in the 1980s. We can only hope it works better this time.

The Pension Protection Act of 2006 was passed to address the growing problem with underfunded and failing pension plans. This legislation provides for stronger pension funding rules, greater transparency, and a stronger pension insurance system.

Individual Retirement Plans

The Pension Reform Act of 1978 updated the Self-Employed Individuals Tax Retirement Act of 1962 to authorize **individual retirement accounts (IRAs)**. IRAs permitted people (such as those who are self-employed) who are not covered by other pension plans to contribute into a tax-deferred savings account. Legislation in 1981 and 1982 expanded the eligibility of these accounts to make them available to almost everyone. IRAs proved extremely popular, to the extent that their use resulted in significant losses of tax revenues to the government. That led Congress to include provisions in the Tax Reform Act of 1986 that sharply curtail eligibility.

Keogh plans are a retirement savings option for the self-employed. Funds can be deposited with a depository institution, life insurance company, or securities firm. The owner of the Keogh is often allowed some discretion as to how the funds will be invested.

On January 1, 1997, the Small Business Protection Act of 1996 went into effect. This act created simplified retirement plans with so-called SIMPLE IRAs and 401(k) plans for businesses with 100 or fewer employees. SIMPLE retirement plans are becoming significantly more popular, especially among the smallest businesses.

The Future of Pension Funds

We can expect that pension funds will continue their growth and popularity as the population continues to grow and age. Workers in their early years of employment often find discussions of retirement investing creeping into their conversations. This heightened attention to providing for the future will result in an increased number of pension funds as well as a greater variety of pension fund options to choose among. We can also expect to see pension funds gain increased power over corporations as they control increasing amounts of stock.

SUMMARY

1. Insurance companies exist because people are risk-averse and prefer to transfer risk away from themselves. Insurance benefits people's lives by reducing the size of reserves they would have to maintain to cover possible loss of life or property.
2. Adverse selection and moral hazard are problems inherent to the insurance business. Many of the provisions of insurance policies—including deductibles, application screening, and risk-based premiums—are aimed at reducing their effects.
3. Insurance is usually divided into two primary types, life insurance and property and casualty insurance. Many life insurance products also serve as savings vehicles. Property and casualty insurance usually has a much shorter term than most life insurance.
4. Because life insurance liabilities are very predictable, these insurers are able to invest in long-term assets. Property and casualty insurance companies must keep their assets more liquid to pay out on unexpected losses.
5. Pension plans are rapidly growing as a longer-lived generation plans for early retirement.
6. There are two primary types of pension plans: defined-benefit and defined-contribution. Defined-benefit plans pay benefits according to a formula that is established in advance. Defined-contribution plans specify only how much is to be saved; benefits depend on the returns generated by the plans.
7. The largest public pension plan is Social Security, which is a pay-as-you-go system. Current retirees receive payments from current workers. Many people are concerned that as the number of retirees increases, the amount paid in to the Social Security system will not be sufficient to cover the sums being paid out.
8. Most private pension plans are insured by the Pension Benefit Guarantee Corporation, which pays benefits when a plan's sponsor goes bankrupt or is otherwise unable to make payments.

KEY TERMS

annuity, p. 509
casualty (liability) insurance, p. 515
certainty equivalent, p. 505
coinsurance, p. 519
deductible, p. 506
defined-benefit plan, p. 522
defined-contribution plan, p. 523
Employee Retirement Income Security Act (ERISA), p. 528
fully funded plan, p. 523
individual retirement accounts (IRAs), p. 530
law of large numbers, p. 510
monoline insurance companies, p. 521
mutual insurance companies, p. 508
named-peril policies, p. 515
open-peril policies, p. 515
overfunded plan, p. 523
Pension Benefit Guarantee Corporation (Penny Benny), p. 528
pension plan, p. 521
private pension plans, p. 524
property insurance, p. 515
public pension plan, p. 525
reinsurance, p. 516
stock company, p. 508
underfunded plan, p. 523
underwriters, p. 507

QUESTIONS

1. Camille is offered two options: (1) receive \$100 or (2) flip a coin and get \$0 if she loses or \$200 if she wins. Assuming Camille prefers the first option; would you say Camille is more or less prone to buy insurance on her house? Why?
2. Why do insurance companies not allow people to buy insurance on personally unrelated risks?
3. Suppose an insurance company decides to insure the earnings obtained by a professional tennis player (in the event of an injury), provided she does not engage in activities like skydiving or skiing. Which asymmetric information problem is the insurance company trying to avoid?
4. Distinguish between adverse selection and moral hazard as they relate to the insurance industry.
5. How do insurance companies protect themselves against losses due to adverse selection and moral hazard?
6. Distinguish between independent agents and exclusive agents.
7. Are most insurance companies organized as mutuals or stock companies?

8. How are insurance companies able to predict their losses from claims accurately enough to let them price their policies such that they will make a profit?
9. What is the difference between term life insurance and whole life insurance?
10. What risks do property and casualty insurance policies protect against?
11. As technology improves over time, fewer workers are needed to produce the same goods as before. Do you think this might have an implication for pay-as-you-go systems?
12. Most rich countries have increasingly aging populations. Discuss the effect of this tendency on pay-as-you-go systems.
13. Why have private pension plans grown rapidly in recent years?
14. What is a pay-as-you-go pension plan?
15. Discuss the effects of a regulation that allows all currently illegal workers to become contributors to Social Security.

QUANTITATIVE PROBLEMS

1. Research indicates that the 1,000,000 cars in your city experience unrecoverable losses of $250,000,000 per year from theft, collisions, and so on. If 30% of premiums are used to cover expenses, what premium must be charged to car owners?
2. Calculate the expected payoff of a game in which you can lose $200 with probability 0.3, win $240 with probability 0.5 and win $700 with probability 0.2.
3. Refer to the previous exercise. Suppose an individual prefers to play the game rather than to accept $200 with certainty. Is this individual risk averse or a risk lover?
4. Assume that the monthly payments faced by an insurance company are normally distributed with a mean of $100,000 and a standard deviation of $12,000. Determine the probability than in a given month the company will have to pay more than $124,000.
5. Kio Outfitters estimated the following losses and probabilities from past experience:

Loss ($)	Probability (%)
30,000	0.25
15,000	0.75
10,000	1.50
5,000	2.50
1,000	5.00
250	15.00
0	75.00

What is the probability Kio will experience a loss of $5,000 or greater? If an insurance company offers a loss policy with a $1,500 deductible, what is the most Kio will pay?

6. A client needs assistance with retirement planning. Here are the facts:
   - The client, Dave, is 21 years old. He wants to retire at 65.
   - Dave has disposable income of $2,000 per month.
   - The IRA Dave has chosen has an average annual return of 8%.

   If Dave contributes half of his disposable income to the account, what will it be worth at 65? How much would he need to contribute to have $5,000,000 at 65?
7. When opening an IRA account, investors have two options. With a regular IRA account, funds added are not taxed initially, but are taxed when withdrawn. With a Roth IRA, the funds are taxed initially, but not when withdrawn. If an investor wants to contribute $15,000 before taxes to an IRA, what will be the difference after 30 years between the two options? Assume that the investor is currently in the 25% tax bracket, and that the IRA will earn 6% per year.
8. An employee contributes $200 a year (at the end of the year) to her pension plan. What would be the total contributions and value of the account after five years? Assume that the plan earns 15% per year over the period.
9. Paul's car slid off the icy road, causing $2,500 in damage to his car. He was also treated for minor injuries, costing $1,300. His car insurance has a $500 deductible, after which the full loss is paid. His health insurance has a $100 deductible and covers 75% of medical cost (total). What were Paul's out-of-pocket costs from the incident?

WEB EXERCISES

Insurance Companies and Pension Funds

1. There are many sites on the Web to help you compute whether you are properly preparing for your retirement. One of the better is offered by Quicken. You will find it at **http://cgi.money.cnn.com/tools**.

   Use the retirement calculator listed under "Retirement." Have you set aside enough retirement money to last your lifetime? The earlier you start, the easier it will be.

   In general, your retirement funds will come from four sources:

   - Pension plans
   - Social Security
   - Tax-deferred savings
   - Basic (taxable) savings

   Use the Retirement Planner to predict the income from the first two, and to determine how much you will need to save to make up the balance for your retirement goals.

2. The Internet offers many calculators to help consumers estimate their needs for various financial services. When using these tools, you must remember that they are usually sponsored by financial intermediaries that hope to sell you products. Visit one such site at **www.finaid.org/calculators/lifeinsuranceneeds.phtml** and calculate how much life insurance you need. Do you have another life insurance policy? Use the calculator to see if that policy is large enough.

CHAPTER

22

Investment Banks, Security Brokers and Dealers, and Venture Capital Firms

> PREVIEW

If you decide to take advantage of that hot stock tip you just heard about from your roommate, you may need to interact with a securities company. Similarly, as the new CFO of WWCF, a candy manufacturer, you may need a securities company if you are asked to coordinate a bond sale or to issue additional stock. If your grandfather decides to sell his firm to the public, you may need to help him by working with investment bankers at that securities company. Finally, if you are looking for capital to grow a small but successful start-up company, you may need the help of a venture capital firm.

The smooth functioning of securities markets, in which bonds and stocks are traded, involves several financial institutions, including securities brokers and dealers, investment banks, and venture capital firms. None of these institutions were included in our list of financial intermediaries in Chapter 2 because they do not perform the intermediation function of acquiring funds by issuing liabilities and then using the funds to acquire financial assets. Nonetheless, they are important in the process of channeling funds from savers to spenders.

To begin our look at how securities markets work, recall the distinction between primary and secondary securities markets discussed in Chapter 2. In a **primary market**, new issues of a security are sold to buyers by the corporation or government agency ultimately using the funds. A **secondary market** then trades the securities that have been sold in the primary market (and so are secondhand). Investment banks assist in the initial sale of securities in the primary market; securities brokers and dealers assist in the trading of securities in the secondary markets. Finally, venture capital firms provide funds to companies not yet ready to sell securities to the public.

Investment Banks

Investment bankers were called "Masters of the Universe" in Tom Wolfe's *The Bonfire of the Vanities*. They are the elite on Wall Street. They have earned this reputation from the types of financial services they provide. Investment banks are best known as intermediaries that help corporations raise funds. However, this definition is far too narrow to accurately explain the many valuable and sophisticated services these companies provide. (Despite its name, an investment bank is not a bank in the ordinary sense; that is, it is not a financial intermediary that takes in deposits and then lends them out.) In addition to underwriting the initial sale of stocks, bonds, and commercial paper, **investment banks** play a pivotal role as deal makers in the mergers and acquisitions area, as intermediaries in the buying and selling of companies, and as private brokers to the very wealthy. Some well-known investment banking firms are Morgan Stanley, Bank of America, Merrill Lynch, Credit Suisse, and Goldman Sachs.

One feature of investment banks that distinguishes them from stockbrokers and dealers is that they usually earn their income from fees charged to clients rather than from commissions on stock trades. These fees are often set as a fixed percentage of the dollar size of the deal being worked. Because the deals frequently involve huge sums of money, the fees can be substantial. The percentage fee will be smaller for large deals, in the neighborhood of 3%, and much larger for smaller deals, sometimes exceeding 10%.

Background

In the early 1800s, most American securities had to be sold in Europe. As a result, most securities firms developed from merchants who operated a securities business as a sideline to their primary business. For example, the Morgans built their initial fortune with the railroads. To help raise the money to finance railroad expansion, J. P. Morgan's father resided in London and sold Morgan railroad securities to European investors. Over time, the profitability of the securities businesses became evident and the securities industry expanded.

Prior to the Great Depression, many large, money center banks in New York sold securities and simultaneously conducted conventional banking activities. During the Depression, about 10,000 banks failed (about 40% of all commercial banks). This led to the passage of the **Glass-Steagall Act**, which separated commercial banking from investment banking.

The Glass-Steagall Act made it illegal for a commercial bank to buy or sell securities on behalf of its customers. The original reasoning behind this legislation was to insulate commercial banks from the greater risk inherent in the securities business. There were also concerns that conflicts of interest might arise that would subject commercial banks to increased risk. For example, suppose that an investment banker working at a commercial bank makes a mistake pricing a new stock offering. After promising the customer that he can sell the stock for $20, no sales materialize. The investment banker might be tempted to go down the hall to the commercial bank's investment department and talk them into bailing him out. This would subject depositors to the risk that the bank could lose money on poor investments.

Regulators thought another problem existed. Suppose the investment banker still cannot sell all of that $20 stock issue. He could call up bank customers and offer to loan them 100% of the funds needed to buy a portion of the stock issue. This would not cause a problem if the stock price rose in the future, but if it fell, the value of the securities would be less than the amount of the loan and the customer might not feel a great obligation to repay the loan. Many industry observers felt that this practice was partially to blame for some of the bank failures that occurred during the Depression. However, bank lobbyists argue that although only large banks were involved in issuing securities, most banks that actually failed were small.

When the Glass-Steagall Act separated commercial banking from investment banking, new securities firms were created, many of which offered both investment banking services (selling new securities to the public) as well as brokerage services (selling existing securities to the public).

The legal barriers between commercial and investment banks have been decaying rapidly since the 1980s. One significant trend has been the acquisition of investment banks by commercial banks. For example, in 1997 Bankers Trust acquired Alex Brown, the oldest investment bank in the nation. Bankers Trust was subsequently acquired by Deutsche Banks, which has been spending enormous amounts of money establishing its own investment banking arm. Bank of America bought Robertson Stephens & Co., while NationsBank acquired Montgomery Securities. During the financial crisis in 2009, Bank of America acquired Merrill Lynch, J.P. Morgan acquired Bear Stearns, and Barclays acquired some of the remaining assets of Lehman Brothers.

Underwriting Stocks and Bonds

When a corporation wants to borrow or raise funds, it may decide to issue long-term debt or equity instruments. It then usually hires an investment bank to facilitate the issuance and subsequent sale of the securities. The investment bank may underwrite the issue. The process of underwriting a stock or bond issue requires that the securities firm *purchase* the entire issue at a predetermined price and then resell it in the market. There are a number of services provided in the process of underwriting.

Giving Advice Most firms do not issue capital market securities very frequently. Over 80% of corporate expansion is financed using profits retained from prior-period earnings. As a result, the financial managers at most firms are not familiar with how to proceed with a new security offering. Investment bankers, since they participate in this market daily, can provide advice to firms contemplating a sale. For instance, a firm may not know if it should raise capital by selling stocks or by selling bonds. The investment bankers may be able to help by pointing out, for example, that the market is currently paying high prices for stocks in the firm's industry (historically high PE ratios), while bonds are currently carrying relatively high interest rates (and therefore low prices).

Firms may also need advice as to *when* securities should be offered. If, for example, competitors have recently released earnings reports that show poor profits, it may be better to wait before attempting a sale: Firms want to time the market to sell stock when it will obtain the highest possible price. Again, because of daily interaction with the securities markets, investment bankers should be able to advise firms on the timing of their offerings.

Possibly the most difficult advice an investment banker must give a customer concerns at what *price* the security should be sold. Here the investment banker and the issuing firm have somewhat differing motives. First, consider that the firm wants to sell the stock for the highest price possible. Suppose you started a firm and ran it well for 20 years. You now wish to sell it to the public and retire to Tahiti. If 500,000 shares are to be offered and sold at $10 each, you will receive $5 million for your company. If you can sell the stock for $12, you will receive $6 million.

Investment bankers, however, do not want to overprice the stock because in most underwriting agreements, they will buy the entire issue at the agreed-upon price and then resell it through their brokerage houses. They earn a profit by selling the stock at a slightly higher price than they paid the issuing firm. If the issue is priced too high, the investment bank will not be able to resell, and it will suffer a loss.

Pricing securities is not too hard if the firm has prior issues currently selling in the market, called **seasoned issues**. When a firm issues stock for the first time in a transaction called an **initial public offering (IPO)**, it is much more difficult to determine what the correct price should be. All of the skill and expertise of the investment banking firm will be used to determine the most appropriate price. If the issuing firm and the investment banking firm can come to agreement on a price, the investment banker can assist with the next stage, filing the required documents.

Filing Documents In addition to advising companies, investment bankers will assist with making the required **Securities and Exchange Commission (SEC)** filings. The activities of investment banks and the operation of primary markets are heavily regulated by the SEC, which was created by the Securities and Exchange Acts of 1933 and 1934 to ensure that adequate information reaches prospective investors. Issuers of new securities to the general public (for amounts greater than $1.5 million in a year and with a maturity longer than 270 days) must file a **registration statement** with the SEC. This statement contains information about the firm's financial condition, management, competition, industry, and experience. The firm also discloses what the funds will be used for and management's assessment of the risk of the securities. The issuer must then wait 20 days after the registration statement is filed with the SEC before it can sell any of the securities. The SEC will review the registration statement, and if it does not object during a 20-day waiting period, the securities can then be sold.

The SEC review in no way represents an endorsement. Their approval merely means that all of the required statements and disclosures are included in the statement. Nor does SEC approval mean that the information is accurate. Inaccuracies in the registration statement open the issuing firm's management up to lawsuits if it incurs losses. In extreme cases, inaccuracies could result in criminal charges.

A portion of the registration statement is reproduced and made available to investors for review. This widely circulated document is called a **prospectus**. By law, investors must be given a prospectus before they can invest in a new security.

While the registration document is in the process of being approved, the investment banker has other chores to attend to. For issues of debt, the investment banker must:

- Secure a credit rating from one or more of the credit-rating agencies, such as Standard & Poor's or Moody's.
- Hire a bond counsel who will issue a statement attesting to the legality of the issue.
- Select a trustee who is responsible for seeing that the issuer fulfills its obligations as stated in the security's contract.
- Have the securities printed and prepared for distribution.

For equity issues, the investment banker may arrange for the securities to appear on one of the stock exchanges. Clearly, the investment banker can be of great assistance to an issuer well before any securities are actually offered for sale.

Underwriting Once all of the paperwork has been completed, the investment banker can proceed with the actual underwriting of the issue. At a prespecified time and date, the issuer will sell all of the stock or bond issue to the investment banking firm at the agreed-upon price. The investment banker must now distribute this issue to the public at a greater price to earn its fee. (The 10 largest underwriters in 2015 are listed in Table 22.1.)

By agreeing to underwrite an issue, the investment banking firm is certifying the quality of the issue to the public. We again see how asymmetric information helps justify the need for an intermediary. Investors do not want to put in weeks and weeks of hard technical study of a firm before buying its stock. Nor can they trust the firm's insiders to accurately report its condition. Instead, they rely on the ability of the investment bank to collect information about the firm in order to accurately establish the firm's value. They trust the investment bank's assessment, since it is backing up its opinion by actually purchasing securities in the process of underwriting them. Investment bankers recognize the responsibility they have to report information accurately and honestly, since once they lose investors' confidence, they will no longer be able to market their deals.

The investment banking firm is clearly taking a huge risk at this point. One way that it can reduce the risk is by forming a **syndicate**. A syndicate is a group of investment banking firms, each of which buys a portion of the security issue. Each firm in the syndicate is then responsible for reselling its share of the securities. Most securities issues are sold by syndicates because it is such an effective way to spread the risk among many firms.

TABLE 22.1 Top 10 U.S. Underwriters of Global Debt and Equity 2015

Global Debt, Equity & Equity-Related (A1)				
	Proceeds per Bookrunner ($ millions)			
Bookrunner	**2015 Rank**	**2014 Rank**	**Proceeds**	**Market Share (%)**
JP Morgan	1	1	461,854.6	7.5
Bank of America Merrill Lynch	2	4	392,425.5	6.4
Citi	3	2	388,192.1	6.3
Barclays	4	5	380,798.6	6.2
Morgan Stanley	5	6	326,217.7	5.3
Deutsche Bank	6	3	325,618.3	5.3
Goldman Sachs & Co.	7	7	325,574.9	5.3
HSBC Holdings PLC	8	8	261,311.2	4.2
Credit Suisse	9	9	246,767.3	4.0
Wells Fargo & Co.	10	11	204,825.6	3.3
Total				53.8

Source: Renaissance Capital.

Investment banks advertise upcoming securities offerings with ads in business journals. The traditional advertisement was a large block ad in the financial section of the paper. These ads were called **tombstones** because of their shape, and they listed all of the investment banking firms included in the syndicate.

The longer the investment banker holds the securities before reselling them to the public, the greater the risk that a negative price change will cause losses. One way that the investment banking firm speeds the sale is to solicit offers to buy the securities from investors prior to the date the investment bankers actually take ownership. Then, when the securities are available, the orders are filled and the securities are quickly transferred to the final buyers.

Most investment bankers are attached to larger brokerage houses (multifunction securities firms) that have nationwide sales offices. Each of these offices will be contacted prior to the issue date, and the sales agents will contact their customers to see if they would like to review a prospectus on the new security. The goal is to **fully subscribe** the issue. A fully subscribed issue is one where all of the securities available for sale have been spoken for before the issue date. Security issues may also be **undersubscribed**. In this case, the sales agents have been unable to generate sufficient interest in the security among their customers to sell all of the securities by the issue date. An issue may also be **oversubscribed**, in which case there are more offers to buy than there are securities available.

It is tempting to assume that the best alternative is for an issue to be oversubscribed, but in fact this will alienate the investment banker's customers. Suppose you were issuing a security for the first time and had negotiated with your investment banker to sell the issue of 500,000 shares of stock at $20. Now you find out that the issue is oversubscribed. You would feel that the investment banker had set the price too low and that you had lost money as a result. Maybe the stock could have sold for $25 and you could have collected an extra $2.5 million [($25 − $20) × 500,000 = $2,500,000]. You, as well as other issuing firms, would be unlikely to use this investment banker in the future.

It is equally serious for an issue to be undersubscribed, since it may be necessary to lower the price below what the investment bankers paid to the issuer in order to sell all of the securities to the public. The investment banking firm stands to lose extremely large amounts of money because of the volume of securities involved. For example, when Google went public, over 24 million shares were offered for sale. If the price was lowered by even $.25 per share, over $6,000,000 would be lost. The high risk taken by investment bankers explains why they tend to be the most elite and highest-paid professionals on Wall Street, many earning millions of dollars per year.

Best Efforts An alternative to underwriting a securities offering is to offer the securities under a *best efforts agreement*. In a best efforts agreement, the investment banker sells the securities on a commission basis with no guarantee regarding the price the issuing firm will receive. The advantage to the investment banker of a best efforts transaction is that there is no risk of mispricing the security. There is also no need for the time-consuming task of establishing the market value of the security. The investment banker simply markets the security at the price the customer asks. If the security fails to sell, the offering can be canceled.

Private Placements An alternative method of selling securities is called the *private placement*. In a private placement, securities are sold to a limited number

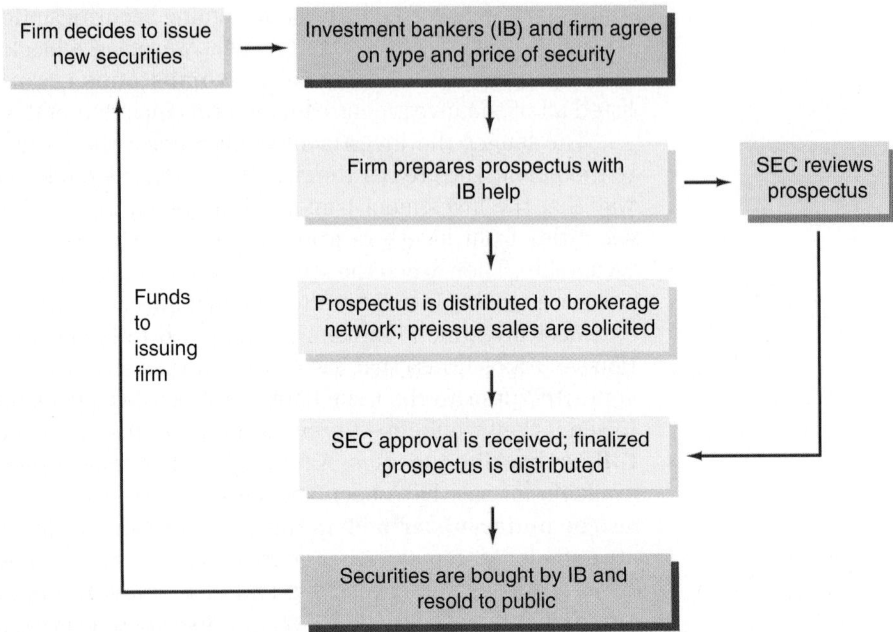

FIGURE 22.1 Using Investment Bankers to Distribute Securities to the Public

of investors rather than to the public as a whole. The advantage of the private placement is that the security does not need to be registered with the SEC as long as certain restrictive requirements are satisfied. Investment bankers are also often involved in private placement transactions. While investment bankers are not required for a private placement, they often facilitate the transaction by advising the issuing firm on the appropriate terms for the issue and by identifying potential purchasers.

The buyers of private placements must be large enough to purchase large amounts of securities at one time. This means that the usual buyers are insurance companies, commercial banks, pension funds, and mutual funds. Private placements are more common for the sale of bonds than for stocks. Goldman Sachs is the most active investment banking firm in the private placement market.

The process of taking a security public is summarized in Figure 22.1.

Equity Sales

Another service offered by investment banks is to help with the sale of companies or corporate divisions. For example, in 1984 Mattel was dangerously close to having its bank loans called when its electronics subsidiary incurred significant losses. Mattel enlisted the help of the investment banking firm Drexel Burnham Lambert. The first step in the firm's restructuring was to sell off all of its non-toy businesses. Mattel returned to health until it again ran into problems in 1999 due to the acquisition of a software company. In 2000 Mattel again used the services of investment bankers to sell this subsidiary.

The first step in any equity sale will be the seller's determination of the business's worth. The investment banker will provide a detailed analysis of the current market for similar companies and apply various sophisticated models to establish company value. Unlike a box of detergent or bar of candy, a going concern has no set price. The company value is based on the use the buyer intends to make of it. If a buyer is interested only in the physical assets, the firm will be worth one amount. A buyer who sees the firm as an opportunity to take advantage of synergies between this firm and another will have a very different price. Despite the elasticity of the yardstick, investment bankers have developed a number of tools to give business owners a range of values for their firms.

How much cash flows will have to be discounted depends very much on who will be bidding on the firm. Again, investment bankers help. They may make discreet inquiries to feel out who in the market may be interested. Additionally, they will prepare a **confidential memorandum** that presents the detailed financial information required by prospective buyers to make an offer for the company. All prospective buyers must sign a confidentiality agreement stipulating that they will not use the information to compete or share it with third parties. The investment bank will screen prospects to ensure that the information goes only to qualified buyers.

The next step in an equity sale is the **letter of intent** issued by a prospective buyer. This document signals a desire to go forward with a purchase and outlines preliminary terms. The investment banker will negotiate the terms of the sale on the seller's behalf and will help to analyze and rank competing offers. The investment banker may even help structure financing in order to obtain a better offer.

Once the letter of intent has been accepted by the seller, the **due diligence** period begins. This 20- to 40-day period is used by the buyer to verify the accuracy of the information contained in the confidential memorandum. The findings shape the terms of the **definitive agreement**. This agreement converts information gathered during the due diligence period and the results of subsequent negotiations into a legally binding contract.

As this discussion demonstrates, a wide variety of skills are required to move a typical corporate sale forward. To meet these needs, investment banks often send in multidisciplined teams of experts to work with clients on their projects. These teams include attorneys, financial analysts, accountants, and industry experts.

Mergers and Acquisitions

Investment banks have been active in the **mergers and acquisitions market** since the 1960s. A merger occurs when two firms combine to form one new company. Both firms support the merger, and corporate officers are usually selected so that both companies contribute to the new management team. Stockholders turn in their stock for stock in the new firm. In an acquisition, one firm acquires ownership of another by buying its stock. Often this process is friendly, and the firms agree that certain economies can be captured by combining resources. It is not unusual that a firm suffering financial stress will even seek out a company to acquire them. At other times, the firm being purchased may resist. Resisted takeovers are called *hostile*. In these cases, the acquirer attempts to purchase sufficient shares of the target firm to gain a majority of the seats on the board of directors. Board members are then able to vote to merge the target firm with the acquiring firm.

Investment bankers serve both acquirers and target firms. Acquiring firms require help in locating attractive firms to pursue, soliciting shareholders to sell their shares in a process called a *tender offer*, and raising the required capital to complete the transaction. Target firms may hire investment bankers to help ward off undesired takeover attempts.

The mergers and acquisitions markets require very specialized knowledge and expertise. Investment bankers involved in this market are highly trained (and, not incidentally, highly paid). The best-known investment banker involved in mergers and acquisitions was Michael R. Milken, who worked at Drexel Burnham Lambert, Inc. Milken is credited with inventing the junk bond market, which we discussed in Chapter 12. *Junk bonds* are high-risk, high-return debt securities that were used primarily to finance takeover attempts. By allowing companies to raise large amounts of capital, even small firms could pursue and take over large ones. During the 1980s, when Milken was most active in this market, merger and acquisition activity peaked. On February 13, 1990, Drexel Burnham Lambert filed for bankruptcy due to rising default rates on its portfolio of junk bonds, a slow economy, and regulations that forced the savings and loan industry out of the junk bond market. Milken pled guilty to securities fraud and was sent to prison.

As a result of the collapse of Drexel and the junk bond market, merger and acquisitions activity slowed during the early 1990s. A healthy economy and regulatory changes caused a resurgence, especially among commercial banks, in the mid and late 1990s. Mergers and acquisitions again slowed during the recessions in 2001 and 2008.

Many of the most well-known investment companies encountered significant financial difficulty during the mortgage and credit crisis in 2008 and 2009. There were several primary causes of their problems. First, some of the investment companies had purchased and held for their own portfolio bonds securitized by subprime mortgages. As the market realized that the quality of these securities did not support their price, the investment companies found that they could not sell them. Second, when the credit markets essentially froze, some investment companies ran into liquidity problems. They had maturing securities that they had to fund but no source of new funds.

Bear Stearns was acquired by J.P. Morgan in April 2008 with $29 billion in federal assistance. In September, Bank of America acquired Merrill Lynch in a deal that led to significant losses to Bank of America in subsequent months. At the same time, Lehman Brothers was the first major investment company to declare bankruptcy. Many of its assets were later acquired by Barclays. Had it not been for aggressive government intervention, it is clear that many more investment firms would have collapsed.

Securities Brokers and Dealers

Securities brokers and dealers conduct trading in secondary markets. *Brokers* are pure intermediaries who act as agents for investors in the purchase or sale of securities. Their function is to match buyers with sellers, a function for which they are paid brokerage commissions.

In contrast to brokers, dealers link buyers and sellers by standing ready to buy and sell securities at given prices. Therefore, dealers hold inventories of securities and make their living by selling these securities for a slightly higher price than they paid for them—that is, on the *spread* between the *bid price*, the price that the broker pays for securities they buy for their inventory, and the *ask price*, the price they receive when they sell the securities. This is a high-risk business because dealers hold securities that can rise or fall in price; in recent years, several firms specializing in bonds have collapsed. Brokers, by contrast, are not as exposed to risk because they do not own the securities involved in their business dealings.[1]

Brokerage Services

Securities brokers offer several types of services.

Securities Orders If you call a securities brokerage house to buy a stock, you will speak with a broker who will take your order. You have three primary types of transactions available: market orders, limit orders, and short sells.

The two most common types of securities orders are the market order and the limit order. When you place a **market order**, you are instructing your agent to buy or sell the security at the current market price. When placing a market order, there is a risk that the price of the security may have changed significantly from what it was when you made your investment decision. If you are buying a stock and the price falls, no harm is done, but if the price goes up, you may regret your decision. The most notable occasion when prices changed between when orders were placed and when they were filled was during the October 19, 1987, stock crash. Panicked investors told their brokers to sell their stocks, but the transaction volume was so great that day and the available technology was such that many orders were not filled until hours after they were placed. By the time they were filled, the price of the stocks had often fallen far below what they were at the time the original orders were placed.

An alternative to the market order is the **limit order**. Here, buy orders specify a *maximum* acceptable price, and sell orders specify a *minimum* acceptable price. For example, you could place a limit order to sell your 100 shares of IBM at $100. If the current market price of IBM is less than $100, the order will not be filled. Unfilled limit orders are reported to the stock specialist who works that particular stock on the exchange. When the stock price moves in such a way that limit orders are activated, the stock specialist initiates the trade.

The **stop loss order** is similar to the limit order but is for stocks you already own. This order tells your broker to sell your stock when it reaches a certain price. For example, suppose you buy a stock for $20 per share. You do not want to suffer a major loss on this stock, so you enter a stop loss order at $18. In the event the stock price falls to $18 the broker will sell the stock. The stop loss order received a great deal of attention in the highly publicized Martha Stewart trial in 2004. She was suspected of trading on insider information about ImClone stock. She argued that the reason for the stock sale was because she had a stop loss order on ImClone at $60. Her conviction suggests that the court did not believe this order was truly in place.

When investors believe that the price of a stock will rise in the future, they buy that stock and hold it until the increase occurs. They can then sell at a profit and capture a gain for their effort. What can be done if an investor is convinced that a stock will *fall* in the future? The solution is to sell short. A **short sell** requires that the investor borrow stocks from a brokerage house and sell them today, with the promise of replacing the borrowed stocks by buying them in the future. Suppose

---

[1]It is easy to remember the distinction between dealers and brokers if you relate to auto dealers and real estate brokers. Auto *dealers* take ownership of the cars and resell them to the public. Real estate *brokers* do not take ownership of the property; they just act as go-betweens.

that you just tried out the new Apple notebook computer and decided that it would sell poorly (in fact, in 1995, Apple had to recall all of its Powerbook computers to fix problems). You might believe that as the rest of the market learned of the poor product, the price of Apple's stock could decline. To take advantage of this situation, you might instruct your broker to short Apple 100 shares. The broker would then borrow 100 shares from another investor on your behalf and sell them at current market prices. You do not own those shares, of course. They are borrowed and at some point in the future, you would be required to purchase those 100 shares at the new market price to replace them. If you were right and the price of Apple declined, you would buy the shares at a lower price than you received for their earlier sale and would earn a profit. Of course, if you are wrong and the price rises, you will suffer a loss.

Market and limit orders allow you to take advantage of stock price *increases*, and short sells allow you to take advantage of stock price *decreases*. Analysts track the number of short positions taken on a stock as an indicator of the number of investors who feel that a stock's price is likely to fall in the future.

Other Services In addition to trading in securities, stockbrokers provide a variety of other services. Investors typically leave their securities in storage with the broker for safekeeping. If the securities are left with the broker, they are insured against loss by the Securities Investor Protection Corporation (SIPC), an agency of the federal government. This guarantee is not against loss in value, only against loss of the securities themselves.

Brokers also provide **margin credit**. Margin credit refers to loans advanced by the brokerage house to help investors buy securities. For example, if you are certain that Intel Corporation stock is going to rise rapidly when its latest computer chip is introduced, you could increase the amount of stock you can buy by borrowing from the brokerage house. If you had \$5,000 and borrowed an additional \$5,000, you could buy \$10,000 worth of stock. Then, if the price goes up as you predict, you could earn nearly twice as much as without the loan. The Federal Reserve sets the percentage of the stock purchase price that brokerage houses can lend (currently 50%). Interest rates on margin loans are usually 1 or 2 percentage points above the prime interest rate (the rate charged large, creditworthy corporate borrowers).

As noted in Chapter 19, the forces of competition have led brokerage firms to offer services and engage in activities traditionally conducted by commercial banks. In 1977 Merrill Lynch developed the cash management account (CMA), which provides a package of financial services that includes credit cards, immediate loans, check-writing privileges, automatic investment of proceeds from the sale of securities in a money market mutual fund, and unified record keeping. CMAs were adopted by other brokerage firms and spread rapidly. Many of these accounts allow check-writing privileges and offer ATM and debit cards. In these ways, they compete directly with banks.

The advantage of brokerage-based cash management accounts is that they make it easier to buy and sell securities. The stockbroker can take funds out of the account when an investor buys a security and put the money into the account when the investor sells securities.

Full-Service vs. Discount Brokers Prior to May 1, 1975, virtually all brokerage houses charged the same commissions on trades. Brokerage houses distinguished themselves primarily on the basis of their research and customer relations. In May

1975, Congress determined that fixed commissions were anticompetitive and passed the Securities Acts Amendment of 1975, which abolished fixed commissions. Now brokerage houses may charge whatever fees they choose. This has resulted in two distinct types of brokerage firms: full-service and discount.

Full-service brokers provide research and investment advice to their customers. Full-service brokers will often mail weekly and monthly market reports and recommendations to their customers in an effort to encourage them to invest in certain securities. For example, when the investment banking department of the brokerage house has an initial public offering available, brokers will contact customers they feel may be interested and offer to send a prospectus. Full-service brokers attempt to establish long-term relationships with their customers and to help them assemble portfolios that are consistent with their financial needs and risk preferences. Of course, this extra attention is costly and must be paid for by requiring higher fees for initiating trades. Bank of America Merrill Lynch is the biggest of the full-service brokers, with about 17,000 financial advisers and $2.2 trillion in client assets.

Discount brokers simply execute trades on request. If you want to buy a particular security, you call the discount broker and place your request. No advice or research is typically provided. Because the cost of operating a discount brokerage firm is significantly less than the cost of operating a full-service firm, lower transaction costs are charged. These fees may be a fraction of the fees charged by a full-service broker. Charles Schwab Corp. is the best-known discount broker. Many discount brokerage firms are owned by large commercial banks, which have historically been prohibited from offering full-service brokerage services.

Regardless of which type of brokerage firm you choose, it will be a member of the major exchanges and have computer links to the NASDAQ (National Association of Security Dealers Automated Quotation System). Suppose that you place an order for 10,000 shares of IBM with your local Merrill Lynch office. Your broker will send an electronic message to the Merrill Lynch traders who work on the floor of the New York Stock Exchange (NYSE) to buy 10,000 shares of IBM in your name. On the floor of the NYSE, there are circular work areas where specialists in each security that is traded on the exchange stand. Each specialist is responsible for several stocks. The Merrill Lynch floor trader will know where the IBM specialist is and will approach that person to fill your buy order. Confirmation of the purchase will then be communicated back to your local broker, who will inform you that the trade has been completed (see the Mini-Case box). Smaller orders will be handled by a computer system that matches buy and sell orders.

Securities Dealers

Securities dealers hold inventories of securities, which they sell to customers who want to buy. They also hold securities purchased from customers who want to sell.

It is impossible to overemphasize the importance of dealers to the smooth functioning of the U.S. financial markets. Consider what an investor demands before buying a security. In addition to requiring a fair return, the investor wants to know that the investment is *liquid*—that it can be sold quickly if it no longer fits into the investor's portfolio. Consider a small, relatively unknown firm that is trying to sell securities to the public. An investor may be tempted to buy the firm's securities, but if these securities cannot be resold easily, it is unlikely that the investor will take a chance on them. This is where the dealers become crucial. They stand ready to make a market in the security at any time—that is, they make sure that an investor

MINI-CASE

Example of Using the Limit-Order Book

Suppose a trader on the New York Stock Exchange was a specialist responsible for Circuit City stock. The limit-order book might look like the following:

Unfilled Circuit City Limit Orders			
Buy Orders		Sell Orders	
37.00	100		
37.12	300		
37.25	100		
		37.37	200
		37.50	500
		37.62	100

Listed under Buy Orders are the highest prices investors are willing to pay to buy the stock. Listed under Sell Orders are the lowest prices investors holding Circuit City are willing to accept to sell. Currently, no transactions occur because there are no cross-over or common prices. In other words, there is currently no one willing to sell Circuit City at a price anyone is willing to pay.

Now suppose the specialist receives a new 200-share market order to buy, an order to be filled at the best market price currently available. The specialist will consult the Sell Orders column and fill the order at 37.37.

Next, the specialist receives a 300-share limit order to sell at 37.12. Again, the specialist will consult the book, but this time will look under the Buy Orders column. The limit order will be filled with 100 shares at 37.25 and 200 shares at 37.12.

Next, suppose that a limit order to buy 500 shares at 36.88 is received. Since there is no sell order for this amount, the order is added to the book, which looks as follows at this point:

Unfilled Circuit City Limit Orders			
Buy Orders		Sell Orders	
36.88	500		
37	100		
37.12	100		
		37.50	500
		37.62	100

can always sell or buy a security. For this reason, dealers are also called **market makers**. When an investor wishes to sell a thinly traded stock (one without an active secondary market), it is unlikely that another investor is simultaneously seeking to buy that security. This nonsynchronous trading problem is solved when the dealer buys the security from the investor and holds it in inventory until another investor is ready to buy it. The knowledge that dealers will provide this service encourages investors to buy securities that would be otherwise unacceptable. In countries with less well-developed financial markets, where dealers will not make a market for less popular securities, it is extremely difficult for small, new, or regional firms to raise funds. Securities market dealers are largely responsible for the health and growth of small businesses in the United States.

Regulation of Securities Firms

Many financial firms engage in all three securities market activities, acting as brokers, dealers, and investment bankers. The largest in the United States is Merrill Lynch; other well-known firms include Morgan Stanley and Salomon Smith Barney (a division of Citigroup). The SEC not only regulates the firms' investment banking operations but also restricts brokers and dealers from misrepresenting securities and from trading on *insider information*, unpublicized facts known only to the management of a corporation.

GO ONLINE

Access the Securities and Exchange Commission Web site, **www.sec.gov**, which contains regulatory actions, concept releases, interpretive releases, and more.

When discussing regulation, it is important to recognize that the public's confidence in the integrity of the financial markets is critical to the growth of our economy and the ability of firms to continue using the markets to raise new capital. If the public believes that there are other powerful players with superior information who can take advantage of smaller investors, the market will be unable to attract funds from these smaller investors. Ultimately, the markets could fail entirely.

Due to asymmetric information, investors will not know as much about securities being offered for sale by firms as firm insiders will. If an average price is set for all securities based on this lack of information, good securities would be withdrawn and only poor and overpriced securities would remain for sale. With only these securities offered, the average price would fall. Now any securities worth more than this new average would be withdrawn. Eventually, the market would fail as the average security offered drops in quality and market prices fall as a result. One solution to the lemons problem is for the government to regulate full disclosure so that asymmetric information is reduced.

The securities laws were designed with two goals: to protect the integrity of the markets and to restrict competition among securities firms so that they would be less likely to fail. Two acts passed in 1933 and 1934 provide the primary basis for regulation of today's securities markets. These acts were passed shortly after the Great Depression and were largely responding to abuses that many people at the time felt were partly responsible for the economic troubles the country was suffering. The principal provisions of the 1933 and 1934 acts are as follows:

- To establish the Securities and Exchange Commission (SEC), which is charged with administering securities laws
- To require that issuers register new securities offerings and that they disclose all relevant information to potential investors
- To require that all publicly held corporations file annual and semiannual reports with the SEC; publicly held corporations must also file a report whenever any event of "significant interest" to investors occurs
- To require that insiders file reports whenever shares are bought or sold
- To prohibit any form of market manipulation

Prior to the passage of these acts, the market was subject to much abuse. For example, a study conducted in 1933 showed evidence of 127 "investment pools" operating during 1932 alone. An investment pool is formed to manipulate the market. A group of investors band together and spread false but damaging rumors about the health of a firm. These rumors drive the price of the firm's stock down. When the price is depressed, the members of the pool buy the stock. Once they all hold shares purchased at artificially low prices, the members of the pool release good news about the company so that the price of the stock rises. Obviously, the members of the pool stand to earn huge profits. Small, uninformed investors lose. Practices such as these were outlawed by the securities acts of 1933 and 1934.

As noted in our discussion of private placements, not all securities issues are subject to SEC oversight. SEC registration is not required if less than $1.5 million in securities is issued per year, if the securities mature in less than 270 days, or if the securities are issued by the U.S. government or most municipalities.

Other legislation of significance to securities firms include the Glass-Steagall Act of 1933, which separated commercial and investment banking (mostly repealed by the Gramm-Leach-Bliley Act); the Investment Advisers Act of 1940, which required investment advisers to register with the SEC; and the Securities Investor Protection Act of 1970, which established the Securities Investor Protection Corporation, which insures customers of securities firms from losses to their cash accounts up to $100,000 and from losses of securities documents up to $500,000. Other regulations related specifically to banks but of interest to securities firms are discussed in Chapter 18.

Relationship Between Securities Firms and Commercial Banks

For many years, commercial banks have lobbied for legislative relief to enable them to compete with securities firms. Consider how the business of banking has been eroded. Prior to the introduction of cash management accounts at Merrill Lynch, the only source of checking accounts was a bank. The Merrill Lynch account not only provided low-cost checking but also paid interest that was higher than the law permitted banks to pay. Securities firms were allowed to make loans, offer credit and debit cards, provide ATM access, and, most important, sell securities. In addition, securities firms could sell some types of insurance. It is not hard to understand why bankers were frustrated. Regulations prevented them from competing with securities firms, but no laws restricted securities firms from competing with banks.

Commercial banks clamored on Capitol Hill for a "level playing field." While the The Gramm–Leach–Bliley Act, also known as the Financial Services Modernization Act of 1999, continued deregulation of banks, banks do not usually sell individual stocks.

Private Equity Investment

When you talk about investing, you are usually discussing stocks and bonds. Both of these securities are sold to the public and have oversight by the SEC. The vast majority of the volume handled by brokers and dealers is in these publicly held securities. However, there is an alternative to public equity investing, which is private equity investing. With private equity investing, instead of raising capital by selling securities to the public, a limited partnership is formed that raises money from a small number of high-wealth investors. Within the broad universe of private equity sectors, the two most common are venture funds and **capital buyouts**. In many cases, the same firms are active in both arenas. Major investors in this industry include KKR (Kohlberg, Kravis, Roberts & Co.), Bain Capital, and Blackstone Group.

Venture Capital Firms

Suppose that you develop and market a new process that you think has a great chance of being a success. However, since it is new and unproven, you cannot get funding from conventional sources. Commercial banks will not loan you money, since there is no established cash flow to use to repay the loan. It will be hard to sell stock to the public through investment bankers because the company is so new and has not yet proven that it can be successful. In the absence of alternative sources of funds, your great idea may not have a true chance to be developed. Venture capital firms provide the funds a start-up company needs to get established.

Description of Industry Venture capital is usually defined as money supplied to young, start-up firms. This money is most frequently raised by limited partnerships and invested by the general partner in firms showing promise of high returns in the future.

Since the mid-1940s, venture capital firms have nurtured the growth of America's high-technology and entrepreneurial communities. Their activities have resulted in job creation, economic growth, and international competitiveness. Venture capitalists backed many of the most successful high-technology companies during the 1980s and 1990s, including Apple Computer, Cisco Systems, Genentech, Microsoft, Netscape, and Sun Microsystems. A number of service firms, such as Staples, Starbucks, and TCBY, also benefited from venture financing. Indeed, much of the growth experienced through the 1980s and 1990s can be traced back to the funding provided by the venture capital industry. Table 22.2 shows the explosive growth in venture capital funding witnessed during the 1990s and the rapid drop in activity after the markets fell in 2000 and 2009.

Venture Capitalists Reduce Asymmetric Information Uncertainty and information asymmetries frequently accompany start-up firms, especially in high-technology communities. Managers of these firms may engage in wasteful expenditures, such as leasing expensive office space, since the manager may benefit disproportionately from them but does not bear their entire cost. The difficulty outside investors have in tracking early-stage high-technology companies leads to other types of costs. For example, a biotechnology company founder may invest in research that brings personal acclaim but little chance for significant returns to investors. As a result of these informational asymmetries, external financing may be costly, difficult, or even impossible to obtain.

Venture capital firms can alleviate the information gap and thus allow firms to receive financing they could not obtain elsewhere. First, as opposed to bank loans or bond financing, venture capital firms hold an equity interest in the firm. The firms are usually privately held, so the stock does not trade publicly. Equity interests in privately held firms are very illiquid. As a result, venture capital investment horizons are long-term. The partners do not expect to earn any return for a number of years, often as long as a decade. In contrast, most investors in stocks are anxious to see annual returns through either stock appreciation or dividend payouts. They are often unwilling to wait years to see if a new idea, process, innovation, or invention will yield profits. Similarly, most investors in bonds are not going to wait years for revenues to grow to a point where interest payments become available. Venture capital financing thus fills an important niche left vacant by alternative sources of capital.

As a second method of addressing the asymmetric information problem, venture capital usually comes with strings attached, the most noteworthy being that the partners in a venture capital firm take seats on the board of directors of the financed firm. Venture capital firms are not passive investors. They actively attempt to add value to the firm through advice, assistance, and business contacts. Venture capitalists may bring together two firms that can complement each other's activities. Venture capital firms will apply their expertise to help the firm solve various financing and growth-related problems. The venture capital partners on the board of directors will carefully monitor expenditures and management to help safeguard the investment in the firm.

TABLE 22.2 Venture Capital Investments Made from 1990–2015

Year	Number of Companies Funded	Investment Total ($ millions)
1990	1,317	3,376.21
1991	1,088	2,511.43
1992	1,294	5,177.56
1993	1,151	4,962.87
1994	1,191	5,351.18
1995	1,327	5,608.30
1996	2,078	11,278.60
1997	2,536	14,903.00
1998	2,974	21,090.60
1999	4,411	54,203.70
2000	6,342	104,986.80
2001	3,787	40,686.70
2002	2,617	21,824.00
2003	2,414	19,678.30
2004	2,571	22,117.40
2005	2,646	22,765.80
2006	3,746	26,315.36
2007	4,027	30,518.26
2008	4,168	29,954.01
2009	3,138	20,231.43
2010	3,625	23,311.33
2011	3,964	29,551.45
2012	3,770	26,874.14
2013	4,295	30,305.00
2014	4,442	50,843.00
2015	4,380	59,066.00

Source: http://www.nvca.org/index.php

One of the most effective ways venture capitalists have of controlling managers is to disburse funds to the company in stages only as the firm demonstrates progress toward its ultimate goal. If development stalls or markets change, funds can be withheld to cut losses.

Implicit to venture capital financing is an expectation of high risk and large compensating returns. Venture capital firms will search very carefully among hundreds of companies to find a few that show real growth potential. Despite this exhaustive search effort, the selected firms usually have little to show initially other than a unique and promising idea. Venture capitalists mitigate the risk by developing a portfolio of young companies within a single fund. Additionally, many venture capital partnerships will manage multiple funds simultaneously. By diversifying the risk among a number of start-up firms, the risk of loss is significantly lowered.

Origins of Venture Capital The first true venture capital firm was American Research & Development (ARD), established in 1946 by MIT president Karl Compton and local business leaders. The bulk of their success can be traced to one $70,000 investment in a new firm, the Digital Equipment Company. This seed money grew in value to $355 million over the next three decades.[2]

During the 1950s and 1960s, most venture capital funding was for the development of real estate and oil fields. By the late 1960s, a shift occurred toward financing technology start-ups. High technology remains the dominant area for venture capital funding.

The source of venture capital funding has shifted from wealthy individuals to pension funds and corporations. In 1979 the U.S. Department of Labor clarified the **prudent man rule**, which restricted pension funds from making risky investments, to explicitly allow investment in some high-risk assets. This resulted in a surge of pension fund dollars going into venture projects.

Corporate funding of venture capital projects increased when many companies reduced their investment in their own in-house R&D in favor of outside start-up companies. If the project was successful, the company could acquire the start-up. This change was fueled by evidence that many of the best ideas from in-house centralized R&D languished unused or were commercialized in new firms started by defecting employees. Salaried employees tend not to be as motivated as entrepreneurs who stand to capture a large portion of the profits a new idea may generate. By investing in start-up firms, corporations can benefit from new discoveries while supporting the entrepreneurial spirit.

Structure of Venture Capital Firms Most early venture capital firms were organized as closed-end mutual funds. A closed-end mutual fund sells a fixed number of shares to investors. Once all of the shares have been sold, no additional money can be raised. Instead, a new venture fund is established. The advantage of this organizational structure is that it provides the long-term money required for venture investing. Investors cannot pull money out of the investment as they could from an open-end mutual fund.

In the 1970s and 1980s, venture capital firms began organizing as limited partnerships. This organizational structure is exempt from securities regulations, including the burdensome disclosure requirements of the Investment Security Act of 1940. While both organizational forms continue to be used, currently most venture capital firms are limited partnerships.

The Life of a Deal Most venture capital deals follow a similar life cycle that begins when a limited partnership is formed and funds are raised. In the second phase, the funds are invested in start-up companies. Finally, the venture firm exits the investment.

Next, we take a more detailed look at this process.

Fundraising A venture firm begins by soliciting commitments of capital from investors. As discussed, these investors are typically pension funds, corporations, and wealthy individuals. Venture capital firms usually have a portfolio target amount that they attempt to raise. The average venture fund will have from just a few investors up to 100 limited partners. Because the minimum commitment is usually so high, venture capital funding is generally out of reach of most average individual investors.

---

[2]Part of this discussion is based on "The Venture Capital Revolution," by Paul Gompers and Josh Lerner, *Journal of Economic Perspectives*, no. 2 (Spring 2001): 145–168.

Once the venture fund begins investing, it will "call" its commitments from the limited partners. These capital calls from the limited partners to the venture fund are sometimes called "takedowns" or "paid-in-capital." Venture firms typically call their capital on an as-needed basis.

The limited partners understand that investments in venture funds are long-term. It may be several years before the first investment starts to pay. In many cases, the capital may be tied up for 7 to 10 years. The illiquidity of the investment must be carefully considered by the potential investor.

Investing Once commitments have been received, the venture fund can begin the investment phase. Venture funds either may specialize in one or two industry segments or may generalize, looking at all available opportunities. It is not uncommon for venture funds to focus investments in a limited geographic area to make it easier to review and monitor the firms' activities.

Frequently, venture capitalists invest in a firm before it has a real product or is even clearly organized as a company. This is called **seed investing**. Investing in a firm that is a little further along in its life cycle is known as **early-stage investing**. Finally, some funds focus on **later-stage investing** by providing funds to help the company grow to a critical mass to attract public financing.

Typically, about 60% of venture capital funds go into seed investments, 25% into early-stage investments, and 15% into later-stage investments.

Exiting The goal of a venture capital investment is to help nurture a firm until it can be funded with alternative capital. Venture firms hope that an exit can be made in no more than 7 to 10 years. Later-stage investments may take only a few years. Once an exit is made, the partners receive their share of the profits and the fund is dissolved.

A venture fund can successfully exit an investment in a number of ways. The most glamorous and visible is through an initial public offering. At the public stock offering, the venture firm is considered an insider and receives stock in the company, but the firm is regulated and restricted in how that stock can be sold or liquidated for several years. Once the stock is freely tradable, usually after two years, the venture fund distributes the stock to its limited partners, who may then hold the stock or sell it. Over the past 25 years, more than 3,000 companies financed by venture funds have had initial public offerings. During the peak years, there were 258 venture-backed initial public offerings.

While not as visible, an equally common type of successful exit for venture investments is through mergers and acquisitions. In these cases, the venture firm receives stock or cash from the acquiring company. These proceeds are then distributed to the limited partners. The number of venture-backed merger and acquisition deals peaked at 269 in 2000.

Venture Fund Profitability Venture investing is extremely high-risk. Most start-up firms do not succeed. Despite the careful monitoring and advice provided by the venture capital firm, there are innumerable hurdles that must be jumped before a new concept or idea yields profits. If venture investing is high-risk, then there must also be the possibility of a high return to induce investors to continue supplying funds.

Historically, venture capital firms have been very profitable, despite their high risk. The 20-year average return is 23.4%. The 1990s were a wonderful time to be a

> E-FINANCE

Venture Capitalists Lose Focus with Internet Companies

Table 22.2 shows that there was a tremendous surge in funds available for venture capitalists in the last half of the 1990s. Much of the investing focus was on the financing of dot-com companies. There are two serious ramifications that result. First, it is likely that there are only a certain number of worthy projects to finance at any one time. When too much money is chasing too few deals, firms are going to obtain financing that would be rejected at other times. As a result, the average quality of venture fund portfolios falls.

A second problem caused by the surge of money into venture funds is that the ability of the partners to provide quality monitoring is reduced. Consider the case of Webvan, an Internet grocer that received more than $1 *billion* in venture financing. Even though it was backed by a group of experienced financiers, including Goldman Sachs and Sequoia Capital, its business plan was fundamentally flawed. In its short life, Webvan spent more than $1 billion building automated warehouses and pricey tech gear. This high overhead made it impossible to compete in the grocery business, where average margins are about 1%. Had the investment bankers been actively monitoring the activities of Webvan, they might have balked at developing an infrastructure that required 4,000 orders per day per warehouse just to break even. Not surprisingly, Webvan declared bankruptcy in July 2001.

Investors in private equity partnerships are well compensated for taking the risk of purchasing poorly performing companies. Partners typically earn a 1.5% fee for managing the equity fund investments. In addition, they get a share of the profits, usually pegged at 20%, when the firm is sold or taken back public. An additional perk is that the profits for both CEOs and the partners are taxed at the 15% capital gains rate, rather than the 35% rate they would suffer if the income were received as salary.

---

venture capitalist. The 10-year average return was 30%. From 1995 to 2000, the average return soared to over 50%.

In the late 1990s, venture capital returns continued to be extraordinary. For example, returns exceeded 165% in 1999. Unfortunately, as the market cooled to technology, so too did venture capital returns. By 2000, average returns were 37.5%, and in 2001 venture firms reported a first-quarter loss of 8.9%. The venture capital market suffered during the 2008–2009 recession as well, posting a 16.5% loss. The E-Finance box discusses possible explanations for the losses suffered by venture capital firms.

Private Equity Buyouts

In the last section, we learned that new start-up companies often fund their growth by raising capital from venture capital firms. The private company is allowed to mature and then, with profitability ensured, it sells shares to the public. In a **private equity buyout**, instead of a private company going public, a public company goes private.

In a typical private equity buyout, the publicly traded shares of a company are purchased by a limited partnership formed for that purpose. Since the public shares are then retired, the firm is no longer subject to the controls and oversight required of publicly held companies, nor does it have to answer to diverse stockholders.

Advantages to Private Equity Buyouts

Private equity partners and the managers of privately held firms cite a number of advantages to the private equity ownership structure. First, as private companies they are not subject to the controversial regulations included in the 2002 Sarbanes-Oxley Act. Many managers and CEOs complain that meeting the requirements of Sarbanes-Oxley is frustrating and takes valuable time away from more productive activities.

Second, CEOs of publicly held firms often feel under pressure to produce quarterly profits. In a private equity scenario, CEOs frequently have more time and flexibility to enact the changes needed to turn around subpar companies. Instead of trying to convince thousands of diverse investors of the wisdom of a particular course of action, the CEO of a privately held company need convince only the managing partners of the private equity firm. This increased freedom has attracted some of the best known corporate leaders in the country, such as Jack Welch (former CEO of GE), Michael Eisner (Former CEO of Disney), Louis Gerstner (former CEO of IBM), and Millard Drexler (former CEO of Ann Taylor and Gap Inc.). One reason top CEOs have been attracted to privately held firms is that they can be compensated more easily with an ownership interest in the firms. Typically, executives are recruited with a small cash salary and an opportunity to invest their own money in the firm, often taking as much as a 20% ownership position. Some believe this more closely aligns the executive's interest with those of the private equity partnership.

Life Cycle of the Private Equity Buyout

In a typical private equity buyout, a partnership is formed and private equity investors are contacted to pledge participation. Each investor usually pledges at least $1 million of capital and agrees to leave the funds under the partnership's control for an extended period of time, often five years or more.

The partnership now identifies an underperforming company that it believes can be turned around by new management. Using the equity contributed by the partners, the firm buys the outstanding public shares of the troubled company. A new CEO and board are elected to run the company. The managing partners tend to be active participants in the management of the firm.

Once the company is revived and showing improved revenues and profitability, it will be either sold to another firm or taken public in an IPO. This is where the investors in the private buyout earn their return. Because the company is now stronger, it is expected to sell for much more than it did when initially purchased and taken private.

SUMMARY

1. Investment banks are firms that assist in the initial sale of securities in the primary market and, as securities brokers and dealers, assist in the trading of securities in the secondary markets, some of which are organized into exchanges. The Securities and Exchange Commission regulates the financial institutions in the securities markets and ensures that adequate information reaches prospective investors.
2. Underwriting involves the investment banking firm's taking ownership of the stock issue by purchasing all of the shares from the issuer and then reselling them in the market. Issues may be oversubscribed, undersubscribed, or fully subscribed, depending on whether the price is set correctly. Investment banks similarly underwrite bond issues.
3. Investment bankers assist issuing firms by providing advice, filing documents, and marketing issues. Investment bankers often assist in mergers and acquisitions and in private placements as well.
4. Securities brokers act as go-betweens and do not usually own securities. Securities dealers do buy and sell securities and by doing so make a market. By always having securities to sell and by always being willing to purchase securities, dealers guarantee the liquidity of the market.

5. Investors may place an order, called a *market order*, to buy a security at the current market price. They may also set limits to the lowest price at which they will sell their security or the highest price they will pay for a security. Orders of this type are called *limit orders*.
6. Some brokerage houses provide research and investment advice in addition to conducting trades on behalf of customers. These are called *full-service brokers*. *Discount brokers* simply place orders. Brokerage houses also store securities, advance loans to buy securities, and offer cash management accounts.
7. Private equity investments include both venture fund investing and capital buyouts of public companies. A typical venture fund investment includes pooling funds from investors to use to support a new company until it is able to go public. In a capital buyout, investors' funds are again pooled, but this time they are used to buy a controlling interest in a public company that is then taken private.

KEY TERMS

capital buyout, p. 548
confidential memorandum, p. 541
definitive agreement, p. 541
due diligence, p. 541
early-stage investing, p. 552
fully subscribe, p. 539
Glass-Steagall Act, p. 535
initial public offering (IPO), p. 537
investment banks, p. 535
later-stage investing, p. 552
letter of intent, p. 541
limit order, p. 543
margin credit, p. 544
market makers, p. 546
market order, p. 543
mergers and acquisitions market, p. 541
oversubscribed, p. 539
primary market, p. 534
private equity buyout, p. 553
prospectus, p. 537
prudent man rule, p. 551
registration statement, p. 537
seasoned issues, p. 537
secondary market, p. 534
Securities and Exchange Commission (SEC), p. 537
seed investing, p. 552
short sell, p. 543
stop loss order, p. 543
syndicate, p. 538
tombstone, p. 539
undersubscribed, p. 539

QUESTIONS

1. What was the motivation behind legislation separating commercial banking and investment banking?
2. Ipora Bank conducts its business mostly by taking in deposits and then lending them out. Pando Bank earns its trade by helping corporations raise funds. If you want to open a checking account, which bank would accept your business? Which bank is not a bank in the ordinary sense?
3. What does it mean to say that investment bankers *underwrite* a security offering? How is this different from a best-efforts offering?
4. What are the primary services that an investment banker will provide a firm issuing securities?
5. Does the fact that a security has passed an SEC review mean that investors can buy the security without having to worry about taking a loss on the investment?
6. Suppose you heard that an investment bank decided not to form a syndicate to underwrite an issue of securities. What does this piece of information tell you about the quality of the securities soon to be offered?
7. Suppose you manage a pension fund and an investment bank contacts you to review the prospectus of a security issue that you know is currently undersubscribed. Assuming your research indicates that this is a good investment, would you offer to buy the security? Why?
8. Consider an equity sale. Suppose Gordon Gekko is interested in buying the company only to dismantle all production and sell the company's assets, including its plant, to real estate investors. Which criterion would Gordon Gekko use to value the firm?
9. What is the difference between a hostile takeover and a merger?
10. What valuable service do dealers provide that facilitates transaction trading and keeping the markets liquid?
11. Suppose that Axel was involved in a short sale of stock of a trucking company. What would happen to Axel's profits if the price of the stock increases?
12. Is it possible to make money if you know that the price of a security will *fall* in the future? How?
13. Why do commercial banks object to brokerage houses being allowed to offer many of the services traditionally reserved for banks?
14. What are the principal advantages often cited as motivation for a private equity buyout?

QUANTITATIVE PROBLEMS

Amazon.com issued an initial public offering in May 1997. Prior to its IPO, the following information on shares outstanding was listed in the final prospectus:

Name and Address	Number of Shares Beneficially Owned	Percentage of Shares Outstanding: Prior to Offering	Percentage of Shares Outstanding: After Offering
Jeffrey P. Bezos c/o Amazon.com, Inc. 1516 Second Avenue, 4th Floor Seattle, WA 98101	9,885,000	7.5%	41.4%
L. John Doerr Kleiner Perkins Caufield & Byers 4 Embarcadero Center, Suite 3520 San Francisco, CA 94111	3,401,376	16.4	14.3
Tom A. Alberg	195,000	*	*
Scott D. Cook	75,000	*	*
Patricia Q. Stonesifer	75,000	*	*
All directors and executive officers as a group (14 persons)	15,688,925	72.5	63.5
Total shares outstanding	20,858,702	100.0	—.–

In the IPO, the firm issued 3,000,000 new shares. The initial price was $18.00/share with investment bankers retaining $1.26 as fees. The final first-day closing price was $23.50.

1. What were the total proceeds from this offering? What part was retained by Amazon? What part by the investment bankers? What percentage of the offering is this?
2. Mr. Doerr of Kleiner Perkins Caufield & Byers owned a significant number of shares. What was the market value of these shares at the end of the first day of trading?
3. What was the market value of Amazon.com following its first day as a publicly held company?
4. Refer back to the IPO of eBay presented in the problems for Chapter 13. What were the fees for eBay as a percentage of funds raised? Does a pattern emerge?
5. Suppose the issue of 5,000,000 shares of stock was originally oversubscribed at a price of $15 per share. Calculate the money "left on the table" if you realize that the stock could have been priced at $17.5 per share.
6. Xavi decides to short sell 10,000 shares of Guiness Co. stock, currently trading at $7.00 per share. Determine Xavi's profits if Guiness stock trades at $5.00 per share at the moment in which Xavi has to buy the shares back.
7. Bluestar Airlines has physical assets valued at $12,500,000, and according to industry experts, the net present value of its future earnings amounts to $40.00 per share. Assuming there are 1,000,000 outstanding shares, determine the maximum price per share that a buyer will pay in an equity sale if this buyer is thinking about dismantling the company and selling its assets.
8. The limit-order book for a security is as follows:

Unfilled Limit Orders			
Buy Orders		Sell Orders	
25.12	100	25.36	300
25.20	500	25.38	200
25.23	200	25.41	200

The specialist receives the following, in order:

- Market order to sell 300 shares
- Limit order to buy 100 shares at 25.38
- Limit order to buy 500 shares at 25.30

How, if at all, are these orders filled? What does the limit-order book look like after these orders?

WEB EXERCISES

Investment Banks, Security Brokers and Dealers, and Venture Capital Firms

1. In initial public offerings (IPOs), securities are sold to the public for the first time. Go to **http://www.renaissancecapital.com/ipohome/marketwatch.aspx**. This site lists various statistics regarding the IPO market.
   - **a.** What was the largest IPO offered recently, ranked by amount raised?
   - **b.** What is the next IPO that will be offered to the public?
   - **c.** How many IPOs were priced in each of the past four years?
2. The Securities and Exchange Commission is responsible for regulating securities firms. Go to **www.sec.gov**. This is the official home page of the SEC. Use this page to answer the following.
   - **a.** What is EDGAR?
   - **b.** What is the stated purpose of the SEC?
   - **c.** Provide a one-sentence summary of the most recently proposed SEC regulation.

PART 7 THE MANAGEMENT OF FINANCIAL INSTITUTIONS

CHAPTER 23

Risk Management in Financial Institutions

> PREVIEW

Managing financial institutions has never been an easy task, but in recent years it has become even more difficult because of greater uncertainty in the economic environment. Interest rates have become much more volatile, resulting in substantial fluctuations in profits and in the value of assets and liabilities held by financial institutions. Furthermore, as we have seen in Chapters 5 and 8, defaults on loans and other debt instruments have also climbed dramatically, leading to large losses at financial institutions. In light of these developments, it is not surprising that financial institution managers have become more concerned about managing the risk their institutions face as a result of greater interest-rate fluctuations and defaults by borrowers.

In this chapter we examine how managers of financial institutions cope with credit risk, the risk arising because borrowers may default on their obligations, and with interest-rate risk, the risk arising from fluctuations in interest rates. We will look at the tools these managers use to measure risk and the strategies they employ to reduce it.

Managing Credit Risk

Access the Web site of the Risk Management Association, **http://www.rmahq.org/**, which offers useful information such as annual statement studies, online publications, and more.

A major part of the business of financial institutions, such as banks, insurance companies, pension funds, and finance companies, is making loans. For these institutions to earn high profits, they must make successful loans that are paid back in full (and so have low credit risk). The concepts of adverse selection and moral hazard (discussed in Chapters 2 and 7) provide a framework for understanding the principles that financial institution managers must follow to minimize credit risk if they are to make successful loans.

Adverse selection in loan markets occurs because bad credit risks (those most likely to default on their loans) are the ones who usually line up for loans; in other words, those who are most likely to produce an *adverse* outcome are the most likely to be *selected*. Borrowers with very risky investment projects have much to gain if their projects are successful, so they are the most eager to obtain loans. Clearly, however, they are the least desirable borrowers because of the greater possibility that they will be unable to pay back their loans.

Moral hazard exists in loan markets because borrowers may have incentives to engage in activities that are undesirable from the lender's point of view. In such situations, it is more likely that the lender will be subjected to the *hazard* of default. Once borrowers have obtained a loan, they are more likely to invest in high-risk investment projects—projects that pay high returns to the borrowers if successful. The high risk associated with these investments, however, makes it less likely that these borrowers will be able to pay back their loans.

To be profitable, financial institutions must overcome the adverse selection and moral hazard problems that make loan defaults more likely. Financial institutions' attempts to solve these problems help explain a number of principles for managing credit risk: screening and monitoring, establishment of long-term customer relationships, loan commitments, collateral, compensating balance requirements, and credit rationing.

Screening and Monitoring

Asymmetric information is present in loan markets because lenders have less information about the investment opportunities and activities of borrowers than borrowers do. This situation leads financial institutions to perform two information-producing activities—screening and monitoring.

Screening Adverse selection in loan markets requires that lenders screen out the bad credit risks from the good ones so loans are profitable to them. To accomplish effective screening, lenders must collect reliable information from prospective borrowers. Effective screening and information collection together form an important principle of credit risk management.

When you apply for a consumer loan (such as a car loan or a mortgage to purchase a house), the first thing you are asked to do is fill out forms that elicit a great deal of information about your personal finances. You are asked about your salary, your bank accounts and other assets (such as cars, insurance policies, and furnishings), and your outstanding loans; your record of loan, credit card, and charge account repayments; and the number of years you've worked and the name of your employers. You also are asked personal questions such as your age, marital status, and number of children. The lender uses this information to evaluate how good a credit risk you are by calculating your "credit score," a statistical measure derived from your answers that predicts whether you are likely to have trouble making your loan payments. Deciding on how good a risk you are cannot be entirely scientific, so the lender must also use judgment. The loan officer, whose job is to decide whether you should be given the loan, might call your employer or talk to some of the personal references you supplied. The officer might even make a judgment based on your demeanor or your appearance.

The process of screening and collecting information is similar when a financial institution makes a business loan. It collects information about the company's profits and losses (income), along with information about its assets and liabilities. The lender also has to evaluate the likely future success of the business. So, in addition to obtaining information on such items as sales figures, a loan officer might ask questions about the company's future plans, the purpose of the loan, and the competition in the industry. The officer may even visit the company to obtain a firsthand look at its operations. The bottom line is that, whether for personal or business loans, financial institutions need to be nosy.

Specialization in Lending One puzzling feature of lending by financial institutions is that they often specialize in lending to local firms or to firms in particular industries, such as energy. In one sense, this behavior seems surprising because it means that the financial institution is not diversifying its portfolio of loans and thus is exposing itself to more risk. But from another perspective, such specialization makes perfect sense. The adverse selection problem requires that the financial institution screen out bad credit risks. It is easier for the financial institution to collect information about local firms and determine their creditworthiness than to collect comparable information on firms that are farther away. Similarly, by concentrating its lending on firms in specific industries, the financial institution becomes more knowledgeable about these industries and is therefore better able to predict which firms will make timely payments on their debt.

Monitoring and Enforcement of Restrictive Covenants Once a loan has been made, the borrower has an incentive to engage in risky activities that make it less likely that the loan will be paid off. To reduce this moral hazard, financial institutions must adhere to the principle for managing credit risk that a lender should write provisions (restrictive covenants) into loan contracts restricting borrowers from engaging in risky activities. By monitoring borrowers' activities to see whether they are complying with the restrictive covenants and by enforcing the covenants if they are not, lenders can make sure that borrowers are not taking on risks at the lenders' expense. The need for financial institutions to engage in screening and monitoring explains why they spend so much money on auditing and information-collecting activities.

Long-Term Customer Relationships

An additional way for financial institution managers to obtain information about their borrowers is through long-term customer relationships, another important principle of credit risk management.

If a prospective borrower has had a checking account or a savings account or other loans with a financial institution over a long time, a loan officer can look at past activity on the accounts and learn quite a bit about the borrower. The balances in the checking and savings accounts tell the loan officer how liquid the potential borrower is and at what time of year the borrower has a strong need for cash. A review of the checks the borrower has written reveals the borrower's suppliers. If the borrower has borrowed previously from the financial institution, the institution has a record of the loan payments. Thus, long-term customer relationships reduce the costs of information collection and make it easier to screen out bad credit risks.

The need for monitoring by lenders adds to the importance of long-term customer relationships. If the borrower has borrowed from the financial institution before, the institution has already established procedures for monitoring that customer. Therefore, the costs of monitoring long-term customers are lower than the cost of monitoring new customers.

Long-term relationships benefit the customers as well as the financial institution. A firm that has a previous relationship with a financial institution will find it easier to obtain a loan from this institution at a low interest rate because the financial institution has an easier time determining if the prospective borrower is a good credit risk and therefore incurs fewer costs in monitoring the borrower.

A long-term customer relationship has another advantage for the financial institution. No financial institution manager can think of every contingency when the institution writes a restrictive covenant into a loan contract; there will always be risky borrower activities that are not ruled out. However, what if a borrower wants to preserve a long-term relationship with the financial institution because it will be easier to get future loans from the bank at low interest rates? The borrower then has the incentive to avoid risky activities that would upset the financial institution, even if restrictions on these risky activities are not specified in the loan contract. Indeed, if the financial institution manager doesn't like what a borrower is doing even when the borrower isn't violating any restrictive covenants, the manager has some power to discourage the borrower from such activity: She can threaten not to give the borrower new loans in the future. Long-term customer relationships therefore enable financial institutions to deal with even unanticipated moral hazard contingencies.

Loan Commitments

Banks have a special vehicle for institutionalizing a long-term customer relationship called a **loan commitment**. A loan commitment is a bank's commitment (for a specified future period of time) to provide a firm with loans up to a given amount at an interest rate that is tied to some market interest rate. The majority of commercial and industrial loans from banks are made under the loan commitment arrangement. The advantage for the firm is that it has a source of credit when it needs it. The advantage for the bank is that the loan commitment promotes a long-term relationship, which in turn facilitates information collection. In addition, provisions in the loan commitment agreement require that the firm continually supply the bank with information about the firm's income, asset and liability position, business activities, and so on. A loan commitment arrangement is a powerful method for reducing the bank's costs for screening and information collection.

Collateral

Collateral requirements for loans are important credit risk management tools. Loans with these collateral requirements are often referred to as **secured loans**. Collateral, which is property promised to the lender as compensation if the borrower defaults, lessens the consequences of adverse selection because it reduces the lender's losses in the case of a loan default. It also reduces moral hazard because the borrower has more to lose from a loan default. If a borrower defaults on a loan, the lender can sell the collateral and use the proceeds to make up for its losses on the loan. Collateral requirements thus offer important protection for financial institutions making loans, and that is why they are extremely common in loans made by financial institutions.

Compensating Balances

One particular form of collateral required when a bank makes commercial loans is called **compensating balances**: A firm receiving a loan must keep a required minimum amount of funds in a checking account at the bank. For example, a business getting a $10 million loan may be required to keep compensating balances of at least $1 million in its checking account at the bank. This $1 million in compensating balances can then be taken by the bank to make up some of the losses on the loan if the borrower defaults.

In addition to serving as collateral, compensating balances help increase the likelihood that a loan will be paid off. They do this by helping the bank monitor the borrower and consequently reduce moral hazard. Specifically, by requiring the borrower to use a checking account at the bank, the bank can observe the firm's check payment practices, which may yield a great deal of information about the borrower's financial condition. For example, a sustained drop in the borrower's checking account balance may signal that the borrower is having financial trouble, or account activity may suggest that the borrower is engaging in risky activities; perhaps a change in suppliers means that the borrower is pursuing new lines of business. Any significant change in the borrower's payment procedures is a signal to the bank that it should make inquiries. Compensating balances therefore make it easier for banks to monitor borrowers more effectively and are another important credit risk management tool.

Credit Rationing

Another way in which financial institutions deal with adverse selection and moral hazard is through **credit rationing**: refusing to make loans even though borrowers are willing to pay the stated interest rate or even a higher rate. Credit rationing takes two forms. The first occurs when a lender refuses to make a loan *of any amount* to a borrower, even if the borrower is willing to pay a higher interest rate. The second occurs when a lender is willing to make a loan but restricts the size of the loan to less than the borrower would like.

Initially, you might be puzzled by the first type of credit rationing. After all, even if the potential borrower is a credit risk, why doesn't the lender just extend the loan but at a higher interest rate? The answer is that adverse selection prevents this from being a wise course of action. Individuals and firms with the riskiest investment projects are exactly those that are willing to pay the highest interest rates. If a borrower took on a high-risk investment and succeeded, the borrower would become extremely rich. But a lender wouldn't want to make such a loan precisely because the credit risk is high; the likely outcome is that the borrower will *not* succeed and the lender will not be paid back. Charging a higher interest rate just makes adverse selection worse for the lender; that is, it increases the likelihood that the lender is lending to a bad credit risk. The lender would therefore rather not make any loans at a higher interest rate; instead, it would engage in the first type of credit rationing and would turn down loans.

Financial institutions engage in the second type of credit rationing to guard against moral hazard: They grant loans to borrowers, but not loans as large as the borrowers want. Such credit rationing is necessary because the larger the loan, the greater the benefits from moral hazard. If a financial institution gives you a $1,000 loan, for example, you are likely to take actions that enable you to pay it back because you don't want to hurt your credit rating for the future. However, if the financial institution lends you $10 million, you are more likely to fly down to Rio to celebrate. The larger your loan, the greater your incentives to engage in activities that make it less likely that you will repay the loan. Because more borrowers repay their loans if the loan amounts are small, financial institutions ration credit by providing borrowers with smaller loans than they seek.

Managing Interest-Rate Risk

With the increased volatility of interest rates that occurred in the 1980s, financial institution managers became more concerned about their exposure to interest-rate risk, the riskiness of earnings and returns that is associated with changes in interest rates. Indeed, the S&L debacle in the 1980s, described in detail in Web Chapter 26, made clearer the dangers of interest-rate risk when many S&Ls went out of business because they had not managed interest-rate risk properly. To see what interest-rate risk is all about, let's take a look at the balance sheet of the First National Bank:

First National Bank

Assets		Liabilities	
Reserves and cash items	$5 million	Checkable deposits	$15 million
Securities		Money market	
Less than 1 year	$5 million	deposit accounts	$5 million
1 to 2 years	$5 million	Savings deposits	$15 million
Greater than 2 years	$10 million	CDs	
Residential mortgages		Variable rate	$10 million
Variable rate	$10 million	Less than 1 year	$15 million
Fixed rate (30-year)	$10 million	1 to 2 years	$5 million
Commercial loans		Greater than 2 years	$5 million
Less than 1 year	$15 million	Fed funds	$5 million
1 to 2 years	$10 million	Borrowings	
Greater than 2 years	$25 million	Less than 1 year	$10 million
Physical capital	$5 million	1 to 2 years	$5 million
		Greater than 2 years	$5 million
		Bank capital	$5 million
Total	$100 million	Total	$100 million

The first step in assessing interest-rate risk is for the bank manager to decide which assets and liabilities are rate-sensitive, that is, which have interest rates that will be reset (repriced) within the year. Note that rate-sensitive assets or liabilities can have interest rates repriced within the year either because the debt instrument matures within the year or because the repricing is done automatically, as with variable-rate mortgages.

For many assets and liabilities, deciding whether they are rate-sensitive is straightforward. In our example, the obviously rate-sensitive assets are securities with maturities of less than one year ($5 million), variable-rate mortgages ($10 million), and commercial loans with maturities of less than one year ($15 million), for a total of $30 million. However, some assets that look like fixed-rate assets whose interest rates are not repriced within the year actually have a component that is rate-sensitive. For example, although fixed-rate residential mortgages may have a maturity of 30 years, homeowners can repay their mortgages early by selling their homes or repaying the mortgage in some other way. This means that within the year, a certain percentage of these fixed-rate mortgages will be paid off, and interest rates on this amount will be repriced. From past experience the bank manager knows that 20% of the fixed-rate residential mortgages are repaid within a year, which means that $2 million of these mortgages (20% of $10 million) must be considered rate-sensitive. The bank manager adds this $2 million to the $30 million of rate-sensitive assets already calculated, for a total of $32 million in rate-sensitive assets.

The bank manager now goes through a similar procedure to determine the total amount of rate-sensitive liabilities. The obviously rate-sensitive liabilities are money market deposit accounts ($5 million), variable-rate CDs and CDs with less than one year to maturity ($25 million), federal funds ($5 million), and borrowings with maturities of less than one year ($10 million), for a total of $45 million. Checkable deposits and savings deposits often have interest rates that can be changed at any time by the bank, although banks often like to keep their rates fixed for substantial periods. Thus, these liabilities are partially but not fully rate-sensitive. The bank manager estimates that 10% of checkable deposits ($1.5 million) and 20% of savings deposits ($3 million) should be considered rate-sensitive. Adding the $1.5 million and $3 million to the $45 million figure yields a total for rate-sensitive liabilities of $49.5 million.

Now the bank manager can analyze what will happen if interest rates rise by 1 percentage point, say, on average from 10% to 11%. The income on the assets rises by $320,000 (= 1% × $32 million of rate-sensitive assets), while the payments on the liabilities rise by $495,000 (= 1% × $49.5 million of rate-sensitive liabilities). The First National Bank's profits now decline by $175,000 = ($320,000 − $495,000). Another way of thinking about this situation is with the net interest margin concept described in Chapter 17, which is interest income minus interest expense divided by bank assets. In this case, the 1% rise in interest rates has resulted in a decline of the net interest margin by 0.175% (= −$175,000/$100 million). Conversely, if interest rates fall by 1%, similar reasoning tells us that the First National Bank's income rises by $175,000 and its net interest margin rises by 0.175%. This example illustrates the following point: ***If a financial institution has more rate-sensitive liabilities than assets, a rise in interest rates will reduce the net interest margin and income, and a decline in interest rates will raise the net interest margin and income.***

Income Gap Analysis

One simple and quick approach to measuring the sensitivity of bank income to changes in interest rates is **gap analysis** (also called **income gap analysis**), in which the amount of rate-sensitive liabilities is subtracted from the amount of rate-sensitive assets. This calculation, *GAP*, can be written as

$$GAP = RSA - RSL \tag{1}$$

where RSA = rate-sensitive assets
RSL = rate-sensitive liabilities

In our example, the bank manager calculates *GAP* to be

$$GAP = \$32 \text{ million} - \$49.5 \text{ million} = -\$17.5 \text{ million}$$

Multiplying *GAP* times the change in the interest rate immediately reveals the effect on bank income:

$$\Delta I = GAP \times \Delta i \tag{2}$$

where ΔI = change in bank income
Δi = change in interest rates

EXAMPLE 23.1

Income Gap Analysis

Using the −$17.5 million gap calculated with Equation 1, what is the change in income if interest rates rise by 1%?

> Solution

The change in income is −$175,000.

$$\Delta I = GAP \times \Delta i$$

where

$GAP = RSA - RSL = -\$17.5 \text{ million}$

Δi = change in interest rate $= 0.01$

Thus,

$$\Delta I = -\$17.5 \text{ million} \times 0.01 = -\$175{,}000$$

The analysis we just conducted is known as *basic gap analysis*, and it suffers from the problem that many of the assets and liabilities that are not classified as rate-sensitive have different maturities. One refinement to deal with this problem, the *maturity bucket approach*, is to measure the gap for several maturity subintervals, called maturity buckets, so that effects of interest-rate changes over a multiyear period can be calculated.

EXAMPLE 23.2

Income Gap Analysis

The manager of First National Bank notices that the bank balance sheet allows him to put assets and liabilities into more refined maturity buckets that enable him to estimate the potential change in income over the next one to two years. Rate-sensitive assets in this period consist of $5 million of securities maturing in one to two years, $10 million of commercial loans maturing in one to two years, and an additional $2 million (20%

of fixed-rate mortgages) that the bank expects to be repaid. Rate-sensitive liabilities in this period consist of \$5 million of one- to two-year CDs, \$5 million of one- to two-year borrowings, \$1.5 million of checkable deposits (the 10% of checkable deposits that the bank manager estimates are rate-sensitive in this period), and an additional \$3 million of savings deposits (the 20% estimate of savings deposits). For the next one to two years, calculate the gap and the change in income if interest rates rise by 1%.

> Solution

The gap calculation for the one- to two-year period is \$2.5 million.

$$GAP = RSA - RSL$$

where

$$RSA = \text{rate-sensitive assets} = \$17 \text{ million}$$

$$RSL = \text{rate-sensitive liabilities} = \$14.5 \text{ million}$$

Thus,

$$GAP = \$17 \text{ million} - \$14.5 \text{ million} = \$2.5 \text{ million}$$

If interest rates remain 1% higher, then in the second year income will improve by \$25,000.

$$\Delta I = GAP \times \Delta i$$

where

$$GAP = RSA - RSL = \$2.5 \text{ million}$$

$$\Delta i = \text{change in interest rate} = 0.01$$

Thus,

$$\Delta I = \$2.5 \text{ million} \times 0.01 = \$25{,}000$$

By using the more refined maturity bucket approach, the bank manager can figure out what will happen to bank income over the next several years when there is a change in interest rates.

Duration Gap Analysis

The gap analysis we have examined so far focuses only on the effect of interest-rate changes on income. Clearly, owners and managers of financial institutions care not only about the effect of changes in interest rates on income but also about the effect of changes in interest rates on the market value of the net worth of the financial institution.[1]

An alternative method for measuring interest-rate risk, called **duration gap analysis**, examines the sensitivity of the market value of the financial institution's net worth to changes in interest rates. Duration analysis is based on Macaulay's concept of *duration*, which measures the average lifetime of a security's stream of

[1]Note that accounting net worth is calculated on a historical-cost (book-value) basis, meaning that the value of assets and liabilities is based on their initial price. However, book-value net worth does not give a complete picture of the true worth of the firm; the market value of net worth provides a more accurate measure. This is why duration gap analysis focuses on what happens to the market value of net worth, and not on book value, when interest rates change.

payments (described in Chapter 3). Recall that duration is a useful concept because it provides a good approximation, particularly when interest-rate changes are small, of the sensitivity of a security's market value to a change in its interest rate using the following formula:

$$\%\Delta P \approx -DUR \times \frac{\Delta i}{1+i} \tag{3}$$

where $\%\Delta P = (P_{t+1} - P_t)/P_t$ = percent change in market value of the security
DUR = duration
i = interest rate

After having determined the duration of all assets and liabilities on the bank's balance sheet, the bank manager could use this formula to calculate how the market value of each asset and liability changes when there is a change in interest rates and then calculate the effect on net worth. There is, however, an easier way to go about doing this, derived from the basic fact about duration we learned in Chapter 3: Duration is additive; that is, the duration of a portfolio of securities is the weighted average of the durations of the individual securities, with the weights reflecting the proportion of the portfolio invested in each. What this means is that the bank manager can figure out the effect that interest-rate changes will have on the market value of net worth by calculating the average duration for assets and for liabilities and then using those figures to estimate the effects of interest-rate changes. To see how a bank manager would do this, let's return to the balance sheet of the First National Bank. The bank manager has already used the procedures outlined in Chapter 3 to calculate the duration of each asset and liability, as listed in Table 23.1. For each asset, the manager then calculates the weighted duration by multiplying the duration times the amount of the asset divided by total assets, which in this case is \$100 million. For example, in the case of securities with maturities of less than one year, the manager multiplies the 0.4 year of duration times \$5 million divided by \$100 million to get a weighted duration of 0.02. (Note that physical assets have no cash payments, so they have a duration of zero years.) Doing this for all the assets and adding them up, the bank manager gets a figure for the average duration of the assets of 2.70 years.

The manager follows a similar procedure for the liabilities, noting that total liabilities excluding capital are \$95 million. For example, the weighted duration for checkable deposits is determined by multiplying the 2.0-year duration by \$15 million divided by \$95 million to get 0.32. Adding up these weighted durations, the manager obtains an average duration of liabilities of 1.03 years.

TABLE 23.1 Duration of the First National Bank's Assets and Liabilities

	Amount (\$ millions)	Duration (years)	Weighted Duration (years)
Assets			
Reserves and cash items	5	0.0	0.00
Securities			
Less than 1 year	5	0.4	0.02
1 to 2 years	5	1.6	0.08
Greater than 2 years	10	7.0	0.70

(continued)

TABLE 23.1 Duration of the First National Bank's Assets and Liabilities (*continued*)

	Amount ($ millions)	Duration (years)	Weighted Duration (years)
Residential mortgages			
Variable rate	10	0.5	0.05
Fixed rate (30-year)	10	6.0	0.60
Commercial loans			
Less than 1 year	15	0.7	0.11
1 to 2 years	10	1.4	0.14
Greater than 2 years	25	4.0	1.00
Physical capital	5	0.0	0.00
Average duration			2.70
Liabilities			
Checkable deposits	15	2.0	0.32
Money market deposit accounts	5	0.1	0.01
Savings deposits	15	1.0	0.16
CDs			
Variable rate	10	0.5	0.05
Less than 1 year	15	0.2	0.03
1 to 2 years	5	1.2	0.06
Greater than 2 years	5	2.7	0.14
Fed funds	5	0.0	0.00
Borrowings			
Less than 1 year	10	0.3	0.03
1 to 2 years	5	1.3	0.07
Greater than 2 years	5	3.1	0.16
Average duration			1.03

EXAMPLE 23.3

Duration Gap Analysis

The bank manager wants to know what happens when interest rates rise from 10% to 11%. The total asset value is $100 million, and the total liability value is $95 million. Use Equation 3 to calculate the change in the market value of the assets and liabilities.

> Solution

With a total asset value of $100 million, the market value of assets falls by $2.5 million ($100 million × 0.025 = $2.5 million).

$$\%\Delta P \approx -DUR \times \frac{\Delta i}{1+i}$$

where

DUR = duration = 2.70

Δi = change in interest rate = $0.11 - 0.10 = 0.01$

i = interest rate = 0.10

Thus,

$$\%\Delta P \approx -2.70 \times \frac{0.01}{1 + 0.10} = -0.025 = -2.5\%$$

With total liabilities of $95 million, the market value of liabilities falls by $0.9 million ($95 million × 0.009 = −$0.9 million).

$$\%\Delta P \approx -DUR \times \frac{\Delta i}{1 + i}$$

where

DUR = duration = 1.03

Δi = change in interest rate = $0.11 - 0.10 = 0.01$

i = interest rate = 0.10

Thus,

$$\%\Delta P \approx -1.03 \times \frac{0.01}{1 + 0.10} = -0.009 = -0.9\%$$

The result is that the net worth of the bank would decline by $1.6 million [−$2.5 million − (−$0.9 million) = −$2.5 million + $0.9 million = − $1.6 million].

The bank manager could have obtained the answer even more quickly by calculating what is called a *duration gap*, which is defined as follows:

$$DUR_{gap} = DUR_a - \left(\frac{L}{A} \times DUR_l\right) \tag{4}$$

where DUR_a = average duration of assets
DUR_l = average duration of liabilities
L = market value of liabilities
A = market value of assets

EXAMPLE 23.4

Gap Analysis

Based on the information provided in Example 3, use Equation 4 to determine the duration gap for First National Bank.

> Solution

The duration gap for First National Bank is 1.72 years.

$$DUR_{gap} = DUR_a - \left(\frac{L}{A} \times DUR_l\right)$$

where

DUR_a = average duration of assets = 2.70

L = market value of liabilities = 95

$$A = \text{market value of assets} = 100$$
$$DUR_l = \text{average duration of liabilities} = 1.03$$

Thus,

$$DUR_{gap} = 2.70 - \left(\frac{95}{100} \times 1.03\right) = 1.72 \text{ years}$$

EXAMPLE 23.5

Duration Gap Analysis

What is the change in the market value of net worth as a percentage of assets if interest rates rise from 10% to 11%? (Use Equation 5 below.)

> Solution

A rise in interest rates from 10% to 11% would lead to a change in the market value of net worth as a percentage of assets of −1.6%.

$$\frac{\Delta NW}{A} = -DUR_{gap} \times \frac{\Delta i}{1 + i}$$

where

$$DUR_{gap} = \text{duration gap} = 1.72$$
$$\Delta i = \text{change in interest rate} = 0.11 - 0.10 = 0.01$$
$$i = \text{interest rate} = 0.10$$

Thus,

$$\frac{\Delta NW}{A} = -1.72 \times \frac{0.01}{1 + 0.10} = -0.016 = -1.6\%$$

To estimate what will happen if interest rates change, the bank manager uses the DUR_{gap} calculation in Equation 4 to obtain the change in the market value of net worth as a percentage of total assets. In other words, the change in the market value of net worth as a percentage of assets is calculated as

$$\frac{\Delta NW}{A} \approx -DUR_{gap} \times \frac{\Delta i}{1 + i} \qquad (5)$$

With assets totaling $100 million, Example 23.5 indicates a fall in the market value of net worth of $1.6 million, which is the same amount that we found in Example 23.3.

As our examples make clear, both income gap analysis and duration gap analysis indicate that the First National Bank will suffer from a rise in interest rates. Indeed, in this example, we have seen that a rise in interest rates from 10% to 11% will cause the market value of net worth to fall by $1.6 million, which is one-third the initial amount of bank capital. Thus, the bank manager realizes that the bank faces substantial interest-rate risk because a rise in interest rates could cause it to lose a lot of its capital. Clearly, income gap analysis and duration gap analysis are useful tools for telling a financial institution manager the institution's degree of exposure to interest-rate risk.

Example of a Nonbanking Financial Institution

So far we have focused on an example involving a banking institution that has borrowed short and lent long so that when interest rates rise, both income and the net worth of the institution fall. It is important to recognize that income gap and duration gap analyses apply equally to other financial institutions. Furthermore, it is important for you to see that some financial institutions have income gaps and duration gaps that are opposite in sign to those of banks, so that when interest rates rise, both income and net worth rise rather than fall. To get a more complete picture of income gap and duration gap analyses, let us look at a nonbank financial institution, the Friendly Finance Company, which specializes in making consumer loans.

The Friendly Finance Company has the following balance sheet:

Friendly Finance Company

Assets		Liabilities	
Cash and deposits	$3 million	Commercial paper	$40 million
Securities		Bank loans	
Less than 1 year	$5 million	Less than 1 year	$3 million
1 to 2 years	$1 million	1 to 2 years	$2 million
Greater than 2 years	$1 million	Greater than 2 years	$5 million
Consumer loans		Long-term bonds and other long-term debt	$40 million
Less than 1 year	$50 million		
1 to 2 years	$20 million	Capital	$10 million
Greater than 2 years	$15 million		
Physical capital	$5 million		
Total	$100 million	Total	$100 million

The manager of the Friendly Finance Company calculates the rate-sensitive assets to be equal to the $5 million of securities with maturities of less than one year plus the $50 million of consumer loans with maturities of less than one year, for a total of $55 million of rate-sensitive assets. The manager then calculates the rate-sensitive liabilities to be equal to the $40 million of commercial paper, all of which has a maturity of less than one year, plus the $3 million of bank loans maturing in less than a year, for a total of $43 million. The calculation of the income gap is then

$$GAP = RSA - RSL = \$55 \text{ million} - \$43 \text{ million} = \$12 \text{ million}$$

To calculate the effect on income if interest rates rise by 1%, the manager multiplies the *GAP* of $12 million times the change in the interest rate to get the following:

$$\Delta I = GAP \times \Delta i = \$12 \text{ million} \times 1\% = \$120{,}000$$

Thus, the manager finds that the finance company's income will rise by $120,000 when interest rates rise by 1%. The reason that the company has benefited from the interest-rate rise, in contrast to the First National Bank, whose profits suffer from the rise in interest rates, is that the Friendly Finance Company has a positive income gap because it has more rate-sensitive assets than liabilities.

Like the bank manager, the manager of the Friendly Finance Company has already calculated the duration of each asset and liability and is interested in what happens to the market value of the net worth of the company when interest rates rise by 1%. So the manager calculates the weighted duration of each item in the balance sheet, adds them up as in Table 23.2, and obtains a duration for the assets of 1.14 years and for the liabilities of 2.77 years. The duration gap is then calculated to be

$$DUR_{gap} = DUR_a - \left(\frac{L}{A} \times DUR_l\right) = 1.14 - \left(\frac{90}{100} \times 2.77\right) = -1.35 \text{ years}$$

Since the Friendly Finance Company has a negative duration gap, the manager realizes that a rise in interest rates by 1 percentage point from 10% to 11% will increase

TABLE 23.2 Duration of the Friendly Finance Company's Assets and Liabilities

	Amount ($ millions)	Duration (years)	Weighted Duration (years)
Assets			
Cash and deposits	3	0.0	0.00
Securities			
Less than 1 year	5	0.5	0.03
1 to 2 years	1	1.7	0.02
Greater than 2 years	1	9.0	0.09
Consumer loans			
Less than 1 year	50	0.5	0.25
1 to 2 years	20	1.5	0.30
Greater than 2 years	15	3.0	0.45
Physical capital	5	0.0	0.00
Average duration			1.14
Liabilities			
Commercial paper	40	0.2	0.09
Bank loans			
Less than 1 year	3	0.3	0.01
1 to 2 years	2	1.6	0.04
Greater than 2 years	5	3.5	0.19
Long-term bonds and other long-term debt	40	5.5	2.44
Average duration			2.77

the market value of net worth of the firm. The manager checks this by calculating the change in the market value of net worth as a percentage of assets:

$$\frac{\Delta NW}{A} = -DUR_{gap} \times \frac{\Delta i}{1 + i} = -(-1.35) \times \frac{0.01}{1 + 0.10} = 0.012 = 1.2\%$$

With assets of $100 million, this calculation indicates that net worth will rise in market value by $1.2 million.

Even though the income gap and duration gap analyses indicate that the Friendly Finance Company gains from a rise in interest rates, the manager realizes that if interest rates go in the other direction, the company will suffer a fall in income and market value of net worth. Thus, the finance company manager, like the bank manager, realizes that the institution is subject to substantial interest-rate risk.

Some Problems with Income Gap and Duration Gap Analyses

Although you might think that income gap and duration gap analyses are complicated enough, further complications make a financial institution manager's job even harder.

One assumption that we have been using in our discussion of income gap and duration gap analyses is that when the level of interest rates changes, interest rates on all maturities change by exactly the same amount. That is the same as saying that we conducted our analysis under the assumption that the slope of the yield curve remains unchanged. Indeed, the situation is even worse for duration gap analysis because the duration gap is calculated assuming that interest rates for all maturities are the same—in other words, the yield curve is assumed to be flat. As our discussion of the term structure of interest rates in Chapter 5 indicated, however, the yield curve is not flat, and the slope of the yield curve fluctuates and has a tendency to change when the level of the interest rate changes. Thus, to get a truly accurate assessment of interest-rate risk, a financial institution manager has to assess what might happen to the slope of the yield curve when the level of the interest rate changes and then take this information into account when assessing interest-rate risk. In addition, duration gap analysis is based on the approximation in Equation 3 and thus only works well for small changes in interest rates.

A problem with income gap analysis is that, as we have seen, the financial institution manager must make estimates of the proportion of supposedly fixed-rate assets and liabilities that may be rate-sensitive. This involves estimates of the likelihood of prepayment of loans or customer shifts out of deposits when interest rates change. Such guesses are not easy to make, and as a result, the financial institution manager's estimates of income gaps may not be very accurate. A similar problem occurs in calculating durations of assets and liabilities because many of the cash payments are uncertain. Thus, the estimate of the duration gap might not be accurate either.

Do these problems mean that managers of banks and other financial institutions should give up on gap analysis as a tool for measuring interest-rate risk? Financial institutions do use more sophisticated approaches to measuring interest-rate risk, such as scenario analysis and value-at-risk analysis, which make greater use of computers to more accurately measure changes in prices of assets when interest rates change. Income gap and duration gap analyses, however, still provide simple frameworks to help financial institution managers to get a first assessment of interest-rate risk, and thus they are useful tools in the financial institution managers' toolkit.

THE PRACTICING MANAGER

Strategies for Managing Interest-Rate Risk

Once financial institution managers have done the income gap and duration gap analyses for their institutions, they must decide which alternative strategies to pursue. If the manager of the First National Bank firmly believes that interest rates will fall in the future, he or she may be willing to take no action, knowing that the bank has more rate-sensitive liabilities than rate-sensitive assets and so will benefit from the expected interest-rate decline. However, the bank manager also realizes that the First National Bank is subject to substantial interest-rate risk because there is always a possibility that interest rates will rise rather than fall, and as we have seen, this outcome could bankrupt the bank. The manager might try to shorten the duration of the bank's assets to increase their rate sensitivity either by purchasing assets of shorter maturity or by converting fixed-rate loans into adjustable-rate loans. Alternatively, the bank manager could lengthen the duration of the liabilities. With these adjustments to the bank's assets and liabilities, the bank would be less affected by interest-rate swings.

For example, the bank manager might decide to eliminate the income gap by increasing the amount of rate-sensitive assets to \$49.5 million, to equal the \$49.5 million of rate-sensitive liabilities. Or the manager could reduce rate-sensitive liabilities to \$32 million so that they equal rate-sensitive assets. In either case, the income gap would now be zero, so a change in interest rates would have no effect on bank profits in the coming year.

Alternatively, the bank manager might decide to immunize the market value of the bank's net worth completely from interest-rate risk by adjusting assets and liabilities so that the duration gap is equal to zero. To do this, the manager can set DUR_{gap} equal to zero in Equation 4 and solve for DUR_a:

$$DUR_a = \frac{L}{A} \times DUR_l = \frac{95}{100} \times 1.03 = 0.98$$

These calculations reveal that the manager should reduce the average duration of the bank's assets to 0.98 year. To check that the duration gap is set equal to zero, the calculation is

$$DUR_{gap} = 0.98 - \left(\frac{95}{100} \times 1.03\right) = 0$$

In this case, using Equation 5, the market value of net worth would remain unchanged when interest rates change. Alternatively, the bank manager could calculate the value of the duration of the liabilities that would produce a duration gap of zero. To do this would involve setting DUR_{gap} equal to zero in Equation 4 and solving for DUR_l:

$$DUR_l = DUR_a \times \frac{A}{L} = 2.70 \times \frac{100}{95} = 2.84$$

This calculation reveals that the interest-rate risk could also be eliminated by increasing the average duration of the bank's liabilities to 2.84 years. The manager again checks that the duration gap is set equal to zero by calculating

$$DUR_{gap} = 2.70 - \left(\frac{95}{100} \times 2.84\right) = 0$$

One problem with eliminating a financial institution's interest-rate risk by altering the balance sheet is that doing so might be very costly in the short run. The financial institution may be locked into assets and liabilities of particular durations because of its field of expertise. Fortunately, recently developed financial instruments, such as financial futures, options, and interest-rate swaps, help financial institutions manage their interest-rate risk without requiring them to rearrange their balance sheets. We discuss these instruments and how they can be used to manage interest-rate risk in the next chapter.

SUMMARY

1. The concepts of adverse selection and moral hazard explain the origin of many credit risk management principles involving loan activities, including screening and monitoring, development of long-term customer relationships, loan commitments, collateral, compensating balances, and credit rationing.
2. With the increased volatility of interest rates that occurred in recent years, financial institutions became more concerned about their exposure to interest-rate risk. Income gap and duration gap analyses tell a financial institution if it has fewer rate-sensitive assets than liabilities (in which case a rise in interest rates will reduce income and a fall in interest rates will raise it) or more rate-sensitive assets than liabilities (in which case a rise in interest rates will raise income and a fall in interest rates will reduce it). Financial institutions can manage interest-rate risk by modifying their balance sheets and by making use of new financial instruments.

KEY TERMS

compensating balances, p. 562
credit rationing, p. 562
duration gap analysis, p. 566
gap analysis (income gap analysis), p. 564
loan commitment, p. 561
secured loans, p. 561

QUESTIONS

1. Can a financial institution keep borrowers from engaging in risky activities if there are no restrictive covenants written into the loan agreement?
2. Why are secured loans an important method of lending for financial institutions?
3. Diego applied for a \$450,000 loan for his local brewing company. However, the bank approved his loan for only \$250,000. Which type of credit risk management strategy was applied by this bank? Which type of asymmetric problem is the bank trying to solve?
4. Why is being nosy a desirable trait for a banker?
5. The following is an excerpt from the Federal Reserve web site, released September 21, 2016: "...the Committee decided to maintain the target range for the federal funds rate at 1/4 to 1/2 percent. The Committee judges that the case for an increase in the federal funds rate has strengthened but decided, for the time being, to wait for further evidence of continued progress toward its objectives." Explain what would be the immediate effect on a bank income if its income gap analysis yields a GAP = −\$500 million. What would happen to bank income if the increase in the federal funds rate finally materializes?
6. "Because diversification is a desirable strategy for avoiding risk, it never makes sense for a financial institution to specialize in making specific types of loans." Is this statement true, false, or uncertain? Explain your answer.

QUANTITATIVE PROBLEMS

1. A bank issues a $100,000 variable-rate 30-year mortgage with a nominal annual rate of 4.5%. If the interest rate drops to 4.0% after the first six months, what is the impact on the interest income for the first 12 months?
2. A bank issues a $100,000 fixed-rate 30-year mortgage with a nominal annual rate of 4.5%. If the interest rate drops to 4.0% immediately after the mortgage is issued, what is the impact on the value of the mortgage?
3. A bank makes a loan with the following characteristics: monthly payments for 20 years, with a nominal annual rate of 4.5%. The amount loaned is $350,000. What is the duration of the loan? Calculate the expected percentage change in value if the interest rate increases 1 percentage point immediately after the loan is approved.
4. Calculate the new interest rate if a bank realizes that the value of a mortgage increases from $450,000 to $471,428.57, if the duration of the mortgage is 10 years and the interest rate used to price this asset was originally 5%.
5. The duration of a bank's portfolio of assets is 9 years; the interest rate has recently decreased by 3/5 of a percentage point, increasing the value of the portfolio 4.5%. If the portfolio is now valued at $6.7 million, determine the value of the portfolio before the change in the interest rate. Determine the interest rate at which the portfolio was originally priced (i.e., the level of the interest rate before its change).
6. A bank manager is worried because the income gap currently equals −$35 million and interest rates are expected to increase by 1.5%. Determine the amount of rate-sensitive assets if rate sensitive liabilities are $467 million. Calculate the change in bank income if interest rates increase by 1.5%.
7. A financial institution has rate-sensitive assets of $392 million. What is the maximum amount of rate-sensitive liabilities this institution will decide to keep in its balance sheet if interest rates are expected to increase by 1% and this institution wants to avoid losses in excess of $450,000.
8. Determine the income gap of a bank with the following assets: reserves ($6 million), short term securities ($8 million), commercial loans maturing in less than 1 year ($20 million), commercial loans maturing in more than 5 years ($30 million); and the following liabilities: federal funds ($9 million), short term borrowings ($10 million), long term borrowings ($7 million), and CDs maturing in more than 2 years ($4 million).
9. The following financial statement is for the current year. From the past, you know that 10% of fixed-rate mortgages prepay each year. You also estimate that 10% of checkable deposits and 20% of savings accounts are rate-sensitive.

   What is the current income gap for Second National Bank? What will happen to the bank's current net interest income if rates fall by 75 basis points?

Second National Bank

Assets		Liabilities	
Reserves	$1,500,000	Checkable deposits	$15,000,000
Securities		Money market deposits	$5,500,000
< 1 year	$6,000,000	Savings accounts	$8,000,000
1 to 2 years	$8,000,000	CDs	
> 2 years	$12,000,000	Variable rate	$15,000,000
Residential mortgages		< 1 year	$22,000,000
Variable rate	$7,000,000	1 to 2 years	$5,000,000
Fixed rate	$13,000,000	> 2 years	$2,500,000
Commercial loans		Federal funds	$5,000,000
< 1 year	$1,500,000	Borrowings	
1 to 2 years	$18,500,000	< 1 year	$12,000,000
> 2 years	$30,000,000	1 to 2 years	$3,000,000
Buildings, etc.	$2,500,000	> 2 years	$2,000,000
		Bank capital	$5,000,000
Total	$100,000,000	Total	$100,000,000

10. Orinoco Bank has the following rate-sensitive assets: Treasury bills ($210 million), commercial loans ($540 million), and consumer loans ($200 million). The duration of each type of asset is 0.65, 1.87 and 6.9 years, respectively. Calculate Orinoco Bank's average duration of the assets if physical capital equals $35 million and the bank holds $15 million in reserves.

11. Determine the duration gap of a financial institution with an average duration of assets of 3.2 years, and an average duration of liabilities of 4.5 years assuming the market value of assets is $405 million and the market value of liabilities equal $382 million.

12. Determine the minimum average duration of assets a bank needs if it wants to tolerate a duration gap not lower than −1.5 years, assuming that the average duration of liabilities is 3 years, that assets are currently valued at $300 million, and that liabilities are $280 million.

13. CNDF Bank has assets totaling $250 million with an average duration of 5 years, and liabilities totaling $225 million, with an average duration of 4 years. CNDF Bank is subject to Basel III requirements, and therefore has to maintain a capital/asset ratio of at least 8%. Determine whether CNDF Bank complies with the requirement if interest rates increase from 6% to 7%.

14. The manager for Tyler Bank and Trust has the following assets and liabilities to manage:

Asset	Value	Duration (years)
Bonds	$75,000,000	9.00
Consumer loans	$875,000,000	2.00
Commercial loans	$700,000,000	5.00

Liability	Value	Duration (years)
Demand deposits	$300,000,000	1.00
Saving accounts	??	0.50

If the manager wants a duration gap of 3.00, what level of saving accounts should the bank raise? Assume that any difference between assets and liabilities is held as cash (duration = 0).

15. The following financial statement for the First National Bank is for the current year. After you review the data, calculate the duration gap for the bank.

First National Bank

Assets		Duration (in years)	Liabilities		Duration (in years)
Reserves	$5,000,000	0.00	Checkable deposits	$15,000,000	2.00
Securities			Money market deposits	5,000,000	0.10
< 1 year	5,000,000	0.40	Savings accounts	15,000,000	1.00
1 to 2 years	5,000,000	1.60	CDs		
> 2 years	10,000,000	7.00	Variable rate	10,000,000	0.50
Residential mortgages			< 1 year	15,000,000	0.20
Variable rate	10,000,000	0.50	1 to 2 years	5,000,000	1.20
Fixed rate	10,000,000	6.00	> 2 years	5,000,000	2.70
Commercial loans			Interbank loans	5,000,000	0.00
< 1 year	15,000,000	0.70	Borrowings		
1 to 2 years	10,000,000	1.40	< 1 year	10,000,000	0.30
> 2 years	25,000,000	4.00	1 to 2 years	5,000,000	1.30
Buildings, etc.	5,000,000	0.00	> 2 years	5,000,000	3.10
			Bank capital	5,000,000	
Total	$100,000,000		Total	$100,000,000	

For problems 16–23, assume that the First National Bank initially has the balance sheet shown above and that interest rates are initially at 10%.

16. If the First National Bank sells $10 million of its securities with maturities greater than two years and replaces them with securities maturing in less than one year, what is the income gap for the bank? What will happen to profits next year if interest rates fall by 3 percentage points?

17. If the First National Bank decides to convert $5 million of its fixed-rate mortgages into variable-rate mortgages, what happens to its interest-rate risk? Explain with income gap and duration gap analyses.

18. If the manager of the First National Bank revises the estimate of the percentage of fixed-rate mortgages that are repaid within a year from 20% to 10%, what will be the revised estimate of the interest-rate risk the bank faces? What will happen to profits next year if interest rates fall by 2 percentage points?

19. If the manager of the First National Bank revises the estimate of the percentage of checkable deposits that are rate-sensitive from 10% to 25%, what will be the revised estimate of the interest-rate risk the bank faces? What will happen to profits next year if interest rates rise by 5 percentage points?

20. Given the estimates of duration in the table above, what will happen to the bank's net worth if interest rates rise by 10 percentage points? Will the bank stay in business? Why or why not?

21. If the manager of the First National Bank revises the estimates of the duration of the bank's assets to four years and liabilities to two years, what is the effect on net worth if interest rates rise by 2 percentage points?

22. Given the estimates of duration in problem 21, how should the bank alter the duration of its assets to immunize its net worth from interest-rate risk?

23. Given the estimates of duration in problem 21, how should the bank alter the duration of its liabilities to immunize its net worth from interest-rate risk?

For problems 24–29, assume that the Friendly Finance Company initially has the balance sheet shown on page 571 and that interest rates are initially at 8%.

24. If the manager of the Friendly Finance Company decides to sell off $10 million of the company's consumer loans, half maturing within one year and half maturing in greater than two years, and uses the resulting funds to buy $10 million of Treasury bills, what is the income gap for the company? What will happen to profits next year if interest rates fall by 5 percentage points? How could the Friendly Finance Company alter its balance sheet to immunize its income from this change in interest rates?

25. If the Friendly Finance Company raises an additional $20 million with commercial paper and uses the funds to make $20 million of consumer loans that mature in less than one year, what happens to its interest-rate risk? In this situation, what additional changes could it make in its balance sheet to eliminate the income gap?

26. Given the estimates of duration in Table 23.2, what will happen to the Friendly Finance Company's net worth if interest rates rise by 3 percentage points? Will the company stay in business? Why or why not?

27. If the manager of the Friendly Finance Company revises the estimates of the duration of the company's assets to two years and liabilities to four years, what is the effect on net worth if interest rates rise by 3 percentage points?

28. Given the estimates of duration found in problem 27, how should the Friendly Finance Company alter the duration of its assets to immunize its net worth from interest-rate risk?

29. Given the estimates of duration in problem 27, how should the Friendly Finance Company alter the duration of its liabilities to immunize its net worth from interest-rate risk?

WEB EXERCISES

Risk Management in Financial Institutions

1. This chapter discussed the need financial institutions have to control credit risk by lending to creditworthy borrowers. If you allow your credit to deteriorate, you may find yourself unable to borrow when you need to. Go to **http://quicken.intuit.com/support/help/managing-your-credit/winning-back-your-finances–how-to-increase-your-credit-score-in-6-months-/INF24303.html**. What factors affect your creditworthiness? What can you do to improve your appeal to lenders?

2. The FDIC is extremely concerned with risk management in banks. High-risk banks are more likely to fail and cost the FDIC money. The FDIC regularly examines banks and rates them using a system called CAMELS. Go to **http://www.frbsf.org/econrsrch/wklyltr/wklyltr99/el99-19.html**. What does the acronym CAMELS stand for? Discuss how CAMELS ratings are used in the supervisory process.

CHAPTER 24

Hedging with Financial Derivatives

> PREVIEW

Starting in the 1970s and increasingly in the 1980s and 1990s, the world became a riskier place for financial institutions. Swings in interest rates widened, and the bond and stock markets went through several episodes of increased volatility. As a result of these developments, managers of financial institutions have become more concerned with reducing the risk their institutions face. Given the greater demand for risk reduction, the process of financial innovation described in Chapter 19 came to the rescue by producing new financial instruments that help financial institution managers manage risk better. These instruments, called **financial derivatives**, have payoffs that are linked to previously issued securities and are extremely useful risk-reduction tools.

In this chapter we look at the most important financial derivatives that managers of financial institutions use to reduce risk: forward contracts, financial futures, options, and swaps. We examine not only how markets for each of these financial derivatives work but also how each can be used by financial institution managers to reduce risk.

Hedging

Access http://www.rmahq.org/. The Web site of the Risk Management Association reports useful information such as annual statement studies, online publications, and so on.

Financial derivatives are so effective in reducing risk because they enable financial institutions to **hedge**, that is, engage in a financial transaction that reduces or eliminates risk. When a financial institution has bought an asset, it is said to have taken a **long position**, and this exposes the institution to risk if the returns on the asset are uncertain. On the other hand, if it has sold an asset that it has agreed to deliver to another party at a future date, it is said to have taken a **short position**, and this can also expose the institution to risk. Financial derivatives can be used to reduce risk by invoking the following basic principle of hedging: ***Hedging risk involves engaging in a financial transaction that offsets a long position by taking an additional short position, or offsets a short position by taking an additional long position.*** In other words, if a financial institution has *bought* a security and has therefore taken a long position, it conducts a hedge by contracting to *sell* that security (take a short position) at some future date. Alternatively, if it has taken a short position by *selling* a security that it needs to deliver at a future date, then it conducts a hedge by contracting to *buy* that security (take a long position) at a future date. We first look at how this principle can be applied using forward contracts.

Forward Markets

Forward contracts are agreements by two parties to engage in a financial transaction at a future (forward) point in time. Here we focus on forward contracts that are linked to debt instruments, called **interest-rate forward contracts**; later in the chapter we discuss forward contracts for foreign currencies.

Interest-Rate Forward Contracts

Interest-rate forward contracts involve the future sale or purchase of a debt instrument and have several dimensions: (1) specification of the actual debt instrument that will be delivered at a future date, (2) amount of the debt instrument to be delivered, (3) price (interest rate) on the debt instrument when it is delivered, and (4) date on which delivery will take place. An example of an interest-rate forward contract might be an agreement for the First National Bank to sell to the Rock Solid Insurance Company, one year from today, $5 million face value of the *6*s of 2037 Treasury bonds (coupon bonds with a 6% coupon rate that mature in 2037) at a price that yields the same interest rate on these bonds as today's, say, 6%. Because Rock Solid will buy the securities at a future date, it has taken a long position, whereas the First National Bank, which will sell the securities, has taken a short position.

THE PRACTICING MANAGER

Hedging Interest-Rate Risk with Forward Contracts

To understand why the First National Bank might want to enter into this forward contract, suppose that you are the manager of the First National Bank and have previously bought $5 million of the *6*s of 2037 Treasury bonds, which currently sell at par value and so their yield to maturity is also 6%. Because these are long-term bonds, you recognize that you are exposed to substantial interest-rate risk and worry that if interest rates rise in the future, the price of these bonds will fall, resulting in a substantial capital loss that may cost you your job. How do you hedge this risk?

Knowing the basic principle of hedging, you see that your long position in these bonds must be offset by an equal short position for the same bonds with a forward contract. That is, you need to contract to sell these bonds at a future date at the current par value price. As a result, you agree with another party, in this case, Rock Solid Insurance Company, to sell them the \$5 million of the 6s of 2037 Treasury bonds at par one year from today. By entering into this forward contract, you have locked in the future price and so have eliminated the price risk First National Bank faces from interest-rate changes. In other words, you have successfully hedged against interest-rate risk.

Why would the Rock Solid Insurance Company want to enter into the forward contract with the First National Bank? Rock Solid expects to receive premiums of \$5 million in one year's time that it will want to invest in the 6s of 2037 but worries that interest rates on these bonds will decline between now and next year. By using the forward contract, it is able to lock in the 6% interest rate on the Treasury bonds (which will be sold to it by the First National Bank).

Pros and Cons of Forward Contracts

The advantage of forward contracts is that they can be as flexible as the parties involved want them to be. This means that an institution like the First National Bank may be able to hedge completely the interest-rate risk for the exact security it is holding in its portfolio, just as it has in our example.

However, forward contracts suffer from two problems that severely limit their usefulness. The first is that it may be very hard for an institution like the First National Bank to find another party (called a *counterparty*) to make the contract with. There are brokers to facilitate the matching up of parties like the First National Bank with the Rock Solid Insurance Company, but few institutions may want to engage in a forward contract specifically for the 6s of 2037. This means that it may prove impossible to find a counterparty when a financial institution like the First National Bank wants to make a specific type of forward contract. Furthermore, even if the First National Bank finds a counterparty, it may not get as high a price as it wants because there may not be anyone else to make the deal with. A serious problem for the market in interest-rate forward contracts, then, is that it may be difficult to make the financial transaction or that it will have to be made at a disadvantageous price; in the parlance of the financial world, this market suffers from a *lack of liquidity*. (Note that this use of the term *liquidity* when it is applied to a market is somewhat broader than its use when it is applied to an asset. For an asset, liquidity refers to the ease with which the asset can be turned into cash, whereas for a market, liquidity refers to the ease of carrying out financial transactions.)

The second problem with forward contracts is that they are subject to default risk. Suppose that in one year's time, interest rates rise so that the price of the 6s of 2037 falls. The Rock Solid Insurance Company might then decide that it would like to default on the forward contract with the First National Bank because it can now buy the bonds at a price lower than the agreed-upon price in the forward contract. Or perhaps Rock Solid may not have been rock solid and will have gone bust during the year and so is no longer available to complete the terms of the forward contract. Because no outside organization is guaranteeing the contract, the only recourse is for the First National Bank to go to the courts to sue Rock Solid, but this process will be costly. Furthermore, if Rock Solid is already bankrupt, the First National Bank will suffer a loss; the bank can no longer sell the *6*s of 2037 at the price it had agreed upon with Rock Solid but instead will have to sell at a price well below that because the price of these bonds has fallen.

The presence of default risk in forward contracts means that parties to these contracts must check each other out to be sure that the counterparty is both financially sound and likely to be honest and live up to its contractual obligations. Because this is a costly process and because all the adverse selection and moral hazard problems discussed in earlier chapters apply, default risk is a major barrier to the use of interest-rate forward contracts. When the default risk problem is combined with a lack of liquidity, we see that these contracts may be of limited usefulness to financial institutions. Although a market for interest-rate forward contracts exists, particularly in Treasury and mortgage-backed securities, it is not nearly as large as the financial futures market, to which we turn next.

Financial Futures Markets

Given the default risk and liquidity problems in the interest-rate forward market, another solution to hedging interest-rate risk was needed. This solution was provided by the development of financial futures contracts by the Chicago Board of Trade, starting in 1975.

Financial Futures Contracts

A **financial futures contract** is similar to an interest-rate forward contract in that it specifies that a financial instrument must be delivered by one party to another on a stated future date. However, it differs from an interest-rate forward contract in several ways that overcome some of the liquidity and default problems of forward markets.

To understand what financial futures contracts are all about, let's look at one of the most widely traded futures contracts, that for Treasury bonds, which are traded on the Chicago Board of Trade. (An illustration of how prices on these contracts are quoted can be found in the Following the Financial News box, "Financial Futures.") The contract value is for $100,000 face value of bonds. Prices are quoted in points, with each point equal to $1,000. This contract specifies that the bonds to be delivered must have at least 15 years to maturity at the delivery date (and must also not be callable, that is, redeemable by the Treasury at its option, in less than 15 years). If the Treasury bonds delivered to settle the futures contract have a coupon rate different from the 6% specified in the futures contract, the amount of bonds to be delivered is adjusted to reflect the difference in value between the delivered bonds and the 6% coupon bond. In line with the terminology used for forward contracts, parties who have bought a futures contract and thereby agreed to buy (take delivery) of the bonds are said to have taken a *long position*, and parties who have sold a futures contract and thereby agreed to sell (deliver) the bonds have taken a *short position*.

> FOLLOWING THE FINANCIAL NEWS

Financial Futures

The prices for financial futures contracts for debt instruments are published daily in newspapers and on Internet sites. A typical entry, like the following one for the Chicago Board of Trade's $100,000 Treasury Bonds contract on June 23, 2016, would have the following information.

	Open	High	Low	Settle	Change	Open Interest
Sept.	131.090	131.090	130.240	130.260	−.170	2,771,629
Dec.	130.235	130.235	130.010	130.020	−.190	3,554,632

Open: Opening price; each point corresponds to $1,000 of face value—131.090 is $131.090 for the September contract.

High: Highest traded price that day—131.090 is $131,090 for the September contract.

Low: Lowest traded price that day—130.240 is $130,240 for the September contract.

Settle: Settlement price, the closing price that day—130.260 is $130,260 for the September contract.

Chg: Change in the settlement price from the previous trading day— −.170 is −$170 for the September contract.

Open Interest: Number of contracts outstanding—2,771,629 for the September contract, with a face value of $277 billion (2,771,629 × $100,000).

To make our understanding of this contract more concrete, let's consider what happens when you buy or sell one of these Treasury bond futures contracts. Let's say that on February 1, you sell one $100,000 June contract at a price of 115 (that is, $115,000). By selling this contract, you agree to deliver $100,000 face value of the long-term Treasury bonds to the contract's counterparty at the end of June for $115,000. By buying the contract at a price of 115, the buyer has agreed to pay $115,000 for the $100,000 face value of bonds when you deliver them at the end of June. If interest rates on long-term bonds rise so that when the contract matures at the end of June the price of these bonds has fallen to 110 ($110,000 per $100,000 of face value), the buyer of the contract will have lost $5,000 because he or she paid $115,000 for the bonds but can sell them only for the market price of $110,000. But you, the seller of the contract, will have gained $5,000 (less commission and expenses) because you can now sell the bonds to the buyer for $115,000 but have to pay only $110,000 for them in the market.

It is even easier to describe what happens to the parties who have purchased futures contracts and those who have sold futures contracts if we recognize the following fact: ***At the expiration date of a futures contract, the price of the contract converges to the price of the underlying asset to be delivered.*** To see why this is the case, consider what happens on the expiration date of the June contract at the end of June when the price of the underlying $100,000 face value Treasury bond is 110 ($110,000). If the futures contract is selling below 110, say, at 109, a trader can buy the contract for $109,000, take delivery of the bond, and immediately sell it for $110,000, thereby earning a quick profit of $1,000. Because earning this profit involves no risk, it is a great deal that everyone would like to get in on. This means that everyone will try to buy the contract, and as a result, its price will rise. Only when the price rises to 110 will the profit opportunity cease to exist and the buying pressure disappear. Conversely, if the price of the futures contract is above 110, say, at 111, everyone will want to sell the contract. Now the sellers get \$111,000 from selling the futures contract but have to pay only \$110,000 for the Treasury bonds that they must deliver to the buyer of the contract, and the \$1,000 difference is their profit. Because this profit involves no risk, traders will continue to sell the futures contract until its price falls back down to 110, at which price there are no longer any profits to be made. The elimination of riskless profit opportunities in the futures market is referred to as **arbitrage**, and it guarantees that the price of a futures contract at expiration equals the price of the underlying asset to be delivered.[1]

Armed with the fact that a futures contract at expiration equals the price of the underlying asset, it is even easier to see who profits and loses from such a contract when interest rates change. When interest rates have risen so that the price of the Treasury bond is 110 on the expiration day at the end of June, the June Treasury bond futures contract will also have a price of 110. Thus, if you bought the contract for 115 in February, you have a loss of 5 points, or \$5,000 (5% of \$100,000). But if you sold the futures contract at 115 in February, the decline in price to 110 means that you have a profit of 5 points, or \$5,000.

THE PRACTICING MANAGER

Hedging with Financial Futures

As the manager of the First National Bank, you can also use financial futures to hedge the interest-rate risk on its holdings of \$5 million of the *6*s of 2037.

To see how to do this, suppose that in March 2017 the *6*s of 2037 are the long-term bonds that would be delivered in the Chicago Board of Trade's T-bond futures contract expiring one year in the future, in March 2018. Also suppose that the interest rate on these bonds is expected to remain at 6% over the next year so that both the *6*s of 2037 and the futures contract are selling at par (i.e., the \$5 million of bonds is selling for \$5 million and the \$100,000 futures contract is selling for \$100,000). The basic principle of hedging indicates that you need to offset the long position in these bonds with a short position, so you have to sell the futures contract. But how many contracts should you sell? The number of contracts required to hedge the interest-rate risk is found by dividing the amount of the asset to be hedged by the dollar value of each contract, as is shown in Equation 1 below.

$$NC = VA/VC \tag{1}$$

where
NC = number of contracts for the hedge
VA = value of the asset
VC = value of each contract

[1]In actuality, futures contracts sometimes set conditions for the timing and delivery of the underlying assets that cause the price of the contract at expiration to differ slightly from the price of the underlying assets. Because the difference in price is extremely small, we ignore it here.

EXAMPLE 24.1

Hedging with Interest-Rate Futures

The *6*s of 2037 are the long-term bonds that would be delivered in the CBT T-bond futures contract expiring one year in the future in March 2018. The interest rate on these bonds is expected to remain at 6% over the next year so that both the *6*s of 2037 and the futures contract are selling at par. How many contracts must First National sell to remove its interest-rate risk exposure from its $5 million holdings of the *6*s of 2037?*

> Solution

$$VA = \$5 \text{ million}$$

$$VC = \$100{,}000$$

Thus,

$$NC = 5 \text{ million}/100{,}000 = 50$$

You therefore hedge the interest-rate risk by selling 50 of the Treasury bond futures contracts.

Now suppose that over the next year, interest rates increase to 8% due to an increased threat of inflation. The value of the *6*s of 2037 the First National Bank is holding will then fall to $4,039,640 in March 2018.** Thus, the loss from the long position in these bonds is $960,360, as shown below:

Value in March 2018 @ 8% interest rate	$4,039,640
Value in March 2017 @ 6% interest rate	−$5,000,000
Loss	−$960,360

However, the short position in the 50 futures contracts that obligates you to deliver $5 million of the *6*s of 2037 in March 2018 has a value equal to the $5 million of these bonds on that date, after the interest rate has risen to 8%. This value is $4,039,640, as we have seen above. Yet when you sold the futures contract, the buyer was obligated to pay you $5 million on the maturity date. Thus, the gain from the short position on these contracts is also $960,360, as shown below:

Amount paid to you in March 2018, agreed upon in March 2017	$5,000,000
Cost of bonds delivered in March 2018 @ 8% interest rate	−$4,039,640
Gain	$960,360

Therefore, the net gain for the First National Bank is zero, showing that the hedge has been conducted successfully.

*In the real world, designing a hedge is somewhat more complicated than the example given here because the bond that is most likely to be delivered might not be a *6*s of 2037.

**The value of the bonds can be calculated using a financial calculator as follows: $FV = \$5{,}000{,}000$, $PMT = \$300{,}000$, $I = 8\%$, $N = 19$, $PV = \$4{,}039{,}640$.

The hedge just described is called a **micro hedge** because the financial institution is hedging the interest-rate risk for a specific asset it is holding. A second type of hedge that financial institutions engage in is called a **macro hedge**, in which the hedge is for the institution's entire portfolio. For example, if a bank has a longer duration for its assets than its liabilities, we have seen in Chapter 23 that a rise in interest rates will cause the value of the bank to decline. By selling interest-rate futures contracts that will yield a profit when interest rates rise, the bank can offset the losses on its overall portfolio from an interest-rate rise and thereby hedge its interest-rate risk.[2]

Organization of Trading in Financial Futures Markets

Financial futures contracts are traded in the United States on organized exchanges such as the Chicago Board of Trade, the Chicago Mercantile Exchange, the New York Futures Exchange, the MidAmerica Commodity Exchange, and the Kansas City Board of Trade. These exchanges are highly competitive, and each organization tries to design contracts and set rules that will increase the amount of futures trading on its exchange.

The futures exchanges and all trades in financial futures in the United States are regulated by the Commodity Futures Trading Commission (CFTC), which was created in 1974 to take over the regulatory responsibilities for futures markets from the Department of Agriculture. The CFTC oversees futures trading and the futures exchanges to ensure that prices in the market are not being manipulated, and it also registers and audits the brokers, traders, and exchanges to prevent fraud and to ensure the financial soundness of the exchanges. In addition, the CFTC approves proposed futures contracts to make sure that they serve the public interest. The most widely traded financial futures contracts and the exchanges where they are traded (along with the number of contracts outstanding, called **open interest**, in May 2016) are listed in Table 24.1.

Given the globalization of other financial markets in recent years, it is not surprising that increased competition from abroad has been occurring in financial futures markets as well.

Globalization of Financial Futures Markets

Because American futures exchanges were the first to develop financial futures, they dominated the trading of financial futures in the early 1980s. For example, in 1985 all of the top 10 futures contracts were traded on exchanges in the United States. With the rapid growth of financial futures markets and the resulting high profits made by the American exchanges, foreign exchanges saw a profit opportunity and began to enter this business. By the 1990s, Eurodollar contracts traded on the London International Financial Futures Exchange, Japanese government bond contracts and Euroyen contracts traded on the Tokyo Stock Exchange, French government bond contracts traded on the Marché à Terme International de France, and Nikkei 225 contracts traded on the Osaka Securities Exchange. All became among the most widely traded futures contracts in the world. Even developing countries have gotten into the act. In 1996 seven developing countries (also referred to as *emerging market countries*) established futures exchanges.

[2]For more details and examples of how interest-rate risk can be hedged with financial futures, see the appendix to this chapter, which can be found on the book's Web site at www.pearsonhighered.com/mishkin_eakins.

TABLE 24.1 Widely Traded Financial Futures Contracts

Type of Contract	Contract Size	Exchange*	Open Interest (May 2016)
Interest-Rate Contracts			
Treasury bonds	$100,000	CBOT	564,537
Treasury notes	$100,000	CBOT	2,629,971
Five-year Treasury notes	$100,000	CBOT	2,556,335
Two-year Treasury notes	$200,000	CBOT	1,007,329
Fed funds	$5 million	CBOT	1,008,414
Eurodollar	$1 million	CME	10,816,515
Stock Index Contracts			
Standard & Poor's 500 Index	$250 × index	CME	83,115
Currency Contracts			
Yen	¥12,500,000	CME	156,605
Euro	€125,000	CME	356,777
Canadian dollar	C$100,000	CME	126,537
British pound	£62,500	CME	243,778
Swiss franc	SF 125,000	CME	57,178
Mexican peso	MXN 500,000	CME	143,577

*Exchange abbreviations: CBOT, Chicago Board of Trade; CME, Chicago Mercantile Exchange.

Source: CME Group: www.cmegroup.com/market-data/volume-open-interest/index.html.

Foreign competition has also spurred knockoffs of the most popular financial futures contracts initially developed in the United States. These contracts traded on foreign exchanges are virtually identical to those traded in the United States and have the advantage that they can be traded when the American exchanges are closed. The movement to 24-hour-a-day trading in financial futures has been further stimulated by the development of the Globex electronic trading platform, which allows traders throughout the world to trade futures even when the exchanges are not officially open. Financial futures trading has thus become completely internationalized, and competition between U.S. and foreign exchanges is now intense.

Explaining the Success of Futures Markets

The tremendous success of the financial futures market in Treasury bonds is evident from the fact that the total open interest of Treasury bond contracts was 2,771,629 on June 23, 2016, for a total value of $277 billion (2,771,629 × $100,000). Several differences can be noted between financial futures and forward contracts and in the organization of their markets that help explain why financial futures markets, like those for Treasury bonds, have been so successful.

Several features of futures contracts were designed to overcome the liquidity problem inherent in forward contracts. The first feature is that, in contrast to forward contracts, the quantities delivered and the delivery dates of futures contracts are standardized, making it more likely that different parties can be matched in the futures market, thereby increasing the liquidity of the market. In the case of the Treasury bond contract, the quantity delivered is $100,000 face value of bonds, and the delivery dates are set to be the last business days of March, June, September, and December. The second feature is that after the futures contract has been bought or sold, it can be traded (bought or sold) again at any time until the delivery date. In contrast, once a forward contract is agreed on, it typically cannot be traded. The third feature is that in a futures contract, not just one specific type of Treasury bond is deliverable on the delivery date, as in a forward contract. Instead, any Treasury bond that matures in more than 15 years and is not callable for 15 years is eligible for delivery. Allowing continuous trading also increases the liquidity of the futures market, as does the ability to deliver a range of Treasury bonds rather than one specific bond.

Another reason why futures contracts specify that more than one bond is eligible for delivery is to limit the possibility that someone might corner the market and "squeeze" traders who have sold contracts. To corner the market, someone buys up all the deliverable securities so that investors with a short position cannot obtain from anyone else the securities that they contractually must deliver on the delivery date. As a result, the person who has cornered the market can set exorbitant prices for the securities that investors with a short position must buy to fulfill their obligations under the futures contract. The person who has cornered the market makes a fortune, but investors with a short position take a terrific loss. Clearly, the possibility that corners might occur in the market will discourage people from taking a short position and might therefore decrease the size of the market. By allowing many different securities to be delivered, the futures contract makes it harder for anyone to corner the market because a much larger amount of securities would have to be purchased to establish the corner. Corners are more than a theoretical possibility, as the Mini-Case box "The Hunt Brothers and the Silver Crash" indicates, and are a concern to both regulators and the organized exchanges that design futures contracts.

Trading in the futures market has been organized differently from trading in forward markets to overcome the default risk problems arising in forward contracts. In both types, for every contract there must be a buyer who is taking a long position and a seller who is taking a short position. However, the buyer and seller of a futures contract make their contract not with each other but with the clearinghouse associated with the futures exchange. This setup means that the buyer of the futures contract does not need to worry about the financial health or trustworthiness of the seller, or vice versa, as in the forward market. As long as the clearinghouse is financially solid, buyers and sellers of futures contracts do not have to worry about default risk.

To make sure that the clearinghouse is financially sound and does not run into financial difficulties that might jeopardize its contracts, buyers or sellers of futures contracts must put an initial deposit, called a **margin requirement**, of perhaps $2,000 per Treasury bond contract into a margin account kept at their brokerage firm. Futures contracts are then **marked to market** every day. What this means is that at the end of every trading day, the change in the value of the futures contract is added to or subtracted from the margin account. Suppose that after buying the Treasury bond contract at a price of 115 on Wednesday morning, its closing price at the end of the day, the *settlement price*, falls to 114. You now have a loss of 1 point,

MINI-CASE

The Hunt Brothers and the Silver Crash

In early 1979, two Texas billionaires, W. Herbert Hunt and his brother, Nelson Bunker Hunt, decided that they were going to get into the silver market in a big way. Herbert stated his reasoning for purchasing silver as follows: "I became convinced that the economy of the United States was in a weakening condition. This reinforced my belief that investment in precious metals was wise . . . because of rampant inflation." Although the Hunts' stated reason for purchasing silver was that it was a good investment, others felt that their real motive was to establish a corner in the silver market. Along with other associates, several of them from the Saudi royal family, the Hunts purchased close to 300 million ounces of silver in the form of either actual bullion or silver futures contracts. The result was that the price of silver rose from $6 an ounce to over $50 an ounce by January 1980.

Once the regulators and the futures exchanges got wind of what the Hunts were up to, they decided to take action to eliminate the possibility of a corner by limiting to 2,000 the number of contracts that any single trader could hold. This limit, which was equivalent to 10 million ounces, was only a small fraction of what the Hunts were holding, and so they were forced to sell. The silver market collapsed soon afterward, with the price of silver declining back to below $10 an ounce. The losses to the Hunts were estimated to be in excess of $1 billion, and they soon found themselves in financial difficulty. They had to go into debt to the tune of $1.1 billion, mortgaging not only the family's holdings in the Placid Oil Company but also 75,000 head of cattle, a stable of thoroughbred horses, paintings, jewelry, and even such mundane items as irrigation pumps and lawn mowers. Eventually both Hunt brothers were forced into declaring personal bankruptcy, earning them the dubious distinction of declaring the largest personal bankruptcies ever in the United States.

Nelson and Herbert Hunt paid a heavy price for their excursion into the silver market, but at least Nelson retained his sense of humor. When asked right after the collapse of the silver market how he felt about his losses, he said, "A billion dollars isn't what it used to be."*

*Quotes are from G. Christian Hill, "Dynasty's Decline: The Current Question About the Hunts of Dallas: How Poor Are They?" *Wall Street Journal*, (November 14, 1984): c28.

or $1,000, on the contract, and the seller who sold you the contract has a gain of 1 point, or $1,000. The $1,000 gain is added to the seller's margin account, making a total of $3,000 in that account, and the $1,000 loss is subtracted from your account, so you now only have $1,000 in your account. If the amount in this margin account falls below the maintenance margin requirement (which can be the same as the initial requirement but is usually a little less), the trader is required to add money to the account. For example, if the maintenance margin requirement is also $2,000, you would have to add $1,000 to your account to bring it up to $2,000. Margin requirements and marking to market make it far less likely that a trader will default on a contract, thus protecting the futures exchange from losses.

A final advantage that futures markets have over forward markets is that most futures contracts do not result in delivery of the underlying asset on the expiration date, whereas forward contracts do. A trader who sold a futures contract is allowed to avoid delivery on the expiration date by making an offsetting purchase of a futures contract. Because the simultaneous holding of the long and short positions means that the trader would in effect be delivering the bonds to itself, under the exchange rules the trader is allowed to cancel both contracts. Allowing traders to cancel their contracts in this way lowers the cost of conducting trades in the futures market relative to the forward market in that a futures trader can avoid the costs of physical delivery, which is not so easy with forward contracts.

THE PRACTICING MANAGER

Hedging Foreign Exchange Risk with Forward and Futures Contracts

As we discussed in Chapter 15, foreign exchange rates have been highly volatile in recent years. The large fluctuations in exchange rates subject financial institutions and other businesses to significant foreign exchange risk because they generate substantial gains and losses. Luckily for financial institution managers, the financial derivatives discussed here—forward and financial futures contracts—can be used to hedge foreign exchange risk.

To understand how financial institution managers manage foreign exchange risk, let's suppose that in January the First National Bank's customer Frivolous Luxuries, Inc., is due a payment of 10 million euros in two months for \$10 million worth of goods it has just sold in Germany. Frivolous Luxuries is concerned that if the value of the euro falls substantially from its current value of \$1, the company might suffer a large loss because the 10 million euro payment will no longer be worth \$10 million. So Sam, the CEO of Frivolous Luxuries, calls his friend Mona, the manager of the First National Bank, and asks her to hedge this foreign exchange risk for his company. Let's see how the bank manager does this using forward and financial futures contracts.

Hedging Foreign Exchange Risk with Forward Contracts

Forward markets in foreign exchange have been highly developed by commercial banks and investment banking operations that engage in extensive foreign exchange trading and so are widely used to hedge foreign exchange risk. Mona knows that she can use this market to hedge the foreign exchange risk for Frivolous Luxuries. Such a hedge is quite straightforward for her to execute. Because the payment of euros in two months means that at that time Sam would hold a long position in euros, Mona knows that the basic principle of hedging indicates she should offset this long position by a short position. Thus, she just enters a forward contract that obligates her to sell 10 million euros two months from now in exchange for dollars at the current forward rate of \$1 per euro.*

In two months, when Mona's customer receives the 10 million euros, the forward contract ensures that it is exchanged for dollars at an exchange rate of \$1 per euro, thus yielding \$10 million. No matter what happens to future exchange rates, Frivolous Luxuries will be guaranteed \$10 million for the goods it sold in Germany. Mona calls her friend Sam to let him know that his company is now protected from any foreign exchange movements, and he thanks her for her help.

---

*The forward exchange rate will probably differ slightly from the current spot rate of \$1 per euro because the interest rates in Europe and the United States may not be equal. In that case, as we saw in Equation A2 in the appendix to Chapter 15, the future expected exchange rate will not equal the current spot rate and neither will the forward rate. However, since interest differentials have typically been less than 6% at an annual rate (1% bimonthly), the expected appreciation or depreciation of the euro over a two-month period has always been less than 1%. Thus, the forward rate is always close to the current spot rate, and so our assumption in the example that the forward rate and the spot rate are the same is a reasonable one.

Hedging Foreign Exchange Risk with Futures Contracts

As an alternative, Mona could have used the currency futures market to hedge the foreign exchange risk. In this case, she would see that the Chicago Mercantile Exchange has a euro contract with a contract amount of 125,000 euros and a price of $1 per euro. To do the hedge, Mona must sell euros as with the forward contract, to the tune of 10 million euros of the March futures.

EXAMPLE 24.2

Hedging with Foreign Exchange Futures Contracts

How many of the Chicago Mercantile Exchange March euro contracts must Mona sell in order to hedge the 10 million euro payment due in March?

> Solution

Using Equation 1:

$$VA = 10 \text{ million euros}$$

$$VC = 125{,}000 \text{ euros}$$

Thus,

$$NC = 10 \text{ million}/125{,}000 = 80$$

Mona does the hedge by selling 80 of the CME euro contracts.

Given the $1 per euro price, the sale of the contract yields 80 × 125,000 euros = $10 million. The futures hedge thus again enables her to lock in the exchange rate for Frivolous Luxuries so that it gets its payment of $10 million.

One advantage of using the futures market is that the contract size of 125,000 euros, worth $125,000, is quite a bit smaller than the minimum size of a forward contract, which is usually $1 million or more. However, in this case, the bank manager is making a large enough transaction that she can use either the forward or the futures market. Her choice depends on whether the transaction costs are lower in one market than in the other. If the First National Bank is active in the forward market, that market would probably have the lower transaction costs, but if First National rarely deals in foreign exchange forward contracts, the bank manager may do better by sticking with the futures market.

Stock Index Futures

As we have seen, financial futures markets can be useful in hedging interest-rate risk. However, financial institution managers, particularly those who manage mutual funds, pension funds, and insurance companies, also worry about **stock market risk**, the risk that occurs because stock prices fluctuate. Stock index futures were developed in 1982 to meet the need to manage stock market risk, and they have become among the most widely traded of all futures contracts.

Stock Index Futures Contracts

To understand stock index futures contracts, let's examine the Standard & Poor's 500 Index futures contract (shown in the Following the Financial News box, "Stock Index Futures"), the most widely traded stock index futures contract in the United States. (The S&P 500 Index measures the value of 500 of the most widely traded stocks.) Stock index futures contracts differ from most other financial futures contracts in that they are settled with a cash delivery rather than with the delivery of a security. Cash settlement gives these contracts the advantage of a high degree of liquidity and also rules out the possibility of anyone's cornering the market. In the case of the S&P 500 Index contract, at the final settlement date, the cash delivery due is $250 times the index, so if the index is at 1,000 on the final settlement date, $250,000 would be the amount due. The price quotes for this contract are also quoted in terms of index points, so a change of 1 point represents a change of $250 in the contract's value.

To understand what all this means, let's look at what happens when you buy or sell this futures contract. Suppose that on February 1, you sell one June contract at a price of 1,000 (that is, $250,000). By selling the contract, you agree to a delivery amount due of $250 times the S&P 500 Index on the expiration date at the end of June. By buying the contract at a price of 1,000, the buyer has agreed to pay $250,000 for the delivery amount due of $250 times the S&P 500 Index at the expiration date at the end of June. If the stock market falls so that the S&P 500 Index declines to 900 on the expiration date, the buyer of the contract will have lost $25,000 because he or she has agreed to pay $250,000 for the contract but has a delivery amount due

> FOLLOWING THE FINANCIAL NEWS

Stock Index Futures

The prices for stock index futures contracts are published daily in newspapers and on Internet sites such as finance.yahoo.com. A typical entry, like the following one for the Chicago Mercantile Exchange's S&P 500 Index contract on June 23, 2016, would have the following information:

	Open	High	Low	Settle	Change	Open Interest
Sept.	2083.00	2112.508	2083.00	2105.80	+29.10	64,616

Information for each contract is given in columns, as follows. (The September S&P 500 Index contract is used as an example.)

Open: Opening price; each point corresponds to $250 times the index—2083.00; that is, 2083.00 × $250 = $520,750 per contract.

High: Highest traded price that day—2112.508, or $528,125 per contract.

Low: Lowest traded price that day—2083.00, or $520,750 per contract.

Settle: Settlement price, the closing price that day—2105.80, or $526,450 per contract.

Chg: Change in the settlement price from the previous trading day— +29.10 points, or $7,275 per contract.

Open Interest: Number of contracts outstanding—64,616, or a total value of $34 billion (= 64,616 × $526,450).

of \$225,000 (900 × \$250). But you, the seller of the contract, will have a profit of \$25,000 because you agreed to receive a \$250,000 purchase price for the contract but have a delivery amount due of only \$225,000. Because the amount payable and due are netted out, only \$25,000 will change hands; you, the seller of the contract, receive \$25,000 from the buyer.

THE PRACTICING MANAGER

Hedging with Stock Index Futures

Financial institution managers can use stock index futures contracts to reduce stock market risk.

EXAMPLE 24.3

Hedging with Stock Index Futures

Suppose that in March 2017, Mort, the portfolio manager of the Rock Solid Insurance Company, has a portfolio of stocks valued at \$100 million that moves percentagewise one-for-one with the S&P Index. Suppose also that the March 2018 S&P 500 Index contracts are currently selling at a price of 1,000. How many of these contracts should Mort sell so that he hedges the stock market risk of this portfolio over the next year?

> Solution

Because Mort is holding a long position, using the basic principle of hedging, he must offset it by taking a short position in which he sells S&P futures. To calculate the number of contracts he needs to sell, he uses Equation 1.

$$VA = \$100 \text{ million}$$

$$VC = \$250 \times 1{,}000 = \$250{,}000$$

Thus,

$$NC = \$100 \text{ million}/\$250{,}000 = 400$$

Mort's hedge therefore involves selling 400 S&P March 2018 futures contracts.

If the S&P Index falls 10% to 900, the \$100 million portfolio will suffer a \$10 million loss. At the same time, however, Mort makes a profit of 100 × \$250 = \$25,000 per contract because he agreed to be paid \$250,000 for each contract at a price of 1,000, but at a price of 900 on the expiration date he has a delivery amount of only \$225,000 (900 × \$250). Multiplied by 400 contracts, the \$25,000 profit per contract yields a total profit of \$10 million. The \$10 million profit on the futures contract exactly offsets the loss on Rock Solid's stock portfolio, so Mort has been successful in hedging the stock market risk.

Why would Mort be willing to forgo profits when the stock market rises? One reason is that he might be worried that a bear market was imminent, so he wants to protect Rock Solid's portfolio from the coming decline (and so protect his job).*

*For more details of how stock market risk can be hedged with futures options, see the appendix to this chapter, which can be found on the book's Web site at www.pearsonhighered.com/mishkin_eakins.

Options

Another vehicle for hedging interest-rate and stock market risk involves the use of options on financial instruments. **Options** are contracts that give the purchaser the option, or *right*, to buy or sell the underlying financial instrument at a specified price, called the **exercise price** or **strike price**, within a specific period of time (the *term to expiration*). The seller (sometimes called the *writer*) of the option is *obligated* to buy or sell the financial instrument to the purchaser if the owner of the option exercises the right to sell or buy. These option contract features are important enough to be emphasized: The *owner* or buyer of an option does not have to exercise the option; he or she can let the option expire without using it. Hence, the *owner* of an option is *not obligated* to take any action but rather has the *right* to exercise the contract if he or she so chooses. The *seller* of an option, by contrast, has no choice in the matter; he or she *must* buy or sell the financial instrument if the owner exercises the option.

Because the right to buy or sell a financial instrument at a specified price has value, the owner of an option is willing to pay an amount for it called a **premium**. There are two types of option contracts: **American options** can be exercised *at any time up to* the expiration date of the contract, and **European options** can be exercised only *on* the expiration date.

Option contracts are written on a number of financial instruments. Options on individual stocks are called **stock options**, and such options have existed for a long time. Option contracts on financial futures called **financial futures options**, or, more commonly, **futures options**, were developed in 1982 and have become the most widely traded option contracts.

You might wonder why option contracts are more likely to be written on financial futures than on underlying debt instruments such as bonds or certificates of deposit. As you saw earlier in the chapter, at the expiration date, the price of the futures contract and of the deliverable debt instrument will be the same because of arbitrage. So it would seem that investors should be indifferent about having the option written on the debt instrument or on the futures contract. However, financial futures contracts have been so well designed that their markets are often more liquid than the markets in the underlying debt instruments. Investors would rather have the option contract written on the more liquid instrument, in this case the futures contract. That explains why the most popular futures options are written on many of the same futures contracts listed in Table 24.1.

The regulation of option markets is split between the Securities and Exchange Commission (SEC), which regulates stock options, and the Commodity Futures Trading Commission (CFTC), which regulates futures options. Regulation focuses on ensuring that writers of options have enough capital to make good on their contractual obligations and on overseeing traders and exchanges to prevent fraud and ensure that the market is not being manipulated.

Option Contracts

A **call option** is a contract that gives the owner the right to *buy* a financial instrument at the exercise price within a specific period of time. A **put option** is a contract that gives the owner the right to *sell* a financial instrument at the exercise price within a specific period of time. Remembering which is a call option and which is a put option is not always easy. To keep them straight, just remember that having a *call* option to *buy* a financial instrument is the same as having the option to *call in* the instrument for delivery at a specified price. Having a *put* option to *sell* a financial instrument is the same as having the option to *put up* an instrument for the other party to buy.

Profits and Losses on Option and Futures Contracts

To understand option contracts more fully, let's first examine the option on the June Treasury bond futures contract that we looked at earlier. Recall that if you buy this futures contract at a price of 115 (that is, $115,000), you have agreed to pay $115,000 for $100,000 face value of long-term Treasury bonds when they are delivered to you at the end of June. If you sold this futures contract at a price of 115, you agreed, in exchange for $115,000, to deliver $100,000 face value of the long-term Treasury bonds at the end of June. An option contract on the Treasury bond futures contract has several key features: (1) It has the same expiration date as the underlying futures contract, (2) it is an American option and so can be exercised at any time before the expiration date, and (3) the premium (price) of the option is quoted in points that are the same as in the futures contract, so each point corresponds to $1,000. If, for a premium of $2,000, you buy one call option contract on the June Treasury bond contract with an exercise price of 115, you have purchased the right to buy (call in) the June Treasury bond futures contract for a price of 115 ($115,000 per contract) at any time through the expiration date of this contract at the end of June. Similarly, when for $2,000 you buy a put option on the June Treasury bond contract with an exercise price of 115, you have the right to sell (put up) the June Treasury bond futures contract for a price of 115 ($115,000 per contract) at any time until the end of June.

Futures option contracts are somewhat complicated, so to explore how they work and how they can be used to hedge risk, let's first examine how profits and losses on the call option on the June Treasury bond futures contract occur. In November our old friend Irving the investor buys, for a $2,000 premium, a call option on the $100,000 June Treasury bond futures contract with a strike price of 115. (We assume that if Irving exercises the option, it is on the expiration date at the end of June and not before.) On the expiration date at the end of June, suppose that the underlying Treasury bond for the futures contract has a price of 110. Recall that on the expiration date, arbitrage forces the price of the futures contract to converge to the price of the underlying bond, so it, too, has a price of 110 on the expiration date at the end of June. If Irving exercises the call option and buys the futures contract at an exercise price of 115, he will lose money by buying at 115 and selling at the lower market price of 110. Because Irving is smart, he will not exercise the option, but he will be out the $2,000 premium he paid. In such a situation, in which the price of the underlying financial instrument is below the exercise price, a call option is said to be "out of the money." At the price of 110 (less than the exercise price), Irving thus suffers a loss on the option contract of the $2,000 premium he paid. This loss is plotted as point A in panel (a) of Figure 24.1.

On the expiration date, if the price of the futures contract is 115, the call option is "at the money," and Irving is indifferent to whether he exercises his option to buy

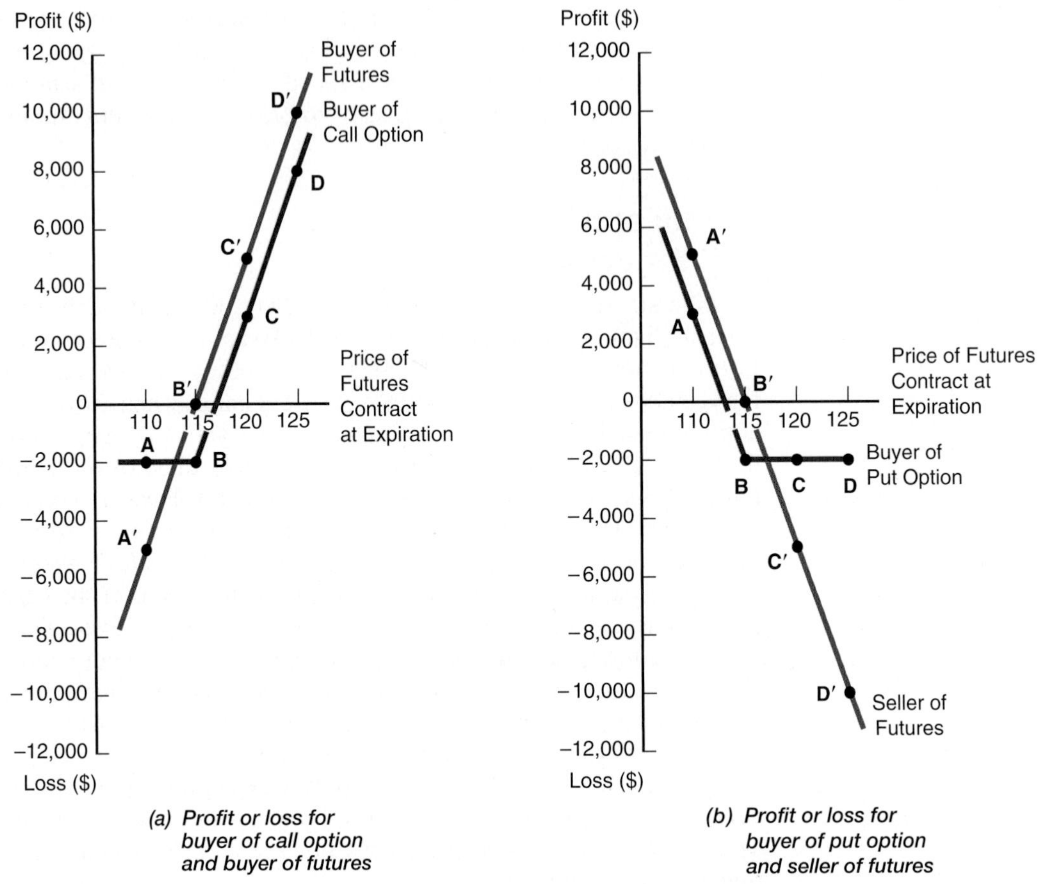

FIGURE 24.1 Profits and Losses on Options Versus Futures Contracts

The futures contract is the $100,000 June Treasury bond contract, and the option contracts are written on this futures contract with an exercise price of 115. Panel (a) shows the profits and losses for the buyer of the call option and the buyer of the futures contract, and panel (b) shows the profits and losses for the buyer of the put option and the seller of the futures contract.

the futures contract or not, since exercising the option at 115 when the market price is also at 115 produces no gain or loss. Because he has paid the $2,000 premium, at the price of 115 his contract again has a net loss of $2,000, plotted as point B.

If the futures contract instead has a price of 120 on the expiration day, the option is "in the money," and Irving benefits from exercising the option: He would buy the futures contract at the exercise price of 115 and then sell it for 120, thereby earning a 5% gain ($5,000 profit) on the $100,000 Treasury bond contract. Because Irving paid a $2,000 premium for the option contract, however, his net profit is $3,000 ($5,000 − $2,000). The $3,000 profit at a price of 120 is plotted as point C. Similarly, if the price of the futures contract rose to 125, the option contract would yield a net profit of $8,000 ($10,000 from exercising the option minus the $2,000 premium), plotted as point D. Plotting these points, we get the kinked profit curve for the call option that we see in panel (a).

Suppose that instead of purchasing the futures *option* contract in November, Irving decides instead to buy the $100,000 June Treasury bond *futures* contract at the price of 115. If the price of the bond on the expiration day at the end of June declines to 110, meaning that the price of the futures contract also falls to 110, Irving suffers a loss of 5 percentage points, or $5,000. The loss of $5,000 on the futures contract at a price of 110 is plotted as point A′ in panel (a). At a price of 115 on the expiration date, Irving would have a zero profit on the futures contract, plotted as point B′. At a price of 120, Irving would have a profit on the contract of 5 percentage points, or $5,000 (point C′), and at a price of 125, the profit would be 10 percentage points, or $10,000 (point D′). Plotting these points, we get the linear (straight-line) profit curve for the futures contract that appears in panel (a).

Now we can see the major difference between a futures contract and an option contract. As the profit curve for the futures contract in panel (a) indicates, the futures contract has a linear profit function: Profits grow by an equal dollar amount for every point increase in the price of the underlying financial instrument. By contrast, the kinked profit curve for the option contract is highly nonlinear, meaning that profits do not always grow by the same amount for a given change in the price of the underlying financial instrument. The reason for this nonlinearity is that the call option protects Irving from having losses that are greater than the amount of the $2,000 premium. In contrast, Irving's loss on the futures contract is $5,000 if the price on the expiration day falls to 110, and if the price falls even further, Irving's loss will be even greater. This insurance-like feature of option contracts explains why their purchase price is referred to as a premium. Once the underlying financial instrument's price rises above the exercise price, however, Irving's profits grow linearly. Irving has given up something by buying an option rather than a futures contract. As we see in panel (a), when the price of the underlying financial instrument rises above the exercise price, Irving's profits are always less than that on the futures contract by exactly the $2,000 premium he paid.

Panel (b) plots the results of the same profit calculations if Irving buys not a call but a put option (an option to sell) with an exercise price of 115 for a premium of $2,000 and if he sells the futures contract rather than buying one. In this case, if on the expiration date the Treasury bond futures have a price above the 115 exercise price, the put option is "out of the money." Irving would not want to exercise the put option and then have to sell the futures contract he owns as a result of exercising the put option at a price below the market price and lose money. He would not exercise his option, and he would be out only the $2,000 premium he paid. Once the price of the futures contract falls below the 115 exercise price, Irving benefits from exercising the put option because he can sell the futures contract at a price of 115 but can buy it at a price below this. In such a situation, in which the price of the underlying instrument is below the exercise price, the put option is "in the money," and profits rise linearly as the price of the futures contract falls. The profit function for the put option illustrated in panel (b) of Figure 24.1 is kinked, indicating that Irving is protected from losses greater than the amount of the premium he paid. The profit curve for the sale of the futures contract is just the negative of the profit for the futures contract in panel (a) and is therefore linear.

Panel (b) of Figure 24.1 confirms the conclusion from panel (a) that profits on option contracts are nonlinear but profits on futures contracts are linear.

Two other differences between futures and option contracts must be mentioned. The first is that the initial investment on the contracts differs. As we saw earlier, when a futures contract is purchased, the investor must put up a fixed amount, the margin requirement, in a margin account. But when an option contract is purchased, the initial investment is the premium that must be paid for the contract. The second important difference between the contracts is that the futures contract requires money to change hands daily when the contract is marked to market, whereas the option contract requires money to change hands only when it is exercised.

Factors Affecting the Prices of Option Premiums

Several interesting facts can be noted about how the premiums on option contracts are priced. The first fact is that when the strike (exercise) price for a contract is set at a higher level, the premium for the call option is lower and the premium for the put option is higher. For example, in going from a contract with a strike price of 112 to one with 115, the premium for a call option for the month of March might fall from 1 45/64 to 16/64, and the premium for the March put option might rise from 19/64 to 1 54/64.

Our understanding of the profit function for option contracts illustrated in Figure 24.1 helps explain this fact. As we saw in panel (a), a lower price for the underlying financial instrument (in this case a Treasury bond futures contract) relative to the option's exercise price results in lower profits on the call (buy) option. Thus, the higher the strike price, the lower the profits on the call option contract and the lower the premium that investors like Irving are willing to pay. Similarly, we saw in panel (b) that a lower price for the underlying financial instrument relative to the exercise price raises profits on the put (sell) option, so that a higher strike price increases profits and thus causes the premium to increase.

Second, as the period of time over which the option can be exercised (the term to expiration) gets longer, the premiums for both call and put options rise. For example, at a strike price of 112, the premium on a call option might increase from 1 45/64 in March to 1 50/64 in April and to 2 28/64 in May. Similarly, the premium on a put option might increase from 19/64 in March to 1 43/64 in April and to 2 22/64 in May. The fact that premiums increase with the term to expiration is also explained by the nonlinear profit function for option contracts. As the term to expiration lengthens, there is a greater chance that the price of the underlying financial instrument will be very high or very low by the expiration date. If the price becomes very high and goes well above the exercise price, the call (buy) option will yield a high profit; if the price becomes very low and goes well below the exercise price, the losses will be small because the owner of the call option will simply decide not to exercise the option. The possibility of greater variability of the underlying financial instrument as the term to expiration lengthens raises profits on average for the call option.

Similar reasoning tells us that the put (sell) option will become more valuable as the term to expiration increases because the possibility of greater price variability of the underlying financial instrument increases as the term to expiration increases. The greater chance of a low price increases the chance that profits on the put option will be very high. But the greater chance of a high price does not produce substantial losses for the put option, because the owner will again just decide not to exercise the option.

Another way of thinking about this reasoning is to recognize that option contracts have an element of "Heads, I win; tails, I don't lose too badly." The greater variability of where the prices might be by the expiration date increases the value of both kinds of options. Because a longer term to the expiration date leads to greater variability of where the prices might be by the expiration date, a longer term to expiration raises the value of the option contract.

The reasoning that we have just developed also explains another important fact about option premiums. When the volatility of the price of the underlying instrument is great, the premiums for both call and put options will be higher. Higher volatility of prices means that for a given expiration date, there will again be greater variability of where the prices might be by the expiration date. The "Heads, I win; tails, I don't lose too badly" property of options then means that the greater variability of possible prices by the expiration date increases average profits for the option and thus increases the premium that investors are willing to pay.

Summary

Our analysis of how profits on options are affected by price movements for the underlying financial instrument leads to the following conclusions about the factors that determine the premium on an option contract:

1. The higher the strike price, everything else being equal, the lower the premium on call (buy) options and the higher the premium on put (sell) options.
2. The greater the term to expiration, everything else being equal, the higher the premiums for both call and put options.
3. The greater the volatility of prices of the underlying financial instrument, everything else being equal, the higher the premiums for both call and put options.

The results we have derived here appear in more formal models, such as the Black-Scholes model, which analyze how the premiums on options are priced. You might study such models in other finance courses.

THE PRACTICING MANAGER

Hedging with Futures Options

Earlier in the chapter, we saw how a financial institution manager like Mona, the manager of the First National Bank, could hedge the interest-rate risk on its $5 million holdings of *6*s of 2037 by selling $5 million of T-bond futures (50 contracts). A rise in interest rates and the resulting fall in bond prices and bond futures contracts would lead to profits on the bank's sale of the futures contracts that would exactly offset the losses on the *6*s of 2037 the bank is holding.

As panel (b) of Figure 24.1 suggests, an alternative way for the manager to protect against a rise in interest rates, and hence a decline in bond prices, is to buy $5 million of put options written on the same Treasury bond futures. Because the size of the options contract is the same as the futures contract ($100,000 of bonds), the number of put options contracts bought is the same as the number of futures contracts sold, that is, 50. As long as the exercise price is not too far from the current price as in panel (b), the rise in interest rates and decline in bond prices will lead to profits on the futures and the futures put options, profits that will offset any losses on the $5 million of Treasury bonds.

The one problem with using options rather than futures is that the First National Bank will have to pay premiums on the options contracts, thereby lowering the bank's profits in order to hedge the interest-rate risk. Why might the bank manager be willing to use options rather than futures to conduct the hedge? The answer is that the option contract, unlike the futures contract, allows the First National Bank to gain if interest rates decline and bond prices rise. With the hedge using futures contracts, the First National Bank does not gain from increases in bond prices because the profits on the bonds it is holding are offset by the losses from the futures contracts it has sold. However, as panel (b) of Figure 24.1 indicates, the situation when the hedge is conducted with put options is quite different: Once bond prices rise above the exercise price, the bank does not suffer additional losses on the option contracts. At the same time, the value of the Treasury bonds the bank is holding will increase, thereby leading to a profit for the bank. Thus, using options rather than futures to conduct the micro hedge allows the bank to protect itself from rises in interest rates but still allows the bank to benefit from interest-rate declines (although the profit is reduced by the amount of the premium).

Similar reasoning indicates that the bank manager might prefer to use options to conduct the macro hedge to immunize the entire bank portfolio from interest-rate risk. Again, the strategy of using options rather than futures has the disadvantage that the First National Bank has to pay the premiums on these contracts up front. By contrast, using options allows the bank to keep the gains from a decline in interest rates (which will raise the value of the bank's assets relative to its liabilities) because these gains will not be offset by large losses on the option contracts.

In the case of a macro hedge, there is another reason why the bank might prefer option contracts to futures contracts. Profits and losses on futures contracts can cause accounting problems for banks because such profits and losses are not allowed to be offset by unrealized changes in the value of the rest of the bank's portfolio. Consider the case when interest rates fall. If First National sells futures contracts to conduct the macro hedge, then when interest rates fall and the prices of the Treasury bond futures contracts rise, it will have large losses on these contracts. Of course, these losses are offset by unrealized profits in the rest of the bank's portfolio, but the bank is not allowed to offset these losses in its accounting statements. So even though the macro hedge is serving its intended purpose of immunizing the bank's portfolio from interest-rate risk, the bank would experience large accounting losses when interest rates fall. Indeed, bank managers have lost their jobs when perfectly sound hedges with interest-rate futures have led to large accounting losses. Not surprisingly, bank managers might shrink from using financial futures to conduct macro hedges for this reason.

Futures options, however, can come to the rescue of the managers of banks and other financial institutions. Suppose that First National conducted the macro hedge by buying put options instead of selling Treasury bond futures. Now if interest rates fall and bond prices rise well above the exercise price, the bank will not have large losses on the option contracts because it will just decide not to exercise its options. The bank will not suffer the accounting problems produced by hedging with financial futures. Because of the accounting advantages of using futures options to conduct macro hedges, option contracts have become important to financial institution managers as tools for hedging interest-rate risk.*

*For more details of how interest-rate risk can be hedged with futures options, see the appendix to this chapter, which can be found on the book's Web site at www.pearsonhighered.com/mishkin_eakins.

Interest-Rate Swaps

In addition to forwards, futures, and options, financial institutions use one other important financial derivative to manage risk. **Swaps** are financial contracts that obligate each party to the contract to exchange (swap) a set of payments it owns for another set of payments owned by the other party. Swaps are of two basic kinds: **Currency swaps** involve the exchange of a set of payments in one currency for a set of payments in another currency. **Interest-rate swaps** involve the exchange of one set of interest payments for another set of interest payments, all denominated in the same currency. We focus on interest-rate swaps.

Interest-Rate Swap Contracts

Interest-rate swaps are an important tool for managing interest-rate risk, and they first appeared in the United States in 1982 when, as we have seen, there was an increase in the demand for financial instruments that could be used to reduce interest-rate risk. The most common type of interest-rate swap (called the *plain vanilla swap*) specifies (1) the interest rate on the payments that are being exchanged; (2) the type of interest payments (variable or fixed rate); (3) the amount of **notional principal**, which is the amount on which the interest is being paid; and (4) the time period over which the exchanges continue to be made. There are many other, more complicated versions of swaps, including forward swaps and swap options (called *swaptions*), but here we will look only at the plain vanilla swap. Figure 24.2 illustrates an interest-rate swap between the Midwest Savings Bank and the Friendly Finance Company. Midwest Savings agrees to pay Friendly Finance a fixed rate of 5% on $1 million of notional principal for the next 10 years, and Friendly Finance agrees to pay Midwest Savings the one-year Treasury bill rate plus 1% on $1 million of notional principal for the same period. Thus, as shown in Figure 24.2, every year the Midwest Savings Bank would be paying the Friendly Finance Company 5% on $1 million while Friendly Finance would be paying Midwest Savings the one-year T-bill rate plus 1% on $1 million.

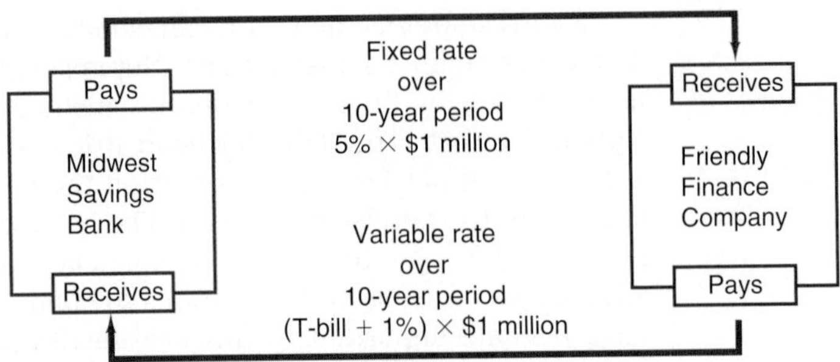

FIGURE 24.2 Interest-Rate Swap Payments

In this swap arrangement, with a notional principal of $1 million and a term of 10 years, the Midwest Savings Bank pays a fixed rate of 5% × $1 million to the Friendly Finance Company, which in turn agrees to pay the one-year Treasury bill rate plus 1% × $1 million to the Midwest Savings Bank.

THE PRACTICING MANAGER

Hedging with Interest-Rate Swaps

You might wonder why the managers of the two financial institutions find it advantageous to enter into this swap agreement. The answer is that it may help both of them hedge interest-rate risk.

Suppose that the Midwest Savings Bank, which tends to borrow short-term and then lend long-term in the mortgage market, has $1 million less of rate-sensitive assets than it has of rate-sensitive liabilities. As we learned in Chapter 23, this situation means that as interest rates rise, the rise in the cost of funds (liabilities) is greater than the rise in interest payments it receives on its assets, more of which are fixed rate. The result of rising interest rates is thus a shrinking of Midwest Savings' net interest margin and a decline in its profitability. As we saw in Chapter 23, to avoid this interest-rate risk, the manager of Midwest Savings would like to convert $1 million of its fixed-rate assets into $1 million of rate-sensitive assets, in effect making rate-sensitive assets equal to rate-sensitive liabilities, thereby eliminating the gap. This is exactly what happens when she engages in the interest-rate swap. By taking $1 million of its fixed-rate income and exchanging it for $1 million of rate-sensitive Treasury bill income, she has converted income on $1 million of fixed-rate assets into income on $1 million of rate-sensitive assets. Now when interest rates increase, the rise in rate-sensitive income on Midwest Savings' assets exactly matches the rise in the rate-sensitive cost of funds on its liabilities, leaving the net interest margin and bank profitability unchanged.

The manager of the Friendly Finance Company, which issues long-term bonds to raise funds and uses them to make short-term loans, finds that he is in exactly the opposite situation to Midwest Savings: He has $1 million more of rate-sensitive assets than of rate-sensitive liabilities. He is therefore concerned that a fall in interest rates, which will result in a larger drop in income from its assets than the decline in the cost of funds on its liabilities, will cause a decline in profits. By doing the interest-rate swap, the manager eliminates this interest-rate risk because he has converted \$1 million of rate-sensitive income into \$1 million of fixed-rate income. Now the manager of the Friendly Finance Company finds that when interest rates fall, the decline in rate-sensitive income is smaller and so is matched by the decline in the rate-sensitive cost of funds on its liabilities, leaving profitability unchanged.*

*For more details and examples of how interest-rate risk can be hedged with interest-rate swaps, see the appendix to this chapter, which can be found on the book's Web site at www.pearsonhighered.com/mishkin_eakins.

Advantages of Interest-Rate Swaps

To eliminate interest-rate risk, both the Midwest Savings Bank and the Friendly Finance Company could have rearranged their balance sheets by converting fixed-rate assets into rate-sensitive assets, and vice versa, instead of engaging in an interest-rate swap. However, this strategy would have been costly for both financial institutions for several reasons. The first is that financial institutions incur substantial transaction costs when they rearrange their balance sheets. Second, different financial institutions have informational advantages in making loans to certain customers who may prefer certain maturities. Thus, adjusting the balance sheet to eliminate interest-rate risk may result in a loss of these informational advantages, which the financial institution is unwilling to give up. Interest-rate swaps solve these problems for financial institutions because in effect they allow the institutions to convert fixed-rate assets into rate-sensitive assets without affecting the balance sheet. Large transaction costs are avoided, and the financial institutions can continue to make loans where they have an informational advantage.

We have seen that financial institutions can also hedge interest-rate risk with other financial derivatives such as futures contracts and futures options. Interest-rate swaps have one big advantage over hedging with these other derivatives: They can be written for very long horizons, sometimes as long as 20 years, whereas financial futures and futures options typically have much shorter horizons, not much more than a year. If a financial institution needs to hedge interest-rate risk for a long horizon, financial futures and option markets may not do it much good. Instead it can turn to the swap market.

Disadvantages of Interest-Rate Swaps

Although interest-rate swaps have important advantages that make them very popular with financial institutions, they also have disadvantages that limit their usefulness. Swap markets, like forward markets, can suffer from a lack of liquidity. Let's return to looking at the swap between the Midwest Savings Bank and the Friendly Finance Company. As with a forward contract, it might be difficult for the Midwest Savings Bank to link up with the Friendly Finance Company to arrange the swap. In addition, even if the Midwest Savings Bank could find a counterparty like the Friendly Finance Company, it might not be able to negotiate a good deal because it couldn't find any other institution to negotiate with.

Swap contracts also are subject to the same default risk that we encountered for forward contracts. If interest rates rise, the Friendly Finance Company would love to get out of the swap contract because the fixed-rate interest payments it receives are less than it could get in the open market. It might then default on the contract, exposing Midwest Savings to a loss. Alternatively, the Friendly Finance Company could go bust, meaning that the terms of the swap contract would not be fulfilled.

It is important to note that the default risk of swaps is not the same as the default risk on the full amount of the notional principal because the notional principal is never exchanged. If the Friendly Finance Company goes broke because $1 million of its one-year loans default and it cannot make its interest payment to Midwest Savings, Midwest Savings will stop sending its payment to Friendly Finance. If interest rates have declined, this will suit Midwest Savings just fine because it would rather keep the 5% fixed-rate interest payment, which is at a higher rate, than receive the rate-sensitive payment, which has declined. Thus, a default on a swap contract does not necessarily mean that there is a loss to the other party. Midwest Savings will suffer losses from a default only if interest rates have risen when the default occurs. Even then, the loss will be far smaller than the amount of the notional principal because interest payments are far smaller than the amount of the notional principal.[3]

Financial Intermediaries in Interest-Rate Swaps

As we have just seen, financial institutions do have to be aware of the possibility of losses from a default on swaps. As with a forward contract, each party to a swap must have a lot of information about the other party to make sure that the contract is likely to be fulfilled. The need for information about counterparties and the liquidity problems in swap markets could limit the usefulness of these markets. However, as we saw in Chapter 7, when informational and liquidity problems crop up in a market, financial intermediaries come to the rescue. That is exactly what happens in swap markets. Intermediaries such as investment banks and especially large commercial banks have the ability to acquire information cheaply about the creditworthiness and reliability of parties to swap contracts and are also able to match parties to a swap. Hence, large commercial banks and investment banks have set up swap markets in which they act as intermediaries.

Credit Derivatives

In recent years, a new type of derivative has come on the scene to hedge credit risk. Like other derivatives, **credit derivatives** offer payoffs linked to previously issued securities, but ones that bear credit risk. In the past 10 years, the markets in credit derivatives have grown at an astounding pace and the notional amounts of these derivatives now number in the trillions of dollars. These credit derivatives take several forms.

[3]The actual loss will equal the present value of the difference in the interest payments that the bank would have received if the swap were still in force as compared to interest payments it receives otherwise.

Credit Options

Credit options work just like the options discussed earlier in the chapter: For a fee, the purchaser gains the right to receive profits that are tied either to the price of an underlying security or to an interest rate. Suppose you buy $1 million of General Motors bonds but worry that a potential slowdown in the sale of SUVs might lead a credit-rating agency to *downgrade* (lower the credit rating on) GM bonds. As we saw in Chapter 5, such a downgrade would cause the price of GM bonds to fall. To protect yourself, you could buy an option for, say, $15,000, to sell the $1 million of bonds at a strike price that is the same as the current price. With this strategy, you would not suffer any losses if the value of the GM bonds declined because you could exercise the option and sell them at the price you paid for them. In addition, you would be able to reap any gains that occurred if GM bonds rose in value.

A second type of credit option ties profits to changes in an interest rate, such as a credit spread (the interest rate on the average bond with a particular credit rating minus the interest rate on default-free bonds such as those issued by the U.S. Treasury). Suppose that your company, which has a Baa credit rating, plans to issue $10 million of one-year bonds in three months and expects to have a credit spread of 1 percentage point (i.e., it will pay an interest rate that is 1 percentage point higher than the one-year Treasury rate). You are concerned that the market might start to think that Baa companies in general will become riskier in the coming months. If this were to happen by the time you are ready to issue your bonds in three months, you would have to pay a higher interest rate than the 1 percentage point in excess of the Treasury rate, and your cost of issuing the bonds would increase. To protect yourself against these higher costs, you could buy for, say, $20,000 a credit option on $10 million of Baa bonds that would pay you the difference between the average Baa credit spread in the market minus the 1 percentage point credit spread on $10 million. If the credit spread jumps to 2 percentage points, you would receive $100,000 from the option (= [2% − 1%] × $10 million), which would exactly offset the $100,000 higher interest costs from the 1 percentage point higher interest rate you would have to pay on your $10 million of bonds.

Credit Swaps

Suppose you manage a bank in Houston called Oil Drillers' Bank (ODB), which specializes in lending to a particular industry in your local area, oil drilling companies. Another bank, Potato Farmers Bank (PFB), specializes in lending to potato farmers in Idaho. Both ODB and PFB have a problem because their loan portfolios are not sufficiently diversified. To protect ODB against a collapse in the oil market, which would result in defaults on most of its loans made to oil drillers, you could reach an agreement to have the loan payments on, say, $100 million worth of your loans to oil drillers paid to the PFB in exchange for PFB paying you the loan payments on $100 million of its loans to potato farmers. Such a transaction, in which risky payments on loans are swapped for each other, is called a **credit swap**. As a result of this swap, ODB and PFB have increased their diversification and lowered the overall risk of their loan portfolios because some of the loan payments to each bank are now coming from a different type of loan.

Another form of credit swap is, for arcane reasons, called a **credit default swap**, although it functions more like insurance. With a credit default swap, one party who wants to hedge credit risk pays a fixed payment on a regular basis, in return for a contingent payment that is triggered by a *credit event*, such as the bankruptcy of a particular firm or the downgrading of the firm's credit rating by a credit-rating agency. For example, you could use a credit default swap to hedge the $1 million of General Motors bonds that you are holding by arranging to pay an annual fee of $1,000 in exchange for a payment of $10,000 if the GM bonds' credit rating is lowered. If a credit event happens and GM's bonds are downgraded so that their price falls, you will receive a payment that will offset some of the loss you suffer if you sell the bonds at this lower price.

Credit-Linked Notes

Another type of credit derivative, the **credit-linked note**, is a combination of a bond and a credit option. Just like any corporate bond, the credit-linked note makes periodic coupon (interest) payments and a final payment of the face value of the bond at maturity. If a key financial variable specified in the note changes, however, the issuer of the note has the right (option) to lower the payments on the note. For example, General Motors could issue a credit-linked note that pays a 5% coupon rate, with the specification that if a national index of SUV sales falls by 10%, then GM has the right to lower the coupon rate by 2 percentage points to 3%. In this way, GM can lower its risk because when it is losing money as SUV sales fall, it can offset some of these losses by making smaller payments on its credit-linked notes.

CASE

Lessons from the Global Financial Crisis: When Are Financial Derivatives Likely to Be a Worldwide Time Bomb?

Although financial derivatives can be useful in hedging risk, the AIG blowup discussed in Chapter 8 illustrates that they can pose a real danger to the financial system. Indeed, Warren Buffet warned about the dangers of financial derivatives by characterizing them as "financial weapons of mass destruction." Particularly scary are the notional amounts of derivatives contracts—around $500 trillion worldwide. What does the recent global financial crisis tell us about when financial derivatives are likely to be a time bomb that could bring down the world financial system?

Two major concerns surround financial derivatives. The first is that financial derivatives allow financial institutions to increase their leverage; that is, these institutions can, in effect, hold an amount of the underlying asset that is many times greater than the amount of money they have had to put up. Increasing their leverage enables them to take huge bets, which if they are wrong can bring down the institution. This is exactly what AIG did, to its great regret, when it plunged into the credit default swap market. Even more of a problem was that AIG's speculation in the credit default swap (CDS) market had the potential to bring down the whole financial system. An important lesson from the global financial crisis is that having one player take huge positions in a derivatives market is highly dangerous.

A second concern is that banks have holdings of huge notional amounts of financial derivatives, particularly interest-rate and currency swaps, that greatly exceed the amount of bank capital, and so these derivatives expose the banks to serious risk of failure. Banks are indeed major players in the financial derivatives markets, particularly in the interest-rate and currency swaps market, where our earlier analysis has shown that they are the natural market makers because they can act as intermediaries between two counterparties who would not make the swap without their involvement. However, looking at the notional amount of interest-rate and currency swaps at banks gives a very misleading picture of their risk exposure. Because banks act as intermediaries in the swap markets, they are typically exposed only to credit risk—a default by one of their counterparties. Furthermore, these swaps, unlike loans, do not involve payments of the notional amount but rather the much smaller payments that are based on the notional amounts. For example, in the case of a 7% interest rate, the payment is only $70,000 for a $1 million swap. Estimates of the credit exposure from swap contracts indicate that they are on the order of only 3% of the notional value of the contracts and that credit exposure at banks from derivatives is generally less than a quarter of their total credit exposure from loans. Banks' credit exposures from their derivative positions are thus not out of line with other credit exposures they face. Furthermore, an analysis by the GAO indicated that actual credit losses incurred by banks in their derivatives contracts have been very small, on the order of 0.2% of their gross credit exposure. Indeed, during the recent global financial crisis, in which the financial system was put under great stress, derivatives exposure at banks has not been a serious problem.

The conclusion is that recent events indicate that financial derivatives pose serious dangers to the financial system, but some of these dangers have been overplayed. The biggest danger occurs in trading activities of financial institutions, and this is particularly true for credit derivatives, as was illustrated by AIG's activities in the CDS market. As discussed in Chapter 18, regulators have been paying increased attention to this danger and are continuing to develop new disclosure requirements and regulatory guidelines for how derivatives trading should be done. Of particular concern is the need for financial institutions to disclose their exposure in derivatives contracts, so that regulators can make sure that a large institution is not playing too large a role in these markets and does not have too large an exposure to derivatives relative to its capital, as was the case for AIG. Another concern is that derivatives, particularly credit derivatives, need to have a better clearing mechanism so that the failure of one institution does not bring down many others whose net derivatives positions are small, even though they have many offsetting positions. Better clearing could be achieved either by having these derivatives traded in an organized exchange like a futures market or by having one clearing organization net out trades. Regulators such as the Federal Reserve Bank of New York have been active in making proposals along these lines.

The credit risk exposure posed by interest-rate derivatives, by contrast, seems to be manageable with standard methods of dealing with credit risk, both by managers of financial institutions and by the institutions' regulators.

New regulations for derivatives markets are sure to come in the wake of the global financial crisis. The industry has also had a wake-up call as to where the dangers in derivatives products might lie. Now the hope is that any time bomb arising from derivatives can be defused with appropriate effort on the part of markets and regulators.

SUMMARY

1. Interest-rate forward contracts, which are agreements to sell a debt instrument at a future (forward) point in time, can be used to hedge (protect against) interest-rate risk. The advantage of forward contracts is that they are flexible, but the disadvantages are that they are subject to default risk and their market is illiquid.
2. A financial futures contract is similar to an interest-rate forward contract in that it specifies that a debt instrument must be delivered by one party to another on a stated future date. However, it has advantages over a forward contract in that it is not subject to default risk and is more liquid. Forward and futures contracts can be used by financial institutions to hedge interest-rate risk.
3. Stock index futures are financial futures whose underlying financial instrument is a stock market index like the Standard and Poor's 500 Index. Stock index futures can be used to hedge stock market risk by reducing systematic risk in portfolios or by locking in stock prices.
4. An option contract gives the purchaser the right to buy (call option) or sell (put option) a security at the exercise (strike) price within a specific period of time. The profit function for options is nonlinear—profits do not always grow by the same amount for a given change in the price of the underlying financial instrument. The nonlinear profit function for options explains why their value (as reflected by the premium paid for them) is negatively related to the exercise price for call options, positively related to the exercise price for put options, positively related to the term to expiration for both call and put options, and positively related to the volatility of the prices of the underlying financial instrument for both call and put options. Financial institutions use futures options to hedge interest-rate risk in a similar fashion to the way they use financial futures and forward contracts. Futures options may be preferred for macro hedges because they suffer from fewer accounting problems than financial futures.
5. Interest-rate swaps involve the exchange of one set of interest payments for another set of interest payments and have default risk and liquidity problems similar to those of forward contracts. As a result, interest-rate swaps often involve intermediaries such as large commercial banks and investment banks that make a market in swaps. Financial institutions find that interest-rate swaps are useful ways to hedge interest-rate risk. Interest-rate swaps have one big advantage over financial futures and options: They can be written for very long horizons.
6. Credit derivatives are a new type of derivatives that offer payoffs on previously issued securities that have credit risk. These derivatives—credit options, credit swaps, and credit-linked notes—can be used to hedge credit risk.
7. There are three concerns about the dangers of derivatives: They allow financial institutions to more easily increase their leverage and take big bets (by effectively enabling them to hold a larger amount of the underlying assets than the amount of money put down), they are too complex for managers of financial institutions to understand, and they expose financial institutions to large credit risks because the huge notional amounts of derivative contracts greatly exceed the capital of these institutions. The last two dangers seem to be overplayed, but the danger from increased leverage using derivatives is real.

KEY TERMS

QUESTIONS

1. In the September 2016 FOMC meeting, governors and voting presidents of the Federal Reserve System agreed not to increase the federal funds rate target, but somewhat let the markets know that there could be a rise in the near future. How do you think that financial managers will react to this news? Which instruments can they use to hedge against a change in interest rates?

2. If the finance company you manage has a gap of +$5 million (rate-sensitive assets greater than rate-sensitive liabilities by $5 million), describe an interest-rate swap that would eliminate the company's income gap.

QUANTITATIVE PROBLEMS

1. Leticia has to hedge the interest-rate risk of her holdings of $6,480,000 in Treasury bonds by buying or selling futures contracts. Determine the type of transaction and the price of each contract if Leticia buys/sells 48 contracts.

2. If the portfolio you manage is holding $25 million of *6*s of 2037 Treasury bonds with a price of 110, what forward contract would you enter into to hedge the interest-rate risk on these bonds over the coming year?

3. Calculate the amount of futures contracts you need to sell to hedge the interest-rate risk on your holdings of $4 million of T-bonds. Assume each contract currently sells for $125,000.

4. Refer to the previous exercise. Determine your profit if at the expiration date the settle price of the contract is 135 points. Calculate the gain or loss in each position.

5. Suppose that the pension you are managing is expecting an inflow of funds of $100 million next year and you want to make sure that you will earn the current interest rate of 8% when you invest the incoming funds in long-term bonds. How would you use the futures market to do this?

6. How would you use the options market to accomplish the same thing as in problem 5? What are the advantages and disadvantages of using an options contract rather than a futures contract?

7. Suppose you buy a call option on a $100,000 Treasury bond futures contract with an exercise price of 105. If the price of the Treasury bond is 115 at expiration, is the option at the money, in the money or out of the money? Determine the premium if the profit equals $8,000.

8. Jason bought a put option on a $100,000 Treasury bond futures contract with an exercise price of 105 for a premium of $2,000. If on expiration the futures contract sells for 110, determine Jason's profits and explain if he will exercise the right to sell the futures contract. How would your answer change if the futures contract sells for 95 on expiration?

9. Refer to the previous exercise. Determine Jason's profits (for both prices on expiration date) if instead of buying a put option on a futures contract he sold a $100,000 Treasury bonds futures contract at par.

10. If the savings and loan you manage has a gap of −$42 million, describe an interest-rate swap that would eliminate the S&L's income risk from changes in interest rates.

11. If your company has a payment of 200 million euros due one year from now, how would you hedge the foreign exchange risk in this payment with 125,000 euros futures contracts?

12. If your company has to make a 10 million euros payment to a German company in June, three months from now, how would you hedge the foreign exchange risk in this payment with a 125,000 euros futures contract?

13. Suppose that your company will be receiving 30 million euros six months from now and the euro is currently selling for 1 euro per dollar. If you want to hedge the foreign exchange risk in this payment, what kind of forward contract would you want to enter into?

14. A hedger takes a short position in five T-bill futures contracts at the price of 98 5/32. Each contract is for $100,000 principal. When the position is closed, the price is 95 12/32. What is the gain or loss on this transaction?

15. A bank issues a $100,000 variable-rate 30-year mortgage with a nominal annual rate of 4.5%. If the interest rate drops to 4.0% after the first six months, what is the impact on the interest income for the first 12 months? Assume the bank hedged this risk with a short position in a 181-day T-bill future. The original price was 97 26/32, and the final price was 98 1/32 on a $100,000 face value contract. Did this work?

16. Laura, a bond portfolio manager, administers a $10 million portfolio. The portfolio currently has a duration of 8.5 years. Laura wants to shorten the duration to 6 years using T-bill futures. T-bill futures have a duration of 0.25 year and are trading at $975 (face value = $1,000). How is this accomplished?

17. Suppose you buy a futures contract at a price of 107 and that the margin requirement is 2 points. Determine the settlement price at which you will receive a margin call if the maintenance margin requirement is 1 point.

18. Chicago Bank and Trust has $100 million in assets and $83 million in liabilities. The duration of the assets is 5.9 years, and the duration of the liabilities is 1.8 years. How many futures contracts does this bank need to fully hedge itself against interest-rate risk? The available Treasury bond futures contracts have a duration of 10 years, have a face value of $1,000,000, and are selling for $979,000.

19. A bank issues a $3 million commercial mortgage with a nominal APR of 8%. The loan is fully amortized over 10 years, requiring monthly payments. The bank plans on selling the loan after two months. If the required nominal APR increases by 45 basis points when the loan is sold, what loss does the bank incur?

20. Assume the bank in the previous question partially hedges the mortgage by selling three 10-year T-note futures contracts at a price of 100 20/32. Each contract is for $1,000,000. After two months, the futures contract has fallen in price to 98 24/32. What was the gain or loss on the futures transaction?

21. Springer County Bank has assets totaling $180 million with a duration of five years, and liabilities totaling $160 million with a duration of two years. Bank management expects interest rates to fall from 9% to 8.25% shortly. A T-bond futures contract is available for hedging. Its duration is 6.5 years, and it is currently priced at 99 5/32. How many contracts does Springer need to hedge against the expected rate change? Assume each contract has a face value of $1,000,000.

22. From the previous question, rates do indeed fall as expected, and the T-bond contract is priced at 103 5/32. If Springer closes its futures position, what is the gain or loss? How well does this offset the approximate change in equity value?

23. A bank issues a $100,000 fixed-rate 30-year mortgage with a nominal annual rate of 4.5%. If the required rate drops to 4.0% immediately after the mortgage is issued, what is the impact on the value of the mortgage? Assume the bank hedged the position with a short position in two 10-year T-bond futures. The original price was 64 12/32 and expired at 67 16/32 on a $100,000 face value contract. What was the gain on the futures? What is the total impact on the bank?

24. A bank customer will be going to London in June to purchase £100,000 in new inventory. The current spot and futures exchange rates are as follows:

Exchange Rates (Dollars/Pound)

Period	Rate
Spot	1.5342
March	1.6212
June	1.6901
September	1.7549
December	1.8416

The customer enters into a position in June futures to fully hedge her position. When June arrives, the actual exchange rate is $1.725 per pound. How much did she save?

25. Suppose a bank has an income gap of −$15 million. How can this bank use interest-rate swaps to hedge against interest rate increases? Determine the amount of the notional principal and propose an interest rate swap.

26. Liverpool Bank has an income gap of −$10 million, Alur Finance Co has an income gap of $25 million and TLBR Bank has an income gap of −$15 million. Propose an interest rate swap that will benefit all three institutions. Determine the amount of notional principal for each interest rate swap.

27. A banker commits to a two-year $5,000,000 commercial loan and expects to fulfill the agreement in 30 days. The interest rate will be determined at that time. Currently, rates are 7.5% for such loans. To hedge against rates falling, the banker buys a 30-day interest-rate floor with a floor rate of 7.5% on a notional amount of $10,000,000. After 30 days, actual rates fall to 7.2%. What is the expected interest income from the loan each year? How much did the option pay?

28. A trust manager for a $100,000,000 stock portfolio wants to minimize short-term downside risk using Dow put options. The options expire in 60 days, have a strike price of 9,700, and have a premium of $50. The Dow is currently at 10,100. How many options should she use? Long or short? How much will this cost? If the portfolio is perfectly correlated with the Dow, what is the portfolio value when the option expires, including the premium paid?

29. Dickey Bank anticipates an increase in interest rates in 2016 and has therefore decided to engage in an interest-rate swap in which it pays 3% over a notional principal of $4 million annually. Fuller Finance Company pays Dickey Bank the interest income generated by applying the T-bill rate plus 2%. Can you determine if the income gap of Dickey Bank is negative or positive? Determine the amount paid by each institution if the T-bill rate is 0.5% or 1.5%.

30. North-Northwest Bank (NNWB) has a differential advantage in issuing variable-rate mortgages but does not want the interest income risk associated with such loans. The bank currently has a portfolio of $25,000,000 in mortgages with an APR of prime +150 basis points, reset monthly. Prime is currently 4%. An investment bank has arranged for NNWB to swap into a fixed interest payment of 6.5% on a notional amount of $25,000,000 in return for its variable interest income. If NNWB agrees to this, what interest is received and given in the first month? What if prime suddenly increased 200 basis points?

WEB EXERCISE

Hedging with Financial Derivatives

1. The following site can be used to demonstrate how the features of an option affect the option's prices. Go to **http://www.hoadley.net/options/bs.htm**. Scroll down to the online options calculator. What happens to the price of an option under each of the following situations?

a. The strike price increases.

b. Interest rates increase.

c. Volatility increases.

d. The time until the option matures increases.

WEB APPENDICES

Please visit our Web site at **www.pearsonhighered.com/mishkin_eakins** to read the Web appendix to Chapter 24:

- **Appendix 1:** More on Hedging with Financial Derivatives

Glossary

advances: See *discount loans*.

adverse selection: The problem created by asymmetric information before a transaction occurs: The people who are the most undesirable from the other party's point of view are the ones who are most likely to want to engage in the financial transaction. 25

agency problem: A moral hazard problem that occurs when the one party (the agents) act in their own interest rather than in the interest of the other party (the principal) due to differing sets of incentives. 174

agency theory: The analysis of how asymmetric information problems affect economic behavior. 141

American depository receipts (ADR): A receipt for foreign stocks held by a trustee. The receipts trade on U.S. stock exchanges instead of the actual stock. 314

American option: An option that can be exercised at any time up to the expiration date of the contract. 594

amortized: Paid off in stages over a period of time. Each payment on a loan consists of the accrued interest and an amount that is applied to repay the principal. When all of the payments have been made, the loan is paid off (fully amortized). 319

anchor currency: The currency to which a country fixes its exchange rate. 373

annuity: An insurance product that provides a fixed stream of payments. 509

appreciation: Increase in a currency's value. 341

arbitrage: Elimination of a riskless profit opportunity in a market. 120, 584

ask price: The price market makers sell the stock for. 301

asset: A financial claim or piece of property that is a store of value. 2, 67

asset-backed commercial paper (ABCP): Short-term commercial paper secured by a bundle of assets, usually mortgages. 264

asset management: The acquisition of assets that have a low rate of default and diversification of asset holdings to increase profits. 396

asset market approach: Determining asset prices using stocks of assets rather than flows. 74

asset-price bubble: An increase in asset prices that are driven above their fundamental economic values by investor psychology. 169

asset transformation: The process by which financial intermediaries turn risky assets into safer assets for investors by creating and selling assets with risk characteristics that people are comfortable with and then use the funds they acquire by selling these assets to purchase other assets that may have far more risk. 24

asymmetric information: The inequality of knowledge that each party to a transaction has about the other party. 25

audits: Certification by accounting firms that a business is adhering to standard accounting principles. 143

automated banking machine (ABM): An electronic machine that combines in one location an ATM, an Internet connection to the bank's Web site, and a telephone link to customer service. 449

automated teller machine (ATM): An electronic machine that allows customers to get cash, make deposits, transfer funds from one account to another, and check balances. 449

balance of payments: A bookkeeping system for recording all payments that have a direct bearing on the movement of funds between a country and all other countries. 372

balance-of-payments crisis: A foreign exchange crisis stemming from problems in a country's balance of payments. 382

balance sheet: A list of the assets and liabilities of a bank (or firm) that balances: Total assets equal total liabilities plus capital. 209, 390

balloon loan: A loan on which the payments do not fully pay off the principal balance, meaning that the final payment must be larger than the rest. 319

bank failure: A situation in which a bank cannot satisfy its obligation to pay its depositors and other creditors and so goes out of business. 416

bank holding companies: Companies that own one or more banks. 446

bank panic: The simultaneous failure of many banks, as during a financial crisis. 170, 416

bank supervision: Overseeing who operates banks and how they are operated.

banker's acceptance: A short-term promissory note drawn by a company to pay for goods on which a bank guarantees payment at maturity. Usually used in international trade. 265

banks: Financial institutions that accept deposits and make loans (such as commercial banks, savings and loan associations, and credit unions). 7

Basel Accord: An agreement that requires that banks hold as capital at least 8% of their risk-weighted assets. 422

Basel Committee on Banking Supervision: A committee that meets under the auspices of the Bank for International Settlements in Basel, Switzerland, and that sets bank regulatory standards. 422

bearer instrument: A security payable to the holder or "bearer" when presented. No proof of ownership is required. 262

behavioral finance: The field of study that applies concepts from other social sciences, such as anthropology, sociology, and particularly psychology, to understand the behavior of securities prices. 131

bid price: The price market makers pay for the stocks. 301

Board of Governors of the Federal Reserve System: A board with seven governors (including the chair) that plays an essential role in decision making within the Federal Reserve System. 187

bond: A debt security that promises to make payments periodically for a specified period of time. 2

bond indenture: Document accompanying a bond that spells out the details of the bond issue, such as covenants and sinking fund provisions. It states the lender's rights and privileges and the borrower's obligations. 281

book entry: A system of tracking securities ownership where no certificate is issued. Instead, the security issuer keeps records, usually electronically, of who holds outstanding securities. 258

branches: Additional offices of banks that conduct banking operations. 463

Bretton Woods system: The international monetary system in use from 1945 to 1971 in which exchange rates were fixed and the U.S. dollar was freely convertible into gold (by foreign governments and central banks only). 373

brokers: Agents for investors who match buyers with sellers. 19

bubble: A situation in which the price of an asset differs from its fundamental market value. 130, 240

call option: An option contract that provides the right to buy a security at a specified price. 594

call provision: A right, usually included in the terms of a bond, that gives the issuer the ability to repurchase outstanding bonds before they mature. 283

capital: Wealth, either financial or physical, that is employed to produce more wealth. 17

capital account: An account that describes the flow of capital between the United States and other countries.

capital adequacy management: Managing the amount of capital the bank should maintain and then acquiring the needed capital. 396

capital buyout: Investors' funds are pooled and used to buy a controlling interest in a public company that is then taken private. 548

capital call: A requirement of limited partners in a venture capital agreement to supply funds per their commitment with the partnership. 552

capital controls: Restrictions on the free movement of capital across the borders. 377

capital market: A financial market in which longer-term debt (maturity of greater than one year) and equity instruments are traded. 20

capital mobility: A situation in which foreigners can easily purchase a country's assets and the country's residents can easily purchase foreign assets. 376

captive finance company: A finance company that is owned by a retailer and makes loans to finance the purchase of goods from the retailer.

cash flow: The difference between cash receipts and cash expenditures. 38

casualty (liability) insurance: Protection against financial losses because of a claim of negligence. 515

central bank: The government agency that oversees the banking system and is responsible for the amount of money and credit supplied in the economy; in the United States, the Federal Reserve System. 7

Central Liquidity Facility (CLF): The lender of last resort for credit unions, created in 1978 by the Financial Institutions Reform Act.

certainty equivalent: An amount that will be received or spent with certainty. An insurance payment is a certainty equivalent, since it removes the risk that unexpected amounts will need to be spent. 505

closed-end fund: A mutual fund that sells a fixed number of shares of stock and does not continue to accept investments. 484

coinsurance: An insurance policy under which the policyholder bears a percentage of the loss along with the insurance company. 519

collateral: Property that is pledged to the lender to guarantee payment in the event that the borrower should be unable to make debt payments. 146

collateralized debt obligation (CDO): Securities that pay out cash flows from subprime mortgage-backed securities. 174

collateralized mortgage obligation (CMO): Securities classified by when prepayment is likely to occur. Investors may buy a group of CMOs that are likely to mature at a time that meets the investors' needs. 333

common bond membership: A requirement that all members of credit unions share some common bond, such as working for the same employer.

common stock: A security that gives the holder an ownership interest in the issuing firm. This ownership interest includes the right to any residual cash flows and the right to vote on major corporate issues. 3

common stockholders: Individuals who have an ownership interest in a firm, with rights to receive dividends and vote on major corporate issues. 298

community banks: Small banks with local roots. 468

compensating balance: A required minimum amount of funds that a firm receiving a loan must keep in a checking account at the bank. 562

competitive bidding: Competing in an auction against other potential buyers of Treasury securities. 258

confidential memorandum: A document that presents detailed financial information required by prospective buyers prior to making an offer to acquire a firm. 541

conflicts of interest: A manifestation of moral hazard in which one party in a financial contract has incentives to act in its own interest, rather than in the interests of the other party. 27, 157

conventional monetary policy tools: Three tools of monetary policy—open market operations, discount lending, and reserve requirements—the Federal Reserve uses to control the money supply and interest rates. 218

conventional mortgages: Mortgage contracts originated by banks and other mortgage lenders that are not guaranteed by the FHA or the VA. They are often insured by private mortgage insurance. 325

costly state verification: Monitoring a firm's activities, an expensive process in both time and money. 148

coupon bond: A credit market instrument that pays the owner a fixed interest payment every year until the maturity date, when a specified final amount is paid. 40

coupon rate: The dollar amount of the yearly coupon payment expressed as a percentage of the face value of a coupon bond. 40, 274

credit-rating agencies: Investment advisory firms that rate the quality of corporate and municipal bonds in terms of the probability of default. 92

credit boom: A lending spree when financial institutions expand their lending at a rapid pace. 169

credit default swap: A transaction in which one party who wants to hedge credit risk pays a fixed payment on a regular basis, in return for a contingent payment that is triggered by a credit event such as the bankruptcy of a particular firm or the downgrading of the firm's credit rating by a credit rating agency. 176, 287, 605

credit derivatives: Derivatives that have payoffs to previously issued securities, but ones that bear credit risk. 604

credit easing: The altering of the composition of the Fed's balance sheet in order to improve the functioning of particular segments of the credit markets. 236

credit-linked note: A type of credit derivative that is a combination of a bond and a credit option. 606

credit options: Options in which for a fee, the purchaser has the right to get profits that are tied either to the price of an underlying risky security or to an interest rate. 605

credit-rating agencies: Investment advisory firms that rate the quality of corporate and municipal bonds in terms of the probability of default. 92

credit rationing: A lender's refusing to make loans even though borrowers are willing to pay the stated interest rate or even a higher rate or restricting the size of loans to less than the amount being sought. 562

credit risk: The risk arising from the possibility that the borrower will default. 396

credit spread: The risk premium: the interest rate on bonds with default risks relative to the interest rate on default-free bonds like U.S. Treasury bonds. 173

credit swap: A transaction in which risky payments on loans are swapped for each other. 605

credit union: A financial institution that focuses on servicing the banking and lending needs of its members, who must be linked by a common bond. 28

Credit Union National Association (CUNA): A central credit union facility that encourages establishing credit unions and provides information to its members.

Credit Union National Extension Bureau (CUNEB): A central credit union facility established in 1921 that was later replaced by the Credit Union National Association.

creditor: A lender or holder of debt. 156

currency board: A monetary regime in which the domestic currency is backed 100% by a foreign currency (say, dollars) and in which the note-issuing authority, whether the central bank or the government, establishes a fixed exchange rate to this foreign currency and stands ready to exchange domestic currency at this rate whenever the public requests it. 378

currency swap: A swap that involves the exchange of a set of payments in another currency. 601

currency union: A situation in which a group of countries decide to adopt a common currency. (Also called a *monetary union*.) 377

current account: An account that shows international transactions involving currently produced goods and services. 372

current yield: An approximation of the yield to maturity that equals the yearly coupon payment divided by the price of a coupon bond. 46, 289

dealers: People who link buyers with sellers by buying and selling securities at stated prices. 19

debt deflation: A situation in which a substantial decline in the price level sets in, leading to a further deterioration in firms' net worth because of the increased burden of indebtedness. 171

deductible: An amount of any loss that must be paid by the insured before the insurance company will pay anything. 506

deep markets: Markets in which there are many participants and a great deal of activity, thus ensuring that securities can be rapidly sold at fair prices. 258

default: A situation in which the party issuing a debt instrument is unable to make interest payments or pay off the amount owed when the instrument matures. 92

default-free bonds: Bonds with no default risk, such as U.S. government bonds. 91

default risk: The risk that a loan customer may fail to repay a loan as promised. 90

defensive open market operations: Open market operation intended to offset movements in other factors that affect reserves and the monetary base. 218

deferred load: A fee on a mutual fund investment that is charged only if the investment is withdrawn. The amount of the deferred load usually falls the longer the investment is left in the fund. 492

defined-benefit plan: A pension plan in which the benefits are stated up front and are paid regardless of how the investments perform. 522

defined-contribution plan: A pension plan in which the contributions are stated up front but the benefits paid depend on the performance of the investments. 523

definitive agreement: A legally binding contract that details the terms and conditions for an acquisition of one firm by another. 541

deleveraging: When financial institutions cut back on their lending because they have less capital. 169

demand curve: A curve depicting the relationship between quantity demanded and price when all other economic variables are held constant. 70

demand deposit: A deposit held by a bank that must be paid to the depositor on demand. Demand deposits are more commonly called *checking accounts*. 262

deposit facility: The European Central Bank's standing facility in which banks are paid a fixed interest rate 100 basis points below the target financing rate. 230

deposit outflows: Losses of deposits when depositors make withdrawals or demand payment. 396

deposit rate ceilings: Restrictions on the maximum interest rates payable on deposits. 455

depreciation: Decrease in a currency's value. 341

devaluation: Resetting of the par value of a currency at a lower level. 375

direct placement: An issuer's bypassing the dealer and selling the security directly to the investor. 263

dirty float: An exchange rate regime in which exchange rates fluctuate from day to day, but central banks attempt to influence their countries' exchange rate by buying and selling currencies. 373

discount: When the bond sells for less than the par value. 293

discount bond: A credit market instrument that is bought at a price below its face value and whose face value is repaid at the maturity date; it does not make any interest payments. (Also known as a *zero-coupon bond*.) 40

discount loans: A bank's borrowings from the Federal Reserve System. (Also known as *advances*.) 209, 391

discount points: Percentage of the total loan paid back immediately when a mortgage loan is obtained. Payment of discount points lowers the annual interest rate on the debt. 321

discount rate: The interest rate that the Federal Reserve charges banks on discount loans. 210, 398

discount window: The Federal Reserve facility at which discount loans are made to banks. 219

discount yield: See *yield on a discount basis*.

discounting: Reduction in the value of a security at purchase such that when it matures at full value, the investor receives a fair return. 256

disintermediation: A reduction in the flow of funds into the banking system that causes the amount of financial intermediation to decline. 455

diversification: Investing in a collection (portfolio) of assets whose returns do not always move together, with the result that overall risk is lower than for individual assets. 24, 481

dividends: Periodic payments made by equities to shareholders. 18

dollarization: A monetary strategy in which a country abandons its currency altogether and adopts that of another country, typically the U.S. dollar. 378

down payment: A portion of the original purchase price that is paid by the borrower so that the borrower will have equity (ownership interest) in the asset pledged as collateral. 323

dual banking system: The system in the United States in which banks supervised by the federal government and banks supervised by the states operate side by side. 445

dual mandate: A central bank mandate in which there are two equal objectives, price stability and maximum employment. 235

due diligence period: A 20- to 40-day period used by the buyer of a firm to verify the accuracy of the information contained in the confidential memorandum. 541

duration: The average lifetime of a debt security's stream of payments. 56

duration gap analysis: A measurement of the sensitivity of the market value of a bank's assets and liabilities to changes in interest rates. 566

dynamic open market operations: Open market operations intended to change the level of reserves and the monetary base. 218

early-stage investing: Investment by a venture capital firm in a company that is in the very beginning stage of its development. 552

easing of monetary policy: A lowering of the federal funds rate. 192

e-cash: A form of electronic money used on the Internet to pay for goods and services. 451

econometric model: A model whose equations are estimated using statistical procedures. 85

economies of scale: Savings that can be achieved through increased size. 24

economies of scope: Increased business that can be achieved by offering many products in one easy-to-reach location. 26, 157, 466

Edge Act corporation: A special subsidiary of a U.S. bank that is engaged primarily in international banking. 475

effective exchange rate index: An index reflecting the value of a basket of representative foreign currencies. 356

efficient market hypothesis: The hypothesis that prices of securities in financial markets fully reflect all available information. 118

e-finance: A new means of delivering financial services electronically. 8

electronic money (or e-money): Money that exists only in electronic form and substitutes for cash as well. 451

emerging market economies: Economies in an earlier stage of market development that have recently opened up to the flow of goods, services, and capital from the rest of the world. 384

Employee Retirement Income Security Act (ERISA): A comprehensive law passed in 1974 that set standards that must be followed by all pension plans. 528

equities: Claims to share in the net income and assets of a corporation (such as common stock). 18

equity capital: See *net worth.*

equity multiplier: The amount of assets per dollar of equity capital. 402

Eurobonds: Bonds denominated in a currency other than that of the country in which they are sold. 20

Eurocurrencies: Foreign currencies deposited in banks outside the home country. 21

Eurodollars: U.S. dollars that are deposited in foreign banks outside of the United States or in foreign branches of U.S. banks. 21

European option: An option that can be exercised only at the expiration date of the contract. 594

excess demand: A situation in which quantity demanded is greater than quantity supplied. 73

excess reserves: Reserves in excess of required reserves. 209, 392

excess supply: A situation in which quantity supplied is greater than quantity demanded. 73

exchange rate: The price of one currency in terms of another. 339

exchanges: Secondary markets in which buyers and sellers of securities (or their agents or brokers) meet in one central location to conduct trades. 19

exercise price: The price at which the purchaser of an option has the right to buy or sell the underlying financial instrument. (Also known as the *strike price.*) 594

expectations theory: The theory that the interest rate on a long-term bond will equal an average of the short-term interest rates that people expect to occur over the life of the long-term bond. 99

expected return: The return on an asset expected over the next period. 67

face value: The specified final amount repaid at the maturity date of a coupon bond. (Also called *par value.*) 40

factoring: The sale of accounts receivable to another firm, which takes responsibility for collections.

fair-value accounting: An accounting principle in which assets are valued in the balance sheet at what they would sell for in the market. 427

Federal Credit Union Act: Law passed in 1934 that allowed federal chartering of credit unions in all states.

federal funds: Short-term deposits bought or sold between banks. 260

federal funds rate: The interest rate on overnight loans of deposits at the Federal Reserve. 211

Federal Home Loan Bank Act of 1932: Law that created the Federal Home Loan Bank Board and a network of regional home loan banks.

Federal Home Loan Bank Board (FHLBB): Agency responsible for regulating and controlling savings and loan institutions, abolished by FIRREA in 1989.

Federal Open Market Committee (FOMC): The committee that makes decisions regarding the conduct of open market operations; composed of the seven members of the Board of Governors of the Federal Reserve System, the president of the Federal Reserve Bank of New York, and the presidents of four other Federal Reserve banks on a rotating basis. 187

Federal Reserve banks: The 12 district banks in the Federal Reserve system. 187

Federal Reserve System (the Fed): The central banking authority responsible for monetary policy in the United States. 7

Federal Savings and Loan Insurance Corporation (FSLIC): An agency that provided deposit insurance to savings and loans similar to the Federal Deposit Insurance Corporation that insures banks. FSLIC was eliminated in 1989.

FICO scores: A credit history of a potential borrower by lenders to determine a borrowers' creditworthiness. 324

financial crisis: A major disruption in financial markets, characterized by sharp declines in asset prices and the failures of many financial and nonfinancial firms. 6, 167

financial derivatives: Instruments that have payoffs that are linked to previously issued securities and are extremely useful risk-reduction tools. 175, 438, 579

financial engineering: The process of researching and developing new financial products and services that would meet customer needs and prove profitable. 174, 447

financial frictions: Asymmetric information problems that act as a barrier to financial markets channeling funds efficiently from savers to households and firms with productive investment opportunities. 167

financial futures contract: A futures contract in which the standardized commodity is a particular type of financial instrument. 582

financial futures options: Options in which the underlying instrument is a futures contract. (Also called *futures options*.) 594

financial globalization: The process of opening up to flows of capital and financial firms from other nations.

financial guarantee: A contract that guarantees that bond purchasers will be paid both principal and interest in the event the issuer defaults on the obligation. 287

financial innovation: The development of new financial products and services. 7, 169

Financial Institutions Reform Act: Law passed in 1978 that created the Central Liquidity Facility as the lender of last resort for credit unions.

Financial Institutions Reform, Recovery, and Enforcement Act: Law passed in 1989 to stop losses in the savings and loan industry. It reversed much of the deregulation included in the Garn–St Germain Act of 1982.

financial instrument: See *security*.

financial intermediaries: Institutions (such as banks, insurance companies, mutual funds, pension funds, and finance companies) that borrow funds from people who have saved and then make loans to others. 6

financial intermediation: The process of indirect finance whereby financial intermediaries link lender-savers and borrower-spenders. 22

financial liberalization: The elimination of restrictions on financial markets. 169

financial markets: Markets in which funds are transferred from people who have a surplus of available funds to people who have a shortage of available funds. 2

financial panic: The widespread collapse of financial markets and intermediaries in an economy. 32

financial supervision: Oversight of who operates financial institutions and how they are operated. (Also called *prudential supervision*.) 423

FINRA: The Financial Industry Regulatory Authority; formerly the National Association of Security Dealers (NASD). 288

fire sales: The quick sale of assets to raise necessary funds. 170

Fisher effect: The outcome that when expected inflation occurs, interest rates will rise; named after economist Irving Fisher. 81

fixed exchange rate regime: Policy under which central banks buy and sell their own currencies to keep their exchange rates fixed at a certain level. 373

fixed-payment loan: A credit market instrument that provides a borrower with an amount of money that is repaid by making a fixed payment periodically (usually monthly) for a set number of years. 40

floating exchange rate regime: An exchange rate regime in which the values of currencies are allowed to fluctuate against one another. 373

foreign bonds: Bonds sold in a foreign country and denominated in that country's currency. 20

foreign exchange intervention: An international financial transaction in which a central bank buys or sells currency to influence foreign exchange rates. 368

foreign exchange market: The market in which exchange rates are determined. 4, 339

foreign exchange rate: See *exchange rate*.

forward contract: An agreement by two parties to engage in a financial transaction at a future (forward) point in time. 580

forward exchange rate: The exchange rate for a forward (future) transaction. 341

forward guidance: A strategy in which the Fed committed to keep the federal funds rate at zero for a long period of time in order to lower the market's expectations of future short-term interest rates, causing the long-term interest rate to fall. 227

forward rate: The interest rate predicted by pure expectations theory of the term structure of interest rates to prevail in the future. 111

forward transaction: An exchange rate transaction that involves the exchange of bank deposits denominated in different currencies at some specified future date. 341

free-rider problem: The problem that occurs when people who do not pay for information take advantage of the information that other people have paid for. 143

fully amortized loan: A fixed-payment loan in which the lender provides the borrower with an amount of funds that must be repaid by making the same payment every period, consisting of part of the principal and interest for a set number of years. 40

fully funded: Describing a pension plan in which the contributions to the plan and their earnings over the years are sufficient to pay out the defined benefits when they come due. 523

fully subscribed: Describing a security issue for which all of the securities available have been spoken for before the issue date. 539

fundamental economic values: The values of assets based on realistic expectations of the assets' future income streams. 169

futures contract: A contract in which the seller agrees to provide a certain standardized commodity to the buyer on a specific future date at an agreed-on price. 448

futures options: See *financial futures options.*

gap analysis: A measurement of the sensitivity of bank profits to changes in interest rates, calculated by subtracting the amount of rate-sensitive liabilities minus rate-sensitive assets. (Also called *income gap analysis.*) 564

general obligation bonds: Bonds that are secured by the full faith and credit of the issuer, which includes the taxing authority of municipalities. 280

generalized dividend model: Calculates that the price of stock is determined only by the present value of the dividends. 304

Glass-Steagall Act: Law that made it illegal for commercial banks to underwrite securities for sale to the public. 535

goal independence: The ability of the central bank to set the goals of monetary policy. 197

Gordon growth model: A simplified model to compute the value of a stock by assuming constant dividend growth. 305

haircuts: Requirements that borrowers have more collateral than the amount of the loan. 178

hedge: To protect oneself against risk. 448, 580

hedge funds: A special type of mutual fund that acquires funds by selling shares but only to very wealthy people, so they are less regulated than mutual funds. 494

hierarchical mandate: A mandate for the central bank that puts the goal of price stability first, but as long as it is achieved other goals can be pursued. 234

hybrid funds: A mutual fund that is composed of both stocks and bonds. 489

impossible trinity: See *policy trilemma.*

incentive-compatible: Aligning the incentives of both parties to a contract. 151

income gap analysis: See *gap analysis.*

index fund: A mutual fund that is composed only of securities that are included in some popular stock index, such as the S&P 500. The fund is designed to mimic the returns generated by the underlying index. 491

indexed bonds: Bonds whose interest and principal payments are adjusted for changes in the price level and whose interest rate thus provides a direct measure of a real interest rate. 51

individual retirement account (IRA): Retirement account in which pretax dollars can be invested by individuals not covered by some other retirement plan. 530

inflation targeting: A monetary policy strategy that involves public announcement of a medium-term numerical target for inflation. 236

initial public offering (IPO): A corporation's first sale of securities to the public. 158, 274, 537

insolvent: A situation in which the value of a firm's or bank's assets have fallen below its liabilities; bankrupt. 170

installment credit: A loan that requires the borrower to make a series of equal payments over some fixed length of time.

instrument independence: The ability of the central bank to set monetary policy instruments. 197

insured mortgage: Mortgages guaranteed by either the Federal Housing Administration or the Veterans Administration. These agencies guarantee that the bank making the loan will not suffer any losses if the borrower defaults. 325

interest parity condition: The observation that the domestic interest rate equals the foreign interest rate plus the expected appreciation in the foreign currency. 363

interest rate: The cost of borrowing or the price paid for the rental of funds (usually expressed as a percentage per year). 2

interest-rate forward contracts: Forward contracts that are linked to debt instruments. 580

interest-rate risk: The possible reduction in returns that is associated with changes in interest rates. 54, 293, 396

interest-rate swap: A financial contract that allows one party to exchange (swap) a set of interest payments for another set of interest payments owned by another party. 601

intermediate target: Any number of variables, such as monetary aggregates or interest rates, that have a direct effect on employment and price level and that the Fed seeks to influence.

intermediate-term: With reference to a debt instrument, having a maturity of between 1 and 10 years. 18

international banking facilities (IBFs): Banking establishments in the United States that can accept time deposits from foreigners but are not subject to either reserve requirements or restrictions on interest payments. 475

International Monetary Fund (IMF): The international organization created by the Bretton Woods agreement whose objective is to promote the growth of world trade by making loans to countries experiencing balance-of-payments difficulties. 373

international reserves: Central bank holdings of assets denominated in foreign currencies. 368

inverted yield curve: A yield curve that is downward sloping. 97

investment banker: A securities dealer who facilitates the transfer of securities from the original issuer to the public. 535

investment banks: Firms that assist in the initial sale of securities in the primary market. 19, 535

January effect: An abnormal rise in stock prices from December to January. 125

junk bonds: Bonds rated lower than BBB by bond-rating agencies. Junk bonds are not investment grade and are considered speculative. They usually have a high yield to compensate investors for their high risk. 93, 285

large, complex banking organizations (LCBOs): Large companies that provide banking as well as many other financial services. 467

later-stage investing: Investment by a venture capital firm in a company to help the firm grow to a critical mass needed to attract public financing. 552

law of large numbers: The observation that when many people are insured, the probability distribution of the losses will assume a normal probability distribution. 510

law of one price: The principle that if two or more countries produce an identical good, the price of this good should be the same no matter which country produces it. 343

leasing: An arrangement whereby one party obtains the right to use an asset for a fee paid to another party for a predetermined length of time.

lender of last resort: Provider of reserves to financial institutions when no one else would provide them to prevent a financial crisis. 220

letter of intent: A document issued by a prospective buyer that signals a desire to go forward with a purchase and that outlines the preliminary terms of the purchase. 541

leverage cycle: A lending boom and then a lending crash. 431

leverage ratio: A bank's capital divided by its assets. 422

liabilities: IOUs or debts. 16

liability management: The acquisition of funds at low cost to increase profits. 396

lien: A legal claim against a piece of property that gives a lender the right to foreclose or seize the property if a loan on the property is not repaid as promised. 323

limit order: An order placed by a customer to buy stock that specifies a maximum price or an order to sell stock that places a minimum acceptable price. 543

liquid: Easily converted into cash. 19

liquid market: A market in which securities can be bought and sold quickly and with low transaction costs. 258

liquidity: The relative ease and speed with which an asset can be converted into cash. 67

liquidity management: The decision made by a bank to maintain sufficient liquid assets to meet the bank's obligations to depositors. 396

liquidity preference framework: A model developed by John Maynard Keynes that predicts the equilibrium interest rate on the basis of the supply of and demand for money. 85

liquidity premium theory: The theory that the interest rate on a long-term bond will equal an average of short-term interest rates expected to occur over the life of the long-term bond plus a positive term (liquidity) premium. 104

liquidity risk: The risk that a firm may run out of cash needed to pay bills and to keep the firm operating.

liquidity services: Services that make it easier for customers to conduct transactions. 24

load fund: A mutual fund that charges a fee when money is added to or withdrawn from the fund. 492

loan commitment: A bank's commitment (for a specified future period of time) to provide a firm with loans up to a given amount at an interest rate that is tied to some market interest rate. 405, 561

loan sale: The sale under a contract (also called a *secondary loan participation*) of all or part of the cash stream from a specific loan, thereby removing the loan from the bank's balance sheet. 405

London interbank bid rate (LIBID): The rate of interest large international banks charge on overnight loans among themselves. 266

London interbank offer rate (LIBOR): The interest rate charged on short-term funds bought or sold between large international banks. 266

long position: A contractual obligation to take delivery of an underlying financial instrument. 580

long-term: With reference to a debt instrument, having a maturity of 10 years or more. 18

longer-term refinancing operations: A second category of open market operations by the European Central Bank that are similar to the Fed's outright purchase of securities. 229

macro hedge: A hedge of interest-rate risk for a financial institution's entire portfolio. 585

macroprudential regulation: Regulatory policy to affect what is happening in credit markets in the aggregate. 242

macroprudential supervision: Supervision that focuses on the safety and soundness of the financial system in the aggregate. 431

main refinancing operations: Operations that involve weekly reverse transactions (purchase or sale of eligible assets under repurchase agreements or credit operations against eligible assets as collateral) that are reversed within two weeks and are the primary monetary policy tool of the European Central Bank. 229

managed float regime: The current international financial environment in which exchange rates fluctuate from day to day, but central banks attempt to influence their countries' exchange rates by buying and selling currencies. (Also known as a *dirty float.*) 373

management advisory services: Auditing and nonauditing consulting services that accounting firms sometimes provide to their clients.

management of expectations: A strategy in which the Fed committed to keep the federal funds rate at zero for a long period of time in order to lower the market's expectations of future short-term interest rates, causing the long-term interest rate to fall.

margin credit: Loans advanced by a brokerage house to help investors buy securities. 544

margin requirement: A sum of money that must be kept in an account (the margin account) at a brokerage firm. 588

marginal lending facility: The European Central Bank's standing lending facility in which banks can borrow (against eligible collateral) overnight loans from the national central bank at a rate 100 basis points above the target financing rate. 230

marginal lending rate: The interest rate charged by the European Central Bank for borrowing at its marginal lending facility. 230

mark-to-market accounting: An accounting method in which assets are valued in the balance sheets at what they would sell for in the market. 427

marked to market: Repriced and settled in the margin account at the end of every trading day to reflect any change in the value of the futures contract. 588

market equilibrium: A situation occurring when the quantity that people are willing to buy (demand) equals the quantity that people are willing to sell (supply). 73

market fundamentals: Items that have a direct effect on future income streams of the security. 130

market maker: Dealers who buy or sell securities from their own inventories, thereby ensuring that there is always a market in which investors can buy or sell their securities. 546

market order: An order placed by a customer to buy stock at the current market price. 543

market segmentation theory: A theory of the term structure that sees markets for different maturity bonds as completely separated and segmented such that the interest rate for bonds of a given maturity is determined solely by supply and demand for bonds of that maturity. 103

matched sale-purchase transaction: An arrangement whereby the Fed sells securities and the buyer agrees to sell them back to the Fed in the near future; sometimes called a *reverse repo*. 218

maturity: Time to the expiration date (maturity date) of a debt instrument. 18

mean reversion: The phenomenon that stocks with low returns today tend to have high returns in the future, and vice versa. 126

mergers and acquisitions market: An informal and unorganized market where firms are bought, sold, or merged with other firms. 541

micro hedge: A hedge for a specific asset. 585

microprudential supervision: Supervision that focuses on the safety and soundness of individual financial institutions. 430

monetary base: The sum of the Fed's monetary liabilities (currency in circulation and reserves) and the U.S. Treasury's monetary liabilities (Treasury currency in circulation, primarily coins). 225

monetary neutrality: A proposition that in the long run, a percentage rise in the money supply is matched by the same percentage rise in the price level, leaving unchanged the real money supply and all other economic variables such as interest rates.

monetary policy: The management of the money supply and interest rates. 7

monetary targeting: A monetary policy strategy in which the central bank announces that it will achieve a certain value (the target) of the annual growth rate of a monetary aggregate.

monetary union: A situation in which a group of countries decide to adopt a common currency. (Also called a *currency union*.) 377

money: Anything that is generally accepted in payment for goods or services or in the repayment of debts. (Also called *money supply*.) 7

money center banks: Large banks in key financial centers. 400

money market: A financial market in which only short-term debt instruments (maturity of less than one year) are traded. 20

money market mutual funds: Funds that accumulate investment dollars from a large group of people and then invest in short-term securities such as Treasury bills and commercial paper. 254

money market securities: Securities that have an original maturity of less than one year, such as Treasury bills, commercial paper, banker's acceptances, and negotiable certificates of deposit. 250

monoline insurance companies: Companies that specialize in credit insurance. 521

money supply: See *money*.

moral hazard: The risk that one party to a transaction will engage in behavior that is undesirable from the other party's point of view. 25

mortgage: A long-term loan secured by real estate. 319

mortgage-backed security: A security that is collateralized by a pool of mortgage loans. (Also called a *securitized mortgage*.) 174, 331

mortgage pass-through: A security that has the multiple borrowers' mortgage payments pass through a trustee before being disbursed to the investors. 332

mutual bank: A bank owned by the depositors.

mutual insurance company: An insurance company that is owned by the policyholders and has the objective of providing insurance for the lowest possible price. 508

named-peril policy: Insurance policy that protects against loss from perils that are specifically named in the policy. 515

National Association of Securities Dealers Automated Quotation System (NASDAQ): A computerized network that links dealers around the country and provides price quotes on over-the-counter securities. 300

national banks: Federally chartered banks. 445

National Credit Union Act of 1970: Law that established the National Credit Union Administration (NCUA), an independent agency charged with the task of regulating and supervising federally chartered credit unions and state-chartered credit unions that receive federal deposit insurance.

National Credit Union Share Insurance Fund (NCUSIF): Agency established by the National Credit Union Act of 1970 that is controlled by the National Credit Union Administration and insures the deposits in credit unions for $100,000 per account. 473

natural rate of unemployment: The rate of unemployment consistent with full employment at which the demand for labor equals the supply of labor. 232

negotiable certificates of deposit: A bank-issued short-term security that is traded and that documents a deposit and specifies the interest rate and the maturity date. 20, 262

net asset value: The total value of a mutual fund's assets minus any liabilities, divided by the number of shares outstanding. 485

net exports: The balance of trade in both goods and services. 372

net interest margin (NIM): The difference between interest income and interest expense as a percentage of assets. 410

net worth: The difference between a firm's assets (what it owns or is owed) and its liabilities (what it owes). (Also called *equity capital.*) 146

no-load fund: A mutual fund that does not charge a fee when funds are added to or withdrawn from the fund. 492

nominal anchor: A nominal variable such as the inflation rate, an exchange rate, or the money supply that monetary policy makers use to tie down the price level. 231

nominal interest rate: An interest rate that is not adjusted for inflation. 48

nonbank banks: Limited-service banks that either do not make commercial loans or do not take in deposits.

noncompetitive bidding: Offering to buy Treasury securities without specifying a price; the securities are ultimately sold at the weighted average of the competitive bids accepted at the same auction. 258

nonconventional monetary policy tools: Three non-interest-rate tools used to stimulate the economy: (1) liquidity provision, (2) asset purchases, and (3) commitment to future monetary policy actions. 223

notional principal: The amount on which interest is being paid in a swap arrangement. 601

off-balance-sheet activities: Bank activities that involve trading financial instruments and the generation of income from fees and loan sales, all of which affect bank profits but are not visible on bank balance sheets. 405, 422

official reserve transactions balance: The current account balance plus items in the capital account.

open-end fund: A mutual fund that accepts investments and allows investors to redeem shares at any time. The value of the shares is tied to the value of investment assets of the fund. 484

open interest: The number of contracts outstanding. 586

open market operations: The buying and selling of government securities in the open market that affect both interest rates and the amount of reserves in the banking system. 190, 209

open-peril policies: See *named-peril policies*. 515

operating expenses: The expenses incurred from a bank's ongoing operations. 409

operating income: The income earned on a bank's ongoing operations. 408

operating instrument: A variable that is very responsive to the central bank's tools and indicates the stance of monetary policy. (Also called a *policy instrument.*)

opportunity cost: The amount of interest (expected return) sacrificed by not holding an alternative asset. 252

options: Contracts that give the purchaser the option (right) to buy or sell the underlying financial instrument at a specified price, called the *exercise price* or *strike price*, within a specific period of time (the *term to expiration*). 594

originate-to-distribute model: A business model in which the mortgage is originated by a separate party, typically a mortgage broker, and then distributed to an investor as an underlying asset in a security. 175, 454

overfunded: Describing a pension plan that has assets greater than needed to make the projected benefit payments owed by the plan. 523

overnight cash rate: The interest rate for very-short-term interbank loans in the euro area. 229

oversubscribed: Having received more offers to buy than there are securities available for sale. 539

over-the-counter (OTC) market: A secondary market in which dealers at different locations who have an inventory of securities stand ready to buy and sell securities to anyone who comes to them and is willing to accept their prices. 19

passbook savings account: An interest-bearing savings account held at a commercial bank.

pecking order hypothesis: The hypothesis that the larger and more established is a corporation, the more likely it will be to issue securities to raise funds. 146

Pension Benefit Guarantee Corporation (Penny Benny): A government agency that performs a role similar to that of the FDIC, insuring pension benefits up to a limit if a company with an underfunded pension plan goes bankrupt. 528

pension plan: An asset pool that accumulates over an individual's working years and is paid out during the nonworking years. 521

perpetuity: A perpetual bond with no maturity date and no repayment of principal that makes periodic fixed payments forever. 45

policy instrument: A variable that is very responsive to the central bank's tools and indicates the stance of monetary policy. (Also called an *operating instrument.*) 197

policy trilemma: A country cannot pursue the following three policies at the same time: (1) free capital mobility; (2) a fixed exchange rate; and (3) independent monetary policy. (Also called *impossible trinity.*) 376

political business cycle: A business cycle caused by expansionary policies before an election. 199

portfolio: A collection of assets. 24

potential output: The level of output that is produced at the natural rate of unemployment. (Also called *natural rate of output.*) 233

preferred habitat theory: A theory that assumes that investors have a preference for bonds of one maturity over another, a particular bond maturity (preferred habitat) in which they prefer to invest. 104

preferred stock: Stock on which a fixed dividend must be paid before common dividends are distributed. It often does not mature and usually does not give the holder voting rights in the company. 299

premium: The amount paid for an option contract. 293, 594

present discounted value: See *present value.* 38

present value: Today's value of a payment to be received in the future when the interest rate is i. (Also called *present discounted value.*) 38

price earnings ratio (PE): A measure of how much the market is willing to pay for $1 of earnings from a firm. 306

price stability: Low and stable inflation. 230

primary dealers: Government securities dealers, operating out of private firms or commercial banks, with whom the Fed's open market desk trades. 209

primary market: A financial market in which new issues of a security are sold to initial buyers. 18, 534

principal–agent problem: A moral hazard problem that occurs when the managers in control (the agents) act in their own interest rather than in the interest of the owners (the principals) due to differing sets of incentives. 147, 175

private equity buyout: When a public company becomes private. 553

private mortgage insurance (PMI): Insurance that protects the lender against losses from defaults on mortgage loans. 323

private pension plan: A pension plan sponsored by an employer, group, or individual. 524

property insurance: Insurance that protects against losses from fire, theft, storm, explosion, and neglect. 515

proprietary trading: Financial institutions that trade with their own money. 438

prospectus: A portion of a security registration statement that is filed with the Securities and Exchange Commission and made available to potential purchasers of the security. 537

prudent man rule: This rule states that those with the responsibility of investing money for others should act with prudence, discretion, intelligence, and regard for safety of capital as well as income. 551

public pension plan: A pension plan sponsored by a government body. 525

put option: An option contract that provides the right to sell a security at a specified price. 594

quantitative easing: Asset purchase programs that lead to an expansion of the Federal Reserve's balance sheet and the monetary base. 235

quotas: Restrictions on the quantity of foreign goods that can be imported. 346

random walk: The movements of a variable whose future changes cannot be predicted because, given today's value, the variable is just as likely to fall as to rise. 122

rate of capital gain: The change in a security's price relative to the initial purchase price. 53

rate of return: See *return.*

real exchange rate: The rate at which domestic goods can be exchanged for foreign goods, meaning the price of domestic goods relative to foreign goods denominated in domestic currency. 344

real interest rate: The interest rate adjusted for expected changes in the price level (inflation) so that it more accurately reflects the true cost of borrowing. 48

real terms: Terms reflecting actual goods and services one can buy. 48

registered bonds: Bonds requiring that their owners register with the company to receive interest payments. Registered bonds have largely replaced bearer bonds, which did not require registration. 282

registration statement: Information about a firm's financial condition, management, competition, industry, and experience that must be filed with the Securities and Exchange Commission prior to the sale to the public of any security with a maturity of more than 270 days. 537

Regulation Z: The requirement that lenders disclose the full cost of a loan to the borrower. (Also known as the "truth in lending" regulation.) 429

regulatory arbitrage: An attempt to avoid regulatory capital requirements by keeping assets on banks' books that have the same risk-based capital requirement but are relatively risky, while taking off their books low-risk assets. 422

regulatory forbearance: Refraining from exercising a regulatory right to put insolvent savings and loans out of business. 530

reinsurance: Allocating a portion of the risk to another company in exchange for a portion of the premium. 516

reinvestment risk: The interest-rate risk associated with the fact that the proceeds of short-term investments must be reinvested at a future interest rate that is uncertain. 55

repossession: The taking of an asset that has been pledged as collateral for a loan when the borrower defaults.

repurchase agreement: A form of loan in which the borrower simultaneously contracts to sell securities and contracts to repurchase them, either on demand or on a specified date. 178, 218

required reserve ratio: The fraction of deposits that the Fed requires to be kept as reserves. 209, 392

required reserves: Reserves that are held to meet Fed requirements that a certain fraction of bank deposits be kept as reserves. 209, 392

reserve account: An account used to make insurance and tax payments due on property securing a mortgage loan. A portion of each monthly loan payment goes into the reserve account. 329

reserve currency: A currency such as the U.S. dollar that is used by other countries to denominate the assets they hold as international reserves. 374

reserve for loan losses: An account that offsets the loan accounts on a lender's books that reflects the lender's projected losses due to default.

reserve requirements: Regulations making it obligatory for depository institutions to keep a certain fraction of their deposits in accounts with the Fed. 209, 392

reserves: Banks' holding of deposits in accounts with the Fed, plus currency that is physically held by banks (vault cash). 209, 392

Resolution Trust Corporation (RTC): A temporary agency created by FIRREA that was responsible for liquidating the assets of failed savings and loans. 434

restrictive covenants: Provisions that specify certain activities that a borrower can and cannot engage in. 138, 283

return: The payments to the owner of a security plus the change in the security's value, expressed as a fraction of its purchase price; more precisely called the *rate of return*. 51

return on assets (ROA): Net profit after taxes per dollar of assets. 402

return on equity (ROE): Net profit after taxes per dollar of equity capital. 402

revaluation: Resetting of the par value of a currency at a higher level. 376

revenue bonds: Bonds for which the source of income that is used to pay the interest and to retire the bonds is from a specific source, such as a toll road or an electric plant. If this revenue source is unable to make the payments, the bonds can default, despite the issuing municipality being otherwise healthy. 280

reverse transactions: Purchase or sale of eligible assets by the European Central Bank under repurchase agreements or credit operations against eligible assets as collateral that are reversed within two weeks. 229

risk: The degree of uncertainty associated with the return on an asset. 24, 67

risk premium: The spread between the interest rate on bonds with default risk and the interest rate on default-free bonds. 91

risk sharing: The process by which financial intermediaries create and sell assets with risk characteristics that people are comfortable with and then use the funds they acquire by selling these assets to purchase other assets that may have far more risk. 24

risk structure of interest rates: The relationship among the various interest rates on bonds with the same term to maturity. 89

roll over: To renew a debt when it matures.

seasoned issues: Securities that have been trading publicly long enough to have let the market clearly establish their value. 537

secondary market: A financial market in which securities that have previously been issued can be resold. 18, 534

secondary reserves: U.S. government and agency securities held by banks. 393

secured debt: Debt guaranteed by collateral. 138

secured loan: A loan guaranteed by collateral. 561

securitization: The process of transforming illiquid financial assets into marketable capital market instruments. 174, 453

securitized mortgage: See *mortgage-backed-security*.

security: A claim on the borrower's future income that is sold by the borrower to the lender. (Also called a *financial instrument*.) 2

seed investing: Investment by a venture capital firm in a company before it has a real product or is even clearly organized as a company. 552

Separate Trading of Registered Interest and Principal Securities (STRIPS): Securities that have their periodic interest payments separated from the final maturity payment and the two cash flows are sold to different investors. 277

shadow banking system: A system in which bank lending is replaced by lending via the securities market. 178, 446

share draft account: Accounts at credit unions that are similar to checking accounts at banks.

shelf registration: An arrangement with the Securities and Exchange Commission that allows a single registration document to be filed that permits multiple securities issues.

short position: A contractual obligation to deliver an underlying financial instrument. 580

short sale: An arrangement with a broker to borrow and sell securities. The borrowed securities are replaced with securities purchased later. Short sales let investors earn profits from falling securities prices. 132, 543

short-term: With reference to a debt instrument, having a maturity of one year or less. 18

simple loan: A credit market instrument providing the borrower with an amount of funds that must be repaid to the lender at the maturity date along with an additional payment (interest). 38

sinking fund: Fund created by a provision in many bond contracts that requires the issuer to set aside each year a portion of the final maturity payment so that investors can be certain that the funds will be available at maturity. 283

smart card: A more sophisticated stored-value card that contains its own computer chip so that it can be loaded with digital cash from the owner's bank account whenever needed. 451

special drawing rights (SDRs): A paper substitute for gold issued by the International Monetary Fund that functions as international reserves.

speculative attack: A situation in which speculators engage in massive sales of a currency. 378

spinning: When an investment bank allocates hot, but underpriced, initial public offerings (IPOs), shares of newly issued stock, to executives of other companies in return for their companies' future business with the investment banks. 158

spot exchange rate: The exchange rate for the immediate (two-day) transaction. 341

spot rate: The interest rate at a given moment. 111

spot transaction: The immediate exchange of bank deposits denominated in different currencies. 341

standard deviation: A statistical indicator of an asset's risk. 68

standing lending facility: A lending facility in which healthy banks are allowed to borrow all they want from a central bank. 220

state banks: Banks chartered by the states. 445

state-owned banks: Banks that are owned by governments. 154

sterilized foreign exchange intervention: A foreign exchange intervention with an offsetting open market operation that leaves the monetary base unchanged. 370

stock: A security that is a claim on the earnings and assets of a corporation. 3

stock company: An insurance company that issues stock and has the objective of making a profit for its shareholders. 508

stock market risk: The risk associated with fluctuations in stock prices. 591

stock option: An option on an individual stock. 594

stop loss order: An order placed with a broker to buy or sell when a certain price is reached; it is designed to limit an investor's loss on a security position. 543

stress testing: Calculating losses under dire scenarios. 426
strike price: See *exercise price*.
structured credit products: Securities that are derived from cash flows of underlying assets and are tailored to have particular risk characteristics that appeal to investors with different preferences. 174
subprime loans: Loans made to borrowers who do not qualify for loans at the usual rate of interest due to poor credit rating or too large of a loan. 334
subprime mortgages: Mortgage loans made to borrowers who do not qualify for loans at the usual rate of interest due to a poor credit history. 174, 454
super display book (SDBK): A computerized system for executing trades very rapidly that removes the specialist from the process. 301
superregional banks: Bank holding companies similar in size to money center banks whose headquarters are not based in one of the money center cities (New York, Chicago, San Francisco). 466
supply curve: A curve depicting the relationship between quantity supplied and price when all other economic variables are held constant. 72
swap: A financial contract that obligates one party to exchange (swap) a set of payments it owns for a set of payments owned by another party. 601
sweep account: An arrangement in which any balances above a certain amount in a corporation's checking account at the end of a business day are "swept out" of the account and invested in overnight repos that pay the corporation interest. 456
syndicate: A group of investment banks that come together for the purpose of issuing a security. The syndicate spreads the risk of the issue among the members. Each participant attempts to market the security and shares in losses. 538
systemic: Financial firms who pose a risk to the overall financial system because their failure would cause widespread damage. 437
systematically important financial institutions (SIFIs): Firms designated by the Financial Stability Oversight Council as systematically important that are subject to additional regulation by the Federal Reserve. 438
T-account: A simplified balance sheet with lines in the form of a T that lists only the changes that occur in a balance sheet starting from some initial balance sheet position. 209
target financing rate: The European Central Bank's target for the overnight cash rate, the interest rate for very-short-term interbank loans in the euro area. 239
tariffs: Taxes on imported goods. 346
term security: A security with a specified maturity date. 262
term structure of interest rates: The relationship among interest rates on bonds with different terms to maturity. 89
theory of efficient capital markets: The theory that prices of securities in financial markets fully reflect all available information. 118
theory of portfolio choice: The theory that tells how much of an asset people want to hold in their portfolio. 70
theory of purchasing power parity (PPP): The theory that exchange rates between any two currencies will adjust to reflect changes in the price levels of the two countries. 343
thrift institutions (thrifts): Savings and loan associations, mutual savings banks, and credit unions. 27
tightening of monetary policy: A rise in the federal funds rate. 192
time-inconsistency problem: The problem that occurs when monetary policy makers conduct monetary policy in a discretionary way and pursue expansionary policies that are attractive in the short run but lead to bad long-run outcomes. 231
tombstone: A large notice placed in financial newspapers announcing that a security will be offered for sale by an underwriter or group of underwriters. 539
too-big-to-fail problem: Quandary in which regulators are reluctant to close down large financial institutions and impose losses on their depositors and creditors because doing so might precipitate a financial crisis. 419
TRACE: A trade reporting and compliance engine created by the Securities and Exchange Trade Commission in 2002. 288
trade association: A group of credit unions organized to provide a variety of services to a large number of credit unions.
trade balance: The difference between merchandise exports and imports. 372
transaction costs: The time and money spent trying to exchange financial assets, goods, or services. 23
Treasury bills (T-bills): Securities sold by the federal government with initial maturities of less than

one year. They are often considered the lowest-risk security available. 256

underfunded: Describing a pension plan in which the contributions and their earnings are insufficient to pay out the defined benefits when they come due. 523

undersubscribed: Having received fewer offers to buy than there are securities available for sale. 539

underwriters: Investment banks that guarantee prices on securities to corporations and then sell the securities to the public. 507

underwriting: Guaranteeing prices on securities to corporations and then selling the securities to the public. 19

unexploited profit opportunity: A situation in which an investor can earn a higher-than-normal return. 120

unsecured debt: Debt not guaranteed by collateral. 138

unsterilized foreign exchange intervention: A foreign exchange intervention in which a central bank allows the purchase or sale of domestic currency to affect the monetary base. 369

U.S. Central Credit Union: A central bank for credit unions that was organized in 1974 and provides banking services to the state central credit unions.

usury: Charging an excessive or inordinate interest rate on a loan.

value at risk (VaR) calculations: Measurements of the size of the loss on a trading portfolio that might happen, say, 1% of the time, over a particular period such as two weeks. 426

vault cash: Currency that is physically held by banks and stored in vaults overnight. 392

venture capital firm: A financial intermediary that pools the resources of its partners and uses the funds to help entrepreneurs start up new businesses. 149

virtual bank: A bank that has no building but rather exists only in cyberspace. 449

wealth: All resources owned by an individual, including all assets. 67

wholesale market: Market where extremely large transactions occur, as for money market funds or foreign currency. 250

World Bank: The International Bank for Reconstruction and Development, an international organization that provides long-term loans to assist developing countries in building dams, roads, and other physical capital that would contribute to their economic development. 374

World Trade Organization (WTO): The organization that monitors rules for the conduct of trade between countries (tariffs and quotas). 374

yield curve: A plot of the interest rates for particular types of bonds with different terms to maturity. 97

yield to maturity: The interest rate that equates the present value of payments received from a credit market instrument with its value today. 41

zero-coupon bond: See *discount bond*. 40

zero-coupon securities: See *Separate Trading of Registered Interest and Principal Securities* (STRIPS). 277

zero-lower-bound problem: Situation in which the central bank is unable to lower the policy interest rate further because it has hit a floor of zero. 223

Index

T

U

Guide to Commonly Used Symbols

Symbol	Page Where Introduced	Term
Δ	61	change in a variable
π^e	48	expected inflation
σ	68	standard deviation
B^d	73	demand for bonds
B^s	73	supply of bonds
C	44	yearly coupon payment
D	70	demand curve
DUR	59	duration
DUR_{GAP}	569	duration gap
E	346	exchange (spot) rate
$(E^e_{t+1} - E_t)/E_t$	364	expected appreciation of domestic currency
EM	402	equity multiplier
GAP	565	income gap
i	38	interest rate (yield to maturity)